T0320236

Economic Developments in Contemporary China

Praise for Ian Jeffries' *China: A Guide to Economic and Political Developments*
2006):

> This book is highly useful not only to casual China watchers ... but also to
> researchers and academics ... an engrossing guide.
>
> (Marc Lanteigne, *International Affairs*)

China's role in global affairs today continues to rise. This book provides an
authoritative, comprehensive and detailed overview of contemporary economic
developments in China. Key topics include agriculture; the market gradually
replacing central planning; the global financial crisis; the reform of state-owned
industrial enterprises; the non-state sectors; the 'open-door' policy (including the
WTO, exchange rate policy, and inward and outward direct foreign investment);
and China's economic performance in general.

The book continues – and adds to – the overview of developments up to May
2006 which were covered in the author's *China: A Guide to Economic and Political Developments* (2006), and is the companion volume to *Political Developments in Contemporary China: A Guide* (2010) – both published by Routledge.

Ian Jeffries is Honorary Professor in the Department of Economics in the School
of Business and Economics at Swansea University, UK. He is the author of
numerous books in the series, *Guides to Economic and Political Developments in
Asia*, including volumes on North Korea, Vietnam, China and Mongolia.

Guides to economic and political developments in Asia

1   **North Korea**
A guide to economic and political developments
Ian Jeffries

2   **Vietnam**
A guide to economic and political developments
Ian Jeffries

3   **China**
A guide to economic and political developments
Ian Jeffries

4   **Mongolia**
A guide to economic and political developments
Ian Jeffries

5   **Contemporary North Korea**
A guide to economic and political developments
Ian Jeffries

6   **Political Developments in Contemporary China**
A guide
Ian Jeffries

7   **Economic Developments in Contemporary China**
A guide
Ian Jeffries

Economic Developments in Contemporary China

A guide

Ian Jeffries

Routledge
Taylor & Francis Group

LONDON AND NEW YORK

First published 2011
by Routledge
2 Park Square, Milton Park, Abingdon, Oxon OX14 4RN

Simultaneously published in the USA and Canada
by Routledge
711 Third Avenue, New York, NY 10017, USA

Routledge is an imprint of the Taylor & Francis Group, an informa business

Typeset in Times by Wearset Ltd, Boldon, Tyne and Wear

British Library Cataloguing in Publication Data
A catalogue record for this book is available from the British Library

Library of Congress Cataloging in Publication Data
Jeffries, Ian.
Economic developments in contemporary China: a guide/Ian Jeffries.
p. cm. – (Guides to economic and political developments in Asia; 7)
Includes bibliographical references and index.

1. China–Economic policy. 2. China–Economic conditions.
3. China–Politics and government. I. Title.
HC427.J44 2010
330.951–dc22

2009050201

ISBN 978-0-415-47866-3 (hbk)
ISBN 0-415-47866-9 (hbk)

ISBN 978-0-203-85083-1 (ebook)
ISBN 0-203-85083-1 (ebook)

Contents

Acknowledgements

I am much indebted to the following individuals (in alphabetical order):

At Swansea University: Robert Bideleux; Siân Brown; Dianne Darrell; Michele Davies; Chris Hunt; Nigel O'Leary; Mary Perman; Ann Preece; Paul Reynolds; Kathy Sivertsen; Fritz Summer, Chris West.

Professors: Nick Baigent, John Baylis; George Blazyca, Steve Brown, Mike Charlton, Steve Cook, Phillip Hanson, Paul Hare, Lester Hunt, Michael Kaser, Phil Murphy and Noel Thompson.

Russell Davies (Kays Newsagency).

At Routledge: Louise Collins, Emma Davis, Alan Jarvis, Eve Setch and Peter Sowden.

Copy-editor: Liz Jones.

At Wearset: Kelly Alderson, Matt Deacon, Claire Dunstan and Allie Waite.

Ian Jeffries
Honorary Professor
Department of Economics and Centre of Russian and East European Studies,
Swansea University

Introduction

> This book is highly useful not only to casual China watchers ... but also to researchers and academics ... Especially interesting was the middle section on political developments and the work of the various government congresses since the early 1990s, which provides an engrossing guide to the political priorities of the National People's Congress and other departments, including both domestic and international issues involving East Asia, the United States and elsewhere in the world. Also noteworthy was the section on China's emerging 'open door' policies which records Beijing's struggles with adapting to a globalized economy, with sections on liberalized trade, engagement with economic institutions, and currency policies, all areas of increasing interest to both analysts and policy communities. Additionally, those interested in the politics of healthcare in China will be especially impressed with the range of topics included ... [including] the SARS crisis ... AIDS and avian influenza ... [Other topics covered include] the transfer of Hong Kong and Macao to Chinese sovereignty ... the Taiwan question ... township elections ... market development, the reform of state enterprises ... [and] agriculture.
>
> (*International Affairs*, 2007, vol. 83, no. 2, p. 409)

I was delighted with these generous comments about *China: A Guide to Economic and Political Developments* (Routledge 2006) by Marc Lanteigne. I can only hope that this companion volume finds equal favour.

Political developments are covered in *Political Developments in Contemporary China: A Guide*, which provides a demographic, historical and political background.

1   Overview

(Developments after November 2009 have not generally been summarized in the Overview. Please see the main text.)

> For 500 years, from the fourteenth century until the 1830s China accounted for a remarkable 30 per cent of world economic output. That is more than the US economy at the height of its global economic dominance after World War II – sustained for a half-millennium! But by 1979 ... China's share of global GDP was barely 1 per cent ... Today China accounts for about 5 per cent of world output.
>
> (Philip Auerswald, *IHT*, 12 August 2008, p. 8)

> Perhaps it would be more accurate to speak of the country's reemergence. In 1820 China accounted for about 30 per cent of the global economy ... The United States then weighed in with less than 2 per cent. But by the 1950s America was dominant and China ... accounted for only about 4 per cent of world economic activity.
>
> (Roger Cohen, *IHT*, 13 April 2005, p. 2)

> Up to the fifteenth century Chinese technological know-how was the most advanced in the world. China has been the largest economy in the world for 1,800 of the past 2,000 years. As recently as 1820 it produced one-third of global output, and it remained the world's largest economy until 1885.
>
> (John Lee, *IHT*, 13 November 2008, p. 8)

> Angus Maddison has calculated that China's share of GDP in 1820 ... was more than 30 per cent ... Between 1820 and 1952 ... China's output per head actually fell while its share of global GDP plunged from one-third to one-twentieth. *Per capita* income fell from level pegging with the world to a quarter of the global average over the period.
>
> (*FT*, 12 November 2009, p. 13)

The economic reforms themselves have been variously described by China, e.g. 'planned socialist commodity economy' has given way to 'socialist market economy' (1992: formally enshrined in the new constitution in March 1993) as the reforms have proceeded and ideological concessions have become more and more accepted.

China is the best example of a generally successful policy of *gradual and partial* economic reform. The Third Plenum of the Eleventh Central Committee in December 1978 was the crucial political event. Since then China, with occasional setbacks, has moved broadly towards a market economy and allowed the non-state sector to gradually play a much greater role. China, however, had no detailed blueprint for economic reform and so groped its way forward.

Those advocating 'big bang'/'shock therapy' for the countries of Eastern Europe and the former Soviet Union generally argue that, despite the country's achievements, China's model cannot be adopted in these cases because circumstances are different. Among other things, China was generally in a more favourable position in 1978 than the countries of Eastern Europe/the former Soviet Union generally were in 1989/1991. For example, China had a relatively low foreign debt, did not suffer from severe inflationary pressures and had substantially reorientated its trade towards the West. (China had quarrelled with the Soviet Union; e.g. in 1960 the Soviet Union withdrew its aid personnel.) The structure of the Chinese economy in 1978 was far more agrarian in nature, allowing a vast flow of cheap labour to the towns to boost the export of manufactured goods, including those produced by foreign companies. China's so-called 'floating population' of rural workers in urban areas is difficult to estimate, but may be of the order of 130 million to 150 million in more recent times. (Woo is an exception in that he argues that 'gradual reform in China was not the optimal reform for China': 1994: 306.)

The discrediting of such extreme and extreme-left policies as the Great Leap Forward (1958–60) and the Cultural Revolution (1966–76) has helped keep the policy of gradual reforms on track. There have been occasional setbacks, but there seems to be no chance of any substantial reversal of the reforms which have been gradually introduced since 1978. China is now a key figure in the global economy, as regards both its exports and imports. Entry into the WTO (the successor to Gatt) on 11 December 2001 helped ensure the irreversibility of the general economic reform process.

The policy of gradualism has been influenced by such factors as the consequences of making drastic mistakes in a poor country with a history of natural and man-made disasters, and disagreements within the ruling elite. The Great Leap Forward (1958–60) and the Cultural Revolution (1966–76; a chaotic and anarchic period and one which was basically a means of reasserting Mao's personal power after his authority had waned in the wake of the disastrous Great Leap Forward) were the result of extreme-left policies. The discrediting of such extreme and extreme-left policies has had a profound effect, both on the decision to implement economic reforms after the watershed year 1978 and on the basic continuity of the reforms.

Economic reforms have sometimes been put on hold or even regressed, e.g. after the Tiananmen crisis in 1989 and the Asian financial crisis (which started with the attack on the Thai baht in July 1997). Periodic worries about inflation or deflation have led to setbacks and there has at various times been resistance to, for example, agricultural tax reform, housing reform and the sale of state assets. Property and bankruptcy laws were slow in coming.

China adopted a policy of gradual and partial price reform. A 'dual' pricing system was used (market prices being allowed for products bought and sold on the market as opposed to state-controlled prices for outputs or inputs forming part of the state plan). Controls have gradually been relaxed over time. Nevertheless, the state still exercises considerable direct and indirect control over price setting. In addition, temporary retrenchment has occurred, such as the reintroduction of price controls to combat inflation (such as in the latter half of 1998, the latter half of 2007 and early 2008) and combat deflation (price floors for a while after October 1997). The unusually severe snowstorms in parts of China that started on 10 January 2008 led to further (temporary) food price controls.

> China lifted its controls on food prices Monday [1 December], the latest sign of how drastically priorities have shifted from earlier this year, when the county was focused on fighting inflation ... Companies would now be free to decide that for themselves, the National Development and Reform Commission said in a statement ... Under the controls manufacturers had to apply for approval for any substantial price increases. Beijing will still keep an eye on prices, however, and work to ensure that no one manipulates them ... 'We must work further on how to address abnormal price movement.' the commission said.
>
> (www.iht.com, 1 December 2008; *IHT*, 2 December 2008, p. 20)

'Starting 1 January [2009] Beijing will allow gasoline and diesel prices to move more regularly in line with the global market' (www.iht.com, 5 December 2008).

> China unveiled a shake-up of its oil pricing system yesterday [5 December], combining a big increase in fuel taxes for consumers with the first steps in liberalizing prices for petrol and diesel. From next year [2009] Beijing will allow prices for refined oil in the Chinese market to 'reflect fluctuations of international oil prices', ending a system of periodic price changes.
>
> (*FT*, 6 December 2008, p. 8)

'China will cut domestic fuel prices on Friday [19 December] for the first time in almost two years' (www.ft.com, 19 December 2008).

'China took a step back from its promise to move towards more market-orientated domestic fuel prices, warning on Friday [8 May] that Beijing would limit petrol, diesel and other fuel price increases when oil prices rose above $80 a barrel' (www.ft.com, 10 May 2009).

'[Companies such as PetroChina have] benefited from two government-sanctioned fuel price increases in June [2009] – part of Beijing's fuel price reforms that guarantee refiners a profit margin if crude oil stays below $80 a barrel' (*FT*, 29 August 2009, p. 15).

Economic success has been achieved on a broad front, in terms of such criteria as output growth, living standards, poverty reduction and inflation. (See Table 1.)

China's rapid expansion of late (the fastest growing large economy) has been of global significance, such as its important contribution to global economic growth and its effects on the world market prices of commodities such as oil. China came through the 1997 Asian financial crisis in good shape and is coping relatively well with the global financial crisis.

But the costs of rapid growth include horrendous levels of pollution. Party leaders are also concerned about increasing inequalities in the distribution of income and wealth.

In December 2005 China announced that it had upwardly revised its official estimate of GDP in 2004 by 16.8 per cent. The main reason given was the considerable underestimation of the private service sector. In January 2006 China presented revised figures for GDP growth rates. From 1993 to 2004 inclusive only the figure for 1998 remained unchanged, while all the others were revised upwards. (See Table 1.)

> China said Tuesday [20 December 2005] that its economy was far bigger than previously estimated and that the new figures suggested that it had probably passed France, Italy and Britain to become the world's fourth largest economy ... trailing only that of the United States, Japan and Germany.
>
> (*IHT*, 21 December 2005, p. 17)

'China could displace Britain as the world's fourth largest economy this year [2005] after Beijing unveiled a 16.8 per cent upward revision to official GDP that pushed it into sixth place in 2004' (*FT*, 21 December 2005, p. 10).

'[China has] the world's fourth largest economy' (*The Economist*, 1 November 2008, p. 67).

'Revised figures published this week show that in 2007 China overtook Germany to become the world's third biggest economy' (www.economist.com, 14 January 2009).

> China on Wednesday [14 January 2009] revised upwards its GDP [growth rate] for 2007 to 13 per cent from 11.9 per cent, which would mean it had passed Germany to become the third largest economy in the world. The revised growth rate, announced by the National Bureau of Statistics, was the fastest since 1993, when the economy expanded 13.5 per cent. The statistics office had already updated its estimate of 2007 growth in April [2008] from an initial reading of 11.4 per cent ... The World Bank uses gross national income converted to dollars using the Atlas method, which takes a three-year moving average for the exchange rate. China now estimates that the total value of goods and services in 2007 was 3.1 per cent higher than previously thought. Applying this increase to the World Bank's published rankings gives China a gross national income of $3.218 trillion for 2007 compared with $3.197 trillion for Germany ... GNI [gross national income]

takes into account all production in the domestic economy plus net flows of income from abroad like profits and wages.

(IHT, 15 January 2009, p. 11)

'Only the United States and Japan [are now] larger than China' (*FT*, 15 January 2009, p. 5). 'Economists were already confident that China overtook Germany during 2008, but it now seems that the change occurred in a year earlier. China took fourth place from Britain in 2005' (www.guardian.co.uk, 14 January 2009).

Purchasing-power parity:

In poorer countries the prices of goods and services that are not internationally traded tend to be lower than those in richer countries. Thus the use of current exchange rates to estimate national output in terms of, say, US dollars gives a lower national income figure for poorer countries than use of purchasing-power parity (PPP). ('Purchasing-power parity [is] the idea that in the long run exchange rates should equalize the prices in any two countries of a common basket of tradable goods and services': *The Economist*, 25 June 2005, p. 100.) Thus China's world ranking in purchasing-power parity terms is higher.

'Using the much stronger "purchasing power" exchange rate of 1.9 renminbi to the dollar used by the World Bank, the figure represents $5.04 trillion, making China's economy the second largest in the world after the United States' (*FEER*, 10 January 2002, p. 29).

'At market prices Japan [is] the world's second largest economy ... [In 2002 it had a] GDP of $4,266 billion, while China's was only $1,210 billion ... [However] at PPP ... China was the world's second largest economy' (*FT*, 22 September 2003, p. 21).

'In dollar terms its GDP is the sixth largest in the world, just smaller than France's. In terms of purchasing-power parity (after adjusting for price differences between economies) it is second only to the United States' (*The Economist*, 15 February 2003, p. 74).

> If China's GDP is converted into dollars using market exchange rates it amounted to $2.7 trillion last year [2006], only one-fifth of America's $13.2 trillion and the fourth largest in the world. But a dollar buys a lot more in China than in America because prices of non-traded goods and services tend to be much lower in poor countries. Converting a poor country's GDP into dollars at market exchange rates therefore understates the true size of its economy ... On a PPP basis the World Bank ranks China as the world's second biggest economy, with a GDP of $10 trillion last year ... The difficulty of measuring PPP is one reason why some economists prefer to compare the sizes of economies using market exchange rates.
>
> (*The Economist*, 1 December 2007, p. 90)

New figures show that China's GDP is 40 per cent smaller than previously thought ... China's GDP in yuan terms remains unchanged. What has happened is that the World Bank has changed the calculations it uses to make international comparisons of the size of economies. Converting a poor country's GDP can understate the true size because a dollar buys more in an emerging market such as China ... Previous estimates of China's GDP were largely guesswork. Now the World Bank has produced new calculations based on a survey of over 1,000 goods and services in 146 countries, including China for the first time. On this basis China's GDP in 2005 was $5.3 trillion, compared with $2.2 trillion using market exchange rates and $8.9 trillion using previous PPP estimates. This was still well below America's $12.4 trillion that year ... The revisions do not reduce China's growth rate – the fastest over thirty years of any large country in history ... It remains ... even on revised figures ... the world's second biggest economy.

(*The Economist*, 22 December 2007, p. 98)

New calculations by the World Bank suggest that the Chinese economy [GDP] may not be as large as previously thought ... The World Bank issued preliminary figures Monday [17 December 2007] that recalculated what would be the economic output of 146 countries – including China ... Purchasing-power parity [PPP] calculations ... showed that China's output was 40 per cent smaller than previous World Bank estimates ... China's economic output [GDP] in 2005 was worth $2.24 trillion at prevailing prices and actual market exchange rates ... The World Bank previously calculated that China's output was worth $8.8 trillion in 2005 if the goods and services produced were valued at American prices. This figure was revised this week down to $5.3 trillion. Even with this revision, China is still the world's second largest economy in PPP terms, after the United States. At market exchange rates it also trails Japan.

(*IHT*, 21 December 2007, p. 11)

Developments in global oil prices:

Oil prices rose above the symbolic level of $100 a barrel for the first time Wednesday [2 January 2008] ... Oil prices, which had fallen to a low of $50 a barrel at the beginning of 2007, have quadrupled since 2003 ... Oil is now within reach of its historic inflation-adjusted high reached in April 1980 in the aftermath of the Iranian revolution, when oil prices jumped to the equivalent of $102 a barrel in today's money. Unlike the oil shocks of the 1970s and 1980s, which were caused by sudden interruptions in oil supplies from the Middle East, the current surge is fundamentally different. Prices have risen steadily over several years because of a rise in demand for oil and gasoline in both developed and developing countries. China has more than doubled its use of oil since New York crude dropped to this century's low of $16.70 a barrel on 19 November 2001.

(*IHT*, 3 January 2008, p. 1)

Crude oil futures for February delivery hit $100 on the New York Mercantile Exchange shortly after noon Wednesday when a single trader bid up the price by buying a modest lot and then selling it immediately at a small loss. Prices eased somewhat in later trading ... The price of a barrel was below $25 as recently as 2003 and below $11 in 1998, a time when there was a glut in the world markets ... Political tensions in countries like Nigeria, Venezuela and Iran have threatened world supplies, while important fields in Mexico, the United States and other countries are ageing and producing less. Big oil companies are having trouble finding promising new fields to bolster supplies. Newly found fields in the deep waters of the Gulf of Mexico and off the coast of Brazil will take years to develop ... Oil is now within reach of its inflation-adjusted high, reached in April 1980 in the aftermath of the Iranian revolution, when oil prices jumped in the equivalent of $102.81 in today's money.

(*IHT*, 4 January 2008, p. 13)

It is true that the global supply of oil has been growing sluggishly, mainly because the world is, bit by bit, running out of the stuff: big oil discoveries have become rare, and when oil is found it is harder to get at. But the reason oil supply has not been able to keep up with demand is surging oil consumption in newly industrializing economies – above all in China. Even now China accounts for only about 9 per cent of the world's demand for oil. But because China's oil demand has been rising along with its economy, in recent years China has been responsible for about a third of the growth in world oil consumption. As a result, oil at $100 a barrel is, in large part, a made-in-China phenomenon.

(Paul Krugman, *IHT*, 5 January 2008, p. 7)

'US crude oil for August delivery hit a record $147.27 a barrel Friday [11 Friday]' (www.iht.com, 15 July 2008).

'ICE August Brent hit a record $147.50 a barrel yesterday [11 July] ... 57.2 per cent higher since the start of the year [2008] ... Nymex August West Texas Intermediate surged to a peak of $147.27 a barrel' (*FT*, 12 July 2008, p. 27).

'International crude oil prices rose more than 50 per cent in the first half of the year, peaking at $147 a barrel on 11 July. They now hover near $114 a barrel' (www.iht.com, 25 August 2008).

Crude oil on the futures market briefly sank below the $100 a barrel mark Friday [12 September] for the first time in five months ... The last time crude traded below $100 a barrel was on 2 April [2008]. Light sweet crude for October delivery fell as low as $99.99 a barrel on the NYMEX floor. It is now trading around $100.20, down 67 cents from yesterday's [12 September] settle price of $100.87 ... In London October crude rose 94 cents to $98.58 a barrel on the ICE Futures exchange, after closing at a six-month low in the previous trading session.

(www.cnn.com, 13 September 2008)

'Oil prices fell below $100 a barrel yesterday [15 September], the lowest level in seven months' (*FT*, 16 September 2008, p. 19).

'After more than six months of closing in triple-digit territory, oil prices dropped sharply Monday [15 September], falling under the symbolic $100 a barrel threshold as financial woes raised concerns about a slowing US economy and slackening oil demand' (*IHT*, 16 September 2008, p. 14).

'Yesterday [19 December] Nymex January West Texas dropped to $33.44 [a barrel], a four-and-a-half-year trough, before recovering at $35.47' (*FT*, 20 December 2008, p. 25).

> Nymex September West Texas Intermediate oil was $2.13 higher by the close of trading [on 3 August] at $71.58 a barrel, having previously hit an intraday high of $71.95 a barrel. ICE September Brent gained $1.85 to $73.55 a barrel, having earlier set a high for 2009 of $73.75 a barrel.
>
> (*FT*, 4 August 2009, p. 28)

'Brent oil prices have surged from February's year-low of $39.35 a barrel to last week's high of $76 on the back of strong Chinese imports' (*FT*, 12 August 2009, p. 29).

'[US] crude hit a ten-month peak of $75 Tuesday [25 August] before beginning a march downward' (*IHT*, 28 August 2009, p. 19).

'Futures touched $82 on Wednesday [21 October], the highest since 14 October 2008' (*IHT*, 23 October 2009, p. 20).

'Crude oil prices ... hit a fresh 2009 high yesterday [21 October] ... Nymex December West Texas Intermediate rose $2.25 to $81.37' (*FT*, 22 October 2009, p. 32).

'On Monday [4 January 2010] oil for February delivery climbed to $81.51 a barrel, the highest settlement price since 9 October 2008. Oil prices have gradually revived since mid-December [2009]' (www.iht.com, 5 January 2010).

> [On Monday 4 January] oil for February delivery rose to close at $81.51 a barrel, the highest settlement since 9 October 2008 ... Prices have spiked 10 per cent in the last seven sessions. They climbed 78 per cent in 2009 and posted the largest annual percentage gain since 1999, when prices humped 112 per cent during the year. Prices surged 134 per cent since hitting an annual low in February [2009].
>
> (www.cnn.com, 5 January 2010)

'[On Wednesday 6 January] benchmark crude rose to $82.90 in the New York Mercantile Exchange after rising as high as $83.15 earlier in the day' (www.iht. com, 6 January 2010). 'US light crude oil rose to $82.68 a barrel' (*IHT*, 7 January 2010, p. 19).

'[On 6 January] Nymex February West Texas Intermediate ... [rose] to $83.15 a barrel – a fresh fifteen-month high' (*FT*, 7 January 2010, p. 34).

> Crude prices passed $82 a barrel this week, about a $10 increase in the past month ... The energy markets have been relatively stable since early

October [2009], with crude prices moving within a narrow range of $70 to $83. That followed years of erratic prices, with oil trading above $147 a barrel in July 2008 and falling below $33 only five months later. Oil prices recovered steadily through most of last year [2009], and peaked in early January [2010] at just under $84 a barrel.

(IHT, 10 March 2010, p. 19)

The government is anxious to maintain social stability by keeping GDP growth to at least 7 per cent, the figure most commonly quoted in the past to keep unemployment from getting out of hand. Labour unrest has been causing increasing concern.

'It is an article of faith among many economists – and a view publicly stated earlier this year [2008] by Chinese prime minister Wen Jiabao – that China needs a growth rate of at least 7 per cent to avoid massive unemployment' (www.economist.com, 10 November 2008). 'The original estimated for China's minimum rate of growth, which was made in the mid-1990s, was 7 per cent' (*The Economist*, 15 November 2008, p. 88).

More recently somewhat higher figures for minimum GDP growth have been mentioned.

'Most economists estimate that 8 per cent growth is needed to prevent urban unemployment from rising, which could trigger demonstrations and undermine the country's social stability' (www.iht.com, 20 October 2008; *IHT*, 21 October 2008, p. 11).

'The government is expected to supply a fiscal stimulus to keep growth above 8 per cent' (*The Economist*, 11 October 2008, p. 110). 'China's own leaders believe they need growth of at least 8 per cent a year to avoid painful unemployment' (*The Economist*, 15 November 2008, p. 14).

It has become an article of faith in China that output needs to grow by at least 8 per cent a year to create enough jobs for the millions of rural Chinese moving to cities. Growth of less than 8 per cent, it is claimed, will lead to rising unemployment and social unrest.

(p. 88)

'Growth below 9 per cent would be unacceptable for a government targeting 10 million new jobs a year, according to Crédit Suisse Group' (www.iht.com, 12 August 2008; *IHT*, 13 August 2008, p. 15).

Officials in Beijing are determined to 'protect eight', shorthand for the goal of achieving 8 per cent growth this year [2009]. That is the minimum rate deemed necessary to maintain social stability and provide jobs for the 15 million-plus people who enter the job market every year.

(www.iht.com, 5 January 2009)

China is pulling out all the stops to keep the economy growing by at least 8 per cent, a pace considered necessary to absorb the millions of migrant workers and graduates who hit the job market every year. But with all its attention focused on the vigorous 'defence of the eight', Beijing risks losing sight of its ultimate goal – creating enough jobs to preserve social peace – and may end up engineering a jobless recovery. It is not only the rate of growth that is important, but also its sources. Expansion led by capital-intensive industries will not be as effective as one driven by more labour-intensive sectors ... Over the years the link between the link between growth and jobs has weakened.

(*IHT*, 8 January 2009, p. 12)

Large-scale, state-determined infrastructure investment programmes (as well as policies such as extended holidays) were employed by the state to help counter the ill effects of the Asian financial crisis (which started in July 1997 with the attack on the Thai baht).

In more recent years China's leaders fretted over GDP growth exceeding set targets. Inflation rates rose and global imbalances caused international friction (see below). The state tried to moderate growth. Deflationary policy was employed. The authorities are still able to issue instructions to the still largely state-owned commercial banks as regards credit volumes, but greater use is being made of more market-orientated instruments such as rising interest rates and increasing reserve ratios. Particular aim was taken at investment in sectors such as steel and cement (both heavy polluters and energy users as well). Increased pressure was placed on local officials to moderate their investment (a long-running problem because their incentives are greatly affected by local economic performance).

Mid-2008 saw a change of emphasis in government policy. Later on in the year the global financial crisis took hold. Although it was the United States and Europe that were particularly hard hit, it soon became apparent that China was by no means immune in that, among other things, the former were important export markets.

A Politburo meeting on 25 July [2008] replaced the previous national economic goal, preventing overheating of the economy and controlling inflation, with a new target. As enunciated by President Hu Jintao in recent appearances, the objective now is to seek fast and sustained economic growth while still keeping inflation under control.

(www.iht.com, 5 August 2008; *IHT*, 6 August 2008, p. 13)

Chinese leaders ... have long been trying to prevent ... the economy ... from growing too fast, but now they fear that growth is slowing too fast and may slow further ... Later in July a meeting of the ruling Politburo signalled a policy shift. The formerly oft-repeated injunction to prevent overheating was dropped. Instead the leadership decided to focus on maintaining 'steady and fast' economic growth, though it said it would continue its efforts to combat inflation.

(*The Economist*, 9 August 2008, p. 53)

'The expansion of the world's fourth biggest economy has slowed for four quarters' (www.iht.com, 12 August 2008; *IHT*, 13 August 2008, p. 15).

After five years of tightening monetary policy to fight inflation, China abruptly reversed course late Monday afternoon [15 September], cutting interest rates and easing bank lending in response to signs that growth of the economy was finally slowing. China's exports have slowed sharply ... Since 2003 China's top priority has been to control inflation. But China's Politburo ... decided at a meeting on 25 July that the top economic goals should shift to sustaining economic development and limiting inflation, in that order.

(www.iht.com, 15 September 2008; *IHT*, 16 September 2008, p. 17)

China's central bank cut the country's benchmark interest rate last night [15 September] for the first time in more than six years, in the face of global financial turmoil and signs of a slowing domestic economy ... The People's Bank of China also said it would reduce the amount smaller domestic banks must hold in reserve with the central bank by one percentage point to 16.5 per cent from 25 September, freeing up funds for those banks to lend. That will be the first drop in the reserve rate requirement since 1999 but does not extend to the five largest banks or the Postal Bank.

(*FT*, 16 September 2008, p. 12)

'China has cut interest rates twice in three weeks, including a move on Wednesday [8 October]' (www.iht.com, 8 October 2008).

China yesterday [8 October] cut interest rates for the second time in less than a month, a move that complemented the co-ordinated easing by global central banks and signalled official determination to support domestic economic growth. While the People's Bank of China gave no reason for its rate cut and did not link it with that of counterparts in the United States, Europe and elsewhere, analysts said there was little doubt the timing was influenced by the international effort to counter the effects of the global financial crisis ... The 0.27 percentage point cut brought the rate for one-year bank loans to 6.93 per cent and followed a reduction of the same size in mid-September. Beijing also reduced the proportion of deposits that banks must hold in reserve by half a percentage point ... A 5 per cent withholding tax levied on interest income would be suspended.

(*FT*, 9 October 2008, p. 10)

China has become the main engine of the world economy, accounting for one-third of global GDP growth in the first half of this year [2008] ... The government is expected to supply a fiscal stimulus to keep growth above 8 per cent ... China has ample room for a stimulus because it boasts the healthiest fiscal position of any big economy ... Compared with many other emerging economies, notably Brazil and Russia, which have recently suffered big capital outflows, China has so far largely shrugged off the global credit crunch ... It has a budget surplus of 2 per cent of GDP, if measured in the same way as in rich countries, and public sector debt is a mere 16 per cent of GDP.

(*The Economist*, 11 October 2008, p. 110)

The State Council, or cabinet, met over the weekend and decided to shift the emphasis of economic policy toward maintaining 'a stable and rapid economic development', state-controlled media reported Monday [20 October]. The previous policy has been 'to ensure growth and control inflation'.

(www.iht.com, 20 October 2008; *IHT*, 21 October 2008, p. 11)

Economic growth in China slowed to 9 per cent in the third quarter of this year [2008], the slowest pace in more than five years, as industrial production and construction slackened because of weak exports, a slumping real estate market and temporary restrictions imposed during the Olympics ... Growth of 9 per cent in the third quarter was slower than most economists expected, with surveys having previously put the average forecast for the quarter at anywhere from 9.1 per cent to 9.7 per cent ... Inflation is slowing at the consumer level ... It was 4.6 per cent in September, down from 4.9 per cent in August and the fifth monthly decline.

(www.iht.com, 20 October 2008)

After five years of growth exceeding 10 per cent, China's growth has decelerated for five consecutive quarters, dropping to about 9 per cent in the third quarter of this year [2008] from 12.6 per cent in the second quarter of 2007 ... Economists expect the economy to expand at an annualized rate of as little as 5.8 per cent in the fourth quarter, down from nearly 11.2 per cent in 2007.

(*IHT*, 7 November 2008, p. 13)

'[There was] 10.6 per cent growth in the first quarter of the year [2008] and 10.1 per cent in the second quarter' (www.independent.co.uk, 20 October 2008).

China's GDP for the first nine months of 2008 increased by 9.9 per cent. 2.3 per cent lower than last year [2007] ... The rate of expansion was the lowest since the second quarter of 2003. when the outbreak of SARS cooled growth to 6.7 per cent ... A fall in the growth of exports due to the global economic slowdown was one of the reasons for the cooling of the economy ... The official Xinhua news agency reported this week that 3,631 toy exporters – 52.7 per cent of the industry's enterprises – went out of business in 2008 ... [owing to] higher production costs, wage increases and the rising value of the yuan.

(www.cnn.com, 20 October 2008)

Slightly more than half the country's toy exporters shut down in the first seven months of this year [2008], mostly very small companies that struggled to cope with new safety standards as well as weakening Western demand, according to China's customs agency.

(*IHT*, 23 October 2008, p. 12)

After five years of growth in excess of 10 per cent, the economy is weakening because of slowing exports and investment growth, declining consumption, and severely depressed stock and property markets. Factory closures in southern China, often dubbed the factory floor of the world, have led to mass lay-offs and even sporadic protests by workers who complained that owners disappeared without paying them their wages.

(www.iht.com, 9 November 2008)

'[Some] 67,000 export-producing factories have closed already this year [2008]' (www.iht.com, 12 November 2008). 'The slowdown in exports contributed to the closing of at least 67,000 factories across China in the first half of the year [2008], according to government statistics. Labour disputes and protests over lost back pay have surged' (www.iht.com, 14 November 2008).

> Guangdong province, in southern China, has been the hardest hit. Thousands of firms making shoes, toys and clothing have been forced to close this year [2008] ... Half of China's toymakers and one-third of its shoe firms have disappeared this year. Yet toys and shoes now account for less than 5 per cent of China's total exports. Exports of machinery and transport equipment [comprise] almost half the total ... UBS, a bank, forecasts that in 2009 net exports will be a negative drag on growth. In 2007 net exports contributed almost 3 percentage points of the 12 per cent increase in GDP.
>
> (*The Economist*, 15 November 2008, pp. 87–9)

> Direct losses by Chinese financial institutions from the US subprime crisis are not huge. Commercial banks have eagerly defended their slight involvement or non-involvement in the crisis. Among the banks Bank of China has the most exposure. In its annual report it said its investment in subprime asset-backed securities was $4.99 last year [2007]. The International Commercial Bank of China, the country's largest commercial lender, suffered a loss of $1.2 billion from the crisis.
>
> (He Fan, *The World Today*, November 2008, p. 7)

'Household debt [is] almost non-existent' (*The Economist*, 25 October 2008, p. 70).

> The government announced a series of measures late Wednesday [22 October] to bolster real estate prices. The central bank ordered commercial banks to reduce mortgage rates and down payments for borrowers obtaining their first mortgage, beginning next Monday [27 October]. And the finance ministry reduced the stamp tax on real estate purchases effective 1 November, but only for first time home buyers acquiring an apartment of less than 90 square metres, or 970 square feet ... Under the rules announced Wednesday mortgage interest rates will be reduced ... Mortgage lending is more tightly regulated than in the West. In China roughly half of all home buyers still pay cash and do not obtain a mortgage at all – although they might borrow some of the cash from friends, families or neighbours. For those who do obtain mortgages, the down payment is 30 per cent for buyers taking out their first mortgage and 40 per cent or more for buyers who have a mortgage on another home. Under the new measures announced Wednesday the

down payment will fall to 20 per cent for buyers seeking their first mortgage. But many cities, including Shenzhen, had already lowered the down payment to 20 per cent for buyers obtaining their first mortgage ... The term of a mortgage must end when the borrower reaches a certain age – fifty-five for a woman and sixty for a man ... It is nearly impossible for Chinese banks to foreclose on homes. Instead, banks tend to renegotiate monthly payments for borrowers who can clearly demonstrate financial strain. Chinese banks hold the mortgages they issue instead of following the US practice of bundling them together as securities and reselling pieces to various investors. The process, known as securitization, is now making it hard for homeowners in the United States to renegotiate their mortgages ... Chinese banks are flush with cash, with capital equal to 12 per cent to 14 per cent of assets, compared with the international regulatory standard of 8 per cent ... Starting in 2004 Beijing officials tried to limit real estate speculation through administrative measures, by setting quotas on real estate lending done by each bank ... In addition to requiring larger down payments for second and third homes, banks charge interest rates that are up to 3 percentage points higher for these homes than for first time home buyers.

(*IHT*, 24 October 2008, pp. 11, 13)

'[In China] if you try to walk away from the mortgage, the bank will come after your personal assets' (*IHT*, 22 December 2008, p. 7).

'The authorities announced rises this week for export rebates on 3,000 products, including textiles, garments, furniture and some electrical machinery. Increased rebates for steel exporters are being considered' (*FT*, 24 October 2008, p. 8).

Asian and European leaders gathered in Beijing for a summit [the seventh such meeting] on 24 and 25 October that was dominated by the global financial crisis ... China proclaimed itself relatively unscathed ... [Prime minister Wen Jiabao] said 'the impact is limited and controllable' ... The crisis is pushing the world's fourth largest economy, with the biggest foreign exchange reserves, to the centre of global summitry ... China has $1.9 trillion in reserves and Japan has nearly $1 trillion ... Chinese leaders told Asem that their priority was to keep their own economy running smoothly. This, said Mr Wen, was 'China's greatest contribution to the world'.

(*The Economist*, 1 November 2008, p. 67)

'Capital controls and a tightly managed exchange rate shielded China from the worst of the 1997–8 financial crisis and are once more offering a large degree of protection' (*IHT*, 28 October 2008, p. 11).

'[On 29 October] the benchmark one-year deposit rate [was cut] from 3.87 per cent to 3.60 per cent' (*FT*, 30 October 2008, p. 7).

'The central bank cut banks' benchmark lending and deposit rates by 0.27 percentage points on Wednesday [29 October], the third cut in six weeks' (www.iht.com, 30 October 2008). 'On 29 October the central bank reduced its benchmark one-year lending rate to 6.66 per cent from 6.93 per cent' (www.iht.com, 2 November 2008).

> Prime minister Wen Jiabao said maintaining the strong economic growth in China was a top priority ... Wen, writing in the Communist Party's ideological journal ... *Qiushi* or *Seeking Truth* ... warned of growing domestic social risks from a global economic downturn. Wen Jiabao: 'Against the current international financial and economic turmoil we must give even greater priority to maintaining our country's steady and relatively fast economic development. We must be crystal clear that without a certain pace of economic growth there will be difficulties with employment, fiscal measures and social development, and factors damaging social stability will grow.'
>
> (www.iht.com, 2 November 2008)

'China announced over the weekend that it was loosening limits on bank lending' (*IHT*, Tuesday 4 November 2008, p. 12). 'Last month [October] Beijing approved a massive $292 billion for the construction of railways and a $19 billion capital infusion for Agricultural Bank of China as part of a restructuring that could eventually cost $100 billion' (www.iht.com, 3 November 2008).

'Prime minister Wen Jiabao said yesterday [10 November]: "Our top task is to maintain steady and relatively fast economic growth"' (*FT*, 11 November 2008, p. 6).

> China announced a massive economic stimulus package Sunday [9 November], aimed at bolstering its weakening economy and fighting the effects of the global economic slowdown. Beijing said it would spend an estimated 4 trillion yuan, or $586 billion, on a wide array of infrastructure and social welfare projects, which would include constructing new railways, subways, airports and rebuilding depressed communities. The package, which was announced by the State Council on Sunday evening [9 November], is the largest economic stimulus ever undertaken by the Chinese government and would amount to about 7 per cent of the country's GDP during each of the next two years. Beijing said it was loosening credit criteria and encouraging lending ... A statement said China's cabinet had approved a plan to invest 4 trillion yuan ($596 billion) in infrastructure and social welfare by the end of 2010. Some of the money will come from the private sector. The statement did not say how much of the spending is on new projects and how much is for ventures already in the pipeline that will be speeded up. China's export-driven growth is starting to feel the impact of the economic slowdown in the United States and Europe ... The statement said the cabinet ... had 'decided to adopt active fiscal policy and moderately easy monetary policies' ... At $586 billion the stimulus package is enormous for any country, let alone one whose GDP was only about $3.3 trillion in 2007. Earlier this year the US Congress passed a $700 billion bailout package in a country with an

economy close to $14 trillion. Analysts were expecting China to announce a big stimulus package but were surprised at the size of it.

(www.iht.com, 9 November 2008; *IHT*, 10 November 2008, pp. 1, 12)

J.P. Morgan in Hong Kong said in a research note on Monday [10 November] that economists had widely expected earlier this year a stimulus package amounting to about 1.5 per cent of Chinese GDP. The package announced Sunday is about ten times as big.

(www.iht.com, 10 November 2008)

[The] 4 trillion ($596 billion) stimulus package [is] the largest in the country's history ... The two-year spending initiative will inject funds into ten sectors, including health care, education, low-income housing, environmental protection, schemes to promote technological innovation, and transport and other infrastructure projects. The government also says that some of the spending will be directed to reconstruction efforts in areas battered by natural disasters, such as Sichuan province which was devastated by a massive earthquake in May. The State Council said: 'Over the past two months, the global financial crisis has been intensifying daily. In expanding investment we must be fast and heavy-handed' ... Officials say that fourth quarter investment for this year will total 400 billion yuan, including 20 billion yuan brought forward from next year's [2009] central government budget. If fully realized the two-year spending spree would amount to about 16 per cent of China's annual GDP. The newly announced measures also include a loosening of credit policies and tax cuts. The plan calls for reforms of the country's value-added tax regime that would save industry 120 billion yuan ... Much remains unclear about the implementation of the stimulus plan – or even its size ... The real size of the package may not be as large as the government has described ... [The view has been expressed that] some of the measures announced in the stimulus package appear to been already introduced or even implemented earlier.

(www.economist.com, 10 November 2008)

The 4 trillion yuan stimulus package ... is to be spent over the next two years. It amounts to 14 per cent of this year's estimated GDP [2008]. The total increase in spending, if genuine, would surely represent the biggest two-year stimulus (outside wartime) by any government in history ... A reform of the VAT system will allow firms to deduct purchases of fixed assets, reducing companies' tax bills by an estimated ... 4 per cent of 2007 industrial profits ... The budget surplus stands at 1 per cent to 2 per cent of GDP (depending on how you measure it) and total public sector debt at less than 20 per cent of GDP [is] one of the smallest of any large economy ... Some commentators have criticized the package for focusing too much on investment (which is already high as a share of GDP in China) rather than spurring consumption through income tax cuts. But in a country like China, where the saving rate is high and confidence is falling, infrastructure investment is much better at boosting growth than tax cuts or welfare payments, which would probably be saved rather than spent ... [In addition] China plainly needs bridges and railways ... But in any case, in contrast to previous fiscal stimuli in China, this package does include some modest measures to boost consumption, such as raising the incomes of farmers and low-income households. Increased spending on health and education should also help to reduce households' worries about how to pay for these services and so encourage them to save less and spend more.

(*The Economist*, 15 November 2008, pp. 87–9)

The State Council, China's cabinet, authorized $586 billion of investment on infrastructure and social welfare over the next two years, although it did not say how much would be on new projects not already in the budget ... The announcement reflects mounting anxiety in Beijing that China's economy is cooling much more quickly than expected in the face of weaker international demand and a slowdown in the local property market ... Some economists believe that growth, which was nearly 12 per cent last year [2007], could fall as low as 6 per cent next year [2009] without a substantial fiscal stimulus.

(*FT*, 10 November 2008, p. 6)

The authorities ... gave no details about how exactly the money would be spent or how much of it would be genuinely new spending not already in the pipeline ... Arthur Kroeber of Dragonomics in Beijing said the extra investment as a result of the fiscal package might be as little as a third of the headline figure, at about 1,300 billion renminbi. That is still about 2 per cent of GDP each year, but much less than the initial reports suggest.

(*FT*, 11 November 2008, p. 6)

'Parts of the scheme have been announced before so the true size of the new stimulus is not clear' (p. 16).

The stimulus is taking the wrong form. Rather than trying to prop up the Chinese economy as it was, this is an opportunity to turn it into an economy China wants – one where consumption at home has more than a cameo role.

(*FT*, editorial, 11 November 2008, p. 16)

China admitted yesterday [14 November] that the central government would provide little more than a quarter of Beijing's planned renminbi 4,000 billion fiscal stimulus package, The news has cast fresh doubts on the likely boost to the economy from public spending. Mu Hong, vice chairman of the National Development and Reform Commission, a government planning agency, said Beijing would increase spending by renminbi 1,189 billion ($172 billion) over the next two years – leaving local government, state-owned banks and companies to provide the rest of the new funds ... Yi Gang, deputy governor of the People's Bank of China, said the risk of inflation had 'basically vanished'. The focus of policy now was to 'avoid potential deflation … and to ensure stable economic growth'. He said China would 'actively participate' in efforts to counter the global financial crisis, including working with the IMF and making bilateral currency swap arrangements.

(*FT*, 15 November 2008, p. 9)

Hints of concern about highly expansionary monetary policy were to be found by the spring of 2009.

'China's central bank on yesterday [12 April] warned it planned to "strictly control" credit to some sectors of the economy after the country recorded a surge in bank loans and money supply on March' (*FT*, 13 April 2009, p. 6).

'The central bank said it will "implement moderately loose monetary policy and maintain the continuity and stability of policy". It also said it would provide "ample liquidity to ensure money supply and loan growth meet economic development needs"' (*The Independent*, 13 April 2009).

China's finance ministry has failed to sell all 28 billion yuan ($4.1 billion) of one-year government bonds it offered at an auction. It is the first undersubscribed government bond auction since 2003 … It comes as the government looks to tighten its monetary policy to prevent the risk of asset bubbles, loan defaults and rapid inflation … The city of Hangzhou has started tightening mortgage lending terms, ahead of any changes to monetary and credit policies by the national government … Chinese property prices nationwide have increased since March, after several months of falls.

(www.bbc.co.uk, 8 July 2009)

Money supply growth surged in June … The broad M2 measure of money supply grew at a record pace of 28.5 per cent in June, blowing past forecasts of a 26 per cent rise and accelerating from a 25.7 per cent increase in May … In a new sign of its worry that rapid lending could fuel spending, the central bank responded with the latest in a series of baby steps to absorb surplus cash washing through the economy by requiring banks to buy 100 billion yuan ($15 billion) in special bills … Traders said the central bank would issue the bills in September at a punitively low interest rate to a clutch of banks that have been responsible for a growing share of new loans. The operation means those banks will have less money to lend out … Other recent steps in recent weeks by the central bank indicating that monetary loosening is over, even if outright tightening has not yet begun, include the resumption of one-year bill sales and an increase in yield on open market operations.

(www.iht.com, 15 July 2009)

The central bank has begun to tug gently at the reins. It has nudged up money market interest rates and warned banks that it intends to increase its scrutiny of new bank loans. The China Banking Regulatory Commission has warned banks to stick to rules on mortgages for second homes, which require a down-payment of at least 40 per cent of a property's value …

Housing starts rose 12 per cent in the year to June, the first growth in twelve months.

(The Economist, 18 July 2009, pp. 57–8)

In the first half of this year [2009] banks lent $1,079 billion, nearly double the total extended in 2008 ... The People's Bank of China has quietly increased inter-bank lending rates in recent weeks, to make it more expensive for small local lenders to access funds.

(FT, 16 July 2009, p. 6)

Chinese regulators on Monday [27 July] ordered banks to ensure unprecedented volumes of new loans are channelled into the real economy and not diverted into equity or real estate markets where officials say fresh asset bubbles are forming. The new policy requires banks to monitor how their loans are spent and comes amid warnings that banks ignored basic lending standards in the first half of this year [2009] as they rushed to extend renminbi 7,370 billion ($1,080 billion) in new loans, more than twice the amount lent in the same period a year earlier.

(www.ft.com, 27 July 2009; *FT*, 28 July 2009, p. 5)

In China there is little debate. The government simply orders banks to lend – and it happens almost instantly ... Last month [July] the central bank called for stricter supervision of bank loans because some stimulus spending appeared to be directed toward wasteful government projects. The China Banking Regulatory Commission also recently took steps to lower risk by ordering Chinese banks to raise their bad-loan reserve rations by the end of the year [2009]. Liu Mingkang (the top banking regulator in late July): 'Rapid expansion of bank loans in the first half year boosted the country's economic growth. But it also increased the possibilities of financial risk' ... At a high level Politburo meeting last month [July] President Hu Jintao called for the country to maintain a 'relatively loose' monetary policy and signalled that the direction of macroeconomic policy 'should be maintained' ... Through June banking regulators said non-performing loans at China's commercial banks accounted for just 1.74 per cent of outstanding loans – down slightly from the beginning of the year. But many experts say that could change in the coming years, as these new loans come due. They suspect that government pressure on banks to make loans will result in loan defaults.

(IHT, 7 August 2009, p. 16)

China's central bank has told the heads of the largest state-controlled banks to slow the pace of new lending, say people familiar with the matter, after new loan volume in the first half of the year tripled from the same period a year earlier. The pressure from the People's Bank of China signals an unstated shift in policy and comes as it steps up its open market operations to control liquidity and slow loan growth. Over the past two weeks China's leaders have emphasized the country will adhere for now to its policy of 'moderately loose' monetary conditions. While there has been no formal change to what is an extremely loose monetary policy, the central bank and regulators have signalled an intention to rein in excessive lending through various policy announcements. The People's Bank of China has raised interest rates in recent weeks on its weekly sales of short-term bills in the interbank market and has ordered the most profligate lenders to buy set amounts of special low-interest, one-year central bank notes, increasing pressure on banks to toe the line ... Officials fear some of the renminbi 7,370 billion ($1.078 billion) in new loans extended in the first half of the year has found its way into the bubbling stock and property markets ... China Construction Bank ... [said it] plans to extend renminbi 200 billion of loans in the second half, down from renminbi 709 billion in the first half. It is usual in China for banks to frontload lending in the first half of the year and extend much less in the latter half but a 70 per cent drop would be extreme ... On Wednesday [5 August] the central bank hinted at shifting priorities when it said in a quarterly report it would carry out 'market-based fine tuning measures' while 'unswervingly implementing the moderately loose monetary policy'.

(www.ft.com, 7 August 2009; *FT*, 8 August 2009, p. 5)

Further tightening measures are likely in the coming months, as the economy continues to recover. In addition, since bank lending in China is typically front-loaded (with most of the lending taking place in the first half of the year), a sharp fall can be expected over the next few months.

(www.economist.com, 7 August 2009)

'Prices continued to fall in July from a year earlier, reducing the likelihood that Beijing will make any significant changes to its policy of boosting growth with fresh liquidity and surging infrastructure spending' (*FT*, 12 August 2009, p. 4).

A sharp sell-off in Chinese shares in late Wednesday [19 August] trading saw the benchmark SCI close 4.3 per cent lower, putting it in sight of a bear market as speculation grew that the Beijing government would tighten its monetary policy ... Beijing is thought to be concerned about illegal lending to property developers and banks are tightening control over the approval of mortgages. New lending in July was down sharply to renminbi 355.9 billion ($52 billion) from renminbi 1,530 billion the previous month [June], raising fears that liquidity would disappear from the stock market.

(www.ft.com, 19 August 2009)

Rumours are rife that banks' capital requirements are being tightened, as are the conditions for various kinds of loans. A decline in new lending in the second half of the year had been expected; the rate of decline has, for many, been a shock.

(*The Economist*, 29 August 2009, pp. 66–7)

New bank lending did indeed slow sharply in July, to 356 billion yuan ($52 billion) from 1.53 trillion yuan in June. But bank lending always slows in the second half of the year; the twelve-month pace of growth is therefore a better measure. On a year-on-year basis bank lending grew by a impressive 34 per cent in July, roughly the same pace as in June.

(p. 67)

The 25–26 September 2009 G-20 meeting took place in the US city of Pittsburg.

The G-20 group of leading and emerging economies is to take on a new role as a permanent body co-ordinating the world economy, a White House statement said. It will take on the role previously carried out by ... the G-8 group ... The G-20 is meeting in the US city of Pittsburgh for a two-day summit. EU officials also announced a deal to shift the balance of voting in the [186-member] IMF towards such growing nations such as China ... A White House statement announced the new role for the G-20: 'The G-20 leaders reached a historic agreement to put the G-20 at the centre of their efforts to work together to build a durable recovery while avoiding the financial fragilities that led to the crisis. Today [25 September] leaders endorsed the G-20 as the premier forum for their international economic co-operation.'

(www.bbc.co.uk, 25 September 2009)

The G-20 would focus on economic issues while the G-8 would deal primarily with international relations and foreign policy ... The G-20 ... was created [in September 1999] at a meeting of G-7 finance ministers in response to the Asian financial crisis of 1997–9 ... The new G-20 Framework for Strong, Sustainable and Balanced Growth aims to work in three stages. First, national leaders agree priorities for the world economy in annual G-20 summits. Second, countries submit reports to show how their domestic policies match those ambitions. Third, the IMF assesses whether national plans mesh together to support global objectives. The enforcement mechanism will be peer review.

(*FT*, 26 September 2009, p. 6)

[The] communiqué said: 'Today we designated the G-20 as the premier forum for our international economic co-operations ... G-20 leaders agreed to: launch a Framework for Strong Sustainable and Balanced Growth'; strengthen financial regulation, via reformed rules on capital adequacy and remuneration of bank employees; reform the global institutional architecture, including reallocation of quotas in the IMF; phase out fossil fuel subsidies; 'bring the Doha round to a successful conclusion in 2010'; reach agreement in Copenhagen on climate change; and meet twice in 2010, first in Canada and then in South Korea.

(*FT*, 28 September 2009, p. 12)

In the short term, the G-20 also agreed to continue with the current stimulus measures, insisting they had been effective in preventing the recession tipping over into a great depression. The IMF is now predicting 3 per cent growth worldwide next year [2010] ... the measure should be continued until a durable recovery had been secured, the communiqué said.

(*Guardian*, 26 September 2009, p. 18)

'The last time the leaders of the G-20 met, in London in April [2009], their task was to steer the world away from a 1930s-style depression' (www.economist.com, 26 September 2009).

[The] communiqué: '[At the April London summit in April] our countries agreed to ensure recovery, to repair our financial systems and to maintain the global flow of capital. It worked ... The process of recovery and repair remains incomplete. In many countries unemployment remains unacceptably high. The conditions for a recovery of private demand are not yet fully in place' ... G-20 leaders agreed to avoid premature withdrawal of stimulus ... [and] plan their exit strategies.

(*FT*, 28 September 2009, p. 12)

'The state-controlled banking system has given out a record $1.27 trillion in new loans this year, and some analysts have warned that too much of that money has ended up in stocks and real estate' (www.iht.com, 22 October 2009; *IHT*, 23 October 2009, p. 19).

Beijing has used its control over banks to engineer a massive increase in lending, with new loans in the first nine months of the year [2009] 149 per cent higher than last year [2008] at renminbi 8,650 billion ($1,270 billion) ... The State Council gave its first clear hint yesterday [21 October] that it was considering a tighter monetary policy when it said strategy should focus on managing inflationary expectations as well as securing stable growth – the first time it has mentioned inflation since the global economic crisis hit the country last year.

(*FT*, 22 October 2009, p. 6)

Li Xiaochao (spokesman for the National Bureau of Statistics: 22 October): 'In the following period we will stick to continuity and stability in our economic policy. According to my understanding, that means no change in policy' ... In spite of yesterday's caution [22 October], the government has given hints that it might be starting to shift strategy. The State Council said on Wednesday [21 October] it would focus on inflationary expectations, its first mention since the crisis started of potential price rises, while a government economist [Chen Daufu of the Development Research Centre] reportedly suggested a stronger currency could be used to limit price rises.

(*FT*, 23 October 2009, p. 10)

The IMF on Thursday [29 October] raised its outlook for growth in Asia for this year and next, reflecting the region's rapid rebound from the depths of the global downturn in recent months ... China will enjoy by far the fastest growth – 8.5 per cent this year and 9 per cent in 2010 ... The Asian Development Bank last month [September] said it now expected China to grow

8.2 per cent this year – 1.2 percentage points higher than what it had forecast in March – and 8.9 per cent next year ... Australia earlier this month
became the first major central bank to start nudging interest rates up again
and Norway followed suit on Wednesday [28 October] with a quarter percentage point increase in its key rate.

(www.iht.com, 20 October 2009)

'The IMF ... raised growth forecasts for 2010 ... [as regards China] from 7.5
per cent to 9 per cent' (*FT*, 30 October 2009, p. 9).

The World Bank on Wednesday [4 November] became the latest major
institution to raise its forecast for growth in China ... though it cautioned
that more policy adjustments would be necessary in the medium term to
ensure that the recovery would be sustained. The World Bank now expects
the economy to grow 8.4 per cent this year [2009] ... up from the 7.2 per
cent it forecast in June. It predicts growth of 8.7 per cent next year
[2010].

(www.iht.com, 4 November 2009; *IHT*, 5 November 2009, p. 18)

Louis Kuijs (the World Bank's chief economist):

We think that now that the government has basically succeeded in dampening the impact of the global crisis, it is a good time to concentrate and focus
effort on rebalancing the economy and getting more growth out of the
domestic economy. This calls for more emphasis on consumption and services and less emphasis on investment and industry.

(www.bbc.co.uk, 4 November 2009)

The G-20 statement (issued after its 7 November meeting in the UK):

The recovery is uneven and remains dependent on policy support, and high
unemployment is a major concern. To restore the global economy and financial system to health, we agreed to maintain support for the recovery until it
is assured.'

(www.bbc.co.uk, 8 November 2009)

New data indicated that economic recovery accelerated last month [October]
... Industrial production rose 16.1 per cent on the same month last year
[2008], the fastest rate of growth since March 2008 ... The robust debate
will intensify the debate about whether the government needs to sharply
scale back its aggressive stimulus policies amid growing fears of asset
bubbles and inflation. The headline rate of new lending in local currency
declined sharply last month to renminbi 252 billion ($37 billion) from ren-
minbi 516.7 billion ... But economists pointed out that the level of medium-
term loans, which are more important for the economy than short-term
credit, remained strong and that foreign exchange loans and capital inflows
were also rising.

(*FT*, 12 November 2009, p. 6)

'Most economists do not expect China to start raising interest rates until well into next year [2010]' (www.iht.com, 11 November 2009). (For later developments, see below.)

GDP growth has been especially driven by exports and investment and encouraging private consumption is seen as helpful in both China and abroad to correct global imbalances (e.g. by increasing Chinese imports). Private consumption is depressed by factors such as much reduced social service provision (such as health) in the new China. China has high saving and investment rates. There are very few alternative outlets to domestic banks. Hence the large savings deposits in banks.

'[The] deputy governor of the People's Bank of China: "The savings rate in China is more than 40 per cent [of GDP]. In the United States it is less than 2 per cent"' (*FT*, 3 November 2004, p. 9).

> The savings rate in China climbed to more than 43 per cent of income in 2004 from about 26 per cent in 1985, according to official figures ... In the United States the savings rate fell to less than 1 per cent in the first quarter of this year [2005], according to the ... [US] Department of Commerce ... In many West European economies savings rates now stand at about 10 per cent or slightly higher, according to the Organization for Economic Co-operation and Development [OECD].
>
> (*IHT*, 14 June 2005, p. 2)

'At more than 40 per cent of GDP, and 25 per cent of household income, it [China's savings rate] is among the world's highest and vastly exceeds existing investment needs' (*FT*, 25 July 2005, p. 15).

'[China] has one of the highest rates of savings in any economy – the gross saving rate approaches half of GDP' (OECD 2005: website Chapter 1).

'Investment accounts for nearly 45 per cent of China's GDP and 90 per cent of that is financed domestically (the national savings rate is 55 per cent of GDP). Foreign direct investment accounts for less than 5 per cent of GDP' (Aziz and Dunaway 2007: 28).

> Personal consumption's share of GDP has fallen by more than 12 percentage points, to about 40 per cent, one of the lowest levels in the world. While household savings are high and their rate has increased somewhat in recent years, this can explain only about 1 percentage point of the drop. Nearly all the decline is attributable to a falling share of national income going to households, including wages, investment income and government transfers. Many countries have seen their wage share decline. But in most countries overall household income has held up reasonably well because rising dividend and interest income have offset the falling wage share. In China, though, household investment income has declined from more than 6 per cent of GDP in the mid-1990s to less than 2 per cent today, mainly because of low deposit rates and limited household equity ownership (directly or through institutional investors). Moreover, in most countries profits of SOEs are transferred to the government, which uses them to provide consumption

goods such as health care and education, and income transfers to households. But in China the government receives no dividends, and transfers to households and public spending on health and education have declined.

(p. 29)

In the 1994 SOE reforms the provision of health care, education and pensions was transferred from companies to local government. However, in general, local governments were not provided with adequate resources to discharge these new responsibilities. Consequently, households have had to bear an increasing portion of the costs of health care and education. Chinese households pay about 80 per cent of health care costs out of their own pockets.

(p. 31)

'Household consumption [in China] last year [2007] came to just 35.3 per cent of GDP, an unprecedented low in peacetime for a major country' (*IHT*, 30 September 2008, p. 8). 'In the 1980s it was over 50 per cent. By comparison, household consumption last year [2007] made up 72 per cent of US GDP' (www.iht.com, 8 December 2008; *IHT*, 9 December 2008, p. 13).

In the mid-1980s Americans saved about 10 per cent of their income. Lately, however, the saving rate has generally been below 2 per cent – sometimes it has even been negative – and consumer debt has risen to 98 per cent of GDP, twice its level a quarter-century ago.

(Paul Krugman, *IHT*, 1 November 2008, p. 9)

'Americans on average stow away 1 per cent of their income. The Chinese on average save more than 25 per cent, giving them the world's most prodigious savers' (*IHT*, 3 December 2008, p. 12).

'In America the household savings ratio (the proportion of disposable income not used for consumption) has been below 2.5 per cent since 1999; in Britain it has been below 3 per cent in each of the past two years' (*The Economist*, 6 December 2008, p. 11).

Consumer spending is just 36 per cent of GDP, half the American shares ... Household savings have been broadly flat. (The rise in China's savings rate comes from firms and the government, not households.) If households are not saving more, why has consumer spending declined as a share of GDP? The answer is that wage incomes have fallen relative to GDP. In China the share of wages dropped from 53 per cent in 1998 to 40 per cent in 2007 ... Even if household saving rates have been falling, they are still high, at around 20 per cent in both China and Taiwan.

(*The Economist*, 31 January 2009, p. 75)

In 2008 private consumption accounted for only 35 per cent of GDP, down from 49 per cent in 1990. By contrast investment had risen from 35 per cent to 44 per cent of GDP. This year [2009] the bulk of the government's stimulus is going into infrastructure, further swelling investment's share ... Consumption as a share of GDP has fallen and is extremely low by international standards: only 35 per cent, compared with 50 per cent to 60 per cent in most other Asian countries and 70 per cent in America. Economists disagree about the main reason why the consumption ration has fallen – and hence the best way to lift it. The most popular explanation is that Chinese households have been saving a bigger slice of their income because of an inadequate social safety net. They have squirrelled away more money to cover the future cost of health care, education and pensions ... [It has been suggested] that the extra saving may owe as much to greater income inequality as to the lack of a welfare state. Rich people save a lot more and their numbers have increased ... The more important reason why consumption has fallen is that the share of national income going to households (as wages and investment income) has fallen, while the share of profits has risen ... [It has been estimated that] households accounted for only one-fifth of the increase in total domestic saving over the period [1998 to 2008]. Most of the increase in saving came from companies.

(*The Economist*, 1 August 2009, pp. 65–6)

'[In China] consumption to GDP in 1981 ... [at] 93.4 per cent ... was higher than America's' (*IHT*, 23 April 2009, p. 23).

Many economists had attributed the increase ... in the national savings rate during the past decade ... to higher corporate profits ... But recently revised statistics showing the flow of funds through China's economy from 1992 to 2007 have reopened the debate. Calla Wiemer with the Center for Chinese Studies at the University of California, Los Angeles, says a leap in the national savings rate to 51.4 per cent of GDP in 2008 – by far the highest level in any major economy in the world – largely reflected increased household savings as a result of changing demographic and income patterns. The flow of funds also shows that government saving surged to 10.6 per cent of national disposable income – which includes GDP plus net income and transfers from abroad – in 2007 from just 4.5 per cent in 2004. Big increases in revenue were either saved or used to pay off debt to the neglect of social welfare spending ... Interpreting Chinese statistics, however, is tricky ... Louis Kuijs ... a World Bank economist in Beijing ... and UBS economist Jonathan Anderson ... both remain of the view that corporations explain the vast share of the jump in national savings.

(*IHT*, 16 February 2010, p. 20)

China's savings help keep interest rates down in the United States (and so globally) through the purchase of vast amounts of US government bonds, but China's ever-rising bilateral trade surpluses with the United States and the EU in particular have ratcheted up the friction level. Even though the yuan has appreciated against the dollar, the United States still considers it undervalued, to China's advantage since its exports are cheaper and its imports dearer. To keep the yuan from appreciating too quickly against the US dollar the Chinese authorities buy dollars at home, adding to the country's ever-growing foreign exchange reserves. To moderate the increase in the money supply (and thus price increases), the Chinese authorities sell bonds in the domestic market. China's foreign exchange reserves exceeded $1 trillion by the end of 2006 and the figure keeps rising.

('China overtook Japan as the world's largest holder of foreign exchange reserves at the end of February [2006]' (www.iht.com, 5 July 2006. 'Foreign [exchange] holdings stood at $1,433 billion in September [2007]': *FT*, 7 November 2007, p. 10. 'Foreign exchange reserves ... hit another high of $1.76 trillion at the end of April [2008]': www.economist.com, 10 June 2008. 'According to leaked official figures, China's foreign exchange reserves jumped by $115 billion during April and May [2008] to $1.8 trillion': *The Economist*, 28 June 2008, p. 95. 'Foreign exchange reserves grew to $1,810 billion at the end of June [2008] ... China's foreign exchange reserves are the biggest in the world': *FT*, 15 July 2008, p. 11. China's foreign exchange reserves increased ... from $1,499 billion at the end of August 2007 to $1,810 billion by the end of June [2008]': *FT*, 12 September 2008, p. 6. 'Figures released this week show that foreign exchange reserves now total $1.9 trillion': www.bbc.co.uk, 20 October 2008. 'Foreign exchange reserves rose by $40.4 billion in the final quarter [of 2008] to $1,946 billion': *FT*, 16 January 2009, p. 6.)

'As of September [2007] ... China owned $396.7 billion of US Treasury securities ... up from $71.4 billion in 2000 ... Among foreign nations, only Japan, with $582.2 billion, owns more US government debt' (*IHT*, 11 December 2007, p. 15).

> In 2004 China bought a fifth of US Treasury securities issued, a proportion that rose to 30 per cent in 2005 and to 36 per cent in 2006. But according to US government figures, in 2007 China has reversed course and become a net seller of Treasury securities. The US Treasury said this week that China had $388 billion of Treasury bonds at the end of October [2007], or $10 billion less than it had at the end of 2006 ... But the figures may be misleading ... The initial estimates are based on reports of transactions in securities and those involving long-term securities, like Treasury bonds and notes, reflect only the initial buyer ... Each June the Treasury does a survey of actual holdings. The survey from June 2007 will be incorporated in the data in February [2008] ... The June 2006 figure was revised up by $62 billion.
>
> (www.iht.com, 23 December 2007)

> China has finally overtaken Japan as the largest holder of US government debt ... China's holdings of Treasury bills, notes and bonds rose to $585 billion in September [2008] from $541.4 billion in August. Japan's holdings fell to $573.2 billion from $586 billion.
>
> (www.ft.com, 19 November 2008)

'Chinese investors – mainly its central bank – have become the biggest foreign holders of US Treasuries, increasing their holdings 15 per cent last year [2008] to nearly $700 billion' (*FT*, 23 February 2009, p. 8).

'About 70 per cent of China's near $2,000 billion foreign exchange reserves are believed to be in US dollar assets' (*FT*, 14 March 2009, p. 6).

'Analysts estimated that nearly half of China's $2 trillion in currency reserves are invested in US Treasuries and notes issued by other government-affiliated agencies' (www.iht.com, 13 March 2009).

'Economists say that half of ... $2 trillion [in foreign exchange reserves] has been invested in Treasury notes and other government-backed debt' (*IHT*, 14 March 2009, p. 11).

China has been diversifying away from the dollar since 2005, when it broke the renminbi's peg to the US dollar and officially marked it to a basket of currencies, but it still holds more than two-thirds in US dollar-denominated assets by most estimate.

(*FT*, 25 April 2009, p. 5)

'China is among the largest purchasers of US government debt, with $767.9 billion as of March [2009], according to Treasury Department data released on Friday [15 May]' (www.iht.com, 16 May 2009).

'[China has] roughly $1,400 billion in dollar assets' (*FT*, 1 June 2009, p. 6).

China reduced its holdings of US government debt by the largest margin in nearly nine years in June [2009], according to date from the US Treasury ... In June China cut its holdings of US securities by about $25 billion, a fall of 3.1 per cent ... China holds more US government debt than any other country ... Japan and the UK – second and third largest holders of US debt – increased their holdings over the same period ... China's holding of US debt is about 7 per cent higher than at the turn of the year ... In 2008 the Chinese increased their holdings in US debt by 52 per cent over twelve months.

(www.bbc.co.uk, 18 August 2009)

'China's foreign exchange reserves ... hit a record high of $2.273 trillion by the end of September 2009' (www.iht.com, 15 October 2009).

The inflation rate has on occasion been in double figures, but inflation has never been the sort of problem experienced by many transitional economies in Eastern Europe and the former Soviet Union. For a few years after late 1997 deflation was something of a problem. Modest inflation was recorded for 2003, but in 2007 and early 2008 there was mounting concern about inflation (especially rising food prices). (Rapidly rising world oil prices have been discussed above.) The inflation rate continued to rise in early 2008, exacerbated by unusually severe snowstorms that began on 10 January and affected large parts of east-central and southern China. The 2008 peak was reached in February. 'The 8.7 per cent figure [for February is] the highest since May 1996' (*FT*, 12 March 2008, p. 8).

'Consumer inflation fell to 4 per cent in October, down from a twelve-month high of 8.7 per cent in February' (*IHT*, 2 December 2008, p. 20).

'China's consumer inflation fell to a twenty-two-month low of 2.4 per cent in November' (www.ft.com, 11 December 2008).

'Inflation at the consumer level fell to a thirty-month low in January [2009] from 1.2 per cent in December [2008]' (www.iht.com, 10 February 2009).

The threat of deflation reappeared.

'Consumer prices were 1.6 per cent lower last month [February] than a year earlier, the first decline since December 2002 ... Prime minister Wen Jiabao set a target of 4 per cent inflation this year [2009]' (*IHT*, 11 March 2009, p. 13).

The old monobank system has given way to a more complicated structure with a central bank, the People's Bank of China, at the apex. Private banks were banned after the communist takeover in 1949.

The central government has long refused to act as an automatic guarantor of debts incurred by regional financial institutions. A start was made in October 1998 when the central bank ordered the closure of the Guangdong International Trust and Investment Corporation after it was unable to repay loans, including foreign ones.

Although things are changing, the banking system is still overwhelmingly state-owned. It is still dominated by four giant banks, which are still largely state-owned (despite some concessions to private ownership in them over time). In market economies the financial system is the means by which saving is transformed into investment. China's financial system, characterized by pervasive state controls, is still relatively inefficient. As regards monetary policy, the emphasis is still on direct control of the volume of credit rather than on using interest rates. Although the liberalization of interest rate setting has been slow, there are signs of change.

As a result of the 'soft budget constraint' applying to many state enterprises, large amounts of bad ('non-performing') bank loans built up, i.e. bank loans that are likely never to be paid back. ('[Non-performing loans are] virtually unrecoverable loans': www.iht.com, 7 March 2005.)

State enterprises have faced increasing competition from non-state enterprises (able to enter an increasing number of markets) and the state is reluctant to see unemployment and enterprise bankruptcies on too large a scale for fear of serious worker unrest. Labour unrest has increased and sometimes takes a violent turn. ('Unity and stability' is a slogan frequently emphasized.) Policies like mergers with healthier state enterprises are preferred to bankruptcy. But many smaller enterprises have been closed down and larger enterprises are not immune from closure these days. A bankruptcy law was not passed by the National People's Congress until 27 August 2006, its provisions applying as of 1 June 2007. Private firms were affected for the first time.

Reforms to try to make state banks more commercially minded have been greatly hindered by, for example, the need to boost spending when deemed necessary by the state; state banks are still not free of central direction as regards the volume of credit. 'In China there is little debate. The government simply orders banks to lend – and it happens almost instantly' (*IHT*, 7 August 2009, p. 16). Although reforms have substantially reduced the proportion of non-performing loans held by the four main banks via so-called Asset Management Companies, the proportion could rise in a recession.

The boosting of the capital resources of major banks has helped to prepare them for initial share offerings (IPOs). The sale of a minority of shares in state banks is meant to improve their commercial attitude towards credit assignment. Bank IPOs proved to be spectacularly popular with Chinese and foreigners alike because of typically large capital gains when the allocated shares went on sale. (See below for later developments.)

> Agricultural Bank of China and China Development Bank are to receive $67 billion of investment from the country's sovereign wealth fund, a sign that the government is nearing completion of a decade-long industry restructuring ... Agricultural Bank, saddled with $100 billion of bad loans, will be the last of the country's four biggest state-owned lenders to be bailed out by the government, paving the way for the company to sell shares for the first time. China has spent about $500 billion recapitalizing its largest banks in the past decade.
>
> (*IHT*, 8 November 2007, p. 14)

'The government has decided to inject $30 billion into Agricultural Bank of China ... The recapitalization would happen "soon"' (*FT*, 2 February 2009, p. 21).

> The price of capital plays a relatively small role in how it is allocated. China has no corporate bond market to speak of and its stock markets, in Shenzhen and Shanghai, are still thin and patchy. Most capital is thus provided by banks, and the most important banks are still owned by the state ... Perhaps two-thirds of the banks' loans serve to prop up state-owned enterprises.
>
> (www.economist.com, 5 November 2004)

> China's banks are mere conduits for pouring money into local governments and state-owned companies, with little regard for risk or profit ... Because China's capital markets are underdeveloped the domestic economy relies on bank loans: bank assets comprise 77 per cent of all financial assets compared with 26 per cent in America ... By end-2003 outstanding loans had surged to 145 per cent of GDP, the highest such ratio in the world. Bad debts to banks at 40 per cent of GDP are a threat to fiscal stability.
>
> (*The Economist*, 6 November 2004, p. 87)

> At present nearly 90 per cent of household savings are held in deposits with state-owned banks, partly because of a lack of alternatives. Most of these deposits are lent to SOEs. By contrast most of the investment in the dynamic, private non-SOE sector that is propelling China's industrial growth is self-financed, or dependent on foreign capital. With few of these non-state growth enterprises being willing – or allowed – to issue shares, trade on domestic stock exchanges is mainly in SOEs, whose non-transparent accounting practices and perceived lack of viability deter households from holding much of their savings in them directly. Hence the

thinness and volatility of the domestic stock markers, as even a little news from the opaque SOEs can trigger big price movements.

(Deepak Lal, *FT*, 29 December 2004, p. 11)

Oversized, undermanaged and enfeebled by long histories of funnelling money to favoured projects without regard to future results, these organizations [banks] are fertile ground for corruption. The traditional Chinese practice of *guanxi*, doing business on the basis of personal relationships instead of objective criteria, have turned these money-laden institutions into gold mines for the sleazy and well connected.

(Seth Kaplan, *IHT*, 22 December 2004, p. 6)

Broadening financial markets is a crucial aspect of improving the allocation of capital. At present such markets have a limited role and this generates a concentration of financial risk in the banking sector to a greater extent than in OECD economies.

(OECD 2005: website Chapter 3)

At 5.5 per cent of all loans at the end of September, non-performers still look high. But the ratio, down from 6.2 per cent at the start of 2008, would be much lower if the state had completed a bailout of Agricultural Bank of China.

(*IHT*, 25 November 2008, p. 11)

'Last week banking regulators began warning about the risk that bad loans would accumulate' (*IHT*, 26 November 2008, p. 15).

'The country has been relatively unaffected by the global crisis so far because its banks are relatively healthy and exports are strong, but "we will see that impact intensify in 2009" [the World Bank said]' (www.cnn.com, 25 November 2008).

'Until recently China had largely avoided the effects of the global crisis because its financial system is insulated from the rest of the world' (www.bbc.co.uk, 25 November 2008).

The government has decided to inject $30 billion into Agricultural Bank of China, the last of the largest state-owned banks to be restructured in preparation for a listing ... China has also begun experimental reforms with underground banks, legalizing three in the Wenzhou area of Zhejiang province in another attempt to stimulate spending to rural enterprises.

(*FT*, 2 February 2009, p. 21)

'China's banks have been largely unscathed by the international financial turmoil (www.iht.com, 18 March 2009).

'[China's] financial system is not yet fully integrated with that of advanced economies ... [China] banned many of the derivative products that caused havoc among financial institutions around the world' (*FT*, Survey, 2 April 2009, p. 2).

As regards agriculture, the Household Responsibility System took root relatively quickly and has been improved by lengthening leases (land is not privately owned), in some cases seemingly indefinite in reality if not law. Private farms are still very small in general, but the state has encouraged the development of larger units in a number of ways: various experiments by the state to lease out larger plots of land; permission given for sub-leasing among farmers; encouragement given to the amalgamation of family plots; and the increasing number of agribusiness companies that lease land from peasants and supply supermarkets. (There have even been cases of forcible reassignment of land from less to more efficient farmers.) The widening gap between urban and rural incomes to the detriment of the latter has caused a mass movement of peasants to the towns (generally put at something like 150 million) and increasing concern to the government. Entry into the WTO has brought real benefits to those farmers willing to switch to products such as those fruits and vegetables in ever greater demand. But there is growing concern about the increasing number of violent protests (sometimes leading to loss of life) in rural areas caused in particular by the takeover of agricultural land by local officials for redevelopment. Such profitable (and often illegal) redesignation of land can lead to corruption and farmers feeling inadequately compensated for loss of land-use rights. There is a debate about whether the new property law (not passed by the National People's Congress until March 2007) will actually protect farmers against illegal land takeovers. The March 2006 session of the National People's Congress outlined a programme of further aid to rural areas, envising a 'new socialist countryside'.

Reforms were adopted by the Third Plenary Session of the Seventeenth Central Committee of the Communist Party at its 9–12 October 2008 meeting.

> In practice many of the more than 150 million rural residents who have migrated to the cities in search of work have already leased their contracted land on an informal basis to neighbours or even some of China's pioneering agribusinesses. But legal protection for these arrangements is lacking, and corruption and abuse by local government officials who oversee the transactions are rife.
>
> (*FT*, 9 October 2008, p. 12)

> State media in recent days have been extolling the 'success' of new farming arrangements in places such as Xiaogang village in Anhui province. Mr Hu recently visited the village, where farmers are leasing their land to other farms or companies to run, for example, a pork farm and a vineyard.
>
> (www.bbc.co.uk, 12 October 2008)

> The most important change would allow China's peasantry to sell land-use contracts to other farmers or to agricultural companies ... A law enacted in 2002 allows limited land-use trades between individual farmers, but does not permit unrestricted trade between farmers and companies, straight sales of land-use rights or the option to use the land as collateral to obtain a loan ... Officials characterize the proposed policy changes as allowing the farmers to lease or trade their thirty-year contracts to individuals or companies ... One point under discussion is whether land contracts should be extended to seventy years from thirty years.
>
> (www.iht.com, 11 October 2008)

Following days of uncertainty, the Communist Party announced a rural reform policy on Sunday [19 October] that for the first time would allow farmers to lease or transfer land-use rights, a step that advocates say would bolster lagging incomes in the countryside. The new policy, announced by the Chinese state media, marks a major economic reform and is also rich in historical resonance, coinciding with the thirtieth anniversary of the land reforms by Deng Xiaoping, which were considered the first critical steps in the market-orientated policies ... Xinhua (the country's official news agency): 'The new measures adopted are seen by economists as a major breakthrough in land reforms initiated by late leader Deng Xiaoping thirty years ago' ... Under the new policy the government will establish markets where farmers can 'subcontract, lease, exchange or swap' land-use rights or join co-operatives. Xinhua reported that giving farmers this latitude would enable them to become more efficient by increasing the size of farms while also providing income that can be used to start new businesses ... In Chengdu a government land market opened last Monday [13 October] ... Reform advocates say that allowing leasing or transfer would enable the creation of larger, more efficient farms that could bolster output. The new programme also pledges to uphold 'the most stringent farmland protection system' and require that local officials maintain 120 million hectares, or 297 million acres, of farmland – the minimum deemed necessary to feed the most populous nation in the world ... Increasing incomes in the countryside is a major part of the government's efforts to bolster domestic output at a time the overall economy is slowing.

(www.iht.com, 19 October 2008)

Sweeping reforms giving China's 730 million rural residents more say over their land [were unveiled on Sunday 19 October] ... Farmers, rather than village authorities, will be able to decide how to use their land, transfer land-use rights and join shareholding schemes.

(*The Times*, 20 October 2008, p. 31)

'The first land use rights exchange was set up on Monday [13 October] in the western city of Chengdu to allow farmers to sell or rent out the rights to use their land' (*FT*, 17 October 2008, p. 12).

China's Communist Party unveiled its plan to double, by 2020, the disposable income of 750 million people in the Chinese countryside. One way it hopes to achieve this is through land reform ... [But] there is less to the new reform than meets the eye ... Much of the 'breakthrough' is already common practice ... The actual reform is minor ... The 'new' proposals are not explicit on this, but a senior official has since suggested that leases may be made longer than thirty years ... The party does not propose lifting the legal ban on farmers' mortgaging their land and houses ... To preserve 'food security' China has set a minimum area for the country's farmland – 120 million hectares, just below the present level ... It is on the non-arable 'construction' land that the latest policy offers something new. It extends an experiment tried in Guangdong province, allowing such land to be traded without first going through government acquisition. In practice, of course, farmers will still be hostage to the whims of the collective.

(*The Economist*, 25 October 2008, p. 14)

State enterprises have gone through a series of complicated reforms to make them more market-orientated and to give management greater authority over decision-making (including at the expense of party officials).

In the original system the enterprise was not just a production unit. It was also, as we have already seen, a social unit. The shift to a more Western-type system of social security (unemployment compensation and pensions), health and housing is a difficult, costly and painful one. Such reforms are needed for state enterprises to compete more effectively with private enterprises in a market economy. State enterprises have become increasingly market-orientated.

Large privatization along Eastern European lines has not been adopted in China. Initially China concentrated on deregulation (i.e. gradually opening up certain sectors to private activity). Later on small enterprises began to be sold off in significant numbers and even some medium-sized and large companies have now been sold. Although the state still dominates ownership in medium-sized and large companies, an increasing number of companies have sold a proportion of their shares to private (including foreign) individuals and companies.

'The dismantling of tens of thousands of state-owned enterprises (SOEs) and the privatization of urban housing did not take off until the late 1990s' (*The Economist*, 13 December 2008, p. 31).

The private sector has been given greater encouragement over time and the constitution has been amended to give it greater protection and status. (The private sector still faces problems relating to such things as finance, property rights, corruption, bureaucracy and state policy as regards entry into particular sectors. It is difficult to measure the importance of the 'private' sector in the economy because of problems such as whether to include collectives in the 'public' sector or in the 'private' sector; it is also, for example, especially difficult to measure the private service sector.) 'Public ownership' remains officially the 'mainstay' of the economy, but the term has been interpreted more liberally (e.g. to include mixed-ownership enterprises). A long-debated property law giving equal protection to private property was not passed by the National People's Congress until 16 March 2007. While the predominance of public property was reaffirmed, critics were concerned, for example, that the law would protect illegally gained assets.

Banks continue to bear the brunt of capital raising in China – about 95 per cent of financing comes through banks – because of the dysfunctional local stock market ... [in turn] because of the poor quality of listed companies and the dominant role still played by the state as a shareholder.

(*FT*, Survey, 7 December 2004, p. 4)

('Some 60 per cent of the average listed company remains in state hands' (*FEER*, 28 October 2004, p. 32).

The year 2006 saw the start of a major debate about the extent to which they depend on reinvested profits to finance investment as opposed to bank credit.

China's stock markets are still dominated by largely state-owned companies. Listings are state controlled.

> The market is off-limits even to many of China's best and biggest companies, such as China Mobile, the world's largest telecom operator, and CNOOC, the top Chinese offshore oil and natural gas producer. They are listed in the offshore market of Hong Kong and, despite their expressed interest to return to the mainland, continue to fail to win the green light from Beijing.
>
> (*IHT*, 21 May 2009, p. 18)

'The Shanghai stock exchange opened in December 1990 and the one in Shenzhen opened in July 1991' (Ma 1998: 386).

'The Shanghai exchange, the largest in mainland China, now lists 857 companies' (*IHT*, 19 November 2007, p. 14).

'The exchange in Shenzhen caters to smaller enterprises' (www.economist. com, 29 December 2007).

'The broader CSI 300 Index of stocks [measures to stock movements] in [both] Shanghai and Shenzhen' (www.iht.com, 21 September 2008).

'In Shanghai and Shenzhen most of the more than 1,400 listed companies are state-controlled firms. China opened another exchange in Shenzhen ... especially for small and medium-sized firms' (www.iht.com, 23 March 2008).

For some years prior to mid-2005 the poor performance of the stock markets was in marked contrast to GDP growth. The value of existing shares was depressed by prospect of the sale of some of the shares still held by the state. 'Some 60 per cent of the average listed company remains in state hands' (*FEER*, 28 October 2004, p. 32).

The revival was stimulated by measures such as schemes effectively compensating existing shareholders when more state shares were listed for sale. Thereafter, the stock markets set off on an astonishing run. Although there were ups and downs in the Shanghai and Shenzhen indexes, the trend was spectacularly upwards, sailing through the global turmoil that produced vast gyrations in global stock markets in 2007 sparked by subprime (low credit-rated) mortgage problems in the United States. Records continued to tumble despite much talk of stock markets 'bubbles' and despite government efforts to dampen speculation (e.g. by raising returns on bank deposits through interest rate rises, reducing taxes on interest earned and increasing taxes on stock transactions).

> After decades where low-interest-rate-bearing accounts in state banks were virtually the only outlet for savings, the soaring stock market has become irresistible to a new generation of Chinese ... Chinese investors have dived

into the markets of Shanghai and Shenzhen, unleasing the huge savings in personal bank accounts.

(*IHT*, 5 November 2007, p. 12)

'Chinese investors can reason that they have little choice but to accept the volatility and the high prices because their alternatives are so limited. Bank deposits pay interest below inflation' (www.economist.com, 6 November 2007).

'After dipping as low as 998.23 in June 2005, the Shanghai stock index has soared over 90 per cent this year [2006], making it the world's best performing major market' (*IHT*, 15 December 2006, p. 19).

'China had the world's best performing stock market last year [2006], with the Shanghai soaring 130 per cent' (www.iht.com, 21 March 2007).

'[On 22 August 2007] the CSI 300 Index ... closed at 5,051.69, a record ... The CSI [is] the best performer among the world's eighty-nine major indexes tracked by Bloomberg' (*IHT*, 23 August 2007, p. 12).

'The benchmark stock index, the CSI 300, has climbed 163 per cent in 2007, the best performer among eighty-nine indexes tracked by Bloomberg' (*IHT*, 27 September 2007, p. 16).

'[On 15 October 2007] the Shanghai composite ... rose above the 6,000 level for the first time' (*FT*, 16 October 2007, p. 44).

'[In October 2007] the Shanghai index peaked at 6,092.06' (*IHT*, 25 April 2008, p. 17).

'The Shanghai Composite Index ... [has reached a] historic closing high of 6,092.06 ... that peak [being] hit on 16 October [2007]' (*FT*, 12 June 2008, p. 39).

'The benchmark Shanghai Composite Index ... [reached a] high of 6,124 in October [2007]' (*FT*, 6 June 2008, p. 41). '[The Shanghai Corporate Index] reached a peak of 6,124 on 16 October last year [2007]' (*FT*, 19 September 2008, p. 21).

'The CSI Index has risen 169.9 per cent this year [2007], the best performance among ninety global benchmarks tracked by Bloomberg' (*IHT*, 30 October 2007, p. 16).

'Mainland shares have risen nearly 600 per cent in two years' (*FT*, 6 November 2007, p. 9).

'[China's] relatively small stock markets in Shanghai and Shenzhen roughly doubled in value during 2007' (*FT*, 2 January 2008, p. 32).

The stock markets peaked in October 2007, followed by often dramatic falls and much greater volatility. Although still volatile, the stock markets responded in and after November 2008 to government measures to stimulate the economy. The first half of 2009 saw a strong recovery, despite some ups and downs.

Movements in the Shanghai Composite Index:

5 November 2007, 5,636;
13 November 2007, 5,158;
20 November 2007, 5,293.70;
22 November 2007, 4,984.16;
23 November 2007, 5,032.13;

3 December 2007, 4,868;
21 January 2008, 4,914.44;
22 January 2008, 4,559.75;
31 January 2008, 4,383.39;
4 February 2008, 4,671.62;
26 February 2008, 4,238.18;
27 February 2008, 4,334.05;
10 March 2008, 4,146.30;
18 March 2008, 3,668.90;
7 April 2008, 3,599.62;
10 April 2008, 3,471.74;
18 April 2008, 3,094.67;
23 April 2008, 3,278.00:

> China slashed the tax on share trading last night [23 April] in an effort to encourage investors to return to a stock market that has fallen by nearly half over the past six months. The government will reduce the tax on each share trade from 0.3 per cent to 0.1 per cent. The announcement effectively reversed a decision last May [2007] when the government tripled the tax.
>
> (*FT*, 24 April 2008, p. 41)

'A stamp duty cut to cut dealing costs gave the flagging Shanghai index a boost ... on the strength of a cut in stamp tax, to 0.1 per cent from 03 per cent' (www. iht.com, 24 April 2008).

24 April 2008, 3,583.03;
28 April 2008, 3,492.78;
30 April 2008, 3,693.11;
5 June 2008, 3,351.65;
10 June 2008, 3,072.33;
11 June 2008, 3,024.24;
17 June 2008, 2,794.00;
18 June 2008, 2,870.29;
20 June 2008, 2,831.74;
1 July 2008, 2,651.61;
3 July 2008, 2,703.53: 'The Chinese index is among the worst performing in the world this year [2008], down some 45 per cent ... [although] the index is now up about 12 per cent from its year low' (*IHT*, 31 July 2008, p. 12).

8 August 2008, 2,605.72;
11 August 2008, 2,470.07;
18 August 2008, 2,319.90;
25 August 2008, 2,413.37:

> Share prices continue to slide in spite of a slew of initiatives by the country's regulator to bolster the stock market ... China's benchmark index [is] down 54 per cent this year [2008] ... Last week the China Securities Regu-

latory Commission published a policy to stop listed companies raising money in secondary offerings unless they have handed out an average of 30 per cent of net profits over the previous three years.

(*FT*, 1 September 2008, p. 17)

1 September 2008, 2,324,39:

[China's] stock market is already the world's weakest performer this year [2008] ... The benchmark Shanghai Composite Index closed down 3 per cent on Monday [1 September], taking the losses from the past year to 55 per cent ... A new unified rate corporate income tax rate for domestic and foreign companies started this year [2008], which cut the rate for local firms to 25 per cent from 33 per cent.

(*IHT*, 2 September 2008, p. 15)

16 September 2008, 1,986.64;

17 September 2008, 1,954.38: '[On 18 September] the Shanghai Composite Index fell 1.7 per cent' (www.iht.com, 18 September 2008). 'The Chinese finance ministry ... said Thursday [18 September] that a 0.1 per cent stamp duty on buying shares would be abolished, although an equivalent tax on share sales would remain' (*IHT*, 19 September 2008, p. 17).

The government on Thursday [18 September] announced dramatic steps to prop up the country's sagging stock market, which has lost 70 per cent of its value since last October [2007]. Stamp duty on stock purchases will be scrapped and a government-controlled investment agency will buy shares in three state-controlled banks.

(www.ft.com, 18 September 2008)

The stamp duty on stock purchases will be scrapped and government money will be used to buy shares ... Central Huijin, an arm of the country's sovereign wealth fund, would buy into listed companies, including state-owned Industrial and Commercial Bank of China, Bank of China and China Construction Bank. Chinese bank shares have fallen steeply in response to the global financial crisis, helping to drive the benchmark Shanghai Composite Index to a twenty-two-month low of 1,896 yesterday [18 September]. The market peaked in October [2007] at 6,092 ... Several Shanghai stockbrokers said they believed government-sanctioned share purchases began the announcement last night, helping Shanghai recover from a 6 per cent early decline to close 1.7 per cent weaker on the day ... The government resisted public pressure to intervene in the stock market during the Beijing Olympics.

(*FT*, 19 September 2008, p. 21)

Last night [18 September] state media announced there would be a cut in stamp duty for buyers but not for sellers of shares. State media also said a branch of the country's sovereign wealth fund would buy shares in three state-owned banks ... and that other state-owned companies would be encouraged to buy back shares in their listed entities ... The Shanghai Composite Index recovered in the afternoon [18 September] to close at 1,896, only 1.72 per cent down on the day. That compares with a peak of 6,124 on 16 October last year [2007].

(p. 42)

19 September 2008, 2,075.09:

[On 19 September] the most spectacular turnaround [in Asia] took place in Shanghai, where the A-share market soared 9.5 per cent ... [It was announced on] Thursday evening [18 September] that a government agency had begun buying shares in three of the mainland's biggest banks.

(www.iht.com, 19 September 2008)

'In Shanghai the Composite Index soared 9.46 per cent to close at 2,075.09. Trading had slowed as many stocks increased by the daily limit of 10 per cent soon after the stock market opened' (www.iht.com, 19 September 2008).

Middle class moms and blue-collar pensioners in mainland China were among the world's most avid and successful investors last year [2007]. Now their record is one of lost fortunes, broken families and protest. Mainland Chinese stock markets are down nearly two-thirds in eleven months and the anger of ordinary citizens has unnerved the stability-obsessed government. On Friday [19 September] announced an unprecedented rescue package that drove up most stocks the maximum permitted 10 per cent. The Shanghai Composite Index closed 9.5 per cent higher at 2,075.091, its biggest daily gain since October 2001. The broader CSI 300 Index of stocks in Shanghai and Shenzhen climbed 9.3 per cent. Yet amateur investors who have been badly burnt may think twice before venturing back into the market.

(www.iht.com, 21 September 2008)

23 September 2008, 2,201.51;
26 September 2008, 2,293.78:

Chinese regulators, seeking to support the equities market in the face of global financial turmoil, said Sunday [5 October] that they would soon allow investors to buy stocks on margin and to short-sell stocks. The changes will initially be made on a trial basis by a small number of brokerage businesses and gradually expanded to other security companies ... By contrast, US, British, French Italian and German regulators in recent weeks temporarily banned short-selling of financial stocks, while Australia, Singapore and Taiwan restricted it ... Since China has been considering the start of margin trading, in which investors borrow money from brokerage businesses to buy shares, and short-selling, in which they borrow stocks from brokers and sell them, hoping to buy them back at lower prices. The changes have been delayed by market volatility, starting with the bull run that lifted the Shanghai Composite Index sixfold from mid-2005 to October 2007 and then a bear market in which the index fell more than 70 per cent.... The index rebounded 21 per cent from a twenty-two-month low hit late last month [September] in response to steps including purchases of shares from the market by a government fund and the abolition of tax on stock purchases ... The China Securities Regulatory Commission said Sunday ... that it expected 'margin buying will greatly exceed short-selling' in the initial stage because brokerage businesses had only a limited amount of stocks available ... Some investors are hoping for the introduction of stock index futures, another change under consideration for years. The commission did not specify exactly when margin trading and short-selling would start or name the brokerage companies that would take part in the initial stages.

(*IHT*, 6 October 2008, p. 6)

6 October 2008, 2,173.74: '[On 6 October] the Shanghai A-share market fell 5.2 per cent after the Shanghai stock exchange, which had been closed for the past week for the National Day holiday, reopened Monday [6 October]' (www.iht.com, 6 October 2008).

China's stock market retreated 3.5 per cent this week. The Shanghai Composite has fallen 68.3 per cent since reaching a peak last October [2007], marking its one-year anniversary by sinking below the 2,000 points level for the first time in almost two years.

(*FT*, 18 October 2008, p. 26)

20 October 2008, 1,974.01: '[On 27 October] the Shanghai Composite Index closed down 6.3 per cent at its lowest level since December 2006' (www.bbc.co.uk, 27 October 2008); 'A giant [$596 billion] economic stimulus package announced [on 9 November] by China lifted stocks in Asia on Monday [10 November] ... The Shanghai Composite Index soared 7.2 per cent to 1,874' (www.iht.com 10 November 2008); '[On 10 November] the Shanghai Composite Index ended 7.3 higher at 1,874.80' (www.bbc.co.uk, 10 November 2008).

25 November 2008, 1.888.71;
6 December 2008, 2,120;
26 December 2008, 1,851.52: 'Shanghai, which was the world's best performing stock market in 2007, dropped 0.7 per cent on Wednesday [31 December] to end at 1,820.8 – a loss of 65.4 per cent this year [2008]' (www.ft.com, 31 December 2008).

The Shanghai Composite Index, which tumbled 65 per cent last year [2008], making China the worst performing major stock market, ended the morning [of 5 January] up 2.14 per cent at 1,859 points ... The Shanghai Composite Index [ended the day up] 3.3 per cent.

(www.iht.com, 5 January 2009)

'The Shanghai Composite Index, which climbed 3.29 per cent on Monday [5 January], ended Tuesday [6 January] up 3 per cent at 1,937 points' (www.iht.com, 6 January 2009).

'[On 7 January] the Shanghai Composite Index closed 0.7 per cent lower at 1,924.02' (www.ft.com, 7 January 2009).

'[On 8 January] the Shanghai Composite Index fell 2.4 per cent' (www.iht. com, 8 January 2009).

21 January 2009 ,1,995.27;

> While the world's stock markets are down 9 per cent this year [2009], China is up by about the same amount. The usual January uplift has eluded almost every major exchange ... [Shanghai was] up 100 per cent in 2007 and down 65 per cent in 2008.
>
> (*FT*, 28 January 2009, p. 16)

'The Shanghai Composite Index has rallied 24 per cent this year [2009], the biggest advance among benchmark equity indexes worldwide ... Last year [2008] the Shanghai index tumbled 65 per cent' (*IHT*, 13 February 2009, p. 15).

> [On 17 February] stocks in mainland China fell for the first time in three days ... The Shanghai Composite Index, which tracks the bigger of the two mainland stock exchanges, was down 0.5 per cent to 2,376 at the mid-day break. The gauge is still up 31 per cent this year [2009], the most among ninety stock gauges worldwide tracked by Bloomberg.
>
> (www.iht.com, 17 February 2009)

> [On 18 February] the Shanghai Composite Index plunged 4.7 per cent to 2,209.86 as reports said regulators were investigating the recent surge in bank lending and whether it raised financial risks. Analysts said there was speculation that some of the lending was being used to place bets on the stock market.
>
> (*IHT*, 19 February 2009, p. 15)

'Share prices have jumped by 30 per cent since November [2008], although they fell sharply this week' (*The Economist*, 21 February 2009, p. 77).

> Some security analysts estimate than loan recipients, mostly state-owned firms, funnelled as much as a third of new loans into stock market trades, which may help to explain a surge in the Shanghai Composite Index this year [2009] despite the deepening gloom. Regulators have asked banks to submit account records in order to track the loans.
>
> (www.iht.com, 4 March 2009)

'The Shanghai stock market ... [its] benchmark index ... gained 6.1 per cent on Wednesday [4 March]' (www.iht.com, 4 March 2009).

'In December [2008] China Investment Corporation, one of the country's sovereign wealth funds, acknowledged buying shares of Chinese banks on the open market. Other government-backed funds are thought to have been buying as well' (*The Economist*, 7 March 2009, p. 70).

'The Shanghai stock exchange is up 22 per cent since 1 January [2009] and added 0.3 per cent on Wednesday [18 March]' (*IHT*, 19 March 2009, p. 15).

'The Shanghai Composite Index stands out as the best performer in the world – up 33 per cent so far this year [2009], despite a 0.2 per cent slip on Friday [3 April]' (www.iht.com, 3 April 2009). 'Anecdotal evidence from corporate treasurers suggests that perhaps a third of the bank loan explosion this year has ended up in stocks' (*FT*, 3 April 2009, p. 16).

'[On 13 April] the Shanghai Composite Index gained 2.8 per cent to reach its highest level in eight months' (*FT*, 14 April 2009, p. 32).

'[On 15 April] the Shanghai Composite Index – the world's best performing market this year [2009] after being the hardest hit in 2008 – held up best [among Asian stocks], dipping just 0.5 per cent' (www.iht.com, 15 April 2009).

'[On 16 April] the Shanghai Composite Index edged down 0.1 per cent 2,534.13' (www.iht.com, 16 April 2009).

'[On 22 April] Shanghai's benchmark fell 2.9 per cent to 2,461.35 – its sharpest one-day drop in two weeks' (www.iht.com, 22 April 2009).

29 April 2009, 2,467.278;
1 May 2009, 2,477.57;
4 May 2009, 2,555.56: '[On 4 May] the Shanghai Composite Index rallied 3.3 per cent to its highest level since August [2008]' (www.iht.com, 4 May 2009).
5 May 2009, 2,560.44: '[On 6 May] the Shanghai Composite Index climbed 1 per cent, taking its rise since 1 January [2009] to 42 per cent' (www.iht.com, 6 May 2009).

7 May 2009, 2,585.86;
11 May 2009, 2,579.78;
14 May 2009, 2,637.00;
15 May 2009, 2,641.97;
16 May 2009, 2,645.26;
18 May 2009, 2,635.58;
19 May 2009, 2,676.68;
20 May 2009, 2,651.41;
22 May 2009, 2,597.60;
25 May 2009, 2,610.01;
26 May 2009, 2,588.57;
2 June 2009, 2,724.30;
3 June 2009, 2,778.59;
4 June 2009, 2,767.24;
5 June 2009, 2,753.89;
8 June 2009, 2,768.34;
9 June 2009, 2,787.89;
10 June 2009, 2,816.25;
11 June 2009, 2,877.35;
12 June 2009, 2,743.76;
15 June 2009, 2,789.55;
16 June 2009, 2,776.02;

17 June 2,810.12;
18 June 2009, 2,853.90;
19 June 2009, 2,880.49;
22 June 2009, 2,896.30;
23 June 2009, 2,892.70;
24 June 2009, 2,922.30;
25 June 2009, 2,925.05;
26 June 2009, 2,928.21;
29 June 2009, 2,975.31;
30 June 2009, 2,959.36;
1 July 2009, 3,008.15;
2 July 2009, 3,060.25:

> The SCI rose 52 points Thursday [2 July] to close at 3,060.25, putting the index up 68 per cent this year [2009] ... Though well off their 2007 highs, Chinese stock markets are again among the world's best performers this year ... The SCI was as low as 1,717 last November [2008] – a 70 per cent drop from its peak in late 2007. Chinese stock markets are known for their volatility, and investors often treat them like casinos. The government pushes and pulls the market by occasionally tweaking regulations. Many listed companies are known for fuzzy or suspect accounting ... Many analysts say the economy is showing signs of improving, but there are also hints that huge, government-initiated bank loans are flowing into the stock and real estate markets now, lifting prices. Speculators, in other words, may be back. In the first half of the year banks operating in China made about $1 trillion in new loans – an astounding figure considering that all of the 2008 bank loans totalled about $620 billion, analysts say.
>
> (www.iht.com, 2 July 2009; *IHT*, 3 July 2009, p. 13)

3 July 2009, 3,088.37;
6 July 2009, 3,124.67;
7 July 2009, 3,089.45;
8 July 2009, 3,080.77;
9 July 2009, 3,123.04:

> China issued rules Monday [9 June] for a new stock exchange to nurture smaller companies ... The rules for the Growth Enterprise Board take effect on 1 July, said the Shenzhen stock exchange, where the board will be located. It gave no details on when companies could apply for listing or when trading would begin.
>
> (*IHT*, 9 June 2009)

10 July 2009, 3,113.93;
13 July 2009, 3,080.56;
14 July 2009, 3,145.16;
15 July 2009, 3,188.55;
16 July 2009, 3,183.74;

17 July 2009, 3,189.74;
20 July 2009, 3,266.92;
21 July 2009, 3,213.21;
22 July 2009, 3,296.62;
23 July 2009, 3,328.49;
24 July 2009, 3,372.60;
27 July 2009, 3,435.21: 'The Shanghai Composite Index added 1.9 per cent
to finish at a thirteen-month high of 3,435.21' (*IHT*, 28 July 2009, p. 17).

> State banks lent nearly $1.1 trillion in the first half of the year [2009] ...
> Somewhere between a fifth and a third of total new lending may have ended
> up in such things as stock market speculation, real estate speculation and
> even a measurable amount may be showing up in the casinos in Macao.
>
> (www.cnn.com, 25 July 2009)

'According to one estimate, 20 per cent of new lending went into the stock
market in the first five months of this year [2009]' (*The Economist*, 18 July 2009,
p. 57).

'Some experts say the stock market has been propped up partly by state-
owned companies that are once again speculating on stocks rather than investing
in their businesses' (*IHT*, 17 July 2009, p. 14).

> According to estimates from UBS, a Swiss investment bank, total new
> inflows into the stock market in the first half of the year [2009] were ren-
> minbi 460 billion, the majority of which would have come from fund manag-
> ers and private investors, rather than bank lending. Moreover, the renminbi
> 460 billion inflow into the stock market compares with total bank lending in
> the first half of the year of $7.4 trillion. The fact that only a small proportion
> of the increase in lending has found its way onto the stock market suggests
> that banks should not be too badly affected by a slump in the stock market.
>
> (www.economist.com, 7 August 2009)

28 July 2009, 3,438.37;
29 July 2009, 3,266.43:

> In response to rumours of a possible curb in lending and liquidity ... Shang-
> hai investors ... bid down shares by more than 5 per cent. China has since
> reassured that it would keep monetary policy 'moderately loose' and shares
> have resumed their upward march.
>
> (*IHT*, 5 August 2009, p. 17)

> At one stage in a trading session late last week, the Shanghai market fell
> almost 8 per cent on a rumour the two biggest state-owned commercial
> banks would cut new lending sharply in the second half [of 2009].
>
> (www.ft.com, 7 August 2009; *FT*, 8 August 2009, p. 5)

30 July 2009, 3,321.56;
31 July 2009, 3,412.06;

3 August 2009, 3,462.59;
4 August 2009, 3,471.44;
5 August 2009, 3,428.50;
6 August 2009, 3,356.33;
7 August 2009, 3,260.69;
10 August 2009, 3,249.76;
11 August 2009, 3,264.73;
12 August 2009, 3,112.72;
13 August 2009, 3,140.56;
14 August 2009, 3,046.97;
17 August 2009, 2,870.63;
18 August 2009, 2,910.88;

19 August 2009, 2,785.58: '[On 19 August] Shanghai stocks tumbled to a two-month low ... yet the Shanghai index is still up some 53 per cent this year' (www.iht.com, 19 August 2009).

> The plunge in the SCI has met the definition of a bear market, which occurs when an index falls more than 20 per cent from a peak, But even with this latest reversal, the Shanghai index is still up about 53 per cent so far this year.
>
> (*IHT*, 20 August 2009, p. 17)

> A sharp sell-off in Chinese shares in late Wednesday [19 August] trading saw the benchmark SCI close 4.3 per cent lower, putting it in sight of a bear market as speculation grew that the Beijing government would tighten its monetary policy ... The SCI fell 4.3 per cent, leaving it 20 per cent [19.8 per cent] below the 2009 high reached on 4 August ... The sudden loss of confidence in the Shanghai market after the mid-day break meant that most Asian indices reversed earlier gains prompted by an over-night US rally ... This year's peak [occurred] on 4 August, when it [the SCI] reached 3,471.44 ... Beijing is thought to be concerned about illegal lending to property developers and banks are tightening control over the approval of mortgages. New lending in July was down sharply to ren-minbi 355.9 billion (\$52 billion) from renminbi 1,530 billion the previous month [June], raising fears that liquidity would disappear from the stock market.
>
> (www.ft.com, 19 August 2009)

> In recent days the sickly Chinese stock market has been blamed for infect-ing markets in other parts of the world. Take yesterday [19 August] ... Other Asian markets dropped sharply and bourses in Europe initially fol-lowed suit before recovering later.
>
> (*FT*, 20 August 2009, p. 31)

20 August 2009, 2,911.58:

> The SCI was up ... helped up reports that the stock regulator had approved new mutual funds this week to help underpin the market ... [One analyst]

said the fact that Chinese shares were having such a big influence on other markets showed how edgy investors were about the global outlook.

(www.iht.com, 20 August 2009)

Stocks rallied worldwide Thursday [20 August] after an equity rebound in China and some solid corporate results … Sentiment improved after the SCI jumped 4.52 per cent, in its second biggest daily percentage gain this year [2009, easing concerns about an almost 20 per cent slide for the Chinese benchmark over the past two weeks.

(*IHT*, 21 August 2009, p. 17)

'A powerful rebound for Chinese stocks offered an encouraging backdrop for global equity markets, although the broader risk environment was more mixed. The SCI leapt 4.5 per cent – its biggest one-day rise since March' (*FT*, 21 August 2009, p. 28).

Anecdotally at least, global stock markets have become more sensitive to Chinese gyrations, on the premise they reflect real shifts in the country's prosperity which have repercussions everywhere. Whether this reputation is deserved is an open question. The market's remarkable rise comes with enough caveats to suggest it is priced as much by madness as by reason … Of even greater concern is that much of the market's strength may be the result of the abundant money sloshing around China, rather than a fundamental change in profit expectations … One source of this liquidity is individuals, usually responsible for about three-quarters of all share purchases in China … More controversially, there is widespread speculation that the tidal wave of bank lending initiated by the government as part of its stimulus plan has made its way into the stock market. The proportion of loans going into shares is hotly debated … After an extraordinary lending binge, the country's leading banks are abruptly pulling back on credit expansion … Rumours are rife that banks' capital requirements are being tightened, as are the conditions for various kinds of loans. A decline in new lending in the second half of the year had been expected; the rate of decline has, for many, been a shock … China's mainland market … is now the world's second largest on most measures, but a second speculative bubble in three years raises real questions about its credibility. The job of a stock market is to provide useful signals to help allocate capital … China's market is a long way from doing that.

(*The Economist*, 29 August 2009, pp. 66–7)

According to one widely quoted estimate, 20 per cent of all new loans this year [2009] have gone into the stock market. Add in property and commodities, and up to half of all lending may have ended up in China's assets markets, it is claimed … [Others] reckon that such estimates are nonsense … Even a small amount going into the stock market (plus the expectation of a lot going in) could have a big impact on prices. But claims about the scale of such risky lending appear exaggerated.

(p. 67)

21 August 2009, 2,960.77;
24 August 2009, 2,993.43;
25 August 2009, 2,915.80; 'The drop had limited fall-out on other markets' (www.iht.com, 25 August 2009).
26 August 2009, 2,967.60;
27 August 2009, 2,946.40;
28 August 2009, 2,860.69;
31 August 2009, 2,667.75:

> China's SCI sank 6.74 per cent to a three-month low on Monday [31 August] and the slump weighed on other Asian shares … The benchmark index lost 192.94 points Monday [31 August] to close at 2,667.75 … the lowest closing figure in more than three months. Shares on the Shanghai exchange had rocketed more than 90 per cent this year until they began to fall back about three weeks ago … The Shenzhen Composite Index of China's second, smaller exchange tumbled 7.2 per cent to 904.14 … The Shanghai index crucially dropped below its 125-day moving average, what is viewed by many domestic investors as the threshold for bear and bull markets. Fears that banks will rein in their lending after a torrid six months of the year and an abundant supply of expected news shares have been knocking Chinese shares for the last month.
>
> (www.iht.com, 31 August 2009)

'Although China's markets ate largely closed to foreign investors, movements in Chinese shares have increasingly been affecting other markets' (*IHT*, 1 September 2009, p. 14).

> A sell-off in the Shanghai markets rippled through other markets on Monday [31 August] with exchanges around the globe trading lower. The SCI plunged 6.75 per cent to close out August with a drop of 21.8 per cent, the worst performance for the month among the world's major exchanges … Shares fell elsewhere in Asia and Europe, and futures indexes in the United States were pointed lower … The volatile market swings in China have given some global analysts pause. The worst falls in Shanghai equities for more than a year pulled the rest of the region lower on Monday [31 August] … The SCI is now trading at its lowest levels since the end of May [2009].
>
> (www.ft.com, 31 August 2009)

1 September 2009, 2,683.72;
2 September 2009, 2,714.97;
3 September 2009, 2,845.02: 'Investor risk confidence [globally] was subdued yesterday in spite of a strong rally for Chinese stocks' (*FT*, 4 September 2009, p. 32).
4 September 2009, 2,861.61:

> China announced new draft rules Friday [4 September] on inbound portfolio investments, increasing the amount institutions can invest in the country's

stock markets. The upward limit for individual institutions' quotas under the Qualified Foreign Institutional Investor programme will be raised to $1 billion from $800 million under the draft rules, the State Administration of Foreign Exchange said. But the overall quota of $30 billion would remain intact, as less than $15 billion has been used so far.

(*IHT*, 5 September 2009, p. 18)

7 September 2009, 2,881.12;
8 September 2009, 2,930.48;
9 September 2009, 2,946.26;
10 September 2009, 2,924.88;
11 September 2009, 2,989.79;
14 September 2009, 3,026.74;
15 September 2009, 3,033.73;
16 September 2009, 2,999.71;
17 September 2009, 3,060.26;
18 September 2009, 2,962.67: 'As much as a third of the extra bank lending in China appears to have gone into real estate and stock market speculation' (www.iht.com, 18 September 2009; *IHT*, 19 September 2009, p. 11).

21 September 2009, 2,967.01;
22 September 2009, 2,897.55;
23 September 2009, 2,842.72;
24 September 2009, 2,853.55;
25 September 2009, 2,838.84;
28 September 2009, 2,763.53;
29 September 2009, 2,754.54
30 September 2009, 2,779.43;
9 October 2009, 2,911.72;
12 October 2009, 2,894.48;
13 October 2009, 2,936.19;
14 October 2009, 2,970.53;
15 October 2009, 2,979.79;
16 October 2009, 2,976.63;
19 October 2009, 3,038.27
20 October 2009, 3,084.45;
21 October 2009, 3,070.59: 'China has 1,631 listed companies, compared with 6,013 in the United States, 4,946 in Mumbai and 2,864 in London' (*IHT*, 22 October 2009, p. 21).

22 October 2009, 3,051.41;
23 October 2009, 3,107.85;
26 October 2009, 3,109.57;
27 October 2009, 3,021.46;
28 October 2009, 3,031.33;
29 October 2009, 2,960.47;
30 October 2009, 2,995.85:

A new stock market, Chi-Next, opened Friday [30 October], making it easier for smaller Chinese companies to raise capital by reducing the requirements for going public. Twenty-eight companies were listed to inaugurate Chi-Next, a side board of the Shenzhen exchange that is modelled on the Nasdaq stock market in the United States, with its large share of technology companies. The shares can be bought only by mainland Chinese and a limited number of foreign institutional investors. The companies together raised 15.5 billion yuan ($2.3 billion) from their initial public offerings ... Until Friday many smaller Chinese companies had been forced to seek funds outside the mainland, with dozens listing on the Growth Enterprise Board in Hong Kong, or on the Nasdaq itself ... Separately, the National Development and Reform Commission said Friday that with the finance ministry it would set up twenty venture capital funds in seven cities across China 'to support the rapid development of innovative enterprises' in high-tech sectors like energy, information technology, biotech and environmental conservation.

(www.iht.com, 31 October 2009)

The highly anticipated opening of China's new Nasdaq-style stock exchange is already being seen as a watershed moment for the country's capital markets, providing new opportunities for Chinese investors and an alternative source of funding for small and medium-sized companies that aim to be innovative ... The Growth Enterprise Market (GEM) ... based in Shenzhen ... is also known as Chi-Next.

(*IHT*, 2 November 2009, p. 15)

On their debut last Friday [30 October] all twenty-eight stocks gained between 76 per cent and 210 per cent ... The speculative nature of China's equity markets was on full display yesterday [2 November] as twenty of the twenty-eight stocks in the newly launched Chi-Next market fell by their 10 per cent daily limit on their second day of trading ... On Chinese stock markets, newly listed companies are free to rise or fall by any amount on their trading debut and are then subject to a daily 10 per cent price fluctuation cap.

(*FT*, 3 November 2009, p. 33)

2 November 2009, 3,076.65;
3 November 2009, 3,114.23;
4 November 2009, 3,128.54;
5 November 2009, 3,155.05;
6 November 2009, 3,164.04;
9 November 2009, 3,175.59;
10 November 2009, 3,178.61;
11 November 2009, 3,175.19;
12 November 2009, 3,172.95;
13 November 2009, 3,187.65;

16 November 2009, 3,275.05;
17 November 2009, 3,282.89;
18 November 2009, 3,303.23;
19 November 2009, 3,320.61;
20 November 2009, 3,308.35;
23 November 2009, 3,338.66;
24 November 2009, 3,223.53;
25 November 2009, 3,290.17;
26 November 2009, 3,170.98;
27 November 2009, 3,096.27;
30 November 2009, 3,195.30;
1 December 2009, 3,235.3;
2 December 2009, 3,269.75;
3 December 2009, 3,264.63;
4 December 2009, 3,317.04;
7 December 2009, 3,331.90;
8 December 2009, 3,296.66;
9 December 3,239,.57;
10 December 2009, 3,254.26;
11 December 2009, 3,247.32;
14 December 2009, 3,302.90;
15 December 2009, 3,274.46;
16 December 2009, 3,255.21;
17 December 2009, 3,179.08;
18 December 2009, 3,113.89;
21 December 2009, 3,122.97;
22 December 2009, 3,050.52;
23 December 2009, 3,073.78;
24 December 2009, 3,153.41;
25 December 2009, 3,141.35;
28 December 2009, 3,188.79;
29 December 2009, 3,211.76;
30 December 2009, 3,262.60;
31 December 2009, 3,277.14;
4 January 2010, 3,243.76;
5 January 2010, 3,282.18;
6 January 2010, 3,254.22;
7 January 2010, 3,192.78;
8 January 2010, 3,196.00:

China has given approval in principle for stock index futures as well as short selling and margin trading ... the securities regulator said on Friday [8 January] ... in major steps offering investors badly needed hedging tools. The reforms, which were approved by the cabinet in 2008 but delayed by the global financial crisis, will initially be conducted on a trial basis and it could take three months before they are launched ... A lack of sophisticated tools to manage risks in China's nascent stock exchanges has been a major shortcoming in the notoriously volatile market, which surged 80 per cent in 2009 after falling 65 per cent in 2008. The government set up the China Financial Futures Exchange in late 2006 to launch derivatives, starting with stock index futures, but the plan was later put on hold because of mounting financial turmoil around the world. Regulators have for several years also been deliberating on whether to allow margin trading, whereby investors borrow from brokerages to buy shares, and short selling, whereby they borrow stocks from brokers and sell them in the hope of buying them back later at a lower price.

(www.iht.com, 8 January 2010)

China took a major step Friday toward making its capital market system more sophisticated and perhaps more stable as it agreed to give investors a new and powerful set of risk-management tools. The government said it had approved, 'in principle', the creation of stock market futures, trading on margin and short selling ... The announcement means that for the first time investors in China have more options than simply buying and selling their favourite stocks. They will soon be able to invest in a stock index (or set of stocks, collectively) and borrow money to trade stocks on margin ... Mainland China's benchmark Shanghai Composite Index almost doubled in 2007, then slumped 65 per cent in 2008 before rebounding about 80 per cent last year [2009] ... In 2006 Beijing established the China Financial Futures Exchange in Shanghai. Since then regulators have been testing stock index futures, short selling and margin trading. But regulators delayed approving the practices because of the global financial crisis and because of worries that such trading could disrupt the volatile stock exchanges in Shanghai and Shenzhen. The Chinese government has worried that short selling and trading on margin in particular could be abused by investors and increase speculation and chaos in the market ... In 2008 the United States and other countries imposed a temporary ban on short selling of financial stocks. The bans were lifted after several months ... Exchanges in Hong Kong have long had such offerings ... Shanghai is eager to establish itself as a financial centre that can compete with Hong Kong and even New York. The city is building a huge financial centre in the Pudong district.

(www.iht.com, 8 January 2010; *IHT*, 9 January 2010, p. 11)

Beijing has approved the launch, on a trial basis, of stock index futures and the short selling of stocks ... Shorting stocks and trading index futures will allow traders to profit from falling as well as rising markets. They will also enable investors to hedge their positions against downturns in China's notoriously volatile markets ... The China Securities Regulatory Commission said yesterday [8 January] that the State Council, China's cabinet, had approved the measures although it might take three months to complete preparations for the launch of index futures. The government also approved margin trading, under which investors borrow money from brokerages to buy shares. In short sales, investors sell stock they do not own, betting that they will be able to buy it back at a lower price and profit from the difference … Chinese investors have been awaiting the introduction of stock index futures for more than three years, since the establishment in 2006 of the China Financial Futures Exchange in Shanghai. The exchange has been conducting mock trading since then and the regulator has been preparing guidelines for index futures and educating investors about risks.

(*FT*, 9 January 2010, p. 23)

11 January 2010, 3,212.75;
12 January 2010, 3,273.97;
13 January 2010, 3,172.66;
14 January 2010, 3,215.55;
15 January 2010, 3,224.15;
18 January 2010, 3,237.10;
19 January 2010, 3,246.87;
20 January 2010, 3,151.85;
21 January 2010, 3,158.86;
22 January 2010, 3,128.59:

China First Heavy Industries, a maker of heavy machinery, said Friday [22 January] that it would start an initial public offer in Shanghai in the coming week to raise at least 8.4 billion renminbi. Along with China First Heavy's share sale, value at $1.23 billion, initial public offerings were announced by five smaller companies that will list on the Shenzhen stock exchange … China First Heavy's announcement comes after China XD Electric, the country's largest maker of electricity transmission and distribution equipment, raised 10.3 billion renminbi in China's first major initial public offering this year [2010].

(www.iht.com, 22 January 2010)

25 January 2010, 3,094.41;
26 January 2010, 3,019.39;
27 January 2010, 2,986.61;
28 January 2010, 2,994.14;
29 January 2010, 2,989.29;
1 February 2010, 2,941.36;
2 February 2010, 2,934.71;
3 February 2010, 3,003.83;
4 February 2010, 2,995.31;
5 February 2010, 2,939.40;
8 February 2010, 2,935.17;
9 February 2010, 2,948.84;

10 February 2010, 2,982.50;
11 February 2010, 2,985.50;
12 February 2010, 3,018.13;
22 February 2010, 3,003.40;
23 February 2010, 2,982.58;
24 February 2010, 3,022.18;
25 February 2010, 3,060.62;
26 February 2010, 3,051.94;
1 March 2010, 3,087.84;
2 March 2010, 3,073.11;
3 March 2010, 3,097.10;
4 March 2010, 3,023.37;
5 March 2010, 3,031.07;
8 March 2010, 3,053.23;
9 March 2010, 3,069.14;
10 March 2010, 3,048.93;
11 March 2010, 3,051.28;
12 March 2010, 3,013.41:

> Beijing permits foreigners to trade the 1,620 stocks on its domestic exchanges in Shanghai and Shenzhen only if they hold special licences. Those licences give them access to quotas of individual stocks, worth on average $100 million to $200 million each … Foreign portfolio investing in mainland-listed shares is allowed only through quotas granted by the state-sanctioned Qualified Foreign Institutional Investor scheme. China had granted QFII quotas with a combined value of about $15.7 billion to seventy-eight foreign groups by the end of September [2009] … Beijing is this year [2010] expected to hand out quotas worth an extra $5 billion… Shares listed on domestic exchanges are classified into two types, A and B. The former, originally for local investors only, are the most common, although a few domestic companies continue to list B shares, previously the only kind foreigners could trade … Foreigners can invest freely in the H shares of companies domiciled on the mainland but listed in Hong Kong … Hong Kong is also home to thirty-four 'Red Chips', mainland companies incorporated outside the mainland but listed in the city … Singapore hosts 124 'S Chips'.
>
> (*FT*, 5 January 2010, p. 9)

15 March 2010, 2,976.94;
16 March 2010, 2,992.84;
17 March 2010, 3,050.48.

Increasing use is being made of the two mainland China stock markets for listings and for initial public offerings (IPOs). But they have not been immune to the ups and downs of the stock markets.

Earlier on, the IPOs were spectacularly popular with Chinese and foreigners alike because of typically large capital gains when the allocated shares have gone on sale. According to Chinese stock market valuation, as of November 2007 China had the world's three largest companies: PetroChina, China Mobile and Industrial and Commercial Bank of China in that order.

[But] the prices set on the Chinese exchanges, still largely isolated from the rest of the world by regulatory barriers that limit the amount of foreign money going into the stock markets and domestic money permitted to go out, bear little relationship to company performance or to markets elsewhere.

(IHT, 5 November 2007, p. 12)

While PetroChina has attracted a lot of scepticism, some of the other Chinese companies on the list have stronger supporting cases. For instance, China Mobile … [and] ICBC … However, even for these consumer-related stocks there are still huge challenges in turning that economic growth into profits … Even optimists acknowledge that the current mainland valuations are partly the product of some technical quirks. Most of the large state-owned companies listed on the Shanghai market have only sold a small percentage of their equity … That means a huge volume of money chasing a small quantity of shares.

(FT, 6 November 2007, p. 26)

'China is home to seven of the twenty-five largest companies by market value in the world … Only PetroChina is among the top twenty-five by profit' *(IHT*, 27 December 2007, p. 14). '[One problem with] the valuations … [is that company] earnings are often influenced by corporate investment in the stock market' (www.economist.com, 29 December 2007).

In 2007 about $90 billion will be raised from initial public offerings (IPOs) in China, almost as much as in New York and London combined … Yet the mood is darkening. Of the fifteen largest offerings to have debuted on the mainland exchanges this year [2007], the share process of eight are below their first-day close … The most vivid example … [is] PetroChina … [It] became the most valuable company in the world when its shares more than doubled on its 5 November debut in Shanghai. Since then its shares have dropped in value by a third … More recently Sinotruck and Sinotrans also fell below their opening prices on the day of listing.

(The Economist, 8 December 2007, p. 68)

Bank financing and the reinvestment of profits do play a huge role in Chinese corporate finance, but equity markets became extraordinarily important last year [2007]. Through initial and secondary offerings Chinese companies raised in excess of $78 billion domestically and more money came in through linked overseas placement … Two big companies recently announced large secondary offerings: Ping An Insurance and Pudong Development Bank. The share prices of both have been slammed, possibly because of the expectation of dilution, but possibly because there is no appetite for new shares. In response to the falling market, the China

Securities Regulatory Commission warned companies against secondary offerings. Ping An is widely expected to reconsider its huge offering.

(www.economist.com, 27 February 2008)

Shares of China Railway Construction rose Monday [10 March] by less than expected in their trading debut in the largest initial public offering of stock this year [2008] ... Analysts had expected a 43 per cent increase ... The company, which has built more than half of China's railroads, rose 28 per cent in Shanghai, but it was the worst debut in the country in more than a year ... It was not unusual for Chinese IPOs to double or even triple in their first day of trading during a stock bull run last year [2007] and the year before [2006].

(*IHT*, 11 March 2008, p. 16)

'New public stock offerings in Hong Kong and Shanghai have also dried up after two years of spectacular initial public offerings' (*IHT*, 19 March 2008, p. 13).

In Shanghai China Pacific Insurance closed [on 26 March] 6.7 per cent below the subscription price for its $4.3 billion floatation in December [2007]. The shares had jumped as much as 73 per cent on their first day of trading and have fallen steadily since.

(*FT*, 27 March 2008, p. 43)

Stocks in three big Chinese companies sank below their initial public offering prices last week ... Investors bought a staggering $100 billion of equity in almost 200 newly issued firms from May 2006, when China lifted a year-long ban on IPOs, in February this year [2008]. The IPO flood, in which deals were greatly oversubscribed by investors, appeared to be a major achievement of China's financial reforms, for the first time making the stock market an important source of funding for many companies. The Shanghai index ... [has plunged] more than 40 per cent below October's [2007] record peak. That plunge led to a virtual halt in IPOs in March [2008]; the only one was the $53 million sale by Fujian Fujing Casttech, a maker of laser equipment. By contrast, five companies raised $300 million in March last year [2007] ... Shares in three large companies – China Shipping Container Lines, China Coal Energy and China Pacific Insurance – have fallen substantially below the prices of their IPOs. They were the first major stock to do so since the ban on offers was lifted. PetroChina has so far escaped that fate, but only just. On Friday morning PetroChina's local currency A shares hit a low of $2.38, the price of its IPO last October [2007], leaving it 62 per cent below its close on its first day of trading in Shanghai. PetroChina ended the day up 5.2 per cent ... but some investors believe authorities or big institutions might have artificially supported it to avert panic in the market.

(www.iht.com, 30 March 2008; *IHT*, 31 March 2008, p. 12)

'Money raised by Chinese firms through initial public offerings shrank nearly 30 per cent from a year earlier to $12 billion, in the first five months of this year [2008]' (*IHT*, 18 June 2008, p. 18).

[There is a] gulf between Shanghai's A shares and the equivalent H shares list in more liberal Hong Kong. The Hong Kong discount, normally about a third, has widened to almost a half in recent weeks. Gaps cannot be arbitraged away as Chinese are, in effect, barred from buying H shares while foreigners are allowed only tiny slivers of A shares. Their quotas amount to less than 2 per cent of China's market capitalization ... At least two-thirds of listed companies' shares [in Shanghai and Shenzhen] are locked up and not exchange-tradable ... Citi is now worth less than one-ninth of ICBC.

(*FT*, 28 January 2009, p. 16)

In 2007 and 2008 hundreds o f Chinese companies worked feverishly with accountants and bankers to prepare for initial public offerings. Their work came to nothing ... Now the companies and bankers that have managed to survive a brutal year are once again seeking capital, through listings on bourses in the mainland and beyond.

(*The Economist*, 27 June 2009, p. 95)

Ten months after halting initial public offerings on Chinese bourses, the government has cleared the way for Guilin Sanjin Pharmaceutical, a maker of traditional Chinese medicines, to list on the Shenzhen exchange. The company plans to raise $133 million with the IPO, which offered subscriptions to retail investors Monday [29 June] ... China Zhongwang raised $1.2 billion when it listed on the Hong Kong exchange in April ... Although the IPO market in China declined last year [2008] with the plunging stock markets, China led the world in IPOs, with 127 deals raising $17.9 billion ... Right now foreign firms are not allowed to list on the Shanghai and Shenzhen stock exchanges.

(www.cnn.com, 29 June 2009)

Enthusiasm for IPOs roared back onto the Shanghai stock exchange on Monday [27 July] as Sichuan Expressway, a toll road operator, made its debut to frenzied buying and two suspensions on its way to tripling the IPO price. But the huge demand after a ten-month moratorium on IPOs that ended last month [2008] raised the spectre of destabilization in the market, with speculators driving a price bubble, analysts said ... The company's IPO raised 1.8 billion yuan in the first share offer on the mainland since a ten-month ban was lifted last month ... Investors' interest in the new listing is expected to be evident again Wednesday [29 July] when trading starts of China State Construction Engineering, which raised $7.3 billion in the world's largest IPO so far this year [2009] ... The Chinese authorities have stepped up approvals of IPOs in hopes of cooling mainland stock markets with additional supplies of equities.

(*IHT*, 28 July 2009, p. 17)

Shares in China's largest home builder soared during their trading debut in Shanghai on Wednesday [30 July] ... China State Construction Engineering's $7.3 billion IPO last week was the world's biggest in more than a year ... The China State Construction listing was the biggest in mainland China since PetroChina's debut at the peak of the market in October 2007 ... It was the largest IPO worldwide since Visa raised more than $19 billion in March of last year [2008] ... On Monday [27 July] the toll road operator Sichuan Expressway, the first company to begin trading in Shanghai in about a year, put in an even more stellar performance.

(www.iht.com, 30 July 2009)

Chinese banks lent 7 trillion yuan ($1 trillion) during the first half of this year [2009], triple the amount lent out during the same period last year [2008]. In comparison, new capital raised through the stock market was merely 10 million yuan ($.46 million), down 50 per cent from last year ... State-owned banks favour large-state-owned firms, which use 84 per cent of GDP and employ merely 25 per cent of the labour force.

(*IHT*, 30 July 2009, p. 19)

Chinese companies listing on the mainland and in Hong Kong have raised four times more than European and US issuers combined to date this year [2009] ... Chinese issuers have raised $21.9 billion this year compared with a combined $5.4 billion raised by European and US issuers ... [China's] government lifted a nine-month IPO ban in June ... The world's two largest IPOs this year were by China State Construction Engineering and Metallurgical Corp of China, the construction and engineering company that yesterday [21 September] made its Shanghai debut after raising $5.12 billion (£3.15 billion) by a dual listing this month ... Metallurgical Corp of China raised renminbi 18.97 billion ($1.7 billion) from Shanghai in the city's second largest listing this year.

(*FT*, 22 September 2009, p. 17)

China XD Electric, the country's largest maker of electricity transmission and distribution equipment, set a modest pricing range in its initial public offering to raise as much as 10.27 billion renminbi in the country's first major offering this year [2010] ... Its Shanghai IPO [gives] the IPO a value of up to $1.5 billion ... XD Electric's lower-than-expected IPO pricing came as several big companies saw their share prices fall below IPO level in recent months, reflecting waning interest in major offerings. China is expected to see a series of new stock offerings in 2010 ... Chinese IPOs may raise more than 320 billion renminbi in 2010, 73 per cent more than in 2009 PriceWaterhouseCoopers forecast. Chinese state-owned enterprises that listed last year [2009], including China Merchant Securities and China CNP, have seen their shares drop below their IPO prices in recent months as regulators sped up approval of new share offers to head off a stock market bubble ... The debut of two IPOs in Shanghai over the past month – the train maker China NR and the state-owned building firm China National Chemical Engineering – were weak, signalling declining investor appetite ... China's stock regulator has been adding huge new share supplies to help the government's campaign to clamp down on excessive asset prices since early December [2009]. Dozens of other forms, including China First Heavy Industries and Huatai Securities, have won regulatory approval and are now on the waiting list for an IPO. The clampdown was partly caused by a 27 per cent jump in the Shanghai Composite Index in less than three months, starting in early September, and has effectively cooled trading.

(www.iht.com, 18 January 2010)

A Chinese regulator's criticisms of the 'irresponsible' pricing of initial public offerings has fuelled speculation that Beijing could temporarily halt the new issue market in order to introduce fresh pricing rules ... Official media quoted Zhu Congjiu, assistant to the chairman of the China Securities Regulatory Commission, as saying institutions were irresponsibly driving up IPO prices. The remarks come as mainland IPOs have met with an increasingly tepid response from the markets. Last week China XD Electric became the first Chinese stock in five years to end its first day of trading below its IPO price ... Mr Zhu said: 'In developed markets 90 per cent of the new shares are subscribed to by institutional investors and they are strongly constrained when offering a price because they have to pay with real money. But in China most new shares are allocated to smaller investors, who are less constrained in the price offering process' ... Last year [2009] Chinese equity raisings accounted for four out of the top ten offerings worldwide by size ... Stock markets analysts said that the China Securities Regulatory Commission was understood to be planning to implement revised IPO pricing and underwriting rules to encourage more rational pricing of new offerings, and that approval of IPOs could be suspended until these take effect. Last week China XD Electric raised $1.5 billion with its float, but saw its new share end their first day of trading down 1.4 per cent at renminbi 7.79. Several recent large offerings have only seen single-digit first-day percentage rises, while others have seen their stocks decline in subsequent sessions.

(*FT*, 1 February 2010)

Over the last five years Chinese companies have raised about $210 billion globally through initial public offerings ... American companies by contrast, have raised $184 billion ... The global economic crisis sharply cut the number of new listings in the United States and around the world last year [2009], with the exception of China: in 2009 eleven of the fourteen foreign public offerings made on United States exchanges were of mainland Chinese companies ... According to *Forbes*, China had seventy-nine billionaires in 2009, up from just one in 2003. Most of that money is tied to shares of newly listed companies ... In 2009 shares of newly listed companies on ... the Shanghai and Shenzhen exchanges ... jumped, on average, 74 per cent on the first day of trading in China. That was the smallest share price increase in three years. In 2007 the average jump was 193 per cent ... Late last month [January] regulators criticized financial institutions for 'irresponsible' pricing of IPOs, saying it had helped fuel stock speculation, even though recent offerings had slumped in early trading.

(www.iht.com, 12 February 2010; *IHT*, 13 February 2010, pp. 8, 12)

China has stuck to its policy of building up conglomerates to compete with the international giants despite the adverse publicity of such organizations as the South Korean chaebols during the Asian financial crisis. Other reforms include separating government administration from enterprise management.

By the end of 1998 the People's Liberation Army had carried out the order to divest itself of most of its substantial commercial operations.

'Township-village enterprises' (TVEs) played a very important role in China's overall growth in the earlier reform period. Their star waned as they came under increasing strain as a result of a more individually orientated society, a more mobile population (the original families in the local communities being averse to sharing the benefits of their TVEs with the newly arrived) and greater competition from private and the more dynamic state enterprises. One response has been the increasing transformation of TVEs into 'shareholding co-operatives'.

As already said, it is difficult to measure the importance of the 'private' sector in the economy because of problems such as whether to include collectives in the 'public' sector or in the 'private' sector; it is also, for example, especially difficult to measure the private service sector. Despite these problems, the dramatic increase in the role played by the non-state sector is indicated by the following figures.

According to the International Finance Corporation (the private sector arm of the World Bank), in 1998 the state sector contributed 37 per cent of GDP. Private businesses generated 33 per cent, while the balance came from agricultural companies and businesses (*Transition*, 2000, vol. 11, no. 2, p. 40).

'The non-state sector now accounts for 75 per cent of GDP if collective and agricultural output is included' (*FEER*, 12 July 2001, p. 49).

> The private sector ... now accounts for half of China's GDP and 75 per cent if the essentially privatized activities of agriculture, rural collectives and shareholding companies are included, according to estimates by the World Bank's ... International Finance Corporation. The figure is expected to rise.
>
> (*FEER*, 30 August 2001, p. 19)

> Non-state enterprises are now producing two-thirds of manufacturing output, SOEs dominate key sectors such as banking, telecoms, energy and the media. Between 2001 and 2006 the number of SOEs fell from 370,000 to 120,000, but this still left assets worth $1.3 trillion in state control ... In the late 1990s around 30 million workers were laid off as a result of SOE reform.
>
> (*The Economist*, 13 December 2008, pp. 31–2)

The 2004 upward revision of GDP (see below) has, of course, implications for estimates of the importance of the non-state sector in GDP.

[There is a] phenomenon known commonly as *guojinmintui*, or 'the state advances as the private sector recedes'. Leaders have repeatedly denied that the government is implementing a policy of renationalizing parts of the economy and most analysts agree there is not formal policy to support *guojinmintui*. But some argue that the government's response to the financial crisis has allowed state-owned enterprises ... partially to reverse the privatization that has occurred in China over the last thirty years.

(*FT*, 25 August 2009, p. 7)

Since 1978 China has gradually opened up its economy to foreign trade, capital and technology (hence the aptly phrased 'open-door' policy). China has illustrated the benefits of globalization in all three respects as a crucial aspect of its developmental model. Unlike export-orientatated Japan in the early decades after the end of the Second World War, China has imported on a grand scale as well. It has become a world ranking attractor of direct foreign investment and is becoming increasingly important as a source.

Since 1978 (when it was number thirty-two exporter) China has climbed rapidly in world trade rankings:

In a little over two decades China has jumped from being an insignificant trading nation to rank fourth behind the United States, Germany and Japan, according to the WTO's 2001 figures. In that year China accounted for 5.6 per cent of global exports and 4.9 per cent of imports. US exports were 11.9 per cent of the world total and imports 18.3 per cent.

(*FEER*, 18 September 2003, pp. 32–3)

'Between 1980 and 2002 China's share in global exports and imports rose from 1.2 per cent and 1.1 per cent to 5.2 per cent and 4.2 per cent, respectively' (*FT*, 12 November 2003, p. 23).

'[China is] the world's ... fifth largest trading power' (*FEER*, 27 September 2001, p. 12).

'[China is] the third largest exporter and importer' (*FT*, 31 August 2005, p. 14).

'Total foreign trade topped $1.4 trillion ... in 2005 ... making China the world's third largest foreign trader after the United States and Germany' (*IHT*, 12 January 2006, p. 11).

'China, the world's fifth largest exporter last year [2002], accounted for 5.1 per cent of global exports' (*FEER*, 17 April 2003, p. 24).

'[In 2004, according to the World Trade Organization China, overtook] Japan as the world's third largest exporter' (*FT*, 15 April 2005, p. 9).

'China's share of the world's exported goods tripled to 7.3 per cent between 1993 and 2005' (*The Economist*, 13 January 2007, pl. 68).

'[In 2007] China's exports ... made up almost 9 per cent of the world's total' (www.iht.com, 1 July 2008).

'China ... was the world's fifth largest importer last year [2000]' (Mike Moore, director-general of the WTO, *IHT*, 19 September 2001, p. 10).

'China is the world's third largest importer' (www.iht.com, 12 July 2004).

China has become a giant in the export of manufactured goods, especially cheap consumer good such as textiles, footwear and toys. Over time China has also moved upmarket from being overwhelmingly an assembler of imported inputs, i.e. there is a lessening of China's reliance on low value-added manufactured exports (towards products such as electronics). China is perceived as a great threat or a great opportunity depending on circumstances.

China became a net importer of both grain and oil in 1993.

Foreign trade as a percentage of GDP has increased to a remarkable extent.

'[China's] trade/GDP ratio is inordinately high for a continental country – more than 40 per cent compared with about 20 per cent for the United States' (*FT*, 8 June 2004, p. 19).

'The trade-to-GDP ratio increased from 10 per cent at the beginning of the reforms to about 40 per cent in the late 1990s' (*Finance and Development*, 2002, vol. 39, no. 3, p. 22).

'China's ... ratio of trade to GDP at market prices was 44 per cent in 2001' (*FT*, 12 November 2003, p. 23).

> The sum of exports and imports – a traditional measure of a country's openness to trade – now amounts to more than 50 per cent, compared with 20 per cent of GDP in 1989 and less than 10 per cent of GDP in 1979.
>
> (Prasad and Rumbaugh 2003: 46–9)

> Last year [2004] the ratio of trade to GDP, at market prices, reached 70 per cent, much the same as in South Korea ... The United States and Japan have ratios of trade to GDP that are below 25 per cent.
>
> (*FT*, 5 September 2005, p. 17)

> For its size ... [China] is unusually open to the rest of the world in terms of trade and foreign direct investment. The sum of its total exports and imports of goods and services amounts to around 75 per cent of China's GDP; in Japan, India and Brazil the figure is 25 per cent to 30 per cent.
>
> (*The Economist*, 30 July 2005, p. 66)

'[China has] a trade-to-GDP ratio of around 70 per cent' (*The Economist*, Survey, 31 March 2007, p. 6).

There are critics of traditional estimates of the importance of exports as a proportion of GDP:

> Up to half of China's exports are made up of intermediate and semi-finished products imported from other countries to be processed and shipped out again. If the double accounting of the import content is stripped out, the ratio of China's exports to its GDP tumbles to about 18 per cent of the 36 per cent seen in the crude data.
>
> (Qu Hongbin, *IHT*, 12 October 2005, p. 8)

> Headline figures show that China's exports surged from 20 per cent of GDP in 2001 to almost 40 per cent in 2007 ... The headline ratio of exports to

GDP [however] is very misleading ... Exports are measured as gross revenue while GDP is measured in value-added terms. Jonathan Anderson, an economist at UBS, a bank, has tried to estimate exports in value-added terms by stripping out imported components, and then converting the remaining domestic content into value-added terms by subtracting inputs purchased from other domestic sectors ... Once these adjustments are made, Mr Anderson reckons that the 'true' export share is just under 10 per cent of GDP.

(*The Economist*, 5 January 2008, p. 67)

'Exports account for 40 per cent of GDP, but those exports have a large import content; only a quarter of the value of China's exports is added locally' (*The Economist*, 21 October 2006, p. 92).

China's exports account for 36 per cent of GDP, but about half of them are 'processing exports', which contain a lot of imported components. Thus the impact of a fall in exports is partially offset if imports fall too. Estimates suggest that domestic value-added from Chinese exports is a more modest 18 per cent of GDP. An alternative measure of the importance of exports is the change in net exports in real terms. Between 2002 and 2007 the increase in net exports contributed only 15 per cent of real GDP growth in China. In contrast, net exports accounted for half of all growth in Singapore and Taiwan. This measure understates the total impact, though, because it ignores the spillover effects of exports on business confidence, investment, employment and consumer spending.

(*The Economist*, 31 January 2009, p. 74)

China has not typically run large foreign trade surpluses (China needs imported inputs), but the surplus surged in and after 2005.

The United States continually complains about its huge bilateral trade deficit with China. US figures are larger than official Chinese ones: 'The United States counts exports through Hong Kong [as Chinese]' (*FEER*, 27 February 2003, 28). The EU also has a large and growing bilateral trade balance with China and complaints have become more vocal.

China has trade deficits with many Asian countries, such as Japan. (Critics of the United States point out that US companies in China export to the United States and that China has taken over the export of goods that would have come from other developing countries in any case.)

'China's trade surplus last year [2006] jumped to a record $177.47 billion' (www.iht.com, 10 January 2007).

'China's trade surplus reached $177.5 billion last year [2006] ... up from $102 billion in 2005 and $32 billion in 2004' (*FT*, 11 January 2007, p. 8).

The United States ran its largest trade deficit in history in 2006 ... For all of 2006 the trade imbalance expanded to a record $763.6 billion – a fifth consecutive annual record ... The deficit with China shot up 15.4 per cent last year [2006] to total $232.5 billion, the largest imbalance ever recorded with any country.

(www.iht.com, 13 February 2007)

'By China's assessment ... China's surplus in bilateral trade [in 2006] ... was $144 billion' (www.iht.com, 13 April 2007).

'China's current account surplus for 2006 was $249.9 billion or 9.5 per cent of GDP, well ahead of consensus predictions of twelve months ago' (*FT*, 12 May 2007, p. 8).

'[China has] rising trade surpluses with the United States and roaring surpluses with Europe. But when it comes to the rest of the world, it is running a trade deficit' (www.iht.com, 15 June 2007).

> [In 2007 China's] annual trade surplus ballooned to $262.2 billion, up 47.7 per cent from 2006 ... [and the bilateral] surplus with the United States rose 19 per cent to $163.3 billion [according to official Chinese figures] ... [China says that its] 2007 trade gap with the EU rose faster, expanding by 46 per cent to $134.3 billion.
>
> (www.iht.com, 11 January 2008)

(In 2005 China's bilateral trade surplus with the EU was $70.1 billion, rising to $91.7 billion in 2006: *IHT*, 29 January 20–07, p. 11.)

The global financial crisis has reduced China's trade surplus.

'[In 2007] the EU replaced the United States as China's largest export market' (*FT*, 12 January 2008, p. 6).

The state monopoly of foreign trade was ended and an increasing number of increasingly market-orientated state enterprises were allowed to conduct foreign trade on their own and to retain a percentage of foreign exchange earnings. Private companies (both domestic and foreign) were allowed to engage in foreign trade. The sector has become increasingly controlled indirectly, e.g. via the exchange rate system and tariffs, although non-tariff barriers to imports such as licensing and regulations (relating to health and safety, for example) are sources of friction with countries exporting to China.

Tariffs (taxes on imports) have generally been reduced over time, a trend encouraged by WTO commitments. (China has used taxes on exports such as steel products to dampen them in response to complaints from countries such as the United States.)

China did not succeed in gaining founder membership of Gatt's successor, the World Trade Organization (WTO), when it was established on 1 January 1995. China's entry into the WTO on 11 December 2001 was delayed by such factors as quotas, an extensive licensing system and large subsidies to state industrial enterprises. It has been argued that WTO entry had implications for the overall economic reform process in China. 'Prime minister Zhu Rongji ... wants to use commitments to the WTO to make it hard for domestic opponents to overturn reforms. Violations of China's commitments to the WTO invite retaliation by China's trade partners' (*The New York Times*, editorial: *IHT*, 4 November 1999, p. 8).

WTO entry did not eliminate trade friction, however. There was, for example, a surge in imports of Chinese textiles into the United States and the EU (to which both responded) after the lifting (on 1 January 2005) of quotas associated with the Multifibre Agreement. Discussions between the EU and China followed. In June 2005 the two sides agreed to a three-year 'transitional arrangement' to control the import of textiles into the EU. The United States also imposed temporary restrictions on some textile imports. In 2006 the EU raised tariffs on imports of leather shoes from China. In the same year China's tariffs on imported car parts from the EU and the United States caused problems. In October of that year the WTO agreed to examine the case, the first time China had referred to the trade body for formal arbitration. The United States and the EU continue to allege that through continuing subsidies China dumps products such as steel and paper products and unfairly impedes imports into China of products such as car parts and films.

Referrals to the WTO are increasing. '[The EU] has begun just one case … [using] the dispute settlement procedures of the WTO … since 2001, while the United States has begun six' (www.iht.com, 6 November 2007).

The global financial crisis has led to protectionist pressures. Although the WTO has helped to ensure that trade skirmishes have not developed into trade wars, warnings have been given, including by the WTO itself. 'Pascal Lamy, WTO director-general, warned last week that the US tyres decision risked provoking a spiral of tit-for-tat retaliation that could weaken the trade impetus for global economic recovery' (*FT*, 23 September 2009, p. 6).

China played an important part in the failure, on 29 July 2008, of the latest round of Doha negotiations. There was disagreement about a so-called 'special safeguard mechanism' to deal with a sudden surge of food imports or food price falls. The main protagonists were China and India (which wanted the import volume triggering the mechanism set relatively low) on the one hand and the United States on the other.

> China is progressing toward receiving the EU's coveted market economy status, something that would help the Asian export powerhouse avoid punitive anti-dumping duties, an EU document showed … Beijing has been seeking such status from the EU since 2004 … The European Commission said in its latest assessment … that China had still met only one of five criteria used to gauge the influence of state intervention on prices and costs. But Beijing had made 'considerable progress' on the four others, it said, providing a 'clear platform' for reaching the target. The report also described the Chinese economy as 'an increasingly modern and market-based system' … It said: 'The conclusion of this report is that China now has in place almost all the legislation which is necessary for granting Market Economy Status. That is a considerable achievement. The focus has now switched to the effective implementation of these laws which are crucial for the functioning of any market economy' … The one criterion that China has met – as determined by Brussels in 2004 – relates to the absence on non-market payment forms like barter. The criteria it has yet to meet include the use of modern accounting standards, on which China had made 'considerable

progress' and bankruptcy, intellectual property and property laws where progress was 'substantial', the report said. There was less progress in redu-cing the state's role in price setting in sectors like energy, a key component for manufacturers and China was slow in improving the independence of its financial system, the Commission said ... If China gets market economy status in the EU, its exporters would probably face lower duties in anti-dumping fights or avoid them altogether. Because China is not classified as a market economy, Brussels considers price data from other countries like Brazil when assessing whether Chinese goods are being dumped, or sold below cost, in the EU. Costs in so-called analogue countries are routinely higher than in China, resulting in findings of high dumping margins and high EU anti-dumping duties for Chinese goods under dispute ... China had a trade surplus of $227 billion with the EU last year [2007], European data show.

(www.iht.com, 18 September 2008; *IHT*, 19 September 2008, p. 20)

The European Chamber of Commerce has highlighted the theft of intellec-tual property rights, an unpredictable mergers and acquisitions regime, and the exclusion of foreign companies from many government procurement contracts as big deterrents to doing business in China. European investment in China dropped from Euro 6 billion in 2006 to Euro 1.8 billion last year [2007], accounting for just 2 per cent of European foreign direct investment.

(*FT*, 2 October 2008, p. 13)

In 2007 the safety of some Chinese foodstuffs and manufactured goods was increasingly called into question. The list of suspect products compiled by other countries included contaminated fish products, excess lead in the paint used in some toys and toxic chemicals in some brands of cough medicine, toothpaste and toy beads. In the case of small magnets not securely attached to toys, however, the problem turned out to be a design fault by a US company. In 2008 milk adulterated by the chemical melamine produced a major scandal. Some babies even died after developing kidney stones. Animal feed contaminated by melamine was also discovered.

Controls on the Chinese economy (such as on capital flows) helped shield China from the worst effects of the Asian financial crisis (which started in July 1997). The crisis had a temporary dampening effect on China's desire to join the WTO.

Exchange rate controls have helped China through the global financial crisis.

Restrictions on capital account transactions are gradually being eased, but they remain extensive and there have been reversals. For example, there was a strengthening of controls on the capital account in July 2008.

Overall, however, policy is to make the yuan (renminbi or 'people's cur-rency') gradually more and more convertible.

The first local foreign exchange markets ('swap centres') were set up in 1985 (a valuable boost to direct foreign investment since profits earned by 'foreign-invested enterprises' could be repatriated without having to export). On 1

January 1994 the official and swap rates were unified, with the yuan subjected to a managed float. On 1 December 1996 China formally accepted Article 8 of the IMF's articles of association on current account convertibility.

The date of full convertibility of the yuan has been continually put back.

> Zhou Xiaochuan, governor of the People's Bank of China, said in Beijing last month [October 2007]: 'The yuan will eventually become a freely convertible currency and China will open its capital account, even if we have not set a clear timetable. China had agreed in principle to make the yuan convertible in the 1990s, but we halted the plan during the 1997 Asian financial crisis.'
>
> (*IHT*, 19 November 2007, p. 14)

But steady progress has been made in making the yuan more convertible on the capital account. '[For example] Chinese banks, insurers and fund managers last year [2006] received approval to invest overseas for the first time through a quota system known as the Qualified Domestic Institutional Investor Scheme' (*FT*, 12 May 2007, p. 8). 'The Chinese government said that it would let banks buy shares outside China for the first time' (www.iht.com, 15 May 2007).

> China's securities brokerages and fund managers will be allowed to invest in overseas stocks and shares for the first time ... New regulations [were issued on 21 June 2007] allowing ... [them] to apply for Qualified Domestic Institutional Investor quotas to invest in offshore securities.
>
> (*FT*, 22 June 2007, p. 9)

Relaxations have also affected individual Chinese citizens.

> Prime minister Wen Jiabao ... warned Monday [19 November 2007] that illicit currency flows ... out of China ... [represent a] 'huge' amount ... Much of the money flowing out of the mainland into Hong Kong is assumed to be entering the Hong Kong stock market.
>
> (www.iht.com, 20 November 2007; *IHT*, 21 November 2007, p. 13)

'In late 1994 Beijing first pegged the yuan to the dollar' (www.iht.com, 22 July 2005).

> China has fixed the value of the yuan at 8.277 to the dollar since 1995 ... The yuan can be freely exchanged only for trade purposes. Restrictions on the capital account, covering investment, prevent foreign investors from moving short-term capital into China and local investors from shifting funds overseas.
>
> (www.iht.com, 2 July 2004; *IHT*, 3 July 2004, p. 11)

> Officially the renminbi is already floating. It is, in theory, allowed to fluctuate 0.3 per cent either side of a reference rate determined each day by the central bank as a weighted average of the previous day's trades. But in practice the renminbi is pegged to the dollar. Normally the central bank is the biggest player on the Shanghai market, buying and selling currency to keep

the exchange rate in a stable range between 8.2770 renminbi and 8.2800 renminbi to the dollar.

(*FEER*, 4 May 2000, p. 58)

'The renminbi ... is now pegged near 8.28 to the dollar within a band of 8.276 to 8.280' (*FEER*, 5 February 2004, p. 23).

China earned considerable respect in the international community for maintaining the exchange rate of the renminbi (and the Hong Kong dollar) and thus not triggering a further round of competitive devaluations in Asia after the financial crisis started in July 1997. Adverse effects included a decline in exports, but China escaped relatively lightly. Long-imposed controls of the capital account were reinforced by increasingly stringent foreign exchange regulations and indirect ways of boosting exports (e.g. tax rebates for exporters). There was a crackdown on smuggling.

As has already been stressed, China has integrated into the world economy to an extraordinary degree – the country exports and imports a great deal. But increasing bilateral trade surpluses with the United States and the EU are creating great friction. Despite some progress, the United States argues that the yuan is still undervalued against the dollar and so encourages China's exports to the United States and discourages its imports from the latter. There is, however, more general disagreement both about how undervalued the yuan is and about how important a factor this is in explaining the growing bilateral surplus.

On 21 July 2005 there was a small revaluation of the yuan against the dollar. There was a controlled appreciation of the yuan until August 2008. But the yuan's appreciation against the dollar has been too small to appease the United States and others have joined in the chorus of criticism. The EU has been increasingly vocal about the Euro's general appreciation against the yuan.

'After letting the currency rise sharply against the dollar in the first half of this year [2008], China's central bank has actually pushed the yuan down against the dollar in each of the past four trading days' (www.iht.com, 5 August 2008; *IHT*, 6 August 2008, p. 13).

'The currency rose 4.2 per cent in the three months through March and 2.3 per cent in the second quarter before stalling in the third' (www.iht.com, 12 August 2008; *IHT*, 13 August 2008, p. 15).

'The central bank has allowed the yuan to decline against the dollar in the past two weeks after a 20 per cent rise since 2005' (*IHT*, 12 August 2008, p. 14).

The Chinese currency has appreciated by 7 per cent against the US dollar this year [2008]. But the pace of appreciation has slowed sharply over the past two months. In August the renminbi even depreciated slightly against the dollar. This is only the second month that this has happened since China moved away from the dollar peg in 2005.

(*FT*, 1 September 2008, p. 8)

'The yuan, after strengthening for twenty-six consecutive months ... actually weakened slightly against the dollar last month [August] ... The yuan has risen

21 per cent against the dollar since China broke its peg to the dollar in July 2005' (*IHT*, 4 September 2008, p. 11).

> The yuan ... has barely budged [against the dollar] over the past four months. But since the dollar has strengthened dramatically of late, the yuan has surged against other currencies, such as the Euro, sterling and most emerging market currencies. Indeed, in trade-weighted terms, against a basket of currencies, it has risen by 12 per cent over the past six months. Since July 2005, when China scrapped its fixed peg to the dollar, the yuan's trade-weighted value has risen by 20 per cent, by far the biggest appreciation of any large economy.
>
> (*The Economist*, 15 November 2008, p. 89)

Developments in the yuan–dollar rate: 'The renminbi [yuan] ... is now pegged near 8.28 to the dollar within a band of 8.276 to 8.280' (*FEER*, 5 February 2004. p. 23). 'China on Thursday [21 July 2005] revalued the yuan to 8.110 for every dollar ... Until the announcement the yuan sold for 8.277 for every dollar' (www.iht.com, 21 July 2005); 13 November 2006; 22 May 2007, 7.6582; 12 November 2007, 7.4108; 28 December 2007, 7.3041; 17 June 2008, 6.8918; '[The yuan appreciated] over 7 per cent against the doallr earlier this year ... [peaking at] 6.8099 in September' (www.iht.com, 3 December 2009); 11 November 2008, 6.8284; 4 December 2008, 6.8741; 'China's yuan trades at about 6.85 to the dollar' (www.iht.com, 30 January 2009); 'In the three years to July 2008 the yuan climbed by 21 per cent against the dollar. But for the last fourteen months it has, in effect, been repegged to the dollar' (www.economist. com, 30 September 2009); 'The government has kept the renmimbi pegged at a rate of 6.82 renmimbi per dollar' (*FT*, 30 October 2009, p. 15); 'The renminbi [has been] held at about 6.8 per cent to the dollar since July last year [2008]' (*FT*, 17 November 2009, p. 18).

'[There is] rising international criticism that China's currency is undervalued' (*FT*, 16 November 2009, p. 6). Although criticism was muted in G-20 meetings and the like in order to encourage co-operation in wider economic and political areas, open criticism was not lacking in 2009.

> [China has an] outrageous currency policy ... The crucial question is whether the target value of the yuan is reasonable. Until around 2001 you could argue that it was: China's overall trade position wasn't too far out of balance. From then onward, however, the policy of keeping the yuan–dollar rate came to look increasingly bizarre. First of all, the dollar slid in value, especially against the Euro, so that by keeping the yuan–dollar fixed, Chinese officials were, in effect, devaluing their currency against everyone else's. Meanwhile, productivity in China's export industries soared; combined with the de facto devaluation, this made Chinese goods extremely cheap on world markets. The result was a huge Chinese trade surplus. If supply and demand had been allowed to prevail, the value of China's currency would have risen sharply. But Chinese authorities didn't let it rise. They kept it down by selling vast

quantities of the currency, acquiring an enormous hoard of foreign assets, mostly in dollars, currently worth about $2.1 trillion. Many economists, myself including, believe that China's asset-buying spree helped inflate the [US] housing bubble, setting the stage for the global financial crisis. But China's insistence on keeping the yuan–dollar rate fixed, even when the dollar declines, may be doing even more harm now ... China has been keeping its currency pegged to the dollar – which means that a country with a huge trade surplus and a rapidly recovering economy, a country whose currency should be rising in value, is in effect engineering a large devaluation instead. And that's a particularly bad thing to do at a time when the world economy remains deeply depressed due to inadequate overall demand. By pursuing a weak currency policy, China is siphoning some of that inadequate demand away from other nations, which is hurting growth almost everywhere ... With the world economy still in a precarious state, beggar-my-neighbour policies by major players can't be tolerated ... US officials have been extremely cautious about confronting the China problem, to such an extent that last week the Treasury Department, while expressing 'concerns', certified in a required report to Congress that China is not ... manipulating its currency.

> (Paul Krugman, www.iht.com, 23 October 2009;
> *IHT*, 24 October 2009, p. 7)

Rather than face up to the need to change their currency policy ... the Chinese ... have taken to lecturing the United States, telling us to raise interest rates and curb fiscal deficits – that is, to make our unemployment problem even worse.

> (Paul Krugman, www.iht.com, 16 November 2009;
> *IHT*, 17 November 2009, p. 6)

(Paul Krugman won the Nobel Prize for Economic Science in 2008. 'In October [2009] the unemployment rate [in the United States] rose to 10.2 per cent, the highest since April 1983': www.cnn.com, 18 November 2009.)

'The World Bank, which has urged China to adopt a stronger currency, said the renminbi had fallen against its main trading partners since March thanks to its informal peg to the US dollar' (*FT*, 5 November 2009, p. 10).

China said Wednesday [11 September] that it would consider major currencies in guiding the yuan, suggesting a departure from an effective peg to the dollar that has been in place since the middle of last year [2008]. The reference to a new set of benchmarks for determining the value of the yuan holds out the possibility of a departure from past practice. The central bank in a monetary policy report said: 'Following the principles of initiative, controllability and gradualism, with reference to international capital flows and changes in major currencies, we will improve the yuan exchange rate formation mechanism' ... It was the first time since a revaluation and establishing of exchange rate changes in July 2005 that the People's Bank of China had strayed from the language of keeping the yuan 'Basically stable at a reasonable and balanced level' when discussing future currency overhauls in such quarterly reports.

(www.iht.com, 11 November 2009)

China's central bank yesterday [Wednesday 11 November] acknowledged the case for a stronger renminbi, days ahead of the arrival in Beijing of President Barack Obama for talks expected to highlight international concern over currency policy. The People's Bank of China said foreign exchange policy would take into account 'capital flows and major currency movements', a pointed reference to the large speculative inflows of capital that China is receiving and US dollar weakness. The bank's new wording, included in its quarterly report on monetary policy, comes on the heels of growing global pressure to strengthen its currency, particularly from the EU and Japan. The IMF said at the weekend that the renminbi, which was in effect repegged to the dollar last year [2008] after being allowed to appreciate by about 20 per cent against the dollar since 2005, was 'significantly undervalued'. The bank's comments contrast with the calls of Chen Deming, commerce minister, at the weekend for the exchange rate to 'create stable expectations' for exporters ... Few economists expect China to abandon its effective peg to the dollar before the middle of 2010.

(*FT*, 12 November 2009, p. 6)

Governments in Asia, Latin America and the EU are already alarmed by the cheap renminbi and say it is hurting domestic manufacturers ... China's exports have plummeted by more than 20 per cent this year [2009] and at least 20 million factory jobs have been lost in the coastal provinces. Beijing does not want to bring more harm to its huge migrant world force by letting the renminbi rise and with it the cost of Chinese goods abroad.

(www.iht.com, 14 November 2009)

'Analysts say currency appreciation will not occur to any significant extent until the middle of next year [2008], largely because too many jobs are at stake' (*IHT*, 16 November 2009, p. 14).

At the Asia-Pacific summit in Singapore, the final communiqué from the twenty-one members was delayed as President Hu Jintao called successfully for the removal of a reference to the desirability of 'market-orientated exchange rates that reflect underlying economic fundamentals'. In a surprise move the reference had been included in a statement by Apec finance ministers on Thursday [12 November], in spite of China's unwillingness to discuss the matter. Mr Hu ignored the subject in his speeches and contributions to debate. Officials confirmed that it has also been included in the final leaders' statement but was removed after a discussion between the US and Chinese leaders.

(*FT*, 16 November 2009, p. 6)

'Since the start of 2008 the yuan has actually risen against every currency except the yen ... China will probably allow the yuan to start rising again early next year [2010]' (www.economist.com, 19 November 2009; *The Economist*, 21 November 2009, pp. 89–90).

China is a magnet for direct foreign investment (FDI) because of factors such as cheap labour.

The deputy governor of the People's Bank of China: 'The cost of labour in China is only 3 per cent of that of US labour' (*FT*, 23 November 2004, p. 1). '[In China wages as a per cent of] the US level ... are only about 3 per cent or 4 per cent' (*IHT*, 29 December 2007, p. 9). 'Chinese manufacturing wages are still less than 10 per cent of those in America' (www.economist.com, 26 December 2008).

Other factors encouraging DFI include a rapidly growing economy and government policy (such as the opening up, at least partially, of an increasing number of sectors – helped by membership of the WTO – and legislation to give greater protection to property rights).

The protection of property rights has much improved, but complaints about counterfeiting (product and trademark piracy) intellectual property theft and contract enforcement still abound. Significant restrictions regarding the degree and area of activity remain (e.g. over sectors considered to be of strategic significance).

There is a crucial distinction between portfolio investment and direct foreign investment (DFI) is that the latter involves control.

The term 'foreign-invested enterprises' refers to both joint ventures and wholly foreign-owned companies.

The law on joint equity ventures was promulgated on 14 July 1979. Foreign ownership was then limited to a maximum 49 per cent and certain sectors were excluded. Over time there have been a considerable relaxation of such restrictions, e.g. 100 per cent foreign ownership in some cases.

Figures for DFI distinguish between contracted (committed or pledged) and utilized (disbursed or actual) totals. Only the latter figures are given below.

Note that there are problems in computing figures for DFI, such as 'round tripping' (domestic capital sent to places like Hong Kong in particular and back again in order to benefit from tax and tariff concessions at home).

'By 1991 ... cumulative [direct foreign] investment ... [amounted to] $22 billion. Some $3.5 billion was invested in 1991 alone' (*The Economist*, Survey, 28 November 1992, p. 18).

In 1995 the world total of utilized DFI was $315 billion. China, with $38 billion, came second only to the USA's $60 billion' (*The Economist*, 13 April 1996, p. 72).

In 1996 utilized DFI was $42.3 billion and in 1997 it was $45.2 billion. In 1997 China received $64 billion in foreign capital, of which $45.3 billion was direct foreign investment. By the end of 1997 the cumulative total of direct foreign investment stood at $225 billion (Lardy 1998: 84). Figures for utilized DFI for subsequent years are as follows: 1998, $45.6 billion; 1999, $40.4 billion; 2000, $40.7 billion; 2001, $46.8 billion; 2002, $52.74 billion; 2003, $53.5 billion (out of a world total of nearly $560 billion); 2004, $60.6 billion; 2005, $60.3 billion; 2006, $63.0; 2007 (first eleven months), $61.67.

It was claimed that in 2002 and 2003 China overtook the United States as the world's number one destination for direct foreign investment, but subsequent upward revisions of US figures showed that this was not in fact the case.

> By 2003 the ratio of China's stock of inward investment to GDP was 35 per cent – against 8 per cent in [South] Korea, 5 per cent in India and just 2 per cent in Japan – while 57 per cent of China's exports came from foreign-invested enterprises in 2004.
>
> (*FT*, 15 September 2005, p. 7)

> [In 2004] global foreign direct investment [amounted to] ... $648 billion ... The UK attracted more foreign direct investment [$78 billion] than China last year [2004], becoming the world's second largest FDI recipient after the United States ... according to the United Nations Conference on Trade and Development (UNCTAD) ... FDI inflows to the United States rose ... $96 billion in 2004, while flows to China increased from $54 billion to $61 billion. The big upward revision in US inflows for 2003, originally estimated at just $30 billion, also shows that, contrary to earlier reports, the United States has never ceded its lead to China as an investment destination.
>
> (*FT*, 30 September 2005, p. 13)

'[China said on 14 December 2004 that it] had attracted $559 billion in [foreign direct] investment since the government opened the country to overseas investors in 1978' (www.iht.com, 14 December 2004). 'The cumulative total ... of FDI ... by the end of last year [2004] reached $562 billion' (*The Economist*, 29 October 2005, p. 77).

'[China] was the third largest recipient of foreign direct investment after the United States and Britain in 2005' (*IHT*, 16 January 2007, p. 13).

> Last year's boom in mergers and acquisitions fuelled a surge in global flows of foreign direct investment of more than a third last year [2006] to top $1,200 billion, according to preliminary United Nations figures released yesterday [9 January 2007]. This was the highest since 2000 when FDI hit a record $1,400. The UN Conference on Trade and Development (UNCTAD) said ... the United States recovered its top position from the UK as the largest recipient of FDI ... France was third at $88 billion. [China came] fourth.
>
> (*FT*, 10 January 2007, p. 10)

'[According to official figures] by the end of 2006 594,000 foreign-funded enterprises had been approved for a total $691.9 billion in investments since China launched its "special economic zones" in 1980' (*FT*, 9 March 2007, p. 6).

'China's ... inward foreign investment stock ... [totals] $876 billion' (*IHT*, 21 July 2009, p. 18).

> In September [2009] ... foreign direct investment rose ... by 19 per cent from a year earlier ... But actual foreign direct investment for the first nine

months of the year totalled $63.8 billion, a 14 per cent decline from the same period of 2008.

(www.iht.com, 15 October 2009)

'In 1991 foreign-invested enterprises [in China] accounted for 16.8 per cent of total exports and 45.8 per cent of the exports of the SEZs' (Kueh 1992: 668).

In 1995 foreign-funded enterprises (including both joint ventures and wholly foreign-owned companies) accounted for 31.5 per cent of exports and 47.6 per cent of imports (*IHT*, Survey, 28 October 1996, p. v).

'[Foreign-invested enterprises increased] their share of total exports from 1 per cent in 1985 to 50.1 per cent in 2001' (*FT*, 29 October 2002, p. 11).

'[Some] 57 per cent of China's exports came from foreign-invested enterprises in 2004' (*FT*, 15 September 2005, p. 7).

'[In 2004] 63.3 per cent of China's export growth ... was produced by foreign-invested enterprises, up from 56.8 per cent in 2000' (*The Economist*, 29 October 2005, p. 77).

'About 60 per cent of China's exports are controlled by foreign-financed companies' (*IHT*, 10 February 2006, p. 6).

'Nearly 60 per cent of Chinese exports are produced by ... companies that have foreign investments or are joint ventures with foreign companies' (*IHT*, 30 November 2007, p. 9).

Four Special Economic Zones (SEZs) were set up in 1980, the State Council having given approval in July 1979. They were 'special' in the sense that concessions such as lower taxes and tariffs and more flexible employment policies were granted in order to attract foreign capital, technology and know-how. The SEZs were essentially built from scratch, a means of experimenting with new ideas in a gradual and partial manner. New ideas and Western influences would only be spread to the remainder of the economy if and when they had proved their worth. It is no coincidence that three of the SEZs (Shenzhen, Zhuhai and Shantou) are in Guangdong province adjacent to Hong Kong and Macao, while the fourth is Xiamen in Fujian province opposite Taiwan. Hainan Island became the fifth (and final) SEZ in 1988. No new SEZs have been approved since then, but there has been a proliferation of economic development zones with various names.

WTO membership includes a commitment to phase out tax concessions for foreign-invested enterprises.

The trend over time has been to improve the conditions for DFI, although foreigners still complain about such problems as the enforcement of property rights (e.g. enforcing contracts where the legal system is not independent of the Communist Party), counterfeiting and quality control by Chinese partners.

Significant developments are as follows:

'Official incentives for FDI are shrinking: the preferential 15 per cent corporation tax rate enjoyed by foreign companies, half the level for their Chinese counterparts, will be phased out by 2006' (*FT*, Survey, 7 December 2004, p. 2).

[On 11 January 2005 China said that it] will maintain preferential tax rates for foreign companies until at least 2007 ... Foreign companies are subject to an average 15 per cent tax rate, less than half of the 33 per cent paid by Chinese companies ... The government [had] planned to unify the corporate tax code as early as 2006 ... [Apart from foreign companies investing in China] Chinese companies that are eligible for tax exemptions are also lobbying for the corporate tax law to be delayed.

(www.iht.com, 11 January 2005; *IHT*, 12 January 2005, p. 13)

'The government said on Tuesday [12 July] that it would keep tax breaks for some foreign investors because rising labour costs and raw material shortages had made the need for technology transfers and management expertise more urgent' (www.iht.com. 13 July 2005).

At the National People's Congress held 5–16 March 2007 legislation was passed to standardize tax rates levied on foreign and domestic companies.

'Chinese companies [currently] pay 33 per cent tax, while foreign investors pay as little as 15 per cent' (*FT*, 5 March 2007, p. 18).

China ended nearly three decades of favourable treatment for foreign companies yesterday [8 March] with the introduction of a measure to equalize tax rates paid by local and overseas enterprises. The long-awaited law ... will see a single tax rate of 25 per cent levied on all companies. Under the current system Chinese companies have been taxed at up to 33 per cent while foreign enterprises have paid as little as 15 per cent ... The new law, to start next year [2008] ... The bill enacting the changes may not affect foreign companies already operating in China fully for up to five years. Because of the way it was being phased in, China would also continue to offer concessionary tax rates to 'low profit enterprises' and to investors offering high-tech projects.

(*FT*, 9 March 2007, p. 7)

On Sunday [4 March] lawmakers said they would unify China's income tax rate at 25 per cent, cutting the rate on local companies from 33 per cent and raising it from 15 per cent on overseas firms, [the] legislature spokesman said.

(*IHT*, 5 March 2007, p. 11)

China's plan to unify tax rates for foreign and domestic companies should raise the total annual tax bill for foreign investors by about $5.5 billion, finance minister Jin Renqing said Friday [9 March] ... If the bill is confirmed next week it will take effect next 1 January [2008]. A measure being considered by China's legislature would end nearly three decades of blanket tax breaks for foreign investors. It would unify tax rates for foreign and Chinese companies at 25 per cent, up from the average of 15 per cent that the government says foreign companies pay now. That increase [is] to be phased in over five years.

(www.iht.com, 9 March 2007)

Tax paid by foreign and domestic firms will be unified at 25 per cent ... Domestic firms currently pay income tax of 33 per cent, while foreign-funded businesses pay between 15 per cent and 24 per cent ... A controversial 50 per cent tax break for foreign firms that focus on exports – which the United States had said was anti-competitive – will be scrapped. High technology will be taxed at 15 per cent under the reforms.

(www.bbc.co,uk, 8 March 2007)

'[China is to unify] the corporate income tax rate for domestic and foreign-invested companies. From 1 January [2008] both will be 25 per cent. This will raise the rate for foreign-invested companies but cut that of domestic ones' (*FT*, 27 December 2007, p. 4).

'On 5 March [2009] Beijing promulgated new regulations to devolve some authority for approving more foreign investment projects to local authorities' (www.iht.com, 17 March 2009).

China's ministry of commerce on Wednesday [18 March] rejected Coca-Cola's $2.4 billion bid for the top Chinese juice maker, Huiyuan Juice, saying the deal would be bad for competition ... The move blocked what would have been the biggest foreign takeover of a Chinese company and suggested Beijing is still uncomfortable with foreign ownership of big Chinese companies ... The deal is considered not only an early test of China's new anti-monopoly law but also whether Beijing will allow foreign companies greater latitude to acquire big Chinese companies.

(www.iht.com, 18 March 2009; *IHT*, 19 March 2009, p. 15)

Regional labour shortages and rising wages were reported prior to the global financial crisis:

'[A] labour shortage in south-east China [especially in Guangdong province] ... has persisted for more than nine months' (www.iht.com, 19 April 2005).

'Reports of labour shortages first emerged in late 2004, when the government identified shortages in two critical provinces in south-eastern China, Guangdong and Fujian' (*IHT*, 3 April 2006, p. 1).

'Labour shortages are very localized and job-specific ... Shortages [of skilled labour] are everywhere' (*IHT*, 8 April 2006, p. 7).

'The country has a surplus labour pool of as many as 300 million people, many living in inland areas with very low wage costs ... The biggest constraint to exploiting that vast labour pool is skill shortages' (*FT*, 20 April 2006, p. 16).

Wages are on the rise. No reliable figures for average wages exist; the government's economic data are notably unreliable. But factory owners and experts who monitor the nation's labour market say that businesses are having a hard time finding able-bodied workers and are having to pay the workers they find more money ... For decades many labour economists said that China's vast population would supply a nearly bottomless pool of workers. So many people would be seeking jobs at any given time, this reasoning went, that wages in this country would be stuck just above subsistence level. As recently as four years ago, some experts estimated that most of the perhaps 150 million underemployed workers in the countryside would be heading to cities. Instead, sporadic labour shortages started to appear in 2003 at factories in the Pearl River delta of southeastern China. Now those shortages have spread to factories up and down the coast, specialists say ... Chinese officials are quick to say that there is no overall shortage of labour – rather there is a shortage of young workers willing to accept the low wages that prevailed in the 1990s. Factories in cities like Guangzhou advertise heavily for young workers, even while employment offices consider it a success if someone over forty can find any job in less than a year. 'Now they're taking workers into their early thirties,' said Jonathan Unger, director of the Contemporary China Centre at Australian National University in Canberra, 'but anything older than that and they think they can't take the conditions, the eleven-hour days', as well as work on weekends and a tedious life in factory-owned dormitories. Plant owners' refusal to hire blue-collar workers over thirty-five to forty is colliding with the demographic reality of China's one-child policy. The number of workers in the twenty-to-twenty-four-year-old range is already shrinking as more of them go to university instead of entering the work force after high school, and the International Labour Organization [ILO] projects that workers in this age will edge slowly downward through at least 2020 ... A separate report by the Chinese Academy of Social Sciences warned of coming labour shortages even in rural areas as soon as 2009 ... Wages are stagnating in the middle of the labour market – workers who consider themselves too educated for entry-level jobs in the garment factory, but lacking the skills or experience to command a premium salary elsewhere.

(Keith Bradsher, www.iht.com, 29 August 2007)

Average wages have risen by around 15 per cent over the past year, but labour productivity in manufacturing has risen even faster. Indeed, wages have been rising at double-digit rates for a decade with no harmful impact on growth, because labour productivity has actually reduced wage costs. There are localized skill shortages, but it is hard to believe that China's labour surplus is exhausted when almost 60 per cent of the population still lives in rural areas. The wide income gap between rural and urban areas will continue to attract workers from farms to factories ... The World Bank argues that China is unlikely to face a labour shortage for many years.

(*The Economist*, 29 September 2007, p. 89)

Employers fear that a new labour law that took effect yesterday [1 January 2008] will intensify growing pressure on manufacturing costs by enhancing the bargaining power of workers ... The new labour law closes a loophole that allowed companies to dismiss workers on temporary or fixed-term contracts without compensation, or even employ them without a formal contract altogether – often through third-party labour agencies. From 1 January workers who have been with a company for ten years – or signed two fixed-term contracts – will be entitled to one month's severance pay for every year worked. The law also requires employers to consult an 'employee representative congress', usually a branch of the official All-China Federation of Trade Unions [ACFTU], on any changes to matters including hours, benefits and compensation ... Labour rights groups, which welcomed the law as a laudable step forward, are worried that patchwork implementation in different localities could water down its protections ... Workers in factories where ACFTU does not have a presence must nevertheless seek the official union's 'direction' or 'guidance'.

(FT, 2 January 2008, p. 6)

Investment overseas by Chinese companies and institutions is becoming increasingly significant in the search for energy and other raw materials, technology, management skills and brand names. The sensitivity of such attempts has led to some deals being frustrated, e.g. the failure to acquire the US oil company Unocal and the failure to acquire a stake in 3Com (a US maker of internet router and networking equipment). In early June 2009 Rio Tinto and BHP Billiton announced that they had formed a fifty–fifty joint venture, with the former pulling out of the deal with Chinalco (announced in February of that year).

The issue of sovereign investment funds (of which China now has one) has become a general global problem, with recipient countries anxious about foreign states possibly having aims other than profit in mind when buying shares.

Sovereign wealth funds [SWFs] are large pools of capital controlled by governments and invested in private markets abroad ... SWFs are government investment vehicles funded by foreign exchange assets and managed separately from official reserves ... From 2000 to 2007 sovereign funds grew dramatically from twenty with assets worth several hundred billion dollars to forty with an estimated worth of $2 trillion to $3 trillion. Current projections forecast an increase in assets to $10 trillion to $15 trillion by 2015 ... SWF assets today are currently larger than the total assets under management by either hedge funds or private equity funds, but are only a fraction of the estimated $190 trillion in global financial assets.

(Robert Kimmitt, IHT, 27 December 2007, p. 4)

China has also been criticized for disregarding human rights and environmental considerations in developing countries.

Until recently Chinese foreign acquisitions generally involved taking majority stakes in oil, gas and commodities companies in developing markets. The largest deal, two years ago, was the acquisition of Petro-Kazakhstan for $4 billion. Forays into the developed world either failed or succeeded only in picking up ailing businesses, as in Lenovo's acquisition of IBM's shrinking personal computer division. Attempts to buy stronger firms such as Unocal and Maytag in America ran aground, mostly for political reasons. But Beijing wants Chinese firms to gain access to foreign technologies, raw materials and skills … So the Chinese have adopted a new approach. Majority control is now less important … Influence and access to skills are regarded as more valuable than control. Small stakes are both educational and more feasible politically. Direct holdings are also less important. Chinese buyers are happy to make investments in intermediate companies [e.g. Blackstone, Bear Stearns and Standard Bank], which can be used to take other, less obvious stakes in other businesses.

(*The Economist*, 3 November 2007, p. 85)

China Development Bank's plan to bid for Dresdner Bank in Germany failed in large part because Chinese leaders refused to agree to the deal in time, a sign of Beijing's increasingly cautious attitude to investments in Western financial institutions. The hesitancy of China's State Council to approve a potential $10 billion bid for a majority stake in Dresdner is another indication of Beijing's caution after investments in Western counterparts last year, most of which have fallen in value. The Chinese government has not approved any major Chinese offshore investment in a financial firm this year [2008] … After a string of high profile overseas acquisitions last year [2007] that seemed to herald the arrival of Chinese financial institutions on the world stage, Beijing has turned cautious and has yet to approve any big offshore investment by the [financial] sector this year … When Citigroup went looking for investors for its giant recapitalization in January [2008], China Development Bank initially offered to provide $5 billion as the anchor investor, but the deal fell through when the government refused to approve it … Almost every high profile Chinese purchase of an overseas financial institution made last year is now deeply in the red … Blackstone … Morgan Stanley … Barclays Bank … Belgo-French insurer Fortis … [China has] foreign exchange reserves of almost $2,000 billion.

(*FT*, 5 September 2008, p, 23)

The State Administration of Foreign Exchange [Safe], the opaque manager of nearly $2,000 billion of reserve, started making huge bets on global stocks … diversifying into equities … early in 2007 and continued this strategy at least until the collapse of the US mortgage finance providers Freddie Mac and Fannie Mae in July 2008, according to … the Council on Foreign Relations in New York … By that point Safe had moved well over 15 per cent of the country's $1,800 billion reserves into riskier assets, including equities and corporate bonds … Judging from the subsequent fall in global stock prices and a conservative estimate that Safe held about $160 billion worth of overseas equities, Chinese losses on those investments would exceed $80 billion.

(*FT*, 16 March 2009, p. 1)

China's ministry of commerce has relaxed rules to make it much easier for Chinese companies to win approval to invest overseas ... Although China is also turning more cautious in overseas investment after the global financial crisis left some firms nursing heavy losses on overseas acquisitions, outbound mergers and acquisitions by Chinese companies still leapt 64 per cent last year [2008] to $47.8 billion ... According to new rules that take effect on 1 May [2009], local authorities under the ministry of commerce will have the power to give approval for most corporate overseas investment projects ... The ministry will retain the power to give approval for corporate investment worth $100 million and above for a single project or investment in a country that does not have diplomatic relations with China ... The rules apply to the establishment, mergers and acquisitions of only non-financial companies ... The official *Shanghai Securities News* said that the changes meant 85 per cent of Chinese foreign investment projects would be approved by local commerce authorities when the new rules come into effect.

(www.iht.com, 17 March 2009)

'China is moving aggressively this year [2009] to acquire foreign assets during the global economic downturn' (www.iht.com, 18 March 2009).

Citing national security, Australia on Friday [27 March] blocked one of several acquisitions China is seeking in the country's natural resources sector, a move that may stoke concerns about rising protectionist tendencies around the globe. The decision to block the purchase of OZ Minerals, a mining company, by state-owned China Minmetals Corporation, coincides with a heated debate concerning a much larger investment that Chinalco is planning to make in British–Australian mining group Rio Tinto ... Australia's treasurer, Wayne Swan, said on Friday that he decided to block the OZ Minerals transaction because the company's Prominent Hill gold and copper mine, its core asset, is near a sensitive defence facility.

(www.iht.com, 27 March 2009; *IHT*, 28 March 2009, p. 14)

Though it remains miniscule by global standards, China's overseas investment has been rocketing upward in the past three years: the 2008 total, $52.2 billion, was double that of the year before. It appears set to rise sharply again in 2009, as the global economic crisis pushes the shares of many companies to bargain levels and foreign companies feel pressure to seek outside investment. Most of the Chinese money has gone into minerals, metals and energy, all areas where China's domestic production falls well short of meeting its industrial needs.

(*IHT*, 4 July 2009, p. 11)

The first half of 2009 may prove to be an inflection point for Chinese outbound foreign direct investment [OFDI] ... [But] the government is not throwing caution to the wind. Beijing blocked Bank of China's purchase of a stake in La Compagnie Financière Edmond de Rothschild, the French investment bank, and has responded tepidly to a bid by Sichuan Tengzhong, a little known machinery maker, for General Motors' Hummer unit ... New government rules issued last week will make it easier for companies to finance outbound foreign direct investment.

(*IHT*, 21 July 2009, p. 18)

The Australian government rejected Chinese investments in two mining projects on Thursday [25 September] ... The Foreign Investment Review Board in Australia said on Thursday that the government preferred that foreign state-owned companies buy less than 50 per cent stakes in small and undeveloped Australian mines, and stakes of less than 15 per cent in big mining operations.

(www.iht.com, 25 September 2009; *IHT*, 26 September 2009, p. 18)

Dimensions of investment overseas by Chinese companies and institutions (outward/outbound direct foreign investment):

'By the end of 1998 Chinese enterprises had invested a total of $6.3 billion overseas' (*FEER*, 15 April 1999, p. 82).

Overseas investment by Chinese companies totalled $2.7 billion last year [2002], the ministry of commerce said ... Total overseas investment by Chinese companies stood at $29.9 billion at the end of 1992. It was the first time that the nation's overseas investment had been officially reported.

(www.iht.com, 17 December 2003)

'China's accumulated direct investment overseas reached $33.4 billion by the end of 2003' (*FEER*, 16 September 2004, p. 32).

'[China's] outward foreign investment was just $2.9 billion in 2003 ... China's stock of outward FDI amounts to $33 billion, less than half a per cent of accumulated world FDI' (*The Economist*, 7 January 2005, p. 58).

'China's government reported $2.85 billion [outward] DFI for 2003, a 5.5 per cent increase from 2002' (www.iht.com, 22 December 2004).

In 2004 'overseas investment by Chinese companies' was $3.6 billion (*FT*, 9 February 2005, p. 6).

'[China's] flows of direct investment abroad grew from $1.8 billion in 2004 to $11.3 billion last year [2005]' (*The Economist*, 21 October 2006, p. 126).

'Worldwide direct investment from China more than tripled in 2005 to about $6 billion, according to the Economist Intelligence Unit' (*IHT*, 3 April 2006, p. 17).

'Chinese outbound foreign direct investment accounts for about 3 per cent of the global total, far below its share of world trade and economic output' (*IHT*, 4 June 2009, p. 19).

'Direct investment originating [in China] ... has leapt from almost nothing six years ago to $52 billion last year [2008]' (*FT*, 8 June 2009, p. 11).

'Chinese offshore investment has surged: from just $143 million in 2002, outbound non-financial direct investment reached $40.7 billion last year [2008] ... In 1998 the figure was $0.1 billion' (*FT*, 12 June 2009, p. 9).

Though it remains miniscule by global standards, China's overseas investment has been rocketing upward in the past three years: the 2008 total, $52.2 billion, was double that of the year before. It appears set to rise sharply again in 2009, as the global economic crisis pushes the shares of many companies to bargain levels and foreign companies feel pressure to seek outside investment.

(*IHT*, 4 July 2009, p. 11)

China's outbound foreign direct investment has increased steadily this decade, and the outflow of $52 billion last year [2008] was a record. Still, the historical stock of the outbound direct investment of $170 billion is puny next to China's foreign exchange reserves and its inward foreign investment stock of $876 billion.

(*IHT*, 21 July 2009, p. 18)

Premier Wen Jiabao in an address to Chinese diplomats on Monday (20 July): 'We should hasten the implementation of our "going out" strategy and combine the utilization of foreign exchange reserves with the "going out" of our enterprises.' The 'going out strategy' is a government slogan for encouraging investment and acquisitions abroad, particularly by state-owned industrial giants such as PetroChina, Chinalco, Bank of China and China Telecom ... Mr Wen did not elaborate on how much of the country's $2,132 billion of reserves would be channelled to Chinese enterprises.

(*FT*, 22 July 2009, p. 6)

'China, which less than two decades ago had just a handful of tiny investments abroad, is now the world's sixth biggest foreign investor' (*IHT*, 19 August 2009, p. 14).

China's outbound direct investment more than doubled last year [2008] from 2007, reaching $56 billion according to the ministry of commerce. But Chatham House, the London-based think-tank, estimates it could have been double that figure. China has gone from annual outward direct investment of just $140 billion in 2002 to being the sixth largest source of outward direct investment last year.

(*FT*, Survey, 1 October 2009, p. 4)

Direct investment abroad doubled to around $50 billion in 2008 – and [is] maintaining a similar level this year [2009] ... A more cautious attitude is shown by the China Investment Corporation, China's sovereign wealth fund, which has been taking stakes to the 7 per cent to 15 per cent range, big enough to be significant but small enough not to raise nationalist hackles.

(*IHT*, 17 November 2009, p. 6)

2   Agriculture

Agriculture has been subject to great policy swings. The land reform of 1950–3 involved a massive redistribution of land and property to poorer peasants. ('Peasants did briefly enjoy private land ownership rights after Mao took over': *The Economist*, 16 February 2008, p. 65.) Learning the lessons of Soviet collectivization of the 1930s, China progressed through increasing degrees of co-operation until 'advanced agricultural producer co-operatives' (AAPC) became dominant.

During the Great Leap Forward (1958–60) an attempt was made to accelerate economic development and the transition to communism. For example, 'Chairman Mao Tse-tung (Zedong) exhorted his countrymen to make enough steel to "overtake Britain in fifteen years and America in twenty years"' (*FT*, 6 May 2003, p. 19). 'People's communes' were set up, reaching an average size of 4,550 households. Pronounced moves towards egalitarianism severely dampened work incentives and the removal of peasants from the land (especially at peak periods) to work in local industry ('backyard' steel furnaces etc.) were factors that contributed to drastic falls in agricultural output and massive loss of life. After the GLF the main unit of production becomes the AAPC and then the team.

'Roughly 10 million people … were killed in Mao's post-1949 political campaigns and the other 30 to 40 million … died as a result of his Great Leap Forward famine of 1958–61' (*FEER*, 13 September 2001, p. 66).

> Chronic soil erosion and extreme poverty [are among] the after-effects of the Great Famine of 1959–61, which flowed from Mao's decision to leave the 1958 harvest unpicked and clear forests to create mega-farms and power 'backyard' steel furnaces … Rivers [have been] polluted by a recent boom in coal mining; this was inspired by Mao's madcap idea that with sufficient coal China's steel industry could surpass Britain's in a year: the so-called Great Leap Forward.
>
> (*FEER*, 27 September 2001, p. 65)

('The countryside was stripped of trees for fuel to fire backyard [steel] furnaces, causing widespread floods': *IHT*, 12 April 2004, p. 6.) 'The Great Leap Forward [left] at least 30 million dead and the Cultural Revolution perhaps 3 million' (*FEER*, 13 March 2003, p. 54). '[Mao's] regime brought about the deaths of perhaps 50 million people during its first calamitous quarter century of rule' (p. 54).

'Jung Chang and Jon Halliday [*Mao: the Untold Story*] … assert that Mao was responsible for upwards of 70 million peacetime deaths, including at least 37 million in the 1959–61 famine that arose from Mao's harebrained economic policies' (Jonathan Mirsky, *IHT*, 6 July 2005, p. 7).

Penny Kane (1988) puts the number of excess deaths in the three years between 1959 and 1961 at between 14 million and 26 million. Some put the upper figure much higher. For example, Roderick MacFarquhar calls it 'the worst man-made famine in history … There were 30 million excess deaths between 1958 and 1961', while Liu Binyan puts the figure at 50 million (cited in *The New York Review of Books*, 5 February 1998, pp. 31–2). 'From 1959 to 1961 probably 30 million died of hunger – the party admits 16 million' (Jonathan Mirsky, *IHT*, 9 January 2004, p. 6).

Chang and Wen (1997) analyse the famine of 1958–61. It resulted in about 30 million additional deaths. Causal factors included bad weather, a reduction in the sown acreage, the government's high grain procurement, forced collectivization, the allocation of resources away from agriculture to heavy industry, bad management, the collapse of the incentive system and the elimination of farmers' withdrawal rights from the collectives (pp. 1–2). There was also a lack of democracy. For example, a free press would have reported correct information about the severity of the crisis. In China local officials tried to please central authorities by providing falsely optimistic news (pp. 28–9).

> The key problem remaining unsolved is that the starvation started actually as early as late 1958 when grain availability was adequate in the suffering regions … While we admit that the magnitude of the catastrophe should be explained by a combination of multidimensional factors, it is the communal dining system that first started and then greatly aggravated the famine.
>
> (p. 2)

In the autumn of 1958 70–90 per cent of peasants were driven into the communal dining system. In this system the entire grain output of a commune (after the deduction of seed, feed and the quota delivered to the state) was sent to the communal dining halls (p. 19). Fearing deprivation, those who had private grain stocks hastily consumed them. The communal dining halls encouraged a huge waste of food and 'the free food supply also induced enormous overconsumption' (p. 20). Incentives were severely damaged since members found that everybody ate the same quantity of food whether whether or not work was done (p. 21). 'Individuals lost their essential consumption rationality required for survival in a poor economy with a limited food supply (p. 28).

> The avoidance of such economic disasters as famines is made much easier by the existence, and the exercise, of various liberties and political rights, including the liberty of free expression. One of the remarkable facts in the history of famine is that no substantial famine has ever occurred in a country

with a democratic form of government and a relatively free press ... It is now estimated that the Chinese famines from 1958 to 1961 killed close to 30 million people ... The so-called Great Leap Forward, initiated in the late 1950s, was a massive failure, but the Chinese government refused to admit it and continued dogmatically to pursue much the same disastrous policies for three more years. It is hard to imagine that this could have happened in a country that goes to the polls regularly and has an independent press. During that terrible calamity the government faced no pressure from newspapers, which were controlled, or from opposition parties, which were not allowed to exist. The lack of a free system of news distribution even misled the government itself. It believed in its own propaganda and the rosy reports of local party officials competing for credit in Beijing. Indeed, there is evidence that just as the famine was moving toward its peak, the Chinese authorities mistakenly believed they had 100 million more metric tons of grain than they actually had. These issues remain relevant in China today. Since the economic reforms of 1979 official Chinese policies have been based on an acknowledgement of the importance of economic incentives without a similar acknowledgement of the importance of political incentives. When things go reasonably well the disciplinary role of democracy might not be greatly missed; but when big policy mistakes are made this lacuna can be quite disastrous.

(Amartya Sen, *IHT*, 16 October 1998, p. 8)

I worked on a farm for half a year in Wu Wei County in 1958 and I know how the county and provincial Party Commission Secretaries disregarded human lives by 'launching satellites' (a nickname for forging astronomically high food production records). This resulted in higher quotas of grain to be handed to the state ... Large numbers ... fled and ... died of starvation.

(Bao Tong, *FEER*, 5 September 2002, www.feer.com)

Yang Jisheng ... has become something of a thorn in the side of the Chinese authorities in recent years ... Yang [is] a Communist Party member ... [He did] a thirty-five-year stint as a journalist for Xinhua, the official Chinese news agency ... His latest book, *Mu Bei* (*Tombstone*), published this year [2008] in Hong Kong, has been hailed as the most comprehensive and authoritative account by a mainland Chinese writer of the Great Famine of late 1958 to 1962, which was precipitated by the calamitous economic policies of Mao's Great Leap Forward ... The title, he writes in the opening passage, has several meanings: 'It is a tombstone for my father, who died of starvation in 1959; it is a tombstone for the 36 million who starved to death; it is a tombstone for the system that led to the Great Famine.' The two-volume, 1,100-page-work is banned in China, as is his previous book, *Political Struggles in China's Age of Reform*, which contains his account of the 1989 military crackdown on student-led pro-democracy demonstrations in Tiananmen Square and three interviews with former prime minister Zhao

Ziyang. Zhao, who was purged for sympathizing with students, met with Yang while under house arrest … Working from official population statistics and his own estimates of under-reported deaths based on his investigations, Yang Jisheng concluded that at least 36 million people died of starvation during the famine … The Chinese government still plays down the man-made disaster as 'three years of natural disasters'.

(www.iht.com, 18 December 2008)

Some general facts and figures about agriculture

China has to support about 22 per cent of the world's population on something like 7 per cent of the world's arable area. 'China has 7 per cent of the world's cultivable land' (*FT*, 27 July 2004, p. 15).

'Agricultural workers accounted for 84.2 per cent of the work force in 1952' (*The Economist*, 19 January 2002, p. 57).

'Agriculture accounted for 71 per cent of employment in 1978 and 49 per cent in 2003' (*FEER*, April 2006, pp. 41–2).

'Agriculture accounts for half of the work force but only 15 per cent of GDP' (*IHT*, 20 November 2001, p. 8).

'According to a report by the OECD … agriculture employed 40 per cent of China's workers, but produced only 15 per cent of economic output' (*FT*, 15 November 2005, p. 10).

'In 1978 a mere 18 per cent of Chinese lived in cities and towns' (www.iht.com, 31 May 2007, p. 2).

'[There are] 900 million peasants, who represent three-quarters of the population but account for only 15 per cent of GDP' (*FEER*, 27 September 2001, p. 66).

'The rural population accounts for 62 per cent of the total population' (www.iht.com, 25 December 2003).

'[In China] 800 million people, about 60 per cent of the population, live in the countryside' (*The Economist*, 9 April 2005, p. 49).

'China keeps its rural and urban populations distinct through population controls, classifying most rural residents as peasants even when they migrate to the cities to find work … [There are] 800 million rural residents' (*IHT*, 3 February 2005, p. 1).

In 1979 80 per cent of the population was classified as rural compared with 58 per cent in 2005 (*The Times*, 4 March 2006, p. 54).

'Currently about 42 per cent of the population is urbanized' (*IHT*, 19 August 2006, p. 4).

'Rural China is still home to about 60 per cent of the country's 1.3 billion people, but agriculture's contribution to GDP has fallen from more than a quarter in 1990 to less than 12 per cent today' (*The Economist*, 13 October 2007, p. 27).

A key feature of the Chinese development model is a huge flow, often put at some 150 million, of migrants from the countryside to the towns. This provides abundant and cheap labour, spurring industry and attracting direct foreign investment. (See 'Migration from the countryside' on the 'floating population', below.)

> Official figures last year [2007] showed that there were 150 million migrant workers. But 737 million Chinese, or 56 per cent of the population, still lived in the countryside at the end of 2006, a high figure compared with other countries at a similar stage of development.
>
> (*IHT*, 5 February 2008, p. 13)

'The hinterland has already dispatched 130 million ... across the country, according to the national agricultural census. The remaining rural labour force ... [is] 530 million' (www.iht.com, 10 March 2008).

> About 250 million farmers ... have left farming in recent years for higher-paid jobs in cities ... Agricultural subsidies [are] expected to reach $19.5 billion this year [2008] ... In the past ten years the government's average purchase price of grain edged up merely 5.3 per cent, according to government figures.
>
> (www.iht.com, 2 July 2008)

'Chinese people work hard because they grew up in a culture built around rice farming. Tending a rice paddy required working up to 3,000 hours a year, and it left a legacy that prizes industriousness' (www.iht.com, 16 December 2008).

Reforms: the Household Responsibility System

Agriculture was the first sector to be reformed.

The Household Responsibility System (HRS) arose from below in the form of local experiments which gained central approval.

> [A] group of peasants in 1978 in a village in central Anhui, who broke up the land into plots farmed by individual households. At the time they seemed to be taking a big risk. But the party itself soon decided that the Mao-era communal farms had failed and households should be allocated plots of land. The Anhui villagers became famous and the new 'Household Responsibility System' pushed up yields and incomes. Land ownership remained unchanged.
>
> (*The Economist*, 16 February 2008, p. 64)

Once generally accepted the HRS was rapidly introduced country-wide. By 1983–4 the HRS had become overwhelmingly dominant (Hartford 1987: 212).

Private (family) farms do not own agricultural land (this is owned by the village community), but are allowed to lease land. Originally leases of three to five years were common, but the length has been increased substantially (some argue indefinitely in reality in some cases). Leases are inheritable and peasants have subsequently been allowed to lease land to one another. Family farms are 'responsible' for meeting quotas for specified products (at state-determined prices), tax obligations and payments for collectively provided services (such as irrigation). But then the private farms are free to determine their own output and to whom to sell (at market prices). Farmers now enjoy wide-ranging production freedom.

'In 1993 only 5 per cent of their production was set by the state plan. Leases are usually fifteen-year ones' (Sachs and Woo 1996: 2; Cao *et al.* 1997: 20).

At the Sixteenth Party Congress held in November 2002 it was announced that peasants would be able to sell land-use rights and that encouragement would be given to larger plots.

> China has secretly launched an experiment ... which has won approval from Beijing ... Several cities will be allowed to sell the usage rights for a certain category of land to construction developers without first obtaining the permission of the central government ... Four cities in central China have so far been chosen to conduct the experiment – Hangzhou and Huzhou in Zhejiang province, Anyang in Henan, and Wuhu in Anhui.
>
> (*FT*, 10 December 2002, p. 13)

'In Shanxi [province] contracts are even longer ... [in some cases] fifty years ... [in some cases] effectively ... permanent ownership [so long as the land is worked]' (Susan Lawrence, *FEER*, 22 October 1998, p. 24).

> Last month [October 1998] a government statement following a legislative review of farm policy made clear that the sector was a vital part of overall economic policy ... confirming the plan to allow farmers thirty-year leases on their land instead of fifteen-year agreements as before.
>
> (*FT*, Survey, 16 November 1998, p. iv)

'Many of the fifteen year leases that were drawn up in 1984 are being renewed for thirty more years' (Wang 1999: 13).

> The adoption of a revised land management law on 29 August 1998 represented a watershed in the reform process. The new law requires that collectively-owned arable land be contracted to collective members for a term of thirty years and that a written contract be executed detailing the rights and obligations of both parties ... The central government called for full implementation of thirty-year land-use rights by the end of 1999 ... The law also restricts land readjustments.
>
> (Brian Schwarzwalder, *Transition*, 2000, vol. 11, no. 5, pp. 21–2)

On 1 March 2003 the Rural Land Contracting Law came into effect:

1   '[In his speech of 8 November 2002 Jiang Zemin] indicated that farmers should be able to sell their land use rights for profit' (*FT*, 13 November 2002, p. 14).

2   '[The law] details the rights of thirty-year contract farmers, attempts to ban reallocation almost completely, and, most radically, allows the transfer of

leases for money' (Stephen Green, *The World Today*, 2003, vol. 59, no. 4, p. 27).

3 'The Rural Land Contracting Law was passed on 1 March [2003]. It helps farmers secure existing rights of tenure for thirty years on their holdings and restricts the ability of local officials to change the size of a holding' (*FEER*, 10 April 2003, p. 47).

4 'In 2003 new legislation gave farmers the right to a thirty-year lease on their land, but this law has not yet been fully implemented' (OECD 2005: website Chapter 1).

(See below for the reforms introduced in October 2008.)

Early agricultural successes

The boost to incentives and other factors (such as higher prices) led to a remarkable improvement in farm incomes during the first half of the 1980s.

Johnson (1988a: 234) estimates that the real income of farm people doubled during the period 1978–86.

The United Nations (1993: 187, 197) estimates that rural income increased at an average annual rate of 12.8 per cent 1978–85, the figure for rural *per capita* income in real terms being 7.5 per cent.

In more recent years there has been considerable peasant discontent, e.g. complaints about the prices they receive for output and have to pay for inputs and the taxes, and charges imposed upon them by local authorities (in some cases illegally; corruption is one commonly cited factor). (Unrest owing to the takeover of agricultural land is discussed below.)

> China [has launched] a sweeping overhaul of rural taxation designed to solve the problem of excessive and arbitrary taxes in the countryside ... The plan, announced at the March [2001] session of the national parliament, calls for all fees and taxes normally levied by the lowest two levels of rural government – the village and the township – to be abolished. Instead a new single tax would be levied by the next highest level – the county – and divided up among the three.
>
> (*FEER*, 5 April 2001, pp. 28–9)

> A leaked text of an address given by Zhu Rongji ... on 5 June [2001 included the statement that] it was necessary to be 'safe and slow down somewhat a few major reforms in light of the current situation'. Mr Zhu indicated that one casualty would be the government's plans to promote badly needed tax reforms in the countryside. The aim of these is to eliminate various fees and levies arbitrarily imposed on farmers by local authorities and rely instead on a single tax based on income from crop production ... These have exacerbated other problems ... [e.g. plummeting] revenues of village-level governments.
>
> (*The Economist*, 16 June 2001, p. 72)

The 'tax-for-fee' reform, as China calls it, has been tried out in the eastern province of Anhui and parts of other provinces in the past two years. The results have been mixed ... China announced this week that a third of its provinces would try out the tax-for-fee system next year [2002], but it was too soon to impose it on the whole country.

(*The Economist*, Saturday 15 December 2001, p. 62)

The gap between urban and rural incomes

The gap between rural and urban incomes has widened considerably in recent years to the detriment of farmers.

In 1978 the annual *per capita* income of urban residents was ... two-and-a-half times the ... average income of rural residents ... In the early 1980s the income gap between urban and rural residents narrowed. In 1984 the income ratio dropped to 1.6:1, a historic low that was never repeated thereafter. The gap narrowed because economic reform focused on rural areas and policies were favourable to the agricultural sector ... Beginning in 1985 the focus of China's economic reform shifted to cities and the income gap grew. In 1994 the ratio of urban to rural incomes reached a record 2.9:1. In 1999 the gap narrowed slightly to 2.7:1.

(*Transition*, 2001, vol. 12, no. 1, p. 13)

'By 2000 ... [the ratio] had risen to 2.8 times and [is] still rising' (*IHT*, 20 November 2001, p. 8).

'In 2000, the fifth straight year of reduced growth, [rural] incomes rose just 2.1 per cent, to an average of $272, compared to $763 in the cities' (*FEER*, 2 May 2002, p. 25).

'The 2003 rise [of 4.3 per cent] resulted in an annual *per capita* net income for rural residents of 2,622 renminbi ($316). Urban residents recorded a 9.3 per cent rise in incomes' (*FEER*, 5 February 2004, p. 22).

'Average rural incomes last year [2003] were 2,622 renminbi; up 4.3 per cent. By comparison urban incomes climbed 9.3 per cent to 8,500 renminbi' (*FT*, 10 February 2004, p. 10).

In 2004 there were signs of a significant improvement in rural incomes owing to such factors as rising prices for agricultural products.

'[But in 2004] average urban income was 3.2 times higher than in rural areas' (*IHT*, 3 February 2005, p. 1).

'*Per capita* disposable income in towns and cities ... rose 7.7 per cent to 9,422 yuan last year [2004], while incomes in rural areas rose 6.8 per cent to 2,936 yuan' (www.iht.com, 14 March 2005).

The agriculture minister ... Du Qinglin [said on 10 March that] average annual incomes for farmers rose 12 per cent last year [2004], but still total just 2,936 yuan, or $355 per person ... By contrast the government says annual incomes in China's booming cities average more than $1,000 per person.

(www.iht.com, 10 March 2005)

'*Per capita* income in the countryside averaged 4,140 yuan last year [2007]. For city dwellers it was 13,786 yuan' (www.iht.com, 21 February 2008).

'The latest official statistics show that *per capita* city incomes are 3.3 times bigger than those in the countryside, the biggest since reforms began in 1978' (*Guardian*, 13 October 2008, p. 25).

'The average farmer's income was 4,140 yuan, or $604, last year [2007], less than one-third the urban average' (www.iht.com, 5 November 2008; *IHT*, 6 November 2008, p. 17).

'The ratio of urban to rural income rose to record level of 3.3 in 2007, government figures show' (*IHT*, 14 April 2009, p. 19).

Migration from the countryside

There is now a huge 'floating population' in the towns and cities as people have left the land. Estimates vary.

An early official figure of 20 million was mentioned, but that figure has climbed considerably.

> Since China's economic reforms of the late 1970s, millions of farmers have left the land to seek work in the cities. The combination of the need for cheap labour and the relative relaxation of state controls over the movement of people has meant that the 'floating population' of Chinese living away from their place of *hukou* registration now amounts to about 120 million, according to the latest official figures ... At birth every Chinese person is assigned to a particular location, called the household registration or *hukou*.
> (Sophia Woodman, *The New York Review of Books*, 11 May 2000, vol. XLVII, no. 8)

(For changes in the *hukou* system, see below.)

Temporary migration to cities was made legal in 1983 (*FEER*, 7 October 1999, p. 64).

'In addition to the 150 million migrant workers, around half ... [of those] currently employed in farming are thought to be surplus to requirements, Chinese academics estimate' (*FT*, 29 October 2002, p. 11). ('[The National Research Institute in Beijing says] there are 300 million to 400 million surplus rural labourers': *FEER*, 1 April 2004, p. 28.)

> Official estimates put the country's floating population, or internal migrants, at 147 million, a number that consists overwhelmingly of adults in their prime who have left the countryside for the booming economies of the eastern coast. Most of them are from provinces in east-central China, like Hubei, Hunan, Anhui and Sichuan. Sichuan, China's most populous province, is its biggest supplier of migrant labour.
> (www.iht.com, 3 November 2006)

> Prime minister Wen Jiabao ... said [on 29 December 2005 that] the government in coming years ... [would do] more to protect migrant workers who

face unsafe and unstable working conditions and are often denied fair wages ... The government promised Thursday [19 January] to improve treatment of rural migrants who move to urban areas to work ... In many parts of China these workers' incomes have stagnated or risen only slightly for the past decade ... Without legal recourse, many go unpaid and are vulnerable to abuse ... In the past twenty years about 140 million farmers and their families have moved to find work in towns and cities, according to estimates from the National Bureau of Statistics.

(www.iht.com, 20 January 2006)

The measures [relating to rural medical insurance] do next to nothing for a huge section of the rural population that has moved to the cities in recent years. These people, perhaps 150 million of them, enjoy neither the recent benefits accorded to those who have stayed on the land nor the far greater subsidies enjoyed by their city-born counterparts ... Only a few million migrant workers enjoy medical insurance provided by their urban employers. From 1 January [2008] it will be compulsory for employers to offer it. But since many migrants are employed informally, without contracts, this will not make much difference.

(*The Economist*, 13 October 2007, pp. 28–9)

Changes in the hukou *system*

[Communist] China had isolated rural and urban economies for about forty years. Such segregation was mainly implemented through two important institutional restrictions. One of them was a strict Household Registration System (HRS) [*hukou* system], which required individuals to register with local authorities to gain residency and thereby determined where people lived and worked. Basically people remained in their place of birth. Accompanying and reinforcing the HRS was the food rationing system, which allowed people to buy food only in the area of their household registration.

(Meng and Zhang 2001: 486)

'Mao Zedong instituted the *hukou* system in 1958' (*FEER*, 14 March 2002, p. 24).

'China announced on 16 August [2001] that it plans to revamp the registration system ... The government is working on a plan that will do away with migration restriction over the next five years' (*The Economist*, 1 September 2001, p. 54).

The changes planned in October [2001] are prompted by economic necessity. The number of excess workers in rural areas already exceeds 150 million, according to conservative official estimates. In addition, farming is expected to become less labour-intensive as the imperative for efficiency grows with China's [prospective] entry into the WTO.

(*FT*, 30 August 2001, p. 9)

A central planning commission in Beijing said that it was working on a scheme to abolish restrictions within five years ... Beijing introduces a tentative reform today [1 October] to grant permanent residency to a small number of rural entrepreneurs who have made good [in terms of taxes paid and jobs provided] in the city.

(*Guardian*, 1 October 2001, p. 17)

China plans to abolish legal distinctions between urban residents and peasant in eleven provinces as the government tries to slow the widening of the country's wealth gap and reduce social unrest, state media said Wednesday [2 November]. Under an experimental programme local governments in the eleven provinces will allow peasants to register as urban residents and enjoy the same rights to housing, education, medical care and social security that city dwellers have ... Shanghai pioneered the concept of a 'blue card' for qualified migrant workers in the mid-1990s, giving them full access to housing and city services if they met certain criteria. The central government first declared that it intended to do away with the *hukou* system at the Sixteenth Party Congress in 2002 and has been making incremental changes since.

(*IHT*, 3 November 2005, p. 3)

China plans to abolish the legal division between urban and rural residents in eleven provinces to protect the rights of migrants needed for labour in booming cities, though a similar experiment failed four years ago, the official media said Wednesday [2 November] ... In 2001 Zhenzhou, a city in Henan province in central China, allowed anyone with relatives in the city to get a free residence permit. Increased pressure on transport, education, health care and a rise in crime forced the city to cancel the measure three years later.

(www.iht.com, 2 November 2005)

Shanghai officials have unveiled plans to relax strict residency rules, making it easier for people from other parts of China to live there permanently. But the new rules are only thought to benefit 3,000 of the city's estimated 6 million migrant workers. Applicants must be professionals who have lived legally for seven years in Shanghai, China's most populous city.

(www.bbc.co.uk, 18 June 2009)

Problems in agriculture

Major problems include the following:

1 The loss of farmland.
2 Inadequate investment in the rural infrastructure as private incentives now dominate in the HRS.
3 Land is distributed relatively equally and the average farm is tiny and divided up into something less than ten plots.
4 The lack of a land ownership system holds back rural development.

5   Land use has not always coincided with state preferences.
6   Male labour has become a more valuable asset on the farm and this has helped undermine the population control programme.
7   Inadequate health provision.

The loss of farmland

'Due to urbanization and desertification its [China's] cultivated land is shrinking by about 2 per cent a year' (www.iht.com, 7 July 2004).

'Last year [2003] alone the amount of farmed land fell by 4.3 per cent due to pressure from development and reforestation, according to the World Bank' (*FEER*, 7 October 2004, p. 27).

> China has said it will keep controls on use of farmland after a six-month development ban ended to prevent a rebound in building projects that have eroded harvests and prompted protests among the nation's rural residents. China has lost 5 per cent of its farmland in the past seven years.
>
> (*FT*, 4 November 2004, p. 12)

'[According to the CIA, there has been an] estimated loss of one-fifth of agricultural land since 1949 [due] to soil erosion and economic development' (*The Spectator*, 8 January 2005, p. 13).

'The government said in 2004 that new factories, housing, offices and shopping malls had consumed about 5 per cent of total arable land in the previous seven years' (*IHT*, 21 January 2006, p. 5).

There is growing concern about the increasing number of violent protests (sometimes leading to loss of life) in rural areas caused in particular by the takeover of agricultural land by local officials for redevelopment. Such profitable (and often illegal) redesignation of land can lead to corruption and farmers feeling inadequately compensated for loss of land-use rights.

'Officials say that the number of "mass protests" taking place throughout China each year has risen from around 10,000 in 1994 to 74,000 in 2004' (*The Economist*, 17 December 2005, p. 63).

'According to official data, 3.8 million people took part in "incidents involving the masses" in 2004. The 74,000 protests represented a sevenfold rise on the 1994 figure' (*Guardian*, 18 January 2006, p. 30).

'Official figures show that the number of mass incidents rose to 74,000 in 2004 from about 10,000 in 1994, with the number of participants increasing from 730,000 to 3.8 million' (www.iht.com, 8 December 2006).

'On Thursday [19 January 2006] the ministry of public security said there were 87,000 protests, riots and other "mass incidents" last year [2005], up 6.6 per cent on 2004' (*Guardian*, 21 January 2006, p. 21).

'The ministry of public security said last month [November] that such [mass] incidents had fallen by 22.1 per cent in the first nine months of the year [2006] to 17,900' (*The Times*, 9 December 2006, p. 49).

'In the past these [grievances] were often to do with the levying of unfair taxes, but more recently they have centred ... on inadequate compensation for the loss of land' (*The Economist*, 17 December 2005, p. 63).

'When land is seized it is often done without adequate compensation. As there is no independent court system, it is usually impossible to seek legal redress' (*Guardian*, 21 January 2006, p. 21).

'Local officials can make huge profits by getting hold of rural land and having it rezoned for industrial use' (*FT*, 21 January 2006, p. 6). 'Conflicts between farmers and governments, mainly over the confiscation of land, have been behind a rapid rise in violent disputes in the countryside in the last two to three years' (*FT*, 6 March 2006, p. 7).

Land grabs by officials ... are provoking mass unrest in the countryside ... Local officials operate with impunity on the one-party state and have little to fear from a legal system that answers to the Communist Party. Endless harangues by central government leaders to pay more attention to inequality have done little to address the root causes of the wealth gap and surging social unrest, analysts say.

(*IHT*, 21 January 2006, p. 5)

Prime minister Wen Jiabao (29 December 2005):

We absolutely cannot commit a historic error over land problems ... Some local governments have taken over farmland illegally without giving reasonable compensation and this has sparked mass incidents in rural areas ... This is still a key source of instability in rural areas and even the whole society ... [The expansion of cities has involved] reckless occupation of farmland.

(*IHT*, 21 January 2006, p. 5; www.iht.com, 20 January 2006; *FT*, 21 January 2006, p. 6; *Guardian*, 21 January 2006, p. 21)

[In August 2005 China] announced that 3.7 million citizens had participated in some 74,000 public protests in 2004. Chinese officials say the number of demonstrations rose to 87,000 in 2005 ... Many analysts conclude that China has a substantial and growing problem with social unrest and that the Communist Party takes that problem very seriously ... President Hu Jintao warns that the social costs have now become unacceptably high ... Hu has built his base of domestic support on promises to solve these problems [of, for example, widening income gaps, environmental damage, unemployment and urban migration] ... Jiang Zemin's government did not publicize data on social unrest. When Hu assumed the presidency protest statistics began to appear ... Data suggesting that unrest is growing as quickly as the country's GDP bolsters Hu's case for reforms.

(Ian Bremmer, *IHT*, 15 July 2006, p. 7)

'Official figures show that there were 87,000 public order disturbances in 2005 alone' (*IHT*, 29 July 2006, p. 13). 'More than 4 million Chinese participated in the 87,000 protests recorded in 2005' (*IHT*, 14 October 2006, p. 2).

China is … drawing up plans to reform the rules governing state requisitions of farmers' land. The reform would introduce a 'market mechanism' for compensation payments for farmland seized for commercial use … [An official spokesman]: 'The basic thinking of the reform is to take a different approach to land requisitions depending on the use to which the land is to be put. If the land is being requisitioned for use for the public good, then there must be a raised standard for compensation. If it is to be used commercially then the market mechanism must be introduced … There certainly is a phenomenon of farmers' interests being harmed by low-price requisitioning of their land' … Under current rules requisition compensation is supposed to be calculated only according to the land's agricultural value, allowing local governments and developers to reap huge profits when converting it to commercial use … [The official spokesman] warned that if both public use and commercial requisition orders continued to be the preserve of local governments it would remain very difficult for farmers to protect their land.

(*FT*, 9 March 2006, p. 9)

'According to Chinese officials, 60 per cent of land acquisitions are illegal' (*IHT*, 14 October 2006, p. 2).

'The government has banned developers from building golf courses, luxury homes and race courses on arable land … The new regulations even restrict the placement of cemeteries' (*The Times*, 19 December 2006, p. 28).

At the National People's Congress held 5–16 March 2007 the property law was finally approved. '[When the property bill was put to the vote on 16 March] 99.1 per cent of the 2,889 legislators attending the National People's Congress backed the property law' (www.bbc.co.uk, 16 March 2007).

Further details can be found below in the section on the private sector, but there were references to agricultural land.

Parliament began debating a landmark private property measure on Thursday [8 March] that would ensure that all forms of property, including the assets of individuals, the state and collectives, have protection under the law … would be given equal protection under the law … At a news briefing on Sunday 4 March], before the opening session, the parliamentary spokesman, Jiang Enzhu, said: 'No matter if it is state, collective or private property', it should be protected equally … The introduction of the proposed law to the National People's Congress follows a rare and long public consultation … In a speech introducing the draft law, Wang Zhaoguo, vice chairman of the Standing Committee, told delegates Thursday that protecting people's property rights was aimed at 'stimulating their vigour to create wealth' and enhancing social stability. 'As the reform and opening-up and the economy develop, people's living standards improve in general and they urgently require effective protection of their own lawful property accumulated through hard work,' Wang said … While all land in China remains the property of the state, legal experts consulted in drafting the law said it would automatically extend the leases that farmers and landowners hold over the land they occupy. But experts say the new law is unlikely to curb the forced reallocation of farming land for commercial or industrial use that has led to widespread unrest and protests in rural areas ... Some economist warn that the law's passage would not significantly enhance the rights of property owners while government officials exerted influence or even outright control over the courts ... Advocates of farmers' rights unsuccessfully urged the authorities to include provisions in the property law that would make it more difficult for local governments to seize farms and sell the rights to use this land to private developers or industry. Under existing law local governments have the power to convert agricultural land to other uses if it is deemed to be in the public interest.

(www.iht.com, 8 March 2007; *IHT*, 9 March 2007, pp. 1, 8)

'It is not clear whether the current version will adequately address the expropriation of collectively owned land from peasants for development – one of the biggest sources of rural unrest' (www.iht.com, 14 March 2007).

[The] new property law ... is the first piece of legislation to cover an individual's right to own assets ... The latest text of the bill state that: 'The property of the state, the collective, the individual and other obligees is protected by law, and no units or individuals may infringe upon it.' But it adds that: 'The nation is in the first stage of socialism and should stick to the basic economic system in which public ownership predominates, co-existing with other kinds of ownership' ... The bill also seeks to address the often illegal land seizures that are taking place, and the government transfer of farmland to developers, frequently without farmers being given adequate compensation ... The bill will also reportedly boost protection against land seizures, which have become a major source of unrest among farmers in rural areas.

(www.bbc.co.uk, 8 March 2007)

Wang Zhaoguo, a vice chairman of the National People's Congress, introducing the bill yesterday [8 March]: 'Effective property of private citizens is not only stipulated by China's constitution ... but is also the general aspiration and urgent demand of the people' ... The wording of the final bill ... includes lengthy references to the primacy of the 'socialist system' and 'state ownership' ... The bill also explicitly rejects any change to the system of 'collective' ownership of rural land, where farmer occupiers have only usage rights over limited contract periods rather than any title that can be bought and sold. Properties in cities, by contrast, can be bought and sold under leases of between fifty and seventy years.

(*FT*, 9 March 2007, p. 7)

'Experts say ... the new property rights bill ... will not give farmers much more protection against unscrupulous officials' (*FT*, 4 April 2007, p. 13).

'Should an underdog try to use the new law to enforce his rights, the corrupt and pliant judiciary would usually ensure he was wasting his time' (*The Economist*, 10 March 2007, p. 11).

Ownership could be challenged, but critics worry that it would be difficult to do so for former state-owned assets or for land-use rights that had been sold off in shady deals ... Farmers ... have something to gain ... The good news is that the latest draft, unlike the 2005 version, gives farmers the right to renew their land-use rights after they expire. Unlike urban land, which is state-owned with usage rights granted for periods of between forty and seventy years, rural land is 'collectively' owned. Farmers are given thirty-year leases (though often no supporting documents) to use plots of land. But the law will put no new limits on the government's powers to appropriate land. It also says that village committees represent the collective. These are supposedly democratically elected but party regulations still give unelected party officials the final say over village affairs. Most important, the ban on mortgaging farmland will remain.

(pp. 25–7)

Land-use conversion regulations have been tightened in an effort to reduce unrest provoked by unfair seizures of land. For example, local governments must now record land sales as 'on-budget' income and certain types of projects – such as golf courses and theme parks – have been banned on undeveloped land. Enforcement efforts have been strengthened by sending out teams of auditors to review land rezoning arrangements by local governments. The NPC will also pass a new private property law which, while stopping short of reforming the rural land-tenure system, reiterates the legal requirements to compensate farmers adequately for the expropriation of their land.

(www.economist.com, 15 March 2007)

The passage last March [2007] of China's first law on property rights ... allowed the renewal on expiry of the thirty-year land use leases most peasants were granted when plots were divided among households. Officials said the process would be automatic, with renewals granted indefinitely. But peasants still cannot sell or mortgage their plots.

(*The Economist*, 16 February 2008, p. 65)

'Farmers will be able to renew their leases, but they will neither be allowed to mortgage land nor to acquire the individual title that would give them property protection against forcible acquisition' (*The Times*, 17 March 2007, p. 20).

'During the next few years the original land lease contracts will start to expire ... the government has said it will extend them by another thirty years' (*FT*, 20 February 2008, p. 11).

The government ... is worried about a fledgling land reform movement that its organizers say is set to spread across the country ... In December [2007] separate groups of peasant farmers in four remote parts of the country published very similar statements on the internet claiming to have seized their collectively owned land from the state and unilaterally privatized it ... [Peasants signed] a declaration posted on the internet claiming 70,000 peasant farmers had seized 10,000 hectares of 'collectively owned' land and divided it among themselves to own privately ... Security agents in the provinces of Heilongjiang, Jiangsu and Shaanxi and the port city of Tianjin quickly rounded up the handful of peasants who signed the documents ... The peasants' statements accused local officials of profiting personally by requisitioning land from farmers without providing adequate compensation and using it for corrupt development projects ... Peasants are allowed to sublet their allotments, which provides huge scope for officials to grant government land free to their friends and relatives, who then lease it for a profit ... [Peasants] say local officials have handed out parcels of free land to friends and relatives, who rent it on to middlemen to lease at exorbitant prices to its original owners ... China's security system deals with close to 100,000 'public order disturbances' every year (according to government statistics, which Chinese political activists believe downplay the true scale of social unrest). But the vast majority of them are localized and uncoordinated and the protagonists usually emphasize their loyalty to the system while appealing to Beijing to address the misdeeds of local officials. This incident was different. Not only were the protesters challenging the party directly, they were also organized at a national level by a loose association of journalists, academics, intellectuals and political activists and its calls for privatization of all rural land were a clear rejection of the current regime ... The authors of the declarations are mostly based in Beijing and have so far evaded capture. They operate in secrecy ... Some are career dissidents while others are solid members of the party ... These organizers, comprised of a core group of about ten people, spent more than two years travelling the country gathering thousands of signatures of peasants involved in land disputes and convincing them that seizing land was the best way to draw attention to their grievances. They say the coordinated release of the four documents is just the beginning of a movement that is set to spread across the country. According to a person who claims to have drafted the original statements (which were all quickly removed from the internet by government censors), thousands more peasant farmers in dozens of other locations have already signed similar declarations and are preparing to seize land.

(*FT*, 20 February 2008, p. 11)

Late last year [2007] groups in different parts of China began claiming land as their own individual private plots ... Of the handful of incidents that have come to light where peasants have taken matters – and land – into their own hands, the first was in the province of Heilongjian. A statement circulated on the internet in December [2007] by leaders claiming to represent 40,000 peasants in seventy-two villages in Jiamusi prefecture called on village representatives 'to pledge to fight to the death' to protect land from seizure by corrupt officials. It said the current system of collective ownership of land had turned peasants into serfs. Peasants, it said, should have the right to negotiate their own price for land appropriated from them. Isolated groups of peasants elsewhere followed suit, some in Shaanxi, Jiangsu, Sichuan and Tianjin ... The flurry of land rights declarations was soon suppressed. Human rights groups report that two peasant leaders in Heilongjiang were sentenced in January [2008] to labour camp. At least two leaders in Shaanxi have also been detained ... [It has been reported] that other villagers are preparing to issue similar declarations.

(*The Economist*, 16 February 2008, pp. 64–5)

China has punished thousands of people for illegal land grabs, following a crackdown on the practice, officials said yesterday [15 April]. But the investigation also showed that the amount of land wrongly seized last year [2007] was almost two-thirds higher than in 2006 – when premier Wen Jiabao warned that China was at risk of an 'historic error' over the practice ... The ministry investigation [was] said by the state news agency Xinhua to be the biggest of recent times ... The ministry of land and resources said it uncovered 31,700 cases of unlawful seizure, involving 225,000 hectares. Of these 43,000 hectares were seized last year. The inquiry focused on local government because officials often side with developers to boost the local economy, as a favour to friends or because of bribes or their own financial interests. The ministry said 2,864 people received disciplinary punishment and 535 criminal penalties, but did not say how many officials were involved.

(*Guardian*, 16 April 2008, p. 22)

Haining [is] a rural town about 100 kilometres, or 60 miles, west of Shanghai in the Yangtze River Delta ... Disputes over land grabs or compensation to make way for a new factory or housing estate periodically turn violent across China. But some places like Haining have started programmes that provide something of a safety net for farmers who quit the land ... [If a farmer] sells part of his land-use rights his family will have the option of putting the proceeds into an insurance plan run by the local government. For an individual payment of 15,000 yuan women above fifty and men above sixty receive a monthly sum of 320 yuan.

(www.iht.com, 17 June 2008)

One Western official said: 'Land use is a huge issue because, in the absence of property taxes, local city authorities have to keep selling land and developing land to stay afloat financially. Chengdu gets about 30 per cent of its city budget from sales of land owned by the state or the military. The government has keep monetizing the land through long-term leases, and of course corrupt officials want to make money by getting bribes and other gifts from the buyers' ... Arthur Kroeber ... an economist ... [said] that as much as 50 per cent of local government revenues came from land sales through China in 2009.

(www.iht.com, 25 January 2010; *IHT*, 26 January 2010, p. 7)

The government has outlined major changes to the way in which land can be seized for redevelopment. Under the draft proposals, using violence and coercion to make people move would be banned and owners would be able to appeal against evictions. Anyone losing land or property would have to be given at least its market value in compensation … China's cabinet said all strong-arm tactics used to force people to leave their properties – including violence and cutting off water or power – would be banned … Local governments would have to ensure public opinion was heard before going ahead with development. In homes deemed to be dangerous – a reason often given for demolition – 90 per cent would have to give approval before they could be taken down. The new proposals are open for public comment until mid-February.

(www.bbc.co.uk, 29 January 2010)

Moving to address a major source of social strife, the government says it plans to toughen regulations significantly to protect and compensate home-owners whose dwellings are singled out for demolition and redevelopment … Homeowners would be entitled to obtain market price compensation for their dwellings on state-owned land and be allowed to file suit, if necessary, to forestall demolition. The use of violence or strong-arm tactics to force people out of their homes would be banned … The regulation would ban the use of violence, illegal coercion and the cut-off of water and power to uproot homeowners … Protests against forced evictions – which are often struggles over compensation – are a leading source of social unrest. Chinese newspapers are filled with stories of powerless homeowners or occupants who have been driven out by officials or developers cashing in on China's property boom. The stories of injustice have multiplied in the past decade as property prices have soared in Beijing and other cities. Only in the past few years has the government begun to build a legal foundation to protect property owners. Until 2004 the constitution gave the state the right to seize private property without compensation, scholars say. In 2007 the government enacted the first explicit protections for property owners. But the perils of homeowners who try to stand up to developers in league with corrupt officials have remained a constant theme. More than a few contests have turned into life and death struggles … Five homeowners set themselves on fire in recent months; one woman died. Some forced evictions have set off riots, especially in rural areas. Many complain that developers or local governments compensate them at artificially low levels that do not reflect the market value of the property, and the court usually declines to hear forced removal cases … Wang Xixin, a Peking University law professor … who helped draft the legislation … said the existing 2001 regulation was unconstitutional … But Professor Cai Dingjian of the China National School of

Administration said the proposal did not go far enough to cover rural areas and should be a law instead of a regulation.

(www.iht.com, 30 January 2010)

Inadequate investment

There is inadequate investment in the (originally collectively provided and extensive) rural infrastructure (such as irrigation and flood control) as private incentives now dominate in the HRS.

China is not only short of water. It has problems on all fronts – pollution, floods, drought, distribution and pricing among them. *Per capita* water reserves are a quarter of the world average and most of the nation's water resources are in the south of the country. In the north deserts and arid land areas are expanding ... [With the HRS] communal duties, including upkeep of the irrigation systems, became more haphazard and competition for water was often fierce ... Small-scale water charges were first introduced to the Chinese countryside in 1983 ... [There have been] experiments with water user associations [WUAs].... [The WUA replaces] the local government as the supplier of water to farmers ... There are about 1,500 WUAs scattered across China ... The associations, whose officials are directly elected by the farmers, are responsible for ensuring the supply of water to all farmers in their areas. That involves organizing the repair and maintenance of irrigation canals and regularly opening locks ... The associations buy water – with funds pooled by their members – from a water supply company ... Supply companies charge WUAs for the volume of water they use. In the past villages were charged for water based on the amount of land they had under cultivation, regardless of the amount of water they used. Under that system there was no incentive to save ... Raising water prices in China in northern China, where the crisis is most serious, and charging by volume rather than by land area, would further encourage conservation, say experts ... Farm holdings in China are small and fragmented. That makes it difficult to impose individual user charges ... Charging individual farmers rather than villages or water user associations for the water they use would further encourage conservation, experts say.

(*FEER*, 24 January 2002, pp. 36–9)

The Chinese government authorized one of the world's biggest engineering projects yesterday [26 November 2002]: to pump water from the flood-prone south to the drought-stricken north ... Mao Zedong ... is credited with first suggesting the project ... Three man-made rivers [canals] will transfer water from the Yangtze ... to the crowded north ... The first imported water could reach Shandong province by 2005 ... The project was trailed tentatively last year [2001] ... Construction was ready to begin on one segment.

(*Guardian*, 27 November 2002, p. 16)

'The projects construction phase is scheduled to run until 2050 and will comprise three separate canals' (*The Times*, 27 November 2002, p. 17).

The State Council gave the go-ahead to a multi-dollar project to divert water from the south to the dry north despite environmental and costs concerns. The project aims to divert water along three canal systems from the nation's largest rivers in the south to northern cities. It is expected to take fifty years to complete and to cost more than $48 billion.

(*FEER*, 5 December 2002, p. 36)

Nearly seven years ago Wen Jiabao, then a vice prime minister, uttered a stark warning: 'The survival of the Chinese nation is threatened by the country's shortage of water' ... Water industry executives say that up to 40 per cent of the population live on supplies that are less than half of international danger levels; and because of severe pollution supplies are often unsafe ... In March [2005] a senior environmental agency official ... said more than 70 per cent of China's rivers and lakes were polluted. Also in March the water resources minister ... said that more than 300 million rural people lacked access to clean drinking water ... In recent years China has lifted most of the protectionist barriers that kept foreign firms out of the water sector. But significant structural obstacles make it hard for companies to [make a] profit. The most basic issue is China's pricing of water. Up until 1985 water was supplied free of charge ... In order to encourage both conservation of water and investment in new projects, the government in recent years has allowed prices to rise, but gradually ... According to China's own estimates, the country uses four times more water per unit of economic output than the global average. Its rate of industrial water reusage stands at only 55 per cent, far below the rate of 80 per cent in most advanced countries.

(www.iht.com, 16 December 2005; *IHT*, 17 December 2005, p. 20)

Since 1980 China's average *per capita* water consumption actually declined by nearly 5 per cent – and not because the country has become an impressively more efficient consumer of irrigation, industrial or residential water ... One of the most frequently cited figures in the Chinese media refers to the country's low average availability of water resources – as of 2005 ... less than a third of the global average and just a quarter of the US rate ... China's [spatial] disparities are particularly large. South China, with roughly 55 per cent of the population and 35 per cent of the cropland, has about 80 per cent of the water resources ... The north ... [has] 45 per cent of the population and nearly 60 per cent of all cropland, but less than 15 per cent of the water ... More than half of China's waste water does not receive even the simplest primary treatment ... In November 2005 the first national inland lakes symposium was told that a recent survey found 70 per cent of the country's rivers contaminated with industrial pollutants and 75 per cent excessively enriched with nitrogen leached from fertilizers.

(*FEER*, November 2005, pp. 30–2)

On 28 September [2008], after more than four years' work on a 307 kilometre-long (191-mile) waterway costing more than $2 billion, Beijing began receiving its top-up ... The channel's inauguration was the most notable achievement so far of what, in the coming years, is intended to become a far more grandiose diversion scheme: bringing water from the Yangtze basin to the parched north, along channels stretching more than 1,000 kilometres ... Controversy has long plagued the South–North Water Diversion Project, as the scheme is formally known. [It was] launched with much fanfare in 2002 ... The stretch from Beijing to Shijiazhuang, Hebei's capital, forms the northernmost end of what is intended to be the central route of three south–north channels ... The authorities had planned to use the new channel before the Olympics began [on 8 August]. But even though it was ready on time they waited until 18 September, one day after the conclusion of the Paralympics, before turning on the spigots. The water took ten days to reach Beijing.... The eastern route has been plagued by delays ... and is not intended to supply Beijing. The western one is still on the drawing board.

(*The Economist*, 11 October 2008, p. 84)

'The US department of agriculture estimates that China feeds 20 per cent of the world's population with just 10 per cent of the world's agricultural land and about 6 per cent of the world's water resources' (*FT*, 17 April 2009, p. 8).

'China faces droughts and floods annually, but it has also seen a recent increase in extreme weather conditions ... Much of the country still relies on rainfall as many of its farming communities have a poor irrigation system' (www.bbc.co.uk, 23 August 2009).

Land distribution

Land is distributed relatively equally and the average farm is not only tiny (something like 0.5 ha) but is also divided up into something less than ten plots (which makes mechanization difficult).

'The average family farm is 0.55 ha and there are, on average, nine plots per farm' (Feder *et al.* 1992: 6).

'Each Chinese worker farms 0.1 ha on average, compared with 1.4 ha in the USA and 0.5 ha in Europe' (*FT*, 16 November 1999, p. 26).

'Holdings average half a hectare in size' (*FEER*, 18 December 2003, p. 33).

'According to a report by the OECD ... fully 200 million of China's 248 million rural households farm on plots of about 0.65 hectares' (*FT*, 15 November 2005, p. 10).

'Because of population growth and the loss of farmland, the average farm size in China ... has fallen from 1.5 hectares in the 1970s to barely 0.5 hectares now' (*The Economist*, 19 April 2008, p. 32).

'Chinese farms now average only about 0.67 hectares, or 1.66 acres, in size, according to the government's agricultural census. Other independent studies say the average farm's size has fallen from 0.6 hectares in 1980 to 0.4 hectares today' (www.iht.com, 9 October 2008).

There have been various experiments by the state to lease out larger plots of land, to encourage the amalgamation of family plots (in forms such as shareholder farms where contributing families share in the output and profit), and even forcibly reassign land from less to more efficient farmers (which shows the limitations of leased land in terms of property rights).

'As many as 70 million farmers have lost their land in the past decade' (*IHT*, 9 December 2004, p. 2). 'As many as 70 million farmers have been left without land' (*IHT*, 22 January 2005, p. 3).

'Forced appropriations by local governments have already deprived as many as 40 million peasants of some or all of their land since the early 1990s' (*The Economist*, 25 March 2006, p. 9). 'Estimates vary, but most agree that tens of millions have lost some or all of their land since the early 1990s, often without compensation' (*The Economist*, Survey, 25 March 2006, p. 6).

'The *Jingji Ribao* (*Economic Daily*) estimated that there might now be 200 million farmers displaced by the rapid conversion of agricultural land for development' (Gallagher 2005: 23).

'Roughly 40 to 50 million peasants have lost their land to commercial development' (*IHT*, 6 March 2007, p. 6).

'According to the land ministry in Beijing, there were more than a million illegal seizures between 1998 and 2005, usually for factories or apartment buildings, and the farmers often received little or no compensation' (*FT*, 4 April 2007, p. 13).

> Of the tens of thousands of peasant protests that occur every year in China, nearly half relate to land grabs, said a report in *Caijing*, an influential Beijing magazine. Tighter procedures introduced in 2006 have simply resulted in local officials forcing peasants to rent their land, instead of seizing it outright. This problem, the report said, was getting 'worse and worse'.
>
> (*The Economist*, 18 October 2008, pp. 77–8)

'Across China ordinary people are losing their land as the country struggles to find space for its expanding cities and attempts to make tiny farm plots more efficient by merging them into large agri-businesses' (*FEER*, 7 February 2002, pp. 57–9).

> There are around 200 million farms with an average size of 1.5 acres … [But] a quiet revolution [is] beginning to spread through Chinese agriculture as farmers try to meet the needs of rapidly expanding supermarket chains. Farms that only a decade ago were merely subsisting are now slowly coming under the influence of agribusiness companies … Supermarkets now rarely deal directly with small farmers. Instead, over the past five years a new generation of companies has emerged to supply them with food … Many are private groups that have leased land from other small farmers, while some are large-scale farms that remained under state control after land reform … Chinese agribusinesses are also beginning to carve out an export sector,

especially in labour-intensive crops such as fruit and vegetables ... The country is a big supplier of apple juice and garlic ... Agribusiness may have grown quickly but it has only begun to nibble at the edges of China's vast farming base. One of the few pieces of academic research on the subject looked at 200 communities in the greater Beijing area last year [2006] and found that the farmers had been only marginally affected by the creation of supply chains for the city's supermarkets.

(*FT*, 4 April 2007, p. 13)

(See the section on agricultural reforms, above, for recent changes in legislation.)

The lack of a land ownership system

The lack of a land ownership system holds back rural development. People cannot sell the land they till; this prevents consolidation into more efficient units. Meanwhile, fear of loss of land use rights is a deterrent to moving off the land permanently.

(Philip Bowring, *IHT*, 20 November 2001, p. 8)

'Farmers do not own the land they work – and they cannot sell it – so larger, more efficient farms have not been created' (www.bbc.co.uk, 5 January 2008).

Land use and state preferences

Land use has not always coincided with state preferences. China has a history of famines and so the state was particularly concerned with the grain harvest.

'Many [farmers] are forced to grow grain crops to feed the Communist Party's paranoia of a Western food embargo' (Bruce Gilley, *FEER*, 29 November 2001, p. 36).

'Chinese peasants are [however] increasingly freed of government orders to grow grain' (*FEER*, 18 December 2003, p. 30).

The value of male labour

Male labour in particular has become a more valuable asset on the farm (to carry on the farm and provide for parents in their old age) and this has helped undermine the population control programme.

Inadequate health provision

[Some] 90 per cent of the 900 million people who live in the countryside ... have no medical insurance ... With health insurance coverage shrinking, while medical costs rise faster than incomes, China faces a humanitarian disaster that threatens to undo one of the country's proudest achievements of the last twenty years: the lifting of an estimated 210 million people out of absolute poverty ...

From the 1950s to the 1970s … China's rural health infrastructure … [there were] set up village health centres, township health centres and county hospitals. At the village level agricultural collectives paid the salaries of so-called 'barefoot doctors' and put money into collective welfare funds for drugs and treatment. Patients paid modest premiums and a nominal fee for consultations and medicines. Local government also contributed … After 1979, however, Deng Xiaoping dismantled the agricultural collectives … Because he did not make any new provisions for funding rural health care, the health infrastructure collapsed … This year [2002] … building a rural health-insurance system has become one of the [health] ministry's top three priorities.

(*FEER*, 13 June 2002, pp. 30–2)

[In] rural areas the former system of free clinics has disintegrated … Until the beginning of the reform period in the early 1980s the socialized medicine system, with 'barefoot doctors' at its core, worked wonders. From 1952 to 1982 infant mortality fell from 200 per 1,000 live births to thirty-four, and life expectancy increased from about thirty-five years to sixty-eight, according to a recent study published by *The New England Journal of Medicine* … In the last several years China has experimented with reforms aimed at improving health care for peasants. The most important is an insurance plan in which participating farmers make an annual payment of a little more than a dollar to gain eligibility for basic medical treatments. Many peasants have complained that even the dollar payment is too big a burden and that in any event the coverage plan theoretically provided is inadequate … The government … recently announced an expansion of this experiment, with increased fees and increased coverage, but it has yet to make an impact on the health crisis. As a result, according to government estimates, in less than a generation, a rural population that once enjoyed universal if rudimentary coverage has become 79 per cent uninsured. More than half urban residents, by comparison, have some kind of coverage, which is supplied by their employers. The near-total absence of adequate health care in much of the countryside has sown deep resentment among the peasantry while helping to spread infectious diseases like hepatitis and tuberculosis and making the country – and the world – more vulnerable to epidemics like SARS and possibly bird flu.

(Howard French, *IHT*, 16 January 2006, p. 4)

The state began cutting hospital subsidies in the early 1980s and by the mid-1990s it covered just 20 per cent of urban state hospitals' costs … About 130 million people in China have health insurance, leaving almost 90 per cent of the population without coverage … The majority of the uninsured – most of them rural residents – avoid going to hospitals for treatment because they cannot afford it.

(*IHT*, 30 March 2006, p. 17)

Mao's system of 'barefoot doctors' for country districts may have been rudimentary, but at least it was readily accessible and practically free. Public health care ... in rural China is now in tatters ... Since 2003 a new medical insurance system, involving for the first time a financial commitment by the central government, has been set up in at least 80 per cent of rural counties in place of the long-discarded barefoot doctor scheme ... The provincial, prefectural and county governments [also contribute] ... At the same time rural children have begun to enjoy free education during their nine years of compulsory schooling – although many have still to pay for their textbooks ... In the case of the medical insurance scheme the biggest beneficiaries are the richest peasants. The poorest are just as likely to choose to die at home rather than risk deeper impoverishment by venturing into hospital ... Without changes in the way rural hospitals are funded, poorer farmers will feel little benefit from the new insurance scheme ... The WHO says the poor would not even be able to find the cash to pay for treatment at first, even though some of it would be reimbursed ... The measures also do next to nothing for a huge section of the rural population that has moved to the cities in recent years. These people, perhaps 150 million of them, enjoy neither the recent benefits accorded to those who have stayed on the land nor the far greater subsidies enjoyed by their city-born counterparts ... Only a few million migrant workers enjoy medical insurance provided by their urban employers. From 1 January [2008] it will be compulsory for employers to offer it. But since many migrants are employed informally, without contracts, this will not make much difference.

(The Economist, 13 October 2007, pp. 27–9)

Recent initiatives on health insurance for the rural population and those outside the formal labour market in urban areas show that the government is ready to move. During 2005–7 rural co-operative medical schemes have expanded coverage to an estimated 80 per cent of China's rural population from less than 24 per cent. An open debate has effectively drawn attention to the schemes' initial failings and gradual improvements are on the agenda.

(FEER, November 2007, p. 52)

China is to dramatically increase funding for a co-operative medical insurance system ... the 'New Co-operative Medical Scheme' ... covering more than 700 million rural residents, with government subsidies for the scheme set to double next year [2008] ... Senior leaders have decided to double standard contributions for each member of the scheme ... [which was] launched on a trial basis four years ago ... China has in the past two years rapidly expanded the co-operative medical scheme, which by the end of September [2007] covered more than 85 per cent of rural areas and had 726 million members. However, officials involved in the scheme – which is based on contributions from the central government, local authorities and members themselves – have said it remains seriously underfunded. Much outpatient treatment is not covered, while less than half the cost of inpatient care at better hospitals is reimbursed ... Standard contributions would be doubled ... for both the central government and local authorities and ... for individuals. Contributions to the scheme varied widely and rich provinces and cities already put much more into it, while poorer provinces might be given more time to meet the new standard.

(*FT*, 22 December 2007, p. 6)

With the collapse and privatization of state-owned enterprises the vast majority of citizens had been left with no insurance. In 2003 the government introduced a new medical insurance scheme in the countryside. This involves contributions from rural residents as well as local governments and, for the first time, the central government. The number of people taking part rose from 80 million that year to more than 730 million now ... All rural residents (about 800 million is the usual official figure) should be insured by the end of the year [2008]. The scheme is only a slight relief, if at all, for the poor. It often does not cover routine outpatient treatment. The average reimbursement rate is only 30 per cent to 40 per cent, and bills have to be paid in full first. So hospital stays are beyond the means of many. There is also a big loophole: those insured can get benefits only in their own localities. Many younger people from the countryside are working in cities where they have to pay all their treatment costs. A new labour contract law introduced this year [2008] requires employers to pay medical insurance for such workers. But migrants are often hired informally, making it easy for employers to evade such requirements ... [One estimate says that] more than half of the urban population has no insurance ... Last year [2007] the government introduced an urban insurance scheme (similar to the rural one) aimed at non-working residents, including children and university students. The aim is to have every urban citizen covered by 2010 ... the government spends a mere 0.8 per cent of GDP on health.

(*The Economist*, 23 February 2008, p. 71)

In the old days healthcare was free or almost free through work units and state enterprises. China had its famous barefoot doctors – an impressive network of rural health workers – farmers with a rudimentary training. Anything complicated they had to refer to proper doctors in hospitals, but they held the health frontline ... Seven hundred million people across China's vast countryside have now signed up for a new rural health scheme whereby a small annual fee from each person is matched by a payment from the state. It gives some cover, but not enough. Only a percentage of medical bills is covered and in some cases a very small percentage.

(www.bbc.co.uk, 29 June 2008)

Changes in agricultural policy since 2005

'The government is trying to improve rural living standards. For example, 'Chinese officials are promising to slash taxes on peasants and increase farm subsidies' (*IHT*, 3 February 2005, p. 1).

Delivering the main opening address to the National People's Congress on Saturday [5 March 2005] prime minister Wen Jiabao ... vowed to eliminate the main tax imposed on China's peasantry for the first time in two millenniums ... Wen emphasized continuing a campaign to cool China's economy and narrow the growing urban–rural wealth gap, which has led to severe social tensions.

(www.iht.com, 6 March 2005)

Prime minister Wen Jiabao on Monday [14 March] ... spoke about China's need to balance its economic growth and to spread its wealth to the vast, impoverished countryside. He said that China had passed into a new era of development in which industrial development has to 'replenish' agriculture. This would involve further reducing taxes on farm products, improving irrigation and farming infrastructure, and improving rural schools and health care, he said.

(*IHT*, 15 March 2005, p. 2)

'Per capita disposable income income in towns and cities ... rose 7.7 per cent to 9,422 yuan last year [2004], while incomes in rural areas rose 6.8 per cent to 2,936 yuan' (www.iht.com, 14 March 2005).

The agriculture minister ... Du Qinglin ... on Thursday [10 March] promised to protect farmers' land rights and spend more on irrigation as China's leaders seek to ease chronic rural poverty, seen as posing their biggest risk of anti-government unrest ... The ministry introduced pilot projects last year [2004] aimed at arbitrating disputes over land contracts ... Average annual incomes for farmers rose 12 per cent last year [2004], but still total just 2,936 yuan, or $355 per person, according to Du. By contrast the government says annual incomes in China's booming cities average more than $1,000 per person ... Premier Wen Jiabao promised [on 5 March] ... to eliminate farm taxes by 2006 – a promise repeated Thursday by the finance ministry ... China said this week that it would start cutting school fees in rural areas this year [2005] in response to growing domestic criticism that the country's education system is corrupt and discriminates against poor, rural students. The new policy will begin with the removal of fees for 14 million students in the country's poorest counties and will continue until 2007.

(www.iht.com, 10 March 2005)

This year's budget calls for more spending on a new rural health care programme aimed at reversing the near collapse of rural medical services in recent years. It also calls for an increase in central government handouts to rural areas, to make up for their loss of revenue as a result of reforms intended to reduce peasants' tax burdens. The government plans to abolish agricultural tax by 2006, two years earlier than it had originally planned. And it also says it will abolish primary school fees for all children in rural areas by 2007.

(*The Economist*, 19 March 2005, p. 72)

Already twenty-seven out of China's thirty-one provinces and municipalities … have abolished agricultural taxes, with the rest soon to follow. 'The agricultural tax will be exempted throughout the country next year [2006],' announced premier Wen Jiabao at the National People's Congress in March 2005.

(*FEER*, November 2005, p. 27)

China's parliament yesterday [29 December 2005] approved a motion phasing out a decades-old agricultural tax from the start of 2006 … The tax raised only 1.5 billion renminbi ($186 million) this year [2005] and amounted to just 1 per cent of China's total tax revenue last year [2004]. It was introduced in 1958 but has long been held to be unfair – farmers had to pay it regardless of how little they earned or even whether they planted crops.

(*FT*, 30 December 2005, p. 6)

Late last year [2005] in Guangdong province, one of China's most affluent regions (and also the scene of some of the most violent peasant protests reported recently), the authorities began allowing villages to trade land that had already been converted to industrial use.

(*The Economist*, Survey, 25 March 2006, p. 9)

The March 2006 session of the National People's Congress paid particular attention to increasing economic inequalities in China, especially between urban and rural areas. A programme of further aid to rural areas was outlined, envisioning a 'new socialist countryside'. (See the entries for 22 February and 5–14 March 2006 in the chronology in Chapter 8 of the companion volume, *Political Developments in Contemporary China*.)

The central government … [decided] in June [2007] to allow the municipality … of Chonqing … to act as a pilot for wide-ranging reforms … Qilin village has made an early start. China's official media have made much of its decision to allow farmers to swap land for shares in a new orange-growing business set up by the entrepreneurial village chief. Farmers are free to sell their shares to other villagers or, with the approval of half the shareholders, to anyone else. It is a far cry from land privatization, which some Chinese say is essential to make permanent the shift of rural residents to cities. Rights to use the land still revert to the original farmer at the end of the thirty-year lease to which all farmland is subject … [But it is claimed that] local officials hope the central government will allow Chonqing to let the leases run much longer.

(*The Economist*, 28 July 2007, p. 62)

Farmers, except for tobacco growers, have been exempted from tax on their land or agricultural production … Since 2004 the government, for the first time, has been giving direct subsidies to grain farmers in an effort to keep them growing grain and to curb grain price rises.

(*The Economist*, 13 October 2007, p. 28)

[China has been running] a pilot programme entitling each rural family in Shandong province and two other provinces to government rebates of 13 per cent when they buy a maximum of two television sets, two refrigerators and two mobile phones. The subsidies are part of central government policies aimed at stimulating domestic consumption and improving the lives of 740 million rural residents.

(www.iht.com, 21 February 2008)

China produces more than 90 per cent of the grain it consumes ... Last month [March] prime minister Wen Jiabao revealed what had been a state secret: that China had grain reserves of 150 million tonnes to 200 million tonnes, equal to 30 per cent to 40 per cent of annual production ... The country's grain policy calls for 95 per cent self-sufficiency.

(*The Economist*, 19 April 2008, p. 69)

Reforms were adopted by the Third Plenary Session of the Seventeenth Central Committee of the Communist Party at its 9–12 October 2008 meeting.

The leadership of China's Communist Party will meet today [9 October] to discuss whether to allow peasant farmers to trade their land titles ... The country's top leaders are expected to enshrine the rights of rural citizens to transfer or rent their thirty-year land leases to other individuals or companies and possibly allow that land to be used for collateral to access loans ... In practice many of the more than 150 million rural residents who have migrated to the cities in search of work have already leased their contracted land on an informal basis to neighbours or even some of China's pioneering agribusinesses. But legal protection for these arrangements is lacking, and corruption and abuse by local government officials who oversee the transactions are rife.

(*FT*, 9 October 2008, p. 12)

A four-day meeting of ... the 204 members of the party's Central Committee ... got underway Thursday [9 October] to discuss agricultural reforms ... The meeting was expected to give farmers formal permission to lease or transfer their land, measures that have already grown common as rural workers move to the city

(www.iht.com, 9 October 2008)

Party leaders began an earnest debate over rural land reform at the Third Plenum of the Seventeenth Central Committee. Policy changes are expected to be announced after the session ends Sunday [12 October] ... The most important change under discussion involves allowing China's farmers to swap or rent out their land-use rights ... Many farmers have abandoned their land ... to move to cities as migrant workers ... *China Daily*: 'The meeting's emphasis on rural issues highlights the top leadership's efforts to reduce the widening urban–rural wealth gap and tap the vast rural market. The meeting is expected to make it easier for farmers to lease or transfer the management rights of their land, measures that have become necessary as many farmers move to cities as migrant workers' ... Officials characterize the proposed changes as allowing farmers to lease or trade their thirty-year land-use contracts to other individuals or companies. One point under discussion is whether the contracts should be extended by decades, scholars say ... On 30 September President Hu Jintao made a highly symbolic visit to Xiaogang village in Anhui province, the site of a bold rejection of communist-style land collectivization in 1978, when several farmers [eighteen families in Xiaogang: www.iht.com, 11 October 2008] divided communal land for personal use. Since then the village has been held up as a precursor to the rural economic reforms enacted under Deng Xiaoping. Hu said during his visit that farmers would soon be allowed to transfer their land contracts, and farms would be allowed to develop larger scale operations. Hu Jintao said: 'Not only will the current land contract relationship be kept stable and unchanged over time, greater and protected land contract and management rights will be given to farmers. Furthermore, if the farmers wish to, they will be allowed to transfer the land contract and management rights in various ways and to develop management on an appropriate scale' ... Some farmers are already leasing out their land use contracts.

(*IHT*, 11 October 2008, p. 6)

Chinese leaders are expected to allow peasants to buy or sell land-use rights for the first time ... The most important change would allow China's peasantry to sell land-use contracts to other farmers or to agricultural companies ... A law enacted in 2002 allows limited land-use trades between individual farmers, but does not permit unrestricted trade between farmers and companies, straight sales of land-use rights or the option to use the land as collateral to obtain a loan ... Officials characterize the proposed policy changes as allowing the farmers to lease or trade their thirty-year contracts to individuals or companies ... One point under discussion is whether land contracts should be extended to seventy years from thirty years ... The Chinese leadership ... is highly unlikely to allow farmers to sell land-use rights for non-agricultural development ... Many party traditionalists strongly favour collective land ownership. They have argued that China's economy is still not robust enough to absorb hundreds of millions of rural labourers full time. They also defend the system of allocating small plots of land to all rural families as guaranteeing farmers at least a subsistence income ... Average income in rural areas lags far behind the average in cities, giving China one of the starkest income gaps in the world, according to government estimates ... Rural land reform has failed to keep pace with urban land reform ... China allows urban residents to trade or sell their land-use contracts freely ... [Deng Xiaoping's] initial economic reforms were unveiled thirty years ago this month [October].

(www.iht.com, 11 October 2008)

The ability to sell the contracts would lead to the establishment of large-scale farms ... Officially, the government claims that 80 per cent to 90 per cent of peasants have proper documentation, but in reality only half do ... [according to] recent statistics compiled by the [Seattle-based] Rural Development Institute.

(IHT, 13 October 2008, p. 4)

A four-day enclave including President Hu Jintao has approved 'major issues' on reform, Xinhua news agency said ... Xinhua: 'The Communist Party of China Central Committee on Sunday [12 October] approved a decision on major issues concerning rural reform and development' ... Reports [about] the Third Plenary Session of the Seventeenth Central Committee ... suggest a key consideration was to enshrine in law the rights of rural citizens to transfer or rent out their land leases to other individuals or companies ... Many farmers swap chunks of land to be held in common by the village. People leaving the village to work in richer coastal areas often lease farming rights to others in informal arrangements. State media in recent days have been extolling the 'success' of new farming arrangements in places such as Xiaogang village in Anhui province. Mr Hu recently visited the village, where farmers are leasing their land to other farms or companies to run, for example, a pork farm and a vineyard.

(www.bbc.co.uk, 12 October 2008)

President Hu Jintao, discussing land transfer problems, said the [the new measures] were aimed at achieving economies of scale ... Sceptics believe that without a social safety net in the countryside the new system will merely persuade indigent farmers to sell cheaply to big agricultural conglomerates. The number of landless farmers, already a problem, could multiply.

(www.guardian.co.uk, 12 October 2008; *Guardian*, 13 October 2008, p. 25)

'[The] Communist Party said yesterday [12 October] it aimed to double the income of the country's farmers in two decades' (*FT*, 13 October 2008, p. 9).

Chinese leaders announced Sunday [13 October] that they would adopt a rural growth policy intended to vastly increase the incomes of farmers by 2020, setting in motion what could be the nation's biggest economic reform in many years ... The [media] reports did not give details of the reform, nor did they say when the plan would take effect. Policy decisions made at the planning session are often given pro forma approval by the National People's Congress in an annual meeting in March before details are unveiled.

(IHT, 13 October 2008, p. 4)

Two years ago ... the party ... decreed that 120 million hectares must be preserved as arable land to ensure food security. That leaves hardly any for conversion to other uses ... Some reports have said reforms could start with free trade in non-arable rural land. Guangdong province in the south has partially allowed this since 2005. But officials in Beijing still worry that the practice could result in swathes of farmland being redesignated as non-arable in order to open it up for sale.

(*The Economist*, 18 October 2008, p. 78)

Chen Xiwen [is] director of the office of the central leading group on rural work. In a party magazine published yesterday [16 October] he wrote: '[The Communist Party will] construct a healthy market for the transfer of land contract rights ... based on the principles of legality, free will and adequate compensation for the peasants ... We cannot change the collective owner-ship status of the land. We cannot change the land-use designation [from arable to commercial, residential or industrial] and we cannot damage the peasants' land-use contracts' ... The first land-use rights exchange was set up on Monday [13 October] in the western city of Chengdu to allow farmers to sell or rent out the rights to use their land ... Under current laws peasant farmers have mostly been given thirty-year land use contracts ... A commu-niqué issued on Sunday [12 October] at the end of the [Central Committee] meeting made only passing mention to perfecting the 'land management system'. Some observers said the omission signalled serious disagreement among China's top rulers over how far the reform should go.

(*FT*, 17 October 2008, p. 12)

Following days of uncertainty, the Communist Party announced a rural reform policy on Sunday [19 October] that for the first time would allow farmers to lease or transfer land-use rights, a step that advocates say would bolster lagging incomes in the countryside. The new policy, announced by the Chinese state media, marks a major economic reform and is also rich in historical resonance, coinciding with the thirtieth anniversary of the land reforms by Deng Xiaoping, which were considered the first critical steps in the market-orientated policies ... Xinhua (the country's official news agency): 'The new measures adopted are seen by economists as a major breakthrough in land reforms initiated by late leader Deng Xiaoping thirty years ago' ... Under the new policy the government will establish markets where farmers can 'subcontract, lease, exchange or swap' land-use rights or join co-operatives. Xinhua reported that giving farmers this latitude would enable them to become more efficient by increasing the size of farms while also providing income that can be used to start new businesses. The fate of the reform programme has been uncertain for the past week. Analysts had expected an announcement last Sunday [12 October] after the conclusion of an important annual Communist Party planning session. But the communi-qué released after the meeting made no mention of land reform, fuelling speculation that opponents may have derailed the plan ... Signs that the reforms may have been approved began to appear as the week wore on. In Chengdu a government land market opened last Monday [13 October]. On Thursday [16 October] a leading Communist Party magazine published an article by one of the country's many senior officials on rural issues in which he said the party would create a market for transferring land-use rights in the countryside ... Reform advocates say that allowing leasing or transfer would enable the creation of larger, more efficient farms that could bolster output. The new programme also pledges to uphold 'the most stringent farmland protection system' and require that local officials maintain 120 million hectares, or 297 million acres, of farmland – the minimum deemed necessary to feed the most populous nation in the world ... On Sunday Xinhua also announced the party's intention to establish a modern rural financial system to extend more credit and investment into the countryside. Chinese banking regulators have been ordered to establish forty more rural banking institutions by the end of the year [2008]. Increasing incomes in the countryside is a major part of the government's efforts to bolster domestic output at a time the overall economy is slowing.

(www.iht.com, 19 October 2008)

Sweeping reforms giving China's 730 million rural residents more say over their land [were unveiled on Sunday 19 October] ... Farmers, rather than village authorities, will be able to decide how to use their land, transfer land-use rights and join shareholding schemes.

(*The Times*, 20 October 2008, p. 31)

China's Communist Party unveiled its plan to double, by 2020, the disposable income of 750 million people in the Chinese countryside. One way it hopes to achieve this is through land reform ... [But] there is less to the new reform than meets the eye ... Much of the 'breakthrough' is already common practice ... The actual reform is minor ... The 'new' proposals are not explicit on this, but a senior official has since suggested that leases may be made longer than thirty years ... The party does not propose lifting the legal ban on farmers' mortgaging their land and houses ... To preserve 'food security' China has set a minimum area for the country's farmland – 120 million hectares, just below the present level ... It is on the non-arable 'construction' land that the latest policy offers something new. It extends an experiment tried in Guangdong province, allowing such land to be traded without first going through government acquisition. In practice, of course, farmers will still be hostage to the whims of the collective.

(*The Economist*, 25 October 2008, p. 14)

In late October [2008] ... a bill board [was erected] in Tawa village, 90 kilometres (56 miles) north-east of the [Beijing] city centre ... [proclaiming] that China's first auction of rural land was going to take place ... [The] auction [was] due to take place on 28 December. In fact, it was delayed ... Forestry cannot be transferred ... Ownership cannot be traded, only 'land use' rights ... [The auction] is hardly path-breaking. Peasants have been legally trading land use rights for years. Moreover, for 'wasteland', like swathes of Tawa's mountain slopes, auctions are common. So peasants have been grumbling less about restrictions on how they sell their rights, than about the shortness of leases and the 'collective' ownership principle covering rural land. Local officials often claim to represent the collective and take big cuts from any deals, leaving little to the land users. Mortgaging rural land or even selling one's own house to non-villagers is banned.

(*The Economist*, 10 January 2009, p. 53)

The global financial crisis sharpened China's interest in microloans … In May 2008 the central bank and the China Banking Regulatory Commission issued a directive expanding to all provinces the establishment of micro-credit companies focused on rural lending and explaining the conditions for raising capital and making loans. That led to an explosion to 500 companies from eight in May 2008, according to GTZ, the German development aid agency, which is conducting a survey with the Chinese central bank.

(*IHT*, 17 June 2009, p. 2)

Agriculture and the World Trade Organization (WTO)

Many [farmers] are forced to grow grain crops to feed the Communist Party's paranoia of a Western food embargo … With WTO entry China's average tariff on agricultural imports will fall to 15 per cent from 22 per cent in trade-weighted terms. More significant is the end of quotas and the state food distribution monopolies that will make China one of the world's most open countries for food imports … The pain will be concentrated in a few sectors – wheat, corn, rice and cotton – where Beijing reckons 13 million people will lose their jobs, most of them in the north … Lower tariffs and a relaxation of state quotas and other controls are expected to bring a surge of food imports that will throw 13 million farmers … [out of] 328 million farmers … out of work, according to official estimates … At the same time WTO membership will bring significant new opportunities for fruit, vegetable and meat producers with access to foreign markets.

(*FEER*, 29 November 2001, pp. 36–8)

Entry to the WTO has brought real benefits to those willing to switch to products such as those fruits and vegetables in ever greater demand.

Grain prices doubled between early 2007 and spring 2008 … Even before a sharp price spike earlier this year [2008], governments in countries from China to Peru to Malawi had begun urging both growing and eating potatoes to ensure food security and build rural income. Production in China rose 50 per cent from 2005 to 2007 … A decade ago the vast majority of potatoes were grown and eaten in the developed world, mostly in Europe and the Americas. Today China and India – neither big potato-eating countries in the past – rank first and third, respectively, in global potato production. And in 2005 developing countries produced a majority of the world's potatoes for the first time … Since they are heavy and do not transport well, they are not generally traded on world financial markets, making their price less vulnerable to speculation. They are generally not used to produce biofuels, a new use for food crops that has helped drive up grain prices. When grain prices skyrocketed potato prices remained stable ... Because potatoes spoil easily and are heavy to ship, groups like the World Food Programme avoid them.

(www.iht.com, 26 October 2008; *IHT*, 27 October 2008, pp. 1, 7)

3 The market gradually replacing central planning

The nearest China came to emulating the traditional Soviet-type command planning system was during the First Five Year Plan (1953–7). But even from the beginning Chinese planning devolved greater powers to the regions (although the degree fluctuated over time), there was no labour market initially (manpower was allocated to enterprises) and greater use was made of consumer good rationing (partly to control population movements). Prior to the 1978 reforms Communist China's development had been erratic, with alternative periods of centralization and decentralization and periods when politics and economics were alternatively in command. For example, the Great Leap Forward (1958–60) and the Cultural Revolution (1966–9/76) were anarchic periods of extreme administrative decentralization when extreme-left politics took priority over economics. These traumatic episodes helped secure the market-orientated reforms of 1978 and after by giving extreme-leftist policies a bad name. The lack of effective medium-term (five years) and long-term planning during the period 1958–76 was reflected in severe bottlenecks in the provision of infrastructure, especially energy, transport and communications. The situation improved. 'Power supply and transportation bottlenecks ... are now seemingly things of the past' (*China Briefing*, January 1998, no. 59, p. 5). But continued rapid growth led to the reappearance of bottlenecks in the early years of the new millennium.

The increasing importance of the market can be judged by the following:

1   'Whereas in 1978 around 700 kinds of producer goods were allocated by the plan, by 1991 the number was below twenty. Even in the case of state enterprises, according to one estimate, in 1989 around 56 per cent of inputs were purchased outside the plan and almost 40 per cent of output was sold outside the plan. Today the market distributes almost 60 per cent of coal, 55 per cent of steel and 90 per cent of cement' (*The Economist*, Survey, 28 November 1992, p. 7).

2   By 1993 central (mandatory) plans controlled only 7 per cent of industrial output (Jefferson and Rawski 1994: 63). The proportion of planned production of total industrial output value fell from 91 per cent in 1978 to 80 per cent in 1984, 16.2 per cent in 1991, 12 per cent in 1992 and 5 per cent in 1993 (Cao *et al.* 1997: 20).

3   'Moving more quickly than political reform ... is China's "marketization" –
     the degree to which its economy is responsive to market forces. The results
     of a study on the topic [in the November 1998 issue of a Chinese journal]
     indicate that after twenty years of reform, half of China's economy is now
     "marketized", with some parts lagging far behind ... Market forces in China
     today influence 70 per cent of labour allocation, 62 per cent of product
     pricing and distribution, 51 per cent of enterprise management, 23 per cent
     of land transfers and 17 per cent of capital distribution ... Bringing China
     up to the level of "countries with relatively developed market economies"
     would take thirty years' (Susan Lawrence, *FEER*, 17 December 1998,
     p. 22).

4   '[China's] extraordinary economic performance has been driven by changes
     in government economic policy that have progressively given greater rein to
     market forces. The transformation started in the agricultural sector more
     than two decades ago and was extended progressively to industry and large
     parts of the service sector' (OECD 2005: website Chapter 1). 'Changes in
     government policies have created a largely market-orientated economy in
     which the private sector plays a key role' (website Chapter 2).

     'During his recent trip to China Hank [Henry] Paulson, the US Treasury
     Secretary, made his first stop in Hangzhou, capital of Zhejiang province.
     This carefully choreographed trip was thought to signal where Mr Paulson
     thinks the country's future lies ... Unlike his predecessors, who liked to tour
     the skyscrapers in Shanghai, Mr Paulson understands the China miracle –
     that its impressive development came from the same dynamics that create
     growth and wealth elsewhere, namely bottom-up entrepreneurship and a
     market-based financial environment ... [i.e.] a bottom-up, entrepreneurial,
     market-orientated model ... Many more people own and operate successful
     small businesses in Zhejiang ... Zhejiang has [according to official figures]
     an entrepreneurial population 3.4 times that of Shanghai on a per household
     basis ... The banks in Zhejiang are the best performing in China ... Banks
     in Zhejiang began to lend to private sector companies long before the rest of
     the country and now Zhejiang has a healthy corporate sector that invests
     wisely and services its debt ... Chinese peasants are extraordinarily entre-
     preneurial. Many of the largest businesses in Zhejiang today were founded
     by rural entrepreneurs in the 1980s ... More than 80 per cent of China's
     poverty reduction occurred in the first five years of the 1980s when China
     had no foreign direct investment and very little trade' (Yasheng Huang, *FT*,
     2 October 2006, p. 19).

5   'China is progressing toward receiving the EU's coveted market economy
     status, something that would help the Asian export powerhouse avoid puni-
     tive anti-dumping duties, an EU document showed ... Beijing has been
     seeking such status from the EU since 2004 ... The European Commission
     said in its latest assessment ... that China had still met only one of five cri-
     teria used to gauge the influence of state intervention on prices and costs.
     But Beijing had made "considerable progress" on the four others, it said,

providing a "clear platform" for reaching the target. The report also described the Chinese economy as "an increasingly modern and market-based system" ... It said: "The conclusion of this report is that China now has in place almost all the legislation which is necessary for granting Market Economy Status. That is a considerable achievement. The focus has now switched to the effective implementation of these laws which are crucial for the functioning of any market economy" ... The one criterion that China has met – as determined by Brussels in 2004 – relates to the absence on non-market payment forms like barter. The criteria it has yet to meet include the use of modern accounting standards, on which China had made "considerable progress" and bankruptcy, intellectual property and property laws where progress was "substantial", the report said. There was less progress in reducing the state's role in price setting in sectors like energy, a key component for manufacturers and China was slow in improving the independence of its financial system, the Commission said' (www.iht.com, 18 September 2008; *IHT*, 19 September 2008, p. 20).

Prices

China adopted a policy of gradual and partial price reform. A 'dual' pricing system was used (market prices being allowed for products bought and sold on the market as opposed to state-controlled prices for outputs or inputs forming part of the state plan). Controls have generally been relaxed over time. Nevertheless, temporary retrenchment has occurred, such as the reintroduction of price controls to combat inflation (price ceilings) and (for some time after October 1997) deflation (price floors).

'Chinese officials like to boast that 96 per cent of all prices are officially set by the market. But that is extremely misleading. The government's influence remains widespread and deeply felt' (*FEER*, 26 August 2004, p. 19).

> Tight regulations on retail prices for diesel and electricity ... have made increasingly profit-orientated refiners and power companies reluctant to sell either. Global markets set wholesale prices for diesel and for heavy fuel oil used by power stations, but the government still insists on setting retail prices.
>
> (*IHT*, 19 April 2005, p. 13)

'Price regulation was essentially dismanted by 2000' (OECD 2005: website Chapter 1). The OECD survey (website Chapter 1) provides information on the share of transactions (per cent of transactions volume) conducted at market prices for the years 1978, 1985, 1991, 1995, 1999 and 2003 for both producer goods and retail sales. For producer goods the respective figures for market prices for the six years are as follows: 0.0 per cent; 13.0 per cent; 46.0 per cent, 78.0 per cent; 86.0 per cent; 87.3 per cent. (The respective figures for state guided and state fixed prices for the six years are as follows: 0.0 per cent and 100.0 per cent; 23.0 per cent and 64.0 per cent; 18.0 per cent and 36.0 per cent;

6.0 per cent and 16.0 per cent; 4.0 per cent and 10.0 per cent; 2.7 and 10.0 per cent.). For retail sales the respective figures for market prices for the six years are as follows: 3.0 per cent; 34.0 per cent; 69.0 per cent; 89.0 per cent; 95.0 per cent; 96.1 per cent. (The respective figures for state guided and state fixed prices are as follows: 0.0 per cent and 97 per cent; 19.0 per cent and 47.0 per cent; 10.0 per cent and 21.0 per cent; 2.0 per cent and 9.0 per cent; 1.0 per cent and 4.0 per cent; 1.3 per cent and 2.6 per cent.)

'Prime minister Wen Jiabao ... said [on 12 September 2006] that about 90 per cent of commodity prices were set by the market' (*IHT*, 13 September 2006, p. 16).

> China said that it had cracked down on price fixing of soybean products, 'hotpot' meals [meat and vegetables cooked in a boiling broth] and other food as the government tackles inflation, which jumped to a ten-year high in July [2007]. Soaring food costs helped push the inflation rate to 5.6 per cent [in August] ... The government's target inflation rate for 2007 is 3 per cent ... Earlier this month [August] China ordered local governments to check food producers, wholesalers and retailers for price fixing or gouging. Food prices account for a third of the Chinese consumer price index ... While the state no longer directly controls the prices of most goods, price edicts from the national government still carry weight. The prices for some basic items, like fuel and rice, are still under formal government control. The pricing department at the National Development and Reform Commission ... an agency of the national State Council ... can issue price directives on any good or service as it deems fit. With the State Council's blessing, local governments have little trouble bringing merchants into line. Even acts like spreading rumours of price increases can draw punishments as severe as the termination of business licences.
>
> (www.iht.com, 28 August 2007)

> The government on Wednesday [19 September] froze prices that it controls for the rest of the year [2007], in the latest sign of Beijing's mounting concern over inflation. Beijing also stressed the importance of holding down market-driven process during the forthcoming holiday period, saying it would have a direct impact on the country's 'development, reform and stability' ... The government still administers a vast array of prices, including those for land, transport, utilities and fuel. The ministries said that, in principle, the government would not introduce any new price changes for the rest of the year ... The statement [by six ministries] said: 'All current rules on goods and service prices controlled by the government should be strictly implemented. Any unauthorized price rise is strictly forbidden' ... The ministries ordered local governments not to raise prices without the approval of the National Development and Reform Commission, the main planning agency ... To keep a lid on pork prices over the holidays, the government would draw if necessary on the country's pork reserves ... Separately, China is set to provide more aid to dairy farmers as

part of an effort to control rising food prices, which have driven consumer price inflation … The State Council, China's cabinet, is to meet Wednesday [19 September] to discuss financial support for dairy farmers after increasing feed costs and low milk prices forced many farmers to stop raising cows.

(www.iht.com, 19 September 2007)

[The government froze] all government-set prices, notably for gasoline, water, electricity and natural gas until at least the end of this year [2007]. It has also banned any increases in the maximum allowed prices for medicines, air and rail trips and certain agricultural commodities like wheat, rice and cotton.

(*IHT*, 26 October 2007, p. 9)

China is to enforce a freeze on all government-controlled prices in a sign of Beijing's alarm at rising public anger over inflation – now at its highest rate for more than a decade. The move will freeze a vast array of prices still under government control, ranging from oil, electricity and water to the cost of parking and entrance fees to public parks. An order was issued jointly by six ministries yesterday [19 September], following a vaguely worded announcement by the State Council, or cabinet, in August [2007] on the need to prevent price rises … The ministries said: 'Any unauthorized price rises are strictly forbidden … and in principle there will be no new price-raising measures this year [2007].'

(*FT*, 20 September 2007, p. 7)

[There is a] low-profile but intense battle between China's government and its increasingly independent oil firms over who should fund fuel subsidies. The showdown has caused diesel shortages in parts of China's booming coastal province of Guangdong for weeks … as refiners seek to staunch losses by reducing sales. The dry pumps are a distant echo of the fuel crisis of the summer of 2005 that sparked long lines and a government crackdown on oil firms' huge exports. Beijing suspended tax incentives and set export quotas to keep more fuel at home … Despite repeated promises to gradually allow fuel prices to catch up with global rates, Beijing has maintained a tight grip on prices, fearful that costlier energy could spark inflation or unrest. Gasoline prices have not been increased since May 2006. The government forces state-owned or state-controlled oil firms to absorb losses that analysts say are now running at up to $10 a barrel on imported crude, although for the past two years Beijing also doled out hefty year-end compensation to Sinopec, the worst hit. In response, refiners trying to limit losses have trimmed processing rates and cut flows to markets, tightening supplies of diesel and cheaper gasoline – particularly in demand hot spots. Major cities, such as Shenzhen and Guangzhou, appear to be better supplied than some other less prosperous areas … US oil prices last month climbed to record levels above $80 a barrel.

(www.iht.com, 1 October 2007)

The worst Chinese fuel crisis in two years [has] spread to the capital and other inland areas ... [such as] Anhui province ... Rationing has already spread along the south-eastern coast from Guangdong through Fujian, Jiangsu and Zhejiang provinces ... State-set diesel and gasoline prices have not been raised since May 2006 ... But with these retail prices most prices can only break even with crude at around $65 a barrel or lower. So as international markets climbed to records near $94 a barrel, they are ever more reluctant to keep markets supplied. The burden has fallen mostly on the state-owned companies. Sinopec, which for the past two years has received hundreds of millions of dollars in year-end compensation from Beijing for losses, has upped imports and refining in November [2007].

(www.iht.com, 31 October 2007)

China raised the price of petrol and diesel [and jet fuel] by almost 10 per cent yesterday [31 October] as crude prices hit a fresh record above $94 a barrel. The move [was] the first increase since May 2006 ... Transport and other fuel-dependent prices would not be raised and industries such as agriculture, forestry, fisheries, public transport and taxis would receive direct subsidies from the government. Government price controls mean Sinopec's break-even oil price is $60 a barrel ... The government gave Sinopec $1.2 billion in 2005 and $640 million in 2006 in 'one-off subsidies' to make up for refining losses ... China imports around 50 per cent of its crude oil needs and with prices surging many small Chinese refiners have stopped production, leaving state-owned firms such as Sinopec, the state's largest refiner, to take up the slack.

(*FT*, 1 November 2007, p. 10)

China has raised fuel prices by almost 10 per cent in an effort to ease the country's worsening supply crisis. Officials hope the extra revenue will make refiners increase production, easing the long queues and rationing at filling stations. The rise is a reversal of policy. In September the government promised to keep fuel prices at current levels ... Oil prices have been sky-rocketing, but Chinese refiners cannot pass those rises on to consumers and so they are losing money. Many have already cut their supplies to limit losses ... The National Development and Reform Commission: 'Prices of railway tickets, natural gas for civilian use and public transportation will not be raised to reduce the impact of price hikes on the public' ... It also added that subsidies would be given to taxi drivers ... However, analysts warned that the companies would still be losing money.

(www.bbc.co.uk, 1 November 2007)

The increase in fuel prices aims to alleviate widespread shortages, especially of diesel, after soaring crude prices prompted refiners to cut output rather than swallow mounting losses at the regulated, below-market prices. The rise will add just 0.05 percentage points to consumer prices, the National

Development and Reform Commission estimates ... One man was killed in a brawl while waiting in a line for gasoline Tuesday [30 October].

(www.iht.com, 1 November 2007)

Low government-controlled oil prices have led to a fuel supply crisis in many parts of the country. Rationing, long queues, bad tempers and violence have become commonplace at filling stations ... This week widespread shortages, which plagued the country two years ago and again in October, have reemerged (if they ever truly abated) ... The severity of shortages varies across the country. Urban Beijing appears unaffected ... The press says some petrol stations have raised prices beyond state-mandated limits to take advantage of frenzied demand ... In 2005 and 2006 the government gave Sinopec (which depends far more than does PetroChina on crude bought at international process) subsidies totalling 15 billion yuan ($2 billion) to offset its refining losses ... Profits at both companies have been rising this year [2007].

(*The Economist*, 24 November 2007, pp. 85–6)

Prime minister Wen Jiabao responded Wednesday [9 January 2008] to growing public anxiety about inflation by announcing that China would freeze prices in the near term, even as international crude oil futures have topped $100 a barrel ... Prices of oil products, natural gas and electricity will be frozen in the near term. Rates for public water bills will also be frozen, as will the cost of public transportation tickets. The edict also called for stabilizing prices on medical services and for certain agricultural fertilizers. It ordered local governments to closely monitor prices and warned that punishments would be strengthened for those who violate government control policies ... The November price increase helped drive consumer prices up 6.9 per cent from a year earlier – a figure that represented an eleven-year high ... Oil futures have continued to rise on world markets and Chinese refiners are again raising the same concerns. Again, lines are forming at service stations, particularly for truckers in southern China.

(www.iht.com, 9 January 2008; *IHT*, 10 January 2008, p. 11)

China has vowed to 'temporarily intervene' in the market to prevent excessive price rises for food and daily necessities ... The announcement said enterprises producing 'general necessities' should register with local price bureaux if they wanted to lift prices. The cabinet did not outline what level of price increase was required to be registered, but some guidelines were separately issued this month [January 2008] by the chief economic planning agency. The National Development and Reform Commission asked for retailers and wholesalers of meat, milk and animal feedstock to register one-off price increases of more than 5 per cent, or accumulated rises of 8 per cent, over October 2007 prices. The local authorities could ask for the prices to be 'readjusted' if they judged them to be 'unreasonable' ... The central government continues to control prices for key economic inputs, including power, oil, gas and water. The wholesale price of grain is also regulated.

(*FT*, 10 January 2008, p. 9)

'Retailers and producers will face heavy fines if they increase the price of basic necessities, the government says. Food prices climbed more than 18 per cent in November' (www.bbc.co.uk, 10 January 2008).

China's cabinet on Monday [14 January] sharply increased penalties for price-fixing, expanding an anti-inflation campaign that has failed to cool a surge in politically sensitive food costs. Fixed costs soared by 18.2 per cent in November [2007], pushing the overall monthly inflation rate to 6.9 per cent, its highest level in eleven years. Companies that hoard goods or try to fix prices can be fined up to 1 million yuan, or $130,000, up to ten times the previous penalty ... The increased penalties are meant to 'strike [at] the activities of driving up prices through hoarding or cheating' ... The government accused Chinese instant noodle makers in August [2007] of pushing up food costs by illegally colluding to raise prices by up to 40 per cent. It has given no indication whether it has evidence of illegal behaviour by other producers ... The surge in food prices has been especially painful for China's poor majority, who spend up to half their incomes on food ... Suppliers of meat, eggs and other food have been ordered to report price increases over 5 per cent to the government. In September [2007] the government froze prices of cooking oil and some other basic food items that are still set by the state. But prices for meat, vegetables, noodles and other processed food are dictated by the market and have risen sharply ... Local authorities have been ordered to pay subsidies to the poor to cushion the blow of higher food costs.

(www.iht.com, 14 January 2008)

'The government imposed complex price controls on 15 January on many foods, from pork and eggs to flour and cooking oil' (*IHT*, 20 February 2008, p. 14).

As food prices gallop upwards the government has asked state-owned agricultural companies to maintain supply at fixed prices. More recently the National Development and Reform Commission has forbidden large food processing companies, fertilizer makers and retailers from raising prices of grain, meat, eggs, dairy products and fertilizers without government approval.

(www.economist.com, 31 January 2008)

In January [2008] the government froze the prices of energy, transport and water, and announced that producers of essential food items, such as meat, grain, eggs and cooking oil must seek approval before raising prices ... Officials say that the measures are only 'temporary', not frozen.

(*The Economist*, 23 February 2008, p. 92)

'The 60 per cent jump in the price of pork over the past year has been largely caused by disease [according to the World Bank]' (p. 94).

Unusually severe snowstorms started in parts of China on 10 January 2008. (For details, see entry in the chronology in Chapter 8 of the companion volume, *Political Developments in Contemporary China*.) '[This is] the worst winter weather in fifty years' (www.cnn.com, 31 January 2008). 'The winter storm [is] China's worst in fifty years' (www.cnn.com, 1 February 2008). 'Many of the worst effects have been in parts of east-central and southern China, which are unaccustomed to serious snowfall' (www.iht.com, 3 February 2008). 'Unusually severe blizzards hit large areas of central and southern China at the beginning of the year, blocking transport links and causing widespread chaos' (www.bbc.co.uk, 18 February 2008). Controls on the prices that power companies can charge exacerbated the problems of electricity supply and food price controls were increased.

'The authorities have capped the prices utilities can charge for power at a time when coal prices have been soaring. Without the incentive of adequate profits, power producers have been reluctant to increase output' (www.iht.com, 31 January 2008; *IHT*, 1 February 2008, p. 14).

'[The severe weather has caused] the government to order a ceiling on food prices' (*Guardian*, 31 January 2008, p. 24).

'The authorities have ordered coal production to be increased and imposed emergency price controls' (www.bbc.co.uk, 1 February 2008).

Power companies – caught between rising coal costs and fixed prices for their output – have been haggling with the coal suppliers, and found themselves short of coal stocks when the snowstorms hit ... China has ordered financial institutions to provide emergency loans to businesses and individuals hit by the snowstorms and power cuts that have paralysed swathes of central and southern China.

(*FT*, 2 February 2008, pp. 8, 10)

A flawed reform has freed fuel prices but left power producers unable to pass on the rising cost of coal to consumers, because electricity prices are fixed. Many producers responded by letting their stocks fall to dangerously low levels, in the hope prices would fall when the weather warms up in the spring ... Power plants that normally stock eighteen-to-twenty days' worth of coal had in some cases run their reserves down to as little as three days' worth ... Electricity prices are fixed and, unable to pass on costs, power producers had been waiting for seasonal price cuts in March before stocking up.

(www.economist.com, 7 February 2008)

'After months of keeping a tight rein on lending by banks in an effort to curb runaway economic growth, China's central bank has ordered provincial banks to speed up loans issued in the worst-hit areas' (*The Independent*, 2 February 2008, p. 37).

China said Friday [28 March] it will pay farmers more for rice and wheat, trying to raise output and cool surging inflation ... Beijing has frozen retail prices of rice, cooking oil and other goods in an effort to curb inflation that saw food prices jump 23.3 per cent in February over the same month last year [2007] ... Minimum grain prices paid to farmers would rise by up to 9 per cent ... Beijing has been prodding farmers to raise production by promising free vaccinations for pigs and other aid ... Under the latest order prices paid for rice will rise by 7 yuan, or $1, for every 50 kg, or 110 lb, to 77 yuan to 82 yuan, depending on the type ... Wheat prices will rise by 3 yuan to 5 yuan, to 72 yuan to 75 yuan per 50 kg. The government regards meeting most of China's grain needs from domestic sources as a matter of national security. It operates a network of grain-buying offices and a grain stockpile. It has been releasing supplies to ease shortages. The exact size of the stockpile is a secret, but premier Wen Jiabao said this month [March] that it is 150 million tonnes to 200 million tonnes.

(www.iht.com, 28 March 2008)

China, the world's second largest consumer of oil, is to raise the price of petrol and diesel by 18 per cent. The move ... caused the [world] price of crude to fall $4. US light, sweet crude fell to $132 on the news, along with confirmation from Saudi Arabia that it will boost the level of its oil production ... Retail fuel prices will increase by 1,000 yuan ($145.40) a tonne from Friday [20 June], while aviation fuel will rise by 1,500 yuan a tonne ... The National Development and Reform Commission said: 'Global crude prices have been rising sharply and Chinese domestic fuel prices have lagged behind. The price difference has highlighted the contradiction between demand and supply' ... The move came as a surprise, as China had ruled out any cuts in subsidies ahead of this summer's Beijing Olympics [August 2008]. It is the first cut in subsidies for eight months and there are fears it will stoke inflation in China.

(www.bbc.co.uk, 20 June 2008)

China raised prices for fuel by as much as 18 per cent on Friday [20 June] ... International oil prices dropped sharply Thursday [19 June] after China said it will raise fuel prices, with light, sweet crude for July delivery falling $4.75 to settle at $131.93 a barrel on the New York Mercantile Exchange ... The *China Daily* newspaper reported Friday that the increase was 'because of the soaring price of crude in the international market'. It said areas in Sichuan province, hit by a massive earthquake last month [12 May], were exempt from the increase. The price increase was announced late Thursday ... by the government's main economic planning agency ... Prices of gasoline and diesel rose by 1,000 yuan ($145) per tonne to 6,980 yuan and 6,520 yuan ($949). Aviation kerosene rose by 1,500 yuan ($218) per tonne to 7,450 yuan ($1,084) ... Electricity prices will also rise for most businesses by 0.025 yuan (0.36 cents) per kilowatt, although residential housing and the farming and fertilizer industries will remain unchanged. Natural gas and liquefied petroleum gas prices will remain unchanged ... The government last hiked fuel prices by about 11 per cent in November [2007] but had kept them frozen since, seeking to avoid fanning inflation, which has touched twelve-year highs since the beginning of the year [2008]. That policy, however, has led to shortages at the pumps as refiners find themselves squeezed by rising world oil and gas prices. To help counter shortages, Shanghai on Monday [16 June] announced an increase in prices for liquefied petroleum gas used by scooters. Earlier this week the economic planning agency said it would look for an opportunity to adjust oil product prices ... [The agency] said high world oil prices had created 'contradictions in the purchasing price of oil higher than the selling price of refined products that were becoming more glaring by the day'. That had led some refiners to halt or suspend production, creating supply interruptions and long lines at some filling stations, it said. Coal prices that have risen 80 yuan ($12) in the past two years have created massive losses for four of the country's five major power producers, it said. Along with the electricity price rise, the government will also continue to provide subsidies to the industry to guarantee supplies [it said].

(www.cnn.com, 20 June 2008)

Faced with increasingly severe fuel shortages and the prospect of power failures during the summer air-conditioning season, the government unexpectedly announced sharp increases late Thursday [19 June] in regulated prices for gasoline, diesel and electricity ... The government has come under intense pressure recently from both environmentalists and other governments to ease up on its fuel subsidies, which are blamed for distorting global markets, encouraging greater consumption and pushing oil prices higher for other nations ... The government, like many others around the world, has struggled to keep up those subsidies as oil prices have spiked in recent months. Finally, despite fears that it will spur inflation, the government raised the retail price of diesel by 18 per cent, to the equivalent of $3.58 a gallon, and the price of gasoline by 16 per cent, to $3.83 a gallon. Electricity prices and the price of jet fuel were also raised ... China is the world's second largest oil consumer, after the United States. With the announcement Thursday China became the eighth Asian country to raise fuel prices in the past month after concluding that low retail prices could not be sustained indefinitely through government subsidies ... Chinese officials have spoken for several years of their desire to move towards a more energy-efficient economy. They have periodically mentioned an intention to impose taxes on energy once world oil prices begin to fall, so as to keep the pressure on Chinese businesses and consumers to improve efficiency. Prices for gasoline and diesel have been fixed since 1 November [2007] even as world oil prices rose 45 per cent in that period ... Until now the government's subsidies have forced the state-controlled refiners to lose money by selling gasoline and diesel for less than the cost of the crude oil needed to make them. Power companies, too, have become reluctant to operate oil-fired stations when they cannot sell the electricity for enough money to cover the cost of oil. As refineries cut back their output this spring [2008], the result has been crippling fuel shortages, particularly for diesel. Those shortages have already produced long lines of trucks at service stations, and might threaten the gathering of the summer harvest. President Hu Jintao and prime minister Wen Jiabao took the highly unusual step on 5 June [2008] of ordering that tractors and other farm vehicles would be given top priority for all supplies of diesel – usually the kind of measure that would be handled by far more junior officials. Farmers were exempted on Thursday night from the latest increase in fuel prices, as were three provinces damaged in earthquakes last month [May]: Sichuan, Shaanxi and Gansu provinces. Power plants that rely on oil have been shutting down because of high oil prices. While China relies mainly on coal and hydroelectric power for electricity generation, oil-fired plants are important in south-eastern China ... China struggles each summer to generate enough electricity, although there have been a few signs that electricity generation capacity is beginning to catch up with demand. The government also announced on Thursday night that it was limiting increases in coal prices, which would help companies afford their fuel – although at the risk of introducing the same kind of price control distortions to the coal market that have already caused problems for diesel users.

(www.iht.com, 20 June 2008)

'On Thursday crude fell almost $5 to settle at below $132 a barrel after China's unexpected decision to increase gasoline and diesel prices by up to 18 per cent' (www.iht.com, 20 June 2008).

The increase took many market watchers by surprise, since Beijing has repeatedly vowed to rule out 'near term' price increases to battle high inflation and avoid social unrest before the Beijing Olympics [in August] ... [It was also] reported that China would also raise some electricity rates on 1 July. The average electricity rate would go up by 0.025 yuan per kilowatt hour, though exemptions will be granted to urban and rural residents along with some farmers and fertilizer producers.

(*IHT*, 20 June 2008, p. 15)

The price of light, sweet crude fell $4.02 to $132.66 per barrel following the fuel price increase announcement ... Huge refining losses have caused the two biggest refiners in the country, Sinopec and PetroChina, to slow production ... Hovering at $3 per gallon, or 79 US cents per litre, with the new increase, gas in China cost 25 per cent less at the pump than it does in the United States ... In 2007 China's subsidy of gasoline alone was $22 billion, close to 1 per cent of its GDP ... With oil prices skyrocketing past $135 per barrel this week, Sinopec and PetroChina shut down many gas stations across the country ... At any point in time Sinopec and PetroChina make up to 16 per cent to 20 per cent of the Shanghai Composite Index ... On Tuesday [17 June] Zhang Xiaoqiang, the deputy head of China's economic planning agency, said China intended to make its energy prices better reflect the market over time but warned it needed to move cautiously because of inflation concerns.

(www.iht.com, 20 June 2008; *IHT*, 21 June 2008, p. 15)

'[On 19 June the government made a decision] to raise the government-set retail price of petrol and diesel by 17 per cent to 18 per cent' (*FT*, 20 June 2008, p. 7).

The decision by China to slash its oil subsidies will cause the country's largest one-off increase in at least a decade in petrol and diesel prices. The increases come into effect today [20 June]. Analysts had expected the authorities to hold off price increases until at least after the August [2008] Olympics. China has been under growing international pressure to reduce its oil subsidies, with Western countries accusing Beijing of artificially stimulating demand for oil by maintaining its price caps. Before the announcement Chinese gasoline prices were about 40 per cent below those of the United States. In the past month India, Taiwan, Malaysia and Indonesia have all cut their subsidies amid mounting fiscal cost and in spite of concern about high prices ... The price caps had caused problems, with the two large state-owned refiners complaining about huge losses and shortages at petrol stations across the country as many small refineries stopped operations ... Fuel shortages have beset China since 2007.

(p. 1)

China unveiled subsidies for fuel users in an effort to prevent unrest and soften the blow of big increases in energy prices that took effect yesterday [20 June]. Beijing announced the subsidies for grain farmers, taxi drivers and low-income groups, and said public transport fares would not go up as a result of the rise in prices. The finance ministry said the targeted subsidies would be worth $2.9 billion ... Petrol costs the equivalent of $0.85 a litre in China compared with $1.08 in the United States and $2.33 in the UK. Long queues built up as rumours of the impending price rises sparked a scramble to fill petrol tanks ... In recent weeks Chinese cities have been affected by significant shortages of fuel, especially diesel, with many petrol stations either rationing sales or operating for only a few hours a day ... The authorities also announced a nationwide cap on coal prices for power companies.

(*FT*, 21 June 2008, p. 7)

Police were called to petrol stations overnight and government officials stood guard at the pumps in Beijing, after angry motorists queued to fill up on learning that petrol and diesel prices were to rise by 18 per cent. The surprise decision by the authorities to remove subsidies prompted drivers to head for petrol forecourts but they were frustrated as many garages refused to serve them until after the price increase took effect at midnight ... The 16.7 per cent increase in gasoline takes the pump rate to about 75 US cents a litre, still a quarter cheaper than in the United States and about a third what British motorists pay. Prices have doubled since 2003 but crude oil has more than quadrupled.

(www.thetimes.co.uk, 20 June 2008)

The 20 June price change was the third increase in twenty-five months, following a 10 per cent rise in both May 2006 and November 2007. Crude prices have nearly tripled during that period ... Between 2003 and 2005 Beijing raised prices eleven times and cut prices twice. Three years ago policy-makers, hopeful that oil prices would halt their ascent at around $60, had managed to bring Chinese prices near to parity with global markets, and introduced a system for keeping them pegged to global crude oil benchmarks ... Prices would need to rise by at least another 20 per cent for refiners simply to break even, analysts say ... Economists say that the price increase should add less than one percentage point to inflation.

(www.iht.com, 30 June 2008)

'Despite an 18 per cent jump in China's domestic fuel prices on 20 June, local prices are still about 18 per cent below US levels' (*IHT*, 17 July 2008, p. 15).

On 20 June the government announced retail price hikes (subsidy reductions) for diesel, gasoline, jet fuel and electricity, and it reestablished price caps on thermal coal, which had already been freed from government control. To prevent coal producers from chasing higher prices abroad, and to hedge against the increased likelihood of coal shortages, the government is expected to ban coal exports (which are already limited) in the near future.

(www.feer.com, 29 June 2008)

A push by China to reopen thousands of small coal mines is failing, deepening its worst power crisis in years as local officials still fear Beijing's wrath if they suffer high profile disasters. Weeks after the central government urged miners to reopen the mines, effectively reversing a years-old policy of shutting them in order to improve safety, local officials are proving reluctant. And Beijing's freeze on coal prices has lowered the incentive for miners ... Six government officials in the Luliang region of Shanxi were fired after a blast at a small mine, approved to reopen just a month earlier, killed thirty-four in June ... China has been pushing forward a safety campaign for three years, shutting down the kind of small, inefficient and often dangerous mines that provided 38 per cent of its coal last year [2007]. Around nine-tenths of Chinese coal mines are classified as small, but they are eight times more deadly per tonne of coal produced than the larger mines. From 1995 to early 2008 the number of coal mines in China had fallen around 80 per cent to about 16,000. Over the same period the death toll is down 40 per cent to 3,786 in 2007, according to the State Administration of Coal Mine Safety. Beijing's goal is to reduce the number of small coal mines to under 10,000 by 2010 and to eliminate them by 2015. But in late May [2008], when coal stocks in key power plants had fallen to critical levels and summer power shortages loomed, prime minister Wen Jiabao called for an increase in coal output, while the cabinet asked local governments to speed up approvals for restarting small coal mines. Some have returned to production in Shanxi, the top producing province, but many are still closed or performing maintenance, traders and analysts say. And in late June [2008] the Shanxi provincial government ordered local governments to shut down illegal coal mines, highlighting the conflicting signals that have kept officials cautious … Beijing last month [June] froze the price miners are paid for thermal coal until the end of the year [2008] as it seeks to cap power prices … In two years power generators have received just a 4.7 per cent increase in state-set prices they can charge, not enough to offset the soaring price of coal, which until the June freeze had been freed to float with the market. Asian benchmark thermal coal prices have tripled in just a year to record highs … The impact of the coal shortage is already being felt. There have been record power shortfalls in Shanxi province, where the government has had to ration power supplies, hurting energy-intensive plants like aluminium smelters. Other industrial provinces, like Shandong and Guangdong, have forecast deep power cuts.

(www.iht.com, 13 July 2008; *IHT*, 14 July 2008, p. 18)

China faces its worst power shortage in at least four years as soaring coal prices and government-set electricity tariffs force dozens of small power plants to shut down rather than face mounting losses. Nearly half of China's provinces have started to ration electricity as the country enters the peak summer season, facing what analysts describe as its worst coal shortage. Analysts warn that this year's electricity shortfall could be more severe than in 2004, when the country was affected by its worst power shortage in decades because of soaring demand for power as the economy boomed … Late last month [June] the government raised fixed electricity tariffs by about 5 per cent but prices are still 30 per cent lower than the current coal price would imply, BNP Paribus estimates. Coal prices in China have doubled since the start of the year [2008]. Beijing last month imposed price controls on thermal coal bought directly from mines but spot market prices continued to rise. About 38 per cent of China's coal supply last year [2007] came from small-scale operations … Power demand has doubled during the past five years.

(*FT*, 17 July 2008, p. 7)

China lifted its controls on food prices Monday [1 December], the latest sign of how drastically priorities have shifted from earlier this year, when the county was focused on fighting inflation … Companies would now be free to decide that for themselves, the National Development and Reform Commission said in a statement … Under the controls manufacturers had to apply for approval for any substantial price increases. Beijing will still keep an eye on prices, however, and work to ensure that no one manipulates them … 'We must work further on how to address abnormal price movement,' the commission said.

(www.iht.com, 1 December 2008; *IHT*, 2 December 2008, p. 20)

'Starting 1 January [2009] Beijing will allow gasoline and diesel prices to move more regularly in line with the global market' (www.iht.com, 5 December 2008).

China unveiled a shake-up of its oil pricing system yesterday [5 December], combining a big increase in fuel taxes for consumers with the first steps in liberalizing prices for petrol and diesel. From next year [2009] Beijing will allow prices for refined oil in the Chinese market to 'reflect fluctuations of international oil prices', ending a system of periodic price changes.

(*FT*, 6 December 2008, p. 8)

China will cut domestic fuel prices on Friday [19 December] for the first time in almost two years ... Beijing announced [on 18 December] a 14 per cent cut in refinery gate gasoline prices and 18 per cent drop in diesel prices, plus a nearly on-third cut in jet fuel.

(www.ft.com, 19 December 2008)

China took a step back from its promise to move towards more market-orientated domestic fuel prices, warning on Friday [8 May] that Beijing would limit petrol, diesel and other fuel price increases when oil prices rise above $80 a barrel ... China is the world's second largest oil consumer and its domestic retail fuel price policy affects global oil prices because the country keeps domestic bills artificially low. The International Energy Agency has pressed Beijing to liberalize its domestic prices to rein in consumption. The National Development and Reform Commission, China's main economic policy-making body, said retail prices would move relatively freely while global crude prices remained below $80 a barrel. In those circumstances Chinese refineries would profit from distilling crude into fuels with a 'normal' refining margin. Above $80 a barrel and up to $130 a barrel domestic prices would also move, but Chinese refineries would not make a profit. The authorities said that above $130 a barrel they would guarantee supplies of retail fuels through 'tax measures', probably supporting refineries with tax rebates, but added that 'petrol and diesel prices will in principle not be raised or not be raised much'. Beijing pledged in November [2008] to allow prices of refined oil to 'reflect fluctuations of international oil prices' from the start of this year [2009]. It had also announced a steep rise in petrol and diesel taxes to replace other fees, such as some road tolls. The new regime replaces a system of periodic adjustments by the government without explanation of the underlying rationale ... The system fails to explain how changes in global crude prices would be calculated. Under new rules, the two state-owned refiners can adjust retail prices if global oil prices change more than 4 per cent from their moving average over twenty-two days. However, they did not indicate what variety of crude oil the authorities would track, nor how the refineries would be compensated above $130 a barrel.

(www.ft.com, 10 May 2009)

'[Companies such as PetroChina have] benefited from two government sanctioned fuel price increases in June [2009] – part of Beijing's fuel price reforms that guarantee refiners a profit margin if crude oil stays below $80 a barrel' (*FT*, 29 August 2009, p. 15).

Earlier this month [September] the government increased petrol prices by 5 per cent, to a record high. This was the seventh adjustment since January [2009], when China introduced a new pricing system that allows local prices to track global crude oil prices more closely than in the past. Petrol prices are adjusted whenever the average of a basket of international crude oil prices rises (or falls) by a daily average of 4 per cent over a twenty-two-day period … The government was reluctant to lift prices fully last year [2008] when inflation was already high, but it has taken advantage of domestic deflation this year [2009] to bring fuel prices more into line with world prices … The [pricing] formula, which has not been published, is still being applied flexibly. The government says that price changes also take account of processing costs, profit margins and domestic supply and demand. If crude oil rises above $80 a barrel, not all the increase will be passed on.

(*The Economist*, 19 September 2009, p. 92)

Monetary policy

(See Jeffries 2006a: 406–41.)

Since 1998 the government has spent almost $283 billion to shift a mountain of bad loans off the books of state-owned banks. In a report last week the OECD said $203 billion more was needed to clean up the rest. Taken together this rescue amounts to more than 30 per cent of GDP for 2004.

(*IHT*, 22 September 2005, p. 13)

An IMF working paper published yesterday [30 March 2006] says that the banks' working practices have hardly changed … The paper reviews the lending of the four big banks in the seven years to the end of 2004 … Not only was the profitability of the enterprises that the banks lent to not taken into account, the big banks' share of lending 'was actually lower in the more profitable provinces' … [The paper] also raises questions about the reported dramatic fall in the new rate of non-performing loans generated in recent years … Only 2 per cent of the loans made since 2000 have gone sour, compared with 45 per cent for the period before 2000.

(*FT*, 31 March 2006, p. 22)

Despite costly efforts to rescue China's major banks, they continue to make high-risk loans to money-losing state-owned enterprises, according to a new IMF working paper. The paper said it was difficult to find evidence in banking data from 1997 to the end of 2004 to show that China's four big state-owned banks had changed their behaviour … About 2 per cent of loans made since 2000 were reported as non-performing, whereas that proportion was as high as 60 per cent for older lending … Banking analysts have warned that bailouts will be wasted if the banks continue to accumulate bad loans.

(*IHT*, 31 March 2006, p. 15)

'A recent paper by economists at the IMF found little evidence that Chinese banks' lending decisions had become more commercial' (*The Economist*, 29 April 2006, p. 82).

> The government will require domestic banks with a 'relatively large number of overseas branches' to adopt the stricter rules of the so-called new Basel Accord starting in 2010–12, according to Liu Mingkang, who heads the China Banking Regulatory Commission ... The rules of the new Basel Accord, also known as Basel II, are scheduled to be phased in from 2008 to 2011. They lay out how banks should set aside capital to protect themselves against sudden shocks like the collapse of major corporate borrowers ... The Basel II rules were drawn up by a committee of international regulators and central bankers and are due to be phased in between 2008 and 2011 ... A total of fifty-three [Chinese] banks, accounting for 75 per cent of banking assets, had met the standard of 8 per cent capital adequacy by the end of 2005, up from eight banks in 2003, Liu said. Most Chinese banks must reach the standard by 2006. Bank of China, China Construction Bank, Industrial and Commercial Bank of China and Bank of Communications, accounting for half of China's total bank assets, had 'basically' resolved their bad loans problems, Liu added.
>
> (www.iht.com, 10 April 2006; *IHT*, 11 April 2006, p. 14)

> A mountain of bad [bank] debts is only the most visible sign of the persistent misallocation of capital. Many more loans do not go bad but yield only negligible returns. In a study to be published on 4 May ... *Putting China's Capital to Work: The Value of Financial System Reform* ... the McKinsey Global Institute, the consultancy's economics think-tank, calculates that China's GDP would be a staggering $320 billion, or 16 per cent, higher if its lenders knew how to lend. Around $60 billion, the think-tank reckons, could be gained from raising the banks' operating efficiency by cutting costs, putting in proper electronic payment systems, and developing bond and equity training. The rest – some $260 billion – would come from redirecting loans to more productive parts of the economy. The banks should switch funds from poorly run state firms to private enterprises [including foreign enterprises], which contribute 52 per cent of GDP but account for only 27 per cent of outstanding loans. This would both increase the efficiency of investment and raise returns for China's army of small savers.
>
> (*The Economist*, 29 April 2006, p. 82)

The McKinsey study provides 2003 figures, respectively, for GDP percentage contribution and corporate bank loans outstanding by type of enterprise: private and foreign enterprises, 52 per cent and 27 per cent; wholly state-owned enterprises, 23 per cent and 35 per cent; shareholding (partly state-owned enterprises), 19 per cent and 27 per cent; collective enterprises, 6 per cent and 11 per cent (ibid.).

> The chief tasks of any good financial system are to attract savings and channel them to productive investments as efficiently as possible. China's

financial system does an outstanding job of mobilizing savings. But there is considerable room for improvements in its capital allocation, and its overall efficiency. Financial system reforms could not only raise GDP by as much as 17 per cent, or $320 billion a year, but also help spread China's new wealth more evenly throughout the country ... Chinese households save a lot by international standards – on average roughly 25 per cent of their disposable income.

(Diana Farrell and Susan Lund, 'Putting China's Capital to Work', McKinsey Global Institute, FEER, May 2006, pp. 5–6)

China has raised the bar for its big state banks, demanding that all five of the country's largest lenders maintain bad debt ratios of less than 5 per cent in the wake of their restructurings. The stricture, which includes a directive that they keep their capital adequacy ratios to at least 8 per cent, previously only applied to the Bank of China and China Construction Bank. The other banks captured by the orders are the Bank of Communications, the Industrial and Commercial Bank of China and the Agricultural Bank of China (ABC) ... They have all managed to get their non-performing loan ratios to near or below 5 per cent in recent years, with the exception of the ABC. ABC's bad debt ratio stood at 26.17 per cent at the end of last year [2005], according to the central bank, and it has yet to be restructured or receive an injection of government funds for a recapitalization.

(FT, 17 May 2006, p. 9)

The savings arm of China's monopoly postal service has begun making loans for the first time, a move intended to help it prepare for its transformation into the country's fifth largest bank. After years of delay officials say Beijing is close to launching reform of the Postal Savings and Remittance Bureau ... The Postal Savings Bureau [has been granted] permission to offer small loans to rural customers on a trial basis ... The bureau is only permitted to lend money to existing rural customers in the three provinces of Fujian, Shaanxi and Hubei.

(FT, 12 April 2006, p. 8)

China's central bank raised official borrowing costs Thursday [27 April] for the first time for a year and a half, trying to slow a spectacular surge in lending and investment that has produced a frenzy of often ill-considered construction and could trigger another wave of bad debts at Chinese banks. From steel mills and auto factories to luxury apartment buildings and plush office complexes, China has been engaged in a nationwide building boom fuelled by easy loans from banks ... The People's Bank of China announced Thursday evening, effective, Friday morning, that it was raising the benchmark lending rates that banks may charge customers by 27-hundredths of a percentage point for loans of all maturities. The increase was the same size it was the last time China raised rates, on 28 October 2004, which in turn was the country's first interest rate increase in nine years ... The central bank left unchanged its caps on the rates that banks can offer on deposits. By raising lending rates while leaving deposit rates untouched, the government allows banks to fatten their profit margins to cover loan defaults ... Prime minister Wen Jiabao had warned on 14 April that China would move to tighten controls over lending and real estate. But most economists had expected China to require banks to hold greater reserves at the central bank, which would have left them with less money to lend.

(www.iht.com, 27 April 2006)

The People's Bank of China ... announced that it was raising the benchmark lending rates that financial institutions may charge customers by 27-hundredths of a percentage point for loans of one year ... The one-year rate rose to 5.85 per cent from 5.58 per cent ... The mostly state-owned banks still make many loans to state-owned companies and politically connected private companies and charge them the lowest rate allowed, which is nine-tenths of the benchmark rate. The yuan strengthened by less than three-hundredths of a per cent in Thursday [27 April] trading, with the dollar slipping to 8.0161 yuan.

(*IHT*, 28 April 2006, pp. 1, 8)

The People's Bank of China raised its benchmark one-year lending rate by a quarter point to 5.85 per cent, from 5.58 per cent ... The central bank also moved to reinforce the rise in interest rates by issuing new guidelines to commercial banks to quell lending to a dozen sectors where excess capacity and investment is at its greatest.

(*The Times*, 28 April 2006, p. 51)

Beijing has again caught the markets by surprise, lifting interest rates for the first time in eighteen months in response to a first quarter surge in banking lending and investment. Many economists had predicted the central bank would respond by raising the amount that banks must set aside in reserves and strengthening administrative controls on lending to rein in credit growth.

(*FT*, 28 April 2006, p. 9)

The one-year benchmark rate will increase by 27 basis points to 5.85 per cent from today [28 April] ... The rate rise is a symbolic opening shot in what is likely to be a sustained official campaign to restrain excessive credit and over-investment in steel, cement, property and other sectors ... The central bank left deposit rates unchanged.

(p. 14)

'China is expected to raise the banks' reserve requirements next month, after China's spring holidays' (*The Economist*, 28 April 2006, p. 82). 'On 16 June the central bank ... demanded that commercial banks increase the ratio of reserves they deposit in its vaults by half a percentage point' (*The Economist*, 24 June 2006, p. 104).

The latest government estimate ... published in March [2006] ... [of] the stock of non-performing [bank] loans ... [is] $164 billion ... Other commentators and consultants have published estimates ranging from $300 billion to $500 billion ... Ernst & Young ... a big auditing and consulting firm ... this week ... withdrew [its estimate of] $911 billion ... admitting it was 'factually erroneous'.

(*The Economist*, 20 May 2006, p. 94)

Outstanding yuan-denominated loans on 30 June stood at 21.5 trillion yuan, or $2.7 billion, 15.2 per cent higher than a year earlier. New yuan lending in the first half [of 2006] totalled 2.18 trillion yuan, approaching the central bank's full-year target of 2.5 trillion yuan. China's banks carry more than 1.3 trillion yuan of non-performing loans, exceeding 8 per cent of those on their books, according to Moody's Investors Services.

(*IHT*, 31 July 2006, p. 15)

'The People's Bank of China has raised both interest rates and reserve requirements for banks and last month [June 2006] ordered regional branches to halt "blind expansion and building of redundant, low value-added industries"' (*IHT*, 31 July 2006, p. 15).

The central government has ordered the provincial authorities and state-owned lenders to review industrial projects, stepping up efforts to curb excess investment and cool the economy's growth. The review covers every project that exceeds 100 million yuan, or $12.5 million, in investment, and steel mills, cement factories, vehicle assembly plants, power stations and aluminium smelters that exceed 30 million yuan in value, according to a statement Tuesday [1 August posted on 3 August] ... China's economy grew 11.3 per cent in the second quarter [of 2006], the fastest since 1994 ... The government will order projects to stop or be postponed if they fail to meet standards for loans, safety or environmental protection, according to the rules announced [on 3 August].

(www.iht.com, 3 August 2006)

The government recently laid out a series of steps designed to slow the economy, including increased reserve requirements for commercial banks in order to reduce the funds available for lending. The government also imposed restrictions on foreign investment in property to curb speculation, and reduced incentives for exporters in a bid to narrow the trade surplus.

(*IHT*, 10 August 2006, p. 13)

China will impose inspections and punishments on local officials as it tries to tame breakneck economic growth, state media said Wednesday [9 August]. A front page commentary in the state-run *People's Daily* newspaper warned officials to clamp down on investment in factories, infrastructure and other fixed assets, which expanded 31.3 per cent in the first half of the year [2006] from a year earlier ... Officials would have clear targets and

deadlines for tempering investment, including inspections and 'tough punishments and rewards', the paper said ... The magnitude of the policy-
makers' task was highlighted in another editorial Wednesday that said local
officials were reporting fake growth numbers. Only three of China's thirty-
one provinces, regions and major municipalities reported growth for the first
half of the year that was slower than the official national total of 10.9 per
cent, state media reported this week. 'Local officials have a reputation for
padding their GDP figures,' the *China Daily* said in an editorial Wednesday.
'The local doctoring of economic figures is detestable and may shake the
authority of the country's statistical work.'

(www.iht.com, 9 August 2006)

'Beijing ordered state enterprises yesterday [15 August] to restrict their
spending in sectors outside their core business to no more than 10 per cent of all
investment' (*FT*, 16 August 2006, p. 7).

China has punished a senior regional leader and his two deputies for allowing the construction of an unauthorized power station ... Local governments, where officials were judged on their ability to attract projects and
bolster local economic output, were responsible for up to 20 per cent of
investment in China ... Trying to control overinvestment in real estate,
China's banking regulator on Thursday [17 August] ordered banks to tighten
credit for property developers ... Under the new guidelines banks would
refuse loans to developers who failed to raise 35 per cent of the project cost
from their own resources.

(www.iht.com, 17 August 2006; *IHT*, 18 August 2006, p. 10)

China's central bank raised interest rates Friday evening [18 August], the
latest in a series of moves by the government to choke off a speculative
lending and investment binge that threatens to saddle the country's banks
with more bad loans if the economy slows. The People's Bank of China
raised interest rates for one-year bank loans and for deposits by 0.27 of a
percentage point each ... China's second [increase] this year [2006] ... The
central bank raised the benchmark rate for one-year bank loans to corporations to 6.12 per cent Friday ... The People's Bank of China said in a statement that the rate increases were intended to 'curb demand for long-term
loans and the overly rapid expansion in fixed-asset investment' ... In
another sign that the central bank may be more worried about speculative
investment than a broader overheating in the economy as a whole, the
People's Bank of China took two steps Friday that appeared aimed at
helping consumers. The central bank gave regulatory approval for commercial banks to offer bigger rate discounts for home buyers seeking mortgages.
And it raised the interest rate that banks can pay on one-year deposits to
2.52 per cent from 2.25 per cent. Higher interest rates are likely to help
households, which save up to half their incomes these days.

(*IHT*, 19 August 2006, p. 11)

The People's Bank of China said it had raised both benchmark lending and deposit rates by 0.27 percentage points, lifting them to 6.12 per cent and 2.52 per cent ... The announcement was different in one significant respect from the last rate rise on 27 April, when the government only lifted lending rates. The government had previously been reluctant to raise deposit rates, fearing that any rise would encourage further capital inflows ... Money kept in banks on low deposit rates currently offers a negative return after inflation and the payment of a tax on interest income.

(*FT*, 19 August 2006, p. 6)

'In 2004 and 2005 the People's Bank of China shifted $60 billion [of non-performing loans] to state banks. The remaining stock of bad loans is now around $250 billion, according to UBS' (*The Economist*, 28 October 2006, p. 105).

'State banking regulators reported in August [2006] that the percentage of bank lending classified as "non-performing" fell by 1.1 percentage points to 7.5 per cent in the first half of this year' (www.iht.com, 29 October 2006).

The central bank on Friday [3 November] for the third time this year [2006] ordered lenders to set aside more money as reserves to curtail a credit-fuelled investment boom ... Banks' reserve ratio requirement was increased in July and August by half a point each time. Banks must set aside 9 per cent of deposits as reserves starting 15 November, up from 8.5 per cent ... the move will cut the amount of money they have available for lending ... Prime minister Wen Jiabao vowed last month [October] to keep controls on lending to cool a spending binge that has created over-capacity in the steel and car industries ... The National Development and Reform Commission, China's top planning body, has identified surplus capacity in the steel, cement, manganese and auto industries ... China's foreign exchange reserves stood at $988 billion on 30 September [2006], making them the world's largest.

(www.iht.com, 3 November 2006)

China's commercial banks officially had a combined estimated $163 billion in non-performing loans, a manageable 7.5 per cent of their total loans in June 2006, according to the China Banking Regulatory Commission. But analysts said they believed that the bad-loan figure could be double the official reports.

(*IHT*, 15 November 2006, p. 16)

China has officially introduced a new Postal Savings Bank that becomes one of its largest banks by outstanding deposits. The new bank will focus on consumer banking and fee-based services with a dedicated rural financial services department ... The introduction of the Postal Savings Bank, with $195 billion of deposits at the end of last June [2006], is part of the restructuring to separate the commercial and regulatory functions of the country's postal services. China is trying to reduce the government's presence in commercial activities.

(*IHT*, 2 January 2007, p. 10)

('China's revamped postal savings system for business yesterday [20 March 2007] as the country's fifth largest bank, pledging to improve its reach in rural areas where financial services are scarce. The launch of China Postal Savings Bank followed years of delay': *FT*, 21 March 2007, p. 9. 'Chinese financial institutions hold $61 billion worth of bad loans, according to the central bank': *IHT*, 23 March 2007, p. 14.)

> China ordered banks to set aside more money for the fourth time since last year [2006] as reserves, in a step to absorb excess funds from the financial system and prevent a rebound in loans and investments. Banks must set aside 9.5 per cent of deposits as reserves starting 15 January [2007], up from the current 9 per cent, the People's Bank of China said. The increase will cut the amount of money they have available for lending.
>
> (*IHT*, 6 January 2007, p. 13)

> Government agencies in Beijing have issued rules barring foreigners from owning more than one house in the capital city as China seeks to curb the speculation that has helped inspire property prices to soar. The rules also apply to residents of Hong Kong, Macao and Taiwan.
>
> (*FT*, 5 February 2007, p. 14)

'China told banks to set aside more money as reserves for the fourth time in seven months to prevent a rebound in lending and investment' (*FT*, 6 January 2007, p. 5).

> China raised the amount of money banks must hold in reserve for the second time this year [2007], reducing the amount available for lending ... The ratio will increase by 0.5 percentage points on Saturday [17 February] the central bank said, meaning banks will be required to keep 10 per cent of their deposits in reserve accounts at the central bank.
>
> (*IHT*, 17 February 2007, p. 15)

> Cities get ten times more loans per head than the countryside, where more than 60 per cent of China's 1.3 billion people live ... Rural China is home to less than one-sixth of all branch branches, which accounted for 15 per cent of the nation's combined deposits and loans as of late 2006 ... To address the issue the government has begun to overhaul Agricultural Bank of China ... and is setting up a new postal bank with a plan to lend principally to farmers and rural enterprises. Beijing will also do more to revamp debt-laden credit co-operatives, now the brittle backbone of rural finance ... In a pilot scheme planned in six provinces individuals will be allowed for the first time to set up privately owned credit co-operatives and other types of financial firms. Policy-makers hope that commercial banks will team up with other private shareholders to set up lenders at county level or below and that farmers or small firms will band together to create new kinds of credit co-operatives, even in small villages. The six provinces and regions – Hubei, Jilin, Sichuan, Qinghai, Gansu and Inner Mongolia – will

also experiment with new lending companies under a relaxed regulatory framework.

(www.iht.com, 19 February 2007)

The ministry of finance will pay for the cleanup of bad loans by the Agricultural Bank of China and take an equity stake in the institution, the bank president, Yang Mingsheng, said Sunday [11 March] ... He said: 'The financial audit will be completed this year. The government will determine the extent of the bailout needed after the audit is completed. The finance ministry will inject funds and become a shareholder' ... A bailout of Agriculture Bank, which is burdened with $95 billion of bad loans, may cost the government up to $140 billion, including the cost of meeting the 8 per cent minimum capital adequacy requirement set by the central bank. China has already spent $452 billion – equal to a fifth of its 2005 GDP – to bail out and recapitalize state-owned banks, according to Moody's Investors Service.

(*IHT*, 12 March 2007, p. 12)

China's central bank said on Saturday [17 March] that it was raising interest rates for the third time in less than a year ... The People's Bank of China said that, effective Sunday, the benchmark one-year yuan lending and deposited rates would rise by 0.27 percentage points each. That brings the one-year deposit rate to 2.79 per cent and the lending rate to 6.39 per cent ... The move follows an increase of lending rates alone on 27 April 2006 and a rise in both rates [on 18 August 2006] ... Prime minister Wen Jiabao said on Friday [16 March] after the end of the annual session of parliament that China needed to do more to address striking imbalances including excessive growth in credit and investment ... The yuan has now appreciated about 4.8 per cent against the dollar since Beijing revalued it by 2.1 per cent ... It touched a post-revaluation high on Friday [16 March] ... Annual consumer inflation ... hit 2.7 per cent in February.

(www.iht.com, 17 March 2007)

The People's Bank of China announced that it was raising by 0.27 per cent the regulated interest rates that banks may charge for loans and may pay for deposits. The benchmark rate for one-year loans to companies with reasonable good credit will become 6.39 per cent, while the one-year deposit rate will become 2.79 per cent.

(*IHT*, 19 March 2007, p. 14)

In China [interest] rate changes are less common: the latest move was only the fourth in three years, a period during which America's Federal Reserve has raised rates seventeen times. China has relied more on quantitative measures, such as direct controls on lending and changes in the amount of reserves that banks must hold at the central bank. The People's Bank of China's reserve requirement ratio has been raised five times since July 2006. One reason for this approach is that the economy has traditionally not been very sensitive to interest rates. Higher borrowing costs deter private sector companies, but do not discourage inefficient state-owned enterprises, because they are less bothered about their return on capital ... Higher reserve requirements have also lost their bite ... Banks' deposits at the PBOC are already much larger than the required ratio, so an increase does little to constrain their ability to lend.

(*The Economist*, 24 March 2007, p. 96)

China has increased the amount of funds it requires commercial banks to keep on deposit with the authorities for the sixth time in less than a year ... The reserve ratio would be increased to 10.5 per cent ... [to] take effect on 16 April.

(www.ft.com, 5 April 2007)

'The renminbi yesterday [6 April] crept to the highest level since it was revalued in 2005, after China increased the proportion of funds commercial banks must keep on deposit with the authorities' (*FT*, 7 April 2007, p. 7).

China for the second time this month on Sunday [29 April] ordered banks to hold more of their deposits in reserve in the latest attempt to prevent credit and investment growth from destabilizing the ... economy. The People's Bank of China said that big banks would have to hold 11 per cent of their deposits in reserve at the central bank starting 15 May, up from 10.5 per cent now ... Policy-makers are also concerned that the ready availability of cheap money is fuelling an unsustainable rally in the domestic stock market.

(www.iht.com, 29 April 2007)

China ordered banks to set aside more money as reserves for the seventh time in eleven months to prevent an accelerating economy from overheating ... Prime minister Wen Jiabao is trying to stop a flood of cash from an export boom from fuelling wasteful investment, inflation and a stock market bubble ... China has raised borrowing costs three times since April last year [2006]. The benchmark one-year lending rate is at an eight-year high of 6.39 per cent. The government has also curbed land use, restricted project approvals and cut export rebates for steel and textiles.

(*IHT*, 30 April 2007, p. 13)

The People's Bank of China is widening the level that the yuan can strengthen or fall against the dollar from 0.3 per cent to 0.5 per cent per day ... The bands determine how far the currency may fluctuate from the parity rate, which is set each day by the central bank ... The yuan rarely approaches the current trading limit of 0.3 per cent ... China has also increased interest rates and the amount of cash that banks have to keep in reserve ... The one-year lending rate is going up by 0.18 percentage points to 3.006 per cent, while the one-year deposit rate is rising by 0.27 percentage points to 6.57 per cent ... Banks' reserve requirements ... have gone up half a percentage point to 11.5 per cent.

(www.bbc.co.uk, 18 May 2007)

The moves are aimed at tightening credit and reducing the risk of overheating in an economy that is growing at more than 11 per cent a year and in mainland Chinese stock markets that have more than tripled since the beginning of last year [2006] ... The People's Bank of China said that it would allow the yuan to rise or fall up to 0.5 per cent in daily trading. The daily limit was 0.3 per cent ... The bank said it would continue to 'keep the exchange rate basically stable at an adaptive and equilibrium level based on market supply and demand with reference to a basket of currencies' ... Since it broke the yuan's peg to the dollar on 21 July 2005 ... the government allowed the yuan to rise 2.1 per ... on 21 July 2005 ... and has only let it inch up by another 5 per cent over the nearly two years since then. By contrast, members of the US Congress from manufacturing states that have lost jobs during the Chinese export boom have been calling for China to revalue by 25 per cent or more ... The People's Bank of China raised the benchmark regulated rate for one-year bank deposits by 0.27 percentage points to 3.06 per cent and increased the benchmark rate for one-year bank loans by 0.18 percentage points to 6.57 per cent. By raising deposit rates more than lending rates the government showed confidence that the banks have put enough of their bad loan problems behind them to survive on slightly narrower profit margins. The central bank also ordered banks to hold 11.5 per cent of assets as reserves, up from 11 per cent. Many banks already have even larger reserves, however, as they have been swamped with deposits from the brisk economic growth and large trade surplus.

(www.iht.com, 18 May 2007; *IHT*, 19 May 2007, p. 17)

The People's Bank of China's decision to widen the daily trading limit to 0.5 per cent has no direct implications for the renminbi's level against the dollar, since the currency has rarely come close to testing the 0.3 per cent limit set in 2005 ... Analysts said the rise in the one-year lending rate by 0.18 of a percentage point and the deposit rate by 0.27 of a percentage point was another step in efforts to tame loan growth and stem the flow of funds into red-hot domestic stocks.

(*IHT*, 19 May 2007, p. 7)

China will allow trust companies, financial leasing firms and insurers to borrow from each other for the first time, as it seeks to develop an interbank market in which trading has surged tenfold over the past decade. Auto financing firms and insurance asset management units will also be allowed in the interbank market, effective 6 August [2007], the People's Bank of China said [on 9 July] ... China established the interbank lending market in 1996 and at the end of last year [2006] it had 730 members, including domestic and foreign banks as well as securities firms. Trading totalled $283 billion in 2006. Banks can borrow for as long as one year while leasing and insurers can borrow for up to three months. For brokerages and trust companies the limit is seven days ... The central bank in January [2007] started publishing a new benchmark for borrowing between banks, known as the

Shanghai interbank offered rate, or Shibor, moving toward a more market-driven financial system. China has been relaxing controls on interest rates as part of a bid to develop its capital market.

(www.iht.com, 9 July 2007)

China raised interest rates Friday [20 July] for the third time since March [2007] to cool the fastest pace of economic growth in twelve years and keep inflation in check. The increase [effective 21 July] came a day after the government reported that annual economic growth accelerated to 11.9 per cent in the second quarter [of 2007] from 11.1 per cent in the first quarter ... Consumer prices rose the most in almost three years in June, and factory and property spending have surged ... Consumer inflation accelerated to 4.4 per cent in the year to June, the fastest pace in thirty-three months ... Urban fixed asset investment climbed 26.7 per cent in the first six months, accelerating from the 24.5 per cent increase for all of 2006 ... The People's Bank of China ordered an increase of 0.27 percentage points on the benchmark one-year deposit and lending rates for commercial banks. That will take the one-year benchmark rate to 3.33 per cent from 3.06 per cent. The one-year lending rate will rise to 6.84 per cent from 6.57 per cent ... The central bank has now raised interest rates five times since 27 April 2006. It has also raised banks' reserve requirements eight times since June 2006.

(www.iht.com, 20 July 2007)

The benchmark one-year lending rate will rise by 0.27 percentage points to an eight-year high of 6.84 per cent ... The deposit rate will increase by the same amount to 3.33 per cent and a tax on interest income will be cut on 15 August to encourage saving ... The tax on interest income will fall to 5 per cent from 20 per cent ... The cut is equivalent to a 0.5 percentage point increase in deposit rates ... Rising food costs [e.g. pork] pushed the inflation costs to 4.4 per cent last month [June].

(*IHT*, 21 July 2007, p. 13)

'The central bank also raised the interest rate on sight deposits to 0.81 per cent from 0.72 per cent, the first time it has adjusted that rate since February 2002' (www.ft.com, 20 July 2007). '[The] tax on interest income ... was introduced in 1999 as part of efforts to reduce individual savings and promote consumption ... [There has been a] recent surge in prices of meat, poultry and eggs' (*FT*, 21 July 2007, p. 6).

Soaring pork prices helped push consumer price inflation to a surprise 4.4 per cent in June ... Pork prices in June were 75 per cent higher than in the same month of 2006, according to state media ... Pork [is] China's most important staple meat.

(*FT*, 25 July 2007, p. 6)

'The rise in inflation [was] driven largely by soaring prices for food, particularly pork and eggs' (*FT*, 26 July 2007, p. 6).

('Pork prices peaked in May and again in early July': www.iht.com, 26 July 2007. 'The recent jump [in inflation] was mainly due to the prices of pork and eggs': *The Economist*, 28 July 2007, p. 79.)

Just over two years after a big unlicensed bank was last found in China, another surfaced this week ... The authorities in Beijing, worried about the surge in the stock market and property prices in the past two years, have tried cooling things down. They had suspected that part of the frothiness in the markets was the result of too much illicit lending. Their investigations appear to have uncovered the bank's existence. Such banks are surprisingly common in China ... A government-funded study by the Central University of Finance and Economics cited by the *South China Morning Post* last year [2006] found that they lent as much as 800 billion yuan a year. Some of this goes to legitimate business. Underground banks provide as much as a third of the loans to small and medium-sized enterprises (SMES) and 55 per cent of the loans to farmers. SMES and farmers are generally poorly served by the larger state banks ... Most of the money these banks lend is for risky investments. As much as 90 per cent of it is used for speculative trades in financial markets. With stock markets around the world jumpy, China's stock market bubble continuing and 3 per cent to 4 per cent of the broad money supply estimated to be flowing underground, it is no wonder the authorities are alarmed. So many unregistered institutions risk the savings of millions being suddenly washed away.

(*The Economist*, 11 August 2007, p. 64)

China's inflation rate accelerated to 5.6 per cent in July – the highest monthly rate in a decade – driven by a 15.4 per cent surge in politically sensitive food prices – over the year-earlier period ... Prices of pork ... China's staple meat ... and other meat surged 45.2 per cent and that of eggs 30.6 per cent ... July's inflation was the highest monthly rate since February 1997 and an increase over June's 4.4 per cent. The next highest monthly rate was 5.3 per cent in August 2004 ... Prices of clothing and other non-food goods rose just 0.9 per cent in July from a year ago ... Consumer prices in the first seven months of the year rose 3.5 per cent compared with the same period of 2006.

(www.iht.com, 13 August 2007)

China raised interest rates on Tuesday [21 August] for the fourth time this year [2007] to stabilize inflation after consumer prices rose in July at the fastest pace in more than a decade ... Consumer process surged 5.6 per cent in the year to July, the fastest pace since early 1997 [February] ... The People's Bank of China (PBOC) said it was raising the rate that banks pay for one-year deposits by 27 basis points to 3.60 per cent [from 3.33 per cent] and the corresponding benchmark for lending rates by 18 basis points, to 7.02 per cent from 6.84 per cent. The increases go into effect on Wednesday [22 August] ... Most economists had forecast an increase, both to anchor inflationary expectations and to reduce the incentive for savers to take money out of the bank – where real deposit rates are deeply negative. .. and pile into the surging stock markets.

(www.ft.com, 21 August 2007)

'The official target for inflation for 2007 is 3 per cent' (*IHT*, 22 August 2007, p. 9).

'The benchmark one-year lending rate rose 0.18 percentage points to 7.02 per cent Wednesday [22 August], and the one-year deposit rate climbed 0.27 percentage points to 3.6 per cent' (*IHT*, 23 August 2007, p. 12).

It was the second time this year that deposit rates increased more than lending rates. The government is trying to make bank savings more attractive to stem the flow of money into property and stock speculation and curb asset bubbles. The increase is to control 'money supply and loans and stabilize inflation expectations', the central bank said.

(www.iht.com, 21 August 2007)

China said that it had cracked down on price fixing of soybean products, 'hotpot' meals [meat and vegetables cooked in a boiling broth] and other food as the government tackles inflation, which jumped to a ten-year high in July [2007]. Soaring food costs helped push the inflation rate to 5.6 per cent [in August] ... The government's target inflation rate for 2007 is 3 per cent ... Earlier this month [August] China ordered local governments to check food producers, wholesalers and retailers for price fixing or gouging. Food prices account for a third of the Chinese consumer price index ... While the state no longer directly controls the prices of most goods, price edicts from the national government still carry weight. The prices for some basic items, like fuel and rice, are still under formal government control. The pricing department at the National Development and Reform Commission ... an agency of the national State Council ... can issue price directives on any good or service as it deems fit. With the State Council's blessing, local governments have little trouble bringing merchants into line. Even acts like spreading rumours of price increases can draw punishments as severe as the termination of business licences.

(www.iht.com, 28 August 2007)

'The authorities ... decided to raise bank reserve requirements by another 0.5 per cent yesterday [6 September]' (*FT*, 7 September 2007, p. 14). 'On 6 September, it [the People's Bank of China] announced it would lift the ratio by another 50 basis points to 12.5 per cent of banks' total deposits' (*FT*, 15 September 2007, p. 7).

Chinese inflation has hit its second ten-year high in two months, led again by a further sharp rise in meat prices. China's rate of consumer price inflation hit 6.5 per cent in the year to August, up from 5.6 per cent in July ... Meat prices have risen 49 per cent over the past year, caused by a shortage of pork after a series of disease outbreaks ... China, the world's biggest consumer of pork, has seen its pig population decline by 10 per cent over the past year due to major outbreaks of blue ear disease ... Non-food prices rose just 0.9 per cent in the year to August.

(www.bbc.co.uk, 11 September 2007)

Food prices were up 18.2 per cent year-on-year in August ... Meat prices were up 49.2 per cent year-on-year for the month, with eggs and vegetables rising by 23.6 per cent and 22.5 per cent respectively ... Prices for durable goods are weakening and for textiles are falling in real terms ... Food prices make up about one-third of the consumer price index ... Producer price inflation, though still comfortably below 2004 levels, rose 2.6 per cent in the year to August.

(www.ft.com, 11 September 2007)

China's inflation rate rose to 6.5 per cent in August – the highest in nearly eleven years ... The August inflation rate was the highest since December 1996 and an increase over July's monthly rate of 5.6 per cent ... The increase in meat prices has been blamed on a shortage of pigs and higher feed costs for poultry and cattle farmers ... The sharp rise in prices for pork, China's staple meat, has been blamed on farmers' reluctance to raise pigs due to high feed prices and an outbreak of blue ear disease that prompted authorities to destroy thousands of animals. Beijing has promised free vaccination for the disease and other aid to farmers to raise pork output ... Among other food items cooking oil was up 34.6 per cent, eggs 23.6 per cent and fresh vegetables 22.5 per cent ... meanwhile the costs of other goods have remained stable. Prices of non-food consumer goods rose just 0.9 per cent.

(www.iht.com, 11 September 2007)

'Food accounts for a third of the consumer price index and housing less than 14 per cent' (*The Economist*, 15 September 2007, p. 76).

Pork alone accounts for around 4 per cent of the basket used for the consumer price index ... although government officials have noted that pork prices have begun to ease since the end of July ... Food accounted for 37 per cent of the average total spending of an urban household in 2005 ... The price of grain has been rising at a steady rate of around 6 per cent to 7 per cent year-on-year since December 2006. This has had a direct impact on meat and poultry costs (and indirectly on eggs), as it has helped force up the cost of animal feed.

(www.economist.com, 18 September 2007)

China raised interest rates Friday [14 September] for the fifth time since March in an attempt to slow the fastest inflation since 1996 and to cool a surging stock market ... [Analysts say] that people get negative returns on bank deposits and that is fuelling investment and bubbles in the stock and property markets ... In the second quarter compared to a year earlier ... the money supply grew at an annual rate of 18.1 per cent, exceeding the central bank's target of 16 per cent for the seventh straight month ... The benchmark one-year lending rate will increase to a nine-year high of 7.29 per cent from 7.02 per cent, starting Saturday [15 September] ... The one-year deposit rate will rise to 3.87 per cent from 3.6 per cent ... The increase contrasts sharply with the paths taken by other major central banks in the world, which are adding to liquidity because of a credit squeeze linked to soured home loans in the United States.

(www.iht.com, 14 September 2007)

China's central bank raised interest rates for the second time in less than a month yesterday [14 September] in an attempt to rein in soaring food prices, excessive bank lending and bubbles in the property and stock markets. The People's Bank of China lifted the one-year benchmark deposit rate by 27 basis points to 3.87 per cent and the one-year lending rate by the same amount to 7.29 per cent, effective immediately ... As well as raising interest rates, the central bank has lifted seven times this year [2007] the amount that banks must hold with it – the so-called reserve requirement ratio. Most recently, on 6 September, it announced it would lift the ratio by another 50 basis points to 12.5 per cent of banks' total deposits. Wu Xiaoling, deputy central bank director, said yesterday Chinese banks were not heeding the central bank's directives to slow lending growth ... The increasing frequency of interest rate rises shows how seriously Beijing takes the issue of food inflation, which has a disproportionate impact on the nation's poor.

(*FT*, 15 September 2007, p. 7)

The government on Wednesday [19 September] froze prices that it controls for the rest of the year [2007], in the latest sign of Beijing's mounting concern over inflation. Beijing also stressed the importance of holding down market-driven process during the forthcoming holiday period, saying it would have a direct impact on the country's 'development, reform and stability' ... The government still administers a vast array of prices, including those for land, transport, utilities and fuel. The ministries said that, in principle, the government would not introduce any new price changes for the rest of the year ... The statement [by six ministries] said: 'All current rules on goods and service prices controlled by the government should be strictly implemented. Any unauthorized price rise is strictly forbidden' ... The ministries ordered local governments not to raise prices without the approval of the National Development and Reform Commission, the main planning agency ... To keep a lid on pork prices over the holidays, the government would draw if necessary on the country's pork reserves ... Separately, China is set to provide more aid to dairy farmers as part of an effort to control rising food prices, which have driven consumer price inflation ... The State Council, China's cabinet, is to meet Wednesday [19 September] to discuss financial support for dairy farmers after increasing feed costs and low milk prices forced many farmers to stop raising cows.

(www.iht.com, 19 September 2007)

China is to enforce a freeze on all government-controlled prices in a sign of Beijing's alarm at rising public anger over inflation – now at its highest rate for more than a decade. The move will freeze a vast array of prices still under government control, ranging from oil, electricity and water to the cost of parking and entrance fees to public parks. An order was issued jointly by six ministries yesterday [19 September], following a vaguely worded announcement by the State Council, or cabinet, in August [2007] on the need to prevent price rises ... The ministries said: 'Any unauthorized price rises are strictly forbidden ... and in principle there will be no new price-raising measures this year [2007].'

(*FT*, 20 September 2007, p. 7)

The most recent in a series of increases in the reserve requirement ratio (the proportion of funds banks have to keep with the central bank) is set to come into effect on 25 September). The government is also using informal guidance to persuade banks to curb speculative loans.

(www.economist.com, 18 September 2007)

Official figures show that non-performing loans had fallen to 7 per cent of all loans early this year [2007] from almost 30 per cent in 2001. But independent analysts suggest the true figure may be closer to 20 per cent (down from over 50 per cent at its peak).

(*The Economist*, 29 September 2007, p. 89)

In 1998 ... the government carved off $170 billion worth of non-performing loans and gave them to specially created Asset Management Companies (AMCs) ... In the following few years another $240 billion or so of bad debt was transferred to the AMCs ... In exchange for the loans the AMCs issued special bonds, earning 2.25 per cent a year, allowing the banks to swap losses for income-generating assets ... The money the AMCs did manage to recover through the resale of bad loans went towards paying the interest on the bonds, although AMC officials admit they will never be able to pay back the principals. The bonds are ultimately guaranteed by the ministry of finance.

(*FT*, Survey, 9 October 2007, p. 2)

The central bank announced Saturday [13 October] that it was raising reserve ratios for the eighth time this year, starting 25 October. The half-percentage point increase takes the ration for big banks to 13 per cent – matching the record rate that applied from September 1988 to March 1998. Analysts said that the raise, in line with market expectations, was a signal to commercial banks that the central bank remained determined to restrain growth in money supply and bank lending.

(www.iht.com, 14 October 2007)

'The People's Bank of China said that it had raised the rate by half a percentage point to 13 per cent, effective 25 October, to "strengthen liquidity management in the banking system and check the excessive credit growth"' (*IHT*, 15 October 2007, p. 12).

'The government, concerned that loans are being used illegally to finance stock purchases, has asked banks to cap lending growth at 15 per cent this year [2007]' (*IHT*, 26 October 2007, p. 16).

'Inflation slowed slightly in September to 6.2 per cent from 6.5 per cent in August' (*IHT*, 26 October 2007, p. 9).

> Bank of China said Tuesday [30 October] that third quarter profits rose 22 per cent, posting the slowest earnings growth among the country's largest lenders after a $322 million loss on US subprime mortgage investments ... Bank of China gets about 35 per cent of profit from outside the mainland, compared with less than 5 per cent for Industrial and Commercial Bank of China. Most Chinese banks have little direct investment in securities linked to US home loans to people with poor credit, compared with their global peers ... The government has told banks to cap loan growth at 15 per cent this year [2007], seeking to prevent bubbles.
>
> (*IHT*, 31 October 2007, p. 19)

> Agricultural Bank of China and China Development Bank are to receive $67 billion of investment from the country's sovereign wealth fund, a sign that the government is nearing completion of a decade-long industry restructuring. China Investment [was] set up to manage $200 billion of the country's currency reserves ... Agricultural Bank, saddled with $100 billion of bad loans, will be the last of the country's four biggest state-owned lenders to be bailed out by the government, paving the way for the company to sell shares for the first time. China has spent about $500 billion recapitalizing its largest banks in the past decade ... China Investment was established in September to seek higher returns on the country's record $1.43 trillion of foreign exchange reserves. The country will use a further third of its assets to buy Central Huijin Investment, a state agency that holds the government's equity stakes in the country's largest banks and invest the rest in financial markets ... Agricultural Bank's cleanup has been delayed because 23 per cent of its loans are not being paid, according to its latest annual report. The bank [was] set up in 1979 to serve China's 800 million farmers ... The ministry of finance and China Investment would each own a third of Agricultural Bank ... A further 20 per cent would be sold to foreign investors with experience in rural lending and about 5 per cent to local corporate investors. The remainder would be offered to the public.
>
> (*IHT*, 8 November 2007, p. 14)

'China ordered banks to put aside more reserves for the ninth time this year [2007] to cool an economy that expanded 11.5 per cent in the third quarter and to damp speculation in stocks and real estate' (*IHT*, 12 November 2007, p. 12).

'The central bank said at the weekend it would raise the proportion of deposits banks must hold in reserve for the ninth time this year [2007], to 13.5 per cent, a record high' (*FT*, 13 November 2007, p. 9).

'The central bank raised the share of deposits that banks are required to hold with it by 0.5 percentage points to 13.5 per cent' (*The Economist*, 17 November 2007, p. 113).

> Consumer prices ... were 6.5 per cent higher in October than a year earlier, accelerating from 6.2 per cent in September ... [and] matching an increase of 6.5 per cent in August, China's highest inflation rate in eleven years ... Food prices rose fastest – they were up 17.6 per cent in October from a year earlier ... while prices of non-food items increased just 1.1 per cent for the month.
>
> (www.iht.com, 13 November 2007)

'Prime minister Wen Jiabao visited the needy Monday [12 November] and promised to stabilize prices' (*IHT*, 14 November 2007, p. 16).

> In a sign of how seriously the government regards inflation, state media reported a stage-managed visit to low-income Beijing families on Monday [12 November] by premier Wen Jiabao, during which he vowed to bring rising prices under control. He blamed global oil and food price increases ... Food prices rose 17.9 per cent in October from a year earlier, with pork up 54.9 per cent, fresh vegetables rising 29.9 per cent and eggs up 14.3 per cent ... Higher oil prices helped push producer price inflation up to 3.2 per cent in October from a year earlier.
>
> (www.ft.com, 13 November 2007)

> China signalled a shift in its monetary policy Wednesday [5 December], saying it would abandon a decade-long 'prudent' policy for a 'tight' one in 2008 ... The change in rhetoric ... [was reached] at an annual economic planning conference of top leaders that closed Wednesday ... The conference, which Communist Party leaders hold every December to draft policy for the coming year, decided to 'strictly control the volume and granting pace of loans so as to better regulate domestic demand and balance international payments' ... The central bank issued a statement Wednesday saying it would 'continue to strengthen and improve the economic control, further implement tight monetary policy ... [and] take forcible measures to strengthen the management of liquidity'.
>
> (www.iht.com, 5 December 2007; *IHT*, 6 December 2007, p. 13)

> China said Saturday [8 December] that for the tenth time this year [2007] it would order banks to raise the amount of reserves they keep on hand in order to curb inflation ... The central bank said it had ordered banks to increase the reserve ratio by a full percentage point to 14.5 per cent in an effort to curb lending. It was the largest single increase in the reserve ratio in four years.
>
> (www.iht.com, 8 December 2007)

'Banks would have to raise their reserve ratios by a percentage point, to 14.5 per cent, in an effort to tighten the supply of money available for loans' (*IHT*, 10 December 2007, p. 13).

Inflation accelerated further last month ... Consumer prices were 6.9 per cent higher in November than a year earlier – the biggest increase in almost eleven years. The big contributors were food prices, which vaulted 18.2 per cent, and fuel, which climbed 5.5 per cent as the government raised regulated retail prices for gasoline and diesel.

(www.iht.com, 11 December 2007)

China raised interest rates Thursday [20 December] for the sixth time this year [2007] ... after inflation accelerated at the quickest pace in eleven years. The benchmark one-year lending rate will increase by 0.18 percentage points to a nine-year high of 7.47 per cent, starting Friday [21 December] ... The one-year deposit rate will rise by 0.27 percentage points to 4.14 per cent ... It was the third time this year that China has raised deposit rates by more than lending rates to encourage people to keep their money in the bank.

(www.iht.com, 20 December 2007)

'The central bank raised one-year benchmark deposit rates by 27 basis points to 4.14 per cent and one-year lending rates by 18 basis points to 7.47 per cent' (*FT*, 21 December 2007, p. 10).

China's central bank will implement a tight monetary policy in 2008, using a range of tools to keep a check on liquidity, the central bank governor, Zhou Xiaochuan, reaffirmed ... He said: '[China must] step up and improve macroeconomic controls, expand the role of monetary policy in economic controls, carry out a tight monetary policy, make co-ordinated use of a range of monetary policy and use effective measures to step up management over liquidity'.... On Sunday [30 December] the finance ministry said that tariffs of 5 per cent to 25 per cent would be imposed on exports of some grains during 2008, in the latest measure aimed at discouraging sales abroad as domestic food prices soar. From 1 January to 31 December [2008] exports of wheat, buckwheat, barley and oats will be taxed at 20 per cent, while for wheat flour and starch the rate will be 25 per cent. Exports of corn, rice, soybeans, sorghum and millet will face a 5 per cent tariff. Those of corn, rice and soybean flour, as well as corn starch, will be taxed at 10 per cent.

(www.iht.com, 30 December 2007)

China will introduce taxes on grain exports in the latest attempt to rein in food-driven inflation that reached an eleven-year high in November ... [of] 6.9 per cent ... Food prices increased 18.2 per cent from a year earlier in November ... Exporters of fifty-seven types of grain ... would have to pay temporary taxes of between 5 per cent and 25 per cent, the finance ministry said yesterday [30 December]. The move comes less than two weeks after China, the world's biggest grain producer, scrapped a 13 per cent rebate on major grain exports in an attempt to increase domestic supply and rein in inflation.

(*FT*, 31 December 2007, p. 4)

Beijing said on Monday [31 December] that a unit of its new $200 sovereign wealth fund would inject $20 billion into China Development Bank ... Central Huijin Investment, an arm of the China Investment Corp., signed a formal agreement on the capital injection on Monday.... While the new sovereign fund's overseas activities have drawn global attention, most of its $200 in initial capital will be tied up in its takeover of Huijin, expected role in other state bank recapitalizations, and planned domestic investments. Only around $70 billion of its funds are earmarked for overseas purchases. Huijin recently injected renminbi 20 billion in China Everbright Bank and is also expected to provide some $40 billion in new funding for Agricultural Bank of China, the nation's sprawling but troubled rural lender. .. Unlike its peers, China Development Bank's role in lending to large state-owned enterprises and infrastructure projects favoured by the central government has left it in sound financial shape. The policy bank had non-performing loans of just 0.68 per cent as of June 2007 ... Beijing has had little trouble financing recent bank recapitalizations using its foreign exchange reserves, which hit $1,445 billion at the end of October.

(www.ft.com, 31 December 2007; *FT*, 2 January 2008, p. 20)

China's remaining two policy lenders, Export–Import Bank of China and Agricultural Development Bank of China, would be the next targets for restructuring, analysts have said ... China Investment Corp. has said it would also provide capital to state-owned Agricultural Bank of China, the only one of China's big state-run commercial banks yet to be restructured.

(www.iht.com, 1 January 2008)

China's central bank announced [on 16 January 2008] it would raise banks' reserve requirement by 50 basis points. From 25 January banks will have to keep 15 per cent of their deposits with the central bank ... [This is] the first rise this year but follows ten increases in 2007 ... Inflation touched 6.9 per cent in November [2007] on the back of soaring food prices.

(*FT*, 17 January 2008, p. 12)

'Inflation hit an eleven-year high in November [2007] ... It fell back in December ... [to] 6.5 per cent' (www.bbc.co.uk, 24 January 2008).

Unusually severe snowstorms started in parts of China on 10 January 2008. (For details, see entry in the chronology in Chapter 8 of the companion volume, *Political Developments in Contemporary China*.) '[This is] the worst winter weather in fifty years' (www.cnn.com, 31 January 2008). 'The winter storm [is] China's worst in fifty years' (www.cnn.com, 1 February 2008). 'Many of the worst effects have been in parts of east-central and southern China, which are unaccustomed to serious snowfall' (www.iht.com, 3 February 2008). 'Unusually severe blizzards hit large areas of central and southern China at the beginning of the year, blocking transport links and causing widespread chaos' (www.bbc.co.uk, 18 February 2008). Controls on the prices that power companies can charge exacerbated the problems of electricity supply and food price controls were increased. 'After months of keeping a tight rein on lending by banks in an effort to curb runaway economic growth, China's central bank has ordered provincial banks to speed up loans issued in the worst-hit areas' (*Independent*, 2 February 2008, p. 37).

> Consumer prices rose 7.1 per cent last month [January 2008], the largest increase in more than a decade … Food prices led the increase again in January, climbing 18.2 per cent … Non-food prices were up 1.5 per cent from a year earlier in January … [As regards] services prices were up 2.6 per cent.
>
> (www.iht.com, 19 February 2008)

'January's [consumer] inflation rate of 7.1 per cent was the highest figure since September 1996, when consumer price inflation hit 7.4 per cent' (www. bbc.co.uk, 19 February 2008).

> Banks in China seem to have dodged a bullet in the US subprime mortgage crisis. Chinese lenders accumulated large amounts of that bad debt. But bankers have assured investors that they are within manageable levels that won't greatly affect their profits … [But] with memories still fresh of Beijing's having injected more than $260 billion into its banks while shifting bad loans off their books, another huge bailout may become necessary if loose lending practices are not halted … The non-performing loan ratio for major Chinese banks rose for the first time in two years, to 6.72 per cent in the fourth quarter [of 2007] from 6.63 per cent in the previous quarter.
>
> (*IHT*, 21 February 2008, p. 17)

> The fifteenth increase in banks' reserve ratio since mid-2006 [was] announced yesterday [18 March]. The 0.5 per cent rise in the ratio, the amount of money banks must leave on deposit with the People's Bank of China, now leaves the reserve requirement for large lenders at 15.5 per cent.
>
> (*FT*, 19 March 2008)

> [On 18 March] the central bank said it would raise the reserve requirement ratio to 15.5 per cent, effective 25 March … The central bank has raised the reserve ratio repeatedly over the past few years, taking it to nearly 16 per cent this year [2008] in its effort to tame inflation.
>
> (*IHT*, 19 March 2008, p. 13)

> Inflation surged in China last month [February] – with consumer prices rising at an annual rate of 8.7 per cent, the fastest pace in more than eleven years – after crippling snowstorms disrupted food supplies … Food prices were the biggest contributor to the acceleration in inflation, up 23.3 per cent from a year earlier … The price of pork soared 63 per cent [63.4 per cent] from a year earlier, vegetables climbed 46 per cent and edible oil rose 41 per cent … Inflation was less pronounced for non-food items, which were up 1.6 per cent in February from a year earlier.
>
> (www.iht.com, 11 March 2008; *IHT*, 12 March 2008, p. 11)

'Despite the recent hike in food prices, they still have a lot of catching up to do. Grain prices have risen barely 5 per cent in the past ten years in China' (*IHT*, 20 March 2008, p. 13).

'The 8.7 per cent figure [for February is] the highest since May 1996' (*FT*, 12 March 2008, p. 8).

Bank of China said it held about $5 billion worth of subprime-related asset-backed securities at the end of 2007 and had booked a $1.3 billion provision to cover potential losses on its US subprime-related securities ... Industrial and Commercial Bank of China said it held US subprime mortgage-backed securities worth $1.23 billion in terms of nominal value by the end of December 2007, the same level as last June [2007] and the lender booked $400 million as an allowance for potential losses on that portfolio.

(www.iht.com, 25 March 2008; *IHT*, 26 March 2008, p. 15)

China said Friday [28 March] it will pay farmers more for rice and wheat, trying to raise output and cool surging inflation ... Beijing has frozen retail prices of rice, cooking oil and other goods in an effort to curb inflation that saw food prices jump 23.3 per cent in February over the same month last year [2007] ... Minimum grain prices paid to farmers would rise by up to 9 per cent ... Beijing has been prodding farmers to raise production by promising free vaccinations for pigs and other aid ... Under the latest order prices paid for rice will rise by 7 yuan, or $1, for every 50 kg, or 110 lb, to 77 yuan to 82 yuan, depending on the type ... Wheat prices will rise by 3 yuan to 5 yuan, to 72 yuan to 75 yuan per 50 kg. The government regards meeting most of China's grain needs from domestic sources as a matter of national security. It operates a network of grain-buying offices and a grain stockpile. It has been releasing supplies to ease shortages. The exact size of the stockpile is a secret, but premier Wen Jiabao said this month [March] that it is 150 million tonnes to 200 million tonnes.

(www.iht.com, 28 March 2008)

Food prices have risen 21 per cent so far this year [in the first quarter of 2008] ... Headline inflation actually slowed slightly in March to 8.3 per cent from 8.7 per cent in February, but higher food prices accounted for the bulk of the figure. The sharp rise in food prices [has been] driven principally by the increased cost of grain.

(www.bbc.co.uk, 16 April 2008)

Consumer prices were 8.3 per cent higher in March from a year earlier ... barely lower than the inflation rate in February [8.7 per cent] ... Food prices have risen 21 per cent in the past year despite price controls imposed in January on cooking oil and some grains.

(www.iht.com, 17 April 2008)

Food prices rose by 21 per cent in the first quarter [of 2008], accounting for 6.8 percentage points of the 8 per cent rise in the consumer price index in that period ... [On 16 April] the People's Bank of China raised the proportion of deposits that large commercial banks must keep with it by 0.5 percentage points to 16 per cent – the sixteenth such increase since mid-2006.

(www.iht.com, 17 April 2008)

'China ordered commercial banks to set aside more of their deposits as reserves for the third time this year [2008], increasing the rate by 0.5 percentage points to 16 per cent [with effect from 25 April]' (*IHT*, 17 April 2008, p. 17).

China produces more than 90 per cent of the grain it consumes ... Last month [March] prime minister Wen Jiabao revealed what had been a state secret: that China had grain reserves of 150 million tonnes to 200 million tonnes, equal to 30 per cent to 40 per cent of annual production ... The country's grain policy calls for 95 per cent self-sufficiency.

(*The Economist*, 19 April 2008, p. 69)

'Consumer price inflation ... is already at the highest level in more than eleven years at an annual rate of 8.3 per cent' (www.iht.com, 9 May 2008).

'Consumer price inflation stood close to a twelve-year high in April ... Annual inflation rose to 8.5 per cent from 8.3 per cent in March ... Food costs rose 22.1 per cent in April from a year earlier' (www.bbc.co.uk, 12 May 2008).

China announced fresh monetary tightening measures yesterday [12 May] after inflation data showed price rises of 8.5 per cent in April, the second highest figure for twelve years. The People's Bank of China lifted the share of funds that commercial banks must leave on deposit with the central bank by 50 basis points [from 16 per cent] to 16.5 per cent, the fourth increase this year [2008] ... Year-on-year [food] price increases ... [hit] 22.1 per cent in April, compared with 21.4 per cent in March.

(*FT*, 13 May 2008, p. 7)

Banks reduced their ratio of non-performing loans to a record low of 5.8 per cent in the first quarter [of 2008]. State-owned banks, joint stock banks, city and rural lenders and foreign banks had a combined $171 billion of soured debts as of 31 March ... The bank loans ratio stood at 6.18 per cent at the end of last year [2007].

(*FT*, 15 May 2008, p. 12)

Chinese banks have emerged relatively unscathed from the credit crisis, which so far has caused nearly $380 billion of losses at Western financial institutions. Apart from Bank of China, which reported a subprime-related writedown of nearly $1.3 billion by the end of last year [2007], no other Chinese bank has been seriously affected.

(*FT*, 28 May 2008, p. 10)

'The central bank on Saturday [7 June] raised the amount lenders must keep in reserve by a full percentage point, the largest increase of the year' (www.iht.com, 9 June 2008).

The People's Bank of China announced on Saturday that it would raise the proportion of assets that banks must hold as reserves by a full percentage point, in two equal steps on 15 June and 25 June. The increase [is] the fifth this year [2008].

(www.iht.com, 10 June 2008)

'[The] central bank raised the reserve ratio to 17.5 per cent' (www.bbc.co.uk, 10 June 2008).

Annual inflation fell in May to 7.7 per cent, the first major break in a year-long surge, as food price increases slowed and other products resisted global commodity costs ... The consumer price index (CPI) showed food inflation had eased to 19.9 per cent in the year to May from the 22.1 per cent pace in April ... Non-food inflation nudged down to 1.7 per cent from 1.8 per cent even though figures showed factory gate prices rose at the fastest rate since late 2004 ... China provides most of its own food, which makes up a third of the consumer price basket ... Officials acknowledge the government's full-year [inflation] target of 4.8 per cent is probably beyond reach ... Beijing is under increasing pressure to raise state-set prices of diesel and gasoline as shortages spread across the country. Currently they are well below international markets, so if the two are brought in line it could push the CPI up again by around 2 percentage points.

(www.iht.com, 12 June 2008)

On 20 June 2008 regulated fuel prices were raised sharply. (For details, see the section on prices.)

A Politburo meeting on 25 July [2008] replaced the previous national economic goal, preventing overheating of the economy and controlling inflation, with a new target. As enunciated by President Hu Jintao in recent appearances, the objective now is to seek fast and sustained economic growth while still keeping inflation under control. He said at a rare news conference on Friday [1 August]: 'We must maintain steady, relatively fast development and control excessive price rises as the priority tasks of macro adjustment' ... After letting the currency rise sharply against the dollar in the first half of this year [2008], China's central bank has actually pushed the yuan down against the dollar in each of the past four trading days, including a drop of 0.13 per cent Monday [4 August] ... In the past several days the Chinese authorities have raised export tax refunds for garment manufacturers – an industry previously slighted by regulators, who remain more interested in promoting high technology industries. Policy-makers have also reportedly moved to ease limits of banks.

(www.iht.com, 5 August 2008; *IHT*, 6 August 2008, p. 13)

Chinese leaders ... have long been trying to prevent ... the economy ... from growing too fast, but now they fear that growth is slowing too fast and may slow further. National income grew by 10.1 per cent in the year to the second quarter [of 2008], compared with 10.6 per cent in the year to the first quarter and 11.2 per cent to the last quarter of 2007 ... Much of the fall results from a decline in net exports ... Manufacturers of low value-added export goods such as clothes and textiles ... are among the hardest hit ... The state-controlled media have reported many closures of small and medium-sized business enterprises in coastal areas. Chinese leaders, previously more eager to nurture high-tech industries, toured textile factories last month [July] in a show of political support ... Later in July a meeting of the ruling Politburo signalled a policy shift. The formerly oft-repeated injunction to prevent overheating was dropped. Instead the leadership decided to focus on maintaining 'steady and fast' economic growth, though it said it would continue its efforts to combat inflation. Since the meeting there have been moves to placate exporters, such as easing controls on lending to small and medium-sized businesses.

(*The Economist*, 9 August 2008, p. 53)

On 1 August [2008] the finance ministry increased export tax rebates on a range of clothing products from 11 per cent to 13 per cent and on bamboo products from 5 per cent to 11 per cent, in an apparent effort to help exporters of cheap goods.

(p. 63)

Inflation cooled for a third month on slower food price gains ... The consumer price index rose 6.3 per cent in July [2008] from a year earlier, after increasing 7.1 per cent in June ... The expansion of the world's fourth biggest economy has slowed for four quarters, prompting officials to emphasize the importance of rapid growth and drop references to maintaining a tight monetary policy. China has already loosened bank lending quotas, raised tax rebates for some exports and halted the yuan's appreciation against the dollar ... The yuan weakened 0.1 per cent to 6.8648 in early trade in Shanghai. The currency rose 4.2 per cent in the three months through March and 2.3 per cent in the second quarter before stalling in the third ... Food prices rose 14.4 per cent in July from a year earlier after gaining 17.3 per cent in June ... Non-food prices increased 2.1 per cent after climbing 1.9 per cent ... Meat prices rose 16 per cent from a year earlier after a 27.3 per cent gain in June. Vegetables gained 8.4 per cent after an 8.3 per cent increase ... Concerns are easing that producer price inflation, which in July accelerated to the fastest pace in twelve years, will stoke a rebound in consumer-price inflation ... Producer prices jumped 10 per cent in the year through July ... China's economy expanded 10.1 per cent in the second quarter from a year earlier, the slowest pace since 2005. Growth below 9 per cent would be unacceptable for a government targeting 10 million new jobs a year, according to Crédit Suisse Group.

(www.iht.com, 12 August 2008; *IHT*, 13 August 2008, p. 15)

'The central bank has allowed the yuan to decline against the dollar in the past two weeks after a 20 per cent rise since 2005' (*IHT*, 12 August 2008, p. 14).

The ministry of finance said on Tuesday [19 August] it would put 3.51 billion yuan this year [2008] into six schemes to encourage small business, up from 2 billion yuan on average in the past eight years … The finance ministry joined forces Monday [18 August] with the central bank and the labour ministry to encourage banks to lend more to small firms by allowing them to charge higher interest. .. And last month [July] the central bank raised banks' lending quotas by 5 per cent and instructed them to channel the extra loans to small firms and to the agricultural sector.

(www.iht.com, 19 August 2008)

The Chinese currency has appreciated by 7 per cent against the US dollar this year [2008]. But the pace of appreciation has slowed sharply over the past two months. In August the renminbi even depreciated slightly against the dollar. This is only the second month that this has happened since China moved away from the dollar peg in 2005.

(*FT*, 1 September 2008, p. 8)

The yuan, after strengthening for twenty-six consecutive months … actually weakened slightly against the dollar last month [August] … The yuan has risen 21 per cent against the dollar since China broke its peg to the dollar in July 2005 … The central bank has tended to favour allowing the yuan to strengthen, which lessens the pressure on it to buy money-losing American securities … By buying US bonds, the government has been investing a large portion of the country's savings in assets earning just 3 per cent a year or so in dollars. And the investments are actually losing as much as 10 per cent a year when inflation and the Chinese currency's appreciation against the dollar are factored in … The interest from the bank's foreign bond holdings barely pays the interest on the money the central bank has borrowed within China to buy the bonds … But the finance ministry, and particularly its allies at the commerce ministry, prefer to keep the yuan weaker to help exports. The bank and the finance ministry are ferocious bureaucratic rivals … Bankers estimate the dollar portion of China's foreign exchange reserves at a little over $1 trillion.

(*IHT*, 4 September 2008, p. 11)

'China's foreign exchange reserves increased … from $1,499 billion at the end of August 2007 to $1,810 billion by the end of June [2008]' (*FT*, 12 September 2008, p. 6).

China's inflation rate eased to 4.9 per cent in August – the lowest in fourteen months … That was down from the 6.3 per cent rise in the consumer price index in July and from a decade high in February … Food prices are still rising rapidly – up 10.3 per cent from a year ago – but not as quickly as before … In July food prices had jumped 14.4 per cent … In August already high wholesale inflation rose further to 10.1 per cent.

(www.cnn.com, 10 September 2008)

Inflation dropped sharply in August for the fourth month in a row, giving more room for policy-makers to take measures to boost the economy if growth begins to slow sharply. Consumer price inflation was 4.9 per cent last month [August], down from 6.3 per cent in July and well below analysts' forecasts. Although factory price inflation nudged up further to 10.1 per cent last month from 10 per cent, the new figures will increase confidence that China has overcome an inflationary problem which saw consumer prices rising earlier this year at their fastest rate in over a decade.

(www.ft.com, 10 September 2008)

After five years of tightening monetary policy to fight inflation, China abruptly reversed course late Monday afternoon [15 September], cutting interest rates and easing bank lending in response to signs that growth of the economy was finally slowing. China's exports have slowed sharply ... Since 2003 China's top priority has been to control inflation. But China's Politburo ... decided at a meeting on 25 July that the top economic goals should shift to sustaining economic development and limiting inflation, in that order ... The central bank said in a statement that the goal of economic policy was: '[To] solve prominent problems in the current economic operation, implement the policy of giving different policies for different needs and optimizing the economic structure, and ensure a steady, rapid and sustained development' ... Effective Tuesday [16 September] the People's Bank of China reduced by 0.27 per cent to 7.2 per cent the regulated benchmark rate that commercial banks may charge for one-year loans to business borrowers with strong credit histories. Rates for shorter-term loans will be generally cut even more, while rates for longer-term loans will be subject to smaller adjustments ... The central bank also reduced, by a full percentage point, the share of assets that small and medium-sized banks must deposit as reserves with the central bank, effective 25 September. [This is] the so-called reserve requirement ratio ... But the People's Bank of China made a point Monday of not reducing the reserve requirement ratio for the country's six largest banks ... [namely] the Industrial and Commercial Bank of China, the Agricultural Bank of China, the Bank of China, the China Construction Bank, the Bank of Communications and the Postal Savings Bank of China. These institutions account for more than two-thirds of the banking market in China. The central bank needs large sums of reserves, for which it pays only 1.89 per cent interest to the banks, so that it can continue buying large sums of foreign exchange reserves. By buying tens of billions of dollars' worth of foreign currency each month, the Beijing authorities have been able to limit the rise of the yuan against the dollar ... The central bank rapidly ratcheted up ... the reserve requirement ratio ... from 6 per cent in August 2003 to 14.5 per cent last December [2007] and 17.5 per cent in June [2008] ... The central bank cut this ratio by 2 percentage points for banks in areas damaged by the Sichuan province earthquake on 12 May.

(www.iht.com, 15 September 2008; *IHT*, 16 September 2008, p. 17)

China's central bank cut the country's benchmark interest rate last night [15 September] for the first time in more than six years, in the face of global financial turmoil and signs of a slowing domestic economy. The People's Bank of China lowered the one-year lending rate by 27 basis points to 7.2 per cent after years of gradual increases aimed at combating inflation and reining in what some saw as an overheating economy. The People's Bank of China also said it would reduce the amount smaller domestic banks must hold in reserve with the central bank by one percentage point to 16.5 per cent from 25 September, freeing up funds for those banks to lend. That will be the first drop in the reserve rate requirement since 1999 but does not extend to the five largest banks or the Postal Bank ... There are signs that the slowdown [in the economy] is accelerating as problems emerge in the export and property sectors.

(*FT*, 16 September 2008, p. 12)

'China has cut interest rates twice in three weeks, including a move on Wednesday [8 October]' (www.iht.com, 8 October 2008).

China yesterday [8 October] cut interest rates for the second time in less than a month, a move that complemented the co-ordinated easing by global central banks and signalled official determination to support domestic economic growth. While the People's Bank of China gave no reason for its rate cut and did not link it with that of counterparts in the United States, Europe and elsewhere, analysts said there was little doubt the timing was influenced by the international effort to counter the effects of the global financial crisis ... The 0.27 percentage point cut brought the rate for one-year bank loans to 6.93 per cent and followed a reduction of the same size in mid-September. Beijing also reduced the proportion of deposits that banks must hold in reserve by half a percentage point ... A 5 per cent withholding tax levied on interest income would be suspended.

(*FT*, 9 October 2008, p. 10)

China has become the main engine of the world economy, accounting for one-third of global GDP growth in the first half of this year [2008] ... The government is expected to supply a fiscal stimulus to keep growth above 8 per cent ... China has ample room for a stimulus because it boasts the healthiest fiscal position of any big economy ... Compared with many other emerging economies, notably Brazil and Russia, which have recently suffered big capital outflows, China has so far largely shrugged off the global credit crunch ... It has a budget surplus of 2 per cent of GDP, if measured in the same way as in rich countries, and public sector debt is a mere 16 per cent of GDP.

(*The Economist*, 11 October 2008, p. 110)

[According to President Gloria Macapagal Arroya of the Philippines] Southeast Asian nations plus Japan, China and South Korea have agreed to set up a multi-billion dollar fund to buy banks' bad debt and support banks ... The

World Bank has committed to provide the Asian fund with $10 billion ...
The Asian development Fund and the IMF may also contribute to the fund
as well as the ten-member Asean and China, Japan and South Korea.

(www.bbc.co.uk, 15 October 2008)

President Gloria Macapagal Arroya [of the Philippines] ... boasted this
week of an agreement to set up a fund to buy toxic debts from banks in
South-east Asia, China, South Korea and Japan. But the World Bank, the
alleged source of some of the money, and the other countries involved,
could not recall such an agreement.

(*The Economist*, 18 October 2008, p. 76)

The State Council, or cabinet, met over the weekend and decided to shift the
emphasis of economic policy toward maintaining 'a stable and rapid
economic development', state-controlled media reported Monday [20
October]. The previous policy has been 'to ensure growth and control
inflation'. As part of the new policy the State Council announced that it
planned to increase export tax rebates for everything from labour-intensive
products like garments and textiles to high-value products like mechanical
and electrical products. Banks will be encouraged to lend more money
to small and mid-size enterprises and a variety of support programmes
will be drafted to help farmers, the government said. Government ministries
will also spend more to rebuild earthquake-damaged areas of south-western
China, to improve transportation links and other infrastructure and to
improve the social welfare system ... Most economists estimate that 8
per cent growth is needed to prevent urban unemployment from rising,
which could trigger demonstrations and undermine the country's social
stability.

(www.iht.com, 20 October 2008; *IHT*, 21 October 2008, p. 11)

China's economic growth rate has fallen for the third quarter in succession
... The National Bureau of Statistics said the economy had grown at a rate
of 9 per cent in the three months to September – down from 10.1 per cent
over the previous quarter ... [A spokesman] said the impact of the global
financial crisis had far exceeded the government's expectations ... The third
quarter growth rate announced on Monday [20 October] marked a significant fall from the 10.4 per cent growth of the first half of 2008 and the 12.2
per cent growth seen in the first three-quarters of 2007 ... Officials said over
the weekend that the government was preparing to announce tax cuts and
increased infrastructure investment ... The National Bureau of Statistics
also announced on Monday that consumer price inflation had cooled to a
fifteenth-month low of 4.6 per cent in September. In February inflation had
hit a twelve-year peak of 8.7 per cent.

(www.bbc.co.uk, 20 October 2008)

Economic growth in China slowed to 9 per cent in the third quarter of this
year [2008], the slowest pace in more than five years, as industrial produc-

tion and construction slackened because of weak exports, a slumping real estate market and temporary restrictions imposed during the Olympics … Growth of 9 per cent in the third quarter was slower than most economists expected, with surveys having previously put the average forecast for the quarter at anywhere from 9.1 per cent to 9.7 percent … Inflation is slowing at the consumer level … It was 4.6 per cent in September, down from 4.9 per cent in August and the fifth monthly decline.

(www.iht.com, 20 October 2008)

After five years of growth exceeding 10 per cent, China's growth has decelerated for five consecutive quarters, dropping to about 9 per cent in the third quarter of this year [2008] from 12.6 per cent in the second quarter of 2007 … Economists expect the economy to expand at an annualized rate of as little as 5.8 per cent in the fourth quarter, down from nearly 11.2 per cent in 2007.

(*IHT*, 7 November 2008, p. 13)

'[There was] 10.6 per cent growth in the first quarter of the year [2008] and 10.1 per cent in the second quarter' (www.independent.co.uk, 20 October 2008).

China's GDP for the first nine months of 2008 increased by 9.9 per cent. 2.3 per cent lower than last year [2007] … The rate of expansion was the lowest since the second quarter of 2003. when the outbreak of SARS cooled growth to 6.7 per cent … A fall in the growth of exports due to the global economic slowdown was one of the reasons for the cooling of the economy … The official Xinhua news agency reported this week that 3,631 toy exporters – 52.7 per cent of the industry's enterprises – went out of business in 2008 … [owing to] higher production costs, wage increases and the rising value of the yuan … Workers at the Smart Union toy factory [which has closed down and which had previously employed 7,000 people in Guangdong and Hong Kong] said that for several months the plant was less busy and pay cheques were arriving late … [About] 100 workers on Friday [17 October] gathered outside the gates of the factory … About 2,000 other labourers protested outside the local government's offices, demanding that the Hong Kong-based company pay their wages, severance and other benefits.

(www.cnn.com, 20 October 2008)

Slightly more than half the country's toy exporters shut down in the first seven months of this year [2008], mostly very small companies that struggled to cope with new safety standards as well as weakening Western demand, according to China's customs agency.

(*IHT*, 23 October 2008, p. 12)

This month [October] alone two big companies – Smart Union Group, a toymaker, and FerroChina, a steel producer – have gone into liquidation …

Early this year [2008] southern China suffered from shortages of workers ...
All that has now reversed. There is a surplus of workers.

(www.economist.com, 20 October 2008)

'Factory gate prices also moderated from 10.1 per cent in August to 9.1 per
cent [in September]' (*FT*, 21 October 2008, p. 11).

'The economic planning agency on Monday [20 October] increased the
minimum purchase price of wheat by up to 15 per cent beginning next year
[2009]' (*IHT*, 23 October 2008, p. 12).

President Hu Jintao expressed concerns over the ailing US financial system
in a phone conversation with US President George W. Bush ... In their conversation Tuesday night [21 October] Chinese time Hu told Bush: '[I hope
US stabilization measures will] take effect as soon as possible, restore investor confidence and prevent further expansion of the crisis. The measures are
conducive to the stability of the world economy and financial markets' ...
[An] Asia–Europe meeting [Asem] begins in Beijing on Friday [24 October]
... China's banks hold relatively little of the toxic mortgaged-related debt
that is wreaking havoc on US institutions and have been largely shielded
from the global shock waves due to strict credit controls.

(www.cnn.com, 22 October 2008)

Direct losses by Chinese financial institutions from the US subprime crisis
are not huge. Commercial banks have eagerly defended their slight involvement or non-involvement in the crisis. Among the banks Bank of China has
the most exposure. In its annual report it said its investment in subprime
asset-backed securities was $4.99 last year [2007]. The International Com-
mercial Bank of China, the country's largest commercial lender, suffered a
loss of $1.2 billion from the crisis.

(He Fan, *The World Today*, November 2008, p. 7)

On 22 October the government announced that the minimum down payment
on first homes would be reduced to 20 per cent from 30 per cent, stamp duty
would be eliminated and mortgage rates cut ... Household debt [is] almost
non-existent.'

(*The Economist*, 25 October 2008, p. 70)

The government announced a series of measures late Wednesday [22
October] to bolster real estate prices. The central bank ordered commercial
banks to reduce mortgage rates and down payments for borrowers obtaining
their first mortgage, beginning next Monday [27 October]. And the finance
ministry reduced the stamp tax on real estate purchases effective 1 November, but only for first time home buyers acquiring an apartment of less than
90 square metres, or 970 square feet ... Under the new rules announced
Wednesday mortgage interest rates will be reduced by 0.27 per cent for first
time buyers, to 4.59 per cent for mortgages of five years or more ... Mortgage lending is more tightly regulated than in the West. In China roughly

half of all home buyers still pay cash and do not obtain a mortgage at all – although they might borrow some of the cash from friends, families or neighbours. For those who do obtain mortgages, the down payment is 30 per cent for buyers taking out their first mortgage and 40 per cent or more for buyers who have a mortgage on another home. Under the new measures announced Wednesday the down payment will fall to 20 per cent for buyers seeking their first mortgage. But many cities, including Shenzhen, had already lowered the down payment to 20 per cent for buyers obtaining their first mortgage ... The term of a mortgage must end when the borrower reaches a certain age – fifty-five for a woman and sixty for a man ... Since the 1950s women have retired at an earlier age, as it was thought necessary to protect women's health ... It is nearly impossible for Chinese banks to foreclose on homes. Instead, banks tend to renegotiate monthly payments for borrowers who can clearly demonstrate financial strain. Chinese banks hold the mortgages they issue instead of following the US practice of bundling them together as securities and reselling pieces to various investors. The process, known as securitization, is now making it hard for homeowners in the United States to renegotiate their mortgages ... Chinese banks are flush with cash, with capital equal to 12 per cent to 14 per cent of assets, compared with the international regulatory standard of 8 per cent ... Starting in 2004 Beijing officials tried to limit real estate speculation through administrative measures, by setting quotas on real estate lending done by each bank ... In addition to requiring larger down payments for second and third homes, banks charge interest rates that are up to 3 percentage points higher for these homes than for first time home buyers.

(*IHT*, 24 October 2008, pp. 11, 13)

'[In China] if you try to walk away from the mortgage, the bank will come after your personal assets.' (*IHT*, 22 December 2008, p. 7).

The government has outlined measures to stimulate the property market, including a reduction in the down payments on house purchases, lower mortgage rates, and a cut in stamp duty and the capital gains tax on property sales. Officials said the construction of low-cost housing would be increased ... The authorities announced rises this week for export rebates on 3,000 products, including textiles, garments, furniture and some electrical machinery. Increased rebates for steel exporters are being considered.

(*FT*, 24 October 2008, p. 8)

'In addition to increasing export tax rebates for many products and making it easier for people to get mortgages, the government has announced that it will spend $292 billion on expanding its railways, greater than what it had previously committed' (www.iht.com, 26 October 2008).

Asian and European leaders vowed Saturday [25 October] to act together to address the global financial crisis, calling for decisive action following a two-day summit in Beijing. The Asem meeting brought together the leaders of forty-three Asian and European nations, along with the heads of the European Commission and Asean ... While the summit is usually a forum for political, economic and cultural issues, it has taken on added significance this year [2008] because of the unfolding crisis ... Friday's statement [24 October] joint statement said there must be more supervision and regulation of all 'financial actors' and that they need to be kept accountable. They said all countries need to strengthen oversight and crisis management mechanisms ... Asian countries have not been as sharply affected by the current crisis as those in Europe, in part because they were not as exposed to the subprime mortgage problems.

(www.cnn.com, 25 October 2008)

Heads of state across Asia and Europe called for a co-ordinated response to the global financial crisis in a two-day [25–26 October] conference in Beijing ... The event in Beijing drew heads of state and other top officials from the twenty-seven member countries of the EU and the ten members of Asean as well as China, Japan, South Korea, India and Pakistan. The concave was the seventh biennial Asia–Europe Meeting, a series of gatherings started in 1996 and last held in Finland two years ago ... [Those attending included] prime minister Wen Jiabao and President Hu Jintao ... But the leaders fell short of offering specific solutions to the current economic troubles ... A joint statement was issued at the conference: 'Necessary and timely measures should be taken ... Leaders were of the view that to resolve the financial crisis it is imperative to handle properly the relationship between financial innovation and regulation and to maintain sound macroeconomic measures. They recognized the need to improve the supervision and regulation of all financial actors, in particular their accountability' ... China said it would attend the international conference on the financial crisis in Washington that President George W. Bush has scheduled for 15 November ... Prime minister Wen Jiabao noted that the effect of global financial turmoil on Chinese financial institutions had been muted. China has moved cautiously in allowing greater financial competition and in permitting money to flow in and out of the country. Wen Jiabao (25 October): 'We need financial innovation, but we need financial oversight even more' ... The statement issued at the conference ... [said the IMF] 'should play a critical role in assisting countries seriously affected by the crisis, upon their request' ... China has been blocking the release of the IMF's annual report on its economy for months because it objects to the IMF's attempt – mainly at the request of the United States – to review whether China is deliberately undervaluing its currency so as to increase exports.

(www.iht.com, 26 October 2008; *IHT*, 27 October 2008, p. 12)

Asian and European leaders gathered in Beijing for a summit [the seventh such meeting] on 24 and 25 October that was dominated by the global financial crisis ... China proclaimed itself relatively unscathed ... [Prime minister Wen Jiabao] said 'the impact is limited and controllable'... The crisis is pushing the world's fourth largest economy, with the biggest foreign exchange reserves, to the centre of global summitry … China has $1.9 trillion in reserves and Japan has nearly $1 trillion … Chinese leaders told Asem that their priority was to keep their own economy running smoothly. This, said Mr Wen, was 'China's greatest contribution to the world'. China's economic growth has recently slowed … [to] 9 per cent in the third quarter [of 2008] … [For the EU] China is the fastest growing market – albeit, as the Europeans like to point out when they complain about Chinese trade barriers, still no bigger than Switzerland. At least European moans about successive years of the yuan's depreciation against the Euro, making European exports costlier, have now been silenced by a reversal of the trend … The most concrete idea discussed by the Asian countries at Asem [Asia–Europe Meeting] was to set up an $80 billion fund by the middle of 2009 to help countries in the region deal with liquidity problems – a plan already agreed in May [2008]. The bulk of the money would come from China, Japan and South Korea.

(*The Economist*, 1 November 2008, p. 67)

'Capital controls and a tightly managed exchange rate shielded China from the worst of the 1997–8 financial crisis and are once more offering a large degree of protection' (*IHT*, 28 October 2008, p. 11).

'[On 29 October] the benchmark one-year deposit rate [was cut] from 3.87 per cent to 3.60 per cent' (*FT*, 30 October 2008, p. 7).

'The central bank cut banks' benchmark lending and deposit rates by 0.27 percentage points on Wednesday [29 October], the third cut in six weeks' (www. iht.com, 30 October 2008). 'On 29 October the central bank reduced its benchmark one-year lending rate to 6.66 per cent from 6.93 per cent' (www.iht.com, 2 November 2008).

Prime minister Wen Jiabao said maintaining the strong economic growth in China was a top priority … Wen, writing in the Communist Party's ideological journal … *Qiushi* or *Seeking Truth* … warned of growing domestic social risks from a global economic downturn. Wen Jiabao: 'Against the current international financial and economic turmoil we must give even greater priority to maintaining our country's steady and relatively fast economic development. We must be crystal clear that without a certain pace of economic growth there will be difficulties with employment, fiscal measures and social development, and factors damaging social stability will grow.'

(www.iht.com, 2 November 2008)

'China announced over the weekend that it was loosening limits on bank lending' (*IHT*, Tuesday 4 November 2008, p. 12). 'Last month [October] Beijing approved a massive $292 billion for the construction of railways and a $19 billion capital infusion for Agricultural Bank of China as part of a restructuring that could eventually cost $100 billion' (www.iht.com, 3 November 2008).

'A spokesman at the central bank: "At present the central bank is no longer applying hard constraints to the lending plans of commercial banks" … A fiscal stimulus plan includes a $292 billion investment in railway infrastructure' (*FT*, 4 November 2008, p. 11).

> After five years of growth in excess of 10 per cent, the economy is weakening because of slowing exports and investment growth, declining consumption, and severely depressed stock and property markets. Factory closures in southern China, often dubbed the factory floor of the world, have led to mass lay-offs and even sporadic protest by workers who complained that owners disappeared without paying them their wages.
>
> (www.iht.com, 9 November 2008)

'[Some] 67,000 export-producing factories have closed already this year [2008]' (www.iht.com, 12 November 2008). 'The slowdown in exports contributed to the closing of at least 67,000 factories across China in the first half of the year [2008], according to government statistics. Labour disputes and protests over lost back pay have surged' (www.iht.com, 14 November 2008).

> Guangdong province, in southern China, has been the hardest hit. Thousands of firms making shoes, toys and clothing have been forced to close this year [2008] ... Half of China's toymakers and one-third of its shoe firms have disappeared this year. Yet toys and shoes now account for less than 5 per cent of China's total exports. Exports of machinery and transport equipment [comprise] almost half the total ... UBS, a bank, forecasts that in 2009 net exports will be a negative drag on growth. In 2007 net exports contributed almost 3 percentage points off the 12 per cent increase in GDP.
>
> (*The Economist*, 15 November 2008, pp. 87–9)

China announced a massive economic stimulus package Sunday [9 November], aimed at bolstering its weakening economy and fighting the effects of the global economic slowdown. Beijing said it would spend an estimated 4 trillion yuan, or $586 billion, on a wide array of infrastructure and social welfare projects, which would include constructing new railways, subways, airports and rebuilding depressed communities. The package, which was announced by the State Council on Sunday evening [9 November], is the largest economic stimulus ever undertaken by the Chinese government and would amount to about 7 per cent of the country's GDP during each of the next two years. Beijing said it was loosening credit criteria and encouraging lending ... A statement said China's cabinet had approved a plan to invest 4 trillion yuan ($596 billion) in infrastructure and social welfare by the end of 2010. Some of the money will come from the private sector. The statement did not say how much of the spending is on new projects and how much is for ventures already in the pipeline that will be speeded up. China's export-driven growth is starting to feel the impact of the economic slowdown in the United States and Europe ... The statement said the cabinet ... had 'decided to adopt active fiscal policy and moderately easy monetary policies' ... The statement said the spending would focus on ten areas. They included picking up the pace of spending on low cost housing ... as well as increased spending on rural infrastructure. Money will also be poured into new railways, roads and airports. Spending on health and education will be increased, as well as on environmental protection and high technology. Spending on rebuilding disaster areas, such as Sichuan province ... will also be speeded up. That includes 20 billion yuan ($2.93 billion) planned for next year [2009] that will be moved up to the fourth quarter of this year [2008] ... Credit limits for commercial banks will be removed to channel more lending to priority projects and rural developments ... Reform of the value-added tax system will cut taxes by 120 billion yuan ($17.5 billion) for enterprises ... At $586 billion the stimulus package is enormous for any country, let alone one whose GDP was only about $3.3 trillion in 2007. Earlier this year the US Congress passed a $700 billion bailout package in a country with an economy close to $14 trillion. Analysts were expecting China to announce a big stimulus package but were surprised at the size of it ... After the Asian financial crisis in 1997 Beijing undertook a similar, but much smaller stimulus package ... Over the weekend the head of the central bank, Zhou Xiao-chuan, said at a meeting of finance ministers in Brazil that China could help stabilize international markets by encouraging consumption at home ... At home Beijing is trying hard to cope with a slowing economy.

(www.iht.com, 9 November 2008; *IHT*, 10 November 2008, pp. 1, 12)

J.P. Morgan in Hong Kong said in a research note on Monday [10 November] that economists had widely expected earlier this year a stimulus package amounting to about 1.5 per cent of Chinese GDP. The package announced Sunday is about ten times as big.

(www.iht.com, 10 November 2008)

[The] 4 trillion ($596 billion) stimulus package [is] the largest in the country's history ... The two-year spending initiative will inject funds into ten sectors, including health care, education, low-income housing, environmental protection, schemes to promote technological innovation, and transport and other infrastructure projects. The government also says that some of the spending will be directed to reconstruction efforts in areas battered by natural disasters, such as Sichuan province which was devastated by a massive earthquake in May. The State Council said: 'Over the past two months, the global financial crisis has been intensifying daily. In expanding investment we must be fast and heavy-handed' ... Officials say that fourth quarter investment for this year will total 400 billion yuan, including 20 billion yuan brought forward from next year's [2009] central government budget. If fully realized the two-year spending spree would amount to about 16 per cent of China's annual GDP. The newly announced measures also include a loosening of credit policies and tax cuts. The plan calls for reforms of the country's value-added tax regime that would save industry 120 billion yuan ... Credit ceilings for commercial banks are to be abolished in the hope of channelling more capital to small enterprises, rural areas and unspecified 'priority projects' ... The State Council decreed that credit spending must be 'rational' and should 'target spheres that would promote and consolidate the expansion of consumer credit'. Finding ways to get Chinese consumers spending should be a priority. Unleashing domestic demand has been a longstanding goal of Chinese policymakers, but Chinese consumers – with few of their healthcare or retirement needs reliably met either by employers or the state – often prefer to save ... It is an article of faith among many economists – and a view stated earlier this year by prime minister Wen Jiabao – that China needs a growth rate of at least 7 per cent to avoid massive unemployment. The country has been hurt in recent months by softening export markets, depressed domestic property values and stock markets, and declining consumer and investor confidence. Much remains unclear about the implementation of the stimulus plan – or even its size ... The real size of the package may not be as large as the government has described ... [The view has been expressed that] some of the measures announced in the stimulus package appear to have been already introduced or even implemented earlier.

(www.economist.com, 10 November 2008)

Total household debt (including mortgages) amounts to only 13 per cent of GDP, against 100 per cent in America. During America's boom it was easy to get a mortgage for 100 per cent or more of the value of a home, but Chinese buyers have had to put down a minimum deposit of 30 per cent ... Measures to encourage home buying have been introduced: the minimum deposit on a mortgage has been cut from 30 per cent to 20 per cent, mortgage rates have been lowered and transactions taxes on homes reduced ... It has become an article of faith in China that output needs to grow by at least 8 per cent a year to create enough jobs for the millions of rural Chinese moving to cities. Growth of less than 8 per cent, it is claimed, will lead to rising unemployment and social unrest ['China's own leaders believe they need growth of at least 8 per cent a year to avoid painful unemployment' p. 14] ... The original estimated for China's minimum rate of growth, which was made in the mid-1990s, was 7 per cent ... The 4 trillion yuan stimulus package ... is to be spent over the next two years. It amounts to 14 per cent of this year's estimated GDP [2008]. The total increase in spending, if genuine, would surely represent the biggest two-year stimulus (outside wartime) by any government in history ... A reform of the VAT system will allow firms to deduct purchases of fixed assets, reducing companies' tax bills by an estimated ... 4 per cent of 2007 industrial profits ... The budget surplus stands at 1 per cent to 2 per cent of GDP (depending on how you measure it) and total public sector debt at less than 20 per cent of GDP [is] one of the smallest of any large economy ... Some commentators have criticized the package for focusing too much on investment (which is already high as a share of GDP in China) rather than spurring consumption through income tax cuts. But in a country like China, where the saving rate is high and confidence is falling, infrastructure investment is much better at boosting growth than tax cuts or welfare payments, which will probably be saved rather than spent ... [In addition] China plainly needs bridges and railways ... But in any case, in contrast to previous fiscal stimuli in China, this package does include some modest measures to boost consumption, such as raising the incomes of farmers and low-income households. Increased spending on health and education should also help to reduce households' worries about how to pay for these services and so encourage them to save less and spend more ... The yuan ... has barely budged [against the dollar] over the past four months. But since the dollar has strengthened dramatically of late, the yuan has surged against other currencies, such the Euro, sterling and most emerging market currencies. Indeed, in trade-weighted terms, against a basket of currencies, it has risen by 12 per cent over the past six months. Since July 2005, when China scrapped its fixed peg to the dollar, the yuan's trade-weighted value has risen by 20 per cent, by far the biggest appreciation of any large economy.

(*The Economist*, 15 November 2008, pp. 87–9)

The State Council, China's cabinet, authorized \$586 billion of investment on infrastructure and social welfare over the next two years, although it did not say how much would be on new projects not already in the budget ... The announcement reflects mounting anxiety in Beijing that China's economy is cooling much more quickly than expected in the face of weaker international demand and a slowdown in the local property market ... Some economists believe that growth, which was nearly 12 per cent last year [2007], could fall as low as 6 per cent next year [2009] without a substantial fiscal stimulus.

(*FT*, 10 November 2008, p. 6)

There will be significant cuts in company tax, while banks will be allowed to lend more to projects involving rural development and technical innovation ... Dominique Strauss-Kahn (managing director of the IMF): 'It's a huge package. It will have an influence not only on the world economy but also a lot of influence on the Chinese economy itself, and I think it is good for correcting imbalances.'

(www.bbc.co.uk, 10 November 2008)

The authorities ... gave no details about how exactly the money would be spent or how much of it would be genuinely new spending not already in the pipeline ... Arthur Kroeber of Dragonomics in Beijing said the extra investment as a result of the fiscal package might be as little as a third of the headline figure, at about 1,300 billion renminbi. That is still about 2 per cent of GDP each year, but much less than the initial reports suggest.

(*FT*, 11 November 2008, p. 6)

'Parts of the scheme have been announced before so the true size of the new stimulus is not clear' (p. 16). 'Standard Charter calculates spending on infrastructure will increase by about renminbi 250 billion a year in 2009 and 2010, an increase of 25 per cent over 2008 levels' (*FT*, Survey, 24 November 2008, p. 2).

> The stimulus is taking the wrong form. Rather than trying to prop up the Chinese economy as it was, this is an opportunity to turn it into an economy China wants – one where consumption at home has more than a cameo role … The problem for China is not whether it can build enough train lines, ports, pipes and houses to weather a global slowdown. It is that the Chinese model needs a substantial redesign. China's growth to date has been phenomenal, but it was based on exports and investment … In 2005 capital investment made up more than half of China's GDP … China has far too little consumer demand. Whereas household consumption made up more than half of China's GDP in the 1980s, it now contributes little more than a third. In the absence of a domestic security net, Chinese household savings have been as high as a quarter of disposable income. In addition corporate or government savings have soared. China has been saving close to 60 per cent of GDP. This contributed to the global savings imbalance. Some of the deepest roots of the current crisis lie in the plugging of Western deficit with Asian savings … In a country with light household taxes, there is room to do much more with cuts. A cash rebate would be most effective. Public spending on schools and health services would also help. Since fears about paying for health and education keep savings high, this would also encourage consumption. China's leaders were right to propose a fiscal stimulus. But they will be missing a chance for meaningful reform if they focus on pouring concrete and do not look at promoting household spending as well. China's problem is more than a mere global downturn. Its development model is no longer sustainable.
>
> (*FT*, editorial, 11 November 2008, p. 16)

'Prime minister Wen Jiabao said yesterday [10 November]: "Our top task is to maintain steady and relatively fast economic growth"' (*FT*, 11 November 2008, p. 6).

> China admitted yesterday [14 November] that the central government would provide little more than a quarter of Beijing's planned renminbi 4,000 billion fiscal stimulus package. The news has cast fresh doubts on the likely boost to the economy from public spending. Mu Hong, vice chairman of the National Development and Reform Commission, a government planning agency, said Beijing would increase spending by renminbi 1,189 billion ($172 billion) over the next two years – leaving local government, state-owned banks and companies to provide the rest of the new funds … Yi Gang, deputy governor of the People's Bank of China, said the risk of inflation had 'basically vanished'. The focus of policy now was to 'avoid potential deflation … and to ensure stable economic growth'. He said China would 'actively participate' in efforts to counter the global financial crisis, including working with the IMF and making bilateral currency swap arrangements.
>
> (*FT*, 15 November 2008, p. 9)

A giant [\$596 billion] economic stimulus package announced [on 9 November] by China lifted stocks in Asia on Monday [10 November] ... Stocks gained in Europe and Asia ... Investors are hoping that [the package] will help take up some of the slack in the world economy amid signs that many countries, including the United States, have slipped into recession ... [The package] also helped push up the price of oil to over \$63 a barrel, from levels below \$60 hit last Friday [7 November] ... Crude oil futures for December delivery rose \$3.68 to \$64.72 a barrel in New York ... The Shanghai Composite Index soared 7.2 per cent to 1,874.

(www.iht.com, 10 November 2008)

'[On 10 November] the Shanghai Composite Index ended 7.3 higher at 1,874.80' (www.bbc.co.uk, 10 November 2008).

'Stocks on Wall Street moved higher on Monday [10 November] joining those in Europe and Asia a day after the Chinese government announced an economic stimulus plan' (www.iht.com, 10 November 2008).

Global stock markets rallied Monday [10 November] after China unveiled a \$586 billion stimulus package that investors hoped would help the world economy stave off a deep recession. But recession worries trumped China's stimulus in the United States, where stock fell in trading on Monday ... Bad company news fuelled the drop.

(www.cnn.com, 11 November 2008)

'Markets in Asia and Europe slumped across the board Tuesday [11 November] ... following disappointing economic news across Europe and the United States' (www.cnn.com, 11 November 2008).

Asian shares declined Tuesday [11 November] and European shares were expected to follow suit as dismal US economic news offset the euphoria created by the huge Chinese fiscal stimulus package ... Bleak news reinforced fears of a long and deep recession in the United States ... [There was] worrying corporate news from the United States ... Stocks fell Tuesday in Europe and Asia as investors speculated the profit slump will worsen.

(www.iht.com, 11 November 2008)

Inflation in mainland China cooled to the slowest pace in seventeen months ... Consumer prices rose 4 per cent in October from a year earlier, the National Bureau of Statistics said Tuesday [11 November] ... The yuan traded at 6.8284 against the dollar in Shanghai, from 6.8280 before the announcement.

(www.iht.com, 11 November 2008)

'October's inflation rate eased to 4 per cent, down from September's 4.3 per cent' (www.cnn.com, 12 November 2008).

'The key one-year lending rate is 6.66 per cent and the deposit rate is 3.6 per cent' (www.iht.com, 11 November 2008).

China ... is to step up support for manufacturers by raising the export tax rebates paid on more than 3,700 types of goods. The initiative, which will take effect from 1 December, is the third such move since July. It was also decided at a meeting yesterday [12 November] of the State Council, China's cabinet, to scrap duties on some steel products, chemicals and grain exports ... Tax rebates [will be raised] on 3,770 types of export goods – 27.9 per cent of the total.

(*FT*, 13 November 2008, p. 12)

[On 14 and 15 November] leaders of the developed and developing world ... gathered to discuss a fast-moving financial crisis ... [at] an expanded conference of G-20 nations ... The most sought-after country at the gathering ... is likely to be China ... Yi Gang (deputy governor of the Chinese central bank) said on 14 November: 'We will actively participate in rescue activities for this international financial crisis' ... It was one of the clearest indications yet that China stood ready to help the IMF aid countries hit by the global financial crisis.

(*IHT*, 15 November 2008, p. 1)

'The decision to broaden the invitation list was made by President George W. Bush ... With the United States the epicentre and, to many of the attendees, the cause of the crisis, the shift in the power has been accentuated' (www.iht.com, 15 November 2008). 'Collectively, the leaders represented countries that account for 85 per cent of the world's economy' (www.iht.com, 16 November 2008).

'Su Ning (deputy governor of the People's Bank of China) said on 14 November: "[Other countries should focus] less attention on monetary policy and more on fiscal policy"' (www.iht.com, 15 November 2008).

The meeting brought together leading industrial powers, such as the United States, Japan and Germany, and also emerging market countries such as China, India, Argentina, Brazil and others – representing 85 per cent of the world economy ... The G-20 group of countries consists of nineteen leading industrialized and developing countries, as well as the EU.

(www.bbc.co.uk, 16 November 2008)

Meeting on the sidelines of the summit the Japanese, Chinese and South Korean finance ministers said they might expand their mutual currency swap arrangements ... UK prime minister Gordon Brown has taken the lead in urging China and other countries with big cash stockpiles to finance the IMF so that it can make more emergency loans. Yi Gang (deputy governor of the Chinese central bank): 'We will actively participate in rescue activities for this international financial crisis.'

(www.bbc.co.uk, 15 November 2008)

'World leaders at the G-20 financial summit pledged to work together to restore global growth. They said they were determined to work together to achieve "needed reforms" in the world's financial systems' (www.bbc.co.uk, 16 November 2008).

'[The meeting] represents 90 per cent of the world's economy and 75 per cent of the world's population' (www.cnn.com, 15 November 2008).

'The leaders of all these rich and emerging economies ... between them represent almost 90 per cent of global GDP' (www.economist.com, 17 November 2008).

> The leaders agreed Saturday [15 November] to work together to revive their economies ... The group planned its next meeting for 30 April [2009] ... In a five-page communiqué that mixed general principles with specific steps, the G-20 pledged a new effort to bolster supervision of banks and credit-rating agencies, scrutinize executive pay and tighten controls on complex derivatives, which deepened the recent market turmoil ... Despite broad support for economic stimulus, the leaders were not able to agree on a co-ordinated global effort.
>
> (www.iht.com, 16 November 2008)

Extracts from the communiqué (www.independent.co.uk, 16 November 2008):

> We, the leaders of the Group of Twenty, held an initial meeting in Washington on 15 November 2008 amid serious challenges to the world economy and financial markets. We are determined to enhance our co-operation and work together to restore global growth and achieve needed reforms in the world's financial systems ... We will ensure that the IMF, World Bank and other multilateral development banks have sufficient resources to continue playing their role in overcoming the crisis ... We are committed to advancing the reform of the Bretton Woods Institutions so that they can more adequately reflect changing economic weights in the world economy in order to increase their legitimacy and effectiveness. In this respect, emerging and developing economies, including the poorest countries, should have greater voice and representation ... We underscore the critical importance of rejecting protectionism and not turning inwards in times of financial uncertainty. In this regard, within the next twelve months, we will refrain from raising new barriers to investment or to trade in goods and services, imposing new export restrictions, or implementing World Trade Organization (WTO)-inconsistent measures to stimulate exports. Further, we shall strive to reach agreement this year on modalities that lead to a successful conclusion to the WTO's Doha Development Agenda with an ambitious and balanced outcome ... Our work will be guided by a shared belief that market principles, open trade and investment regimes, and effectively regulated financial markets foster the dynamism, innovation and entrepreneurship that are essential for economic growth, employment and poverty reduction ... Policy-makers, regulators and supervisors, in some advanced countries, did not adequately appreciate and address the risks building up in financial markets, keep pace with financial innovation, or take into account the systematic ramifications of domestic

regulatory actions ... We will: continue our vigorous efforts and take whatever further actions are necessary to stabilize the financial system; recognize the importance of monetary policy support, as deemed appropriate to domestic conditions; use fiscal policy measures to stimulate domestic demand to rapid effect, as appropriate, while maintaining a policy framework conducive to fiscal sustainability ... We will implement reforms that will strengthen financial markets and regulatory regimes so as to avoid future crises. Regulation is first and foremost the responsibility of national regulators who constitute the first line of defence against market instability. However, our financial markets are global in scope; therefore, intensified international co-operation among regulators and strengthening of international standards, where necessary, and their consistent implementation is necessary to protect against adverse cross-border, regional and global developments affecting international financial stability ... Supervisors should collaborate to establish supervisory colleges for all major cross-border financial institutions, as part of efforts to strengthen the surveillance of cross-border firms. Major global banks should meet regularly with their supervisory college for comprehensive discussions of the firm's activities and assessment of the risks it faces. Regulators should take all steps necessary to strengthen cross-border crisis management arrangements, including on co-operation and communication with each other and with appropriate authorities, and develop comprehensive contact lists and conduct simulation exercises, as appropriate ... We commit to ... strengthening transparency and accountability ... We will strengthen financial market transparency ... Regulators should develop enhanced guidance to strengthen banks' risk management practices ... Regulators should take steps to ensure that credit-rating agencies meet the highest standards of the international organization of securities regulators and that they avoid conflicts of interest, provide greater disclosure to investors and to issuers, and differentiate ratings for complex products ... We request our finance ministers to formulate additional recommendations ... [including] reviewing and aligning global accounting standards, particularly for complex securities in times of stress ... The key global accounting standards bodies should work intensively toward the objective of creating a single high quality global standard ... We recognize that these reforms will only be successful if grounded in a commitment to free market principles, including the rule of law, respect for private property, open trade and investment, competitive markets, and efficient, effectively regulated financial systems ... Recognizing the necessity to improve financial sector regulation, we must avoid over-regulation that would hamper economic growth and exacerbate the contraction of capital flows, including to developing countries. We underscore the critical importance of rejecting protectionism and not turning inwards in times of financial uncertainty ... Emerging and developing economies should have a greater voice and representation in these [Bretton Woods] institutions.

'Companies in two provinces, Shandong and Hubei, have been told they must seek official consent if they want to lay off more than forty people' (www.bbc. co.uk, 18 November 2008).

[On 20 November] Yin Weimin (minister of human resources and social security) said: '[The global economic slowdown has resulted in a] grim [employment situation in China]. This is particularly the case for labour-intensive small and medium-sized companies. It is extremely important to maintain employment stability.'

(www.bbc.co.uk, 20 November 2008)

Yin Weimin (minister of human resources and social security) said on 20 November: 'Stabilizing employment is the top priority for us right now. The current situation is grim and the impact is still unfolding. Since October our country's employment situation has been affected along with changes in international economic conditions' ... This week two provincial governments announced measures aimed at deterring businesses from laying off workers. Hubei and Shandong said companies trying to lay off more than forty staff would need prior approval from the local authorities.

(*FT*, 21 November 2008)

The nation's minister of human resources and social security ... Yin Weimin ... said Thursday [20 November] ... China's job outlook is 'grim' and the global financial crisis could cause more layoffs and more labour unrest until the country's economic stimulus kicks in next year [2009] ... Xinhua said Yin has predicted unemployment will rise in the first quarter of 2009. After that, he said, the stimulus package and other steps China has taken to boost the financial sector should boost employment, according to Xinhua.

(www.cnn.com, 21 November 2008)

Projects planned by provincial governments in China will add an additional $1.46 trillion to the value of the Chinese economic stimulus package, state television said Sunday [23 November]. The spending, worth 10 trillion yuan, comes on top of the 4 trillion yuan stimulus package that the national government announced earlier this month ... Central China Television: 'Within the last week provincial governments have announced accompanying stimulus programmes amounting to 10 trillion yuan ... The spending plans will emphasize rural infrastructure' ... Among the largest investment plans are that of Yunnan province at 3 trillion yuan and Guangdong at 2.3 trillion yuan ... The central government has allocated 4.8 billion yuan to building rural health care, particularly hospitals and clinics, Xinhua said Sunday, as part of its commitment to increase spending on rural medical care in 2008. Still, the funding mechanism for many of the announced projects is unclear, while reported numbers are often in flux. Officials in Sichuan province said Friday [21 November] that most of the estimated 3 trillion yuan needed for the three-year reconstruction of towns devastated by a 12 May earthquake would come from non-government sources like banks and businesses. The central government would provide 200 billion yuan and the provincial government 300 billion yuan.

(www.iht.com, 23 November 2008)

Governments of provinces have proposed more than $1.4 trillion in spending on roads and other projects after the central government announced a huge national stimulus package this month to shield China from a global slowdown, state television reported Sunday [23 November]. The central government's announcement electrified investors ... But as details were released it became clear that the programme, whose value was put at 4 trillion yuan ($586 billion) included less new spending than initially thought. Similar concerns are already being raised about the provincial governments' proposals. The key to the success of the national package will be its ability to reassure consumers, which makes its emotional impact as important as its actual size and gives communist leaders an incentive to embellish figures. On Sunday China Central Television [CCTV] said plans announced during the past week by provincial governments totalled 10 trillion yuan. But it gave few details and no indication how much of that figure represents new spending, as opposed to plans announced earlier. The CCTV report said: 'Within a week the governments of various provinces announced massive-scale investment blueprints. Based on a rough calculation the current total investment by all the provinces and cities has already exceeded 10 trillion yuan' ... The biggest proposal came from Yunnan province, which plans to invest 3 trillion yuan over the next five years, CCTV said. Guangdong province proposed 2.3 trillion yuan in investments ... But *The 21st Century Business Herald*, a Chinese business newspaper, said few investments announced by the provinces were new. It said most were either already under construction, had been under discussion for some time or had been planned but not begun because of a lack of money. Provinces may have revived some of those defunct projects in the hope that the difficult financial times would persuade Beijing to finance them ... Analysts have suggested that Beijing filled its stimulus programme with as many projects as possible, including many already under way, to produce a big yuan figure that would encourage consumers and companies to spend. The programme, announced on 9 November, was aimed at increasing domestic consumer spending to reduce Chinese reliance on the cooling global export market. Analysts have said that the package includes projects already covered by its five-year plan that runs through 2010 ... [But] J.P. Morgan Chase says it still calls for about 1.6 trillion yuan in spending on top of previously announced projects. Beijing has said it will provide 1.8 trillion yuan of the stimulus spending, while local governments will supply the rest. On Sunday [23 November] prime minister Wen Jiabao called for companies to bolster confidence and adapt to market changes to weather the global crisis.

(www.iht.com, 23 November 2008)

[There was no indication in the state television] report how much of the provincial spending, if any, was new, or whether officials were announcing earlier plans in an effort to reassure the public and investors that the government was taking action ... Beijing puts the total value of its plan at 4 trillion yuan ($586 billion), but only 1.2 trillion yuan is coming from the central government. The rest is expected to come from local governments and state companies. The plan also includes previously announced projects ... CCTV gave no indication of whether the provinces would get financial support from the central government. But according to a report Friday [21 November] by *The 21st Century Business Herald*, a major Chinese business newspaper, much of the proposed provincial spending is still awaiting approval by Beijing. The newspaper said few investments announced by the provinces were new. Most are either already under construction, have been under discussion for some time or had been planned but not begun due to lack of money, it said.

(www.cnn.com, 23 November 2008)

'Local governments are already facing their own cash problems because of declining land [use] sales, one of their main sources of finance, and are not allowed to issue debt to fund investment' (*FT*, Survey, 24 November 2008, p. 2) 'Around 30 per cent of bank credit is either to housebuyers or property developers' (p. 4).

Leaders from Asia-Pacific countries ... [at an] Asia-Pacific Economic Co-operation (Apec) summit ... have pledged not to respond to the global financial crisis by raising trade barriers over the next year ... Apec countries account for half the world's economic activity. Their joint statement: 'There is a risk that slower world economic growth could lead to calls for protectionist measures which would only exacerbate the current economic situation ... We strongly support the Washington Declaration and will refrain within the next twelve months from raising new barriers to investment or to trade in goods and services [and from] imposing new export restrictions.'

(www.bbc.co.uk, 23 November 2008)

Leaders of nations around the Pacific Rim promised to work together to combat the global economic crisis and pledged to refrain from forming new barriers to trade and investment. Leaders of the twenty-one-nation Asia-Pacific Economic Co-operation group (Apec), which includes the United States, China and Japan, also called for improved corporate governance and supported efforts to thaw frozen credit markets. The group said: 'We have already taken urgent and extraordinary steps to stabilize our financial sectors and strengthen economic growth and promote investment and consumption. We will continue to take such steps and work closely, in a co-ordinated and comprehensive manner, to implement future actions' ... Apec members also said their governments were committed to reaching an agreement on the Doha round of WTO negotiations next month [December]. The talks began in 2001 and negotiations have failed year after year to agreeing on even the outlines of a deal ... The leaders called for a tightening of standards on corporate governance and risk management in the financial industry.

(www.iht.com, 23 November 2008)

At 5.5 per cent of all loans at the end of September, non-performers still look high. But the ratio, down from 6.2 per cent at the start of 2008, would be much lower if the state had completed a bailout of Agricultural Bank of China ... With banks requiring minimum down payments of 20 per cent, only 1 per cent of home mortgages is non-performing ... Banks have been scaling back lending to developers, which account for about 7 per cent of all bank loans. Mortgages make up a further 12 per cent of the loan book. In the United States about half of bank loans are property related.

(*IHT*, 25 November 2008, p. 11)

'Last week banking regulators began warning about the risk that bad loans would accumulate' (*IHT*, 26 November 2008, p. 15).

The World Bank cut its 2009 growth forecast for China on Tuesday [25 November], projecting the slowest pace of expansion since 1990 ... The bank lowered its outlook for 2009 GDP growth to 7.5 per cent from 9.2 per cent, a forecast it had made in June before the international financial crisis took a serious turn for the worse. It already expected growth this year [2008] to moderate to 9.4 per cent, the first single-digit pace of expansion since 2002, from 11.9 per cent in 2007 ... If the bank's forecast proves to be correct, it would be China's weakest GDP growth since 1990, when the economy expanded just 3.8 per cent; growth in 1999 was 7.6 per cent ... [The World Bank] said China is going to face a difficult coming six months ... Heavy industries, such as steel and cement, had already slowed remarkably ... The bank expected consumer prices to rise just 2.0 per cent next year [2009] after a 6.5 per cent increase in 2008 ... The bank expected government-influenced spending to account for more than half of next year's growth. Net export, by contrast, are likely to lop 1 percentage point off GDP growth as overall imports substantially outpace exports ... It would be the first time in many years that net external trade has subtracted from growth, the report said.

(www.iht.com, 25 November 2008)

The country has been relatively unaffected by the global crisis so far because its banks are relatively healthy and exports are strong, but 'we will see that impact intensify in 2009' [the World Bank said] ... Beijing's stimulus plan announced on 9 November should help shield China from the global downturn by buoying growth and employment ... [The World Bank said] Beijing is talking with the World Bank about providing financing for loans to other developing countries ... directly or indirectly.

(www.cnn.com, 25 November 2008)

'Until recently China had largely avoided the effects of the global crisis because its financial system is insulated from the rest of the world' (www.bbc. co.uk, 25 November 2008).

> The World Bank said Beijing should accelerate steps to rebalance the economy away from exports and investment towards more domestic consumption ... [The World Bank said]: 'The impact of the international financial and economic turmoil on China's economy has been manageable so far but is expected to intensify. Prospects are for a sharp reduction in export growth' ... Even the reduced growth rate next year [2009] would rely heavily on higher public spending, the bank said ... While government spending contributed 1.5 percentage points of growth last year [2007], it would add 4 percentage points in 2009 ... The bank said net exports were likely to reduce the growth rate by one percentage point in 2009.
>
> (*FT*, 26 November 2008, p. 8)

'Economists are forecasting that after growing nearly 12 per cent last year [2007], growth could slow to a 5.5 per cent annualized rate in the fourth quarter of this year [2008]' (*IHT*, 26 November 2008, p. 15).

> The People's Bank of China announced late Wednesday [26 November] that it was lowering by 1.08 percentage points the one-year lending rate and deposit rates that banks are allowed to charge, effective Thursday [27 November]. The central bank had already cut the benchmark rate three times since 16 September and the benchmark deposit rate twice, by 0.27 percentage points each time. The one-year lending rate is important in China because banks use it to calculate other interest rates, based on the maturity of the loan and the creditworthiness of the borrower. The latest reduction was the largest since the central bank cut the rate by 1.44 points in October 1997, at the height of the Asian financial crisis ... The bank also reduced the percentage of assets that large banks must hold as reserves by one percentage point, and cut the reserve requirement by 2 percentage points for smaller banks ... To give banks an extra incentive to lend money instead of hoarding reserves, the central bank also lowered by 0.27 percentage points the interest rates that it pays banks for reserves deposited with it.
>
> (www.iht.com, 26 November 2008)

'The rate cut, to 5.58 per cent for loans and 2.52 per cent for deposits, was the fourth reduction since September' (*FT*, 27 November 2008, p. 6).

'The rate will fall to 5.58 per cent on a one-year loan' (www.thetimes.co.uk, 26 November 2008).

> The downturn in the economy accelerated over the past month and could lead to high unemployment and social unrest, the country's top economic planner warned yesterday [27 November]. Zhang Ping, chairman of the National Development and Reform Commission, said the government needed to take

'forceful' measures to limit the slowdown in the economy ... Mr Zhang gave no fresh details about economic activity over the past month. Industrial production grew by 8.2 per cent in October, the lowest level in seven years ... Mr Zhang provided the first breakdown of how the money would be spent, indicating that nearly three-quarters of the renminbi 4,000 billion ($596 billion) investment over two years would go to infrastructure. He said that renminbi 1,800 billion would be spent on railways, roads and airports, with a further renminbi 1,000 billion on disaster reconstruction, especially in the region of Sichuan province, hit by an earthquake in May. About renminbi 370 billion would be spent on rural development and renminbi 40 billion on health and education. Mr Zhang said that the extra spending would add about 1 percentage point to economic growth next year [2009], less than most private sector economists had forecast. He added that there were no plans to allow local governments to issue bonds to pay for new investments.

(*FT*, 28 November 2008, p. 7)

President Hu Jintao ... [gave a] warning at a Saturday [29 November] meeting of the Politburo, the party's twenty-five-member inner council: 'In this coming period we will starkly confront the effects of the sustained deepening of the international financial crisis and pressure as global economic growth clearly shows ... [The slowdown of growth is] clearly reducing external demand and exerting pressure to steadily weaken our country's traditional competitive advantages ... Whether we can turn this pressure into momentum, turn challenges into opportunities, and maintain steady and relatively fast economic development is a test of our party's capacity to govern ... Under current conditions we must keep an even tighter focus on economic development ... China is under growing tension from its large population, limited resources and environmental problems, and needs faster reform of its economic growth pattern to achieve sustainable development'... Last week a state research institute forecast that annual economic growth will slow to 8 per cent this quarter from 9 per cent in the third quarter.

(www.iht.com, 30 November 2008, and 1 December 2008)

China lifted its controls on food prices Monday [1 December], the latest sign of how drastically priorities have shifted from earlier this year, when the country was focused on fighting inflation ... Companies would now be free to decide that for themselves, the National Development and Reform Commission said in a statement ... Under the controls manufacturers had to apply for approval for any substantial price increases. Beijing will still keep an eye on prices, however, and work to ensure that no one manipulates them ... 'We must work further on how to address abnormal price movement,' the commission said ... Consumer inflation fell to 4 per cent in October, down from a twelve-month high of 8.7 per cent in February. Food prices, which make up a third of the consumer price index, rose 8.5 per cent in October, down from a 23.3 per cent increase in February ... The easing of food price controls came the same day that data showed that China's manufacturing industry had slumped in November as new orders, especially from abroad, tumbled ... Indexes released Monday, based on two surveys of hundreds of executives across China, plumbed record lows ... The readings Monday were the weakest since the surveys began in 2004 and 2005.

(www.iht.com, 1 December 2008; *IHT*, 2 December 2008, p. 20)

'On Monday [1 December] the government introduced a subsidy in fourteen provinces that will make it cheaper for people to buy cellphones, washing machines and flat-screen televisions' (*IHT*, 3 November 2008, p. 12).

China urged the United States on Thursday [4 December] to spare no effort to stabilize its economy and financial markets to help avert a global recession. Speaking at the start of a fifth meeting of the cabinet-level 'strategic economic dialogue' between the United States and China, the deputy prime minister, Wang Qishan, said Beijing was doing its part by pursuing fast growth ... Zhou Xiaochuan (central bank governor): 'Over-consumption and a high reliance on credit is the cause of the US financial crisis. As the largest and most important economy in the world, the United States should take the initiative to adjust its policies, raise its savings ratio appropriately and reduce its trade and fiscal deficits.'

(www.iht.com, 4 December 2008)

The United States and China will provide $20 billion in loans to finance trade by developing countries amid a global crisis that has battered credit markets ... In a closing statement after the fifth round of the cabinet-level Sino-American 'strategic economic dialogue' US Treasury Secretary Henry Paulson said Friday [5 December] that the export–import banks of China and the United States had made an additional $20 billion for trade finance available, particularly for credit-worthy importers in developing countries. The US Export–Import Bank will provide $12 billion and the Export–Import Bank of China will provide $8 billion to help finance the export of more US and Chinese goods ... Paulson: 'Both nations reiterated the importance of completing a successful Doha round and meaningful progress toward that goal by the end of this year [2008] ... As in the past we discussed the importance of domestic-led growth, and the importance of a market-determined currency in promoting balance growth in China and that will contribute to a healthy global economy' ... [Paulson was] referring to the WTO's long-running Doha round of market-opening talks.

(www.iht.com, 5 December 2008)

[There is] a pending nationwide expansion of a successful pilot programme offering a 13 per cent tax break to rural buyers of electrical appliances ... Health care and education ... are the two largest out-of-pocket expenses for most Chinese, yet only 1 per cent of China's new 4 trillion yuan, or $586 billion, stimulus plan is earmarked for the two sectors.

(www.iht.com, 8 December 2008; *IHT*, 9 December 2008, p. 13)

Exports declined in November from the same period a year ago for the first time since 2001 ... Exports dropped by 2.2 per cent, while imports shrank by a massive 17.9 per cent ... China reported a record monthly trade surplus of $40.1 billion.

(www.bbc.co.uk, 10 December 2008)

'Exports dropped 2.2 per cent in November from a year earlier ... a stunning reversal from the 19.2 per cent growth seen as recently as October' (www.iht.com, 10 December 2008).

On the shelves of Chinese shops is the usual assortment of toys, clothing, appliances and cookware. But over the past month the quality of many of the goods on offer has improved. In part this is because scandals over toxic paint and poisoned milk have brought closer scrutiny from inspectors ... But it is also partly because of falling demand for Chinese goods from America, Europe and the Middle East, which has given China's manufacturers and local governments a big incentive to work around the country's formidable export-promotion policies and to sell at home ... Exports fell by a startling 2.2 per cent in November, compared with a year earlier. Analysts had expected an increase of around 15 per cent; it was the first fall in exports for seven years. The news followed a government survey, released on 1 December, that showed a precipitous decline in the fortunes of export manufacturers, confirming lots of anecdotal evidence. Every week brings fresh reports of factory closings, particularly in the industrial belt around the Pearl River delta in southern China. Unpaid workers have been staging violent protests ... China encourages the import of industrial commodities, such as oil, base metals and even quality fabrics and industrial machinery – provided goods made with them are sent abroad. Accordingly, a tax is imposed on imports, and is then mostly reimbursed when finished goods are exported. (Products brought into special zones devoted to manufacturing for markers abroad avoid the tax altogether.) As a result of pressure from China's trading partners, these tax rebates on exports have been contracting. But in November a new stimulus plan was announced that increased the rebates on more than 3,000 items.

(*The Economist*, 13 December 2008, p. 79)

The credit crunch turned into a full-blown financial crisis in September when Lehman Brothers, one of Wall Street's big investment banks, declared bankruptcy and American officials seized control of American International Group [AIG] to prevent the giant insurer's collapse. As panic spread governments engineered the rescue of distressed banks or took them over directly. By the end of the month the remaining big Wall Street houses had either been absorbed by others or become bank holding companies.

(*The Economist*, 20 December 2008, p. 13)

'Labour disputes almost doubled in the first ten months of 2008' (www.economist.com, 10 December 2008).

'Shenzhen officials hope the crisis might also catalyse a welcome transformation ... to upgrade the industrial structure' (*FT*, 12 December 2008, p. 7).

'Top leaders ended a three-day meeting Wednesday night [10 December] promising to increase public spending and cut taxes, but gave no details' (www. iht.com, 10 December 2008).

China aims to increase its money supply by 17 per cent in 2009, according to the State Council, part of a broad blueprint for easing financial conditions ... The directive by the State Council, China's cabinet, was dated 8 December but posted on the central government's website late Saturday [13 December] ... It follows a pledge by leaders last week to take measures to stimulate domestic demand ... The new target for growth in the broad M2 measure of money supply is a substantial increase from the 15 per cent pace in the year to October. Among other measures to revive growth, the cabinet said the central bank would stop issuing three-year bills and reduce its issuance of one-year and three-month bills, providing more liquidity in the financial system. The cabinet said: '[the steps are intended to] diligently implement the active fiscal policy and appropriately loose monetary policy and expand the support of the financial sector, so as to promote stable, rapid economic growth' ... The thirty-point directive mandated a range of policy changes aimed at making it easier for companies and investment projects to obtain the credit they need, though most of them will have to be followed up with more specific implementation rules. The cabinet said it would give banks more flexibility on the minimum allowable lending rates they could charge, and it could loosen other rules to give them more leeway in making lending decisions. Beijing currently maintains a floor on lending rates and a ceiling on deposit rates. The State Council called on banks to provide more credit to companies with sound fundamentals and to offer refinancing to such companies if they hit short-term cash flow problems. It also told them to lend more in support on investment projects in line with the government's priorities, like high technology, environmental technology and rural development, while limiting their loans to industries like the processing trade, which Beijing has been trying to discourage. The cabinet said: 'Banks must do a good job of balancing their roles in boosting economic growth with that of guarding themselves against risks; they should not be blindly reluctant to lend during an economic downturn' ... Other measures by the State Council included [the following] ... It reiterated its longstanding commitment to making the yuan's exchange value more flexible while keeping it 'basically stable at a reasonable, balanced level'. It pledged a series of capital market innovations, including new types of steel and grain futures and an expanded corporate bond market, especially for companies involved in key infrastructure projects. It said it would approve Nasdaq-style stock markets for start-up companies when appropriate and develop real estate investment trusts on a pilot basis. The cabinet said the government would closely monitor global and domestic financial conditions and offer emergency liquidity support if needed.

(www.iht.com, 14 December 2008; *IHT*, 15 December 2008, p. 14)

China urged its troubled state-owned airlines on Wednesday [10 December] to cancel or defer new aircraft purchases amid the global economic turmoil – a move that could hurt American and European aircraft makers. The Civil Aviation Administration of China said that it also encouraged carriers to retire old aircraft and would not approve new airlines before 2010 ... Last month [November] China started to provide financial aid for its airlines hit badly by weak air traffic demand and hefty losses in fuel price hedging [global oil prices having fallen] ... Chinese airlines have been battered – first by high fuel prices and later by low demand.

(www.iht.com, 10 December 2008; *IHT*, 11 December 2008, p. 12)

'China's consumer price inflation fell to a twenty-two-month low of 2.4 per cent in November ... Economists had expected inflation to moderate to 3.0 per cent from 4.0 per cent in the year to October' (www.ft.com, 11 December 2008). 'Consumer price inflation, running at a twelve-year high in February, receded to 2.4 per cent in November' (www.iht.com, 22 December 2008).

The leaders of China, Japan and South Korea held their nations' first three-way summit Saturday [13 December] in a meeting [held in Japan] intended to overcome political animosities that instead focused on a joint Asian response to the global economic crisis ... The leaders ... promised new stimulus spending to lift domestic demand and pick up the slack in global growth left by the US slowdown. Japan and China also agreed to open lines of foreign currency credit to South Korea, whose economy has been hit hardest by the crisis ... The summit meeting was originally planned months ago, before the turmoil in financial markets began in September, with the vague goals of building good will and establishing political dialogue. The nations' leaders have held three-way meetings in the past, but only on the sidelines of larger international conferences ... The leaders agreed to increase dialogue by holding three-way summits on a regular basis. The statement said the nations will hold a second summit meeting next year [2009] in China, and a third in South Korea ... Prime minister Taro Aso of Japan: 'It is the first time historically for the three countries to hold an independent summit. It is epoch-making progress for the leaders of the three countries to hold meetings regularly and strengthen ties' ... Among the summit's few concrete results were agreements by Japan and China to lend foreign currency to South Korea to shore up the won, which has dropped by one-third against the dollar since the current crisis began. The agreements will expand so-called currency swap deals in which the South Korean central bank is allowed to borrow foreign currency from the other nations' central bank using won as collateral. Tokyo promised to make available the equivalent of $20 billion, while Beijing pledged $26 billion. Seoul has sought the agreements after depleting its foreign currency reserves trying to defend the won.

(www.iht.com, 13 December 2008; *IHT*, 15 December 2008, p. 14)

'Growth in industrial production slowed to 5.4 per cent in November [compared with November 2007] from 8.2 per cent in October [compared with October 2007]. This was well below what analysts had expected' (*IHT*, 16 December 2008, p. 17).

The IMF could cut its forecast for Chinese 2009 economic growth to around 5 per cent in its next revision ... said the managing director, Dominique Strauss-Kahn [on 15 December], In its previous forecast, released in November, the IMF had predicted that China's growth would fall to 8.5 per cent in 2009 from 9.7 per cent this year [2008]. November's forecast for 2009 was 0.8 percentage points lower than the IMF's previous forecast.

(*IHT*, 16 December 2008, p. 14)

'Dominique Strauss-Kahn, the managing director of the IMF, said [on 15 December] that next year [2009] "China will probably grow at 5 per cent or 6 per cent"' (*FT*, 16 November 2008, p. 5).

China yesterday [17 December] announced new measures to stimulate the domestic property market ... Beijing said it would lower taxes, make it easier for property developers to obtain credit and reduce the lock-up period for home sales during which owners are unable to sell without paying stiff taxes ... The State Council said it would shorten to two years the lock-up period during which homeowners are subject to a business tax if they resell their homes ... The government called on lenders to increase loans to developers of low-priced housing ... The National Development and Reform Commission said in a separate statement that it would offer renminbi 10 billion of subsidies. The People's Bank of China said that developers building low-rent housing could enjoy a 10 per cent discount on lending rates, effective from January [2009]. Beijing will allow some local governments, on a trial basis, to tap housing funds to build more modest homes.

(*FT*, 18 December 2008, p. 7)

'President Hu Jintao praised the achievements made by his country during thirty years of reforms ... One recent Chinese news report quoted an official as saying more than 10 million migrant workers have lost their jobs' (www.bbc.co.uk, 18 December 2008).

President Hu Jintao ... has vowed to continue the economic reforms ... Speaking on the thirtieth anniversary of China's decision to open itself up to the outside world, President Hu Jintao told a crowd of 6,000 at Beijing's Great Hall of the People: 'Standing still and regressing will lead only to a dead end' ... The first policies were approved on 18 December 1978. Hu said: 'Reform and opening up are the fundamental causes of all achievements and progress we have made ... [Deng Xiaoping's vision three decades ago was] completely correct' ... Hu warned the Chinese people not to grow complacent, especially in the midst of the global economic crisis. He said China must continue to concentrate on economic development and diversification.

(www.cnn.com, 18 December 2008)

President Hu Jintao: 'We must be clearly aware that development is of over-riding importance and stability is our overriding task. If there is no stability, then nothing can be achieved, and what achievements we have made will be lost ... [China has] achieved positive results in responding to the international financial crisis. We must earnestly implement various measures to further boost domestic demand and promote economic growth, properly address the global financial crisis and other risks from the international economic world and do our best to keep relatively fast and stable growth' ... The World Bank estimates China's plans to cut taxes and boost spending on infrastructure will add up to 3 percentage points of GDP in genuine fiscal stimulus.

(FT, 19 December 2008, p. 8)

'Factory output expanded by just 5.4 per cent in the year to November, the weakest pace for a non-holiday month on record, and its exports declined for the first time in more than seven years' (www.iht.com, 22 December 2008).

The government plans to spend 4 trillion yuan ... If just 40 per cent of that is new money, it should lift GDP growth by about 3 percentage points in 2008 and 2009 ... Unemployment is rising. Urban joblessness is already at 9.4 per cent, according to the Chinese Academy of Social Sciences. The real figure may be higher, and the official national unemployment figure of 4 per cent is almost certainly too low. Export sectors alone account for 50 million employers, and about 4 million have been laid off this year [2008].

(www.iht.com, 24 December 2008)

Prime minister Wen Jiabao told students at the Beijing University of Astro-nautics at the weekend: 'We have made finding jobs for university students our top priority and will come out with some measures to make sure all graduates have somewhere constructive to direct their energy' ... Mr Wen said the government was also extremely concerned about migrant workers who had been made redundant. By the end of November [2008] 10 million migrant workers had lost their jobs nationwide and 4.85 million of those had returned home, according to government figures. A survey last week by a government think-tank estimated the number of recent graduates who have been unable to find work at 1.5 million. Tertiary institutions are expected to churn out another 6.5 million graduates next year [2009] ... The State Council, China's highest governing body, issued a decree to local governments over the weekend ordering them to create jobs for migrant workers who had returned to their home towns.

(FT, 22 December 2008, p. 1)

The government ... has ordered all necessary steps to 'ensure 8 per cent growth' next year ... The government estimates more than 10 million migrants have lost their jobs so far, while 6.5 million university students will enter the work force next year. But even if China achieves 8 per cent growth, it will only be able to create a maximum of 9 million jobs next year, prime minister Wen Jiabao said at the weekend. He also said Beijing was closely watching the effects of the crisis and would 'redouble efforts' to boost growth if current measures were not adequate.

(*FT*, 23 December 2008, p. 6)

'More than 6 million students will try to enter China's work force during 2009, half a million more than last year [2007]' (www.bbc.co.uk, 22 December 2008).

China cut interest rates for the fifth time in three months yesterday [22 December] ... The benchmark one-year lending rate was cut by 27 basis points to 5.31 per cent, while the one-year deposit rate was lowered by the same amount to 2.25 per cent. The People's Bank of China also reduced the amount of money banks must hold in reserve by cutting the required reserve ratio by 50 basis points, a move that analysts say will release $43.8 billion for the banks to lend ... China's foreign exchange reserves ... apparently fell in October for the first time in five years, according to an official from the State Administration of Foreign Exchange.

(*FT*, 23 December 2008, p. 6)

China's central bank cut interest rates for the fifth time in four months ... The one-year lending rate will fall by 0.27 percentage points to 2.25 per cent, effective Tuesday [23 December] ... The reduction came just four weeks after China's biggest rate cut in eleven years.

(*IHT*, 23 December 2008, p. 14)

The central bank trimmed interest rates Monday [22 December] for the fifth time since mid-September ... though the cut was smaller than many analysts had expected. The People's Bank of China cut the one-year lending rate by 27 basis points, to 5.31 per cent, and the deposit rate also by 27 basis points, to 2.25 per cent – far smaller than its last move in late November, when it cut rates by 1.08 percentage points. A basis point is one-hundredth of a percentage point. Analysts said the move ... looked timid compared with action taken by the [US] Federal Reserve and the Bank of Japan in cutting rates to almost zero last week ... The Chinese central bank also lowered the amount of money that commercial lenders must keep on deposit with it, cutting their required reserve ratio by half a percentage point.

(www.iht.com, 22 December 2008)

China has said it is to allow some trade with its neighbours to be settled with its currency, the yuan. The pilot scheme was announced in a package of measures designed to help exporters hit by the global downturn. It means if the two parties to a trade have yuan available, they need not enter world exchange markets to pay. Most of China's foreign trade is settled in US dollars or the Euro, leaving exporters vulnerable to exchange rate fluctuations ... Officials did not say when the trial scheme would start. When it does the yuan could be used to settle trade between parts of eastern China (Guangdong and the Yangtze River delta) and the territories of Hong Kong and Macao, and between south-west China (Guangxi and Yunnan) and the Asean group of countries (Brunei, Cambodia, Indonesia, Laos, Malaysia, the Philippines, Singapore, Thailand and Vietnam). Analysts told the Chinese media that the yuan was already being used in some South-east Asian countries and that China was happy to see such use extended. They also agreed that the measure was intended to help companies cope with the global financial meltdown, even though buying and selling the currency require the presentation of legitimate trade documents to banks. The latest measure follows Beijing's announcement earlier this month [December] of a thirty-point directive in which it vowed to 'support the development of yuan business in Hong Kong' and expand the use of the currency to settle trade with neighbouring countries ... Central bank governor Zhou Xiaochuan ... said that Guanxi, a province in southern China, had already been settling trade with Vietnam in yuan for some time. A document released after a meeting of China's State Council on Wednesday [24 December] announced more measures to stimulate domestic consumption. These include subsidies to rural households for the purchase of household appliances and other goods, and the setting up of new stores and distribution centres in rural areas. The document called for the renovation of urban food markets, the provision of more variety of goods for sale, the setting up of more second-hand markets, incentives for distribution companies to merge and consolidate, and support of small and medium-sized enterprises. The state news agency Xinhua said the government intended to raise export tax rebates for high technology products, to encourage foreign investment, extend customs and inspection services, lower inspection fees for exports and strengthen trade relations in emerging markets.

(www.bbc.co.uk, 25 December 2008)

The exports of ... some of the smaller [Asian] economies, such as Singapore and Hong Kong ... amount to 20 per cent to 30 per cent of GDP – compared with only 8 per cent for China ... China accounted for about one-third of global growth in 2008 ... Chinese manufacturing wages are less than 10 per cent of those in America.

(www.economist.com, 26 December 2008)

Officials estimate that more than 10 million migrant labourers have already returned to the countryside ... The social security ministry says 10 per cent of all migrants have already gone back to the countryside ... Over the past three decades about 130 million people ... known as the 'floating population' ... have left the countryside for the ... cities ... Unveiling its rural policy for next year [2009] the government said Sunday [28 December] that it would encourage unemployed people who return home to start their own businesses. Officials in the Sichuan city of Chongqing and Henan province, two big sources of migrants, have already pledged to lend seed money.

(www.iht.com, 30 December 2008; *IHT*, 31 December 2008, p. 13)

In the past two weeks Chinese officials have announced a series of measures to help exporters. State banks are being directed to lend more to them, particularly to small and midsize exporters. Government research funds are being set up ... Particularly noteworthy have been the government's steps to help labour-intensive sectors like garment production, one of the industries China has been trying to get away from in an effort to climb the ladder of economic development, moving to more skilled work that pays higher wages. But now China has become reluctant to yield the bottom rungs of the ladder to countries with even lower wages, like Vietnam, Indonesia and Bangladesh. China has been restoring export tax rebates for its textile sector, for instance, which it had been phasing out ... Municipal governments have also stopped raising the minimum wage, which had doubled over the last two years in some cities, reaching a peak of $146 a month in Shenzhen. Li Yizhong (minister of industry and information technology on 19 December): 'China will resort to tariff and trade policies to facilitate export of labour-intensive and core technology-supported industries' ... American quotas on the import of a wide range of Chinese garments expired on Thursday [1 January 2009]. Even before the Chinese began announcing their latest programmes for exporters, the United States filed a legal challenge on 19 December [2008] at the WTO, accusing China of having already provided illegal subsidies to exporters in a long list of industries as part of a programme of trying to build recognizable export brands. China denied on 23 December that there were any illegal subsidies, saying that many countries tried to help exporters and that its actions were no different ... Shifting toward a greater reliance on domestic demand is not easy. Chinese households have one of the world's highest savings rates ... Important bureaucratic obstacles also exist. Chinese factories are allowed to import equipment while paying little or no duty provided that the equipment will only be used to produce goods for export; obtaining approval to switch the same equipment to making goods for the domestic market can take two years and requires the payment of much of the import duties that were previously avoided, a payment that many factories cannot afford. China's measures to help exporters are starting to cause concern in other Asian countries that compete with it, and raises the risk of a protectionist backlash against China.

(www.iht.com, 1 January 2009; *IHT*, 2 January 2009, pp. 11, 14)

'The downturn has been devastating to China's toy manufacturing hub, Guangdong province. Customs statistics showed that 1,554 toy companies were exporting at the end of September 2008 – a drop of 3,266 from 2007' (www.cnn.com, 9 January 2009).

'Prime minister Wen Jiabao ... said the auto industry's current difficulties concerned him the most because the industry had a long supply chain' (*IHT*, 8 January 2009, p. 12).

'Fewer than one in ten cars is sold on credit in China' (*FT*, 2 January 2009, p. 17).

> The urban registered jobless rate stood at 4.0 per cent at the end of September [2008], not counting migrant workers. The real unemployment is closer to 9.4 per cent, the social science academy estimates ... The Chinese Academy of Social Science [is] a top government think-tank.
>
> (*IHT*, 8 January 2009, p. 12)

> Officials in Beijing are determined to 'protect eight', shorthand for the goal of achieving 8 per cent growth this year [2009]. That is the minimum rate deemed necessary to maintain social stability and provide jobs for the 15 million-plus people who enter the job market every year.
>
> (www.iht.com, 5 January 2009)

> China is pulling out all the stops to keep the economy growing by at least 8 per cent, a pace considered necessary to absorb the millions of migrant workers and graduates who hit the job market every year. But with all its attention focused on the vigorous 'defence of the eight', Beijing risks losing sight of its ultimate goal – creating enough jobs to preserve social peace – and may end up engineering a jobless recovery. It is not only the rate of growth that is important, but also its sources. Expansion led by capital-intensive industries will not be as effective as one driven by more labour-intensive sectors. Statistics of the past three months show that with the focus on investment, rise of heavy industries and China's wish to move up the value chain, more and more economic growth has been needed to create the same number of jobs. The latest efforts to shield the economy from the global financial crisis, including a nearly $600 billion stimulus, also focus on capital-heavy infrastructure projects ... Most migrant workers are employed by small private exporters ... Traditionally, China's development policies have favoured capital-intensive industries like autos, steel and machinery, which are seen as crucial to modernization and sustained economic growth. In recent years the authorities have tried to move away from low value-added light industries, even though they have played a big part in the boom of the past three decades and have the potential to create more jobs, especially for unskilled workers. China reckons it needs to add about 9 million jobs every year – about 3 per cent of its urban work force – for the estimated 8.4 million villagers moving to the cities every year. Since the early 1990s, however, it has met the goal only when growth has exceeded 10 per cent. And over the years the link between growth and jobs has weakened. In the 1980s each 1 per cent increase in GDP led to a rise of 0.3 per cent in employment. This has dropped to a mere 0.1 per cent jobs gain ... Two World Bank economists, Jianwu He and Louis Kuijs, have suggested that China should shift its focus to the services sector from industry and that it should let consumption, instead of investment and exports, play a bigger role in the economy.
>
> (*IHT*, 8 January 2009, p. 12)

China's government is using the collapse in commodity prices to further its domestic agenda, with support for stricken sectors tailored to speed up plans to overhaul operations rather than to rescue ailing companies or prop up prices ... China's policy-makers ... are favouring the strongest in each industry as part of a drive toward consolidation [e.g. in steel-making], and at the same time using low prices as a chance to stock up on supplies [such as sugar, rubber, oil, corn and industrial metals] ... The government [for example] is refusing to prop up small coal mines in line with its philosophy of allowing small, less efficient commodity producers to go under ... The stimulus package has ruled out any direct investment in polluting or energy-intensive industry.

(www.iht.com, 7 January 2009)

'Prime minister Wen Jiabao was quoted Sunday [11 January] ... as saying that the economy had performed "better than expected" in December and that the country should be confident of becoming the first to recover from the global financial crisis' (*IHT*, 12 January 2009, p. 15).

'Prime minister Wen Jiabao declared China's efforts to offset the global economic downturn an "initial success" on Sunday [11 January] as the economy performed "better than expected" last month [December 2008]' (www.ft.com, 11 January 2009).

Exports and imports shrank at an accelerating rate last month [December 2008] ... Measured in dollars exports were 2.8 per cent lower in December than a year earlier, while imports were down 21.3 per cent, according to figures released on Tuesday [13 January 2009] by China's customs agency. The decline in exports followed a drop of 2.2 per cent in November, and was the steepest fall since April 1999. China's trade surplus narrowed slightly, to $39 billion from $40 billion in November ... The slowdown mainly reflects slumping demand in China's two biggest export markets, the EU followed by the United States ... China releases its trade figures in dollars.

(www.iht.com, 13 January 2009; *IHT*, 14 January 2009, p. 11)

December imports ... declined 21.3 per cent ... That was a bigger decline than November's 17.9 per cent drop. With exports in December worth $111.2 billion and imports worth $72.2 billion, that made December's trade surplus $39 billion. That is the country's second highest trade surplus ever, just short of November's record $40.1 billion ... December's export decline was the sharpest since April 1999.

(www.bbc.co.uk, 13 January 2009)

Exports tumbled by 13 per cent (in dollar terms) in the fourth quarter [of 2008], leaving them 3 per cent lower in December than a year earlier. In the first half of 2008 China's trade surplus did shrink. But since then, although exports stumbled, its imports fell by much more – down by 21 per cent in the twelve months to December (compared with over 30 per cent in the first half) ... Following interest rate cuts and the government's scrapping of tight restrictions on bank lending, total bank loans jumped by 19 per cent in the twelve months to December, up from growth of 14 per cent last summer ... The yuan has been held broadly constant since July.

(www.economist.com 14 January 2009)

China yesterday [14 January] cuts sales tax on small cars ... The State Council said in a statement that it would halve to 5 per cent the sales tax on purchases of cars with engine sizes of less than 1.6 litres. Beijing will also give cash subsidies to owners of high emission vehicles who trade them in for cleaner ones ... The government also announced some longer-term measures to support the sector, including a renminbi 10 billion fund to promote new technology vehicles ... Beijing also said it would encourage consolidation in the crowded car industry ... and in the steel sector, where overcapacity has been depressing prices. The State Council said it would allow no new steel capacity expansion projects and would adopt a flexible tax policy on steel exports to 'stabilize' the country's share of the global market.

(*FT*, 15 January 2009, p. 5)

The economic downturn hit the export industry first, and factories have been shutting down and putting migrant workers on the street for months. Now Chinese white-collar businesses are starting rounds of lay-offs, dropping salaries and cutting the year-end bonuses that employees prize so highly ... On Monday [19 January] prime minister Wen Jiabao said at a cabinet meeting that 'this year's employment situation is very grave' ... Earlier a government ordered state-owned companies not to lay off people ... The official urban unemployment rate for the end of 2008 was 4.2 per cent, up from 4 per cent in 2007; it was the first time the official rate had risen after five consecutive years of decline ... Migrant workers and newly graduated college students were not included in the government count ... The Chinese Academy of Social Sciences did a study last year [2008] that put the urban unemployment rate at 9.4 per cent. That number included migrant workers in the city ... About 670,000 businesses shut down and 6.7 million jobs 'evaporated' last year [2008] ... This month [January] the ministry of civil affairs announced that it would dole out a total of $1.3 billion to 74 million people as a one-time living subsidy – people living in the countryside would get about $15 each, and those in the city would get about $22. The ministry said the money would be given out before the Lunar New Year [which starts on 26 January] ... Of the 5.59 million Chinese college graduates in 2008, an estimated 27 per cent were unable to find jobs by the end of the year, according to the Chinese Academy of Social Sciences ... The People's Liberation Army, a force of 2.3 million, has had increasing success in recruiting college students, through the promise of large cash stipends ... Last year 10,000 college students joined the military, many more than in previous years ... Last November [2008] nearly a million students took the civil service exam to compete for government jobs, a jump of 25 per cent from a year earlier.

(*IHT*, 24 January 2009, p. 15)

Growth in the first quarter of last year [2008] was 10.6 per cent, but that had slowed to just 6.8 per cent in the last three months ... Ma Jiantang ... head of the National Bureau of Statistics ... revealed that millions of migrant workers ... had already lost their jobs. He did not give an absolute figure for the number of migrants who are now jobless, but he said a survey showed about 5 per cent had lost work. China's Academy of Social Sciences recently said that there were about 200 million migrant workers – meaning about 10 million migrants are now unemployed.

(www.bbc.co.uk, 22 January 2009)

'Economic growth slowed sharply during the last quarter of 2008, to 6.8 per cent, and to 9 per cent for all of 2008, down from 13 per cent in 2007, the Chinese Bureau of Statistics reported [on 22 January 2009]' (www.iht.com, 22 January 2009; *IHT*, 23 January 2009, p. 14).

China said its economy expanded by 6.8 per cent in the fourth quarter [of 2008] compared with the same period the year before ... For the year as a whole the economy grew 9 per cent, down from the revised 13 per cent growth rate in 2007 ... China releases GDP figures on a year-to-year basis, but does not provide data from one quarter to another ... The government said that factory gate prices fell 1.1 per cent in December, while consumer price inflation halved to 1.2 per cent.

(*FT*, 23 January 2009, p. 6)

China announced Wednesday [21 January] that it intended to spend $123 billion by 2011 to establish universal health care for the country's 1.3 billion people. The plan was passed Wednesday at a session of the State Council, the Chinese cabinet. Prime minister Wen Jiabao presided. Xinhua, the state news agency, said the authorities would 'take measures within three years to provide basic medical security to all Chinese in urban and rural areas, improve the quality of medical services and make medical services more accessible and affordable for ordinary people'. Providing universal health care is seen by some economists as a way to stimulate domestic spending during the current economic downturn. The Chinese have a high savings rate, and one of the reasons usually cited is their worry about possible medical expenses because China lacks a social safety net, including affordable health care ... Xinhua reported that the plan approved Wednesday would aim to provide some form of medical insurance for 90 per cent of the population by 2011. Each person covered by the system would receive an annual subsidy of more than $17 starting in 2010. Medicine would also be covered by the insurance, and the government would begin a system of producing and distributing necessary drugs this year [2009]. The plan also aims to improve health centres in rural areas and remote areas as well as equalize health services between urban and rural areas. Furthermore, the government would begin this year to reform the operations of public hospitals.

(www.iht.com, 22 January 2009; *IHT*, 23 January 2009, p. 5)

'China announced Wednesday [21 January] that, separately from its stimulus programme, it would spend $123 billion to provide universal health care within two years. The previous goal had been to do this within eleven years' (*IHT*, 23 January 2009, p. 14).

'The government will spend renminbi 850 billion ($124 billion) over the next three years on healthcare reform, in what appears to be a substantial increase in the health budget' (*FT*, 23 January 2009, p. 6).

Insurers have recently been given the authority to start lending to infrastructure projects ... China requires that any arable land converted from farming to other uses must be offset by bringing other land in China into cultivation. But the stimulus plan calls for construction on nearly three times as much arable land this year [2009] and next year [2010] as can readily be brought into cultivation elsewhere. The Ministry of Planning and Resources said at the end of December [2008] that it was studying ways to 'borrow' land that was supposed to be brought into cultivation in 2011 and 2012 and use it for economic stimulus projects now.

(*IHT*, 23 January 2009, p. 14)

There are no signs of unhappiness and dissent becoming organized. Last November [2008] a taxi strike in Chongqing prompted stoppages by drivers across the country, including Guangzhou. But it was copycat, not co-ordinated, action ... Some 35 million urban workers were laid off between 1997 and 2002, yet no major unrest resulted.

(www.guardian.co.uk, 25 January 2009)

China's state-run Xinhua news agency announced on Monday [26 January] that the government is to help train as many as 1 million jobless college graduates over the next three years. Graduates will also be offered small loans to help them start their own businesses.

(www.bbc.co.uk, 26 January 2009)

Speaking on condition that he not be quoted, a researcher at the Central Communist Party School, a top level official research institution, estimated that out of the 130 million Chinese migrants who crossed provincial lines for work, 20 per cent to 30 per cent will find themselves jobless after the [Lunar New Year] holiday.

(*IHT*, 27 January 2009, p. 12)

[China has an] estimated 150 migrant workers ... Violations of the rights of migrants have been well documented by the Chinese government as well as non-governmental organizations including Human Rights Watch long before the current economic crisis. Migrant workers, particularly construction workers, have been prone to exploitation by employers who deny them legally stipulated labour contracts. Many employers routinely refuse to comply with laws requiring monthly salaries and instead make migrants wait for an annual salary payment ahead of the Lunar New Year. Such payments are often below official minimum wage standards, and in some cases employers cheat migrants of the entirety of their yearly wages ... Research by the Chinese Academy of Social Sciences indicates that migrants are the front-line victims of the country's economic downturn through mass lay-offs in migrant-dominated export manufacturing ... Ministry of Human Resources and Social Security data indicate that up to 10 million migrants lost their jobs in 2008 due to the financial crisis. A recent study by China's Tsinghua University suggests that up to 50 million migrant workers will lose their urban jobs in 2009 if the downturn continues ... Migrants from the countryside have long been denied social welfare benefits available to residents with urban *hukou* [household registration system], including state-sponsored retirement pensions and medical care. Although some municipalities have temporary urban *hukou* programmes, the majority of migrant workers remain deprived of urban *hukou*-related rights and benefits ... Migrant remittances to their families in rural areas ... hit $30 billion in 2005 ... [according to] a World Bank study.

(Phelim Kine, Human Rights Watch, *IHT*, 27 January 2009, p. 6)

No one seems to know for sure how many migrant workers there are, but there could be around 200 million – perhaps more ... The government has announced a six-point plan to help migrant workers who find themselves without a job. It will provide retraining, give them priority in construction jobs and guarantee land rights for those who remain in their villages.

(www.bbc.co.uk, 30 January 2009)

Officials believe that of more than 200 million non-agricultural workers from the countryside, more than 80 million work close to their villages. The proportion working closer to home has increased in recent years, as more jobs have appeared inland ... Zhang Jianmin of Minzu University in Beijing reckons that around 10 per cent of Chinese workers from the countryside who are employed beyond their home areas will be out of a job this year [2009] – about 15 million people ... The central government ... has made it easier for farmers to register new businesses and has encouraged banks to lend them money. Local authorities say they are providing free job training for returning migrants ... In the late 1990s, even amid the Asian financial crisis in 1997–8, China resolutely carried out a massive restructuring of its state-owned enterprises (SOEs). Some 40 million lost their jobs. As many people lost their jobs as the number forecast for migrant labourers this year [2009] ... But there are important differences between then and now ... [For example] at the same time as closing down, selling and merging SOEs, the government virtually gave away the housing stock attached to them. This ensured that laid-off workers still had somewhere affordable to live (they also got subsistence payments that today's migrants would envy) ... The government's target for the year is to keep the [official urban unemployment] rate below 4.6 per cent – the highest figure since 1980 ... A record 5.6 million graduated last year [2008], nearly 650,000 more than the year before. Another 6.1 million will graduate in 2009. Around 1.5 million, however, were jobless at the end of last year [2008] ... The government said it would give loans to graduates to help them start businesses as well as to companies that employ them ... There has been little sign of political activism among students in recent years. They have taken to the streets only to make nationalist points and in support of the government ... Just before the Lunar New Year [which started on 26 January] the government announced unprecedented one-off payments totalling 9.7 billion yuan to 74 million people living close to the poverty line ... In January 2008 a law was implemented that made it harder to fire employees. Now some complain that it is being widely ignored.

(*The Economist*, 31 January 2009, pp. 27–9)

'After correcting for double-counting and unrealistic measures, China, Singapore, South Korea and Taiwan will all enjoy a fiscal stimulus of at least 3 per cent of GDP' (pp. 74–5). 'Weaker domestic spending – mainly the result of a collapse in housing construction – accounted for more than half of the country's slowdown in 2008' (p. 73).

China's exports account for 36 per cent of GDP, but about half of them are 'processing exports', which contain a lot of imported components. Thus the impact of a fall in exports is partially offset if imports fall too. Estimates suggest that domestic value-added from Chinese exports is a more modest 18 per cent of GDP. An alternative measure of the importance of exports is the change in net exports in real terms. Between 2002 and 2007 the increase in net exports contributed only 15 per cent of real GDP growth in China. In contrast, net exports accounted for half of all growth in Singapore and Taiwan. This measure understates the total impact, though, because it ignores the spillover effects of exports on business confidence, investment, employment and consumer spending.

(p. 74)

Consumer spending is just 36 per cent of GDP, half the American share ... Household savings have been broadly flat. (The rise in China's savings rate comes from firms and the government, not households.) If households are not saving more, why has consumer spending declined as a share of GDP? The answer is that wage incomes have fallen relative to GDP. In China the share of wages dropped from 53 per cent in 1998 to 40 per cent in 2007 ... Even if household saving rates have been falling, they are still high, at around 20 per cent in both China and Taiwan.

(p. 75)

At this year's annual meeting of the World Economic Forum [in Davos, Switzerland] ... prime minister Wen Jiabao said Wednesday [28 January] that the pervasive global financial meltdown has had a 'big impact' on his country, adding that growth would slow this year [2009]. In a speech at the meeting he said: the global financial crisis was causing 'rising unemployment in urban areas' ... In the fourth quarter [of 2008] growth slowed to 6.8 per cent ... But Wen said the robustness of the Chinese economy, which grew at 9 per cent last year [2008], could help restore confidence in global markets and stem the financial one. He said: 'China remains on the track of steady and fast development' ... For 2009 he said China had set a target of 8 per cent economic growth. He said: 'We think that that is obtainable ... [but it is] a tall order' ... [Wen Jiabao was] speaking as the first of forty heads of government or state scheduled to take the stage in Davos this week.

(www.iht.com, 28 January 2009)

'[According to the IMF] China's economy will likely expand 6.7 per cent this year [2009] ... reducing its estimate for the world's fastest growing major economy from 8.5 per cent in November [2008]' (www.iht.com, 28 January 2009).

Wen Jiabao, in a rare appearance by a top Chinese official at Davos, said the government had set a goal of 8 per cent economic growth in 2009, which he called 'an attainable target through hard work' ... Wen Jiabao said: 'We are facing severe challenges, including notably shrinking external demand, overcapacity in some sectors, difficult business conditions for enterprises, rising unemployment in urban areas and greater downward pressure on economic growth' ... [As regards international co-operation] Wen said: 'Only with closer co-operation and mutual help can we overcome the crisis.'

(*IHT*, 29 January 2009, pp. 1, 5)

Prime minister Wen Jiabao called for greater co-operation between developed and developing nations in tackling the global financial crisis and building a ... 'new world international financial order' ... [including] the reform of supra-national financial institutions to grant more power to developing nations ... He also warned that further action was needed internationally to 'restore market confidence' and continue world economic growth ... Wen Jiabao: 'In tackling the crisis practical co-operation is the effective way. The financial crisis is a test of the readiness of the international community to enhance co-operation and a test of our wisdom' ... Wen admitted that the economic crisis had severely affected China's businesses, notably because of falling demand for Chinese exports. But he said the fundamentals of China's economy remained in 'good shape', predicting 8 per cent growth in 2009.

(www.cnn.com, 28 January 2009)

Prime minister Wen Jiabao said: '[China has] the confidence, conditions and ability to maintain steady and fast economic growth and continue to contribute

> to world economic growth' ... He added that, while it would be difficult for China to meet forecasts of 8 per cent GDP growth in 2009, it was 'attainable with hard work' ... He said that 'a confrontational relationship' with the United States 'will make both losers'... Mr Wen argued that Western countries had been dangerously negligent in their policies towards their financial institutions and that this failure, coupled with a culture of 'low savings and high consumption', was behind the [global economic] crisis ... Mr Wen yesterday [28 January] insisted China was helping global growth through measures to keep its economy healthy in spite of the 'rather big impact' of the global crisis.
>
> (*FT*, 29 January 2009, pp. 1, 7)

(The reference to the United States relates to the comments of Timothy Geithner on 22 January about currency manipulation: see the section on yuan convertibility and exchange rate policy, below.)

> [Prime minister Wen Jiabao said] that China's economy was in good shape 'on the whole'. Mr Wen said that among the reasons behind the current global downturn were 'inappropriate macroeconomic policies in some economies, characterized by [a] low savings rate and high consumption'. He also pointed to a 'failure of financial supervision and regulation to keep up with innovation which allowed financial derivatives to spread' ... Wen Jiabao: 'The Chinese economy is now under mounting downward pressure. We are targeting a growth rate of about 8 per cent in 2009. It will be a tall order, but I hold the conviction that through hard work we can reach the goal' ... As the demand for China's exports shrinks he said that as part of relaunching the economy, the country had to focus now on expanding domestic consumer demand ... Wen Jiabao: 'Will China's economy continue to grow fast and steady? Some people may have doubts about it, yet I can give you a definite answer. Yes, it will, we are full of confidence ... [China will] take prompt, forceful and effective measures [to ensure the health of the economy].'
>
> (www.bbc.co.uk, 29 January 2009)

'[On 28 January] prime minister Wen Jiabao voiced concern about protectionism' (*FT*, 29 January 2009, p. 1).

'Both leaders [prime minister Vladimir Putin and prime minister Wen Jiabao] rejected protectionism' (www.bbc.co.uk, 29 January 2009). '[During his three-day visit to the UK, starting on 31 January] prime minister Wen Jiabao would be seeking reassurance that the UK will join China's fight against global protectionism ... China says this is damaging to its export trade' (www.bbc.co.uk, 1 February 2009).

'[On 1 February during a visit to London] Wen Jiabao spoke out about a "dangerous trend" towards protectionism as countries around the world struggle to respond to the crisis' (www.iht.com, 2 February 2009).

> China will set up 'procurement missions' to buy goods and technologies in Europe in an effort to stem protectionist sentiment in the region against its exports. Prime minister Wen Jiabao, who was talking in London on Monday

[2 February] at the end of a five-day trip to Europe, said the procurement trips would be established as soon as possible ... He said Chinese companies had signed contracts totalling $15 billion during his trip to Europe. The announcement underlines Beijing's anxiety that the global financial crisis will prompt a new wave of protectionism which would be damaging to a country such as China which is the second largest exporter in the world. Europe is China's largest trading partner ... Gordon Brown, the British prime minister, said the UK planned to double annual exports to China in the next eighteen months, from £5 billion to £10 billion ($14.2 billion). He said a planned expansion of bilateral trade could be an example to the rest of the world, demonstrating that the downturn could be confronted by open trade rather than protectionism.

(www.ft.com, 2 February 2009; *FT*, 3 February 2009, p. 6)

Last week [India] suddenly banned Chinese toy imports for six months, after the Consumer Welfare Association filed a public interest lawsuit. The body cited health concerns posed by Chinese toys, which are suspected of having a high content of lead and other potentially dangerous chemicals ... India's own toy industry has watched China grab 60 per cent of the domestic toy market.

(*FT*, 3 February 2009, p. 6)

Chinese premier Wen Jiabao ... and British prime minister Gordon Brown ... presented the planned expansion of bilateral trade as an example to the rest of the world, demonstrating that the slump could be combated by free trade rather than protectionism ... The need to head off protectionism, in the EU but particularly in the United States, has been at the top of Wen Jiabao's agenda during his three-day visit to the UK.

(www.guardian.co.uk, 2 February 2009)

'Prime minister Wen Jiabao: "It is completely confusing right and wrong when some countries that have been overspending then blame those that lend them money for their spending"' (*FT*, 2 February 2009, p. 7).

Prime minister Wen Jiabao said on Sunday [1 February] that he saw signs of recovery in the final days of 2008 ... but indicated that further stimulus might be needed ... He said (addressing business leaders at a dinner during a visit to London): 'During the last ten days of December it started to get better. The goods piled up in port started to decrease and the price of industrial goods started to rise' ... The government has already pledged $585 billion over the next two years to help boost domestic demand. Work on projects including rebuilding the earthquake-hit south-west and improving road and rail links is under way ... Wen Jiabao: 'We may take further new, timely and decisive measures. All these measures have to be taken pre-emptively before an economic retreat' ... Wen told an audience of business figures ... that he would unveil stimulus measures for shipbuilding and textiles when he returns home ... He said: 'The financial sector in China has in the face of this crisis been affected to a certain extent, but generally speaking remains sound, healthy and stable.'

(www.iht.com, 2 February 2009)

An estimated 20 million workers from rural areas who had been working in cities have lost their jobs, according to a senior official. A survey carried out in fifteen provinces suggests about 15 per cent of the total migrant labour pool is now unemployed ... The Chinese government researchers visited 165 villages across the country to try to build an accurate picture ... The data they collected suggests the number of migrant workers now unemployed is 20 million – far higher than had been announced previously ... The government has said the economic downturn in China first started to be felt in the provinces where many exporters were based in the east and south of the country. But now the effects are being felt west as migrant workers see their wages cut or lose their jobs and are forced to return home.

(www.bbc.co.uk, 2 February 2009)

According to a survey conducted by the agriculture ministry ... about 20 million out of China's total estimated 130 million migrant workers ... have been forced to return to rural areas because of lack of work ... One in seven rural migrant workers have been laid off or are unable to find work, twice as many as estimated just five weeks ago ... In late December employment officials estimated that at least 10 million migrant workers had lost their jobs in the third quarter of 2008 as waves of factories and businesses shut their doors ... Chen Xiwen, a senior rural planning official, released the joblessness estimate at Monday's briefing [2 February] ... The military called upon its forces Sunday [1 February] to exercise strict obedience in the face of challenges to social stability. In a joint report issued Sunday China's cabinet and the Communist Party's Central Committee warned 2009 will be 'possibly the toughest year' since the Asian economic bubble burst in the late 1990s for economic growth and rural development.

(www.iht.com, 2 February 2009)

The government has not released annual figures on social unrest – what it terms 'mass incidents' – for several years [since 2005], but foreign media reports suggest that protests are growing as unemployment spreads. An article last month [December 2008] in *Outlook Weekly*, a magazine published by the government news agency Xinhua, predicted a record year for mass protests. Chen Xiwen: 'It is fair to say that the Chinese government takes very seriously the issue of employment of migrant workers. Guaranteeing employment and livelihood is to guarantee social stability.'

(*IHT*, 3 February 2009, pp. 1, 10)

More than 20 million rural migrant workers in China have lost their jobs and returned to their home villages or towns as a result of the global economic crisis, government figures released yesterday [2 February]. By the start of the New Year festival on 25 January 15.1 per cent of China's 130 million migrant workers had lost their jobs and left coastal manufacturing centres to return home, said officials quoting a survey from the agriculture ministry. The job losses were a direct result of the global economic crisis and its impact on export-orientated manufacturers, said Chen Xiwen, director of the Central Rural Work Leading Group. He warned that the flood of unemployed migrants would pose challenges to social stability in the countryside. The figure of 20 million unemployed migrants does not include those who have stayed in cities to look for work after being made redundant and is substantially higher than the figure of 12 million that premier Wen Jiabao gave to the *Financial Times* in an interview on Sunday [1 February]. Speaking on a visit to the UK yesterday [2 February] Mr Wen said there had been signs at the end of last year [2008] that the Chinese economy might have started to recover. But in a speech at Cambridge University later he warned that the global economy could face further problems: 'The crisis has not yet hit the bottom, and it is hard to predict what other problems there will be down the path' … Mr Wen's speech was interrupted by a protester who called him a 'dictator' and threw a shoe at the stage – an act reminiscent of the Iraqi journalist who threw shoes at George W. Bush, former US president, last year [2008] … In the past decade 6 million to 7 million rural migrant workers a year have left the countryside … [to go the] booming cities … According to a rough calculation, one percentage point of Chinese GDP growth creates about 1 million jobs … A government-backed project aims to kick-start sales in rural areas of the country by offering television sets, washing machines, refrigerators and mobile phones at controlled prices with an additional 13 per cent rebate … The Home Appliances to the Countryside scheme has been running in twelve provinces since December [2008] but officially launched on 1 February … The government has set a renminbi 2,000 retail price ceiling for television sets under the programme … China, the world's largest grain producer, will raise direct subsidies for planting grain and oilseed crops to a record level. Stockpile buying will also be increased to support farmers amid a decline in prices of food staples. Beijing plans to increase subsidies 17 per cent to renminbi 120 billion ($17.5 billion) this year [2009], Chen Xiwen said yesterday.

(*FT*, 3 February 2009, p. 5)

The figure [of 20 million], based on a survey of 150 villages and extrapolated across the country, was twice that calculated by the human resources ministry at the end of last year [2008] … In raising the alarm that 20 million unemployed migrants might soon be on the march – joined by perhaps 7 million new entrants to the itinerant work force – Mr Chen was putting on alert the Chinese bureaucracy, every level of which has been focused on making the migrants job hunt as 'harmonious' as possible … Localized disturbances are a common occurrence and these are only likely to multiply in the months ahead. But Chinese workers focus their anger first on the factories and bosses that fire them, with local government officials quick to adopt an empathetic and supportive pose when disputes flare up.

(www.ft.com, 8 February 2009; *FT*, 9 February 2009, p. 8)

'[Measures taken include] pay rises for 12 million schoolteachers and spending subsidies to low-income consumers' (*FT*, 5 February 2009, p. 34).

The party Central Military Commission issued an order for complete obedience from the People's Liberation Army in the face of multiple security threats ... China's most senior official on agricultural policy revealed that 15.3 per cent of the 130 million migrants moving from farms and villages to cities and factories – about one in seven – had returned to the countryside jobless. With some 6 to 7 million new entrants expected to join the rural labour market this year [2009], more than 25 million people could find themselves without a job ... Chen Xiwen: 'Protecting employment and protecting people's welfare is protecting rural social stability.'

(www.thetimes.co.uk, 2 February 2009)

A recent government survey showed that more than 15 per cent of China's 130 million migrant workers have returned to their home towns recently, where they are now unemployed, said Chen Xiwen, director of the Central Rural Work Leading Group. Another 5 to 6 million new migrants enter the work force each year Mr Chen added: 'So if we put these figures together we have roughly 25 to 26 million rural migrants who are now coming under pressure for employment. So ensuring job creation and maintenance is ensuring the stability of the countryside' ... China's official jobless tally, which only counts registered urban workers, was estimated last November [2008] at 8.3 million. This rate is believed to under-represent the true number of unemployed because it leaves out large swathes of the private or informal economy ... The government already has policies to help rural workers returning, including help in setting up businesses, Mr Chen said.

(www.independent.co.uk, 3 February 2009)

'The People's Bank of China reckons remittances from migrant workers in the rich cities account for nearly two-thirds of an average rural family's income' (www.independent.co.uk, 22 February 2009).

Economic growth slowed to 6.8 per cent in the year to the fourth quarter of 2008 ... China's lowest rate of growth since the fourth quarter of 2001 ... The Labour Contract Law ... introduced at the start of 2008 ... is widely acknowledged to have added approximately 20 per cent to employers' labour costs.

(www.economist.com, 3 February 2009)

The government has decided to inject $30 billion into Agricultural Bank of China, the last of the largest state-owned banks to be restructured in preparation for a listing ... The recapitalization would happen 'soon' ... The eventual capital injection is substantially higher than the $20 billion that the bank was expected to receive ... Chinese official media said Agricultural Bank of China is planning to restructure its operations along the lines of a commercial bank and is considering applying for stock market listings in Shanghai and Hong Kong ... China has also begun experimental reforms with underground banks, legalizing three in the Wenzhou area of Zhejiang province in another attempt to stimulate spending to rural enterprises.

(*FT*, 2 February 2009, p. 21)

After declaring a drought emergency China's government on 5 February quadrupled the amount of money set aside for relief to renminbi 400 million ($58.5 million) from renminbi 100 million. The drought, brought on by abnormally low winter rainfall, is different from previous dry spells because it covers large swathes of central and northern China. This region includes several major grain producer provinces. The agriculture ministry says water shortages are affecting up to 43 per cent of the country's wheat producing area and around 3.7 million people, from Shandong province on the east coast to Gansu province far inland.

(www.economist.com, 6 February 2009)

Severe drought now plagues Henan and six other provinces in northern and central China. After 100 days without precipitation in the region, the government has declared a 'Level 1' emergency for the worst drought in fifty years, authorizing an extra $44 million in special drought-relief spending.

(*The Economist*, 14 February 2009, p. 69)

Since November [2008] northern and central China has had little precipitation. Many places have not had rainfall for more than 100 days. State-run media reports 4.4 million and 2.1 million livestock are facing water shortages. China's winter wheat crop is most seriously threatened. The drought has hit almost half the country's winter wheat fields. Rice crops are also affected.

(www.cnn.com, 9 February 2009)

'Winter wheat is the nation's second largest crop, behind rice' (*IHT*, 25 February 2009, p. 4).

'Since 1 February all China's more than 200,000 rural households have been eligible for a government-financed discount on such purchases ... [as] televisions and fridges ... From next month [March] they will be entitled to subsidized cars as well' (*The Economist*, 19 February 2009, p. 59).

More than 4,000 Chinese toy companies closed last year [2008] as the global recession cut demand and some countries tightened safety standards ... Forty-nine per cent of Chinese export-orientated toy companies closed last year, leaving 4,388 of the businesses still functioning.

(www.iht.com, 8 February 2009)

Incidents of social unrest are not uncommon across the Chinese hinterland. Last year [2008] there were an estimated 120,000 strikes, protests or riots, most of them sparked by popular discontent over government corruption, the illegal confiscation of land, or workers agitating for unpaid wages.

(www.iht.com, 9 February 2009; *IHT*, 10 February 2009, p. 2)

Inflation at the consumer level fell to a thirty-month low in January ... Annual consumer price inflation slowed to 1 per cent last month [January] from 1.2 per cent in December [2008], close to market expectations of an increase of 0.9 per cent ... It was the ninth consecutive monthly drop in consumer inflation, which is now well below the twelve-month high of 8.7 per cent reached last February [2008] ... The National Bureau of Statistics ... also said producer prices had fallen 3.3 per cent in January from a year earlier. The decline, the biggest since 2002, was steeper than the 1.1 per cent fall in December from a year earlier and the 2.6 per cent drop forecast by economists.

(www.iht.com, 10 February 2009)

Exports plummeted in January ... The fall of 17.5 per cent from a year earlier was worse than most analysts had projected ... [The fall] was far worse than the 2.8 per cent decline recorded in December [2008] ... [and was] exacerbated by the timing of the Chinese New Year holiday. The week-long festival took place in January this year; last year it was in February ... About 70 per cent of [imports] ... are raw materials and capital goods for the industrial sector.

(www.iht.com, 11 February 2009)

'Exports dropped 17.5 per cent in January compared with the same month the year before ... Imports declined by a dramatic 43.1 per cent' (www.ft.com, 11 February 2009).

China has done little to rebalance its economy away from exports and heavy industry towards domestic consumption, entrenching income inequality and increasing its vulnerability to the financial crisis, the World Bank said on Thursday [12 February]. The bank's researchers said that 'limited strengthening' of the exchange rate had also created an unsustainable current account surplus. They called for increased spending on social services. The verdict on China's economic strategy was contained in a World Bank mid-term evaluation of China's later five-year plan, which was launched in 2006, with a rebalancing of the economy as one of its main goals. The report underlines the case that China needs decisive steps to boost domestic consumption, both as a strategy for overcoming the present crisis but also to ensure sustainable long-term growth once the global economy has recovered. China has launched a renminbi 4,000 billion ($586 billion) investment plan over the next two years in response to the slump in economic growth, but some economists fear the proposals place too much emphasis on infrastructure spending, which could exacerbate the existing bias towards polluting heavy industry. The World Bank said China had made 'significant progress' in some areas of the five-year plan's objectives. Growth had been higher than forecast and public services had improved. However, the economy's heavy reliance on capital-intensive and export-related industry had not shifted, making it harder to improve energy efficiency and reduce pollution and leading to 'unavoidable' widening of social inequalities. The report said: 'Little progress has been made in rebalancing the overall pattern of growth' … The Chinese central bank said on Thursday that new loans extended in January reached a record renminbi 1,600 billion, more than double the amount seen in the same period last year [2008] and the third month in a row of substantial new lending.

(www.ft.com, 15 February 2009)

[A] G7 conference [took place in Rome] … over the weekend … Veering sharply from his past testimony before the US Congress, where he used harsh language in criticizing China's reluctance to let the yuan appreciate, the new US Treasury Secretary, Timothy Geithner, was quick to commend China for its 4 trillion yuan ($585 billion) stimulus package. He said during a news conference Saturday [14 February]: 'We very much welcome the steps China has taken to strengthen domestic demand and its commitment to further exchange rate reform' … This view was echoed by the G7's communiqué, which added that the yuan was 'expected to appreciate in effective terms' … Geithner emphasized the [US] administration's commitment to open markets.

(www.iht.com, 15 February 2009; *IHT*, 16 February 2009, pp. 1, 12)

The Obama administration has said Timothy Geithner's description of China's currency policy was 'not making any determinations' as to whether the country was manipulating its currency – a judgement the Treasury has to make in April in a formal currency report.

(*FT*, 16 February 2009, p. 6)

China's official news agency Xinhua slammed the 'Buy American' requirement of the US economic stimulus package, saying that trade protectionism is a 'poison' that will harm poor countries … The remarks [were made] on Saturday [14 February] … The US Congress approved the $787 billion plan to jump start the world's biggest economy on Friday [13 February], stipulating that public works and building projects funded by the stimulus use only US-made goods, including iron and steel. The plan does require that procurement be carried out in a manner consistent with US obligations under multilateral and bilateral trade pacts, potentially giving Canada, the EU, Japan and some other countries the chance to benefit from the additional spending. But countries like China, India, Brazil and Russia, which are not members of an international government procurement agreement, would be shut out.

(www.iht.com, 15 February 2009)

'Xinhua: "History and economic theory show that in facing a financial crisis trade protectionism is not a way out, but rather could become just the poison that worsens global economic hardships"' (*FT*, 16 February 2009, p. 6).

> Russia has won $25 billion in loans from China in return for agreeing to supply oil from new fields in eastern Siberia for the next twenty years as Moscow seeks funds to see its oil industry through the financial crisis. Transneft, Russia's oil pipeline monopoly, said yesterday [17 February] China had agreed to lend it $10 billion and Rosneft, Russia's state-controlled oil group, $15 billion in return for twenty years' worth of oil supplies.
>
> (*FT*, 18 February 2009, p. 6)

> Earlier this week Russia's national oil company, Rosneft, and national pipe-line operator, Transneft, completed a deal for $25 billion in loans from the China Development Bank. In exchange the Russian companies agreed to provide an additional 300,000 barrels or so a day of oil to China over twenty years, along a trans-Siberian oil pipeline that is scheduled to reach China in 2010.
>
> (www.iht.com, 18 February 2009)

'The supply of 300,000 barrels of oil a day ... [represents] about 10 per cent of China's current oil imports' (*The Economist*, 21 February 2009, p. 8).

> [Some] 45 per cent of its $586 billion stimulus package announced in November of last year [2008] is devoted to the development of highways, railways, airports and power grids, while another 25 per cent will go to post-earthquake construction in Sichuan ... This week more than 3,000 public security directors from across the country are gathering in the capital to learn how to neutralize rallies and strikes before they blossom into so-called mass incidents.
>
> (www.iht.com, 23 February 2009)

'Before the crisis China had tended to invest approximately 10 per cent of GDP in infrastructure' (www.feer.com, 22 February 2009).

> Leaving aside the attraction of its first-world infrastructure and well-oiled supply chains, China's labour markets are responding with a flexibility that should underpin the country's competitiveness when global demand recovers. Migrants looking for new work after the Lunar New Year holidays report that jobs are available, but at lower wages. What is more, some local authorities have suspended mandatory minimum wage increases and government inspectors are no longer enforcing a year-old labour law that businesses said added hugely to their costs ... Prices of US imports from China fell 0.7 per cent in January, the fifth successive monthly decline ... Multinationals had flirted with shifting labour-intensive manufacturing to cheaper locations like India and Vietnam when costs were rising sharply. Now China

is being judged favourably again because it is perceived as less volatile and growing cheaper.

(www.iht.com, 2 March 2009; *IHT*, 3 March 2009, p. 13)

China's hopes for a speedy export recovery from the global crisis could be undermined by the weakest links in its powerful supply chain – smaller companies too damaged by the downturn and credit crisis to get goods to the market. As collapsing sales to recession-hit Western markets weigh on China's economy, bankruptcies pose a growing risk to its export machine, threatening everyone from suppliers of crucial parts and materials to companies that transport finished products ... PriceWaterhouse-Coopers estimates that 670,000 small companies have closed across China because of the global crisis. In addition to tumbling exports, companies have been hit by a squeeze in credit markets. About 90 per cent of world merchandise trade is funded by trade finance, such as letters of credit. A report Wednesday [4 March] showed that factory output and new orders had returned to mild growth in February after shrinking for four months, though analysts cautioned about reading too much into the rise ... While rising bankruptcies are raising the risk of doing business in China, the country is unlikely to lose its status as a low-priced global trade centre, not least because many companies are focused on the country's huge market in the long run.

(www.iht.com, 7 March 2009)

Last November [2008] Beijing announced a 4 trillion yuan ($594 billion) stimulus package ... On Wednesday [4 March] a senior planning official said China would increase spending over and above the 4 trillion yuan by an unspecified amount ... The official also said China would spend more on welfare to strengthen the country's social welfare net ... A senior economic planning official ... [said] the government will increase spending in areas such as infrastructure and manufacturing on top of the 4 trillion yuan ($584.7 billion) stimulus package announced in November ... On Sunday [1 March] a senior central planning agency official said the government would publicize project details after the ... 4 trillion yuan ... plan was approved.

(www.iht.com, 4 March 2009)

In its $585 billion economic stimulus package the central government is contributing just a quarter of the funds needed, leaving the rest of the tab to banks, local governments and the private sector ... China's budget deficit is expected to swell ... to 3 per cent in 2009] from 0.6 per cent last year [2008]. In contrast, the US federal deficit will shoot up to 12.3 per cent this year [2009] from 3.2 per cent.

(www.iht.com, 11 March 2009; *IHT*, 12 March 2009, p. 14)

'The National Development and Reform Commission – the government body that is directing much of the stimulus spending – announced that it would post details of its spending plans on the internet' (*IHT*, 5 March 2009, p. 11).

China will reduce export taxes to zero and give more financial support to exporters ... the country's commerce minister ... Chen Deming ... announced yesterday [9 March] ... Mr Chen said the government would gradually reduce export taxes to zero while following international trade rules and restricting industries that were highly polluting, energy intensive or wasteful of natural resources.

(*FT*, 10 March 2009, p. 9)

Just as America watered down the buy-local clause in its own financial bail-out package, China quietly removed one from its own industry-support bill a few weeks ago. This had instructed 'governments of different levels to give priority to home-grown light industry products' ... Although Beijing publicly continues to rally against protectionism [however], China's provinces are busily erecting internal barriers. Farmers in Hangzhou now get a 13 per cent subsidy if they buy Hangzhou-made refrigerators, televisions, mobile phones and washing machines. Officials in Henan and Hubei must give priority to local suppliers of buses, cars, farming equipment, software and medicines. In the province of Anhui publicly funded infrastructure projects must use Anhui-made steel, concrete, doors and windows, glass wiring and electrical equipment. Appliance makers and two carmakers based in the province, Chery and Jianghuai Automobile, must buy locally made steel. In return state-owned businesses, taxi operators and government officials will buy their cars. From next month [April] power plants will also have to buy locally mined coal. Similarly, in Changchun city, in the Jilian province, inspection fees for new vehicles made by First Auto Works (FAW), a local carmaker, are being waived, giving the company a price advantage over rivals. Government officials have been told to consider FAW vehicles first; farmers will get a 10 per cent discount on locally made tractors. At least 50 per cent of the equipment for officially sanctioned 'large projects' must be bought locally, too.

(www.economist.com, 12 March 2009)

'Consumer prices fell 1.6 per cent ... in February ... compared to a year ago, while the producer price index dropped 4.5 per cent from a year earlier' (www. cnn.com, 10 March 2009).

Consumer prices were 1.6 per cent lower last month [February] than a year earlier, the first decline since December 2002 ... Producer prices were 4.5 per cent lower last month than a year earlier ... Prime minister Wen Jiabao set a target of 4 per cent inflation this year [2009] ... China lost 3 million jobs in the fourth quarter [of 2008], labour minister Yin Weimin said on Tuesday [10 March] ... About 11 million migrant labourers who travelled to cities from rural areas in search of work after the Lunar New Year are still unemployed, he said.

(www.iht.com, 10 March 2009; *IHT*, 11 March 2009, p. 13)

China's exports fell much more sharply than expected in February ... Exports dropped 25.7 per cent from a year earlier, compared to a forecast of a 5 per cent decline. Imports fell 24.1 per cent, against a forecast of a 25.9 per cent drop. The country's trade surplus shrivelled to $4.84 billion last month [February], a three-year low, from $39.1 billion in January. Economists had expected a surplus of $27.3 billion.

(www.iht.com, 11 March 2009)

'The sharp drop in exports [in February], compared with a year ago, was unexpected – economist has been predicting little change' (*IHT*, 12 March 2009, p. 12).

'The country's trade surplus stood at $4.8 billion in February, compared with $39.1 billion the month before' (www.bbc.co.uk, 11 March 2009).

'Exports were hard hit starting in late 2008 because of the global economic crisis' (www.cnn.com, 11 March 2009).

A session of the National People's Congress was held 5–13 March 2009.

Prime minister Wen Jiabao (speech at the National People's Congress delivered on 5 March):

> We are facing unprecedented difficulties and challenges ... [The year 2009 will be one of] arduous tasks ... The global financial crisis continues to spread and get worse ... In projecting the economic growth target of about 8 per cent, we have taken into consideration both our need and ability to sustain growth ... As long as we adopt the right policies and appropriate measures and implement them effectively, we will be able to achieve this target ... Maintaining a certain rate of growth for the economy is essential for expanding employment for urban and rural residents, increasing people's incomes and ensuring social stability ... We will improve the early warning system for social stability to actively prevent and properly handle all types of mass incidents ... [Bolstering consumer demand must become] a long-term strategic principle and a basic point of departure for stimulating economic growth.
>
> (www.iht.com, 5 March 2009; www.bbc.co.uk, 5 March 2009;
> www.cnn.com, 5 March 2009; *Independent*, 6 March 2009, p. 25;
> *FT*, 6 March 2009, p. 6)

> Prime minister Wen Jiabao did not announce fresh economic stimulus as some investors had hoped ... Wen did not explicitly announce any new spending ... beyond the $585 billion that China committed to spend in November [2008] ... But Wen did re-label the government's stimulus plan, worth nearly $585 billion, as an investment plan ... He said that China's budget deficit this year [2009] would be equal to about 3 per cent of GDP, a modern record.
>
> (www.iht.com, 5 March 2009)

'The previous record, of about 2.6 per cent [of GDP], was recorded in 2002' (*IHT*, 5 March 2009, p. 9).

> China's national budget deficit will jump more than seven-fold this year [2009] to over 1 trillion yuan. But that will still be less than 3 per cent of national income. The United States, by comparison, is budgeting a deficit of 12.3 per cent of GDP.
>
> (www.iht.com, 6 March 2009)

Prime minister Wen Jiabao said the budget deficit this year [2009] would rise to 950 billion yuan. According to the official press, this would be nearly three times bigger than the previous record deficit in 2003. Mr Wen said that at less than 3 per cent of GDP it would still be 'safe'. (America's budget deficit is likely to rise to more than 12 per cent of GDP this year.)

(*The Economist*, 7 March 2009, p. 64)

'Prime minister Wen Jiabao ... [said] that the budget deficit would reach renminbi 950 billion ($138.8 billion) – almost 3 per cent of GDP. This compares with a deficit of renminbi 180 billion in 2008' (*FT*, 6 March 2009, p. 6).

'The government deficit currently sits at 750 billion yuan ($109 billion) – 570 billion yuan ($83 billion) more than last year [2008]' (www.cnn.com, 5 March 2009).

'The Chinese [budget] deficit [will] balloon ... from 0.4 per cent of national income last year [2008] to 3 per cent this year [2009]' (www.guardian.co.uk, 5 March 2009).

Prime minister Wen Jiabao said yesterday [5 March] that ... [the November 2008] stimulus package ... was an 'investment plan' – an indication that some of the spending would have taken place anyway ... He failed to outline the new stimulus package many investors had been expecting ... Mr Wen did not announce additional measures beyond the $585 billion 'investment plan' unveiled in November ... He provided only a few extra details to help clarify how much of that investment would be new spending and where the money would be allocated.

(*FT*, 6 March 2009, p. 6)

'Much of the planned investment was already in the pipeline, but has been accelerated' (*FT*, 7 March 2009).

'The premier said he hoped to create 9 million jobs in the cities and increase local government spending budgets by almost 25 per cent' (www.bbc.co.uk, 5 March 2009).

'Many economists estimate that China may see growth of only 5 per cent or 6 per cent this year [2009]. This would be markedly below the 8 per cent the government is projecting' (www.iht.com, 4 March 2009).

'A number of analysts say they believe a 2009 growth rate of 6.5 per cent or 7 per cent ... is increasingly likely' (*IHT*, 5 March 2009, p. 9).

The World Bank has cut its prediction for China's economic growth in 2009 to 6.5 per cent from 7.5 per cent ... Falling demand for Chinese goods abroad – which the bank said could cost up to 25 million jobs – is the main reason for the projected slowdown ... The World Bank said: 'As the global crisis has intensified China's exports have been hit badly, affecting market-based investment and sentiment, notably in the manufacturing sector.'

(www.bbc.co.uk, 18 March 2009)

'The World Bank lowered its forecast of China's GDP growth this year [2009] to 6.5 per cent, down from 7.5 per cent it predicted at the end of November last year [2008]' (www.ft.com, 18 March 2009).

> The global economy is set to shrink 1 per cent to 2 per cent this year [2009], Robert Zoellick, the president of the World Bank said Saturday [21 March], adding that the depth of the slowdown was unprecedented since the Great Depression of the 1930s ... [He] referred to an IMF forecast that the world economy would shrink 0.5 per cent to 1 per cent this year.
>
> (www.iht.com, 22 March 2009)

'The World Bank, forecasting growth of only 6.5 per cent, still notes that China is "a relative bright spot in an otherwise gloomy global economy"' (www.economist.com, 19 March 2009).

> The IMF says ... the global slowdown is so severe that the worldwide economy will contract for the first time in sixty years ... The total of goods and services produced around the world is projected to slump by 1 per cent in 2009, compared with a 3.2 per cent growth rate the year before ... Japan's economy is forecast to shrink by 5.8 per cent in 2009, while Europe's is expected to decline 3.2 per cent and the United States' 2.6 per cent ... The IMF thinks the world's emerging and developing economies will continue to grow this year [2009], but by no more than 2.5 per cent, after a 6.1 per cent growth rate in 2008. Global recovery won't come until 2010, according to the IMF report. The world's economic powers will struggle to break even in the new year, while developing nations' economies will surge by up to 4.5 per cent.
>
> (www.cnn.com, 20 March 2009)

'China's central bank chief, Zhou Xiaochuan, said Friday [6 March] that he saw signs of the economy recovering and that officials would err on the side of acting sooner rather than later to revive growth' (www.iht.com, 6 March 2009).

> China's economic leaders struck a note of quiet confidence that the economy was already reviving ... But comments Friday by a trio of top officials suggested that while Beijing stands ready to prime the pump further, extra measures might prove unnecessary because substantial fiscal and monetary stimuli are already coursing through the economy. Zhou Xiaochuan (central bank governor): 'The economic figures are stabilizing and recovering, which demonstrates that the policies have begun to show an impact ... We must err on the side of being quick and decisive' ... Zhang Ping, head of the National Development and Reform Commission, the main planning agency, said Beijing would keep tracking the flow of economic date before deciding whether extra stimulus was necessary.
>
> (www.iht.com, 6 March 2009)

Zhang Ping (chairman of the National Development and Reform Commission): 'Whether we need to adopt new measures will depend on changing circumstances ... Some numbers are showing signs of containing the down-turn or of a revival' ... Zhou Xiaochuan (central bank governor): 'We have to avoid being too slow-handed or light-handed in responding. We must err on the side of being quick and decisive' ... There were signs that China's economy was responding to measures undertaken so far, he added, and policies to date had 'achieved significant results' ... He added: 'We are also seeing that the economic figures are stabilizing and recovering, which demonstrates that the policies have begun to show an impact.'

(www.bbc.co.uk, 6 March 2009)

Prime minister Wen Jiabao (13 March):

I expect that next year [2010] both China and the world will be better off ... I admit it will be a difficult job [to reach the 8 per cent growth target]. This being said I also believe that with considerable efforts it is possible for us to attain this goal ... I really believe we will be able to walk out of the shadow of the financial crisis at an early date. After this trial I believe the Chinese economy will show greater vitality ... [China's budget deficit is under control and the debt level is still safe] ... We already have our plans ready to tackle even more difficult times, and to do that we have reserved adequate ammunition. That means that at any time we can introduce new stimulus policies ... We can launch new economic stimulus policies at any time ... We now have more leeway to run a larger fiscal deficit and take on more debt. The most direct, powerful and effective way to deal with the current financial crisis is to increase fiscal spending – the quicker the better ... The unemployment issue is a very serious one ... [Confidence is] more important than gold or money [in overcoming the world's financial troubles] ... Only when we have confidence can we have courage and strength, and only when we have courage and strength can we overcome difficulties ... We have made a huge amount of loans to the United States. Of course we are concerned about the safety of our assets. To be honest I am a little bit worried ... I would like to call on the United States to honour its words, stay a credible nation and ensure the safety of China's assets.

(www.cnn.com, 13 March 2009; www.bbc.co.uk, 13 March 2009, and
14 March 2009; www.iht.com, 13 March 2009; www.independent.co.uk,
13 March 2009; www.guardian.co.uk, 13 March 2009'
FT, 14 March 2009, p. 6)

China [is] the world's biggest holder of United States government debt ... Analysts estimated that nearly half of China's $2 trillion in currency reserves are invested in US Treasuries and notes issued by other government-affiliated agencies ... During her visit to China last month [February] Secretary of State Hillary Rodham Clinton sought to reassure Beijing that those holdings remained a reliable investment ... China has the world's largest reserves of foreign exchange ... Prime minister Wen Jiabao did not specify China's concerns about the safety of its investment in American debt. But some economists have cited fears that the dollar's value will depreciate over time, lowering the value of China's holdings ... [Others argue that] if the American stimulus package is financed mainly by borrowing this may affect the future value of Treasury securities. Some experts also cite fears that inflation will erode the dollar's value.

(www.iht.com, 13 March 2009)

Economists ... said China could face steep losses in the event of a sharp rise in interest rates or a plunge in the value of the dollar ... Economists say that half of ... $2 trillion [in foreign exchange reserves] has been invested in US Treasury notes and other government-backed debt.

(*IHT*, 14 March 2009, pp. 1, 11)

'[There is the argument that the Chinese] are worried about forever-rising deficits [in the United States], which may devalue Treasuries by pushing interest rates higher' (www.independent.co.uk, 13 March 2009).

'Nearly half of China's $2 trillion in currency reserves is invested in US Treasury bills and other government-affiliated notes' (www.bbc.co.uk, 13 March 2009).

'About 70 per cent of China's near $2,000 billion foreign exchange reserves are believed to be in US dollar assets' (*FT*, 14 March 2009, p. 6).

Few new details of the stimulus were revealed at the congress. The government said that details of a separate massive spending programme on health care reform (850 billion yuan over three years) would be finalized only after the parliamentary session ... It revealed that spending on welfare projects would be increased from 1 per cent to 4 per cent of the stimulus package. Spending on infrastructure would drop from 45 per cent to 38 per cent. But spending on environmental projects would also be cut from 9 per cent to 5 per cent.

(*The Economist*, 21 March 2009, p. 32)

'Prime minister Wen Jiabao ... promised to focus on job creation and give more help to smaller companies, which he said generate 90 per cent of Chinese new employment' (www.independent.co.uk, 13 March 2009).

The country is using its nearly $600 billion economic stimulus package to make its companies better able to compete in markets at home and abroad, to retrain migrant workers on a vast scale, and to rapidly expand subsidies for research and development ... With subsidies from Beijing, provincial governments have already embarked on large-scale vocational training programmes.

(*IHT*, 17 March 2009, pp. 1, 12)

Prime minister Wen Jiabao said this month [March] that China must make domestic demand 'a basic point of departure for stimulating economic growth' ... But ... Chinese consumers ... save for good reason: at least one-fourth of the population has no health insurance at all, according to official statistics. Hundreds of millions of others face crippling bills for treatment of serious illnesses that are not covered by rudimentary insurance programmes.

Public pensions cover less than one-third of workers. An estimated 130 million migrant workers are not protected by unemployment insurance. Payments to the poor reach only a fraction of those eligible, according to the China Development Research Foundation, a non-profit group ... The government has pledged more social spending, led by a $123 billion three-year initiative to deliver basic, universal health care to nine in ten Chinese. That follows a three-year drive to provide compulsory, free education to students through ninth grade.

(www.iht.com, 19 March 2009; *IHT*, 20 March 2009, p. 4)

'China's banks have been largely unscathed by the international financial turmoil' (www.iht.com, 18 March 2009).

On 13 March, at the end of the parliamentary session, prime minister Wen Jiabao said that to counter the crisis China 'would rather speed up reforms'. He said it should 'give full play to market forces in allocating resources' and encourage the development of the private sector.

(*The Economist*, 21 March 2009, p. 32)

Finance ministers from the G-20 group of rich and emerging nations [including China, gathered in the UK on 14 March] ... A joint statement was issued: 'We are committed to deliver the scale of sustained effort necessary to restore growth' ... The outline agreements released in the joint communiqué include a commitment to fighting all forms of protectionism, and the restoration of banking. The finance ministers have also pledged to continue with economic stimulus packages and low interest rates, and to increase IMF funding ... The key two agreements were the pledge to increase the funds to the IMF, and the commitment to guard against protectionism ... [In April there will be a] meeting of G-20 leaders in London ... The G-20 includes the world's biggest industrial and developing countries, making up 85 per cent of the world economy.

(www.bbc.co.uk, 15 March 2009)

A statement was issued after the meeting Saturday (14 March): 'We have taken decisive co-ordinated and comprehensive action to boost demand and jobs and we are better prepared to take whatever action is necessary until growth is restored' ... The G-20 finance leaders said they had agreed to increase financing to the IMF 'very substantially' to aid smaller economies ... But the ministers of the so-called Group of 20 nations, representing about 85 per cent of the world economy, stopped short of announcing any details ... The meeting was a precursor to the coming G-20 meeting to be held on 2 April in London.

(www.iht.com, 15 March 2009)

'The G-20 finance leaders ... failed to offer specifics about the size or timing of a co-ordinated economic stimulus ... The United States and China have undertaken the most vigorous stimulus programmes' (*IHT*, 16 March 2009, pp. 1, 15).

The G-20 financiers recommended substantial increases in support for the IMF and Asian Development Bank. In a communiqué they said an expansion of the IMF's membership should be considered ... Action must be taken, the financiers said, to ensure that all major 'financial institutions, markets and instruments are subject to an appropriate degree of regulation and oversight, and that hedge funds or their managers are registered and disclose appropriate information to assess the risks they pose'.

(www.cnn.com, 15 March 2009)

The participants represent 85 per cent of the world's economic output ... The communiqué contained a commitment 'to deliver the scale of sustained [fiscal stimulus] effort necessary to restore growth' and it called on the IMF 'to assess the actions taken and the actions required' ... The G-20 agreed to bring forward the next review of voting power at the IMF to 2011 from 2013 and to end the traditional carving up of the heads of the World Bank and the IMF between Europe and the United States. The communiqué said: 'The heads of the international financial institutions should be appointed through open, merit-based selection processes' ... [The United States says that it has a] 2 per cent of national discretionary fiscal stimulus.

(www.ft.com, 15 March 2009)

'Their communiqué said they would ensure that "all systematically important financial institution, markets and instruments are subject to an appropriate degree of regulation and oversight"' (*FT*, 16 March 2009, p. 6).

This week [on 23 March] the WTO predicted that the volume of global merchandise trade would shrink by 9 per cent this year [2009] ... [This will be the steepest drop ... in world trade ... since the Second World War: p. 14] ... This will be the first fall in trade flows since 1982. Between 1990 and 2006 trade volumes grew by more than 6 per cent a year, easily outstripping the growth rate of world output, which was about 3 per cent. Now the global economic machine has gone into reverse: output is declining and trade is tumbling at a faster rate ... According to the World Bank, seventeen members of the [G-20] group have taken a total of forty-seven trade-restricting steps since November [2008 when the G-20 leaders met in the United States] ... A few tariffs have been raised, but tighter licensing requirements, import bans and anti-dumping (imposing extra duties on goods supposedly dumped at below cost by exporters) have also been used. Rich countries have included discriminatory procurement provisions in their fiscal stimulus bills and offered subsidies to ailing national industries ... Most countries are able to raise tariffs, because their applied rates are below the maximum allowed by their WTO commitments ... In the World Bank's study tariff increases accounted for half of the protective measures by these countries. Ecuador raised duties on 600 goods. Russia increased them on used cars. India put them up on some kinds of steel ... Two-thirds of the trade-restricting measures documented by the World Bank are non-tariff barriers of various kinds. As with tariffs, developing countries are the principal wielders of these weapons. Indonesia has specified that certain categories of goods, such as clothes, shoes and toys, may be imported through only five ports. Argentina has imposed discretionary licensing requirements on car parts, textiles, televisions, toys, shoes and leather goods; licenses for all these used to be granted automatically. Some countries have imposed outright import bans, often justified by a tightening of safety rules or by environmental concerns. For example, China has stopped imports of a wide range of European food and drink, including Irish pork, Italian brandy and Spanish dairy products. The Indian government has banned Chinese toys ... Rich countries' weapon of choice so far is neither tariff nor non-tariff barriers to imports. They have been keen users instead of subsidies to troubled domestic industries, particularly carmakers ... The EU has regulations to limit state aid, and is looking into its members' assistance to carmakers ... Some governments have inserted discriminatory conditions into their fiscal programmes, the prime example being the 'Buy American' procurement rules. These were weakened after protests and threats of retaliation from abroad ... Subsidies in agriculture are being used with greater vigour, especially as farm prices fall. The EU, for example, has announced new export subsidies for butter, cheese and milk powder.

(*The Economist*, 28 March 2009, pp. 72–4)

Recovery measures come with a high risk of protectionism – not of the traditional sort in the form of higher tariffs, but the more subtle type like subsidies to local purchases that favour domestic industries at the expense of competitors in other countries ... When G-20 leaders gathered last November [2008] in Washington, they declared ... 'the critical importance of rejecting protectionism' and pledged to refrain from raising new barriers to investment or to trade in goods and services ... [Since then the World Bank has reported] that seventeen of the G-20 have implemented forty-seven different measures whose effect is to restrict trade at the expense of other countries. The United States has itself drawn much ire for the inclusion of 'buy America' provisions in the stimulus bill.

(www.iht.com, 26 March 2009)

A gradual build-up of protectionist measures threatens to strangle international trade and hamper global recovery, the WTO said in its latest report ... Pascal Lamy (WTO director-general): 'There is no indication of an imminent descent into high intensity protectionism, involving widespread resort to trade restriction and retaliation. The danger today is of an incremental build-up of restrictions that could slowly strangle international trade and undercut the effectiveness of policies to boost aggregate demand and restore sustained growth globally' ... Though most of the WTO's 153 members seemed to be keeping those pressures under control at the start of this year [2009], when Mr Lamy produced his first report on protectionism, 'since then there has been significant slippage'. The WTO catalogued higher tariffs, new non-tariff barriers and more resort to trade defence measures such as anti-dumping actions, which jumped by a quarter in 2008. It named nine major traders, the EU as one, that have taken steps to restrict imports of footwear, eleven that are discouraging steel imports, and twelve offering special help to their domestic car industries ... Instead of subsidies to industry and anti-import measures, such as the 'Buy American' provisions in the United States, governments should put money in the hands of consumers and leave them free to choose what they spend it on. Tariffs and subsidy cuts for trade in goods already on the table in the Doha global trade talks were equivalent to a new stimulus package of $150 billion and other trade liberalizing moves under discussion could more than double that, the WTO estimated. However, in the absence of a Doha deal, average tariffs could legally be doubled, slashing the value of world trade. Earlier this week the WTO forecast that the volume of global goods trade will slump by 9 per cent this year, the worst contraction for sixty years.

(www.ft.com, 27 March 2009)

China on Monday [23 March] proposed a sweeping overhaul of the global financial system, outlining how the dollar could eventually be replaced as the world's main reserve currency by the IMF's Special Drawing Right. The SDR is an international reserve asset created by the IMF in 1969 that has the potential to act as a super-sovereign reserve currency, Zhou Xiaochuan, governor of the People's Bank of China, said in remarks published on the central bank's website ... Zhou did not refer explicitly to the dollar.

(www.iht.com, 23 March 2009; *IHT*, 24 March 2009, p. 13)

China's central bank on Monday [23 March] proposed replacing the US dollar as the international reserve currency with a new global system controlled by the IMF ... Although Zhou Xiaochuan did not mention the US dollar, the essay gave a pointed critique of the current dollar-denominated monetary system ... To replace the current system, Mr Zhou suggested expanding the role of Special Drawing Rights, which were introduced by the IMF in 1969 to support the Bretton Woods fixed exchange rate regime but became less relevant once that system collapsed in the 1970s. Today the value of SDRs is based on a basket of four currencies – the US dollar, the yen, the Euro and the pound sterling – and they are used largely as a unit of account by the IMF and some other international organizations ... China's proposal would expand the basket of currencies forming the basis of SDRs valuation to all major economies and set up a settlement system between SDRs and other currencies so they could be widely used in international trade and financial institutions. Countries would entrust a portion of their SDR reserves to the IMF to manage collectively on their behalf and SDRs would gradually replace existing reserve currencies.

(www.ft.com, 23 March 2009; *FT*, 24 March 2009, p. 8)

'To enable and encourage take-up ... Zhou Xiaochuan ... proposes wider uses for the SDR and giving some surplus countries' reserves to the IMF for it to manage' (*FT*, 25 March 2009, p. 10).

Currently the SDR is backed by a 'basket' of the world's leading currencies, of which the American dollar is the most important, accounting for 44 per cent of its weight. The Euro (34 per cent), the pound and the yen (11 per cent each) make up the rest.

(www.independent.co.uk, 24 March 2009)

The governor of the People's Bank of China ... Zhou Xiaochuan ... suggests the international financial system, which is based on a single currency (he does not actually cite the dollar), has two main flaws. First, the reserve currency status of the dollar helped to create global imbalances. Surplus countries have little choice but to place most of their spare funds in the reserve currency since it is used to settle trade and has the most liquid bond market. But this allowed America's borrowing binge and housing bubble to persist for longer than it otherwise would have. Second, the country that issues the reserve currency faces a trade-off between domestic and international stability. Massive money printing by the Fed to support the economy makes sense from a national perspective, but it may harm the dollar's value ... The SDR was created in 1969, during the Bretton Woods fixed exchange rate system, because of concerns that there was insufficient liquidity to support global economic activity. It was originally intended as a reserve currency, but is now mainly used in the accounts for the IMF's transactions with member countries. SDRs are allocated to IMF members on the basis of their contribution to the fund ... The total amount of SDRs outstanding is equivalent to only $32 billion, or less than 2 per cent of China's foreign exchange reserves, compared with $11 trillion of American Treasury bonds ... Losing its [America's] reserve currency status would raise the cost of financing its budget and current account deficits.

(www.economist.com, 27 March 2009)

China's ICBC, the world's largest bank by market value, has said its net profit for 2008 rose by 35 per cent ... The size of its bad loans on its books fell to 2.29 per cent from 2.74 per cent in 2007, ICBC said.

(www.bbc.co.uk, 25 March 2009)

'[China's] financial system is not yet fully integrated with that of advanced economies ... [China] banned many of the derivative products that caused havoc among financial institutions around the world' (*FT*, Survey, 2 April 2009, p. 2).

According to recent official Chinese statements only $173 billion of the [$587 billion] stimulus is actually new spending. How much will be central government funded remains unclear: local government, banks and enterprises are expected to contribute 70 per cent of the stimulus, though which stimulus, the previously announced $587 billion or just the new spending, is equally unclear ... Spending on healthcare and education is a meagre 4 per cent of the entire stimulus (raised from 1 per cent in an earlier version.

(www.feer.com, 2 April 2009)

'Anecdotal evidence from corporate treasurers suggests that perhaps a third of the bank loan explosion this year has ended up in stocks' (*FT*, 3 April 2009, p. 16).

Extracts from the statement issued by the G-20 meeting in London on 2 April 2009 (www.bbc.co.uk, 2 April 2009):

> We face the greatest challenge in the world economy in modern times, a crisis which has deepened since we last met … A global crisis requires a global solution.

> We have today, therefore, pledged to do whatever is necessary to: restore confidence, growth and jobs; repair the financial system to restore lending; strengthen financial regulation to rebuild trust; fund and reform our international financial institutions to overcome this crisis and prevent future ones; promote global trade and investment and reject protectionism, to underpin prosperity; and build an inclusive, green, and sustainable recovery. By acting together to fulfil these pledges we will bring the world economy out of recession and prevent a crisis like this from recurring in the future.

> The agreements we have reached today, to treble resources available to the IMF to $750 billion, to support a new SDR [Special Drawing Rights] allocation of $250 billion, to support at least $100 billion of additional lending by the MDBs [Multilateral Development Banks], to ensure $250 billion of support for trade finance [through our export credit and investment agencies and through the MDBs], and to use the additional resources from agreed IMF gold sales for concessional finance for the poorest countries, constitute an additional $1.1 trillion programme of support to restore credit, growth and jobs in the world economy. Together with the measures we have each taken nationally, this constitutes a global plan for recovery on an unprecedented scale.

> We are undertaking an unprecedented and concerted fiscal expansion, which will save or create millions of jobs which would otherwise have been destroyed, and that will, by the end of next year [2010], amount to $5 trillion, raise output by 4 per cent and accelerate the transition to a green economy. We are committed to deliver the scale of sustained fiscal effort necessary to restore growth.

> Our actions to restore growth cannot be effective until we restore domestic lending and international capital flows. We have provided significant and comprehensive support to our banking systems to provide liquidity, recapitalize financial institutions, and address decisively the problem of impaired assets. We are committed to take all necessary actions to restore the normal flow of credit through the financial system and ensure the soundness of systemically important institutions, implementing our policies in line with the agreed G-20 framework for restoring lending and repairing the financial system.

> We call on the IMF to assess regularly the actions taken and the global actions required.

We will ... refrain from competitive devaluation of our currencies and promote a stable and well-functioning international monetary system. We will support, now and in the future, to candid, even-handed, and independent IMF surveillance of our economies and financial sectors, of the impact of our policies on others, and or risks facing the global economy.

We each agree to ensure our domestic regulatory systems are strong. But we also agree to establish the much greater consistency and systematic cooperation between countries and the framework of internationally agreed high standards.

We agree: to establish a new Financial Stability Board (FSB) with a strengthened mandate, as a successor to the Financial Stability Forum (FSF), including all G-20 countries, FSF members, Spain and the European Commission; that the FSB should collaborate with the IMF to provide early warning of macroeconomic and financial risks and the actions needed to address them ...; to extend regulation and oversight to all systematically important financial institutions, instruments and markets – this will include, for the first time, systemically important hedge funds; to endorse and implement the FSF's tough new principles on pay and compensation and to support sustainable compensation schemes and the corporate social responsibility of all firms ...; to take action against non-co-operative jurisdictions, including tax havens ...; to extend regulatory oversight and registration to Credit Rating Agencies.

We will not repeat the historic mistakes of protectionism of previous eras.

We agree that the heads and senior leadership of the international financial institutions should be appointed through an open, transparent, and merit-based selection process.

'China is expected to contribute $40 billion [to the IMF], following the lead of Japan and the EU, which each pledged $100 billion' (*IHT*, 3 April 2009, p. 4).

'[British prime minister] Gordon Brown claimed that China had agreed a $40 billion contribution to IMF funds' (*FT*, 3 April 2009, p. 1). 'Japan unilaterally gave $100 billion last November [2008], while the EU pledged $101 billion. Gordon Brown said China had pledged $40 billion but Beijing has not confirmed the figure' (p. 4).

'Officials [in China] said the details of China's contribution [to the IMF] were still under discussion' (*FT*, 4 April 2009, p. 7).

'France and other European countries also pressed China to accept action against tax havens, a step it has resisted because of the possible consequences for its coastal banking centres, Hong Kong and Shanghai' (*IHT*, 3 April 2009, p. 4).

'There were no new [fiscal stimulus] announcements' (*FT*, 3 April 2009, p. 5).

'President Barack Obama ... did not get much of what American officials were hoping for, notably failing to persuade other countries to commit more fiscal stimulus spending' (www.iht.com, 3 April 2009).

'New funding pledges ... [included] $100 billion that international development banks can lend to the poorest countries ... [and a] $6 billion increase in lending for the poorest countries' (www.bbc.co.uk, 2 April 2009).

'[The United States was] fiercely resistant to the idea of a global regulator' (www.iht.com, 3 April 2009). 'China is expected to kick in $40 billion, which it may do by buying bonds issued by the IMF ... [The United States is] committed to $100 billion' (www.iht.com, 7 April 2009).

In recent weeks the government has announced various measures to cushion the blow for graduates. They can get loans of up to 50,000 yuan ($7,300) to start their own businesses. Companies that employ them can also qualify for loans and earn tax breaks. Graduates who join the army or who take up jobs in poor, remote areas of western China will get their university tuition fees refunded by the government. Most cities have been told that for graduates they should waive residency requirements that restrict hiring from beyond their own municipalities.

(*The Economist*, 11 April 2009, p. 57)

[The World Bank estimates that China will achieve] a growth rate of 6.5 per cent this year [2009]. The World Bank said: 'A ray of hope may be emerging with signs of China's economy bottoming out by mid-2009. A recovery in China, fuelled largely by the country's huge economic stimulus package, is likely to begin this year and take full hold in 2010, potentially contributing to the region's stabilization, and perhaps recover.'

(www.guardian.co.uk, 7 April 2009)

'The World Bank ... predicts that the Chinese economy will bottom out by the middle of the year [2009]' (www.economist.com, 14 April 2009).

Executives of state-owned banks and insurers in China have been told to cut their salaries to ease the disparity between themselves and Chinese workers ... Executive pay in China is modest by Western standards, but is many times that of ordinary workers. The average employee in one of China's top financial institutions earns $58,000 – with those at the very top of these firms earning considerably more. In Chinese cities the average employee earns about $2,200 a year ... Executive pay packages for 2008 still being calculated should be no more than 90 per cent of the level of the year before, the finance ministry said ... Most of China's major banks, insurers, stock exchanges and other financial institutions are government owned. The people who run these institutions will have their pre-tax income reduced by 10 per cent ... [There are] further 10 per cent reductions for those companies which are losing money ... Executive pay is set by each company's board of directors.

(www.bbc.co.uk, 10 April 2009)

Exports were 17.1 per cent lower in March [2009] than a year earlier ... That marked a fifth consecutive month of declines ... Imports to China fell

25.1 per cent from a year ago, a slide that was steeper than that in February and than economists had expected. But the drop in exports was below what economists had projected and less severe than the 25.7 per cent plunge recorded the previous month.

(www.iht.com, 10 April 2009)

'Exports and imports fell steeply for the fourth month in March from a year earlier but by less than most analysts had predicted' (www.ft.com, 10 April 2009).

China's exports increased last month [March], but were still down 17 per cent year-on-year. Exports totalled $90.3 billion in March – a $25 billion increase from the previous month ... Imports to China dropped 25 per cent year-on-year to $72 billion ... Total trade was $162 billion in March, compared to about $142 billion in January ... China's trade ... has been decelerating in recent years, with an annual growth rate of 17.8 per cent last year [2008] compared to 35.7 per cent in 2004, according to the National Bureau of Statistics.

(www.cnn.com, 10 April 2009)

Economists have long argued about the role of exports ... Jonathan Anderson, an economist at UBS, argues that only about 8 per cent of the work force is actually employed in export industries and that, even at the peak of recent trade expansion, net exports accounted for only about a sixth of growth ... Although China's headline export figures are huge, some researchers believe this greatly exaggerates the importance of the sector, because many export factories only assemble parts manufactured elsewhere.

(*FT*, 16 April 2009, p. 6)

'Exports count for nearly 40 per cent of GDP, but they use a lot of imported components, and make up about 18 per cent of domestic value-added. Fewer than 10 per cent of jobs are in the export sector' (www.economist.com, 16 April 2009; *The Economist*, 18 April 2009, p. 83).

Suddenly reversing its role as the world's fastest growing buyer of US Treasuries and other foreign bonds, the Chinese government actually sold bonds heavily in January and February before resuming purchases in March, according to data released this weekend by China's central bank. Foreign reserves in China grew in the first quarter of this year [2009] at the slowest pace in nearly eight years ... China has lent vast sums to the United States – roughly two-thirds of the central bank's $1.95 trillion in foreign reserves are believed to be in American securities. But the Chinese government now finances a dwindling percentage of new American mortgages and government borrowing.

(www.iht.com. 12 April 2009; *IHT*, 13 April 2009, p. 15)

Prime minister Wen Jiabao has said the economy is showing 'positive changes' but still faces 'very big difficulties' ... Mr Wen also said he would spend more if necessary to boost the economy ... The economy showed 'better than expected positive changes in the first quarter [of

2009]', Mr Wen said. Citing improved investment, consumption and trade figures, he said that some sectors of the economy 'are in the process of gradual recovery'. He added that while the global crisis was deepening, China had perhaps seen the worst of it. He said: 'As the crisis has not touched the bottom, we can hardly say that the Chinese economy alone has got out of the crisis' ... But he explained that China was prepared to implement further measures to ensure that the economy continued to stabilize: 'What we should do is exert our utmost efforts to minimize the effects of the crisis' ... On Sunday [12 April] the People's Bank of China also said it would ensure the financial system has sufficient liquidity for economic development.

(www.bbc.co.uk, 12 April 2009)

China's central bank on yesterday [12 April] warned it planned to 'strictly control' credit to some sectors of the economy after the country recorded a surge in bank loans and money supply on March ... Money supply data appeared to confirm that Beijing's stimulus measures are revitalizing the domestic economy but raised credit risk and inflation concerns ... The central bank said yesterday: '[The central bank will] maintain liquidity in the banking system, and ensure that monetary supply is sufficient to meet the needs of economic development ... [There is need to] give more support to the agricultural sector, small and medium enterprises and other weak links ... [and] concretely resolve some financing difficulties faced by companies ... [But there is need to] strictly control lending to high-polluting, high-energy consuming and to those with overcapacity.'

(*FT*, 13 April 2009, p. 6)

'The central bank said it will "implement moderately loose monetary policy and maintain the continuity and stability of policy". It also said it would provide "ample liquidity to ensure money supply and loan growth meet economic development needs"' (*The Independent*, 13 April 2009).

'China's real state investment grew 4.1 per cent in the first quarter [of 2009] from a year earlier' (www.ft.com, 13 April 2009).

China has unveiled plans to establish a $10 billion investment fund for South-east Asian countries. It has also offered credit of $15 billion to the Association of South-east Asian Nations [Asean] ... Over the next three to five years China planned to offer $15 billion in credit, including loans with preferential terms of $1.7 billion in aid for co-operation projects.

(www.bbc.co.uk, 13 April 2009)

'Recently the central government has allowed local governments to issue bonds for the first time' (www.iht.com, 14 April 2009, p. 19).

China's economy grew 6.1 per cent in the first quarter [of 2009], the lowest year-on-year reading since quarterly GDP data was first published in 1992 ...

Fixed asset investment, which accounted for more than 42 per cent of GDP in 2008, showed a marked acceleration in March, rising 28.8 per cent in the first quarter, 4.2 percentage points higher than the growth in the same period last year [2008] ... Industrial production accelerated to grow 8.3 per cent in March and 5.1 per cent in the first quarter from a year earlier, down from 16.4 per cent growth in the first quarter of 2008 ... Consumer prices remained in deflationary territory in March, with the benchmark consumer price index dropping 1.2 per cent from a year earlier and falling 0.3 per cent from February.

(www.ft.com, 16 April 2009)

China does not publish quarter-on-quarter comparisons ... Using quarter-on-quarter comparisons, Goldman Sachs and J.P. Morgan both estimated growth rebounded sharply to 5.8 per cent on a seasonally adjusted basis, up from 2.2 per cent in the fourth quarter of last year ... Figures released yesterday [16 April] showed consumer prices falling 0.6 per cent in the first quarter and 1.2 per cent in March from a year earlier ... Industrial use of electricity ... fell 8.38 per cent in the first quarter from a year before ... [The National Bureau of Statistics said it] had no explanation for the discrepancy between falling power consumption and rising industrial production but insisted that both figures were accurate and the issue required 'further study'.

(*FT*, 17 April 2009, p. 6)

[GDP] was 6.1 per cent greater in the first quarter of this year [2009] than a year earlier, the National Bureau of Statistics said, warning in a statement that this had led to some increase in unemployment. But retail sales, industrial production and urban fixed asset investment were all stronger than expected in March ... Urban fixed asset investment jumped 30.3 per cent in March from a year earlier ... Using another measure of economic growth – the annualized rate of growth from one quarter to the next – China's economy actually accelerated during the first quarter of this year ... [HSBC] calculated that using this measure the economy was growing at an annual rate of 6.2 per cent in the first quarter, compared with just 2.5 per cent in the fourth quarter of last year [2008].

(www.iht.com, 16 April 2009)

'The National Bureau of Statistics said Thursday [16 April] that next year [2010] it would start releasing the annualized rate from one quarter to the next' (*IHT*, 17 April 2009, p. 15).

This [6.1 per cent] is the weakest [GDP] growth since quarterly records began in 1992 ... Industrial output expanded 5.1 per cent in the first quarter. It was up 8.3 per cent year-on-year in March, against 3.8 per cent in January and February. Fixed asset investments on items such as new factories and equipment was up 28.6 per cent in March from 26.5 per cent in February ... The National Bureau of Statistics said: 'The overall national economy showed positive changes, with better performance than expected.'

(www.bbc.co.uk, 16 April 2009)

Comparing the first quarter [of 2009] with the previous three months. GDP rose at an estimated annualized rate of around 6 per cent, after nearly stalling in the fourth quarter [of 2008]. By March the economy was gaining more speed, with the year-on-year increase in industrial production rising to 8.3 per cent from an average of 3.8 per cent in the previous two months ... Banks have an average loan-to-deposit ratio of only 67 per cent, low by international standards, and less than 5 per cent of banks' loans are non-performing, down from 40 per cent in 1998.

(www.economist.com, 16 April 2009; *The Economist*,
18 April 2009, p. 83)

In the rush to invest 4 trillion yuan ($585 billion) in economic stimulus money, China has relaxed some of the environmental restraints introduced during the long economic boom ... A portion of the stimulus package that had been earmarked for sustainable environmental projects, like water sanitation, has been slashed from 350 billion yuan to 210 billion yuan.

(*IHT*, 16 April 2009, pp. 1, 18)

The [US] Treasury Department said on Wednesday [16 April] that China was not manipulating its currency ... Treasury Secretary Timothy Geithner: 'China has taken steps to enhance exchange rate flexibility' ... He said the yuan had climbed 16.6 per cent against other currencies from June [2008] through February [2009], even as the financial crisis intensified and other currencies lost value against the dollar ... Mr Geithner ... also praised China for its stimulus plan ... Treasury officials placed even greater emphasis on China's $586 billion fiscal stimulus programme. They couched the entire discussion of currency manipulation in the context of fighting the global downturn, adding that China's stimulus programme was bigger than that of any other country except the United States.

(www.iht.com, 16 April 2009; *IHT*, 17 April 2009, p. 15)

'China's registered urban jobless rate ... rose to 4.3 per cent at the end of the first quarter [of 2009] from 4.2 three months earlier' (www.iht.com, 22 April 2009).

Thirteen East and South-east Asian countries agreed Sunday [3 May] to set up a $120 billion emergency fund for use in the economic downturn, the first independent effort by Asia to shield itself from financial crisis. Japan also announced a plan to supply up to $60.5 billion to support its neighbours in a downturn. While Asian banks largely avoided the credit crisis that tore through Wall Street and much of Europe, the region has since been hit by the downturn in the West, which has eroded demand for Asian automobiles, electronics and other exports.

(*IHT*, 4 May 2009, p. 17)

[There was] agreement among the ten members of the Association of South-east Asian Nations [Asean] and China, Japan and South Korea (known as the Asean-Plus-3 Group) on the creation of a $120 billion currency pool – to which China and Japan would contribute $38.4 billion – from which smaller countries could borrow.

(www.iht.com, 6 May 2009; *IHT*, 7 May 2009, p. 7)

Japan offered $100 billion yesterday [3 May] to help Asian states hit by the financial crisis ... Tokyo announced at a meeting of the finance ministers of the ten countries of Asean in Indonesia [Bali] that it would set up a $60.5 billion bilateral currency swap scheme, on top of a $38.4 billion commitment to the multilateral Chiang Mai initiative. The Chiang Mai deal, a $120 billion currency scheme that has been under discussion for years, was formally agreed yesterday by the Asean countries during a meeting with the finance ministers of Japan, China and South Korea ... The Chiang Mai scheme, which had originally been envisaged as a series of bilateral currency swaps limited to $80 billion, is due to come into force before the end of the year [2009] ... The thirteen countries have also agreed to put $500 million as initial capital into a new trust fund to guarantee local currency bond issues by Asian countries.

(*FT*, 4 May 2009, p. 8)

China and the EU ... should ... demonstrate their common, clear commitment against trade protectionism at the second China–EU high level economic dialogue. Trade liberalization is the engine of economic growth ... The world economy paid a heavy price for the prevalence of trade protectionism during the Great Depression in the 1930s, which led to the contraction of global trade by two-thirds. We should make sure that the same mistake is not repeated ... China is firmly committed to reform and to opening up. Since its accession to the WTO China's market has become much more open and its trade greatly liberalized. The current overall tariff level of China is only 9.8 per cent. Its average tariff level on industrial products is only 8.9 per cent, the lowest among all developing countries. Its tariff on imported agricultural products is only 15.2 per cent, which is not only lower than other developing countries but also far below that of many developed countries. The openness of China's trade in services has reached a level close to that of an average developed country ... The Chinese government recently sent Chinese enterprises on procurement missions to Europe and the United States ... The EU is now China's largest trading partner and China is the second largest trading partner of the EU.

(Wang Qishan, vice premier of the State Council of China, www.iht.com, 5 May 2009; *IHT*, 6 May 2009, p. 8)

Consumer prices fell 1.5 per cent in the year to April ... from a year earlier ... marking the third consecutive month of deflation after a 1.2 per cent fall in the twelve months to March ... Factory gate prices fell 6.6 per cent in the year to April, the rate of decline accelerating from a 6.0 per cent drop in the twelve months to March. Both falls were one-tenth of a percentage point deeper than markets had expected ... In April consumer prices fell 0.2 per cent, following a 0.3 per cent drop in March.

(www.iht.com, 11 May 2009)

Exports fell more steeply than expected in April, overshadowing strength in capital spending ... Exports were down 22.6 per cent last month from a year earlier ... That was steeper than March's 17.1 per cent decline and greater than the 18 per cent drop that economists had expected ... Imports [in April] fell 23 per cent ... Economists had expected a 22 per cent fall in imports after a 25.1 per cent drop in March ... the annual pace of fixed asset investment growth in urban areas surged to 30.5 per cent in the first four months [of 2009] ... Economists had expected a reading of 29.1 per cent following a 28.6 per cent increase in the first quarter.

(www.iht.com, 12 May 2009)

'J.P. Morgan said it estimated that month-on-month exports fell 2.8 per cent on a seasonally adjusted basis after gaining 6.1 per cent month-on-month in March' (*FT*, 13 may 2009, p. 8).

'Industrial production rose less than expected in April ... rising 7.33 per cent from a year earlier ... [This was] below the 8.3 per cent recorded in March and below what analysts had expected for April' (www.iht.com, 13 May 2009).

'China's first quarter [of 2009] economic data showed 6.1 per cent year-on-year GDP growth' (www.economist.com, 14 May 2009).

China's renminbi 4,000 billion economic stimulus package is being delayed by local governments unable to raise their share of financing, according to a report from the state auditor ... the National Audit Office ... Central government has pledged renminbi 1,200 billion ($175 billion) for infrastructure and public works projects to boost flagging growth, with the rest of the renminbi 4,000 billion expected to come from local governments, state-owned enterprises and private companies ... In spite of its complaints that local authorities are delaying the stimulus package, the audit office concluded that no serious abuse of stimulus funding had occurred and the stimulus plan had no big problems.

(*FT*, 19 May 2009, p. 6)

'In April the State Council (the cabinet) announced that it planned to lower the capital ratio required for lending to infrastructure projects' (www.economist. com, 1 June 2009).

'US Treasury Secretary Timothy Geithner arrived Sunday [31 May] in Beijing for two days of talks with Chinese leaders ... China is America's biggest creditor, holding $768 billion in Treasury securities' (www.iht.com, 31 May 2009; *IHT*, 1 June 2009, p. 15).

[On Monday 1 June] the Treasury Secretary just briefly touched on currency issues ... Mr Geithner did urge China to move toward a more flexible exchange rate ... Under President George W. Bush, Treasury Secretary

Henry Paulson held regular meetings with officials in Beijing as part of the so-called strategic economic dialogue. The Obama administration has decided to broaden these discussions, with Secretary of State Hillary Clinton taking part, in what is now being called the strategic and economic dialogue.

(www.iht.com, 1 June 2009).

'In a speech at Peking University Timothy Geithner said: "We will cut our [budget] deficit and we will eliminate the extraordinary government support that we have put in place to overcome the crisis"' (*IHT*, 2 June 2009, p. 12).

In remarks to an audience at Peking University [on 1 June] that set the tone for two days of talks with Chinese leaders, Timothy Geithner reiterated President Barack Obama's pledge to lower the US fiscal deficit to about 3 per cent of GDP once the economy was on a stable recovery path ... He tried to reassure his audience at Peking University that the United States would do what was necessary to bring its budget under control, reducing the fiscal deficit to about 3 per cent of GDP. He said: 'The president in his initial budget to Congress made it clear that, as soon as recovery is firmly established we are going to have to bring our fiscal deficit to a level that is sustainable over the medium term' ... But Mr Geithner also named a long list of tasks the Chinese government had to address to make its contribution to a more balanced global economy. These included expanding its social safety net, spending more on education and encouraging changes in industry structure through market mechanisms. Mr Geithner said: 'An important part of this strategy is the government's commitment to continue progress toward a more flexible exchange rate regime' ... He also said: 'In the United States saving rates will have to increase, and the purchases of US consumers cannot be as dominant a driver of growth as they have been in the past. Growth [in China] that is sustainable will require a very substantial shift from external to domestic demand' ... Such a shift would require a more flexible currency regime.

(*FT*, 2 June 2009, p. 6)

'Timothy Geithner said: "Our common challenge is to recognize that a more balanced and sustainable global recovery will require changes in the composition of growth in our two economies"' (www.ft.com, 1 June 2009).

'China is among the largest purchasers of US government debt, with $767.9 billion as of March [2009], according to Treasury Department data released on Friday [15 May]' (www.iht.com, 16 May 2009).

'[China has] roughly $1,400 billion in dollar assets' (*FT*, 1 June 1009, p. 6).

'Data for May showed consumer prices falling 1.4 per cent from a year earlier, reflecting the decline of food and energy prices from their unusually high levels last year [2008]' (www.iht.co, 10 June 2009).

[On 10 June] the consumer price index fell 1.4 per cent last month [May] from a year earlier, compared with a 1.5 per cent decline in April ... On a month-on-month basis the National Bureau of Statistics said the consumer price index dropped 0.3 per cent from April's level. The decline in food prices eased significantly, from 1.3 per cent in April to 0.6 per cent in May. Non-food prices, however, fell 1.7 per cent last month, more than April's 1.5 per cent ... The producer price index, which measures prices paid at the factory gate, fell 7.2 per cent in May. This was sharper than the 6.6 per cent fall in April.

(www.ft.com, 11 June 2009)

China's exports plunged by a record 26.4 per cent in May from a year earlier ... China's imports fell a little more slowly than exports, dropping 25.2 per cent from a year-earlier period ... Imports were down 25.2 per cent from a fairly weak level a year ago.

(www.iht.com, 11 June 2009)

'Industrial production rose 8.9 per cent in May from a year earlier, higher than April's 7.3 per cent year-on-year growth' (*FT*, 13 June 2009, p. 7).

China has introduced a 'Buy Chinese' policy as part of its economic stimulus efforts ... In an edict released jointly by nine governments, Beijing said government procurement must use only Chinese products unless they are not available within China or cannot be bought on reasonable commercial terms or legal terms ... A few months ago Beijing was raging against a proposed 'Buy American' clause included in the US economic rescue package ... Foreign companies operating in China argue that they have been largely cut out of procurement related to the government's stimulus package.

(*FT*, 17 June 2009, p. 8)

China has imposed a requirement for its stimulus projects to use domestically made goods ... projects must obtain permission to use imported goods, said an order issued by China's main planning agency and eight other bodies ... China criticized Washington for a provision that favoured US suppliers of steel, iron and manufactured goods in projects financed by the US stimulus package.

(*IHT*, 18 June 2009, p. 21)

The World Bank has raised its forecast for growth in China this year from 6.5 per cent to 7.2 per cent ... It predicted in March that the Chinese economy would grow by 6.5 per cent in 2009 ... The World Bank believes the global economy, excluding China, will shrink by about 3 per cent this year [2009].

(www.bbc.co.uk, 18 June 2009)

The World Bank's June quarterly update ... forecasts economic growth at 7.2 per cent in 2009 ... For such an open economy to cope with a fall in the rate of real export growth from 20 per cent in 2007 to 8 per cent last year [2008] and a forecast of minus 10 per cent this year [2009] is remarkable. Nevertheless, the impact of China's stimulus on the rest of the world will be modest: the country generates only 7 per cent of global output, at market prices; moreover, the World Bank also forecasts a decline of 5 per cent in real imports this year. The net stimulus China will give to the rest of the world will only be around 0.1 per cent of global output in 2009 ... The fiscal deficit is forecast at a mere 5 per cent of GDP in 2009 and the risk of an upsurge in inflation is quite small.

(FT, editorial, 22 June 2009, p. 10)

'[According to the OECD] GDP is forecast to rise 7.7 per cent in 2009 and 9.3 per cent in 2010, up from forecasts [in March] of 6.3 per cent and 8.5 per cent, respectively' (www.iht.com, 24 June 2009).

Of the 4 trillion yuan economic stimulus package announced last November [2008] 300 billion has now been reallocated from infrastructure projects to welfare schemes. Critics say China could afford to do much better. Its public finances are in good shape, with its public debt at less than 20 per cent of GDP and its fiscal balance improving rapidly. Saving, at over 40 per cent of GDP, is high by international standards.

(The Economist, Special Report on Ageing Populations, 27 June 2009, p. 15)

There is huge potential for higher consumption in the countryside as incomes rise: only 30 per cent of rural households have a refrigerator, for example, compared with virtually all urban households ... On 19 June ... the government ... ordered all state-owned firms that had listed on the stock market since 2005 to transfer 10 per cent of their shares to the national Social Security Fund to shore up its assets ... In most Asian economies household debt is less than 50 per cent of GDP, compared with around 100 per cent in many developed economies; in China and India it is less than 15 per cent ... The Chinese bank regulator announced draft rules in May to allow domestic and foreign institutions to set up consumer finance firms to offer personal loans for consumer goods purchases.

(The Economist, 27 June 2009, p. 94)

The World Bank said on 22 June that world trade volumes ... will shrink by nearly 10 per cent this year [2009]. That would be the sharpest fall since the [Great] Depression, and the first decline in trade since a small dip in 1982.

(The Economist, 27 June 2009, p. 96)

'Consumer prices ... [fell] by 1.4 per cent in June from a year earlier. Factory gate prices were down 7.2 per cent' *(IHT*, 2 July 2009, p. 17).

China's finance ministry has failed to sell all 28 billion yuan ($4.1 billion) of one-year government bonds it offered at an auction. It is the first under-subscribed government bond auction since 2003 ... It comes as the government looks to tighten its monetary policy to prevent the risk of asset bubbles, loan defaults and rapid inflation ... The city of Hangzhou has started tightening mortgage lending terms, ahead of any changes to monetary and credit policies by the national government ... Chinese property prices nationwide have increased since March, after several months of falls.

(www.bbc.co.uk, 8 July 2009)

[On 8 July G-8 leaders, meeting in Italy] failed to agree a concerted strategy to boost the global economy, in the face of diverging views on the state of the recovery and what to do next. In a gloomy prognosis, the G-8 communiqué said: 'We note some signs of stabilization in our economies. However, the economic situation remains uncertain and significant risks remain to economic and financial stability ... The situation is still uncertain and risks do remain in the economic and financial sectors ... Exit strategies will vary from country to country depending on domestic economic conditions and public finances' ... Angela Merkel, German Chancellor, wanted the G-8 talks to focus on an 'exit strategy' – plotting an unwinding of a massive fiscal and monetary stimulus ... Other leaders, such as Gordon Brown, Britain's prime minister, argued that such talk was premature when the world still faced economic dangers, while Barack Obama, US president, kept open the prospect of a further stimulus ... Working sessions today [9 July] will be open to the G-5 countries (Brazil, India, China, Mexico and South Africa) and to Egypt, plus the United Nations and the World Bank Hu Jintao, the Chinese president, [decided] to return home on the eve of the summit to deal with the crisis caused by ethnic strife in Xinjiang.

(*FT*, 9 July 2009, p. 7)

The IMF said on Wednesday [8 July] ... the global economy would probably contract 1.4 per cent this year [2009], a touch steeper than the 1.3 per cent decline it expected in April. It now sees world economic growth of 2.5 per cent in 2010, however, compared with an April projection of 1.9 per cent.

(www.iht.com, 9 July 2009)

'The IMF ... now expects output to grow by 8.5 per cent in China' (*The Economist*, 11 July 2009, p. 9).

China's exports fell again in June for the eighth consecutive month, but the declines were much less severe than in May. Exports fell 21.4 per cent in June from a year earlier, a moderation from May's record 26.4 per cent decline. Imports were down 13.2 per cent, much better than the 20 per cent forecast and followed a 25.2 per cent [fall] in May.

(www.bbc.co.uk, 10 July 2009)

Exports rose 7.5 per cent last month [June] from May ... Exports were down 21.4 per cent on a year-on-year basis though they were the highest monthly tally since December [2008] ... Imports rose 15.6 per cent from May, while declining 13.2 per cent year-on-year.

(www.ft.com, 10 July 2009)

'Property prices rose in June for the first time in seven months, official data show ... House prices in seventy cities rose 0.2 per cent in June from a year earlier. Prices rose 0.8 per cent from May' (www.bbc.co.uk, 10 July 2009).

> Money supply growth surged in June ... The broad M2 measure of money supply grew at a record pace of 28.5 per cent in June, blowing past forecasts of a 26 per cent rise and accelerating from a 25.7 per cent increase in May ... In a new sign of its worry that rapid lending could fuel spending, the central bank responded with the latest in a series of baby steps to absorb surplus cash washing through the economy by requiring banks to buy 100 billion yuan ($15 billion) in special bills ... Traders said the central bank would issue the bills in September at a punitively low interest rate to a clutch of banks that have been responsible for a growing share of new loans. The operation means those banks will have less money to hand out ... Other recent steps in recent weeks by the central bank indicating that monetary loosening is over, even if outright tightening has not yet begun, include the resumption of one-year bill sales and an increase in yield on open market operations ... The central bank reported that its foreign exchange reserves leapt by $177.9 billion in the second quarter [of 2009] to $2.13 trillion. China is the only country to have amassed more than $2 trillion in currency reserves.
>
> (www.iht.com, 15 July 2009)

'Currency reserves rose 17.8 per cent from June 2008 to a record $2.13 trillion. Its currency stockpile is twice the size of Japan's – the second biggest holder' (www.bbc.co.uk, 15 July 2009).

> The central bank has begun to tug gently at the reins. It has nudged up money market interest rates and warned banks that it intends to increase its scrutiny of new bank loans. The China Banking Regulatory Commission has warned banks to stick to rules on mortgages for second homes, which require a down-payment of at least 40 per cent of a property's value ... Housing starts rose 12 per cent in the year to June, the first growth in twelve months.
>
> (*The Economist*, 18 July 2009, pp. 57–8)

> In the first half of this year [2009] banks lent $1,079 billion, nearly double the total extended in 2008 ... The People's Bank of China has quietly increased inter-bank lending rates in recent weeks, to make it more expensive for small local lenders to access funds.
>
> (*FT*, 16 July 2009, p. 6)

> The economy grew by 7.1 per cent so far this year [2009, compared with the first half of 2008] ... GDP grew 7.9 per cent alone in the April to June quarter [compared with April to June 2008]. That is close to the government's target rate of 8 per cent – an auspicious number in Chinese culture.
>
> (www.cnn.com, 16 July 2009)

> GDP ... grew at an annual rate of 7.9 per cent between April and June, up from 6.1 per cent in the first quarter of the year [2009] ... Economists had

forecast a second quarter growth rate of 7.5 per cent ... Industrial output grew by more than 10 per cent year-on-year in June ... Urban fixed asset investment rose by more than 35 per cent over the same period ... China's consumer price index fell 1.7 per cent in June compared with the same month a year earlier, the fifth consecutive monthly decline. Exports in June were down 21.4 per cent compared with a year earlier.

(www.bbc.co.uk, 16 July 2009)

Fixed asset investment, the prime engine of growth, [was] up 33.5 per cent in the first half of the year [2009] compared with the same period last year [2008] ... Retail spending expanded 15 per cent in the first six months of the year.

(*FT*, 17 July 2009)

A breakdown of the 7.1 per cent GDP growth for the first half of 2009 showed that investment accounted for 6.2 percentage points ... Consumption added 3.8 percentage points to GDP, but net exports subtracted 2.9 percentage points ... Factory output growth rose 10.7 per cent in June, faster than May's 8.9 per cent.

(www.guardian.co.uk, 16 July 2009)

Chinese regulators on Monday [27 July] ordered banks to ensure unprecedented volumes of new loans are channelled into the real economy and not diverted into equity or real estate markets where officials say fresh asset bubbles are forming. The new policy requires banks to monitor how their loans are spent and comes amid warnings that banks ignored basic lending standards in the first half of this year [2009] as they rushed to extend renminbi 7,370 billion ($1,080 billion) in new loans, more than twice the amount lent in the same period a year earlier.

(www.ft.com, 27 July 2009; *FT*, 28 July 2009, p. 5)

In China there is little debate. The government simply orders banks to lend – and it happens almost instantly ... Last month [July] the central bank called for stricter supervision of bank loans because some stimulus spending appeared to be directed toward wasteful government projects. The China Banking Regulatory Commission also recently took steps to lower risk by ordering Chinese banks to raise their bad-loan reserve rations by the end of the year [2009]. Liu Mingkang (the top banking regulator in late July): 'Rapid expansion of bank loans in the first half year boosted the country's economic growth. But it also increased the possibilities of financial risk' ... At a high level Politburo meeting last month [July] President Hu Jintao called for the country to maintain a 'relatively loose' monetary policy and signalled that the direction of macroeconomic policy 'should be maintained' ... Through June banking regulators said non-performing loans at China's commercial banks accounted for just 1.74 per cent of outstanding loans – down slightly from the beginning of the year. But many experts say that could change in the coming years, as these new loans come due.

They suspect that government pressure on banks to make loans will result in loan defaults.

(*IHT*, 7 August 2009, p. 16)

The strong rebound in China's economy in the second quarter [of 2009] – pushing GDP 7.9 per cent higher than a year ago – came entirely from domestic demand ... Net exports (exports minus imports) contributed 2.6 percentage points of the country's GDP growth in 2007, but shaved almost three points off its growth in the first half of this year ... Its current account surplus did soar from 2005 onwards, but until then was rather modest ... Over the past ten years net exports accounted, on average for only one-tenth of its growth.

(*The Economist*, 1 August 2009, p. 65)

'Private consumption contributed just 2.8 percentage points of China's annual average GDP growth of 10.2 per cent from 2000 to 2008' (*IHT*, 4 August 2009, p. 18).

In response to rumours of a possible curb in lending and liquidity ... Shanghai investors ... bid down shares by more than 5 per cent. China has since reassured that it would keep monetary policy 'moderately loose' and shares have resumed their upward march ... There are already reports that large banks reduced lending in July.

(*IHT*, 5 August 2009, p. 17)

On 27 July ... America and China ... will hold their first Strategic *and* Economic Dialogue attended, unlike previous conjunctionless ones, by America's Secretary of State ... The new forum tweaks the Strategic Economic Dialogue launched by President George W. Bush in 2006 which was led on the American side by the Treasury Secretary. It also absorbs a security-focused forum called the Senior Dialogue which began in 2005.

(www.economist.com, 23 July 2009)

[US] Treasury Secretary Timothy Geithner and [US] Secretary of State Hillary Clinton co-host the talks [in Washington]. The meeting, called the US–China Strategic and Economic Dialogue, is the first formal negotiation between the United States and China since President Barack Obama took office ... China has sent vice premier Wang Qishan and State Councillor Dai Bingguo.

(www.bbc.co.uk, 27 July 2009)

The so-called Strategic and Economic Dialogue is a successor to a wide-ranging consultation begun during the [George W.] Bush administration by the former Treasury Secretary, Henry [Hank] Paulson ... The discussions in Washington represent the continuation of a dialogue begun in the George W. Bush administration, which focused on economic tensions between the two nations. President Barack Obama chose to expand the talks to include foreign policy issues as well as economic disputes over trade and currency values ... President Barack Obama: 'The relationship between the United States and China will shape the twenty-first century, which makes it as important as any bilateral relationship in the world ... Just as we respect China's ancient culture and remarkable achievements, we also strongly believe that the religion and culture of all peoples must be respected, and all people should be free to speak their minds. That includes ethnic and religious minorities in China, as surely as it includes minorities within the United States' ... Vice premier Wang Qishan oversees economic policy, and State Councillor Dai Bingguo oversees foreign policy.

(www.iht.com, 27 July 2009; *IHT*, 28 July 2009, p. 8)

[US] Treasury Secretary Timothy Geithner said Tuesday [28 July] that the United States and China have reached agreement on the need to work toward more balanced global growth once the current economic crisis has ended. Geithner spoke as the two countries were wrapping up two days of discussions aimed at seeking to narrow differences on a wide range of economic and foreign policy issues. In his opening comments Chinese vice premier Wang Qishan voiced support for a key US goal that China shift to a more domestic-led growth rather than depending so much on exports that drive up the US trade deficit. Wang said: 'China will focus on boosting domestic demand and in particular consumer demand.'

(www.iht.com, 28 July 2009)

China sought and received assurances from the Obama administration that the United States would reduce its budget deficit once an economic recovery was under way, a senior Chinese official said Tuesday at the end of two days of high-level talks between the countries. Xie Xuren (the Chinese finance minister): 'Attention should be given to the fiscal deficit' ... He said Treasury Secretary Timothy Geithner had assured the Chinese that once the economy rebounded the deficit would gradually come down from its current record levels. Timothy Geithner: 'As we put in place conditions for a durable recovery led by private demand we will bring down our fiscal position to a more sustainable level over time' ... For China the rising American deficit is a concern because it could weaken the dollar and put at risk China's vast holdings of Treasury securities and other dollar-based assets. China holds an estimated $1.5 trillion in such securities, making it the United States' largest foreign creditor.

(www.iht.com, 29 July 2009)

Treasury Secretary Timothy Geithner said on Tuesday [28 July] the United States will emphasize fiscal discipline on both the federal and personal levels, while China will encourage more domestic spending instead of relying on foreign demand ... He called the agreement on complementary economic strategies the 'most important strategic achievements' of the [two-day] talks ... Timothy Geithner: 'We want to be very careful, as we work together to help remove the ... global economy back from crisis to growth, that we don't lay the seeds of future crises. So ... as we move to put in place a more stable, more resilient financial system in the United States, we need to see actions in China and in other countries to shift the source of growth more to domestic demand.'

(www.cnn.com, 29 July 2009)

Timothy Geithner: 'The United States and China are among the biggest beneficiaries of the global trading system and share a common interest in ensuring that global trade and investment remain open and rules-based' (www.bbc.co.uk, 29 July 2009).

'At the Strategic and Economic Dialogue meeting between American and Chinese officials on 27 and 28 July in Washington, DC, the yuan's exchange rate was barely discussed' (www.economist.com, 30 July 2009).

'According to figures released on Tuesday [4 August], although the country's jobless rate remains unchanged, some 3 million graduates have not yet found work' (www.bbc.co.uk, 5 August 2009).

> China's central bank has told the heads of the largest state-controlled banks to slow the pace of new lending, say people familiar with the matter, after new loan volume in the first half of the year tripled from the same period a year earlier. The pressure from the People's Bank of China signals an unstated shift in policy and comes as it steps up its open market operations to control liquidity and slow loan growth. Over the past two weeks China's leaders have emphasized the country will adhere for now to its policy of 'moderately loose' monetary conditions. While there has been no formal change to what is an extremely loose monetary policy, the central bank and regulators have signalled an intention to rein in excessive lending through various policy announcements. The People's Bank of China has raised interest rates in recent weeks on its weekly sales of short-term bills in the inter-bank market and has ordered the most profligate lenders to buy set amounts of special low-interest, one-year central bank notes, increasing pressure on banks to toe the line ... Officials fear some of the renminbi 7,370 billion ($1.078 billion) in new loans extended in the first half of the year has found its way into the bubbling stock and property markets ... China Construction Bank ... [said it] plans to extend renminbi 200 billion of loans in the second half, down from renminbi 709 billion in the first half. It is usual in China for banks to frontload lending in the first half of the year and extend much less in the latter half but a 70 per cent drop would be extreme ... On Wednesday [5 August] the central bank hinted at shifting priorities when it said in a quarterly report it would carry out 'market-based fine tuning measures' while 'unswervingly implementing the moderately loose monetary policy'.
>
> (www.ft.com, 7 August 2009; *FT*, 8 August 2009, p. 5)

Further tightening measures are likely in the coming months, as the economy continues to recover. In addition, since bank lending in China is typically front-loaded (with most of the lending taking place in the first half of the year), a sharp fall can be expected over the next few months.

(www.economist.com, 7 August 2009)

'Comparing the second quarter [of 2009] with the first at an annualized rate, GDP grew by 15 per cent' (*The Economist*, 15 August 2009, p. 57).

'With the fall in exports, investment has accounted for about 80 per cent of growth so far this year [2009]' (*FT*, 10 August 2009, p. 4).

'Trade data published by the customs office showed exports in July dropped 23 per cent from a year earlier, a slightly smaller decline than economists had expected' (www.iht.com, 11 August 2009).

> Prices continued to fall in July from a year earlier, reducing the likelihood that Beijing will make any significant changes to its policy of boosting growth with fresh liquidity and surging infrastructure spending. China's consumer price index fell 1.8 per cent while the producer price index was down 8.2 per cent from a year earlier ... In July the volume of new lending fell 77 per cent from a month earlier.
>
> (*FT*, 12 August 2009, p. 4)

'New loans nearly tripled in the first seven months from the same period last year [2008]' (www.ft.com, 11 August 2009).

> Total new lending in the month of July fell to renminbi 356 billion from renminbi 1,530 billion in June as the government ordered banks to slow the pace of loan growth that many believe has contributed to renewed bubbles in the property and stock markets.
>
> (www.ft.com, 14 August 2009)

> The global economic downturn has severely hurt the [iron and steel] sector ... Faced with a glut of steelmaking capacity and many small steel companies vying to buy iron ore, Beijing officials on Thursday [13 August] ordered a three-year moratorium on the construction of any new steel mills or the expansion of existing ones.
>
> (www.iht.com, 16 August 2009; *IHT*, 17 August 2009, p. 16)

> A sharp sell-off in Chinese shares in late Wednesday [19 August] trading saw the benchmark SCI close 4.3 per cent lower, putting it in sight of a bear market as speculation grew that the Beijing government would tighten its monetary policy ... Beijing is thought to be concerned about illegal lending to property developers and banks are tightening control over the approval of mortgages. New lending in July was down sharply to renminbi 355.9 billion ($52 billion) from renminbi 1,530 billion the previous month [June], raising fears that liquidity would disappear from the stock market.
>
> (www.ft.com, 19 August 2009)

> Rumours are rife that banks' capital requirements are being tightened, as are the conditions for various kinds of loans. Although a decline in new lending in the second half of the year had been expected; the rate of decline has, for many, been a shock.
>
> (*The Economist*, 29 August 2009, pp. 66–7)

New bank lending did indeed slow sharply in July, to 356 billion yuan ($52 billion) from 1.53 trillion yuan in June. But bank lending always slows in the second half of the year; the twelve-month pace of growth is therefore a better measure. On a year-on-year basis bank lending grew by an impressive 34 per cent in July, roughly the same pace as in June.

(p. 67)

The worst global recession since the 1930s may be over. Led by China, Asia's emerging economies have revived fastest, with several expanding at annualized rates of more than 10 per cent in the second quarter [of 2009]. A few rich economies also returned to growth, albeit far more modestly, between April and June. Japan's output rose at an annualized pace of 3.7 per cent, and both Germany and France notched up annualized growth rates of just over 1 per cent ... [But] a gloomy U [shaped recovery] with a long, flat bottom of weak growth is the likeliest share of the next few years.

(*The Economist*, 22 August 2009, pp. 8–9)

'The American economic stimulus plan requires any project receiving money to use steel and other construction materials ... from countries that have signed the WTO's agreement on free trade in government procurement. China has not' (www.iht.com, 25 August 2009).

China is buying the equivalent of $50 billion of the first bond sale by the IMF, a purchase that might raise Beijing's standing in the fund and help the government's quiet campaign to expand the reach of its tightly controlled currency. The sale is part of an effort by the IMF to raise $500 billion to finance lending to help economies battered by the global downturn ... China is the first country to buy the five-year bond: Russia and Brazil have also expressed interest. EU governments said Wednesday [2 September] they would contribute $175 billion, or more than a third of the amount sought by the IMF. China took the unusual step of paying for the IMF bonds with 341.2 billion yuan ... rather than dollars ... The new bonds are denominated in Special Drawing Rights, a quasi-currency used by the IMF in its dealings with member governments ... Beijing had been promoting ... the use of the yuan abroad ... China signed a currency swap deal with Argentina in March [2009] and has agreed to lend yuan to the central banks of South Korea, Malaysia, Indonesia and Belarus in the event of emergencies.

(*IHT*, 4 September 2009, p. 14)

'Yin Weimin, China's labour minister, said there had been a modest increase in the number of jobs in the economy during June, July and August, reversing the sharp slump in employment which began last October [2008]' (*FT*, 10 September 2009, p. 7).

'Chinese exports began declining last November [2008] and the government reckons that poor export performance knocked 2.9 percentage points off the growth rate in the first half of this year [2009]' (*The Economist*, 12 September 2009, p. 78).

Industrial output grew at a twelve-month high of 12.3 per cent in August from a year earlier, jumping from 10.8 per cent in July and beating expectations of a 12.0 per cent rise, data issued by the National Bureau of Statistics showed on Friday [11 September]. Annual urban fixed-asset investment growth also picked up, reaching 33.0 per cent for the first eight months, notching up from 32.9 per cent in January to July [2009], and beating forecasts of 32.5 per cent … Premier Wen Jiabao on Thursday [10 September] said the government would unswervingly apply its policy mix of massive government spending and loose money because the economic recovery remains fragile. Zhang Xiaoqiang, vice chairman of the National Development and Reform Commission, carried out that refrain on Friday, telling reporters at a meeting of the World Economic Forum that the recovery was not yet solid, even though growth picked up to an annual 7.9 per cent in the second quarter … Deflationary pressures eased as food prices rose. Consumer prices fell only 1.2 per cent in August from a year earlier compared with a decline of 1.8 per cent in July, tempering the pace of deflation.

(www.iht.com, 11 September 2009)

Premier Wen Jiabao said on Thursday (10 September]: 'The stabilization and recovery of the Chinese economy is not yet steady, solid and balanced. Some of the stimulus measures will see their effect wane, and it will take time before those long-term policies show effect.'

(www.bbc.co.uk, 11 September 2009)

'Premier Wen Jiabao said on Thursday (10 September): "China's economic rebound is unstable, unbalanced and not yet solid. We cannot and will not change the direction of our policies when the conditions are not appropriate"' (*FT*, 12 September 2009, p. 7).

'Exports continued to decline in August, down from 23 per cent from the same month last year [2008]' (www.bbc.co.uk, 11 September 2009).

August exports fell 23.4 per cent from a year ago, though shipments rose to a seasonally adjusted 3.4 per cent from July … Industrial output expanded by 12.3 per cent from a year earlier, the fastest pace in twelve months … Fixed asset investment rose 33 per cent on the year, nearly flat with July's growth.

(*FT*, 12 September 2009, p. 7)

Government agencies have been told not to buy imported goods with money from economic stimulus programmes unless no domestic alternative is available. Washington has imposed a less restrictive rule, misleadingly known as 'Buy American', requiring that construction materials for the stimulus programme be bought from any of the thirty-nine countries that have agreed to free trade in government procurement – which China has not.

(www.iht.com, 18 September 2009)

The 25–26 September 2009 G-20 meeting took place in the US city of Pittsburg.

> President Barack Obama will announce Friday [25 September] that the once elite club of rich industrial nations known as the G-7 will be permanently replaced as a global forum for economic policy by the much broader G-20 that includes China, Brazil, India and other fast-growing developing countries.
>
> (www.iht.com, 25 September 2009)

> Global leaders were set to announce on Friday that the elite club of rich industrial nations known as the G-7 would be permanently replaced as a global forum for economic policy by the G-20 ... For more than three decades the main economic group was the G-7 ... Russia was gradually added [to make the G-8] ... The group will still meet twice a year to discuss security matters.
>
> (*IHT*, 26 September 2009, p. 1)

> The G-20 group of leading and emerging economies is to take on a new role as a permanent body co-ordinating the world economy, a White House statement said. It will take on the role previously carried out by ... the G-8 group ... The G-20 is meeting in the US city of Pittsburgh for a two-day summit. EU officials also announced a deal to shift the balance of voting in the [186-member] IMF towards such growing nations such as China. Currently China wields 3.7 per cent of IMF votes compared with France's 4.9 per cent ... A White House statement announced the new role for the G-20: 'The G-20 leaders reached a historic agreement to put the G-20 at the centre of their efforts to work together to build a durable recovery while avoiding the financial fragilities that led to the crisis. Today [25 September] leaders endorsed the G-20 as the premier forum for their international economic co-operation.'
>
> (www.bbc.co.uk, 25 September 2009)

> One year after a financial crisis that began in the United States tipped the world into a severe recession, [G-20] leaders ... agreed on Friday [25 September] to a far-reaching effort to revamp the economic system. The agreements, if carried out by national governments, would lead to a much tighter regulation over financial institutions, complex financial instruments and executive pay. They could also lead to big changes and more outside scrutiny over the economic strategies of individual countries, including the United States ... The leaders pledged to rethink their economic policies in a co-ordinated effort to reduce the immense imbalances between export-dominated countries like China and Japan and debt-laden countries like the United States, which has long been the world's most willing consumer. The United States will be expected to increase its savings rate, reduce its trade deficit and address its huge budget deficit. Countries like China, Japan and Germany will be expected to reduce their dependence on exports by promoting more consumer spending and investment at home. The ideas are not

new, and there is no enforcement mechanism to penalize countries if they stick to their old habits. But for the first time ever, each country agreed to submit its policies to a 'peer review' from the other governments as well as monitoring by the IMF.

(www.iht.com, 26 September 2009)

The G-20 would focus on economic issues while the G-8 would deal primarily with international relations and foreign policy ... The G-20 ... was created [in September 1999] at a meeting of G-7 finance ministers in response to the Asian financial crisis of 1997–9 ... The new G-20 Framework for Strong, Sustainable and Balanced Growth aims to work in three stages. First, national leaders agree priorities for the world economy in annual G-20 summits. Second, countries submit reports to show how their domestic policies match those ambitions. Third, the IMF assesses whether national plans mesh together to support global objectives. The enforcement mechanism will be peer review.

(*FT*, 26 September 2009, p. 6)

[The] communiqué said: 'Today we designated the G-20 as the premier forum for our international economic co-operations ... G-20 leaders agreed to: launch a Framework for Strong Sustainable and Balanced Growth'; strengthen financial regulation, via reformed rules on capital adequacy and remuneration of bank employees; reform the global institutional architecture, including reallocation of quotas in the IMF; phase out fossil fuel subsidies; 'bring the Doha round to a successful conclusion in 2010'; reach agreement in Copenhagen on climate change; and meet twice in 2010, first in Canada and then in South Korea.

(*FT*, 28 September 2009, p. 12)

There was agreement that macroeconomic policies should be harmonized to avoid the imbalances – America's spendthrift ways and deficits; Asia's savings glut – that made the financial crisis so much worse. But strengthening co-operation, through the Framework for Strong, Sustainable and Balanced Growth will not be easy, even with the IMF knocking heads together ... The governance structure of the IMF will change, with 'underrepresented' (mostly developing) countries getting at least 5 per cent more of the voting rights by 2011 ... The other big institutional change is the ascension of the Financial Stability Board, a club of central bankers and financial regulators, which has also been broadened to include the big developing countries. From now on it will take a lead role in co-ordinating and monitoring tougher financial regulations and serve (along with the IMF) as an early warning system for emerging risks.

(www.economist.com, 26 September 2009)

In the short term, the G-20 also agreed to continue with the current stimulus measures, insisting they had been effective in preventing the recession tipping over into a great depression. The IMF is now predicting 3 per cent growth worldwide next year [2010] ... the measure should be continued until a durable recovery had been secured, the communiqué said.

(*Guardian*, 26 September 2009, p. 18)

The last time the leaders of the G-20 met, in London in April [2009], their task was to steer the world away from a 1930s-style depression. They succeeded ... But while stability has returned, much more needs to be done to put economies, and particularly their banking sectors, on a sounder footing ... The leaders pledged not to withdraw stimulus measures until a durable recovery is in place. They agreed to co-ordinate their exit strategies, while also acknowledging that timing will vary from country to country depending on the forcefulness of measures in place.

(www.economist.com, 26 September 2009)

'The Pittsburg summit agreed that the $1.1 trillion boost to the global economy agreed at the last G-20 meeting in April [2009] had prevented the recession turning into a depression. The leaders' communiqué: "It worked"' (*Independent*, 26 September 2009, p. 6).

[The] communiqué: '[At the London summit in April] our countries agreed to ensure recovery, to repair our financial systems and to maintain the global flow of capital. It worked ... The process of recovery and repair remains incomplete. In many countries unemployment remains unacceptably high. The conditions for a recovery of private demand are not yet fully in place' ... G-20 leaders agreed to avoid premature withdrawal of stimulus ... [and] plan their exit strategies.

(*FT*, 28 September 2009, p. 12)

Chinese insurance companies will be allowed to invest directly in commercial real estate for the first time under new regulations ... [which] come into force tomorrow [1 October], although details on investment limits and what types of property insurers can buy will not be released for another month at least ... Chinese insurers are currently allowed to invest up to 10 per cent of their total assets directly in equities and another 10 per cent in equity investment funds ... Most Chinese insurers are directly owned by the state.

(*FT*, 30 September 2009, p. 17)

China has issued a stark warning about the risk from rising overcapacity in the economy, saying it could hamper recovery and lead to a surge in non-performing bank loans. The State Council, the country's cabinet, issued a new plan to combat overcapacity in seven industries, barring new aluminium smelters for three years and criticizing 'blind expansion' in parts of the steel and cement industries. The cabinet statement, which came late on Tuesday [29 September] in Beijing, follows a crescendo of warnings from senior officials. It also outlined measures to restrict manufacturing of equipment for 'green' industries of wind and solar power ... In the past three months many government officials have begun to warn publicly that the credit binge could create overcapacity in heavy industry, which could produce a new round of bad bank loans. The State Council said: 'Some regions act illegally, give approvals in violation of regulations or allow building before approval is granted.'

(*FT*, 1 October 2009, p. 7)

As for bank lending, which grew 34 per cent in the year to August, the government has repeatedly signalled that it will maintain its easy monetary policy because it is still concerned about the sustainability of the recovery. But it is also trying to curb speculative excesses and to tighten bank supervision. The banking regulator strengthened the rules on mortgages for investment properties this summer, and has told banks to raise their capital ratios to 10 per cent and to hold provisions equal to 150 per cent of projected loan losses by the end of the year [2009].

(*The Economist*, 8 October 2009, p. 82)

IMF members said in a statement issued Sunday [4 October]: 'We recognize that the distribution of quota shares should reflect the relative weights of the fund's members in the world economy, which have changed substantially in view of the strong growth in dynamic emerging market and developing countries.' IMF members endorsed a general plan to transfer 5 per cent of the IMF's quotas away from the industrialized world to emerging market economies, and directed senior officials to work out the details by January 2011 ... The IMF did not address one of the most contentious issues, that of the effective US veto at the organization. With a 17 per cent voting share in a body that requires 85 per cent for major decisions, the United States can block any significant move.

(www.iht.com, 4 October 2009; *IHT*, 5 October 2009, p. 17)

In a statement earlier this month [October] finance ministers from the G-7 [said]: 'We welcome China's continued commitment to a more flexible exchange rate, which should lead to continued appreciation of the renminbi in effective terms and help promote more balanced growth in China and in the world economy.'

(*IHT*, 16 October 2009, p. 200)

Exports in September fell 15.2 per cent year-on-year ... while imports declined by 3.5 per cent ... Both declines were improvements over August, when exports contracted 23 per cent and imports fell 17 per cent.... Exports in September rose 6.3 per cent compared with the previous month, while imports were up 8.3 per cent month-on-month ... after adjusting for seasonal factors.

(www.iht.com, 14 October 2009)

'Exports fell ... 15.2 per cent from September 2008, but [this] was the smallest fall in nine months ... Imports fell 3.5 per cent ... the smallest decline since imports began to slide in November 2008' (www.bbc.co.uk, 14 October 2009).

With the global recession making consumers and businesses more price conscious, China is grabbing market share from its export competitors ... China's exports this year [2009] have already vaulted past Germany to become the world's biggest exporter ... China is winning a larger piece of a shrinking pie ... World trade declined this year because of the recession.

(www.iht.com, 13 October 2009; *IHT*, 14 October 2009, p. 1)

'Economic growth rose to 7.9 per cent over a year earlier in the quarter ending 30 June, up from 6.1 per cent the previous quarter, and analysts say the recovery is gathering strength' (www.iht.com, 15 October 2009).

In the third quarter [of 2009] ... the economy expanded 8.9 per cent from a year earlier, speeding up from 7.9 per cent growth in the second quarter, the National Statistics Bureau said Thursday [22 October. [GDP] growth for the first nine months of the year was 7.7 per cent and officials have said they expect the economy to at least reach the annual growth target of 8 per cent ... Investment in factories, construction and other fixed assets rose by one third in January–September ... China's auto market has surged ahead to become the world's biggest, with sales up 34 per cent to 9.66 million vehicles in the first nine months of the year ... Retail sales growth was 15.1 per cent higher in the first three quarters ... Despite surging share and property prices, consumer prices fell, with inflation at negative 1.1 per cent so far this year ... Industrial output rose 8.7 per cent in the first three quarters of the year, and 12.4 per cent in July–September.

(www.iht.com, 22 October 2009)

'GDP increased 8.9 per cent in the third quarter [of 2009] ... The growth was in line with expectations ... China's economy ... grew at 6.1 per cent in the first quarter and 7.9 per cent in the second quarter' (www.cnn.com, 22 October 2009).

The state-controlled banking system has given out a record $1.27 trillion in new loans this year, and some analysts have warned that too much of that money has ended up in stocks and real estate. Property values in mainland China have soared 73 per cent this year. And the country's stock market rose 80 per cent during the first seven months of 2009 before falling back in recent months ... The Shanghai stock market is still up nearly 67 per cent so far this year ... Earlier this year Australia became the first major economy to raise interest rates again ... The rate increase, on 6 October, was by a modest quarter of a percentage point.

(www.iht.com, 22 October 2009; *IHT*, 23 October 2009, p. 19)

'GDP growth was up 8.9 per cent ... in the third quarter ... from 7.9 per cent in the previous quarter. It is the fastest growth since the third quarter of last year [2008]' (www.bbc.co.uk, 22 October 2009).

Fixed asset investment in urban areas, the main driver of economic growth in recent years, increased by 33.3 per cent in the first three quarters, up from 33 per cent in the January–August period. Infrastructure spending rose 52.6 per cent in the first nine months and social spending was 72.9 per cent higher. Retail sales rose 15.5 per cent in the twelve months to September … Retail sales increased in real terms by 16.5 per cent in the first three-quarters of 2009.

(*FT*, 23 October 2009, p. 10)

'Over the first nine months the economy grew 7.7 per cent. Of that, investment accounted for 7.3 percentage points and consumption 4 percentage points. The decline in net exports lopped off 3.6 percentage points' (p. 20).

Beijing has used its control over banks to engineer a massive increase in lending, with new loans in the first nine months of the year [2009] 149 per cent higher than last year [2008] at renminbi 8,650 billion ($1,270 billion) … The State Council gave its first clear hint yesterday [21 October] that it was considering a tighter monetary policy when it said strategy should focus on managing inflationary expectations as well as securing stable growth – the first time it has mentioned inflation since the global economic crisis hit the country last year.

(*FT*, 22 October 2009, p. 6)

Li Xiaochao (spokesman for the National Bureau of Statistics: 22 October): 'In the following period we will stick to continuity and stability in our economic policy. According to my understanding, that means no change in policy … In spite of yesterday's caution [22 October], the government has given hints that it might be starting to shift strategy.' The State Council said on Wednesday [21 October] it would focus on inflationary expectations, its first mention since the crisis started of potential price rises, while a government economist [Chen Daufu of the Development Research Centre] reportedly suggested a stronger currency could be used to limit price rises.

(*FT*, 23 October 2009, p. 10)

The IMF on Thursday [29 October] raised its outlook for growth in Asia for this year and next, reflecting the region's rapid rebound from the depths of the global downturn in recent months … China will enjoy by far the fastest growth – 8.5 per cent this year and 9 per cent in 2010 … The Asian Development Bank last month [September] said it now expected China to grow 8.2 per cent this year – 1.2 percentage points higher than what it had forecast in March – and 8.9 per cent next year … Australia earlier this month became the first major central bank to start nudging interest rates up again and Norway followed suit on Wednesday [28 October] with a quarter percentage point increase in its key rate.

(www.iht.com, 20 October 2009)

'The IMF said the recoveries in China, India and Australia had been so rapid that conditions were now right for some policy adjustments. Elsewhere, however, recovery remains tentative, inflation risks low and asset price increases muted' (*IHT*, 30 October 2009, p. 18).

'The IMF … raised growth forecasts for 2010 … [as regards China] from 7.5 per cent to 9 per cent' (*FT*, 30 October 2009, p. 9).

The World Bank on Wednesday [4 November] became the latest major institution to raise its forecast for growth in China ... though it cautioned that more policy adjustments would be necessary in the medium term to ensure that the recovery would be sustained. The World Bank now expects the economy to grow 8.4 per cent this year [2009] ... up from the 7.2 per cent it forecast in June. It predicts growth of 8.7 per cent next year [2010] ... China's rebound stems mostly from a huge spending package of 4 trillion yuan ($585 billion) that the government announced a year ago ... Export growth is likely to resume, helped by strong fundamental competitiveness and the recent depreciation of the nominal effective exchange rate, the World Bank said. It said: 'Net exports are likely to stop being a drag on growth' ... But the challenge, according to the institution, would be to continue weaning China off its reliance on exports and stimulate domestic demand. Although the World Bank said that China had already seen broad-based domestic demand growth, it said that more was needed. The World Bank said: 'Following on earlier initiatives, some steps have been taken in recent months to rebalance and boost domestic demand, including increasing the presence of the government in health, education and social safety [and other measures like improving small and mid-sized companies' access to financing] ... But more policy measures will be needed to rebalance growth in China, given the strong underlying momentum of the traditional pattern. Structural reforms to unleash more growth and competition in the service sector and stimulate more successful, permanent migration would be particularly welcome' ... Louis Kuijs (the main author of the World Bank's update): 'In our view macroeconomic conditions in the real economy do not yet call for a major tightening. However, risks of asset price bubbles and misallocation of resources in the face of abundant liquidity are real and the overall monetary stance will have to be tightened eventually.'

(www.iht.com, 4 November 2009; *IHT*, 5 November 2009, p. 18)

Louis Kuijs (the World Bank's chief economist):

We think that now that the government has basically succeeded in dampening the impact of the global crisis, it is a good time to concentrate and focus effort on rebalancing the economy and getting more growth out of the domestic economy. This calls for more emphasis on consumption and services and less emphasis on investment and industry.

(www.bbc.co.uk, 4 November 2009)

The rebound had been fuelled by 'very large' fiscal and monetary surplus, the World Bank said ... There have been signs that the recovery has been broadening, while export growth was likely to resume next year [2010]. Although there were risks that loose monetary policy could spill over into asset price bubbles, China did not yet need to embark on a major tightening, the World Bank said ... China's current account surplus will fall by almost half this year [2009], the World Bank predicted yesterday [4 November] ... The current account was likely to drop from 9.8 per cent of GDP last year

[2008] to 5.6 per cent this year, and to 4.1 per cent in 2010. In absolute terms the World Bank forecast that the surplus would fall from $426 billion in 2008 to $261 billion this year and $213 billion in 2010. At its peak in 2007 ... the current account surplus was equivalent to 11 per cent of GDP.

(*FT*, 5 November 2009, p. 10)

The G-20 statement (issued after its 7 November meeting in the UK):

The recovery is uneven and remains dependent on policy support, and high unemployment is a major concern. To restore the global economy and financial system to health, we agreed to maintain support for the recovery until it is assured.

(www.bbc.co.uk, 8 November 2009)

'The finance ministers agreed on a detailed timetable to achieve balanced economic growth and reiterated a pledge not to withdraw any economic stimulus until a recovery was certain' (www.iht.com, 8 November 2009).

Finance ministers and central bankers of the G-20 countries talked only in general terms about rebalancing economies and implied they might not be able to agree before the end of next year [2010] on specific policies for the individual countries to adopt ... The G-20 did not press China on the sensitive issue [of the yuan] ... The G-20 did publish a detailed, unprecedented timetable for countries to discuss the economic rebalancing that could eventually bring more stability to global currency markets. In an appendix to the communiqué, the G-20 members were asked to submit descriptions of their monetary, fiscal and other policies to the IMF by the end of January [2010]. The IMF said it would produce an analysis of the global economy by April. The G-20 members would then 'develop a basket of policy options' in June, and their leaders would consider recommendations for policies at a meeting next November.

(*IHT*, 10 November 2009, p. 19)

'Leaders of G-20 countries ... called on their finance ministers to make progress ... on ensuring the global recovery was strong, sustained and balanced' (*FT*, 9 November 2009, p. 2). 'The G-20 agreed a timetable for the new "framework for strong, sustainable and balanced growth" ... with finance ministers committing to "more specific policy recommendations" in place by November' (www.ft.com, 8 November 2009).

'Saturday's agenda focused on three main areas: structural reform of economies, stimulus and exit strategies for the current downturn and financing of climate change' (www.cnn.com, 8 November 2009).

'Finance minister Xie Xuren said at the G-20 meeting: "There are still many uncertain factors in the global economic recovery. So all countries should maintain the continuity and stability of macroeconomic policy"' (*IHT*, 10 November 2009, p. 20).

Industrial output and retail sales for October both topped analysts' expectations, with rises of 16.1 per cent and 16.2 per cent, respectively, from a year earlier. The increases in October were also higher than those recorded in September, indicating that the recovery is continuing to pick up steam. Urban fixed investment climbed ... 33.1 per cent in the first ten months of the year [2009] ... Exports in October dropped 13.8 per cent below levels from a year ago, while imports fell 6.4 per cent, which was more than expected by analysts ... Most economists do not expect China to start raising interest rates until well into next year [2010] ... Bank lending had slowed to 253 billion yuan in October, from 516.7 billion yuan in September.

(www.iht.com, 11 November 2009)

Industrial production rose 16.1 per cent [in October] from the same month a year before, up from a rate of 13.9 per cent in the year to September ... Retail sales gained 16.2 per cent over a year earlier, accelerating from a 15.5 per cent increase the month before, while fixed asset investment increased 33.1 per cent year-on-year ... Consumer prices fell 0.5 per cent year-on-year and were down 0.1 per cent compared to September. Prices at the factory gate fell 5.8 per cent compared to the same month last year [2008].

(www.cnn.com, 11 November 2009)

New data indicated that economic recovery accelerated last month [October] ... Industrial production rose 16.1 per cent on the same month last year [2008], the fastest rate of growth since March 2008 ... The robust debate will intensify the debate about whether the government needs to sharply scale back its aggressive stimulus policies amid growing fears of asset bubbles and inflation. The headline rate of new lending in local currency declined sharply last month to renminbi 252 billion ($37 billion) from renminbi 516.7 billion ... But economists pointed out that the level of medium-term loans, which are more important for the economy than short-term credit, remained strong and that foreign exchange loans and capital inflows were also rising.

(*FT*, 12 November 2009, p. 6)

'Thanks to its monetary and fiscal stimulus, domestic demand has contributed 12 percentage points to GDP growth this year, while net exports subtracted almost 4 percentage points' (www.economist.com, 19 November 2009; *The Economist*, 21 November 2009, p. 89).

GDP growth forecasts by the Organization for Economic Co-operation and Development (OECD): 2009. 8.3 per cent; 2010, 10.2 per cent (www.bbc.co.uk, 19 November 2009).

China's role in the international policy debate has been rising in tandem with its growing economy. As a key member of the G-20, China is helping guide global policy priorities and devise solutions to global problems ... While the global outlook has improved, we still face considerable policy challenges. The biggest risk is a premature withdrawal of policy stimulus. While it is prudent to plan for so-called 'exit strategies', policy-makers should keep supportive measures in place until a recovery is firmly established, and particularly until conditions are in place for unemployment to decline. In China the government's commitment to maintain fiscal stimulus into 2010 will be important for supporting growth. As the government also recognizes, however, the time has come to begin slowing the very rapid pace of loan growth, which raises risks of overinvestment, overcapacity and ultimately bad loans. With the recovery emerging, a key medium-term policy challenge for the global economy is how to achieve a more stable distribution of demand across economies. This is the challenge of what we have come to call global economic rebalancing … In economies that have run large current account surpluses, domestic demand needs to be stronger … In emerging Asia, rebalancing means increasing domestic demand – investment in many countries, and in China an emphasis on private consumption. China's leadership has already articulated a clear vision for how to boost private consumption. Consumer spending is growing faster than the economy as a whole. Moreover, as noted by President Hu Jintao, China will be taking further steps to boost household spending – and reduce reliance on exports – in the period ahead. Much is already being done. For example, the bold new initiative to provide quality health care for most of the Chinese people. Reform of the rural pension system is also moving forward. But more can be done to secure a lasting, structural shift toward consumption, by expanding the scope of social services, moving ahead on financial sector reform and undertaking corporate governance reforms. A stronger currency is part of the package of necessary reforms. Allowing the renminbi and other Asian currencies to rise would help increase the purchasing power of households, raise the labour share of income and provide the right incentives to reorientate investment. At the end of the day, higher Chinese domestic demand, along with higher US saving, will help rebalance world demand and assure a healthier economy for us all.

(Dominique Strauss-Kahn, managing director of the IMF, www.iht.com, 20 November 2009; *IHT*, 21 November 2009, p. 6)

[On 24 November] Dominique Strauss-Kahn said that the Euro appeared 'somewhat overvalued' while the yuan was 'still undervalued'. A rise in the value of the Chinese currency would be a logical element in the country's 'shift from an export-driven economy to one that was more dependent on domestic demand', he said.

(*IHT*, 25 November 2009, p. 14)

Chinese banking regulators are putting pressure on the country's banks to raise more capital and temper their rapid growth in lending, in the clearest signs yet of official concern about the sustainability of the nation's credit boom, senior Chinese bankers said Monday [23 November] … As bank lending has soared this year, banks' capital has risen less quickly, so the banks' capital adequacy ratios have begun to slip. While China's regulators are comfortable with current capital adequacy levels at the nation's major banks, they want them to have plenty of capital to be able to continue lending briskly next year [2010] without difficulty if needed to sustain economic growth, bankers said … Chinese banks lent more money in the first seven months of this year [2009] than in the two previous years combined. They have only gradually begun to moderate their pace of new loans this autumn … Reuters, citing a source, reported Monday that the China Banking Regulatory Commission was asking big banks to raise their capital adequacy ratios to 13 per cent by the end of next year, compared to a broad industry average of 11 per cent in China now. But the commission denied this … saying that it had not set a 13 per cent target and had not imposed limits on lending. The commission did say, however, that banks were being discouraged from engaging in any extra push to lend money before the end of the year … Industrial Bank, based in Fujian province, announced Monday that it planned to raise 18 billion yuan ($2.6 billion) in a share sale next year. China Minsheng Banking raised $3.8 billion through the sale of shares in Hong Kong last week, while China Merchants Bank has said that it intends to raise 22 billion yuan through a rights offering by the end of the year. Chinese banks' capital adequacy rations look high by comparison with the rations at Western banks, many of which are struggling to meet an international standard of 8 per cent. But the Chinese banks' ratios are not necessarily directly comparable, bank analysts caution, because Chinese banks are sometimes slow to acknowledge that delinquent loans may not be collectible.

(www.iht.com, 23 November 2009; *IHT*, 24 November 2009, p. 17)

A surge in spending on investment will create excess capacity … The European Chamber of Commerce in China lays out the challenge in six sectors: aluminium, where the capacity utilization rate is forecast to be 67 per cent in 2009; wind-power, on 70 per cent; steel, on 72 per cent; cement, on 78 per cent; chemicals, on 80 per cent; and refining, on 85 per cent. Yet vast additional capacity is on the way … At the end of 2008 China's steel capacity was 660 million tonnes against demand of 470 million tonnes … Yet, notes the report, 'there are currently 58 million tonnes of new capacity under construction in China'.

(*FT*, 30 November 2009, p. 12)

'China will expand programmes that give consumers a discount if they trade in old cars and household appliances for new ones' (*IHT*, 30 November 2009, p. 17).

China will extend into next year [2010] stimulus measures that have driven car and home appliances sales to record levels, while reining in some incentives in a move to curb excesses, especially in the property market. The decision by the State Council is the first big adjustment of the series of pro-consumption policies that Beijing unveiled last year [2008].

(*FT*, 10 December 2009, p. 16)

On Friday [11 December] data for November showed industrial output had soared 19.2 per cent from a year earlier ... its highest since June 2007 ... while imports jumped 26.7 per cent ... their first rise in thirteen months. Exports were 1.2 per cent below November 2008, but the drop was slight compared to the double-digit year-over-year declines in previous months ... Still, Friday's output and import data topped analysts' expectations ... Retail sales climbed 15.8 per cent over a year earlier, slightly less than in October ... Urban fixed-asset investment rose 32.1 per cent in the January-to-November period from a year earlier, after climbing 33.1 per cent through October ... Consumer prices rose 0.6 per cent in November, the first increase since January [2009].

(www.iht.com, 11 December 2009)

Economists thought [industrial] output would rise by 18 per cent. Instead it rose by 19.2 per cent in November compared to 16.1 per cent in October ... Consumer prices grew year-on-year in November for the first time in ten months. The index rise of 0.6 per cent beat expert expectations of 0.4 per cent ... November's year-on-year fall in exports of 1.2 per cent was the slowest of 2009, although growth had been expected.

(www.bbc.co.uk, 11 December 2009)

Consumer prices rose by 0.6 per cent last month [November] from a year ago, after falling 0.5 per cent the month before, while prices at the factory gate fell by 2.1 per cent last month compared with a 5.8 per cent decline the month before ... Exports declined 1.2 per cent compared with the year before, bettering the 13.7 per cent drop posted in October. On a sequential basis, exports were up only 0.7 per cent last month over October.

(*FT*, 12 December 2009, p. 6)

China has reintroduced a nationwide real estate sales tax in an attempt to reduce speculation and cool the bubbling property market after price rises accelerated across the country in November. The new policy is the first concrete response from Beijing to growing fears that an unsustainable bubble has formed in the real estate market ... The new tax policy requires anyone selling a second-hand apartment or house within five years of its purchase to pay a sales tax of 5.5 per cent, extending the period from the previous two years ... The new policy essentially returns the market to the situation a year ago ... Chinese leaders have pledged in recent days to increase support for affordable low-end housing projects in big cities.

(www.cnn.com, 11 December 2009)

Chinese banks extended renminbi 9,210 billion in new loans in the first eleven months of this year [2009], far more than the average of renminbi 3,000 billion to renminbi 4,000 billion in recent years ... Beijing has set a target of renminbi 7,000 billion to renminbi 8,000 billion for next year [2010] ... With more than renminbi 1,000 billion of this year's loans remaining unspent in the banking system, the target in effect means that the

Beijing government is planning to maintain lending at its current rate next year ... The ratio of non-performing loans at all China's commercial banks decreased to 1.6 per cent at the end of November.

(*FT*, 22 December 2009, p. 21)

'China revised its 2008 growth rate to 9.6 per cent, taking it well above the originally reported 9.0 per cent, after calculating that the service sector had been more productive than originally thought' (www.ft.com, 25 December 2009).

China revised its 2008 growth rate to 9.6 per cent Friday [25 December], taking it well above the originally reported 9 per cent. It made the revision after calculating that the service sector had been more productive than previously believed ... In 2009 China's economy grew 7.7 per cent in the first three quarters, compared with the same period a year earlier ... The service sector accounted for 41.8 per cent of GDP last year [2008], up from the previously reported 40.1 per cent. In developed economies services often contribute more than 70 per cent of GDP ... China's central bank reaffirmed earlier in the week its long-standing commitment to maintain an 'appropriately loose' monetary policy. The government also pledged this week to deliver the second half of its promised two-year stimulus package in 2010. The package is worth a total of 4 trillion renminbi ($585 billion). Yet beneath this headline stability, Beijing has started to wind down some parts of its stimulus. Over the past month it has scaled back a tax exemption on property sales, increased tax on automobile purchases, vowed to crack down on speculation in the sizzling housing market and outlined how it would more strictly control bank lending. The revisions also showed that China used 5.2 per cent less energy per GDP unit in 2008, a bigger drop than the previously reported 4.6 per cent ... The country set a goal of cutting energy by 20 per cent over the five years to 2010.

(*IHT*, 26 December 2009, p. 12)

China streaked ahead of its Western and Asian rivals at the weekend by unveiling the world's fastest long-distance passenger train service. The *Harmony* express raced 1,100 kilometres in less than three hours on Saturday [26 December], travelling from Guangzhou, capital of southern Guangdong province, to the central city of Wuhan. The journey previously took at least eleven hours ... The *Harmony* express, which reached a top speed of 394 kilometres per hour in pre-launch trials, travelled at an average rate of 350 kilometres per hour on its debut. This compared with a maximum service speed of 300 kilometres per hour for Japan's *Shuinkansen* bullet trains and France's TGV service ... In total the railways ministry intends to complete 18,000 kilometres of high-speed rail lines by 2012, allowing passengers to travel between most Chinese provincial capitals in eight hours or less.

(www.cnn.com, 28 December 2009)

China's lavish new rail system is a response to a failure of central planning six years ago. After China joined the WTO in November 2001 exports and manufacturing soared. Electricity generation failed to keep up because the railway ministry had not built enough rail lines or purchased enough locomotives to haul coal needed to run new power plants. By 2004 the government was turning off the power to some factories up to three days a week to prevent blackouts in residential areas. Officials drafted a plan to move much of the nation's passenger traffic on to high-speed routes by 2020, freeing existing tracks for more freight. Then the global financial crisis hit in late 2008. Faced with mass lay-offs at export factories, China ordered that the new rail system be completed by 2012 instead of 2020, throwing more than $100 billion in stimulus at the projects ... [In September 2009 it was said] that the government planned forty-two lines by 2012, with 5,000 miles of track for passenger trains travelling at 215 miles an hour and 3,000 miles of track for passenger and fast freight trains travelling at 155 miles an hour ... Without retreating from their goals yet, Chinese officials have hinted in the last several weeks that stimulus spending may slow. Some transportation experts predict that a few of the forty-two routes may not be finished until 2013 or 2014 as a result.

(www.iht.com, 12 February 2010; *IHT*, 13 February 2010, pp. 1, 10)

Prime minister Wen Jiabao [27 December]: 'We will not yield to any pressure of any form forcing us to appreciate. As I have told my foreign friends, on the one hand, you are asking for the yuan to appreciate, and on the other hand, you are taking all kinds of protectionist measures' ... The true purpose of these calls is to contain China's development, he said ... Mr Wen also repeated an oft-made declaration that the stable renminbi had contributed to the global economic recovery. He gave a cautious outlook for the domestic economy in 2010, saying that it was too early to pare down the government's stimulus policies but that officials needed to be attentive to surging real estate prices and incipient inflation. Although China will continue to encourage citizens to buy homes for their own use, differentiated interest rates will be used as a tool to fight property market speculation, Mr Wen said. He was apparently referring to a proposal that China keep offering preferential mortgages – at a discount of as much as 30 per cent from benchmark lending rates – for people buying their first homes but eliminate such mortgages for additional home purchases. More broadly, Mr Wen warned of rising imbalances from too much bank lending while defending China's use of a stimulus package worth 4 trillion renminbi ($586 billion) to limit the effects of the global economic crisis. 'Parts of the economy are not balanced, not co-ordinated and not sustainable,' Mr Wen said, repeating previous statements. He added that it would be better if lending by Chinese banks were not on such a large scale. China's overall lending situation improved in the second half of the year [2009], when banks drastically slowed their pace of credit issuance after a record surge in the first half, Mr Wen said. Chinese banks are on course to lend an unprecedented 9.5 trillion renminbi this year, double the total of last year.

(www.iht.com, 27 December 2009; *IHT*, 28 December 2009, p. 17)

The Chinese currency has depreciated by about 9 per cent against a basket of currencies representing its main trading partners since early this year [2009] ... However, Beijing argues its exchange rate against its trading partners is roughly in line with its level at the start of the global financial crisis in September 2008, when the US dollar at first strengthened ... The government was worried property prices in some parts of China had risen too quickly, prime minister Wen Jiabao said, and that bank lending this year had been excessive, though he added the authorities were already taking measures to moderate activity ... There were no immediate signs of inflation, he said, but the government had to be watchful because 'inflation may emerge'.

(*FT*, 28 December 2009, p. 4)

'When the time came for the AMCs [Asset Management Companies] to repay the principal on the 1990s vintages this autumn [2009], banks simply rolled over the bonds for another decade' (p. 14).

Chinese authorities have found that 234.7 billion renminbi in public funds was misused in the first eleven months of 2009, with much tied to the government's massive stimulus package [it was reported on Monday 28 December] ... Next year's audit would focus on government debt issuance, particularly local government financing ... [There was a call] for greater oversight of big projects.

(*IHT*, 29 December 2009, p. 15)

Chinese officials misused or embezzled about $35 billion in government money in the first eleven months of the year, according to a national audit released this week ... The National Audit Office did not disclose the size of the budgets reviewed this year. But the agency said it surveyed nearly 100,000 government departments and state-owned companies, and that more than 1,000 officials were facing prosecution or disciplinary action because of the audits. Auditors said government officials engaged in everything from money laundering and issuing fraudulent loans to cheating the government through the sale or purchase of state land or mining rights ... In 2005 the National Audit Office reported finding about $35 billion worth of government funds misused or embezzled. That was the last year the office gave a national figure covering its audits.

(www.iht.com, 29 December 2009)

China's central bank raised a key interest rate slightly Thursday [7 January] for the first time in nearly five months, in what economists interpreted as the beginning of a broader move to tighten monetary policy and forestall inflation ... The People's Bank of China announced Thursday that the yield from its weekly sale of three-month central bank bills had inched up to 1.3684 per cent. The yield had been stuck at 1.328 per cent since 13 August [2009] ... Top officials at the People's Bank of China concluded an annual two-day policy review on Wednesday [6 January] with a lengthy statement that had particularly strong cautions against bank lending to sectors of the economy with overcapacity or excessive energy use ... After cutting interest rates on the same three-month central bank bills by 2.4 percentage points in the last quarter of 2008 ... the People's Bank of China nudged up interest rates by 0.363 [percentage points] from late June to early August last year [2009] in a series of increasingly large weekly increases. But the central bank has been on hold ever since ... Thursday's increase appeared to confirm that the central bank was starting to become concerned again about rising prices, economists said ... The central bank sells its bills mainly to banks, which pay in renminbi that the central bank then effectively takes out of circulation, slowing the growth in the money supply. Weekly sales of central bank bills are part of a process that economists describe as 'sterilization' of China's extensive intervention in currency markets. As US dollars and other foreign currencies pour into China from its trade surplus and foreign investment, the central bank prints vast amounts of renminbi and issues them to buy those dollars and other currencies. To prevent all those extra renminbi from feeding inflation, the central bank then claws back the renminbi from the market through a series of measures that include the sale of central bank bills ... The goal of sterilization is to keep inflation under control while keeping the renminbi weak ... The central bank is already buying more than $300 billion a year of foreign currencies, mainly dollars, to keep the renminbi weak and preserve the competitiveness of Chinese exports.

(www.iht.com, 7 January 2010; *IHT*, 8 January 2010, p. 14)

China has finally arrived at the top of the rankings of global exporters, displacing Germany. China exported $957 billion of goods in the first ten months of 2009, compared with $917 billion for Germany ... [As regards imports] China ranks second, with imports of $797 billion between January and October. It overtook Germany, which imported goods worth $774 billion in this period ... but it still lagged behind the United States, with imports of $1,269 billion.

(*FT*, 7 January 2010, p. 16)

'German exports were worth $1,020 billion in the eleven months to November [2009], versus $1,070 billion for China' (*FT*, 9 January 2010, p. 6)

Figures due out on 11 January [2010] are expected to show that China's exports in December [2009] were higher than a year ago, after thirteen months of year-on-year declines. China's exports fell by around 17 per cent in 2009 as a whole, but other countries' slumped by even more. As a result China overtook Germany to become the world's largest exporter and its share of world exports jumped to almost 10 per cent, up from 3 per cent in 1999. China takes an even bigger slice of America's market. In the first ten months of 2009 America imported 15 per cent less from China than in the same period of 2008, but its imports from the rest of the world fell by 33 per cent, lifting China's market share to a record 19 per cent. So although America's trade deficit with China narrowed, China now accounts for almost half of America's total deficit, up from less than one-third in 2008 ... Projections in the IMF's *World Economic Outlook* imply that exports will account for 12 per cent of world trade by 2014. Its 10 per cent slice this year [2010] will equal that achieved by Japan at its peak in 1986 ... China's current account surplus has fallen from 11 per cent to an estimated 6 per cent of GDP. In 2007 net exports accounted for almost 3 percentage points of China's GDP growth; last year [2009] they were a drag on its growth to the tune of 3 percentage points. In other words, rather than being a drain on global demand, China helped pull the world economy along during the course of last year ... China's imports have been stronger than its exports, rebounding by 27 per cent in the year to November [2009], when its exports were still falling.

(*The Economist*, 9 January 2010, pp. 69–70)

Figures due out on Monday 11 January are expected to show that China's exports in December were higher than a year ago, after thirteen months of year-on-year declines. China's exports fell by around 17 per cent in 2009 as a whole, but other countries' slumped by even more.

(www.economist.com, 10 January 2010)

China overtook Germany as the world's top exporter after December [2009] exports jumped 17.7 per cent for their first increase in fourteen months ... Exports for the last month of 2009 were $130.7 billion ... That raised total 2009 exports to $1.2 trillion, ahead of the Euro 816 billion ($1.17 trillion) forecast for Germany ... [Germany] supplies the factory equipment used by top Chinese manufacturers ... China's trade surplus shrank by 34.2 per cent in 2009 to $196.07 billion ... Total 2009 Chinese trade fell 13.9 per cent from 2008.

(www.iht.com, 10 January 2010; *IHT*, 11 January 2010, p. 13)

China's exports rose 17.7 per cent in December ... The rise, compared with a year earlier, breaks a thirteen-month decline in trade ... Total exports for 2009 were $1.2 trillion, but total trade over the year was down 13.9 per cent ... Exports overall in the year were $1.2 trillion, down 16 per cent from 2008, while imports were 11.2 per cent down from a year earlier at $1.01 trillion.

(www.bbc.co.uk, 10 January 2010)

[China's economy] showed the strength of its recovery with exports rising for the first time in fourteen months and imports soaring by a staggering 56 per cent in December from a year earlier ... China's exports leapt 17.7 per cent in December from a year earlier, far outstripping the expected 4 per cent rise to break thirteen months of decline ... [There was] an even bigger leap in December's imports, which rose 55.9 per cent year-on-year to $112.3 billion, much more than the expected 31.0 per cent rise. That squeezed China's trade surplus down to $18.4 billion compared with $19.1

billion in November and $39 billion in December 2008 ... Germany releases full-year figures on 9 February.

(www.thetimes.co.uk, 10 January 2010)

China's exports rose in December for the first time in fourteen months ... Exports to China's biggest markets rebounded last month, with sales to the United States increasing 15.9 per cent and to the EU 10.2 per cent. However, the year-on-year comparisons were inflated by the low base of the previous year's figures. Economists said some of the improvement was due to restocking by companies that had run down inventories ... Beijing also signalled at the weekend that there would be no near-term tightening in fiscal or monetary policies. President Hu Jintao told a seminar attended by officials that China should continue 'pro-active' fiscal policies and 'moderately loose' monetary policies. He said: '[priority should go] to policies that support domestic consumption expansion, economic growth, economic structure adjustments and projects concerning people's livelihood'.

(*FT*, 11 January 2010, p. 1)

The December trade figures also showed a 51 per cent year-on-year increase in processing imports, the imported components assembled into consumer goods in China. Economists said this was a sign exporters were becoming more confident of likely demand. The previous improvement in Chinese exports had been put down partly to retailers in the United States and Europe rebuilding inventories.

(*FT*, 12 January 2010, p. 5)

'Chinese exports ... are now only 4.4 per cent below their peak ... Imports are largely of raw materials and basic manufactured goods' (p. 15).

'The World Bank economists point out that China's share of world imports has grown from around 10 per cent in mid-2008 to over 12 per cent last year [2009]' (www.economist.com, 28 January 2010).

China sold more than 13.5 million vehicles in 2009, Xinhua said on Friday [8 January], overtaking the United States to become the world's largest auto market as government policy initiatives spurred demand. The final figure compared with annual sales of 10.4 million cars and light trucks sold in the United States, the lowest level in twenty-seven years. It was also well above the 10 million in vehicle sales that China had originally targeted for 2009. The Chinese tally, which also includes heavy vehicles, is still higher than that of the United States after deducting roughly 650,000 units of heavy trucks ... The market was likely to return to a slower ... rate of growth of roughly 10 per cent in 2010 on continued policy support from the government even though the renewed tax incentives for small cars were not as aggressive as expected, analysts said.

(www.iht.com, 8 January 2010)

'China surged past the United States to become the world's largest automobile market – in units, if not dollars' (www.iht.com, 12 January 2010).

> China has overtaken the United States to become the biggest car market in the world as government policy initiatives spur demand … China's market grew by 45 per cent year-on-year in 2009 … Total industry sales fell 21 per cent in the formerly dominant US market … China was not expected to exceed the US market until 2020 but the speed with which the recession affected consumers in the United States combined with incentives from the Beijing government to help buyers accelerated the trend, China's government cut sales taxes on smaller, fuel-efficient cars and spent $730 million on subsidies for buyers of larger cars, pickup trucks and minivans. Stimulus spending on building highways and other public works also helped to boost sales of trucks used in construction.
>
> (www.guardian.co.uk, 8 January 2010)

'[The ministry of industry and information technology warned that vehicle sales may slow to 15 per cent this year [2010], partly because the tax break on small cars has been reduced' (www.cnn.com, 11 January 2010).

> China said Sunday [10 January] that it would strengthen its monitoring of lending by banks and try to counter the arrival of speculative capital from abroad as risks increase of price bubbles in real estate markets … Government agencies will increase monitoring of loan flows from illegally entering the property market, the State Council said.
>
> (*IHT*, 11 January 2010, p. 17)

'Yesterday [11 January] state media reported that bank loans in just the first week of this year [2010] reached renminbi 600 billion ($88 billion), twice the monthly average of last year [2008]' (*FT*, 12 January 2010, p. 5).

> Loans in the first week of 2010 reached renminbi 600 billion ($88 billion), not far short of the monthly average last year [2009] … Lending more than doubled from renminbi 4,200 billion in 2008 to above renminbi 9,000 billion last year [2009].
>
> (*FT*, 13 January 2010, p. 6)

> China on Tuesday [12 January] raised the proportion of deposits that banks must hold in reserve, the clearest sign yet that it has started to tighten monetary policy. The 0.5 percentage point increase in the reserve requirement ratio will take effect on 18 January and will apply to all banks except rural credit co-operatives … It was the first time that the central bank has adjusted the ratio since it lowered the ratio in December 2008 … The move came far earlier than expected … The increase followed two other tightening steps taken by the central bank. The central bank raised the yield on its 20 billion renminbi ($2.9 billion) in one-year bills by eight basis points to 1.8434 per cent after holding it steady in the previous twenty auctions. It also drained a record 200 billion renminbi via twenty-eight-day bond repurchase agree-

ments, ensuring it will draw net funds from the market this week … the tightening steps come after reports that bank lending surged in the first week of the year to 600 billion renminbi.

(www.iht.com, 12 January 2010)

The central bank raised the reserve requirement for major banks to 16 per cent as of 18 January, an increase of half a percentage point from the current rate. Smaller banks would jump to 14 per cent, from 13.5 per cent. Xinhua reported on Tuesday that banks had made new loans totalling almost 600 billion renminbi ($87.9 billion) in the first week of January alone. At that rate Chinese banks would lend almost 50 per cent more money this January than in January 2009 … Chinese bank lending in the first eleven months of 2009 – 9.2 trillion renminbi – was twice as much as had been lent the previous year.

(*IHT*, 13 January 2010, p. 15)

'The central bank's action came earlier than investors had expected' (p. 17).

'Chinese banks must now keep more money back in reserves, the first such increase since June 2008' (www.bbc.co.uk, 12 January 2010).

China has increased the amount banks must set aside as reserves in the clearest sign yet that the central bank is trying to tighten monetary conditions amid mounting concerns of overheating and inflation … The People's Bank of China also raised interest rates modestly in the inter-bank market yesterday [12 January] for the second time in less than a week … Reserve requirements were raised by 0.5 percentage points, while rates on one-year paper increased by 0.08 per cent and on three-month paper by 0.04 per cent.

(*FT*, 13 January 2010, p. 6)

Tao Wang … an economist at UBS … calculates that if 20 per cent of all new lending last year [2009] and another 10 per cent of this year's lending turned bad, this would create new bad loans equivalent to 5.5 per cent of GDP by 2012, on top of 2 per cent now. That is far from trivial, but well below the 40 per cent of GDP that bad loans amounted to in the late 1990s.

(*The Economist*, 16 January 2010, p. 69)

Chinese banks doled out 9.6 trillion yuan in new loans last year [2008], data showed on Friday [15 January], far exceeding the government's minimum target of 5 trillion yuan and amounting to nearly 30 per cent of 2008 GDP … Government bond yields edged higher, with the one-year yield rising to 1,5691 from 1.5555 on Thursday … China saw a 103 per cent rise in foreign direct investment in December [2009] compared with a year earlier, though full year inflows shrank for the first time since 2005.

(www.iht.com, 15 January 2010)

The central bank said yesterday [15 January] bank loans rose by renminbi 380 billion ($55.6 billion) in December, bringing the total amount of new loans issued last year [2008] to renminbi 9,590 billion. That was more than double the amount of new loans extended in 2008.

(*FT*, 16 January 2010, p. 7)

The authorities signalled Wednesday [20 January] that bank lending would slow significantly this year [2010] and reportedly instructed some banks to curb loans – the latest in a series of moves designed to forestall inflation and stave off bubbles in the stock and property markets. Liu Mingkang, chairman of the China Banking Regulatory Commission, said he expected the nation's banks to extend loans totalling about 7.5 trillion renminbi ($1.1 trillion) – down nearly 22 per cent from the record 9.6 trillion renminbi doled out last year [2009] ... He added that regulators were paying special attention to loans for local government projects and real estate ... The official *China Securities Journal* cited unidentified sources Wednesday as saying that some banks had been told to stop all lending for the rest of the month.

(www.iht.com, 20 January 2010; *IHT*, 21 January 2010, p. 19)

Many analysts predict that total bank lending may pull back by about 20 per cent, to no more than 8 trillion renminbi this year [2010] ... Jing Ulrich ... managing director of China equities in Hong Kong for J.P. Morgan ... in a 12 January research note ... predicted a 20 per cent to 30 per cent cut in bank lending growth for this year, compared with 2009.

(www.iht.com, 24 January 2010)

China said on Thursday [21 January] that its economy rose by 10.7 per cent in the fourth quarter [of 2009] compared with a year ago ... Over the whole year GDP grew 8.7 per cent, surpassing the 8 per cent growth rate benchmark that Chinese leaders assert is necessary to maintain social stability. If China keeps up that rate of growth, it will very likely replace Japan as the world's second largest economy by the end of this year [2010]. The National Bureau of Statistics also announced on Thursday that industrial production in December increased by 18.5 per cent and retail sales rose by 17.5 per cent. The December consumer price index grew by 1.9 per cent and the producer price index by 1.7 per cent. The numbers were generally in line with earlier predictions ... Economic numbers released on Thursday also showed China's export industry was still responsible for much of the growth.

(www.iht.com, 21 January 2010)

China is expected to keep growing at a rapid clip this year [2010], and possibly overtake Japan as the world's second largest economy, after that of the United States. The 10.7 per cent expansion ... in the final quarter of 2009 ... was measured against the fourth quarter of 2008 and was an acceleration from the third quarter, when the expansion was put at 9.1 per cent, according to revised figures.

(*IHT*, 22 January 2010, p. 14)

China beat its target of 8 per cent economic growth comfortably last year [2009] … the economy expanded 10.7 per cent year-on-year in the fourth quarter and 8.7 per cent in 2009 … GDP reached $4,900 billion, short of the $5,100 billion Japan is expected to register after last year's contraction … Consumer price inflation jumped again last month [December 2009], from 0.6 per cent in November year-on-year to 1.9 per cent … Factory gate prices also rose 1.7 per cent in December, reversing November's 2.1 per cent fall … Industrial production slowed from a 19.2 per cent rise year-on-year in November to 18.5 per cent [in December] … Regulators have ordered some banks to stop new loans until the end of the month [January] … China's banks extended renminbi 9,590 billion ($1,404 billion) in new loans last year, more than double the amount in 2008 … The M1 measure of money supply … rose by nearly 35 per cent last year … The government has targeted new bank loans this year [2010] of renminbi 7,500 billion ($1,097 billion), down from last year but a big increase on pre-crisis levels.

(*FT*, 22 January 2010, p. 9)

[Compared with a year ago GDP grew] at 6.2 per cent in the first quarter, 7.9 per cent in the second quarter, and 9.9 per cent in the third quarter … The government had set a growth target rate of 8 per cent last year [2009] … Retail sales rose 16.9 per cent in 2009 as China encouraged domestic spending … Foreign trade dropped 13.9 per cent. China still holds a significant trade surplus – $196 billion – though the surplus slipped more than 34 per cent.

(www.cnn.com, 21 January 2010)

Figures published on Thursday 21 January showed that real GDP grew by 10.7 per cent year-on-year in the fourth quarter [of 2009]. Industrial production jumped by 18.5 per cent in the year to December, while retail sales increased by 17.5 per cent … In real terms the rise in retail sales last year [2009] was the biggest for over two decades … The twelve-month rate of consumer price inflation rose to 1.9 per cent in December, an abrupt change from July when prices were 1.8 per cent lower than a year before … The growth in bank credit slowed to 32 per cent in the year to December.

(www.economist.com, 21 January 2010)

Contributions to economic growth in 2009 [have been published] … Ninety-two per cent of last year's 8.7 per cent growth came from spending on fixed assets … Last week President Hu Jintao called for 'no delay' in boosting service industries, consumption and technology, at the expense of exports and investment.

(*FT*, 8 February 2010, p. 16)

Consumer prices increased by 1.9 per cent in December from a year earlier … Ma Jiantang (head of the National Bureau of Statistics): '[Price rises were] mild and under control … According to the UN standard – that is $1 a day – there are still 150 million poor people in China.'

(www.bbc.co.uk, 21 January 2010)

A decade ago Chinese banks staggered under a load of bad debt, reported by the Bank of China at nearly 40 per cent of their total lending in 1999. In 2000 the non-performing loan rate for the major commercial banks in China stood at 29 per cent, according to official statistics, and in the view of many Western analysts who questioned Chinese accounting standards it was probably far higher. Non-performing loans are defined as those loans on which repayments are more than three months in arrears. The government vowed to bring the rate down to 15 per cent by 2005, and by the end of 2007 it had dropped below 7 per cent ... Sceptics say the clean-up was largely based on sleight of hand, involving specially established Asset Management Companies, speculative bonds and fuzzy government guarantees that together did little more than kick the problem down the road. Even the least cynical analysts acknowledge that lower ratios reflected the dilution of bad loans in a vast sea of new lending, some of which would go bad but was still too recent to register as non-performing. Yet such doubts and qualifications notwithstanding, few deny that some degree of bad debt reduction was genuine and that overall loan quality among Chinese banks has improved from the worst of times. Now, however, new concerns are emerging over the state of Chinese banks and their balance sheets. Zhou Xiaochuan, governor of the People's Bank of China spoke publicly of such worries in early January, and hinted at a lending slowdown. Mr Zhou said: '[Large credit flows] will not only go against the objective of economic structural adjustment, but will pose bank lending quality risks' ... As recently as November [2009] senior Chinese bankers spoke confidently of their ability to avoid loan quality problems ... About the same time, the Banking Regulatory Commission reported that during the first ten months of 2009 the non-performing loan ratio for commercial banks had fallen by 0.76 percentage points from the end of 2008, to a mere 1.66 per cent.

(www.iht.com, 24 January 2010)

Fears of more policy tightening by China rattled investors Tuesday [26 January] after Beijing ordered some banks to comply immediately with a planned increase in reserves and a report suggested that earlier attempts at curbing lending had failed ... China implemented a planned increase in required reserves for some banks Tuesday ... Five major banks suggested that they had received instructions from the authorities last week to slow new lending, but not to stop it ... The increase in the amount of reserves some banks have to set aside, which was ordered last week, came after a newspaper report said China's efforts to curb bank lending had been meeting with mixed success, fuelling fears that policy-makers might take tougher action soon. Chinese banks extended 1.45 trillion renminbi ($212 billion) in new loans during the first nineteen days of the year.

(www.iht.com, 26 January 2010)

China showed a government budget surplus for the first eleven months of last year [2009], but Western economists still expect a small deficit for the entire year because agencies tend to go on spending binges every December to avoid returning unspent money.

(www.iht.com, 8 February 2010)

In an update of its *World Economic Outlook*, the IMF said that the global economy would expand 3.9 per cent this year [2010], sharply higher than the 3.1 per cent it had predicted as recently as October [2009]. The IMF's analysts expect economic growth worldwide of 4.3 per cent next year [2011] … The IMF expected growth of 10 per cent in China this year, up from 8.7 per cent last year [2009] … Advanced economies are expected to return to a growth rate of 2.1 per cent this year, after a contraction of 3.2 per cent in 2009 … The IMF predicted that the advanced countries would grow by 2.4 per cent in 2011, down from its October estimate of 2.5 per cent growth.

(www.iht.com, 26 January 2010)

'Emerging economies in Asia are likely to grow at an average 8.4 per cent pace this year and next, a strong improvement over last year's 6.5 per cent' (*IHT*, 27 January 2010, p. 20).

China's vice president, Li Keqiang, told the World Economic Forum in Davos [Switzerland] that domestic demand is key for China's economic growth … He said China had been 'excessively reliant on investment and export'. Mr Li pointed out that domestic spending improved in 2009, with sales of consumer goods up 15.5 per cent last year. He said the government had already taken successful steps to boost consumer demand. For example, they had introduced a plan to subsidize home appliances, such as televisions and fridges, for farmers … Mr Li, who is tipped to replace premier Wen Jiabao, also said it was vital to raise the living standards of poorer rural communities … Nearly 10 million people move from countryside to cities every year, according to Mr Li. He said income in the central and western areas was still very low.

(www.bbc.co.uk, 28 January 2010)

In easily his most high profile speech abroad since his elevation to vice premier two years ago, Li Keqiang … the man poised to become China's next premier in 2010 … resolutely defended China's record in pursuing balanced growth, implicitly rejecting criticism that Beijing had not done enough to mend its export-led model. He said: 'China's contribution to the world's economic recovery is obvious' … [He added] that its 8.7 per cent growth in output last year [2009] came in spite of falling exports that shaved nearly 4 per cent off the headline rate. Growing domestic demand, both through government-led investment and consumption, contributed more than 12.5 per cent to the growth of GDP, he said. Li Keqiang: 'While promoting growth, we spared no effort in rebalancing the structure of the economy' … [He criticized] countries that preached free trade but adopted protectionist practices … Mr Li, who has a doctorate in economics, peppered his speech with data aimed at proving that China was shifting to more balanced and sustainable growth. Sales of consumer goods had risen 15.5 per cent last year, while income grew in tandem with GDP, increasing disposable income, he said. Li Keqiang: '[While acknowledging that China remains] excessively dependent on exports, I am confident that consumption will play a bigger and better role to drive China's economic development.'

(*FT*, 29 January 2010, p. 7)

Li Keqiang, widely expected to be the next prime minister [in 2012], vowed that his country would act swiftly to shift from an over-reliance on exports toward greater domestic consumption ... Mr Li said: 'As we stand at a historic juncture, we must change the old way of inefficient growth and transform the current development model that is excessively reliant on investment and exports. We will focus on boosting domestic demand ... The growth in domestic consumption in China will not only drive growth in China but also provide greater markets for the world' [He listed] a number of initiatives from providing a stronger health care safety net, which would lessen the need for families to set aside large amounts of savings, to subsidizing farmers who buy household appliances ... At the same time, Mr Li repeatedly emphasized the importance of international co-operation, from continued co-ordination on fiscal stimulus to a global accord on climate change ... His speech to the world's political and business elite in Davos was his first high profile international appearance. A year ago it was prime minister Wen Jiabao who took the podium [in Davos] ... He said he would press ahead with pro-market changes, break monopolies and introduce more competition. He said: '[China will] allow the market to play a primary role in allocation of resources ... Efforts will be made to improve intellectual property rights ... Trade protectionism will only exacerbate the economic crisis ... The international financial crisis is not over and the foundations of economic recovery are still weak' ... He noted that more than half of Chinese exports were manufactured by foreign companies in China and that China had now become the second biggest importer in the world ... He said: '[China needs to] strike a balance between steady and fast growth and properly managing inflationary risks.'

(*IHT*, 29 January 2010, p. 16)

China needs to run a continued budget deficit and let its real exchange rate rise to rebalance its economy towards domestic demand and thus sustain the impressive growth of recent years, the OECD said on Tuesday [2 February]. In only its second full-length study of non-member China, the Organization for Economic Co-operation and Development (OECD) maintained its November [2009] forecast of an acceleration in GDP growth to 10.2 per cent in 2010 from 8.7 per cent last year [2009]. The report highlights major challenges facing China, including [the following]: the ageing of the population; income inequalities; fragmented social safety nets; the inability of small firms to access financing; and a lack of incentives for innovation due to weak protection of intellectual property rights ... Despite its bullish 2010 GDP forecast, which is in line with the 10 per cent growth projected by the

IMF, the OECD said near-term economic overheating was unlikely as the economy had ample spare capacity. Consumer prices would rise 1.8 per cent in 2010, an upward revision from its November forecast of a 0.1 per cent increase. The OECD said the fiscal deficit remained small despite Beijing's 4 trillion yuan ($585.9 billion) stimulus programme and advised against a return to the conservative spending policies that left the general government budget in surplus to the tune of over 5 per cent of GDP in 2007 on the eve of the global downturn. The report said: 'Further out, maintaining strong domestic demand will require a continued fiscal deficit' ... Durably lower government saving was needed to keep reducing China's current account surplus and to pay for further reforms in areas such as education, welfare assistance, pensions and health.

(www.iht.com, 2 February 2010)

The IMF and the World Bank have long called for China to increase social spending so its citizens have less need to save and can consume more ... The OECD said: 'Looking ahead at the exit from the ongoing stimulus programmes, it will be important not to revert to budget surpluses. China's public finances position is remarkably strong and can readily accommodate a permanently high level of government spending' ... China may have rapidly increased outlays on welfare pensions and health, but it has barely scratched the surface. The OECD said: 'Greater public spending on education in particular can help both to boost productivity and to reduce inequality' ... Despite having implemented a stimulus programme worth $585 billion, the government has a budget deficit last year [2009] of just 2.2 per cent of GDP, below its target of 3 per cent. If spending slows as the pump-priming ends, the OECD fears that surpluses could return and lead to a renewed widening of China's current account surplus ... Whereas the OECD advocates more education spending, a new IMF study concludes that, to reduce precautionary savings, the priority should be on public health care. Each additional renminbi in government health spending increases urban consumption by 2 renminbi.

(*IHT*, 16 February 2010, p. 2)

China should jettison its fiscal conservatism and shift spending to social welfare as its economy rebounds from the global crisis, the OECD said. Richard Herd (head of the OECD's China and India economics department): 'Once this fiscal stimulus starts to ease, the Chinese government should not move back to the very conservative fiscal policy [that it had from 2000 to 2007] ... Higher levels of social spending need to be sustained.'

(*FT*, 3 February 2010, p. 6)

China will not experience serious inflation this year [2010] and the government can prevent any asset bubbles, a top financial official said on Monday [8 February] ... Dai Xianglong [is] the chairman of China's National Council for Social Security Fund ... The fund Mr Dai controls, the government's pension fund, has more than $100 billion in assets ... Mr Dai, a former governor of the People's Bank of China, said Monday that radical fiscal policy changes were unlikely ... The Chinese government expects to keep consumer price inflation at around 3 per cent this year, while continuing the 'moderately loose monetary policy' it has pursued to date, he said. The government is unlikely to increase interest rates anytime soon, Mr Dai added ... He added that while China recognized the leading role of the dollar, it was necessary to 'promote diversification of international currencies'. The world's new international monetary system should be made up of the US dollar, the Euro and an Asian currency he said. The internationalization of the renminbi may take twenty years to complete, Mr Dai said. Ultimately it will be convertible with other currencies and account for a portion of global reserves, and the Chinese government will 'take appropriate responsibilities for the stability of international currencies', he said.

(*IHT*, 9 February 2010, p. 17)

'The central bank governor insisted on Tuesday [9 February] that price rises seen so far this year [2010] remain relatively low, but acknowledged his officials were keeping a close eye on the inflation data' (www.bbc.co.uk, 10 February 2010).

Germany lost its status as the world's leading exporter, as China's surging economy pushed it into first place last year [2009], according to official German data published Tuesday [9 February]. Chinese exports amounted to $1.2 trillion in 2009, while German exports totalled $1.1 trillion (Euro 797 billion] ... Germany became the top world exporter in 2003, surpassing the United States.

(*IHT*, 10 February 2010, p. 14)

[According to official German figures] German exports last year [2009] were equivalent to $1,121.3 billion, which compared with the $1,201.7 billion exported by China ... China's goods exports ... fell by 16 per cent over the course of the year, the first time they had declined since 1978 ... China's trade surplus dropped 34 per cent last year to $196 billion.

(www.cnn.com, 10 February 2010)

China said Wednesday [10 February] that its exports climbed 21 per cent in January from a year earlier, while imports surged 85.5 per cent ... Imports rose impressively, and in line with economists' expectations, because imports a year ago were so weak ... China's exports showed a somewhat smaller increase than expected ... Imports in January rose impressively, in line with economists' expectations, because imports a year ago were so weak. Many export factories nearly stopped buying raw materials then as their orders dried up, but they have been restocking since late spring [2009]. Exports and imports both benefited this year [2010] from the timing of Chinese New Year, which will be Sunday [14 February]. It fell on 26 January last year, and a weeklong holiday at the end of January last year helped curtail economic activity ... Auto sales surged 143 per cent from a year earlier and production leapt 124 per cent.

(www.iht.com, 10 February 2010)

The figures were distorted by the timing of Chinese New Year holidays, which meant the economy operated for one week less last January [2009]. The import figures were also flattered by the fact that imports at the start of last year were at their lowest level since 2005. In terms of volume of trade, the January numbers were actually below December's, with exports down from $130.7 billion in December to $109.5 billion, and imports falling from $112.3 billion to $95.3 billion. RBS calculated that exports were down 2 per cent on a seasonally adjusted basis month-on-month.

(www.ft.com, 10 February 2010)

'Reports this week suggested some of the provinces where lots of exporters are based have already or are planning to raise their minimum wages' (www.bbc.co.uk, 10 February 2010).

The rate of inflation at factories and other producers more than doubled last month [January] ... with producer prices climbing at their fastest pace in fifteen months while money supply continued to grow briskly. The sudden acceleration partly reflects the very low level of commodity prices a year ago ... Producer prices were up 4.3 per cent in January from a year earlier ... In December [2009] the increase from a year earlier was just 1.9 per cent. As recently as last October [2009] China was still suffering from gradual deflation at the producer level. However, consumer prices were up 1.5 per cent from a year earlier, compared with a year-on-year increase of 1.9 per cent in December ... Data showed that banks lent 1.39 trillion renminbi ($204 billion) of loans in January, more than the 1.35 trillion renminbi that economists had forecast.

(www.iht.com, 11 February 2010)

New bank loans reached renminbi 1,390 billion ($203 billion) in January, more than the previous three months combined ... New loans in January were a sharp increase from the renminbi 379.8 billion issued in December [2009] but the figure was down from renminbi 1,620 billion in the same month last year [2009] The new data provided a mixed picture, with consumer price inflation actually dropping to 1.5 per cent in January from 1.9 per cent the month before, while factory gate inflation rose faster than expected to 4.3 per cent from 1.7 per cent ... [There has been a] slowdown in lending since the middle of January ... In a report issued yesterday [11 February] the central bank said that policy remained 'moderately loose' but hinted at slow tightening when it said monetary conditions would 'gradually move toward a normal situation from an anti-crisis situation'.

(*FT*, 12 February 2010, p. 10)

For the second time in less than five weeks, China's central bank has moved to limit lending to consumers and businesses by ordering big commercial banks to park a larger share of their deposits at the central bank. The step, announced Friday [12 February], came earlier than most economists had expected and was aimed at forestalling inflation by controlling a rapid expansion in bank loans ... The People's Bank of China ordered an increase in banks' reserve requirement ratio, which is the share of deposits that commercial lenders must park at the central bank, earning very little interest ... The central bank pushed up the ratio by half a percentage point, to 16.5 per cent, for large banks, effective 25 February. But it left the ratio unchanged at 14 per cent for smaller financial institutions, such as rural co-operatives, which have been less active in a frenzy of lending to big state-owned enterprises in particular this winter ... The latest increase ... in the ratio ... is to take effect after the week-long Lunar New Year holiday next week ... The increase in the reserve ratio will not actually require banks to curtail lending immediately, because the commercial banks have typically been keeping about 18 per cent of their assets at the central bank – more than the reserve requirement. But raising the minimum makes it less likely that big banks will take this money back and start lending it elsewhere.

(www.iht.com, 12 February 2010; *IHT*, 13 February 2010, p. 8)

Analysts had expected the central bank to increase reserve levels again, but were surprised it ordered a second increase so soon after January's move ... Lending by Chinese banks hit 1.4 trillion yuan ($205 billion) in January [2010], one of the highest monthly totals on record.

(www.bbc.co.uk, 12 February 2010)

Economists in China point out the authorities have not reduced the planned target for new lending this year [2010] of renminbi 7,500 billion ($1,098 billion). Instead, they have been trying to prevent banks from frontloading a substantial part of their annual lending quota into the early months of the year, which could lead to overheating of the economy.

(*FT*, 13 February 2010, p. 6)

Chinese moves to restrain credit growth ... rattled global markets ... Nigel Rendell (senior emerging markets strategist at RBC Capital Markets): 'The Chinese move hit markets because it is now the economy that everyone is looking at to gauge the strength of the recovery. The United States is no longer the lead economy.'

(*FT*, 13 February 2010, p. 6)

Japan's economy grew at an annualized rate of 4.6 per cent in the final quarter of 2009, preliminary numbers showed Monday [15 February] ... It was the third consecutive quarter of growth ... Still, economists forecast that growth will slow this year and that Japan is likely to be overtaken by China as the world's second largest economy, behind the United States ... Since mid-2009 Japan has limped back into recovery, helped by exports and capital investment. The growth in exports has been buoyed by a recovery in China and the rest of Asia.

(www.iht.com, 15 February 2010)

'Growth in the October–December quarter came to 1.1 per cent above that of the third quarter … which translates to 4.6 per cent over the course of a year' (*IHT*, 16 February 2010, p. 16).

Japan's 2009 GDP was $5.27 trillion, according to figures released by the government on Monday [15 February], compared to the $4.9 trillion Chinese economy last year [2009] … Two factors led to Japan's better than expected financial results – growth in export demand (especially from China and the rest of Asia) as well as stronger government consumption drive by stimulus funding … Japan has been the world's second largest economy since 1968, when it passed the economy of the former West Germany … The United States remains the world's largest economy, with a value of about $14 trillion.

(www.cnn.com, 15 February 2010)

Japan's economy grew by a better-than-expected 1.1 per cent in the final quarter of last year [2009]. This is the equivalent of an annualized increase of 4.6 per cent. However, despite the growth in October to December, the economy contracted by 5 per cent over the whole of 2009 … Japan's return to growth has been led by exports, particularly to China, which is now its largest overseas market. Consumer spending, which accounts for about 60 per cent of the Japanese economy, rose 0.7 per cent from the previous quarter as shoppers took advantage of government incentives on cars and home appliances. However, consumer spending remains weak in general. Corporate capital spending rose by 1 per cent in the quarter, seeing the first expansion since the three months to March 2008. Public investment fell 1.6 per cent, while exports jumped 5 per cent.

(www.bbc.co.uk, 15 February 2010)

Japan's GDP grew 1.1 per cent in the last quarter of 2009 compared with the previous three months … Japan remains highly reliant on external demand, with net exports accounting for 0.5 percentage points in the fourth quarter GDP growth … Net exports accounted for 0.5 percentage points of the 1.1 per cent in seasonally adjusted quarter-on-quarter growth reported for the fourth quarter … GDP declined 1.2 per cent in 2008 and 5 per cent in 2009 … Yet Japan remained the second largest economy in 2009, with GDP of about $5,080 billion compared with China's $4,900 billion … Exports to China rose 43 per cent year-on-year in December [2009] alone.

(*FT*, 16 February 2010, p. 7)

Foreign demand for US Treasury securities fell by a record amount in December [2009] as China purged some of its holdings of government debt, the US Treasury department said on Tuesday [16 February]. China sold $34.2 billion in US Treasury securities during the month, the US Treasury said on Tuesday, leaving Japan as the biggest holder of US government debt with $768.8 billion. China overtook Japan as the largest holder in September 2008. The shift in demand comes as countries retreat from the 'flight to safety' strategy they embarked upon during the worst of the global financial crisis and could mean the United States will have to pay more to service its debt interest. For China the shedding of US debt marks a reversal that it signalled last year [2009] when it said it would begin to reduce some of its holdings.

(www.cnn.com, 17 February 2010)

China is facing a shortage of workers in the Pearl River Delta manufacturing hub in southern China. Some estimates suggest factories need 2 million more migrant workers from other parts of China. The shortages have been highlighted in Chinese media as the country gets back to work after the week-long Spring Festival, or Lunar New Year holiday ... Factories in southern China started reporting that it was hard to find enough workers last August [2009], as orders picked up after the financial crisis. Now, the country's media report, the shortages are becoming significant.

(www.bbc.co.uk, 22 February 2010)

China's banking regulator has told commercial lenders to restrict new lending they provide to the financing arms of local governments ... Last month [January] Liu Mingkang, chairman of the China Banking Regulatory Commission, said he expected the nation's banks to extend credit totally about 7.5 trillion renminbi ($1.1 trillion) – more than one-fifth less than the record 9.6 trillion renminbi doled out last year [2009]. On Wednesday [24 February] the state-run *Shanghai Securities News* newspaper reported that the commission had ordered banks to inspect their existing loans to companies used by local government to raise funds, and to stop lending to those projects that are backed only by expected fiscal revenues.

(www.iht.com, 24 February 2010)

Regulators have ordered Chinese banks to step up lending to private businesses while restricting credit to local government projects. Banks were ordered to lend more to small businesses this year [2010] than they did in 2009 ... Small businesses account for most of China's economic growth and new jobs, but largely missed out on a major stimulus package last year. Chinese banks last year extended loans totalling 9.6 trillion renminbi ($1.4 trillion), with lending to companies accounting for 5.7 trillion renminbi. Of that 24.8 per cent went to small enterprises, according to the central bank.

(*IHT*, 24 February 2010)

'Chinese banks have been told by their regulators to lend more to small businesses and less to the financing arms of local governments' (www.economist. com, 25 February 2010).

Zhu Min, one of the most prominent financial officials in China, is to become a special adviser to the head of the IMF ... Mr Zhu, who will start work at the IMF in May [2010], will work as a special adviser to Dominique Strauss-Kahn ... Mr Zhu has been one of the deputy governors of the Chinese central bank since October [2009]. Before that he was a senior executive at Bank of China and spent six years working for the World Bank. His move to the role at the IMF follows the selection in 2008 of Justin Yifu Lin, a Chinese academic, as chief economist of the World Bank ... In December [2009] Mr Zhu said the sharp fall in China's exports last year [2009] had given Beijing reason to depreciate rather than appreciate the renminbi.

(*FT*, 25 February 2010, p. 6)

At the World Economic Forum in Davos, Switzerland, last month [January] Zhu Min defended his country's policy of maintaining a stable exchange rate for its currency and warned that dollar volatility was threatening a global economic recovery ... Mr Zhu received a doctorate in economics from Johns Hopkins University in the United States and joined Bank of China in 1996 ... Before that he was an economist at the World Bank for six years ... The appointment of Mr Zhu came just two years after the World Bank picked a Peking University professor, Justin Lin, as its first chief economist from outside Europe and the United States ... The IMF softened its rhetoric last year [2009] on China's renminbi policy as it reached out to Chinese officials on policy issues.

(*IHT*, 26 February 2010, p. 18)

China reaffirmed its determination Thursday [25 February] to keep steady the value of the renminbi ... Yao Jian (a spokesman for the commerce ministry): 'The yuan's exchange rate is not the main reason triggering China's trade surplus, America's trade deficit or global economic imbalances' ... He said there had not been a clear rebound in external demand despite two consecutive months of year-on-year gains in exports, including a 21 per cent increase in January. Overseas shipments will not regain full momentum for an additional two or three years, he said. Yao Jian: 'Many exporters are still struggling for survival. So I think a stable exchange rate for the yuan will remain a prime target of China's current economic policies' ... Exports fell 16 per cent in 2009 ... and Mr Yao said any sharp year-on-year growth in the first half of 2010 would simply reflect the low comparison base of a year earlier. He said: 'So we should not read too much into it' ... China's trade surplus fell 34 per cent last year [2009] to $196.1 billion.

(*IHT*, 26 February 2010, p. 18)

Just a year after laying off millions of factory workers, China is facing an increasingly acute labour shortage ... The immediate cause of the shortage is that millions of migrant workers who travelled home for the long Lunar New Year earlier this month [February] are not returning to the coast. Thanks to a half-trillion-dollar government stimulus programme, jobs are being created in the interior. But many economists say the recent global downturn also obscured a longer-term trend: China has drained its once vast reserves of unemployed workers in rural areas and is running out of fresh labourers for its factories ... The official *China Daily* newspaper said on Thursday [25

February] that surveys of employers showed that one in twelve migrant workers was not expected to return to Guangdong province. Cities farther north along China's coast are also running low on labour; Wenzhou alone posted a shortage of up to 1 million workers ... Rising wages suggest the re-emergence of a worker shortage that was becoming evident before the financial crisis. A government survey three years ago of 2,749 villages in seventeen provinces found that in 74 per cent of them there was no one left who was fit to go to work in city factories – the labour pool was dry. Mass lay-offs in late 2008 and early 2009 because of the global financial crisis temporarily masked the developing shortage of industrial workers. But two powerful trends were still working to reduce the supply of young people headed for factories. For one, the Chinese government has rapidly expanded secondary education. Universities and other institutions of higher learning enrolled 6.4 million new students last year [2009], compared with 5.7 million in 2007 and just 2.2 million in 2000. At the same time China's birth rate has been sliding steadily ever since the introduction of the 'one child' policy in 1977. Labour shortages have returned quickly in recent weeks as these long-term trends have collided with a recovery in overseas demand for Chinese goods. Far more jobs are available these days in China's interior. Government projects like rail and highway construction have absorbed millions of workers, particularly after Beijing allocated nearly $600 billion to economic stimulus in 2009 and 2010. Consumer spending is also rising briskly.

(www.iht.com, 27 February 2010; *IHT*, 1 March 2010, p. 18)

In a major speech at the start [on 5 March] of China's annual parliamentary session [of the National People's Congress] ... premier Wen Jiabao said China must reverse its widening income gap between rich and poor ... [He] also said the economy needed restructuring. He wants Chinese firms to improve their ability to innovate, producing high-tech and high-quality products ... He said: 'We will not only make the "pie" of social wealth bigger by developing the economy, but also distribute it well ... [We will] resolutely reverse the widening income gap' ... As part of that project, the premier said China would reform the household registration system that classifies people as either city or rural dwellers ... He said: '[We will] gradually ensure that they [migrant workers] receive the same treatment as urban residents in areas such as pay, children's education, healthcare, housing and social security' ... He said reforms would only be carried out in towns and smaller cities ... Premier Wen said China needed to concentrate on restructuring the economy. He said: 'This is crucial for ... accelerating the transformation of the pattern of economic development' ... He wants future growth to be fuelled by innovation. China should also expand consumer demand by getting people to spend on such things as tourism, fitness and other services ... Many people across China are currently concerned about rising house prices that mean many cannot afford a home. Mr Wen said China would do something about it.

(www.bbc.co.uk, 5 March 2010)

Premier Wen Jiabao promised increased spending on welfare and rural areas, aiming to halt the growth of the gap between rich and poor, maintain stability and spur domestic demand. His annual policy speech set a steady course for the country – with a growth target of 8 per cent, as in previous years – but left the government room for flexibility as he cautioned that the global economic outlook remained uncertain ... The 11.4 per cent increase will take total spending to 8.45 trillion yuan, but is less than half of last year's 24 per cent rise ... He said: 'We must not interpret the economic turnaround as a fundamental improvement in the economic situation. There are insufficient internal drivers of economic growth ... We can ensure that there is sustained impetus for economic development, a solid foundation for social progress, and lasting stability for the country only by working hard to ensure and improve people's well-being' ... In an online chat on Saturday [27 February] he said that a society was 'doomed to instability' if wealth was concentrated in the hands of a few. Today's [5 March] two-hour speech announced increases of 8.8 per cent on social spending and 12.8 per cent on rural programmes – well above the unexpectedly low 7.5 per cent rise in the military budget announced yesterday [4 March] ... He reiterated Beijing's pledge to keep its currency basically steady ... Wen Jiabao also said Beijing would maintain an appropriately easy monetary stance and an active fiscal policy. He set the inflation target at around 3 per cent and said the [budget] deficit would be kept below 3 per cent of national income. He pledged to curb the 'precipitous rises in housing prices' in some cities ... The government will boost funding for low income housing by 14.8 per cent ... The premier said ... a special effort would be made to raise living standards of minority ethnic communities.

(www.guardian.co.uk, 5 March 2010)

Prime minister Wen Jiabao said Friday [5 March] that the nation would expand social spending, bolster lending, curb inflation and meet its traditional 8 per cent growth target in 2010, but he cautioned that China still confronted 'a very complex situation' in the wake of the global financial crisis ... Mr Wen said that 'destabilizing factors and uncertainties' in the world economy posed a challenge to China's continued growth. But he effectively said that China's plan to ease away from last year's [2009] enormous stimulus programme ... would continue unchanged ... China managed an 8.7 per cent increase in its GDP ... He pledged to clamp down on speculative real estate purchases, which some analysts say are creating a bubble in China's housing market. He also said the state would take measures to rein in an explosive rise in urban land prices. He warned that some Chinese industries ... had developed serious overcapacity problems. And even as he committed to expand the nation's money supply by 17 per cent this year [2010], increasing lending by 7.5 trillion renminbi ($1.1 trillion). Mr Wen warned that 'latent risks in the banking and public finance sectors are increasing' ... Mr Wen said the government would run a budget deficit of $154 billion in 2010, which is in line with economists' expectations. As a share of GDP the projected deficit is unchanged from last year [2009]. Overall, spending will rise about 11.4 per cent this year [2010], half of the increase in spending during the recession last year ... Last year, he said, the government's stimulus measures helped increase auto sales by 46.2 per cent, housing by 42.1 per cent, as measured in square metres, and retail sales of consumer goods by 16 per cent. Mr Wen said that China would pour money into strategic industries, increasing research and development and infrastructure spending to 'capture the economic, scientific and technological high ground'. Among the areas he singled out were biomedicine, energy conservation, information technology and high-end manufacturing ... Mr Wen pledged to increase environmental protection measures ... Wen Jiabao: 'At the same time as we keep our reforms orientated toward a market economy, let market forces play their basic role in allocating resources and stimulate the market's vitality, we must make best use of the socialist system's advantages, which enable us to make decisions efficiently, organize effectively and concentrate resources to accomplish large undertakings.'

(www.iht.com, 5 March 2010)

'Premier Wen Jiabao said the government hopes to hold overall consumer price rises to 3 per cent this year [2010]' (www.iht.com, 11 March 2010).

China's economy, prime minister Wen Jiabao said in a two-hour speech, had been the first in the world to make a turnaround ... He spoke of socialism's 'advantages': quick decision-making, effective organization and an ability to 'concentrate resources to accomplish large undertakings' ... China's economic planning agency, the National Development and Reform Commission, acknowledged in a report to the National People's Congress that house prices were 'overheating' in some cities, consumer spending was unlikely to grow significantly this year [2010] and the effect of stimulus measures 'might wear off'. Yet the government says it wants to keep the budget deficit to 2.8 per cent of GDP this year, about the same as last year [2009].

(www.economist.com, 5 March 2010)

Premier Wen Jiabao ... said that to meet the target of 8 per cent growth, Beijing would maintain a 'proactive fiscal policy and moderately easy monetary policy' ... He said: 'The launching of new projects must be strictly controlled ... [Government investment] should be used mainly for carrying on and completing projects' ... Mr Wen also warned that 'latent risks in the banking and public finance sectors are increasing' ... Mr Wen, who last week referred to property markets in some cities as being like a 'wild horse', said the government would increase spending on low-income housing and rein in property speculation ... He said: 'We will resolutely curb the precipitous rise of housing prices in some cities' ... The budget deficit is forecast to be 2.8 per cent of GDP this year [2010], compared with 2.2 per cent of GDP in 2009 ... [There is] a marked slowdown in the rate of growth of government spending, from 21 per cent last year [2009] to 11 per cent this year.

(*FT*, 6 March 2010, p. 7)

'There was still "insufficient internal impetus driving economic growth"' (*FT*, 8 March 2010, p. 12).

'Premier Wen Jiabao ... said the exchange rate would remain 'basically stable at an appropriate and balanced level' ... The premier announced a series of measures to help small and medium-sized companies, including tax breaks and bank guarantees' (www.cnn.co, 6 March 2010).

> [On Saturday 6 March] the central bank head, Zhou Xiaochuan, said China should be 'very cautious' about revaluing the yuan as long as major economies remained mired in slow growth. He called China's practice of pegging the renminbi to the dollar a 'special foreign exchange mechanism' made to respond to the world financial crisis. Such mechanisms will be abandoned 'sooner or later', he said, but 'we must be very cautious and discreet in choosing the timing' ... Mr Zhou offered no timetable for allowing the renminbi to resume its rise against the dollar, but he noted that it could take two or three years for global export markets to recover from the financial collapse ... A slowdown in exports did shave roughly 4 percentage points off the growth rate of China's GDP last year [2009], economists say. But the currency stabilization and a large stimulus programme kept China's economy on track so that it exceeded the 8 per cent target that the government has set for economic growth in 2009.
>
> (www.iht.com, 7 March 2010; *IHT*, 8 March 2010, p. 19)

> China's central bank chief Zhou Xiaochuan [6 March]: 'This is part of our package for dealing with the global financial crisis. Sooner or later we will exit the policies. If we say we withdraw from non-conventional policy and return to conventional economic policy, we must be very cautious and discreet in choosing the timing. This also includes the renminbi exchange rate policy' ... Chen Deming, commerce minister, said the outlook for international trade remained 'uncertain and unstable' and it would take two or three years before Chinese exports recovered to pre-crisis levels.
>
> (*FT*, 8 March 2010, p. 6)

> China's exports grew strongly in February ... Exports were up 45.7 per cent in February over a year earlier ... beating forecasts by private sector analysts of 35 per cent to 40 per cent growth. Imports were also up strongly, rising by 44.7 per cent in February from a year earlier ... China's trade figures can be distorted by the week-long Lunar New Year holiday, which falls at varying times in January and February. Combining data from the two months, which analysts say produces a more accurate picture of trade conditions, shows exports surged 31.4 per cent in the January–February period over the same period last year [2009].
>
> (www.iht.com, 10 March 2010)

It was the third consecutive month of increases in Chinese exports and the fastest growth in three years. Orders from the United States, the EU and

Japan accounted for almost half the growth, following a pickup in demand from emerging markets in the previous two months.

(www.iht.com, 10 March 2010)

'Last year [2009] the New Year festival fell in January ... [One analyst said that since] there were five fewer business days in February this year [2010] than last year ... [this] makes the export number pretty impressive' (www.bbc.co.uk, 10 March 2010).

The rate of increase of imports from South-east Asia and South America was between 80 per cent and 100 per cent in February, more than double the rate of increase of ... trade partners such as the United States and Europe. Compared with January [2010] exports fell 2.2 per cent on a seasonally adjusted basis, while imports rose 6.3 per cent ... Zhua Guangyao, assistant minister of finance, warned yesterday [10 March] of an unpredictable global economic situation, despite the strong trade performance. He said China must wait until at least the third quarter [of 2010] to decide whether to withdraw stimulus policies, including the renminbi's peg against the dollar.

(*FT*, 11 March 2010, p. 7)

Investment in real estate rose 31.1 per cent in the first two months of the year [2010], compared with a year earlier ... Property inflation in seventy major cities rose to 10.7 per cent in February from a year earlier, compared with 9.5 per cent in January ... China unveiled strict new rules Wednesday [10 March] governing bankers' pay that are designed to limit risk taking ... Payment of 40 per cent or more of an executive's salary must be delayed for a minimum of three years and could be withheld if the bank performs poorly, the China Banking Regulatory Commission said in a statement on its website.

(www.iht.com, 10 March 2010; *IHT*, 11 March 2010, p. 17)

'Housing price inflation also accelerated in February, with costs in seventy cities rising by 10.7 per cent over a year earlier, up from January's 9.5 per cent' (www.iht.com, 11 March 2010).

China's banking regulator has issued guidelines linking bonus pay of bank executives and employees to performance ... The guidelines would require at least 40 per cent of executive bonuses to be deferred for at least three years ... Banks could then hold back money from the retained bonuses if executives perform badly. The criteria for bonuses would be based on a range of factors, such as a bank's business performance, social responsibility and risk management, which includes bad loans. The guidelines issued Wednesday [10 March] would also limit an executive's bonus to no more than three times their annual base salary. For rank-and-file employees, bonuses could not exceed 35 per cent of base pay.

(www.ccn.com, 12 March 2010)

Chinese data showed ... inflation hit a sixteen-month high ... Consumer prices rose 2.7 per cent in February over a year earlier, up from January's

1.5 per cent increase, the National Bureau of Statistics reported Thursday [11 March]. That exceeded most analysts' forecasts and was driven by a 6 per cent jump in food costs ... The statistics bureau blamed the latest jump on bad weather that hurt food production and said pressure should ease once spring harvests come in ... Poor families spend up to 40 per cent of their incomes on food ... Total lending by Chinese banks in February fell to 700 billion yuan ($102 billion), down by half from January's level after credit controls were tightened, the central bank reported Thursday ... Data showed February's wholesale inflation accelerating to 5.4 per cent, up from January's 4.3 per cent.

(www.iht.com, 11 March 2010)

Consumer prices rose 2.7 per cent in February over the year earlier period ... partly attributable to the Lunar New Year holiday ... when families tend to splurge on food and gifts ... but also to rising inflationary pressures ... The harsh winter hurt food production ... China's leaders insist that inflation is firmly in check, below the government's target of 3 per cent.

(www.iht.com, 11 March 2010; *IHT*, 12 March 2010, p. 16)

'For the combined January to February period, which factors out distortions from the Lunar New Year holidays, industrial output expanded by 20.7 per cent and retail sales rose 18 per cent compared to a year ago' (www.iht.com, 11 March 2010; *IHT*, 12 March 2010, p. 16).

Inflation jumped to a sixteen-month high in February ... Consumer prices rose by 2.7 per cent last month [February] over the year before, up from 1.5 per cent in January ... Factory gate prices rose 5.4 per cent in February against 4.3 per cent the month before. Consumer and factory gate inflation have been on an upward trend since November [2009] ... Industrial production ... rose by 20.7 per cent in January and February over the year before, above forecasts and December's 18.5 per cent rise ... Retail sales grew in line with forecasts, rising 17.9 per cent year-on-year in January and February, up from 15.8 per cent in December, while fixed asset investment surged 26.6 per cent in the first two months of the year, from 20.5 per cent in December.

(*FT*, 12 March 2010, p. 7)

In recent weeks a number of the country's senior leaders and regulators have signalled an end to the practice of local governments extending guarantees on loans taken out by their special financing entities. This could spell big trouble for Chinese banks. The comments have focused attention on research done by Victor Shih, a professor of Northwestern University in America, into China's local investment companies. These financing vehicles allow municipalities to circumvent central government restrictions on direct borrowing. As many as 8,000 of these investment companies may exist, estimates Mr Shih ... He reckons that these entities have outstanding debt of 11.4 trillion yuan ($1.7 trillion), and commitments for a further 12.7 trillion yuan, much of it tied to infrastructure projects designed to stimulate the economy. For comparison, China's national stimulus plan was worth 4 trillion yuan, 1 trillion yuan of which came from the central government.

(The Economist, 13 March 2010, p. 82)

'Local governments … enjoy huge windfalls when they sell land-use rights … Some analysts believe that in many places fees from land transfers make up more than 30 per cent of local government revenues' (p. 62).

'Local authorities are barred by law from borrowing directly' (*IHT*, 16 March 2010, p. 19).

Prime minister Wen Jiabao (speaking on 14 March, the final day of the annual session of the National People's Congress):

> I do not think the renminbi is undervalued. We oppose all countries engaging in mutual finger-pointing or taking strong measures to force other nations to appreciate their currencies. That is not in the interest of reform of the renminbi or the renminbi's exchange rate regime. We will continue to reform the renminbi exchange rate regime and will keep the renminbi basically stable at an appropriate and balanced level. Since the outbreak of the international financial crisis, we have made strong efforts to keep the renminbi exchange rate at a stable level. This has played an important role in facilitating the global economy … [Protecting the dollar is a matter of] national credibility [for the United States]. Any fluctuation in the value of the US currency is a big concern for us … We are very concerned about the lack of stability in the US dollar … In the press conference last year I said I was a bit concerned [about the security of US Treasuries that China holds] … This year I make the same remark. I am still concerned. We cannot afford any mistake, however slight, when it comes to financial assets … I hope the United States will take concrete measures to reassure international investors … It is not only in the interests of the investors, but also the United States itself … I understand some economies want to increase their exports, but what I do not understand is the practice of depreciating one's own currency and attempting to force other countries to appreciate their own currencies, just for the purpose of increasing their own exports. In my view that is a protectionist measure. All countries should be fully alarmed by such developments.
>
> (www.iht.com, 14 March 2010; www.bbc.co.uk, 14 March 2010;
www.guardian.co.uk, 14 March 2010; www.cnn.com, 14 March 2010;
www.ft.com, 14 March 2010; www.thetimes.co.uk, 14 March 2010;
IHT, 15 March 2010, pp. 1, 16; FT, 15 March 2010, p. 1)

Prime minister Wen Jiabao argued that the renminbi is not unfairly valued, citing government calculations that suggested that, measured in real terms, China's currency had actually risen in value at the height of the economic crisis … Analysts expect Beijing to let the yuan rise against the dollar some time this year [2010]. But they foresee a gradual increase of no more than 5 per cent this year.

(www.iht.com, 14 March 2010; *IHT*, 15 March 2010, p. 16)

Prime minister Wen Jiabao pointed out that around half of China's exports were processing trade – where imported components are assembled at factories in China – and 60 per cent were made by foreign companies or joint ventures with a foreign partner. He said: 'If you restrict trade with China, you are hurting your own countries' firms.'

(www.ft.com, 14 March 2010; *FT*, 15 March 2010, p. 1)

Prime minister Wen Jiabao insisted that inflation must be managed while maintaining rapid economic growth and carrying out state-led economic restructuring, a goal that he conceded would be 'extremely difficult' ... Prime minister Wen Jiabao: 'If there is inflation, plus unfair income distribution and corruption, that could be strong enough to affect social stability and even the consolidation of state power ... It will be an extremely difficult task for us to promote steady and fast economic growth, adjust our economic structure and manage inflation expectations all at the same time, but it is imperative for us to accomplish these three tasks' ... Mr Wen said other countries faced the prospect of inflation, which he said was a big factor contributing to the risk of a double-dip global recession. Mr Wen said: 'As a result of inflation expectations, some countries are facing difficulties in making the right policy decisions. Should we encounter setbacks [in China's economic recovery] much is at stake and the cost will be too high ... [China aims to maintain an] appropriate and sufficient money supply, keep our interest rates at a reasonable level and manage inflation expectations.'

(*FT*, 15 March 2010, p. 8)

'Inflation in February was higher than expected but not by enough to force a change in strategy, the central bank governor, Zhou Xiaochuan, said Sunday [14 March]' (*IHT*, 15 March 2010, p. 17).

Beijing called yesterday [16 March] for US multinationals to lobby the Obama administration against taking protectionist measures over the renminbi ... The Chinese commerce ministry said: 'We hope that US companies in China will express their demands and points of view in the United States, in order to promote the development of global trade and jointly oppose trade protectionism.' ... The comments came as the political heat surrounding China's currency policy intensified in Washington. Led by Chuck Schumer, the New York Democrat, and Lindsey Graham, the South Carolina Republican, a group of senators said Beijing's refusal to let its currency appreciate was damaging the US recovery and hurting American competitiveness ... The senators have proposed a bill that would require the [US] Treasury to identify countries with 'fundamentally aligned currencies' as well as those that needed to be tackled with 'priority action'. Those countries would have nearly a year to adjust the value of their currency before the administration was required to bring a case against them at the WTO, according to the proposal. The Treasury would also have to 'consult' with the Federal Reserve and other central banks about 'remedial intervention in currency markets'. Some measures could be taken earlier, including forbidding Chinese companies from participating in US government contracts. Mr Schumer and Mr Graham have been leading the charge in Congress against China's currency policy for several years and have periodically presented similar proposals.

(*FT*, 17 March 2010, p. 7)

China could face duties on some of its exports to the United States if it does not take steps to realign its currency, according to the draft text of legislation that was to be introduced Tuesday [16 March] in the Senate. The draft bill by Charles Schumer and Lindsey Graham would require the US Treasury Department to identify countries with fundamentally misaligned currencies each September and March. It would authorize the Commerce Department to take currency misalignment into its calculation of import injury duties for specific products if a targeted country had not begun steps within ninety days to realign its currency, according to the text of the bill … Several years ago Mr Schumer and Mr Graham co-authored a bill that threatened China with a 27.5 per cent across-the-board tariff if it did not revalue the renminbi. That bill was passed by the Senate but its authors eventually abandoned it when Beijing began making some movement toward revaluing the renminbi. Many US lawmakers, with strong backing from economists, believe that China's currency is undervalued by 25 per cent to 50 per cent, giving Chinese companies an unfair price advantage in trade by effectively subsidizing exports and taxing competing imports.

(*IHT*, 17 March 2010, p. 19)

Members of Congress from both parties sought on Tuesday [16 March] to put more pressure on China to allow an increase in the value of its currency, saying Beijing's policy of holding the value down to give China an edge in export markets was holding back job creation in the United States … Five senators [three others joining Charles Schumer and Lindsey Graham] introduced a bill that would all but compel the administration to act. A manipulation finding could prompt retaliatory efforts by the United States. In addition, 130 House members sent a letter on Monday [15 March] calling on the Treasury to issue a finding of manipulation and on the Commerce Department to impose countervailing duties to protect American manufacturers. The Senate bill would require the Treasury to identify 'fundamentally misaligned currencies' based on specific criteria. The bill would seek to address one reason that the United States has not cited China for manipulation since 1994, which is that a finding of manipulation requires intent. If the Treasury designated such a misaligned currency 'for priority action', that would set off other steps, including an investigation by the Commerce Department that could result in import duties to counter the effects of foreign export subsidies.

(www.iht.com, 17 March 2010)

The World Bank on Wednesday [17 March] recommended higher interest rates and a stronger currency for China as it raised its growth forecasts for the country ... The World Bank raised its forecast to 9.5 per cent growth [GDP] from the 8.7 per cent it had projected in November [2009]. It also estimated that growth would slow somewhat next year [2011] to 8.7 per cent ... The World Bank singled out the looming property bubble and strained local government finances as 'macroeconomic risks'. The report said: 'Inflation expectations can be contained by a tighter monetary stance and a stronger exchange rate. The case for a larger role for interest rates in monetary policy is strong. If policy-makers remain concerned about interest rate sensitive capital flows, more exchange rate flexibility would help ... The monetary policy stance needs to be tighter than last year [2009] and the case for exchange rate flexibility and more monetary independence from the United States is strengthening. It would also be helpful to increase the tolerance for modest inflation, to ensure room for desirable relative price changes. Strengthening the exchange rate can help reduce inflationary pressures and rebalance the economy. Over time more exchange rate flexibility can enable China to have a monetary policy independent from US cyclical conditions, which is increasingly necessary ... [With output in China once again] close to potential ... [the country now needs] a different macro stance than most other countries.'

(www.iht.com, 17 March 2010)

'Separately, Dominique Strauss-Kahn, the managing director of the IMF, said: "Some currencies in Asia are undervalued, especially the renminbi" ' (www.iht. com, 17 March 2010).

The World Bank now expects consumer prices to rise by 3.7 per cent on average this year [2010], up from 2 per cent in November [2009], and by 2.8 per cent in 2011. The World Bank report said: 'We think that inflation risks remain modest, in large part because of the global context. Nonetheless, the macro stance needs to be noticeably tighter than in 2009 to manage inflation expectations and contain the risk of a property bubble' ... [The World Bank] highlighted higher asset prices and strained local government finances as the biggest risks.

(www.guardian.co.uk, 17 March 2010)

The 'Beijing consensus':

The country's economic miracle, the *People's Daily* boasted last week, exists because its leaders – unlike those in other, unnamed nations – can make quick decisions and ensure underlings carry them out ... Some experts fear that too much of the stimulus money was put into unprofitable projects and bad loans that will be exposed in a few years ... In Beijing officials said *per capita* GDP is expected to exceed $4,000 this year [2010], a 10 per cent jump from 2009.

(www.iht.com, 12 January 2010)

As developing countries everywhere look for a recipe for faster growth and greater stability than that offered by the now-tattered 'Washington consensus' of open markets, floating currencies and free elections, there is growing talk of a 'Beijing consensus' ... China is a Confucian–Communist–capitalist hybrid under the umbrella of a one-party state that has so far resisted giving greater political freedom to a growing middle class ... What exactly is the Beijing consensus? Some see it as a form of economic management with greater government involvement that is on the rise across the world. Others interpret it to mean more strictly controlled capital markets, which have made an appearance even in previously open countries like Brazil. Policy-makers in Malaysia and Dubai focus on replicating China's special economic zones, which afford generous terms to foreign investors in manageable geographical areas. Some suggest that China's lack of democracy is an advantage in making unpopular but necessary changes.

(Katrin Bennhold, *IHT*, 27 January 2010, pp. 1, 13)

'Many Chinese now feel they have little to learn from the rich world. On the contrary, a 'Beijing consensus' has been gaining ground, extolling the virtues of decisive authoritarianism over shilly-shallying democratic debate' (*The Economist*, 6 February 2010, p. 12).

4 The reform of state industrial enterprises

It was during the First Five Year Plan (1953–7) that the operation of the typical Chinese state industrial enterprise came nearest to its Soviet counterpart (including soft budget constraints). But even then the Chinese enterprise differed from the latter in significant ways. Thus manpower was allocated to the Chinese enterprise, virtually all profits were transferred to the state budget and management bonuses were much less important. The *danwei* (workplace) provided housing, health and social welfare services and the party took an increasingly important role in running the enterprise. Chaotic conditions prevailed during the Cultural Revolution.

Experimental reforms began in 1978 but general reforms in the industrial sector did not begin to be implemented until October 1984. (See Jeffries 2006a: 441–3.)

The discarding of social functions

In the original system the enterprise was not just a production unit. It was also, as we have already seen, a social unit. The shift to a more Western-type system of social welfare (unemployment compensation and pensions), health and housing is a difficult, costly and painful one. Such reforms are needed for state enterprises to compete more effectively with private enterprises in a market economy.

(For experiments to provide unemployment compensation, see Jeffries 2006a: 443–4.)

(For experiments to shift the pensions, housing and health burdens away from enterprises and towards various levels of government and/or individuals, see Jeffries 2006a: 444–50.)

> Since the nationwide reform of 1997 the public pension system, which covers only 14 per cent of the active population, has been a two-part system. The first part provides a basic flat rate pension, while the second part provides a pension proportional to contributions.
>
> (OECD 2005: website Chapter 4)

'About 173 million people, or less than a quarter of China's workers, are covered by basic pensions. The government said it aimed to increase the insured population to 220 million by 2010' (www.iht.com, 22 December 2005).

'For the last year state-owned companies listing overseas have had to allocate 10 per cent of the new shares to the National Council for Social Security Fund, the central government-run pension fund' (*FT*, 25 October 2006, p. 8).

> The pension system covered 205 million people as of March 2008, according to the ministry of human resources and social security, or about 15 per cent of the population. The government aims to lift that figure to 223 million by the end of next year [2010], it said last week ... A pension programme that started in the 1990s covers only about 10 per cent of the rural labour forces, the World Bank says. Participants dropped by a third between 1999 and 2004 ... prime minister Wen Jiabao pleaded last month [March 2009] to expand urban and rural pension coverage and develop a system that would allow migrant workers who change jobs frequently to shift retirement benefits.
>
> (*IHT*, 22 April 2009, p. 2)

'Just 31 per cent of the work force, mainly in the state sector, receives public pensions. Most of the fast-growing private sector is excluded, as are migrant workers. As for rural China, pensions are virtually non-existent' (*IHT*, 28 April 2009, p. 19).

> Until about twenty years ago the vast majority of urban workers were covered by a system known as the 'iron rice bowl'. People who worked for the state, in state-owned companies or in state-approved collectives, enjoyed cradle-to-grave benefits ranging from housing, education and health care to a generous pension scheme, with an official retirement age of fifty-five for men and fifty for women for manual workers (but five years more for white-collar workers) and a replacement rate of about 80 per cent of final salary. Most people retired about five years before the official age ... Average life expectancy at birth, at seventy-four, is now twenty-five years higher than it was fifty years ago, yet the retirement age has remained at the same low level. Unless it goes up, any comprehensive pension system that China might eventually introduce will be hideously expensive ... Whereas civil servants and employees in state-owned firms used to make up nearly 80 per cent of all urban workers, their share is now down to 20 per cent. The government is committed to honouring the pension promises left over from the old system, but the 'iron rice bowl' has gone. That has left a huge gap in urban workers' social security provision. Workers in rural areas, who still make up about half the total labour force, never had much coverage of any kind anyway ... the pensions system is in flux. In the early 1990s the government announced a three-pillar scheme along the lines of those in many developed countries: a basic pay-as-you go pension to which both employers and employees make mandatory contributions; funded individual accounts, also with contributions from employers and workers; and individuals' private savings. This is work in progress. Reforms are being announced 'almost annually', says Wang Yanzhong, who heads the Centre

of Labour and Social Security Studies at the Chinese Academy of Sciences. So far only about a third of the population is covered by any kind of pension scheme. The funded individual accounts envisaged under the government's plans have been set up, but so far there is little money in them. Because of restrictions on investment abroad and a dearth of high-yielding instruments at home, such money as has been accumulated has been invested mainly in the domestic banking system, where it earns a rate of return far too low to meet the government's pension promises.

(*The Economist*, Special Report on Ageing Populations, 27 June 2009, pp. 14–15)

The government is to introduce a new pension scheme for the country's hundreds of millions of rural workers. The minister for social security announced that a trial scheme would be extended across China by October [2009]. The government will pay for basic insurance for rural workers and farmers will contribute to a pension pot … The government already operates a basic pension plan for urban workers. Hu Xiaoyi: 'The new system is paid for by farmers, collective benefits and government subsidy, which is totally different from the old system, paid for by farmers themselves, with no subsidy from the government' … The scheme will be valid for all farmers over sixty. Anyone over the age of sixteen who does not take part in the government's existing urban pension scheme is eligible to pay into the pro-gramme. A pilot version of the scheme is currently being trialled across some parts of China, including in Tangwei county, in Suzhou … The payment will vary regionally and be based on average local income.

(www.bbc.co.uk, 5 August 2009)

'[China] is reforming the pension system, which now leaves out over half of urban workers and 90 per cent of their rural counterparts' (*The Economist*, Survey on the World Economy, 3 October 2009, p. 9).

'Only one-tenth of the population has health insurance; more than half of the people who get sick cannot afford professional medical care' (*IHT*, 6 March 2007, p. 6).

China announced Monday [6 April] the outlines of a thorough reform of the health care system that pledges to provide services to all citizens by 2020 … The first stage of the plans calls for extending some form of basic health insurance to 90 per cent of the population by the end of 2011. Currently only 30 per cent of China's population of 1.3 billion is covered. Further improvements in funding and oversight will then provide 'safe, effective, convenient and affordable' health services for all citizens by the end of the next decade, according to the plan approved by the State Council, China's cabinet. Hospitals and clinics in the poor countryside and less developed cities would be improved and the price of essential medicines would be capped. Disease prevention and control, maternal health, mental health and first aid services would also receive greater attention … At present insurance is mainly provided to working-age urban residents, often through their employers or government agencies. Xinhua said the reforms envisioned 'diversified medical insurance systems' to give coverage to employees in the private sector, non-working urbanites and residents of the countryside ... Financial details of the reforms were not given, although the government announced in January [2009] plans to spend 850 billion yuan ($124 billion) on the first three years of the programme ... Health care spending by both the private and public sector in China amounts to just 5 per cent of GDP, significantly less than the 17 per cent spent in the United States ... More than twenty government agencies have a stake in the health care system.

(www.iht.com, 6 April 2009)

China will build or maintain a clinic in every one of the country's 700,000 villages over the next three years, the government announced today [8 April 2009], as part of a 850 billion yuan revamp of the healthcare system ... The government will also extend basic medical coverage and insurance to 90 per cent of China's 1.3 billion people, almost a third of whom currently have to meet treatment cost entirely out of their own pockets ... The health ministry will train 1.4 million doctors, nurses and other medical practitioners to staff village clinics, in addition to half a million healthcare workers in towns and cities ... Under plans unveiled this week the government will also build 2,000 county hospitals and build or renovate 3,700 community clinics and 11,000 health service centres in urban areas within three years. The central government will pay 40 per cent of the costs, leaving the reminder to be covered by local authorities. Prices of essential medicines will be capped and the medical insurance scheme will be extended to nine in ten people by 2011 ... In a comparison of health systems in 2000, China was ranked 144th out of 191 states. In terms of access to medical care it was fourth from bottom, beating only Sierra Leone, Brazil and Burma.

(www.guardian.co.uk, 8 April 2009; *Guardian*, 9 April 2009, p. 24)

After years of dithering ... the government has a plan ... It was only in 2006 that work began on drawing up a comprehensive plan for healthcare reform ... Two documents issued on 6 and 7 April [2009] set out reform targets through to 2020 as well as more specific objectives for the next three years. The broad goals remain unchanged from draft proposals released last October [2008] after a delay of several months. Officials say 200 million Chinese have no insurance now. But by 2020 China is to have a 'relatively robust' government-financed health insurance system, with more than 90 per cent of citizens covered by 2011. Also unchanged is the figure of 850 billion yuan ($125 billion), which the government said in January it intended to spend on these reforms during 2009 and the two subsequent years ... The recent documents ... give no clear target even by 2020 for how much citizens can expect to be reimbursed for hospital treatment. Even for those with government insurance a substantial amount still usually has to be paid out of the patient's own pocket. In the countryside, despite the government's rapid rolling out of a new insurance scheme in the past few years, many peasants still shy away from hospitals. A big objective of the reforms is to break the dependence of government-owned hospitals on the payments exacted from patients for tests, medicine and other treatments. Government subsidies account for a tiny amount of hospitals' revenue. Reports in the state-run press say more than 90 per cent of their income comes from charges (poorly regulated and often excessive) for providing services and medicine ... The government's plan is to publish a list this month of essential medicines. Over the next three years government-run medical facilities will be required to give preference to drugs on this list and profits made on them by healthcare providers will be phased out. They will receive extra subsidies to make up for their losses. But hospitals have often profited from illegal mark-ups on medicines and from commissions from manufacturers on the sales of their drugs. The new subsidies are unlikely to take this into account, so hospitals could see their revenues shrink. Hospitals have also proven adept in the past at evading price controls on particular drugs by prescribing other medicines or unnecessary extra tests and treatments. Another big obstacle to reform could be a lack of enthusiasm among local governments. Of the planned 850 billion yuan in spending, officials say only 40 per cent will come from the central government. Provincial and lower level authorities may be reluctant to divert resources to areas that do not produce immediate benefits in terms of boosting employment and GDP growth. How much of an extra burden local governments will have to bear is still unclear.

(*The Economist*, 18 April 2009, p. 61)

The health ministry is to introduce rules to try and prevent hospitals from making a profit on drug sales. In rural areas a fixed salary scheme for doctors is being tried out, taking away the link between drug sales and their salaries ... Coverage under the insurance plans is limited – for rural residents it will be renminbi 120 a year, compared with an average in-patient hospital bill of renminbi 4,000. Most local governments provide additional subsidies, especially for serious illness, but patients usually end up with substantial bills ... A drawback of the current system – that patients need to pay the hospital up front in cash, being reimbursed only later – will still be in place.

(*FT*, 13 May 2009, p. 13)

A survey carried out in 2000 by the China Research Centre on Ageing, a think-tank, found that more than half the over-sixties' medical expenses came out of their own pockets and a big chunk of the rest was paid for by their families ... In April [2009] the government set out its plan for a comprehensive reform to build a 'safe, effective, convenient and affordable' healthcare system by 2020. Over the next three years it intends to spend 850 billion yuan. By 2011 more than 90 per cent of the population is meant to be covered by the system. In rural areas that figure has already been reached, but the scheme usually covers only in-patient treatment and the reimbursement rate remains very low.

(*The Economist*, Special Report on Ageing Populations, 25 June 2009,
p. 14)

Since the New Rural Co-operative Medical System was started in 2003, coverage has expanded to 830 million people and the average reimbursement rate of hospital bills has increased to 41 per cent from 25 per cent, according the ministry of health ... In a new study of rural health reform in China, the World Bank said total out-of-pocket spending on health care in the countryside fell from 80 per cent in 2004 to 69 per cent in 2006. But the report said the share financed out of pocket was unlikely to drop much below 60 per cent ... China spends almost 5 per cent of GDP on health services, but the government accounts for less than a fifth of that, according to the United Nations ... The United States spends ... 17.6 per cent of GDP ... on health.

(*IHT*, 4 August 2009, p. 18)

A pilot scheme is under way where patients in small villages receive healthcare for just 1 renminbi ($0.15) ... The villagers pay an annual insurance premium, a little less than $3, and the clinic is limited to treating just thirty medical conditions, like coughs and colds ... [Doctors] also can prescribe only seventy-four different medicines ... This type of basic healthcare is similar to what were known as the 'barefoot doctors', who, during the days of Chairman Mao, went door to door, village to village ... But economic reforms during the 1980s meant an end to the barefoot doctors.

(www.cnn.com, 6 August 2009)

Following extensive privatization during the past decade a residential housing market has emerged, with the owner occupation rate approaching 70 per cent in urban areas. Nonetheless, the short length of commercial and residential leases (fifty and seventy years, respectively) may constitute a barrier to effective improvement of land, as property on the land reverts to the state at the end of a lease.

(OECD 2005: website Chapter 1)

[Some] 80 per cent of China's urban households now own their home (in America the national figure is 69 per cent), compared with only around 10 per cent owning shares ... Over half of Chinese owners obtained their homes at well below market rates during the housing privatization from the late 1990s onwards.

(*The Economist*, 7 July 2007, p. 83)

Later reform periods

(For an analysis of the 1994–7 reforms, see Jeffries 2006a: 450–1.)

Shareholding and privatization

(See Jeffries 2006a: 451–82.)

Large privatization along Eastern European lines has not been adopted in China. Initially China concentrated on deregulation (i.e. gradually opening up certain sectors to private activity). Later on small enterprises began to be sold off in significant numbers and even some medium-sized and large companies have now been sold. Although the state still dominates ownership in medium-sized and large companies, an increasing number of companies have sold a proportion of their shares to private (including foreign) individuals and companies.

'H' shares are traded on the Hong Kong stock exchange – the first company involved was the Tsingtao Brewery in July 1993 – while 'N' shares are traded in New York's Wall Street. 'B' shares were supposed to be purchased for hard currencies such as the US dollar by foreigners only. In reality they were bought by Chinese citizens, but the state periodically clamped down on the practice. On 19 February 2001 it was announced that Chinese citizens would be allowed to buy 'B' shares and in November 2002 there was a relaxation of controls on foreign purchases of 'A' shares in Chinese companies.

' "Red chips" [are] Hong Kong-listed companies based on the mainland but incorporated overseas that have not yet been allowed to list domestically' (www. ft.com, 28 December 2007). ' "Red chips" ... [are] offshore Chinese companies' (*FT*, 29 August 2009, p. 22).

'Public ownership' formally remains the 'mainstay' of the economy, but the term has been interpreted more liberally (e.g. to include mixed-ownership enterprises).

> The government launched Shanghai's [stock] exchange in 1990 (and Shenzhen's a year later) ... The mainland's stock market is in dismal slump. On 1 February [2005] the domestic A-share indices in Shanghai and on the junior exchange in Shenzhen hit their lowest level for more than five years. Even after recovering a little since then, they are still down by more than 40 per cent and 50 per cent, respectively, from the record highs of June 2001 ... At that point the government got greedy and tried to sell its remaining holdings, a plan that started the current decline. Even though it was hastily withdrawn the threat of another mass sell-off of state shares continues to spook the market. Four years after the first sell-off a full two-thirds of the market's $460 billion capitalization remains tied up in non-tradable or 'legal person' shares held by state-controlled entities ... And the market's inexorable decline has pole-axed the Chinese broking industry, which not only guaranteed investors double-digit returns but also often speculated corruptly with their funds. Most of the 130-odd securities firms are, in effect, insolvent ... China has private savings of at least 12 trillion yuan ($1.4 trillion) sitting unproductively in banks. The country also has thousands of entrepreneurial firms crying out for funds. If the stock market were allowed to bring the two together, it could, through better allocation of capital, both raise the efficiency of the economy and help maintain its growth rate. Instead, much of

that fallow cash has found its way into property, inflating a bubble. Better still, developing China's capital markets would reduce the primacy of the banks ... On 21 February ... [China] announced a fund worth up to $6 billion to compensate investors for the bankruptcy or incompetence of local broking firms. Last weekend regulators launched a test allowing commercial banks to set up mutual funds arms and the week before selected insurers received the green light to invest up to $7 billion in shares ... In December [2004] Goldman Sachs [was allowed] to buy 33 per cent of Gao Hua Securities with management control and the right to raise its stake.

(The Economist, 26 February 2005, pp. 81–2)

China plans to let China Life Assurance, Ping An Insurance (Group) and other insurers buy controlling stakes in fund managers and other financial institutions ... Insurers will also be allowed to invest in public works projects and real estate, according to rules drafted by the China insurance regulatory commission ... The country's insurers hold more than 80 per cent of their assets in bonds and bank deposits ... Foreign insurers ... more than tripled their share of the Chinese insurance market to 8.9 per cent last year [2005] from 2.6 per cent a year earlier ... The government allowed overseas insurers to start selling health, pension and group policies in December 2004 to meet WTO obligations.

(IHT, 21 February 2006, p. 19)

Stock market regulators said yesterday [17 April] new share offerings would begin again 'soon', after a year-long freeze. It also said foreign funds might be allowed to invest more on mainland markets ... A rally in the mainland market [has taken place] this year [2006] The Shanghai composite exchange, which has risen 17 per cent so far this year after a four-year slump, closed 1.4 per cent higher.

(FT, 18 April 2006, p. 6)

China plans to allow investors to take out loans to buy shares and to sell borrowed stock for the first time aimed at tapping the country's $4 trillion of bank deposits and bolstering trading ... [China] is considering plans to select five brokerage firms to start margin-lending and short-selling services this year [2006] ... The pilot programme may be expanded to more firms later ... [It has been argued that the plan] will alleviate concern that the market will be weighed down by listings of big companies ... The plan arrives as the government prepares to end a year-long ban [since May 2005] on public share sales ... An investor buying on margin pays only a percentage of the cost of the stock, with the brokerage house financing the rest through a loan. In short sales investors sell stock they have borrowed in anticipation that they can buy it back later at a lower price and profit from the difference ... The Shanghai Composite Index has risen 36 per cent from its July [2005] low and the Shenzhen Composite Index has jumped 46 per cent since 18 July [2005]. On Monday [17 April] the Shanghai index rose

19.08 points, or 1.4 per cent, to close at 1,378.61 points, the highest level since November 2004. The government will initially allow companies to sell shares through placements, then by public sales of additional shares and finally through initial offerings … [The plan is] to set up a company, called China Securities Finance, this year to provide loans for brokerage firms to finance margin trading … It is also proposed to let brokerage firms borrow directly from banks to finance client subscriptions to initial public offerings.

(*IHT*, 18 April 2006, p. 17)

Chinese stock surged Monday [8 May] after Beijing lifted a one-year ban on share sales, giving publicly traded companies more financing operations to expand in a booming economy. But regulators left in doubt when initial public offerings might resume. To be eligible to again sell stock the companies must now meet thirty-four criteria, including three successive years of profit and dividend payments equal to at least 20 per cent of income … The government halted sales in May 2005 to avoid a glut of equity as it sought to make more than $200 billion of mostly state-owned stock tradable … The benchmark Shanghai Composite Index rose to its highest level in almost two years, climbing 4 per cent to close at 1,497.10 points. The index has risen 27 per cent this year [2006] after falling to a eight-year low in 2005 … China published proposed rules for resuming public offerings on 28 April, without setting a timetable … About 200 to 2,000 of 1,365 publicly traded companies in China will be eligible to sell more shares … Under the new rules, which took effect Monday, share sales cannot be bigger than 30 per cent of a company's capital before the offering. Companies selling convertible bonds should set a cap of their total debt after the sale at less than 40 per cent of the previous financial year.

(*IHT*, 9 May 2006, p. 17)

China reopened its market for initial public offerings on Thursday [18 May] after a year-long suspension … [It was] also said that a set of rules governing new IPOs proposed at the end of last month [April] would take effect immediately, with slight revisions … [For example] candidates for offerings must have been profitable for three consecutive years … New offerings were halted last year [2005] to allow China's two stock markets, which had been mired in a four-year slump, time to absorb $250 billion in previously issued shares in listed companies. Companies accounting for 70 per cent of the value of the two stock markets have now made arrangements to convert their non-tradable shares into regular stock … The Shanghai Composite Index jumped 17.3 per cent in the past month and has advanced 54 per cent since hitting an eight-year low in July [2005]. The stock markets remain dominated by small, state-owned manufacturers because the best and largest corporations have listed abroad.

(www.iht.com, 18 May 2006)

A rally has made the Shanghai stock market the world's best performer in the past month … The Shanghai Composite Index rose 17.3 per cent in the past month, and has advanced 54 per cent since hitting an eight-year low in July [2005]. On Thursday [18 May] the benchmark fell 0.5 per cent to 1,617.28 points as indexes across Asia retreated.

(*IHT*, 20 May 2006, p. 17)

Bank of China ... raised $9.7 billion Wednesday [24 May] in the world's biggest share offering in six years ... Bank of China, the second of China's four big state-run banks to go public, attracted an avalanche of funds as the sale of a 10.5 per cent stake was heavily oversubscribed ahead of its stock listing in Hong Kong next Thursday. The proceeds could swell to about $11.15 billion if Bank of China sells extra shares set aside to meet demand ... China Construction Bank went public in October [2005] ... The Bank of China public offering was the biggest on international markets since AT&T's wireless unit was floated in 2000 ... Bank of China said that during 2005 the proportion of bad loans on its books fell to 4.9 per cent from 5.5 per cent ... In a paper in March ... Richard Podpiera ... an analyst at the IMF ... said: 'The pricing of credit risk remains rather undifferentiated and bank lending continues to be driven by availability of funds and does not appear to take enterprise profitability into account when making lending decisions' ... In a report released this month [May] ... the international accounting firm Ernst & Young said China's big four banks could have piled up an estimated $845 billion in bad loans over the past fifteen years. The report said that after all the bailouts and transfers, the combined amount of bad loans remaining on their books could still total $358 billion, or more than double the official figure of $133 billion. After a furious response from China's central bank ... Ernst & Young, which audits Industrial and Commercial Bank of China, withdrew the report and apologized.

(www.iht.com, 24 May 2006; *IHT*, 25 May 2006, pp. 1, 14)

'On Wednesday [7 June] the Bank of China said it was exercising an option to sell 3.84 billion additional shares, increasing the initial public offering of last month by 15 per cent to $11.2 billion' (*IHT*, 8 June 2006, p. 22).

Bank of China said Wednesday [28 June] that it had attracted $84.6 billion in bids for the biggest domestic initial public offering in China, thirty-three times the stock on offer ... [The bank] sought 20 billion yuan, or $2.5 billion, selling local currency shares ... The stock was priced at between 3.05 and 3.15 yuan, a discount to its Hong Kong share price, which has risen 15 per cent since shares started trading on 1 June after raising $11.2 billion.

(www.iht.com, 28 June 2006)

Regulators said Sunday [2 July] that beginning in August they would allow investors to sell borrowed stock and take out loans to buy shares. The moves are a way to tap China's $4 trillion of bank deposits and to increase trading ... [There are conditions laid down for obtaining] a licence to offer the services ... China halted share sales in May 2005 to avoid a flood of equity as companies pursued plans to make more than $200 billion of mostly state-owned stock tradable. As of May [2006] companies accounting for about 70 per cent of the value of China's market had joined the programme. The Shanghai Composite Index, which covers yuan-denominated Class A shares and foreign currency Class B shares, has risen 44 per cent this year [2006], while the Shenzhen Composite Index has jumped 55 per cent. An investor buying on a margin pays only a percentage of the cost of the stock, with the brokerage financing the rest through a loan. In short sales investors sell stock they have borrowed in anticipation that they can buy it back later at a lower price and profit from the difference ... The government also wants to shore up a brokerage industry hurt by falling stock prices, mismanagement and corruption. The top fifty Chinese brokerages posted a combined net loss of $562 million in 2004.

(*IHT*, 3 July 2006, p. 13)

'The rules will take effect on 1 August [2006] ... The news lifted the Shanghai Composite Index 1.5 per cent to 1,697.28 points, its highest close since 13 April 2004. The Shenzhen composite rose 1.6 per cent to 440.13 points' (www.iht. com, 3 July 2006).

Starting Tuesday [1 August] China's biggest brokerages can apply for regulatory approval to lend money and shares to customers, paving the way for them to offer margin financing and short-term selling for the first time on the nation's stock exchanges. Brokerages with net assets of at least $150 million will be eligible to apply.

(*FT*, 2 August 2006, p. 17)

China said Thursday [14 September] it had halted acquisitions of domestic brokerages by international firms, delaying Wall Street's expansion in the world's fastest growing stock market. The China Securities Regulatory Commission also said it would stop issuing licences and approving new branches for Chinese brokerages to give domestic firms time to improve profitability. The ban ... appears to alter plans by Beijing to draw on foreign investor capital and management expertise to help clean house in a sector plagued for years by corruption, poor management and heavy losses. The Chinese regulator said exceptions would be made only for deals judged to be capable of reducing risk. The decision leaves Goldman Sachs Group and UBS as the only firms with their own brokerage ventures in the country ... The action also threw up further evidence of what appears to be efforts by Beijing policy-makers to restrict certain sectors of the economy from foreign investment, especially banking and finance ... The brokerage issue would only be looked at again after China completed its overhaul of the industry ... by the end of October next year [2007] ... Under its WTO commitments China must allow foreign investors to hold up to 49 per cent stakes in local brokerages five years after succession to the trading body, or by December 2006. The current ceiling is capped at 33 per cent. The government began a campaign three years ago to clean up the brokerage sector, shutting down many small and medium-sized houses in hopes of taming a sprawling industry that included more than 130 companies ... About 100 brokerages remain ... Global firms want access to China's stock markets, where the average number of shares traded each day more than doubled in the past year. The Shanghai Composite Index has surged 41 per cent this year [2006], the tenth best performing in the world ... UBS in June [2006] won approval to set up UBS Securities in China after a nine-month wait. The Zurich-based firm plans to buy Beijing Securities. New York-based Goldman won approval in 2004 to set up a venture with Beijing Gao Hua Securities ... China's top fifty brokerages reported a combined net loss of $562 million in 2004 ... The government has been forcing brokerages to merge or close, with the number falling to 143 registered with the Shanghai stock exchange as of last month [August], from 154 at the end of 2004.

(www.iht.com, 14 September 2006; *IHT*, 15 September 2006, p. 13)

China's stock market regulator announced yesterday [14 September] that it had placed a temporary ban on investment by foreign brokerages in the domestic securities industry – a key target for international banks ... The ban was likely to remain in place for just over a year, by when [October 2007] the government hoped to have completed a reform of the shareholder structure of listed companies ... Although it is widely known that such a ban has been informally in place since the end of last year [2005], the state-ment published yesterday ... was the first official acknowledgement by the regulator. UBS agreed last September [2007] to buy a 20 per cent stake in Beijing Securities for $200 million ... However, the deal was held up by regulatory delays as opposition to foreign investment in the sector grew. UBS said in July [2006] that it had been granted 'preparatory approval' by regulators to pursue its investment in Beijing Securities ... Although the owners of many of China's struggling brokers would be happy to sell out, senior figures in the industry have lobbied the regulator against permitting more deals for fear that they would be unable to compete.

(FT, 15 September 2006, p. 26)

'On 14 September China's stock market regulator made official a long-rumoured ban on foreign acquisitions of domestic stockbrokers and investment banks – which many of their international rivals are keen to snap up' (*The Econ-omist*, 23 September 2006, p. 88).

China Merchants Bank, the most profitable lender in China, raised 18.8 billion Hong Kong dollars, selling shares in Hong Kong after investors ordered fifty-three times more stock than was available in the sale, bankers involved in the deal said Sunday [17 September]. Merchants Bank, which is based in Shenzhen, sold 2.2 billion shares at 8.55 dollars, or $1.10, each, the top end of the range marketed to investors ... The sale is the second over-seas this year [2006] by a Chinese lender after Bank of China raised $11.2 billion in June.

(IHT, 18 September 2006, p. 16)

China Merchants Bank made a strong debut Friday [22 September] on the Hong Kong stock market as another Chinese lender – the country's biggest – got ready for what could be the world's largest initial public offering ... Industrial and Commercial Bank got approval to list in Hong Kong. The bank is planning its $19 billion IPO to take place simultaneously in Hong Kong and Shanghai in late October. That valuation would make the offering the world's largest since the company that is now NTT DoCoMo raised $18.4 billion in 1998.

(www.iht.com, 22 September 2006)

'Industrial and Commercial Bank of China ... China's largest ... plans to list on the stock exchanges of Hong Kong and Shanghai on 27 October [2006] in the first initial public offering [IPO] to be introduced simultaneously on both' (*IHT*, 16 October 2006, p. 12). 'The ICBC offering is the first ever dual listing on both domestic and overseas bourses. The yuan-denominated "A shares" issued in Shanghai will be available only to Chinese investors and so-called qualified foreign institutional investors' (www.iht.com, 23 October 2006).

Industrial and Commercial Bank said Monday [23 October 2006] that it would sell 15 per cent more shares in its domestic IPO to individual investors because of additional demand, raising the total to 46.6 billion yuan ... ICBC, the biggest Chinese bank, completed the simultaneous offering in Hong Kong and China, raising a record $19.1 billion last week in the largest ever IPO. Investors ordered more than $500 billion of stock.

(www.iht.com, 24 October 2006)

ICBC made history by simultaneously conducting its IPO in Shanghai and Hong Kong in parallel listings that enabled both domestic and foreign investors to participate. The stock sale raised up to $21.9 billion, beating the previous record $18.4 billion IPO staged by NTT DoCoMo Inc. in 1998. The bank raised a minimum of $19.1 billion, but the bank was expected to soon increase its offering to $21.9 billion by exercising the so-called greenshoe option to meet extra demand ... ICBC received a $15 billion injection from the government to clean up its balance sheet last year [2005] ... More than 72.5 per cent of ICBC is held in equal shares by the ministry of finance and the state's asset management arm, Central Safe Investments Ltd. The national pension fund holds a 5.4 per cent stake and foreign strategic investors a combined 7.4 per cent. That leaves about 15 per cent of the bank's equity in the form of Hong Kong and Shanghai trade shares.

(www.iht.com, 27 October 2006)

Bad loans represented 4.1 per cent of ICBC's total in June [2006], down from 4.7 per cent at the end of last year [2005]. The China banking regulatory commission said the country's five biggest banks should cut bad loans to less than 5 per cent.

(*IHT*, 9 October 2006, p. 16)

The benchmark Shanghai index tumbled from 2,245 points in mid-2001 to a low of 998 points in mid-2005. It closed Friday [27 October 2006] at 1,807, just below a five-year high of 1,842 ... Reforms started last year [2005] set in place a process for swapping non-tradable government shares in listed companies into tradable shares, and compensating existing shareholders with cash and tradable shares for any consequent decline in existing share values. More than 900 companies – more than 70 per cent of listed companies – have so far followed this process. Market sentiment improved toward the end of last year as the restructuring gathered momentum. The markets were further energized in January [2006] with a rule change that made it easier for foreign strategic investors to buy stakes in yuan-denominated shares – the so-called A shares – of listed companies. Previously the only investors allowed to buy A shares, the primary class of listed stock, were a limited group of institutional investors approved by China's regulator and known as Qualified Institutional Investors. The new rule allowed strategic investors greater latitude in purchasing A shares as long as they bought a minimum stake of 10 per cent and held it for a minimum of three years. As the market began further momentum in the second quarter the China Securities Regulatory Commission allowed the resumption of domestic initial public offerings, which had been halted in the middle of 2005 while that tradable share reform was pushed through ... Chinese banks have raised more than $40 billion from share sales since the middle of last year [2005], including ICBC's sale of a 15 per cent stake to the public – mainly through the Hong Kong market – for $21 billion ... Insurance companies [have been allowed] to buy equity directly ... Anti-speculative measure [in real estate] – like the imposition of a 20 per cent capital gains tax – prompted many investors to cash out of the property market, and much of this liquidated capital had probably been channelled into the stock market ... One major shortcoming is that stock markets remain closed to the small and mid-size companies in the private sector that are the drivers of the economy ... According to the brokerage CLSA, the Chinese private sector is now responsible for more than 70 per cent of GDP and employs about 75 per cent of the total work force ... Only 10 per cent of listed equity on the markets is from the private sector.

(www.iht.com, 29 October 2006)

'The Shanghai A-share index is up more than 52 per cent from the beginning of the year [2006]' (www.iht.com, 23 October 2006).

'China Communications Construction, the largest Chinese port builder, raised $2.1 billion in its initial public offering [in Hong Kong] ... The company sold ... a 24.5 per cent stake' (*IHT*, 11 December 2006, p. 16).

The consumer banking market was opened to international lenders Monday [11 December] ... After a $400 billion government bailout and $44 billion of share sales, Chinese banks are profitable, growing and confident ... The government has bought up $400 billion of bad loans since 1998 and four of the country's five biggest lenders have held initial public offerings. The banks are still overhauling their management and risk controls.

(*IHT*, 12 December 2006, pp. 14, 17)

'Tianjin [is] a northern port city that was chosen for a pilot programme in which companies will be allowed to convert some of their yuan earnings into foreign currencies through banks in the district' (www.iht.com, 11 December 2006).

The main [Shanghai] stock index jumped Thursday [14 December] to close at 2,249.11 points, beating a 2001 record. The surge added to a powerful rally in which Chinese stock prices have nearly doubled in 2006, ending an ugly and debilitating four-year-long bear market ... After dipping as low as 998.23 in June 2005, the Shanghai stock index has soared by over 90 per cent this year [2006], making it the world's best-performing major market.

(*IHT*, 15 December 2006, p. 19)

'The Shanghai and Shenzhen A share indices were up by 130.57 per cent and 127.85 per cent respectively in 2006, making them the world's best performing markets after Caracas' (*FT*, 3 January 2007, p. 20).

The value of the Chinese stock market has topped $1 trillion for the first time ... The value of shares on the Shanghai and Shenzhen stock exchanges more than tripled in the past year and reached $1.1 trillion as of the close on Wednesday [10 January 2007].

(*IHT*, 12 January 2007, p. 13)

From 1 January 2007 China has decreed that the 1,200 companies listed on the Shanghai and Shenzhen stock exchanges must comply with a new set of accounting rules that are based on – but not identical to – the IASB's standards. The move is designed to improve the credibility of Chinese accounting, which is seen as vital to promoting market stability and attracting continued investment ... A landmark agreement [was signed] last year [2005] between China and the International Accounting Standards Board [IASB]. It points out that some parts of China's new accounting standards deserve to be studied by international accounting standards ... In July [2006] ... the IASB announced that it would review a standard that Beijing said was unworkable ... [China] followed a Soviet accounting system until 1993 ... The country's accountants are in short supply.

(*FT*, Special Report on Chartered Accountancy, 4 September 2006, p. 1)

At the beginning of this year [2007] China made its biggest move yet when the ministry of finance required the 1,200 companies listed on the Shenzhen and Shanghai stock markets to adopt, with important exceptions, norms similar to the International Financial Reporting Standards (IFRS) ... Countries all over the world are embracing them. China has given all its other firms the option of complying with them 'voluntarily' ... The decision to adopt international accounting standards was made in November 2005 ... Certain conditions, such as 'related-party' transactions, are almost impossible to bring into line with international standards, so they will be fudged. Under international accounting norms, deals between companies with overlapping ownership are supposed to be clearly disclosed. This is a sound principle in general and particularly appropriate for companies in countries where the government owns a piece of almost everything, and presses companies to take steps that may be bad for them (such as buying from troubled suppliers to protect jobs). But because overlapping ownership is so common in China (the government still owns shares in almost every large company), detailing each transaction would overwhelm a financial report. For 'purely state-controlled enterprises' there will be no disclosure requirement. An equally large problem is the lack of accountants to process the raw numbers. In no other place in the world, and probably at no other time in history, have accountants been so sought after as they are in China.

(*The Economist*, 13 January 2007, pp. 63–4)

Stock markets around the world plunged Tuesday [27 February] after share indexes in China plummeted nearly 9 per cent, their biggest decline in a decade, a day after reaching record highs ... Analysts had cautioned for months that the markets in China, which soared almost non-stop for more than a year, appeared vulnerable. Some investors say the drop was triggered by concern that the government would clamp down on illegal share offerings ... The possibility of tighter investments controls in China also scared shareholders in companies that get a large proportion of their shares from there ... The benchmark Shanghai Composite Index, which passed the 3,000-point milestone Monday [26 February] after the week-long Chinese New Year holiday, lost 268 points, or 8.8 per cent, to close at 2,771.79. The Shenzhen Composite Index fell 66.31 points, or 8.5 per cent, to 709.81 ... But the declines Tuesday were not all because of China, as investors said negative news on the US economy exacerbated stock declines in America and Europe.

(*IHT*, 28 February 2007, p. 1)

The Chinese stock market was rife with rumours that the government was considering new measures to tame the world's hottest stock market before a bubble developed ... None of the world's major stock markets has been as volatile as in China, where people tend to refer to the stock market as *dubo ji*, or the slot machine ... Government officials began cautioning several weeks ago against 'blind optimism' in the stock market ... Stock prices fell sharply for four consecutive days in early February [2007] as investors seemed to contemplate the possibility of an overheated stock market. After a brief pause they rushed in again. Foreign money is also piling in ... Regulators are seeing a growing number of stock scams targeting small investors.

(www.iht.com, 27 February 2007)

'The market tumble sent the Shanghai Composite Index down 8.8 per cent to 2,771 – just about where it was on 1 February [2007] ... Some investors blamed the market nosedive on rumours of new capital gains taxes' (www.iht.com, 28 February 2007). 'The government stepped in, creating the task force to address unauthorized share sales and other unspecified activities. The decision followed an order last month [January] that banks should prevent the illegal use of personal loans for stock purchases' (*IHT*, 1 March 2007, p. 20).

US stocks suffered their steepest drop since the invasion of Iraq in 2003, after the biggest fall in Chinese shares for a decade and slides in other global stock markets triggered a sharp rise in risk aversion ... Mainland Chinese shares fell nearly 9 per cent amid fears that the authorities were planning a crackdown to cool the market's exuberance. Traders said it was highly unusual for events in Chinese markets to have a global impact, but saw it as a sign of China's increasing influence on the global economy.

(*FT*, 28 February 2007, p. 1)

The carnage began on Tuesday [27 February] after the Shanghai stock market fell 9 per cent. It came amid concerns over the state of the US economy and subprime mortgage market and followed comments from Alan Greenspan, former chairman of the Federal Reserve, about a possible US recession.

(*FT*, 3 March 2007, p. 1)

There was much surprise that China could have had such an impact, despite its fast-growing influence on the world economy. In truth it was merely one of several catalysts. Investors are becoming more worried about the state of America's mortgage market ... They were also unnerved by a warning from Alan Greenspan, former chairman of the Fed, that America could possibly be sliding towards recession; a fall in durable-goods orders added to the broader economic concerns.

(www.economist.com, 28 February 2007)

The Shanghai stock market rallied Wednesday [28 February] from the biggest drop in a decade to gain a hefty 109 points, or 3.9 per cent, closing at 2,881.07 – about where it was on 14 February. No other Asian stock market did as well Wednesday ... With the rebound on Wednesday the index is still up 121 per cent from a year ago ... The Chinese government closely monitors the markets ... The government has an obvious incentive to prop up the market and to prevent steep sell-offs ... The government is, of course, worried about a stock market bubble. And recently officials have warned investors about 'blind optimism' in the stock market. But nothing could be worse than a market crash ... Instability is the government's biggest fear. In 1992 people hurled stones at the Shenzhen stock exchange after officials were accused of colluding with brokers to manipulate IPOs. And two years ago, when stocks were mired in a protracted bear market, angry investors protested outside the offices of regulators. There is also what investors call the Olympics factor.

(www.iht.com, 28 February 2007)

Wall Street showed signs of recovery Wednesday ... Most Asian countries closed down ... In China both mainland stock markets rebounded sharply Wednesday ... These indexes rose Wednesday nearly 4 per cent after state-controlled media reported that the Chinese government might allow greater foreign investment in Chinese stocks and would not impose capital gains taxes on stocks soon ... Government regulations have kept foreign investment in these markets to an insignificant level ... One factor behind the rebound Wednesday in mainland markets was a report in the Shanghai media that the government might increase the cap on foreign investment to 10 per cent of the market ... That report, together with signs that the government would not move quickly to impose capital gains taxes, helped offset continuing nervousness about the Chinese central bank's campaign to put the brakes on the economy by pushing banks to slow down their rapid growth in lending ... Markets elsewhere in Asia continued to slump.

(*IHT*, 1 March 2007, pp. 1, 17)

Wall Street rallied [on 28 February] after its worst slide since 2001 ... European shares fell heavily ... Asian markets suffered heavy losses, although China – which triggered Tuesday's global rout after falling 9 per cent – rebounded almost 4 per cent. This was after regulators scotched talk of a capital gains tax, which had helped to unsettle the market on Tuesday and after Wen Jiabao, Chinese prime minister, said the government aimed to ensure the country's financial stability and safety.

(*FT*, 1 March 2007, p. 1)

'Financial markets swung wildly yesterday [1 March] in frenzied trading ... The Shanghai Composite fell a further 2.9 per cent' (*FT*, 2 March 2007, p. 1).

'Asian stock markets continued to slide Thursday [1 March] amid concerns that a slowing US economy could hurt the region's export-dependent economies ... The benchmark Shanghai Composite Index shed 2.91 per cent' (www.iht. com, 1 March 2007). 'Markets in Japan, Hong Kong and Taiwan [fell on 2 March] ... Stock in China also dropped, with one benchmark index [Shanghai] falling roughly 2.79 per cent' (*IHT*, 2 March 2007, p. 15).

'On Friday [2 March] markets closed up in Shanghai and Shenzhen, while Japan's slipped again. European markets edged down' (*IHT*, 3 March 2007, p. 15).

'Global investors remained on edge yesterday [2 March] at the end of a turbulent week in which UK and European markets suffered their heaviest losses for four years ... Wall Street remained under pressure' (*FT*, 3 March 2007, p. 1).

'Chinese share prices rose across the board on Friday [2 March], led by real estate. The Shanghai Composite Index ended at 2,831.526 points' (www.iht. com, 4 March 2007).

China's tax authority has denied speculation that it is planning a capital gains tax on stock market earnings ... [It said] the government had no plans for taxing gains made trading in domestic stock markets ... China stopped taxing gains from stock markets in 1994 to promote its markets.

(*IHT*, 5 March 2007, p. 10)

Asian stock markets continued a meltdown Monday [5 March] ... European stock markets also started the day lower. Every stock market index in Asia except Vietnam's ended the day lower, and the drops were severe in many [e.g. in Japan, Hong Kong and India].

(www.iht.com, 5 March 2007)

'Stock markets around the world entered a second week of volatility Monday ... The decline was pronounced in Asia and Europe' (*IHT*, 6 March 2007, p. 1).

'Stocks rebounded across the globe Tuesday [6 March]' (*IHT*, 7 March 2007, p. 14).

'The Shanghai and Shenzhen 300 index has regained more than two-thirds of its losses from last week' (*IHT*, 9 March 2007, p. 18).

China's securities regulator on Tuesday [20 March] barred publicly traded companies from using proceeds from their stock sales, in an attempt to hold back speculative buying. Companies are also banned from buying derivative products and convertible bonds with share sale proceeds ... China wants to curb speculation in the real estate and stock markets ... China's cabinet approved a task force last month [February] to clamp down on illegal share sales and other banned activities ... Since January the nation's banking watchdog has also cracked down on bank loans used to invest in property and shares ... In December [2006] China's banking regulator sent out a statement urging banks to stop lending for stock investments and to recall outstanding share loans. In January the regulator told domestic banks to strengthen efforts to rein in property loans to help slow growth. Publicly traded companies must use share-sale proceeds as outlined in their prospectuses unless their stockholders approve changes, the securities regulator said Tuesday.

(*IHT*, 1 March 2007, p. 16)

Shanghai stocks, whose drop in February began a global sell-off, reached a record level Wednesday [21 March]. The Shanghai Composite Index, which tracks the bigger of the two Chinese stock exchanges, rose 0.8 per cent to 3,057.38, its highest ever close. An 8.8 per cent decline in the index on 27 February sent stocks plunging, erasing $3.3 trillion of value in stock markets worldwide. Chinese stocks, after more than doubling last year [2006], plunged when the government announced that it was forming a task force to clamp down on illegal lending. As much as 20 billion yuan, or $2.6 billion, in personal bank loans was used illicitly to buy stocks last year ... The Shenzhen component index gained 10.77 points to reach 805.68.

(*IHT*, 22 March 2007, p. 22)

'China had the world's best performing stock market last year [2006], with the Shanghai soaring 130 per cent' (www.iht.com, 21 March 2007).

Shares of more than 90 per cent of the 1,400 companies covered by the new rules have received government and shareholder approval for sale, although most are bound by lock-up periods ranging from one to three years. The shares freed up by the regulatory changes for sale in 2007, worth 600 billion yuan, or almost $78 billion, come in addition to an expected 300 billion yuan of new shares from initial public offerings and rights issues. In 2006, though nearly 100 billion yuan of government-owned shares went up for sale, actual sales totalled less than one-tenth of that amount ... State agencies have given the green light to sell ... some $78 billion of shares ... equal to one-sixth of the free float on China's bourses, as part of a programme to gradually remove a supply overhang of $250 billion of shares held by government entities ... But few major shareholders actually intend to sell, officials and company executives say. The state is unlikely to relinquish control of major companies.

(www.iht.com, 22 March 2007)

The value of stocks listed on the Chinese mainland surpassed that of Hong Kong for the first time this week ... The combined capitalization of shares listed on the Shanghai and Shenzhen exchanges totalled $1.81 trillion on Tuesday [10 April] ... surpassing the Hong Kong market's capitalization of $1.79 trillion ... The CSI 300 Index, which tracks the yuan-denominated shares listed on the two mainland exchanges, has gained 53 per cent so far this year, after jumping 117 per cent in 2006.

(*IHT*, 12 April 2007, p. 14)

China Citic Bank sold $5.4 billion of stock ... the maximum it targeted ... Citic Bank raised $1.7 billion selling ... new yuan-denominated shares in Shanghai ... [and the remainder in Hong Kong] ... China has spent almost $500 billion bailing out state-owned banks ... since 1998. Citic Bank has not received a state bailout. Citic Bank was the seventh largest Chinese bank by assets at the end of 2005 ... It fell to eighth last month [March 2007] after the Postal Savings Bank of China was established.

(www.iht.com, 20 April 2007)

'China Citic Bank raised $5.4 billion in the world's biggest initial public offering so far this year' (*IHT*, 30 April 2007, p. 14).

China Citic Bank ... said Wednesday [2 May] that it increased the sale by 15 per cent to $5.95 billion after individual investors in Hong Kong ordered 230 times the number of shares available to them. The lender, a unit of Citic Group, China's biggest state-run investment company, said it had raised an additional $548 million selling shares in Hong Kong.

(*IHT*, 3 May 2007, p. 18)

News that the economy had grown by 11.1 per cent in the first quarter raising fears that the country would lift interest rates further, sparked a sell-off not only in Shanghai but also in Japan and Hong Kong ... The Shanghai composite slumped 4.52 per cent ... its biggest daily drop since a 9 per cent one-day plunge at the end of February.

(www.ft.com, 19 April 2007)

'Growth accelerated to 11.1 per cent year-on-year, above expectations' (*FT*, 20 April 2007, p. 14).

GDP increased 11.1 per cent in the first quarter compared with 10.4 per cent in the final three months of 2006 ... Inflation was higher, reaching 3.3 per cent in March ... The prospect [was heightened] of further interest rate rises and monetary tightening ... [On 19 April] the Shanghai Composite Index, which measures the larger of the two exchanges, dropped 4.5 per cent ... The Shanghai Shenzhen 300 Index, which covers the largest companies on both the Shanghai and Shenzhen exchanges, fell 4.7 per cent ... Global markets wobbled ... The correction helped trigger market falls around the region and weighed on US and European equities.

(p. 6)

'The correction helped trigger market falls around the region and weighed on US and European equities' (pp. 1, 6).

'Despite the big drop the Shanghai Composite Index's close, at 3,449.02, reflects a nearly 200 per cent gain during the past sixteen months' (*IHT*, 20 April 2007, p. 14). 'The economy expanded at a faster than expected 11.1 per cent in the first quarter from a year earlier' (p. 17). '[There] was a 2.7 per cent quarterly jump in consumer prices' (www.iht.com, 19 April 2007).

'Consumer prices rose 3.3 per cent in March' (*The Economist*, 21 April 2007, p. 121).

'Markets fell in Frankfurt, Paris and London' (www.bbc.co.uk, 19 April 2007).

'The next day [20 April] markets rebounded' (www.economist.com, 24 April 2007). 'The bulls have quickly returned' (*The Economist*, 28 April 2007, p. 72).

The benchmark Shanghai Composite Index, which tracks both dollar and yuan-denominated shares, ended up 1.6 per cent at 4,013.09, an all-time high. The Shenzhen Composite Index rose 0.3 per cent to 1,111.29, also a record close. Chinese shares have surged this week despite the central bank governor's expression of anxiety Sunday [6 May] that they might be headed for a bubble ... Investors shrugged off official warnings of a possible market bubble amid soaring corporate profits ... So far this year [2007] the Shanghai index is up 50 per cent ... after a 130 per cent gain last year [2006]. In just over four months the Shenzhen Composite Index is up 100 per cent this year [2007] ... Two years ago the Shanghai Composite was hovering around 1,200 points ... Shenzhen was even more depressed.

(www.iht.com, 9 May 2007; *IHT*, 10 May 2007, p. 11)

China's stock market fell 0.7 per cent Friday [11 May] on fears the country's raging bull market could be headed for a government-induced correction ... Investors are worried the government is preparing to issue a new policy to dampen irrational exuberance ... The Shanghai Composite ... finished the day at 4,021.68.

(www.ft.com, 11 May 2007)

Alan Greenspan, [former] chairman of the US Federal Reserve ... [said on 23 May] that the Chinese [stock] market was 'clearly unsustainable' and could undergo a 'dramatic contraction'. After setting records on Monday, Tuesday and Wednesday [21, 22 and 23 May] shares slipped Thursday [24 May] in Shanghai and Shenzhen. The warning was nothing new for Zhou Xiaochuan, chairman of the People's Bank of China, and other Chinese officials. The central bank, securities regulators and prominent business executives have all been cautioning investors.

(*IHT*, 25 May 2007, p. 11)

'Remarks by Alan Greenspan ... sent a shiver through European markets, which declined Thursday for the first time in three days ... The Dow Jones Stoxx 600 fell' (p. 15). 'China's securities regulator has ordered [Wednesday] brokerages to step up a programme of educating investors, adding to the central bank's warnings ... A recent warning [has also been given by] ... the richest man in Asia, Li Ka-shing' (p. 17).

After setting records on Monday, Tuesday and Wednesday, the A shares, those traded in yuan, fell 0.47 per cent in Shanghai and 0.6 per cent in Shenzhen on Thursday [24 May] ... On Wednesday [23 May] ... the Shanghai A share index closed at 4,354.

(www.iht.com, 25 May 2007)

'Li Ka-shing, the tycoon known to generations of Hong Kong investors as Superman ... [said] that it "must be a bubble"' (*IHT*, 1 June 2007, p. 12).

Chinese shares have continued rising at a breakneck pace, pushing Shanghai's main stock index through the 4,000 mark for the first time. Shanghai's benchmark CSI 300 Index closed up 2.6 per cent at 4,090.57. It has doubled in value this year [2007] and quadrupled since the start of 2006 ... Marshall Gittler, Deutsche Bank's chief Asian strategist, told the BBC's World Business Report that buying shares was the new Chinese national pastime.

(www.bbc.co.uk, 28 May 2007)

The [Shanghai] CSI 300 climbed 2.2 per cent to close at 4,072.58 ... The index fell 0.5 per cent the day after Alan Greenspan's comment. It resumed its gains the next day, closing 1.7 per cent higher ... Chinese regulators last week ordered brokerages to make investors sign a declaration that they are aware of the risks when opening stock-trading accounts.

(*IHT*, 29 May 2007, p. 12)

China's main share index fell 6.5 per cent in Wednesday [30 May] trading following a decision to triple the tax on stock transactions ... The stamp duty on share trading rose from 0.1 per cent to 0.3 per cent. The Shanghai

Composite Index had risen 62 per cent this year to Tuesday's [29 May] record close and had quadrupled in value since the start of 2006.

(www.bbc.co.uk, 30 May 2007)

The two major stock exchanges [were] sharply lower. The Shanghai Composite Index plunged 6.5 per cent to close at 4,053.09. The Shenzhen Composite Index dropped 7.2 per cent to close at 1,199.45 ... But shares in other parts of Asia fell only modestly Wednesday [30 May] ... Despite the drop Shanghai's benchmark index is still up 52 per cent for the year, following a 130 per cent jump in 2006 ... Since July 2005, when a bearish market turned bullish, share prices have soared more than 300 per cent in Shanghai and 400 per cent in Shenzhen, despite the sell-off Wednesday. But the decline was especially sharp given regulations requiring that no single stock may rise or fall more than 10 per cent in a single trading day ... During a long bear market in 2001–2005 the main market index fell from 2,300 to under 1,000 points ... The stamp tax was set at 0.6 per cent when it was introduced in the early 1990s but has since been cut repeatedly to encourage the Chinese public to invest in stocks. It fell to 0.1 per cent in 2005 ... [On 30 May 2007] the 'stamp tax' on stock trades ... tripled ... from 0.1 per cent to 0.3 per cent.

(www.iht.com, 30 May 2007)

'Markets elsewhere reacted calmly ... Shares in other parts of Asia and in Europe fell only modestly Wednesday [30 May] ... In New York stock were little changed' (*IHT*, 31 May 2007, p. 11).

'The Shanghai and Shenzhen 300 index, which covers both bourses, dived 6.8 per cent to 3,859.9 ... Mainland share prices [have] increased by around 60 per cent this year [2006] on top of 130 per cent last year [2006]' (www.ft.com, 30 May 2007). 'World financial markets largely shrugged off a sharp tumble in [China]' (*FT*, 31 May 2007, p. 1). 'A steep fall for the Chinese stock market triggered only a modest ripple around the world' (p. 44).

'China's benchmark CSI 300 Index plunged 6.8 per cent ... Shares recovered slightly Thursday [31 May], with the index closing 1.1 per cent higher' (*IHT*, 1 June 2007, p. 12).

'On 30 May prices on the Shanghai Composite Index dropped by 6.5 per cent. But they promptly regained 1.4 per cent by the end of the following day' (*The Economist*, 2 June 2007, p. 86).

Stock markets in China tumbled again Monday [4 June] in one of the biggest sell-offs in years ... The benchmark Shanghai stock exchange fell 330 points, or 8.3 per cent, to close at 3,670.40. The country's second major index, the Shenzhen Composite, plunged 7.9 per cent to finish at 1,039.89 ... Stock markets in other parts of Asia, however, shrugged off the news ... The Shanghai bourse saw shares tumble 6.5 per cent the day the new rules went into effect, then bounced back Thursday [31 May] before falling again Friday [1 June] ... The downturn Monday [4 June] ... left the Shanghai

Composite down 15.3 per cent from its high of 4,334.92 in just four sessions.

(*IHT*, 5 June 2007, p. 15)

Chinese shares plunged another 7 per cent Tuesday morning [5 June] ... But the panic selling abruptly gave way to frenzied buying early Tuesday afternoon, as rumours circulated that the government might defer the introduction of a capital gains tax for up to three years. State-controlled newspapers also reported that the government had authorized four large funds to raise money for the purchase of stocks. The Shanghai A share market ended the day with a gain of 2.58 per cent, while the Shenzhen A share market gained 2.34 per cent. Investors outside China have barely reacted to the sharp drop and considerable volatility of Chinese shares since last Wednesday [30 May], when the government tripled its tax on share transactions ... The government authorized the creation of four funds that will be allowed to raise up to $1.3 billion each from investors for the purchase of stocks, the official *China Daily* newspaper reported [on 5 June].

(*IHT*, 6 June 2007, p. 12)

'The Shanghai stock market fell sharply on Thursday [14 June]. The Shanghai Composite Index closed down 1.47 per cent at 4,115.209 points, after dropping as much as 2.18 per cent at one stage' (www.iht.com, 14 June 2007).

The stock market has become the quickest way for officials, as insiders, to get rich quick – and to do so legally. Even the normally very discreet World Bank recently noted the losses to public coffers resulting from the underpricing of initial public offerings of Chinese shares ... Of course, every company listing on every exchange wants its shares to go to a premium when trading begins. China also had reason to want to spread acceptance of the stock market as a place for investment, as a proper location for household savings. It needs a proper market if it is to continue to sell down its stakes and gradually privatize the economy. However, there is another reason why the China Securities Regulatory Commission, which oversees the market, and officials in general, likes to see underpricing: the people who mainly benefit are the insiders, the directors, managers, underwriters and other insiders who are favoured with share allotments and, if necessary, provided with cheap loans with which to acquire stock ... The way it works for dozens of relatively small mainland listings has been seen on a grand scale with listings of major mainland enterprises in Hong Kong. In addition to well-placed mainlanders themselves, very large blocks of stock are first offered to local tycoons and their companies. These placements to anchor investors help ensure the success of the offering, even though the price has already been pitched at a level which is most likely to ensure success. The end result is that relatively few shares are available to the public. One consequence is a massive oversubscription leading to a stampede for stock when trading begins.

(Philip Bowring, *IHT*, 13 June 2007, p. 4)

The main Chinese stock index rose to a record Monday [18 June], having taken less than two weeks to rebound from a rout that erased more than $400 billion of market value, after an anticipated rise in interest rates did not take place ... The CSI 300 climbed 128.19, or 3.1 per cent, to close at 4,227.57 ... The Shanghai Composite Index ... gained 2.9 per cent to 4,253.35. The Shenzhen Composite Index ... rose 2.8 per cent to 1,257.75.

(*IHT*, 19 June 2007, p. 19)

'Shanghai fell almost 4 per cent' (*FT*, 26 June 2007, p. 42).

'Citic Securities led the CSI 300 to its biggest drop in three weeks after the governor of the central bank ... said that Chinese shares might be overvalued and interest rate increases could not be ruled out' (*IHT*, 26 June 2007, p. 13).

'The China Banking Regulatory Commission fined six banks this month [June] for granting loans that it said had been illegally used to finance speculation in the stock and property markets' (*IHT*, 27 June 2007, p. 14).

Auditors have found [it was reported on 27 June] misconduct involving 15.5 billion yuan at three of China's biggest banks ... The latest inquiry found violations, involving the equivalent of $2 billion, at Bank of China, the country's number two commercial lender, Bank of Communications and Merchants Bank ... Contraventions included lending for real estate development in defiance of government efforts to slow speculation in the industry ... On Tuesday [26 June] the State Administration for Foreign Exchange said it punished nineteen Chinese and ten foreign banks for 'assisting speculative foreign capital to enter the country disguised as trade or investment'. Last week China's bank regulator announced it was punishing eight banks for making improper loans used by two state companies to speculate in stocks and estate. Investigations at other banks have revealed embezzlement, bribery and violations of regulations on the size and purpose of loans.

(www.iht.com, 28 June 2007)

'The legislature approved a bill that allows the cabinet to suspend a 20 per cent tax on interest from bank savings ... encouraging investors to keep their money in banks rather than shifting funds to the surging stock market' (*IHT*, 30 June 2007, p. 14).

'[Some] 80 per cent of China's urban households now own their home (in America the national figure is 69 per cent), compared with only around 10 per cent owning shares' (*The Economist*, 7 July 2007, p. 83).

Chinese stocks tumbled Thursday [5 July] on waning confidence and government worries about government steps to cool the markets ... The benchmark Shanghai Composite Index fell 5.3 per cent to 3,615.87. The Shenzhen Composite Index, China's smaller, second market, plunged 5.8 per cent to 1,015.85 ... The drop Thursday, after a 2.1 per cent decline Wednesday [4 July], also reflected concern that plans for the issuance of

... $200 billion ... in special government bonds to capitalize a state invest-
ment agency might further pressure the amount of funds available in the
market.

(www.iht.com, 5 July 2007)

Chinese stocks fell Thursday by the most in a month on concern that $20
billion of planned sales will overwhelm demand for equities ... The CSI
300 Index slumped 206.15 points, or 5.8 per cent, to close at 3,537.44, the
biggest percentage move among markets included in global benchmarks
... China Construction Bank, China Shenhua and PetroChina ... have in
the past month announced plans to sell shares valued at about $20 billion
on the mainland ... The absence of a capital-gains tax on equity investments has made short-term trading more attractive than holding stocks
[China says].

(*IHT*, 6 July 2007, p. 13)

'The CSI 300 Index tumbled on concern that new share sales would drain as
much as $40 billion from the market' (p. 14).

'A tax on interest income will be cut on 15 August [2007] to encourage
saving ... The tax on interest income will fall to 5 per cent from 20 per cent'
(*IHT*, 21 July 2007, p. 13). '[The] tax on interest income ... was introduced in
1999 as part of efforts to reduce individual savings and promote consumption'
(*FT*, 21 July 2007, p. 6).

'In China the Shanghai Composite Index [on Thursday 26 July] climbed 0.5
per cent to a record high' (*FT*, 27 July 2007, p. 40).

Stock markets across Asia suffered one of the worst days of the year Friday
[27 July] as contagion spread from a sell-off on Wall Street ... The heavy
selling in Asia was sparked by a [heavy] fall on Wall Street on Thursday
[26 July] ... Losses were comparable in Europe ... But China's stock
indexes were mainly flat [on Friday 27 July] ... [The] Shanghai composite
eased lower by 0.03 per cent.

(www.iht.com, 27 July 2007)

'The CSI Index in China managed a small gain' (*IHT*, 28 July 2007, p. 1).

'[On 31 July] the Shanghai Composite Index edged up to another record' (*FT*,
1 August 2007, p. 38).

'[On Thursday 2 August] China's Shanghai Composite Index rallied 2.5 per
cent after Wednesday's 3.8 per cent slump' (*FT*, 3 August 2007, p. 38).

'[On 2 August] the CSI 300 in China jumped 3.4 per cent for Asia's biggest
advance' (*IHT*, 3 August 2007, p. 14).

'[On 3 August] Shanghai bucked the trend [in Asia] as it climbed to a record
high' (*FT*, 4 August 2007, p. 32).

Many Asian and European stock markets fell Monday [6 August] after Wall
Street plunged [on Friday 3 August] ... Chinese stocks meanwhile shrugged
off the drops elsewhere to lift key indexes to record highs for the second

straight session. The benchmark Shanghai Composite Index rose 1.5 per cent to a record 4,628.11.

(www.iht.com, 6 August 2007)

'Chinese stocks maintained their record-breaking run. The Shanghai Composite Index climbed another 1.5 per cent, taking its year-to-date gain to 73 per cent' (*FT*, 7 August 2007, p. 36).

'Asian stock bounced back Wednesday [8 August] from an eight-week low ... Markets rose, except in New Zealand and China' (*IHT*, 9 August 2007, p. 15).

'With stock markets around the world jumpy, China's stock market bubble [is] continuing' (*The Economist*, 11 August 2007, p. 64).

Asian stock markets edged higher Monday [13 August] following their biggest drop in five months Friday [10 August] ... In China the CSI 300 fell 5.49 points to 4,721.19 ... European stocks posted their biggest gain in more than a year Monday.

(*IHT*, 14 August 2007, p. 15)

The European central bank has been a hive of activity since Thursday [9 August] when the bank thrust itself into a market rattled by fears of a credit crisis ... A rally in Asia paved the way for rising markets in Europe and the United States after a week of steady losses.

(p. 1)

'Asian financial markets fell Tuesday [14 August] ... The Chinese CSI 300 rose 74.38 points to 4,795.57, a record level' (*IHT*, 15 August 2007). 'The booming China stock market keeps defying gravity' (www.iht.com, 15 August 2007).

The contagion sweeping through the global markets hit Asia with typhoon-like force yesterday [16 August] ... Even markets in China, which until mid-week seemed oblivious to the rest of the region's sub-prime concerns, had the jitters. Shanghai fell 2.1 per cent, although that leaves the market trading 78 per cent higher than at the beginning of the year [2007].

(*FT*, 17 August 2007)

US stocks rose the most in two weeks on Friday [17 August] after the Federal Reserve unexpectedly cut its discount lending rate ... The Fed's decision to lower the interest rate on direct loans to banks by 0.5 percentage points also spurred a rebound in Europe.

(*IHT*, 18 August 2007, p. 14)

'Asian markets [including those in China], which closed before they could benefit from yesterday's Fed move, were hardest hit' (*FT*, 18 August 2007, p. 32).

Asian stock markets rebounded sharply on Monday [20 August] ... Shares in mainland China continued to rally, after pausing briefly last week when investors there finally began to notice the credit-crunch worries that beset the rest of the region. The Shanghai Composite Index closed 5 per cent higher at 4,904.85, representing a gain of 83.3 per cent since the start of the year [2007].

(www.ft.com, 20 August 2007)

'Asian stock markets produced their biggest rally in three years Monday [20 August]' (*IHT*, 21 August 2007, p. 13). 'The Shanghai A share stock market climbed 5.34 per cent' (p. 9).

The key CSI 300 Index has climbed 144 per cent this year [2007] after more than doubling in 2006, while the main Shanghai share index [Shanghai Composite Index] is up 80 per cent this year, on top of a 130 per cent leap in 2006.

(www.iht.com, 21 August 2007)

'Asian stocks rose for a second consecutive day Tuesday [21 August]. The Chinese CSI Index rose 87.28 points to a record level of 4,972.71' (*IHT*, 22 August 2007, p. 13).

'Asian equities largely built on Monday's powerful rallies [20 August] ... In Shanghai the Composite Index rose 1 per cent [on 21 August] to a fresh record close' (*FT*, 22 August 2007, p. 36).

'Stocks rallied worldwide Wednesday [22 August]' (*IHT*, 23 August 2007, p. 1).

Chinese stocks rose Wednesday, driving the benchmark CSI 300 Index above the 5,000 level for the first time ... The CSI 300 advanced 78.98 points, or 1.6 per cent, to close at 5,051.69, a third successive record. The benchmark, which tracks yuan-denominated 'A' shares listed on the exchanges in Beijing and Shanghai has risen about 150 per cent since the start of the year. It is up 13 per cent this month [August] alone, making the CSI the best performer among the world's eighty-nine major indexes tracked by Bloomberg.

(*IHT*, 23 August 2007, p. 12)

'In Shanghai investors ... pushed the composite index to a record close just short of the 5,000 level' (*FT*, 23 August 2007, p. 40).

'[On 23 August] Asian stocks had another day of strong gains ... Chinese stocks had another record breaking session, with the Shanghai Composite Index climbing above the 5,000 level for the first time to end 1.1 per cent higher' (*FT*, 24 August 2007, p. 36).

After appearing immune to the turmoil unleashed on world markets from high-risk home lending in the United States, China suffered its first serious setback Friday [24 August] from the meltdown in subprime loans. Investors [in Hong Kong] punished China's flagship lender, Bank of China, after it disclosed the biggest exposure revealed so far of any bank in Asia to this segment of the USA mortgage market ... Shares in the bank, the second largest in China, fell 5.4 per cent to close at 3.87 Hong Kong dollars, or $0.50, after it reported holding almost $9.7 billion in securities backed by subprime mortgages. That is about 3.5 per cent of its total securities portfolio. Industrial and Commercial Bank of China, the biggest Chinese lender, also suffered at the hands on investors Friday after it disclosed that it was holding $1.23 billion in securities backed by these mortgages ... Despite plunging in Hong Kong, shares in Bank of China and ICBC gained ground Friday in Shanghai ... China's CSI 300 benchmark index added 81.65, or 1.6 per cent, to close Friday at 5,217.58, a record.

(*IHT*, 25 August 2007, p. 13)

A new sort of financial crisis [is] unfolding in the United States subprime mortgage market ... China's financial institutions ... have little exposure to the higher-yielding debt securities that have come under pressure, particularly in comparison to their total asset bases.

(*FEER*, September 2007, p. 18)

'US and European equities were hit by a new bout of nerves yesterday [28 August]. Asian equities also moved broadly lower ... Shanghai climbed to a fresh record close' (*FT*, 29 August 2007, p. 36).

The New York Stock Exchange has become the first foreign bourse to win approval to set up a representative office in Beijing ... The NYSE's Beijing office would be allowed to carry out communication, promotion and research activities. Other foreign stock exchanges have applied to open offices in China following a rule change in July [2007].

(*IHT*, 5 September 2007, p. 12)

The Chinese market hit a new high yesterday [6 September] ... China's market has doubled since the start of the year [2007], but earnings growth – running at levels of as much as 75 per cent – has almost kept up ... [But] while declared earnings growth is 75 per cent, growth in operating earnings, profit from actually running a business, is 33 per cent. Most of the rest comes from property and other investments ... This difference between net and operating profit means there can be no doubt: companies have been speculating in the stock market.

(*FT*, 7 September 2007, p. 14)

'Asian markets were lower [on 10 September] ... [but] Shanghai ended 1.5 per cent higher' (*FT*, 11 September 2007, p. 42).

'US stocks ... European stocks ... [and] Asian stocks fell Monday [10 September] ... [but] the CSI 300 Index in China rose' (*IHT*, 11 September 2007, p. 15).

China's inflation rate rose to 6.5 per cent in August – the highest in nearly eleven years [it was announced on 11 September] ... The August inflation rate was the highest since December 1996 and an increase over July's monthly rate of 5.6 per cent.

(www.iht.com, 11 September 2007)

'Stocks in China, which have gained 151 per cent this year [2007], fell sharply Tuesday [11 September] ... The benchmark CSI 300 Index fell 4.7 per cent' (*IHT*, 12 September 2007, p. 12). 'Asian stocks rose Tuesday ... [but] the CSI 300 Index fell the most in two months after the inflation rate to near an 11-year high, raising concerns that interest rates would rise again' (p. 17).

'Chinese stocks had their biggest fall since 5 July' (*FT*, 12 September 2007, p. 8).

> Global stock markets recouped some of the losses of the past two sessions ... Asian stock markets were broadly higher ... But the Shanghai Composite Index tumbled 4.5 per cent, its biggest one-day drop for two months, as a sharp rise in consumer price inflation last month [August] sparked fears of further interest rate rises.
>
> (p. 46)

CNN television reported on 13 September that the Shanghai composite had risen 1.95 per cent.

'European stocks declined Monday [17 September] ... US stocks dropped ... Asian stocks dropped Monday ... except for China, South Korea, the Philippines, Pakistan and Sri Lanka' (*IHT*, 18 September 2007, p. 17).

'[On 19 September] European stocks climbed the most in more than four years ... US stocks extended their biggest rally in four years ... Asian stocks had their steepest rise in a month' (*IHT*, 20 September 2007, p. 16).

> China Construction Bank raised 58 billion yuan in the second biggest share sale in the world this year [2007] ... One of the largest banks in the country [it] sold 9 billion shares in Shanghai in the $7.7 billion deal ... [It is considered] the best managed among the state-owned banks ... Construction Bank, established in 1954 to finance building infrastructure, is the country's largest mortgage and real estate lender. It provides 22 per cent of Chinese mortgages and about 13 per cent of overall loans ... Bank of America, which paid $2.5 billion for a 9 per cent stake in the bank in 2005, will see its holding diluted to 8.2 per cent. Central Huijin Investment, a government investment arm, will control 59.1 per cent of the bank.
>
> (*IHT*, 19 September 2007, p. 20)

> China Construction Bank raised 58.05 billion yuan in mainland China's biggest initial public offering ever, state media reported Wednesday [19 September] ... The bank already has shares traded in Hong Kong ... The shares are due to begin trading on 25 September. The sale [in Shanghai] raised the equivalent of $7.7 billion.
>
> (www.iht.com, 19 September 2007)

'Benchmark indexes retreated from record levels in Hong Kong, China and India' (*IHT*, 26 September 2007, p. 15).

'The benchmark stock index, the CSI 300, has climbed 163 per cent in 2007, the best performer among eighty-nine global equity indexes tracked by Bloomberg' (*IHT*, 27 September 2007, p. 16).

'China, where the CSI 300 Index closed on 28 September at a record, was shut for a week-long holiday' (*IHT*, 5 October 2007, p. 17).

> Equities account for less than 20 per cent of households' total financial assets, compared with half in America, so price swings have less impact on spending ... According to a study by Morgan Stanley, one-third of listed companies' profits in the first half of 2007 came from share-price gains and other investment income. If share prices sink, so will profits ... Chinese banks are officially not allowed to lend to investors to buy shares, but anecdotal evidence suggests that households and firms have taken out loans disguised as mortgages to buy shares. If so, the effect of the bubble bursting could be larger than the direct impact on consumers' wealth ... The ratio of house prices to average income has fallen by 25 per cent since 1999. A collapse in house prices therefore seems unlikely.
>
> (*The Economist*, 29 September 2007, pp. 88–9)

> China's benchmark Shanghai Composite Index rose 2.5 per cent to a record close Monday [8 October] as investors indulged in a post-holiday buying spree. The index gained 140.46 points to 5,692.96, beating the previous record close of 5,552.30 hit on the last pre-holiday trading day Friday [28 September]. In intraday trade the Shanghai index hit an all-time high of 5,729.96. The Shenzhen Composite Index of China's smaller, second market rose 0.5 per cent to 1,541.35 ... China's markets were closed all last week for the 1 October National Day holiday ... [In] Hong Kong and the United States [stocks in] banks [had] surged over the holidays ... The Shanghai Composite Index has gained 113 per cent since the beginning of the year.
>
> (www.cnn.com, 8 October 2007)

'The CSI 300 rose 72.32 points, or 1.3 per cent, to 5,653.14 points on the first day of trading this month [October] after the National Day period' (*IHT*, 9 October 2007, p. 19).

'Benchmarks in China ... set new highs [on 11 October]' (*IHT*, 12 October 2007, p. 15).

'On Friday [12 October] the stock market swung wildly in heavy volume, with the index plunging more than 4.30 per cent at one stage before closing just 0.17 per cent lower' (www.iht.com, 14 October 2007).

'[On 15 October] the Shanghai composite rose 2.2 per cent to close above the 6,000 level for the first time' (*FT*, 16 October 2007, p. 44).

'Asian stocks were broadly lower [on 17 October] ... Shanghai fell 0.9 per cent' (*FT*, 18 October 2007, p. 44).

'In Asia the focus was on China [on 18 October] as the Shanghai Composite Index suffered its worst drop for five months on reports that Beijing was studying plans to arbitrage dual-listed shares on the Hong Kong and mainland exchanges' (*FT*, 19 October 2007, p. 44).

The stock market in Taipei [Taiwan] is up 49 per cent from the end of 2005 through the close of trading Friday [19 October], whereas the Hang Seng index in Hong Kong has risen 98 per cent and the CSI 300, which includes major companies in the Shanghai and Shenzhen exchanges, has soared 496 per cent ... Stock markets in China overtook it [Taiwan] in capitalization on 14 May [2007] and have kept on rising ... Estimates of total Taiwan holdings on the mainland run as high as $280 billion ... At least 1.2 million of the ... people of Taiwan have moved to the mainland, providing a wealth of management expertise ... [The 1.2 million] is 5 per cent of the population, but much larger than 5 per cent ... [for] key people aged twenty-five to forty-five.

(*IHT*, 20 October 2007, p. 19)

On 22 October the Shanghai index fell 2.59 per cent (www.cnn.com, 22 October 2007).

'[On 24 October] the CSI 300 Index rose after the yuan climbed past 7.5 to the dollar for the first time' (*IHT*, 25 October 2007). 'The CSI 300 rose 0.9 per cent Wednesday [24 October] and reached a record high on 17 October' (p. 21).

'[On 25 October] the Shanghai Composite Index tumbled 4.8 per cent, its biggest one-day drop since July' (*FT*, 26 October 2007, p. 42).

'The Shanghai stock market [was] 4.8 per cent lower Thursday [25 October] on fears that the central bank will continue raising interest rates to limit inflation' (*IHT*, 26 October 2007, p. 9).

On Friday 26 October the Shanghai index rose 0.49 per cent (www.cnn.com, 26 October).

'The government, concerned that loans are being used illegally to finance stock purchases, has asked banks to cap lending growth at 15 per cent this year [2007]' (*IHT*, 26 October 2007, p. 16).

'Over the week ... the Shanghai Composite Index shed 3.9 per cent – its worst week since July' (*FT*, 27 October 2007, p. 34).

'The Shanghai Composite added 2.8 per cent to 5,748' (*FT*, 30 October 2007, p. 42).

'The CSI Index has risen 169.9 per cent this year [2007], the best performance among ninety global benchmarks tracked by Bloomberg. The Hang Seng index in Hong Kong, which is dominated by Chinese companies, has gained 58.2 per cent' (*IHT*, 30 October 2007, p. 16).

'[On 30 October] most Asian equity indices gave up some of their recent gains, although Hong Kong's Hang Seng edged 0.2 per cent higher, its fourth straight record close, and China's Shanghai Composite ... advanced 2.6 to 5,77.19' (*FT*, 31 October 2007, p. 44).

For many years the world's fastest growing major economy had one of the world's quietest stock markets. But beginning a couple of years ago investors began to return to the stock market after a series of reforms improved protections for minority shareholders. At the same time many Chinese companies rose to become global giants – Industrial and Commercial Bank of China, China Life Insurance Company and China Mobile are all the largest companies in the world within their respective sectors, by market capitalization. As China's leading companies are now listing at home, investors are queuing to buy their shares.

(Jing Ulrich, *IHT*, 31 October 2007, p. 8)

China has the biggest bank [Industrial and Commercial Bank of China], insurance company, telecommunications carrier and airline by market capitalization … Soon after the [5 November 2007] listing analysts expect PetroChina to surpass the US energy giant Exxon Mobil, as the world's largest company by market capitalization … [But] the prices set on the Chinese exchanges, still largely isolated from the rest of the world by regulatory barriers that limit the amount of foreign money going into the stock markets and domestic money permitted to go out, bear little relationship to company performance or to markets elsewhere.

(Donald Greenlees and David Lague, *IHT*, 5 November 2007, p. 12)

'Equity markets tumbled … in the United States and Europe' (*FT*, 2 November 2007, p. 1). 'Turbulence hit global financial markets yesterday [1 November] … Asian equities were mixed' (p. 40).

'Asian stocks rose Thursday [1 November]' (*IHT*, 12 November 2007, p. 16).

PetroChina makes its debut Monday [5 November] on the Shanghai stock exchange … PetroChina and a string of other state-controlled A-share mainland listings. The oil and gas company raised $8.9 billion before its Monday listing … the largest amount ever raised in a mainland initial offering. But only 13 per cent of the company has been floated.

(www.iht.com, 4 November 2007)

With China's economy continuing to grow at double-digit rates and no sign that investors are losing their appetite for the share markets, this price bubble has so far been unaffected by low-credit-rated borrowers [subprime borrowers] in the United States … After decades where low-interest-bearing accounts in state-owned banks were virtually the only outlet for savings, the soaring stock market has become irresistible to a new generation of Chinese … Chinese investors have dived into the markets of Shanghai and Shenzhen, unleashing the huge savings in personal bank accounts.

(*IHT*, 5 November 2007, p. 12)

PetroChina became the world's first company to pass $1 trillion in market capitalization when it debuted on the Shanghai stock exchange on Monday [5 November] … It trebled in value on its opening day and surpassed US energy behemoth Exxon Mobil as the world's most valuable company … At its intra-day high in Shanghai trading it was valued at almost $1.2 trillion, compared with Exxon Mobil's market capitalization at Friday's market close [2 November] of $487 billion … [But PetroChina] is about half as profitable as its rival. In the first half of 2007 PetroChina's net income was $10.9 billion, compared to $19.5 billion for Exxon Mobil … On the Hong

Kong stock exchange PetroChina dropped 8.2 per cent, its biggest decline since November 2000.

(www.iht.com, 5 November 2007)

Superheated markets in China on Monday drove the value of PetroChina above $1 trillion, giving it the highest market capitalization in corporate history and underscoring worries about a fast growing stock bubble on the mainland. On PetroChina's first day of trading on the Shanghai stock exchange, it surpassed the combined capitalization of Exxon Mobil and General Electric, the world's next two most valuable companies. Pet-roChina's shares ... almost tripled in price in an initial offering ... [But] in Hong Kong, where PetroChina's shares have been trading since 2000 ... PetroChina's Hong Kong-listed H-share dropped 8.1 per cent ... Only 13 per cent of PetroChina is listed, while the remainder is held by its state-owned parent, China National Petroleum ... In the first half of 2007 Pet-roChina had revenue of less than a third of Exxon Mobil. The US energy giant had net profit of $19.5 billion, compared with $10.9 billion for PetroChina.

(*IHT*, 6 November 2007, p. 13)

'PetroChina raised $8.9 billion in the world's biggest share sale this year [2007]' (p. 17).

On Monday [5 November], the first day PetroChina listed shares on the Shanghai stock exchange, its market valuation – the value of all its stock combined, assuming that the value of a share in Shanghai translates to all shares globally – ran up to more than $1 trillion.

(*IHT*, 7 November 2007, p. 1)

[PetroChina] raised $9 billion from the world's biggest IPO so far this year [2007] ... The PetroChina listing is the largest ever in the mainland, sur-passing China Shenhua Energy's September IPO, which raised ... Pet-roChina sold 4 billion shares on Shanghai, equivalent to just 2.2 per cent of its expanded share capital ... The company's mainland shares are now trading at a premium of around 150 per cent to its Hong Kong shares.

(www.ft.com, 5 November 2007)

[PetroChina was] worth more than $1,000 billion at yesterday's closing [5 November] – the first company to break that barrier ... Three of the most valuable companies in the world are now Chinese – PetroChina, China Mobile and Industrial and Commercial Bank of China [ICBC] – while two are from the United States, Exxon Mobil and General Electric ... [But Pet-roChina's] annual earnings are only half those of Exxon ... Part of the jump in PetroChina's shares ... [a] 163 per cent bounce ... was attributable to the company's decision to sell only 2.2 per cent of its expanded share capital. The small float failed to satisfy huge investor demand ... the company's mainland shares are now trading at a premium of about 150 per cent to its

Hong Kong shares … While PetroChina has attracted a lot of scepticism, some of the other Chinese companies on the list have stronger supporting cases. For instance, China Mobile, which is worth twice as much as the UK's Vodaphone, now has 350 million subscribers and added 48 million in the first nine months of the year [2007] … While Citigroup is still trying to work out the extent of its subprime losses, ICBC … saw profits increase 61 per cent in the first half of the year. Although ICBC's profits are still only about half of Citigroup's … [one prediction was that] its earnings could catch up with Citigroup by 2010] … However, even for these consumer-related stocks there are still huge challenges in turning that economic growth into profits … Even optimists acknowledge that the current mainland valuations are partly the product of some technical quirks. Most of the large state-owned companies listed on the Shanghai market have only sold a small percentage of their equity … That means a huge volume of money chasing a small quantity of shares.

(*FT*, 6 November 2007, p. 26)

'In terms of profit, though, Asia's top oil and gas producer does not even make it into the world's top fifty companies' (www.bbc.co.uk, 5 November 2007).

'China is home to seven of the twenty-five largest companies by market value in the world … Only PetroChina is among the top twenty-five by profit' (*IHT*, 27 December 2007, p. 14).

'[One problem with] the valuations … [is that company] earnings are often inflated by corporate investment in the stock market' (www.economist.com, 29 December 2007).

'The Shanghai market dropped 2.48 per cent to 5,634 points' (www.ft.com, 5 November 2007). 'The Shanghai Composite Index fell 2.5 per cent' (*FT*, 6 November 2007, p. 9).

'[On 5 November] the benchmark Hang Seng index tumbled … 5 per cent … its biggest one-day loss' (www.iht.com, 5 November 2007).

'In mainland China share prices have increased almost six fold over the past two years' (www.ft.com, 5 November 2007). 'Mainland shares have risen nearly 600 per cent in two years' (*FT*, 6 November 2007, p. 9).

'The Chinese stock market … has gained 110 per cent already this year' (www.bbc.co.uk, 5 November 2007).

'Chinese investors can reason that they have little choice but to accept the volatility and the high prices because their alternatives are so limited. Bank deposits pay interest below inflation; property comes with suspect ownership rights' (www.economist.com, 6 November 2007).

'[On 8 November] the CSI 300 Index [was] off 4.8 per cent' (www.ft.com, 8 November 2007).

'The CSI 300 tumbled 4.8 per cent [on 8 November]' (*IHT*, 9 November 2007, p. 13).

'In Shanghai the composite index ended 2.4 per cent weaker, but well off its low for the day' (*FT*, 13 November 2007, p. 48).

'China's benchmark CSI 300 Index [has] soared as much as 188 per cent this year ... [But] the CSI 300 has lost 16 per cent since peaking on 16 October' (*IHT*, 13 November 2007, p. 16).

'[On 13 November] Chinese shares ended lower after initially rising for the first time in two weeks ... The Shanghai Composite fell to its lowest in two months, finishing down 0.6 per cent at 5,158.12' (www.ft.com, 13 November 2007).

'During the span of the last eighteen months the Shanghai stock exchange rose 400 per cent, from around 1,400 to 6,000. After the last ratings came out in early October [2007] the Shanghai stock exchange shed 10 per cent' (www.iht. com, 16 November 2007).

'The Chinese and Indian markets rose strongly [on 14 November]' (*FT*, 15 November 2007, p. 46).

'The CSI Index rose the most since 20 August' (*IHT*, 15 November 2007, p. 16).

> Eighty per cent of the Chinese stock exchange listings are state-owned enterprises restructured in the 1990s into stock holding companies, managed by top party officials and their family members. The restructuring process allowed children of top party officials, known as the 'princelings' to take over China's most strategic and profitable industries: banking, insurance, transportation, power generation, natural resources, media and weapons. Princelings can get loans from government-controlled banks, acquire foreign partners and list their companies on stock exchanges. Before going public they often divvy up large blocks of shares for themselves, mid-range managers, and their families.
>
> (Peter Kwong, www.iht.com, 16 November 2007;
> *IHT*, 17 November 2007, p. 7)

> The [corruption] clean-up effort has extended to stock market listings, hitherto the easiest way for well-placed officials to become overnight multi-millionaires by being allotted shares at low pre-listing prices. According to a World Bank report, the sale of shares in state assets at artificially low prices in just one year has cost China $9.5 billion, more than Beijing spends on rural education.
>
> (Philip Bowring, www.iht.com, 22 November 2007)

'The Shanghai exchange, the largest in mainland China, now lists 857 companies' (*IHT*, 19 November 2007, p. 14).

> [On 20 November] the benchmark Shanghai Composite Index gained 0.5 per cent to 5,293.70 ... Asian stocks have been among the world's best-performing this year, but trading has been extremely volatile in recent months amid persistent worries over defaults in risky, or subprime, mortgages in the United States, and their wider fallout.
>
> (www.iht.com, 20 November 2007)

'Asian stocks rose [on 20 November] ... Benchmarks in Hong Kong, China and Australia climbed' (*IHT*, 21 November 2007, p. 19).

'Asian stocks slumped [on 21 November] ... All Asian markets fell except New Zealand and Pakistan' (*IHT*, 22 November 2007, p. 19).

This month [November] ... the nation's benchmark CSI 300 Index ... [has fallen] ... 12 per cent ... The CSI has risen in just three trading days this month [November] ... China's CSI 300 Index has surged 145 per cent this year [2007], the world's best return. The benchmark tracks the 300 biggest companies on the yuan-denominated A-share markets in Shanghai and Shenzhen.

(*IHT*, 22 November 2007, p. 17)

'China's Shanghai Composite slumped 4.4 per cent to 4,984.16, its first close below 5,000 in three months [since August]' (*FT*, 23 November 2007, p. 19).

Asia stocks declined [on 22 November] ... The CSI 300 fell 225, or 4.5 per cent, to 4,772.62 in Shanghai, its biggest drop since 8 November. The benchmark has slumped 19 per cent since reaching a record on 16 October. Only eleven of the index's 300 stocks rose on Thursday.

(*IHT*, 23 November 2007, p. 19)

'China's Shanghai index ... closed yesterday [23 November] at 5,032.13 after losing more than 17 per cent since its record high in mid-October' (*FT*, 24 November 2007, p. 34).

'Benchmarks gained [in Asia] ... except for China and Sri Lanka' (*IHT*, 27 November 2007, p. 17).

'Asian stocks fell Tuesday [27 November] ... Benchmarks dropped in most markets' (*IHT*, 28 November 2007, p. 15).

'Benchmarks declined in South Korea, China, India, Taiwan and Australia, and rose in Hong Kong' (*IHT*, 29 November 2007, p. 16).

'The main Chinese stock index tumbled 20 per cent since tripling in the first ten months of the year ... The benchmark CSI 300 Index has slumped from the October peak' (*IHT*, 29 November 2007, p. 18).

'[On 29 November] the Shanghai Composite climbed 4.2 per cent' (*FT*, 30 November 2007, p. 42).

China Railway Group raised $3 billion in its Shanghai initial public offering, one of the mainland's biggest ... [Its shares] rose 69 per cent on their Shanghai debut Monday [3 December] ... It raised another $2.5 billion from an initial public offering in Hong Kong, where it will have its debut Friday [7 December].

(www.iht.com, 3 December 2007)

In 2007 about $90 billion will be raised from initial public offerings (IPOs) in China, almost as much as in New York and London combined ... Yet the mood is darkening. Of the fifteen largest offerings to have debuted on the mainland exchanges this year [2007], the share process of eight are below their first-day close ... The most vivid example ... [is] PetroChina ... [It] became the most valuable company in the world when its shares more than doubled on its 5 November debut in Shanghai. Since then its shares have dropped in value by a third ... More recently Sinotruck and Sinotrans also fell below their opening prices on the day of listing.

(*The Economist*, 8 December 2007, p. 68)

Shares in China Railway rose as much as 30 per cent Friday [7 December] in their Hong Kong debut, beating forecasts, after one of the largest construction contractors in the world raised $5.5 billion in an initial public offering in Hong Kong and Shanghai ... The Shanghai shares of the company ... closed up 1 per cent Friday [7 December] ... [There is] a railroad investment boom in China ... China Railway builds railroads, highways, ports and other big-ticket projects ... The Chinese government gives the bulk of its rail construction work to China Railway and the state-owned China Railway Construction, which is expected to go public next year [2008].

(www.iht.com, 7 December 2007)

'The benchmark Shanghai Composite Index ended down 0.07 per cent at 4,868 points Monday [3 December] and has dropped by more than a fifth from a record high in mid-October' (www.iht.com, 3 December 2007).

'The CSI Index climbed' (*IHT*, 5 December 2007, p. 16).

'The Shanghai stock market's main index ... is still up 88.5 per cent this year [2007]' (www.iht.com, 5 December 2007).

Over the past twelve months prices on the Hong Kong, Shanghai and Shenzhen stock exchanges have leapt by 45 per cent, 83 per cent and 132 per cent respectively ... [But] the Shanghai and Shenzhen exchanges are both 19 per cent below their October heights; the Hong Kong index has dipped by 9 per cent.

(*The Economist*, 8 December 2007, p. 87)

'In recent weeks Chinese stocks have dropped more than 15 per cent, but they stabilized in the past week and regained some ground. Over the past few years Chinese stock prices have risen by more than 300 per cent' (www.iht.com, 8 December 2007).

The Shanghai Composite Index fell 20 per cent from its peak in October to 30 November ... The CSI 300 has rebounded 7.2 per cent in December [to date] ... The Shanghai index plunged more than 50 per cent from June 2001 to July 2005. It has jumped almost fivefold since then ... Institutional investors, including mutual funds, held shares worth 44 per cent of the total value of the tradable stocks on the Shanghai and Shenzhen exchanges, Xinhua, the official Chinese news agency, reported last month [November].

(*IHT*, 13 December 2007, p. 15)

'[On 10 December] China's CSI 300 Index was the biggest gainer in Asia' (*IHT*, 11 December 2007, p. 16).

'[On 17 December] all ... Asian benchmarks ... fell' (*IHT*, 18 December 2007, p. 16).

'[On 18 December] most Asian benchmarks slipped' (*IHT*, 19 December 2007, p. 19).

'[The] domestic stock market has dropped 17 per cent from a 16 October peak' (*IHT*, 19 December 2007, p. 17). 'Most Asian stocks rose Wednesday [19 December]' (*IHT*, 20 December 2007, p. 21).

'[On 20 December] the CSI 300 Index climbed 1.8 per cent' (www.iht.com, 20 December 2007).

'[On 20 December] the Shanghai Composite Index rose 2.1 per cent' (*FT*, 21 December 2007, p. 38).

'After soaring 188 per cent in the year through 16 October [2007] the benchmark CSI 300 Index has since fallen 13 per cent' (*IHT*, 24 December 2007, p. 14).

'This year [2007] ... the Shanghai Composite is up 95.6 per cent' (*FT*, 27 December 2007, p. 32).

'The CSI is up 171 per cent this year in dollar terms, even after slumping 11 per cent from its 16 October close' (*IHT*, 27 December 2007, p. 14).

'[On 26 December] China's Shenzhen Composite Index rose 1.7 per cent' (*FT*, 27 December 2007, p. 32).

'[In Shanghai there was] a rise of 1.4 per cent [on 27 December]' (*FT*, 28 December 2007, p. 34).

'[On 28 December] stock markets fell across China ... The Shanghai A share index declined 0.89 per cent ... The Shenzhen A share index fell 0.44 per cent' (*IHT*, 29 December 2007, p. 18). ('The exchange in Shenzhen caters to smaller companies': www.economist.com, 29 December 2007.)

'[China's] relatively small stock markets in Shanghai and Shenzhen roughly doubled in value during 2007' (*FT*, 2 January 2008, p. 32).

'Official figures show that more than 100 million people have invested in equities, mostly during the recent bull market run' (*FT*, 22 January 2008, p. 15).

'Global shares fell Wednesday [16 January] ... The CSI 300 Index in China declined 3.4 per cent' (www.iht.com, 16 January 2008).

'Shares rose Thursday [17 January] in Asia and Europe ... But Chinese stocks fell 2 per cent' (www.iht.com, 17 January 2008).

'[There was] a rout in Asian and European equity markets. Many indices suffered their biggest one-day falls since September 2001. Wall Street was closed for [a holiday] ... Shanghai [fell by] 5.1 per cent' (*FT*, 22 January 2008, p. 42).

'Global stock markets plunged Monday [21 January] ... Shanghai's Composite Index closed down 5.1 per cent at 4,914.44' (www.iht.com, 21 January 2008).

US markets were closed [for a holiday] ... Worries about China are adding to Asia's uneasiness. Its private property market is in the midst of a shakeout, and scores of small developers have gone out of business. Chinese banks were hard hit Monday [21 January], in part because they hold the bulk of Asia's exposure to subprime mortgages ... While Asia has been less buffeted by the crisis than Europe, the Bank of China now appears vulnerable, with analysts predicting that it will have to write down the value of its America mortgage holdings.

(*IHT*, 22 January 2008, pp. 1, 15)

'Stock markets [globally] have been in retreat this year [2008] … Many indexes are now more than 20 per cent below their recent cycle peaks' (p. 18).

As well as hitting exports, America's troubles could affect Asia through various financial channels. Asia's exposure to the subprime mess is thought to be much smaller than that of American or European banks. Even so, Chinese bank shares tumbled this week on rumours that they would have to make much bigger write-downs on their holdings of American subprime securities … Some Asian economies are more vulnerable than others: Singapore, Hong Kong and Malaysia have exports to America equivalent to 20 per cent or more of their GDPs, compared with only 8 per cent in China and 2 per cent in India.

(www.economist.com, 23 January 2008)

'Stocks plummeted across Asia for a second day on Tuesday [22 January] … In Shanghai the composite index sagged 7.2 per cent to 4,559.751' (www.ft.com, 22 January 2008).

'[On 22 January] the Shanghai market closed with a loss of 7.22 per cent' (www.iht.com, 22 January 2008). 'China's main index tumbled 7.2 per cent to a five-month low' (www.iht.com, 23 January 2008).

The Shanghai Composite Index dropped 7.2 per cent Tuesday [22 January] to close at 4,559.75 points and the Shenzhen Composite fell 7.7 per cent … [The sell-off] has seen share prices here [in Shanghai] plummet more than 10 per cent over the past two days … The heavy selling, which is believed to be tied to global fears about a recession in the United States, came after two years of spectacular stock gains … But after reaching record highs in recent months, the major stock indexes in China have plunged 15 per cent to 30 per cent.

(*IHT*, 23 January 2008, p. 12)

'As Chinese stocks plunge in the global equity rout, a slump in home sales in some major cities suggests that Beijing's efforts to cool an overheated property market may be taking hold' (p. 10).

'[On 23 January] the Shanghai Composite ended up 4.65 per cent' (www.iht.com, 23 January 2008).

'[On 23 January] Shanghai gained 3.1 per cent' (*FT*, 24 January 2008, p. 38).

'The main Shanghai stock index fell 7.19 per cent on Monday [28 January]' (www.iht.com, 28 January 2008).

'European and Asian stocks saw further heavy falls yesterday [28 January] … The Shanghai Composite fell 7.2 per cent' (www.ft.com, 28 January 2008; *FT*, 29 January 2008, p. 42).

'Stocks [were buoyed] in Asia and Europe on Tuesday [29 January] … The CSI Index of mainland shares rose 0.6 per cent' (www.iht.com, 29 January 2008).

'[On 30 January] Shanghai's Composite Index bounced 0.9 per cent after Monday's [29 January] 7.2 per cent tumble' (*FT*, 30 January 2008, p. 42).

'[On 30 January] stocks in Asia were weaker ... The Shanghai Composite Index fell about 1 per cent' (www.iht.com, 30 January 2008).

[On 31 January] Asian shares managed to end Thursday's session on a generally positive note ... [But] Shanghai's Composite Index [was] down 0.8 per cent to a five-month low of 4,383.39. That took January's losses to 16.7 per cent, the market's second worst monthly performance since 2000.

(www.ft.com, 31 January 2008)

'Chinese stocks fell Friday [1 February]' (www.iht.com, 1 February 2008).

[On 4 February China's] stock markets surged ... The benchmark Shanghai Composite Index gained 8.1 per cent, or 350.85 points, to 4,671.62. The Shenzhen Composite Index jumped 7.9 per cent to 1,375.73 ... Stocks rose 8 per cent in Shanghai, their biggest daily gain since June 2005, as the government approved two new stock funds created by domestic mutual firms in an apparent attempt to prevent the local stock market from sliding further.

(www.iht.com, 4 February 2008)

'The Shanghai Composite Index, which had been down 30 per cent from the high it reached in October [2007], rose 8.1 per cent to close at 4,671.6 points' (www.ft.com, 4 February 2008).

'European markers were slightly lower Wednesday [6 February] after Asian markets slumped ... [But] markets in South Korea, Taiwan and mainland China [were] already closed for the rest of the week for the Lunar New Year holiday' (www.iht.com, 6 February 2008).

'The Shanghai Composite Index rose 2.1 per cent' (*FT*, 20 February 2008, p. 44).

'The Chinese stock market [is] down 25 per cent in the past four months' (www.iht.com, 20 February 2008).

'[On 22 February] Shanghai's Composite ... [lost] more than 1 per cent' (www.iht.com, 22 February 2008).

'[On 25 February] Asian markets were mostly higher ... [but] Shanghai bucked the trend as it fell to a seven-month low' (*FT*, 26 February 2008, p. 40).

'Hong Kong blue chips and shares in China fell as tumbling mainland stock markets unnerved investors' (*IHT*, 26 February 2008, p. 18).

'[On 26 February] the Shanghai Composite Index closed up 1.1 per cent on 4,238.18' (www.ft.com, 26 February 2008).

'[On 27 February] the Shanghai Composite Index gained 2.3 per cent to 4,334.05' (www.ft.com, 27 February 2008).

On Wednesday [27 February] the country's two stock exchanges shrugged off Monday's blues [25 February], when both indices dropped by about 4 per cent, and gained a bit instead ... China's stock markets have been suffering from a protracted slide. Shanghai is already down by more than a third since October last year [2007] ... Foreign participation in the Chinese market has been strictly curtailed. As a result, global losses are limited and so news of the financial destruction that has accompanied the massive share-price losses has failed to stir interest beyond the country's borders. Exactly a year ago a 9 per cent tumble of Shanghai's stock market sent a shockwave around the world ... Now, perhaps, with damage spreading through the global credit market, there is a sense that there are bigger things to worry about. There are also reasons to believe that the losses – in excess of $1 trillion – are not as devastating as they first appear. Much of the capitalization of the Chinese markets is tied up in shares held by the government, so whatever the extent of the losses less than half has been borne by private investors. China has a huge number of brokerage accounts – upward of 115 million and 70,000 new ones are established every day – but many are inactive. And, unlike in many Western countries, the stock market appears to play a relatively small role in providing for companies, with bank loans and retained earnings statistically far more important. But even with these caveats, the losses are still wrenching. Estimates of active brokerage accounts range from 10 million to 15 million and an equal number of people have invested in mutual funds. Bank financing and the reinvestment of profits do play a huge role in Chinese corporate finance, but equity markets became extraordinarily important last year [2007]. Through initial and secondary offerings Chinese companies raised in excess of $78 billion domestically and more money came in through linked overseas placement ... Two big companies recently announced large secondary offerings: Ping An Insurance and Pudong Development Bank. The share prices of both have been slammed, possibly because of the expectation of dilution, but possibly because there is no appetite for new shares. In response to the falling market, the China Securities Regulatory Commission warned companies against secondary offerings. Ping An is widely expected to reconsider its huge offering. In a further move to bolster prices, the government is rumoured to be on the verge of reducing a stamp duty tax on transactions ... In the past many companies earned substantial profits from gains on stock market investments. A repetition is unlikely. More realistically, given the market's decline, profits will suffer, depressing results and pulling share prices further down in a vicious circle.

(www.economist.com, 27 February 2008)

'The Shanghai A Share market rose 2.07 per cent on Monday [3 March] even as most other Asian stock markets fell' (www.iht.com, 3 March 2008).

Chinese stocks have fallen as a result of some bigger problems; the life insurer Ping An Insurance stands accused of pouring salt on the market's wounds in January [2008] by announcing plans for a $17 billion share offering. Ping An shares sank, pulling the Chinese stock market down with them to a one-year low, amid concern that the market could not absorb the new capital. Officials at the China Securities Regulatory Commission, seeking to revive the sagging index, declared that companies should 'on no account maliciously seize money from the market' and vowed to 'strictly' examine fund-raising applications.

(www.iht.com, 5 March 2008)

'Shanghai's Composite Index dropped 3.6 per cent to 4,146.30' (www.ft.com, 10 March 2008). 'Asian stocks suffered hefty losses ... Shanghai lost 3.6 per cent' (*FT*, 11 March 2008, p. 42).

Shares in China fell Monday [10 March] with the CSI 300 Index dropping 4.1 per cent, bringing its decline to 24.6 per cent since its peak in October [2007] ... Shares of China Railway Construction rose Monday by less than expected in their trading debut in the largest initial public offering of stock this year [2008] ... Analysts had expected a 43 per cent increase ... The company, which has built more than half of China's railroads, rose 28 per cent in Shanghai, but it was the worst debut in the country in more than a year ... It was not unusual for Chinese IPOs to double or even triple in their first day of trading during a stock bull run last year [2007] and the year before [2006].

(*IHT*, 11 March 2008, p. 16)

'[On 17 March] the Shanghai market was down 3.6 per cent ... and the Shenzhen A share market was down 6.4 per cent' (www.iht.com, 17 March 2008).

Shares on the Shanghai stock exchange fell nearly 4 per cent Tuesday [18 March], with the Shanghai Composite Index closing at 3,668.90. The Shanghai index is down nearly 40 per cent from its record high last October [2007]. In the mainland's second bourse, the Shenzhen Composite Index fell even more sharply, dropping 6.6 per cent to close at 1,080.28 ... After frenzied investing that sent the Shanghai Composite over 350 per cent during the past few years, the market has gone into a tailspin. New public stock offerings in Hong Kong and Shanghai have also dried up after two years of spectacular initial public offerings.

(*IHT*, 19 March 2008, p. 13)

'[On 19 March] shares in Shanghai surged 3.6 per cent' (www.iht.com, 19 March 2008).

'[On 19 March] Shanghai ... gained 2.5 per cent' (*FT*, 20 March 2008, p. 40).

The benchmark Shanghai Composite Index has fallen nearly 40 per cent since October [2007] ... In Shanghai and Shenzhen most of the more than 1,400 listed companies are state-controlled firms. China opened another exchange in Shenzhen ... especially for small and medium-sized firms.

(www.iht.com, 23 March 2008)

'The CSI 300 has slumped 27 per cent since 31 December [2007]' (www.iht.com, 25 March 2008).

'[On 24 March] Shanghai fell 4.5 per cent' (*FT*, 25 March 2008, p. 36).

'Since the beginning of the year [2008] the Shanghai Composite, one of last year's best performers, has lost 31.5 per cent' (*FT*, 27 March 2008, p. 43).

In Shanghai China Pacific Insurance closed [on 26 March] 6.7 per cent below the subscription price for its $4.3 billion floatation in December [2007]. The shares had jumped as much as 73 per cent on their first day of trading and have fallen steadily since.

(*FT*, 27 March 2008, p. 43)

'[On 27 March] the Shanghai Composite Index fell 5.4 per cent and is down 44 per cent from its peak last year' (*FT*, 28 March 2008, p. 40).

Stocks in three big Chinese companies sank below their initial public offering prices last week ... Investors bought a staggering $100 billion of equity in almost 200 newly issued firms from May 2006, when China lifted a year-long ban on IPOs, in February this year [2008]. The IPO flood, in which deals were greatly oversubscribed by investors, appeared to be a major achievement of China's financial reforms, for the first time making the stock market an important source of funding for many companies. The Shanghai index ... [has plunged] more than 40 per cent below October's [2007] record peak. That plunge led to a virtual halt in IPOs in March [2008]; the only one was the $53 million sale by Fujian Fujing Casttech, a maker of laser equipment. By contrast, five companies raised $300 million in March last year [2007] ... Shares in three large companies – China Shipping Container Lines, China Coal Energy and China Pacific Insurance – have fallen substantially below the prices of their IPOs. They were the first major stock to do so since the ban on offers was lifted. PetroChina has so far escaped that fate, but only just. On Friday morning PetroChina's local currency A shares hit a low of $2.38, the price of its IPO last October [2007], leaving it 62 per cent below its close on its first day of trading in Shanghai. PetroChina ended the day up 5.2 per cent ... but some investors believe authorities or big institutions might have artificially supported it to avert panic in the market.

(www.iht.com, 30 March 2008; *IHT*, 31 March 2008, p. 12)

'In the first quarter of 2008 ... the Shanghai Composite Index dropped 34 per cent' (*FT*, 1 April 2008, p. 40).

The Shanghai Composite Index has plunged 45 per cent from its high, reached last October [2007]. The first quarter of this year [2008], which ended Monday [31 March] with a huge sell-off, was the worst ever for the market ... The Shenzhen Composite Index ... [is] down 38 per cent ... By some estimates 15 per cent to 20 per cent of the profits reported last year [2007] by publicly listed companies in Shanghai that are not involved in banking or finance (which usually invests in stocks) came from stock trading gains ... J.P. Morgan estimates that 150 million people in China were invested in the Chinese stock market as of the end of last year.

(www.iht.com, 2 April 2008)

'[On 3 April] shares in Shanghai gained 2.3 per cent, recovering from a 7 per cent drop over the previous two sessions' (www.iht.com, 3 April 2008).

'[On 3 April] Shanghai rallied 2.9 per cent' (*FT*, 4 April 2008, p. 38).

'[On 7 April] Shanghai rose 4.45 per cent' (www.cnn.com, 7 April 2008).

'[On 7 April] China's Shanghai Composite rose 4.5 per cent to 3,599.62' (*FT*, 8 April 2008).

'[On 9 April] the Shanghai Composite Index fell 5.5 per cent' (www.iht.com, 9 April 2008).

'China's main stock index tumbled ... 5.5 per cent ... on Wednesday [9 April] ... ending a four-day rebound off eleven-month lows' (www.ft.com, 9 April 2008).

'[On 10 April] the Shanghai Composite Index – which has fallen by 34 per cent in value so far this year [2008] ... gained 1.7 per cent to 3,471.74' (www.ft.com, 10 April 2008).

'[On 11 April] the Shanghai Composite rallied 1.4 per cent' (*FT*, 12 April 2008, p. 34).

'[On 14 April] the Shanghai Composite Index plunged 5.6 per cent' (www.iht.com, 14 April 2008).

[On 15 April] the Shanghai Composite Index rallied 1.6 per cent' (*FT*, 16 April 2008, p. 44).

'[On 18 April] the Shanghai Composite Index slid 4 per cent to close at 3,094.668, a twelve-month low' (www.ft.com, 18 April 2008).

'[On 18 April] China's CSI Index dropped 3.4 per cent, extending its decline this week to 14 per cent' (www.iht.com, 18 April 2008).

'Over the week ... Shanghai's decline of 11.4 per cent took its loss from a record high in October [2007] to nearly 50 per cent' (*FT*, 19 April 2008, p. 34).

'The Shanghai Composite Index closed with a gain of less than 1 per cent, after falling at one stage to a new low for the year, with 0.2 per cent of halving in value since its all-time hit 16 October [2007]' (www.ft.com, 21 April 2008).

'[On 22 April] the Shanghai Composite Index ... ended 1 per cent higher' (*FT*, 23 April 2008, p. 42).

> China slashed the tax on share trading last night [23 April] in an effort to encourage investors to return to a stock market that has fallen by nearly half over the past six months. The government will reduce the tax on each share traded from 0.3 per cent to 0.1 per cent. The announcement effectively reversed a decision last May [2007] when the government tripled the tax ... The Shanghai Composite Index fell from 6,124 points in October [2007] to below 3,278 yesterday. Despite the slump the benchmark index has still risen threefold since late 2005.
>
> (*FT*, 24 April 2008, p. 41)

'Shanghai jumped 4.2 per cent ... after touching a thirteen-month low on Tuesday [22 April]' (p. 42).

A stamp duty cut to cut dealing costs gave the flagging Shanghai index a boost ... The Shanghai Composite Index opened up 8 per cent on the strength of a cut in stamp tax, to 0.1 per cent from 0.3 per cent. The Shanghai market has fallen 51 per cent from its October [2007] peak.

(www.iht.com, 24 April 2008)

China's main share index saw one of its biggest gains after the government cut taxes on share trading. The Shanghai Composite Index rose 9.3 per cent, or 304.7 points, to close at 3,583.0 ... Thursday's [24 April] rise was close to the biggest possible, because individual Shanghai shares are limited to 10 per cent daily increases.

(24 April 2008)

The price surge was one of the biggest ever recorded in Shanghai and came after a similar rally Wednesday [23 April], producing a two-day gain of nearly 14 per cent ... On Sunday [20 April] Beijing announced new trading rules making it more difficult for large blocks of shares to come to the market ... The Shanghai Composite Index, which had recorded its worst quarter ever at the end of March, rose 9.3 per cent on Thursday [24 April] to close at 3,583.03. The Shenzhen Composite Index also soared, climbing 8.7 per cent to close at 1,043.80 ... Since October [2007], when the Shanghai index peaked at 6,092.06, share prices have fallen dramatically and also turned volatile, sometimes rising sharply and then falling sharply ... From 2001 to 2005 stock prices fell sharply in China.

(www.iht.com, 24 April 2008; *IHT*, 25 April 2008, p. 17)

'[On 28 April] the benchmark Shanghai Composite Index ... was down 1.83 per cent at 3,492.777 ... The index soared 15 per cent last week in its biggest weekly gain since 1996' (www.iht.com, 28 April 2008).

'Asian shares were mixed on Tuesday [29 April] with Hong Kong and Shanghai lifted' (www.ft.com, 29 April 2008). 'Shanghai gained 1.4 per cent' (*FT*, 30 April 2008, p. 42).

'[On 30 April] Shanghai's Composite Index surged 4.8 per cent to close at 3,693.106' (www.ft.com, 30 April 2008).

'[On 6 May] Shanghai slipped 0.7 per cent' (*FT*, 7 May 2008, p. 44).

'[On 7 May] Shanghai fell sharply' (*FT*, 8 May 2008, p. 40).

'[On 8 May] the Shanghai Composite Index rose 2.2 per cent' (www.iht.com, 8 May 2008).

'[On 12 May] Chinese stocks ended slightly firmer' (*FT*, 13 May 2008, p. 40).

'[On 13 May] shares ... [were] pushed down in Shanghai ... The benchmark stock index fell 1.5 per cent' (www.iht.com, 13 May 2008). 'The CSI 300 Index fell 1.4 per cent' (www.iht.com, 13 May 2008).

'[On 13 May] Shanghai fell 1.8 per cent' (*FT*, 14 May 2008, p. 42).

'[On 14 May] Shanghai rallied 2.7 per cent' (*FT*, 15 May 2008, p. 42).

'[On 15 May] Shanghai gained less than 1 per cent' (www.iht.com, 15 May 2008).

'[On 20 May] Shanghai tumbled 4.5 per cent' (*FT*, 21 May 2008).

'[On 26 May] major stocks in Japan and China dropped more than 2 per cent' (www.iht.com, 26 May 2008).

'[On 28 May] Shanghai ... [advanced] 2.5 per cent' (*FT*, 29 May 2008).

'The benchmark Shanghai Composite Index fell 0.54 per cent yesterday [5 June] to end at 3,351.65, far below the high of 6,124 it reached in October [2007]' (*FT*, 6 June 2008, p. 41).

'[On 10 June] China's main index fell 7.7 per cent ... The benchmark Shanghai Composite Index fell 257.34 points to close at 3,072.33, the biggest single-day percentage loss in more than a year' (www.bbc.co.uk, 10 June 2008).

'China's main stock market fell 7.7 per cent, its biggest fall for a year' (*FT*, 11 June 2008, p. 9). '[Shanghai fell] 7.7 per cent to a fourteenth-month low, its biggest one-day decline for a year' (p. 38).

Chinese stocks ... in the Shanghai and Shenzhen markets ... plummeted 8.1 per cent on Tuesday [10 June], their biggest single-day drop in nearly sixteen months ... Chinese stock markets have lost 45 per cent of their value since setting a record last October [2007].

(www.iht.com, 10 June 2008)

'[On 11 June there was a] 2 per cent decline in the Shanghai Composite Index' (www.iht.com, 11 June 2008).

[On Wednesday 11 June] shares continued their slide ... The Shanghai Composite Index fell 1.6 per cent to finish at 3,024.24 – its lowest close since 19 March 2007 – after dropping 7.7 per cent on Tuesday [10 June] in the biggest one-day fall in percentage terms since 4 June last year [2007]. It has plunged by 50.4 per cent since its historic closing high of 6,092.06. That peak, hit on 16 October [2007], marked the end of an extraordinary eight-month rally of 141 per cent.

(*FT*, 12 June 2008, p. 39)

The Shanghai Composite Index fell 2.21 per cent to a new low Thursday [12 June]. It has lost 11 per cent in the past three days and 52 per cent since reaching a high in October [2007]. About $1.9 trillion of value in the Shanghai and Shenzhen markets has been erased since December [2007] ... A small group of angry investors demonstrated outside the Shanghai stock exchange on Thursday [12 June] as the market hit a fourteen-month low. The protest ... underlined the fury and despair among the millions of individual Chinese investors as the stock market fell.

(*IHT*, 13 June 2008, p. 16)

'Shares in Shanghai lost 14.4 per cent in value during the week' (www.ft.com, 13 June 2008). 'This week ... Shanghai lost 13.8 per cent and set its lowest close for fifteen months' (*FT*, 14 June 2008, p. 26).

The Shanghai Composite Index has tumbled 19 per cent so far this month
[June] ... The index ended at a fifteen-month low of 2,794 points on
Tuesday [17 June], down 54 per cent from the peak last October [2007].
About $2.2 trillion of value on the Shanghai and Shenzhen exchanges has
been lost since last October ... Money raised by Chinese firms through
initial public offerings shrank nearly 30 per cent from a year earlier to $12
billion, in the first five months of this year [2008].

(IHT, 18 June 2008, p. 18)

'[On 18 June] the Shanghai Composite Index jumped by 2.7 per cent to
2,870.29, the first rise after falling for ten days in a row' (www.ft.com, 18 June
2008). '[On 18 June] Shanghai broke a ten-session losing run as the Composite
Index jumped 5.2 per cent' (*FT*, 19 June 2008, p. 42).

'[On 19 June] Shanghai stocks eased 1.3 per cent in early trade and are now
down 45 per cent this year [2008]' (www.iht.com, 19 June 2008).

'[On 19 June] Shanghai slid 6.5 per cent, extending the loss this year [2008]
to 48 per cent and leading the index at its lowest point since February 2007' (*FT*,
20 June 2008, p. 42).

'The Shanghai market plunged 6.5 per cent in Thursday [19 June] trading'
(www.iht.com, 20 June 2008).

'[On 20 June] the Shanghai index gained 3 per cent to 2,831.74' (*IHT*, 21
June 2008, p. 15).

'[On 23 June] shares in ... Shanghai were down more than 1 per cent' (www.
iht.com, 23 June 2008).

'[On 23 June] Shanghai fell 2.5 per cent, extending its loss this year [2008] to
47.5 per cent' (*FT*, 24 June 2008, p. 40).

'[On 24 June] Shanghai ... [was] down less than 1 per cent' (www.iht.com,
24 June 2008).

'[Shanghai] rose 3.6 per cent and closed higher for the second day in a row'
(*FT*, 26 June 2008, p. 40).

'[On 27 June] the Shanghai stock index fell 4 per cent' (www.iht.com, 27
June 2008).

'[On Friday [27 June] ... China's main index fell nearly 4.5 per cent' (www.
bbc.co.uk, 27 June 2008).

'[On 30 June] Shanghai fell 0.4 per cent' (*FT*, 1 July 2008, p. 42).

'[On 1 July] the Shanghai Composite Index fell 3.1 per cent' (www.iht.com,
1 July 2008).

'[On 1 July] the Shanghai Composite Index slumped 3.1 per cent to
2,651.605, the lowest in seventeen months' (www.ft.com, 1 July 2008).

'[On 3 July] the Shanghai Composite Index rose almost 2 per cent' (www.iht.
com, 3 July 2008).

'[On 3 July] Shanghai shares bucked the trend gaining for a second day. The
Shanghai Composite Index closed the day 2 per cent higher at 2,703.529' (www.
ft.com, 3 July 2008).

'[On Monday 7 July] the Shanghai Composite Index jumped 4.2 per cent ...

bouncing from a seventeen-month low plumbed last week' (www.iht.com, 7 July 2008).

'[On 9 July] Shanghai jumped 3.8 per cent' (*FT*, 10 July 2008, p. 40).

'[On 15 July] Shanghai was off 2.5 per cent' (www.cnn.com, 15 July 2008).

'[On 17 July] Shanghai slipped' (*FT*, 18 July 2008, p. 36).

'Shanghai stocks ... rose 1.3 per cent Monday [28 July]' (*IHT*, 29 July 2008, p. 14).

'The Chinese index is among the worst performing in the world this year [2008], down some 45 per cent ... [although] the index is now up about 12 per cent from its year low' (*IHT*, 31 July 2008, p. 12).

'[On 31 July] some markets fell, including Shanghai' (*IHT*, 1 August 2008, p. 14).

'When [stock market] trading resumed in 1991 only domestic firms could list. But many foreign ones have been eager to join them, and after a change in securities laws announced on 6 August [2008] some may now have the chance' (*The Economist*, 16 August 2008, p. 67).

> Asia-Pacific shares fell on Friday [8 August] ... on the day the Beijing [Olympic] Games were due to start ... Mainland shares made their worst close this year [2008] ... The Shanghai Composite has halved in value so far this year and plunged 57.5 per cent since their peak in October 2007 to close at 2,605.72.
>
> (www.ft.com, 8 August 2008)

'Shares have fallen to their lowest level for nineteen months ... The Shanghai Composite tumbled 5.2 per cent to close at 2,470 points, down 60 per cent from last October's peak [2007]' (www.bbc.co.uk, 11 August 2008).

'Shanghai shares fell more than 5 per cent on Monday [11 August] to their lowest close since December 2006' (www.ft.com, 11 August 2008). 'The Shanghai Composite Index tumbled 5.2 per cent to a fresh nineteen-month low' (*FT*, 12 August 2008, p. 38).

'[On 11 August] the Shanghai Composite Index finished at 2,470.07, down 135.65 points, its lowest close in nineteen months' (*IHT*, 12 August 2008, p. 14).

'[On 12 August] the main Shanghai index, which is down 60 per cent from a record high reached in October [2007], fell 0.5 per cent to close at a nineteen-month low' (*IHT*, 13 August 2008, p. 15).

> China's main index fell by 5.3 per cent on Monday [18 August] to a twenty-month closing low ... The Shanghai Composite Index ended at 2,319.9 points. It has lost 15 per cent over the past seven trading days and fallen 62 per cent from last October's record peak [October 2007].
>
> (www.bbc.co.uk, 18 August 2008)

'[On 20 August] the Shanghai Composite Index leapt 7.6 per cent' (*FT*, 21 August 2008, p. 38).

'[On 21 August] the Shanghai Composite Index slipped 1.7 per cent' (www. iht.com, 21 August 2008).

'[On 25 August] the Shanghai Composite Index closed 0.3 per cent higher at 2,413.374' (*FT*, 26 August 2008, p. 36).

> Share prices continue to slide in spite of a slew of initiatives by the country's regulator to bolster the stock market ... China's benchmark index [is] down 54 per cent this year [2008] ... Last week the China Securities Regulatory Commission published a policy to stop listed companies raising money in secondary offerings unless they have handed out an average of 30 per cent of net profits over the previous three years.
>
> (*FT*, Monday 1 September 2008, p. 17)

'The Shanghai Composite Index sank 3 per cent Monday [1 September] ... Just before the midday break the index was at 2,324.338 in thin turnover' (www. iht.com, 1 September 2008). 'The Shanghai Composite Index tumbled 3 per cent ... extending its drop this year [2008] to just over 50 per cent' (www.iht.com, 1 September 2008).

> [China's] stock market is already the world's weakest performer this year [2008] ... The benchmark Shanghai Composite Index closed down 3 per cent on Monday [1 September], taking the losses from the past year to 55 per cent ... A new unified rate corporate income tax rate for domestic and foreign companies started this year [2008], which cut the rate for local firms to 25 per cent from 33 per cent.
>
> (*IHT*, 2 September 2008, p. 15)

'[On 5 September] the Shanghai A-share market dropped 3.3 per cent' (www. iht.com, 5 September 2008).

'Bucking the regional [Asian] trend [on 8 September] was China's Shanghai Composite Index, which was down more than 2 per cent' (www.cnn.com, 8 September 2008).

'[On 10 September] the Shanghai Composite Index rose 2.3 per cent' (www. cnn.com, 10 September 2008).

'China's stock market has fallen more than 60 per cent this year [2008]' (*FT*, 16 September 2008, p. 12).

> Asian shares plunged on Tuesday [16 September] ... Markets in Japan, Hong Kong, China and South Korea lost between 5 per cent and 7 per cent as they opened for business for the first time this week following a holiday long weekend. The Shanghai Composite Index closed below 2,000 for the first time since 17 November 2006, meaning it has lost just over two-thirds in value since peaking in October last year [2007] ... The Shanghai Composite Index spent most of the session below 2,000 – the first drop below this level since 29 November 2006, as trading resumed after a market holiday on Monday [15 September]. It closed down 4.5 per cent lower at 1,986.64.
>
> (www.ft.com, 16 September 2008)

The Shanghai Composite Index was down as much as 1.8 per cent [on Wednesday 17 September], adding to Tuesday's 4.5 per cent loss, to reach its lowest level since 17 November 2006 ... [On 17 September] the Shanghai Composite Index was 1.6 per cent lower at 1,954.38.

(www.ft.com, 17 September 2008)

'[On 18 September] the Shanghai Composite Index fell 1.7 per cent' (www.iht.com, 18 September 2008). 'The Chinese finance ministry ... said Thursday [18 September] that a 0.1 per cent stamp duty on buying shares would be abolished, although an equivalent tax on share sales would remain' (*IHT*, 19 September 2008, p. 17).

The government on Thursday [18 September] announced dramatic steps to prop up the country's sagging stock market, which has lost 70 per cent of its value since last October [2007]. Stamp duty on stock purchases will be scrapped and a government-controlled investment agency will buy shares in three state-controlled banks.

(www.ft.com, 18 September 2008)

The stamp duty on stock purchases will be scrapped and government money will be used to buy shares ... Central Huijin, an arm of the country's sovereign wealth fund, would buy into listed companies, including state-owned Industrial and Commercial Bank of China, Bank of China and China Construction Bank. Chinese bank shares have fallen steeply in response to the global financial crisis, helping to drive the benchmark Shanghai Composite Index to a twenty-two-month low of 1,896 yesterday [18 September]. The market peaked in October [2007] at 6,092 ... Several Shanghai stockbrokers said they believed government-sanctioned share purchases began the announcement last night, helping Shanghai recover from a 6 per cent early decline to close 1.7 per cent weaker on the day ... The government resisted public pressure to intervene in the stock market during the Beijing Olympics.

(*FT*, 19 September 2008, p. 21)

Last night [18 September] state media announced there would be a cut in stamp duty for buyers but not for sellers of shares. State media also said a branch of the country's sovereign wealth fund would buy shares in three state-owned banks ... and that other state-owned companies would be encouraged to buy back shares in their listed entities ... The Shanghai Composite Index recovered in the afternoon [18 September] to close at 1,896, only 1.72 per cent down on the day. That compares with a peak of 6,124 on 16 October last year [2007].

(p. 42)

[On 19 September] the most spectacular turnaround [in Asia] took place in Shanghai, where the A-share market soared 9.5 per cent ... [It was announced on] Thursday evening [18 September] that a government agency had begun buying shares in three of the mainland's biggest banks.

(www.iht.com, 19 September 2008)

'In Shanghai the Composite Index soared 9.46 per cent to close at 2,075.09. Trading had slowed as many stocks increased by the daily limit of 10 per cent soon after the stock market opened' (www.iht.com, 19 September 2008).

Middle-class moms and blue-collar pensioners in mainland China were among the world's most avid and successful investors last year [2007]. Now their record is one of lost fortunes, broken families and protest. Mainland Chinese stock markets are down nearly two-thirds in eleven months and the anger of ordinary citizens has unnerved the stability-obsessed government. On Friday [19 September] it announced an unprecedented rescue package that drove up most stocks the maximum permitted 10 per cent. The Shanghai Composite Index closed 9.5 per cent higher at 2,075.091, its biggest daily gain since October 2001. The broader CSI 300 Index of stocks in Shanghai and Shenzhen climbed 9.3 per cent. Yet amateur investors who have been badly burnt may think twice before venturing back into the market.

(www.iht.com, 21 September 2008)

'[On 23 September] the mainland Chinese CSI 300 Index dropped 3 per cent, after rising to a two-week high Monday [22 September] following a Beijing rescue package plan to salvage stock prices' (www.iht.com, 23 September 2008).

'[On 23 September] the benchmark Shanghai Composite Index declined 1.56 per cent to 2,201.51' (www.cnn.com, 23 September 2008).

'[On 25 September] the Shanghai Composite Index closed 3.6 per cent higher' (www.iht.com, 25 September 2008).

'[On 26 September] Shanghai's Composite Index [was] down 0.2 per cent on the day at 2,293.78' (www.ft.com, 26 September 2008).

Chinese regulators, seeking to support the equities market in the face of global financial turmoil, said Sunday [5 October] that they would soon allow investors to buy stocks on margin and to short-sell stocks. The changes will initially be made on a trial basis by a small number of brokerage businesses and gradually expanded to other security companies ... By contrast, US, British, French, Italian and German regulators in recent weeks temporarily banned short-selling of financial stocks, while Australia, Singapore and Taiwan restricted it ... Since China has been considering the start of margin trading, in which investors borrow money from brokerage businesses to buy shares, and short-selling, in which they borrow stocks from brokers and sell them, hoping to buy them back at lower prices. The changes have been delayed by market volatility, staring with the bull run that lifted the Shanghai Composite Index sixfold from mid-2005 to October 2007 and then a bear market in which the index fell more than 70 per cent .... The index rebounded 21 per cent from a twenty-two-month low hit late last month [September] in response to steps including purchases of shares from the market by a government fund and the abolition of tax on stock purchases ... The China Securities Regulatory Commission said Sunday ... that it expected 'margin buying will greatly exceed short-selling' in the initial stage because brokerage businesses had only a limited amount of stocks available ... Some investors are hoping for the introduction of stock index futures, another change under consideration for years. The commission did not specify exactly when margin trading and short-selling would start or name the brokerage companies that would take part in the initial stages.

(*IHT*, 6 October 2008, p. 6)

'[On 6 October] the Shanghai A-share market fell 5.2 per cent after the Shanghai stock exchange, which had been closed for the past week for the National Day holiday, reopened Monday [6 October]' (www.iht.com, 6 October 2008).

Shanghai shares joined the fray after a week-long holiday, declining 5.2 per cent to 2,173.738. The China Securities Regulatory Commission said it would introduce trial margin trading and short-selling of shares to develop the stock markets, despite moves across the globe to curb short selling in the wake of the financial crisis.

(www.ft.com, 6 October 2008)

'[On 7 October] the Shanghai Composite Index slipped 0.7 per cent' (www.iht.com, 7 October 2008).

'[On 8 October] the Shanghai Composite Index fell 3 per cent' (www.iht.com, 8 October 2008).

'[On 9 October] Shanghai's index was down 3.8 per cent' (www.bbc.co.uk, 10 October 2008).

'[On 23 October] Shanghai's benchmark index rose 3.65 per cent after falling earlier' (www.bbc.co.uk, 13 October 2008).

'[On 15 October] the Shanghai Composite Index ... was down about 1.5 per cent' (www.iht.com, 15 October 2008). 'The Shanghai A-share market fell 1.2 per cent Wednesday [15 October]' (www.iht.com, 15 October 2008).

'[On 16 October] the Shanghai Composite Index closed 4.3 lower' (*FT*, 17 October 2008, p. 42).

China's stock market retreated 3.5 per cent this week. The Shanghai Composite has fallen 68.3 per cent since reaching a peak last October [2007], marking its one-year anniversary by sinking below the 2,000 points level for the first time in almost two years.

(*FT*, 18 October 2008, p. 26)

'[On 20 October] the Shanghai Composite Index gained 2.3 per cent to 1,974.006' (www.ft.com, 20 October 2008).

'[On 27 October] the Shanghai Composite Index closed down 6.3 per cent at its lowest level since December 2006' (www.bbc.co.uk, 27 October 2008).

'A giant [$596 billion] economic stimulus package announced [on 9 November] by China lifted stocks in Asia on Monday [10 November] ... The Shanghai Composite Index soared 7.2 per cent to 1,874' (www.iht.com 10 November 2008).

'[On 10 November] the Shanghai Composite Index ended 7.3 higher at 1,874.80' (www.bbc.co.uk, 10 November 2008).

'Chinese stocks ended 2.2 per cent higher. The Shanghai Composite Index has notched up strong gains in the past week, after the fiscal stimulus announced by Beijing a week ago, and yesterday [17 November] closed at a one-month high' (*FT*, 18 November 2008, p. 42).

'[On 18 November] the Shanghai Composite Index tumbled more than 6 per cent' (*FT*, 19 November 2008, p. 44).

'[On 19 November] the Shanghai Composite Index ... rose 6.1 per cent' (www.iht.com, 19 November 2008).

'[On 19 November] The Shanghai Composite Index ... showed a gain of 3.1 per cent' (www.cnn.com, 19 November 2008].

'[On 21 November] the Shanghai Composite Index overcame early losses to rise about a per cent' (www.cnn.com, 21 November 2008).

'By early afternoon [24 November] ... the Shanghai Composite Index was down 2 per cent' (www.iht.com, 24 November 2008).

'[On 25 November] the benchmark Shanghai Composite Index ... ended the day down 0.44 per cent at 1,888.71' (www.guardian.co.uk, 25 November 2008).

'[On 26 November] in Shanghai the A share index rose 0.48 per cent' (*IHT*, 27 November 2008, p. 13).

'The Shanghai Composite Index was up nearly 4 per cent by early afternoon [27 November]' (www.iht.com, 27 November 2008).

'[On 1 December] the Shanghai Composite Index rose 1.3 per cent' (*IHT*, 2 December 2008, p. 21).

'[On 3 December] the Shanghai Composite Index rose 4.01 per cent' (www. cnn.com, 3 December 200).

'[On 5 December] markets in China and Australia were little changed' (www. iht.com, 5 December 2008).

'[On 6 December] the Shanghai Composite Index rose 0.9 per cent to 2,120' (www.cnn.com, 6 December).

'[On 8 December] the Shanghai Composite Index rose 3.6 per cent' (www. iht.com, 8 December 2008).

'[On 9 December] the Shanghai Composite Index lost 2.5 per cent' (*IHT*, 10 December 2008, p. 15).

'[On 10 December] the Shanghai Composite Index gained 2 per cent' (*IHT*, 11 December 2008, p. 14).

'[On 11 December] the Shanghai Composite Index was off 2.27 per cent' (www.cnn.com, 11 December 2008).

'[On 12 December] shares in Shanghai were 4.8 per cent lower' (*IHT*, 13 December 2008, p. 16).

'[On 15 December] the Shanghai Composite Index advanced 0.5 per cent' (www.iht.com, 15 December 2008).

'[On 16 December] the Shanghai Composite Index rose 0.5 per cent' (*IHT*, 17 December 2008, p. 15).

'[On 18 December] the Shanghai Composite Index closed up 2 per cent' (*IHT*, 19 December 2008, p. 14).

'[On 23 December] the Shanghai Composite Index fell 2.2 per cent' (www. iht.com, 23 December 2008).

'[On 25 December the] CSI 300 Index, which tracks yuan-denominated A shares on the nation's two exchanges, fell 0.9 per cent, to 1,870.77, the lowest level since 2 December' (www.iht.com, 25 December 2008).

'[On 26 December] the Shanghai Composite Index was 0.12 per cent lower shortly after the open' (www.iht.com, 26 December 2008).

'[On 26 December] the Shanghai Composite Index lost recent gains and fell to a six-week low of 1,851.52' (*FT*, 27 December 2008, p. 22).

> Chinese exchanges raised just $22 billion in initial public offerings [IPO's] in 2008. The slowdown means China will not finish the year as the leading centre for IPOs, falling behind New York for the first time since 2005. Mainland companies last year [2007] raised $109 billion on global exchanges, largely in Shanghai and Hong Kong ... Listings of Chinese companies this year [2008] raised $14.6 billion on the mainland and $7.4 billion in Hong Kong – the lowest total in three years – plus $1 billion on other global exchanges ... Floatations raised $25.4 billion on the New York stock exchange, propelled by the $19.8 billion of Visa in March, while $9.3 billion was raised on the London stock exchange.
>
> (*FT*, 29 December 2008, p. 13)

'Shanghai, which was the word's best performing stock market in 2007, dropped 0.7 per cent on Wednesday [31 December] to end at 1,820.8 – a loss of 65.4 per cent this year [2008]' (www.ft.com, 31 December 2008).

> The Shanghai Composite Index, which tumbled 65 per cent last year [2008], making China the worst performing major stock market, ended the morning [of 5 January] up 2.14 per cent at 1,859 points ... The Shanghai Composite Index [ended the day up] 3.3 per cent.
>
> (www.iht.com, 5 January 2009)

'The Shanghai Composite Index, which climbed 3.29 per cent on Monday [5 January], ended Tuesday [6 January] up 3 per cent at 1,937 points' (www.iht. com, 6 January 2009).

'[On 7 January] the Shanghai Composite Index closed 0.7 per cent lower at 1,924.02' (www.ft.com, 7 January 2009).

'[On 8 January] the Shanghai Composite Index fell 2.4 per cent' (www.iht. com, 8 January 2009).

'[On 13 January] the Shanghai Composite Index fell 2 per cent' (*IHT*, 14 January 2009, p. 15).

'[On 14 January] shares in Shanghai posted modest gains' (www.iht.com, 14 January 2009).

'[On 20 January] the Shanghai Composite Index recovered most of its earlier losses, tracking down 0.37 per cent' (www.cnn.com, 20 January 2009).

'Stock markets in China were largely flat with the Shanghai Composite Index inching up 0.06 per cent, the fourth consecutive day of gains in a row ... [The index] ended the morning at 1,995.266 points after opening lower' (www.iht. com, 21 January 2009). '[On 21 January] the Shanghai Composite Index fell 0.5 per cent' (*IHT*, 22 January 2009, p. 13).

'[On 22 January] Shanghai gained 1 per cent to close at a one-month high' (*FT*, 23 January 2009, p. 36).

> While the world's stock markets are down 9 per cent this year [2009], China is up by about the same amount. The usual January uplift has eluded almost every major exchange ... [But] there is a gulf between Shanghai's A shares and the equivalent H shares list in more liberal Hong Kong. The Hong Kong discount, normally about a third, has widened to almost a half in recent weeks. Gaps cannot be arbitraged away as Chinese are, in effect, barred from buying H shares while foreigners are allowed only tiny slivers of A shares. Their quotas amount to less than 2 per cent of China's market capitalization ... At least two-thirds of listed companies' shares [in Shanghai and Shenzhen] are locked up and not exchange-tradable ... [Shanghai was] up 100 per cent in 2007 and down 65 per cent in 2008 ... Citi is now worth less than one-ninth of ICBC.
>
> (*FT*, 28 January 2009, p. 16)

(See summary.)

Conglomerates

China has encouraged the growth of large manufacturing companies to help them compete internationally:

Qingdao Haier, well known for the quality of its home appliances such as washing machines and fridges, has just become one of a half-dozen 'national-level experimental enterprises', model companies expected to rank among the world's giants in a few years' time. The South Korean *chaebol* has been influential. But the government still pressurizes these companies to take on problem enterprises (*The Economist*, 20 December 1997, pp. 119–20). (The *kieretsu* is the Japanese equivalent.)

China had second thoughts about foreign models after the Asian financial crises began in July 1997, which, for example, exposed the weaknesses of organizations like the *chaebol*. But the National People's Congress held in March 1998 confirmed the move towards conglomerates.

'The state economic and trade commission has been charged with creating vast ... conglomerates in the all-important steel, energy, chemicals, motor and textile industries' (*FT*, Survey, 16 November 1998, p. vi).

'[On 27 June 2001] China unveiled a five-year plan to restructure its auto industry by building two or three domestic giants while forcing dozens of smaller manufacturers out of business' (*IHT*, 28 June 2001, p. 19). '[China] has 120 automakers, most of them surviving on various forms of local protectionism' (*FEER*, 12 July 2004, pp. 17–19). 'China has more than 100 automakers' (*IHT*, 19 November 2004, p. 15).

> Anshan Iron and Steel, the second largest steel maker in China by output, said Monday [15 August 2005] that it would merge with a smaller rival, the biggest move so far in the government's effort to make the steel industry competitive. Anshan Iron and Steel is combining with Benxi Iron and Steel Group, the nation's fifth biggest producer, to form Anben Steel Group, which will have an annual output of almost 20 million tonnes. Shanghai Baosteel Group [is] the biggest.
>
> (www.iht.com, 15 August 2005)

> The long delay in finalizing the deal led to suggestions the talks were foundering. The companies, both based in the north-east province of Liaoning, are the listed arms of Anshan Steel and Benxi Steel. The news that the merger is to go ahead comes a month after Beijing launched a sweeping blueprint for the steel sector which included a plan for rapid consolidation and the creation of two or three companies to rank in size with the global top ten.
>
> (*FT*, 16 August 2005, p. 24)

> The government said Tuesday [19 December 2006] that it planned to nurture as many as fifty state-owned enterprises to become globally competitive companies while maintaining control of companies engaged in key industries. The government wants to continue its oversight over companies engaged in national defence, petrochemicals, power transmission, telecommunications, coal, civil aviation and shipping, said Li Rongrong, director of the State-Owned Assets Supervision and Administration Commission, which acts as a warden of government assets ... Li Rongrong: 'The central government must maintain absolute control over industries that concern national security and economic safety ... [The government will] foster the growth of between thirty and fifty internationally competitive business groups with their own intellectual property rights and brands' ... The State Assets Commission wants to model itself on Singapore's Temasek Holdings, prodding mergers for companies to grow, improve their management and enhance their capital ... The Assets Commission will reduce its own companies to between eighty and 100 by 2010 from the current 161, closing companies that are unprofitable or insolvent ... Li Rongrong: 'Compared with leading foreign companies the gap in management quality is obvious, so a key goal for the second period of reforms is to improve management.'
>
> (www.iht.com, 19 December 2006; *IHT*, 20 December 2006, p. 12)

'The 161 enterprises under Sasac supervision include China's largest and most powerful oil, telecommunications, power and airline companies, many of which have listed subsidiaries on overseas stock markets. In addition, provincial offices of Sasac control scores of separate companies' (*FT*, 5 December 2006, p. 10).

In December [2006] the government announced that state-owned enterprises under the central government would remain in control of industrial sectors crucial to national security and economic welfare: military equipment, electric power, oil and petrochemicals, telecommunications, coal, aviation and shipping. But the number of centrally owned state enterprises would continue to decline from 161 at the end of last year [2006] to between eighty and 100 in 2010. Among these the government hopes that thirty to fifty internationally competitive conglomerates will emerge. State-owned enterprises with no hope of turning a profit will 'exit the market' by 2008. In other words, sell-offs to the non-state sector will continue.

(*The Economist*, 10 March 2007, p. 27)

Shanghai Automotive Industry, China's largest automaker, has agreed to buy Nanjing Automobile Group's auto-assembly and component-making businesses as China urges its carmakers to consolidate ... to compete with overseas rivals like Toyota and Volkswagen ... SAIC Motor, the listed unit of Shanghai Auto, will pay $286 million to buy the assets, the two state-owned companies said in a joint statement Wednesday [26 December] ... China, the world's third largest vehicle producers, has forty-seven carmakers, including foreign companies, with operating plants, compared with fifteen in the United States ... Nanjing Auto will own 25 per cent of Dong Hua, a joint venture with SAIC ... Nanjing Auto, the country's oldest carmaker, will terminate its joint venture with Fiat ... Fiat and Nanjing will continue to co-operate in commercial vehicle making and parts production ... Shanghai Auto has 17.44 per cent of the Chinese auto market ... The country has more than tripled automobile output and sales since 2001 and overtook Japan last year [2006] as the world's second largest vehicle market after the United States.

(www.iht.com, 26 December 2007; *IHT*, 27 December 2007, p. 12)

Shanghai Automotive Industrial Corporation (SAIC), China's largest carmaker, is to take over the vehicle and assembly and parts operations of Nanjing Automobile ... SAIC's Shanghai-listed SAIC Motor will pay $286 million for the core operations of Nanjing Auto, which include the British MG brand ... The two companies bought different parts of UK's Rover when it went bankrupt and sell almost identical versions of the old Rover 75 under rival MG and Roewe brands ... Nanjing Auto's parent will also get a stake of just under 5 per cent in SAIC Motor.

(*FT*, 27 December 2007, p. 17)

China yesterday [11 May 2008] unveiled a state-owned aircraft manufacturer intended to eventually challenge Boeing and Airbus's control of the global market in large airliners. The creation of the Commercial Aircraft Corporation of China (CACCC) is a significant step in Beijing's drive to create an advanced civil aviation manufacturing sector able to help meet the country's rapidly growing demand for regional and larger jets ... Beijing has made the development of an airliner with more than 150 seats by 2020 part of its national industrial policy ... Highlighting the difficulties, China recently delayed the first flight of a pioneering ARJ21 regional jet under development by China Aviation Industry Corporation I, better known as AVIC I ... The new company's main shareholders include the government's state-owned Assets Supervision and Administration Commission, AVIC I and its sister company. AVIC II, as well as Baosteel Group, the Aluminium Corporation of China (Chinalco) and Sinochem.

(*FT*, 12 May 2008, p. 28)

China on Sunday [11 May 2008] formally established a company to build regional commercial jets, with a goal of eventually reducing the country's reliance on Boeing and Airbus ... Commercial Aircraft Corporation of China has a capitalization of 19 billion yuan, or $2.72 billion, with 6 billion yuan coming from the state-owned Assets Supervision and Administration Commission, giving it the single largest stake at 30 per cent ... A consortium made up of the municipal government of Shanghai, where the ARJ21 regional jet is being developed, and two state aircraft manufacturers, China Aviation Industry Corporation I, or AVIC I, and AVIC II, will have a 25 per cent share for 5 billion yuan ... The ninety-seat ARJ-700 was presented by AVIC I last year [2007] and would be the first regional jet developed and produced by China. It is to be test flown later this year and deliveries are scheduled to begin in 2009 ... General Electric and Parker Hannifin supply parts for ARJ21. The project is not the first attempt by China to build a commercial passenger jet. Other attempts have included separate deals with McDonnell Douglas and Airbus, but all have failed ... The longer-term Chinese goal is to make large passenger jets with more than 150 seats or freighters capable of handling more than 100 tonnes of cargo ... Major state-owned Chinese firms, including the parent groups of Aluminium Corporation of China, Baoshan Iron and Steel and the state oil trader Sinochem International will each invest 1 billion yuan in Commercial Aircraft Corporation of China. Chinese airlines, which Airbus estimates will need about 2,650 new passenger jets in the next twenty years, have been placing big orders with Boeing and its European rival in recent years.

(*IHT*, 12 May 2008, p. 13)

China's aviation industry has learned a lot from making increasingly sophisticated parts for Boeing and Airbus over the past twenty years. China makes doors and some wing parts for the A320. It is also expected to build around 5 per cent of the airframe of the new A350. Boeing sources not only doors and tailfins for the 737 from China, but also the rudder of its new 787 Dreamliner. Within a few months AVIC I and its smaller state-owned rival AVIC II will take an important next step. In a joint venture with Airbus they will start producing up to four A320s a month on a final assembly line in the northern port city of Tianjin.

(*The Economist*, 17 May 2008, p. 85)

In a statement at the weekend [24 May 2008] the government unveiled the long-awaited restructuring of China's four big operators and a pair of also-rans into three major telecoms intended to have 'national network resources and relatively comparable strength and scale'. Beijing said the reform would also clear the way for the long-delayed introduction of third generation high-speed state services, with '3G licences to be issued following the completion of restructuring' ... Under the scheme the two networks operated by number two wireless group China Unicom are to be divided, with its CDMA operations sold to leading fixed-line operator China Telecom and its GSM network to be merged with trailing fixed-line company China Netcom ... Officials hope to foster potent competition for the runaway champion China Mobile, which has 70 per cent of the wireless market and is signing up new subscribers at the rate of 7 million a month ... China has ordered 'strong support' for the development and use of domestic technology in its telecoms industry amid a restructuring of the country's telephone operators and the approaching launch of third generation wireless services ... In a statement at the weekend the government said its planned reorganization of telecoms operators should be accompanied by a raft of measures to promote home-grown technology ... The statement said: 'Relevant government departments will make use of favourable overseas loans, aid grants and other export policies to promote the globalization of products featuring autonomous innovation' ... The government shied away from mentioning its current flagship project: telecoms technology based on the Beijing-backed 3G standard TD-SCDMA ... [which] lags far behind the more established international 3G standards, WCCDMA and CDMA2000 ... Officials have been pushing China Mobile to adopt the home-backed TD-SCDMA standard, creating a potential handicap for the company if it fails to match up to more mature technology adopted elsewhere ... Consultancy BDA says official support for TD-SCDMA may be weakening.

(*FT*, 26 May 2008, p. 20)

The market boasts more than 584 mobile users ... As part of the executive reshuffle ... Zhang Chunjiang, chairman of Netcom, was yesterday [Thursday 22 May] named a China Mobile vice president. However, Mr Zhang was also named China Mobile's Communist Party secretary, meaning he will be junior to China Mobile chairman and president Wang Jianzhou in operational terms, while outranking him politically.

(*FT*, 24 May 2008, p. 20)

China Unicom is to merge with China Netcom and the new company is likely to be licensed to build a 3G network based on the European-supported WCDMA standard ... China Telecom is widely expected to introduce 3G services based on the US-favoured CDMA2000 standard. WCDMA and CDMA2000 networks are already in commercial operation around the world, meaning their technology is relatively mature ... TD-SCDMA, by contrast, already risks being labelled as an also-ran.

(FT, 27 May 2008, p. 21)

China will issue three licences for high speed third generation, or 3G, mobile phone services and is calling for a merger of China Unicom and China Netcom, two of its four biggest providers, in a long-awaited industry overhaul. The government said Saturday [24 May 2008] that it would also call on China Telecom, the country's biggest fixed-line telecommunications carrier, to purchase the CDMA network of the wireless telecommunications company China Unicom ... The move is expected to foster competition in China's mobile sector, where China Mobile, the world's largest mobile service provider by subscribers, has long overshadowed Unicom. The sector has been hobbled by a split between the two different networks: CDMA and GSM ... China announced an initial series of moves Friday [23 May], including leadership changes and a directive for China Mobile to take over a small fixed-line operator, China Railway Communication.

(IHT, 26 May 2008, p. 12)

The country's telecoms industry, with nearly 600 million mobile subscribers, 360 million fixed-line customers and $244 billion in revenue, will be reconfigured. Six companies will be collapsed into three, each spanning mobile, fixed and broadband services. China Mobile, the world's largest mobile operator by subscribers, will merge with China TieTong, the smallest fixed-line operator. China Telecom, the country's biggest fixed-line operator, will acquire one of the mobile networks run by China Unicom, which will merge its remaining mobile operations with China Netcom, another fixed-line operator. A sixth operator, China Satcom, will be taken over by China Telecom ... The main purpose of the plan is to create a more competitive industry – which means, in practice, taking China Mobile down a peg or two. It will gain a fixed-line arm, but that is no recompense for what it will give up: its lock on the massive mobile market, encompassing two-thirds of Chinese customers and an even higher share of new subscribers. Under the new rules, which have yet to be spelled out, it will face regulatory pressure to allow rivals into its market ... The reorganization is the fourth since China first opened its telecoms industry to limited, state-orchestrated competition.

(The Economist, 31 May 2008, p. 80)

China announced two big deals on Monday [2 June] as the government overhauls the world's largest telecommunications industry, with the mobile operator China Unicom taking over a fixed-line peer and unloading an underperforming network. Unicom, the smaller rival of China Mobile, said it would issue new shares and swap 1.5 shares for every share in Netcom, the smaller of China's two fixed-line carriers. Unicom said it would pay a total of more than $55 billion for China Netcom ... Unicom also agreed to sell a wireless network to the fixed-line leader, China Telecommunications, and its parent for $15.2 billion ... Analysts say China Telecom is paying a high price for a network that only broke even in 2006 after years of losses and which is a third the size of Unicom's Global System for Mobile Communications network.

(www.iht.com, 2 June 2008)

China Unicom would acquire a fixed-line provider while selling off an under-performing mobile business. Unicom, the country's number two mobile operator after China Telecom, said it would buy China Netcom Group in a share swap valuing the fixed-line operator at $23.8 billion ... Separately, China Unicom and its parent said they would sell the 'code division multiple access', or CDMA, mobile network and accompanying business to China telecom and its parent for $15.9 billion. The moves were expected as part of a government-mandated shake-up of the telecommunications sector introduced last month [May]. That plan called for the country's six telecom companies to combine into three groups in a bid to create a more competitive industry and prevent a dominant operator from monopolizing the market ... Under the transactions revealed Monday [2 June] each existing China Netcom share would be swapped for 1.508 new China Unicom shares ... In a separate statement to the Hong Kong stock exchange, China Telecom said its parent, China Telecommunications, would acquire the CDMA network from China United Telecommunications ... and would buy China's Unicom's CDMA operations ... The CDMA technology is popular in the United States and Asia ... China Unicom is the only CDMA service provider in China, with 42 million subscribers by the end of 2007.

(*IHT*, 3 June 2008, p. 14)

China Unicom said Friday [28 August] it will sell Apple Inc.'s iPhone in China this year [2009], ending months of rumours about when the hit phone would make its long-delayed debut in the world's most populous mobile market. The phones are expected to go on sale in the fourth quarter under a multi-year deal struck between the two companies ... Unicom, one of three state-owned carriers, would be the first Chinese phone company to formally support the iPhone ... China's mobile market trails the United States, Japan and some others in financial size but it has 650 million mobile phone accounts and is seen as a major prize for foreign firms ... The companies will not share revenues, with Unicom instead buying the phones in batches from iPhone and offering them subsidies ... Unicom says it had 133 million accounts as of 31 December [2008], while China Mobile, the world's biggest phone company by subscribers, says it has more than 450 million. The third competitor is China Telecom, with a small mobile unit.

(www.iht.com, 28 August 2009)

China Unicom yesterday [28 August] said it would start selling the 3G iPhone in the fourth quarter [of 2009] after signing a non-exclusive three-year contract with Apple. The company said it would not use Apple's traditional revenue-sharing model and would instead pay the group on a wholesale basis ... The move will put China Unicom and Apple in direct competition with China Mobile, which is set to launch a range of smart phones based on Google's Android operating system. The world's largest telecoms operator by subscribers will launch smart phones made by Dell, the US computer manufacturer, China's Lenovo and Taiwan's HTC. China Telecom, meanwhile, is in talks with Research In Motion, maker of the BlackBerry, and Palm to offer services ... Analysts doubt how much of a boost the iPhone would provide to China Unicom as grey market iPhones not tied to any operator are widely available. Analysts estimate 1 million to 2 million iPhones are in use in China, which has nearly 700 million mobile users.

(*FT*, 29 August 2009, p. 14)

Vested interests are thwarting consolidation. There are more than 100 Chinese auto manufacturers and many of them are regional players propped up or partly owned by local governments. That leaves a legacy of wasteful investments in excess capacity, while frustrating plans by Beijing to build up national champions that could compete globally ... Analysts expect the foot-dragging on consolidation to continue at least in the near term ... [One argument is that] there is little incentive at the local government level to hand over jobs and tax revenue to outsiders ... Recent months have brought a handful of rare news media reports on acquisition talks ... Combinations could ease the fragmentation that has built up heavy overcapacity in the auto sector ... But despite the increased talk of deals in China, few have actually been completed ... Analysts doubted the recent slowdown in the Chinese car market would provide much impetus for mergers and acquisitions.

(www.iht.com, 15 October 2008)

China will concentrate more power in the hands of fewer automobile and steel companies, the government has said in unveiling its most concrete plans yet for reform of the two industries. The State Council, or cabinet, said it would push five steel makers and two or three car companies to take dominant positions in their respective industries ... The cabinet also named which companies China would encourage to lead the consolidation. Among automakers China called on FAW, Dongfeng, Shanghai Automotive Industry Corp. and Changan to make acquisitions nationwide. It said that Beijing Automotive Industry, Guangzhou Automobile Group, Chery Automobile and China National Heavy Duty Truck should spearhead regional efforts ... In steel Baosteel, Anben Iron and Steel and Wuhan Iron and Steel were tapped to be the three biggest players ... The government said that more than 45 per cent of steel output in China, the world's biggest steel producer, should come from the top five companies.

(www.iht.com, 22 March 2009)

Detailing plans announced in January [2009] to support the automobile and steel sectors in the face of the global financial crisis, the State Council pledged to increase the degree of concentration in both industries ... The cabinet's blueprint said that it would seek major progress in restructuring the industry during the next three years and wanted 'to create two to three big car making groups with an output of more than 2 million vehicles a year, [and] four to five car making groups with output of more than 1 million vehicles' by the end of 2011. In addition, the number of dominant players that control a combined 90 per cent share of the market should drop from fourteen to ten ... The government said that within three years it wanted to see 45 per cent of the market in the hands of the top five steelmakers, up from 28.5 per cent now.

(*FT*, 23 March 2009, p. 23)

('The head of a privately owned Chinese airline has disappeared after takeover talks with flag-carrier Air China broke down and Beijing grounded its fleet. The case is raising fears of a trend towards renationalization in some sectors in China as state groups use their clout to swallow struggling private competitors ... China's civil aviation authority suspended operations of East Star Airlines, a private regional airline, over the weekend, a day after East Star made a public statement that it was no longer for sale and alleged it had been subjected to strong-arm tactics in negotiations with Air China ... East Star's chairman and chief executive has been missing since last Friday [13 March] ... Some claim he has been taken into custody ... The airline has been hit by falling passenger numbers and a debt burden ... State companies have been gobbling up smaller private participants in steel, textiles, coal and oil': www.ft.com, 18 March 2009.)

China Eastern Airlines said it would buy its smaller rival Shanghai Airlines in a share swap. In a statement Sunday [12 July] China Eastern said it would give Shanghai Airlines shareholders 1.3 of its shares for every A share of Shanghai Airlines ... the combined airline will dominate air travel in and out of Shanghai ... China Eastern is one of the three state-owned carriers, alongside China Southern and Air China.

(www.iht.com, 13 July 2009)

(See the section in direct foreign investment on outward investment by Chinese companies.)

A chronology of developments in ownership policy and state enterprise reform

(See Jeffries 2006a: 486–503.)

A proposed law that would be the first to protect private property rights before parliament, after being withdrawn five months ago amid ideological disputes, state media said Wednesday [23 August]. The legislation, admitted Tuesday [22 August], would give private property the same protection as government assets while affirming the 'dominant role' of state industry ... The law was withdrawn in March [2006] during the annual session of the National People's Congress after complaints that its protections were too sweeping and that they would shield corrupt officials who took bribes or stole public property. Such anxiety has been magnified by mounting public anger at the ... growing gap between rich and poor ... China's constitution was amended in March 2004 to enshrine the right to own private property, a first since its revolution of 1949.

(www.iht.com, 23 August 2006)

At the National People's Congress held 5–16 March 2007 the property law was finally approved. '[When the property bill was put to the vote on 16 March] 99.1 per cent of the 2,889 legislators attending the National People's Congress backed the property law' (www.bbc.co.uk, 16 March 2007).

Originally scheduled for March 2006 the passage of the [property rights] law was delayed after Peking University law professor Gong Xiantian issued an open letter arguing that the draft law violated Article 12 of the constitution (which declares that state property is inviolable) and basic principles of socialism. This appeal, which was published on the internet, ignited considerable controversy. In late 2006 Professor Gong issued a second letter, this one signed by hundreds of scholars and former officials, again attacking the draft law.

(*FEER*, May 2007, p. 17)

Old-style Marxists oppose the property rights bill, which they warned would worsen inequalities in society and legitimize the theft of state assets by corrupt officials ... In a survey by the Chinese Academy of Social Sciences, half of the respondents believed the rich had acquired their wealth through illegal means. Critics of the bill say it will legitimize what they see as a mass theft from the people ... Most representatives in the National People's Congress [they say] are high-level officials from the provinces. They have personally benefited from privatization so they support the new law ... Although details [of the bill] have yet to be made public, it is expected to include a passage that states: 'Ownership rights of the state, groups and individuals are protected by law, and no individual or organization may violate these rights' ... Building owners are expected to be offered an automatic extension of their leases.

(*Guardian*, 5 March 2007, p. 14)

'The law ... has drawn criticism from lawmakers and some senior officials who fear it could protect the gains of those who misappropriate state-owned assets' (*IHT*, 5 March 2007, p. 1).

Perhaps the most important clause is the one that gives urban residents full effective ownership of their homes. City housing must currently be bought under a seventy-year lease that has to be reregistered. Yin Tian, a professor

at Peking University and one of those who drafted the law, said that ownership would be extended automatically. 'Before this there was no legal
answer in China as to what would happen to your property after the seventy
years' [he said].

(*The Times*, 8 March 2007, p. 38)

Parliament began debating a landmark private property measure on Thursday
[8 March] that would ensure that all forms of property, including the assets of
individuals, the state and collectives, have protection under the law ... would
be given equal protection under the law ... At a news briefing on Sunday 4
March], before the opening session, the parliamentary spokesman, Jiang
Enzhu, said: 'No matter if it is state, collective or private property', it should
be protected equally ... The introduction of the proposed law to the National
People's Congress follows a rare and long public consultation ... In a speech
introducing the draft law, Wang Zhaoguo, vice chairman of the Standing
Committee, told delegates Thursday that protecting people's property rights
was aimed at 'stimulating their vigour to create wealth' and enhancing social
stability. 'As the reform and opening-up and the economy develop, people's
living standards improve in general and they urgently require effective protection of their own lawful property accumulated through hard work,' Wang said
... While all land in China remains the property of the state, legal experts consulted in drafting the law said it would automatically extend the leases that
farmers and landowners hold over the land they occupy. But experts say the
new law is unlikely to curb the forced reallocation of farming land for commercial or industrial use that has led to widespread unrest and protests in rural
areas ... A leading Chinese Marxist economist, Gong Xiantian, has been a
key figure in rallying opposition to the draft law. After a government call for
public comment in 2005 Gong wrote an open letter to the chairman of the
Standing Committee, Wu Bangguo, warning that putting private property on
the same legal basis as public assets would 'undermine the legal foundation of
China's socialist economy'. 'This means that people who become rich by
preying on state-owned assets and bribes could be shielded from prosecution,'
Gong wrote in the letter, which included the signatures of 3,274 people,
including retired senior officials and military officers. 'Such a law would pose
a serious violation against China's constitution, which stipulates that socialist
public property is deemed sacrosanct and shall be free from encroachment,'
he wrote ... Some economists warn that the law's passage would not significantly enhance the rights of property owners while government officials
exerted influence or even outright control over the courts ... Advocates of
farmers' rights unsuccessfully urged the authorities to include provisions in
the property law that would make it more difficult for local governments to
seize farms and sell the rights to use this land to private developers or industry. Under existing law local governments have the power to convert agricultural land to other uses if it is deemed to be in the public interest.

(www.iht.com, 8 March 2007; *IHT*, 9 March 2007, pp. 1, 8)

'It is not clear whether the current version will adequately address the expropriation of collectively owned land from peasants for development – one of the
biggest sources of rural unrest' (www.iht.com, 14 March 2007).

> [The] new property law ... is the first piece of legislation to cover an indi-
> vidual's right to own assets ... The latest text of the bill states that: 'The
> property of the state, the collective, the individual and other obligees is pro-
> tected by law, and no units or individuals may infringe upon it.' But it adds
> that: 'The nation is in the first stage of socialism and should stick to the
> basic economic system in which public ownership predominates, co-existing
> with other kinds of ownership' ... The bill also seeks to address the often
> illegal land seizures that are taking place, and the government transfer of
> farmland to developers, frequently without farmers being given adequate
> compensation ... The bill will also reportedly boost protection against land
> seizures, which have become a major source of unrest among farmers in
> rural areas.
>
> (www.bbc.co.uk, 8 March 2007)

Wang Zhaoguo, a vice chairman of the National People's Congress, introducing the bill yesterday [8 March]: 'Effective property of private citizens is
not only stipulated by China's constitution ... but is also the general aspiration and urgent demand of the people' ... The wording of the final bill ...
includes lengthy references to the primacy of the 'socialist system' and
'state ownership' ... The bill also explicitly rejects any change to the system
of 'collective' ownership of rural land, where farmer occupiers have only
usage rights over limited contract periods rather than any title that can be
bought and sold. Properties in cities, by contrast, can be bought and sold
under leases of between fifty and seventy years.

> (*FT*, 9 March 2007, p. 7)

'Experts say ... the new property rights bill ... will not give farmers much more
protection against unscrupulous officials' (*FT*, 4 April 2007, p. 13).

> Living up to one's name poses something of a problem for the Communist
> party ... whose name in Chinese literally means 'the public property
> party' ... Should an underdog try to use the new law to enforce his rights,
> the corrupt and pliant judiciary would usually ensure he was wasting his
> time.
>
> (*The Economist*, 10 March 2007, p. 11)

[The] new law on property rights is mainly intended to reassure the country's fast growing middle class that their assets are secure. Three years ago
China added a clause to its constitution saying that private property was 'not
to be encroached upon' ... A vocal body of intellectuals and retired officials
has denounced the property law as a betrayal of the country's socialist principles. It will, they say, protect the fortunes of corrupt officials and the ill-
gotten gains of crooked businessmen. Further, it will hasten the demise of

China's remaining state-owned industries and the creation of a plutocracy ... Among the more than 3,200 signatories ... [of] a recent petition to the NPC ... are seven former government ministers or deputy ministers, five former provincial leaders, a sprinkling of retired senior military officers and about fifty professors at the party's Central School, an academy for top officials ... Ownership could be challenged, but critics worry that it would be difficult to do so for former state-owned assets or for land-use rights that had been sold off in shady deals. The timing of the earlier draft's publication in 2005 was bad for the bill's supporters. It followed an upsurge of debate about the frequent sale of state-owned enterprises at rock-bottom prices to their managers. In response, the government banned management buy-outs of large state enterprises. But there was also concern about its sales of strategic stakes in state-owned banks to foreign investors ... The leadership itself invited discussion by publishing a draft of the law in 2005 – a very unusual move in a country that normally keeps its legislative processes shrouded in secrecy ... Sweeping privatization of housing since the late 1990s has radically changed the social and political fabric of urban China. Property rights have become a topic of critical interest to urban residents anxious to protect their new assets from the whims of the state ... Farmers ... have something to gain ... The good news is that the latest draft, unlike the 2005 version, gives farmers the right to renew their land-use rights after they expire. Unlike urban land, which is state-owned with usage rights granted for periods of between forty and seventy years, rural land is 'collectively' owned. Farmers are given thirty-year leases (though often no supporting documents) to use plots of land. But the law will put no new limits on the government's powers to appropriate land. It also says that village committees represent the collective. These are supposedly democratically elected but party regulations still give unelected party officials the final say over village affairs. Most important, the ban on mortgaging farmland will remain.

(pp. 25–7)

Land-use conversion regulations have been tightened in an effort to reduce unrest provoked by unfair seizures of land. For example, local governments must now record land sales as 'on-budget' income and certain types of projects – such as golf courses and theme parks – have been banned on undeveloped land. Enforcement efforts have been strengthened by sending out teams of auditors to review land rezoning arrangements by local governments. The NPC will also pass a new private property law which, while stopping short of reforming the rural land-tenure system, reiterates the legal requirements to compensate farmers adequately for the expropriation of their land.

(www.economist.com, 15 March 2007)

China on Friday [16 March] enacted its first law to protect private property ... [There was] a ban on news media discussion of the proposal ... When one popular financial magazine, *Caijing*, defied the propaganda department's ban on reporting on the matter and published a cover story on the law last week, it was ordered to halt distribution and reprint the magazine without the offending story ... [Neither Hu Jintao or Wen Jiabao] has spoken publicly about [the property law]. Wen Jiabao's two-hour address to the nation on the opening day of the annual two-week session did not mention property rights ... The leadership did not so much overcome opposition to the property law as forbid it. Unlike in 2005, when leaders invited broad discussion about property rights, the latest drafts of the law were not widely circulated. Several left-leaning scholars ... said they had come under pressure from their universities to stay silent ... Hundreds of scholars and retired officials signed a petition in February against the law, which they said 'overturns the basic system of socialism'. The petition claimed the law did too little to distinguish between private property gained legally through hard work and public property that falls into private hands through corruption. They also argued that China could not give state-owned property and private property the same legal status and still call itself socialist ... Supporters of the law dispute the assertion that it will protect the ill-gotten gains of corruption, arguing that it protects only legally held property ... China's urban middle class has fuelled a real estate boom, even though all land is owned by the state and purchasers trade only the right to use property on it for up to seventy years. The disposition of property after that term expires is one of many unsettled issues that property law is intended to address, but the details have yet to be publicized ... The final wording of the law remains unclear – as does the nature of any compromises that may have been necessary to build a consensus within the party to pass it.

(www.iht.com, 16 March 2007; *IHT*, 17 March 2007, p. 6)

'Farmers will be able to renew their leases, but they will neither be allowed to mortgage land nor to acquire the individual title that would give them property protection against forcible acquisition' (*The Times*, 17 March 2007, p. 20).

Anti-monopoly (anti-trust) law

In August [2008] a new anti-monopoly law takes effect in China, extending its economic influence far beyond its borders. The law, which goes into effect on 1 August, is intended to strengthen an existing set of anti-trust regulations originally established in 1993 ... Formally enacted by the National People's Congress last year [2007], the measure gives Chinese regulators authority to examine foreign mergers when they involve acquisitions of Chinese companies or foreign businesses investing in Chinese companies' operations. Beijing could also consider national security issues.

(www.iht.com, 28 March 2008; *IHT*, 29 March 2008, p. 11)

After fourteen years of wrangling China will introduce a comprehensive anti-trust law on 1 August [2008] ... At the moment competition is governed by a set of regulations from 2006, along with three other laws – the

Anti-Unfair Competition Law, the Price Law and the Consumer Rights and Interests Protection Law. These various rules are scattered throughout China's bureaucracy, and are universally condemned as toothless and lacking clarity ... After a series of drafts included and then excluded state-owned monopolies, a compromise was reached. The law applied to them, but with an exemption when economic or national security is threatened – a loophole almost as big as China itself ... [There is] a suspicion that rather than going after the big monopolies, the law's initial targets will be foreign companies.

(The Economist, 19 July 2008, p. 79)

China yesterday [4 August] published new merger control regulations that lawyers believe could delay or prevent some high profile cross-border deals. China's State Council published turnover thresholds that will trigger merger filings under a new anti-monopoly law, which took effect on Friday [1 August 2008].

(FT, 5 August 2008, p. 6)

Two pioneering legal actions in China involving high profile companies have been concluded with one case highlighting the fresh powers handed to consumers under the country's new anti-monopoly laws. China Mobile, the world's largest mobile phone group with 500 million subscribers, has agreed to pay renminbi 1,000 ($146) to settle a lawsuit filed by a customer who alleged it had abused its monopoly position to extract unfair revenue from subscribers ... The settlement, mediated by a Beijing court, agreed without accepting liability ... A Shanghai court has thrown out a case against Nasdaq-listed Shanda Interactive Entertainment because the plaintiff had insufficient evidence to prove its allegations. The Shanda ruling is the first legal judgement from a mainland court under China's revamped competition regime, which was introduced in August 2008.

(FT, 27 October 2009, p. 23)

Bankruptcy law

The National People's Congress ... adopted a bankruptcy law Sunday [27 August 2006] that for the first time includes private companies as well as state-owned ones, in the hope of boosting investor confidence. The corporate bankruptcy law will apply to foreign companies as well as to Chinese businesses and will protect the rights of both creditors and workers ... The law, which will come into effect next 1 June [2007], allows creditors or financial supervision agencies to initiate bankruptcy proceedings against companies whose managements are unwilling to do so.

(www.iht.com, 27 August 2006; *IHT*, 28 August 2006, p. 10)

Parliament adopted a long-awaited corporate bankruptcy law yesterday [27 August 2006], aimed at protecting creditors and workers of bankrupt enterprises. It also passed two bills dealing with joint ventures and supervision of local governments. The bankruptcy law, which will come into effect on 1 June 2007, has taken twelve years to make its way through the legislative process in the National People's Congress.

(*IHT*, 28 August 2006, p. 4)

The bankruptcy law [was] passed in August after more than a decade of debate ... However, the law, which is due to come into effect in June 2007, will not apply to 2,116 state-owned enterprises considered at financial risk by the authorities until at least the end of 2008.

(*FT*, 25 September 2006, p. 9)

China has introduced a new bankruptcy law [1 June 2007] that gives creditors precedence over workers when it comes to claiming the assets of failed companies. The law also means that, for the first time, private Chinese firms that have failed will be allowed to collapse. Previously they existed in legal limbo – their assets could not be released and their debts could not be struck from their creditors' books ... The new law further means that failed enterprises can also now be officially liquidated for the first time. Until now studies estimate that there are about 30 million Chinese people listed on the employment rolls of public companies that are no longer operational.

(www.bbc.co.uk, 1 June 2007)

There is a good chance that on 1 June ... at least one Chinese company will declare bankruptcy or have bankruptcy thrust upon it ... After over a decade of contentious debate China has finally enacted a law that allows worthless private companies to die ... In 1986 a law was passed for state-owned companies, allowing only their government supervisor to put them into bankruptcy. First claim to any remaining assets belonged to the workers. No explicit provisions existed for private companies ... In the future the claims of workers will take precedence over unsecured creditors ... The new bankruptcy law will apply to Chinese companies overseas and to many foreign companies operating in China.

(*The Economist*, 2 June 2007, p. 86)

Last year [2007] a new bankruptcy law came into effect, but it is incomplete and poorly understood. Even firms that might recover by restructuring under court jurisdiction are reluctant to use it ... In the past bosses often preferred to run a business into the ground before acknowledging problems, at which point there was little to reorganize. Even under the new law it is unclear whether lenders who step in after a bankruptcy have priority over old claims, undermining any incentive for a would-be backer to give the firm a second chance ... More than thirty companies on the national stock markets have recently failed ... But in many cases control has been acquired by other firms to engineer a 'backdoor listing', without the lobbying and delays common in China. Evidently some Chinese entrepreneurs continue to believe that a listed firm's ability to raise public capital is worth having.

(*The Economist*, 11 October 2008, p. 90)

The new labour law

China passed a new contract law on Friday [29 June 2007] in a bid to improve basic worker rights amid widespread complaints of unpaid wages, forced labour and other abuses ... The approval follows eighteen months of deliberation and a rare government request for public comment on the law. It is expected to be the most significant change in labour rules in more than a decade by setting standards for labour contracts, use of temporary workers and severance pay ... The law was approved Friday by the Standing Committee of the National People's Congress and is to take effect on 1 January [2008] ... The new law 'is expected to improve protection of employees' legal rights following exposure of forced labour scandals in brick kilns in central and north China', Xinhua said. Nearly 1,000 workers have been released following police raids in recent months, prompted in part by accusations posted on the internet that authorities were ignoring such practices. The law was proposed in December 2005 amid complaints that companies were mistreating workers by withholding pay, requiring unpaid overtime or failing to provide written contracts.

(www.iht.com, 29 June 2007)

China's legislature passed a sweeping new labour law that strengthened protections for workers ... rejecting pleas from foreign investors who argued that the measure would reduce China's appeal as a low-wage, business-friendly industrial base ... Foreign executives said that they were especially worried about new labour regulations because their companies tend to comply with existing laws more rigorously than some of their Chinese competitors do ... The law, which is to take effect in 2008, also enhances the role of the Communist Party's monopoly union and allows collective bargaining for wages and benefits. It softens some provisions for wages and benefits that foreign companies said would hurt China's competitiveness, but retained others that American multinationals had lobbied vigorously to exclude ... While the new law will do little to eliminate violations of existing laws, it does require that employers treat migrant workers as they do other employees. All will have written employment contracts that comply with minimum wage and safety regulations. It also moves China closer to European-style labour regulations that emphasize fixed- and open-term employment contracts enforceable by law. It requires that employees with short-term contracts become full-time employees with lifetime benefits after a short-term contract is renewed twice. Perhaps most significant, it gives the state-run union and other employee representative groups the power to bargain with employers. Many multinational corporations had lobbied against provisions in an earlier draft of the labour law. The early draft, circulated widely in business and legal circles, more sharply limited the use of temporary workers and required obtaining approval from the state-controlled union for layoffs. Companies argued that the rules would substantially increase labour costs and reduce flexibility ... International labour experts said several of the most delicate clauses had been watered down. But lawyers representing some global companies doing business … [in China] complained the new law still imposes a heavy burden. The National People's Congress released a summary that said companies must 'consult' the state-backed union if it plans workforce reductions, suggesting a softening from earlier drafts that gave unions the right to approve or reject layoffs before they could take place. But it retained language that limits 'probationary contracts' that many employers use to deny employees full-time status. It also states that severance pay will be required for many workers, and tightens the conditions under which an employee can be fired. Moreover, the law empowers company-based branches of the state-run union or employee representative committees to bargain with employers over salaries, bonuses, training and other work-related benefits and duties. In the past workers have had to negotiate wages with their employers individually.

(*IHT*, 30 June 2007, p. 11)

In response to the scandal … of children and adults abducted and working as slaves in brick factories and mines across central provinces … a clause was added to the legislation mandating punishment for state officials who overlook or tolerate labour rights violations. The law, which takes effect on 1 January [2008] sets standards for mandatory labour contracts, lay-offs and severance payments, and grants more power to China's state-sanctioned labour unions … Companies in China would have to award permanent contracts to employees after they had completed a probationary period as, under Chinese law, the circumstances for laying off workers were very limited, helping employees gain long-term, secured employment contracts … [Critics point to the problem of] implementation of the law … [There is] poor implementation of existing legislation … Foreign companies often complain they are put at a disadvantage by complying with laws that are ignored by domestic rivals.

(*FT*, 2 July 2007, p. 6)

A sweeping new labour law [was] passed on 29 June … It does not go into effect until 1 January 2008 … The new law replaces one put into effect in 1995 … Companies will need written contracts with all full-time employees, and anyone who works for more than four hours a day is likely to be considered a full-time employee. Once they are full-time, employees who are laid off must be bought out at a multiple of their average monthly salary. Making more than twenty employees or 10 per cent of the labour force redundant is allowed, but it must be done on the basis of seniority not merit, China's trade unions could be transformed by the law. Previously they focused on social welfare; now they will be able to act more like Western trade unions, weighing in on discipline, safety, remuneration and working hours. The new law also grants them the right to litigate … The law is full of inconsistencies. It does not, for example, apply to foreign representative offices, yet since these offices must hire their workers through official staffing agencies, it will apply to their employees. Worse, since foreign firms cannot hire directly, they are required to offer the kind of short-term contracts the new law bars. And although the new law should standardize practices throughout the country, it will inevitably be interpreted differently in every region.

(*The Economist*, 28 July 2007, p. 72)

A new labour law, coming into effect on 1 January [2008], will in theory improve workers' lots, but it is creating more headaches. The law is supposed to provide greater job security. Workers with ten years or more of service will have open-ended contracts and companies will have to inform unions before sacking anyone. Employers fear the law will mean bigger severance payments. The unions will also have the power to negotiate collective contracts ... The Chinese press has cited numerous attempts to circumvent the law. Huawei, China's best known maker of telecommunications equipment has attracted special notice. It has been accused of asking some 7,000 employees with more than eight years of service to resign to compete for new short-term posts. The aim, allegedly, was to reclassify them as new employees. The new law has been a boon to the All-China Federation of Trade Unions (ACFTU), an umbrella for all China's unions that is in effect an arm of government ... After persuading Huawei, which denied trying to evade the law, to revise its plans, the ACFTU this week issued a stern warning to other companies not to try anything similar. It said a 'small number' were laying off workers in advance of the new law ... [Critics say] that the new law does nothing to improve the lot of tens of millions of migrant workers from the countryside ... China's official trade unions have yet to build a network among such workers ... Poor enforcement [is an issue] ... Critics say many companies will continue efforts to evade the law or else simply ignore it ... China has no plans to reintroduce the right to strike, which it abolished in 1982 as it began to fret about the example set by the Solidarity trade union movement in Poland.

(*The Economist*, 8 December 2007, pp. 67–8)

China on Tuesday [1 January 2008] introduced a labour law that enhances rights for mainland workers, including open-ended work contracts and severance pay ... The new law will make it more difficult for companies to hire temporary workers, a practice favoured by exporters to cope with fluctuations in orders ... The Labour Contract Law aims to improve job security for workers, making open-ended terms of employment for those who have completed two fixed terms. The legislation limits overtime, sets minimum wages and requires one month's pay for each year worked for dismissed employees ... Some companies have been terminating contracts and asking employees to resign before the introduction of the new law. Huawei Technologies, the largest Chinese maker of telecommunications equipment, recently offered about 7,000 workers new contracts with benefits if they terminated their old agreements ... [The company said that] some employees accepted, while others chose not to sign and left … [and that] the move was not aimed at evading legislation.

(www.iht.com, 1 January 2008)

Employers fear that a new labour law that took effect yesterday [1 January 2008] will intensify growing pressure on manufacturing costs by enhancing the bargaining power of workers … The new labour law closes a loophole that allowed companies to dismiss workers on temporary or fixed-term contracts without compensation, or even employ them without a formal contract altogether – often through third-party labour agencies. From 1 January workers who have been with a company for ten years – or signed two fixed-term contracts – will be entitled to one month's severance pay for every year worked. The law also requires employers to consult and 'employee representative congress', usually a branch of the official All-China Federation of Trade Unions [ACFTU], on any changes to matters including hours, benefits and compensation … Labour rights groups, which welcomed the law as a laudable step forward, are worried that patchwork implementation in different localities could water down its protections … Workers in factories where ACFTU does not have a presence must nevertheless seek the official union's 'direction' or 'guidance'.

(*FT*, 2 January 2008, p. 6)

Many younger people from the countryside are working in cities where they have to pay all their treatment costs. A new labour contract law introduced this year [2008] requires employers to pay medical insurance for such workers. But migrants are often hired informally, making it easy for employers to evade such requirements … [One estimate says that] more than half of the urban population has no insurance … Last year [2007] the government introduced an urban insurance scheme (similar to the rural one) aimed at non-working residents, including children and university students. The aim is to have every urban citizen covered by 2010 … the government spends a mere 0.8 per cent of GDP on health.

(*The Economist*, 23 February 2008, p. 71)

'The new law mandates contracts for all employees, open-ended contracts for long-term employees, and health insurance and other benefits. Unlike past labour laws, it provides more channels for workers to bring complaints against employers' (*FEER*, March 2008, p. 32).

A year and a half after a landmark labour law took effect, experts say conditions have actually deteriorated in southern China's export-orientated factories … With China's exports reeling and unemployment rising because of the global slowdown, there is growing evidence that factories are ignoring or evading the new law, and that the government is reluctant to enforce it … The number of labour disputes in China doubled to 693,000 in 2008, the first year the law was in effect, and are sharply rising this year [2009], the government says … The law requires that all employees have a written contract that complies with minimum wage and safety requirements. It also strengthens the monopoly state-run labour union and makes it more difficult for companies to use temporary workers or to dismiss employees ... Lawyers say some local governments have issued their own competing rules or interpretations of the law that weaken it, to aid factory owners ... [It is claimed that] many exporters evade the law by subcontracting to so-called shadow factories, which operate under illegal conditions.

(www.iht.com, 23 June 2009; *IHT*, 24 June 2009, p. 14)

Financing investment: the debate

State enterprises have generally grown more profitable over time and the year 2006 saw the start of a major debate about the extent to which they depend on reinvested profits to finance investment as opposed to bank credit.

Imprudent banks, aggrandizing officials, avid foreign investors; many culprits are blamed for China's overheating economy. Yet those most responsible are rarely fingered: Chinese companies ... Firms' investment in fixed assets ... is largely financed by companies' retained earnings: indeed, firms, not China's thrifty households, are now the country's biggest savers. Both the rate of retention and the furious pace of investment could be cut if companies were made to pay dividends. At the moment China's state-owned enterprises (SOEs), which most of the biggest still are, do not pay dividends to their main shareholder, the state. Louis Kuijs, an economist with the World Bank in Beijing who has studied the issue, calls this 'remarkable'. The reasons are historic. Before economic reforms began state firms simply received all financing from the government budget and remitted any profit. In the 1980s SOEs were gradually given more independence and allowed to keep some profits in order to motivate managers and staff ... This system broke down in practice as every state firm – after several rounds of consolidation there are still 169,000 today – haggled over the precise share of earnings it could retain. China's 1994 tax reform cleared all that up, by setting a non-negotiable corporate tax rate (now around 33 per cent, about double that for foreign firms). In return, companies could keep all their post-tax profits. This mattered little in the early 1990s, when most SOEs made no money and needed any cash they generated to restructure themselves and repay debt. Nowadays, however, they are rather profitable. China's 169 biggest industrial state firms – a list that includes PetroChina, China Mobile and Baosteel – declared net profits of 600 billion yuan ($75 billion) last year [2005], up from 400 billion yuan in 2004. A wider group of 450 big SOEs made 331 billion yuan in the first five months of this year [2006], according to the State-owned Asset and Administration Commission (SASAC), which oversees them ... Profits [in 2004 were] estimated at 6.5 per cent of GDP ... In February SASAC officials said that a plan was being drawn up ... [for] state firms to pay dividends ... Extracting some of the profit in the form of dividends would force these firms to be more circumspect in how they spend the remainder, improving capital allocation and cutting back the wasteful investment and over-capacity so prevalent in China. It would also reduce the cash available for speculating in property and equity markets for expansion into new, usually unrelated business lines ... Forcing greater financial discipline on SOEs should reduce pro-cyclical investment.

(The Economist, 29 July 2006, pp. 73, 76)

Fixed-asset investment [is] now more than 40 per cent of GDP ... Because of a remarkable rise in profits, retained earnings now account for more than half of capital spending. Only 27 per cent comes from the banks – though the bank contribution to real estate investment is much higher. Overall return on capital for the once-derided state-owned enterprises rose from 2 per cent in 1998 to 12.7 per cent in 2005, and for other enterprises from 7 per cent to 16 per cent. Corporate sector savings now account for a massive 20 per cent of GDP ... While China does not need more fiscal stimulus, a policy to push for dividends from state-owned enterprises and spending on social needs would do much to rein in economic excesses and reduce domestic imbalances. If state-owned enterprises paid out 50 per cent of profits as dividends, government health and education spending could be nearly doubled, according to the World Bank. Manufacturing and construction investment would be lower, but probably wiser.

(Philip Bowring, *IHT*, 1 August 2006, p. 7)

According to the World Bank ... in its quarterly report ... [said that] 'One reason for the resilience of fixed-asset investment to tightening measures is that profits, which finance over half of investment, picked up momentum' ... The World Bank says that local governments are responsible for 10 per cent to 20 per cent of investment, propelled largely by officials still judged by how fast their economy grows and their dependence on land sales for revenue.

(FT, 16 August 2006, p. 7)

'More than half of all industry investment is financed ... [by] reinvesting profits ... and only a fifth by bank loans' *(FT*, 17 August 2006, p. 12).

Contrary to conventional wisdom, the frugality of Chinese households is not the chief explanation for China's surplus savings. As Jonathan Anderson of UBS notes, the principal explanation is China's huge corporate savings. Between 2000 and 2005 China's gross domestic investment rose from 33.7 per cent to 41.2 per cent of GDP. Over the same period, however, its gross savings rate rose from 37.9 per cent to 49.5 per cent ... Corporate savings (that is, undistributed corporate profits) jumped from 22.1 per cent of GDP to 30.2 per cent over the same period, while household savings rose from 12.9 per cent to 16.8 per cent of GDP. Overall, some 70 per cent of the increase in gross savings was generated by the rising profitability of the corporate sector. Certainly, Chinese household savings are high by international standards. As the IMF noted recently, they were an impressive 32 per cent of household disposable income in 2004. Nevertheless, household savings generate only a third of China's overall savings. The undistributed profits of corporations are far more important. Corporations still need to borrow from banks, as Jonathan Anderson stresses, since they invest even more than they save … China's corporations are generating vast savings. This does not mean that they are sensationally profitable, however, since the capital they use is also, as the investment rate shows, very large.

(*FT*, 4 October 2006, p. 17)

The World Bank claims that there has been a huge increase in corporate profitability so that now two-thirds of China's huge investment in capital stock (nearly 50 per cent of GDP) is being paid for out of retained earnings and new equity, not bank loans.

(*IHT*, 24 October 2006, p. 7)

It is well known that China's high growth has been driven to a considerable extent by high and rising investment, which now accounts for more than 40 per cent of GDP. How investment has been financed, or the composition of economy-wide saving, is less well known. The conventional wisdom has long been that China's enterprise investment was financed largely by bank credit, with banks channelling the savings of China's exceptionally frugal households to unprofitable firms. To some extent this was true a decade to fifteen years ago, although even then the picture was more nuanced than this. Regardless, since then things have changed: firms have become more profitable and more of their investment is financed by enterprise saving (retained earnings plus depreciation). What makes China stand out, compared to other countries, is high saving by enterprises and, to a lesser extent, the government. As shown by the national accounts, enterprise saving in China is now over 20 per cent of GDP (after tax), higher than household saving and significantly higher than in most other countries. Moreover, only about one-third of enterprise investment is now financed externally, largely by banks, while more than half is financed by enterprise saving. Using 2005 as an example, China's investment reached over 40 per cent of GDP in 2005, of which around 31 per cent of GDP was done by enterprises, 6 per cent of GDP by households and 3 per cent of GDP by the government. Of the enterprise investment about 10 per cent of GDP (one-third of total enterprise investment) was financed externally, the majority by banks … Chinese households are still fairly frugal, saving over 25 per cent of their income in recent years, or around 16 per cent of GDP … However, household saving is only about 35 per cent of the economy-wide total.

(Bert Hofman and Louis Kuijs, chief economist and economist respectively at the World Bank office in Beijing, *FEER*, October 2006, pp. 40–1)

A story has been going around that Chinese firms, state-owned or otherwise, are highly profitable and retain too much of their earnings. It is these profits, rather than bank loans – the story goes – that have financed China's surging capacity and rapid economic growth. Most recently the World Bank sought to lend credence to this tale by running it in its *China Economic Quarterly* … The Bank concludes that China's rapid growth in capacity expansion and fixed asset investment poses no particular danger to the country's banking system. That is because, it says, the majority of China's investment is not financed by bank loans, but, rather, by retained earnings … The fact is [however] that bad loan problems have plagued Chinese banks for years, which is why the Chinese leadership has recently made a vigorous effort to reform the system. How can there be a significant non-performing loan problem if banks finance only a small proportion of growth behind so much equity? Indeed, if investments in general are generating as much as double-digit returns, why should banks worry about getting paid even if all the investments are financed by bank loans? If firms are so profitable, where do all the hundreds of billions of dollars of China's reported bad loans come from? Of course, the reality is quite different from the World Bank story. In recent years Chinese manufacturers have been caught in 'biflation' – soaring raw materials costs coupled with either flat or declining prices for finished products … Profit margins must be severely eroded. So how can Chinese firms appear to be so profitable? To get to the root of the problem I [Weijian Shan] went back to the same data that the World Bank used to derive its results. What I was able to find tells a quite different story … [There are various ways to] exaggerate the profit number … The true profitability number for Chinese industrial firms could be as much as 6 to 7 percentage points less than the 15.2 per cent number from the World Bank results. The average profitability of Chinese industrial firms after such adjustments comes down to no more than 8 per cent to 9 per cent … Chinese firms, of course, borrow much more than they deposit. Much of their deposits, in fact, are not for the purpose of saving, but rather to secure bank credit … There is no question that China's growth continues to be financed by banks. In fact, total investment by industrial firms likely accounts for no more than 20 per cent of the country's annual fixed asset investment. Bank loans, on the other hand, are greater than China's GDP.

(Weijian Shan, *FEER*, September 2006, pp. 29–32)

At issue is not whether the profits of Chinese firms have grown, as the World Bank researchers suggest … At issue is whether China allocates and uses capital efficiently enough so that it produces a return on capital at par or better than international markets. The question is: by international stand-ards how efficient is China in using its capital? My own analysis of the same data used by the World Bank concludes that the return-on-equity numbers reported by it are significantly overstated because they do not net out such items as corporate income taxes. The World Bank does not dispute this. But

it insists that Chinese firms are now making so much profit that undistributed profits or retained earnings finance more than half of their investments,
whereas bank loans finance only one-third or as little as one-sixth. If this is
true it suggests that Chinese firms finance their investments with much less
debt in proportion to equity on average than probably all their international
peers, and, therefore, by implication, they must have been more profitable.
For evidence, the World Bank points to the increase in the proportion of
corporate savings, now accounting for more than 20 per cent of GDP ... The
World Bank researchers tell us that corporate savings, as a macroeconomic
concept, are equal to undistributed profits or retained earnings *by definition*
... [But] as a macroeconomic concept corporate savings include depreciation, amortization (both of which are treated as costs in any corporate
income statement) and other things (including government subsidies).
Depreciation alone is a big number ... [By my calculation] depreciation
alone (11 per cent of net asset value) is more than 1.2 times as large as
undistributed profits (9 per cent of net asset value) or at least 55 per cent of
corporate savings. Undistributed profits at most represent about 45 per cent
of corporate savings ... There is absolutely no way anyone can draw any
inference on how firms finance their investments in aggregate from corporate or national savings data. Even if the amount of corporate savings
exceeds corporate investments, as in the United States, bank loans can still
finance as much as 100 per cent of corporate investments. The key to
knowing who provides financing is to understand who bears the risk of providing money to enable investment ... The bank is a provider of risk capital
... Chinese industrial firms, at least those in the NBS [National Bureau of
Statistics] database, finance 60 per cent of their investments with bank
loans. Therefore, regardless of the fact that corporate savings are mathemat-
ically equal to 60 per cent or 100 per cent of corporate investments, bank
loans still finance the majority of China's corporate investments ... There is
no evidence that Chinese banks have begun to price their loans correctly. In
fact, to date there is hardly any differential pricing between banks. This year
[2006] the central bank has had to impose restrictions on banks from lending
to eleven major industries which are deemed to have suffered overcapacity
or overheated. If banks adequately control or price their own risks such
restrictive measures would have been unnecessary.

(Weijian Shan, *FEER*, November 2006, pp. 23–7)

State enterprises are likely to pay dividends for the first time in more than a
decade next year [2007] ... according to the head of the state industries
agency [SASAC] ... Li Rongrong [said] ... he hoped a proposal to reintroduce dividend payments would be approved early next year [2007] ...
Beijing stopped collecting dividends in 1994 when many were technically
bankrupt and could not afford to pay returns to the government, their main
shareholder ... Huge profits ... [have been made by] state enterprises in
recent years ... The 161 enterprises under SASAC supervision include

China's largest and most powerful oil, telecommunications, power and airline companies, many of which have listed subsidiaries on overseas stock markets. In addition, provincial offices of SASAC control scores of separate companies.

(*FT*, 5 December 2006, p. 10)

'About 60 per cent of private sector investment is funded from companies' own profits and another 20 per cent from banks; issuing shares accounts for only 10 per cent' (*The Economist*, 26 March 2007, p. 100).

Businesses in China remain overwhelmingly dependent on banks to raise money, counting on them for 85 per cent of their external financing last year [2006], while raising just 10 per cent of their money from bond issuance and 5 per cent from sales of stock.

(*IHT*, 25 May 2007, p. 11)

Household consumption is the lowest of any major economy. It fell to 36.4 per cent of GDP in 2006 from 37.7 per cent in 2005, when the comparable figures for the United States and India were 70 per cent and 61 per cent, respectively. The downward trend is not new: in 1990 China's ratio was 49 per cent.

(www.iht.com, 17 September 2007)

'The official *China Securities Journal* estimated that more than 60 per cent of last year's profits [2006] from state-owned enterprises were generated by just nine companies, including PetroChina, Baosteel and China Mobile' (www.iht.com, 18 December 2007).

The market in corporate bonds [is] a mainstay of any advanced economy, but tiny in China, where firms rely mainly on state-owned banks for credit ... Prospects for the bond market brightened last year [2007] when the securities regulator was empowered to authorize listed firms to issue bonds. Previously, the economic planning agency had been the gatekeeper, imposing strict quotas and conditions that stifled issuance. But then things got messy. The banking regulator, worried that banks were being exposed to undue risk, ordered them to stop guaranteeing corporate bonds. The insurance regulator concluded that if banks had to be shielded from risk, so did insurers. So it barred them from buying non-guaranteed bonds. The result? Still next to no corporate bond issues. Frustrated at the deadlock the People's Bank of China this month [April] created a new bond market at the stroke of a pen by extending, to five years, the maximum twelve-month tenor of commercial bills traded among banks. Seven companies duly sold an initial batch of $5.6 billion of medium-term notes last Tuesday [22 April]. But fund management companies were not among the investors: they were warned off by the securities regulator, which, according to market sources, said it needed time to evaluate the fledgling market.

(www.iht.com, 28 April 2008)

Trade union branches in enterprises

The first labour union at a Wal-Mart store in China has been formed following a lobbying campaign by the country's official union group ... Thirty employees at a Wal-Mart store in the south-eastern city of Quanzhou in Fujian province voted Saturday [29 July 2006] to form a union ... The official All-China Federation of Trade Unions has been lobbying Wal-Mart for two years in an attempt to organize the employees of its sixty stores in China and it has accused the company of obstructing its efforts. Wal-Mart opened its first outlet in China in 1996 and says it has 28,000 employees in China ... China does not allow independent unions ... There are official unions at 39,000 of China's 100,000 foreign companies.

(www.iht.com, 30 July 2006)

According to China's trade union law, enterprises or institutions with twenty-five employees and above should establish trade unions ... Wal-Mart has long battled to bar unions from its stores, particularly in the United States ... [In] the United States ... no employees are union members ... [Wal-Mart says] some Wal-Mart employees in Argentina, Brazil, Mexico, Britain and Germany are union members.

(*IHT*, 31 July 2006, p. 11)

After years of fighting unionization efforts at its stores, Wal-Mart, the world's largest retailer, said Wednesday [9 August] that it would work closely with Chinese officials to establish labour unions at its outlets here [China] ... The announcement came less than two weeks after Wal-Mart employees established their first union in China. Since then four more Wal-Mart stores in the country have formed unions ... The company has about sixty retail outlets and 30,000 employees here.

(*IHT*, 10 August 2006, p. 11)

Wal-Mart ... is allowing the establishment of a Communist Party committee in one of its Chinese stores. The news comes weeks after the world's biggest retailer accepted trade unions in its Chinese outlets ... The party branch has been set up in Wal-Mart's store in Shenyang in the north-east ... The committee had been set up on 12 August ... Companies qualify to form a committee only if at least three employees are already party members. Relatively few foreign multinationals, however, have party committees. Party committees are mandatory in state-owned enterprises, but differ in their role – some run political education campaigns while others are confined to human resources issues. The party has been pushing for years to extend its reach into private companies ... but with mixed success. A senior party official recently disclosed that 85 per cent of private companies eligible to have a committee had established them.

(*FT*, 25 August 2006, p. 5)

This month [August] Communist Party and Communist Youth League branches and a trade union were set up at a Wal-Mart outlet in the north-eastern industrial city of Shenyang [it was announced on 24 August] ... Wal-Mart, which has sixty stores in thirty Chinese cities ... [and] 30,000 ... resisted for two years before employees in the south-eastern city of Quanzhou successfully voted to set up a union in late July. The Shenyang Wal-Mart has only two party members and sixteen Communist Youth League members out of 389 employees, according to the official news agency Xinhua. But the Xinhua report stressed that the branch's basic function would be to promote better business. The party and youth league branches 'will encourage members to play an exemplary role in doing a good job and that will be helpful to business development', Xinhua quoted a Communist Party district leader in Shenyang as saying ... [he] said the groups would not interfere with management operations of the retailer ... China aims to unionize employees at 60 per cent of its foreign companies by the end of the year [2006].

(www.iht.com, 25 August 2006)

An official survey conducted two years ago found that trade unions had been established in a mere 10 per cent of half a million foreign-invested enterprises then registered in China ... The right to strike was removed from China's constitution in 1982 ... Since the 1990s the rapid growth of private, including foreign, enterprise and the widespread closure of state-owned firms has gutted unions from the urban workforce. It has also stripped the party of its own network of cells in workplaces, each of which once had both a union and a party committee ... Party rules require a cell in any enterprise with three or more party members ... By 1999 union membership had fallen to 87 million, down from a peak of 104 million in 1995 ... Official figures suggest the party is making headway. By the end of 2004 there were 55 million union members in non-state-owned enterprises, 35 per cent more than a year earlier and a more than fourfold increase compared with the late 1990s. In foreign-invested enterprises progress has been particularly striking. About one-third now have unions, official reports say. In some areas with large concentrations of such firms [such as Shanghai and Zhejiang province] unionization is even more widespread ... Two-thirds of Wal-Mart's supermarkets now have unions. In August the company's first two openly declared Communist Party cells were set up in the north-eastern city of Shenyang. Since unions are usually led by senior party members in a firm, it is likely there are others.

(*The Economist*, 23 September 2006, pp. 65–6)

Wal-Mart workers have set up unions in all sixty-six outlets [in China] ... capping what a senior Chinese union official described Thursday [12 October 2006] as the beginning of a wider campaign aimed at other foreign companies in China that are seen as traditionally anti-union ... [The official trade union body in China says that] about 6,000 of Wal-Mart's 30,000 employees in China were now union members ... The official All-China Federation of Trade Unions ... [said that] the success in unionizing Wal-Mart stores would be a springboard to similar campaigns aimed at foreign companies including Foxconn Electronics, Eastman Kodak and Dell ... The authorities will concentrate on high-profile foreign companies in densely populated areas. Companies that have a history of opposing unions will also be a top priority ... There are now more than 100,000 foreign companies operating in China, including businesses from Taiwan and Macao ... Employees are barred from organizing independent unions ... The official union already boasts 150 million members ... Some labour market analysts and human rights groups say establishing branches of the official union was aimed more at allowing Chinese authorities to tighten control over the rapidly expanding private sector work force ... Labour unrest is now common, particularly among the 150 million-strong army of migrant workers, and some experts suggest that an improved network of unions could assist the authorities in defusing protests that could potentially pose a threat to Communist Party rule ... Other political analysts have suggested that the authorities also want to expand the reach of the official union ... because of the decline of the state-owned sector ... China has been attempting to unionize workers in foreign companies for more than three years ... But reports in the official media suggested that efforts were intensified this year [2006] after President Hu Jintao in March issued instructions to accelerate the establishment of Communist Party organizations and trade unions in foreign companies. The official union later set a target of 60 per cent of foreign-funded enterprises to be unionized by 2006 and 80 per cent or more by the end of 2007 ... [The official trade union body says] that the target for 2006 would be met.

(www.iht.com, 12 October 2006; *IHT*, 13 October 2006, p. 14)

'[On 5 January 2007] the All-China Federation of Trade unions ... set a target of organizing unions at 70 per cent of foreign companies this year [2007] after meeting its goal of 60 per cent in a campaign begun last year [2006]' (*IHT*, 6 January 2007, p. 13).

The US fast-food giants McDonald's and KFC said Thursday [5 April] they were working with the Chinese authorities to resolve allegations that the companies underpay their part-time workers, as a labour investigation expanded to other cities ... The All-China Federation of Trade Unions, the national umbrella group for government-approved unions, is in the midst of a campaign to bolster the group's presence in foreign companies, which employ some 25 million people in China but until recently resisted allowing labour organizing.

(www.iht.com, 5 April 2007)

A year after Wal-Mart unionized all its stores in China ... McDonald's is co-operating with ... the All-China Federation of Trade Unions ... to allow

the formation of more union locals in its 670 outlets here ... The announcement came nearly two weeks after a state-controlled newspaper in Guangdong reported that some McDonald's, KFC and Pizza Hut restaurants in
Guangdong were violating the law by paying employees less than minimum
wage and denying some benefits. Officials at McDonald's and Yum!
Brands, which operates nearly 2,000 KFC and Pizza Hut outlets in
China, said they obey the law ... A McDonald's spokesman said the fast-
food chain has unionized some of its outlets in China and that even
before the pay allegations, the company had been co-operating with the official union in Guangzhou, the capital of Guangdong ... The All-China Federation of Trade Unions says its goal by the end of this year [2007] is to
have unions active in 70 per cent of the foreign-invested companies operating here ... [The union is] helping prepare a new draft labour law, expected
to pass sometime this year, that could expand the role of labour
organizations.

(*IHT*, 10 April 2007, p. 13)

'Worker abuse is common today in many of the Chinese factories that supply
Western companies goods for export to the United States and Europe, according
to labour rights groups and interviews with Chinese workers' (*IHT*, 5 January
2008, p. 15).

The All-China Federation of Trade Unions (ACFTU) [is] a monopoly that
claims 193 million members ... In January [2008] China imposed one of the
most far-reaching labour laws in the world ... The ACFTU ... has used the
new law as the basis for a huge registration drive by the ACFTU that began in
June [2008] and is intended to sign up 80 per cent of the largest foreign companies by the end of September [2008]. And that, in turn is a prelude to the
stated goal of having trade unions in all of China's non-state-owned companies by 2010 ... Firms that are willing to co-operate receive two critical
benefits: the ability to influence who their union chairman will be, and some
negotiating freedom around a 2 per cent payroll 'tax' to the national union,
much of which is remitted back to the municipal and company branches and,
in the best circumstances, may then be used to pay for social functions,
medical benefits and bereavement leave ... The ability to negotiate on the
payroll levy can mean, for example, that expatriate salaries are excluded from
the payroll figure, or that a smaller figure from a previous year is used as the
basis of the calculation ... Companies that resist ... will be subject to endless
audits, tax examinations and ... accusations of employment law violations
Two foreign fast-food chains Yum! Brands and McDonald's, agreed to worker
representation in 2007 after being slammed in the Chinese press for breaking
the law in their payments of students (the charges turned out to be false).

(*The Economist*, 2 August 2008, p. 68)

The role of the party in enterprises

[On 13 July 2006 it was announced] that a substantial number of new party members have been set up inside private companies. In a rare public disclosure one of the party's most senior officials said that 85 per cent of private companies eligible to have a committee had established them. Companies qualify to form a committee only if at least three employees are already party members ... Party committees are mandatory in state enterprises but vary greatly in their role, with some playing an active role in running political education campaigns, while others simply manage human resources. In a sign of the evolving partnership between business and the party, a group of entrepreneurs in Shenzhen, a city near Hong Kong dominated by the private sector, formed an official delegation to the city's annual party congress last year [2005], the first time that has happened, according to the local media. The entrepreneurs promised in return to help the party establish itself in many companies that had hitherto spurned it.

(FT, 14 July 2006, p. 9)

Wal-Mart ... is allowing the establishment of a Communist Party committee in one of its Chinese stores. The news comes weeks after the world's biggest retailer accepted trade unions in its Chinese outlets ... The party branch has been set up in Wal-Mart's store in Shenyang in the north-east ... The committee had been set up on 12 August ... Companies qualify to form a committee only if at least three employees are already party members. Relatively few foreign multinationals, however, have party committees. Party committees are mandatory in state-owned enterprises, but differ in their role – some run political education campaigns while others are confined to human resources issues. The party has been pushing for years to extend its reach into private companies ... but with mixed success. A senior party official recently disclosed that 85 per cent of private companies eligible to have a committee had established them.

(FT, 25 August 2006, p. 5)

An official survey conducted two years ago found that trade unions had been established in a mere 10 per cent of half a million foreign-invested enterprises then registered in China ... The right to strike was removed from China's constitution in 1982 ... Since the 1990s the rapid growth of private, including foreign, enterprise and the widespread closure of state-owned firms has gutted unions from the urban workforce. It has also stripped the party of its own network of cells in workplaces, each of which once had both a union and a party committee ... Party rules require a cell in any enterprise with three or more party members ... By 1999 union membership had fallen to 87 million, down from a peak of 104 million in 1995 ... Official figures suggest the party is making headway. By the end of 2004 there were 55 million union members in non-state-owned enterprises, 35 per cent more than a year earlier and a more than fourfold increase compared with the late 1990s. In foreign-invested enterprises progress has been particularly striking. About one-third now have unions, official reports say. In some areas with large concentrations of such firms [such as Shanghai and Zhejiang province] unionization is even more widespread ... Two-thirds of Wal-Mart's supermarkets now have unions. In August the company's first two openly declared Communist Party cells were set up in the north-eastern city of Shenyang. Since unions are usually led by senior party members in a firm, it is likely there are others.

(*The Economist*, 23 September 2006, pp. 65–6)

A Communist Party branch ... was set up Friday [15 December 2006] at Wal-Mart headquarters in Shenzhen ... as part of a campaign by the party to expand at foreign companies ... [Wal-Mart has] 36,000 employees and sixty-eight stores ... The Communist Party has about 70 million members ... The party branch at Wal-Mart headquarters is its sixth in China. The first was set up on 12 August in Shenyang ... Party officials there vowed not to interfere with the management of the store ... Many foreign companies in China already have party branches, either officially or unofficially. One of the earliest was at Motorola in Tianjin. That branch was officially set up in 1997, but news reports have said it was set up as early as 1990 and kept secret to avoid alarming Motorola management. The All-China Federation of Trade Unions ... has announced a goal of setting up unions at 60 per cent of China's 150,000 foreign companies by the end of this year [2006] ... Wal-Mart resisted the creation of unions at its Chinese stores for two years before agreeing in August [2006] to help the federation organize its workers ... The party has not disclosed its own expansion target.

(*IHT*, 19 December 2006, p. 15; www.iht.com, 18 December 2006)

The economic activities of the People's Liberation Army

(See Jeffries 2006a: 503–6.)

The economic activities of party and state officials

(See Jeffries 2006a: 506–7.)

The non-state non-agricultural sectors

The non-state sector includes:

1   the private sector, although in China the distinction is made between 'individual' enterprises (employing fewer than eight people) and 'private' enterprises (employing eight or more people);
2   foreign-invested enterprises (dealt with below);
3   collectives, mainly 'township-village enterprises' (TVEs).

The percentage of industrial output contributed by various sectors

In 1978 the state sector accounted for 78 per cent of industrial output (TVEs 21 per cent and the private sector 1 per cent). But the non-state sector has grown much more rapidly than the state sector. The share of the non-state sector in total industrial output increased from 24.5 per cent in 1980 (0.0 per cent for category 1, 0.5 per cent for category 2 and 24 per cent for category 3, respectively) to 47 per cent in 1991 (5.7 per cent, 5.7 per cent and 36 per cent, respectively) and 57 per cent in 1994. TVEs accounted for 10.9 per cent of total exports in 1987, 44.4 per cent in 1993 and 32.6 per cent in 1994 (Sachs and Woo 1996: 3).

During the period 1980 to 1997 the state's share of industrial output fell from 76 per cent to 25.5 per cent, while collectively owned enterprises saw their share increase from 23.6 per cent to 38.1 per cent. 'Other', including private firms and foreign joint ventures, increased from 0.5 per cent to 36.4 per cent (Smyth 2000: 724).

In 1994 state enterprises accounted for 43 per cent of industrial output (compared with 78 per cent in 1978) and employed about 70 per cent of industrial workers (*The Economist*, 10 June 1995, p. 69). In 1995 state enterprises accounted for less than one-third of industrial output, compared with over three-quarters in 1978 (*The Economist*, 14 December 1996, p. 87).

State enterprises generate 30 per cent of total industrial output (*FEER*, 21 May 1998, p. 14).

The share of state enterprises in industrial output fell from 77.6 per cent in 1978 to 28.8 per cent in 1996, although they still employed 57.4 per cent of urban workers in 1996 (Lin *et al.* 1998: 422).

The state sector's share of industrial output has fallen as follows: 1978, 78.0 per cent; 1988, 57.0 per cent; 1995, 34.0 per cent; 2000, 23.5 per cent (Hirschler 2002: 7).

In 1994 collectives accounted for 39 per cent of industrial output (*IHT*, 19 June 1995, p. 2).

In 1996 rural industrial enterprises contributed 26 per cent of GDP, 44 per cent of gross industrial output and 35 per cent of total earnings from exports (Smyth 1998: 784).

'Foreign-owned companies' share in the gross output of industrial enterprises rose from nothing in the early 1980s to 12 per cent in 1995 and 29 per cent in 2002' (*FT*, 9 December 2003, p. 21).

> Until the late 1970s China did not even keep official statistics on private enter-prises because they were illegal and negligible in number ... Before 1988 it was illegal for 'individual businesses' to hire more than eight workers because Karl Marx's *Das Kapital* indicated that businesses with more than eight employees were 'exploitative capitalist producers'. Private entrepreneurs found a way of getting around this restriction by simply registering their busi-nesses as 'collective enterprises'. This adaptive strategy became commonly known as 'wearing a red hat' ... [Some] 19.8 per cent of entrepreneurs sur-

veyed by official entities in 2000 indicated that they were already Communist Party members ... Today there are over 29 million private businesses, which employ over 200 million people and generate two-thirds of China's industrial output ... According to official surveys, 33.9 per cent of private entrepreneurs are now members of the Communist Party and, conversely, 2.86 million, or 4 per cent of party members, work in the private sector.

(Tsai 2008: 13–15)

The private sector as a whole as a percentage of GDP

In 1992 ... a survey by *The Economist* [28 November 1992] put the state sector at no more than 25 per cent of the economy ... Most analysts today guess that the private sector [as a whole] accounts for around 25 per cent of total output ... Fresh work in the latest *China Economic Quarterly* (CEQ), an independent publication, concludes that both guesses are way out ... Since 1978 [in agriculture] ... the transformation has nearly been completed ... Since half of China's 700 million workers are engaged in farm-related work, the privatization of farming is the biggest reason why three-quarters of China's workforce is today in private employment. The private contribution to ... construction, industry and mining is harder to measure, in part because many 'collectives' are private firms in disguise. But CEQ's educated guess is that 51 per cent of industrial GDP is now in private hands (including foreigners) ... Private firms [account for] just 37 per cent of services output. Rolling ... [all] sectors together gives an estimate for the private share of the whole economy of ... 53 per cent ... If agriculture and foreign-invested companies are stripped out the private sector shrinks to less than two-fifths of GDP.

(*The Economist*, 19 June 1999, p. 104)

'State enterprises that account for less than one-third of the country's output command more than two-thirds of all credit' (*The Economist*, 9 September 2000, p. 125).

Only about a third of China's economy is still directly controlled by the government through state-owned enterprises. But these are concentrated in key areas like defence and utilities. While many of the biggest state firms have publicly quoted subsidiaries on international stock markets, the government retains ultimate ownership ... The top 190 or so state-owned enterprises are directly controlled by the State Assets Supervision and Administration Commission – set up in 2003 to restructure these often moribund firms ... Two-thirds of the economy is in private hands ... [but] private companies are often beholden to state banks for capital and to local officials for favours and contracts.

(*The Economist*, 3 September 2005, pp. 63–4)

The OECD estimates that in 2003 private companies accounted for 63 per cent of China's business sector output (which in turn accounts for 94 per cent of GDP). This compares with 54 per cent in 1998 and virtually nothing in the 1970s. If you add in 'collective' enterprises, which are officially controlled by local government but in practice operate more like private firms, the private sector's share was 71 per cent in 2003.

(The Economist, 17 September 2005, p. 91)

[The] private sector accounts for some two-thirds of GDP ... Even outside agriculture it is often unclear whether a 'private' enterprise is really owned by individuals or by a local government or party unit. Conversely, some 'collective' or 'state' enterprises operate in ways indistinguishable from the private interests of their bosses.

(The Economist, 10 March 2007, p. 11)

Official figures show investment by the private sector in fixed assets such as factory buildings and machinery grew nearly threefold between 2000 and 2005. As a proportion of total fixed-assets investment the figures suggest little change (14 per cent to 16 per cent). But if investments by collective enterprises (many of which are private) are included in the private share, it has risen from 42 per cent to 60 per cent.

(p. 26)

'The non-state sector now accounts for 75 per cent of GDP if collective and agricultural output is included' (*FEER,* 12 July 2001, p. 49).

The private sector ... now accounts for half of China's GDP and 75 per cent if the essentially privatized activities of agriculture, rural collectives and shareholding companies are included, according to estimates by the World Bank's ... International Finance Corporation. The figure is expected to rise.

(FEER, 30 August 2001, p. 19)

The OECD (2005: website Chapter 2) provides information on the percentage of GDP contributed by the various sectors (value-added by firm ownership) in 1998 and 2003. The private sector accounted for 50.4 per cent and 59.2 per cent, respectively, for the two years. The public sector is split into state-controlled and collectively controlled firms (figures in brackets). In 1998 the public sector accounted for 49.6 per cent of GDP (36.9 and 12.7 percentage points, respectively), while the 2003 figure was 40.8 per cent (33.7 and 7.1 percentage points, respectively).

'According to the brokerage CLSA, the private sector is now responsible for more than 70 per cent of GDP and employs about 75 per cent of the total work force' (www.iht.com, 20 October 2006).

The private, non-agricultural sector as a percentage of GDP

The International Finance Corporation estimates that nearly half of the companies that call themselves collective should in fact be called private (*FT,* 11 May 2000, p. 14).

According to the International Finance Corporation (the private sector arm of the World Bank), in 1998 the state sector contributed 37 per cent of GDP. Private businesses generated 33 per cent, while the balance came from agricultural companies and businesses (*Transition*, 2000, vol. 11, no. 2, p. 40).

> By 1998 the domestic private sector had grown to about 27 per cent of GDP, making it second only to the state sector in economic importance. (The other sectors are the foreign, collective and agriculture sectors.) Despite its growing importance, at the end of 1999 the private sector accounted for only 1 per cent of bank lending and only 1 per cent of the companies listed on the Shanghai and Shenzhen stock exchanges were non-state firms ... Chinese firms rely more on internal sources of financing than do firms in transition and developed economies.
>
> (Neil Gregory and Stoyan Tenev, *Finance and Development*, 2001, vol. 38, no. 1, pp. 14–15)

'About 20 per cent of ... GDP last year [2000] came from its 1.2 million purely private enterprises' (*IHT*, 2 July 2001, p. 4).

> The private sector, concentrated on the country's south-eastern coast, remains a small slice of an economy still dominated by government-owned enterprises. Even the 800 million ostensibly independent farmers grow crops on state-owned land and sell grain to state-owned grain companies. Private companies, excluding those controlled by foreigners, accounted last year [1999] for less than 20 per cent of economic output.
>
> (Craig Smith, *IHT*, 13 July 2000, p. 16)

> Though many people cite figures that show China's economy is now mostly private, those data include foreign-owned and collectively owned businesses, most of which are still controlled at some level by the government. True private companies, those that are majority-owned by individuals, still account for less than 20 per cent of economic output and for only about 50 million jobs.
>
> (Craig Smith, *IHT*, 4 June 2001, p. 11)

'China's private sector is now responsible for 33 per cent of economic output, state-controlled media reported' (*IHT*, 8 April 2002, p. 11).

> Private firms now produce a third of China's GDP – just a few percentage points less than the state sector. In the first quarter of this year [2002] they created almost 30 per cent of new jobs. Many others came from what are known as 'collective enterprises', which in practice are often also privately run.
>
> (*FEER*, 16 May 2002, p. 24)

> China's private sector provides 25 per cent of GDP and is set to boom over the next few years ... the official *China Daily* quoted a National Bureau of Statistics report as saying. Some Western economists, however, estimate

that the non-state sector, including foreign firms, accounts for 50 per cent to 70 per cent of China's GDP.

(FEER, 17 October 2002, p. 28)

A Beijing think-tank reckons that the private sector contributes just over 60 per cent of GDP, counting TVEs and businesses with foreign investors (worth about 15 per cent). Yet the World Bank's report in January 2003 put the share as low as a third.

(The Economist, Survey, 20 March 2004, p. 15)

'While small and mid-sized private enterprises account for nearly 50 per cent of GDP, they only receive 10 per cent to 15 per cent of China's total commercial loans' *(FEER,* 18 September 2003, p. 48). 'According to the Asian Development Bank, SMEs account for 60 per cent of industrial output ... Most of these companies are now privately run' *(FEER,* 17 June 2004, p. 34).

The Chinese government estimates that the private sector now accounts for a third of the economy, up from less than 1 per cent in 1978. Analysts say the private sector's share is much higher than official figures suggest. However, assessing that share is complicated by the opaque ownership of many companies and their shareholding structures.

(FT, Money and Business, 25 February 2005, p. 6)

'[According to the OECD] the private sector now generates between 57 per cent and 65 per cent of non-farm GDP, depending on how it is measured' *(FT,* 17 September 2005, p. 6).

Precise measurement of the size of the private sector is difficult, but a definition which considers as private all companies that are controlled neither by state nor collective shareholders suggests that the private sector was responsible for as much as 57 per cent of the value-added produced by the non-farm business sector in 2003. Even amongst larger companies in the industrial sector the private sector produced over half of value-added in 2003 and that share appears to have risen even further in the following two years.

(OECD 2005: website Chapter 2)

The OECD (website Chapter 2) provides information on the percentage of value-added by firm ownership for 1998 and 2003. The non-farm business sector (79 per cent of GDP) is divided into the private sector (43.0 per cent and 57.1 per cent, respectively, for the two years) and the public sector (57.0 per cent and 42.9 per cent respectively: this is further split into state-controlled firms and collectively-controlled firms – 40.5 percentage points and 16.5 percentage points respectively for 1998, and 34.1 percentage points and 8.8 percentage points respectively for 2003).

Small and medium enterprises ... [were] virtually non-existent in 1979 ... [They] numbered around 1 million by 1990 and 8 million by 2001. Today they total around 60 million. The smallest have just a handful of workers, and the largest of the medium-sized ones, according to the government's definitions, employ no more than 2,000 people. Yet together they account for 60 per cent of China's GDP and half its tax revenues. More than 95 per cent are privately owned ... They are responsible for 66 per cent of the country's patent applications and more than 80 per cent of its new products. They are also responsible for 68 per cent of China's exports, and it is this last figure that has made the current hard times especially difficult for them ... In the short term smaller firms' fortunes are lagging ... Much of ... the 4 trillion yuan ($586 billion) stimulus package launched last November [2008] ... has been directed toward the sort of infrastructure projects that are dominated by large state-owned enterprises ... Of more than 7 trillion yuan loaned out in the first half of this year [2009] by Chinese banks, only an estimated 10 per cent has gone to smaller firms. Much of China's bank lending remains politically driven, putting state enterprises at a great advantage. Smaller firms have fared little better with lending decisions made on commercial terms ... There are fresh signs that officials recognize the need to level the field. State news media this month [September] reported plans for new measures aimed at improving access to capital for smaller businesses, including the establishment of two dedicated investment funds totalling 4 billion yuan.

(*The Economist*, 12 September 2009, pp. 78–9)

'Last year [2008], on official figures, state-controlled firms accounted for 28.4 per cent of output by larger industrial enterprises' (*The Economist*, 14 November 2009, p. 74).

(The 2004 upward revision of GDP has, of course, implications for the above estimates of the importance of the non-state sector in GDP. The main reason given for the upward revision was the considerable underestimation of the private service sector.)

[There is a] phenomenon known commonly as *guojinmintui*, or 'the state advances as the private sector recedes'. Leaders have repeatedly denied that the government is implementing a policy of renationalizing parts of the economy and most analysts agree there is not formal policy to support *guojinmintui*. But some argue that the government's response to the financial crisis has allowed state-owned enterprises ... partially to reverse the privatization that has occurred in China over the last thirty years ... [There is the argument] that China's enormous credit-fuelled rescue plan has been focused on supporting the state sector, leaving many smaller private companies to go under, even though they make up the most dynamic part of the economy and provide the most jobs ... Analysts say struggling, privately owned petrol stations are being rapidly acquired by state monopolies such as PetroChina, while many private real estate developers are unable to compete with well-funded state giants.

(*FT*, 25 August 2009, p. 7)

[There are] claims that there has been creeping renationalization during the last year ... Critics say that the stimulus measures have been accompanied by the state reasserting control over some sections of the economy ... The dominance of state-owned enterprises is being reasserted in a range of industries, including airlines, steel and coal mining at the expense of private ownership – a phenomenon that has been called *guojinmintui*, translated as 'the state advances as the private sector recedes'. Most of the country's privately owned airlines that were set up in recent years have been absorbed by loss-making state competitors in virtual hostile takeovers, while Rizhao Steel, a prominent private steel company, agreed to sell a majority stake to a state-owned rival under strong political pressure ... Rizhao Steel, one of the largest privately owned companies, sold a majority stake to a state-owned rival in September [2009] under heavy political pressure. Most privately owned airlines have been absorbed by state-owned rivals ... While Beijing has not advocated renationalization as a goal, officials and businesspeople say the government's policies have had that effect, particularly since the onset of the global financial crisis last year [2008].

(*FT*, 26 November 2009, p. 7)

China Mobile said Wednesday [10 March 2010] it would pay $5.8 billion for 20 per cent of Shanghai Pudong Development Bank as part of a strategy to achieve dominance in the country's nascent mobile e-commerce market. China Mobile, which has more than 500 million subscribers, said it would develop mobile finance and e-commerce services with the bank. Such services, which allow customers to buy and pay for products and services using their cellphones, are seen as a crucial future source of revenue for telecommunications companies.

(*IHT*, 11 March 2010, p. 21)

The underground economy

'According to recently published official figures ... the underground economy is the equivalent of 20 per cent of GDP (actually twice that, say independent estimates)' (*FEER*, 21 June 2001, p. 60). 'The chief economist at CLSA in Hong Kong ... argues that China's underground economy is worth anywhere between 50 per cent and 100 per cent of official GDP' (*FEER*, 17 June 2004. p. 35).

Township-village enterprises (TVEs)

'The larger villages or small rural towns are known ... [as] townships' (*The Economist*, 20 July 2002, pp. 67–8).

TVEs have aroused the greatest interest. They have to survive in a competitive atmosphere and face hard budget constraints.

Weitzman (Weitzman and Xu 1993: 550–5) describes the TVE as the driving force of the Chinese model. The TVE is a vaguely defined co-operative ... a communal organization about as far removed from having a well-defined ownership structure as can be imagined ... Legally, the TVE is collectively owned by all the people in the community where it is located. There is no stipulation of any individual owners nor does anyone have rights to appropriate assets of the firm. There are no shares at all, formally speaking ... Reward structures are extremely vague and informal.

Naughton (1994: 266–70) says that TVEs are controlled by township and village governments. In most cases that have been studied township and village officials in their official capacity possess all the key components of property rights.

Bolton (1995: 7) suggests possible advantages of township-village governments in terms of corporate control (they appoint and monitor managers). But critics of TVEs point to weaknesses of township-village governments in terms of short time horizons (they may be moved on) and local corruption and the limited role of workers in decision-making. In the long term the importance of TVEs is likely to decline as a more individually orientated society develops and conventional property rights become more important.

Chow (1997: 322) notes the advantages possessed by TVEs stemming from 'the local government's power to enforce contracts and from the credibility of such a "public" enterprise in raising funds as compared with an entirely private enterprise'.

In the mid-1980s the commune structure was dismantled and townships and villages assumed responsibilities for rural enterprises (Smyth 1998: 786). Commune and brigade enterprises were renamed township and village enterprises (TVEs) (p. 285).

Woo is sceptical of some of the reasons put forward to explain the importance of TVEs, such as culture, a lack of entrepreneurs, the raising of capital and reducing the principal-agent problem. He favours explanations such as the early restrictions on private ownership, tax and other benefits endowed upon TVEs and early low labour mobility (Woo 1997: 316–17).

Many of China's once-booming township enterprises are being privatized in an effort to revive flagging rural industry ... In recent years ... the township enterprise miracle has started to fade ... With so many domestic and foreign companies rushing to get a piece of China's booming market in the first half of the 1990s, China today has a surplus of just about everything, especially the low-value-added, labour-intensive items ... In this intensely competitive environment only the best-managed and most efficient companies will survive. While some township enterprises have made the changes necessary to remain contenders, many have not, underscoring the limitations of the township-owned model. Low-skilled labour, unsophisticated management and capital shortages make it difficult for many of these firms to upgrade quality, move into higher-value types of manufacturing and increase their scale of production ... [Local] government intervention [means] ... that town-appointed managers are not held responsible for failures ... Ideological objections to private ownership have relaxed over the past few years – a trend formally sanctioned at September's Fifteenth Party Congress.

(Pamela Yatsko, *FEER*, 5 February 1998, pp. 52–3)

'The township and village enterprises that fuelled China's economic growth for most of the past fifteen years are flagging as their low-tech, low-wage approaches reach their limits' (Steven Mufson, *IHT*, 13 April 1998, p. 13).

'Increasingly sophisticated urban corporations with easy access to capital have driven many TVEs to the brink of financial collapse' (*FT*, 25 July 2000, p. 22).

'Township enterprises that brought wealth and jobs to millions of rural Chinese are faltering in many areas' (*IHT*, 5 September 2000, p. 5).

Since 1988 there have been experiments with 'shareholding co-operatives':

1   The 'shareholding co-operative system' is an experiment which has been running since 1988 'in order to improve some of the TVEs' internal drawbacks: to define the property rights of the TVE, to improve the incentive system and democratic management, strengthen the role of entrepreneurs and to attract scarce resources'. By May 1995 the number of 'shareholding co-operatives' had increased to 204,000 or 12.4 per cent of all TVEs. 'The main idea of a co-operative is participation, democracy and the principle of one and equal voice for each member. The main idea behind "shareholding" is the preference of capital (on workers) and allocation according to one's shares' (Amir Helman, *The CEA (UK) Newsletter*, December 1996, vol. 8, no. 4, pp. 24–5).

2   TVEs face problems in terms of interference by local governments, decreased incentives to invest locally when labour mobility increases, the attractions of risk diversification, increasing difficulties of raising outside capital and restrictions on managerial autonomy (Woo 1997: 317–19). 'In addition to the above five problems, there has been a recent development that has pushed the TVEs to "clarify" their property rights. The capacity expansion of many of the coastal TVEs in southern China has forced them to rely increasingly on migrant labour from the poorer provinces. The original inhabitants want to prevent the new residents from having an automatic share in the dividends of the collective-owned enterprises, and so they have corporatized the TVEs and divided the shares among themselves' (p. 320). 'Many TVEs have transformed themselves into shareholding corporations in the search for a more efficient organizational form, but their shares are legally not transferable' (p. 300). 'The fact that there are informal markets for these legally non-transferable shares speaks volumes about popular expectations about the future institutional basis of economic transactions in China' (p. 322).

3   'As rural enterprises have started to get bigger and become more marketized, informal relationships are no longer sufficient. For example, in the start-up phase in southern Jiangsu it was common for the township or village government (TVG) to provide either financial assistance or a guarantee to the lending organization to help the rural enterprise to raise capital. Toward the

end of 1997 the ministry of agriculture issued "proposals for expanding the reform of township enterprises". As a result, China has started to experiment with such alternative forms as joint stock companies and shareholding co-operatives as well as mergers, outright sales and bankruptcies' (Smyth 1998: 785). 'The downside of TVEs with strong TVG involvement is that it is difficult to know who is the true owner. This places the TVG in a powerful position to use profits from TVEs to finance municipal government budgets or cross subsidize unprofitable enterprises under its control' (p. 791). 'Many large rural enterprises have formed enterprise groups and/or converted to joint stock limited liability companies ... Large firms are being encouraged to form enterprise groups with both other rural enterprises and entities with different ownership forms such as private firms, local SOEs and research institutions like universities ... In addition, a number of larger rural enterprises have been converted into joint stock or limited liability companies in which each shareholder's liability is proportionate to his/her investment' (pp. 792–4). 'The major avenue for reforming small and medium-sized rural enterprises has been to transform them into shareholding co-operatives ... Under the shareholding (or Shandong) model, management and workers are sold shares in the enterprise.' At the end of 1995 there were over 3 million shareholding co-operatives accounting for more than 10 per cent of rural enterprises (p. 795). 'A number of benefits have been claimed for shareholding co-operatives ... It is argued that it clarifies the relationship between TVE and TVG through creating a "government share" in the enterprise ... In most instances it accounts for about 20 per cent to 25 per cent of total shares, but in some cases it is higher ... Issuing shares provides a means provides a means to raise capital from management and workers' (p. 796). 'Other approaches that have been used in small enterprise reform include auction or sale to private investors and joint ventures with domestic and foreign investors' (p. 797). 'While recent reforms have brought a range of benefits there are still a number of problems ... In some instances workers have been forced to invest their savings in purchasing shares ... One of the objectives of introducing shareholding co-operatives is to make the workers the true owners of the enterprise. It is thought that if ownership is clarified internal management will be improved; however, in practice in many cases shareholding co-operatives have not reduced the power of local government ... In some cases local government continue to exercise tight control over the appointment of managers even after the reforms' (pp. 797–8).

Along the eastern seaboard these ... rural industries ... developed rapidly from the mid-1980s to the mid-1990s (far less in inland areas such as Henan) ... By the end of 1996 they employed 135 million people, contributing nearly half of China's exports, compared with one-sixth at the beginning of the decade. But since then they have gone into decline. Last year [2001 the number of] rural enterprises fell by 620,000 and employment was down 5 million on the 1996 peak ... Many were, in effect, under the control of township and village governments ... resulting in poor management and irrational investment decisions. Many of these have now been privatized, but the private sector is especially starved of capital ... Many small and isolated rural enterprises will be unable to compete as larger-scale private businesses develop in urban areas.

(The Economist, Survey, 15 June 2002, p. 11)

'Entry occurred rapidly in China [in the period 1979–84]. Most of the new entrants were not private firms, but rural enterprises run by local governments, called township and village enterprises' (McMillan and Woodruff 2002: 157).

These firms were publicly owned, by communities of a few thousand people. They were managed by village government, and the profits were shared between villagers and local government by explicit rules. Around 60 per cent of profits were reinvested, and the remainder was paid as bonuses to workers or used for local public goods such as education, roads and irrigation. Managerial discipline ... came from the fact that these enterprises had no access to government subsidies to cover any losses and faced intensely competitive product markets ... [They] received some benefits from having village government as a partner. Access to state banks and to rationed inputs was eased [for example] ... After a decade and a half of growth they began to be privatized. By the late 1990s more than a half of them were partially or fully privately owned [citing Hongbin Li and Scott Rozells, *Agricultural Economics*, 2000, vol. 23, no. 3, pp. 241–52].

(p. 165)

5   The 'open door' policy

In 1978 the policy was announced of opening up the economy to foreign trade, capital, technology and know-how in order to modernize and speed up the growth of the economy:

Foreign trade

The importance of foreign trade to the Chinese economy has increased substantially, as the following indicators show:

1   China has climbed rapidly in the world ranking of exporters from its position at number thirty-two in 1978.
2   Foreign trade as a percentage of GDP has increased to a remarkable extent and of late there are signs that China's exports are improving as regards value-added.
3   China became a net importer of both grain and oil in 1993.
4   China has not typically run large foreign trade surpluses, but the surplus surged in and after 2005.
5   Tariffs have been reduced, a trend encouraged by WTO commitments.
6   The state monopoly of foreign trade was ended and an increasing number of state enterprises were allowed to conduct foreign trade on their own and to retain a percentage of foreign exchange earnings.

China's rapid climb in the world ranking of exporters

China has climbed rapidly in the world ranking of exporters from its position at number thirty-two in 1978.

'[China is] the world's ... fifth largest trading power' (*FEER*, 27 September 2001, p. 12).

'By 2000 China was the seventh largest trading nation' (Nicholas Lardy, *Foreign Policy*, March–April, 2002, p. 20).

'China ... was the world's fifth largest importer last year [2000]' (Mike Moore, director-general of the WTO, *IHT*, 19 September 2001, p. 10).

'China, the world's fifth largest exporter last year [2002], accounted for 5.1 per cent of global exports' (*FEER*, 17 April 2003, p. 24).

> In a little over two decades China has jumped from being an insignificant trading nation to rank fourth behind the United States, Germany and Japan, according to the WTO's 2001 figures. In that year China accounted for 5.6 per cent of global exports and 4.9 per cent of imports. US exports were 11.9 per cent of the world total and imports 18.3 per cent.
>
> (*FEER*, 18 September 2003, pp. 32–3)

'Between 1980 and 2002 China's share in global exports and imports rose from 1.2 per cent and 1.1 per cent to 5.2 per cent and 4.2 per cent, respectively' (*FT*, 12 November 2003, p. 23).

'[In 2004, according to the World Trade Organization China, overtook] Japan as the world's third largest exporter' (*FT*, 15 April 2005, p. 9).

'[China is] the third largest exporter and importer' (*FT*, 31 August 2005, p. 14).

'Total foreign trade topped $1.4 trillion ... in 2005 ... making China the world's third largest foreign trader after the United States and Germany' (*IHT*, 12 January 2006, p. 11).

'China's share of the world's exported goods tripled to 7.3 per cent between 1993 and 2005' (*The Economist*, 13 January 2007, p. 68).

'[In 2007] China's exports ... made up almost 9 per cent of the world's total' (www.iht.com, 1 July 2008).

The remarkable increase of foreign trade as a percentage of GDP

Foreign trade as a percentage of GDP has increased to a remarkable extent and of late there are signs that China's exports are improving as regards value-added.

It is important to stress that *both* exports and imports have grown rapidly, a sign of increasing overall integration into the world economy that contrasts with the experience of Japan (which stressed exports).

> Through foreign direct investment China runs a huge processing operation for the world on behalf of multinational corporations. This is one reason why its trade/GDP ratio is inordinately high for a continental country – more than 40 per cent compared with about 20 per cent for the United States.
>
> (*FT*, 8 June 2004, p. 19)

> Exports are ... worth around 20 per cent of GDP and the value-added is low, with about half of all exports consisting of processed imports ... The preponderance of low-technology consumer exports like toys and shoes has protected China from the plunge in electronics demand that has hammered Taiwan and [South] Korea.
>
> (*FEER*, 25 October 2001, p. 68)

> While the ratio of exports to GDP for China is relatively high (22 per cent), the impact of slowing external demand on China's overall economic growth

is unlikely to be as large as that for many other Asian economies. One reason is that a substantial proportion of China's exports consists of simple processing of imported materials with low value-added.

(United Nations, World Economic and Social Survey 2001, p. 108)

'The trade-to-GDP ratio increased from 10 per cent at the beginning of the reforms to about 40 per cent in the late 1990s' (*Finance and Development*, 2002, vol. 39, no. 3, p. 22).

'China's ... ratio of trade to GDP at market prices was 44 per cent in 2001' (*FT*, 12 November 2003, p. 23).

'The sum of exports and imports – a traditional measure of a country's openness to trade – now amounts to more than 50 per cent, compared with 20 per cent of GDP in 1989 and less than 10 per cent of GDP in 1979' (Prasad and Rumbaugh 2003: 46–9).

'Last year [2004] the ratio of trade to GDP, at market prices, reached 70 per cent, much the same as in South Korea ... The United States and Japan have ratios of trade to GDP that are below 25 per cent' (*FT*, 5 September 2005, p. 17).

For its size ... [China] is unusually open to the rest of the world in terms of trade and foreign direct investment. The sum of its total exports and imports of goods and services amounts to around 75 per cent of China's GDP; in Japan, India and Brazil the figure is 25 per cent to 30 per cent.

(*The Economist*, 30 July 2005, p. 66)

'[China has] a trade-to-GDP ratio of around 70 per cent' (*The Economist*, Survey, 31 March 2007, p. 6).

'Exports make up 38 per cent of China's economy, World Bank data say' (*IHT*, 9 July 2007).

'Exports' share of GDP has doubled in the past decade to 40 per cent – more than twice that of the United States or Japan' (www.iht.com, 17 September 2007).

Innovation has become a national buzzword and Chinese leaders have been tossing it into their speeches since the beginning of the year, when President Hu Jintao started an ambitious campaign to drive China's economy up the value chain ... In launching their National and Medium-term Programme for Scientific and Technological Development (2006–20), President Hu, prime minister Wen Jiabao and other top officials have vowed to spend more on science and technology, and to insist on business reforms. Their goal is to move China beyond its dependence on natural resources and cheap labour, and stake its place among the economies that depend on education and information technology ... One target is to reduce China's dependence on imported technology to 30 per cent or less by 2020 ... The plan also calls for an increase in research and development from its current 1.23 per cent of GDP to 2.5 per cent by 2020, putting it in the same range as OECD countries' current scores.

(*The Economist*, 5 August 2006, pp. 50–1)

'The mainland spent ten years from 1990 until 2000 taking over low-end markets, and for the last five years has been rapidly gaining market share in electronics' (Jonathan Anderson, *FEER*, September 2006, p. 14).

> A surge in high-tech exports (in 2005, telecoms equipment, electronics and computers accounted for 43 per cent of China's exports by value) might look like a leap up the value chain. Yet assembling many 'high-tech' products is not that different from making ... [for example a] talking toy ... After all, laptops [for example] are simply assembled from foreign components ... Most of the firms involved are foreign, accounting for three-fifths of all Chinese exports, four-fifths of exports assembled from imported parts and components and nearly nine-tenths of the high-tech stuff.
>
> (*The Economist*, Survey, 31 March 2007, p. 11)

'Elecronic products accounted for 42 per cent of total manufactured exports in 2006, up from 18 per cent in 1995' (*The Economist*, 5 January 2008, p. 67).

'[On 18 March 2007] the government made public a decision to step up efforts to make [large] passenger aircraft, a first step in challenging Boeing and Airbus, the world's dominant plane makers' (www.ijht.com, 20 March 2007). 'China's recent announcement of its intention to produce large jets and Intel's plans to set up a chip plant ... [are cited] as examples of how hard Beijing is working to shift manufacturing and exports to higher value-added products' (*IHT*, 10 April 2007, p. 14).

> China plans to rely more on its own designs and technology as it expands the world's third longest rail network, which would hand market share to Chinese makers at the expense of Alstrom of France and Siemens of Germany, the world's biggest producers of locomotives and rolling stock.
>
> (www.iht.com, 20 March 2007)

> China is now going through a more subtle phase. It is becoming a giant test bed for manufacturing ideas, building on its existing strengths in low-cost production by using efforts of engineers and developers not just in China but from around the world ... [For example] in Nanjing engineers working for BASF are finalizing ambitious plans ... A joint venture between the German chemicals manufacturer and Sinopec, the Chinese energy group ... [is] intended [not only] to boost output ... [but also to] gain expertise in combining China's famed low costs with the development of new design and production skills ... This will involve importing ideas from BASF's operations around the world and linking these with concepts developed by BASF's 6,000-strong staff in China, including a team of 100 research and development engineers.
>
> (*FT*, 29 May 2008, p. 13)

> Chinese companies are moving up the value chain ... The government is ... using incentives to encourage companies to innovate, but also moving to discourage low-end manufacturers from operating in south-eastern China ... By introducing tougher labour and environmental standards and ending tax

breaks for thousands of factories, the government has sent a powerful signal about its desire to have Chinese companies move up the value chain, and also helped fuel an exodus of factories from an area long considered the shop floor of the world ... In some ways the government is only riding the currents that come with strong economic growth. For instance, many manufacturers in south-east China are moving to the interior, where land and labour costs are cheaper, or expanding operations in lower costs countries like India, Vietnam or Bangladesh.

(*IHT*, 31 July 2008, pp. 1, 10)

There are critics of traditional estimates of the importance of exports as a proportion of GDP:

Up to half of China's exports are made up of intermediate and semi-finished products imported from other countries to be processed and shipped out again. If the double accounting of the import content is stripped out, the ratio of China's exports to its GDP tumbles to about 18 per cent of the 36 per cent seen in the crude data.

(Qu Hongbin, *IHT*, 12 October 2005, p. 8)

Headline figures show that China's exports surged from 20 per cent of GDP in 2001 to almost 40 per cent in 2007 ... The headline ratio of exports to GDP [however] is very misleading ... Exports are measured as gross revenue while GDP is measured in value-added terms. Jonathan Anderson, an economist at UBS, a bank, has tried to estimate exports in value-added terms by stripping out imported components, and then converting the remaining domestic content into value-added terms by subtracting inputs purchased from other domestic sectors ... Once these adjustments are made, Mr Anderson reckons that the 'true' export share is just under 10 per cent of GDP.

(*The Economist*, 5 January 2008, p. 67)

'Exports account for 40 per cent of GDP, but those exports have a large import content; only a quarter of the value of China's exports is added locally' (*The Economist*, 21 October 2006, p. 92).

China's exports account for 36 per cent of GDP, but about half of them are 'processing exports', which contain a lot of imported components. Thus the impact of a fall in exports is partially offset if imports fall too. Estimates suggest that domestic value-added from Chinese exports is a more modest 18 per cent of GDP. An alternative measure of the importance of exports is the change in net exports in real terms. Between 2002 and 2007 the increase in net exports contributed only 15 per cent of real GDP growth in China. In contrast, net exports accounted for half of all growth in Singapore and Taiwan. This measure understates the total impact, though, because it ignores the spillover effects of exports on business confidence, investment, employment and consumer spending.

(*The Economist*, 31 January 2009, p. 74)

Economists have long argued about the role of exports … Jonathan Anderson, an economist at UBS, argues that only about 8 per cent of the work force is actually employed in export industries and that, even at the peak of recent trade expansion, net exports accounted for only about a sixth of growth … Although China's headline export figures are huge, some researchers believe this greatly exaggerates the importance of the sector, because many export factories only assemble parts manufactured elsewhere.

(*FT*, 16 April 2009, p. 6)

'Exports count for nearly 40 per cent of GDP, but they use a lot of imported components, and make up about 18 per cent of domestic value-added. Fewer than 10 per cent of jobs are in the export sector' (www.economist.com, 16 April 2009; *The Economist*, 18 April 2009, p. 83).

China as a net importer of grain and oil

China became a net importer of both grain and oil in 1993.

'Since 1993 China has become a net oil importer' (*IHT*, 12 April 2005, p. 6).

'China overtook Japan last year [2003] to become the world's second largest oil consumer' (*FEER*, 10 June 2004, p. 27). 'Last year [2003] China surpassed Japan to become the world's second largest consumer of oil after the United States' (*FEER*, 17 June 2004, p. 31).

'China imports 35 per cent [of its oil], of which 60 per cent is from the Gulf' (*IHT*, 9 February 2006, p. 8). 'China … relies on the Middle East for nearly 60 per cent of its imports [of oil], energy experts say, and that dependence is expected to grow in the years ahead' (*IHT*, 20 September 2006, p. 3). 'Oil imports from Saudi Arabia … account for 14 per cent of China's total oil imports' (*IHT*, 24 January 2006, p. 12).

'For the first time in twenty years China became a net importer of food last year [2004]' (*FT*, 28 July 2005, p. 10).

(Further statistics on China's impact on world commodity markets are given in the section on economic performance.)

The surge in China's foreign trade surpluses

China has not typically run large foreign trade surpluses, but the surplus surged in and after 2005.

'After a sharp rise in China's overall trade surplus during 1993–7 the surplus has remained relatively stable in the range of about $35 billion to $45 billion since 1997' (Prasad and Rumbaugh 2003: 49).

'China ran a trade surplus in 2004 of $31.9 billion, the highest since 1998 (*The Economist*, 15 January 2005, p. 102).

China said Wednesday [11 January 2006] that its trade surplus with the rest of the world tripled in 2005 to a record $102 billion … [China's official estimate of its] trade surplus with the United States reached a record $114.7

billion ... Excluding the United States, China actually had a trade deficit with the rest of the world of about $12 billion in 2005, largely with Japan and oil exporting countries.

(*IHT*, 12 January 2006, p. 11)

('[China's] current account surplus doubled last year [2005] to $125 billion: www.iht.com, 27 February 2006.)

The United States continually complains about its huge bilateral trade deficit with China. (The United States has exerted pressure on China to revalue its currency against the dollar: see below.)

'China said its trade surplus with the United States was $42.7 billion last year [2002] ... while the United States, which counts exports through Hong Kong, estimates its deficit at about $100 billion' (*FEER*, 27 February 2003, p. 28).

'The United States puts the trade surplus at $103 billion (*FT*, 24 February 2003, p. 7).

'In 2002, according to the United States, China's trade surplus was $103 billion. China said it was only $43 billion' (*FT*, 30 October 2003, p. 2). The figure of $103 billion 'surpassed the size of Japan's surplus for the first time' (*FT*, 3 September 2003, p. 11).

The United States said that in 2003 the surplus was $124 billion compared with China's figure of $58.6 billion (*The Economist*, 17 April 2004, p. 60).

[The United States claims that] the US deficit with China in 2004 was $162 billion ... China says the deficit is only $80 billion ... The United States counts exports from Hong Kong as Chinese exports, and China does not include exports from the mainland to the United States from China-based American companies.

(*FT*, 22 March 2005, p. 10)

[China's official estimate of its] trade surplus with the United States reached a record $114.7 billion ... in 2005 ... up from $80 billion a year earlier and $28 billion in 2001 ... [According to the United States] through October 2005 China already had a trade surplus of over $166 billion.

(*IHT*, 12 January 2006, p. 11)

Despite the big shift to China, US imports from Asia as a whole have hardly changed in the last fifteen years ... Asia's share of imports into the United States has held remarkably steady, at 38 per cent ... While China now has an estimated $200 billion trade surplus with the United States, it also has a $137 billion trade deficit with the rest of Asia.

(*IHT*, 10 February 2006, pp. 1, 6)

'[According to the United States, in 2005 the] US trade deficit with China [increased] to a record $201.6 billion' (*IHT*, 16 February 2006, p. 18). '[The] US trade deficit [as a whole in 2005 reached a] record $725.8 billion' (*IHT*, 15 February 2006, p. 13).

'The US ... balance of payments ... deficit with mainland China accounts for only a quarter of its overall deficit ... [China] ran a current account surplus of about $150 billion last year [2005]' (*FT*, 19 April 2006, p. 15).

'China's trade surplus last year [2006] jumped to a record $177.47 billion' (www.iht.com, 10 January 2007).

> China's trade surplus reached $177.5 billion last year [2006] ... up from $102 billion in 2005 and $32 billion in 2004 ... The bilateral deficit with the United States is even higher according to the Washington's measure, reaching an all-time high of $214 billion in the eleven months to November [2006]. The gap between Beijing's and Washington's measure of the value of their bilateral trade is explained in large part by the US classification of value-added exports from Hong Kong as Chinese.
>
> (*FT*, 11 January 2007, p. 8)

> The United States ran its largest trade deficit in history in 2006 ... For all of 2006 the trade imbalance expanded to a record $763.6 billion – a fifth consecutive annual record ... The deficit with China shot up 15.4 per cent last year [2006] to total $232.5 billion, the largest imbalance ever recorded with any country.
>
> (www.iht.com, 13 February 2007)

'By China's assessment ... China's surplus in bilateral trade [in 2006] ... was $144 billion' (www.iht.com, 13 April 2007).

'China's trade surplus with America increased to $233 billion last year [2006], accounting for almost 30 per cent of America's total deficit' (*The Economist*, 19 May 2007, p. 79).

'China's total current account surplus reached an estimated $250 billion [in 2006], or 9 per cent of GDP, up from only 1 per cent in 2001' (*The Economist*, 19 May 2007, p. 79).

'China's current account surplus for 2006 was $249.9 billion or 9.5 per cent of GDP, well ahead of consensus predictions of twelve months ago' (*FT*, 12 May 2007, p. 8).

> [China has] rising trade surpluses with the United States and roaring surpluses with Europe. But when it comes to the rest of the world, it is running a trade deficit ... Chinese statistics show surpluses with individual countries far smaller than those shown by figures released by China's trade partners. For 2005, the US Treasury reported this week, the total deficits reported by all of China's trade partners came to $423 billion, while China reported a surplus of only $117 billion. The American report concluded that most, but not all, of the discrepancy could be explained by two factors. First, China, like most countries, includes the costs of shipping and insurance in their import figures, but not their exports. Second, many exports to Hong Kong are reexported to other countries, and show up as Chinese imports in those countries' figures.
>
> (www.iht.com, 15 June 2007)

[In 2007 China's] annual trade surplus ballooned to $262.2 billion, up 47.7 per cent from 2006 ... [and the bilateral] surplus with the United States rose 19 per cent to $163.3 billion [according to official Chinese figures] ... [China says that its] 2007 trade gap with the EU rose faster, expanding by 46 per cent to $134.3 billion.

(www.iht.com, 11 January 2008)

(In 2005 China's bilateral trade surplus with the EU was $70.1 billion, rising to $91.7 billion in 2006: *IHT*, 29 January 2007, p. 11.)

'[In 2007] the EU replaced the United States as China's largest export market' (*FT*, 12 January 2008, p. 6).

'[The EU's] trade deficit with China hit nearly $250 billion last year [2008]' (*The Economist*, 18 April 2009, p. 42).

(See: 'Is the yuan overvalued?' *The Economist*, 19 May 2007, pp. 79–81.)

The reduction in tariffs

Tariffs have been reduced, a trend encouraged by WTO commitments (see below).

The average tariff rate fell from 43 per cent in 1992 to 17 per cent on 1 October 1997. On 1 July 1999 China announced that it would reduce the average tariff on imported goods from 17 per cent to 15 per cent in 2000. It also indicated that it would fulfil its promise to cut the average tariff on imported capital goods to 10 per cent by 2005 (*FT*, 2 July 1999, p. 4).

By last year [2001] quotas and licensing requirements restricted only 5 per cent of all imports, compared with about half a little more than a decade ago. China has pledged to eliminate the remaining import quota and licence restrictions by 2005, a pace of opening that is actually less rapid than the recent past. Restrictions on trading rights, which at one time gave a single or small number of state companies a monopoly on the right to import all goods, have been slashed and now apply to little more than a dozen products. The government has committed itself to phasing out restrictions on trading rights for about half of these commodities over a three-year period.

(Nicholas Lardy, *FT*, Survey, 15 March 2002, p. ii)

(See the section on the WTO, below, for later developments.)

The ending of the state monopoly of foreign trade

The state monopoly of foreign trade was ended and an increasing number of state enterprises were allowed to conduct foreign trade on their own and to retain a percentage of foreign exchange earnings. Private companies (both domestic and foreign) have been allowed to engage in foreign trade. The sector has become increasingly controlled indirectly, e.g. via the exchange rate system and tariffs (although, for example, licensing still exists).

China's foreign trade ministry was to allow overseas companies for the first time to set up foreign trade joint ventures with Chinese partners (*IHT*, 1 October 1996, p. 17).

In November 1995 it was announced that three or four foreign trading joint ventures would be approved in Shanghai and other locations. In July 1996 four applications were approved by the Shanghai authorities, while the first joint venture was approved by the central authorities in late October 1996. The regulations include high levels of trade turnover, location in Shanghai's Pudong zone or the Shenzhen SEZ, and a minority shareholding for the foreign partner (*China Briefing*, January 1997, p. 3).

The first joint-venture foreign trade company has been set up (*IHT*, 12 July 1997, p. 15).

The first three joint-venture trading enterprises began operation in Shanghai on 28 August 1997, foreign companies taking stakes of 49 per cent in each case (*FEER*, 11 September 1997, p. 64).

On 14 October 1998 it was announced that China would open its export trade (currently restricted to state enterprises) to private enterprises by 1 January 1999 (*IHT*, 15 October 1998, p. 19).

> China said yesterday [5 January 1999] that it had allowed twenty private companies to engage directly in foreign trade in an effort to boost the country's flagging export performance ... Private companies have previously been allowed to import and export only through state-run trading houses ... Exports in 1998 fell slightly against 1997, failing to meet a trade ministry target of 10 per cent growth, and falling far short of 1997's 20.9 per cent year-on-year increase.
>
> (*FT*, 6 January 1999, p. 6)

> State media reported that China had cleared twenty privately owned companies to conduct foreign trade as part of a move to increase exports ... The ministry of foreign trade and economic co-operation issued trade licences to twenty companies, including the [New] Hope Group, China's biggest animal feed producer. 'This is the first time that private firms have been allowed to enter foreign trade,' said an official of the ministry. Until now only state-run trading companies, selected state-owned manufacturers and Chinese companies in which foreigners have a stake have had the right to conduct foreign trade.
>
> (*IHT*, 6 January 1999, p. 15)

The WTO

China did not succeed in gaining founder membership of Gatt's successor, the World Trade Organization (WTO), when it was established on 1 January 1995. China's entry into the WTO was delayed by such factors as quotas, an extensive licensing system and large subsidies to state industrial enterprises.

It was argued that WTO entry had implications for the overall economic reform process in China.

Controls on the Chinese economy (such as on capital flows) helped shield China to some extent from the effects of the Asian financial crisis (which started in July 1997). This had a temporary dampening effect on China's desire to join the WTO.

China had to negotiate first with individual member countries or trading blocs, such as the EU.

China became a member of the WTO on 11 December 2001.

(See Jeffries 2006a: 522–43.)

WTO developments since April 2006

China has agreed to hold talks over tariffs on car parts, the commerce secretary said Sunday [9 April 2006] ... China's ambassador to the WTO ... sent letters to his US and EU counterparts informing them that Beijing had accepted their requests for a meeting.

(www.iht.com, 9 April 2006)

The EU, the United States and Canada said late Friday [15 September] that they planned to ask the WTO at a meeting on 28 September to set up a panel to investigate whether China had unfairly raised tariffs on imported auto parts. That plan, if followed through, would result in the first request for a panel against China since it joined the global trade body in 2001. But by announcing their plans, trade negotiators left nearly two weeks to try to reach a deal that would eliminate the need for such a panel ... Washington sought consultations with Beijing through the WTO in 2004 to resolve a disagreement over China's rebates of value-added taxes but the move Friday was the first publicly announced plan to request a panel. China has begun assessing its 25 per cent tariff for imported vehicles, instead of its 10 per cent tariff for imported auto parts, on the parts themselves if automakers bring a large number of them into the country ... According to the EU, the Chinese rules assess the tariff for an entire vehicle if an automaker imports as little as a car's roof, doors, cylinder head and fuel pump ... The new Chinese rules classify parts as a whole vehicle if they are two adjoining parts of the structure and at least two parts of the engine.

(*IHT*, 16 September 2006, p. 19)

The EU, the United States and Canada ... said Friday that the time for consultation had run out in a dispute with Beijing over rules that assign a higher full-vehicle tariff to imported auto parts if the account for 60 per cent or more of the value of a final vehicle.

(*IHT*, 18 September 2006, p. 15)

'The carmaking market in China has grown rapidly and it is now second only to that of the United States. But manufacturers have to buy 40 per cent of the spare parts by their value in China to avoid the tax' (*IHT*, 29 June 2006, p. 12).

'Last week the EU imposed anti-dumping duties on plastic bags from China and Thailand' (*IHT*, Tuesday 3 October 2006, p. 15).

> EU nations agreed Wednesday [4 October] to impose long-term tariffs on leather footwear from China and Vietnam. But the deal bitterly divided the EU, which will now look into changing the way it imposes such duties ... The shoe issue opened a rift in the EU between North and South, with countries like Germany, Britain and the Nordic members opposing the tariffs, while Italy along with France, Spain and Portugal lobbied hard for them. The Italians argued that their shoemakers – small-scale and often family-run businesses with high labour costs – were being unfairly smothered by their huge-scale Asian counterparts. The northern European faction – with backing from shoe sellers hungry for low-cost products – contended that the measures were not protection but protectionism. After tough negotiations the twenty-five EU member states reached a compromise Wednesday, agreeing to tariffs on the shoes for two years rather than the full five-year period that the European Commission ... had recommended ... An EU study this year said that China and Vietnam were dumping – or selling at below-cost prices to win market share – in Europe by unfairly helping their leather shoe manufacturers with favourable financing deals and low rents ... The Commission had imposed temporary tariffs, but those expire Friday [6 October]. The new tariffs, of 16.5 per cent against China and 10 per cent against Vietnam, go into effect Saturday [7 October] on most categories of leather shoe imports.
>
> (*IHT*, 5 October 2006, p. 16)

'China supplied about half of the 2.5 billion pairs of shoes sold in Europe last year [2005]. China has about 9 per cent of the EU market for leather shoes' (*IHT*, 6 October 2006, p. 16).

> Imports of leather shoes from China and Vietnam to Europe will continue to face steep punitive tariffs under a deal reached by EU governments on Wednesday [4 October]. In future imports from China will face tariffs of 16.5 per cent and imports from Vietnam will face a 10 per cent levy ... Earlier this year [2006] ... the European Commission ... said there was 'compelling evidence of serious state intervention in the leather footwear sector in China and Vietnam' ... Wednesday's compromise deal means that the new tariffs will enter force for just two years and not the five recommended by the Commission.
>
> (www.bbc.co.uk, 4 October 2006)

> The WTO agreed Thursday [26 October] to examine China's duties on imported car parts in the first case against the Asian nation to reach arbitration ... Until now China has only been involved in full WTO disputes as a complainant, joining in 2002 a case launched by several trading powers against the United States over tariffs Washington imposed on steel parts. In 2004 the United States started a WTO case against Beijing over duties on

semi-conductors but dropped it before the panel stage when the two countries negotiated a settlement.

(IHT, 27 October 2006, p. 12)

The United States on Friday [2 February 2007] started legal action at the WTO against a wide range of Chinese subsidies, saying that efforts to resolve the issue bilaterally had failed. The complaint filed in Geneva alleged that Beijing was using Chinese government support and tax policies to bolster Chinese firms in competition against US and other foreign companies in a wide range of industries, from steel to paper to computers. 'The United States believes that China uses its basic tax laws and other tools to encourage exports and to discriminate against imports of a variety of American manufactured goods,' the US trade representative, Susan Schwab, said, announcing that Washington was seeking consultations with China under WTO rules ... 'The subsidies at issue are offered across the spectrum of industry sectors in China – whether in steel, wood products, information technology or others,' Schwab said ... A request for consultations [the consultation period lasting up to sixty days] is the first step in what could be a lengthy process to determine whether Chinese subsidies violate WTO rules. First the two countries must try to negotiate a solution. If those talks fail the United States could then request a dispute settlement panel to arbitrate its subsidy complaint against China. A victory by the Bush administration would clear the way for the United States to impose economic sanctions against China if Beijing still refused to change its subsidy programme ... China scrapped a rebate on a value-added tax on semiconductors after the United States took a similar step in 2005, and a dispute over anti-dumping duties on kraft linerboard, a type of heavy-duty paper used in cardboard boxes and other shipping applications, was settled the day the United States was to file its complaint to the WTO. Last year [2006] the United States, the EU and Canada filed a joint complaint against China's policy on auto parts tariffs. There has been no ruling yet in that case.

(www.iht.com, 2 February 2007; IHT, 3 February 2007, p. 11)

The Bush administration, in a major escalation of trade pressure on China, announced Friday [30 March] that it would adopt a new policy of imposing potentially steep tariffs on Chinese manufactured goods on the grounds that its government subsidies of exports are illegal.

(IHT, 31 March 2007, p. 1)

[The United States said] that it would impose potentially steep tariffs on Chinese manufactured goods, with a move to protect American paper producers from unfair Chinese government subsidies. The action reverses twenty-three years of US trade policy by treating China, which is classified as a 'non-market economy', in the same way that other US trading partners are treated in disputes involving government subsidies ... The action means that China's imports of glossy paper will be subjected to tariffs ranging from

10.9 per cent up to 20.4 per cent as a penalty for subsidies that the Chinese government is providing for its own companies. Those extra duties will be imposed immediately on a preliminary basis, pending further review in the coming months to set the final penalty margin ... High-gloss, coated paper [is] the kind used in the making of brochures, catalogues, movie posters and other high-end paper products ... Industry officials say they hope that future tariffs could be imposed on steel, plastics, machinery, textiles and many other Chinese products sold in the United States ... The ruling could be far reaching ... It could set a precedent for duties to be imposed on steel, machinery, plastics, furniture and other goods from China ... For two decades the US government has held that American companies did not have the right to challenge government subsidies granted to their foreign competitors if those companies were in non-market economies like China ... China suffered a defeat on Thursday [29 March] in an effort to derail the administration's change in policy when the US Court of International Trade, a federal court which handles trade matters, ruled that the administration did have the right to proceed with sanctions ... US companies have always had the right to file dumping cases against China, which can result in penalty duties if Chinese companies are found to be selling products in the United States below cost. But the ability to file subsidy cases could significantly expand the level of penalties that Chinese imports could face, giving American producers more protection ... Anti-dumping duties are small compared with the duties under separate regulation against subsidies. In the 1980s the US government adopted the rationale that it was impossible to tell what was a subsidy in a non-market economy like China ... China would have the right to appeal the decision of the trade court ... to the US Court of Appeals.

(www.iht.com, 30 March 2007)

Washington announced Friday a preliminary countervailing duty of 10.9 per cent on Shandong Chenming Paper ... and of 20.35 per cent on Gold East Paper ... The United States is imposing a preliminary countervailing duty rate of 18.16 per cent on all other glossy paper exports.

(www.iht.com, 2 April 2007)

The duties announced by the [United States] ... average around 18.16 per cent but Gold East Paper in eastern Jiangsu province was slapped with a 20.35 per cent duty, the highest penalty ... The new duties against Chinese glossy paper are countervailing anti-subsidy tariffs, intended to offset the alleged advantage that manufacturers enjoy as a result of the support they get from the Chinese government.

(www.ft.com, 1 April 2007)

'[The United States has accused the Chinese companies of] receiving subsidies in the form of tax breaks, low-cost loans and debt forgiveness' (*FT*, 3 April 2007, p. 6). ('Textiles, electronics and machinery account for 60 per cent of [China's] exports': *FT*, 27 Februaury 2007, p. 8.)

The United States confirmed Monday [9 April] that it was filing a pair of cases against China at the WTO over widespread piracy of American movies, music, books and software, but said it still hoped to resolve the issue through talks ... The two US cases focuses on China's failure to stop widespread piracy of American copyright goods, as well as market access barriers that prevent Chinese consumers from buying legitimate versions of the entertainment and business products ... [The United States said that] because bilateral dialogue has not resolved its concerns, it was taking the next step in requesting WTO consultations.

(*IHT*, 10 April 2007, p. 1)

'Beijing has recently announced a range of measures to try to damp exports, the latest yesterday [10 April] being the removal of export rebates on most steel products' (*FT*, 11 April 2007, p. 7).

The Bush administration announced on Monday [9 April] that it would file complaints with the WTO. The complaints, which were actually lodged with the trade body on Tuesday, accuse China of tolerating widespread violations of trademarks and copyrights and of unfairly limiting the import of books, journals, movies, videos and music to state-owned companies.

(*IHT*, 11 April 2007, p. 11)

'On 9 April the United States ... filed two complaints against China with the WTO – one over the Chinese government's failure to protect US copyrights and trade marks, the other over barriers to trade in books, music, movies and videos' (*IHT*, 17 May 2007, p. 6).

'In early April the Bush administration filed two more complaints: one of Chinese pirating of DVDs and CDs, and the other over restrictions on the sale of foreign films and music in China' (*The Economist*, 19 May 2007, p. 79).

China will remove or reduce tax rebates on nearly 3,000 export categories, including some metals products, textiles, shoes and other manufactured goods, the finance ministry said Tuesday [19 June]. The long-anticipated changes could temporarily stem a flood of exports, particularly of steel and aluminium ... The changes will take effect starting 1 July ... China usually balanced lower rebates on low-end products with higher rebates to encourage exports from higher value-added industries. China has cut export rebates three times this year [2007]. The tax bureau in April reduced tax breaks on seven products, including stainless steel and cold-rolled coils. On 28 March China eased import rules for 338 products to forestall trade disputes that may come from the nation's record surplus. This time Beijing also issued a modest list of exports that would enjoy tax-free status, including uncooked peanuts, some artwork and stamps.

(www.iht.com, 19 June 2007)

China said Tuesday [19 June] that it would reduce export rebates on 2,831 products to curb a record trade surplus, ease friction with other countries and spur industries to use less energy. From 1 July rebates will be removed on 553 types of goods that require a lot of energy to produce and are polluting, including fertilizers, cement, salt and leather ... Rebates will be pared for 2,268 other exports, while ten products will be made tax free.

(*IHT*, 20 June 2007, p. 16)

The government said that it would slash the refund of value-added tax on about 37 per cent of its export categories on 1 July. Rebates will be scrapped on 553 products and cut by 5 to 13 percentage points on another 2,268 lines, including steel, toys, plastic and rubber products and apparel ... China started to reduce tax rebates in 2004. It has also taxed the export of some energy-intensive polluting products.

(www.iht.com, 26 June 2007)

China has cut and, in some cases, abolished export tax rebates for some of its largest categories ... The rebate, which can be as high as 17.5 per cent, the level of China's value-added tax, has been abolished for some leather products, fertilizer and some wood products. The finance ministry said the cuts were aimed at energy-intensive industries ... Beijing, meanwhile, continues to complain about US restrictions on high-technology exports to China. The United States on Monday [18 June] introduced new regulations that will tighten the sales of some goods overseas, including some aircraft and engines, and space communications systems.

(*FT*, 20 June 2007, p. 8)

('The United States is imposing new export controls on high-tech goods ranging from aircraft to space communications systems that could be used by China's rapidly expanding military ... The new regulation, which takes effect Tuesday [19 June], also creates a "trusted customer" programme that will allow approved companies in China to import certain high-tech goods without having to get an individual licence': *IHT*, 18 June 2007, p. 4.)

Business groups in North America and Europe say onerous technical standards create unfair barriers to entering the Chinese market and now rank as one of their top concerns, along with intellectual property rights and access to service industries ... For its part the Chinese ministry of commerce said last week that technical barriers to trade in other countries had cost its exporters $75.8 billion last year [2006] ... China and its main trading partners are at loggerheads over technical barriers to trade that both sides say are costing them billions of dollars in lost business a year.

(www.iht.com, 18 July 2007; *IHT*, 19 July 2007, p. 13)

China said Wednesday [25 July] that it would curb exports of cheap, labour-intensive products to force manufacturers into making higher quality goods, in a move to smooth relations with its major trading partners and mitigate the country's worsening environmental crisis. The ministry of commerce will expand a catalogue of goods subject to mandatory export limits in the second half of 2007 ... The commerce ministry said: 'The new policy will add cost and affect the cash flow of exporters, especially those engaged in the labour-intensive part of the industry' ... China said Monday [23 July] that it would implement a tax on companies that import metals, plastic and textiles into China for use in products that will in turn be shipped abroad. Some goods that include copper, lead, zinc and cloth will be added to the category ... The Chinese economy ... has been driven mostly by the so-called processing trade, in which companies import tax-deductible raw materials to turn into export products. The processing trade has surged over the past quarter-century and accounted for 45 per cent of China's total value of imports and exports in the first six months of this year [2007], according to trade ministry data ... Manufacturers can be exempted from the exports limit if they shift their production to inland provinces, including Shaanxi, Xinjiang and Gansu farther away from the coast ... The ministry of commerce said: 'Processing trade manufacturers can alternatively move to central or western regions from the south and east coasts to be exempted from the export restrictions. Production and labour costs are relatively low' ... The latest moves to restrict exports also strikes at energy-intensive industries with high amounts of emissions and effluents, in an attempt to reduce China's energy dependence and improve the country's environmental record ... The National Development and Reform Commission ... said that it would 'unswervingly' curb expansion in industries that consume large amounts of energy, pollute heavily and face over-capacity.

(www.iht.com, 25 July 2007)

Moves to dismantle EU duties on low-energy light bulbs from China were delayed by a year Wednesday [29 August] because of a split within the European Commission over a case seen as a significant test of free trade. Peter Mandelson, the EU trade commissioner, had sparked a fierce rift by proposing an end to duties up to 66 per cent on Chinese light bulb imports that were imposed five years ago. At a Wednesday meeting the European Commission agreed to recommend the removal of the duties but to delay the move until next year [2008] ... The proposal to lift the tariffs next year needs approval from EU member states.

(www.iht.com, 29 August 2007)

'The EU imposed duties in 2001 and the twenty-seven member countries must decide by mid-October whether to accept the commission's recommendation ... European production can meet only 25 per cent of demand for energy-saving bulbs, the commission estimates' (*IHT*, 30 August 2007, p. 1).

'Less than 20 per cent of energy-saving bulbs on sale in Europe are made within the EU, with more than two-thirds imported from China' (www.bbc.co.uk, 29 August 2007).

The WTO opened a formal investigation Tuesday [25 September] into allegations China is providing a safe haven for product piracy and counterfeiting, the most far-reaching of four current trade disputes between Washington and Beijing. The US complaint over China's enforcement of intellectual property rights is the culmination of years of agitation in Washington and elsewhere over one of the world's biggest sources of illegally copied goods, ranging from DVDs, CDs and designer clothes to sporting goods and medications ... The WTO panel's scope will be limited to whether Beijing has taken sufficient action to protect intellectual property rights, but it could ultimately authorize US trade sanctions against China worth billions of dollars annually – the amount the United States claims its companies lose because of China's lax enforcement. Such a panel often takes years to reach a final decision ... A WTO panel is currently examining a complaint by the United States and the EU on whether China maintains an illegal tax system to block imports of foreign-made auto parts into China. A first decision in the dispute – which came as a five-year transition period following Beijing's 2001 entry into the WTO ended – is expected late this year [2007] or early 2008 ... [In August 2007 the WTO] launched an investigation into US and Mexican allegations that China is providing illegal subsidies for a range of industries.

(www.iht.com, 25 September 2007; *IHT*, 26 September 2007, p. 9)

The EU and China have agreed to monitor Chinese clothing exports to Europe until the end of 2008, the European Commission said Tuesday [9 October] ... [The Commission] said it would run 'joint import surveillance' with the Chinese foreign trade ministry for the next year for some types of clothing instead of lifting all quotas on Chinese textiles as originally planned for the start of 2008 ... Authorities will check both Chinese export licences and European export permits for T-shirts, pullovers, men's trousers, dresses, bras, bed linen and flax yarn to make sure that trade is not surging.

(www.iht.com, 9 October 2007)

Chinese textile imports will be monitored next year [2008] under a system announced Tuesday, as the EU seeks to avoid a repeat of the debacle in 2005 that followed a surge in goods from China. Export licences to the twenty-seven EU countries will be tracked by both the European Commission and the Chinese ministry of foreign trade under a system of joint import surveillance that will stay in place during 2008 ... Though no textiles quotas will be imposed during 2008, the announcement leaves open the technical possibility that the EU could revert to using safeguard measures if imports rise dramatically before the end of the year ... The monitoring system will cover eight of the ten categories of imports in the 2005 agreement: T-shirts, pullovers, men's trousers, blouses, dresses, bras, bed linen and flax yarn ... Under the 2005 pact China agreed to limit exports of ten types of textiles to the EU until the end of this year [2007], restricting their annual growth to a maximum of 12.5 per cent.

(*IHT*, 10 October 2007, p. 9)

'[The EU] has begun just one case … [using] the dispute settlement procedures of the WTO … since 2001, while the United States has begun six' (www.
iht.com, 6 November 2007).

[A] directive issued in June [2007] called for burdensome new safety
inspections for foreign-made medical services – but not for those made in
China … the Chinese directive seems typical of a pattern over the last year
of new regulations aimed at favouring Chinese industries over foreign competitors … Beyond the medical device sector there were many other examples cited in a report in September [2007] by the US Chamber of Commerce,
drawing on the experience of business operating in China. China, the report
said, had become 'increasingly sophisticated at developing and wielding
industrial policies' in procurement, standards and anti-monopoly laws to the
disadvantage of foreign investors and exporters. Among the sectors cited are
standards for wireless technology, mobile phones and mobile phone batter-
ies that favour Chinese firms, as well as anti-monopoly laws that exempt
Chinese government enterprises.

(*IHT*, 16 November 2007, pp. 1, 15)

'China has made "considerable progress" in improving the safety of the toys
it exports, a European Commission report has found' (www.bbc.co.uk, 22
November 2007).

Beijing has responded harshly to a US congressional panel's warnings about
Chinese spying … The warning came from the US–China Economic and
Security Review Commission, which said in its annual report to Congress
last week that Chinese espionage represented the greatest threat to US technology. It called for counter-intelligence efforts to stop China from stealing
US manufacturing expertise and warned that small and medium manufacturers 'faced the full brunt of China's unfair trade practices, including currency
manipulation and illegal subsidies for Chinese exports'.

(www.iht.com, 20 November 2007)

The US International Trade Commission … ruled against the American
glossy paper industry's request for tariffs on imported Chinese paper. The
decision Tuesday [20 November] threw out duties that had been authorized
by the Bush administration early this year … [The ruling found that] makers
of glossy or coated paper had not been 'materially injured' or 'threatened
with material injury' from Chinese subsidies. The ruling did not dispute that
the subsidies might be improper or illegal, only that the paper producers had
not been harmed by them. It thus left intact efforts by American steel, tyre
and chemical manufacturers to obtain relief on the basis that they are
harmed by Chinese subsidies of exports. Also left intact was the Bush
administration policy, adopted in March, that imposed potentially steep
tariffs on Chinese manufactured goods on the ground that China illegally
subsidizes some of its exports, including paper … The Bush administration's decision to seek potentially high tariffs on Chinese manufactured

goods deemed to have been illegally subsidized reversed more than twenty years of US policy. Previously Washington held that subsidies could not be illegal in a country that was not a market economy, including China.

(www.iht.com, 21 November 2007)

The WTO opened an investigation Tuesday [27 November] into Chinese restrictions on the sale of American movies, music and books ... It is Washington's fourth commercial complaint against Beijing in little over a year ... Washington expanded the scope of its complaint in July to include censorship rules that it says unfairly single out Hollywood movies and foreign suppliers of music recordings in China ... The WTO is expected to make three rulings next year [2008]: on claims by the United States and the EU that China maintains an illegal tax system to block imports of foreign made auto parts; on a US and Mexican complaint over Chinese industrial subsidies; and on claims by Washington that Beijing is effectively providing a safe haven for product piracy and counterfeiting through excessively high thresholds for criminal prosecution.

(*IHT*, 28 November 2007, p. 13)

Bowing to American pressure ... China agreed Thursday [29 November] to terminate a dozen different subsidies that promote exports and discourage imports of steel, wood products, information technology equipment and other manufactured goods. The Chinese actions affect exports by companies that have foreign investments or are joint ventures with foreign companies. Nearly 60 per cent of Chinese exports are produced by these businesses.

(*IHT*, 30 November 2007, p. 9)

China and the United States ... signed an agreement Tuesday [11 December] calling for a greater US role in certifying and inspecting Chinese food exports, including an increased presence of American officials at Chinese production plants. The accord ... would impose new registration and inspection requirements on Chinese food exporters for ten specific products ... US officials said that the agreement was less than sweeping, in that it did not cover all the food products sought for tighter inspections. But they said the accord was a start and could be expanded. It is to cover some preserved foods, pet foods and farm-raised fish, all products that have been the focus of charges of being tainted ... Officials are already allowed to inspect Chinese facilities under limited conditions, but the agreement signed Tuesday will expand that role ... The food and feed accord was the centrepiece of a flurry of fourteen different agreements worked on over the last several months and completed in the last couple of days ... The other new agreements would impose new registration and certification requirements on imported Chinese drugs, active ingredients in pharmaceuticals and medical devices to avoid counterfeiting and safety problems. There were also accords on promoting American tourism for Chinese visitors, joint development of bio-fuels and expanded science and technology exchanges. As part of these accords ... China agreed not to impose, at least for now, an inspection requirement on imported medical devices like heart monitors and surgical implants, which had been the focus of complaints by [US companies] ... because that restriction was to be directed at imported medical devices, not ones made in China.

> (www.iht.com, 11 December 2007; *IHT*, 12 December 2007, p. 15)

'In return, under a series of bilateral agreements, the United States will allow Chinese tour groups easier access to the United States. Tourism visas to the United States are, at present, difficult to obtain for Chinese' (*FT*, 12 December 2007, p. 9).

'Both countries [are to be allowed] ... to make surprise safety inspections of each other's factories producing food, medical devices and drugs' (*The Economist*, 15 December 2007, p. 86).

> There were new reports of the Chinese barring, at least temporarily, US films from release in China, apparently in retaliation at the WTO suit ... China has stopped granting permission to show American films in its cinemas in an apparent trade dispute with the United States, according to several Hollywood executives and US government officials. The Chinese government has not announced any ban, but American movies are no longer being approved for release early next year [2008].
>
> (www.iht.com, 11 December 2007; *IHT*, 12 December 2007, pp. 1, 17)

'China and the United States ended three days of intense economic talks Thursday [14 December] ... under the heading of the "strategic economic dialogue" ... There was a deal to let foreign companies issue stocks and bonds denominated in Chinese currency' (*IHT*, 14 December 2007, p. 14).

'More than 40 per cent of Chinese exports go the United States and Europe' (*FT*, 5 February 2008, p. 9).

> China did agree to allow foreign investors in China to list on local stock markets and to issue local currency bonds ... A communiqué included, at Beijing's request, a commitment from the United States that Chinese banks would be treated like other foreign lenders if they wished 'to acquire stakes' in US banks.
>
> (*FT*, 14 December 2007, p. 12)

> [On 26 December China announced that it] was to scrap import duties on copper, coal and aluminium, and halve tax on oil products from the beginning of next year [1 January 2008]. Export taxes on some steel products, coking coal and coke will also be raised to curb profits on exports of polluting products ... Export taxes on semi-finished steel products will be raised as much as 25 per cent and a 15 per cent export tax will be imposed on some stainless steel welded pipes and other steel products in an effort to cool investment in the steel sector.
>
> (www.ft.com, 26 December 2007)

China said Wednesday [26 December] that it would introduce export tariffs on some steel products, effective 1 January [2008] and increase rates on other items ... China would also remove import duties on alumina, refined copper and coal ... In an effort to cool investment in the steel sector, export taxes on semi-finished steel products will be raised to as much as 25 per cent and a 15 per cent export tax will be imposed on some stainless steel, welded pipes and other steel products ... Existing tariffs on the export of other products, including carbon steel billets and pig iron will be raised. The current import tax for alumina is 3 per cent while the import tax for refined copper is 2 per cent. Imports from Chile, a major exporter with a bilateral free trade agreement with China, are already duty-free. China had already cut tax rebates and raised duties on some steel shipments this year [2007] ... China will cut imports tariffs on 1 January on a range of other goods as well, from sporting goods to coffee-brewing machines and automobile gear boxes [as well as pianos and audio loudspeakers].

(*IHT*, 27 December 2007, p. 9)

'[On 28 December] China submitted its application to join the WTO's government procurement agreement, which lays out rules aimed at making purchases by governments more transparent and ensuring they do not favour domestic products or suppliers' (*IHT*, 29 December 2007, p. 18).

The US Commerce Department set preliminary anti-dumping duties Wednesday [6 February 2008] of up to 210 per cent [the range being 10.98 per cent to 210.48 per cent on various Chinese companies] on millions of off-road tyres from China it said were being sold in the United States at unfairly low prices ... They were the sixth Chinese product to be hit with US anti-dumping duties since the start of the year [2008]. The others include nails, certain steel pipe, a teeth-whitening ingredient and laminated woven sacks used to package items such as dog food and bird seed ... The US International Trade Commission must make a final determination that US producers have been materially harmed, or are threatened with material harm, for final duties to go into effect. The decision is expected in August. Altogether the United States has more than sixty anti-dumping orders in force against China. Many date back for years ... The Commerce Department responded in December [2007] by setting preliminary countervailing duties ranging from 2.38 per cent to 6.59 per cent.

(www.iht.com, 7 February 2008)

The WTO on Wednesday [13 February] issued its first official condemnation of Chinese commercial practices, siding with the United States, EU and Canada in a dispute over car parts. The WTO found that China was breaking trade rules by taxing imports of auto parts at the same rate as foreign-made finished cars ... The three-member panel found against China on nearly every point of contention with the United States, the EU and Canada. The three trade powers argued that the tariff was discouraging automakers from using imported car parts for the vehicles they assemble in China. The ruling [is] to be officially released in March ... The decision is officially only an 'interim ruling'. But no panel has ever changed its findings between interim and final decision. China, which will be able to appeal, claims the tariffs are intended to stop whole cars being imported in large chunks, allowing companies to avoid the higher tariff rates for finished vehicles ... But the United States and the EU say that China promised not to treat parts as whole cars when it joined the WTO in 2001 ... WTO cases tend to take years before retaliatory sanctions can be authorized. After the ruling is released Beijing will be given a 'reasonable period of time' to make legislative changes. A separate panel would then have to find that Beijing was still breaking the rules.

(*IHT*, 14 February 2008, p. 15)

('China yesterday [18 July 2008] since joining the WTO seven years ago after the global trade body ruled against Beijng's import tariffs for car parts. A WTO dispute panel confirmed an interim judgement in February, which upheld complaints by the United States, the EU and Canada that China violated fair trade rules by discriminating against imported parts ... China is expected to appeal, postponing any definitive decision until later this year [2008]. However, if the appeal goes against it Beijing will have to remove the offending measures or face swingeing trade sanctions ... The $19 billion Chinese vehicle market is the world's third largest after the United States and Japan ... Beijing still has three other cases outstanding. The United States has challenged China's enforcement of intellectual property rules and alleged discrimination against US films, music and books. And last month [June 2008] Canada joined the United States and the EU in a complaint over Chinese restrictions on foreign financial news agencies': *FT*, 19 July 2008, p. 5.)

The EU and China plan to open a high level trade dialogue in April [2008] the EU said Monday [25 February] ... [called] the EU–China High Level Economic and Trade Mechanism ... The United States and China started a similar high level economic dialogue in 2006 ... The two sides meet twice a year.

(www.iht.com, 25 February 2008)

'Brussels said Monday that the EU's trade deficit with China had swollen to Euro 159 billion, or $235 billion, in 2007, the large majority of an overall deficit of Euro 185.7 billion' (*IHT*, 26 February 2008, p. 14).

The EU and the United States have decided to file a joint complaint against China at the WTO over how Beijing regulates foreign financial information providers ... Both Brussels and Washington object to rules that Xinhua, the Chinese state news agency, issued in September 2006 that preclude foreign companies from directly providing financial information to Chinese clients. Instead, foreign companies like Reuters, Dow Jones and Bloomberg must go through Xinhua, which is also China's domestic regulator of financial information services and offers a financial news service of its own ... Washington has won a victory against Chinese government subsidies at the WTO and settled two other cases involving semiconductors and kraft liner board before getting to the litigation stage. US trade officials have also confirmed a recent win against China that challenged China's treatment of foreign auto parts. That ruling is expected to be made public in the coming weeks. Washington is also pressing ahead with two other cases aimed at reducing piracy and counterfeiting in China and lowering the barriers to imports of legitimate films, music, books and software. Away from the WTO, the European Commission has initiated anti-dumping investigations into claims that Chinese manufacturers are selling a range of products, from steel to candles, in the EU market at prices that do not even cover their production costs.

(www.iht.com, 2 March 2008; *IHT*, 3 March 2008, p. 12)

The United States and EU on Monday [3 March] filed a WTO case against China, demanding that Beijing loosen restraints on foreign companies vying for a greater slice of the country's market for financial information. The United States and the EU said they were challenging rules announced eighteen months ago that undermine the ability of Reuters Group, Dow Jones and Bloomberg to sell financial information to banks, government agencies and other customers in China ... Xinhua went into direct competition with foreign financial information in June [2007] by starting its own service ... The new regulations make Xinhua both a competitor and regulator to its foreign rivals, requiring that data, videos and photos be funnelled through Xinhua-approved distributors. The only currently approved distributor is a Xinhua subsidiary. Under the terms of its WTO entry, China undertook not to close markets that it had already opened. Xinhua has promised not to abuse its position as regulator to help its commercial activities ... The United States urged Beijing to set up an independent regulator and to return to conditions of 1996–2006, allowing foreign suppliers to have direct business relations with clients.

(www.iht.com, 3 March 2008; *IHT*, 4 March 2008, p. 12)

'China's commerce ministry yesterday [4 March] reacted in unusually mild fashion to a WTO action brought by the EU and the United States ... The ministry said in a statement: "As a WTO member, China respects other members' choices"' (*FT*, 5 March 2008, p. 6).

China and New Zealand signed a sweeping free-trade agreement [FTA] on Monday [7 April 2008], China's first such pact with a developed country ... The deal came after fifteen rounds of negotiations over three years ... Two-way trade between China and New Zealand currently is worth more than $6.1 billion a year, with Chinese exports making up about 75 per cent, according to Statistics New Zealand. When the deal goes into effect on 1 October, tariffs on New Zealand exports to China that are currently set at 5 per cent or less will be cut to zero. For New Zealand exports that face larger tariffs there will be a staggered timeframe for cuts, with 31 per cent of New Zealand's exports to China slated for tariff-free status by 2013. Tariffs on dairy products, a primary New Zealand export, will be phased out over a longer period of time, taking until 2019 when almost all of the country's current exports to China will be tariff free. The FTA provides for elimination over time of tariffs on 96 per cent of New Zealand's current exports to China ... Beyond trade in goods, the agreement covers the services sector, from insurance and banking to education and labour supply. The agreement also calls for up to 1,800 Chinese to enter New Zealand each year to work in areas such as traditional Chinese medicine, language teaching and food service.

(www.iht.com, 7 April 2008)

Under the agreement New Zealand will phase out all tariffs on imports from China by 2016. In return China will remove tariffs on 96 per cent of its imports from New Zealand by 2019 ... Agricultural produce makes up nearly half of New Zealand exports to China, but prime minister Helen Clark of New Zealand said that prime minister Wen Jiabao had expressed particular interest in harnessing New Zealand expertise in reducing carbon emissions to tackle climate change ... The accord will take effect on 1 October when China will end tariffs of 5 per cent or less on New Zealand goods, covering 35 per cent of those imports. Duties on an additional 31 per cent of imports will be phased out over five years. For China 70 per cent of its exports to New Zealand will be duty free in five years, up from 37 per cent now. The trade agreement is the sixth for China and another six are being negotiated with countries that include Australia. Peru and South Africa ... Talks on the Beijing–Wellington agreement started in 2004 after New Zealand became the first rich country to grant China market economy status, a precondition Beijing sets for negotiating a free-trade pact. The EU and the United States still designate China as a non-market economy, making it easier for them to impose stiffer penalties on goods they judge China is exporting below their production costs.

(*IHT*, 8 April 2008, p. 15)

US steel pipe manufacturers, who have been battling a surge in imports from China, won a major victory Friday [20 June] when the International Trade Commission cleared the way for the imposition of stiff penalty tariffs for the next five years. The commission voted five to zero that the US industry was being harmed by the import of circular steel pipe. The decision marked the first time a US industry has won a decision to impose tariffs on a Chinese product based on the argument that the Chinese government was unfairly subsidizing a Chinese industry. The commission ruling means penalty tariffs ranging from 99 per cent to 701 per cent will be imposed on Chinese imports of circular welded pipe, a form of pipe used in a variety of construction jobs, such as home plumbing and sprinkler systems. For more than two decades the US government had refused to consider subsidy cases against the Chinese government because China was classified as a non-market economy. But the administration of President George W. Bush, facing increasing anger over soaring trade deficits with China, reversed course last year [2007] and announced that it would treat China in the same way as other countries in disputes involving government subsidies. The pipe case is the first to clear all government hurdles for the tariffs to go into effect. Last year the Commerce Department imposed penalty tariffs on imports of glossy paper, but the trade body blocked the tariffs by ruling that the domestic industry had not proven it was being materially harmed by the imports.

(www.iht.com, 21 June 2008)

Last week the director-general of the WTO, Pascal Lamy, invited China into a new Group of 7 comprised also of the United States, the EU, India, Brazil, Australia and Japan. Not long ago global trade talks were steered largely by the so-called 'quad' made up of the United States, the EU, Canada and Japan.

(*IHT*, Tuesday 29 July 2008, p. 11)

A high level summit meeting to salvage a global trade pact collapsed Tuesday [29 July] after the United States, China and India failed to compromise on farm import rules ... Started in 2001 in Qatar the so-called Doha Development Agenda aims to open up world trade by cutting tariffs while reducing agricultural subsidies in the developed world ... Trade officials from 153 countries have been talking in Geneva for nine consecutive days ... Negotiators were hoping for a deal this week on farm and industrial trade so that crisis-ridden WTO talks could be saved ... A United States trade dispute with China and India over farm import safeguards effectively ended any hope of a breakthrough ... The talks foundered on a relatively technical issue of a new 'special safeguard mechanism'. This would have allowed developing countries like India to protect their subsistence farmers against sudden surges of imported food products like rice. While farm import safeguards exist in rich and poor countries, they are rarely used. The dispute over the proposals concerned the threshold for when developing nations could raise their tariffs and how high those taxes could rise. That violated the spirit of the trade round, the United States and other agricultural exporters argued, because it was supposed to help poorer countries develop their economies by bolstering their exports of farm produce. The United States accused India and China of seeking to backtrack on an agreement in principle made Friday [25 July]. Washington accused the two emerging powers of insisting on allowances to raise farm tariffs above even their current levels. India denied that it ever approved the previous text ... At present India does not have a safeguard mechanism for its farmers, though developed countries can invoke special measures to protect some of their goods if imports climb sharply.

(www.iht.com, 29 July 2008)

World trade talks collapsed here [in Geneva] on Tuesday [29 July] after seven years of on-again, off-again negotiations, in the latest sign of India's and China's growing might on the world stage and the decreasing ability of the United States to impose its will globally … Supporters of the so-called Doha round of talks, which began in 2001, say a deal would have been a bulwark against protectionist sentiments that are likely to spread as economic growth falters in much of the world … One official said that the relatively technical nature of the cause of the breakdown underlined a lack of political will to reach an agreement that would be a tough sell in many countries.

(www.iht.com, 30 July 2008)

The strong Chinese stance on farm goods comes at a time of rapidly rising worry in Beijing about food security. Food prices have soared around the globe in recent months, particularly for rice, and many countries with a food surplus have imposed limits on exports to retain supplies for their own populations. China has become increasingly focused on making sure that its farmers can continue to produce most of the food needed for the 1.3 billion people in that country, and leery of having to rely on imports. President Hu Jintao made that point when he met with leaders from the G8 nations in Japan on 9 July. According to a Chinese government statement issued afterwards, 'Hu said China attaches great importance to agriculture and especially the food issue' and he noted that China 'pursues a food security policy of relying on domestic supply, ensuring basic self-sufficiency and striking a balance through appropriate import and export' … Chinese officials … [who] have held domestic grain prices well below international levels through heavy subsidies … have been aggressively chasing smugglers who try to buy cheap Chinese rice and other grain and ship it to neighbouring countries for resale … Reducing agricultural tariffs has been an important part of the global talks. Food exporting nations argued that in imposing safeguard tariffs developing countries could only let their tariffs bounce back up to current levels – in other words, they could revoke whatever tariff reductions they endorse in the current trade talks and no more. China, with support from India, demanded that safeguard tariffs be allowed that would actually be higher than prevailing tariffs now – a demand that the United States and other food exporters found unacceptable.

(www.iht.com, 30 July 2008)

The talks saw India and China reverting to the very food security arguments used in the past to justify European subsidies … After a long period of keeping a low profile at the Doha talks, Beijing revealed its protectionist colours by pressing for special deals for key items like rice, sugar and cotton, all products in which other developing countries – including India, Brazil, South-east Asian nations and some African countries – are competitive.

(www.iht.com, 30 July 2008)

'The issue concerned a "special safeguard" developing countries led by China and India have demanded to deal with a sudden surge of imports or drop in prices' (www.cnn.com, 29 July 2008).

The United States and the EU want greater access to provide services to the fast growing emerging countries, including China and India. Meanwhile, developing countries want greater access for their agricultural products in Europe and the United States ... The talks in Geneva were complicated by recent increases in the price of food and fuel ... with food prices doubling over the past year ... Higher prices have prompted protests in both developed and developing nations, making it harder for negotiators to reach a compromise on opening up their markets to greater competition ... The main stumbling block was farm import rules, which allow countries to protect poor farmers by imposing a tariff on certain goods in the event of a drop in prices or a surge in imports. India, China and the United States could not agree on the tariff threshold for such an event.

(www.bbc.co.uk, 29 July 2008)

The present food price crisis has led to a shortage of produce in international markets, not a glut. But many emerging-market countries seem to have drawn the conclusion from the food crisis that they need to keep more production at home ... China broke cover on Monday [28 July], publicly accusing the United States of hypocrisy for heavily subsidizing its own cotton farmers ... while asking other countries to submit theirs to harsh competition.

(*FT*, 30 July 2008, p. 4)

Ministers ... ultimately stumbled over an apparently small detail of new rules on agricultural trade ... An American presidential election [is] looming ... Congress may have little appetite for more open trade ... At the onset the likeliest stumbling block seemed to be America's unwillingness to reduce the ceiling on its agricultural subsidies to somewhere near to the amount it actually spends ... WTO members negotiate over maximum tariffs and subsidies, not actual rates and sums ... In the end it was a dispute over protection for developing countries' farmers that proved the deal-breaker. The draft text envisaged a 'special safeguard mechanism' – a right for developing countries to raise tariffs to protect their farmers against a surge of imports. America wanted the import volume that triggered the mechanism set relatively high; India and China wanted it low. Deadlock ensued ... Another contentious issue – cotton – was not formally dealt with.

(www.economist.com, 30 July 2008)

The government has found another way of to reduce the flow of expensive automotive imports. On 13 August the government announced a new 'green' tax that will come into effect on 1 September. The new tax is meant to reduce fuel consumption and fight pollution. Rather than further raising the tax on fuel, which increased by almost 20 per cent in June, the government is taxing gas-guzzling cars ... Most such cars are foreign made. Cars with engine capacity larger than 4.1 litres will now incur a 40 per cent sales tax –

twice the previous level. Cars with engines between 3 litres and 4 litres will be taxed at 25 per cent, up from 15 per cent. The tax on the smallest cars, with engines smaller than 1 litre, will fall from 3 per cent to 1 per cent. The 8 per cent and 10 per cent taxes on other cars will not change. The government says the new tax will encourage a shift to more fuel-efficient cars. It will also help Chinese carmakers, as they tend to make cars with engines smaller than 2.5 litres.

(The Economist, 23 August 2008, p. 56)

China is progressing toward receiving the EU's coveted market economy status, something that would help the Asian export powerhouse avoid punitive anti-dumping duties, an EU document showed ... Beijing has been seeking such status from the EU since 2004 ... The European Commission said in its latest assessment ... that China had still met only one of five criteria used to gauge the influence of state intervention on prices and costs. But Beijing had made 'considerable progress' on the four others, it said, providing a 'clear platform' for reaching the target. The report also described the Chinese economy as 'an increasingly modern and market-based system' ... It said: 'The conclusion of this report is that China now has in place almost all the legislation which is necessary for granting Market Economy Status. That is a considerable achievement. The focus has now switched to the effective implementation of these laws which are crucial for the functioning of any market economy' ... The one criterion that China has met – as determined by Brussels in 2004 – relates to the absence on non-market payment forms like barter. The criteria it has yet to meet include the use of modern accounting standards, on which China had made 'considerable progress' and bankruptcy, intellectual property and property laws where progress was 'substantial', the report said. There was less progress in reducing the state's role in price setting in sectors like energy, a key component for manufacturers, and China was slow in improving the independence of its financial system, the Commission said ... If China gets market economy status in the EU, its exporters would probably face lower duties in anti-dumping fights or avoid them altogether. Because China is not classified as a market economy, Brussels considers price data from other countries like Brazil when assessing whether Chinese goods are being dumped, or sold below cost, in the EU. Costs in so-called analogue countries are routinely higher than in China, resulting in findings of high dumping margins and high EU anti-dumping duties for Chinese goods under dispute ... China had a trade surplus of $227 billion with the EU last year [2007], European data show.

(www.iht.com, 18 September 2008; *IHT*, 19 September 2008, p. 20)

The European Chamber of Commerce has highlighted the theft of intellectual property rights, an unpredictable mergers and acquisitions regime, and the exclusion of foreign companies from many government procurement contracts as big deterrents to doing business in China. European investment in China dropped from Euro 6 billion in 2006 to Euro 1.8 billion last year [2007], accounting for just 2 per cent of European foreign direct investment.

(FT, 2 October 2008, p. 13)

The United States has begun legal action at the WTO aimed at halting Chinese government subsidy programmes to lift the sale of Chinese-branded goods around the world, the US trade representative's office said Friday [19 December]. The subsidies to help develop and promote 'famous brands' include cash grants for exporting, preferential loans for exporters, research and development financing to develop new products and payments to lower the cost of export-credit insurance, the US trade office said.

(IHT, 20 December 2008, p. 14)

The Chinese ministry of commerce has begun an anti-dumping review of some screws and washers made in Europe, in apparent retaliation for the EU's decision to impose heavy duties on screws and fasters made in China. An EU predatory pricing committee voted in December to impose duties of as much as 87 per cent on Chinese steel screws, a move Chinese producers regarded as particularly unfair because it excluded China-based units of some European manufacturers.

(IHT, 2 January 2009, p. 13)

The WTO agreed yesterday [20 January] to rule on a dispute launched by China over US curbs on imports of steel pipes, tyres and woven sacks. It is the first case that China has pushed to a dispute panel since it joined the WTO at the end of 2001 ... The case involves four sets of parallel anti-dumping and anti-subsidy duties imposed by the United States on two types of steel pipe, pneumatic off-road tyres and laminated woven sacks ... The case is the third China has taken against the United States in the WTO, while the United States has brought seven WTO cases against China.

(FT, 21 January 2009, p. 10)

The United States said Monday [26 January] that it had won a WTO dispute with China over patent and copyright protections arising from complaints by makers of movies, music and software that their products are being pirated. A WTO panel of judges ruled Monday that China's intellectual property laws were inconsistent with its obligations to [the WTO] ... But the United States failed to persuade the WTO panel on one main point of its case: that Chinese copyright pirates and counterfeiters had no fear of criminal prosecution because the government's threshold for bringing a case was too high ... Under WTO rules, China must change its laws to conform to the judges' ruling. If it does not the United States can petition to retaliate against Chinese products. China's copying of movies, music and software cost companies $2.2 billion in 2006 sales, according to an estimate by lobby groups representing Microsoft, Walt Disney and Vivendi. The WTO complaint, brought in 2007, is the first by the United States against China for breaching intellectual property rights.

(IHT, 27 January 2009, p. 1)

'China has launched a formal challenge at the WTO to a new US law banning imports of processed Chinese poultry. Beijing says the ban is "discriminatory and protectionist", and cannot be justified on safety grounds' (*FT*, 18 April 2009, p. 7).

> China and the EU ... should ... demonstrate their common, clear commitment against trade protectionism at the second China–EU high level economic dialogue. Trade liberalization is the engine of economic growth ... The world economy paid a heavy price for the prevalence of trade protectionism during the Great Depression in the 1930s, which led to the contraction of global trade by two-thirds. We should make sure that the same mistake is not repeated ... China is firmly committed to reform and to opening up. Since its accession to the WTO China's market has become much more open and its trade greatly liberalized. The current overall tariff level of China is only 9.8 per cent. Its average tariff level on industrial products is only 8.9 per cent, the lowest among all developing countries. Its tariff on imported agricultural products is only 15.2 per cent, which is not only lower than other developing countries but also far below that of many developed countries. The openness of China's trade in services has reached a level close to that of an average developed country ... The Chinese government recently sent Chinese enterprises on procurement missions to Europe and the United States ... The EU is now China's largest trading partner and China is the second largest trading partner of the EU.
>
> (Wang Qishan, vice premier of the State Council of China, www.iht.com, 5 May 2009; *IHT*, 6 May 2009, p. 8)

> The United States and the EU accused China of unfair trade practices on Tuesday [23 June], saying the Chinese government was restricting exports of raw materials to give manufacturers in that country a competitive advantage ... The United States said China had imposed quotas, export duties and other costs on raw materials used in the production of steel, chemicals and aluminium ... The United States and the EU filed complaints with the WTO, the first step in what could be a years-long process of trying to resolve grievances against China ... Since China joined the WTO in 2001, it has filed four complaints against the United States, and has been the subject of seven other complaints by the United States and two by the EU ... On Monday [22 June] China announced that it would cut or eliminate export taxes on some metals, steel wire, fertilizer, soybeans and wheat.
>
> (www.iht.com, 23 June 2009)

> Chinese exporters have been given large tax rebates worth as much as 17 per cent of the value of their products, generous loans from state-owned banks and government-paid trips to trade shows all over the world ... Provincial governments appear to have cut back on their enforcement of counterfeiting laws and other intellectual property protections ... When China joined the WTO in late 2001, it never actually signed the WTO document

barring discrimination in government procurement ... Under the rules of the WTO, discrimination by nationality in the purchasing of goods is prohibited – except for government procurement, which is covered by a separate WTO agreement that virtually all industrialized countries have signed. When China joined the WTO in November 2001 and gained full access for its exports to foreign markets, it pledged to join the agreement on government procurement 'as soon as possible'. Subsequent talks in Geneva produced no progress.

(IHT, 24 June 2009, pp. 1, 14)

The EU and the United States complained to the WTO that China's export quotas and duties on raw materials such as coking coal were distorting the global market and hurting manufacturers of steel and other products ... Ron Kirk (US trade representative): 'We are most troubled that this appears to be a conscious effort to create unfair preferences for Chinese industries by making raw materials cheaper for Chinese companies to get and goods more economical for them to produce' ... Catherine Ashton (EU trade commissioner): 'The Chinese restrictions on raw materials distort competition and increase global prices' ... EU officials have been complaining about China's treatment of natural resources for some time, arguing that Beijing in effect grants unfair subsidies to manufacturers of steel, chemicals and thousands of finished goods.

(FT, 24 June 2009, p. 8)

On Wednesday [24 June] the Chinese ministry of commerce rejected the charges. It said in a statement: 'The main objective of China's relevant export policies is to protect the environment and natural resources. China believes the policies in question are in keeping with WTO rules ... Following the WTO procedures for dispute resolution, China will appropriately handle the request for consultations' ... Beijing also retaliated with its own request on Wednesday for the WTO to set up a panel of experts to investigate restrictions on the import of Chinese poultry products. China first requested talks with the United States at the WTO over the ban on Chinese poultry imports on 17 April, but those discussions failed to satisfy Beijing, which is now requesting further investigation by the WTO ... The United States and China banned each other's poultry in 2004 after outbreaks of bird flu, but China lifted its ban in September last year [2008] while the United States has refused to do so because of lingering concerns over the spread of the virus and numerous other health and safety scandals in China. The EU lifted its six-year ban on Chinese poultry imports at the end of last year [2008].

(www.iht.com, 24 June 2009)

China defended the practice Wednesday [24 June] on environmental and conservation grounds ... China defended its policies as necessary 'to protect the environment and natural resources', but said it would enter into consultation with the EU and the United States on the matter. Consultation is the first step in a WTO dispute resolution process ... the complaint involves the export of bauxite, coke, fluorspar, magnesium, manganese, silicon metal, silicon carbide, yellow phosphorous and zinc ... Catherine Ashton (EU trade commissioner): 'Restrictions on raw materials give Chinese companies an unfair advantage, as downstream industries in China have access to cheaper materials than their competitors outside China' ... The claim suggests China sets minimum prices and tariffs of up to 70 per cent on some of these raw materials in violation of WTO fair trading rules.

(www.cnn.com, 24 June 2009)

'The US and EU complaints now trigger a sixty-day consultation period' (www.bbc.co.uk, 24 June 2009).

When the United States' top energy and commercial officials arrive in China on Tuesday [14 July], they will land in the middle of a building storm over China's protectionist tactics to become the world's leader in renewable energy. Calling renewable energy a strategic industry, China is trying hard to make sure that its companies dominate globally ... China is shielding its clean energy sector while it grows to a point where it can take on the world ... Steven Chu [is] the American energy secretary and Gary Locke [is] the commerce secretary ... WTO rules ban countries from using local content requirements to force companies like the wind turbine manufacturers to set up factories in a country instead of exporting to it. But much of China's power industry, although publicly traded, is majority owned by the government. While China promised to sign the WTO side agreement on government procurement 'as soon as possible' when it joined the free trade group in 2001 and won low-tariff access to foreign markets, it has never actually signed the side agreement. So its huge state sector remains largely exempt from international trade rules.

(www.iht.com, 14 July 2009; *IHT*, 15 July 2009, pp. 14–15)

The US energy secretary, Steven Chu, concluded his first official visit to Beijing on Thursday [16 July] with a memorandum of understanding with Chinese officials for joint studies on ways to improve the energy efficiency of buildings ... China now accounts for half the square footage of buildings under construction around the world.

(www.iht.com, 16 July 2009)

China yesterday [30 July] expressed regret over an EU decision to apply permanent penalties on Chinese steel pipes, saying the tariffs were not necessary. The duties will replace a series of provisional six-month duties. Permanent or definitive EU trade duties usually last for five years.

(*FT*, 31 July 2009, p. 6)

China has sparked a row with the EU after complaining to the WTO that EU anti-dumping duties on Chinese screws and bolts are breaking global commerce rules ... [China] lodged its first complaint against the EU with the WTO yesterday [31 July], protesting that EU tariffs of up to 85 per cent were 'neither impartial nor transparent' and were damaging hundreds of Chinese companies ... Duties [were] imposed in January [2009] on goods worth $812 million ... The dispute comes after EU trade officials approved penalties on imports of steel pipe from China ... [China said the EU measure] 'infringes the legitimate commercial interests of over 1,700 Chinese fastener producers' ... It said the EU has been inconsistent in its application of the rules given that two Chinese subsidiaries of European firms – Italy's Agrati and Celo of Spain – were exempt from the duties ... Between last September [2008] and June [2009] other WTO members, particularly the United States, India and European countries, brought seventy-seven cases worth a total of $9.8 billion against China, more than double the number of cases in the same period a year earlier ... Until recently China has been reluctant to use the WTO to defend its interests ... The move [relating to screws and bolts] signals Beijing's willingness to defend its trade-related interest more aggressively through multilateral institutions.

(*FT*, 1 August 2009, p. 5)

The WTO has ruled against China and for the United States in a blockbuster decision that could provide massive market opportunities for American makers of everything from CDs and DVDs to music downloads and books. The ruling on Wednesday [12 August] finds definitively against China for forcing American media producers to route their business in China through Chinese state-owned companies. It could set a larger precedent for others, such as automakers claiming to be hampered by cumbersome Chinese distribution rules ... The United States filed its complaint in March of last year [2008], after months of negotiations to get China to lift its requirement that these suppliers distribute their data and news reports through Xinhua, the Chinese government news agency.

(www.iht.com, 12 August 2009)

Responding to a petition filed by the United States in early April 2007, and joined two weeks later by the EU, the panel urged China to remove its extensive administrative restrictions on the import and distribution of a wide range of books, movies, DVDs and music recordings ... The panel stopped short of endorsing a US request for a ruling on whether Chinese censorship has unfairly restricted imports. The panel said that this question was outside its purview; for the same reason, the panel also declined to rule on whether China's approval processes were too onerous for would-be distributors of imported entertainment ... In its petition to the WTO the United States criticized the requirement that most copyrighted material be imported through a few government-designated companies. The WTO condemned this, saying that 'it also appears that foreign individuals and enterprises, including those not invested or registered in China, are accorded treatment less favourable than that accorded to enterprises in China with respect to the right to trade'

... The Chinese government has not removed heavy taxes on imported auto parts that were condemned by another WTO panel in July 2008.

(www.iht.com, 12 August 2009; *IHT*, 13 August 2009, pp. 1, 15)

By 1 September [2009] China must comply with a WTO ruling in a case brought by the United States against illicit taxes on imported auto parts. By March [2010] it must comply with another ruling on a case brought by the United States about its lax enforcement of counterfeiting laws.

(www.iht.com, 14 August 2009)

The decision from the WTO organization settlement dispute panel said China was breaching international trade rules by blocking foreign-owned companies from acting as importers and wholesalers of US films, music and printed material. The WTO upheld China's limits on the distribution of US films and made no ruling on censorship ... The WTO also said China was breaking trade rules by preventing US music download firms from offering their services directly to Chinese customers. Its ruling covers the export of US books, magazines and computer games to China.

(www.bbc.co.uk, 13 August 2009)

China expressed regret at the ruling and rejected its findings. A spokesman for the commerce ministry said that ... China may choose to appeal ... This is the third time the WTO has ruled against China in just over a year and the other cases – one on imported automobile parts and another on counterfeiting – have not yet led to substantial changes in the way business is done. But the latest ruling adds pressure in an especially sensitive area ... Although China's markets have liberalized hugely over the years, the information-based industries remain something of a special case. Virtually all print and broadcast media are government-run or supervised, and subject to censorship by Communist Party propaganda officials. The internet is closely monitored and a great deal of content is blocked ... The WTO dispute resolution machinery turns slowly. America made this complaint in April 2007. It was later joined by the EU, Japan, Australia and others. Having taken so long to reach this point, the WTO will take a great deal longer to force compliance, especially if China does appeal.

(*The Economist*, 15 August 2009, p. 47)

China said Monday [17 August] it would challenge a WTO ruling against its restrictions on imported films, Books and audiovisual products ... The US trade deficit with China totalled $103 billion in the first half of 2009, down 13 per cent from last year [2008].

(www.iht.com, 17 August 2009)

'The American economic stimulus plan requires any project receiving money to use steel and other construction materials ... from countries that have signed the WTO's agreement on free trade in government procurement. China has not' (www.iht.com, 25 August 2009).

China promised when it joined the WTO that it would approve as quickly as possible the WTO side agreement on government procurement, which bans countries from discriminating against imports for government purchases. But Beijing officials have not acted on the side agreement since then. China's top economic planning agency barred government agencies this spring [2009] from buying any imports with the country's nearly $600 billion economic stimulus programme unless no comparable domestic goods were available.

(www.iht.com, 30 August 2009)

After four years of negotiations and WTO reviews the Chinese government announced Friday [28 August] that it would comply with the WTO's ruling that China must reduce its steep tax on imported auto parts that do not meet certain local content standards. The Chinese decision had been widely awaited because it marked the first time that China has had to comply with a WTO decision, having failed in an appeal, China had faced the possibility of American trade sanctions if it did not comply by Tuesday [1 September] ... The Chinese action comes after lengthy negotiations during which automakers have moved production to China on a very large scale anyway. Foreign automakers with assembly plants in China have largely stopped using imported auto parts, partly to avoid paying the steep taxes on these parts and partly because international auto parts manufacturers have moved production to China ... Beijing officials are still considering what to do about two more recent rulings against them at the WTO. In those rulings the WTO declared that China had failed to enforce laws against counterfeiting and had unfairly limited imports of movies, music, books and other copyrighted materials. General Motors, the automaker that accounts for three-quarters of American brand vehicle sales in China, now manufactures or purchases in China so many of its auto parts for vehicles sold in China that the government decision to comply with the WTO ruling makes little difference ... China reduced its prohibitive taxes on imported cars and car parts when it joined the WTO in November 2001. But even after the reduction, the taxes have stayed higher than in most markets – 25 per cent for imported cars and 10 per cent for imported parts. Four years ago China tightened its rules and declared that importers of car parts would have to pay the higher tax for imported cars, unless only a few imported parts were being installed in cars built mostly with Chinese parts ... Negotiations with China moved slowly, so the United States began formal consultations at the WTO with China in March 2006. The WTO set up a dispute resolution panel on 26 October 2006, and the panel ruled on 18 July 2008 that China had broken its commitments by charging the higher tax rate on imported parts instead of the 20 per cent rate that it had pledged. China appealed but lost the appeal last December [2008], which meant that it had until 1 September [2009] to comply or else the United States could impose penalties ... Chinese auto parts exports back to the United States have soared, almost doubling during the first three years after the Chinese imposed the tax before receding slightly in the past year as auto production has slumped in the United States because of the recession there.

(www.iht.com, 30 August 2009; *IHT*, 31 August 2009, p. 16)

In a break with the trade policies of his predecessor, President Barack Obama announced on Friday [11 September] that he would impose a 35 per cent tariff on automobile and light-truck tyres from China ... The United States, which already imposes a 4 per cent tariff on Chinese tyres, would impose an additional tariff of 35 per cent for one year. The tariff will be reduced to 30 per cent in the second year and 25 per cent in the third year. The tariff is to take effect on 26 September [2009] ... The decision signals the first time that the United States has invoked a special safeguard provision that was part of its agreement to support China's entry into the WTO in 2001. Under that safeguard provision, American companies or workers harmed by imports from China can ask the government for protection simply by demonstrating that American producers have suffered a 'market disruption' or a 'surge' in imports from China. Unlike more traditional anti-dumping cases, the govern-ment does not need to determine that a country is competing unfairly or selling its products at less than their true cost. The International Trade Com-mission had already determined that Chinese tyre imports were disrupting the $1.7 billion market and recommended that the president impose new tariffs. Members of the commission, an independent government agency, voted four-to-two on 29 June, to recommend that President Obama impose tariffs on Chinese tyres for three years ... American imports of Chinese tariffs tripled between 2004 and 2008, and China's share of the American market grew to 16.7 per cent, from 4.7 per cent ... The trade commission proposed higher tariffs than the president actually imposed, recommending an initial levy of 55 per cent ... President George W. Bush received four similar rec-ommendations from the trade commission, the most recent one involving steel pipe in December 2005, but he rejected all of those recommendations.

(www.iht.com, 12 September 2009)

'The International Trade Commission recommended tariffs in only four out of six cases' (www.iht.com, 13 September 2009).

The Chinese authorities said in a statement: 'In line with national laws and WTO rules, the commerce ministry has started an anti-dumping and anti-subsidy examination of some imported US car products and chicken meat ... [The commerce ministry says there are concerns the US imports have] dealt a blow to domestic industries' ... It comes a day after the US imposed tariffs on Chinese tyre imports in order 'to remedy a market disruption caused by a surge in tyre imports' ... The US trade deficit with China totalled $103 billion in the first half of 2009, down 13 per cent from the same period last year [2008].

(www.bbc.co.uk, 13 September 2009)

The Chinese government said Sunday [13 September] that it was opening investigations into whether the United States was subsidizing and dumping automotive and chicken meat exports to China ... The Chinese commerce ministry did not mention the tyre dispute in its announcement, taking pains to portray the investigations as 'based on the laws of our country and on WTO rules' ... The website of Xinhua prominently linked together its reports on the tyre dispute and the Chinese investigations without actually mentioning the tyre issue in its description of the coming investigations ... The commerce ministry issued ... criticism of the tyre decision Saturday [12 September].

(IHT, 14 September 2009, p. 1)

China exported $1.3 billion in tyres to the United States in the first seven months of 2009, while the United States shipped about $800 million in automotive products and $376 million in chicken meat to China ... Agriculture is one of the very few trade categories in which the United States runs a trade surplus with China. Chickens are a longstanding issue in Sino-American trade relations ... Congress, worried about low-cost Chinese chickens at a time of international worries about food safety in China, has banned the agriculture department for the last several years from spending money to certify China's procedures as equivalent. The Senate budget bill, expected to come up for a vote next week, would remove the ban. So China's latest move could represent an attempt to influence that vote ... China has rapidly increased its share of the auto parts market in the United States over the past three years ... The [US] trade deficit with China was a record $268 billion in 2008 ... China surpassed Germany in the first half of this year [2009] as the world's largest exporter.

(www.iht.com, 14 September 2009)

America's trade unions have complained that a 'surge' in imports of Chinese-made tyres had caused 7,000 job losses among US factory workers ... Official US figures show an increase in imports by volume from 14.6 million tyres in 2004 to 46 million in 2008. The US data shows that the value of tyre imports from China increased from $453.3 million in 2004 to $1.8 billion in 2008.

(FT, 14 September 2009, p. 1)

[On Monday 14 September] China requested talks, under WTO rules, with the United States over its trade dispute. The United States imposed tariffs on Chinese tyre imports on Friday [11 September]. China responded with an 'anti-dumping' probe into US car parts and chicken meat imports. China's commerce ministry said the tyre duties were in 'violation of WTO rules' ... China has called the moves 'protectionist'.

(www.bbc.co.uk, 14 September 2009)

In 2004 China and the United States banned each other's poultry imports after an outbreak of avian flu. China restored imports from the United

States, but the United States has continued to block processed Chinese poultry on health grounds … In response to a two-year-old US ban on processed chicken imports from China, Beijing has banned imports of US chickens from several states.

(*FT*, 15 September 2009, p. 7)

The duties are to be imposed on 26 September under a part of American trade law known as 'Section 421'. The American government argues that these tyres are being imported into America from China in 'such increased quantities and under such conditions as to cause or threaten to cause market disruption to domestic producers' of competing tyres. America imported tyres worth $1.3 billion from China between January and the end of July this year [2009]. Under the terms of China's accession to the WTO in 2001, countries have the right to impose tariffs in response to a 'surge in imports' from China. But there is always dispute about what constitutes enough of an export surge to justify the use of tariffs, and China has already notified the WTO of its intention to file a case against America. It is also said that it is considering the imposition of retaliatory tariffs on American exports of car parts and chicken meat … [There is the argument that] the American action and Chinese retaliation may presage more protectionist measures to come from both sides … [There are] worries that this could lead to a slew of other American industries demanding protection against competition from Chinese imports.

(www.economist.com, 14 September 2009)

Last week the [US] commerce department, concurring with a US International Trade Commission finding of improper subsidies, said it was imposing duties ranging from 10.9 per cent to 30.6 per cent on imports of Chinese pipes used to transport oil. The department is also investigating a complaint that Chinese steel manufacturers are selling pipe in the United States at unfairly low prices, with a decision due in November [2009] … Fred Bergson, director of the Petersen Institute for International Economics … criticized President Barack Obama's tyres decision … [but Bergson] said China had violated trade rules by requiring some foreign-owned tyre factories to export a high percentage of their output.

(www.iht.com, 15 September 2009)

The Chinese commerce ministry said: 'We do not want to see anything bad happen to bilateral relations' … China has called America's move on tyres 'protectionist'. Under WTO rules Beijing and Washington will try to solve the dispute over the next sixty days through negotiations. If that fails, China can ask for a WTO panel to make a ruling on tyre imports.

(www.bbc.co.uk, 15 September 2009)

'Pascal Lamy, WTO director-general, warned last week that the US tyres decision risked provoking a spiral of tit-for-tat retaliation that could weaken the trade impetus for global economic recovery' (*FT*, 23 September 2009, p. 6).

China yesterday [22 September] filed a last-minute appeal against a WTO ruling that it unfairly restricts the sale of US films, music and books, reviving an argument that its restrictions were needed to protect public morals and Chinese culture ... Although WTO rules permit governments to justify trade barriers on the grounds of protecting public morality, the panel said China's measures were more restrictive than they needed to be to attain its objectives. The WTO ruling did reject the import quota of twenty foreign films a year that are funnelled through China Film, a state company, nor did it challenge China's right to censor foreign films and publications.

(FT, 23 September 2009, p. 6)

The EU yesterday [25 September] imposed anti-dumping duties of nearly 40 per cent on imports of steel pipe from China. The decision, which followed a preliminary ruling earlier in the year [2009], broke new ground by imposing tariffs based only on the threat of damage to European groups from low-priced imports rather than requiring them to show actual lost sales.

(FT, 26 September 2009, p. 6)

China dominates the global production of rare earths, a collection of seventeen chemical elements in the periodic table that are used in making hybrid cars, wind turbines and smartphones. This is unusual as China depends on imports from abroad for most of its raw materials ... China's reserves are being used up rapidly. They now account for only half of the world's total, down from almost 90 per cent in 1990. In response, China has started to impose quotas and duties on rare earth exports ... Since 2004 exports from China have shrunk by about 10 per cent each year. But the move has angered China's trading partners ... The United States and the EU both filed complaints with the WTO earlier this year [2009].

(IHT, 8 October 2009, p. 22)

'Rare earths' [are] seventeen obscure chemical elements ... Most rare earths are not that rare, but they are difficult to find in concentrations worth mining that are untainted by uranium. About 95 per cent of the world's supply comes from China ... Chinese industry now consumes about two-thirds of rare earth production. Analysts expect domestic demand to lap up all of China's output within a few years. To safeguard its dwindling surpluses, the Chinese government has been stockpiling rare earths, taxing them and imposing ever smaller exports quotas. Earlier this year [2009] a Chinese government report suggested an outright export ban for the scarcest rare earths.

(The Economist, 10 October 2009, pp. 73–4)

The EU's executive is proposing extending anti-dumping duties on Chinese and Vietnamese shoe exports for a minimum of fifteen months, a compromise that aims to satisfy shoemakers and retailers alike in Europe. The European Commission, under pressure from shoe-making countries like

Italy, first imposed duties on imports in 2006 for two years ... But the issue has divided the bloc, with countries such as Sweden ... arguing the duties hurt consumers by pushing up prices. The Commission reimposed the tariffs on a temporary basis last October [2008] pending a review ... The proposal is expected to be adopted by the full Commission in the next few weeks, and then goes to national governments, which must decide whether to accept or reject it ... The Commission recommended that most Chinese shoes continue to face duties of 16.5 per cent, while it said 10 per cent duties would be applied to products of all Vietnamese companies. The Commission could have proposed an extension of up to five years, but limited it to fifteen months – for now ... If approved by EU members states, the new measures would take effect from 3 January.

(www.iht.com, 13 October 2009; *IHT*, 14 October 2009, p. 14)

The Chinese ministry of commerce issued a preliminary ruling Monday [19 October] that imposed a 36 per cent tariff on American-made Nylon 6, a synthetic filament that ends up in a wide array of products, including toothbrushes, auto parts, socks and the handles of Glock handguns. Nylon 6 from Taiwan and Russia would also be taxed, but at much lower rates ... The ministry said it would begin collecting the tariff immediately, though the money would be kept as a deposit and returned, should the decision be reversed. The ruling was the latest in a series of punitive measures that started last month [September], when the administration of Barack Obama imposed a 35 per cent tariff on Chinese-made tyres. Beijing quickly followed up with a threat to increase tariffs on American exports of chicken meat and car parts ... According to the commerce ministry's website, imports of Nylon 6 more than doubled from 2005 to 2007; in the first nine months of 2008, the website said, imports grew by nearly 21 per cent, much of them from the United States. The ministry said imports had harmed six Chinese enterprises.

(www.iht.com, 19 October 2009)

China is preparing to launch a trade investigation into whether US carmakers are being unfairly subsidized by the US government ... Through a 'countervailing duties' investigation, China would assess whether the United States was open to the charge ... of unfairly subsidizing its exporters ... China had notified the United States it had received anti-dumping and countervailing duty petitions on cars ... General Motors [GM] and Chrysler have received about $60 billion in government bail-out funds, though Ford has received nothing. Washington has also provided substantial aid to US and foreign carmakers, as well as parts suppliers, to encourage investment in 'green' technology. The wildly popular 'cash-for-clunkers' sales incentive scheme this summer was also a boon for both US and foreign manufacturers ... Few vehicles are actually exported from the United States to China ... The United States exports about 30,000 vehicles to China ... of which GM, Chrysler and Ford account for 7,000 to 9,000.

(www.cnn.com, 20 October 2009)

Trade talks between top Chinese and US officials opened on a discordant note Thursday [29 October] as fresh friction surfaced over American auto exports ... China plans to investigate dumping allegations against auto exports by the three big Detroit automakers ... Ford, General Motors and Chrysler export only about 9,000 cars to China a year, though they manufacturer millions more inside China in the joint venture they are required to operate with local partners ... Mercedes-Benz, BMW and Nissan also export cars to China from plants in the United States, but these won't be included in the investigation ... GM and Chrysler have received billions of dollars in aid from the [US] government's $700 billion bail-out fund, though Ford has not.

(www.iht.com, 20 October 2009)

Chinese officials said Thursday [29 October] that Beijing will lift a ban on imports of US pork that was imposed last spring due to swine flu fears. China's agriculture minister and commerce minister, speaking after a day of trade talks with US officials, emphasized that the decision was based on scientific analysis ... The ban ... had continued despite insistence by international health officials that pork is safe and the country's hogs are not to blame for the epidemic.

(www.iht.com, 29 October 2009)

At a high level meeting of officials from both countries ... China said it would permit US pork and relax restrictions on wind power components and government procurement ... Chinese officials said Beijing would lift a ban on imports of pork from the United States which had been in place since the outbreak of swine flu in the spring, although they did not say exactly when imports would start ... China would remove its local content requirement in tenders for wind power equipment ... [The United States] said China had agreed to treat joint venture companies involving the two countries as local businesses in government procurement contracts ... China would also submit an offer to join the WTO's government procurement agreement by 2010.

(*FT*, 30 October 2009, p. 12)

'China agreed to remove local-content requirements on wind turbines' (*IHT*, 2 November 2009, p. 18).

China will impose anti-dumping duties on adipic acid imported from the United States, the EU and South Korea starting Monday [2 November], the Chinese commerce ministry said Sunday [1 November]. The taxation is valid for five years, the ministry said in a statement. It said that Chinese producers of adipic acid, which is used to make nylon, were 'suffering substantial harm' from dumping.

(*IHT*, 2 November 2009, p. 17)

The United States, Mexico and the EU have asked that a WTO panel review China's restraints on raw material exports after talks with Beijing failed to settle the dispute, US trade officials said Wednesday [4 November]. China imposes quotas on exports of bauxite, coke, fluorspar, silicon carbide and zinc, as well as certain intermediate products incorporating some of these commodities ... The office of the US trade representative said: 'We believe the restraints at issue significantly distort the international market and provide preferential conditions for Chinese industries that use these raw materials.'

(*IHT*, 5 November 2009, p. 20)

The US Commerce Department has imposed anti-dumping tariffs of up to 99 per cent on imports of Chinese tubular goods ... The US Commerce Department said it has 'determined that Chinese producers/exporters have sold OCTG (oil country tubular goods) in the United States at prices ranging from zero to 99.14 per cent less than normal value' ... The department said that imports of OCTG from China were valued at an estimated $2.6 billion in 2008 ... Beijing has filed a WTO challenge to US anti-dumping duties on certain types of steel pipes, pneumatic off-road tyres and woven sacks.

(www.bbc.co.uk, 6 November 2009)

China denounced new US anti-dumping duties on steel pipes as protectionist on Friday [6 November] and opened an investigation into imports of US-made automobiles ... On Thursday [5 November] Washington imposed preliminary anti-dumping duties on Chinese-made pipes used in the US oil and natural gas industry. That followed US countervailing duties on the pipes, announced in September ... The Chinese investigation into possible US auto export subsidies would target sedans with engine capacities of 2 litres or more, as well as sport vehicles, the Chinese commerce ministry said. It issued a list of incentives and tax breaks that it said had been granted by the US government and the state of Michigan ... Beijing also called for the swift recognition by the United States that China was a market economy – a designation that would make it harder for countries to declare that Chinese products were being dumped at prices below market value ... In meetings with US trade officials in China last month [October] the Chinese side pressed for recognition as a market economy before the 2016 deadline that was negotiated when China entered the WTO. Washington promised to set up a panel to consider the issue. As long as China has no recognition as a market economy, its trade partners, when considering whether or not products have been dumped, can compare its products with those of other countries that have different cost structures for labour or transportation. Pipes that can carry highly corrosive oil and natural gas presented an opportunity for Chinese steel producers to move up the value chain. Exports to the United States, their biggest market, tripled to $2.63 billion in 2008 from 2007 ... The US International Trade Commission was to vote on Friday on whether to approve three more investigations into Chinese exports, covering coated paper, some standard steel fasteners, and sodium and potassium phosphate salts. China said Thursday that it would study policies in Arkansas, Alabama and Texas as part of its anti-subsidy investigation into chicken parts imported from the United States.

(www.iht.com, 6 November 2009)

Chinese officials criticized a US decision to impose anti-dumping duties on Chinese-made pipes used by the oil and natural gas industry and appealed to Washington on Wednesday [25 November] to avoid protectionism. The commerce industry accused US officials of improperly calculating the market value of the pipes when it announced Tuesday [24 November] it would impose duties of 10.36 per cent to 15.78 per cent. The US Commerce Department said it was acting to counter the effects of improper loans, tax breaks and other subsidies extended to Chinese manufacturers.

(*IHT*, 26 November 2009, p. 20)

China could face a protectionist backlash next year [2010] as a huge over-expansion of industrial capacity built up in recent months threatens to turn into a new surge of cheap exports, a European business group said yesterday [26 November]. Beijing's huge stimulus measures to revive the economy had exacerbated the already serious problem of over-capacity, the European Chamber of Commerce in China said in a report. Industries such as steel and plastics were still 'blindly expanding'. By the second half of 2010 there will be far more dumping cases against China ... Last month [October] the State Council, China's cabinet, announced it was taking steps to limit capacity increases in seven sectors ... The stimulus ... has caused continued expansion in steel, aluminium, cement and chemicals. The wind-power equipment and oil refining sectors were also facing over-capacity, the chamber said.

(*FT*, 27 November 2009, p. 10)

'Producers of wind power sell the electricity they generate to China's power distributors at prices fixed by the state ... The government obliges distributors to buy all wind power at preferential tariffs' (www.economist.com, 3 December 2009; *The Economist*, 5 December 2009, p, 74).

China said Thursday [10 December] that it would impose provisional duties on some US and Russian steel imports after anti-dumping and subsidy investigations ... Flat-rolled electrical steel products from steel makers including AK Steel Holding Corp., OAO Novolipetsk Steel and Allegheny Ludlum would attract duties of as much as 25 per cent starting Friday [11 December] ... The steel is used to make power transformers ... The United States and Russia last year [2008] exported a combined $602 million of the designated steel products to China ... Baosteel Group Corp. and Wuhan Iron and Steel Group [are] the only two producers of transformer steel in China ... US steel producers will face two types of duties, one for subsidies and the other for dumping, the Chinese said ... Russian companies will pay tariffs only for violating anti-dumping rules ... A final ruling will be decided later ... China's commerce ministry: 'This is the first time China has conducted an anti-subsidy and anti-dumping investigation' ... It said the imports have hurt the Chinese steel industry ... The Chinese commerce ministry in October made a preliminary ruling that US, European, Russian and Taiwanese chemical companies had dumped nylon fibres at below-cost prices in the Chinese market.

(www.iht.com, 10 December 2009)

Beginning Friday [11 December] US and Russian exporters will be required to pay cash deposits, but the ministry did not specify the amount, adding that its decision was a preliminary ruling. The ministry said the duties would be as high as 25 per cent ... The ministry said it was the first time that China had conducted an anti-subsidy investigation against imported products, although it has previously undertaken many anti-dumping investigations ... Grain-orientated electrical steel, a high-value, specialized product used in transformers, motors and power generators, makes up only a tiny proportion of total steel production in Russia. Novolipetsk (NLMK) is the only major producer of this particular steel product in Russia.

(*IHT*, 11 December 2009, p. 21)

China imposed duties yesterday [10 December] on imports of certain speciality steel products from the United States and Russia ... The Chinese commerce ministry said the duties were a response to the dumping of products in the Chinese market by companies from the two countries. Beijing also alleged the US companies were receiving what in effect were subsidies as a result of 'Buy American' legislation ... The decision is a further sign the steel industry is emerging as the most politically sensitive area of trade relations between China and its trading partners ... The Chinese commerce ministry said US steel companies had benefited from higher domestic prices because of the 'Buy American' provisions in the US stimulus package. As a result, they were able to tolerate charging lower prices on exported goods, the ministry said. Imports of these speciality steel products had grown sharply in the past two years, while domestic production had slumped.

(*FT*, 11 December 2009, p. 8)

'China agreed to end dozens of subsidies that promote its exports to resolve a US WTO complaint ... Washington accused China of providing cash grants, loans and research funding to makers of so-called famous-brand products, including apparel and high-tech electronics' (*FT*, 19 December 2009, p. 44).

Arbitrators at the WTO upheld a ruling on Monday [21 December] that China was illegally restricting imports of American music, films and books, and Washington pushed forward with a new case accusing China of manipulating the prices for key ingredients in steel and aluminium production ... The WTO made no finding that implies it is illegal for Beijing to review foreign goods for objectionable content. But it said China cannot limit the distribution of American goods to Chinese state-owned companies, and said the Asian country's burdensome restrictions were not 'necessary' to protect public morals ... The enquiry initiated Monday by the WTO – at the request of the United States, Mexico and the EU – focuses on the other half of the equation by examining China's treatment of domestic and foreign manufacturers with regards to its vast wealth of minerals. Washington and Brussels claim that China unfairly favours domestic industry by setting export quotas on materials such as coke, bauxite, magnesium and silicon metal. Export quotas are contentious under trade rules because they can cause a glut on the domestic market, driving down prices for local producers, while leading to scarcity and higher prices for competitors abroad. Beijing, however, claims that the curbs are an effort to protect the environment, and say they comply with WTO rules. For its part, China is challenging American trade rules on several issues like poultry, and asked the WTO at the dispute body meeting Monday for a new investigation into American import taxes on Chinese tyres ... Last week the two countries settled a dispute initiated by the Bush administration in December over subsidies that China allegedly provides to exporters of famous Chinese merchandise. Beijing agreed out-of-court to eliminate the subsidies.

(www.iht.com, 21 December 2009)

Monday's verdict, which is final, also opens the way for US and other foreign companies to sell mobile ring tones and music over the internet in China. This rapidly growing market, already worth half a million dollars annually, is currently barred to non-Chinese companies ... China has brought six cases to the WTO since joining in 2001, five against US measures ... China will be given time to comply with the latest ruling, but if it fails to do so it could be liable for US trade sanctions equivalent to the estimated value of trade lost. The WTO has not challenged China's right to censor foreign firms and publications, nor is Beijing required to lift the quota it imposes of just twenty foreign films a year. But it will now have to allow US and other foreign companies to import films, music and books into China, rather than channel all imports through state-owned entities, and permit US/Chinese joint ventures to distribute music over the internet.

(www.cnn.com, 22 December 2009)

The EU has voted to extend tariffs on shoes from China and Vietnam ... The tariffs, which were first introduced in 2006, will last for a further fifteen months ... The tariffs on Chinese shoes will remain at [a maximum of] 16.5 per cent, and those on Vietnamese shoes will remain at 10 per cent ... A number of countries in the EU were opposed to the extension ... The extension has also proved unpopular among some retail groups in Europe ... UK business secretary Lord Mandelson: 'A small majority of member states did not oppose the measures.'

(www.bbc.co.uk, 22 December 2009)

The charges add 9.7 per cent to 16.5 per cent to the import price of Chinese shoes and 10 per cent to Vietnamese shoes ... European importers and retailers had called for an end to the charges ... European governments said that they had voted by a majority to extend the duties at a meeting Tuesday [22 December]. They did not say how the twenty-seven member countries had voted. The EU introduced the trade charges in October 2006.

(www.iht.com, 22 December 2009)

The extension of the duties, as high as 16.5 per cent on leather shoes, was a compromise with a group of Northern European countries, which opposed extending the levies for the usual five-year period ... The trade protectionism, begun in 2006, helped reduce Chinese and Vietnamese exporters' combined share of the EU shoes market to 28.7 per cent in the twelve months through June 2008 from 35.5 per cent in 2005. The 2006 decision to impose the levies for two years was itself a compromise because such anti-dumping measures usually last five years. The levies are 16.5 per cent against all Chinese exporters except Golden Step, which faces a 9.7 per cent duty, and 10 per cent against all Vietnamese exporters. In April 2008 the EU extended the 16.5 per cent duty to Macao after finding that Chinese exporters were shipping leather shoes to Europe via Macao or were assembling them there to evade the duty.

(*IHT*, 23 December 2009)

China imposed anti-dumping duties on imports of carbon steel fasteners from the EU on Wednesday [23 December] ... A review found that Chinese production of certain types of fasteners like screws and washers had been materially injured by dumping by EU firms ... Beijing will start enforcing the anti-dumping duties, ranging from 16.8 per cent to 24.6 per cent, on Monday [28 December].

(*IHT*, 24 December 2009, p. 17)

The US government is imposing new duties on imports of steel pipes from China ... The case is the largest steel dispute in US history and will affect about $2.7 billion worth of Chinese imports. The US International Trade Commission [ITC] voted Wednesday [30 December] to impose duties of 10.36 per cent to 15.78 per cent on the pipes, which are mostly used in the oil and gas industries. The duties are intended to offset government subsidies that the US government says China is providing its steel makers ... the move Wednesday only addresses the US industry's concern that Chinese imports benefit from government subsidies. The ITC will also vote in the spring [of 2010] on whether to impose additional tariffs of up to 99 per cent to penalize the Chinese steel makers for dumping.

(*IHT*, 31 December 2009, p. 15)

The case is the biggest against China brought before the International Trade Commission ... The ruling will be passed on to the commerce department, which will impose the additional tax. In November the commerce department imposed separate anti-dumping duties of up to 99 per cent on imports of some Chinese pipes.

(*FT*, 31 December 2009, p. 8)

When the clock strikes midnight on New Year's Eve, China and the Asean nations will usher in the world's third largest free trade area ... Trade between China and the ten states that make up Asean has soared in recent years, to $192.5 billion in 2008, from $59.6 billion in 2003. The new free trade zone will remove tariffs on 90 per cent of traded goods ... The zone will rank behind only the European Economic Area and the North American Free Trade Area in trade volume. It will encompass 1.9 billion people ... Existing tariffs are already low ... Some manufacturers in South-east Asia are concerned that cheap Chinese goods may flood their markets once import taxes are removed ... Indonesia, for example, is so worried that it plans to ask for a delay in removing tariffs from some items like steel products, textiles, petrochemicals and electronics ... Asean and China have gradually reduced many tariffs in recent years. However, under the free trade agreement – which was signed in 2002 – China, Indonesia, Thailand, the Philippines, Malaysia, Singapore and Brunei will have to remove almost all tariffs in 2010. Asean's newest members – Cambodia, Laos, Vietnam and Myanmar – will gradually reduce tariffs in coming years and must eliminate them entirely by 2015. Most of the goods that will become tariff-free in January [2010] – including manufactured items – are currently subject to imports taxes of about 5 per cent. Some agricultural products and parts for motor vehicles and heavy machinery will still face tariffs in 2010, but those will gradually be phased out. In recent years China has overtaken the United States to become Asean's third largest trading partner after Japan and the EU. The overall trade balance has shifted slightly in China's favour, although there are significant differences among South-east Asian countries' trade balances ... Singapore, Malaysia and Thailand have only small trade deficits with China, while Vietnam's has grown substantially in recent years. In 2008 Vietnam exported items worth $4.5 billion to China but imported about $15.7 billion worth of Chinese goods ... [It has been argued that] countries like Vietnam that focus on the production of inexpensive consumer goods are more likely to be hurt ... [but that] China will import more agricultural goods, like, tropical fruit, from countries like Thailand, Malaysia and Vietnam when the trade area takes effect.

(www.iht.com, 28 December 2009; *IHT*, 29 December 2009, p. 14)

'The free trade area is expected to help Asean nations increase exports, particularly those with commodities that resource-hungry China desperately wants' (www.iht.com, 1 January 2010).

The China–Asean deal takes effect following the completion last summer [2009] of an agreement on investment rules, the last leg of an eight-year negotiating marathon that produced earlier agreements on goods and services. Tariffs have been falling since 2005, with 90 per cent of goods due to be tariff-free from yesterday [1 January 2010] for the six core members ... The target is 2015 for the other four (Laos, Cambodia, Burma and Vietnam) ... The deal remains short of genuine free trade. The trade in goods agreement provides for each country to register hundreds of sensitive goods on which tariffs will continue to apply, in many case until 2020. Sensitive goods include various types of electronic equipment, motor vehicles and automotive parts and chemicals, as well as items such as popcorn, snow-boarding equipment and toilet paper ... The deal creates the third largest regional trading agreement by value after the EU and the North American Free Trade Agreement, covering countries with mutual trade flows of $231 billion in 2008 ... China is already South-east Asia's third largest trading partner, with about 11 per cent of total two-way trade ... Indonesia led opposition to the pact, seeking to delay its implementation because of fears that sectors from steel to petrochemicals to cosmetics and herbal medicines would face overwhelming competition from cheap Chinese imports.

(*FT*, 2 January 2009, p. 6)

China launched an unfair trade case against the EU on Thursday [4 February], accusing the EU of imposing illegal duties on Chinese shoes, the WTO said ... Documents outlining China's case, which Vietnam did not participate in, were not immediately available. Its official complaint initiates a sixty-day consultation period, after which Beijing can ask the WTO to establish an investigative panel. If the WTO rules against Brussels, it can authorize China to target European goods with higher tariffs or other penalties in retaliation, though cases generally take years to reach that point.

(www.iht.com, 4 February 2010)

China, which joined the WTO in 2001, filed its first unfair trade case against the EU last July [2009], also involving anti-dumping duties ... In 2009, when the EU applied anti-dumping tariffs on imports of iron and steel fasteners from China, Beijing dragged the EU into the WTO dispute settlement process for the first time ... The latest move appeared designed to increase pressure on the EU, which itself had been sharply divided over extending the shoe tariffs.

(*IHT*, 5 February 2010, p. 14)

'It is only the second time that Beijing has taken the EU to the WTO's formal dispute resolution process' (*FT*, 5 February 2010, p. 12).

China is to enforce anti-dumping duties on US chicken imports, accusing American poultry firms of exporting the meat at unfairly low prices ... The tariffs will start from 13 February [2010]. China launched an investigation into US chicken in September [2009] ... The duties will vary across the various main US chicken farms ... The Chinese commerce department said its ruling was a preliminary one, but did not give any indication of when it will make its final decision.

(www.bbc.co.uk, 5 February 2010)

'China's commerce ministry announced it had decided to impose anti-dumping duties of up to 105.4 per cent on US poultry imports' (*FT*, 6 February 2010, p. 6).

China will levy initial anti-dumping duties ranging from 43.1 per cent to 105.4 per cent on US chicken products, the commerce ministry said Friday [5 February] ... The duties take effect Saturday [6 February] ... The ministry's initial investigation showed that US companies had dumped chicken products.

(*IHT*, 6 February 2010, p. 110)

China ... accounts for 97 per cent of the global supply of rare earth elements – a list of seventeen elements of the periodic table for which demand is growing fast ... Concerns about China's dominance were aggravated by market rumours last year [2009] that Beijing was about to tighten its rare earth elements export quota further, extending a policy that has seen a notable cut in exportable quantities in the past decade. However, the traders' chatter proved false: Beijing eased its quotas recently, allowing exports of 16,300 tonnes of strategically important rare earth metals for the first half of this year [2010], up by more than 8 per cent from the same period in 2009.

(*FT*, 29 January 2010, p. 12)

The United States yesterday [24 February] said it would impose preliminary anti-subsidy duties on steel pipe from China ... The decision, by the commerce department, needs to be confirmed' (*FT*, 25 February 2010, p. 8).

Yuan convertibility and exchange rate policy

The yuan (renminbi or 'people's currency') has gradually been made more and more convertible.

The first local foreign exchange markets ('swap centres') were set up in 1985 (a valuable boost to direct foreign investment since profits earned by 'foreign-invested enterprises' could be repatriated without having to export).

On 1 January 1994 the official and swap (market exchange) rates were unified, with the yuan subjected to a managed float.

'In late 1994 Beijing first pegged the yuan to the dollar' (www.iht.com, 22 July 2005).

China has fixed the value of the yuan at 8.277 to the dollar since 1995 ... The yuan can be freely exchanged only for trade purposes. Restrictions on the capital account, covering investment, prevent foreign investors from moving short-term capital into China and local investors from shifting funds overseas.

(www.iht.com, 2 July 2004; *IHT*, 3 July 2004, p. 11)

Officially the renminbi is already floating. It is, in theory, allowed to fluctuate 0.3 per cent either side of a reference rate determined each day by the central bank as a weighted average of the previous day's trades. But in practice the renminbi is pegged to the dollar. Normally the central bank is the biggest player on the Shanghai market, buying and selling currency to keep the exchange rate in a stable range between 8.2770 renminbi and 8.2800 renminbi to the dollar.

(*FEER*, 4 May 2000, p. 58)

'The renminbi ... is now pegged near 8.28 to the dollar within a band of 8.276 to 8.280' (*FEER*, 5 February 2004, p. 23).

In the Asian financial crisis (see below) there was relief that China did not devalue the yuan. More recently there has been the opposite pressure to revalue the yuan. The United States (with its large bilateral trade deficit with China) is particularly keen that China's currency strengthens against the US dollar in order to make Chinese exports less competitive. (While it is generally thought that the yuan is undervalued, there is considerable disagreement as to the extent to which this is so. See, for example, *The Economist*, 25 June 2005, p. 100.)

'China's central bank bought about $180 billion of US Treasuries last year [2004] to maintain the value of the yuan as foreign currency flowed into the economy' (www.iht.com, 13 January 2005).

China and other Asian countries have – because of massive dollar purchases to prevent their currencies appreciating – emerged as the financiers of the US's [large] current account and fiscal deficits, providing cheap capital that has kept the dollar's decline orderly and helped bring economic growth and low interest rates ... Foreign central banks, mainly from Asia, buy US Treasury paper ... [Asian countries] face capital losses on their reserves as the dollar declines ... Economists estimate that three-quarters of China's foreign reserves of more than $600 billion are held in US dollar assets ... A shift in exchange rate policy would allow the government to use monetary policy for domestic goals, rather than subordinating interest rate decisions to the management of the renminbi [the government having to buy dollars with renminbi in order to maintain the exchange rate, thus increasing the money supply] ... The government has been able to offset the impact of the accumulation of reserves on the domestic economy by selling Chinese government securities – a process called sterilization. Reserves increased last year [2004] but the central bank drained about two-thirds of this out of the system through sterilization, ensuring that the impact on the money supply was minimal.

(*FT*, 14 April 2005, p. 17)

Money is pouring into China, both because of its rapidly rising trade surplus and because of foreign investment. Normally this inflow would be self-correcting: both China's trade surplus and the foreign investment pouring in would push up the value of the yuan ... making China's exports less competitive and shrinking its trade surplus. But the Chinese government, unwilling to let that happen, has kept the yuan down by shipping incoming funds right back out again, buying huge quantities of dollar assets – about $200 billion worth in 2004, and possibly as much as $300 billion worth this year ... This money flowing in from abroad has kept US interest rates low despite the enormous [US] government borrowing required to cover the [US] budget deficit.

(Paul Krugman, *IHT*, 21 May 2005, p. 6)

'Reports in the official Chinese media say that Beijing has invested about two-thirds of its $750 billion of foreign currency reserves in US government and corporate debt' (*IHT*, 7 November 2005, p. 14).

> China's foreign currency reserves of $660 billion are rising by $17 billion or so a month. To mop up the liquidity created from buying these reserves, China's central bank has to issue ever more domestic currency bonds. With more than 1 trillion yuan of these bonds now outstanding, the country's commercial banks are becoming more reluctant to buy them.
>
> (*The Economist*, 21 May 2005, pp. 85–6)

> The combination of a rising current account surplus and foreign direct investment inflows has led to a need to purchase dollar assets to stabilize the exchange rate. The authorities have been able to sterilize much of this inflow through changes in reserve ratios, open market operations and window guidance to restrain the growth of bank lending without raising interest rates ... Reliance on window guidance to limit bank lending goes against the government's policy of increasing the use of market-based instruments to control monetary developments.
>
> (OECD 2005: website Chapter 1)

> Massive, sustained one-way intervention in the foreign exchange market (averaging 12 per cent of GDP in 2003 and 2004 and rising in 2005) has kept the renminbi from appreciating against the dollar in nominal terms and has induced moderate depreciation in China's real effective exchange rate.
>
> (Morris Goldstein and Michael Mussa, *FT*, 3 October 2005, p. 19)

On 21 July 2005 there was a small revaluation of the yuan against the dollar, with the peg against the dollar scrapped in favour of the yuan moving within a daily trading band of 0.3 per cent either way against a basket of currencies (including the dollar). (For details, see the section below.)

On 1 December 1996 China formally accepted Article 8 of the IMF's articles of association on current account convertibility (restrictions remaining on capital account transactions).

Developments in yuan convertibility and exchange rate policy since April 2006

(See Jeffries 2006a: 546–76 for earlier developments.)

On 21 July 2005 there was a small revaluation of the yuan against the dollar. There has been a controlled appreciation of the yuan since then. But the yuan's appreciation against the dollar has been too small to appease the United States and others have joined in the chorus of criticism. The EU has been increasingly vocal about the Euro's general appreciation against the yuan.

'Chinese currency remains at least 25 per cent below its fair market value' (*FT*, 7 April 2006, p. 14).

Analysts say that China has been gradually diversifying away from dollar assets in its foreign exchange reserves, but fears of a collapse in the currency will prevent Beijing from making any dramatic shift ... China held $262.6 billion of US Treasury securities as of January [2006], which is dwarfed by Japan's holding of $668.3 billion.

(www.iht.com, 4 April 2006)

The European Commission is proposing ... to a meeting of EU finance ministers [15–16 April] ... that Europe back China's policy of switching to a more flexible exchange rate system at its own pace – rebuffing the US call for faster steps to raise the value of the currency ... The commission warned that sudden moves to strengthen the yuan, as demanded by US officials, could further weaken the dollar against the Euro ... The European Commission: 'China should introduce greater exchange rate flexibility in a gradual manner ... [A gradual move would lessen the risk of the dollar, Euro and yen] overshooting [on the markets] ... [An abrupt move to stop pegging the yuan and possibly other Asian currencies to the dollar] could give rise to a sudden reversal of Asian capital flows into the United States, which might risk an excessive additional downward of the dollar against the Euro' ... The twelve countries using the Euro posted a trade deficit with China of $90 billion in 2005. The US deficit with China was $201.6 billion.

(*IHT*, 4 April 2006, p. 13)

'The EU [as a whole] posted a ... $128 billion trade deficit with China last year [2006]' (*IHT*, 10 April 2006, p. 10).

European finance ministers steered clear of public confrontation with China over the value of its currency as a two-day meeting between EU and Asian finance ministers drew to a close [in Vienna on 9 April] ... Nevertheless, a main concern at the talks was the divisive issue of the yuan's valuation. The United States has called strongly for China to allow its currency to appreciate. But European leaders were more guarded Sunday [9 April], noting that Beijing had allowed the yuan to rise, albeit gradually, with some adding that a sudden revaluation could lead to turmoil in currency markets.

(www.iht.com, 9 April 2006)

EU finance ministers called Sunday [9 April] for China to allow its currency to appreciate, but they couched their demands in a gentle tone that contrasted sharply with the tough-talking approach taken by American officials and the US Congress. During a meeting of EU finance ministers with their Asian counterparts in Vienna, EU officials highlighted the need for China to allow the yuan ... to float more freely. But they pointedly avoided giving the Chinese formal advice in a high-profile diplomatic setting ... The final communiqué from the meeting included no mention of the exchange rate issue, though it cited global imbalances as a risk to economic growth ... European diplomacy appears to have embraced the concept that the outside world can do little but try to convince the Chinese that letting the yuan strengthen is in their own interest.

(IHT, 10 April 2006, p. 10)

Beijing announced a broad package of currency changes Friday [14 April] that will allow Chinese individuals and institutions unprecedented access to foreign currencies ... The new rules may relieve upward pressure on the yuan to strengthen and may open up foreign stock markets to Chinese individuals for the first time by allowing qualified Chinese brokerage firms and fund managers to purchase foreign securities, including stocks, on behalf of individual clients. Domestic banks and insurance companies will be able to buy US Treasury securities and other overseas fixed-income securities with foreign currency purchased in China ... The real level of capital outflows from China could be constrained by quotas and other barriers contained in implementing guidelines Beijing has yet to issue ... [It is not known] whether the quotas are going to be small or a few billion dollars ... Beijing will increase the amount of foreign currency Chinese individuals can buy when they leave the country. From 1 May Chinese travellers abroad will be permitted to take up to $20,000 a year out of the country, up from $8,000 now ... Until recently China made its companies sell to the government all of the foreign money they earned overseas and it maintained strict limits on the amount of foreign cash Chinese citizens could buy when they left the country.

(IHT, 15 April 2006, p. 11)

China is to relax restrictions on companies and individuals making financial investments overseas in the latest stage of the government's gradual efforts to loosen capital controls ... The package of changes, which comes into effect in May, allows individuals to buy up to $20,000 of foreign exchange every year – up from $8,000 – and simplifies the procedures. Certain banks will be allowed to convert clients' deposits into foreign currency to be invested in overseas bond markets, while insurance companies will be allowed to buy overseas fixed income instruments. Some fund managers will be permitted to use funds raised in foreign currencies to buy overseas equities ... Beijing announced yesterday [14 April] that foreign exchange reserves increased by $56.2 billion in the first quarter to $875.1 billion.

(FT, 15 April 2006, p. 7)

The yuan rose a tenth of a per cent on Wednesday [19 April] in Shanghai trading to 8.0163 ... China revalued the yuan by 2.1 per cent on 21 July [2005] and has let it creep up by another 1.2 per cent since then ... Chinese businesses across a range of industries [such as clothing, shoes, ceramics and automobiles] say that their main response to a strengthening currency and rising wages has been to accelerate their move toward higher-end products, from shoes to cars ... Chinese exporters are nervous that their country's currency will keep appreciating and are responding with a race to sell higher-value goods.

(www.iht.com, 19 April 2006)

'On Wednesday [19 April] the yuan had its biggest gain against the dollar since its July 2005 revaluation, rising as much as 0.14 per cent. The dollar eased to 8.0128 yuan' (www.iht.com, 19 April 2006).

National productivity improvements have broadly matched nominal wages growth for more than a decade. Of course, rising costs squeeze manufacturers of highly labour-intensive products, such as T-shirts ... Industrialization is all about shifting continuously from basic products to more advanced ones. The changing composition of China's surging exports shows how successfully it has done so. Textiles and clothing, which generated 28 per cent of the total in 1993, accounted for 9 per cent last year [2005], while the share of machinery and electrical goods trebled to 56 per cent.

(*FT*, 20 April 2006, p. 16)

'The US Treasury [on 10 May] ... stopped short of accusing China of manipulating the value of its currency, but said Beijing had made "far too little progress" in adopting a flexible exchange rate' (*FT*, 11 May 2006, p. 11).

China allowed its currency to strengthen Monday [15 May] past the psychologically significant level of 8 yuan to the dollar for the first time since 1994 ... The actual rise was tiny: not quite one-tenth of a percent from Friday's level ... Monday's appreciation of the yuan marked the first time that it has breached 8 to the dollar since China unified a series of separate official rates in 1994 into a single exchange rate. The rate was initially set at 8.7 yuan to the dollar ... The People's Bank of China set a rate of 7.9982 yuan to the dollar at the opening of heavily regulated trading in Shanghai [on Monday], and the yuan strengthened a little further during the day to close at 7.9976 ... The yuan actually weakened on Thursday and Friday [when it was 8.0063] before rallying on Monday. China revalued the yuan by 2.1 per cent on 21 July [2005] and has allowed it to creep up 1.4 per cent since then, including Monday's increase. The yuan meanwhile has actually been losing ground against the Euro and the yen as the dollar has slipped sharply against them in the past month. The yuan has fallen 5.3 per cent against the Euro and 6.1 per cent against the yen since 1 April.

(www.iht.com, 15 May 2006; *IHT*, 16 May 2006, pp. 1, 18)

China's central bank on Friday [19 July] ordered commercial lenders to put aside 8.5 per cent of deposits as reserves, raising the requirement for the second time in two months to curb inflation and excessive investment. The reserve ratio will be raised from 15 August ... The central bank on 16 June raised the reserve ratio by 0.5 percentage points to 8 per cent, effective 5 July ... Every 0.1 percentage point rise in the reserve ratio reduces available loans by 150 billion yuan, according to the central bank's estimate ... Second quarter [of 2006] economic growth of 11.3 per cent [was] the faster pace in more than a decade.

(www.iht.com, 21 July 2006)

The central bank tried Friday for the second time in five weeks to curb excessive lending in a bid to cool a surging economy ... 'Investment in fixed assets is increasing too fast and credit is growing too rapidly,' the central bank said ... On Friday the yuan traded at 7.982 to the dollar ... Senior officials, including prime minister Wen Jiabao, have acknowledged in recent weeks that the sharp increase in spending on luxury apartments, shopping malls, steel mills and mines could lead to excess capacity and waste.

(*IHT*, 22 July 2006, pp. 11–12)

'In the most recent quarter [of 2006] GDP grew by 11.3 per cent over the year earlier, the fastest pace since 1994, when the economy was one-fourth its current size' (*IHT*, 31 July 2006, p. 15).

China is to cut tax rebates on exports of energy-consuming and resource-intensive products within the next three months as it seeks to curb a record trade surplus [it was reported on 23 July] ... Sectors including textiles, iron and steel would see their tax rebates cut by an average of 2 per cent in a policy designed to take effect in September or October ... High-tech industries would have their tax rebates increased, reflecting the government's desire to move the economy away from exports with low value-added ... The government paid rebates last year [2005] of 0.4429 yuan for every dollar of commodities exported. Scrapping the rebates would have been equivalent to strengthening the yuan to 7.7 per dollar at the end of 2005 ... The actual exchange rate then was 8.07 per dollar ... The yuan closed Friday [21 July] at 7.98 per dollar, the strongest finish yet. On Friday China authorized three banks to invest $4.8 billion in overseas securities in the first phase of a programme designed to provide an escape valve for some of the foreign currency flooding into the financial system from the trade surplus. The approval marked the first time that the state administration of foreign exchange has allowed state commercial banks to invest funds in overseas investment projects on behalf of their clients ... The Bank of China was given $2.5 billion in quotas; the Commercial Bank of China $2 billion; and the Bank of East Asia $300 million ... Other banks have also applied.

(*IHT*, 24 July 2006, p. 9)

Beijing will trim export rebates for a range of products as part of a series of measures aimed at rebalancing and restraining economic growth and swelling trade and current account surpluses ... The rebates will be cut by about 2 per cent in industries that are 'energy consuming' and 'resource intensive' ... The long expected rebate is expected to hit sectors such as textiles and steel, parts of which have seen exports surge in recent months in anticipation of the change. China has been a net exporter of all steel products for the last two months ... The rebate for steel could fall from about 13 per cent to as low as 8 per cent to 9 per cent ... The measures buttress the two stated pillars of economic policy: to have trade policy broadly balanced and reduce over-investment in heavy and resource-intensive industries. Despite this, China's economy continues to be propelled by the two 'strong horses' of trade and investment, with what the local press calls the 'weak donkey' of consumption lagging behind ... Beijing introduced export rebates in 1985 and increased them in the late 1990s during the Asian financial crisis, when the currencies of China's regional competitors fell. Since 2003 they have been trimmed a number of times and abolished for some products. Local experts ... said the gradual reduction of the rebates amounted to an effective revaluation of the renminbi to 7.7 to the dollar at the end of 2005 ... China dropped its decade-long peg to the US dollar in July last year [2005] and allowed a one-off 2.1 per cent revaluation. Since then the currency has risen by only another 1.6 per cent, to 7.98 to the dollar.

(*FT*, 24 July 2006, p. 8)

China on Monday [24 July] announced rules to limit foreign investment in real estate amid quickening efforts to cool the surging economy ... Under the new rules foreigners would face 'restrictions on residential property pur-chases' ... Developers would be required to invest more of their own money in projects to reduce heavy borrowing ... [It was not said when the rules] would take effect ... The regulations are similar to a draft published this month [July], but they add a requirement that foreign individuals must have worked or studied in China for at least a year to be eligible to buy a home ... The rules stipulate that only foreign entities with offices in China and foreign individuals who meet the residency requirement may purchase property on their own, and that it must be for their own use. Foreign companies or indi-viduals that want to buy property not for their own use must establish a locally registered investment company and buy through that company. Foreign prop-erty firms investing more than $10 million must have registered capital of at least 50 per cent of the investment ... Investment from Hong Kong and other sources outside China's mainland has poured into real estate ... Investors apparently hope to profit from rising prices and an anticipated rise in the yuan, which would lift the value of mainland assets in foreign currency terms.

(www.iht.com, 24 July 2006; *IHT*, 25 July 2006, p. 62)

The yuan rose 0.1 per cent against the dollar in Shanghai on Thursday [27 July], the most since China scrapped a peg against the currency last summer after US lawmakers threatened trade sanctions unless gains accelerated by 30 September ... The dollar fell to 7.9768 yuan. The lawmakers, Senators Charles Schumer and Lindsey Graham ... [said on Wednesday 26 July] that they wanted to see the yuan appreciate or they would push ahead with legis-lation to impose a 27.5 per cent duty on Chinese goods.

(www.iht.com, 27 July 2006)

The yuan set a post-revaluation high against the dollar for the second con-secutive day on Friday [28 July] amid continued speculation that the central bank would allow the Chinese currency to appreciate faster ... Over the past few days ... the central bank has stayed out of the market ... The dollar finished at 7.9705 yuan, the strongest close for the Chinese currency since its 2.1 per cent revaluation in July 2005 ... The dollar's previous post-revaluation low had been 7.9740 on Thursday. The Chinese currency has now gained a further 1.75 per cent against the dollar since the revaluation.

(www.iht.com, 28 July 2006)

'The Chinese currency has since [July 2005] appreciated by about 3.8 per cent' (*IHT*, 31 July 2006, p. 15).

[China holds] more than $300 billion in US government debt, or 8 per cent of the total that is publicly held ... The overall US deficit in its current account last year [2005 was] $800 billion ... [In July] Senator Lindsey Graham ... and Senator Charles Schumer ... declared that if China did not revalue its currency by 30 September they would reintroduce legislation to raise taxes on Chinese imports ... After a 2.1 per cent revaluation against the dollar a year ago, the currency has only climbed another 1.6 per cent. The central bank lets the currency trade within a tight range each day. The bank allowed a slight appreciation on Thursday [10 August], setting the centre of the range at 7.9688 yuan to the dollar, compared with 7.9772 at the end of trading on Wednesday.

(www.iht.com, 10 August 2006; *IHT*, 11 August 2006, p. 12)

'[On 16 August] China permitted the biggest gain in the yuan since ending a peg to the dollar in July last year [2005], a day after allowing the largest decline, suggesting the central bank is easing controls over the exchange rate' (www.iht. com, 16 August 2006).

The Chinese currency has recorded its biggest single-day rise against the US dollar ... to close trading at renminbi 7.98 to the dollar ... The rise yesterday [16 August] followed a relatively sharp weakening of the renminbi on Tuesday [15 August] for the first time hitting the 0.3 per cent daily fluctuation limit against the dollar set last year [2005] ... The renminbi has appreciated by only about 1.7 per cent against the greenback since [July 2005].

(*FT*, 17 August 2006, p. 5)

The Chinese currency 0.28 per cent fall on 15 August was its biggest in a day since China revalued the yuan in July 2005. The next day it gained 0.24 per cent at one point, before closing 0.16 per cent up; only three times has it risen by more in a day ... Over the past few months the yuan's exchange rate has been getting more volatile, by its own modest standards ... The rate is allowed to vary by 0.3 per cent either side of a parity set daily by China's central bank ... From 8.11 to the dollar after revaluation it has risen only to around 8.00.

(*The Economist*, 19 August 2006, p. 65)

'The yuan rose Friday [18 August] ... 0.15 per cent to 7.9765 against the dollar in Shanghai from its closing price Thursday [17 August]' (*IHT*, 19 August 2006, p. 11).

'Since July 2005 ... the yuan has gained nearly 2 per cent against the US currency. It was at 7.9543 to the dollar Monday [11 September] in Shanghai' (www. iht.com, 12 September 2006).

China's foreign currency reserves, already the world's largest, grew ... to $925 billion as of the end of May [2006] ... The reserves totalled $875.1 billion at the end of March ... China overtook Japan as the world's largest holder of foreign exchange reserves at the end of February [2006].

(www.iht.com, 5 July 2006)

'Foreign exchange reserves were ($954.4 billion at the end of July [2006]' (*IHT*, 5 July 2006, p. 14).

China will use a trade and financial zone under development ... the Binhai area ... at the northern port of Tianjin to ease restrictions on the convertibility of the yuan on a trial basis [its was reported on 11 September 2006] ... The yuan will become convertible on the capital account within a certain geographical area and up to certain monetary amounts ... [No] details [were given] of plans for the trial currency or when it might occur ... But the reform would be broad, with Chinese residents and companies permitted to buy foreign currencies freely, and qualified institutions allowed to expand foreign investment activities.

(www.iht.com, 12 September 2006)

China's national welfare fund will start investing overseas soon, with European markets among potential destinations, the top fund official said Thursday [21 September]. The fund had assets of 23 billion yuan, or $29.02 billion, invested in financial assets including bank deposits, bonds and trust funds at the end of August [2006] ... Overseas investment will be in instruments including stocks and bonds ... The amount to be invested would depend on market conditions, with no fixed quota to meet. The fund had planned to invest between $500 million and $800 million outside the mainland by the end of this year [2006], state media [reported in June] ... At the time it was said that the fund would select managers and trust companies in the third quarter and start investment in Hong Kong in the fourth quarter ... A separate programme, known as the Qualified Domestic Institutional Investor Plan, grants certain financial institutions quotas to invest abroad. At home the fund planned to spend an initial 1 billion yuan in the Bohai Industrial Investment Fund being set up in the Binhai New Area in the northern port of Tianjin ... If the Bohai fund, which will be the first such equity fund in China, proves a success, the national security fund will look to expand into other such investment fund ... The fund also planned more investment in industrial projects in China ... [e.g.] a 3 billion yuan trust loan to the railway ministry at the end of last year [2005].

(www.iht.com, 21 September 2006)

Significant sections of China's policy-making elite remain convinced that Japan's lengthy recession had its roots in a large revaluation of the yen forced on it by the United States in the mid-1980s ... Within the next few weeks China's [foreign currency] reserves are due to top $1,000 billion – a record for any country ... The composition of China's reserves is secret, but analysis of global funds data suggests that Beijing has not been able to diversify in any meaningful senses its reliance on [the US dollar] ... [One estimate suggests that] about 70 per cent of the reserves are in dollars, mainly US Treasury bills but increasingly in instruments such as mortgage-backed securities and even emerging market bonds.

(FT, 25 September 2006, p. 15)

The government allowed the country's currency to rise Thursday [29 September], with the yuan falling below 7.9 to the dollar for the first time, the latest in a series of daily highs as its pace of appreciation has mysteriously accelerated ... The yuan rose 0.07 per cent in Shanghai trading on Thursday to trade at 7.8965 at 5.30 p.m., and has climbed at an annual rate of 17 per cent in the last two weeks ... Beijing's leaders have long bridled at foreign criticism, prompting some China watchers to suggest that quiet diplomacy may be more productive in bringing about an appreciation of the yuan than confrontation. [US] Treasury Secretary Henry Paulson Jr, with decades of experience in dealing with China while at Goldman Sachs, has pursued a much more low key approach to the currency issue this summer than his predecessors or US lawmakers, preferring to raise the issue in private with Chinese leaders .... The People's Bank of China said when it revalued the currency in July 2005 that it would start setting the value of the yuan based on a basket of foreign currencies, and would no longer peg it just to the dollar. But in practice the central bank has allowed the yuan to appreciate at a fairly steady pace against the dollar; statistical analyses of changes in the yuan's value have shown almost no correlation to currencies other than the dollar. Through capital controls and other measures the People's Bank of China has made sure that spot trading of the yuan is conducted only in Shanghai, where the central bank is heavily involved in trading and sets the benchmark exchange rate between the yuan and the dollar each morning.

(IHT, 29 September 2006, p. 12)

China welcomed the decision by US senators Charles Schumer and Lindsey Graham to abandon a 27.5 per cent tariff on US-bound Chinese goods unless Beijing significantly raised the value of the yuan within six months. The senators said Thursday [28 September] that they had accomplished their goal of focusing more attention on China's exchange controls.

(IHT, 30 September 2006, p. 15)

('The 27.5 per cent tariff proposed in the Schumer–Graham bill is the middle range, from 15 per cent to 40 per cent, of estimates of the yuan's undervaluation against the dollar that the two senators knew about': *The Economist*, 1 April 2006, p. 73.)

The yuan has picked up the pace over the past couple of months, rising at an annual rate of almost 7 per cent against the American dollar since September [2006] – four times as fast as over the previous fourteen months since it broke its link with the dollar ... On 13 November the yuan hit a new high of 7.864 to the dollar, putting it within a whisker of the Hong Kong dollar's trading band of HK$ 7.75–7.85.

(*The Economist*, 18 November 2006, p. 92)

The Chinese currency rose to another high against the dollar Monday [27 November] as the central bank set its rate at 7.8402 yuan per dollar ... The rise, just 0.16 per cent above the close Friday [24 November], brought the yuan to its highest level against the dollar since the exchange system was established in 2005, in keeping with China's policy of allowing a steady but incremental move towards a more market-driven valuation of the currency ... Beijing has allowed the yuan's value to rise by about 3.3 per cent since it revalued the currency by 2.1 per cent in July 2005, when it severed the yuan's virtual peg with the dollar. China allows the dollar–yuan rate to move no more than 0.3 per cent above or below the daily parity rate each day. Other currency pairs – the yuan's values against the yen, the Euro, the Hong Kong dollar and the pound – are allowed to move within 3 per cent of the parity rate each day.

(www.iht.com, 27 November 2006)

China's currency gained 0.11 per cent in Shanghai, with the dollar at 7.8436 yuan, bringing its appreciation to 3.3 per cent since ... 21 July 2005 ... The People's Bank of China fixed the reference rate for yuan trading at 7.8402 against the dollar on Monday.

(*IHT*, 28 November 2006, p. 16)

'Over the past year-and-a-half the yuan has gained just 3.74 per cent against the dollar, reaching a new high of 7.8185 on Friday [15 December]' (www.bbc.co.uk, 15 December 2006).

On Thursday [14 December] the yuan closed at 7.8185 to the dollar, reflecting a 5.9 per cent increase in the last year and half [the 5.9 per cent including the 2.1 per cent increase in July 2005] ... Many economists say a free-floating yuan would rise 20 per cent or more.

(www.iht.com, 15 December 2006)

The Bush administration, softening its tone of criticism, has reported to Congress that the Chinese had made strides in revaluing their currency, but that the progress was 'considerably less than is needed' ... In May [2006] the Treasury's report on China said the administration was 'extremely dissatisfied' with Beijing's progress on the currency issue. The Treasury secretary at the time, John Snow, criticized China even while declining to label it a currency manipulator, because such a ruling would have required a finding of intent on the part of the Chinese.

(www.iht.com, 20 December 2006)

Insurers in China may be allowed to invest up to 15 per cent of their 1.89 trillion yuan of total assets in overseas stocks, fixed-income products and currency market funds, according to draft rules by the regulator published on Thursday [21 December 2006] ... The commission is seeking public comment. The new rules give Chinese insurers additional investment options up to $242 billion, and longer return periods on their assets to match liabilities that stretch to thirty years for life insurance and other policies ... To qualify for the QDII programme ... the domestic institutional investor programme ... the insurers' funds must be handled by asset management companies operating within rules and risk controls that meet the regulator's standards.

(*IHT*, 22 December 2006, p. 18)

The yuan rose past the Hong Kong dollar Thursday [11 January 2007] ... The yuan climbed to more than one per Hong Kong dollar for the first time in thirteen years ... The yuan rose to 1.0004 per Hong Kong dollar and 7.7949 to the US dollar on Thursday in Shanghai. The currency has advanced 6.2 per cent since China ended a decade-old peg to the dollar in July 2005.

(*IHT*, 12 January 2007, p. 13)

'The Hong Kong Monetary Authority pegged the Hong Kong dollar at 7.8 to the United States dollar in 1983 and maintained that policy with few changes until June 2005. It then moved to a narrow trading band of 7.75 to 7.85 to the dollar' (*IHT*, 6 January 2007, p. 13).

'China has let the yuan rise just 3.9 per cent since it was revalued by 2.1 per cent against the dollar in July 2005' (www.iht.com, 10 January 2007).

'The yuan ... [experienced a] 3.4 per cent rise in 2006 ... The yuan has gained 4.3 per cent against the dollar on top of the 2.1 per cent revaluation that occurred ... in July 2005' (www.iht.com, 20 January 2007).

'The yuan ... [has] risen by a further 4 per cent against the dollar since the government first revalued the currency by 2.1 per cent in July 2005' (*The Economist*, 13 January 2007, p. 69).

[On 24 January 2007 it was reported that] Bank of Beijing, which is 19.9 per cent owned by Dutch bank ING, has won official approval to invest $300 million of client money under the Qualified Domestic Institutional Investor programme ... The Chinese bank is the first city commercial bank in mainland China to win the right to invest in overseas capital markets ... Including the $300 million quota allocated to Bank of Beijing, China has granted a total quota of $13.2 billion to mainland commercial banks.

(www.iht.com, 24 January 2007)

Chinese officials have periodically hinted they might widen the limit on how much the yuan can trade up and down within a single day, currently set at three-tenths of a per cent. But officials have given little sign that they are willing to allow faster appreciation of the yuan, which has crept up by 6.7 per cent since China broke the yuan's peg to the dollar in July 2005.

(*IHT*, 13 March 2007, p. 10)

('At present ... the yuan [is allowed] to climb or fall a maximum of 0.3 per cent from a daily fixed rate': www.bbc.co.uk, 12 March 2007.)

China is creating an investment company to get better returns of its foreign currency reserves worth $1 trillion ... [At the National People's Congress held 5–16 March 2007] finance minister Jin Renqing [on 9 March] gave no details when the fund would be set up or how it would manage the money. However, he pointed to Singapore's state investment firm Temasek as a possible model.

(www.bbc.co.uk, 9 March 2007)

People close to the state administration of foreign exchange, which is controlled by the People's Bank of China and manages the country's reserves, estimated that the agency already held about $100 billion worth of American mortgage-backed securities ... The People's Bank of China discloses few details about its holdings. But experts estimate that it holds another $600 billion or so worth of US Treasury securities that it lends actively to generate extra profit, as well as at least $200 billion worth of Euro-denominated bonds. The remainder is thought to be held in bonds denominated in yen and other currencies.

(*IHT*, 6 March 2007, p. 14)

Finance minister Jin Renqing ... announced the formation of a new agency on Friday [9 March] to oversee investment of the country's massive $1 trillion in foreign currency reserves ... [although] he offered no specifics about how much of China's currency reserves would be made available to the investment agency. China already has the world's largest foreign exchange holdings and they are growing at a rapid pace ... The government said one of the models for the new agency is Temasek Holdings, the Singapore government's hugely successful investment agency, which manages an $84 billion global portfolio of investments. China's currency exchange reserves are now held by ... the People's Bank of China and most of the reserves are expected to continue to be held there in safe, conservative investments in government securities. But a large sum is expected to be shifted to the new agency or investment group, which could ... invest it for higher returns ... Jin Renqing said the new agency would answer directly to the State Council.

(www.iht.com, 9 March 2007)

China's currency exchange reserves are now held by the People's Bank of China and most of the reserves are expected to continue to be held there, in safe, conservative investments in government securities ... Jin Renqing: 'The biggest priority is safety and under the principle of security we will try to increase the efficiency of management and the investments' returns.'

(*IHT*, 10 March 2007, pp. 1, 17)

'The State Council has already made research into separating the management of normal foreign exchange reserves and a portion allocated for investment,' Jin Renqing said ... 'This company is now under construction' [he said] ... Mr Jin said the aim of the new agency was to manage the reserves prudently, but also more 'profitably' and 'efficiently'. The government is under increasing pressure over managing the reserves, which reached $1,066 billion by the end of last year [2006] and have risen by about $20 billion a month, fuelled mainly by China's trade surplus ... Mr Jin said the new agency would report to the State Council, China's cabinet, but he shed no light on its structure, which has been the subject of extensive debate. Nor did he give any detail on how much of the reserves would be put under the management of the new agency. Chinese officials and local press reports have suggested a sum of up to $300 million. However, this amount is unlikely to be transferred in a single tranche for immediate investment, either domestic or offshore ... The bulk of the reserves will continue to be managed by the present custodian, the state administration for foreign currency, an agency under the central bank. The make-up of the investment portfolio is secret, but its mandates for foreign banks investing money on its behalf have generally been conservative, focusing on Treasury bills and mortgaged-backed securities. About three-quarters of the reserves are believed to be in US dollar-denominated assets. In recent years the state administration for foreign currency has also given mandates to foreign mutual funds but they are relatively small compared to the huge amounts of money under its management.

(*FT*, 10 March 2007, p. 9)

Prime minister Wen Jiabao said Friday [16 March] that China's creation of a new company to invest a portion of its $1 trillion in foreign exchange reserves would have no impact on Beijing's holdings of US dollar-denominated assets ... Wen Jiabao: 'Our purchases of US dollars are mutually beneficial. Setting up of the new agency won't affect the value of the US dollar assets' ... China is believed to keep as much as 70 per cent of its reserves in US Treasuries and other dollar-denominated assets.

(www.iht.com, 16 March 2007)

Wen said that even as China explored new ways to invest more than $1 trillion in foreign currency reserves in overseas assets, Beijing still amounted to a small player in world financial markets and would 'not have any impact on US dollar-denominated assets' globally.

(*IHT*, 17 March 2007, p. 6)

Wen Jiabao ... said at the press conference to close the National People's Congress [on 16 March] that investments by the ... new state investment agency ... 'would not have any impact on US dollar-denominated assets'. Mr Wen's comments were reinforced by the People's Bank of China, which said in a report hours later that it would not make 'frequent, major adjustments to the structure of the reserves in response to market movements' ...

Chinese leaders have been cautious in what they say about the reserves, especially regarding the US dollar, for fear of encouraging speculation that Beijing is reducing its holdings of the currency. Mr Wen's reassurance on the US dollar is also in China's self-interest, since any dollar sell-off would leave huge capital losses for Beijing's existing holdings. The precise make-up of China's holdings is a state secret, but about 75 per cent are believed to be held in dollar-denominated assets. Mr Wen said: 'I can assure you that by instituting such a foreign exchange reserve investment company, it will not have any adverse impact on US dollar-denominated assets.' He acknow-ledged that China held the majority of its reserves in US dollar instruments, which he said had been purchased 'on the basis of mutual benefit'.

(*FT*, 17 March 2007, p. 5)

'The currency has remained basically stable against the dollar since the start of March' (*FT*, 11 April 2007, p. 7).

'The yuan was virtually unchanged against the dollar in March, after rising steadily through January and February' (*IHT*, 11 April 2007, p. 11).

The yuan is now trading at about 7.7 to the dollar, up by a little over 7 per cent since the Chinese currency went off its fixed peg in mid-2005 ... It is not clear how much ... a more freely floating currency ... would really have on exports. For many of the products it exports China is merely an assem-bler of parts made elsewhere, which is why its trade surplus with the rest of the world is less impressive than its bilateral one with America. Should the yuan rise it will make those inputs cheaper for Chinese firms, so export prices will rise less than the yuan-bashers might hope.

(www.economist.com, 24 April 2007)

The yuan rose on Tuesday [8 May] to 7.6942 to the dollar, the highest since ... July 2005 ... Banks must keep 5 per cent of their foreign currency depos-its as reserves, up from 4 per cent ... The increase will take effect on 15 May ... The ruling will make less of the $165 billion in foreign currency deposits that were held as of 31 March [2007] available for lending.

(www.iht.com, 8 May 2007)

Beijing yesterday [11 May 2007] unveiled new rules that would allow Chinese banking clients to access overseas stock markets for the first time, in a move that could trigger a massive inflow of investments into financial centres such as Hong Kong ... Under the new rules Chinese banking clients can gain exposure to foreign equity funds authorized by overseas regulators such as Hong Kong's Securities and Futures Commission. Chinese banks are expected to offer these funds in the form of wealth management prod-ucts, which are allowed to invest up to half of their net asset value in over-seas equities. The products, requiring a minimum investment of $39,000, can only invest up to 5 per cent of net asset value in individual stocks. Inter-national fund managers are set to benefit from this important liberalization of the tightly regulated market for overseas Chinese investments. The new

rules, in effect, let foreign groups tap China's $2,000 billion in bank depos-
its without forming mandatory fund joint ventures with local partners.
Chinese banks, insurers and fund managers last year [2006] received
approval to invest overseas for the first time through a quota system known
as the Qualified Domestic Institutional Investor scheme. More than $100
billion of investments could be channelled through the QDII programme
during the next two years [according to one estimate] ... Several lenders,
including six international banks, have been allowed to invest up to $18.5
billion abroad on behalf of Chinese clients. But only a fraction of this QDII
quota has been used.

(FT, 12 May 2007, p. 8)

The new rules, in effect, let foreign fund managers tap China's $2,000
billion in retail bank deposits, without forming mandatory domestic operations ... The latest rule change suggests that overseas fund products would
remain exempt from Chinese regulations so long as they bear the stamp of
an overseas regulator such as Hong Kong's Securities and Futures Commission, which recently signed a memorandum of understanding with the
Chinese banking watchdog ... However, analysts said the China Banking
Regulatory Commission would retain significant control, because banks had
to seek individual approval for their new wealth management products, in
which overseas equity funds could not account for more than half of the net
asset value. Moreover, fund managers seeking to participate in the new
scheme will almost certainly have to sign a memorandum of understanding
with the CBRC, based on a strict vetting process.

(FT, 14 May 2007, p. 26)

'The Chinese government said that it would let banks buy shares outside
China for the first time' (www.iht.com, 15 May 2007). 'The government
announced last week that it would let banks buy shares overseas to divert
money flows from the domestic stock market. Most of the $7 billion freed up by
the move may go into Hong Kong stocks initially' (www.iht.com, 16 May
2007).

The People's Bank of China is widening the level that the yuan can
strengthen or fall against the dollar from 0.3 per cent to 0.5 per cent per day
... The bands determine how far the currency may fluctuate from the parity
rate, which is set each day by the central bank ... The yuan rarely
approaches the current trading limit of 0.3 per cent.

(www.bbc.co.uk, 18 May 2007)

The People's Bank of China said that it would allow the yuan to rise or fall up
to 0.5 per cent in daily trading. The daily limit was 0.3 per cent ... The bank
said it would continue to 'keep the exchange rate basically stable at an adaptive and equilibrium level based on market supply and demand with reference
to a basket of currencies' ... Since it broke the yuan's peg to the dollar on 21
July 2005 ... the government allowed the yuan to rise 2.1 per cent ... on 21

July 2005 ... and has only let it inch up by another 5 per cent over the nearly two years since then. By contrast, members of the US Congress from manufacturing states that have lost jobs during the Chinese export boom have been calling for China to revalue by 25 per cent or more ... The People's Bank of China's decision to widen the daily trading limit to 0.5 per cent has no direct implications for the renminbi's level against the dollar, since the currency has rarely come close to testing the 0.3 per cent limit set in 2005.

(www.iht.com, 18 May 2007; *IHT*, 19 May 2007, p. 7)

Beijing broke a direct link between the yuan and the dollar in July 2005 and revalued the currency by 2.1 per cent. Since then it has allowed the currency to rise 5.3 per cent against the dollar in tightly controlled trading ... A rise of 10 per cent in the yuan would lead to the loss of 5.5 million jobs in China, according to a report by the Chinese central bank. The bank also said that the companies that would most suffer are those that make textiles, furniture, shoes and toys for export.

(www.iht.com, 20 May 2007)

'The yuan has gained 7.9 per cent against the dollar since July 2005' (*IHT*, 21 May 2007, p. 16).

'Since July 2005, when the yuan's direct peg to the dollar was cut and revalued 2.1 per cent, the Chinese currency has risen 5.6 per cent. On Tuesday [22 May] the dollar was trading at 7.6582 yuan' (www.iht.com, 22 May 2007).

[It was announced on 20 May that] the government is to use $3 billion of its vast foreign exchange reserves to buy a 9.9 per cent stake in Blackstone, the US buy-out company, in an unprecedented move ... The government has taken the unusual step of giving up its voting rights associated with the stake in Blackstone. The move appears aimed at defusing any US political opposition to the deal ... The investment will come through a new China agency charged with managing part of the country's $1,200 billion in foreign exchange reserves ... Beijing has agreed to keep the stake for at least four years. It is understood that China's foreign reserve agency has agreed not to invest in rival private equity groups for twelve months ... China's decision to buy a stake in Blackstone's IPO rather than in one of its buy-out funds, which are more volatile and risky, is a sign of Beijing's cautious approach to private equity.

(*FT*, 21 May 2007, p. 19)

[The to-be-established] state investment company will buy non-voting shares ... in the private equity firm Blackstone Group ... concurrent with Blackstone's planned $4 billion initial public offering. China will buy the shares for 95.5 per cent of the public offering price ... [China] has agreed to hold its investment for at least four years, the two groups said.

(*IHT*, 21 May 2007, p. 13)

China sought Monday [21 May] to offer assurances that it was looking only to improve returns on overseas investments – not to take control of foreign companies ... The Chinese government is setting up a new state investment company to diversify the country's overseas investments beyond its holdings in US Treasuries and other bonds ... Jesse Wang [is] the chairman of the Chinese government agency that is managing the transaction on behalf of a new state investment company, which has yet to be set up. But the new state investment company is not currently negotiating for further stakes in overseas companies, Wang added ... [He said that] the main goal of the investment company is to accumulate a broad portfolio of small stakes in lots of companies, instead of purchasing controlling stakes in a few companies ... [He said] the new investment company would be more interested in investments paralleling funds that buy shares in most or all of the stocks in indexes that track the overall performance of overseas stock markets ... Jesse Wang: 'We hope it will be in operation before the end of the year.'

(www.iht.com, 21 May 2007; *IHT*, 22 May 2007, pp. 1, 13)

'The government ... is to begin creating a so-called sovereign wealth fund: a government-owned investment company that issues yuan-denominated bonds in China and uses the proceeds to buy dollars for overseas acquisitions' (www.iht. com, 3 August 2007).

'Blackstone said Monday [21 May] that it planned to raise as much as $7.75 billion from selling stakes to the public and to China' (*IHT*, 22 May 2007).

The yuan on Tuesday [12 June] posted its largest gain against the US dollar since its July 2005 revaluation, rebounding from a three-day slide ... Traders said that by engineering a big drop in the yuan and the causing a rebound, the central bank appeared to be trying to make the market accustomed to greater volatility. Creating a more active foreign exchange market is a long-standing policy goal.

(*IHT*, 13 June 2007, p. 13)

The yuan has appreciated about 8 per cent in relation to the dollar since July 2005. But economists say that the yuan has stayed at about the same value in relation to an aggregation of the dollar and all other currencies. With China's currency levels artificially low, especially against European currencies, European leaders have also begun warning China over its trade practices.

(*IHT*, 14 June 2007, p. 12)

China's securities brokerages and fund managers will be allowed to invest in overseas stocks and bonds for the first time ... The China Securities Regulatory Commission issued new regulations yesterday [21 June] allowing the country's 110-odd securities firms and fifty-seven fund management companies to apply for Qualified Domestic Institutional Investor (QDII) quotas to invest in offshore securities ... Until now only one fund manager, Shanghai-based Hua-an, had been allowed to invest overseas, alongside eighteen banks and three large insurers, under a pilot programme begun last year [2006]. Beijing has handed out nearly $19 billion of QDII quotas to these institutions but just a fraction has been used.

(*FT*, 22 June 2007, p. 9)

'The yuan rose 0.15 per cent last week to 7.6037 to the dollar, and gained 8.9 per cent since China ended its peg to the US currency in July 2005' (*IHT*, 9 July 2007, p. 15).

('In spite of a substantial accumulated realignment of the yuan against the US dollar, on a trade-weighted basis China's currency is actually losing value': *FEER*, September 2007, p. 13.)

China has scrapped a set of rules that provided incentives for exporters to bring home as much foreign currency as they could, signifying another step in its efforts to ease capital inflows. In the wake of the Asian financial crisis in the late 1990s China introduced a series of measures encouraging exports and inflows of foreign exchange ... Its capital and current account surpluses have since soared, and Beijing is now trying to reverse the situation to ease the upward pressure on the yuan created by such inflows. The state administration of foreign exchange said on Monday [9 July] that it had rescinded, as of 1 July, a set of rules dating back to 1999 that had provided incentives for exporters to exchange their foreign exchange earnings with banks in a timely manner, as well as punishments for those that did not ... The rules had allowed for preferential treatment in customs procedures and bank lending for export firms with good track records in remitting foreign exchange, and penalties as severe as revocation of export licences for the worst offenders. The removal of such incentives complements initiatives to encourage capital outflows, such as the Qualified Domestic Institutional Investor programme, which allows financial institutions to invest client funds overseas ... The regulator last year [2006] designated 5,300 firms as 'needing special attention' because they were suspected of engaging in currency speculation through transactions disguised trade flows.

(www.iht.com, 9 July 2007)

Beijing raised the limits for overseas investment by Chinese insurance companies yesterday [25 July], potentially making up to $50 billion (£24 billion) available. The country's insurance regulatory commission said it was raising the cap on insurers' overseas investments from 5 per cent to 15 per cent of their assets with immediate effect. Chinese insurers have a combined 2,500 billion renminbi (£161 billion) in assets and the total is growing at 25 per cent to 30 per cent a year. Since 2004 some insurers have been allowed to invest foreign exchange earned by overseas share sales on offshore fixed income securities. The government also allowed some groups to buy limited amounts of foreign exchange last year [2006] to invest in the Hong Kong initial public share offerings of some mainland Chinese companies. By the end of last year fifteen insurance companies had been approved to invest a combined $5.8 billion. They had invested $2.6 billion overseas by the end of last month [June 2007], according to official figures.

(*FT*, 26 July 2007, p. 1)

China further loosened its capital controls Monday [20 August ... Residents will be permitted for the first time to invest directly in the Hong Kong securities market under a pilot programme to be started in the northern port city of Tianjin ... Rules limiting the purchase of foreign exchange by individuals to $50,000 a year will not apply for the pilot scheme: investors will be able to convert an unlimited amount of yuan into foreign currency and invest it in Hong Kong ... Until now individuals have been allowed to invest overseas only through banks, brokers, insurers and fund managers licensed under the Qualified Domestic Institutional Investor programme. To spur capital outflows China recently relaxed the rules of the programme so investors could buy overseas shares as well as less risky bonds. Now, investors wanting to bypass the plan's intermediaries will have to open an account with Bank of China's Tianjin branch and with Bank of China International Securities in Hong Kong. Although restricted to the port city, any Chinese resident can participate in the pilot programme by opening an account with a Bank of China branch that has signed an agreement with the Tianjin branch ... Foreign exchange reserves [were] $1.33 trillion at the end of June [2007].

(www.iht.com, 20 August 2007)

The State Administration of Foreign Exchange ... did not specify when the policy would start ... [and] did not specify how long the trial would last ... The agency released the text of a new regulatory proposal that it described as having been approved. The proposal allows Chinese citizens to open accounts at the Tianjin branch of the Bank of China, and then sell yuan and buy Hong Kong dollars for the purpose of buying shares in Hong Kong. Chinese citizens will also be allowed to use their foreign exchange savings to buy shares in Hong Kong, using the Tianjin branch. Located 96 kilometres, or 60 miles, from Beijing in north-eastern China, Tianjin is an industrial port that Beijing officials are trying to develop into a third financial centre to rival Hong Kong and Shanghai. Chinese citizens will need to show their national identity cards and transactions will be monitored for any sign of money laundering ... Previous regulations had allowed individuals to transfer up to $50,000 in a single day to Hong Kong. But transfers to securities companies in Hong Kong are banned ... With the steep rise in the Shanghai stock market over the past two years, essentially identical shares in mainland companies now sell for considerably more in Shanghai than in Hong Kong, and some mainland Chinese may now choose to buy the less expensive shares in Hong Kong.

(*IHT*, 21 August 2007, p. 9)

'While the change will enable Chinese citizens to invest directly in all Hong Kong traded securities, investors are expected to focus on Chinese companies, which trade at an average 50 per cent discount to the mainland' (*FT*, 21 August 2007, p. 4).

Forty-two Chinese companies have listed H-shares in Hong Kong and A-shares on either the Shanghai or Shenzhen stock exchange. Even after Monday's rally [20 August] in Hong Kong, such dual-listed shares were still trading at an average 78 per cent premium domestically as compared with Hong Kong. The expectation is that once they are unleashed on the Hong Kong market, retail investors will chase H-shares higher.

(*FT*, 22 August 2007, p. 4)

The government will delay allowing investors in the mainland to buy Hong Kong shares directly until rules have been introduced to limit capital outflows, according to three officials at the country's banking regulator. The State Council, China's cabinet, blocked the introduction of the share-purchasing programme, announced on 20 August by the State Administration of Foreign Exchange, after objections by securities and banking regulators ... Easing controls too rapidly may lead to an exodus of investors from the Shanghai and Shenzhen stock markets and increase financial risks ... Hong Kong-listed shares are surging on speculation ... All forty-two Chinese companies whose shares are listed in both Hong Kong and the mainland are less expensive to buy in Hong Kong ... China last year [2006] started allowing banks and brokerage houses to invest outside of the mainland under the so-called qualified domestic institutional investor, or QDII, programme. These investments will also be subject to any new policy regulating capital outflows ... The Chinese foreign exchange regulator said last month [August] that it would allow individuals holding accounts at Bank of China's branch in Tianjin to buy Hong Kong stocks for the first time. It did not specify an investment quota or say when the plan can start.

(*IHT*, 6 September 2007, p. 16)

China is to impose a quota on investments on the Hong Kong stock market – which will reduce capital outflows to a fraction of the $100,000-plus forecast when its outward investment scheme was announced last month [August] ... Liu Mingkang, chairman of the China Banking Regulatory Commission, said there would be no limit on individuals. But he said there would be tight controls on the total amount. Mr Liu said there would be a 'quota in general' and when that is reached the State Administration of Foreign Exchange would reassess market activity. 'They can lift and read-just the quota if necessary and appropriate – it is a flexible ceiling,' he [said].

(*FT*, 21 September 2007, p. 1)

China will limit the amount that individuals can invest in Hong Kong equities, Xia Lingwu, a spokesman in Beijing for the China Banking Regulatory Commission, said [on 21 September] ... He was confirming comments made by chairman of the regulator, Liu Mingkang, which appeared in *The Financial Times* on Friday [21 September].

(www.iht.com, 21 September 2007)

'As of September [2007] ... China owned $396.7 billion of US Treasury securities ... up from $71.4 billion in 2000 ... Among foreign nations, only Japan, with $582.2 billion, owns more US government debt' (*IHT*, 11 December 2007, p. 15).

('China has in effect frozen a proposal to allow mainland citizens to buy shares in Hong Kong ... Wen Jiabao, the premier, has attached four conditions to final approval for the scheme, all of which are so open-ended that Beijing could take months, if not longer, to permit it to go ahead': *FT*, 5 November 2007, p. 6. 'Prime minister Wen Jiabao's comments on a plan to allow Chinese investors to buy Hong Kong stocks may signal a delay in its implementation ... The government needs to study the risks, increase knowledge among Chinese investors and prepare regulations to protect the stock markets in Hong Kong and at home before starting the programme, Wen said Saturday [3 November]': *IHT*, 5 November 2007, p. 13. 'The introduction of a programme to allow individuals to invest directly in Hong Kong equities will be delayed until the second quarter of next year [2008]. Crédit Suisse said Monday [12 November] ... The programme, introduced by the State Administration of Foreign Exchange, has been pushed back amid objections from the China Securities Regulatory Commission and the China Banking Regulatory Commission ... [Crédit Suisse said that] China may impose a ceiling of $30 billion for the entire pilot programme ... [and] that the government may also require each investor to put up at least $40,473 to participate': *IHT*, 13 November 2007, p. 16.)

China Investment, the $200 billion sovereign wealth fund, formally started operating Saturday [29 September] as the government sought to increase returns on its foreign exchange reserves, the biggest in the world ... China Investment incorporates the former investment arm of the central bank, Central Huijin Investment, which holds controlling stakes in the four biggest Chinese banks ... Surging trade surpluses helped push its currency reserves to a record level of $1.33 trillion ... The agency [is] to be financed by special government bond sales totalling $206.5 billion that will be used to buy foreign exchange reserves from the central bank ... The State Administration of Foreign Exchange, a regulatory branch under the central bank, is still managing most of China's foreign exchange reserves, which are largely invested in low risk assets like US government debt. China owns $405 billion, or 18 per cent, of foreign-held US Treasury securities, the second largest amount in the world after Japan.

(*IHT*, 1 October 2007, p. 17)

Eurozone finance ministers said the renminbi's exchange rate should more accurately reflect China's vast and growing current account surplus ... The EU is frustrated with the Euro–renminbi exchange rate not only because of

China's ever increasing trade surplus with China, but also because the dollar's decline means that the Euro is bearing the brunt of China's reluctance to allow an appreciation of the renminbi … The thirteen-nation Eurozone's ministers broke new ground on Monday night [8 October] with a statement that for the first time identified the renminbi's level as a greater source of concern to Europe than the level of the dollar or yen … The renminbi has fallen by at least 5 per cent against the Euro over the past two years.

(www.ft.com, 9 October 2007)

Failing to find unity over the Euro's strength against the dollar, European finance ministers sought instead to put pressure on China, urging it to allow the yuan to appreciate against other global currencies. A meeting of the finance ministers from the thirteen countries that use the Euro issued a statement making a rare reference to China's exchange rate policy, a statement Europeans usually leave to Washington to pursue with Beijing … The European ministers' statement argued that in 'emerging economies with large and growing current account surpluses, especially China, it is desirable that their effective exchange rate move so that necessary adjustments will occur'.

(www.iht.com, 9 October 2007; *IHT*, 10 October 2007, p. 9)

In some of its strongest language to date, IMF officials call on China to let its currency appreciate … The *World Economic Outlook* argued: 'Further upward flexibility of the renminbi, along with measures to reform the exchange rate regime and boost consumption, would also contribute to a necessary rebalancing of demand and to an orderly unwinding of global imbalances.'

(www.ft.com, 17 October 2007)

'As China's trade surplus with the United States and Europe has accelerated, the G7 [Group of Seven: the United States, Japan, Germany, the UK, France, Italy and Canada] language has become ever more explicit' (www.ft.com, 19 October 2007).

In April [2007] the G7 said: 'In emerging economies with large and growing current account surpluses, especially China, it is desirable that their effective exchange rates move so that necessary adjustments will occur' … Beijing's relations with the IMF have cooled since the Washington-based organization adopted the new currency surveillance mechanism, which China believes is directed at forcing a faster appreciation of the renminbi.

(*FT*, 20 October 2007, p. 5)

After a four-year campaign to win more foreign exchange flexibility from China, governments in Canada and Europe are now warning as well that their economies are being hurt by the yuan's failure to rise against their currencies … The dollar's slide to its weakest level since 1997 this month [October] has been lopsided. The yuan has advanced 3.9 per cent on the dollar so far this year [2007], less than half the Euro's gain and a fraction of the Canadian dollar's 20 per cent climb ... The yuan has fallen 4.1 per cent versus the Euro.

(*IHT*, 20 October 2007, p. 17)

'[On 24 October] the CSI 300 Index rose after the yuan climbed past 7.5 to the dollar for the first time' (*IHT*, 25 October 2007).

Zhou Xiaochuan, governor of the People's Bank of China, said in Beijing last month [October 2007]: 'The yuan will eventually become a freely convertible currency and China will open its capital account, even if we have not set a clear timetable. China had agreed in principle to make the yuan convertible in the 1990s, but we halted the plan during the 1997 Asian financial crisis.'

(*IHT*, 19 November 2007, p. 14)

'The yuan reached its highest level Thursday [1 November], 7.4518, since it was depegged in July 2005' (www.iht.com, 1 November 2007).

'The renminbi has risen by nearly 11 per cent against the US dollar since mid-2005 [the 11 per cent including the initial 2.1 per cent rise]' (*FT*, 7 November 2007, p. 10).

'Foreign holdings stood at $1,433 billion in September [2007]' (*FT*, 7 November 2007, p. 10).

'The yuan traded at 7.4103 against the dollar Friday [9 November], the strongest level since the end of a fixed exchange rate in July 2005. It has gained 11.5 per cent versus the dollar since then' (www.iht.com, 13 November 2007).

'Beijing has let the yuan rise 9.5 per cent against the dollar since it was revalued by 2.1 per cent in July 2005 ... The yuan scaled a post-revaluation peak of 7.4108 per dollar Monday [12 November]' (www.iht.com, 12 November 2007).

'The central bank has been buying foreign currency, mainly dollars, at a pace of $1 billion a day to slow the rise of its currency' (*IHT*, 14 November 2007, p. 16).

European finance ministers [from Cyprus and Spain] pressed China to let its currency strengthen so that their economy no longer bears the brunt of the drop in the US dollar. The officials are stepping up complaints just two weeks before an EU delegation arrives in Beijing to make the case for a stronger yuan ... While the currency has gained 5.1 per cent against the dollar this year [2007], it has dropped 4.7 per cent against the Euro, hurting Europe's exporters ... [However], not every European official is worried by the Euro's gains, which have amounted to a 7 per cent jump against the dollar since August ... José Barroso, president of the European Commission, said [on 13 November] a strong Euro is preferable to a weak one and is a 'signal of confidence in the European economy'.

(www.iht.com, 13 November 2007)

Money changers across the border in Hong Kong's free wheeling neighbour Shenzhen have accepted deposits in yuan at local currency exchange bureaus and then withdrawals of the equivalent in Hong Kong dollars on the other side of the border. It spawned a vast enterprise that quietly went on for years, as mainlanders happily subverted their country's strict currency controls and illegal currency dealers pocketed tidy commissions. That is until last June. The authorities in Shenzhen delivered a blow to the illicit foreign currency trade by arresting a businesswoman they said was behind one of the biggest underground operations ... [She] had allegedly supervised currency transactions worth $578 million going back to 2005. The arrest, disclosed last week ... has thrown a spotlight on the extent of illegal currency flows out of China into Hong Kong. It has also highlighted the difficulty mainland authorities have in restraining investors who clearly want more options than pumped-up Chinese share and property markets or low-interest-bearing bank accounts ... Prime minister Wen Jiabao ... warned Monday [19 November] that the illicit currency flows could have an adverse impact on the financial stability of both the mainland and Hong Kong. Wen said Shenzhen 'alone accounts for almost half' of the fund flows out of China, which he called a 'huge' amount ... The Hong Kong Monetary Authority has not expressed concern about a risk of financial instability from illegal currency transfers, but it has noted the potential for money laundering through underground banking. Hong Kong tightened controls over remittance agents and money changers last January ... Much of the money flowing out of the mainland into Hong Kong is assumed to be entering the Hong Kong stock market. Analysts said that between 10 per cent and 20 per cent of the turnover of the market is mainland money, although precise figures are impossible to determine.

(www.iht.com, 20 November 2007; *IHT*, 21 November 2007, p. 13)

'Beijing has announced a move to halve the flow of money from the mainland to Hong Kong and Macao by closing a grey market currency swap centre and cracking down on the export of currency notes' (www.iht.com, 22 November 2007).

'As part of the November [2007] crackdown under instructions from the Shenzhen branch of China's central bank, limits were placed on cash withdrawals to stop illicit funds from being carried over the border' (*The Economist*, 24 November 2007, p. 106).

The yuan strengthened Friday [23 November] beyond 7.4 to the dollar for the first time since a fixed exchange rate was scrapped in 2005 ... The currency advanced 0.18 per cent, the biggest gain in two weeks, to 7.4010 against the dollar in Shanghai, from 7.4257 a week ago ... The yuan took a month to rise to 7.4 per dollar from 7.5, compared with more than three months for the previous 0.10 increment. The central bank signalled Friday that it wanted the yuan to gain by setting the reference rate for the day's trading at 7.3992 from the close of 7.4145 Thursday. The yuan is not allowed to fluctuate more than 0.5 per cent from the daily rate ... China tempers advances in the currency by buying dollars to protect exporters, limiting gains so far this quarter to 1.4 per cent compared with 4.5 per cent in the Philippine peso and 2.8 per cent in the Singapore dollar ... While the yuan has risen about 5 per cent on the dollar this year [2007], it has weakened by almost 7 per cent versus the Euro.

(www.iht.com, 23 November 2007)

In the first visit of its kind, a delegation from the European single currency zone will press China on Tuesday [27 November] to allow the yuan to appreciate as the EU adopts a more assertive tone with Beijing over the Euro's strength ... Brussels has been content to let the United States do the tough talking on currency issues in Beijing, preferring instead to put pressure on Washington over the weakness of the dollar. Now Europe and the United States have joined forces ... At the meeting of finance ministers and central bankers of the Group of Seven [G7] industrialized countries last month [October], the Eurozone broke new ground by shifting the focus of its currency concerns from the weakness of the dollar to the status of the yuan. The switch of emphasis was politically convenient because it papered over tensions between Paris and Berlin over how much pressure to exert on Washington over currency issues, with France wanting a more proactive stance than Germany ... [There is concern that] the Euro is rising against the dollar and against Asian currencies, so the Europeans are bearing the burden of the adjustment.

(www.iht.com, 23 November 2007)

Two days of planned meetings starting Tuesday, the first of their kind between representatives of China and the EU, will focus on the future of the yuan ... Long content to let the United States take the lead, Europe changed its tune at the meeting of finance ministers and central bankers of the Group of Seven industrialized countries in October. After months of political pressure – notably from France – to address the weak dollar, European officials endorsed the theory that China, rather than the United States, was critical to stopping the rise of the Euro.

(*IHT*, 24 November 2007, p. 1)

'While the Chinese currency has climbed 9 per cent against the dollar since its landmark 2.1 per cent revaluation in July 2005, it has fallen about 11 per cent in total against the Euro' (www.iht.com, 25 November 2007). 'In addition to a 2.1 per cent increase in the value of the yuan against the dollar, Beijing has allowed the currency to appreciate by almost 10 per cent' (*IHT*, 28 November 2007, p. 11).

Chinese and European policy-makers agreed to co-operate in preventing big exchange rate fluctuations, as the first high level economic talks between Beijing and the thirteen-nation Eurozone began [on 27 November]. China's central bank said the two groups had expressed a willingness to 'take comprehensive measures to enhance structural economic adjustments, avoid big swings in currency movements and make respective contributions to an orderly adjustment of global imbalances'.

(*FT*, 28 November 2007, p. 7)

China and the EU have agreed to set up a high level 'mechanism' to discuss economics and trade issues … Beijing already has a top level Strategic Economic Dialogue with the United States and will this weekend hold its first ministerial economic dialogue with Japan.

(*FT*, 29 November 2007, p. 8)

Europe's disquiet is likely to grow. Last year [2006] its trade deficit with China reached Euro 131 billion ($164 billion), say EU figures. This year [2007] it is expected to grow to Euro 150 billion to Euro 160 billion … That is more disturbing for Europeans because they are not used to it: for years their trade deficit with China was modest.

(*The Economist*, 1 December 2007, p. 71)

China is to treble the amount of money that foreigners can invest in the mainland capital market … The quota for registered foreign investors would be increased from $10 billion to $30 billion. It could take several months before institutional investors secure fresh quotas … Beijing agreed in principle to expand the quota for Qualified Foreign Institutional Investors in May.

(*FT*, 10 December 2007, p. 8)

'The yuan has strengthened 11.9 per cent [against the dollar] since … July 2005' (*IHT*, 11 December 2007, p. 15).

'The renminbi has depreciated about 25 per cent against the Euro since 2000' (*FT*, 12 December 2007, p. 17).

The American strategy lately has been to avoid the contention that currency appreciation would alter the trade balance. Rather, Treasury Secretary Henry Paulson said he had argued that China's policy of keeping currency values low requires keeping interest rates low and that this contributes to an overheated economy and inflation.

(*IHT*, 13 December 2007, p. 12)

Paulson reiterated calls for a faster yuan appreciation, saying it would help China deal more effectively with rising inflation and asset bubbles amid signs its economy was overheating. But he said people were 'misinformed' if they thought the trade imbalance could be significantly affected simply by a rise in the yuan's value.

(www.iht.com, 13 December 2007)

China is encouraging investment in foreign securities through its Qualified Domestic Institutional Investor programme. As of 12 December Chinese financial institutions had received approval to invest $42.2 billion overseas, of which about $27 billion had already been invested. Market estimates put the total at $80 billion to more than $100 billion by the end of 2008.

(*IHT*, 24 December 2007, p. 14)

'[On 20 December] the yuan closed at 7.3694 versus the dollar (www.iht. com, 20 December 2007).

Cheng Siwei, vice chairman of the Standing Committee of the National People's Congress, caused financial markets to tremble when he said that China – which currently holds $1.4 trillion in dollar reserves and is accumulating dollars at a rate that will add about $500 billion in 2007 – would invest outside the dollar. Cheng's comments were 'clarified' a few days later by Chinese financial officials.

(www.iht.com, 14 December 2007)

The yuan rose Tuesday [25 December] to its highest level since [July 2005] ... after the central bank reiterated its aim to all greater exchange rate flexibility ... The yuan gained 0.06 per cent to 7.265 per dollar ... bringing its advance this year [2007] to about 6.4 per cent. The currency has appreciated more than 12 per cent against the dollar since July 2005. The yuan is currently trading within a 0.5 per cent band either side of the daily reference rate ... The central bank set the reference rate for yuan trading at 7.3261 per dollar Tuesday, the highest since the end of the fixed exchange rate.

(*IHT*, 26 December 2007, p. 14)

The yuan has risen faster against the dollar this week than at any time since the end of the Chinese currency's peg to the dollar in 2005, feeding speculation that the government has begun allowing a brisker pace of appreciation ... The renminbi rose 0.9 per cent this week. That included an increase of 0.18 per cent on Friday [28 December] to close at 7.3041 to the dollar ... The increase Friday also followed a jump of 0.37 per cent Thursday [27 December] that was the largest one-day increase since Beijing abandoned the peg on 21 July 2005 ... [According to] a member of the central bank's monetary committee until last year [2006] ... rising inflation was making it easier for the government to accept a stronger currency ... to slow the rise of food and fuel prices ... the latest in a series of hints from current and former officials that the country's leadership is beginning to see some advantages in a stronger currency.

(www.iht.com, 28 December 2007; *IHT*, 29 December 2007, pp. 15, 18)

[On Thursday 27 December] the yuan gained 0.37 per cent, closing at 7.3175 to the dollar. The central bank encouraged the jump by setting a very strong daily reference rate or mid-point of 7.3079 ... In July 2005 China freed the yuan from its tight peg to the US dollar, by allowing it to float within a narrow 0.15 per cent band either side of a level set by a basket of currencies. The central bank's reference rate defines the day's trading band, which extends 0.5 per cent on either side of the rate. On Monday [24 December] the central bank set such a high mid-point that the previous trading day's close was outside the trading band.

(www.bbc.co.uk, 29 December 2007)

Since the beginning of October [2007] the yuan has climbed at an annual rate of 13 per cent against the dollar – its fastest pace since China stopped pegging to the dollar in July 2005. Since 2005 it has appreciated by a total of 14 per cent ... It may appear as if Beijing has caved in to Washington's demands. But the main reason why China is allowing the yuan to rise faster is because its policymakers believe the benefits to China from a rising currency now outweigh the costs. Beijing's top concern today is inflation, which rose to 6.9 per cent in November [2007] ... A faster pace of currency appreciation offers a more powerful weapon: it will help reduce imported inflation, especially of food and raw materials. By reducing the need to intervene to hold down the currency, it will also curb the build-up of foreign exchange reserves and hence monetary growth. Another reason for the shift in policy is that the costs of holding down the yuan are rising. The People's Bank of China [PBOC] has so far succeeded in 'sterilizing' most foreign exchange inflows – printing yuan to buy incoming dollars and then selling bonds to bankers in order to mop up the resulting excess liquidity. It has even made a profit on this activity, because the return on its dollar reserves exceeded the rate it paid out on sterilizing bonds. Now, however, the PBOC is losing money. Thanks to falling interest rates in America and rising rates in China, Chinese rates are now higher than those in America and the gap is likely to widen this year [2008]. Since the shrinking yuan value of China's dollar reserves also has to be reported at a loss, the cost of currency intervention is higher still ... The slide in the dollar since 2005 means the yuan has risen by only 5 per cent in trade-weighted terms, according to the Bank for International Settlements.

(*The Economist*, 12 January 2008, p. 69)

'Foreign exchange reserves ... passed the $1.5 trillion mark at the end of last year [2007]' (*The Economist*, 2 February 2008, p. 106).

[It was announced on 23 January that] China will let its commercial banks invest in Singapore stocks and funds ... It reached the agreement under the so-called qualified domestic institutional investor programme ... China will 'soon' sign similar agreements with the US, German and Japanese governments ... The Chinese government is expanding investment destinations for its QDII programme after four funds offered by fund houses posted combined losses of renminbi 11.8 billion (£838 million) in the fourth quarter of 2007.

(*FT*, 24 January 2008, p. 5)

The yuan has appreciated 4.5 per cent against the dollar since late October [2007], for an annual rate of 15 per cent. Foreign exchange dealers expect the full-year pace of appreciation to be 8.5 per cent to 10 per cent, compared with 6.9 per cent in 2007 and 3.4 per cent in 2006 ... During the past four months the yuan's rise has exceeded the dollar's depreciation on global markets, with the result that it has also strengthened against a basket of currencies, including the Euro.

(www.iht.com, 26 February 2008)

'The yuan has risen 11 per cent against the dollar since the start of 2007'
(*IHT*, 26 March 2008, p. 16).

The renminbi closed trading in China on Friday [28 March] at 7.017 renminbi to the dollar ... After rising by about 14 per cent over the thirty
months since mid-2005, when the dollar peg was dropped, the renminbi has
accelerated at an annualized pace of about 15 per cent to 20 per cent against
the US currency in the opening months of 2008 ... But other trading
partners have ... seen the Euro appreciate by more than 3 per cent this
year [2008] against the Chinese unit. The Japanese yen, in turn, had
strengthened by more than 7 per cent in 2008 by the end of last week. As a
result, the renminbi's effective exchange rate, the yardstick advocated by
bodies such as the IMF, has not moved at all this year against its leading
trading partners.

(*FT*, 31 March 2008, p. 7)

China has made substantial progress toward adopting a more flexible currency that will help it cope with inflation pressures from rising food prices,
the US Treasury Secretary Henry Paulson said Wednesday [2 April in
Beijing] ... Paulson: 'I acknowledge to President Hu the very material
progress that they've made with their currency, because they have a currency that more accurately reflects underlying economic fundamentals' ...
He added that a more flexible currency would give China 'a very important
tool' in its bid to keep food price rises in check ... A major reason for Paulson's visit was to meet Wang Qishan, a newly promoted deputy prime
minister who is taking charge of Beijing's part in the so-called Strategic
Economic Dialogue, which Paulson helped start in 2006.

(www.iht.com, 2 April 2008)

Paulson and Wang have a long-standing relationship. The two worked
closely together years ago, when Paulson was serving as chairman of
Goldman Sachs and pushing the Wall Street bank to expand in China. At
the time Wang held government posts with oversight of banks ... Paulson
said he was pleased with the sharp rise of the yuan against the dollar in
recent months. Since Beijing ended its long-standing peg to the dollar in
mid-2005 the yuan has climbed about 18 per cent against the dollar, which
now stands close to 7 yuan ... Paulson: 'I won't be satisfied until there's a
market-determined currency.'

(*IHT*, 4 April 2008, p. 14)

The yuan traded stronger than 7.00 against the US dollar on Thursday [10
April] for the first time in over a decade ... The central bank, which tightly
controls the foreign exchange market, paved the way for the rise by fixing
the yuan's daily mid-point, or reference rate, at a fresh high of 6.9920 before
trade began. The yuan opened at 6.9920 against the dollar compared to
7.0017 at Wednesday's close. It was the first trade above 7.00 since China
devalued the yuan to 8.7 from 5.8 at the start of 1994, creating a modern

foreign exchange rate market. Since the yuan's peg to the dollar was abolished in July 2005 its appreciation against the US currency has accelerated each year, from 2.6 per cent in 2005 to 3.4 per cent in 2006 and 6.9 per cent in 2007. So far this year [2008] it is up 4.5 per cent … Last November [2007] the central bank declared for the first time that it would use the exchange rate actively to fight mounting inflation, which rose to an eleven-year high of 8.7 per cent in February this year [2008].

(www.iht.com, 10 April 2008)

For the first time in more than a decade a dollar bought less than 7 yuan, ending the day close to 6.9920 yuan … In July 2005 a dollar bought about 8.3 yuan … The yuan has now gained about 16 per cent against the dollar since the peg ended.

(www.iht.com, 10 April 2008)

The People's Bank of China fixed the renminbi's daily mid-point, or reference rate, at a fresh high of renminbi 6.9916 per dollar before trading opened in Shanghai. The currency appreciated to renminbi 6.9910 to the dollar in the first hour of trading, from a close of renminbi 7.0017 on Wednesday [9 April], before ending the day at 6.9916.

(www.ft.com, 10 April 2008)

'The yuan has now gained more than 18 per cent against the dollar since … July 2005' (www.iht.com, 11 April 2008).

'On 16 April the renminbi was trading at renminbi 6.99: $1' (www.economist.com, 25 April 2008).

'Beijing has kept the yuan on a tight leash, letting it rise just 0.9 per cent against the dollar over the past two months' (*IHT*, 29 May 2008, p. 16).

'Foreign exchange reserves … hit another record high of $1.76 trillion at the end of April [2008]' (www.economist.com, 10 June 2008). 'According to leaked official figures, China's foreign exchange reserves jumped by $115 billion during April and May [2008] to $1.8 trillion' (*The Economist*, 28 June 2008, p. 95).

'The yuan has appreciated nearly 20 per cent since mid-2005' (www.iht.com, 11 June 2008).

'China's State Administration of Foreign Exchange [Safe] has agreed to invest more than $2.5 billion in the latest TPG fund [in the United States], it what could be the largest commitment made to a private equity fund' (*FT*, 11 June 2008, p. 17).

'[On 17 June] the yuan rose to a high of 6.8918 per dollar – a gain of some 20 per cent since it ditched the fixed exchange rate' (www.bbc.co.uk, 17 June 2008).

On 4 May [2008] the finance ministers of thirteen East Asian countries agreed on the sidelines of the annual meeting of the Asian Development Bank in Madrid to set up a pool of foreign exchange reserves. The members of the Association of South-east Asian nations [Asean] together with China, Japan and South Korea decided that at least $80 billion of the region's foreign reserves are to be funnelled into a regional fund to protect regional currencies against speculative attacks and provide countries in crisis with liquidity. Of the funds 20 per cent are to be provided by the ten Asean members and the remaining 80 per cent by the 'Plus Three' countries (China, Japan and South Korea) ... To ease concerns that the IMF's position would be damaged, the ministers agreed to include an 'IMF link', which allowed only 10 per cent of the credit lines to be disbursed without the borrowing country having a lending programme with the IMF. In 2005 the portion that could be disbursed without an IMF programme was increased to 20 per cent.

(www.feer.com, 18 June 2008)

China announced a major strengthening of capital controls last night [2 July] in an attempt to limit the amount of speculative 'hot money' entering the economy.... The State Administration of Foreign Exchange said exporters would be required to park revenues in special accounts while the authorities verified the funds were the result of genuine trade ... Exporters will now be required to provide documentary evidence that their invoices are based on genuine transactions if they wish to change dollars into renminbi. The regulator said the new computer system for checking invoices would be introduced from 4 August [2008]. A trial period begins on 14 July. Recent leaked figures showed record inflows of capital entering China over the past two months. Officials believe some money came in illegally after companies exaggerated export revenues. China has become an attractive country for investors and companies because interest rates are now above US levels and the renminbi is expected to appreciate ... China's foreign exchange reserves increased by a record $114.8 billion in April and May [2008] to $1,800 billion. Although it is impossible to calculate how much of that inflow is short-term, speculative capital, the figures were substantially higher than the combined numbers for the trade surplus and foreign direct investment. The capital inflows have made economic management more difficult because, even though domestic inflation has been high in recent months, the central bank has been reluctant to raise interest rates for fear of attracting more hot money. Authorities have so far prevented the inflows from causing money supply to grow too sharply by issuing bonds and ... [raising] bank reserve requirements.

(*FT*, 3 July 2008, p. 1)

'Foreign exchange reserves grew to $1,810 billion at the end of June [2008] ... China's foreign exchange reserves are the biggest in the world' (*FT*, 15 July 2008, p. 11).

'The yuan [is] now trading at around 6.82 per cent' (*IHT*, 29 July 2008, p. 14).

A Politburo meeting on 25 July [2008] replaced the previous national economic goal, preventing overheating of the economy and controlling inflation, with a new target. As enunciated by President Hu Jintao in recent appearances, the objective now is to seek fast and sustained economic growth while still keeping inflation under control. He said at a rare news conference on Friday [1 August]: 'We must maintain steady, relatively fast development and control excessive price rises as the priority tasks of macro adjustment' ... After letting the currency rise sharply against the dollar in the first half of this year [2008], China's central bank has actually pushed the yuan down against the dollar in each of the past four trading days, including a drop of 0.13 per cent Monday [4 August] ... In the past several days the Chinese authorities have raised export tax refunds for garment manufacturers – an industry previously slighted by regulators, who remain more interested in promoting high technology industries. Policymakers have also reportedly moved to ease limits of banks.

(www.iht.com, 5 August 2008; *IHT*, 6 August 2008, p. 13)

Chinese leaders ... have long been trying to prevent ... the economy ... from growing too fast, but now they fear that growth is slowing too fast and may slow further. National income grew by 10.1 per cent in the year to the second quarter [of 2008], compared with 10.6 per cent in the year to the first quarter and 11.2 per cent to the last quarter of 2007 ... Much of the fall results from a decline in net exports ... Manufacturers of low value-added export goods such as clothes and textiles ... are among the hardest hit ... The state-controlled media have reported many closures of small and medium-sized business enterprises in coastal areas. Chinese leaders, previously more eager to nurture high-tech industries, toured textile factories last month [July] in a show of political support ... Later in July a meeting of the ruling Politburo signalled a policy shift. The formerly oft-repeated injunction to prevent overheating was dropped. Instead the leadership decided to focus on maintaining 'steady and fast' economic growth, though it said it would continue its efforts to combat inflation. Since the meeting there have been moves to placate exporters, such as easing controls on lending to small and medium-sized businesses.

(*The Economist*, 9 August 2008, p. 53)

On 1 August [2008] the finance ministry increased export tax rebates on a range of clothing products from 11 per cent to 13 per cent and on bamboo products from 5 per cent to 11 per cent, in an apparent effort to help exporters of cheap goods.

(p. 63)

Inflation cooled for a third month on slower food price gains ... The consumer price index rose 6.3 per cent in July [2008] from a year earlier, after increasing 7.1 per cent in June ... The expansion of the world's fourth biggest economy has slowed for four quarters, prompting officials to emphasize the importance of rapid growth and drop references to maintaining a tight monetary policy. China has already loosened bank lending quotas, raised tax rebates for some exports and halted the yuan's appreciation against the dollar ... The yuan weakened 0.1 per cent to 6.8648 in early trade in Shanghai. The currency rose 4.2 per cent in the three months through March and 2.3 per cent in the second quarter before stalling in the third.

(www.iht.com, 12 August 2008; *IHT*, 13 August 2008, p. 15)

'The central bank has allowed the yuan to decline against the dollar in the past two weeks after a 20 per cent rise since 2005' (*IHT*, 12 August 2008, p. 14).

The Chinese currency has appreciated by 7 per cent against the US dollar this year [2008]. But the pace of appreciation has slowed sharply over the past two months. In August the renminbi even depreciated slightly against the dollar. This is only the second month that this has happened since China moved away from the dollar peg in 2005.

(*FT*, 1 September 2008, p. 8)

The yuan, after strengthening for twenty-six consecutive months ... actually weakened slightly against the dollar last month [August] ... The yuan has risen 21 per cent against the dollar since China broke its peg to the dollar in July 2005 ... The central bank has tended to favour allowing the yuan to strengthen, which lessens the pressure on it to buy money-losing American securities ... By buying US bonds, the government has been investing a large portion of the country's savings in assets earning just 3 per cent a year or so in dollars. And the investments are actually losing as much as 10 per cent a year when inflation and the Chinese currency's appreciation against the dollar are factored in ... The interest from the bank's foreign bond holdings barely pays the interest on the money the central bank has borrowed within China to buy the bonds ... But the finance ministry, and particularly its allies at the commerce ministry, prefer to keep the yuan weaker to help exports. The bank and the finance ministry are ferocious bureaucratic rivals ... Bankers estimate the dollar portion of China's foreign exchange reserves at a little over $1 trillion.

(*IHT*, 4 September 2008, p. 11)

'China's foreign exchange reserves increased ... from $1,499 billion at the end of August 2007 to $1,810 billion by the end of June [2008]' (*FT*, 12 September 2008, p. 6).

'China's inflation rate eased to 4.9 per cent in August – the lowest in fourteen months' (www.cnn.com, 10 September 2008).

'Inflation dropped sharply in August for the fourth month in a row, giving more room for policy-makers to take measures to boost the economy if growth begins to slow sharply.' (www.ft.com, 10 September 2008).

After five years of tightening monetary policy to fight inflation, China abruptly reversed course late Monday afternoon [15 September], cutting interest rates and easing bank lending in response to signs that growth of the economy was finally slowing. China's exports have slowed sharply ... Since 2003 China's top priority has been to control inflation. But China's Politburo ... decided at a meeting on 25 July that the top economic goals should shift to sustaining economic development and limiting inflation, in that order ... The central bank said in a statement that the goal of economic policy was: '[To] solve prominent problems in the current economic operation, implement the policy of giving different policies for different needs and optimizing the economic structure, and ensure a steady, rapid and sustained development' ... Effective Tuesday [16 September] the People's Bank of China reduced by 0.27 per cent to 7.2 per cent the regulated benchmark rate that commercial banks may charge for one-year loans to business borrowers with strong credit histories. Rates for shorter-term loans will be generally cut even more, while rates for longer-term loans will be subject to smaller adjustments ... The central bank also reduced, by a full percentage point, the share of assets that small and medium-sized banks must deposit as reserves with the central bank, effective 25 September. [This is] the so-called reserve requirement ratio ... But the People's Bank of China made a point Monday of not reducing the reserve requirement ratio for the country's six largest banks ... [namely] the Industrial and Commercial Bank of China, the Agricultural Bank of China, the Bank of China, the China Construction Bank, the Bank of Communications and the Postal Savings Bank of China. These institutions account for more than two-thirds of the banking market in China. The central bank needs large sums of reserves, for which it pays only 1.89 per cent interest to the banks, so that it can continue buying large sums of foreign exchanger reserves. By buying tens of billions of dollars' worth of foreign currency each month, the Beijing authorities have been able to limit the rise of the yuan against the dollar ... The central bank rapidly ratcheted up ... the reserve requirement ratio ... from 6 per cent in August 2003 to 14.5 per cent last December [2007] and 17.5 per cent in June [2008] ... The central bank cut this ratio by 2 percentage points for banks in areas damaged by the Sichuan province earthquake on 12 May.

(www.iht.com, 15 September 2008; *IHT*, 16 September 2008, p. 17)

'China's central bank cut the country's benchmark interest rate last night [15 September] for the first time in more than six years, in the face of global financial turmoil and signs of a slowing domestic economy' (*FT*, 16 September 2008, p. 12).

The yuan ... has barely budged [against the dollar] over the past four months. But since the dollar has strengthened dramatically of late, the yuan has surged against other currencies, such the Euro, sterling and most emerging market currencies. Indeed, in trade-weighted terms, against a basket of currencies, it has risen by 12 per cent over the past six months. Since July 2005, when China scrapped its fixed peg to the dollar, the yuan's trade-weighted value has risen by 20 per cent, by far the biggest appreciation of any large economy.

(*The Economist*, 15 November 2008, p. 89)

'[On 11 November] the yuan traded at 6.8284 against the dollar in Shanghai' (www.iht.com, 11 November 2008).

After keeping its currency almost entirely in the range of 6.82 to 6.85 against the dollar for four months, even as the global financial crisis caused most other currencies to plunge against the dollar, China's central bank let the yuan drop steeply. On Monday [1 December] it set an unusually weak mid-point for the yuan and stood back without intervening as the currency fell to the bottom of its permitted daily trading band, which extends 0.5 per cent on either side of the midpoint, for the first time. The yuan hit the bottom of its band again on Tuesday [2 December] and Wednesday [3 December]. Trading almost ground to a halt Wednesday morning because so few banks were willing to sell dollars, traders said ... [The yuan appreciated] over 7 per cent against the dollar earlier this year ... [peaking at] 6.8099 in September.

(www.iht.com, 3 December 2008; *IHT*, 4 December 2008, p. 14)

Beijing holds more than 60 per cent of its $2 trillion of reserves in dollar assets, with a big chunk in debt issued by the Treasury and the troubled mortgage lenders, Fannie Mae and Freddie Mac, which have effectively been taken over by the US government.

(www.iht.com, 4 December 2008)

Sharp downward moves by the renminbi against the dollar in recent days have been interpreted by some analysts as a sign that China has shifted policy. The country's foreign exchange market was dominated again yesterday [3 December] by expectations that Chinese authorities are now eager to see the renminbi depreciate against the US dollar. Trading in the renminbi almost dried up at one stage yesterday, market-makers said, owing to fears that banks would run out of dollars to meet demand from Chinese investors, prompting the central bank to sell dollars into the market ... China's State Council, the country's cabinet, also announced measures yesterday to stimulate lending ... The council said it would ... allow the country's three 'policy' banks – China Development Bank, China Export and Import Bank and China Agricultural Development Bank – to make a further renminbi 100 billion ($14.5 billion) of loans.

(*FT*, 4 December 2008, p. 11)

[There were] relatively large renminbi movements in Monday's trading. The currency, which trades between narrow bands managed by the authorities, fell by 0.73 per cent – its biggest one-day drop in three years – as traders speculated that Beijing wanted to help exporters. The volatile trading follows mounting calls for more help for exporters ... It remains unclear whether Beijing was signalling a shift in policy towards a weaker renminbi on Monday. The dollar–renminbi rate set by the central bank appreciated slightly yesterday, leading some economists to play down talk of a significant policy change ... In 2005 China moved from an exchange rate fixed to the US dollar to a managed float in which the central bank sets a daily parity against the US dollar. The renminbi trades up to 0.5 per cent either side of this rate. Economists believe the authorities are increasingly targeting a basket of currencies rather than just focusing on the US dollar.

(p. 11)

The United States urged China on Friday [5 December] not to 'roll back' the appreciation of its currency that has taken place over the last two years ... Hank Paulson, Treasury Secretary, said that the main reason for job losses among Chinese exporters was slowing global demand, not currency appreciation. Paulson: 'Some people in China, looking at the slowing global economy and seeing what is happening to exports, might blame it on currency appreciation and seek to roll that back. China understands, as do we, how important currency reform is to rebalancing growth in China' ... Mr Paulson was speaking at the end of the two-day 'strategic economic dialogue', a bi-annual meeting of US and Chinese ministers and officials. The meeting has been accompanied, after a relatively large drop in the renminbi earlier this week, by considerable speculation the Chinese central bank is weakening the currency against the dollar to help exporters ... The renminbi appreciated modestly on Friday as speculation about a shift in currency policy receded. Chen Deming, China's commerce minister, said the recent weakening of the currency against the dollar was not aimed at helping exporters.

(www.ft.com, 5 December 2008)

The renminbi posted a record one-day drop against the dollar on Monday [1 December] ... as speculation grew that the Chinese authorities would allow the pegged currency to weaken in order to boost exports. Over the week the renminbi lost 0.6 per cent against the dollar, trading at renminbi 6.8741.

(*FT*, 6 December 2008, p. 27)

The week began with the news that the renminbi had depreciated by 0.73 per cent on Monday [1 December] The renminbi is a tightly managed currency and this was by far its greatest daily move since the Chinese authorities opted to allow the renminbi to start to float in 2005. Moreover, it was in a new direction ... The renminbi's drop on Monday brought it to its lowest against the dollar since June, but still 20 per cent stronger than in 2005.

(p. 28)

'The yuan has been held broadly constant since July' (www.economist.com 14 January 2009).

'Foreign exchange reserves rose by $40.4 billion in the final quarter [of 2008] to $1,946 billion' (*FT*, 16 January 2009, p. 6).

China's decision to let foreign banks trade corporate bonds may give a lift to the market and help it develop into a major fund-raising source for Chinese companies. The change gives foreign banks a new investment channel in China. They were previously limited to buying bonds issued by the government and other banks, which offer much higher yields ... The China Banking Regulatory Commission told some foreign institutions last week they could enter the inter-bank market for corporate bonds.

(*IHT*, Thursday 15 January 2009, p. 13)

'On a trade-weighted basis, China's currency has appreciated by about 10 per cent since August [2008]' (www.iht.com, 27 January 2009; *IHT*, 28 January 2009, p. 7). 'China limited yuan gains against the dollar in July 2008 after the currency rose 21 per cent following the end of a peg three years earlier ... China's yuan trades at about 6.85 to the dollar' (www.iht.com, 30 January 2009).

'In 2008 the renminbi appreciated by 9.5 per cent against the US dollar, and by even more against most of China's Asian neighbours' (www.economist.com, 3 February 2009).

[In his] statement Thursday [22 January] ... to the Senate Finance Committee ... Timothy Geithner, who is expected to be confirmed soon as US Treasury Secretary, [said] that President Barack Obama believed that China was 'manipulating' its currency ... Geithner: 'President Obama – backed by the conclusions of a broad range of economists – believes that China is manipulating its currency' ... [Geithner] stopped short of charging that China is manipulating its currency intentionally to gain an unfair trade advantage, as the 1988 law requires for an official citation of currency 'manipulation' ... It remained unclear whether Geithner was signalling that Obama would officially declare this spring [2009], when the administration is required by the twenty-year-old law to report to Congress on exchange rate issues, that China was engaging in currency manipulation ... The Bush administration purposely did not use the term 'currency manipulator' ... even when it was criticizing China's trade policy ... When Obama was a senator he supported legislation as recently as last year [2008] that would open the door to trade sanctions against China for currency manipulation ... In his written statement to the Senate panel Geithner further noted that Obama's support as a senator for 'tough legislation to overhaul the US process for determining currency manipulation and authorizing new enforcement measures so countries like China cannot continue to get a free pass for undermining fair trade principles' ... An administration official said that Geithner was only repeating what Obama had said during the campaign, and pointed out that his statement also emphasized that Obama intended to use 'all the diplomatic avenues available to him' to address the currency question ... Geithner's statement was in response to a written question about the new administration's stance that was submitted by Senator Charles Schumer, Democrat, of New York, a vocal critic of China's currency policies ... In his statement Geithner said the administration would move deliberately in dealing with China: 'The question is how and when to broach the subject in order to do more good than harm. The new economic team will forge an integrated strategy on how best to achieve currency realignment in the current economic environment.'

(www.iht.com, 23 January 2009; *IHT*, 24 January 2009, p. 16)

Rather than sending a high level message, China's commerce ministry responded to Geithner's comments with a low key statement that said Beijing had not manipulated the value of its currency to promote exports, adding that accusations of government tampering in foreign exchange would only fuel US protectionism. The official statement was released early Saturday [24 January]: 'China will keep its currency stable and will not depreciate the currency to support exports.'

(*IHT*, 24 January 2009, p. 1)

Every six months America's Treasury must publish a list of countries which it deems to be currency manipulators. Once a country appears on that list, formal negotiations to end the manipulation must begin. The Treasury under George [W.] Bush, particularly in recent years preferred a softer, behind-the-scenes approach and refused to brand China a manipulator. Although Timothy Geithner did not commit himself to any specific action, the use of the m-word suggests Team Obama will take a tougher line ... [President Barack Obama's] advisers see tough words as a ... warning that Beijing must not be tempted to prop up its staggering economy by weakening the yuan ... Sino-American economic tensions are already rising as Chinese officials hotly dispute the idea that their savings surplus had anything to do with the current global mess. An official at China's central bank recently called the idea 'ridiculous' and an example of 'gangster logic'.

(www.economist.com, 24 January 2009)

The IMF is caught in a stand-off between members over whether to label China's currency as 'fundamentally misaligned' ... The issue is so controversial the IMF's executive board has not discussed the Chinese economy since 2006, in spite of rules saying it should regularly assess member economies. The decision touches directly on one of the most divisive issues among governments worldwide: the extent to which huge current account deficits and surpluses and artificially managed exchange rates have contributed to the financial crisis.

(*FT*, 26 January 2009, p. 5)

[In Brussels on 30 January] Prime minister Wen Jiabao ... brushed aside the US criticism that the Chinese authorities were 'manipulating' the renminbi's exchange rate and should let the currency appreciate faster against the dollar. He made clear its present exchange rate policies were appropriate for the world economy ... Mr Wen said: 'To maintain the stability of the Chinese currency on a reasonable and balanced basis at this moment will play a positive role in stabilizing international finance and the economy' … EU officials said they regarded the need to boost Chinese domestic demand as more important than the exchange rate issue, in terms of the specific measures Beijing could take to help pull the world out of its downturn … China and the EU … agreed to hold a summit soon and to co-operate more closely on overcoming the world economic downturn … [It was] agreed that high level trade and economic officials from the EU and China should reconvene in April in a forum which met for the first time since last year [2008] … The most concrete outcome was the signature of an EU–Chinese accord on strengthening intellectual property rights to combat the counterfeiting of goods.

(www.ft.com, 30 January 2009; *FT*, 31 January 2009, p. 8)

The argument … that China is 'manipulating' its currency [is] 'completely unfounded' he [Wen Jiabao] says … Wen Jiabao: 'I want to make it very clear that maintaining the stability of the renminbi at a balanced and reasonable level is not only in the interest of China but also in the interests of the world. Many people have yet to come to see this point that if we have drastic fluctuation in the exchange rate of the renminbi, it would be a big disaster.'

(*FT*, 2 February 2009, p. 7)

[A] G7 conference [took place in Rome] … over the weekend … Veering sharply from his past testimony before the US Congress, where he used harsh language in criticizing China's reluctance to let the yuan appreciate, the new US Treasury Secretary, Timothy Geithner, was quick to recommend China for its 4 trillion yuan ($585 billion) stimulus package. He said during a news conference Saturday [14 February]: 'We very much welcome the steps China has taken to strengthen domestic demand and its commitment to further exchange rate reform' … This view was echoed by the G7's communiqué, which added that the yuan was 'expected to appreciate in effective terms' … Geithner emphasized the [US] administration's commitment to open markets.

(www.iht.com, 15 February 2009; *IHT*, 16 February 2009, pp. 1, 12)

The Obama administration has said Timothy Geithner's description of China's currency policy was 'not making any determinations' as to whether the country was manipulation its currency – a judgement the Treasury has to make in April in a formal currency report.

(*FT*, 16 February 2009, p. 6)

'The yuan … is now the strongest in trade-weighted real terms since 1993' (*FT*, 12 March 2009, p. 22).

Since mid-December [2008] China has sealed currency swap accords totalling 650 billion yuan ($95 billion) with the central banks of South Korea, Malaysia, Indonesia, Hong Kong, Belarus and, in a deal announced Monday [30 March 2009], Argentina … Financial diplomats say more agreements are in the pipeline. The proximate purpose is to grease the wheels of trade, which have been gummed up by the global credit crunch. Importers in the six entities involved will be able to pay for Chinese goods in yuan instead of dollars, the principal export–import currency ... [A] programme, due to be started soon, is to allow trade between Hong Kong and the mainland province of Guangdong to be settled in yuan rather than in US or Hong Kong dollars. The 200 billion yuan swap that Beijing signed with Hong Kong in January [2009] will provide an initial pool of Chinese currency needed for paying export and import invoices in yuan.

(*IHT*, 31 March 2009, p. 21)

China has agreed to a renminbi 70 billion ($10.24 billion) currency swap with Argentina that will allow it to receive renminbi instead of dollars for its exports to the Latin American country ... The deal was signed on Sunday [29 March] ... Beijing has signed renminbi 650 billion ($95 billion) of deals since December [2008] with Malaysia, South Korea, Hong Kong, Belarus and Indonesia and now Argentina in an attempt to unblock trade financing that has been severely curtailed by the [global financial] crisis ... China has suggested replacing the dollar with an enhanced version of the IMF's unit of account, the Special Drawing Right (SDR) ... Economists say the SDR plan is infeasible for now but see Beijing's currency swap deals as pieces in a jigsaw designed to promote wider international use of the renminbi, starting with making it more acceptable for trade and aiming at establishing it as a reserve currency in Asia.

(www.ft.com, 31 March 2009)

The [US] Treasury Department said on Wednesday [16 April] that China was not manipulating its currency ... Treasury Secretary Timothy Geithner: 'China has taken steps to enhance exchange rate flexibility' ... He said the yuan had climbed 16.6 per cent against other currencies from June [2008] through February [2009], even as the financial crisis intensified and other currencies lost value against the dollar ... Mr Geithner ... also praised China for its stimulus plan ... Treasury officials placed even greater emphasis on China's $586 billion fiscal stimulus programme. They couched the entire discussion of currency manipulation in the context of fighting the global downturn, adding that China's stimulus programme was bigger than that of any other country except the United States.

(www.iht.com, 16 April 2009; *IHT*, 17 April 2009, p. 15)

[In southern China] at the Boao Forum for Asia ... China's riposte to the annual World Economic Forum in Davos [Switzerland] ... China moved to boost the international profile of ... the renminbi ... signing bilateral swap agreements totalling renminbi 650 billion ($95 billion) and announced a trade settlement pilot allowing selected companies in Hong Kong, Shanghai and Guangdong to settle cross-border transactions in renminbi.

(*FT*, 20 April 2009, p. 5)

'China said over the weekend it would allow Hong Kong banks on the mainland to issue yuan-denominated bonds' (www.iht.com, 20 April 2009).

> China has been diversifying away from the dollar since 2005, when it broke the renminbi's peg to the US dollar and officially marked it to a basket of currencies, but it still holds more than two-thirds in US dollar-denominated assets by most estimates.
>
> (*FT*, 25 April 2009, p. 5)

'Many American economists say that the renminbi still appears to be undervalued by about 10 per cent to 20 per cent' (*IHT*, 16 May 2009, p. 2).

'US Treasury Secretary Timothy Geithner arrived Sunday [31 May] in Beijing for two days of talks with Chinese leaders' (*IHT*, 1 June 2009, p. 15). '[On Monday 1 June] the Treasury Secretary just briefly touched on currency issues ... Mr Geithner did urge China to move toward a more flexible exchange rate' (*IHT*, 2 June 2009, p. 12).

> China has taken another step towards internationalizing its currency and reducing its reliance on the US dollar with the announcement of new rules to allow select companies to invoice and settle trade transactions in renminbi. The regulations released by the People's Bank of China will allow approved companies to settle transactions through financial institutions in Shanghai and other cities in southern China ... Offshore, the trial scheme will allow transactions to be settled in renminbi in Hong Kong and Macao ... and later in limited fashion in south-east Asia as well. Importers and exporters will be able to place orders with authorized Chinese companies, and settle payments for them, in renminbi.
>
> (*FT*, 3 July 2009, p. 6)

> China has officially opened a pilot programme to allow companies to settle imports and exports in renminbi in selected regions ... Three pairs of Shanghai companies with their Hong Kong companies and Indonesian counterparts signed contracts on Monday [6 July] to be the first to settle business deals in the Chinese currency. Executives said the move would save costs and avoid exchange rate risks. Bank of China and Bank of Communications were the first lenders to clear transactions in renminbi ... Hong Kong also kicked off the long-awaited yuan settlement programme on Monday, HSBC said it completed its first renminbi trade settlement with Shanghai and its first cross-border credit transaction.... In announcing the renminbi settlement programme in April, Beijing said it would initially be confined to certain areas, including Hong Kong, which are outside mainland China, and to Shanghai and China's key export province of Guangdong in the south. The programme would also be used between the Association of South-east Asian Nations [Asean] and Yunnan and Guangxi regions in southern China before it is launched elsewhere. Although the total amount in the first batch of deals signed on Monday was small, less than 14 million renminbi ($2 million), state media said around 400 Chinese companies had already won

approval to conduct renminbi business and predicted that the programme would have huge potential ... China revalued the renminbi by 2.1 per cent against the dollar in July 2005 ... The renminbi has appreciated by a further 19 per cent against the dollar since then.

(www.iht.com, 6 July 2009; *IHT*, 7 July 2009, p. 15)

Banks in China and Hong Kong began wiring Chinese renminbi directly to one another on Monday [6 July] to settle payments for imports and exports ... The Chinese government is accelerating the process of making its own currency more readily convertible into other currencies, which gives it the potential over the long term to be used widely for trade and as a reserve currency ... Almost all payments for China's imports and exports, as well as international investment in China and Chinese investment abroad, are made in dollars. Smaller sums cross China's borders as Euros and yen, but seldom renminbi ... Three people who have discussed the issue ... [of] full convertibility ... with China's central bank ... said that China's recently announced goal to turn Shanghai into an international financial centre by 2010 meant that China probably wants a renminbi that is fully convertible into other currencies by then ... Currency specialists and economists estimate that China still holds close to three-quarters of its $2 trillion in foreign reserves in the form of dollar-denominated assets. But these assets have nearly stopped growing since the global financial crisis began last September [2008], as Chinese authorities have also shifted away from the longer-maturity bonds and the securities of government-sponsored enterprises like Fannie Mae and toward shorter-date securities, especially Treasury bills.

(www.iht.com, 7 July 2009)

Six Shanghai companies have signed contracts with counterparts in Hong Kong and Indonesia to settle deals in yuan. It means if the two sides have yuan available, they need not enter world exchange markets to pay. Executives said the move would save costs and avert exchange rate risks. Most of China's foreign trade is settled in US dollars or the Euro, leaving exporters vulnerable to exchange rate fluctuations ... The trial is expected to be limited to Hong Kong and Macao outside of mainland China, and to Shanghai and Guangdong province. However, it is expected to be extended so that the yuan could be used to settle trade between parts of eastern China (Guangdong and the Yangtze River delta) and the Asean group of countries: Brunei, Burma, Cambodia, Indonesia, Laos, Malaysia, the Philippines, Singapore, Thailand and Vietnam.

(www.bbc.co.uk, 6 July 2009)

Starting on 6 July selected firms in five Chinese cities are now allowed to use yuan to settle transaction with businesses in Hong Kong, Macao and Asean countries. Foreign banks will be able to buy or borrow yuan from mainland lenders to finance such trade. In June Russia and China agreed to expand the use of their currencies in bilateral trade; Brazil and China are discussing a similar idea. The People's Bank of China has also signed currency swap agreements with Argentina, Belarus, Hong Kong, Indonesia, Malaysia and South Korea. The central bank will make yuan available to pay for imports from China if these countries are short of foreign exchange. In another recent move Hong Kong banks are now allowed to issue yuan-denominated bonds, a step towards building an offshore yuan market ... The dollar accounts for 65 per cent of the world's foreign exchange reserves, only slightly less than a decade ago and well ahead of the Euro's 26 per cent share. Three-quarters of all reserves are in the hands of emerging economies; China alone holds one-third of the global stash ... World foreign exchange reserves by currency in the first quarter of 2009: dollar, 65 per cent; Euro 26 per cent; pound 4 per cent; yen 3 per cent; other 3 per cent. China's foreign exchange reserves (total $2.2 trillion) by asset (latest estimate): US treasuries 35 per cent; US agencies (including Fannie Mae and Freddie Mac) 23 per cent; Other US 8 per cent; non-dollar assets 35 per cent.

(*The Economist*, 11 July 2009, pp. 67–8)

'The central bank reported that its foreign exchange reserves leapt by $177.9 billion in the second quarter [of 2009] to $2.13 trillion. China is the only country to have amassed more than $2 trillion in currency reserves' (www.iht.com, 15 July 2009).

'Currency reserves rose 17.8 per cent from June 2008 to a record $2.13 trillion. Its currency stockpile is twice the size of Japan's – the second biggest holder' (www.bbc.co.uk, 15 July 2009).

'Beijing called a halt to the appreciation last July [2008]. The renminbi has been stable against the greenback ever since' (*FT*, 27 July 2009, p. 7).

'The yuan, after rising in value about 22 per cent since 2005, has scarcely budged in the past year' (www.iht.com, 27 July 2009).

From July 2005 (when China abandoned its dollar peg) to February 2009 the yuan rose by 28 per cent in real trade-weighted terms, according to the Bank for International Settlements. But alarmed by the collapse of exports, China has virtually pegged the yuan to the dollar over the past twelve months. As the greenback fell this year [2009] it dragged the yuan down with it. Since February the yuan's real trade-weighted value has lost 8 per cent. Economists disagree about the extent to which the yuan is undervalued. In the IMF's 'Article IV' assessment of China, published on 22 July, officials were split over whether the currency was 'substantially undervalued'. Morris Goldstein and Nicholas Lardy ... estimate that the yuan is undervalued by 15 per cent to 25 per cent, based on the adjustment needed to eliminate the current account surplus.

(*The Economist*, 1 August 2009, p. 66)

The ministry of finance said Tuesday [8 September] that it would issue 6 billion yuan worth of government bonds in Hong Kong, a major step to internationalize its currency ... The bond issue [is] worth about $879 million

... The finance ministry said ... the yuan bond issue ... will 'promote the yuan in neighbouring countries ... [and] improve the yuan's international status' ... While domestic banks like Bank of China and the Export–Import Bank of China have issued yuan-denominated bonds in Hong Kong for a couple of years ... this is the first time that government bonds are to be issued ... In July the People's Bank of China started a programme for local companies to settle trade in yuan, but it has so far spurred little trade.

(www.iht.com, 8 September 2009; *IHT*, 9 September 2009, p. 15)

'Intervention in currency markets has prevented the value of the yuan from moving appreciably against the dollar in more than fourteen months, and has pushed the yuan down by 18 per cent against the Euro since March [2009]' (*IHT*, 19 September 2009, p. 11).

China started selling yuan-denominated sovereign bonds in Hong Kong for the first time on Monday [28 September], testing international demand for its currency with the $879 million issue as it moved to widen the yuan's exposure and appeal to markets abroad ... The debt sale ... is limited to investors who have renminbi accounts in Hong Kong banks ... Results will be announced on 22 October ... In July China made three government bond sales, and fell short of its targets each time.

(www.iht.com, 28 September 2009)

In the three years to July 2008 the yuan climbed by 21 per cent against the dollar. But for the last fourteen months it has, in effect, been repegged to the dollar. As a result the slide in the greenback has dragged down the yuan's trade-weighted value by almost 10 per cent since the start of this year [2009]. Morris Goldstein and Nicholas Lardy of the Petersen Institute for International Economics in July estimated that the yuan was undervalued by 15 per cent to 25 per cent.

(www.economist.com, 30 September 2009)

'Since ... the summer of 2008 ... the Chinese currency has been flat against the dollar' (*IHT*, 16 October 2009, p. 20).

'The government has kept the renminbi pegged at a rate of 6.82 renminbi per dollar' (*FT*, 30 October 2009, p. 15). 'The renminbi [has been] held at about 6.8 per cent to the dollar since July last year [2008]' (*FT*, 17 November 2009, p. 18).

'The yuan has been pegged at about 8.83 to the dollar since July 2008' (www. thetimes.co.uk, 17 November 2009).

'China's foreign reserves ... hit a record high of $2.273 trillion by the end of September [2009]' (www.iht.com, 15 October 2009).

[China has an] outrageous currency policy ... The crucial question is whether the target value of the yuan is reasonable. Until around 2001 you could argue that it was: China's overall trade position wasn't too far out of balance. From then onward, however, the policy of keeping the yuan–dollar rate came to look increasingly bizarre. First of all, the dollar slid in value, especially against the Euro, so that by keeping the yuan–dollar fixed, Chinese officials were, in effect, devaluing their currency against everyone else's. Meanwhile, productivity in China's export industries soared; combined with the *de facto* devaluation, this made Chinese goods extremely cheap on world markets. The result was a huge Chinese trade surplus. If supply and demand had been allowed to prevail, the value of China's currency would have risen sharply. But Chinese authorities didn't let it rise. They kept it down by selling vast quantities of the currency, acquiring an enormous hoard of foreign assets, mostly in dollars, currently worth about \$2.1 trillion. Many economists, myself included, believe that China's asset-buying spree helped inflate the [US] housing bubble, setting the stage for the global financial crisis. But China's insistence on keeping the yuan–dollar rate fixed, even when the dollar declines, may be doing even more harm now ... China has been keeping its currency pegged to the dollar – which means that a country with a huge trade surplus and a rapidly recovering economy, a country whose currency should be rising in value, is in effect engineering a large devaluation instead. And that's a particularly bad thing to do at a time when the world economy remains deeply depressed due to inadequate overall demand. By pursuing a weak currency policy, China is siphoning some of that inadequate demand away from other nations, which is hurting growth almost everywhere ... With the world economy still in a precarious state, beggar-my-neighbour policies by major players can't be tolerated ... US officials have been extremely cautious about confronting the China problem, to such an extent that last week the Treasury Department, while expressing 'concerns', certified in a required report to Congress that China is not ... manipulating its currency.

(Paul Krugman, www.iht.com, 23 October 2009; *IHT*, 24 October 2009, p. 7)

In recent months China has carried out what amounts to a beggar-thy-neighbour devaluation, keeping the yuan–dollar exchange rate fixed even as the dollar has fallen sharply against other major currencies. This has given Chinese exporters a growing competitive advantage over their rivals, especially producers in other developing countries. What makes China's currency policy especially problematic is the depressed state of the world economy. Cheap money and fiscal stimulus seem to have averted a second Great Depression. But policy-makers have not been able to generate enough spending, public or private, to make progress against mass unemployment. And China's weak currency policy exacerbates the problem, in effect siphoning much needed demand away from the rest of the world into the pockets of artificially competitive Chinese exporters ... Rather than face up to the need to change their currency policy ... the Chinese ... have taken to lecturing the United States, telling us to raise interest rates and curb fiscal deficits – that is, to make our unemployment problem even worse.

(Paul Krugman, www.iht.com, 16 November 2009; *IHT*, 17 November 2009, p. 6)

('In October [2009] the unemployment rate [in the United States] rose to 10.2 per cent, the highest since April 1983': www.cnn.com, 18 November 2009.)

'The World Bank, which has urged China to adopt a stronger currency, said the renminbi had fallen against its main trading partners since March thanks to its informal peg to the US dollar' (*FT*, 5 November 2009, p. 10).

> A few years ago we came up with the term 'Chimerica' to describe the combination of the Chinese and American economies, which together had become the key driver of the global economy ... We called it Chimerica for a reason: we believed this relationship was a chimera – a monstrous hybrid like the part-lion, part-goat, part-snake of legend ... In its heyday Chimerica consisted largely of the combination of Chinese development led by exports and American over-consumption ... For a time Chimerica seemed not a monster but a marriage made in heaven ... China made a sustained effort to control the value of its currency, the renminbi, which resulted in a huge accumulation of reserve dollars ... The Chimerica era is drawing to a close ... Right now Chimerica serves China better than America. Call it the 10:10 deal: the Chinese get 10 per cent growth, America gets 10 per cent unemployment ... It is in China's interest to kick its currency intervention habit. A heavily undervalued renminbi is the key financial distortion in the world economy today. If it persists for much longer, China risks losing the very foundation of its economic success: an open global trading regime. And this is exactly what President Barack Obama can offer in return for a substantial currency revaluation of, say, 20 per cent to 30 per cent over the next twelve months: a clear commitment to globalization and free trade, and an end to the nascent Chinese–American trade war.
>
> (Niall Ferguson and Moritz Schularick, www.iht.com, 16 November 2009)

> China said Wednesday [11 September] that it would consider major currencies in guiding the yuan, suggesting a departure from an effective peg to the dollar that has been in place since the middle of last year [2008]. The reference to a new set of benchmarks for determining the value of the yuan holds out the possibility of a departure from past practice. The central bank in a monetary policy report said: 'Following the principles of initiative, controllability and gradualism, with reference to international capital flows and changes in major currencies, we will improve the yuan exchange rate formation mechanism' ... It was the first time since a revaluation and establishing of exchange rate changes in July 2005 that the People's Bank of China had strayed from the language of keeping the yuan 'basically stable at a reasonable and balanced level' when discussing future currency overhauls in such quarterly reports.
>
> (www.iht.com, 11 November 2009)

> China's central bank yesterday [Wednesday 11 November] acknowledged the case for a stronger renminbi, days ahead of the arrival in Beijing of President Barack Obama for talks expected to highlight international concern

over currency policy. The People's Bank of China said foreign exchange policy would take into account 'capital flows and major currency movements', a pointed reference to the large speculative inflows of capital that China is receiving and US dollar weakness. The bank's new wording, included in its quarterly report on monetary policy, comes on the heels of growing global pressure to strengthen its currency, particularly from the EU and Japan. The IMF said at the weekend that the renminbi, which was in effect repegged to the dollar last year [2008] after being allowed to appreciate by about 20 per cent against the dollar since 2005, was 'significantly undervalued'. The bank's comments contrast with the calls of Chen Deming, commerce minister, at the weekend for the exchange rate to 'create stable expectations' for exporters ... Few economists expect China to abandon its effective peg to the dollar before the middle of 2010.

(*FT*, 12 November 2009, p. 6)

Finance ministers from the Asia Pacific Economic Co-operation [Apec] group ended a meeting in Singapore [on 12 November] with a strong endorsement of 'market-orientated exchange rates that reflect economic fundamentals' ... Zhu Guangyao, assistant finance minister, said that one of China's contributions to the recovery had been maintaining 'currency stability'.

(*FT*, 13 November 2009, p. 8)

'[China] signed up at the end of a meeting of Asia Pacific finance ministers in Singapore on Thursday [12 November] to a statement that promised "monetary policies consistent with price stability in the context of market-orientated exchange rates"' (www.iht.com, 13 November 2009).

President Hun Jintao told the Asia Pacific Economic Co-operation summit on Friday [13 November]: 'The inherent problems of the international economic system have not been fully addressed and a comprehensive world economic recovery still faces many uncertainties ... We are making a great effort to expand the domestic market, especially the rural market, control total discharge of pollutants and ensure both a sound natural eco-system and a sound socio-economic system ... The international financial crisis has given rise to trade and investment protectionism of various forms. Protectionism will not help any country move out of the crisis. It can only pose a threat to the fragile momentum of the economic recovery ... We must continue to promote trade and investment liberalization and oppose protectionism in all its manifestations, particularly the unreasonable trade and investment restrictions placed on developing countries.'

(www.iht.com, 13 November 2009; www.cnn.com, 13 November 2009)

Governments in Asia, Latin America and the EU are already alarmed by the cheap renminbi and say it is hurting domestic manufacturers ... China's exports have plummeted by more than 20 per cent this year [2009] and at least 20 million factory jobs have been lost in the coastal provinces. Beijing does not want to bring more harm to its huge migrant world force by letting the renminbi rise and with it the cost of Chinese goods abroad.

(www.iht.com, 14 November 2009)

Analysts say currency appreciation will not occur to any significant extent until the middle of next year [2008], largely because too many jobs are at stake ... Chinese exports have plummeted more than 20 per cent this year [2009], and at least 20 million factory jobs have been lost in the coastal provinces. Beijing does not want to bring more harm to its huge migrant work force by letting the yuan rise, and with it the cost of Chinese goods abroad.

(*IHT*, 16 November 2009, p. 14)

Discord surfaced at a summit of the Asia Pacific Economic Co-operation (Apec) forum in Singapore when a reference to 'market-orientated exchange rates' was cut from a communiqué issued at the end of two days of talks. An Apec delegation official said Washington and Beijing could not agree on the wording ... An earlier draft pledged Apec's twenty-one members to maintain 'market-orientated exchange rates that reflect underlying economic fundamentals'. That statement had been agreed at a meeting of Apec finance ministers on Thursday [14 November], including China, although it made no reference to the yuan.

(www.independent.co.uk, 15 November 2009)

At the Asia-Pacific summit in Singapore, the final communiqué from the twenty-one members was delayed as President Hu Jintao called successfully for the removal of a reference to the desirability of 'market-orientated exchange rates that reflect underlying economic fundamentals'. In a surprise move the reference had been included in a statement by Apec finance ministers on Thursday [12 November], in spite of China's unwillingness to discuss the matter. Mr Hu ignored the subject in his speeches and contributions to debate. Officials confirmed that it had also been included in the final leaders' statement but was removed after a discussion between the US and Chinese leaders.

(*FT*, 16 November 2009, p. 6)

Beijing has been the most critical of US fiscal policy, urging Washington to spend less ... [On 15 November] Liu Mingkang, China's chief banking regulator, said the US Federal Reserve's policy of maintaining low interest rates, together with the weak dollar, posed a threat to the global economic recovery. He said: '[It] is boosting speculative investment in stock and property markets and will pose new, real and insurmountable risks to the recovery in emerging markets. The situation has already encouraged a huge dollar carry trade and had a massive impact on global assets prices' ... The comments were made ... amid rising international criticism that China's currency is undervalued.

(*FT*, 16 November 2009, p. 6)

'Since the start of 2008 the yuan has actually risen against every currency except the yen ... China will probably allow the yuan to start rising again early next year [2010]' (www.economist.com, 19 November 2009; *The Economist*, 21 November 2009, pp. 89–90).

'On 25 November China tightened the rules on foreign currency transfers by individuals in a bid to control flows of hot money into the country' (*The Economist*, 28 November 2009, p. 88).

> The Eurozone's top economic officials pressed China on Sunday [29 November] to let the yuan resume its gradual rise. The Eurogroup includes the finance ministers from the sixteen countries that use the Euro ... The yuan rose 21 per cent against the dollar in the three years after Beijing ended a peg to the US currency in 2005. At that time Beijing said it would let the yuan float within a controlled band that tracked a basket of currencies. This July, however, China effectively repegged the exchange rate at around 6.83 to the dollar.
>
> (*IHT*, 30 November 2009, p. 16)

Luxembourg prime minister Jean-Claude Juncker, who heads economic talks in the Eurozone, said (on 29 November): 'We think an orderly and gradual appreciation of the renminbi would be in the best interest of China and of the global economy' (www.iht.com, 30 November 2009).

> European officials on Sunday [29 November] failed to persuade Beijing to begin strengthening its currency ... EU exports to China fell 5.3 per cent in the first half of the year [2009] ... The Euro has gained 15 per cent against the Chinese currency in the past year ... Eurozone officials argued that a gradual, orderly rise in the renminbi was in the interests of both China and the world economy ... Beijing insists China needs a stable exchange rate against the dollar to assist its economic recovery, which it says has benefited the world.
>
> (www.cnn.com, 30 November 2009)

> Premier Wen Jiabao, following a summit Monday [30 November] with EU leaders, said: 'To maintain the basic stability of the renminbi exchange rate is conducive to the economy and the recovery of the world economy ... Some countries demand change while practising trade protectionism against developing countries. This is unfair. We will maintain the stability of the renminbi at a reasonable and balanced level.'
>
> (www.iht.com, 30 November 2009)

> Wen Jiabao told the European financial leaders that China would keep the yuan stable while continuing to gradually make the yuan more flexible, the state-run *China Daily* reported Monday. He said: 'China hopes all major reserve currencies will maintain stability. The stability of Chinese currency is an important contribution to world financial stability.'
>
> (www.iht.com, 30 November 2009)

Prime minister Wen Jiabao: 'In this international financial crisis of a kind rarely seen in history, maintaining the basic stability of the renminbi exchange rate has benefited China's economic development and benefited the world economic recovery. Now some countries, on the one hand, want the renminbi to appreciate but, on the other hand, engage in brazen trade protectionism against China. This is unfair. In fact, it amounts to restricting China's development' ... The EU is China's biggest market, absorbing 20 per cent of its exports, and runs a large bilateral trade deficit with China.

(*IHT*, 1 December 2009, p. 21)

'[China's] real exchange rate is no higher than in early 1998 and has appreciated by 12 per cent over the past seven months' (*FT*, 9 December 2009, p. 15).

Zhu Min, a deputy governor of the Chinese central bank, said this week that: '[During the financial crisis China had] good reason [to weaken the renminbi because exports were falling sharply] ... But we took the same policy as we did in the Asian financial crisis, we decided to stabilize the exchange rate.'

(*FT*, 11 December 2009, p. 8)

The first Chinese overseas investment fund in seventeen months is expected to receive a lukewarm reception from mainland investors because of their unhappy experience with such products and the growing appeal of alternatives, based on strong domestic stock markets ... The main Chinese stock market [is] up about 75 per cent this year [2009], one of the world's top performers ... E Fund Management's Asia-focused stock fund under China's Qualified Domestic Institutional Investor programme (QDII) is seen as testing investors' demand for a line of products that some analysts see rising tenfold in assets to $100 billion in five years. Chinese regulators lifted in October [2009] a nearly one-and-a-half-year ban on the creation of new funds under the programme ... China introduced the programme in 2006 to allow domestic funds to be invested abroad but halted new fund approvals in May 2008 after heavy losses on QDII products ... as the financial crisis sent global markets tumbling. Since lifting the ban in October regulators have granted a combined $6 billion in QDII quotas to seven firms ... E Fund Management, which is allowed to raise as much as $1 billion, had raised about 500 million renminbi ($73 million) as of 23 December ... Analysts expect it may eventually raise less than half the $1 billion target ... So far this year the nine existing QDII funds have gained an average of 55.69 per cent in net asset value, lagging behind the 69.44 per cent rise for domestic equity funds ... Current investor wariness contrasts sharply with the public mania surrounding QDII products in 2007, when multi-billion-dollar funds sold out in a single day as global stock markets surged ... In the long run QDII products are expected to prosper as investors seek to diversify their assets and China seeks to ease pressure for a stronger renminbi ... Less than 5 per cent of China's mutual fund assets are invested overseas, but may rise to 10 per cent in five years and 20 per cent in a decade, according to [one estimate] ... [with] total QDII fund assets under management increasing tenfold over the next five years to 700 billion renminbi.

(IHT, 29 December 2009, p. 17)

'China's foreign exchange reserves grew 23 per cent in 2009 ... [They] rose to $126.5 billion in the fourth quarter to $2.4 trillion ... in line with market expectations' (www.iht.com, 15 January 2010).

'Foreign exchange reserves rose by $126.5 billion in the fourth quarter of last year [2009] to hit $2,399 billion ... For the year [2009] China added $453 billion to the reserves. $35 billion more than the increase in 2008' *(FT,* 16 January 2010, p. 7).

An increase of $453 billion last year [2009] in foreign exchange reserves partly reflected currency valuation effects and was not solely the result of inflows of speculative funds, the Chinese currency regulator said Tuesday [19 January] ... The State Administration of Foreign Exchange rejected media reports that the difference between the funds from the trade surplus and foreign direct investment, on the one hand, and the total increase in reserves, on the other hand, had been caused by speculative 'hot money'. The agency said it had sufficient information to explain the gap last year of $167 billion. The agency said: 'It is absolutely not right to do simple subtractions and declare that the gap is unexplainable, or even label it as hot money' ... But it acknowledged that speculative money was entering China in the form of disguised trade and investment and that low interest rates in the United States were encouraging the flow of money into China. For these reasons, the agency said, China needed to retain controls on capital flows, even though it reaffirmed the longstanding policy to move toward the full convertibility of the renminbi, and to give individuals and institutions in mainland China more opportunities to invest abroad. *Caijing* magazine, a Chinese business publication, reported Tuesday that Shanghai was considering allowing its residents to invest outside mainland China ... The programme would not limit investors to Hong Kong. The report did not provide details on the scope or timing of any such move. The foreign exchange agency did not provide any information about the currency composition of China's $2.4 trillion in foreign exchange reserves ... Analysts said about two-thirds of the reserves are in dollars. The Foreign Exchange agency said: 'We cannot release details of investment returns and currency changes, but we can use some relevant figures as references' ... The Foreign Exchange agency cited the 8.5 per cent fall in the dollar index in 2009 and data from the IMF showing that non-dollar assets accounted for about 40 per cent of global foreign exchange reserves. The agency said: 'The appreciation of non-dollar currencies against the dollar in 2009 has definitely led to growth in outstanding foreign exchange reserves calculated in dollars' ... Investment returns also increased the Chinese reserves, it said. As an example, it cited the annual average return of 4.8 per cent in the Barclays Global Investors bond index from 2005 to 2009.

(www.iht.com, 19 January 2010)

The US government borrowed more money than ever in 2009, but its largest lender – China – sharply reduced the amount it was willing to lend. The US Treasury estimated this past week that during the first eleven months of 2009 China raised its holdings of Treasury securities by just $62 billion. That was less than 5 per cent of the money the Treasury had to raise. That raised China's holdings to $790 billion, leaving it the largest foreign holder of US Treasury securities. (Japan is second, at $757 billion, and Britain a distant third at $278 billion.) But China's holdings at the end of November [2009] were lower than they were at the end of July [2009]. Not since 2001, when China was a relatively minor investor in Treasury securities, had the country shown a decline in holdings over a six month period ... China is on course to lend just 4.6 per cent of the money the government raised during the year, compared with 20.2 per cent in 2008 and a peak of 47.4 per cent in 2006 ... Some economists have feared what could happen if China were to decide to sell the Treasury securities it owns, but the reduction probably did not result from any decision to do that, said Robert Barbera, the chief economist of ITG, an investment advisory firm. Instead, he said, China's main determination now is to prevent the rise of its currency against the dollar and the country needed to buy fewer dollar-based securities to accomplish that goal as the Chinese trade surplus with the United States declined. The figures on foreign holdings by the Treasury Department include both official and private holdings. In China that is mostly official, but in some countries many of the holdings are owned by investors or money managers who could be managing portfolios on behalf of people from yet another country. It is possible that some Chinese purchases appear to be from other countries.

(*IHT*, 23 January 2010, p. 12)

President Barack Obama (3 February): 'One of the challenges we're got to address internationally is currency rates and how they match up to make sure our goods are not artificially inflated in price and their goods are artificially deflated in price' (www.bbc.co.uk, 4 February 2010).

President Barack Obama (3 February): '[The United States needs] to make sure our goods are not artificially inflated in price and their goods are not artificially deflated in price; that puts us at a huge competitive disadvantage' (www.iht.com, 4 February 2010). 'Mr Obama stopped short of saying China manipulates its currency, but his words on China's economic policies were harsh' (www.iht.com, 4 February 2010; *IHT*, 5 February 2010, p. 1).

At a meeting with Senate Democrats on Wednesday [3 February] President Barack Obama was asked whether the United States would cut ties with Beijing over continuing trade disputes. He said he would continue to make sure that China and other countries abided by trade agreements, but warned that it would be a mistake for the United States to become protectionist. He said: 'The approach that we're taking is to try to get much tougher about the enforcement of existing rules, putting constant pressure on China and other countries to open up their markets in reciprocal ways. But what I don't want to do is for us, as a country or as a party, to shy away from the prospects of international competition. Our future is going to be tied up with our ability to sell products all around the world, and China is going to be one of our biggest markets. To close us off from that market would be a mistake.'

(www.bbc.co.uk, 4 February 2010)

Ma Zhaoxu (foreign ministry spokesman): 'Judging from the international balance of payments and the currency market's supply and demand, the value of the renminbi is getting to a reasonable and balanced level' (www.iht.com, 4 February 2010).

Ma Zhaoxu: 'At the moment, looking at international balance of payments and foreign exchange market supply and demand, the level of the yuan is close to reasonable and balanced ... Criticism and pressing obviously is not helpful to solving problems' ... Ma said the exchange rate of the yuan was not the main reason for the US trade deficit with China. He added 'We hope the US side could objectively and rationally see a number of problems in the Chinese–US economic and trade co-operation and appropriately deal with them via negotiations' ... China reported a $196 billion global trade surplus last year [2009].

(www.guardian.co.uk, 4 February 2010)

'Ma Zhaoxu said the Chinese currency is not the main reason for China's trade surplus with the United States' (www.guardian.co.uk, 5 February 2010).

Dai Xianglong [is] the chairman of China's National Council for Social Security Fund ... [and] a former governor of the People's Bank of China, said Monday that radical fiscal policy changes were unlikely ... [On Monday 8 February he said that] while China recognized the leading role of the dollar, it was necessary to 'promote diversification of international currencies'. The world's new international monetary system should be made up of the US dollar, the Euro and an Asian currency, he said. The internationalization of the renminbi may take twenty years to complete, Mr Dai said. Ultimately it will be convertible with other currencies and account for a portion of global reserves, and the Chinese government will 'take appropriate responsibilities for the stability of international currencies', he said.

(*IHT*, 9 February 2010, p. 17)

China does not want to politicize its purchases of US Treasury bonds and continues to buy Treasuries 'every day', according to the official in charge of managing China's $2,400 billion foreign exchange reserves. Yi Gang (director of the States Administration of Foreign Exchange [Safe] said on Tuesday [9 March]: '[Chinese investments in US Treasuries are] market investment behaviour and we do not wish to politicize them. We are a responsible investor and in the process of these investments we can definitely achieve a mutually beneficial result' ... Despite the financial crisis and Safe's ill-timed 2008 diversification into global equities, Mr Yi said his agency had achieved 'relatively good' returns from its management of the reserves over the last two years ... The composition of China's reserves is a state secret but the apparent decline in Beijing's direct holdings of US Treasuries in recent months has led to speculation that it may be deliberately cutting its holdings in retaliation for worsening US–China relations. But analysts say the monthly Treasury data that show a dip in Chinese Treasury holdings do not capture the extent of Safe's purchases through international banks and overseas financial centres such as London and Hong Kong. When the data are revised at the end of the second quarter China is likely to have continued purchasing US Treasuries although it may have allowed some short-term debt to mature as it buys more long-term US government securities ... Despite the secrecy surrounding China's reserves, around two-thirds are invested in US-denominated assets, according to analysts and people who work closely with Safe ... Mr Yi said China would be 'cautious' about adding more gold to its foreign exchange reserves and gold would never become a big part of Safe's portfolio ... China is the world's biggest gold producer and Safe has been quietly adding to its gold holdings by buying from state-owned domestic producers, raising its total from 600 tonnes in 2003 to 1,054 tonnes by the middle of last year [2009] ... Last month [February] the US Treasury published preliminary data showing that China cut its holdings of Treasuries by $34.2 billion in December [2009]. Total holdings, according to revised figures, stood at $895 billion at year end ... ... Safe is known to route purchases through its offices in London and Hong Kong ... Taking this into account, Standard Chartered Bank estimates that China's US Treasury holdings actually stood at about $1,020 billion at the end of 2009 ... Overall it looks like China's USA holdings, as a ratio of its total holdings, are still within the normal historical range of about 68 per cent of its total reserves by the end of 2009.

(www.ft.com, 9 March 2010)

President Barack Obama (11 March):

For too long America served as the consumer engine for the entire world. But we are rebalancing. We're saving more. We all need to rebalance ... Countries with external deficits need to save and export more. Countries with external surpluses need to boost consumption and domestic demand. As I've said before, China moving to a more market-orientated exchange rate would make an essential contribution to that global rebalancing effort.

(www.bbc.co.uk, 12 March 2010)

Prime minister Wen Jiabao (speaking on 14 March, the final day of the annual session of the National People's Congress):

I do not think the renminbi is undervalued. We oppose all countries engaging in mutual finger-pointing or taking strong measures to force other nations to appreciate their currencies. That is not in the interest of reform of the renminbi or the renminbi's exchange rate regime. We will continue to reform the renminbi exchange rate regime and will keep the renminbi basically stable at an appropriate and balanced level. Since the outbreak of the international financial crisis, we have made strong efforts to keep the renminbi exchange rate at a stable level. This has played an important role in facilitating the global economy ... [Protecting the dollar is a matter of] national credibility [for the United States]. Any fluctuation in the value of the US currency is a big concern for us ... We are very concerned about the lack of stability in the US dollar ... In the press conference last year I said was a bit concerned [about the security of US Treasuries that China holds] ... This year I make the same remark. I am still concerned. We cannot afford any mistake, however slight, when it comes to financial assets ... I hope the United States will take concrete measures to reassure international investors ... It is not only in the interests of the investors, but also the United States itself ... I understand some economies want to increase their exports, but what I do not understand is the practice of depreciating one's own currency and attempting to force other countries to appreciate their own currencies, just for the purpose of increasing their own exports. In my view that is a protectionist measure. All countries should be fully alarmed by such developments.

(www.iht.com, 14 March 2010; www.bbc.co.uk, 14 March 2010; www.guardian.co.uk, 14 march 2010; www.cnn.com, 14 March 2010; www.ft.com, 14 March 2010; www.thetimes.co.uk, 14 March 2010; *IHT*, 15 March 2010, pp. 1, 16; *FT*, 15 March 2010, p. 1)

Prime minister Wen Jiabao argued that the renminbi is not unfairly valued, citing government calculations that suggested that, measured in real terms, China's currency had actually risen in value at the height of the economic crisis ... Analysts expect Beijing to let the yuan rise against the dollar some time this year [2010]. But they foresee a gradual increase of no more than 5 per cent this year.

(www.iht.com, 14 March 2010; *IHT*, 15 March 2010, p. 16)

Prime minister Wen Jiabao pointed out that around half of China's exports were processing trade – where imported components are assembled at factories in China – and 60 per cent were made by foreign companies or joint ventures with a foreign partner. He said: 'If you restrict trade with China, you are hurting your own countries' firms.'

(www.ft.com, 14 March 2010; *FT*, 15 March 2010, p. 1)

Twice a year, by law, [the US] Treasury must issue a report identifying nations that 'manipulate the rate of exchange between their currency and the US dollar for purposes of preventing effective balance of payments adjustments or gaining unfair competitive advantage in international trade' … The next report [is] due on 15 April.

(www.iht.com, 15 March 2010)

One hundred and thirty … members of the US Congress called on the Obama administration yesterday [15 March] … [to] officially designate China a currency manipulator when it issues its regular report on exchange rate policies [on 15 April] … The congressmen called for countervailing duties to be imposed on Chinese imports.

(*FT*, 16 March 2010, p. 7)

A spokesman for President Barack Obama [16 March]: 'You saw the president mention just a few days ago that he wished and hoped that China approached their currency using a more market-based interpretation' … [The spokesman] was reacting to a bipartisan effort in the US Senate that would slap duties on some Chinese exports to the United States if it does not realign its currency.

(www.iht.com, 16 March 2010)

Beijing called yesterday [16 March] for US multinationals to lobby the Obama administration against taking protectionist measures over the renminbi … The Chinese commerce ministry said: 'We hope that US companies in China will express their demands and points of view in the United States, in order to promote the development of global trade and jointly oppose trade protectionism' … The comments came as the political heat surrounding China's currency policy intensified in Washington. Led by Chuck Schumer, the New York Democrat, and Lindsey Graham, the South Carolina Republican, a group of senators said Beijing's refusal to let its currency appreciate was damaging the US recovery and hurting American competitiveness … The senators have proposed a bill that would require the [US] Treasury to identify countries with 'fundamentally aligned currencies' as well as those that needed to be tackled with 'priority action'. Those countries would have nearly a year to adjust the value of their currency before the administration was required to bring a case against them at the WTO, according to the proposal. The Treasury would also have to 'consult' with the Federal Reserve and other central banks about 'remedial intervention in currency markets'. Some measures could be taken earlier, including forbidding Chinese companies from participating in US government contracts. Mr Schumer and Mr Graham have been leading the charge in Congress against China's currency policy for several years and have periodically presented similar proposals.

(*FT*, 17 March 2010, p. 7)

China could face duties on some of its exports to the United States if it does not take steps to realign its currency, according to the draft text of legislation that was to be introduced Tuesday [16 March] in the Senate. The draft bill by Charles Schumer and Lindsey Graham would require the US Treasury Department to identify countries with fundamentally misaligned currencies each September and March. It would authorize the Commerce Department to take currency misalignment into its calculation of import injury duties for specific products if a targeted country had not begun steps within ninety days to realign its currency, according to the text of the bill ... Several years ago Mr Schumer and Mr Graham co-authored a bill that threatened China with a 27.5 per cent across-the-board tariff if it did not revalue the renminbi. That bill was passed by the Senate but its authors eventually abandoned it when Beijing began making some movement toward revaluing the renminbi. Many US lawmakers, with strong backing from economists, believe that China's currency is undervalued by 25 per cent to 50 per cent, giving Chinese companies an unfair price advantage in trade by effectively subsidizing exports and taxing competing imports.

(*IHT*, 17 March 2010, p. 19)

Members of Congress from both parties sought on Tuesday [16 March] to put more pressure on China to allow an increase in the value of its currency, saying Beijing's policy of holding the value down to give China an edge in export markets was holding back job creation in the United States ... Five senators [three others joining Charles Schumer and Lindsey Graham] introduced a bill that would all but compel the administration to act. A manipulation finding could prompt retaliatory efforts by the United States. In addition, 130 House members sent a letter on Monday [15 March] calling on the Treasury to issue a finding of manipulation and on the Commerce Department to impose countervailing duties to protect American manufacturers. The Senate bill would require the Treasury to identify 'fundamentally misaligned currencies' based on specific criteria. The bill would seek to address one reason that the United States has not cited China for manipulation since 1994, which is that a finding of manipulation requires intent. If the Treasury designated such a misaligned currency 'for priority action' that would set off other steps, including an investigation by the Commerce Department that could result in import duties to counter the effects of foreign export subsidies.

(www.iht.com, 17 March 2010)

The World Bank on Wednesday [17 March] recommended higher interest rates and a stronger currency for China as it raised its growth forecasts for the country ... The World Bank raised its forecast to 9.5 per cent growth [GDP] from the 8.7 per cent it had projected in November [2009]. It also estimated that growth would slow somewhat next year [2011] to 8.7 per cent ... The World Bank singled out the looming property bubble and strained local government finances as 'macroeconomic risks'. The report said: 'Inflation expectations can be contained by a tighter monetary stance and a stronger exchange rate. The case for a larger role for interest rates in monetary policy is strong. If policy-makers remain concerned about interest rate sensitive capital flows, more exchange rate flexibility would help ... The monetary policy stance needs to be tighter than last year [2009] and the case for exchange rate flexibility and more monetary independence from the United States is strengthening. It would also be helpful to increase the tolerance for modest inflation, to ensure room for desirable relative price changes. Strengthening the exchange rate can help reduce inflationary pressures and rebalance the economy. Over time more exchange rate flexibility can enable China to have a monetary policy independent from US cyclical conditions, which is increasingly necessary ... [With output in China once again] close to potential ... [the country now needs] a different macro stance than most other countries.'

(www.iht.com, 17 March 2010)

'Separately, Dominique Strauss-Kahn, the managing director of the IMF, said: "Some currencies in Asia are undervalued, especially the renminbi"' (www.iht. com, 17 March 2010).

China's currency is pegged by official policy at about 6.8 yuan to the dollar. At this exchange rate, Chinese manufacturing has a large cost advantage over its rivals, leading to huge trade surpluses ... My back-of-the-envelope calculations suggest that for the next couple of years Chinese mercantilism may end up reducing US employment by around 1.4 million jobs ... [If the Chinese dump] their hoard of dollars ... [they] would inflict large losses on themselves ... The world is awash in cheap money. So if China were to start selling dollars, there's no reason to think it would significantly raise US interest rates. It would probably weaken the dollar against other currencies – but that would be good, not bad, for US competitiveness and employment ... There's the claim that protectionism is always a bad thing, in any circumstances ... [But] when unemployment is high and the government can't restore full employment, the usual rules don't apply ... The victims of mercantilism have little to lose from a trade confrontation. So I'd urge China's government to reconsider its stubbornness. Otherwise the very mild protectionism it's currently complaining about will be the start of something much bigger.

(Paul Krugman, www.iht.com, 1 January 2010; *IHT*, 2 January 2010, p. 6)

China's policy of keeping the renminbi undervalued has become a significant drag on global economic recovery ... Widespread complaints that China was manipulating its currency – selling renminbi and buying foreign currencies, so as to keep the renminbi weak and China's exports artificially competitive – began around 2003. At that point China was adding about $10 billion a month to its reserves, and in 2003 it ran an overall surplus on its current account – a broad measure of the trade balance – of $46 billion. Today, China is adding more than $30 billion a month to its $2.4 trillion hoard of reserves. The IMF expects China to have a 2010 current surplus of more than $450 billion – ten times the 2003 figure. This is the most distortionary exchange rate policy any major nation has ever followed. And it's a policy that seriously damages the rest of the world. Most of the world's large economies are stuck in a liquidity trap – deeply depressed, but unable to generate a recovery by cutting interest rates because the relevant rates are already near zero. China, by engineering an unwarranted trade surplus, is in effect imposing an anti-stimulus on these economies which they can't offset ... The Peterson Institute for Economics estimates that the renminbi is undervalued by between 20 per cent and 40 per cent ... In 1971 the United States dealt with a similar but much less severe problem of foreign undervaluation by imposing a temporary 10 per cent surcharge on imports, which was removed a few months later after Germany, Japan and other nations raised the dollar value of their currencies. At this point, it's hard to see China changing its policies unless faced with the threat of similar action – except that this time the surcharge would have to be much larger, say 25 per cent.

(Paul Krugman, www.iht.com, 15 March 2010; *IHT*, 16 March 2010, p. 7)

'China's exchange rate ... is mercantilist trade policy, whose costs are borne more by countries competing with China – namely other developing and emerging market countries – than by rich countries' (Arvind Subramanian, *FT*, 4 February 2010, p. 13).

Economists estimate that the renminbi is undervalued by at least 25 per cent and as much as 40 per cent, relative to the dollar and other currencies. That gap, they say, is wider than at any time since 2005, when Beijing, under pressure from the Bush administration, allowed the renminbi to rise modestly.

(www.iht.com, 4 February 2010)

'Economists ... say the renminbi is undervalued by 25 per cent to 40 per cent compared with the dollar and other currencies' (*IHT*, 5 February 2010, p. 1).

Eswar Prasad: 'Maintaining an undervalued exchange rate certainly benefits China, but at the expense of other countries that lose their relative competitiveness in foreign trade' (www.iht.com, 7 March 2010).

IMF policies call for it to disclose documents and information on a timely basis, with the deletion only of market-moving information. But under the rules a member country may decide to withhold a report ... China allowed the release of its reports until the IMF's executive board decided in June 2007 that reports should pay more attention to currency policies. China has quietly blocked release of reports on its policies ever since, without providing its specific reasons to the IMF. A person who has seen copies of the most recent report last summer said that the IMF staff concluded the renminbi was 'substantially undervalued'. The IMF regards a currency undervalued if it is more than 20 per cent below its fair market value.

(www.iht.com, 15 March 2010; *IHT*, 16 March 2010, p. 14)

The Asian financial crisis and subsequent developments

China did not nominally devalue the renminbi (effectively pegged to the US dollar) during the Asian financial crisis, although there was some real devaluation because of factors such as deflation and export subsidies. China was highly praised for not starting off another round of competitive devaluations.

(See Jeffries 2006a: 560–76.)

Direct foreign investment (DFI)

The crucial distinction between portfolio investment and direct foreign investment (DFI) is that the latter involves control.

The term 'foreign-invested enterprises' refer to both joint ventures and wholly foreign-owned companies.

The law on joint equity ventures was promulgated on 14 July 1979. Foreign ownership was then limited to a maximum 49 per cent and certain sectors were excluded. Over time there has been a considerable relaxation of such restrictions, e.g. 100 per cent foreign ownership in some cases.

The volume of DFI and other indicators of its importance

China has become a magnet for direct foreign investment (DFI) owing to such factors as its abundant and cheap labour.

The deputy governor of the People's Bank of China: 'The cost of labour in China is only 3 per cent of that of US labour' (*FT*, 23 November 2004, p. 1).

'[In China wages as a percentage of] the US level ... are only about 3 per cent or 4 per cent' (*IHT*, 29 December 2007, p. 9).

Other factors encouraging DFI include a rapidly growing economy and government policy (such as the opening up, at least partially, of an increasing number of sectors – helped by membership of the WTO – and legislation to give greater protection to property rights).

Figures for DFI distinguish between contracted (committed or pledged) and utilized (disbursed or actual) totals.

Note problems such as 'round tripping', i.e. domestic capital sent to places like Hong Kong and back again.

The Economist talked of a 'good quarter' of total DFI and 'between a quarter and a third' (26 August 1995, p. 60, and 8 March 1997, Survey, p. 12, respectively). 'Maybe more than half of what is counted as "foreign investment" is actually domestic, recycled through Hong Kong' (*The Economist*, 19 June 1999, p. 103). 'A large amount of China's FDI is money that has been earned in mainland China but then booked to accounts in Hong Kong for tax reasons' (*The Economist*, 15 February 2003, p. 75).

> At least 25 per cent of China's 'foreign' cash inflows likely represent investment by domestic companies. Firms routinely funnel money out of the country to tax havens such as Hong Kong and the Caribbean and then move the cash back to China, where it is counted as 'foreign' investment.
>
> (*FEER*, 15 May 2003, p. 39)

'By 1991 there were roughly 20,000 foreign ventures, with a cumulative investment of $22 billion. Some $3.5 billion was invested in 1991 alone' (*The Economist*, Survey, 28 November 1992, p. 18).

'In 1991 the figure for direct foreign investment was $4.2 billion' (*FEER*, 24 December 1992, p. 72).

'In 1995 the world total of utilized DFI was $315 billion. China, with $38 billion, came second only to the USA's $60 billion' (*The Economist*, 13 April 1996, p. 72).

In 1996 utilized DFI was $42.3 billion and in 1997 it was $45.2 billion. Figures for utilized DFI for subsequent years are as follows: 1998, $45.6 billion; 1999, $40.4 billion; 2000, $40.7 billion; 2001, $46.8 billion; 2002, $52.74 billion; 2003, $53.5 billion (out of a world total of nearly $560 billion); 2004, $60.6 billion; 2005, $60.3 billion; 2006, $63.0.; 2007 (first eleven months), $61.67 billion.

'Foreign direct investment into China: 2008, $92.4 billion … [In 1998 the figure was] $45.5 billion' (*FT*, 12 June 2009, p. 9).

'Foreign direct investment to China dropped 18 per cent to $43 billion in the first half of the year [2009], according to Chinese government figures' (www.ft. com, 12 August 2009).

[In 2004] global foreign direct investment [amounted to] … $648 billion … The UK attracted more foreign direct investment [$78 billion] than China last year [2004], becoming the world's second largest FDI recipient after the United States … according to the United Nations Conference on Trade and Development (UNCTAD) … FDI inflows to the United States rose … to $96 billion in 2004, while flows to China increased from $54 billion to $61 billion. The big upward revision in US inflows for 2003, originally estimated at just $30 billion, also shows that, contrary to earlier reports, the United States has never ceded its lead to China as an investment destination.

(*FT*, 30 September 2005, p. 13)

'[Foreign-invested enterprises increased] their share of total exports from 1 per cent in 1985 to 50.1 per cent in 2001' (*FT*, 29 October 2002, p. 11).

About 60 per cent of China's exports are controlled by foreign-financed companies, according to the latest Chinese customs data. In categories like computer parts and consumer electronics, foreign companies command an even greater share of control over the exports, analysts say.

(*IHT*, 10 February 2006, p. 6)

'Nearly 60 per cent of Chinese exports are produced by … companies that have foreign investments or are joint ventures with foreign companies' (*IHT*, 30 November 2007, p. 9).

'According to NDRC [National Development and Reform Commission] data … China attracted $383 billion in overseas investment in the five years to 2005, including $286 billion in foreign direct investment and $38 billion through share issues' (*FT*, 11 October 2006, p. 9).

'[According to official figures] by the end of 2006 594,000 foreign-funded enterprises had been approved for a total $691.9 billion in investments since China launched its "special economic zones" in 1980' (*FT*, 9 March 2007, p. 6).

'China's … inward foreign investment stock … [totals] $876 billion' (*IHT*, 21 July 2009, p. 18).

(For foreign-invested companies' contribution to industrial output, see the section on the importance of the private sector above.)

Investment overseas by Chinese companies (outward/outbound direct foreign investment)

'By the end of 1998 Chinese enterprises had invested a total of $6.3 billion overseas' (*FEER*, 15 April 1999, p. 82).

'Chinese companies had invested only $6.7 billion overseas by the end of 1998, puny compared with the $276 billion worth of foreign investment that flooded the mainland, according to the ministry of foreign trade and economic co-operation' (*FT*, 6 May 1999, p. 7).

'Several industries were chosen ... such as those industries in which China lacked its own resources or those already possessing mature technology which could use overseas investment to implement technology transfer to other developing countries, thereby stimulating export growth' (Wu and Chen 2001: 1235).

'China has invested heavily in foreign oil fields in a bid to guarantee supply' (*FEER*, 20 June 2002, pp. 15–16).

'[China is seeking] the kind of management and technologies needed in China ... technology and know-how that would take years to build up organically' (*FT*, 18 December 2003, p. 32). '[The main aims of outward investment are] to secure raw materials ... and to bring local management skills up to international standards' (*FT*, 8 March 2005, p. 12).

> Overseas investment by Chinese companies totalled $2.7 billion last year [2002], the ministry of commerce said ... Total overseas investment by Chinese companies stood at $29.9 billion at the end of 2002. It was the first time that the nation's overseas investment had been officially reported.
>
> (www.iht.com, 17 December 2003)

> Chinese companies invested $2.7 billion abroad in 2002, according to the ministry of commerce ... Outward investment still requires official approval. Projects that exceed $30 million must go to the State Council ... Beijing in 2003 gave more leeway to Chinese companies to invest overseas ... [It] raised to ten the number of regions from which companies may invest outside China ... The ceiling on outward investments for each approved region is just £200 million ... The bulk of China's investments overseas remain resource-based.
>
> (*FEER*, 5 February 2003, pp. 25–7)

'China announced rules to make it easier for its companies to invest overseas' (*FEER*, 21 October 2004, p. 28).

> China's accumulated direct investment overseas reached $33.4 billion by the end of 2003, according to the commerce ministry in its first report on overseas investment excluding the financial sector. The ministry said that

such investment was $2.85 billion in 2003, which was 5.5 per cent greater than in 2002.

(*FEER*, 16 September 2004, p. 32)

'[China's] outward foreign investment was just $2.9 billion in 2003 ... China's stock of outward FDI amounts to $33 billion, less than half a per cent of accumulated world FDI' (*The Economist*, 7 January 2005, p. 58).

'China's government reported $2.85 billion [outward] DFI for 2003, a 5.5 per cent increase from 2002' (www.iht.com, 22 December 2004).

In 2004 'overseas investment by Chinese companies' was $3.6 billion (*FT*, 9 February 2005, p. 6).

'[China's] flows of direct investment abroad grew from $1.8 billion in 2004 to $11.3 billion last year [2005]' (*The Economist*, 21 October 2006, p. 126).

'Worldwide direct investment from China more than tripled in 2005 to about $6 billion, according to the Economist Intelligence Unit' (*IHT*, 3 April 2006, p. 17).

While Chinese outbound investments have more than doubled to $46 billion so far this year [2008], stakes in overseas financial institutions plunged as a percentage of total investments to 14.3 per cent from 73.1 per cent in 2007, according to Thomson Reuters data.

(www.iht.com, 3 November 2008)

'Chinese outbound foreign direct investment accounts for about 3 per cent of the global total, far below its share of world trade and economic output' (*IHT*, 4 June 2009, p. 19).

'Direct investment originating [in China] ... has leapt from almost nothing six years ago to $52 billion last year [2008]' (*FT*, 8 June 2009, p. 11).

'Chinese offshore investment has surged: from just $143 million in 2002, outbound non-financial direct investment reached $40.7 billion last year [2008] ... In 1998 the figure was $0.1 billion' (*FT*, 12 June 2009, p. 9).

Though it remains miniscule by global standards, China's overseas investment has been rocketing upward in the past three years: the 2008 total, $52.2 billion, was double that of the year before. It appears set to rise sharply again in 2009, as the global economic crisis pushes the shares of many companies to bargain levels and foreign companies feel pressure to seek outside investment. Most of the Chinese money has gone into minerals, metals and energy, all areas where China's domestic production falls well short of meeting its industrial needs.

(*IHT*, 4 July 2009, p. 11)

China's outbound foreign direct investment has increased steadily this decade, and the outflow of $52 billion last year [2008] was a record. Still, the historical stock of the outbound direct investment of $170 billion is puny next to China's foreign exchange reserves and its inward foreign investment stock of $876 billion.

(*IHT*, 21 July 2009, p. 18)

'China, which less than two decades ago had just a handful of tiny investments abroad, is now the world's sixth biggest foreign investor' (*IHT*, 19 August 2009, p. 14).

Direct investment abroad doubled to around $50 billion in 2008 – and [is] maintaining a similar level this year [2009] ... A more cautious attitude is shown by the China Investment Corporation, China's sovereign wealth fund, which has been taking stakes to the 7 per cent to 15 per cent range, big enough to be significant but small enough not to raise nationalist hackles.

(*IHT*, 17 November 2009, p. 6)

Developments in outward (outbound) direct foreign investment

The sale [has taken place] of IBM's personal computer business to Lenovo, China's largest maker of PCs ... Under Lenovo's ownership the IBM personal computer business will continue to be based in the United States and run by its current management team. IBM will take a stake of 18.9 per cent in Lenovo, which is based in Beijing but now plans to have its headquarters in New York ... Lenovo ... partly owned by the Chinese government ... is paying ... the relatively modest amount ... of $1.75 billion in cash, stock and debt.

(*IHT*, 9 December 2004, p. 11)

Lenovo ... is owned mainly by public shareholders. But a government institution, the Chinese Academy of Sciences, owns 37 per cent. If the acquisition is completed the government's holding will fall below 30 per cent and IBM will have an 18.9 per cent stake.

(www.iht.com, 7 January 2005)

In 2003 Lenovo changed its English name from the Legend Group, which it was called soon after its inception in 1984. It chose a distinctly non-Chinese name, explaining that it had appended the first syllable of 'legend' to the word *novo* from Latin, meaning new.

(*IHT*, 20 June 2008, p. 15)

'[The Lenovo takeover is the] biggest overseas acquisition by a Chinese company' (*FT*, 27 January 2005, p. 1). 'Executives at Lenovo ... have made it clear that [their planned purchase] ... is aimed at learning the skills to protect their diminishing market dominance at home' (*FT*, 8 March 2005, p. 12).

Lenovo ... is majority-owned by the Chinese Academy of Sciences ... [Another Chinese company called TCL is] the most profitable television producer ... Buying the television business of France's Thomson in early 2004 turned it into the world's biggest volume television maker.

(*The Economist*, 8 January 2005, p. 58)

'Lenovo acquired the right to use the IBM name on its computers for five years' (www.economist.com, 23 June 2005). 'Lenovo had the right to use the IBM brand for five years, but dropped it two years ahead of schedule, such was its confidence in its own brand' (www.economist.com, 18 September 2008).

> China intends to create world-class companies ... The central government decided some years ago that thirty to fifty of its best state firms should be built into 'national champions' or 'globally competitive' by 2010 ... Over the past decade China has created some quite large companies. More than a dozen [e.g. Baosteel] are in the *Fortune 500* list, though almost all of those are domestic monopolies or near monopolies, such as telecom operators or big commodity producers. A handful of others are starting to compete internationally, though mostly in niche markets and on price rather than with technology or brands. But the global footprint of Chinese companies is still rather faint [see figures above] ... China has so far failed to build world-class companies. Even the natural monopolies and resources companies are mostly just big rather than particularly efficient. In manufacturing, technology and consumer areas a few companies are groping towards international competitiveness, but none are there yet ... Unless China institutes far-reaching political and structural reforms that give Chinese managers the confidence to invest in long-term technological development, it cannot readily build a globally competitive corporate sector ... The most impressive [Chinese companies] are the resources groups. Three big oil companies, PetroChina, Sinopec and CNOOC, are aggressively buying overseas and building pipelines across central Asia to satisfy China's fuel demands. They are in more than a dozen countries: CNOOC, for example, is Indonesia's largest offshore oil producer. Baosteel [is] China's top steel producer ... Chalco [is] China's leading aluminium group ... Yanzhou Coal [is] the largest listed coal producer ... Lenovo [is] in personal computers ... TCL [is] in televisions ... Huawei [telecoms equip-ment] ... insists it is a private company owned by its employees ... [but there is] speculation that it is really controlled by the military.
>
> (*The Economist*, 8 January 2005, pp. 57–9)

(See the section on conglomerates for earlier material.)

> On 20 June [2005] Haier, China's leading white-goods maker, launched a $1.3 billion cash offer for Maytag, an ailing American rival ... Haier teamed up with two American buy-out firms to bid $1.3 billion for Maytag ... On 23 June China National Offshore Oil Corporation (CNOOC) ... made an offer of $18.5 billion (excluding debt) for Unocal, a California-based oil and gas company ... The Chinese offer is in cash – the shares even of a well-run Chinese firm are not yet acceptable as takeover currency ... [The offer is a] contested one. On 4 April Unocal agreed to be acquired by Chevron, the second biggest American oil firm, in a deal worth $17 billion (excluding debt).
>
> (*The Economist*, 25 June 2005, p. 86; www.economist.com, 23 June 2005)

'In 2004 TCL, its [China's] leading television producer, bought most of the tele-vision manufacturing business of France's Thomson plus a mobile handset making business from Alcatel' (*The Economist*, 2 July 2005, p. 70).

'Unocal [is] a California oil and gas company with extensive fields in Asia's (*IHT*, 25 June 2005, p. 16). '[Unocal has] natural gas reserves, most of which are in Asia' (*IHT*, 27 June 2005, p. 8).

> CNOOC [is] China's third largest company ... [and] Haier Group its largest appliance maker ... [China desires] Western brand names ... By acquiring household names China wants to bolster global sales and distribution capabilities ... China has a dearth of internationally known companies that operate on a global scale and market their products abroad.
>
> (www.iht.com, 27 June 2005)

> [Maytag would be a way] to acquire a brand name and a distribution network to serve Haier's growing manufacturing capability ... CNOOC, a company that is 70 per cent owned by the Chinese government, is seeking to acquire control of Unocal, an energy company with global reach ... Unocal has a history ... of doing business with problematic regimes in difficult places, including the Burmese junta and the Taliban.
>
> (*IHT*, 28 June 2005, p. 9)

> China's ministry of commerce issued a report this month [June] that said that even though China's exports were dominated by consumer products, there were few famous Chinese brands involved in the export trade. Most goods were shipped abroad with foreign brand labels ... The ministry called on Chinese companies to start exporting their own 'famous brands'. Every region was ordered to produce its own famous brands ... By acquiring well-known brand names, experts say, Chinese companies are hoping to get access to global distribution networks, sophisticated research and development and recognizable brand names ... TCL became the world's biggest maker of television sets last year [2004] after it acquired the television set business of Thomson, the French technology company that also owned the old RCA brand ... Earlier this month [there] was $1.4 billion bid [unsuccessful] by China Mobile, a huge state-owned telecommunications company, for control of Pakistan Telecommunication.
>
> (*IHT*, 29 June 2005, p. 8)

('China Mobile was outbid by a competitor from the United Arab Emirates. China Minmetals failed in its $7 billion offer for Canada's Noranda': *The Economist*, 6 August 2005, p. 53.) 'The takeover bid by CNOOC for the US oil and gas company Unocol is under review by a US government national security panel' (www.iht.com, 11 July 2005). 'CNOOC is 70 per cent owned by the government-controlled China National Offshore Oil Corporation ... The shareholders of Unocol will vote [on 10 August]' (www.iht.com, 21 July 2005).

> CNOOC's $19.6 billion bid for Unocal, Haier's $1.28 billion approach to Maytag and Lenovo's $1.75 billion acquisition last month of IBM's personal computer business are proof that Chinese corporations intend to buy

companies that help produce the world's oil, assemble its PCs and manufacture its washing machines. Cars and microchips may follow.

(*FT*, 25 June 2005, p. 12)

'Something like half of Unocal's reserves are in Asia' (*FT*, 27 June 2005, p. 19).

'[On 19 July] Haier Group ... abandoned its $1.28 billion bid for the appliance maker Maytag ... saying the group was not prepared for a takeover battle with Whirlpool, a rival bidder' (www.iht.com, 20 July 2005). 'Haier ... was backed in its bid by Blackstone Group and Bain Capital' (*IHT*, 21 July 2005, p. 5). ('Whirlpool ... [is] America's biggest white goods maker': *The Economist*, 23 July 2005, p. 64.)

> CNOOC said Tuesday [2 August that it had] to end its $18.5 billion takeover bid for ... Unocal because of fierce political opposition in Washington. The decision ended a hotly contested battle between CNOOC and Chevron, the second largest US oil company ... The move by CNOOC clears the way for Chevron to finalize its acquisition of Unocol for about $17 billion in cash and stock. Unocol shareholders are expected to vote whether to accept Chevron's bid on 10 August. CNOOC's all-cash bid for Unocol was the largest takeover attempt ever made in the United States by a Chinese company. It came just two months after Chevron had already agreed to a merger, sparking a takeover battle that eventually forced Chevron to sweeten its bid to $17.6 billion in cash and stock from $16.8 billion.
>
> (*IHT*, 3 August 2005, p. 1)

> CNOOC ... said that it had 'given active consideration to further improving the terms of its offer and would have done so but for the political environment in the United States' ... The political resistance to CNOOC's bid culminated in the insertion into an energy bill of a clause requiring a four-month study of China's energy policy before the bid could continue ... China is intent on creating up to fifty state-controlled 'global Champions'.
>
> (www.economist.com, 4 August 2005)

> A few weeks ago the government folded the assets of China National Petroleum Corporation (CNPC) and its listed affiliate, PetroChina, into a new, as yet unnamed firm. This new entity's express purpose is to be a 'platform for international business development' and to 'establish significant overseas operations'.
>
> (*The Economist*, 6 August 2005, p. 53)

> The fate of Unocol was finally settled on Wednesday [10 August] when a majority of the company's shareholders approved a takeover offer of about $18 billion by Chevron ... [on] the same day as the vote crude oil prices touched a new high of $65 a barrel in New York.
>
> (www.iht.com, 11 August 2005)

> State-owned companies in China and India are trying to buy a Canadian company with oil fields in Kazakhstan ... A joint venture of China National

Petroleum, China's biggest oil company, and PetroChina, its publicly traded subsidiary, offered roughly $3.2 billion late Monday [15 August] for PetroKazakhstan ... whose shares are traded in Toronto ... [and which has] headquarters in Calgary ... Oil and Natural Gas, India's main government oil company, has already submitted a bid of $3.6 billion in co-operation with the steel maker Mittal Group ... China National Petroleum already has substantial oil investments of its own in Kazakhstan and has been trying to build a pipeline to carry the oil to China.

(*IHT*, 17 August 2005, p. 14)

China National Petroleum Corporation ... would be able to pump its production through its 1,000 kilometre pipeline linking Atasu in Kazakhstan to the Alataw Pass in the north-western Chinese region of Xinjiang. The pipeline is currently working below its 20 million tonnes capacity.

(*FT*, 16 August 2005, p. 24)

China National Petroleum Corporation ... agreed on Monday [22 August] to pay $4.18 billion for ... PetroKazakhstan ... [outbidding] the Indian state-owned company Oil and Natural Gas ... PetroKazakhstan has had a series of legal skirmishes with the Russian company Lukoil, its main partner in the oil fields. Lukoil's main pipeline from Kazakhstan into Russia is already full, but CNPC is expected to finish a pipeline from Kazakhstan into western China at the end of this year [2005] ... PetroKazakhstan previously operated as Hurricane Hydrocarbons ... [which] bought Yuzhneftegaz, a Kazakh state-owned oil company ... for $120 million in 1996.

(www.iht.com, 22 August 2005; *IHT*, 23 August 2005, pp. 1, 4)

'CNPC bid $4.18 billion for PetroKazakhstan ... The deal, which is expected to be approved by PetroKazakhstan shareholders on 18 October, would mark the largest cross-border acquisition by a Chinese company' (*FT*, 5 October 2005, p. 29).

Vladimir Shkolnik, the Kazakh energy minister said yesterday [4 October]: 'The question of the sale of PetroKazakhstan to CNPC is very serious – we are talking about a strategic project. What shape the deal will take has not been decided, but the government of Kazakhstan will do everything to ensure that strategic control remains with the company. Our national oil company KazMunaiGaz, will have a stake in this company' ... It had been reported earlier that Beijing-based CNPC was in talks to sell part of PetroKazakhstan to KazMunaiGaz, the national oil and gas company in Kazakhstan.

(*FT*, 5 October 2005, p. 29)

On Saturday [15 October] President Nursultan Nazarbayev of Kazakhstan signed changes to a law, changes that would let the government block sales in oil and gas companies ... The bill was approved by parliament on 12 October ... CNPC said Monday [17 October] that it had agreed to sell a

33 per cent stake in PetroKazakhstan to the state-owned KazMunaiGaz in an attempt to ease the Kazakh government's opposition to the purchase ... Another potential obstacle may come from legal actions by Lukoil, Russia's largest oil company. Lukoil is asking an Alberta court to postpone the take-over until its case in a Stockholm arbitration court is resolved. Lukoil said it had filed with the Stockholm chamber of commerce, claiming that a share-holders' agreement gave it the right to buy out PetroKazakhstan's half-ownership of a joint venture that produces oil in Kazakhstan.

(www.iht.com, 19 October 2005)

Under Kazakh law the state oil company, KazMunaiGaz, has a pre-emptive right to buy oil fields. That right was asserted during the sale this fall of PetroKazakhstan, a Canadian-owned company, to China National Petro-leum, the biggest oil deal in Kazakhstan this year [2005]. The deal was only approved after the Chinese company agreed to sell assets, including a refin-ery, to KazMunaiGaz.

(www.iht.com, 23 December 2005)

The leading oil companies of China and India have agreed to jointly acquire Petro-Canada's petroleum interests in Syria ... [it was] reported on Wednes-day [22 December 2005] ... China National Petroleum and Oil and Natural Gas have agreed to pay $576 million for the assets ... The companies, both state-owned, are buying Petro-Canada's interests in Al Furat Petroleum. The transaction requires the approval of Syria's government.

(*IHT*, 22 December 2005, p. 13)

A Chinese government drive to secure reliable supplies of foreign energy has been dealt a setback by shareholders in one of China's top oil com-panies. The oil company, the Hong Kong-listed CNOOC, said Tuesday [3 January 2006] that independent shareholders had blocked a proposal that would have allowed the company's parent, which is owned by the Chinese government, to invest in overseas oil and gas reserves. Energy industry ana-lysts said the proposal suggested that the Chinese government was worried about the country's long-term energy security and wanted CNOOC's parent to have the freedom to make politically sensitive investments in countries like Sudan or Iran, or offer higher than market prices for reserves ... At present the parent, China National Offshore Oil Corp., is barred from investing in foreign petroleum reserves as part of a non-competition agree-ment offered as a sweetener when CNOOC went public in 2001 ... Under the 2001 non-competition agreement CNOOC was to specialize in offshore domestic oil and gas production and downstream processing. However, in December [2005] the listed company's management asked for shareholder approval to overturn the agreement so that the parent could make invest-ments in oil and gas reserves without fear of a backlash from investors over price or political risk. If these investments were successful the listed company could buy them from the parent, the management explained ...

CNOOC said it regretted that 59 per cent of independent shareholders had opposed the proposal in the Saturday [31 December 2005] vote.

(www.iht.com, 3 January 2006)

CNOOC, China's biggest offshore oil producer, said Monday [9 January 2006] that it would pay $2.3 billion in cash for a stake in a Nigerian oil field ... CNOOC [China National Offshore Oil Corp.] will buy a 45 per cent stake in Nigeria's OML 130 oil area, also known as the Akpo field, from the privately owned Nigerian company South Atlantic Petroleum ... China is competing with India, whose government blocked the state-run Oil and Natural Gas from buying the Akpo stake in December [2005] because of concern over ownership at South Atlantic ... The Indian cabinet rejected the proposal because of a lack of clarity in ownership at South Atlantic Petroleum ... Nigeria is among the world's eight most corrupt nations, according to Transparency International, based in Berlin.... The Akpo field ... will pump 225,000 barrels a day after 2008, or 9 per cent of Nigeria's current production ... Total, based in Paris, holds 24 per cent of the field and Brazil's Petroleo Braasileiro owns 16 per cent. The rest is held by South Atlantic and the state-owned Nigeria National Petroleum.

(www.iht.com, 9 January 2006)

CNOOC said it had agreed to pay nearly $2.3 billion ... $2.28 billion ... to acquire a large stake in a Nigerian oil and gas field ... The oil field is located in the Niger Delta, one of the world's largest oil and gas basins. The field ... is now operated by the French oil company Total, which also has a large stake in the field. CNOOC has also committed to spend $2.25 billion over the next few years to help develop the Nigerian project ... An Indian company, Oil and Natural Gas, last month [December 2005] won the contest for the Nigerian assets with a bid of about $2 billion, but it was blocked from making the deal by India's cabinet. The deal was blocked over concerns about the transparency of the Nigerian ownership, according to Bloomberg News ... Pending the approval from the Nigerian authorities, the deal Monday would be the biggest ever for CNOOC and one of the largest overseas acquisitions ever made by a Chinese company ... CNOOC, one of China's most aggressive energy companies, has spent nearly $2 billion over the past few years acquiring overseas oil and gas exploration assets in such countries as Australia, Indonesia, Vietnam, Thailand, Bangladesh and Azerbaijan.

(*IHT*, 10 January 2006, p. 11)

'CNOOC ... bought a block that a rival energy consumer, India, had shunned after an initial bid. The stake was sold by a former Nigerian defence minister, who was awarded it when Nigeria was under military rule' (*The Economist*, 21 January 2006, p. 58).

China and India ... yesterday [12 January] ... agreed to co-operate in securing crude oil resources overseas ... Under their agreement Chinese and

Indian oil companies will establish a formal procedure to exchange information about a possible bid target, before agreeing to co-operate formally.
Their memorandum of understanding also covers possible co-operation
across the energy industry, from exploration to marketing. But India and
China's national oil companies could still compete in third countries.

(FT, 13 January 2006, p. 1)

India's minister for petroleum and natural gas ... said the two countries
would exchange information in bids for overseas assets ... Some analysts
said they believed that India's bargaining power with the Chinese would be
limited ... [Other critics said they believed] that India and China would
succeed jointly only in going after assets that were not attractive to Western
companies.

(IHT, 21 January 2006, p. 13)

'Before the ink was even dry on the Beijing agreement, Indian oil ministry
officials found out that Myanmar had agreed to sell natural gas from a field
partly owned by an Indian company exclusively to China' (*IHT*, 24 January
2006, p. 7).

China and Saudi Arabia signed an agreement Monday [23 January] on energy
co-operation ... on 'co-operation in oil, natural gas and minerals' ... during a
milestone visit by King Abdulla of Saudi Arabia ... The visit is the first by a
Saudi king since the two nations established diplomatic relations in 1990 ...
[China] reported that the two sides were hoping to reach agreement to build
an oil reserve facility on the southern island of Hainan to store 100 million
tonnes of oil ... China's oil imports from Saudi Arabia have already risen
from 8.8 million tonnes in 2001 to about 20 million tonnes last year [2005] ...
Oil imports from Saudi Arabia ... account for 14 per cent of China's total oil
imports ... Among the bilateral deals already in the works Sinopec of China is
drilling for gas in the Saudi desert and building a refinery with the Saudi oil
firm Saudi Aramco in China's Fujian province. Aramco is also beginning
engineering work with Sinopec in the Chinese city of Qingdao.

(www.iht.com, 23 January 2006; *IHT*, 24 January 2006, p. 12)

Iran in 2004 agreed in principle to sell China 250 million tonnes of liquefied
natural gas over thirty years, a deal valued at $70 billion. China already
imports 14 per cent of its oil from Iran. Sinopec ... hopes to develop Iran's
enormous Yadavaran oil field.

(IHT, 25 January 2006, p. 6)

Japan, South Korea and Taiwan import all their oil, of which 75 per cent is
from the Gulf. India imports 75 per cent, of which 80 per cent is from the
Gulf. China imports 35 per cent, of which 60 per cent is from the Gulf.

(IHT, 9 February 2006, p. 8)

China's biggest oil company said Wednesday [19 July] that a $500 million
stake it had bought in Russia's newly listed petroleum giant, Rosneft, would

help its efforts to secure energy for the Chinese market. The state-owned China National Petroleum said in a statement published on its website that the investment would build on earlier agreements between the two companies to extract, refine and process Russian oil for shipment to China ... Chinese demand is a major factor behind the current high oil prices ... Imports account for almost half of China's oil consumption ... Rosneft allocated the Chinese oil company a stake in its $10.4 billion initial public offering on Friday [14 July] on Moscow and London – the biggest in Europe in seven years. China National bought those shares at the offer price of $7.55 ... The Chinese company had been seeking a bigger stake to gain more influence over Rosneft's exploration and production plans ... Rosneft also sold shares worth $1 billion to British Petroleum and $1.1 billion to Malaysia's state-owned oil company, Petronas ... [When] Russia's president, Vladimir Putin, [visited] Beijing in March [2006] ... China National signed a memorandum of understanding with the Russian energy giant Gazprom to build two gas pipelines from Siberia to China. The two pipelines were expected to deliver 80 billion cubic metres of gas a year to China beginning in 2011. Russia also agreed in March to work with China on a technical feasibility study for an oil pipeline from eastern Siberia to China ... China's second biggest oil company, China Petrochemical, last month [June] teamed up with Rosneft to pay $3.5 billion for a BP joint venture oil producer in Russia.

(www.iht.com, 19 July 2006)

China Construction Bank ... agreed Thursday [24 August] to buy the Hong Kong and Macao retail banking operations of Bank of America for $1.25 billion – the first big Chinese bank of significant operations from an American one ... In June 2005 ... [there took place] the Bank of America's $3 billion stake in China Construction Bank ... As part of its purchase Bank of America agreed not to compete on its own in mainland China.

(*IHT*, 25 August 2006, p. 9)

Overseas investment by Chinese companies in industries including textiles, shoes and computers surged to $12.3 billion in 2005, bringing the accumulated investment to $57.2 billion in 163 countries. Half of the investment went through mergers and acquisitions ... To make overseas acquisitions easier, the government on 1 July [2006] removed limits on how much foreign currency Chinese companies can buy.

(www.iht.com, 4 September 2006)

CITIC, the government investment company, will pay $1.9 billion to buy the oil assets in Kazakhstan held by Nations Energy Canada ... Completion of the transaction is planned for December [2006] ... The Kazakh government has yet to decide whether to waive its pre-emptive rights on the assets.

(*IHT*, 27 October 2006, p. 16)

CITIC, the state investment arms, has completed a $1.9 billion deal to buy oil assets in Kazakhstan from Nations Energy, dispelling speculation that the purchase might be blocked by Kazakh authorities. The acquisition was finalized at the weekend after months of negotiations ... CITIC first announced in October 2006 that it was buying the rights to develop the Karazhanbas field ... CITIC Group, parent of Hong Kong-listed CITIC Resources Holdings, has previously only dabbled in relatively small energy-related investments abroad. It is a powerful conglomerate that is also active in finance, real estate and other industries. Nations Energy is an Indonesian-owned Canadian company.

(FT, 2 January 2007, p. 18)

Larry Yung ... the third richest man in China ... has bought an $800 million stake in resources group Anglo American held by the Oppenheimer dynasty, a landmark deal in China's aggressive acquisition of African resources ... The sale [involves] 17 million shares by the family which founded Anglo ... Anglo American was founded [by] Ernest Oppenheimer in 1917 ... The Oppenheimers remain Anglo American's largest single non-institutional shareholder with a 2 per cent stake, valued at $1.6 billion ... Larry Yung, chairman of CITIC, the Chinese state-owned industrial holding company, bought the shares in his personal capacity ... Rong Yiren [Larry Yung's father] ... was China vice president.

(FT, 11 November 2006, pp. 1, 9)

Industrial and Commercial Bank of China, the second biggest bank in the world by market value, said it planned to press ahead with the purchase of a 90 per cent stake in Indonesia's Bank Halim – its first acquisition outside China. The transaction requires final approval from the China banking and regulatory commission and Indonesia's central bank ... ICBC, which raised $21.2 billion in a dual initial public offering in Hong Kong and Shanghai in October [2006], last week passed Bank of America to become the world's biggest bank by capitalization after Citigroup ... ICBC said it expected to have the option to purchase the remaining 10 per cent of Bank Halim in three years.

(FT, 2 January 2007, p. 19)

Nanjing Automobile is about to begin producing MGs ... Nanjing Auto paid just over $100 million for the MG assets two years ago ... The planned revival of the British sports car is the latest ... example of how China's growing economic might is carefully reaching into foreign markets, buying troubled companies with established brands and using them to build bridge-heads for the billions of dollars the country has to invest overseas ... It began in 2002 when TCL, a Chinese maker of televisions and mobile phones, brought the German company Schneider Electronics. The Chinese computer maker Lenovo acquired IBM's personal computer business in 2004. Qiangjiang Group, the largest Chinese motorcycle manufacturer, now owns Benelli, the oldest motorcycle maker in Italy. Shenyang Machine Tool Group has bought Schiess, a longtime maker of German machine tools. Xinjiang Chalkis even owns a French tomato cannery and sells Chinese tomato sauce in Provence. All of those acquired companies were facing financial problems. Many of China's foreign purchases have been focused on energy resources, dominated by big state-owned enterprises like PetroChina and CNOOC, which have spent billions in recent years in acquiring oil and natural gas fields. Those deals have helped swell the value of China's outbound acquisitions from $18.6 million in 1990 to nearly $14 billion on more than 100 deals last year [2006] … China's experience of acquiring high profile natural resources and the political backlash that has foiled some of those attempts, have made a cautious entry with smaller Chinese companies … [Examples include autos, auto parts, furniture and news bureaux] … Still, the acquisitions are but a trickle at this stage.

(*IHT*, 13 March 2007, pp. 1, 14)

[The British] Barclays [Bank] on Monday [23 July 2007] increased its offer for the Dutch bank ABN AMRO to Euro 67.5 billion [£45.6 billion] after securing a direct cash infusion from a state-owned Chinese bank and the investment company of the government of Singapore. China Development Bank and Temasek Holdings agreed to buy a combined Euro 3.6 billion [$4.9 billion; £2.4 billion] worth of new Barclays shares and pledged to invest a further Euro 9.8 billion [£6.5 billion] if the bid for ABN AMRO succeeded … China Development Bank agreed to invest Euro 2.2 billion [£1.5 billion] in Barclays and another Euro 7.6 billion should it win the bidding for ABN AMRO. Temasek said it would invest Euro 1.4 billion in Barclays now and an additional Euro 2.2 billion if the ABN AMRO bid succeeded … China Development Bank, which was created in 1994 to help finance Beijing's top development priorities, has provided financial backing for multi-billion-dollar infrastructure projects like the Three Gorges Dam, the north–south water diversion project, and major ports and airports. The bank may see benefits from allying with Barclays as it expands its lending in development countries, especially in Africa, where Barclays has a major presence … Despite China Development Bank's mission to carry out state directives, on paper it is one of the healthiest banks in the country … The bank operates directly under the State Council, or cabinet, and has ministry-level status in China's bureaucracy … The investment in Barclays would not draw directly on China's foreign exchange reserves … Two months ago China invested $3 billion [£1.5 billion] in the initial public offering of Blackstone Group.

(*IHT*, 24 July 2007, pp. 1, 13)

'This is the first time a mainland bank has taken a stake in a European or American [bank]' (*IHT*, 7 August 2007, p. 12).

ICBC and Bank of China have been dipping their toes in Asian waters with, respectively, the January [2007] acquisition of Bank Halim, a small

Indonesian bank, and the 2006 acquisition of Singapore Aircraft Leasing Enterprise, the biggest aircraft leasing operation in Asia.

(IHT, 7 August 2007, p. 12)

'The initial Euro 2.2 billion by China Development Bank will happen regardless of the bid going through, as will Temasek's injection of Euro 1.4 billion. Both investors will take a seat on the board of Barclays' (*FT*, 24 July 2007, p. 23).

> China Development Bank and Temasek ... would spend up to a combined $18.5 billion for a 10.6 per cent stake in the merged Barclays and ABN AMRO, provided the merger is successful. If the deal fails, China Development Bank and Temasek will still retain a combined 5.2 per cent in the British bank.
>
> (p. 23)

'China Development Bank brings access to Chinese industrial companies, but it does not have a meaningful retail customer base' (p. 20).

> [It is] involved in infrastructure and international trade finance ... It does not take deposits but raises money by issuing long-term bonds and lends only to government-approved [mostly infrastructure] projects ... [In June 2007 it] announced it was forming a $5 billion China Africa Development Fund to provide cheap financing to domestic companies investing in Africa, particularly in the oil and minerals sectors.
>
> (p. 23)

'Chinese representation on the Barclays board is limited to one non-executive ... [The] Barclays stake ... is limited by agreement to 10 per cent in the next three years' (p. 15).

> If Barclays acquires ABN, the Chinese state would emerge with a shareholding of 7.7 per cent in the enlarged group. It has pledged not to raise its stake to more than 9.9 per cent of the group over the next three years. A smaller stake of about 3 per cent would be taken by Temasek – which is owned by the Singapore government but says all investment decisions are made independently ... China Development Bank is state-owned, though it is seen by analysts as one of the country's most commercial banks, financing industries including petrochemicals and railways.
>
> (www.bbc.co.uk, 23 July 2007)

'The mission of China Development Bank (CDB) is to support "the state's policies to implement disciplined development and build a harmonious society" ... Barclays says that CDB's stake will increase business opportunities for the bank in China' (*The Economist*, 28 July 2007, pp. 77–8).

(Note that the Barclays Bank's bid for ABN AMRO was not successful.)

> The Chinese National Petroleum Corporation has broken into the Russian oil industry winning an auction with Rosneft, the state oil company, for two fields

in eastern Siberia, not far from the Chinese border. After years of deliberation Moscow has signalled approval for a pipeline to carry Russian oil exports direct to China. CNPC will finance and build the 69 kilometre pipeline.

(*FT*, 15 August 2007, p. 8)

China's NOCs [National Oil Companies] ... pumped a combined total of 685,000 barrels per day of oil abroad in 2006 – less than 1 per cent of world oil production – and appear to have sold at least two-thirds of it on the international market.

(*FEER*, September 2007, p. 54)

On Monday [22 October] Bear Stearns [the established Wall Street firm founded in 1923] and Citic Securities [China's largest investment bank and one of the top underwriters of China's public offering market] announced a partnership – with Citic investing $1 billion in Bear for a 6 per cent stake and Bear taking a similar position in Citic. The firms will also start a joint venture in Hong Kong to provide investment banking services throughout Asia ... Citic's investment comes in the form of forty-year convertible securities, which will translate into a 6 per cent stake with an option to go as high as 9.9 per cent. Bear's investment is through a six-year convertible instrument with a five-year option to secure additional shares.

(www.iht.com, 23 October 2007)

Bear Stearns and Citic Securities, China's largest listed brokerage, on Monday [22 October] agreed to invest $1 billion in each other ... underpinned by a landmark Hong Kong-based joint venture ... The establishment of a fifty–fifty joint venture [is] the first of its type involving a US and Chinese firm. The two sides said the new company would offer a broad range of capital markers on a pan-Asia basis, including cross-border merger and acquisitions advisory and international offerings of Chinese companies. The cross-investment is one of the largest of its kind to involve a US and Chinese financial institution ... Five-year options [are involved] to acquire additional shares.

(www.ft.com, 22 October 2007)

China's largest securities firm said on 22 October that it would take a 6 per cent stake in Bear Stearns, an embattled American investment bank, via a capital and equity swap; Bear Stearns will get 2 per cent of Citic in return.

(*The Economist*, 3 November 2007, p. 85)

China's biggest bank said Thursday [25 October] it will buy a 20 per cent stake on South Africa's biggest lender for $5.5 billion amid a rapid foreign expansion by Chinese investors. The deal between Industrial and Commercial Bank of China and Standard Bank Group Ltd is one of China's biggest foreign corporate acquisitions to date ... ICBC's decision in South Africa to take a minority stake instead of acquiring a bank outright was in line with a Chinese strategy of trying to avoid possible political frictions over buying assets abroad ... Chinese companies invested $21 billion abroad last year [2006], according to the government.

(www.iht.com, 25 October 2007; *IHT*, 26 October 2007, p. 9)

The deal disclosed yesterday [25 October] ... [was] between Asia's largest lender and Africa's biggest bank by assets ... [This] is the largest foreign acquisition by a Chinese commercial bank and the biggest direct investment in South Africa since the end of apartheid ... The two banks ... said they would establish a global resources fund ... [which] would capitalize at $1 billion ... to invest in mining, metals, and oil and gas in emerging markets.

(*FT*, 26 October 2007, p. 1)

A takeover is not on the cards: ICBC's investment is capped at 20 per cent ... This is the largest foreign investment by a Chinese bank anywhere in the world ... [It is] the largest foreign direct investment in South Africa ... The deal ... still needs the nod from shareholders and regulators ... The South African bank, which has a small presence in China, now expects to operate in the Chinese market more easily. Both banks are keen to join forces to expand their presence in other emerging markets as well. They are also planning to create a common $500 million fund to invest in oil and mining ... Angola [is] now the largest single supplier of oil to China.

(www.economist.com, 26 October 2007)

Until recently Chinese foreign acquisitions generally involved taking majority stakes in oil, gas and commodities companies in developing markets. The largest deal, two years ago, was the acquisition of PetroKazakhstan for $4 billion. Forays into the developed world either failed or succeeded only in picking up ailing businesses, as in Lenovo's acquisition of IBM's shrinking personal computer division. Attempts to buy stronger firms such as Unocal and Maytag in America ran aground, mostly for political reasons. But Beijing wants Chinese firms to gain access to foreign technologies, raw materials and skills ... So the Chinese have adopted a new approach. Majority control is now less important ... Influence and access to skills are regarded as more valuable than control. Small stakes are both educational and more feasible politically. Direct holdings are also less important. Chinese buyers are happy to make investments in intermediate companies [e.g. Blackstone, Bear Stearns and Standard Bank], which can be used to take other, less obvious stakes in other businesses.

(*The Economist*, 3 November 2007, p. 85)

Kazakhstan has agreed to share its uranium resources with China in exchange for equity in Chinese nuclear power facilities in a strategic deal that brings together the world's fastest growing uranium and nuclear energy producers. Moukhtar Dzhakishev, the president of Kazatomprom, Kazakhstan's state-owned nuclear power company, said: 'We will sway shares in uranium production for shares in Chinese atomic facilities ... This is the first time China has allowed any foreign company to become a shareholder in its atomic power industry enterprises' … China National Nuclear Corp. and China Nuclear Guangdong Power Corp., China's leading nuclear power companies, would team up to take a 49 per cent stake in a uranium mining venture in Kazakhstan with Kazatomprom retaining a 51 per cent stake … In exchange, Kazatomprom would take equity in Chinese fuel processing or electricity generation plants. Details of the agreement signed by the Chinese government are expected by next month [December 2007] … Kazakhstan bought a 10 per cent stake in Westinghouse, the US nuclear technology company, from Toshiba for $540 million this year [2007]. The partnership mirrors the Chinese deal, with providing Westinghouse with a guaranteed source of uranium and Kazakhstan with access to fuel processing know-how and technology.

(*FT*, 19 November 2007, p. 8)

A state-owned Chinese company has won the right to develop a large copper deposit in Afghanistan after agreeing to invest $3 billion in the project [it was announced on 20 November 2007] … The deal is the largest foreign invest-ment in Afghanistan's history and will give China Metallurgical Group (MCC) the right to extract high quality copper from the Aynak copper field near Kabul. The company will pay the Afghan government $400 million a year to exploit what some geologists think could be the world's biggest copper deposit … MCC will first have to build a power station to run power to the mine and find coal deposits to fuel the power station. Excess electricity from the station will power Kabul, which, at present, enjoys only a few hours of electricity a day … Some analysts were expecting the tender to go for less than $2 billion … MCC … has invested $1 billion in overseas mining opera-tions in countries including Brazil and Pakistan and in resources ranging from iron ore and copper to gold and nickel. Its largest division is in equipment manufacturing … MCC bid for the contract in Afghanistan in collaboration with two other Chinese mining companies.

(*FT*, 21 November 2007, p. 9)

A Chinese mining company has won a tender to develop one of the world's largest copper mines … It is in a relatively safe area, not far from the capital [Kabul] … The $3 billion that the China Metallurgical Group is to invest in Aynak compares with a total of $4 billion which the Afghan government says foreign companies have invested in the country since the overthrow of the Taliban six years ago … The Aynak tender was hotly contested by com-panies from Canada, Australia and Russia as well as China … Apart from copper, there is coal, iron, gas and oil … [as well as] a sparkling assortment of gemstones [in Afghanistan].

(www.bbc.co.uk, 20 November 2007)

Ping An Insurance Group has bought a 4.2 per cent stake in Fortis, the largest Belgian financial services company, in the biggest overseas purchase ever by a Chinese insurer … [The] $2.7 billion purchase makes Ping An its

[Fortis's] biggest investor ... Chinese state-owned companies have spent almost $17 billion on overseas financial purchases in 2007, buying stakes in companies like Barclays, Bear Stearns, Blackstone Group and Standard Bank Group.

(*IHT*, 30 November 2007, p. 13)

Up to 2006, 800 Chinese companies invested $1 billion in Africa, establishing 480 joint ventures and employing 78,000 workers from China, according to the European Commission. Beijing imports 32 per cent of its oil from Africa and oil-related investment in recent years amount to $16 billion, according to the European Commission.

(www.iht.com, 8 December 2007)

'Chinese investment in Africa hit $6.4 billion at the end of last year [2007] as firms from giant telecoms gear maker Huawei Technologies to small players like Zhejiang Huayou Cobalt Nickel Materials made inroads around the continent' (*IHT*, 9 January 2008, p. 11).

Iran has signed a $2 billion oil contract with Sinopec of China yesterday [9 December] ... The contract to partly develop the giant Yadavaran oil field in south-west Iran is one of the biggest Tehran has signed and is the first with a Chinese company ... The contract involves production of only 85,000 barrels per day by the time the field is developed in four years. The second phase, to produce another 100,000 barrels per day, will be decided later. Sinopec is obliged to give 51 per cent of its sub-contracts to Iranian companies.

(*FT*, 10 December 2007, p. 1)

China's biggest refiner, Sinopec, and Iran have signed a $2 billion agreement on developing the Yadavaran oil field ... The long-awaited agreement signed Sunday [9 December] in Tehran completes a 2004 memorandum of understanding for state-owned Sinopec Group to help develop the huge oil field ... [Iran has] estimated the cost of the project at $2 billion ... The field will produce 85,000 barrels a day in four years and a further 100,000 barrels a day three years after that. Under the 2004 agreement China would pay Iran as much as $100 billion over twenty-five years for liquefied natural gas and oil and a 51 per cent stake in Yadavaran. Sinopec Group hopes to talk about liquefied natural gas supplies 'later' ... Iran's constitution bars the sale of equity in the nation's oil and gas fields. Investors are compensated for their spending in oil and gas, a method known as 'buyback'.

(www.iht.com, 10 December 2007; *IHT*, 11 December 2007, p. 13)

A consortium including State Grid of China ... China's largest electricity provider ... won the right to operate the Philippine power grid with a $3.95 billion bid Wednesday [22 December] in what would be the biggest privatization in the history of the country. The winning offer [was] from the group led by the Philippines' Monte Ore Grid Resources.

(www.iht.com, 12 December 2007)

Morgan Stanley posted its first quarterly loss ever Wednesday [19 December] after taking an additional $5.7 billion write-down related to subprime mortgages. The [US] investment bank also said it would sell a $5 billion stake to China Investment Corp., China's sovereign investment fund ... The sale, which would give China a 9.9 per cent stake in one of Wall Street's biggest investment banks, is the latest example of a foreign investor aiding a Western financial firm after the housing meltdown ... In taking a major investment from the Chinese sovereign wealth fund, Morgan Stanley is following a model set by Citigroup and UBS, two other financial giants badly damaged by their exposure to securities backed by risky home loans. Citibank sold a 4.9 per cent stake to Abu Dhabi's investment arm, while UBS sold stakes to the Singapore government [via Temasek] and an unidentified Middle Eastern investor. The stake taken by the Chinese investment firm will be passive and give it no special rights to name directors, Morgan Stanley said. China Investment Corp., also known as CIC, will purchase equity units that will be converted into common shares on 17 August 2010. The units will pay a fixed annual rate of 9 per cent quarterly ... The deal marks a strategic shift for the $200 billion China Investment Corp. and underlines the extent to which the government fund is under the direct control of China's leaders ... China Investment Corp. is under the control of the Chinese finance ministry, with some influence as well from the People's Bank of China, the central bank. Lou Jiwei, chairman of the fund, said in a speech last month [November] that it sought liquidity and would mainly invest in financial instruments like index products. Lou also said that the fund ... would start hiring foreign experts before making more overseas investments. Officials familiar with the fund also said two-thirds of its money would be used to shore up China's domestic banking sector, leaving only a third for overseas investments ... The investment fund bought a $3 billion stake in the initial public offering last June [2007] of Blackstone Group, the US private equity group – only to lose more than $600 million over the last six months as Blackstone shares plunged ... There has been discussion in the Chinese government over whether more foreign currency should be put in the investment fund.

(www.iht.com, 19 December 2007)

The issue of sovereign investment funds (of which China now has one) has become a general global problem, with recipient countries anxious about foreign states possibly having aims other than profit in mind when buying shares. 'Sovereign wealth funds [SWFs] are large pools of capital controlled by governments and invested in private markets abroad ... SWFs are government investment vehicles funded by foreign exchange assets and managed separately from official reserves ... From 2000 to 2007 sovereign funds grew dramatically from twenty with assets worth several hundred billion dollars to forty with an estimated worth of $2 trillion to $3 trillion. Current projections forecast an increase in assets to $10 trillion to $15 trillion by 2015 ... SWF assets today are currently larger than the total assets under management by either hedge funds or private equity funds, but are only a fraction of the estimated $190 trillion in global financial assets.

(Robert Kimmitt, *IHT*, 27 December 2007, p. 4)

China's State Administration of Foreign Exchange [Safe] ... is starting to diversify its holdings, buying up stakes in three Australian retail banks during the past two months ... [Its] Hong Kong subsidiary ... has bought minority stakes of less than 1 per cent in ANZ Bank, Commonwealth Bank of Australia and National Australia Bank. The Safe purchases were first reported in the Australian press in December [2007] ... Each stake would be worth less than $176 million ... China Investment Corp. has about $70 billion to invest in foreign assets and it seems to have developed a taste for overseas financial stocks, particularly in the wake of the subprime problems that have depressed prices across the financial sector in the United States and elsewhere.

(www.iht.com, 4 January 2008; *IHT*, 5 January 2008, p. 15)

After a scramble by China's big oil companies to secure energy reserves overseas, they seem to have found their best prospects in the most unexpected place: under their own feet. China is turning inward for energy resources to feed its economy as it faces increasingly nationalist governments from Venezuela to Russia that want bigger oil profits and competition for remote deep-water fields or unconventional resources, like Canada's oil sands ... Already the world's sixth largest producer, China is accelerating oil exploration at home, using advanced technologies to squeeze more out of existing fields and hurrying development of its huge but under-explored reserves of natural gas.

(www.iht.com, 28 January 2008; *IHT*, 29 January 2008, p. 14)

Chinalco and Alcoa of the United States teamed up to buy a 12 per cent stake in the Anglo-Australian mining group Rio Tinto ... [in an] audacious share raid ... Chanalco and Alco ... [acquired a] 12 per cent stake of Rio Tinto's London-listed shares, which equates to about 9 per cent of the whole company. People close to the deal said it was the largest ever Chinese outbound investment and the largest ever cross-border deal involving a Chinese company ... Chinalco is the parent company of Chalco, China's largest aluminium maker and alumina miner.

(www.ft.com, 1 February 2008)

China ... launched the largest ever dawn raid to snap up a 9 per cent stake in Rio Tinto ... Chinalco, a state-owned mining company, in a joint exercise with Alcoa, the US aluminium group, spent $14 billion ... Together they secured up to 12 per cent of Rio's London-listed shares, giving them a 9 per cent overall stake ... BHP Billiton had been expected to launch an offer of three BHP shares for each Rio share on Wednesday [6 February], the deadline set by the UK Takeover Panel ... Rio, the UK-listed company, owns

some of the best iron ore, copper and aluminium mines and is a big supplier
to China.

(*FT*, 2 February 2008, p. 1)

The Shining Prospect consortium [is] 95 per cent owned by Chinalco ...
Alcoa invested $1.2 billion in the vehicle acquiring the shares ... [Alcoa]
has the right to increase its investment in Shining Prospect ... [and] has had
a close relationship with Chinalco since 2001, when it bought 8 per cent of
Chalco ... [China's contribution] was part financed by China Development
Bank.

(p. 17)

The state-owned Aluminium Corp. of China on Friday [1 February 2008]
joined the US company Alcoa in taking a 12 per cent stake in Rio Tinto in
an apparent move to head off a huge mining industry merger that China
feared could drive up soaring prices for raw materials. The move came after
Chinese officials expressed concern over BHP Billiton's plans to link up
with Rio Tinto in a merger that would give the combined company a dominant position in iron ore. Less than a week before the deadline for BHP to
make a formal offer for Rio, Chinalco, as the state-owned company is
called, described the $14.05 billion shareholding in the Anglo-Australian
miner as China's biggest foreign investment ever. The company said it did
not intend to make an offer for the whole of Rio, but reserved the right to do
so if another party made a firm bid ... China has been strongly opposed to
BHP's proposed merger with Rio, fearing that a merger of the world's two
biggest resources companies would give the combined company the power
to dictate the price of commodities, particularly iron ore ... Chinalco is one
of the biggest Chinese mining and metals companies involved in exploration, extraction and processing of aluminium, copper and other metals. It
operates in twenty-one provinces in China and has investments in Australia,
Canada, Peru, Fiji, Guinea and Myanmar.

(www.iht.com, 1 February 2008; *IHT*, 2 February 2008, p. 11)

'Chinalco and Alcoa bought 12 per cent in Rio's London-listed shares on Friday
[1 February], giving them a holding of over 9 per cent in the overall company,
which includes an Australia stock listing' (www.iht.com, 4 February 2008).

The acquisition by Aluminium Corp. of China, along with Alcoa, of a 12
per cent stake in Rio Tinto, the largest foreign investment ever by China,
was financed by a state-owned bank ... [Of] the Rio Tinto stake ... $12.8
billion was financed by China Development Bank and $1.2 billion by Alcoa
... Settling for a minority stake showed a recognition of political realities
abroad and management limitations at home.

(*IHT*, 6 February 2008, p. 17)

Chinalco's president, Xiao Yaqin, [later] said ... that the company had no
plans to increase its stake or play a role in management ... he said: 'We are

satisfied with our 12 per cent stake' ... Xiao also said Chinalco would consider selling its stake for the right price if BHP went ahead with its bid.

(*IHT*, 5 February 2008, p. 13)

('The Chinese aluminium giant Chinalco and its US partner Alcoa agreed to buy
as much as 14.9 per cent of Rio Tinto this month and had as much as $24 billion
to spend, according to a memo dated 30 January [2008]': *IHT*, 15 February
2008, p. 17.)

Chinalco paid for the bulk of the $15 billion investment ... Chinalco's bid
vehicle, Shining Prospect, has been set up in Singapore. Alcoa has committed $1.2 billion by way of a convertible instrument to the bid vehicle. It has
a long-standing relationship with Chinalco having invested in the floatation
of its subsidiary Chalco, the Chinese steel company, on the Shanghai
exchange in 2001 ... Chinalco is the nation's biggest producer of the light-
weight metal ... Its biggest asset is a 38.56 per cent stake in Chalco ... Last
year [2007] it expanded into copper, acquiring Peru copper and Yunnan
Copper Group for a combined $1.9 billion, as it seeks to diversify. BHP and
Rio together are the world's second and third largest producers of iron ore.

(www.thetimes.co.uk, 1 February 2008)

'The battle over Rio Tinto intensified Wednesday [6 February] when BHP
Billiton, the world's biggest mining company, increased its takeover offer to
about $147 billion' (www.iht.com, 6 February 2008).

'Rio Tinto's board on Wednesday [6 February] unanimously rejected an
improved takeover by BHP Billiton of about $147 billion' (*IHT*, 7 February
2008, p. 15).

The head of China's $200 billion government investment fund, seeking to
reassure Americans nervous about the possibility of foreign takeovers, said
this week that China would invest mostly in portfolios rather than individual
companies, except when a 'big fat rabbit' like the investment bank Morgan
Stanley came along ... Lou Jiwei [is] chairman of China Investment Corp.,
a so-called sovereign wealth fund established last year [2007] to invest some
of China's foreign exchange reserves ... Lou said that only a third of the
fund's $200 billion in assets would be used to buy up foreign assets. The
other two-thirds are to be used to shore up three Chinese commercial banks,
he said.

(*IHT*, 2 February 2008, p. 12)

[Wednesday 21 February saw] the apparent collapse of a Chinese company's effort to purchase a stake in 3Com, an American maker of internet
router and networking equipment in the face of Bush administration questions about the deal's national security risks. The proposed $2.2 billion deal
had called for Bain Capital, a private equity firm based in Boston, to join
with a Chinese company, Huawei Technologies, to acquire 3Com ... The
3Com deal involved a stake of more than 16 per cent by the Chinese

company ... The snag was that 3Com makes anti-hacking computer software for the military, among other things, and Huawei Technologies has ties to the Chinese military ... The concern in Washington was that the Chinese company would be able to alter the electronic equipment and computer software sold to the military in a way that could make it less than 100 per cent effective ... 3Com ... withdrew once concerns were raised ... though it hinted that it might still try to win approval later.

(www.iht.com, 21 February 2008)

'The [3Com] deal fell foul of national security concerns ... It became clear that it would not win approval from a Washington committee that scrutinizes foreign investments in sensitive sectors' (*FT*, 22 February 2008, p. 9).

The unravelling of the plan by Citic Securities to link up with Bear Stearns may prove to be the latest example of a Chinese deal gone bad ... Over the weekend Citic's $1 billion venture with Bear was thrown into serious doubt. Facing a collapse, [on 16 March] Bear agreed to be bought by J.P. Morgan Chase for a mere $2 a share, a tiny fraction of its worth only a few months ago. Citic on Tuesday [18 May] confirmed that it was scrapping its proposed investment in Bear Stearns ... Chinese stakes in Wall Street firms, including Blackstone to Morgan Stanley, have fared poorly ... Last spring [2007] China agreed to buy a $3 billion stake in Blackstone, the private equity firm that later went public at $31 per share. Its stock is now at $15.68 after the credit crunch dried up loans for private equity deals. Last October [2007] Bear and Citic announced plans to invest about $1 billion in each other and form a joint banking venture in Asia. Citic was to obtain a stake of about 6 per cent in Bear, with Bear getting about 2 per cent of Citic. The same month Industrial and Commercial of China (ICBC), the biggest Chinese lender, agreed to buy 20 per cent of Standard Bank, which is based in South Africa, for $5.6 billion in cash, the biggest foreign acquisition by a Chinese commercial bank. Bank shares have slid 19 per cent since the deal was announced. China's deal with Morgan Stanley has also been disappointing. China Investment Corp. agreed to pump $5 billion into the Wall Street bank after it posted $9.4 billion of losses in subprime mortgages and other assets. The bank's shares have since fallen 25 per cent.

(*IHT*, 19 March 2008, p. 14)

'Chinese companies invested more than $30 billion in foreign companies from 1996 to 2005, nearly $10 billion in 2004 and 2005 alone' (*IHT*, 18 March 2008, p. 15).

China Investment Corp., the country's $200 billion sovereign wealth fund, has signed a deal with the US firm J.C. Flowers to start a $4 billion private equity fund to focus on investments in US financial assets ... The Beijing-based fund, known as CIC, will become a limited partner of the new private equity fund, in which CIC will provide about 80 per cent of the contributions ... J.C. Flowers, a private equity firm based in New York, will offer about 10 per cent of the capital ... There will be several other general partners who will cover about 10 per cent of the capital ... It will be the first private equity fund to be started by CIC since it was established by the Chinese government in late 2007 as part of Beijing's plan to diversify the investments of its huge foreign exchange reserves and to seek better returns from global markets. The deal also makes J.C. Flowers the first overseas private equity fund manager appointed by CIC ... J.C. Flowers eventually agreed to accept tougher than usual conditions for the partnership ... Usually private equity fund managers may be asked to contribute only a symbolic 1 per cent or 2 per cent of the capital to a new fund. CIC required J.C. Flowers to invest more money, with the aim that it share more responsibility and risk ... Besides investments in private equity funds, CIC is also looking for more than a dozen global asset managers for both the equity and fixed-income investments ... The new $4 billion private equity fund will be run by J.C. Flowers and while CIC will not be involved in regular management it will be briefed by J.C. Flowers on some significant investments in advance ... So far CIC's investments in the Wall Street banker Morgan Stanley and the US private equity house Blackstone Group have both fallen sharply since it became involved.

(www.iht.com, 4 April 2008)

Beijing is asking Chinese banks and other financial services companies to seek permission from the cabinet before making major investments in the struggling US finance sector. Concerns are growing that the value of some Chinese investments in US banks and private equity companies has dropped significantly as the credit crisis has worsened.

(www.iht.com, 6 April 2008)

Since its formation last September [2007] China's sovereign wealth fund, China Investment Corp. (CIC) has been beset by suspicion and criticism from abroad, and recrimination from officials and the public at home, over its investment decisions ... CIC has [now] found itself running into another, unforeseen, obstacle ... the State Administration of Foreign Exchange (Safe) ... Safe is both competing with CIC for investments and complicating the sovereign fund's attempts to defuse criticism of the way it operates and makes investment decisions Safe, which is under the central bank, has long conservatively managed China's rapidly swelling foreign reserves, which stood at about $1,660 billion at the end of February [2008]. For a long time that meant investing largely in US Treasuries. Even now about 70 per cent of its assets are in dollars, say bankers. But in recent months Safe has emerged as a powerful and more aggressive investor, chasing the kind of returns that CIC was mandated to go after. Safe has built up a 1.6 per cent stake in the French oil firm Total, worth about $2.8 billion ... It has bought stakes in Australian banks and considered investing in private equity funds. Bankers familiar with its operations believe that it is also considering investing in international real estate ... Only CIC is under any pressure to disclose its dealings ... CIC has only about $70 billion to $80 billion to invest directly at the moment. Moreover, the head of Safe sits on the CIC board, with access to sensitive information about its planned investments ... CIC has sought to tackle its critics head on, conducting its business in a frank and straightforward manner. Lou Jiwei, its head, has toured global investment capitals to make his case. By contrast, Safe has a reputation for secrecy, whether its investments originate out of a Hong Kong subsidiary or a newly established office for alternative investments out of Beijing. Its secrecy complicates life for CIC, which is trying to be more transparent in response to concerns from governments that are suspicious of sovereign funds ... Safe is controlled by the People's Bank of China, while the CIC has ministry status and is closer to the finance ministry.

(FT, 5 April 2008, p. 10)

China has accumulated a stake of just less than 1 per cent in BP, the British oil company, the company confirmed Tuesday [15 April] ... BP said it was aware of the Chinese stake, which is worth about $2 billion ... The British company declined to identify the specific investor, but China operates the State Administration of Foreign Exchange [Safe], an arm of the central bank that manages the country's $1.68 trillion on currency reserves ... China also controls the China Investment Corp. [CIC], a $200 billion sovereign wealth fund that Beijing set up last September [2007] to increase the returns on its reserves by taking greater risks ... Some academics believe that CIC has been put in an awkward position from day one because of rivalry between the finance ministry and the central bank over who should control China's foreign exchange reserves. CIC was funded with part of the central bank's reserves. But it is headed by Lou Jiwei, a former deputy finance minister who has come under fire for the poor performance of the fund's investments in the US private equity group Blackstone and the investment bank Morgan Stanley ... [There is the argument] that China's senior leaders may intend to use competition to incentivize better performance by each agency ... Safe, which invests mostly in lower risk bonds, came on to the equity market's radar in January [2008] with reports that it has taken small stakes in Australia and New Zealand Banking Group. ANZ confirmed Safe had bought a stake of under 1 per cent.

(www.iht.com, 15 April 2008)

A Chinese government entity has acquired a sizeable stake in BP, one of the world's largest oil companies, for about $2 billion ... [BP said] that over the past six months an unidentified Chinese entity had acquired a 1 per cent stake ... Experts say the investment most likely came from Safe ... A spokesman for Total confirmed that a Chinese entity had acquired about 1.3 per cent of the French company recently. The spokesman declined to identify the entity, but said that the stake was worth more than $1.5 billion.

(IHT, 16 April 2008, p. 11)

A senior official, who declined to be identified by name, said that because of a communications gaffe the first time prime minister Wen Jiabao knew of CIC's $5 billion stake in Morgan Stanley was when he heard about it on the television. Wen, the official said, was not amused.

(www.iht.com, 28 April 2008)

A bid [for 3Com Corp.] ... the [US] telecommunications equipment maker ... was blocked by US regulators. Bain Capital Partners put together a $2.2 billion deal in which Huwei Technologies would acquire a 16 per cent stake in 3Com. But the plan came under fire from members of Congress because the TippingPoint business makes network security gear used by US government agencies, including the military. Huwei has close ties to China's military. Critics worried that it might share technical details of TippingPoint products with Chinese intelligence services, helping them to break into US government computer networks.

(www.iht.com, 1 May 2008)

Chinese engineers are coming to the rescue of the Russian electricity sector under a five-year expansion plan that will rival the efforts of Lenin and Stalin to electrify the Soviet Union. An estimated 41,000 megawatts of new generating capacity is expected by 2011, much of it powered by coal rather than natural gas. This goal is out of reach for Russian machine builders and even threatens to swamp the order books of global companies like General Electric and Siemens. In search of an alternative supplier, the Russian power producer OGK-2 turned to a consortium of Chinese engineering companies, led by Harbin Turbine, granting them a tender to build two 660 megawatt coal-powered turbines by 2012. It was the first such deal between Russian and Chinese companies.

(www.iht.com, 5 May 2008; *IHT*, 6 May 2008, p. 15)

In the past year Chinese banks have bought tiny foreign operations, or made minority investments in larger institutions. But on 2 June China Merchants Bank ... which is private ... became the first to launch a big takeover: it said it would buy Hong Kong's Wing Lung Bank [founded in 1933] for $4.7 billion.

(*The Economist*, 7 June 2008, p. 90)

Car ownership [in Russia], at about 200 per 1,000 people, is still very low by developed-world standards. In most of Western Europe it is over 500 and in America it is around 800 ... The growth and size of the Russian market has confounded every forecast. In 2007 ... sales of passenger cars exceeded 2.7 million ... Renaissance Capital, an investment bank, thinks Russia could outstrip Germany as Europe's biggest market this year [2008], with sales reaching around 3.3 million. By 2012 Russian will be buying more than 5 million, of which nearly 90 per cent will be foreign brands, predicts Ernst & Young, a consultancy ... Domestic producers have found it hard to compete, first with imported second-hand cars and more recently with new imports and foreign brands made in Russia ... In 2002 the government slapped a 25 per cent duty on imported used cars. But the local firms failed to take advantage of the breathing space. As the sale of used imports fell new imports took their place ... The government's response was not to raise import duties again, but to pass a measure intended to persuade foreign makers to revive the Russian car industry by setting up local assembly plants. The terms were simple: to qualify for relief from import duty, foreign carmakers had to build a factory with a capacity of more than 25,000 vehicles a year – a minimum investment of at least $100 million. Within five years of production starting, the local content in each car had to reach 30 per cent. Unlike in China, firms did not have to establish partnerships with local producers. This triggered a scramble by ten of the world's biggest car firms to build factories in Russia [including Renault, Volkswagen, Toyota, Ford, General Motors, Nissan, Suzuki and Hyundai] ... In 1990 ... domestic carmakers ... built 1.2 million passenger vehicles, but last year [2007] they sold just 756,000. AvtoVAZ, which makes more than 90 per cent of the Russian-brand passenger cars, is the most exposed. Its Ladas still sell in provincial Russia because there are lots of dealers, the cars are cheap and there are few alternatives. The main threat to Lada comes from very cheap Chinese cars. So the authorities have refused the like of Chery and Great Wall permission to set up in Russia ... AvtoVAZ's main hope lies in the 25 per cent stake recently acquired by Renault for $1 billion.

(*The Economist*, 7 June 2008, pp. 73–4)

China's $200 billion sovereign wealth fund intends to be a socially responsible global investor by shunning industries such as gambling, tobacco and arms manufacturing, the fund's president said yesterday [13 June 2008]. Gao Xiqing (president of China Investment Corp.): 'We are looking at clean energy and environmentally friendly investment ... [CIC will look at] everything cross-border except for casinos, tobacco companies or machine-gun factories' ... As far as is known the fund has primarily invested in financial services ... Of its $200 billion in assets the fund has $80 billion to $90 billion to invest overseas. The rest is being used to recapitalize state-owned banks and absorb Central Huijin, which manages state holdings in Chinese financial institutions.

(*FT*, 14 June 2008, p. 8)

China's largest offshore oil services group agreed on Monday [7 July] to buy a Norwegian drilling rig company, Awilco Offshore, for about $2.5 billion to increase its drilling capacity and expand in overseas markets ... China Oilfield Services [is] an arm of China's top offshore oil and gas producer, CNOOC ... Buying Awilco would expand China Oilfield's overseas operations, which accounted for just 18 per cent of the state-run company's revenue last year [2007] ... The acquisition is China Oilfield's first successful overseas purchase after it failed to seal a small deal for the Russian oil services business STU from TNK-BP ... Cross-border acquisitions by China have more than quadrupled so far this year [2008] to $41.1 billion worth of announced deals.

(IHT, 8 July 2008, p. 16)

The Chinese metal giant Sinosteel ... [which is] controlled by the Chinese government ... has succeeded in its bid to take over Midwest, an Australian iron ore producer in China's passage from taking stakes in individual resource projects to taking full control of non-Chinese mining companies ... The company controls 50.97 per cent of the stock of Midwest ... Sinosteel is the first Chinese company to win a hostile takeover battle ... Australian company Murchison Metals, which owns 10 per cent of Midwest, pulled out of the battle.

(IHT, 12 July 2008, p. 13)

Australia has approved Chinalco's recent purchase of a minority stake in the miner Rio Tinto, but warned the state-run Chinese aluminium giant against buying more shares without prior approval. Aluminium Corp. of China, backed by its US peer Alcoa, began amassing shares this year [2008] with the aim of taking up to 14.9 per cent of Rio, the target of a $127 billion takeover from BHP Billiton ... [Australia] said Chinalco had already promised to meet these conditions by pledging to not raise its stake above 14.99 per cent without receiving fresh government approval and to not seek to appoint a director to Rio Tinto's board.

(www.iht.com, 24 August 2008)

China's state-owned oil firm CNPC has agreed a $3 billion oil services contract with the government of Iraq. The two parties negotiated a 1997 deal to pump oil from the Ahdab oilfield ... The deal is the first major oil contract with a foreign firm since the US-led war in Iraq ... Production is set to begin at the Ahdab oilfield three years from now and the contract will run for twenty years ... CNPC would own 75 per cent of a joint venture to be set up for the contract, with the remainder held by Iraq's Northern Oil Company.

(www.bbc.co.uk, 30 August 2008)

The contract with the China National Petroleum Corporation could be worth up to $3 billion. It would allow the CNPC to develop an oil field in southern Iraq's Wasit province for about twenty years ... The Chinese company will provide technical advisers, oil workers and equipment to develop the al-Ahdab oil field ... As it did with other international companies, the Saddam regime had a partnership contract with CNPC, signed at the end of the 1990s that entitled the company to share profits. The current contract, however, will only be a 'service contract' under which CNPC is simply paid for its services.

(www.cnn.com, 30 August 2008)

CNPC [is] the parent company of PetroChina ... Iraq changed the contract to a set-fee service deal from the oil production-sharing agreement signed under Saddam. Under a service contract oil companies are paid a flat fee for their services, rather than gaining a share of the profits.

(FT, 3 September 2008, p. 8)

China Development Bank's plan to bid for Dresdner Bank in Germany failed in large part because Chinese leaders refused to agree to the deal in time, a sign of Beijing's increasingly cautious attitude to investments in Western financial institutions. The hesitancy of China's State Council to approve a potential $10 billion bid for a majority stake in Dresdner is another indication of Beijing's caution after investments in Western counterparts last year, most of which have fallen in value. The Chinese government has not approved any major Chinese offshore investment in a financial firm this year [2008] ... After a string of high profile overseas acquisitions last year [2007] that seemed to herald the arrival of Chinese financial institutions on the world stage, Beijing has turned cautious and has yet to approve any big offshore investment by the [financial] sector this year ... When Citigroup went looking for investors for its giant recapitalization in January [2008], China Development Bank initially offered to provide $5 billion as the anchor investor, but the deal fell through when the government refused to approve it ... Almost every high profile Chinese purchase of an overseas financial institution made last year is now deeply in the red ... Blackstone ... Morgan Stanley ... Barclays Bank ... Belgo-French insurer Fortis ... [China has] foreign exchange reserves of almost $2,000 billion.

(FT, 5 September 2008, p. 23)

China has the cash and ambition to be a major player in the world's biggest sale of financial assets in half a century, but politics, a lack of expertise and an aversion to risk will relegate it largely to the sidelines for now ... Ping An Insurance bought 5 per cent of Fortis, the struggling Belgian–Dutch financial group, for $2.67 billion last year [2007]. But Fortis said earlier this month [September] that the Chinese authorities had delayed approval of the $3.3 billion sale of its asset management arm to Ping An ... China Development Bank bought a 3.1 per cent stake in Barclays of Britain last year, but China's cabinet rejected a request in July to increase that stake when Barclays was raising fresh capital.

(IHT, 9 September 2008)

China quietly announced plans last month [September 2008] to invest $100 billion building roads and railways to open up remote Central Asia to the rest of the world. More than 20,000 kilometres of rail track will be built in the coming decade to bring Chinese goods into central Asia and carry back oil and metals to China.

(FT, Survey on Central Asia, 30 October 2008, p. 1)

The chairman of the Chinese sovereign wealth fund said Wednesday [3 December] that China had no plans for further investments in Western financial institutions, nor did it have any plans to 'save' the world through economic policies. The comments by Lou Jiwei, chairman and chief executive of China Investment Corp., are the clearest signals yet that after sustaining heavy losses on investments in Blackstone, Morgan Stanley and Barclays, state-run Chinese institutions and the nation's leaders are turning their attention inward. Lou Jiwei: 'Right now we do not have the courage to invest in financial institutions because we do not know what problems they may have ... If China can do a good job domestically that is the best thing it can do for the world' ... China Investment Corp. has $200 billion and was initially expected to invest all of it outside of China. But the fund has since made its largest investments shoring up the capital of banks in China ... Lou said the sheer pace of new initiatives and new rules issued by Western regulatory agencies was disconcerting and made it even harder for him to choose worthwhile investments. He asked: 'It is changing every week, how can you expect me to have confidence?' ... he did not rule out overseas investments entirely, however, noting that 'right now the value of many investments is underestimated'. But he suggested that China may find some of its best opportunities in low income countries. He said: 'We do not want to look at only the advanced or developing countries; we also want to look at emerging markets' ... China Investment Corp.'s first investment, in Blackstone Group, has attracted considerable criticism in China. The fund spent $3 billion buying shares at $29.605; the stock closed Tuesday [2 December] in New York at $5.34. That is a loss of $2.46 billion, or 82 per cent. The sovereign wealth fund has also had heavy losses on its investment in the British bank Barclays' plunge.

(www.iht.com, 3 November 2008)

Rio Tinto confirmed on Thursday [12 February 2009] that Aluminium Corp. of China will invest $19.5 billion in the mining group, a move that Rio hopes will help pay down debt, but that is likely to set off opposition from politicians worried about the Chinese group's influence on the miner. Under the deal Aluminium Corp. of China, known as Chinalco, will take stakes in various Rio assets for a total of $12.3 billion and buy $7.2 billion of convertible bonds, which will allow the Chinese company to secure supplies of raw materials at a time when asset prices are depressed because of the global economic slowdown ... Under the deal, the biggest foreign investment by a Chinese company, Chinalco will buy $7.2 billion worth of bonds convertible into Rio stock and pay $12.3 billion in cash for stakes in Rio's aluminium, iron ore and copper assets in the United States, Australia and Chile ... The state-controlled Chinalco would own 18 per cent of Rio if the bonds are converted ... The transaction is subject to the approval of regulators in five countries ... Some analysts have criticized Rio's willingness to allow Chinalco to raise its existing stake in it, saying it will limit Rio's flexibility in the future and upset some shareholders, whose investments suffered after Rio's stock plummeted 64 per cent over the last twelve months ... Rio Tinto risks upsetting its loyal investor base by seeking investments from China instead of offering shares to all investors … through a rights issue … [Rio says that the Chinese] investment comes at a premium of 124 per cent to the current enterprise value … [and that] Rio would retain operational control of the joint venture assets … Rio Tinto, which is based in London, needs to raise money to reduce $39 billion of debt amassed through its 2007 pur-chase of the Canadian aluminium maker Alcan. About $9 billion of debt is due for repayment in October [2009]. Rio has already started to sell assets, cut almost 13 per cent of jobs, reduced capital spending plans and con-sidered a rights issue to repay debt.

(www.iht.com, 12 February 2009; *IHT*, 13 February 2009, p. 11)

On 12 February the Aluminium Corporation of China (Chinalco), a state-owned enterprise, announced it would invest $19.5 billion in Rio, in two tranches. Chinalco will pay $12.3 billion for stakes of up to 50 per cent in nine of Rio's mining assets, and will also buy $7.2 billion of bonds convertible into shares, in effect giving it the right to own just under 20 per cent of Rio. The total … is sufficient to pay off debts maturing over the next two years … Rio's shareholders are likely to have mixed feelings. The price offered for the assets was as much as 124 per cent above their market value, according to the firm, though it is probably just a fraction of what could have been achieved only months ago when BHP Billiton was pursuing a takeover.

(*The Economist*, 14 February 2009, p. 75)

Anglo-Australian miner Rio Tinto announced that China's state-owned Chi-nalco was to invest a further $19.5 billion in the business. The move – China's largest in a foreign company – could see Chinalco increase its stake in Rio to 18 per cent from the current level of 9 per cent … Chinalco's $19.5 billion investment is made up of $12.3 billion being spent on stakes in nine of Rio's mining assets, and $7.2 billion on Rio bonds that can be con-verted into shares … Rio is securing a sixty-year loan from the Chinese. It is selling a right to buy its shares in the future at a massive premium to the prevailing price.

(www.bbc.co.uk, 12 February 2009)

'Heavily indebted Rio has proposed selling minority stakes in some of its best assets, including the Hamersley iron ore mine in Australia and the Escondida copper mine in Chile, to Chinalco to raise $12.3 billion' (*FT*, 13 February 2009, p. 1).

China Minmetals … rode to the rescue of OZ Minerals, an Australian mining company saddled with debt, offering to pay $1.7 billion for the world's second largest producer of zinc. As with the Rio Tinto/Chinalco deal, Australian regulators will examine rules on foreign ownership.

(*The Economist*, 21 February 2009, p. 8)

'Hunan Valin hopes to acquire a 16.5 per cent stake in Fortescue' (*FT*, 3 March 2009, p. 25).

Beijing said Friday [20 February] that ... China Development Bank agreed to lend Petrobas, the Brazilian oil giant, $10 billion in exchange for a long-term supply of oil. That investment came after similar deals were signed this week with Russia and Venezuela, bringing China's total oil investments this month [February] to $41 billion. This month Chinalco agreed to invest $19.5 billion in Rio Tinto of Australia ... And on Monday [16 February] China Minmetals bid $1.7 billion to acquire Oz Minerals, a huge Australian zinc company ... Venezuela got a $6 billion loan from China and agreed to increase its oil exports in the country, bringing China's total investment in the country to $12 billion. In Brazil China signed a $10 billion 'loan-for-oil' deal that guaranteed the country up to 160,000 barrels a day at market prices ... In Brazil the $10 billion loan will be used to finance a deep-water oil reserve that Brazil hopes will help turn the country into a major oil producer ... In Beijing this week prime minister met his Russian counterpart after China agreed to loan Russia's struggling oil giant Rosneft and the Russian oil pipeline company Transneft $25 billion in exchange for 15 million tonnes of crude oil a year for twenty years.

(www.iht.com, 20 February 2009; *IHT*, 21 February 2009, pp. 1, 15)

When Shanghai Automotive Industry Corp., China's largest carmaker, set its sights on overseas expansion in 2004, it took a small hop across the Yellow Sea. It bought a controlling stake in SsangYong Motor of South Korea, the most ambitious foreign venture for China's surging auto industry. Five years later Shanghai Auto's marriage with SsangYong, a milestone of China's rising industrial clout and South Korea's deepening economic ties with its neighbour, is falling apart in acrimony and criminal investigations ... SsangYong filed for bankruptcy protection last month [January]. Its combative trade unions and some South Korean commentators have vilified Shanghai Auto as an exploitative owner that siphoned off SsangYong's technology, reneged on promises to invest and dumped the company when the market turned sour. Shanghai Auto has a different account of what went wrong ... [saying] its troubles in South Korea revealed a deep-seated Korean bias against the Chinese ... Modern-day failures like SsangYong – and a similarly acrimonious break-up between BOE Technology Group, a Chinese electronics company, and Hydis of South Korea – loom large in Korean minds.

(www.iht.com, 24 February 2009; *IHT*, 25 February 2009, pp. 11–12)

The State Administration of Foreign Exchange [Safe], the opaque manager of nearly $2,000 billion of reserve, started making huge bets on global stocks ... diversifying into equities ... early in 2007 and continued this strategy at least until the collapse of the US mortgage finance providers Freddie Mac and Fannie Mae in July 2008, according to ... the Council on Foreign Relations in New York ... By that point Safe had moved well over 15 per cent of the country's $1,800 billion reserves into riskier assets, including equities and corporate bonds ... Judging from the subsequent fall in global stock prices and a conservative estimate that Safe held about $160 billion worth of overseas equities, Chinese losses on those investments would exceed $80 billion ... Total holdings of US equities by all Chinese entities reached $100 billion by the end of June last year [2008], more than triple the total of Chinese holdings in June 2007, according to an annual survey published by the US Treasury. In mid-2006 Chinese holdings of US equities totalled just $4 billion. Chinese investors are mostly barred from investing abroad and Safe is the only entity with the resources and the authority to make such large-scale offshore portfolio investments ... Safe uses a Hong Kong subsidiary when investing in offshore equities in the United States and other countries. This arm took small stakes last year in dozens of UK groups including Rio Tinto, Shell, BP, Barclays and Tesco.

(*FT*, 16 March 2009, p. 1)

Chinese holdings of US equities tripled to $100 billion between mid-2007 and mid-2008, just before the economic crisis took hold and global equity markets began to tumble ... China Investment Corporation, the fledgling $200 billion sovereign wealth fund, has been savaged domestically for losing more than $4 billion with misjudged investments in Blackstone and Morgan Stanley.

(p. 8)

China's ministry of commerce has relaxed rules to make it much easier for Chinese companies to win approval to invest overseas ... Although China is also turning more cautious in overseas investment after the global financial crisis left some firms nursing heavy losses on overseas acquisitions, outbound mergers and acquisitions by Chinese companies still leapt 64 per cent last year [2008] to $47.8 billion ... According to new rules that take effect on 1 May [2009], local authorities under the ministry of commerce will have the power to give approval for most corporate overseas investment projects ... The ministry will retain the power to give approval for corporate investment worth $100 million and above for a single project or investment in a country that does not have diplomatic relations with China ... The rules apply to the establishment, mergers and acquisitions of only non-financial companies ... The official *Shanghai Securities News* said that the changes meant 85 per cent of Chinese foreign investment projects would be approved by local commerce authorities when the new rules come into effect.

(www.iht.com, 17 March 2009)

'China is moving aggressively this year [2009] to acquire foreign assets during the global economic downturn' (www.iht.com, 18 March 2009).

Citing national security, Australia on Friday [27 March] blocked one of several acquisitions China is seeking in the country's natural resources sector, a move that may stoke concerns about rising protectionist tendencies around the globe. The decision to block the purchase of OZ Minerals, a mining company, by state-owned China Minmetals Corporation, coincides with a heated debate concerning a much larger investment that Chinalco is planning to make in British–Australian mining group Rio Tinto ... Australia's treasurer, Wayne Swan, said on Friday that he decided to block the OZ Minerals transaction because the company's Prominent Hill gold and copper mine, its core asset, is near a sensitive defence facility. Wayne Smith: 'The government has determined that Minmetals' proposal for OZ Minerals cannot be approved if it includes Prominent Hill ... [Discussions are continuing] in relation to OZ Minerals' other businesses and assets, and the government is willing to consider alternative proposals relating to those other assets and businesses ... OZ Minerals is scheduled to repay more than $900 million in debt next week, and must now renegotiate the deal or obtain a loan extension ... The attempted OZ Minerals takeover, and a separate bid by the Chinese manufacturer Hunan Valin Iron for a 17.5 per cent stake in Fortescue Metals Group, another Australian company, are much smaller – $1.7 billion in the case of OZ Minerals.

(www.iht.com, 27 March 2009; *IHT*, 28 March 2009, p. 14)

China's Minmetals ... has submitted a fresh bid [for OZ Minerals] that excludes a mine whose location was cited by Canberra as the reason for rejecting the offer on national security concerns ... OZ Minerals' Prominent Hill copper and gold mine [is] located in the Woomera Prohibited Area. The fresh proposal from Minmetals, which could be valued at A$1.5 billion ($1 billion), according to one industry source, comes as OZ Minerals is locked in talks with its banking syndicate over extending debt repayments on the bulk of its A$1.3 billion of borrowings which expire tonight [31 March] ... Apart from Prominent Hill, a fresh takeover deal would be likely to exclude OZ Minerals' Martabe gold and silver mine in Indonesia and Australia's Golden Grove zinc and copper mine assets that the Australian mining group has been trying to sell for some time to pay down its debts ... Australia's Foreign Investment Review Board is also examining Hunan Valin Iron and Steel of China's planned A$1.2 billion investment in Fortescue Metals, Australia's third biggest iron ore group.

(*FT*, 31 March 2009, p. 26)

Minmetals submitted a revised offer for OZ Minerals on Tuesday [31 March] that excluded Prominent Hill and other assets ... A statement from Minmetals: 'China Minmetals has made an incomplete proposal for all of OZ Minerals' assets except for Prominent Hill, Martabe and the company's portfolio of listed assets, including Toro Energy Limited ... [Minmetals and OZ Minerals] did not disclose the value of the new bid.

(www.iht.com, 31 March 2009; *IHT*, 1 April 2009, p. 17)

'Treasurer Wayne Swan of Australia approved [on Tuesday 31 March] a bid by Hunan Valin Iron and Steel Group to take a stake of as much as 17.55 per cent in the iron ore miner Fortescue, for $438 million' (www.iht.com, 31 March 2009; *IHT*, 1 April 2009, p. 17).

Australia approved a $438 million Chinese investment in iron ore producer Fortescue Metals Group on Tuesday [31 March] ... Treasurer Wayne Swan said he had given foreign investment approval for Chinese state-owned steelmaker Hunan Valin Iron and Steel Group to take up to 17.55 per cent of the country's third largest iron ore miner, subject to several conditions. These included a condition that any Fortescue board member nominated by Hunan Valin must formally declare his or her potential conflict of interest regarding Fortescue iron ore sales. Swan also capped Hunan Valin's stake at 17.55 per cent. Hunan Valin is a major customer of Fortescue ... Fortescue is quadrupling iron ore sales to an arm of Hunan Iron and Steel Group, which will become the company's second largest shareholder after company founder Andrew Forest ... Under the deal Fortescue has agreed to issue new shares to Hunan Valin to raise funds to help pay for its next expansion phase. The Chinese steel maker is also buying shares from some existing shareholders.

(www.ft.com, 31 March 2009)

OZ Minerals agreed to sell most of its assets to China's Minmetals for $1.21 billion on Wednesday [1 April] ... [The deal] gives Minmetals all but two of OZ Minerals' main assets ... Minmetals said the Australian government's foreign investment review process on the new offer was underway ... Minmetals would pick up the Century, Golden Grove, Rosebery and Avebury mines in Australia, the Sepon operations in Laos, mines in Canada and other exploration and development assets ... OZ Minerals ... careened to the brink of collapse in January [2009] when it secured a lifeline from its bankers.

(www.ft.com, 1 April 2009)

OZ Minerals agreed to sell most of its assets to Minmetals for $1.2 billion Wednesday [1 April] ... The new deal excludes Prominent Hill ... The new deal also excludes the Martabe gold and silver prospect in Indonesia and OZ Minerals' stakes in listed companies, including Toro Energy, which has uranium assets ... As a result of the new deal, OZ Minerals' lenders have extended a debt payment deadline on $825.1 million (A$1.2 billion) by a month to 30 April.

(www.iht.com, 1 April 2009)

[China has agreed] to lend Kazakhstan $10 billion and buy into a major oil field. The agreements, signed during a five-day visit by Nursultan Nazarbayev, the Kazakh president, in Beijing this week, underscores Chinese determination to exploit the global financial crisis to acquire foreign natural resources, especially energy. They also mark a significant advance into the oil business in Kazakhstan where Russia, the United States, Europe and Asia are competing for resources. China National Petroleum Corporation will lend $5 billion to KazMunaiGaz, the Kazakh state oil company, to help finance the purchase of privately owned MangistauMunaigaz, Kazakhstan's fourth biggest oil producer. CNPC has beaten competition from

Russian and Indian companies to gain equity in MangistauMunaigaz while agreeing to help Kazakhstan's domestic gas pipeline network. China's Exim Bank will lend $5 billion to the state-owned Development Bank of Kazakhstan to support telecommunications, transport, agriculture and education projects to diversify the Kazakh economy away from oil and gas. .. Kazakhstan's economy boomed while oil prices were high, but is expected to enter recession this year [2009]. The government is tapping the national oil fund, a stash of windfall oil profits, to bail out the banking sector burdened by $40 billion of foreign debts about half of which fall due this year ... China is already a major stake holder in the Kazakh oil industry and has built a pipeline linking an oilfield it owns in central Kazakhstan with its north-western Xinjiang province.

(www.ft.com, 17 April 2009)

'PetroChina said on Friday [17 April] it would pay up to $1.4 billion for a stake in an oil group in neighbouring Kazakhstan' (*FT*, 20 April 2009, p. 23).

The head of China's flagship sovereign wealth fund is looking to invest in Europe after expressing relief that snubs from the continent saved Beijing from embarrassing investment losses last year [2008]. Lou Jiwei, head of China Investment Corp., said he was pleased he did not make any trips to Europe in 2008 after EU officials expressed concerns about his fund's transparency and intentions.

(*FT*, 20 April 2009, p. 5)

'Chinese companies are falling victim to Chinese trademark pirates ... In one of the most dramatic cases, two Chinese individuals have applied for trademark registration in Canada for the names and logos of more than sixty Chinese companies' (*FT*, 22 April 2009, p. 10).

Having kept a relatively low profile after big paper losses on its early overseas investments, China's fledgling sovereign wealth fund, China Investment Corporation (CIC), is hunting for acquisition targets once more ... Comments by the CIC's chairman, Lou Jiwei, in mid-April underlined the firm's renewed appetite for foreign investment ... As foreign financial institutions sold stakes in China's largest state-owned commercial banks, the CIC stepped in. The fund began purchasing sizeable quantities of share in domestic banks from September 2008 and continued to do so in January 2009 ... The bolder strategy ... [of] industrial state-owned enterprises ... is being encouraged by the central government's 'go global' policy (also referred to as the 'going out' policy), the aim of which is to establish a larger Chinese presence in the international arena. The policy focuses on foreign acquisitions, brand building and boosting international competitiveness.

(www.economist.com, 29 April 2009)

The Bank of America, under pressure to raise additional cash, is selling a 5.8 per cent stake in the China Construction Bank for about $7 billion, a person briefed on the sale said Tuesday [12 May]. The sale of the stake is Bank of America's second as it tries to shore up its finances – it raised $2.83 billion in January by selling ... Construction Bank shares ... After the sale Bank of America will still own a stake in the Chinese bank.

(www.iht.com, 12 May 2009)

Bank of America agreed to a private placement sale of about a third of its 16 per cent stake in China Construction Bank ... Chinese banks were largely insulated from the kinds of mortgage and derivatives investments made in the United States and Europe.

(*IHT*, 13 May 2009, p. 14)

'Bank of America yesterday [12 May] raised $7.3 billion after selling a stake in China Construction Bank ... representing a third of its holdings ... Bank of America's stake is now down to 10.6 per cent' (*FT*, 13 May 2009, p. 24).

A deal [was] unveiled on 24 May in which PetroChina, a partially state-owned oil firm, will buy a big stake in Singapore Petroleum ... PetroChina, China's largest energy company, will pay $1 billion for the 45 per cent stake in Singapore Petroleum held by Keppel Corp., a conglomerate in which Temasek, Singapore's state investment fund, owns a big shareholding ... PetroChina has offered a substantial premium to the stock market price ... Over the past three months the state-owned China Development Bank has agreed to lend billions of dollars to state-controlled Brazilian and Russian oil firms in exchange for long-term supplies of crude. Meanwhile China National Offshore Oil Corporation (CNOOC) and PetroChina have each done multi-billion-dollar deals tied to the development of specific gas projects in Australia, blurring the line between investments and supply contracts.

(*The Economist*, 30 May 2009, p. 72)

'This week China's sovereign wealth fund agreed to spend more than $1 billion to increase its already significant share in Morgan Stanley, the Wall Street investment bank' (www.iht.com, 4 June 2009; *IHT*, 5 June 2009, p. 18).

[China's] largest investment ever in a Western company, a proposed $19.5 billion stake in the Australian–British mining giant Rio Tinto Group, collapsed early Friday [2 June 2009] ... The board of Rio Tinto announced the decision after meeting in London on Thursday, saying it had ended the deal it struck in February to sell the stake to Chinalco ... The China deal, which would have effectively expanded Chincalco's stake of 9.3 per cent in Rio to 18.5 per cent, had drawn stiff political opposition in Australia ... The board said in a statement early Friday that it had ended the deal with Chinalco and would raise about $20 billion by issuing new stock and forming a joint venture with its long-time rival, the Australian mining giant BHP Billiton, the world's largest mining company ... Rio Tinto said in a statement that it had agreed to raise $5.8 billion by forming a joint venture with BHP Billiton and that it planned to raise $15.2 billion more through a stock offering ... The tentative agreement [with Chinalco] had come under increasing fire as the global economy bounced back, pushing metal prices and Rio's own stock price up considerably from their earlier lows ... Global financial markets have strengthened in recent weeks and commodity prices have rebounded ... The Australian Foreign Investment Review Board ... was expected to rule on the China investment this month [June] or early next month ... Rio said it would continue to work with Chinalco and had agreed to pay Chinalco a $195 million break-up fee.

(www.iht.com, 5 June 2009)

Institutional shareholders had complained that Rio should raise money through a new stock issue instead of selling a dominant stake to the Chinese government, which they argued had an interest in keeping the price of ores as low as possible. Chinalco insisted it was independent of the government, and Australian regulators ruled that the Chinese would not be able to affect iron ore prices, a main Rio product, even with the proposed stake.

(*IHT*, 6 June 2009, p. 14)

'Rio and BHP have signed an agreement to set up a fifty–fifty joint venture ... The move is likely to upset the Chinese steel makers, who have said that Australian iron ore miners have too much power to decide prices' (www.bbc.co.uk, 5 June 2009).

The proposed deal between Rio and Chinalco, the largest overseas investment ever by a Chinese company, had provoked political opposition in Australia ... Beijing said consistently that the investment was purely a commercial affair, but its hands-off stance was undermined when Xiao Yaqin, the Chinalco president and chief architect of the deal, was appointed to the State Council, China's cabinet, immediately after the deal was announced ... Australia's prime minister, Kevin Rudd, met with Xiong Weioping, Chinalco president, in Canberra on Friday [5 June] and assured him that Australia remained open to Chinese investment. He said it was government policy to consider foreign investment based on 'national interest' tests ... Mr Rudd said that 'national interest' would also be relevant when it considered an application from BHP Billiton to combine its iron ore operations with Rio's in the Pilbara region of Western Australia.

(www.iht.com, 5 June 2009)

Rio Tinto completed its $15.2 billion rights issue, the fifth biggest on record. Chinalco took part, maintaining its 9 per cent holding in the mining company. Chinalco had been on course to invest $20 billion in Rio. Heavily indebted Rio chose instead to raise money by selling new shares and combining its iron ore operations in Australia with BHP Billiton. This led the official Chinese media to dub Rio a 'dishonourable woman'.

(*The Economist*, 4 July 2009, p. 7)

A Chinese steel executive detained along with four Rio Tinto employees is being investigated for leaking China's 'bottom line' on iron ore prices, a source with knowledge of the probe said on Friday [10 July]. Tan Yixin, the head of iron ore imports for state-owned steelmaker Shougang, is suspected of 'revealing China's negotiating strategy' to Anglo-Australian miner Rio Tinto, the source [said] ... Shanghai's state security bureau accused three local Rio Tinto staff and senior Australian executive Stern Hu of bribing unidentified Chinese steelmakers during tense iron ore price negotiations this year [2009]. Xinhua: 'This seriously damaged China's economic security and interests. The activities of Stern Hu and the others violated Chinese law as well as international business morality' ... China dominates the steel industry, making as much as the next eight biggest steel producing countries put together ... Chinese security authorities detained the four Rio employees on Sunday [5 July], alleging they were involved in stealing state secrets. They were later formally arrested ... The detentions came after the two sides missed a 30 June deadline in the iron ore talks and Rio ditched a $19.5 billion tie-up with Chinalco last month [June].

(www.iht.com, 10 July 2009)

Several other executives in the iron ore trade in China are also under investigation and at least one Chinese executive has been detained ... Some of the major steel producing nations, like Japan and South Korea, have already accepted a price [for iron ore] 33 per cent lower than last year's. China, which imports about half the world's supply of iron ore each year, has dug in its heels and is holding out for an even larger reduction, of as much as 45 per cent.

(www.iht.com, 10 July 2009)

Early Friday [10 July] ... a website controlled by the Shanghai government said that the investigation was linked to the pricing of iron ore and that the Chinese authorities were looking into whether Rio employees paid bribes to Chinese officials in exchange for confidential government documents.

(*IHT*, 11 July 2009, p. 10)

China has 'conclusive evidence' that four employees of the world's second largest mining company were stealing state secrets, the foreign ministry said. Four employees of Rio Tinto – one Australian and three Chinese – have been arrested on suspicion of espionage and stealing state secrets. Australian Stern Hu is the general manager of Rio Tinto's Shanghai office, where all the employees work. A Chinese government statement: 'As understood from the Shanghai state security bureau, during China's iron ore negotiation with foreign miners in 2009 Stern Hu gathered and stole state secrets from China via illegal means, including bribing staff of Chinese steel companies.'

(www.cnn.com, 10 July 2009)

The ministry of foreign affairs on Thursday [9 July] said the authorities had obtained evidence which proves they stole – for a foreign country – Chinese state secrets, which hurt China's economic interests and economic security ... Iron ore price negotiations between China and miners including Rio Tinto have been particularly contentious this year [2009].

(www.ft.com, 10 July 2009)

'While Japanese, Korean and Taiwanese steel companies have agreed contract prices with iron ore suppliers, The Chinese have yet to do so, demanding larger price cuts' (www.ft.com, 7 July 2009).

The Chinese authorities have detained or questioned at least seven Chinese steel industry executives in a broadening corruption investigation connected to the detentions last week of four employees of the mining giant Rio Tinto, the state-controlled news media reported Monday [13 July]. The investigation, which began with accusations that the four Rio Tinto workers had conspired to steal state secrets, has rapidly widened ... It now includes accusations of widespread bribery in business dealing, as well as allegations that the four workers paid for detailed government trade and manufacturing data to give Rio Tinto executives an edge in iron ore negotiations with Chinese state-controlled steelmakers. The reports said that senior managers at five steel factories were giving the authorities information ... Experts on China's large steel and iron ore industry say an array of corrupt practices have gone on for years, including iron ore deals off the books and the exchange of confidential market data that Beijing now considers state secrets.

(www.iht.com, 13 July 2009; *IHT*, 14 July 2009, pp. 1, 14)

One of the tricks is widely discussed. Big, government-owned steel makers would use their import licences to buy more iron ore than they needed. Then they would turn around and profit by illegally selling excess ore to small producers that did not have a licence to import iron ore ... Smaller steel producers are not supposed to buy supplies from big steelmakers with long-term contracts and volume discounts. They are supposed to buy on the open market, where prices can be volatile. It is a system that smaller producers have long complained favours big state-owned companies ... A government-controlled website ... alleged that the Rio employees bribed steel executives to get access to confidential government documents that detailed production and inventory levels at state-owned steel mills. Such data could have given Rio Tinto an edge in its annual iron ore negotiations with Chinese mills.

(www.iht.com, 14 July 2009; *IHT*, 15 July 2009, p. 15)

China has extended its investigations into alleged spying and bribery by Rio Tinto employees to executives of five Chinese steelmakers. Baosteel Group, Anshan Iron and Steel Group. Laigang Group and Jigang Group are being probed, the *China Daily* said. An executive at another major producer, Shougang Group, was detained last week ... Rio Tinto was acting as lead negotiator for global iron ore producers in talks with Chinese mills on the price for annual supply contracts. The Rio employees are accused of bribing Chinese steel company personnel to obtain summaries of the negotiators' meetings, according to Chinese news reports.

(www.bbc.co.uk, 14 July 2009)

China stepped up its campaign against Rio Tinto on Wednesday [15 July] by saying the company had bribed virtually every one of China's big steel makers ... *China Daily* said Rio Tinto bribed sixteen large Chinese steel companies, all members of the China Steel and Iron Association ... Wednesday's report is the first time a government publication has alleged that many of the country's biggest steel companies may have been involved in the scandal ... In the past week China has questioned or detained at least ten steel executives.

(www.iht.com, 15 July 2009; *IHT*, 16 July 2009, p. 15)

Sam Walsh (Rio Tinto's iron ore chief executive): 'Rio Tinto believes that the allegations in recent media reports that employees were involved in bribery of officials at Chinese steel mills are wholly without foundation. We remain fully supportive of our detained employees, and believe that they acted at all times with integrity and in accordance with Rio Tinto's strict and publicly stated code of ethical behaviour.'

(www.bbc.co.uk, 17 July 2009, p. 7)

China's State Secrets Bureau website Rio Tinto had spied on Chinese steel mills for six years and helped to inflate iron ore prices. It said Chinese steelmakers had lost 700 billion yuan ($102 billion; £61.2 billion) through overpaying for imported iron ore ... The report said: 'This six-year espionage case involved corruption, information gathering and spying.'

(www.bbc.co.uk, 10 August 2009)

[A] report issued by China's National Administration for the Protection of State Secrets said Rio Tinto's commercial spying involved 'winning over and buying off, prying out intelligence, routing one by one, and gaining things by deceit' over six years ... The new report said Rio's spying meant Chinese steel makers paid over 700 billion yuan (£61 billion) more for imported iron ore than they otherwise would have ... The report said the case should force Chinese officials and companies to do more to protect sensitive commercial information, and foreign businesses in China must come under stricter controls to deter them from spying ... The report and others on the state secrets website said the government should spell out more clearly what commercial data count as official secrets. Contacts between local officials, experts and managers should also be more strictly controlled, said the report on Rio.

(www.iht.com, 9 August 2009)

China said Sunday [9 August] that it had evidence showing that for at least six years, employees working for the British–Australian mining giant Rio Tinto had engaged in commercial espionage, costing the country about $100 billion. The sensational allegation was published on a website affiliated with China's State Secrets Bureau, which detained four Rio Tinto employees ... The new allegations, published by the National Administration for the Protection of State Secrets in China, named only Rio Tinto but suggested that all foreign iron ore suppliers had benefited from fraud. The major iron ore producers generally follow the same benchmarks price set during annual negotiations ... The article said: 'The computer data Rio Tinto staff held showed that they have gained extensive, detailed inside information on the steel industry and were definitely spying on China's economic interests and security' ... China contends that the price was manipulated, costing the government-controlled steel industry an additional $100 billion.

(*IHT*, 10 August 2009, pp. 14, 16)

[The] bounce-back in iron ore prices [is] due in large part to Chinese demand ... China's total imports of iron ore over that period were only $168 billion, of which about 20 per cent was from Rio. China was paying the same negotiated prices as Japanese, Korean and other importers. And China's own mines, which provide more than 50 per cent of its needs, were using similar benchmarks, or selling on the spot market, where prices have been mostly higher than the negotiated ones.

(www.iht.com, 11 August 2009; *IHT*, 12 August 2009, p. 7)

'[Rio Tinto's] entire global revenue over the six years to 2008 is some $162 billion, of which less than a third has come from iron ore' (www.economist.com, 10 August 2009).

China has accused Rio Tinto of spying on its steel industry, costing the country renminbi 700 billion (£61.3 billion) in excessive charges for the iron ore ... The remarks [were] contained in an editorial in the magazine of the National Administration for the Protection of State Secrets [NAPSS] ... The NAPSS said: 'From the large amounts of intelligence data that was found on Rio Tinto computers ... it is clear that the economic spies, using bribes for six years, forced the Chinese steel companies ... to pay more than renminbi 700 billion more for imported iron ore than they would otherwise' ... The report said the Rio case was only the tip of the iceberg ... The watchdog argues that the law needs to be defined clearly and narrowly and that responsibility for guarding secrets should be assigned clearly in government and the corporate sector. The watchdog also called for the creation of a new regulatory framework for the registration, auditing and supervision of foreign companies and their representative in China.

(*FT*, 10 August 2009, p. 1)

'China's vague legislation stipulates that any information on defence, foreign policy, economic and social development, science and technology, criminal investigations or "other matters" can be classified as a state secret – even if it is already in the public domain' (*FT*, 11 August 2009, p. 5).

'China has levelled new allegations ... saying Rio Tinto overcharged Chinese steel mills by $100 million over six years' (www.cnn.com, 10 August 2009).

'An article published online ... alleged that Rio spied on Chinese mills for six years, resulting in the mills overpaying $102 billion for iron ore' (www.iht.com, 11 August 2009).

China appeared on Monday [10 August] to step away from allegations made over the weekend that Rio Tinto had engaged in commercial espionage for six years ... The allegations were published late Saturday or early Sunday [8–9 August] on www.baomi.org, a website affiliated with China's State Secrets Bureau, but the article was removed on Monday ... During interviews with Bloomberg News and Dow Jones, the author of that article, a government official, said Monday that he was simply expressing his own opinion and did not know details of the case ... Since late June, after China broke off acrimonious iron ore negotiations with Rio Tinto and other big mining companies, its state-controlled media and websites have published a series of damaging reports about Rio Tinto, bribery and corruption in China's steel and iron ore industry. The negotiations have recently resumed. The author of the www.baomi.org, article, Jiang Ruqin, is an official with the State Secrets Bureau. In an interview on Monday with the Bloomberg and Dow Jones news agencies, he said that he had not been assigned to write the article, but was expressing his own opinion ... Mr Jiang said his main accusation – that because of Rio's spying China's steel industry was overcharged by about $100 billion – came from China Central Television ... An official at the propaganda department of the National Administration for the Protection of State Secrets told Dow Jones Newswires on Monday that the agency had not authorized anyone to release comments on the case.

(www.iht.com, 10 August 2009; *IHT*, 11 August 2009, p. 13)

Rio Tinto said Tuesday [11 August] it has yet to be presented with any evidence to support the detention of four of its China-based staff on suspicions of stealing state secrets ... The four have yet to be officially charged ... Australian diplomats had made a fresh appeal for China to grant legal representation to Stern Hu ... an Australian citizen.

(www.iht.com, 11 August 2009; *IHT*, 12 August 2009, p. 17)

Negotiations between suppliers and China's steelmakers, which should have concluded by April [2009], are at an impasse ... Secret annual discussions with one iron ore producer (in this case Rio) and a leading steelmaker (Baosteel for China) result in a price that is, by tradition, accepted by the other miners and the world's steelmakers. This year [2009] China has been pushing for big price cuts, in response to a waning world economy. Although steelmakers in Japan and South Korea had made a deal to pay 33 per cent less than last year [2008], China has demanded a deeper discount. But as talks continued spot prices, a determinant of contract prices, began to rise, and many of China's steelmakers looked for supplies on the open market to fill hungry blast furnaces. China's negotiating position worsened even as it made increasingly belligerent noises.

(www.economist.com, 10 August 2009)

Four employees of Rio Tinto have been formally arrested on charges of trade secrets infringement and bribery, China's state media reported Tuesday [11 August] ... [The Australian government] received notification late Tuesday from the Chinese ministry of public security of the formal arrest of the four 'on suspicion of violating commercial secrets and taking bribes from individuals not employed by state organizations' ... China's Supreme People's Protectorate said in a statement that preliminary investigations had shown that the four employees had obtained commercial secrets of China's steel and iron industry through illegal means and were involved in bribery, Xinhua reported ... Obtaining commercial secrets comes with a maximum sentence of seven years.

(www.cnn.com, 12 August 2009)

The four employees have been charged with using 'improper means' to obtain 'commercial secrets' about China's steel and iron industry, said Xinhua ... There was no mention of charges of stealing state secrets ... which carry tougher sentences ... China is Australia's biggest trade partner, worth $53 billion in 2008. Of this, $14 billion came from iron ore exports, powered by Rio Tinto and BHP Billiton.

(www.bbc.co.uk, 12 August 2009)

China formally arrested an Australian citizen and three other employees of Rio Tinto early Wednesday [12 August] on suspicion of commercial bribery and trade secrets infringement ... In the filing ... China backed away from the much more serious charge of espionage or violation of the country's state secrets law, which Beijing had earlier alleged ... Prosecutors said that the four Rio Tinto employees used 'improper means' to gain access to information about China's state-controlled steel industry and that they engaged in commercial bribery ... The prosecutor's office said Wednesday [12 August] that the investigation was continuing and that the four employees had not yet been indicted ... Australian officials added more detail Wednesday, saying Chinese officials had informed them that the Rio employees had given bribes but had also taken bribes from 'individuals not employed by state organizations' ... In a statement released Wednesday, the company's chief executive, Sam Walsh, said: 'Rio Tinto will strongly support its employees in defending these allegations. From all the information available to us, we continue to believe that our employees have acted properly and ethically in their business dealings in China' ... In the first half of this year [2009] alone Beijing says 9,000 government officials were found guilty of graft, and about 24,000 officials were investigated ... State-run media have published articles saying the iron and steel industry is plagued by bribery and corruption.

(www.iht.com, 12 August 2009; *IHT*, 13 August 2009, p. 13)

In a statement published on Wednesday [12 August] in official state media, China's Supreme People's Procuratorate said prosecutors had gathered sufficient evidence to formally approve their arrest for 'obtaining commercial secrets of China's steel and iron industry through improper means', in violation of the country's criminal law. The statement said prosecutors had also found evidence the four were involved in commercial bribery. If convicted, the four face a fine and up to seven years in jail. They would have faced the death penalty if convicted of violating China's vaguely worded state secrets law ... The four will now be allowed to meet with lawyers and receive visitors.

(www.ft.com, 12 August 2009)

The Australian miner Fortescue Group broke ranks with its larger rivals Monday [17 August] to agree on a slightly lower iron ore price with Chinese steel mills in exchange for up to $6 billion in funding ... But analysts said it was unlikely that the surprise deal to sell ore to China at 35 per cent below last year's price – touted by the Chinese side as a new 'reference' for price negotiations with the top three suppliers – would coax a compromise out of the larger miners, which are insisting on the 33 per cent cut agreed upon earlier. Rio Tinto said the Fortescue deal was not relevant to its pricing for this year ... The price [is] effectively 3 per cent lower than the benchmark that Rio set with Japanese and South Korean mills in May ... The Fortescue price cut is well short of the 40 per cent to 45 per cent reduction that the China Iron and Steel Association (CISA) had hoped to win from miners when negotiations began nearly a year ago ... Unlike its Australian rivals, Fortescue sells its ore only to China, is part-owned by a Chinese mill and will now turn to China to raise the financing it desperately needs to expand. The deal is conditional on the completion of a $5.5 billion to $6 billion in Chinese financing by 30 September ... Fortescue signed the pact with CISA and with Baosteel, China's top steel mill ... [The sides agreed] on prices for only the second half of the year [2009] ... Analysts were doubtful that the price would hold up as a reference, with spot market prices having surged 50 per cent since the initial 33 per cent deal and a number of Chinese steel mills having already broken away from CISA to reach their own agreements.

(www.iht.com, 17 August 2009)

The Australians recalled their Chinese ambassador to the capital, Canberra, for talks on Wednesday [19 August], after a week in which Beijing's state-controlled news media excoriated Australia's 'Sinophobic politicians' and suggested that China's billions were better spent trading with friendlier nations. The Chinese cancelled planned visits by vice premier Li Keqiang, the heir apparent to prime minister Wen Jiabao, and the vice foreign minister, He Yafei, who was supposed to attend a meeting of Asian nations.

(www.iht.com, 22 August 2009)

General Motors has reached a preliminary agreement for the sale of its Hummer brand of large sport utility vehicles and pickup trucks to a machinery company in western China with ambitions to become a carmaker, a person with knowledge of the Chinese government approval process said Tuesday [2 June]. The Sichuan Tengzhong Heavy Industrial Machinery Company Ltd, based in Chengdu, concluded the agreement with GM ... Sichuan Tengzhong is a privately owned company, but Tuesday's deal required preliminary vetting by Beijing officials, who retain the right to veto any effort at an overseas acquisition by a Chinese company and who give special attention to deals over $100 million ... Even before the Hummer deal the company has been moving into heavy-duty trucks, including tow trucks and oil tankers ... If the purchase is completed it would be the first acquisition of a well known American automotive brand by a Chinese company ... Chinese automakers have already purchased the MG and Rover brands, two of the most famous names in British automotive history.

(www.iht.com, 2 June 2009)

General Motors, newly bankrupt and struggling to raise cash, agreed to sell its Hummer division ... Hummer [is] maker of the gas-guzzling behemoths who trace their provenance to the US military ... The state media reported Friday [5 June] that the deal has hit regulatory hurdles ... Sales of passenger cars in China have grown by 20 per cent to 30 per cent a year since 2005. In January [2009], for the first time ever, China's monthly vehicle sales exceeded those in the United States ... China is moving to impose fuel efficient standards tougher than those in the United States while developing hybrid cars. And most car owners favour smaller, less expensive models.

(*IHT*, 8 June 2009, p. 16)

A Chinese firm's bid to buy the gas-guzzling Hummer car will be blocked on environmental grounds ... Hummers were originally built as military off-road vehicles ... Sichuan Tengzhong Heavy Industrial Machinery emerged as the surprise buyer for the brand earlier in the year ... China National Radio said Hummer is at odds with the country's planning agency's attempts to decrease pollution from Chinese manufacturers. The acquisition from General Motors would need Chinese regulatory approval. The value of the bid was not disclosed at the time, but analysts say that GM would have made about $100 million from the sale. National Development and Reform Commission will also block Sichuan Tengzhong from buying Hummer because the Chinese construction equipment maker lacks expertise in car production, state radio added.

(www.bbc.co.uk, 26 June 2009)

Vietnam's great war hero, General Vo Nguyen Giap, has stood up to defend his country once again, this time against what he says would be a huge mistake by the government – a vast mining operation run by a Chinese company. Now ninety-seven, the commander who led his country to victory over both France and the United States has emerged as the most prominent voice in a broad popular protest that is challenging the secretive workings of the country's Communist leaders. In an unusual step, the government has taken note of the criticisms in recent weeks and appears to be making at least gestures of response, saying it will review the project's environmental impact and slow its full implementation. The project, approved by the Communist Party's decision-making Politburo in late 2007, calls for an investment of $15 billion by 2025 to exploit reserves of bauxite – the key mineral in making aluminium – that by some estimates are the third largest in the world. The state-owned mining group Chinalco has already put workers and equipment to work in the remote Central Highlands under contract to Vinacomin, the Vietnamese mining consortium that is aiming for up to 6.6 million tonnes of aluminium production by 2015. General Giap and other opponents say the project will be ruinous to the environment, displace ethnic minority populations and threaten national security with an influx of Chinese workers and economic leverage … As the outlines of the project have emerged, a loose coalition of scientists, academics, environmentalists, war veterans and leaders of unofficial Buddhist and Catholic groups have come together to challenge what prime minister Nguyen Tan Dung has called 'a major policy of the party and the state'. Their voices have been amplified in the echo chamber of political blogs, a new voice in public discourse here [in Vietnam] … In a petition to the National Assembly in April [2009] 135 scholars and intellectuals opposed the plan, saying: 'China has been notorious in the modern world as a country causing the greatest pollution and other problems' … State-owned Vinacomin [said] … construction will end in two years and only a small number of Chinese will remain to run the operations … The government opened itself to its critics in April, convening a seminar at which scientists and economists voiced strong opposition to what one of them said could become a 'major disaster'. Responding at the seminar, deputy prime minister Hoang Trung Hai assured critics that the government would not consider developing the mines without regard to the larger impact and would readjust the projects in an effort to protect the environment. The government now says it will begin with only two of the four planned mining operations, and it is allowing a debate in the National Assembly … The government might well have brushed off its critics if General Giap had not spoken up, first in January [2009] and twice afterwards, saying the project 'will cause serious consequences to the environment, society and national defence' … General Giap is the last living comrade of the country's founding father, Ho Chi Minh … Vietnam was a tributary state of China for 1,000 years and was invaded by China in 1979, and the two countries continue to joust for sovereignty in the South China Sea.

(www.iht.com, 28 June 2009)

Sinopec has made a $7.22 billion takeover bid for Canadian oil and gas company Addax Petroleum, the companies announced Wednesday

[24 June]. The takeover would give Sinopec access to Addax's stakes in oil fields off the coast of West Africa, as well as in Iraq. Sinopec already has interests in Gabon as well as Sudan. Its parent, Sinopec Group, is wholly owned by the Chinese government.

(www.iht.com, 24 June 2009; *IHT*, 25 June 2009, p. 19)

'Addax last year [2008] produced 137,000 barrels of oil per day, all of which was from Africa, although the group's Taq Taq field in Kurdish northern Iraq began production earlier this month [June]' (www.ft.com, 24 June 2009).

Addax Petroleum [is] a Swiss company which has listings in Toronto and London and drilling rights in Iraq, Gabon and Nigeria ... The deal is worth $9 billion including the assumption of debt ... If it succeeds ... it will be the biggest takeover of a foreign firm by a Chinese one ... In December [2008] another Sinopec subsidiary spent $2 billion to acquire Tanganyika Oil, which, like Addax, trades on the Toronto exchange. Tanganyika produces 23,000 barrels a day, one-sixth of Addax's current production.

(*The Economist*, 27 June 2009, p. 84)

China emerged as the early winner Tuesday [30 June] in the long-awaited auction to develop Iraq's huge oil reserves ... [Iraq's] oil reserves [are] the third largest in the world after Saudi Arabia and Iran ... [The day] ended with the awarding of only one contract ... The three main Chinese oil companies all bid in partnership with Western firms, and a pairing of BP and China National Petroleum Corp. won the contract for the largest field on offer: Rumaila, near the southern city of Basra. Once the bid is accepted by the oil minister ... the Iraqi parliament must issue final approval ... Under the twenty-year service contracts on offer in Tuesday's auction, the oil companies would be paid a per barrel fee for any crude they produce in excess of a minimum production target ... China National Petroleum Corp. started drilling in the spring [of 2009] in the Ahdab oil field in south-eastern Iraq.

(*IHT*, 1 July 1009, pp. 1, 14)

Scores of Chinese, Russian, American and British oil executives, representing eight of the world's top ten non-state oil companies ... listened closely on headphones to translations as bids for six oil fields and two natural gas fields were read out.

(www.iht.com, 30 June 2009)

Iraq's first big effort to attract foreign investment to its oil sector met stiff resistance from companies yesterday [30 June]. Only BP of the UK and China's CNPC were willing to agree to Baghdad's tough terms, allowing them to win a bid to turn the country's Rumaila field into the world's second largest ... BP was forced to halve its fee – to $2 a barrel from $3.99 – to secure the contract ... CNOOC, Sinopec and CNPC of China [were involved in the bidding process] ... The [year] 2003 ... [saw] the toppling of Saddam Hussein ... [This] is the biggest oil frontier to be opened up since the fall of the Soviet Union ... Only Saudi Arabia and Iran hold more oil [reserves than Iraq].

(*FT*, 1 July 2009, p. 6)

The Iraqi government rejected bids for five other oil fields and a natural gas field because the bidders did not agree to the service charge set by the ministry of oil ... Iraq did not say how much the BP–CNPC bid was worth. It runs for twenty years ... [The oil minister] said the government was satisfied with the auction, even though only one contract was awarded, because the contract was for Iraq's largest oil field. Iraq plans to open bidding this year [2009] on ten more oil fields and one natural gas field, all of which are underdeveloped ... Iraq has some of the largest oil reserves in the world, with an estimated 115 billion barrels – tying Iran for second place, behind Saudi Arabia's 264 billion barrels.

(www.cnn.com, 1 July 2009)

Besides the Addax purchase, China has spent $5.4 billion this year for petroleum assets in Syria, Kazakhstan and Singapore. The government has also sealed loan-for-oil deals this year [2009], in which it has lent billions of dollars at discounted rates to finance oil projects in exchange for a share of production, in Russia, Kazakhstan, Brazil and Venezuela.

(*IHT*, 4 July 2009, p. 11)

The first half of 2009 may prove to be an inflection point for Chinese outbound foreign direct investment [OFDI] ... [But] the government is not throwing caution to the wind. Beijing blocked Bank of China's purchase of a stake in La Compagnie Financière Edmond de Rothschild, the French investment bank, and has responded tepidly to a bid by Sichuan Tengzhong, a little known machinery maker, for General Motors' Hummer unit ... New government rules issued last week will make it easier for companies to finance outbound foreign direct investment.

(*IHT*, 21 July 2009, p. 18)

General Motors is to press ahead with talks with Magna International and RHJ International for a stake in its Opel business, after throwing out a bid from China's Beijing Automotive Industry Corporation ... The Berlin government, which will play a decisive role in the final decision, is backing the bid by Magna International, the Canadian parts supplier, and Russia's Sberbank. In its statement GM said it had also 'agreed to continue talks' with RHJ International, the Brussels-listed industrial investment group. Berlin will provide the bulk of roughly Euro 4 billion in government guarantees needed to finance the spin-off ... The Chinese company would have used the acquisition of Opel as an opportunity to expand its operations in China and had outlined plans to spend $2 billion on what would have been Opel's first factory in the country. However, those plans could have put it on a collision course with GM, which would have been wary of a new competitor in one of its most important growth markets.

(www.ft.com, 23 July 2009)

'General Motors did not mention Beijing Automotive Industry Corp. in the statement Thursday [23 July]' (*IHT*, 24 July 2009, p. 15).

Premier Wen Jiabao in an address to Chinese diplomats on Monday (20 July): 'We should hasten the implementation of our "going out" strategy and combine the utilization of foreign exchange reserves with the "going out" of our enterprises.' The 'going out strategy' is a government slogan for encouraging investment and acquisitions abroad, particularly by state-owned industrial giants such as PetroChina, Chinalco, Bank of China and China Telecom ... Mr Wen did not elaborate on how much of the country's $2,132 billion of reserves would be channelled to Chinese enterprises.

(*FT*, 22 July 2009, p. 6)

In the ten months since Lehman imploded, Chinese companies have gone on an unprecedented buying spree. Chinese bidders have announced fifty outbound offers worth $30 million or more, according to Dealogic, totalling just over $50 billion. Setting aside Chinalco's thwarted approach to Rio Tinto, and Beijing Automotive's failed bid for Opel, the success rate has been high. Just three deals have been withdrawn, and one of those – Minmetals' bid for OZ Minerals – was resurrected in an acceptable form. Twenty-four deals worth a combined $17 billion have been completed; twenty-one, worth almost $18 billion, are pending ... Rio seemed to have served as a lesson ... Since then the focus has stayed constant: more than two-thirds of offers have been in mining or energy. Deals have also been smaller and simpler.

(*FT*, 27 July 2009, p. 16)

Chinese money is helping drive infrastructure investment in many developing countries, but in its wake has also come a big rise in Chinese immigrants and overseas workers that has proved less popular ... The number of attacks on Chinese citizens and property increases.

(www.economist.com, 11 August 2009)

Yanzhou Coal of China has reached a deal to buy the Australian coal miner Felix Resources, a person with knowledge of the deal said Monday [10 August], in a deal worth as much as 4 billion Australian dollars ... The $3.3 billion takeover comes with asset valuations rebounding ... Still, the takeover by state-owned Yanzhou, one of the top Chinese coal producers, could face political opposition in Australia ... So far this year [2009] Chinese companies have invested about $2.2 billion in Australian energy and resources companies.

(www.iht.com, 10 August 2009)

Baosteel, China's largest steelmaker, plans to invest $241.2 million for a 15 per cent stake in Aquila Resources, an Australian iron ore and coal company ... Baosteel said the Aquila purchase was its first large strategic investment in a foreign public company ... A flurry of Chinese companies have invested in Australian mining groups in the past year, led by Hunan Valin's purchase of a more than 17 per cent stake in Fortescue Metals, Australia's third biggest iron ore producer behind Rio Tinto and BHP Billiton … The [Baosteel] investment must be cleared by the Australian government and is also subject to Chinese regulatory approval.

(*FT*, 30 August 2009, p. 15)

China Investment Corp. is investing as much overseas each month this year [2009] as it did in the whole of 2008, Lou Jiwei, the chairman of the $298 billion wealth fund, has said. The fund is counting on handsome returns this year and might one day ask the government to hand it more of the country's hoard of foreign reserves to manage, Mr Lou, a former vice finance minister, said during an interview Saturday [29 August]. The fund invested a relatively small $4.8 billion outside China last year [2008] as it kept its powder dry during the financial crisis. At the end of the year [2008] it held 87.4 per cent of its overseas investments in cash or cash equivalent.

(*IHT*, 31 August 2009, p. 17)

'On 31 August [2009] PetroChina agreed to pay $1.7 billion for a majority stake in two tar-sands projects [in Canada]' (*The Economist*, 5 September 2009, p. 72).

Chinese state-owned companies expanded their footprint in Australia's mining industry Tuesday, agreeing to help fund two iron ore explorers in return for supply contracts and taking a controlling stake in a uranium prospector … China Railway Materials forged separate alliances with the explorers FerrAus and United Minerals … China Guangdong Nuclear Power agreed to the takeover of a uranium prospector, Energy Metals.

(*IHT*, 9 September 2009, p. 15)

China National Petroleum Corp., parent of the state-run oil and natural gas giant PetroChina, announced Wednesday [9 September] that it had received a low-interest $30 billion loan to finance overseas acquisitions. The five-year loan [is] from the China Development Bank, state-run lender … This year [2009] China has spent $12 billion on overseas oil and refining assets alone … The country had to import about 3.6 million barrels a day last year [2008] to meet a little less than half its needs.

(www.iht.com, 9 September 2009; *IHT*, 10 September 2009, p. 16)

As the global economic crisis ebbs, China is focusing on building up its domestic financial firms and banks rather than investing in Western companies, the chairman of Lloyds of London said Tuesday [15 September]. Having made investments in 2007 and 2008 that soured as the financial crisis set in, China's sovereign wealth fund is turning inward, Peter Levene said … [He] also sits on the board of China Construction Bank.

(www.iht.com, 15 September 2009; *IHT*, 16 September 2009, p. 17)

'Venezuela has announced a $16 billion investment deal with China for oil exploration in the Orinoco River … The deal with China is over three years' (www.bbc.co.uk, 17 September 2009).

The China Investment Corporation, the country's $300 billion sovereign wealth fund, invested $1.9 billion on Wednesday [23 September] in securities issued by PT Bumi Resources, the largest Indonesian producer of coal for electric utilities. And the Corporation agreed on Tuesday to pay $850 million for a 15 per cent stake in the Nobel Group, a diversified commodities company based in Hong Kong with stakes around the world in enterprises like iron ore and sugar mills.

(www.iht.com, 25 September 2009)

The Australian government rejected Chinese investments in two mining projects on Thursday [25 September] ... The Foreign Investment Review Board in Australia said on Thursday that the government preferred that foreign state-owned companies buy less than 50 per cent stakes in small or undeveloped Australian mines, and stakes of less than 15 per cent in big mining operations ... Two Australian government agencies chose different reasons on Thursday for rejecting investments in Australian mines by companies controlled by the Chinese government. The Foreign Investment Review Board demanded that the China Nonferrous Metal Mining Company reduce its $220 million investment in the Lynas Corporation and acquire less than 50 per cent of the company, instead of a planned 51.6 per cent [agreed on 1 May 2009], and receive fewer seats on the board. The Chinese company responded by pulling out of the deal ... Lynas is developing one of the world's largest mines outside China for the production of so-called rare earths, a group of chemical elements that are crucial for things as varied as missiles, cellphones and wind turbines ... Australia's defence department blocked plan by Wuhan Iron and Steel Group of China to invest $40 million in a fifty–fifty joint venture with Western Plains Resources to develop an iron ore project directly under the flight path of Australia's missile tests.

(www.iht.com, 25 September 2009; *IHT*, 26 September 2009, p. 18)

The Chinese state-owned chemical firm Sinochem bid $2.5 billion on Monday [28 September] for the Australian farm chemicals groups Nufarm ... Nufarm is in the manufacturing industry where the foreign investment regime [in Australia] has generally been more liberal ... So far this year [2009] Chinese companies have invested about $5 billion in Australian companies ... Last month [August] China's biggest steelmaker, Baosteel, agreed to buy a 15 per cent stake in iron ore explorer Aquila Resources for $240 million. China is Australia's biggest export market, with two-way trade worth $53 billion last year [2008].

(www.iht.com, 28 September 2009)

China's outbound direct investment more than doubled last year [2008] from 2007, reaching $56 billion according to the ministry of commerce. But Chatham House, the London-based think-tank, estimates it could have been double that figure. China has gone from annual outward direct investment of just $140 million in 2002 to being the sixth largest source of outward direct investment last year.

(*FT*, Survey, 1 October 2009, p. 4)

General Motors (MG) agreed to sell its Hummer brand to Chinese firm Sichuan Tengzhong Heavy Industrial Machinery for an undisclosed fee ... Tengzong will take an 80 per cent stake in the company, with the remaining 20 per cent going to Hong Kong entrepreneur Suolong Duoji. The current Hummer management team will continue to run the company.

(www.bbc.co.uk, 10 October 2009)

General Motors said Friday [9 October] that it would sell its Hummer brand, once a crucial part of its strategy to expand its line-up of sport utility vehicles, to a Chinese heavy equipment maker and a private investor. The sale ... is another step in GM's rapid downsizing after an emergency from a government-financed bankruptcy ... The automaker is 60 per cent owned by the [US] government ... GM's talks with Sichuan Tengzhong were disclosed in June [2009], and the agreement is still subject to regulatory approvals by the Chinese government. No terms were announced, but people with knowledge of the deal estimated the price at $150 million.

(www.iht.com, 10 October 2009)

'GM's earlier estimate [was] that the brand could fetch more than $500 million' (www.iht.com, 12 October 2009).

Iraq's cabinet has ratified a new deal with two foreign energy companies to develop the giant southern oilfield in Rumaila. The contract with Britain's BP and CNPC of China is the first major deal with foreign firms since the international auction in June ... Iraq has the world's third largest oil reserves, but production lags behind the potential due to a lack of investment ... BP and CNPC agreed to run the Rumaila field – near the southern city of Basra – after the US giant Exxon Mobil turned it down ... The British company will hold a 38 per cent stake in the venture, compared to CNPC's 37 per cent share, while Iraq's State Oil Marketing organization will control the remaining 25 per cent.

(www.bbc.co.uk, 18 October 2009)

'China satisfies just 14 per cent of its [oil] needs through its overseas production' (*FT*, 4 November 2009, p. 12).

Estimates of Chinese investment in Africa range upward from $6 billion as China tries to lock up oil, natural gas and other key resources ... Estimates for total loans, investment and aid donations – often difficult to distinguish from each other – run closer to $50 billion ... Trade has soared ten times since 2001, passing the $100 billion mark last year [2008], according to the Chinese trade ministry.

(*IHT*, 28 October 2009, p. 18)

A consortium of Chinese and American companies announced a joint venture on Thursday [29 October] to build a 600 megawatt wind farm in West Texas, using turbines made in China. Construction of the $1.5 billion wind farm will be financed largely by Chinese banks, with the help of loan guarantees and cash grants from the US government ... The wind farm will be the first instance of a Chinese manufacturer exporting wind turbines to the United States.

(www.iht.com, 30 October 2009)

Suntech, China's largest solar panel manufacturer, plans to open its first American plant near Phoenix, the company announced on Monday [16 November]. The plant is to begin production in the third quarter of 2010 and will initially employ seventy-five people, probably rising over time to 200 ... [Suntech] would not say how much it would cost to build the plant ... [but] the company has applied for a 30 per cent investment tax credit from the stimulus package that applies to solar manufacturing in the United States ... The Phoenix plant will make the panels out of solar cells shipped in from China. Suntech estimates that it already has about 12 per cent to 13 per cent market share in the United States ... with a goal of reaching 20 per cent by the end of 2010 ... Suntech has been under scrutiny as American manufacturers fear being overwhelmed by cheap Chinese panels. Suntech's chief executive, Shi Zhengrong, told *The New York Times* in August that his company was selling panels to American customers for less than the cost of the materials, assembly and shipping, in an effort to build market share. But he swiftly reversed his comments.

(www.iht.com, 16 November 2009)

Huawei Technologies ... a Chinese equipment maker ... [is] the rising star of the mobile equipment industry, whose low-cost, multipurpose networks have catapulted it to number two in the world behind Ericsson ... Supplying gear to China's three big operators – China Mobile, China Telecom and China Unicom – helped Huawei almost double its share of the $38 billion global mobile equipment market to 20.1 per cent in the third quarter [of 2009] from 11 per cent a year earlier ... Huawei moved past Nokia Siemens, at 19.5 per cent, and trails Ericsson, which has 32 per cent. ZTE, China's second largest maker of networking equipment, is also growing rapidly as Chinese operators roll out mainland China's first 3G network this year [2009] ... Huawei has grown beyond China's borders, with foreign orders accounting for 75 per cent of its $18.3 billion in 2008 sales, up 43 per cent from a year earlier ... [Huawei says it is] owned by its 80,000 employees and has no links to Chinese officialdom ... A 2007 report by the Rand Corp., a policy research group, for the US Air Force, said Huawei 'maintains deep ties with the Chinese military, which serves a multifaceted role as an important customer, as well as Huawei's political patron and research development partner' ... Security concerns motivated the Committee on Foreign Investment, a US government panel, to reject Huawei's joint $2.2

billion bid with Bain Capital in 2008 for 3Com, a US communications equipment maker that produces anti-hacking software for the US military.

(www.iht.com, 29 November 2009; *IHT*, 30 November 2009, p. 14)

General Motors [GM] has reached an agreement to sell about half of its India operations and a small stake in its China business to its main joint venture partner in China, people with a detailed knowledge of the transaction said on Thursday [3 December]. GM's main partner in China [is] the Shanghai Automotive Industry Corporation, better known as SAIC … GM has become the second largest automaker in China mainly through a fifty–fifty venture with SAIC that makes a wide range of GM-designed cars. Under the deal being completed, GM would sell a 1 per cent stake in the venture to SAIC, raising the Chinese automaker's share to 51 per cent, although GM would retain equal voting rights in company decisions and have an option to buy back the stake later … GM is separately putting its Indian operations into a new joint venture with SAIC, effectively selling about half of the operations to SAIC as well.

(www.iht.com, 3 December 2009)

GM's sale Friday [4 December] of a 1 per cent stake in its main joint venture in China, coupled with a new India venture with its China partner, should provide the US automaker with about $400 million at a time when its overseas operations need cash to restructure and expand. GM said it would sell the 1 per cent stake in its main joint venture in China, Shanghai Automotive Industry Corp., for $85 million. It also said it would put its wholly owned India operations into a fifty–fifty venture with SAIC, with the Chinese company contributing $300 million to $350 million … GM began setting up a series of ventures with it in 1997 to enter the Chinese market. SAIC has learned a lot from GM since then and has started to build its own cars outside the alliance with GM. It also has a venture with Volkswagen. The Chinese government has long limited foreign automakers to no more than a 50 per cent stake in auto assembly plants in the country, and it shows no signs of lifting that limit … [GM] said Friday that the 51 per cent stake would give SAIC the right to approve the venture's budget, future plans and senior management. But the venture has a co-operative spirit in which SAIC has already been able to do so … In a separate transaction, GM and SAIC will set up an equally owned investment company based in Hong Kong. GM will put in its India assets, and SAIC will be the main provider of the $300 million to $350 million in extra investment for expansion needed to make the overall venture worth $650 million.

(www.iht.com, 4 December 2009)

Even as other potential buyers circle Saab, Beijing Automotive Industry Holding [BAIC] has struck a tentative agreement for the right to produce several of the beleaguered Swedish manufacturer's models. If completed, people close to the negotiations said Sunday [13 December], the agreement would allow Beijing Automotive to produce older versions of the Saab 9-3 and 9-5 in China, but not prevent a separate deal for the entire company, a unit of GM ... The deal would not cover Saab's brand-new version of the 9-5, a luxury sedan, which is scheduled to arrive in showrooms in April [2010]. It is the first update of Saab's top-end car in twelve years ... A new version of the 9-3 was also in the works, but the timing of its debut was uncertain ... The fate of Saab's 3,500 workers in Sweden was uncertain following the unexpected collapse last month [November] of a deal between GM and high-end automaker Koenigsegg for Saab ... Beijing Automotive was one of Koenigsegg's backers in the earlier acquisition plan, potentially contributing $200 million to $300 million toward the deal ... In October [2009] Ford announced that China's Zhejiang Geeling Holding Group was its preferred bidder for Volvo, Saab's more successful Swedish archrival. Volvo sells about 400,000 cars globally compared with Saab's 100,000 each year.

(www.iht.com, 13 December 2009; *IHT*, 14 December 2009, pp. 1, 16)

'BAIC is acquiring "certain Saab 9-3, current 9-5 and powertrain technology and tooling", the companies said in a statement' (www.iht.com, 15 December 2009; *IHT*, 15 December 2009, p. 20).

'GM emerged from bankruptcy protection in July this year [2009] ... The company is now 62 per cent owned by the US government' (www.bbc.co.uk, 20 December 2009).

GM announced Friday [18 December] that it would wind down Saab operations after talks to sell the company collapsed ... GM said that after the withdrawal of Koenigsegg Group last month [November], GM had been in discussions with Spyker Cars about its interest in acquiring Saab. But during the talks certain issues arose that both parties believe could not be resolved, leading to a decision to end the discussions.

(www.iht.com, 18 December 2009)

Spyker Cars, the tiny Dutch automaker ... came back Sunday [20 December] with a renewed offer ... Publicly, GM executives declined to identify their problems with Spyker, but several officials familiar with the negotiations said GM was troubled by Spyker's reliance on Russian loans to finance the deal, as well as the fate of its proprietary technology under Spyker. The biggest investor in Spyker is the Russian bank Convers Group, which is controlled by Alexander Antonov, a tycoon who was shot seven times and reportedly lost a finger in a failed assassination attempt in Moscow in March. His son, Vladimir, is a top executive at Convers and chairman of Spyker. In the first half of 2009 Spyker borrowed Euro 11.6 billion ($16.6 million) from Bank Snoras, a Lithuanian bank also controlled by the Antonovs. Another snag had been the question of whether Spyker could win a Euro 400 million ($573 million) loan from the European Investment Bank that had been part of a previous plan to sell Saab to Koenigsegg, a Swedish maker of high-end sports cars ... [On Sunday Spyker said it] could complete the deal without the European Investment Bank's help.

(*IHT*, 21 December 2009, p. 13)

GM said Tuesday [26 January] that it had struck a preliminary deal to sell Saab to Spyker Cars, a tiny Dutch maker of high-end sports cars ... Spyker will give GM $74 million in cash and $326 million in preferred shares of the new, combined Saab–Spyker entity ... A previous bid from Spyker was rejected by GM in late December [2009] because GM was uncomfortable with Spyker's Russian backers, according to several people familiar with the negotiations ... The biggest investor in Spyker is the Russian bank Convers Group, which is controlled by Alexander Antonov. In March [2009] Mr Antonov was shot seven times and reportedly lost a finger in an attempt on his life in Moscow. His son Vladimir is a top official at Convers and the chairman of Spyker. In the first half of 2009 Spyker borrowed $16.3 billion from Bank Snoras, a Lithuanian bank also controlled by the Antonovs ... [The new package does] not rely as heavily on Russian finance and addresses GM's fears that Saab's latest technology could fall into the hands of its Russian competitors.

(*IHT*, 27 January 2009, pp. 1, 22)

'The Swedish government has agreed to guarantee a Euro 400 million ($563 million) loan Saab had requested from the European Investment Bank' (www. bbc.co.uk, 27 January 2009).

GM can claim to be getting $500 million for Saab. Spyker will pay about $74 million in cash. In addition, GM will receive preference shares worth $326 million in Saab–Spyker Automobiles and will keep about $100 million from Saab's operating capital ... Spyker's chief executive Victor Muller's investment company Tenaci Capital BV agreed to buy out the 29 per cent holding in Spyker of Vladimir Antonov, a Russian investor. Mr Antonov will also leave Spyker's supervisory board. One reason GM decided at the last moment not to sell its Opel/Vauxhall division to a consortium involving Sberbank, a state-owned Russian bank, was the fear of intellectual property finding its way to Russia.

(www.economist.com, 28 January 2010: *The Economist*, 30 January 2010, p. 82)

The Russian investor Vladimir Antonov has sold his stake in Spyker Cars and resigned as chairman after the Dutch automaker completed the purchase of GM's Saab unit ... The shares were sold to Tenaci Capital, a company controlled by the Spyker chief executive, Victor Muller ... GM's agreement to sell Saab to Spyker called for Mr Antonov to sell his 29.9 per cent stake in Spyker and resign as chairman.

(*IHT*, 24 February 2010, p. 21)

On Friday [11 December] Royal Dutch Shell, in partnership with Malaysia's Petronas, won the right to develop Majnoon, one of the world's biggest untapped oilfields. CNPC, China's largest oil and gas producer, with

Petronas and France's Total were also awarded a contract to extract oil from Halfaya beating off competition from other European, American and Asian oil companies. On Saturday [12 December] Russia's Lukoil and Norway's Statoil got their hands on the biggest prize on offer, West Qurna-2. Although several of the fields under the hammer on Friday and Saturday failed to find buyers this latest auction of Iraq's oil is already more successful than the previous effort ... The fields that attracted little or no interest were the ones located in the more dangerous eastern parts of Iraq, near Baghdad or near Mosul in the north of the country.

(www.economist.com, 12 December 2009)

'Shell will operate the [Majnoon] project and hold a 45 per cent share, with Petronas (Malaysia's state oil company) having a 30 per cent share and the rest being held by Iraq' (www.cnn.com, 12 December 2009).

Lukoil of Russia and Statoil of Norway on Tuesday [29 December] formally signed a contract with Iraqi authorities to develop the West Qurna 2 oil field. The untapped reserves are seen as critical to Iraqi reconstruction efforts ... The field [is] in Basra province, in the south of the country ... Lukoil was originally granted rights to develop West Qurna 2 in 1997 by Saddam Hussein, but he rescinded the contract early this decade ... Statoil said Tuesday that it had renegotiated the terms of the deal to give it a somewhat larger stake than was originally foreseen. Under the new terms Statoil will eventually hold 18.75 per cent of the consortium, with Lukoil holding 56.25 per cent and a partner from the Iraqi state holding the remainder.

(www.iht.com, 30 December 2009)

The return will be fairly negligible ... Firms like Lukoil and Statoil are eager to snap up fields in Iraq – even on terms that may offer little immediate reward – to deepen their involvement in a country that appears poised to become a top-tier producer ... Iraq ranks third in the world in terms of proven reserves, behind Saudi Arabia and Russia but ahead of Iran.

(*IHT*, 30 December 2009, p. 14)

China ... is increasingly known for shipping out inexpensive labour. These global migrants often toil in factories or on Chinese-run construction and engineering projects, though the range of jobs across 180 countries is astonishing ... But a backlash against them has grown. Across Asia and Africa incidents of protest and violence against Chinese workers have flared. Vietnam and India are among the countries that have moved to impose new labour rules this year [2009] for foreign companies and to restrict the number of Chinese workers allowed to enter, straining diplomatic relations with Beijing ... From Angola to Uzbekistan, and Iran to Indonesia, some 740,000 Chinese workers were abroad at the end of 2008, with 58 per cent sent out last year [2008] alone ... The numbers going abroad this year are on track to roughly match that rate. Chinese workers are not always less expensive, but they tend to be more skilled and easier to manage than local workers, Chinese executives say … Vietnam had a $10 billion trade deficit with China last year. In July a senior [Vietnamese] official … said that 35,000 Chinese workers were in Vietnam … A half-million Vietnamese are working in fourteen countries and territories … Populist anger erupted this year over a contract that the Vietnamese government gave to Aluminium Corp. of China to mine bauxite, one of Vietnam's most valuable natural resources, using Chinese workers. Dissidents, intellectuals and environmental advocates protested. General Vo Nguyen Giap, the revered ninety-eight-year-old military leader, wrote three open letters criticizing the Chinese presence to Vietnamese party leaders … Over the summer the central government shut down critical blogs, detained dissidents and ordered Vietnamese newspapers to cease reporting on Chinese labour and the bauxite issue. But in a nod to public pressure, the government also tightened visa and work permit requirements for Chinese and deported 182 Chinese labourers from a cement plant in June, saying they were working illegally. Hanoi generally bans the import of skilled workers from abroad and requires foreign contractors to hire Vietnamese for civil works projects, though that rule is sometimes violated by Chinese companies – well placed bribes can persuade officials to look the other way, Chinese executives say.

(*IHT*, 21 December 2009, p. 16)

A company controlled by the Chinese government has notified the Obama administration that it is withdrawing its application to buy a Nevada gold mining company to avoid a conflict after federal officials raised 'serious, significant and consequential national security' concerns. The decision by Northwest Nonferrous International Investment Company, at least for now, eliminates a showdown over the tiny company, the Firstgold Corporation. The Treasury Department on Monday [21 December] was prepared to recommend that President Obama block the deal … Officials at the Treasury Department, which oversees the review panel known formally as the Committee on Foreign Investment in the United States, have not publicly said what the explicit cause of the security concern is, as the process is confidential. But in meetings with Firstgold executives the federal officials cited the proximity of the company's four Nevada properties – most of which operate on leased federal land – to the Fallon Naval Air Station, as well as 'other sensitive and classified security and military assets that cannot be identified', according to a summary of a conference call held last week. Northwest Nonferrous is a giant Chinese-run mining company, with more than 6,000 employees, that is in the midst of a push to expand its global presence by buying up mines, or investment in mining operations, including in the south-west Yukon section of Canada.

(www.iht.com, 21 December 2009)

The decision by Northwest International Investment averts a showdown over its proposed $26 million purchase of a 51 per cent stake in Firstgold … US government officials have repeatedly cited the proximity of Firstgold's four Nevada properties to the Fallon Naval Air Station, where pilots test laser-guided weapons.

(*IHT*, 23 December 2009, p. 17)

Ford Motor and Zhejiang Geely Holding Group said Wednesday [23 December] that they had settled 'all substantial commercial terms' on a sale of Volvo, clearing the way for the Chinese automaker to purchase the Swedish business early next year [2010] ... The companies did not disclose a price ... Ford paid $6 billion in 1999 to buy Volvo; unconfirmed reports have said that Zhejiang Geely could pay $2 billion for the unit in the currently depressed market for automakers ... Geely is the largest private automaker in China ... Ford said it would continue to co-operate with Volvo in several areas, but it did not intend to retain a stake in the Swedish company ... Ford was the only Detroit automaker to avoid bankruptcy this year [2009], as GM and Chrysler were bailed out by taxpayers, with the latter ending up under the wing of Fiat.

(www.iht.com, 23 December 2009)

Neither company would comment on the price, though sources close to the deal say it is in the region of $1.8 billion to $2 billion ... Geely will take over Volvo's international manufacturing and sales network, but will also manufacture Volvos in China.

(www.cnn.com, 23 December 2009; *IHT*, 24 December 2009, p. 14)

Two years ago the China Metallurgical Group Corporation [MCC], a state-owned conglomerate, bid $3.4 billion – $1 billion more than any of its competitors from Canada, Europe, Russia, the United States and Kazakhstan – for the rights to mine deposits near the village of Aynack ... about twenty miles south-east of Kabul ... [This is] the single largest investment in Afghan history ... The Chinese bid far more for the mining rights to the Aynack project and promised to invest hundreds of millions more in associated infrastructure projects than other bidders ... MCC will build a 400-megawatt generating plant to power both the copper mine and blackout-prone Kabul. MCC will dig a new coal mine to feed the plant's generators. It will build a smelter to refine copper ore, and a railroad to carry coal to the power plant and copper back to China. If the terms of the contract are to be believed, MCC will also build schools, roads, even mosques for the Afghans ... To minimize corruption, the Afghan government decided, on the advice of American advisers, to ask the World Bank and a Colorado geological consulting firm to help oversee the bidding ... China promised to staff the entire venture with Afghan labourers and managers – many of whom must be trained from scratch in a country with little mining expertise. [It is claimed that] after five years it's only Afghan engineers ... Only in administration do the Chinese stay.

(www.iht.com, 30 December 2009; *IHT*, 31 December 2009, pp. 1, 16)

Canada's industry minister, Tony Clement, has given PetroChina the go-ahead for a $1.7 billion acquisition of two oil sand projects. The deal gives the Chinese company 60 per cent control of Athabasca Oil Sands Corporation's MacKay and Dover oil sands deposits in Alberta province. The two are projected to yield 5 million barrels of oil ... The sands contain the second biggest store of oil in the world. They are estimated to hold 175 billion barrels of oil. Only Saudi Arabia holds more. But it is tricky – and costly – to extract oil from such sands ... The Chinese company made a commitment to contribute more than $250 million to cover its share of developing the oil sands projects over the next three years.

(www.bbc.co.uk, 30 December 2009)

Australia and China ... signed a $3 billion coal deal Wednesday [6 January 2010] Felix Resources [was purchased] by Yanzhou Coal Mining ... The buy-out was the biggest by a Chinese company in Australian mining history and among the top ten mergers and acquisitions in Australia in 2009.

(www.iht.com, 6 January 2010)

By the end of 2008 China's total overseas assets reached $2,920 billion, of which only 6 per cent, or $169.4 billion, was overseas direct investments. Almost 70 per cent, or $2,000 billion, was held in foreign exchange reserves, while 9 per cent was portfolio investments and 18 per cent was other investments such as trade finance and bank loans.

(*FT*, 18 December 2009, p. 13)

China's sovereign wealth fund quietly snapped up more than $9 billion worth of shares last year [2009] in some of the biggest American corporations, including Morgan Stanley, Bank of America and Citigroup. Although most of the stakes were small, China Investment Corp. [CIC], the government's $300 billion investment fund, now owns stock in some of the best known American brands, including Apple, Coca-Cola, Johnson & Johnson, Motorola and Visa. The detailed list, which contained holdings totalling $9.6 billion as of 31 December 2009, was disclosed Friday [5 February] in a filing with the US Securities and Exchange Commission; it lists stakes only in companies traded in the United States ... CIC, already one of the world's largest sovereign funds, was formed in 2007 with about $200 billion. It now has assets of nearly $300 billion and ... is expecting another large injection of funds ... Analysts said the filing showed that the fund had invested only a small portion of its $300 in American stocks and the fund seemed to be following a cautious strategy to diversify globally after initially having put its biggest investments into shoring up the capital of Chinese banks ... The sovereign fund got off to a rocky start in 2007 and early 2008 by acquiring a $3 billion non-voting stake in the American private equity firm Blackstone and paying another $5 billion for a 9.9 per cent stake in Morgan Stanley. Shares of both plummeted in 2008 during the financial crisis, leading to a storm of criticism directed at CIC. But analysts say the fund performed well in 2009, particularly because it was buying aggressively as the market recovered ... CIC's acquisition of non-voting units of Blackstone and its early stake of preferred shares in Morgan

Stanley are not listed in the filing. The Blackstone and Morgan Stanley stakes are not listed, apparently because they are not traded equities … Most sovereign funds, with the exception of Norway's, disclose few details about their holdings.

(www.iht.com, 8 February 2010; *IHT*, 9 February 2010, p. 16)

Hostility from Chinese regulators and bank financing problems have raised two potentially insurmountable obstacles to plans by an obscure Chinese machinery company to buy GM's Hummer division, people close to the negotiations said Tuesday [24 February] … Privately owned Sichuan Tengzhong Heavy Industrial Machinery Co. has failed to win regulatory approval for the transaction at a time when senior Chinese officials are trying to put new emphasis on environmental responsibility.

(www.iht.com, 23 February 2010)

'GM's deal to sell its Hummer brand … fell through Wednesday [25 February] and the company said it now plans to shut down the brand' (www.cnn.com, 25 February 2010).

GM said on Wednesday [25 February] that it would shut down Hummer … after a deal to sell it fell apart … Sichuan Tengzhong Heavy Industrial Machines said that it had withdrawn its bid because it was unable to receive approval from the Chinese government, which was trying to put a new emphasis on limiting China's dependence on imported oil and protecting the environment. Tight financial markets also hurt the deal. When the commerce ministry did not bless the transaction, Chinese banks became reluctant to lend money to Tengzhong, even though it tried to set up an overseas subsidiary to buy Hummer. That left Tengzhong trying to borrow money from Western banks … A spokesman for Hummer … said GM had no specific timetable for completing its wind-down, but left open the possibility that GM would be open for new bids.

(www.iht.com, 25 February 2010; *IHT*, 26 February 2010, p. 18)

'Government officials in Beijing said they had never received the necessary application for approval and thus could not grant it' (*IHT*, 27 February 2010, p. 6).

China's state-owned energy company CNOOC is to take a 50 per cent stake in Argentina's Bridas in a $3.1 billion deal that marks the latest move by Beijing to secure energy resources … The deal will make CNOOC a partner of Britain's BP in Pan American Energy, a joint venture with coveted oil and gas exploration and production activities across Latin America and in which Bridas has a 40 per cent stake … The transaction will add about 3 per cent to CNOOC's reserves.

(*FT*, 15 March 2010, p. 15)

'Bridas holds a 40 per cent stake in oil business Pan American Energy, which is 60 per cent owned by UK group BP' (www.bbc.co.uk, 15 March 2010).

'Bridas also has gas operations in Turkmenistan' (*IHT*, 17 March 2010, p. 21).

China and Taiwan

Under the ... policy imposed in 1996 ... businesses in Taiwan are not allowed to undertake any mainland-bound investment project worth more than $50 million and infrastructure sectors are also banned ... Many companies skirt this ban by channelling investments through third countries ... Taiwan entrepreneurs are estimated to have invested more than $40 billion in China since the commencement of civil contacts in late 1987.

(*IHT*, 6 September 2000, p. 20)

'The government on Friday [29 March 2002] eased a ban on computer-chip investments in China ... Companies would be allowed to produce less advanced computer chips in China as long as they are making more sophisticated ones in Taiwan' (*IHT*, 30 March 2002, p. 12).

Taiwan's parliament approved measures to allow mainland Chinese to invest in the island's property, the latest in a string of steps to encourage mainland companies to put money into Taiwan. Lawmakers also approved the final reading of regulations exempting profits and dividends earned by local companies in China from domestic taxes when repatriated. The property move comes after Taiwan lifted a ban on local [micro] chip makers building plants on the mainland but set tough rules for what is considered a strategic industry by limiting construction to three plants by 2005.

(*FEER*, 11 April 2002, p. 25)

'Taiwan's accumulated investment in China [amounted] to $29.32 billion by the end of 2001' (*FEER*, 21 February 2002, p. 29).

Taiwan relaxed restrictions on direct trading with mainland China and lifted a ban on importing 2,000 Chinese farm and industrial products. In addition, Taiwanese and Chinese banks will be allowed to make direct remittances, but they will be restricted to currencies other than the new Taiwan dollar and Chinese renminbi.

(*FEER*, 28 February 2002, p. 26)

Taiwan's state-owned Chinese petroleum and its Chinese counterpart, China Offshore Oil, signed a landmark pact $25 million yesterday [16 May 2002] to explore jointly for oil and natural gas in the Taiwan Strait, which separates the island from China. This is the first big joint venture between state-run companies since ... 1949.

(*FT*, 17 May 2002, p. 11)

[In May 2002] state-owned oil companies from both sides signed a landmark joint exploration deal. Chinese Petroleum Corporation of Taiwan and China National Offshore Oil Corporation, China's biggest offshore-energy company, will set up a 50–50 joint venture to look for oil and gas in the Tainan Basin between Taiwan and China.

(*FEER*, 30 May 2002, p. 24)

'With or without government approval, Taiwan businessmen have poured an estimated $70 billion of investment into the mainland since Taipei relaxed restrictions in 1987' (*IHT* 26 August 2002, p. 9).

'China last year [2001] replaced the United States as Taiwan's biggest export market' (*FEER*, 20 June 2002, p. 21).

Taiwan's cabinet ... yesterday [13 April 2005] passed draft technology protection legislation ... If the legislature adopts the bill the transfer or export of advanced technology by individuals or companies to China will require approval by [the government] ... At present investments from $50 million upwards are subject to approval.

(*FT*, 14 April 2005, p. 11)

Taiwanese government-approved direct investment on the mainland stands at a cumulative $48 billion, ranking Taiwan alongside Japan and the United States as an investor in China. However, the island's central bank estimates that the total is in fact as high as $70 billion and private estimates put the amount at more than $100 billion – in either case placing it second only to Hong Kong in the scale of its exposure. But under measures announced last month [March] the island's government will approve mainland investments larger than $100 million, or those of any size that relate to sensitive technology, only if the company allows on-the-ground checks in China by Taiwanese state-appointed auditors, negotiates the remittance of profits and undertakes also to invest within Taiwan ... [The Taiwanese government says that] '70 per cent of our foreign direct investment went to the mainland last year [2005]' ... Taipei has opened up many sectors but bans remain in banking and parts of the technology, infrastructure and petrochemical industries. The most widely used loophole – one that the latest regulations seek to block – is for Taiwanese businesspeople to invest in China in a personal capacity.

(*FT*, 12 April 2006, p. 15)

'Total Taiwanese investment in China has been estimated at more than $100 billion and the island has a $58 billion trade surplus with the mainland' (www. iht.com, 14 April 2006).

'According to official [Chinese] data ... from 1991 to September of this year [2006] companies from Taiwan invested $53 billion in China' (www.iht.com, 7 November 2006).

Taiwan chipmakers will gain government approval before the end of the year [2006] to use the same level of technology in their factories in China as their global competitors. The Taipei government's long-awaited move to relax restrictions on operations that its semiconductor companies run on the

Chinese mainland is intended to prevent companies such as Taiwan Semi-conductor Manufacturing, the world's largest chip maker, from losing global market share.

(*FT*, 13 November 2006, p. 16)

Estimates of total Taiwan holdings on the mainland run as high as $280 billion ... At least 1.2 million of the ... people of Taiwan have moved to the mainland, providing a wealth of management expertise ... [The 1.2 million] is 5 per cent of the population, but much larger than 5 per cent ... [for] key people aged twenty-five to forty-five.

(*IHT*, 20 October 2007, p. 19)

'Cumulative Taiwanese investment in China ... by one [Taiwanese] government estimate ... has reached $150 billion' (*FEER*, March 2008, p. 34).

The government [of Taiwan] in February [2008] approved Fubon Bank's purchase of 20 per cent of Xiamen Commercial Bank through Fubon's Hong Kong subsidiary. This would be the first acquisition of a stake in a Chinese financial institution by a Taiwan bank. Fubon still needs the approval of Beijing's State Council and Taiwan Affairs Office ... Recently the government [of Taiwan] lifted a ban on mainland firms investing in commercial property in Taiwan ... In 2007 bilateral trade was worth $125 billion, an increase of 15.4 per cent over 2006 ... Taiwan had a surplus of $77 billion. China is also Taiwan's number one foreign investment destination. According to mainland figures, Taiwan firms had, as of September 2007, set up 74,327 projects in China with total investment of $45.1 billion. But unofficial estimates, including investment via third countries, put the figure at $100 billion, making Taiwan the top foreign investor in China ... [There is at present] a Democratic Progressive Party government limit of 1,000 mainland tourists a day.

(www.economist.com, 17 March 2008)

Taiwanese investment on the mainland has dropped by nearly half during Chen Shui-bian's nearly eight years in office, to about $2 billion a year, as he enforced limits on how much capital could be invested by Taiwanese companies on the mainland – limits that [President-elect] Ma Ying-jeou said he would lift.

(*IHT*, 25 March 2008, p. 12)

China is already Taiwan's largest trading partner and investment destination for Taiwanese companies ... Cumulative investment FDI ... in China ... might be close to $300 billion, according to the [Taiwanese] government's latest estimates – which would make Taiwan China's largest source of FDI ... [Critics say that] the ceiling [set by Taiwan] which limits companies' investments in China at 40 per cent of their net worth has failed to discourage them from mainland investments. It has just discouraged them from repatriating profits to Taiwan for fear of not being able to use the funds for further expansion on the mainland ... The government [currently] bans the sale on the island of mutual funds that invest more than a tiny portion in China-linked equities.

(*FT*, 26 March 2008, p. 13)

Government initiatives to promote cross-strait business opportunities, such as tourism, have had little success so far. Beijing's concern over allowing too many of its citizens to visit democratic Taiwan has meant there was just a trickle of tourists last year [2008], when Taiwan's public and its aggressive media were expecting a flood of wealthy Chinese spenders. Only last month [April 2009] did tourist numbers finally reach the daily quota of 3,000 visitors ... The [Chinese] government-owned China Mobile proposed to take a 12 per cent stake in FarEasTone, a Taiwanese mobile operator, in the first mainland investment in a Taiwan-listed company.

(*FT*, 7 May 2009, p. 15)

[On 29 April China mobile said that it would buy 12 per cent of FarEasTone Telecommunications, a big Taiwanese mobile operator ... The deal will need government approval ... The number of [regular] flights increased from thirty-six a week to more than 100 a week in December [2008], and again to 270 from 26 April. Taiwan is pushing for the number to double again. Along with closer ties in aviation and telecoms, several other potential agreements have come from the thaw between Taipei and Beijing, starting with direct discussions between Chinese and Taiwanese financial regulators on greater co-operation. Taiwan will also open up to direct Chinese investment in services, manufacturing, property and rail projects. Taiwan has invested in China for decades, and by some reckoning more than 5 per cent of Taiwan's population now lives on the mainland in order to do business there. But Taiwan itself has long felt that it was too small, and China too threatening, to allow reciprocal ownership.

(*The Economist*, 9 May 2009, pp. 71–2)

China Mobile's bid for a 12 per cent stake in Taiwan's FarEasTone was dealt a blow yesterday [12 May] when Taiwan's economics minister said the island would not immediately allow Chinese investment into its telecommunications operators ... Sixty-five manufacturing sectors would be opened to Chinese investors in the first phase of liberalization. These include the automobile, textiles and rubber industries, but not more sensitive sectors such as telecommunications, semiconductors or flat panels.

(*FT*, 13 May 2009, p. 24)

Commenting on China Mobile's plans to take a stake in FarEasTone, the Taiwan mobile operator ... which would be the first Chinese investment in a listed Taiwan company ... the island's premier ... Liu Chao-shiuan ... said the two companies 'must amend their plans' when the economics ministry announces its detailed rules for Chinese investment next month [June].

(*FT*, 21 May 2009, p. 7)

Taiwan has invested about $150 billion in the mainland since the 1980s, according to one Taiwan government estimate. Mainland China has until now been barred from directly investing in Taiwan ... [On] 26 April representatives from Taipei and Beijing met in the mainland city of Nanjing and signed a statement on financial co-operation. Three days later Taiwan said it would allow mainland investment in nearly 100 sectors. It also said it would permit mainland investment in construction projects that are part of President Ma Ying-jeou's multibillion dollar economic stimulus package ... On 1 May China formally approved Taiwan-bound investment by qualified domestic institutional investors. Four days later it announced a plan to ramp up development of a cross-strait economic zone in Fujian province ... Taiwan will likely allow mainland investment in ninety-eight industries during the first phase, including automobiles, textiles, rubber and retailing, with detailed rules probably coming at month-end, the Taiwan minister of economic affairs, Yiin Chii-ming, told reporters this weekend. But flat panel and contract chip manufacturing will be shut to mainland investors for now ... Some media reports have portrayed ... the ballyhooed tie-up between China Mobile and FarEasTone ... as a done deal ... But the economy minister said this week that telecommunications would not be one of the first sectors opened to mainland investment ... For now Beijing is capping Taiwan-bound investment at about $219 million.

(www.iht.com, 13 May 2009; *IHT*, 14 May 2009, p. 17)

China and Taiwan agreed on the substance of a financial co-operation deal signed this week .... On the mainland about 1 million Taiwanese live and work, and Taiwanese firms have invested at least $15 billion ... Until now Taiwanese banks have been allowed to set up only representative offices that cannot do business. After the new deal takes effect in January [2010] Taiwanese banks ... will eventually be able to upgrade those offices into branches, allowing them to lend to Taiwanese firms on the mainland and do other business ... It paves the way for securities firms to open branches on the opposite side of the strait. And it will permit China's qualified domestic institutional investors to invest in Taiwanese stocks, bonds and futures ... The agreement on insurance was mostly symbolic, and the two sides have not discussed market access ... The Taiwanese government has said it does not need legislative approval for most cross-Strait deals. But it has agreed to seek such approval before signing a broader trade deal with Beijing, which it hopes to do next year [2010].

(www.iht.com, 19 November 2009)

Conditions for FDI in China

The trend over time has been to improve the conditions for DFI, although foreigners still complain about such problems as the enforcement of property rights

(e.g. enforcing contracts where the legal system is not independent of the Communist Party), counterfeiting and quality control by Chinese partners.
   (See Jeffries 2006a: 591–2.)

The opening up of an increasing number of sectors to FDI

An increasing number of sectors have been made eligible for at least joint ventures. Some of the earlier examples can be found in Jeffries (2006a: 593–601).

More recent chronological developments regarding conditions
affecting FDI

(See Jeffries 2006a: 601–15.)

> [It is said that] UBS, a Swiss bank, has won final approval for a landmark $212 million agreement to take control of troubled brokerage Beijing Securities – the first high-profile deal involving a foreign group to be cleared in months ... The China Securities Regulatory Commission [CSRC] ... [has] approved UBS's purchase of a 20 per cent stake in Beijing Securities ... However, its right to control the management of the venture is believed to have been sanctioned in writing by the State Council, China's powerful cabinet ... An official announcement could come over the next few weeks ... The deal ... would enable the Swiss bank to become the first foreign investment firm to buy directly into one of China's ailing brokerage firms. The regulatory approval follows months during which the authorities hardened their attitude to foreign takeovers of domestic companies in important sectors such as finance and manufacturing ... The CSRC has taken on a sterner, less welcoming attitude to foreign investment in recent months in line with the national mood of increasing antagonism towards overseas buyouts.
>
> (*FT*, 5 April 2006, p. 25)

> The government said Thursday [29 June] that control of major equipment makers should remain in domestic hands, calling into question a planned takeover by the Carlyle Group ... a buy-out fund based in Washington ... of Xugong Group Construction Machinery, the nation's biggest maker of building machinery ... Carlyle has yet to receive the approval of the Chinese government after agreeing to buy 85 per cent of Xugong for $375 million in October [2005] ... Caterpillar, the world's largest maker of earth-moving equipment, entered China in 1996 and now has thirteen jointly or wholly owned companies in the country.
>
> (*IHT*, 30 June 2006, p. 18)

> China said foreign investment in the industrial machinery sector must be approved by the government ... Carlyle ... and Caterpillar ... have both made bids for Chinese makers of construction machinery and both have

been held up by regulatory delays ... Caterpillar's bid for Xiamen Engineering machinery has been held up by disagreements over control of the state-owned company ... The Carlyle bid, which would be the largest private equity deal in China, has come under attack recently after Sany Heavy Industry, another equipment maker, said it would offer a premium for Xugong to keep it in Chinese hands.

(*FT*, 30 June 2006, p. 26)

Kazakhstan's national oil company bought from China's largest oil company a 33 per cent share in a major oil producer operating in the oil-rich Central Asian nation. KazMunaiGaz said it paid China National Petroleum $55 a share for the stake in Canada-based PetroKazakhstan but gave no total value for the deal.

(*IHT*, 6 July 2006, p. 16)

A strip of industrial sprawl and barren semi-wasteland that stretches for 150 kilometres (90 miles) along the northern coast is being turned into a development zone far bigger than either Shanghai's or Shenzhen's. And its planners have been given the central government's blessing to experiment with a wide range of economic and bureaucratic reforms. The government has high hopes for this venture. The Binhai New Area, as the zone is called, is intended to help a swathe of northern China, including Beijing and the provinces around the Bohai Gulf ... Officials want Tianjin city to regain its pre-communist era status as north China's financial capital. Binhai's port, already north China's largest, is due to double its container-handling capacity by 2010 ... Tianjin's leaders established the [Binhai] zone in 1994 but it was not until last year [2005] that the central government gave a clear signal that it regarded this as a project of national importance, not just a local venture ... On 6 June [2006] a central government document declared Binhai to be an 'experimental zone for comprehensive reform'. Hitherto only Pudong New Area, Shanghai's flagship development zone, had enjoyed this title, which it acquired last year. Binhai has emerged as the development zone darling of President Hu Jintao and prime minister Wen Jiabao (himself a native of Tianjin), just as Shenzhen was to ... Deng Xiaoping in the 1980s and Pudong was to ... Jiang Zemin ... Binhai hopes another $20 billion of foreign capital will be invested in the zone by 2010, compared with $15.9 billion between 1994 and the end of last year (most of it in the Tianjin Economic-Technological Development Area, a long-established foreign investment enclave within Binhai).

(*The Economist*, 23 June 2006, p. 77)

The government is drawing up rules that will make it more difficult for overseas investors to buy Chinese assets, a move aimed at curbing inflows of foreign capital to cool China's soaring economic growth. The ministry of commerce will be added to a list of government agencies that must review foreign takeovers and purchases of Chinese assets by offshore shell companies, according to a draft dated 30 June. The government will ban the sale of assets that threaten 'China's economic safety', the document said.

(www.iht.com, 27 July 2006)

The government is strengthening its influence over acquisitions by foreign companies. The planned takeover by the US private equity firm the Carlyle Group of Xugong Group Construction Machinery, the biggest company in its sector in China, is on hold, pending regulatory approval, as the government seeks to restrict the sale of assets to foreigners in some strategic industries.

(*IHT*, 31 July 2006, p. 12)

Foreign investors will be invited to join a $27 billion rail project to connect Beijing with Shenzhen, the state news media reported Thursday [3 August] ... Work on some sections of the railroad has already begun [in 2004] and the entire project is expected to be completed by 2010 ... The new railroad will be solely for passengers, leaving the old track to carry cargo. The project is separate from another multi-billion railroad project to be built between Beijing and Shanghai. This project is also expected to be completed by 2010 and be open to foreign investment.

(www.iht.com, 3 August 2006)

In 2005 58 per cent of exports were produced by companies with either part or total foreign ownership, a statistic some economists believe is inflated when Chinese capital is funnelled through foreign companies to take advantage of tax breaks ... Foreign companies account for as much as one-third of total manufacturing, according to Nicholas Lardy ... In the United States, one of the world's most open economies, about 20 per cent of manufacturing is done by foreign companies.

(www.iht.com, 3 August 2006)

China's new laws make it almost impossible for foreigners to buy investment properties ... The new rules, announced on 24 July by six core economic departments and agencies, closed an investment window that had been open to foreigners for barely more than three years ... There are some exceptions. Chinese living overseas and citizens of Hong Kong and Macao will be allowed to own second homes on the mainland. And a foreigner who has studied or worked in China for at least a year will be allowed to buy a home, but not to become a landlord ... In contrast with the absolute ban on new foreign landlords, the new rules do not block foreign companies from building residential or commercial properties – as long as they meet equity, residence and licensing rules.

(*IHT*, 4 August 2006, p. 17)

China's ministry of commerce yesterday [10 August 2006] published new rules on foreign takeovers designed to ensure standard treatment for acquisitions while protecting 'national economic security' ... The regulations, an expansion on temporary 2003 rules, will for the first time allow foreign companies to use shares as payment for stakes in Chinese ventures, opening a potentially important new financing option. But it is unclear whether the rules will make it harder or easier for foreign takeovers, since officials will retain substantial leeway to block or approve any deals. The ministry said the rules will take effect on 8 September.

(*FT*, 11 August 2006, p. 6)

China plans to impose restrictions on foreign banks gearing up to compete for local currency deposits worth $2 trillion despite a pledge to open this sector to overseas lenders from December [2006] ... Under the terms of China's entry to the WTO, Beijing agreed to open its banking sector to full foreign competition from 11 December, but the Chinese authorities are proposing new regulations that could hamper overseas banks in their efforts to attract retail customers. Representatives of about thirty foreign banks last month opened talks with the China Banking Regulatory Commission on the proposed regulations. The proposed rules would require foreign banks to incorporate in China with a minimum of 1 billion yuan, or $123.3 million, in capital before they could compete with domestic banks for retail customers ... Beijing also plans to stipulate that foreign banks could accept only fixed deposits of more than 1 million yuan from individual local customers, a sum beyond the reach of most Chinese savers ... Some banking specialists say the regulations, while not technically in breach of WTO undertakings, will clearly prevent foreign banks competing with local banks on a level footing. China's cabinet, the State Council, has to approve the draft regulations before they come into force ... China has permitted the sale of minority stakes in its big state-owned banks but the ruling Communist Party maintains tight control over the operations of these lenders ... There are now more than seventy foreign banks in China operating about 230 outlets. Current regulations restrict these banks to foreign currency loans and deposits. They can also offer local currency services to enterprises and companies in twenty-five major cities.

(*IHT*, 6 September 2006, p. 16)

'The draft rules contain restrictive measures the [foreign] banks had not expected. They would require, for example, foreign banks to incorporate in China – posing additional legal and bureaucratic hurdles' (www.iht.com, 5 September 2006).

The national development and reform commission's five-year plan ... [intends] to guide China's use of foreign investment between 2006 and 2010 ... [It] highlights the need to combat overseas-controlled monopolies that could threaten 'national economic security' ... [and] complains that local governments have failed to focus on the 'quality' of foreign funding ... The policy document states: 'In some industries increasing numbers of leading enterprises are being acquired by foreign investment; in some sectors there are foreign-invested monopolies or signs of the rapid creation of monopolies. This may become a threat to national economic security and particularly industrial security' ... The warning against emerging monopolies and accompanying complaints about international companies' 'abuse of intellectual property rights' reflect concerns among Chinese officials that foreign companies are winning too much economic influence ... Such concerns have repeatedly been expressed by individual officials and other government departments in recent months ... Such concerns have already had an impact on some prominent deals, including a proposed takeover of Xugong Construction Machinery by Carlyle Group, the US private equity group, that has been stalled for more than a year because of nationalist objections. The ministry of commerce in August published new rules on foreign takeovers of local companies that are explicitly intended to protect economic security by reviewing acquisitions in sensitive sectors and blocking the transfer of 'famous trademarks' or 'old brands' ... The five-year plan calls for more effort to ensure officials focus not on the amount of overseas investment attracted but on the degree to which it contributes to development. The plan says priority should be given to investment that brings China advanced technology, management expertise and high quality talent, while stressing environmental protection and more efficient use of resources.

(*FT*, 11 November 2006, p. 9)

The State Council has approved long-awaited draft rules on foreign banks operating in the country, the government said Thursday [9 November 2006]. The rules were approved at a meeting presided over by prime minister Wen Jiabao on Wednesday. No details were given of the draft regulations.

(www.iht.com, 9 November 2006)

China will expedite the passing of a proposed anti-monopoly law to prevent overseas capital from controlling businesses that are critical to its security, according to the National Development and Reform Commission. The government will gradually reduce tax exemptions for foreign companies and try to prevent tax evasion by them, the panel said Saturday [11 November 2006]. The government is adjusting its policy on foreign investment under its five-year plan to emphasize the quality of overseas capital rather than quantity.

(*IHT*, 13 November 2006, p. 12)

China yesterday [15 November] issued landmark rules allowing foreign banks to offer a full range of services to local customers – a liberalization promised as part of its 2001 entry to the WTO. The regulations were broadly in line with recent drafts ... but did include operating fund requirements for local branches of overseas banks that were considerably lower than some had feared. The rules take effect on the 11 December anniversary of China's WTO entry ... To offer the full range of renminbi services for local customers, foreign-funded and joint venture banks must, like Chinese rivals, incorporate locally with registered capital of 1 billion renminbi ($128 million) and operating capital of 100 million renminbi for each branch ... Chinese branches of foreign banks without a local subsidiary will be barred from accepting individual deposits of less than 1 million renminbi, excluding them from most retail business. But the rules said the operating capital requirement for each branch would be only 200 million renminbi, far less than the 500 million renminbi executives had been led to expect by draft rules ... More than seventy foreign banks from twenty countries had set up 238 operating branches in China by the end of last year [2005], but they accounted for only 0.55 per cent of local currency loans.

(*FT*, 16 November 2006, p. 8)

China defended new rules allowing foreign banks into the lucrative retail banking market, with officials saying that the regulations' stringent requirements meet promises on opening the long-protected retail banking sector to foreign competition. The rules, announced Wednesday [15 November] but known for months to be under consideration, require foreign banks to incorporate locally if they want to offer local currency services to individual Chinese. Beyond that foreign banks must put up 1 billion yuan, or $127 million, for the incorporated bank and set aside 100 million yuan for each branch. The rules will take effect on 11 December [2006] ... For more than a decade major foreign banks have sought to gain access to the retail banking market in China, where people on average save about a quarter of their incomes ... Under current regulations foreign banks can handle loans and deposits in foreign currencies, but they can provide services in the local currency only to enterprises in twenty-five cities. Foreign banks were allowed to run their China branches from their overseas headquarters. The new regulations drop the geographical restrictions and allow services to ordinary Chinese as well as enterprises ... Under the new rules foreign banks that choose not to incorporate in China are allowed only to accept term deposits of at least 1 million yuan, effectively restricting their services to all but the wealthiest residents of China. That condition, regulators suggested, went even further than what the WTO required.

(www.iht.com, 16 November 2006)

Under the new rules foreign banks are required, like their domestic competitors, to incorporate their Chinese subsidiaries locally, commit a minimum capital of 1 billion yuan ($127 million) and hold at least 100 million yuan of operating capital in each branch. To be sure, foreign banks are still hampered by rules that limit total loans they issue to no more than 75 per cent of the deposits they attract. And they have to have operated in China for at least three years and be profitable for two consecutive years before they become eligible for a domestic retail banking licence.

(*FEER*, March 2007, p. 50)

Citigroup, the biggest US financial services company, plans to sign an agreement Thursday [16 November] to take control of Guangdong Development Bank for about $3 billion, two people with knowledge of the decision said Wednesday. Citigroup's bidding group topped offers from Société Générale in France and Ping An Insurance (Group) of China in the sixteen-month race to acquire 85 per cent of Guangdong Development ... Citigroup, based in New York, will buy 20 per cent of the bank, based in Guangdong province bordering Hong Kong. International Business Machines [IMB] will buy 5 per cent of the bank, while China Life Insurance [a state-run insurance company] and State Grid Corporation [an electric utility] of China will each own 20 per cent ... Other investors include CITIC Trust and Development and Puhua Investment ... Guangdong Development Bank has bad loan problems ... Bad loans accounted for 21.9 per cent of total lending at the end of 2003, the latest figure from the company ... The bank is to receive about $7.6 billion from the sale of problem loans ... the bank has forecast it will ... reduce its bad loan ration to around 4 per cent this year [2006] ... Guangdong Development, established in 1988, has offices mainly in Guangdong, a province of 110 million people ... Citibank initially wanted to buy 40 per cent of Guangdong Development, but the Chinese government refused to relax the rules that restrict foreign companies from owning more than 20 per cent of a Chinese bank. Despite its minority interest Citibank will have operating control ... the only other overseas business with that distinction is Newbridge Capital, based in Texas, which bought 17.9 per cent of Shenzhen Development Bank for $1,499 million in December 2004. The stake gave Newbridge the right to appoint the chairman and senior executives at the bank, which is also based in Guangdong province.

(*IHT*, 16 November 2006, p. 16)

Citigroup established its first office in China in 1902 and bought 5 per cent of Shanghai Pudong Development Bank in 2003. It has won approval to increase the stake in Pudong Bank to 19.9 per cent ... A group of investors led by Citigroup agreed Thursday [16 November] to pay about $3.1 billion to acquire a controlling stake in Guangdong Development Bank, the first time a foreign-led consortium has won the right to manage a major Chinese bank ... The bank is owned by the Guangdong provincial government ... Despite widespread concerns about weak risk management controls and bad loans in the Chinese banking system, global financial giants like Bank of America, HSBC, Goldman Sachs, UBS and Royal Bank of Scotland have lined up to acquire multi-billion dollar stakes in the biggest state-owned banks in China.

(www.iht.com, 16 November 2006)

Citigroup ... is teaming up with IBM and a group of powerful Chinese state-owned companies to take control of 85.6 per cent of the ailing mid-size lender, which is expected to undergo massive restructuring ... IBM, the computer services company ... has agreed to acquire a 4.7 per cent stake ...

Citigroup, the only investor with banking experience, is expected to assume significant management control over the bank.

(www.iht.com, 16 November 2006; *IHT*, 17 November 2006, p. 11)

[Guangdong Development Bank's] most recent audited statement in 2003 showed that non-performing loans represented an alarming 22 per cent of its portfolio. A report in the government-backed *China Daily* agency put non-performing loans at 25 per cent in 2005 … Citigroup initially bid for out-right control [of Guangdong Development Bank] at the request of the local authorities. The offer was withdrawn under national government pressure because of limits on the stake of any foreign investor in a Chinese bank to 20 per cent, and of total foreign investment to 25 per cent … Citigroup is thought to have the first right of repurchase for IBM's shares.

(*The Economist*, 18 November 2006, p. 92)

Banco Bilbao Vizcaya Argentina, one of the largest Spanish banks, agreed Wednesday [22 November] to buy stakes in units of the Citic Group for Euro 989 million … BBVA will pay Euro 501 million, or $647 million, for a 5 per cent stake in China Citic Bank and Euro 488 million for a 15 per cent holding in Citic International Financial Holdings … The total purchase is the equivalent of $1.27 billion. The agreement includes an option allow-ing BBVA to raise its stake in China Citic Bank to 9.9 per cent … The transactions will be completed by March 2007 … The sale of the stake to BBVA paves the way for Citic Bank in Beijing to raise $2 billion in an initial public offering in Hong Kong … [Citic Bank's] non-performing loan ratio stood at 2.79 per cent as of 30 September [2006].

(www.iht.com, 22 November 2006; *IHT*, 23 November 2006, p. 18)

The government said Wednesday [6 December 2006] that overseas com-panies would be allowed to sell refined oil products as of 1 January 2007, as China Petroleum and Chemical and other refiners prepare for competition under WTO rules … The rule breaks the government monopoly and allows BP, Exxon Mobil and other overseas companies in sales of kerosene, gaso-line and diesel in China. Beijing will maintain a foreign ownership limit on retailers with more than thirty service stations in the country, banning over-seas control. The wholesale oil business in China … is dominated by China National Petroleum and China Petroleum, with smaller private sellers gaining market share.

(www.iht.com, 6 December 2006; *IHT*, 7 December 2006, p. 18)

China said Thursday [7 December 2006] that overseas companies would be allowed to sell crude oil in the country beginning 1 January [2007], pushing PetroChina and other producers to compete under WTO rules … The rule breaks the government monopoly and allows BP, Exxon Mobil and other overseas companies to supply crude oil to the world's second largest con-sumer of the fuel, after America.

(*IHT*, 8 December 2006, p. 13)

China has closed the door on new foreign investment in television and film production, telling international media companies to work instead through individual projects with local partners. Zhu Hong of the State Administration of Radio, Film and Television (Sarft) ... [said] that Beijing had put aside landmark rules issued in 2004 allowing foreign investors to take minority stakes in local production units ... He said: 'Our policy is to temporarily not approve the creation of new joint companies. People can jointly invest in filming individual movies and individual television dramas, but we are not going to approve the creation of programme production companies' ... Last year [2005] Sarft limited most foreign companies to just one such venture and banned any considered 'unfriendly' to China ... By forcing international media companies to work through individual projects, Beijing hopes to give local companies the chance to absorb the management and technology they need to become globally competitive while keeping control firmly in Chinese hands.

(*FT*, 8 December 2006, p. 9)

'Rules announced on 8 September [2006] require overseas buyers of Chinese assets to get clearance from the ministry of commerce for deals that involve a strategic industry, a well known trademark or an "old Chinese brand"' (*IHT*, 18 December 2006, p. 381).

At the National People's Congress held 5–16 March 2007 legislation was passed to standardize tax rates levied on foreign and domestic companies. '[When the property bill was put to the vote on 16 March] 99.1 per cent of the 2,889 legislators attending the National People's Congress backed the property law. The tax legislation ... was passed with only slightly less support' (www. bbc.co.uk, 16 March 2007).

Chinese companies [currently] pay 33 per cent tax, while foreign investors pay as little as 15 per cent ... Many of the supposedly foreign investors profiting from tax concessions are ... Chinese investors 'round-tripping' their money via the British Virgin Islands and other tax havens.

(*FT*, 5 March 2007, p. 18)

China ended nearly three decades of favourable treatment for foreign companies yesterday [8 March] with the introduction of a measure to equalize tax rates paid by local and overseas enterprises. The long-awaited law ... will see a single tax rate of 25 per cent levied on all companies. Under the current system Chinese companies have been taxed at up to 33 per cent while foreign enterprises have paid as little as 15 per cent ... The biggest winners will be China's large state banks, according to [the company] J.P. Morgan, because income and revenue tax – the last of which only banks have to pay – now eat up nearly 50 per cent of their pre-tax profit ... [J.P. Morgan] expected the 5 per cent revenue tax to be gradually phased out ... The new law, to start next year [2008], also targets so-called 'fake' foreign companies – local companies that move money out of and back into China to earn a tax break. The bill enacting the changes may not affect foreign companies already operating in

China fully for up to five years. Because of the way it was being phased in, China would also continue to offer concessionary tax rates to 'low profit enterprises' and to investors offering high-tech projects.

(*FT*, 9 March 2007, p. 7)

'On Sunday [4 March] lawmakers said they would unify China's income tax rate at 25 per cent, cutting the rate on local companies from 33 per cent and raising it from 15 per cent on overseas firms, [the] legislature spokesman said' (*IHT*, 5 March 2007, p. 11).

China's plan to unify tax rates for foreign and domestic companies should raise the total annual tax bill for foreign investors by about $5.5 billion, finance minister Jin Renqing said Friday [9 March] ... If the bill is confirmed next week it will take effect next 1 January [2008]. A measure being considered by China's legislature would end nearly three decades of blanket tax breaks for foreign investors. It would unify tax rates for foreign and Chinese companies at 25 per cent, up from the average of 15 per cent that the government says foreign companies pay now. That increase [is] to be phased in over five years.

(www.iht.com, 9 March 2007)

Tax paid by foreign and domestic firms will be unified at 25 per cent ... Domestic firms currently pay income tax of 33 per cent, while foreign-funded businesses pay between 15 per cent and 24 per cent ... A controversial 50 per cent tax break for foreign firms that focus on exports – which the United States had said was anti-competitive – will be scrapped. High technology will be taxed at 15 per cent under the reforms.

(www.bbc.co.uk, 8 March 2007)

Carlyle, the US buy-out group, has bowed to Chinese political pressure and agreed to acquire a minority stake in China's biggest construction machinery maker. It was announced at the weekend that Carlyle had signed an agreement to acquire 45 per cent of Xugong Construction Machinery ... The development follows a saga that began in October 2005, when Carlyle agreed to pay $375 million for an 85 per cent stake in Xugong, whose parent is controlled by the local government of Xuzhou city, after a year-long public auction. But the deal was caught in a backlash over foreign investment and the merits of private equity investment. It became a benchmark of Beijing's attitude towards open access to key industrial assets. Carlyle tried to restructure the deal in October [2006] as a fifty–fifty joint venture, paying about $230 million, but Beijing rejected this because of the sector's 'strategic importance'. It was argued that Xugong, the industry leader, owned advanced technologies and the sale of such companies could result in China losing its technology to overseas rivals ... The government does not believe the entire construction machinery sector is off limits. Volvo completed the purchase of 70 per cent of Lingong Construction Machinery this year [2007] with regulatory approval.

(*FT*, 19 March 2007, p. 27)

Chinese authorities have issued new rules making it harder for foreigners to invest in the property market in another attempt to cool the nation's heated real estate market. In a statement dated 23 May [2007] but published Monday [11 June] China's foreign exchange regulator and the commerce ministry said foreigners needed to obtain land-use rights before developing property projects ... Existing foreign-funded firms need to seek additional approvals from the authorities to start new development schemes ... The new regulations come nearly one year after Beijing issued controversial rules restricting foreign purchases of property.

(www.iht.com, 11 June 2007)

China is tightening controls on foreign takeovers, adding a requirement for national security reviews to a proposed anti-monopoly law ... Beijing stepped up scrutiny of foreign takeovers after an uproar in 2005 over an offer by Carlyle Group, a US fund, to buy a Chinese maker of construction equipment. The latest step would be the first time a requirement for a national security review has been enshrined in law ... Lawmakers took up the new version of the law for the first time during the weekend.

(www.iht.com, 26 June 2007, p. 10)

Chinese regulators have rejected the US investment fund Carlyle Group's bid to buy a portion of a small bank ... Regulators rejected Carlyle's bid for 8 per cent of Chongqing Commercial Bank because it 'does not meet current relevant rules and regulations' ... It was not clear whether Chinese regulators would consider Carlyle an appropriate partner for a bank, due to its lack of banking experience ... Carlyle and Dah Sing Bank in Hong Kong agreed in December [2006] to buy a combined 24 per cent stake in the bank, which is located in the south-western industrial city of Chongqing. The Dah Sing purchase of a 17 per cent stake was approved by regulators in April [2007] ... China has stepped up scrutiny of foreign corporate acquisitions following an uproar over Carlyle's 2005 bid to buy a company that manufactures construction equipment ... Acquisitions of even minority stakes in existing companies are still unusual and politically sensitive. Critics complain that China might be selling important assets too cheaply or endangering its economic security. A provision in a proposed anti-monopoly law under investigation by China's legislature would require a national security review for foreign takeovers of Chinese companies.

(www.iht.com, 3 July 2007)

Singapore Airlines and Singapore's state investment agency [Temasek] have agreed to pay $923 million for 24 per cent of struggling China Eastern Airlines in a long-awaited deal that signals the opening of the Chinese mainland's aviation sector to outside investors. SIA would pay $602 million for a 15.7 per cent stake in CEA, while Temasek, the government investment company that owns nearly 55 per cent of SIA, would pay $321 million for 8.3 per cent ... SIA and Temasek will have three seats on CEA's fourteen-member boards and SIA will be involved in CEA's long-haul routes, marketing and daily operations. But analysts have warned it may be hard for SIA to have any real influence on CEA in the short term if Cathay's experience in dealing with Air China is anything to go by ... Last year [2006] Air China agreed to a complicated shareholding arrangement with Cathay Pacific, SIA's main regional competitor, in which the two companies hold 17.5 per cent stakes in each other ... After more than a year, the two sides are yet to co-operate on anything more than a few code-share flights, according to Air China officials.

(FT, 3 September 2007, p. 24)

Singapore Airlines and its parent company, Temasek Holdings, have agreed to pay about $918 million for a 24 per cent stake on China Eastern Airlines ... The shares cannot be sold within three years of the contract's closing date ... But Temasek is allowed to transfer its shares to Singapore Airlines during this period. China Eastern, the third largest carrier in China behind China Southern and Air China, will expand its board to fourteen members from eleven members ... China Eastern's parent company, China Eastern Air Holding, will buy 1.1 billion new shares, giving it a 51 per cent stake.

(IHT, 3 September 2007, p. 13)

The government said Thursday [6 September] it would lift a one-year moratorium on foreign investment in the securities industry, now that local brokerage firms have strengthened their finances ... Shang Fulin: 'After the completion of a three-year restructuring of the domestic brokerage industry, we will resume reviewing the applications for joint ventures.' Foreign investment banks will be allowed to buy stakes in fully licensed domestic brokerage firms, Shang said. Overseas banks are allowed a maximum stake of 33 per cent in local ventures. Shang did not say whether the limit would be increased. Among global securities firms only Goldman Sachs and UBS currently wield management control over local investment banking ventures.

(IHT, 7 September 2007, p. 12)

China will issue twenty licences next month [October] to select fund managers and financial institutions to help manage the country's 90 billion yuan company pensions market. The government is assessing applications from fund houses, banks and other financial firms to manage the funds in the market, worth $11 billion, and will announce the companies selected in six weeks ... The government ... [is opening] the industry to professional money managers, hoping to raise returns while the nation dismantles its welfare system. The market was valued at about 90 billion yuan at the end of 2006 and is expected to grow by between 30 billion and 50 billion yuan in 2007 ... China will transfer more than 70 billion yuan in company pension plans to fund professionals by the end of [2007 it was said in April] ... The twenty approvals to be issued in six weeks will include licences to serve as investment managers, trustees, account administrators and custodians for China's company pension plans ... China requires a separate licence for each of these four roles ... China now allows thirty-seven firms to handle enterprise annuities, as the plans are known. Of these four are joint-venture fund houses ... The government awarded the last batch of licences in 2005. China may also allow fund professionals to handle some of the enterprise annuities held by Shanghai's pension agency ... In May Shanghai's government set up Changjiang Pension Insurance to manage 15 billion yuan of company pension funds held by its labour and social security bureaux. Changjiang Pension was set up after abuses found in Shanghai's government-run pension fund led to the September 2006 firing of the city's highest ranking Communist Party official, Chen Liangyu.

(*IHT*, 10 September 2007, p. 12)

China will prevent foreign investors from taking control of domestic brokerages ... Overseas companies would be limited to owning stakes in publicly traded brokerages, with the foreign holding capped at 20 per cent ... The China Securities Regulatory Commission has submitted the draft rules to the State Council, the highest decision-making body in China ... Goldman Sachs and UBS are the only global securities companies that control investment banking units in China ... China only allows domestic brokerages to trade shares; direct investment is the only way that non-Chinese firms can tap that trading revenue ... UBS and Goldman are special cases ... While foreign ownership of Chinese brokerages would be capped at 20 per cent, overseas firms could hold as much as 33 per cent of their investment banking ventures with Chinese partners ... That would allow them to engage directly in underwriting stock and bond sales ... Morgan Stanley helped set up China International Capital eleven years ago, taking a 34 per cent stake in the first investment bank in China. The New York-based firm surrendered management responsibilities at CICC in 2000 following a dispute with the Chinese company's management. UBS won approval last year [2006] to set up UBS Securities. Goldman has a 33 per cent-owned investment banking venture with Beijing Gao Hua Securities.

(www.iht.com, 4 October 2007; *IHT*, 4 October 2007, p. 19)

Lawmakers in Beijing are about to pass legislation limiting acquisitions in China on national security grounds. After thirteen years of debate and various drafts, the National People's Congress is poised to pass a broad anti-monopoly law this week. But while Western companies have welcomed many of the law's provisions, including limits on monopolistic behaviour by state-owned enterprises, the final draft also has a last-minute addition: acquisitions by foreign companies 'should go through national security checks' ... National security concerns have been raised more often lately as a reason to delay deals in industries that would not be seen as security risks in the United States. Carlyle Group, a US private equity company, has been trying for nearly three years to buy a construction equipment manufacturer, with government approval still on hold as some Chinese officials have mentioned national security worries; even a French purchase of a Chinese cookware company was delayed this year [2007] for a national security review, although the commerce ministry eventually gave its approval ... Many experts say that Chinese officials have long made national security a key consideration in their reviews of foreign purchases and that the new legislation simply formalizes this. Various Chinese rules and regulations also require that national security be taken into account during government reviews of mergers and acquisitions ... The new legislation has numerous provisions long sought by Western companies. While earlier drafts referred to protecting the rights of businesses, and could be cited by state-owned enterprises seeking to avoid being purchased by multinationals, the latest draft calls for protecting consumers. Mergers and acquisitions accounted for only 5 per cent of foreign direct investment in China before 2004, but this proportion rose to 11 per cent in 2004 and almost 20 per cent in 2005, the official newspaper *China Daily* said in its weekend edition. No figure was provided for last year [2006]. The government has eased controls in some industries and now allows foreign companies to own 100 per cent of factories in industries like auto parts, where joint ventures with Chinese businesses were previously required. But in other industries, like car assembly, multinationals are still limited to 50 per cent stakes.

(*IHT*, 28 August 2007, p. 10)

[China] issued a new set of guidelines limiting foreign direct investment. China will bar foreigners from projects mining rare minerals and will prohibit investing in small and mid-size refineries. The new regulations also state that foreign companies will be banned from investing in news websites, internet audio-visual services and web cafés.

(*IHT*, 8 November 2007, p. 13)

Kazakhstan has agreed to share its uranium resources with China in exchange for equity in Chinese nuclear power facilities in a strategic deal that brings together the world's fastest growing uranium and nuclear energy producers. Moukhtar Dzhakishev, the president of Kazatomprom. Kazakhstan's state-owned nuclear power company, said: 'We will swap shares in uranium production for shares in Chinese atomic facilities ... This is the first time China has allowed any foreign company to become a shareholder in its atomic power industry enterprises' ... China National Nuclear Corp. and China Nuclear Guangdong Power Corp., China's leading nuclear power companies, would team up to take a 49 per cent stake in a uranium mining venture in Kazakhstan with Kazatomprom retaining a 51 per cent stake ... In exchange, Kazatomprom would take equity in Chinese fuel processing or electricity generation plants. Details of the agreement signed by the Chinese government are expected by next month [December 2007] ... Kazakhstan bought a 10 per cent stake in Westinghouse, the US nuclear technology company, from Toshiba for $540 million this year [2007]. The partnership mirrors the Chinese deal, providing Westinghouse with a guaranteed source of uranium and Kazakhstan with access to fuel processing know-how and technology.

(FT, 19 November 2007, p. 8)

'[China is to unify] the corporate income tax rate for domestic and foreign-invested companies. From 1 January [2008] both will be 25 per cent. This will raise the rate for foreign-invested companies but cut that of domestic ones' (*IHT*, 27 December 2007, p. 4).

> The northern port of Tianjin ... nearly 100 kilometres (60 miles) east of Beijing ... long overshadowed by other booming cities in China ... is in pole position to lead the country's next wave of financial advancement, and seemingly local decisions are taking on national significance. In an approach pioneered in the 1980s, the Chinese authorities have chosen the city, which has a population of 11 million, as a proving ground for policy experiments that may be carried out nationwide if they are successful ... City leaders are promoting Tianjin to deliver the same stimulus to the national economy that the development of Shenzhen and the Pudong area of Shanghai provided in the 1980s and 1990s. Deputy mayor Cui Jindu (11 January 2008): 'We want Tianjin to be northern China's gateway to the outside world, a high-value manufacturing and research and development base, an international centre for shipping and logistics' ... The city has made a tentative start to fulfil its loudly voiced ambitions. For example, in late 2006 it began the Bohai Industrial Investment Fund, with 20 billion yuan ($2.75 billion), the first equity fund of its kind in a country heavily reliant on bank lending. At the same time officials suggested that they might use the Tianjin Binhai New Area to experiment with making the yuan freely tradable, though talk of that quickly died down. Last July [2007] Tianjin was designated as the sole gateway for a landmark programme that would permit Chinese residents to invest directly in Hong Kong equities, but this 'through train' plan has remained on hold since then. An important question is whether the recently appointed acting mayor, Huang Xingguo, will continue the efforts of his predecessor, Dai Xianglong, a former central bank governor who was seen as a force for change. While they state strong support for financial reform, Tianjin's leaders seem firmly focused on industrial development, which is already well under way. International companies like Motorola and Samsung have big operations in Tianjin.
>
> (www.iht.com, 14 January 2008)

'Banking and insurance regulators will agree this week to allow banks to invest in insurers, and Bank of Communications, the Chinese partner of HSBC, could be the first to win approval for such a move' (*IHT*, Wednesday 16 January 2008, p. 11).

> China is the source of 80 per cent of the fake goods in the world and holds the key to stopping the trade, José Barroso, president of the European Commission, said last month [March] ... A spokesman for the [Chinese] State

Intellectual Property Office said 17 April): 'The Chinese government has taken concrete steps and success is there for all to see ... China is a country which has only had an intellectual property rights protection system for a short period of time, just twenty years or so, and people do not know as much about the matter as in Western nations.'

(www.iht.com, 17 April 2008)

Crédit Suisse said that it had won approval from regulators to set up a securities joint venture in China that would allow it to underwrite domestic stock and bond offerings in the country. Crédit Suisse is to own 33.3 per cent of its Beijing-based joint venture with China's Founder Securities. The approval, which came Saturday [14 March 2008], is the first by the China Securities Regulatory Commission since new rules were adopted on Sino-foreign securities in December [2007]. The Swiss bank joins rivals, UBS and Goldman Sachs, as foreign investment banks with domestic joint ventures in the fast growing but restrictive Chinese market. Morgan Stanley owns a stake in China International Capital, a leading mainland investment bank.

(*IHT*, 16 June 2008, p. 13)

The western region has been allowed to maintain the 15 per cent preferential tax rate for foreign enterprises which was removed in other areas on 1 January [2008] ... Over half of China's GDP and 82 per cent of foreign direct investment remain concentrated in the east, according to the government.

(www.economist.com, 7 July 2008)

China has opened its market to financial information providers, ending an attempt to give the official Xinhua news agency tight control over its foreign competitors and resolving a trade dispute with the United States, the EU and Canada. Under a deal signed by the four parties in Geneva yesterday [13 November] China agreed to transfer Xinhua's role in overseeing foreign financial information suppliers to an independent regulator and to allow such suppliers to set up commercial operations. The agreement, reached after seven months of WTO consultations, removes a big operation risk for financial information providers such as Thomson Reuters, Dow Jones and Bloomberg ... Xinhua sparked the debate by issuing tough new rules on the foreign agencies in September 2006. China has required foreign news agencies to distribute to media clients only through Xinhua for more than fifty years. The agencies do not challenge these restrictions, which help the Chinese government ensure news does not reach the public uncensored. But the agencies' financial information services had been relatively unrestricted until the 2006 rules, which demanded that they censor their own content and distribute to non-media clients only through an agent wholly owned by Xinhua ... So far they [foreign news agencies] have been allowed only to maintain representative offices in China.

(*FT*, 14 November 2008, p. 8)

The United States and the EU filed a case against China at the WTO in March, arguing that China unfairly required foreign news and financial information providers to be licensed by Xinhua ... a direct competitor of the foreign news companies. Canada later filed its own complaint against China ... An independent regulatory agency [will be set up] to oversee all financial news and information providers.

(*IHT*, 14 November 2008, p. 14)

UBS has made a profit of about $350 million from selling its stake in Bank of China, as Switzerland's biggest bank continues to repair the damage done to its balance sheet by the credit crisis. The sale to institutional investors [was] completed late on Tuesday [30 December] ... The move follows the expiry of a three-year lock-up period that had prevented UBS and other non-Chinese investors, including Royal Bank of Scotland and Singapore's Temasek, from selling the BoC shares they acquired in 2005 ... UBS sold shares at a slight discount to the market price, generating proceeds of about $850 million. It bought the stake for about $500 million in 2005 ... Earlier in December Bank of America shelved a $3 billion sale of China Construction Bank stock following [unspecified] objections from Beijing.

(www.ft.com, 31 December 2008; *FT*, 2 January 2008, p. 16)

UBS has become the first overseas investor to offload its holding in a major Chinese bank ... Switzerland's largest bank raised $835 million by selling its share in the Hong Kong-listed arm of Bank of China in a discounted institutional placing. It acquired the 1.3 per cent stake for $500 million in 2005, a year before it advised on the stock market listing of the mainland lender ... UBS has offices in Beijing and Guangzhou, is licensed to trade renminbi-denominated A-shares, and is a leading mergers and acquisitions adviser to Chinese companies ... Royal Bank of Scotland, which holds a 4.3 per cent stake in BoC, was recently bailed out by the UK government and is tipped by dealmakers to follow UBS and decide that the holding is non-core.

(www.ft.com, 1 January 2009; *FT*, 2 January 2008, p. 16)

Bank of America, the US lender that is seeking to raise cash to weather a dismal market at home, sold a $2.83 billion portion of its holdings in China Construction Bank on Wednesday [7 January 2009] ... Western financial giants ... are now under pressure to find cash as the global financial crisis ravages the banking industry ... Bank of America sold more ... nearly 13 per cent of its holdings in the bank ... Bank of America made a profit of about $1.13 billion on the stake sale, based on Construction Bank's initial public offering price. It sold the stake at a 12 per cent discount to the Tuesday close of the Hong Kong-listed shares. The bank's shares are also listed in Shanghai. The stake represents about 2.5 per cent of Construction Bank's share capital, and will leave Bank of America with a 16.6 per cent holding in the Beijing-controlled lender. Bank of America first bought shares of Construction Bank before its initial public offering in 2005, and built its holding up to just over 19 per cent ... The share sale Wednesday was handled by UBS ... the embattled Swiss bank [that] recently sold its shareholdings in Bank of China ... and Merrill Lynch, which Bank of America acquired last year [2008].

(*IHT*, 8 January 2009, p. 12)

'China Construction Bank is the world's second most valuable bank in stock market terms' (www.ft.com, 7 January 2009).

A court in southern China convicted eleven people on Wednesday [31 December] of violating national copyright laws and participating in a sophisticated counterfeiting ring that for years manufactured and distributed pirated Microsoft software throughout the world. The men were sentenced by a court in the city of Shenzhen to between one-and-a-half and six-and-a-half years in prison ... Microsoft applauded the sentence ... saying they were the stiffest sentences ever handed down in this type of Chinese copyright infringement case. Microsoft has called the group part of 'the biggest software counterfeiting organization we have ever seen, by far' and estimated its global sales at more than $2 billion. This case is considered by some legal experts to be a landmark because it involved a joint anti-piracy effort by the US Federal Bureau of Investigation and China's Ministry of Public Security. Law enforcement officials said it was also notable because the group operated like a multinational corporation, producing and distributing high quality counterfeit software that was created and packaged almost identically to the real products, despite Microsoft's anti-piracy measures. The counterfeit goods, such as Windows XP and Office 2007, were marketed using the internet and exported from China, mostly shipped to the United States and Europe, where they commanded relatively high prices ... [Microsoft said it] found their products in thirty-six countries ... American and Chinese officials say they broke up the criminal ring in July 2007 with the arrest of twenty-five people in China, the dismantling of several manufacturing facilities and the confiscation of counterfeit software valued at more than $500 million ... A separate trial involving nine suspects in Shanghai has not yet reached a verdict. That group has been accused of counterfeiting Microsoft and Symantec software and distributing it worldwide ... Even customs officials have been fooled by the counterfeits, which contained hologram markings and Microsoft's difficult to replicate 'certificate of authenticity' ... Counterfeiting experts say the ring appeared to be less interested in selling its products inside of China, where counterfeit Microsoft software can be purchased for as little as $3. They were seeking the higher value export market. Microsoft says its seventy-five-member anti-piracy team had been tracking the ring since 2001. The FBI began its own operation ... in 2005 and co-operated with Chinese officials ... Software piracy is rampant in China, where about 80 per cent of computers are believed to use counterfeit software, according to the Business Software Alliance ... While the FBI and Chinese officials say hundreds of millions of dollars' worth of material were seized in a variety of international raids, the Shenzhen court found on Wednesday that the suspects on trial there had sold less than $200,000 of counterfeit products overseas. It is unclear whether others pocketed much greater sums or whether many more ring-leaders are still at large.

(www.iht.com, 31 December 2008; *IHT*, 2 January 2008, p. 13)

After years of delay the government said late Wednesday [31 December] that it would issue licences for next-generation 3G wireless services, which could fuel growth in what is already the world's biggest market for wireless services. China's State Council, or cabinet, made the announcement on its website saying the government would back three standards, including one chiefly developed in China [based on technology developed by the German firm Siemens]. The move has been expected for much of the year ... China said it would issue licences for each of the three major standards, the home-grown TD-SCDMA standard, as well as two international 3G standards that are favoured in the United States [CDMA 2000] and Europe [WCDMA] ... To prepare for the move to 3G, China restructured its telecommunications industry into three major players earlier this year [2008] ... The country now has more than 600 million cellphone subscribers, by far the largest number in the world ... China's telecommunications industry is still not fully open to competition. International telecommunications equipment makers and cellphone producers are thriving here [in China], but only Chinese state-controlled companies can offer telephone services to regular customers.

(www.iht.com, 1 January 2009)

Royal Bank of Scotland, the UK lender, has raised about $2.4 billion (£1.65 billion) by offloading its stake in Bank of China. RBS became the leading foreign shareholder in the Chinese lender after acquiring a 4.3 per cent stake in 2005. It had been expected to offload the holding after it was rescued by the UK government as a result of the financial crisis ... The bank's balance sheet last year [2008] received a £20 billion capital injection from the government. RBS bought its Bank of China shareholding for £800 in December 2005 as the leading partner in a consortium that included Merrill Lynch and Temasek of Singapore. The three-year lock-in period on the investment expired last month [December 2008] ... RBS will retain an interest in China through the eighteen-branch network it acquired as part of ABN Amro ... Li Ka-shing, the Hong Kong tycoon, last week raised more than $500 million by selling part of his charitable foundation's Bank of China stake.

(*FT*, 14 January 2009, p. 17)

'The bail-out left the UK government with a 57 per cent shareholding in the bank' (www.ft.com, 13 January 2009).

'A single foreign investor is permitted to hold no more than 19.9 per cent of a Chinese bank' (*IHT*, 16 January 2009, p. 14).

On 5 March [2009] Beijing promulgated new regulations to devolve some authority for approving more foreign investment projects to local authorities … Under these regulations merger deals involving foreign investment in China in most sectors with a price tag below $100 million only need approval from local commerce authorities, rather than the ministry [of commerce]. Sectors where foreign investment is 'forbidden' or 'restricted' are excluded from the changes.

(www.iht.com, 17 March 2009)

China yesterday [18 March] rejected a $2.4 billion Coca-Cola deal that would have been the country's biggest foreign takeover, stoking fears of protectionism and warnings that the decision could scupper Beijing's push to invest in overseas mining companies … Publication of the decision followed a report in the *Financial Times* that the regulator had demanded Coke relinquish the Huiyuan brand after the acquisition, a request that was refused.

(*FT*, 19 March 2009, p. 17)

Hong Kong-listed Huiyuan Juice has a 42 per cent share of the domestic market in pure fruit juice and is a nationally recognized brand. Coke has long sold carbonated drinks in China but lacked a presence in the pure juice segment. It would have been the largest foreign takeover of a domestic company … The country has introduced vague but sweeping economic and national security laws that can be used to stop foreign investors from buying 'national brands' in virtually any industry … FDI is expected to fall further this year [2009] after dropping 21 per cent in 2008. The government will introduce a new law in May that requires sales of state-owned companies or assets to be based on market prices, imposing an additional regulatory hurdle for acquisitions in China.

(p. 23)

'Huiyuan has about a 40 per cent share of the Chinese juice market' (www. bbc.co.uk, 18 March 2009).

China's ministry of commerce on Wednesday [18 March] rejected Coca-Cola's $2.4 billion bid for the top Chinese juice maker, Huiyuan Juice, saying the deal would be bad for competition. The acquisition would have been the largest ever takeover of a Chinese company by a foreign rival. The proposed purchase was rejected on anti-monopoly grounds, the commerce ministry said … China Huiyuan Juice Company … [is] one of China's biggest beverage makers. The move blocked what would have been the biggest foreign takeover of a Chinese company and suggested Beijing is still uncomfortable with foreign ownership of big Chinese companies … The deal is considered not only an early test of China's new anti-monopoly law but also whether Beijing will allow foreign companies greater latitude to acquire big Chinese companies … Bankers and investors had eagerly anticipated the ministry's ruling as a litmus test of China's attitudes towards overseas investment in the wake of last year's promulgation of a tough anti-monopoly law ... Very few foreign companies have taken full control of a major Chinese company. But legal analysts said they had expected the deal to be approved because China itself is moving aggressively this year [2009] to acquire foreign assets during the global economic downturn ... Chinese anti-trust regulators [had] indicated that Coca-Cola would have to relinquish the China Huiyuan Juice brand after the acquisition ... Huiyuan Juice ... is one of China's biggest producers of fresh apple, orange and pear juice. The company is privately owned and two foreign companies hold minority stakes: Groupe Danone of France and Warburg Pincus, the American private equity firm. The bid by Coke was part of the company's aggressive expansion effort in China, where it already has a large presence. The company sells over a billion bottles of Coke annually, and markets its Sprite and Minute Maid brands here. Just a week ago Coke pledged to further expand its presence in China ... by investing an additional $2 billion in China over the next three years.

(www.iht.com, 18 March 2009; *IHT*, 19 March 2009, p. 15)

Last August [2008], after fourteen years of debate, the government finally passed ... a broad anti-monopoly law for a country rife with state-imposed monopolies. In the subsequent months people have wondered how the law would be applied, and whether it would advance China's transformation into a market economy, or serve as an impediment to genuine competition. On Wednesday 18 March an answer emerged with the rejection of the largest outright acquisition by a foreign company, a $2.3 billion offer by Coca-Cola for China Huiyuan, the country's largest juice distributor. When the deal was announced last September [2008] it was at a price three times Huiyuan's valuation at the time. Since then, as global markets have collapsed, it has only become more appealing. Huiyuan is a private company and juice has previously been free of government control ... The Coca-Cola company holds as much as half of the domestic Chinese market for carbonated beverages, but the juice business is highly fragmented. Estimates are not particularly reliable, but various accounts suggest that the two companies would control more than 20 per cent of the juice business ... Adding irony to the decision, it comes just as the Chinese government is indicating that it is actively encouraging, if not forcing, consolidation and greater market concentration in a number of areas, including steel, cars and airlines, and just after it imposed a new oligopoly in telecommunications. No domestic Chinese transaction appears to have been subjected to the new monopoly law. Signs that foreign companies might be the primary targets of the law began to emerge in November [2008], when a merger between two brewers, America's Anheuser-Busch and Belgium's InBev, was endorsed by Chinese regulators only on the condition that the combined firm's existing interest in several domestic breweries be frozen. In particular, Anheuser-Busch's non-controlling stake in Tsingtao, a leading Chinese brewer, was largely liquidated in January [2009] after what is presumed to be pressure from the government ... Deepening the gloom, another new Chinese law comes into effect on 1 May [2009], subjecting any transfer of a state-controlled asset to yet another layer of review, this time by a local commission.

(www.economist.com, 18 March 2009)

'At Asia Aluminium non-Chinese bondholders face losing all their investment after a local government reneged on its offer to buy them out ... Asia Aluminium [is] a metals group based in the province of Guangdong' (*IHT*, 23 March 2009, p. 15).

'Direct investments from foreigners in 2008 were just $28 billion' (*IHT*, 23 March 2009, p. 15).

> Foreign investors in Chinese banks will in future be forced to accept a lock-up period of at least five years ... [as opposed to the current] three-year period ... Beijing would not reconsider current ownership limits for Chinese banks, which restricts single foreign investors to a 20 per cent holding and all foreign investors to no more than a combined 25 per cent stake in any Chinese bank ... Only Goldman Sachs has made a public commitment to hold the majority of its stake in IBBC for at least another year.
>
> (*FT*, 2 April 2008, p. 24)

'In five years China wants 60 per cent of car parts in new Chinese vehicles to be locally made' (*The Economist*, 18 April 2009, p. 42).

> Although *shanzhai* [black market] cellphones have only been around for a few years, they already account for more than 20 per cent of sales in China, which is the biggest mobile phone market, according to the research firm Gartner. They are also being illegally exported to Russia, India, the Middle East, Europe, even the United States ... Even Chinese mobile phone producers are losing market share to underground companies.
>
> (www.iht.com, 28 April 2009; *IHT*, 29 April 2009, p. 17)

> China yesterday [30 April] unveiled new rules governing foreign providers of financial information, demanding that they not furnish domestic clients with information that could destabilize markets or stir up social tension. The rules will affect the operations of companies such as Bloomberg, Dow Jones and Thompson Reuters ... Foreign financial information providers must not distribute data that 'contravenes the basic principles of the constitution of the People's Republic of China', the rules state. They come into effect on 1 June.
>
> (*FT*, 1 May 2009, p. 6)

> Beijing is offering multinational companies subsidies and tax benefits if they set up regional headquarters in the capital. The move signals growing competition among main cities for investment as the financial crisis has forced many multinationals to suspend or slow investment. It could make Beijing a more serious rival for cities such as Singapore or Hong Kong.
>
> (*IHT*, 1 July 2009, p. 6)

The Fiat Group announced a fifty–fifty joint venture on Monday [6 July] with the Guangzhou Automobile Group to make cars and engines for the Chinese market … The companies said they would build a … plant in Changsha, in Hunan province, at a cost of more than $556 million, with production set to begin by the end of 2011 … Fiat has been looking for a new Chinese partner since it terminated a venture with Nanjing Auto in late 2007. A planned joint venture with Chery Automobile, China's largest domestic carmaker, had been scheduled to start production this year [2009], but that project was put on indefinite hold in March … Fiat has been a very small player in China.

(www.iht.com, 6 July 2009; *IHT*, 7 July 2009, p. 15)

Microsoft said it had won a major battle against software piracy in China after four people were on Thursday [20 August] sentenced to jail for illegal reproduction and distribution of the Windows XP software through a website called 'Tomato Garden'. The US company said the court victory was the first successful criminal prosecution against large-scale software privacy in China … 'Tomato Garden' allowed the public to download pirated software for free, in return for advertising revenues, according to Microsoft … A Chengdu-based company, which operates 'Tomato Garden', was ordered to turn in renminbi 2.92 million it made illegally and pay a fine three times that amount.

(www.ft.com, 21 August 2009)

The founders and main executives of 'Tomato Garden' … [were sentenced] to three-and-a-half years in prison and a fine of renminbi 1 million ($146,000) each. Others involved got smaller fines and jail sentences … The defendants can appeal … Security authorities launched the investigation into 'Tomato Garden' after a complaint [in 2008] from the Washington-based Business Software Alliance, the industry's main global lobbying group … Since 2004 China's software market's piracy rate – the proportion of counterfeit software sales out of total software sales – has dropped from 90 per cent to 80 per cent, said the Business Software Alliance. Even so it put losses from software piracy at $6.68 billion.

(*FT*, 22 August 2009, p. 4)

A court in eastern China has sentenced four people to prison and imposed about $1.6 million in fines for distributing pirated versions of Microsoft's Windows XP and other software … [Two] were sentenced to three-and-a-half years in prison … [while the other two] received sentences of two years … The court also fined the Chengdu Share Software Net Co., which operated 'Tomato Garden', more than 8.7 million yuan and confiscated nearly 3 million yuan of its revenue … Authorities moved against 'Tomato Garden' after receiving complaints from the Business Software Alliance. The Alliance, an industry trade group, lauded the court's decision as the first successful prosecution of large-scale, online software piracy in China.

(www.iht.com, 21 August 2009)

General Motors China and state-owned automaker FAW Group Corp. launched a 2 billion yuan ($293 million) joint venture Sunday [30 August] to make light-duty trucks and vans, initially for the fast-growing Chinese market ... [It is a] fifty–fifty joint venture ... Adding truck production will help the company's [GM's] exposure in one of the few major markets that continues to grow.

(www.iht.com, 30 August 2009)

'The Chinese market now accounts for more than half the world's sales of ... light delivery trucks ... as entrepreneurial small businesses flourish.... GM has been closing factories in the United States' (www.iht.com, 30 August 2009).

The vehicles will initially be sold in China under the FAW brand, but could in future be exported under the GM brand ... GM has recently emerged from bankruptcy in the United States and has seen its sales fall year-on-year on most of its Western markets, so China is a key area of growth.

(www.bbc.co.uk, 30 August 2009)

China is backsliding on overhauls to open up its economy to foreign business, thereby hindering competition and imperilling its shift to a new model of sustainable growth, the EU Chamber of Commerce in China said Wednesday [2 September]. In its annual position paper, the chamber said that government intervention in industrial policy and restrictions on foreign investment had been on the rise in the past three years, making China less attractive to European companies. The failure of the world's five largest wind energy operators to have a single national development project in China is one of the examples the chamber gave in arguing that foreign companies face discrimination.

(*IHT*, 3 September 2009, p. 19)

Telefonica, the Spanish telecom operator, and China Unicom, China's second largest telecom company, on Sunday [6 September] said they would swap stock in each other worth $2 billion as the companies deepened a strategic alliance to include the joint purchasing of mobile networks and phones ... Each operator will buy shares worth $1 billion in the other. The purchase will boost Telefonica's stake in China Unicom to 8 per cent from 5.4 per cent, making the Spanish operator the largest single investor in China Unicom. China Unicom, which trails only China Mobile in the domestic market, will acquire a 0.88 per cent stake in Telefonica, the former Spanish phone monopoly that owns mobile operator O2 in Europe and is the largest mobile operator in Latin America. Together the two companies will have about 550 million customers ... The agreement would also extend to network roaming and the sharing of technical research. Managers would also be swapped through an exchange programme ... Telefonica has been a financial investor in China's telecom market since 2005, when it bought a 2.99 per cent stake, which it later raised to 5.4 per cent, in China Netcom, an operator that was merged into China Unicom last year [2008].

(www.iht.com, 6 September 2009; *IHT*, 7 September 2009, p. 14)

China Unicom and Spain's Telefonica are to broaden the alliance deal to buy equity in each other worth $1 billion apiece. It is the first time a China telecoms group has taken an equity stake in a European operator. The Spanish company, the third largest telecommunications group by market capitalization, said in a regulatory filing on Sunday [6 September] that it would increase its holding in the Chinese operator to just above 8 per cent from 5.4 per cent ... Unicom hopes to use its strengthening alliance with the Spanish group to enter Latin America, where China is forging relationships to secure supplies of metals and hydrocarbons. Telefonica is keen to diversify outside the mature domestic market, where recession has hit demand. Vodaphone, among its competitors, has a 3.3 per cent stake in China Mobile, the country's largest mobile operator ... The companies said on Sunday they had reached agreement on a 'broad strategic alliance that includes co-operation in infrastructure and equipment purchasing, joint development of mobile services platforms, the provision of services to multinational clients, roaming and research and development'.

(www.ft.com, 6 September 2009; *FT*, 7 September 2009, p. 23)

Police [in Shanghai] have detained a former Coca-Cola bottling plant employee they accuse of corruption and bribery while working at the company. The detention of the employee from the Shanghai Shen-Mei Beverage and Food Company, a bottling plant partly owned by Coca-Cola, was reported over the weekend by China's state-run news media, which said the employee took about $1.5 million in bribes ... A female middle manager at the plant was detained by Shanghai police earlier this year [2009] and then dismissed by the bottling company ... The detention is the second high profile bribery case this year involving a global company. In July four Shanghai-based employees of Rio Tinto were detained ... Even though corruption is pervasive in China, very few executives working for global companies have been detained or arrested by Chinese police ... Earlier this year the company's (Coca-Cola's] move to pay $2.4 billion to acquire one of China's biggest juice makers, Huiyuan Juice Group, was blocked by the government, which cited anti-trust concerns.

(www.iht.com, 13 September 2009; *IHT*, 14 September 2009, p. 16)

Coca-Cola said Tuesday [15 September] that a second manager who worked in the company's Shanghai bottling plant has been detained by police on suspicion of accepting bribes or kickbacks ... A Coca-Cola spokesman said ... [that the] matter does not involve bribery of government officials but instead allegations that the former employees extracted kickbacks from suppliers and embezzled from the bottler. Coca-Cola said both former employees are Chinese citizens and worked as middle managers at the bottling operation, which is partly owned by Coke. One left the company in January 1998, and the other was dismissed by Coke after being detained by investigators in May of this year [2009].

(www.iht.com, 15 September 2009)

Groupe Danone of France resolved a long-running dispute with its Chinese joint venture partner Wednesday [30 September], agreeing to exit the venture by selling its 51 per cent stake in the Wahaha Group, one of China's largest beverage companies … the two companies agreed to drop legal proceedings that have dragged on for years, ending a high profile joint venture between the French food giant and a Chinese company that grew into a $2 billion beverage behemoth and one of China's best known brands. The terms of the sale were not disclosed, but analysts estimated that Danone could receive over $500 million for its 51 per cent … The dispute erupted in 2007, when Danone accused its Chinese partner, Wahaha, which is based in Hangzhou, of secretly operating a set of parallel companies that mirrored the joint venture's operations with virtually identical products and siphoned off as much as $100 million from the partnership … On Wednesday the two sides said they reached an 'amicable settlement that was awaiting Chinese government approval'.

(www.iht.com, 30 September 2009)

In September … foreign direct investment rose … by 19 per cent from a year earlier … But actual foreign direct investment for the first nine months of the year totalled $63.8 billion, a 14 per cent decline from the same period of 2008 … The September rise in foreign direct investment compared with a 7 per cent year-on-year increase in August, and declines of 35.7 per cent in July and 6.8 per cent in June.

(www.iht.com, 15 October 2009)

After a courtship of about twenty years, the Walt Disney Company [said on 4 November that it] has won approval from the central government to build a Disneyland-style theme park in Shanghai … [The] courtship began in July 1990, when Zhu Rongji, then the mayor of Shanghai, made a trip to the original Disneyland in Los Angeles with four other Chinese mayors and came home determined to have a Disneyland in his city. Mr Zhu rose through the ranks to become premier of China from 1998 to 2003 … The agreement for a Shanghai Disneyland is a landmark deal that carries enormous cultural and financial implications. Analysts estimate the initial park – not including hotels and resort infrastructure – will cost $3.5 billion, making it one of the largest ever foreign investments in China … Disney will own about 40 per cent of the Shanghai resort, with the remainder owned by a holding company formed by a consortium of Chinese companies selected by the government … Disney [already] has more than 600 employees in Beijing, Shanghai and Guangzhou … Hong Kong Disneyland opened four years ago … in September 2005.

(www.iht.com, 4 November 2009)

'The Hong Kong government owns a majority stake in Hong Kong Disneyland' (*IHT*, 5 November 2009, p. 18).

The US embassy in Beijing confirmed today [20 November] that it is pressing China to release an American held for two years on state secrets charges.

Xue Feng, a Chinese-born geologist, was detained after negotiating the sale of an oil industry database to his US-based employer.

(www.iht.com, 20 November 2009)

The Chinese government has held an American oil geologist on suspicion of stealing state secrets for nearly two years, prompting President Barack Obama to raise the issue during his visit to Beijing this week, the American embassy in Beijing said Friday [20 November] ... Chinese prosecutors indicted Xue Feng on a charge of theft of state secrets for having signed a contract on behalf of his employer at the time, IHS Inc., for the purchase of an oil industry database from a Chinese company ... Xue Feng's arrest received no public attention until this week and remained mired in a lengthy legal proceeding in Beijing ... [His] detention was first reported Thursday [19 November] by the Associated Press ... [He] left the company six months before his arrest.

(www.iht.com, 21 November 2009)

Beijing this month [November] fired a warning shot to acquisition-hungry chief executives across the globe when it demanded that Panasonic divest several coveted assets in Japan, in return for granting local anti-trust approval for its proposed takeover of Sanyo Electric, a domestic rival ... China cleared Panasonic's $9 billion takeover of Sanyo, but ordered production plant divestments in Japan and the halving of a 40 per cent Panasonic stake in a coveted battery joint venture with Toyota ... The ruling marks the first time that China has used powers introduced in August 2008 to compel disposals outside the mainland as part of an anti-monopoly review ... China is hardly alone in taking such actions. The United States and the EU have used the lure of access ... to impose conditions on outside companies ... Beijing has used the anti-monopoly laws to force global companies engaged in mergers and acquisitions to sell mainland assets or, in the case of Coca-Cola, to block an acquisition of a local company ... In March 2009 China blocked Coca-Cola's $2.4 billion bid for China Huiyuan Juice on competition grounds ... In November 2008 China cleared InBev's $52 billion takeover of Anheuser-Busch, but imposed restrictions to stop the Belgian brewer acquiring interests in four Chinese companies.

(*FT*, 30 November 2009, p. 11)

New Chinese rules for government procurement, which reportedly favour products with some parts designed in China, were being reassessed yesterday [15 December] after protests from foreign businesses and the United States following their publication last week. Some lawyers now believe that it should be possible for foreign companies to qualify.

(*FT*, 16 December 2009, p. 8)

Gazprom signalled yesterday [21 December] it would fight to retain influence over central Asia's gas exports, settling an eight-month trade dispute with Turkmenistan and saying it would build new pipelines to bring Turkmen gas to Europe … [Gazprom] said Russia had agreed to buy up to 30 billion cubic metres a year of gas from Turkmenistan starting next year [2010]. Gazprom would also build a new pipeline to link untapped gas reserves in east Turkmenistan with a new pipeline running along the Caspian coast from central Asia to Russia … the dispute erupted in April [2009] after a pipeline explosion halted Turkmenistan's gas exports to Russia … Turkmenistan accuse Gazprom of causing the blast – a charge the Russian company denied … Gazprom, facing a drop in Russian and European gas demand, ordered Turkmenistan to renegotiate a contract signed last year [2008] to supply Russia with 50 billion cubic metres of gas in 2009. Turkmenistan refused, turning instead to China and Iran with offers of extra gas supplies. It also stepped up talks with the EU to join the planned Nabucco pipeline project to bring Caspian and central Asian gas to Europe, via the Caucasus and Turkey.

(*FT*, 23 December 2009)

Western companies contend that they face a lengthening list of obstacles to doing business in China, from 'buy Chinese' government procurement policies and growing restrictions on foreign investments to widespread counterfeiting. These barriers generally fall into two broad categories. Some relate to China's desire to maintain control over internal dissent. Others involve its efforts to become internationally competitive in as many industries as possible … Foreign companies have long complained of being cheated by joint venture partners who set up parallel businesses on the side or abscond with assets … On 4 June [2009] … national, provincial and local government agencies … [were ordered] to buy Chinese-made products as part of the nearly $600 billion economic stimulus programme; imports were only allowed when no suitable Chinese products were available … China has also restricted exports of a long list of minerals for which it mines much of the world's supply, like zinc for making galvanized steel and so-called rare earth elements for manufacturing hybrid gasoline–electric cars. Those restrictions … [include] steep export tariffs to tonnage quotas and even export bans.

(www.iht.com, 13 January 2010)

China allows twenty foreign films a year to be shown on local screens, splitting revenue among producers, theatres and local distributors. Chinese distributors purchase the local rights to show other foreign firms without sharing profits with the producers, industry sources say.

(www.iht.com, 30 January 2010)

'In recent weeks China has been left out of annual iron ore negotiations by global mining companies, in part because of fears of retribution if talks collapse' (*FT*, 14 January 2010, p. 2).

In the world of iron ore … Vale of Brazil, Rio Tinto and BHP Billiton recently began talking to Japanese companies about setting a benchmark price for the metal. That price will be presented to Beijing on a 'take it or leave it' basis, executives said … Chinese customers, led by Baosteel, account for more than half of the seaborne market.

(p. 15)

Last year [2009] the China Iron and Steel Association, which took over representing iron ore buyers in the negotiations, failed to reach agreement on term prices with top suppliers and left mills to pay spot prices. China has tried to strengthen its position with the government unifying the price for iron ore imports, curbing the number of mills permitted to import ore and forcing small mills to buy via a licensed importer.

(www.thetimes.co.uk, 10 February 2010)

'Last year's iron ore contract price talks failed to set a price for China, because of differences between China's steel industry association and foreign miners' (*FT*, 11 February 2010, p. 17).

A Chinese prosecutor handed down indictments on Wednesday [10 February] against an Australian citizen and three Chinese employees of British–American mining giant Rio Tinto, charging them with accepting bribes and stealing trade secrets … The indictments [were] announced through Xinhua … According to Xinhua, the four employees 'requested and received' huge bribes from state-owned steel producers and gained trade secrets from Chinese steel companies by 'luring with valuable goods and other illegal methods'.

(*IHT*, 11 February 2010, p. 19)

The prosecutor's office also said the Rio Tinto employees had badly harmed the Chinese steel makers … The announcement suggests that prosecutors are not pressing forward with allegations that the Rio employees bribed steel industry officials, something that was alleged earlier.

(www.iht.com, 10 February 2010)

The prosecutor appeared to accuse the men of giving and of taking bribes: 'Many times they used personal inducements and other improper means to obtain commercial secrets to obtain secrets from Chinese steel firms, causing serious consequences for the steel firms.'

(*FT*, 11 February 2010, p. 17)

The prosecutor's office said: 'The accused four, including Stern Hu, exploited their positions to seek gain for others, and numerous times either sought or illegally accepted massive bribes from a number of Chinese steel firms. Many times they used personal inducements and other improper means to obtain commercial secrets from Chinese steel firms, causing serious consequences for the steel firms concerned.'

(www.bbc.co.uk, 10 February 2010)

Kohlberg Kravis Roberts and Company and TPG Capital have tentatively agreed to pay close to $1 billion to acquire Morgan Stanley's 34 per cent stake in China's leading investment bank ... The deal for a stake in the China International Capital Corporation would be one of the largest single foreign investments ever made in China's financial services industry ... Morgan Stanley and one of this country's biggest banks, the China Construction Bank, helped form China International Capital in 1995. But for more than a year Morgan Stanley has been trying to sell its stake to focus on establishing a Chinese joint venture that would give Morgan Stanley more management control. The deal has not been finalized and must still meet the approval of regulators ... A report that KKR and TPG are close to a deal with Morgan Stanley was reported on Tuesday [23 February] in *The Wall Street Journal* ... The Blackstone Group, the Carlyle Group and other firms are even forming private equity funds denominated in the renminbi. China International Capital, which is run by Levin Zhu, the son of former prime minister Zhu Rongyi, generates hundreds of millions of dollars in revenue and usually tops the list of Chinese stock underwriters. But for years Morgan Stanley has had little or no role in the company's management decisions, having lost much of its control after rocky relations in the earliest years of the venture.

(www.iht.com, 23 February 2010)

Carlyle Group, one of the world's biggest private equity firms, said Wednesday [24 February] that it had formed a partnership with one of the largest non-state-owned Chinese conglomerates to invest in China and around the world. The deal with Fosun Group of Shanghai, which has holdings in steel, mining, pharmaceuticals and real estate, is Carlyle's latest push into ... China ... and another indication of the growing role Chinese companies are seeking to play in global deal-making. At a news conference Wednesday executives from the two companies ... said the partners had already set up a $100 million fund denominated in the renminbi to invest in emerging Chinese companies. But there are plans, they said, to raise substantially more money from wealthy Chinese to bolster the size of the fund. The announcement comes just weeks after Carlyle said it had agreed to form a separate renminbi-denominated fund with the help of the Beijing government, thereby joining Blackstone Group and other global equity firms in the scramble to tap Chinese investors. Carlyle has not disclosed the size of the fund it is forming with Beijing's help ... Carlyle has invested about $2.5 billion in the country over more than a decade ... In the deal announced Wednesday Carlyle and Fosun executives said that in addition to searching for deals in China, the two companies would look for overseas acquisition targets and help Chinese companies 'go global' to acquire assets or brands.

(www.iht.com, 24 February 2010; *IHT*, 24 February 2010, p. 21)

The [global] flow of direct foreign investment (FDI) fell by 39 per cent in 2009 to just over $1 trillion, from a shade under $1.7 trillion in 2008,

according to the UN Conference on Trade and Development [Unctad] ...
FDI into China ... declined by only 2.6 per cent.

(*The Economist*, 13 February 2010, p. 106)

Special Economic Zones (SEZs)

Four Special Economic Zones (SEZs) were set up in 1980, the State Council
having given approval in July 1979. They were 'special' in the sense that concessions such as lower taxes and tariffs and more flexible employment policies
were granted in order to attract foreign capital, technology and know-how.
('[There] are tax breaks for foreign companies in five SEZs, fourteen "open
coastal cities" and some fifty development zones. Foreign investors pay corporate tax at a maximum 15 per cent in SEZs and 24 per cent in open coastal cities
and development zones. Chinese companies in the same locations pay a
maximum of 33 per cent': *FT*, 18 September 2002, p. 20.)

The SEZs were essentially built from scratch, a means of experimenting with
new ideas in a gradual and partial manner. New ideas and Western influences
would only be spread to the remainder of the economy if and when they had
proved their worth. It is no coincidence that three of the SEZs (Shenzhen, Zhuhai
and Shantou) are in Guangdong province adjacent to Hong Kong and Macao,
while the fourth is Xiamen in Fujian province opposite Taiwan. Hainan Island
became the fifth SEZ in 1988.

> The industrial sector was placed at the centre stage of SEZ economies ...
> Domestic enterprises, state- and non-state-owned alike, were purposely
> allowed to operate alongside foreign-invested firms. Firms in the zone were
> encouraged to establish connections of various sorts with their counterparts
> in the rest of the domestic economy in order to foster technology transfers
> and to promote growth through the expanded economic links ... [But] as a
> precaution taken to minimize possible negative impacts on the rest of the
> economy, should the SEZ efforts later fail, all four zones were set up in
> backward areas.
>
> (Ge 1999: 1269)

> As the testing ground for developing a market-oriented, open economy
> numerous reform measures have first been experimented in the SEZs
> and those useful ones are later introduced into the rest of the economy ...
> One example of these reforms has been the SEZ effort in revitalizing
> state-owned enterprises ... [e.g.] employment is now based on labour
> contracts ... Ownership structure is changing from a pure state ownership to
> a mixed one; private and foreign investors may have a piece of pie by owning
> enterprise stocks ... Foreign direct investment in the tertiary sector, such as
> retailing, insurance, banking and other financial and information services, are
> expanding. Stock, bond and futures markets are developing. Experimentation
> with utilizing foreign portfolio investment is already underway.
>
> (pp. 1281–2)

No new SEZs have been approved since 1988, but there has been a proliferation of economic development zones with various names. In 1984 fourteen major east coast cities (including Shanghai) were opened to foreign investment. Governed by regulations similar to those in the SEZs, several hundred economic and technological development zones were set up in these open areas. Shortly afterwards open areas were extended to the Pearl, Yangtzi and South Fujian deltas, as well as the Liaoning and Jiaodong peninsulas. In 1988 the 'coastal area economic development strategy' was approved, almost the entire coastal area being opened to the outside world. In April 1990 the Pudong New Area was established in Shanghai. Since the early 1990s the entire border area of China and many inland regions have been opened up (Ge 1999: 1282).

The SEZs did not have a smooth ride. For example, in 1985 Deng Xiaoping described Shenzhen as 'an experiment that remains to be proved' (e.g. the volume of exports and the level of technology attracted were disappointing). Deng visited Shenzhen and Zhuhai in early 1992 and gave his approval. But in early 1993 the central government clamped down on the spread of other zones, often set up without central government approval, in order to dampen the construction boom. Although their immediate future is secure, the concessions granted to all development zones are to be gradually phased out over the longer term. (This was a requirement for WTO membership. The section on the WTO, above, includes material on the conditions relating to DFI.)

Authorities have already begun dismantling some of the useless projects that officials build in pursuit of GDP growth and promotions. These include thousands of 'development zones', which local governments carved out of requisitioned farmland to build villas, golf courses and resorts, leaving farmers landless and jobless. A report in November [2004] by the ministry of land resources said local governments had cut the number of development zones from 5,658 to 3,612 and frozen approval of new zones.

(*FEER*, 1 April 2004, p. 31)

China has 6,749 registered industrial and investment zones ... The central government has tried to control their growth but has largely failed because provinces, cities, towns and villages are all competing with each other for business to create local employment.

(*FT*, Survey, 7 December 2004, p. 3)

WTO membership included a commitment to phase out tax concessions for foreign-invested enterprises.

'Official incentives for FDI are shrinking: the preferential 15 per cent corporation tax rate enjoyed by foreign companies, half the level for their Chinese counterparts, will be phased out by 2006' (*FT*, Survey, 7 December 2004, p. 2).

[On 11 January 2005 China said that it] will maintain preferential tax rates for foreign companies until at least 2007 ... Foreign companies are subject to an average 15 per cent tax rate, less than half of the 33 per cent paid by Chinese companies ... The government [had] planned to unify the corporate tax code as early as 2006 ... [Apart from foreign companies investing in China] Chinese companies that are eligible for tax exemptions are also lobbying for the corporate tax law to be delayed.

(www.iht.com, 11 January 2005; *IHT*, 12 January 2005, p. 13)

'The government said on Tuesday [12 July] that it would keep tax breaks for some foreign investors because rising labour costs and raw material shortages had made the need for technology transfers and management expertise more urgent' (www.iht.com, 13 July 2005).

The [18 December] 1978 political meeting [is] known as the Third Plenum ... Two years later Deng Xiaoping pointed at a sleepy fishing village in coastal southern China and ordained it the country's first Special Economic Zone to experiment with foreign investment and export manufacturing. Today Shenzhen is a city of more than 10 million people.

(*IHT*, 19 December 2008, p. 7)

6   Economic performance

China still has a relatively low *per capita* GDP.

'Despite all the progress since 1978, China is still a much poorer country than most people realize – it is not even in the top 100 in the IMF's GDP *per capita*' (*FT*, 23 October 2008, p. 15).

'Nationwide *per capita* income is only about $2,000' (*IHT*, 23 October 2008, p. 12).

> One of the more surprising statistics about the Chinese economy is that, in terms of *per capita* GDP, it is still not in the top 100 countries. According to the IMF, China ranked behind Cape Verde and Armenia in 2008, and only just ahead of Iraq and the Republic of Congo. Despite the remarkable reduction in poverty, daily life for most Chinese families is still a struggle to get by.
>
> (*FT*, 27 September 2009, p. 11)

'*Per capita* income on a purchasing power parity [PPP] basis has hit $6,000. That still makes China a lower middle income country' (*FT*, 1 October 2009).

Since 1978 economic performance has generally been very impressive. (See Table 1: the table presents the earlier official Chinese figures for rates of growth of GDP, whereas the section below entitled 'The upward revision of 2004 GDP' gives the revised figures.)

'[China's is] one of the largest and most sustained expansions in history' (Larry Rohter, www.iht.com, 19 November 2004).

> The pace of economic change in China has been extremely rapid since the start of economic reforms just over twenty-five years ago. Economic growth has averaged 9.5 per cent over the past two decades and seems likely to continue at that pace for some time. Such an increase in output represents one of the most sustained and rapid economic transformations seen in the world economy in the past fifty years. It has delivered higher incomes and a substantial reduction of those living in absolute poverty ... A marked evolution of economic policies over the past two decades has led to a long period of sustained economic expansion. National income has been doubling every eight years and this has been reflected in the reduction of the poverty rate to

Table 1 China: selected economic indicators

Economic indicator	1990	1991	1992	1993	1994	1995	1996	1997	1998	1999	2000	2001	2002	2003	2004	2005	2006	2007	2008	2009
Rate of growth of GDP (%) (revised figures in brackets)	3.8	9.2	14.2	13.5 (14.0)	12.6 (13.1)	10.5 (10.9)	9.6 (10.0)	8.8 (9.3)	7.8 (7.8)	7.1 (7.6)	8.0 (8.4)	7.3 (8.3)	8.0 (9.1)	9.5 (10.0)	9.5 (10.1)	10.2	11.1	11.9	9.6	8.7
Rate of growth of industrial output (%)	7.8	12.9	20.8	23.6	18.0	13.9	12.1	10.8	8.8	9.9			12.6	18.1						
Rate of growth of agricultural output (%)	7.6	3.0	3.7	4.0	3.5	5.0	5.1	3.5	3.5											
Grain output (million tonnes)	435.0	435.3	442.6	456.4	444.5				512.0	508.0		450.0		430.6	469.5	484.0				
Retail or consumer inflation rate (%)	2.1	2.7	5.4	13.0	21.7	14.8	6.1	1.5	-2.6	-2.9	-1.5		-0.8	1.2	3.9	1.8	1.5	4.8		
Population (billion)		1.158	1.170							1.259	1.265	1.272			1.300					
Balance of trade ($ billion)													25.50	31.90		117.0	177.47	262.2		
Foreign exchange reserves ($ billion)				21.2				139.9			154.67	165.6	212.2	286.4	403.25	609.9	819.9	1,066.0	1,500.0	1,946.0

Source: Various issues of IMF, *World Economic Outlook*; United Nations, *World Economic and Social Survey*; United Nations Economic and Social Commission for Asia and the Pacific, *Economic and Social Survey of Asia and the Pacific*; *FEER*; OECD, *Economic Outlook*; FT; and *IHT*; Jeffries (1996a: 696).

much lower levels. Indeed, by some accounts, over half of the reduction in absolute poverty in the world between 1980 and 2000 occurred in China.

(OECD 2005: website Chapter 1)

During their industrial revolutions America and Britain took fifty years to double their real incomes per head; today China is achieving that in a single decade ... Until the late nineteenth century China and India were the world's two biggest economies.

(*The Economist*, 21 January 2006, pp. 12–13)

'China's growth rate [is] the fastest over thirty years of any large country in history' (*The Economist*, 22 December 2007, p. 98). 'The past thirty years ... have witnessed the most astonishing economic transformation in human history' (*The Economist*, 13 December 2008, p. 13).

China both came through the 1997 Asian financial crisis in good shape and is coping relatively well with the global financial crisis (as has already been discussed).

China's rapid expansion of late (the fastest growing large economy) has been of global significance.

Using GDP converted at market rates China has accounted for only 17 per cent of the total increase in global GDP over the past three years; but measured on a purchasing-power parity (PPP) basis it has contributed almost one-third of global GDP growth, much more than America's 13 per cent.

(*The Economist*, Survey, 2 October 2004, p. 8)

'China accounted for 13 per cent of global growth in 2004, according to the IMF' (*IHT*, 16 January 2006, p. 13).

'China's economy accounted for about a quarter of the world's economic growth last year [2007]' (www.iht.com, 12 November 2008).

'In recent years China has contributed around a quarter of global GDP growth' (www.ft.com, 20 October 2008).

'China has become the main engine of the world economy, accounting for one-third of global GDP growth in the first half of this year [2008]' (*The Economist*, 11 October 2008, p. 110).

In past global slowdowns the United States invariably led the way out, followed by Europe and the rest of the world. But now, for the first time, the catalyst is coming from China and the rest of Asia, where resurgent economies are helping the still-shaky West recover from the deepest recession since World War II ... China overtook the United States as Japan's leading trading partner in the first half of 2009, while in Europe manufacturers are looking east instead of west.

(*IHT*, 24 August 2009, pp. 1, 16)

China has affected world market prices of commodities such as oil (see below), coal, iron ore, steel and cement.

China has become one of the world's foremost destination for direct foreign investment.

China's global significance can also be gauged from the following:

'China overtook Japan last year [2003] to become the world's second largest oil consumer [after the United States]' (*FEER*, 10 June 2004, p. 27).

'Last year [2003] China overtook Japan and the EU to become the world's largest importer of iron ore' (www.iht.com, 5 March 2004).

> Cie Vale do Rio Doce, the world's biggest iron ore maker, and Baosteel Group of China agreed Thursday [21 December] to raise iron ore prices next year [2007] by 9.5 per cent, setting a benchmark price increase that would affect steel makers worldwide. The deal marks the first time that the industry's benchmark has been set with a Chinese steel maker. Historically, the first steel maker to settle with CVRD, BHP Billiton or Rio Tinto set the price for the global steel industry. The three mining companies control two-thirds of global iron ore trade ... CVRD is the largest supplier of iron ore to China and supplies about a third of exports ... Baosteel was charged with leading the negotiations for all the Chinese steel makers – some 260 in all ... China produces more than 40 per cent of the world's steel ... Baosteel, the top Chinese steel maker threatened not to observe a 19 per cent rise for 2006 set by CVRD and ThyssenKrupp.
>
> (www.iht.com, 22 December 2006)

> China moved last year [2005] from being a massive importer of steel to being a modest net exporter ... [China] produces three times as much [steel] as Japan, the second placed country, and output has doubled over the last five years.
>
> (*FT*, 3 August 2006, p. 11)

'In 2005 China consumed 31 per cent of the world's steel and, as a result, 41 per cent of iron ore, 35 per cent of coal and 23 per cent of refined copper' (*FT*, 8 March 2007, p. 8).

> In 1996 China and the United States each accounted for 13 per cent of global steel production. By 2005 the US share had dropped to 8 per cent, while China's share had risen to 35 per cent ... China now makes half of the world's cement and flat glass, and about a third of its aluminium. In 2006 China overtook Japan as the second largest producer of cars and trucks after the United States.
>
> (*IHT*, 27 August 2007, p. 4)

'Steel production ... is now about 40 per cent of the world's output' (*IHT*, 11 December 2007, p. 13).

'China, with about a fifth of the world's population, now consumes half of its cement, a third of its steel and over a quarter of its aluminium' (*The Economist*, Survey, 15 March 2008, p. 4).

'China was a net importer of coal in January 2007 for the first time' (*IHT*, 16 July 2007, p. 13).

China and world prices, especially oil prices

Oil prices rose above the symbolic level of $100 a barrel for the first time Wednesday [2 January 2008] … Crude oil futures for February delivery hit $100 on the New York Mercantile Exchange shortly after noon New York time, before falling back slightly … Around mid-day in New York futures were trading at $99.15, up $3.17. Oil prices, which had fallen to a low of $50 a barrel at the beginning of 2007, have quadrupled since 2003 … Oil is now within reach of its historic inflation-adjusted high reached in April 1980 in the aftermath of the Iranian revolution, when oil prices jumped to the equivalent of $102 a barrel in today's money. Unlike the oil shocks of the 1970s and 1980s, which were caused by sudden interruptions in oil supplies from the Middle East, the current surge is fundamentally different. Prices have risen steadily over several years because of a rise in demand for oil and gasoline in both developed and developing countries. China has more than doubled its use of oil since New York crude dropped to this century's low of $16.70 a barrel on 19 November 2001. That has soaked up most of the world's spare production capacity amid supply cuts in Nigeria, Iraq and Venezuela. The 11 per cent slide of the dollar last year [2007] against the Euro also fed into higher oil prices because it made commodities cheaper for buyers outside the United States and attracted investors as a hedge against inflation.

(*IHT*, 3 January 2008, p. 1)

Crude oil futures for February delivery hit $100 on the New York Mercantile Exchange shortly after noon Wednesday when a single trader bid up the price by buying a modest lot and then selling it immediately at a small loss. Prices eased somewhat in later trading, settling at $99.62 at the end of Wednesday. In early NYMEX trading Thursday [3 January] prices reached $99.90 a barrel. The $100 mark was a long-anticipated milestone in an era of rapidly escalating energy demand and tightening supplies … The price of oil had been flirting with $100 for months … There is no shortage of explanations for the escalation of oil prices by about 60 per cent over the last year. The price of a barrel was below $25 as recently as 2003 and below $11 in 1998, a time when there was a glut in the world markets … Political tensions in countries like Nigeria, Venezuela and Iran have threatened world supplies, while important fields in Mexico, the United States and other countries are ageing and producing less. Big oil companies are having trouble finding promising new fields to bolster supplies. Newly found fields in the deep waters of the Gulf of Mexico and off the coast of Brazil will take years to develop … Oil is now within reach of its inflation-adjusted high, reached in April 1980 in the aftermath of the Iranian revolution, when oil prices jumped in the equivalent of $102.81 in today's money. The brief stab at $100 on Wednesday broke the previous intraday trading record of $99.29, reached on 21 November. The price at the end of the day, $99.62, surpassed the record close of $98.18, set on 23 November.

(*IHT*, 4 January 2008, p. 13)

It is true that the global supply of oil has been growing sluggishly, mainly because the world is, bit by bit, running out of the stuff: big oil discoveries have become rare, and when oil is found it is harder to get at. But the reason oil supply has not been able to keep up with demand is surging oil consumption in newly industrializing economies – above all in China. Even now China accounts for only about 9 per cent of the world's demand for oil. But because China's oil demand has been rising along with its economy, in recent years China has been responsible for about a third of the growth in world oil consumption. As a result, oil at $100 a barrel is, in large part, a made-in-China phenomenon.

(Paul Krugman, *IHT*, 5 January 2008, p. 7)

The immediate catalysts for the rising prices were ongoing turmoil in places like Nigeria and Pakistan and the continuing slump of the dollar. To those holding Euros or yen, the weakening dollar makes oil and gold look cheaper; they can bid up prices in dollar terms without spending any more of their own currency. Moreover, gold, and nowadays oil too, is seen as a haven when the dollar is weak ... Demand for oil continues to rise quickly in booming spots such as China and the Gulf states. These countries make matters worse by artificially inflating demand for petrol through subsidies or price caps, which leave consumers with little incentive to drive less even as the oil price surges. Western oil companies, saddled with rising prices for everything from engineers to truck tyres – and in some cases, outright shortages – are struggling to pump more oil. They have also been excluded from the most promising terrain for exploration by nationalist regimes, which are increasingly reluctant to share their wealth with outsiders. Those same regimes seem in no hurry to increase their output, partly because they realize that their sluggishness is helping keep prices high. But publicly, at least, the Organization of the Petroleum Exporting Countries [OPEC] argues that oil at $100 is the result not of a shortage of supply but of financial speculation. There might be some truth in that: in recent years the volume of oil traded on markets such as New York's Mercantile Exchange (NYMEX) has risen out of all proportion to the amount consumed. Hedge and pension funds and even individual investors have been piling into commodities of late. This influx of money could be exaggerating the market's gyrations. Indeed, oil topped $100 in a single transaction before falling back.

(www.economist.com, 3 January 2008)

Setting an all-time record, prices rose to nearly $104 a barrel on Monday [3 March], exceeding the inflation-adjusted high reached in the early 1980s during the second oil price shock. Oil futures rose as much as $2.11 to $103.95 on the New York Mercantile Exchange. That level tops the record set in April 1980 of $39.50 a barrel, which would translate to $103.76 in today's money ... The surge in oil prices is markedly different from the energy crises of the 1970s and 1980s, which were brought about by sudden interruptions in oil supplies. Since the year 2000 oil prices have more than quadrupled as strong growth in demand from the United States and Asia outstripped the ability of oil producers to increase their output ... In London Brent crude futures rose $2.07 to $102.17 a barrel.

(www.iht.com, 3 March 2008)

'On the New York Mercantile Exchange, crude for April delivery was up $1.76 at $103.60 a barrel, after reaching a record high of $103,95' (*IHT*, 4 March 2008, p. 15).

> Despite its exporting prowess, China remains a 'price taker' on global markets. Wal-Mart and other big buyers still dictate terms to China's legions of manufacturers of mainly low value-added goods ... Jim O'Neill (chief global economist with investment bank Goldman Sachs in London): 'Pricing power comes when you make something that the rest of the world is desperate to buy. I can't think of a single industry where you can say that about China' ... Nor is China's insatiable appetite for raw materials increasing its bargaining power with big mining companies. Witness China's distress at the possibility that BHP Billiton might take over Rio Tinto and squeeze ever higher prices for iron ore from the country's steel makers.
>
> (Alan Wheatley, www.iht.com, 7 January 2008)

> Shortages and soaring prices for palm oil, soybean oil and many other types of vegetable oils are the latest, most striking example of a developing global problem: costly food ... A startling change is unfolding in the world's food markets. Soaring fuel prices have altered the equation for growing food and transporting it across the globe. Huge demand for biofuels has created tension between using land to produce fuel and using it for food.
>
> (www.iht.com, 20 January 2008)

> [Globally] the primary cause of the stubbornly high food and energy prices is demand from fast growing emerging economies like China, along with the rise of ethanol, which is gobbling up a big chunk of the US corn crop and diverting acreage from wheat.
>
> (*IHT*, 3 March 2008, p. 14)

> Consumption of meat and other high quality foods – mainly in China and India – has boosted demand for grain for animal feed. Poor harvests due to bad weather in this country [the United States] and elsewhere have contributed. High energy prices are adding to the pressures. Yet the most important reason for the price shock is the rich world's subsidized appetite for biofuels. In the United States 14 per cent of the corn crop was used to produce ethanol in 2006 – a share expected to reach 30 per cent by 2010.
>
> (www.iht.com, 3 March 2008; *IHT*, 4 March 2008, p. 4)

'The country that discovered the soya bean has to import most of its needs' (www.bbc.co.uk, 5 January 2008).

> Lately traders have taken notice of flat or declining output from non-OPEC producers like Mexico and Britain ... In Russia, the world's number two

producer after Saudi Arabia, output failed to grow for a third month in a row in March [2008]. But in China, where a decline might be expected at old fields like Daqing, growth has been small but steady. Output climbed 2.2 per cent in the first quarter [of 2008] ... China's oil companies have channelled vast amounts of cash into high- and low-tech methods of extracting extra barrels of crude. While surging oil demand in China grabs the headlines, its upstream, or production, sector has quietly become the world's fifth biggest at 3.76 million barrels a day, displacing Mexico and closing in on Iran, which pumps just under 4 million barrels a day ... With its reliance on imported crude heading towards 50 per cent of its needs, Beijing has urged its state-owned companies Sinopec, PetroChina and CNOOC to pump out every possible drop of oil ... Pessimists thought the decline of China's oil output could have begun as early as the middle of this decade, but cash from higher oil prices and an intensive exploration and production drive have staved off that date for at least a few years. China is optimistic it can increase or maintain oil output for several decades ... [A] deputy minister for energy resources ... [said] last year [2007] that China thought it could maintain oil output at 200 million tonnes – well above current levels – for at least thirty years ... But even those with a positive outlook warn that Beijing may be shooting itself in the foot by charging a windfall tax on oil production and requiring its majors to use upstream profits to subsidize low, state-set prices for oil products.

(*IHT*, 22 April 2008, p. 15)

(See the relevant section in the summary for more recent figures on oil prices.)

GDP growth

There are various estimates of GDP growth. It was once generally thought that official figures exaggerated performance. Since October 2003, however, there have been increasing reports that the official estimated growth rate for the year might actually have been underestimated. (See Jeffries 2006a: 618–21.)

China claims that its economy is growing at 10 per cent to 11 per cent a year ... Don't believe it ... Economic growth can be inferred from electricity consumption. In every country in the world electricity use has generally grown faster than GDP ... If we consider China's actual electricity use ... we come up with this estimate: GDP in China has been growing somewhere between 4.5 per cent ... to 6 per cent a year.

(Lester Thurow, *IHT*, 21 August 2007, p. 1)

Growth of 7 per cent is considered the minimum required to generate the 10 million new jobs needed each year over the next five years to cover the increase in the work force and absorb surplus farm labour as well as workers idled as a result of state factory closures.

(*IHT*, 8 November 2001, p. 10)

'Employment in China is growing by only 1 per cent a year' (www.iht.com, 19 October 2007).

'Anything [less than 8 per cent growth], experts say, and the economy cannot create enough jobs to keep up with the mass of humanity, at least 15 million people, entering the labour market every year' (www.iht.com, 5 November 2008; *IHT*, 6 November 2008, p. 17).

Prior to the global financial crisis, the actual GDP growth rate in recent years exceeded the annual state-set target, despite restrictive monetary policy (such as rising interest rates and increases in bank reserve ratios) and central government pressure on banks to slow the expansion of credit and on local authorities to slow investment. The global financial crisis has already been discussed.

The upward revision of 2004 GDP

(See Jeffries 2006a: 621–6.)

> China has revised its rate of economic growth for 2007 from 11.4 per cent to 11.9 per cent, saying it had underestimated the output from the service sector ... The National Bureau of Statistics also raised its measure of 2006 growth from 11.1 per cent to 11.6 per cent.
>
> (www.iht.com, 10 April 2008)

The upward revision of 2007 GDP

'Revised figures published this week show that in 2007 China overtook Germany to become the world's third biggest economy' (www.economist.com, 14 January 2009).

> China on Wednesday [14 January 2009] revised upwards its GDP [growth rate] for 2007 to 13 per cent from 11.9 per cent, which would mean it had passed Germany to become the third largest economy in the world. The revised growth rate, announced by the National Bureau of Statistics, was the fastest since 1993, when the economy expanded 13.5 per cent. The statistics office had already updated its estimate of 2007 growth in April [2008] from an initial reading of 11.4 per cent ... The World Bank uses gross national income converted to dollars using the Atlas method, which takes a three-year moving average for the exchange rate. China now estimates that the total value of goods and services in 2007 was 3.1 per cent higher than previously thought. Applying this increase to the World Bank's published rankings gives China a gross national income of $3.218 trillion for 2007 compared with $3.197 trillion for Germany ... GNI [gross national income] takes into account all production in the domestic economy plus net flows of income from abroad like profits and wages.
>
> (*IHT*, 15 January 2009, p. 11)

Only the United States and Japan [are now] larger than China ... According to the IMF, Germany's GDP was $3,321 billion in 2007, using exchange rates for that year. By the latest estimate China's GDP was $3,382 billion, the US's was $13,807 billion and Japan's $4,382 billion. China is also close to surpassing Germany as the world's biggest exporter ... It was the second time China had revised upwards the growth figures for its 2007 GDP, first calculated to be 11.4 per cent. Some suspect Chinese authorities of massaging the figures to underplay economic volatility, exaggerating growth when conditions are tough and underestimating it when the economy is booming.

(*FT*, 15 January 2009, p. 5)

'Economists were already confident that China overtook Germany during 2008, but it now seems that the change occurred in a year earlier. China took fourth place from Britain in 2005' (www.guardian.co.uk, 14 January 2009).

'GDP expanded 13 per cent [in 2007], up from an earlier estimate of 11.9 per cent, to $3.5 trillion ... Germany's GDP per person was $38,800 in 2007 compared with $2,800 in China' (www.bbc.co.uk, 14 January 2009).

Purchasing-power parity (PPP)

'Purchasing-power parity (PPP) [is] the idea that, in the long run, exchange rates should equalize the prices in any two countries of a common basket of tradable goods and services' (*The Economist*, 25 June 2005, p. 100).

China's world ranking in terms of GDP and GDP per head in purchasing-power parity (PPP) terms is higher:

'Using the much stronger "purchasing power" exchange rate of 1.9 renminbi to the dollar used by the World Bank, the figure represents $5.04 trillion, making China's economy the second largest in the world after the United States' (*FEER*, 10 January 2002, p. 29).

In dollar terms its GDP is the sixth largest in the world, just smaller than France's. In terms of purchasing-power parity (after adjusting for price differences between economies) it is second only to the United States with an 11.8 per cent share of world GDP.

(*The Economist*, 15 February 2003, p. 74)

'At market prices Japan [is] the world's second largest economy ... [In 2002 it had a] GDP of $4,266 billion, while China's was only $1,210 billion ... [However] at PPP ... China was the world's second largest economy' (*FT*, 22 September 2003, p. 21).

If China's GDP is converted into dollars using market exchange rates it amounted to $2.7 trillion last year [2006], only one–fifth of America's $13.2 trillion and the fourth largest in the world. But a dollar buys a lot more in China than in America because prices of non-traded goods and services tend to be much lower in poor countries. Converting a poor country's GDP into dollars at market exchange rates therefore understates the true size of its economy ... On a PPP basis the World Bank ranks China as the world's second biggest economy, with a GDP of $10 trillion last year ... The difficulty of measuring PPP is one reason why some economists prefer to compare the sizes of economies using market exchange rates.

(*The Economist*, 1 December 2007, p. 90)

New figures show that China's GDP is 40 per cent smaller than previously ... China's GDP in yuan terms remains unchanged. What has happened is that the World Bank has changed the calculations it uses to make international comparisons of the size of economies. Converting a poor country's GDP can understate the true size because a dollar buys more in an emerging market such as China ... Previous estimates of China's GDP were largely guesswork. Now the World Bank has produced new calculations based on a survey of over 1,000 goods and services in 146 countries, including China for the first time. On this basis China's GDP in 2005 was $5.3 trillion, compared with $2.2 trillion using market exchange rates and $8.9 trillion using previous PPP estimates. This was still well below America's $12.4 trillion that year ... The revisions do not reduce China's growth rate – the fastest over thirty years of any large country in history ... It remains ... even on revised figures ... the world's second biggest economy.

(*The Economist*, 22 December 2007, p. 98)

New calculations by the World Bank suggest that the Chinese economy [GDP] may not be as large as previously thought ... The World Bank issued preliminary figures Monday [17 December 2007] that recalculated what would be the economic output of 146 countries – including China ... Purchasing-power parity [PPP] calculations ... showed that China's output was 40 per cent smaller than previous World Bank estimates ... The average Chinese has an economic output worth $1,721 at China's low market prices. That works out to the buying power of someone consuming $4,091 worth of goods and services valued at the prices of an industrialized economy – a level of consumption that would leave an American struggling in poverty ... China's economic output [GDP] in 2005 was worth $2.24 trillion at prevailing prices and actual market exchange rates ... The World Bank previously calculated that China's output was worth $8.8 trillion in 2005 if the goods and services produced were valued at American prices. This figure was revised this week down to $5.3 trillion. Even with this revision, China is still the world's second largest economy in PPP terms, after the United States. At market exchange rates it also trails Japan ... The World Bank declared Monday that prices in China were closer to world levels than it had previously assumed. So the bank calculated that the PPP of China's economy was closer to the market exchange value than previously thought ... [so] the new figures strengthen somewhat Beijing's contention that the yuan is not seriously undervalued ... Some economists question whether the World Bank has now over-stated prices in China ... [noting] that the bank looked mainly at affluent cities in coastal provinces with big export industries ... The World Bank used data that the Asian Development Bank had obtained from the Chinese government's National Bureau of Statistics, which in turn gathered data in the administrative regions of eleven large, mostly prosperous Chinese cities. The World Bank calculated prices for the three-fifths of China's population who live in rural areas by using prevailing prices in agricultural areas at the fringes of the eleven cities. While the World Bank made some adjustments ... [critics] questioned whether the final figures still overstated average rural prices across all of China. This would then understate the true size of China's economy ... The bank's figures had previously been based on prices first calculated by two Chinese economists in 1986 and only crudely updated for inflation since then.

(*IHT*, 21 December 2007, p. 11)

Manufacturing output

According to the Vienna-based United Nations Industrial Development Organization ... [over the decade 1995–2005 China's manufacturing] output rose by 156 per cent ... with its share of world manufacturing output rising from 4.2 per cent to 8 per cent. Accordingly, it increased its place in the world's league table from fifth to third ... In spite of the UK's relative decline in its share of world production ... from 3.8 per cent to 3 per cent ... the country is still in eighth position in the world in terms of the overall size of its manufacturing output, only one place lower than the seventh position it occupied in 1995 ... Over this period [1995–2005] global manufacturing output expanded 34 per cent ... while UK production rose by only 6 per cent. Britain's much slower rate of growth illustrates why the country's share of manufacturing value-added output measured in constant 1995 prices has declined. The UK's performance has been significantly worse than that of the United States – which has kept its share of global manufacturing value-added roughly constant in this period at just over 20 per cent. Japan, the second biggest manufacturer after the United States, increased its manufacturing output over the decade by 12.6 per cent ... Its share of the [world] total dropped to 17.7 per cent from 21.1 per cent in 1995.

(*FT*, 22 May 2006, p. 3)

'[As regards] manufacturing output ... China doubled its share of global production to almost 7 per cent in the decade to 2003' (*The Economist*, 13 January 2007, p. 68).

According to Global Insight, a US economic consultancy, it [China] accounted for 5 per cent of global manufacturing value-added in 1995; by last year [2007] this share had risen to 14 per cent, putting the country in joint second place – with Japan – in the world league table of manufacturers ranked by production. Both countries are well behind the United States, which in 2007 accounted for a quarter of global manufacturing output, but a long way ahead of Germany and Britain, whose shares have dwindled to 7 per cent and 3 per cent respectively.

(*FT*, 29 May 2008, p. 13)

The sources of growth

(See Jeffries 2006a: 627.)

> The basic formulation ... [of] the traditional [economic] growth model ... offers three ways for an economy to expand: add more labour, invest more capital, or combine labour and capital in new and better ways, which allows for more growth at every level of physical input. This last element is productivity ... 'total factor productivity' [TFP] ... Over the last twenty-five years the mainland economy recorded an average real growth rate of more than 9.5 per cent per annum, making it the new world record holder among major economies. Does this make China different? Or is this just one more example of an Asian high-growth economy in action? Most casual observers would respond that China is very different indeed – but the broad bulk of serious research on the mainland economy says they are wrong ... The mainland economy looks almost exactly like its Asian predecessors [such as Japan, Hong Kong, Singapore, South Korea and Taiwan] ... Even if we bring those headline figures down a notch (most economists assume an average growth rate of perhaps 8.5 per cent to 9 per cent over the past few decades), the Chinese growth story is hauntingly familiar to anyone studying the earlier Asian experience: a reasonable but respectable TFP role, another modest share coming from labour force growth, and an overwhelming contribution from capital investment. As it turns out, the only reason mainland growth has exceeded the rest of Asia is because China saves and invests even more than its neighbours ... Nearly every academic study shows that the TFP contribution to overall growth in China has been slightly higher than the Asian average ... In part this is a reflection of the rapidly growing private sector; the state accounted for two-thirds of the economy fifteen years ago, but only one-third today. And in part it reflects the mainland government's surprising commitment to some core market principles.
>
> (Jonathan Anderson, *FEER*, September 2006, pp. 10–13)

'Total factor productivity growth in China has been even faster than in the rest of Asia. Over the past quarter-century it has averaged 3 per cent a year, accounting for roughly the same amount of GDP growth as capital investment' (*The Economist*, Survey of the World Economy, 16 September 2006, p. 12).

> Official figures last year [2007] showed that there were 150 million migrant workers. But 737 million Chinese, or 56 per cent of the population, still lived in the countryside at the end of 2006, a high figure compared with other countries at a similar stage of development. Speeding up urbanization would tap a rich seam of growth because the productivity of Chinese agriculture is just

one-sixth of the expansion rate in the rest of the economy ... Louis Kuijs [is] a senior economist in Beijing with the World Bank ... Work by Kuijs sheds light on the relatively small role played by migration so far in China's industrial revolution. From 1993 to 2005 shifting labour from the farm sector contributed only 1.1 percentage points to annual GDP growth of 9.6 per cent. Overall employment growth also accounted for just 1.1 percentage points. By far the largest driver of growth was capital accumulation, accounting for 5.3 percentage points, a far higher proportion than in other countries ... China has done better than most in increasing 'total factor productivity' – finding ways to work smarter so output increases even without adding labour or machinery. The problem, as Beijing recognizes, is that its capital-intensive growth model is not sustainable. Investment has already increased to 45 per cent of GDP in 2006 from 35 per cent in 2000 ... The household registration system has slowed rural–urban migration and partly dictated why firms have relied more on capital than labour to grow ... Labour shortages in southern China would be less severe if people were more free to move to cities without encountering discrimination. Migrant workers pay more to send their children to school and have limited access to welfare and social services.

(*IHT*, 5 February 2008, p. 13)

Poverty

There has been a dramatic reduction in poverty, despite some recent adjustments in the figures.

(See Jeffries 2006a: 628–9.)

[One US dollar] a day [is a] standard long used by the World Bank. Last month [December 2007] the World Bank's estimate of the number of poor people in China was tripled to 300 million from 100 million, after a new survey on prices altered the picture of what a dollar could buy. The new standard was set according to what economists call purchasing-power parity. By the new calculations, estimates of the overall size of the Chinese economy shrank by 40 per cent.

(www.iht.com, 13 January 2008; *IHT*, 14 January 2008, p. 2)

The World Bank recently revisited its 'dollar a day' global poverty yardstick and came to a startling conclusion: it was wrong when it said some 250 million people in China had escaped from severe poverty between 1990 and 2004. Instead, by its latest count, some 407 million Chinese citizens rose out of poverty during those fourteen years – roughly one-third of the entire population of the most populous country on the planet.

(William Amelio, *IHT*, 26 June 2008, p. 8)

A pilot project with a difference is making a dent in rural poverty and, more significantly, giving villagers a voice in the development of a pocket of southern China bypassed by the country's economic boom. What sets the project apart is that public funds to tackle poverty are being channelled through non-governmental organizations, a first in China. In a country where NGOs have long been regarded with suspicion, this is nothing short of a seismic shift, according to the Asian Development Bank, which is financing the project's overhead costs with a modest grant ... The sums involved in the project are small: the NGOs, working in co-operation with local governments, have $73,000 to spend in each of sixteen mountain villages in the interior province of Jiangxi. But the stakes are potentially high: if the project works its backers hope it can become a model for some 148,000 poor villages concentrated in central and western China. The trial runs until October [2008], but the initial evaluation is positive ... More than 20 million people live under China's official poverty line. Many of them live in hard-to-reach clusters that require targeted help and the government wants to find out whether civil groups can be harnessed to tackle the problem.

(*IHT*, 5 August 2008, p. 11)

The World Bank reported in August [2008] that in 2005 there were 1.4 billion people [in the world] living below the poverty line – that is, living on less than $1.25 a day. That is more than a quarter of the developing world's population and 430 million more people living in extreme poverty than previously estimated ... Forty-two per cent of India's people live below the World Bank's poverty line, as do 16 per cent of China's ... Fast growth slashed the number of Chinese living in extreme poverty by three-fourths in less than twenty-five years ... India has more people in extreme poverty than it did twenty-five years ago.

(*IHT*, 3 September 2008, p. 8)

Inflation

Retail price inflation reached a peak in the 1990s of 21.7 per cent in 1994, but this was low relative to many transitional economies in Eastern Europe and the former Soviet Union in the early years of transition. (See Table 1.) (This is explained by such factors as control over money supply growth, the high rate of growth of output, a high propensity to save, and the relatively small size of the state sector of industry compared with transitional countries in Eastern Europe and the former Soviet Union, which helps keep subsidies down.)

'The CPI (consumer price index) ... excludes housing costs and [so] understates inflation' (*FT*, 26 January 2005, p. 18). 'The prices of ... [things] such as health care, education and housing are not reflected in the CPI' (www.iht.com, 24 March 2005).

'The retail price index ... measures a narrower basket of commodities than the consumer price index' (*FT*, 14 March 2000, p. 14). 'The retail price index (RPI) ... includes readings from sought-after services such as education' (*FT*, 23 May 2001, p. 12).

There was deflation in China for some time after October 1997, i.e. prices actually fell.

During 2003 modest inflation started to be recorded.

During 2007 there was mounting concern about inflation, about rising food prices in particular. 'The government's target inflation rate for 2007 is 3 per cent' (www.iht.com, 28 August 2007).

> Inflation has hit its second ten-year high in two months, led again by a further sharp rise in meat prices. China's rate of consumer price inflation hit 6.5 per cent in the year to August [2007], up from 5.6 per cent in July ... Meat prices have risen 49 per cent over the past year, caused [especially] by a shortage of pork.
>
> (www.bbc.co.uk, 11 September 2007)

'China's inflation rate rose to 6.5 per cent in August ... the highest since December 1996 ... [There was a] sharp rise in prices for pork, China's staple meat ... Prices of non-food consumer goods rose just 0.9 per cent' (www.iht.com, 11 September 2007).

The inflation rate continued to rise in early 2008, exacerbated by unusually severe snowstorms that began on 10 January and affected large parts of east-central and southern China. The 2008 peak was reached in February. 'The 8.7 per cent figure [for February is] the highest since May 1996' (*FT*, 12 March 2008, p. 8).

(The global financial crisis has already been discussed.)

Unemployment

(See Jeffries 2006a: 630–4.)

'The official Chinese jobless rate, the so-called urban registered unemployment rate, fell to 4.1 per cent at the end of last year [2006] as the country added 11.8 million jobs, according to government data' (www.iht.com, 5 February 2007).

> Over the past couple of years protests by demobilized soldiers have become a potent challenge to local governments trying to keep the lid on unrest ... The ex-servicemen's main grievance is the difficulty of settling back into the civilian sector when they leave the army. But this has become increasingly difficult because of the dismantling of state-owned enterprises (SOEs) in recent years and the resentment of surviving SOEs at having ex-soldiers foisted on them. Rural soldiers – the bulk of the non-officer ranks – are being sent back to villages where there is next to nothing to do ... In addition to the regular turnover, hundreds of thousands have been demobilized in recent years as a result of efforts to trim the military's enormous size. In the decade up to 2004 some 7 million enlisted people left the military. Another 600,000 officers were given jobs in the civilian sector. Between 2003 and 2005 the army was trimmed by some 200,000 people, leaving it

2.3 million strong. Local governments are supposed to find jobs for ex-officers. Since 2001, in response to dwindling opportunities in the state sector, the central government has been encouraging officers to accept cash pay-outs and find their own work. But local governments do not have enough cash to provide much of a cushion.

(*The Economist*, 10 November 2007, pp. 81–2)

After five years of growth exceeding 10 per cent, China's growth has decelerated for five consecutive quarters, dropping to about 9 per cent in the third quarter of this year [2008] from 12.6 per cent in the second quarter of 2007 … Economists expect the economy to expand at an annualized rate of as little as 5.8 per cent in the fourth quarter, down from nearly 11.2 per cent in 2007.

(*IHT*, 7 November 2008, p. 13)

Officially China's urban jobless rate was 4.0 per cent at the end of September [2008], unchanged over the past twelve months. The problem is that the figure measures only legal residents who actually report that they are out of work and register for unemployment benefits. It excludes the tens of millions of migrants labouring in cities. Economists think China's jobless rate could be twice as high as the government's figure.

(www.iht.com, 5 November 2008; *IHT*, 6 November 2008, p. 17)

(The global financial crisis has already been discussed.)

Pollution

(See Jeffries 2006a: 634–7.)

'An estimated 70 per cent of China's rivers are polluted and 300 million people have no access to clean water, according to government estimates' (www. iht.com, 1 August 2006).

China has blamed fraud in project approvals and failure to apply emission control measures for rising pollution, state media reported Monday [21 August 2006] … China's senior environmental official also said a government investigation into pollution control approvals for construction projects worth more than $12.5 million had found violations in almost 40 per cent of cases, according to the report … China, which burns more than 2 billion metric tons of coal a year to produce about 80 per cent of its electricity, leads the world in emissions of sulphur dioxide, which causes acid rain … The State Environmental Protection Administration … said that in some counties only 30 per cent of projects had been checked for compliance with pollution controls before they were granted construction licences … And almost half of the companies, including those that passed environmental appraisals, failed to carry out required emission control measures … The country now has some of the world's most polluted air, water and soil. China has sixteen of the world's twenty cities with the most polluted air, according to the Worldwatch Institute, based in Washington ... According to reports in the official media, 90 per cent of waterways that flow through China's cities and 75 per cent of lakes are contaminated ... On 18 July official media reported that the government planned to spend $175 billion on environmental protection over the next five years.

(*IHT*, 22 August 2006, p. 13)

Water pollution is worsening in cities across China, in spite of heavy investment in new wastewater treatment facilities, a government official said yesterday [22 August 2006] ... [He said] that urban areas need to do more to conserve and treat water if they are to avoid crises ... During the next five years China expected to spend renminbi 1,000 billion ($125 billion), which included renminbi 330 billion to construct urban wastewater treatment facilities and renminbi 320 billion for two main lines of the south–north water diversion project. China's water problems, specifically high pollution levels and persistent droughts, are set to continue in spite of Beijing's plans to expand water-related infrastructure. Shortages of water supplies, especially in the north, have long been a serious problem. In recent weeks scorching temperatures have caused a drought in the south-west – mainly Sichuan province and Chongqing municipality – that has ruined crops and caused drinking water shortages ... China's urban wastewater treatment rate jumped from 34 per cent in 2000 to 52 per cent last year [2005]. However, the ministry of construction admitted that many wastewater plants were operating at only partial capacity; the collection of wastewater fees is often irregular; and pipeline networks are often old or incomplete ... Beijing is a positive example of a city that has significantly cut its water use ... [The official] said the central government needed to intensify its supervision of water-related industries while allowing the market to become less state-dominated as it opened itself to foreign and private investment ... Foreign investment in China's urban water sector is less than 10 per cent of the total.

(*FT*, 23 August 2006, p. 6)

The government plans to spend 1 trillion yuan by 2010 to build water treatment plants and upgrade water distribution systems, the ministry of construction said Thursday [22 August 2006]. Of that amount, which is equivalent to $125.5 billion, as much as 330 billion yuan will be spent on the water projects in urban centres. As many as 278 cities lack proper treatment facilities and at least thirty cities have plants that operate at less than 30 per cent capacity, the ministry said. China wants to tap the technology of overseas companies ... Shortages of natural water, worsened by rampant industrial pollution, plague the central and western provinces, which are facing China's worst drought in fifty years ... Foreign financing in the industry is less than 10 per cent ... The government has set a goal of treating 70 per cent of urban waste water by the end of 2010, up from 50 per cent ... In 150 cities no waste water treatment fees were collected last year

[2005] ... Overuse of water resources ... has caused the ground to sink in fifty cities, while irreparable damage has already been done to the ecology of some natural water resources ... The government is building a $62 billion network of canals to move water to arid northern provinces, and it has pledged to increase spending in rural areas ... Factories and urban residents used 34 per cent of the nation's water in 2004, up from 25 per cent in 1998 ... Water in China is priced at '20 per cent of replacement', Elizabeth Economy said in June [2006].

(www.iht.com, 22 August 2006)

There is no shortage of environmental laws and regulations in China, many of them passed in recent years by a central government trying to address one of the worst pollution problems in the world. But those problems persist, in part, because environmental protection is often subverted by local protectionism, corruption and regulatory inefficiency ... Despite its rising profile, the State Environmental Protection Administration [SEPA] remains one of the weakest agencies in the central government bureaucracy and has sought to increase its regulatory powers. For years it has complained that local environmental protection bureaus are accountable to local officials rather than the state agency. This has meant that local regulators had to answer to mayors or other local officials who may have had financial or other interests in protecting polluting industries. In early August [2006] SEPA announced that it would establish eleven regional offices to monitor pollution problems better. The agency also announced that local officials eligible for promotion would be judged on their pollution track record, in addition to how well they deliver economic growth. Public disgust over pollution is growing. In May [2006] the official English language newspaper *China Daily* reported that more than 50,000 disputes and protests arose in 2005 over pollution. Public complaints to the national environmental administration rose by 30 per cent.

(Jim Yardley, www.iht.com, 4 September 2006)

An estimated 70 per cent of China's lakes and rivers are now polluted, according to environmental experts. Official figures show that only half of the urban and industrial waste-water is treated in sewage plants before discharge. In rural areas ... sewage treatment is virtually non-existent.

(*IHT*, 10 October 2006, p. 15)

The *China Daily* reported this week that at least 24 million acres of cultivated land in China – one-tenth of the country's total arable land – is now polluted, posing a 'grave threat' to China's food safety. More than half its rivers are also polluted, which is why less than 9 per cent of 'drinkable water' met government standards for bacteria in 243 rural supply stations recently tested. Many wells have excessive nitrates that can cause diabetes or kidney damage.

(www.iht.com, 15 November 2006)

'China's environmental protection administration recently estimated the annual number of premature deaths caused by air pollution at 358,000' (*IHT*, 18 November 2006, p. 5).

On 8 September 2006 a Chinese newspaper reported that China's environmental protection agency and its National Bureau of Statistics had re-examined China's 2004 GDP number. They concluded that the health problems, environmental degradation and lost workdays from pollution had actually cost China … 3.05 per cent of its total economic output for 2004. Some experts believe the real number is closer to 10 per cent.

(*IHT*, 14 April 2007, p. 7)

'The cost of pollution to China, in terms of extra health care expenditures, destruction of natural resources and premature deaths, is at least 8 per cent of GDP' (Minxin Pei, *IHT*, 6 March 2007, p. 6).

'The true cost of China's environmental mess is hard to assess, but the official government figure, which puts it at about 3 per cent of GDP, is certainly a gross underestimate' (*The Economist*, Survey, 31 March 2007, p. 13).

'More than 10 per cent of China's farmland is polluted, posing a "severe threat" to the nation's food production, state media reports … Excessive fertilizer use, polluted water, heavy metals and solid wastes are to blame, the reports said' (www.bbc.co.uk, 23 April 2007).

'In September 2006 … the first ever report [was published by China] on the economic costs of pollution. This study estimates that environmental pollution still costs China \$64 billion, or 3.05 per cent of GDP in 2004' (*FEER*, June 2007, p. 36).

China released its first comprehensive strategy for addressing climate change Monday [4 June 2007], a plan calling for improving energy efficiency and controlling greenhouse gas emissions but rejects mandatory caps on emissions that could harm the sizzling economy … Ma Kai (head of the economic and planning agency, the National Development and Reform Commission): 'Our general stance is that China will not commit to any quantified emission reduction targets, but that does not mean that we will not assume responsibilities in responding to climate change … The ramifications of limiting the development of developing countries would be even more serious that those from climate change' … Under the Kyoto Protocol, which took effect in 2005, industrialized nations are subject to caps on certain industrial emissions, while developing countries, including China and India, are exempt. The Bush administration pulled out of the agreement … China is heavily dependent on coal, which accounts for roughly 68 per cent of its energy. But under the climate change programme China is planning a major expansion of nuclear power, as well as renewable energy sources. The plan calls for renewable energy to account for 10 per cent of the country's power by 2010. China is also in the midst of a nationwide reforestation programme to help absorb greenhouse gases … China is strongly encouraging domestic research on new clean technologies, but has also called on developed countries to transfer technology and provide financial assistance to help developing countries.

(www.iht.com, 4 June 2007; *IHT*, 5 June 2007, pp. 1, 4)

China has unveiled its first national plan for climate change, saying it is intent on tackling the problem but not at the expense of economic development. The report reiterated China's aim to reduce energy use by a fifth before 2010 and increase the amount of renewable energy it produces ... [China] stressed that the country's first priority remained 'sustainable development and poverty eradication'.

(www.bbc.co.uk, 4 June 2007)

China overtook the United States in 2006 as the world's biggest emitter of carbon dioxide, the greenhouse gas blamed for the bulk of global warming, a policy group that advises the Dutch government said. China produced 6,200 million tonnes of carbon dioxide from burning fossil fuels and making cement last year [2006], the Netherlands Environmental Agency said Tuesday [19 June] ... Rapid industrialization in China has long prompted predictions that it would overtake the United States as the world's biggest emitter ... The International Energy Agency ... said in April [2007] that China would become the biggest emitter this year [2007] or next [2008], an advance on the IEA's previous forecast of 2009 ... The Dutch figures do not include emissions from flaring gas during oil and gas extraction, from underground coal fires or from deforestation.

(www.iht.com, 20 June 2007)

While China was 2 per cent below the United States in carbon dioxide emissions in 2005, voracious coal consumption and increased cement production caused the numbers to rise rapidly, the Netherlands Environmental Assessment Agency said Tuesday. China overtook the United States by about 7.5 per cent in 2006, the agency said ... It is hypocritical to criticize China's greenhouse gas emissions while simultaneously buying products from its booming manufacturing sector, Beijing said Thursday [21 June] ... [China] would not confirm that China had overtaken the United States in carbon dioxide emissions ... [and] said China's efforts to combat greenhouse gas emissions include energy conservation measures, increasing forest coverage and family planning policies that have slowed population growth ... [China] also repeated the argument Chinese officials have made in the past, that while total emissions are going up they are still less than one quarter of those of the United States on a *per capita* basis ... China signed the 1997 Kyoto Protocol, which caps the amount of carbon dioxide that can be omitted in industrialized countries. But because China is considered a developing country it is exempt from emission reductions – a situation often cited by the United States and Australian governments for not accepting the treaty.

(www.iht.com, 21 June 2007; *IHT*, 22 June 2007, p. 14)

Beijing engineered the removal of nearly a third of a World Bank report on pollution in China because of concerns that its findings on premature deaths could provoke 'social unrest' ... The excised material, about 30 per cent of the original report, detailed the number of premature deaths in China each year from air and water pollution ... The report, produced in co-operation with Chinese government ministries over several years, found about 750,000 people die prematurely in China each year, mainly from air pollution in large cities. China's State Environmental Protection Agency (Sepa) and health ministry asked the World Bank to cut the calculations of premature deaths from the report when a draft was finished last year [2006], according to bank advisers and Chinese officials ... Missing from this report are the research project's findings that high air pollution levels in Chinese cities are leading to the premature deaths of 350,000 to 400,000 people each year. A further 300,000 people die each year from exposure to poor air indoors, but little of this issue survived in the report ... Another 60,000-odd prema- ture deaths were attributable to poor quality water, largely in the countryside.

(*FT*, 3 July 2007, p. 6)

'Yesterday [17 July] a senior Chinese official defended Beijing's decision [to remove mortality calculations from the World Bank report], arguing that the data were based on faulty methodology' (*FT*, 18 July 2007, p. 6).

Despite the apparent dispute over figures, the preliminary World Bank report published in March [2007] suggests air and water pollution do lead to an increased number of deaths in China. It also says the total cost of air and water pollution in the country amounts to about 5.8 per cent of GDP.

(www.bbc.co.uk, 3 July 2007)

China denied Thursday [5 July] that government officials had pressed the World Bank into removing estimates of the number of premature deaths linked to pollution from a World Bank report ... A person involved in draft- ing the report said the Chinese authorities wanted the information removed because they had doubts about the method use to estimate the deaths and they were worried about the social consequences of making such statistics public ... A draft of the report, 'Cost of Pollution in China', was released at a conference in Beijing in March. In a statement issued Tuesday [3 July] the World Bank did not deny that some data had been removed from the draft report at the request of China. But a World Bank spokeswoman in Washing- ton said that the matter was under review.

(*IHT*, 6 July 2007, p. 4)

[The OECD's] eighteen-month review of China's environmental perform- ance confirms that China's severe pollution has resulted in 'significant damage to human health', which would affect its prospects for continued economic growth ... No specific figure for the cost of China's pollution [was given] ... The Chinese government said last year [2006] that pollution had cost the country $64 billion in economic losses, about 3 per cent of its economy that year. It has not given updated figures. The OECD report was released Tuesday [17 July 2007]. It cited an earlier World Bank report as saying that by 2020 pollution will cause 600,000 premature deaths in urban areas and 20 million cases of respiratory illness a year. The overall cost of health damage will be equal to 13 per cent of GDP. Some 190 million people are estimated to be suffering from illnesses related to dirty drinking water and more than 30,000 children die every year from diarrhoea due to polluted water, it said. China's pollution had cut into productivity, driven up health care costs and triggered social unrest ... China's poor record on environmental issues also threatened to damage its reputation as an exporter ... [e.g. in products such as] pharmaceuticals, food and feed.

(www.iht.com, 17 July 2007)

By 2020, the [OECD] report forecast, pollution would cause '600,000 premature deaths in urban areas, 9 million person-years of work lost due to pollution-related illness, 20 million cases of respiratory illness a year, 5.5 million cases of chronic bronchitis and health damage', which would cost 13 per cent of GDP.

(*FT*, 18 July 2007, p. 6)

The OECD report [was] prepared at China's request ... It says up to 300 million people are drinking contaminated water every day, and 190 million are suffering from water-related illnesses each year. If air pollution is not controlled, it says, there will be 600,000 premature deaths in urban areas and 20 million respiratory illnesses a year within fifteen years ... One-third of the length of all China's rivers is now 'highly polluted' as are 75 per cent of its major lakes and 25 per cent of all its coastal waters. Nearly 30,000 children die from diarrhoea due to polluted water each year ... More than 17,000 towns have no sewage works and the human waste from nearly 1 billion people is barely collected or treated. 'A majority of the water flowing through China's urban areas is unsuitable for drinking or fishing,' says the report ... Many of ... its cities ... have some of the worst pollution in the world ... The burning of more than 2 billion tonnes of the dirtiest coal is costing the economy the equivalent of 3 per cent to 7 per cent of GDP, according to the report ... The report estimates that 27 per cent of China's land mass is now becoming desertified. Much of the country already suffers from water shortages.

(*Guardian*, 18 July 2007, p. 18)

China has about 7 per cent of the world's water resources and roughly 20 per cent of its population. It also has a severe regional water imbalance, with about four-fifths of the water supply in the south ... The $62 billion South-to-North Water Transfer Project ... [involves] three routes from the Yangtze river basin, where water is more abundant. The project, if fully built, would be completed in 2050. The eastern and central line are already under construction; the western line, the most controversial because of environmental concerns, remains in the planning stages ... The western line may never be built: plans would require huge dams and tunnels through remote mountains.

(*IHT*, 27 September 2007)

One recent World Bank report found that sixteen of the world's twenty most polluted cities were in China; and a draft version of another puts the total economic cost of outdoor air and water pollution at around $100 billion a year, or 5.8 per cent of China's GDP. By some estimates China has now overtaken America to become the world's largest producer of greenhouse gases. Environmental protests such as one that took place in Xiamen last month [June 2007] in response to a plan to build a chemical plant in the city, are on the rise.

(*The Economist*, 21 July 2007, p. 68)

The toll pollution has taken on human health remains a delicate topic in China. The leadership has banned publication of data on the subject for fear of inciting social unrest, said scholars involved in the research. But the results of some research provide alarming evidence that the environment has become one of the biggest causes of death. An internal, unpublicized report by the Chinese Academy of Environmental Planning in 2003 estimated that 300,000 people die each year from ambient air pollution, mostly of heart disease and lung cancer. An additional 110,000 deaths could be attributed to indoor air pollution caused by poorly ventilated coal and wood stoves or toxic fumes from shoddy construction materials, said a person involved in that study. Another report, prepared in 2005 by Chinese environmental experts, estimated that annual premature deaths attributable to outdoor air pollution were likely to reach 380,000 in 2010 and 550,000 in 2020. This spring [2007] a World Bank study done by Sepa, the national environmental agency, concluded that outdoor pollution was already causing 350,000 to 400,000 premature deaths a year. Indoor pollution contributed to the deaths of an additional 300,000 people, while 60,000 died from diarrhoea, bladder and stomach cancer and other diseases that can be caused by water-borne pollution. China's environmental agency insisted that the health statistics be removed from the published version of the report, citing the possible impact of 'social stability', World Bank officials said. But other international organizations with access to Chinese data have published similar results. For example, the WHO found that China suffered more deaths from water-related pollutants and fewer from bad air, but agreed with the World Bank that the total death toll had reached 750,000 a year. In comparison 4,700 people died last year [2006] in China's notoriously unsafe mines, and 89,000 people were killed in road accidents, the highest number of automobile-related deaths in the world. The ministry of health estimates that smoking takes a million Chinese lives each year. Studies of Chinese environmental health mostly use statistical models developed in the United States and Europe and apply them to China, which has done little long-term research on the matter domestically ... Chinese officials say that, if any-

thing, the Western models probably understate the problems ... [since, for example] China's pollution is worse, the density of its population is greater and people do not protect themselves as well ... Only 1 per cent of China's urban population of 560 million now breathes air considered safe by the EU, according to a World Bank study of Chinese pollution published this year [2007] ... China has only one-fifth as much water *per capita*, as the United States. But while southern China is relatively wet, the north, home to about half of China's population, is an immense, parched region that now threatens to become the world's biggest desert ... Chinese industry uses four to ten times more water per unit of production than the average in industrialized nations, according to the World Bank ... China's environmental monitors say that one-third of all river water, and vast sections of China's great lakes, the Tai, Chao and Dianchi, have water rated Grade V, the most degraded level, rendering it unfit for industrial or agricultural use.
(www.iht.com, 26 August 2007; *IHT*, 27 August 2007, pp. 1, 4)

('About 100,000 Chinese died annually from diseases associated with passive smoking, while more than 500 million on the mainland suffered from the smoke exhaled from cigarettes, according to the Xinhua China news agency. China's ministry of health said 1 million people died from smoking-related diseases each year in China, the world's largest tobacco producing and consuming country': *FT*, 30 May 2007, p. 8. 'Nearly 1 million Chinese die every year from smoking-related diseases, and 100,000 from passive smoking, according to the first survey of its kind by the ministry of health. China has more than 350 million smokers': *The Times*, 30 May 2007, p. 42. 'Cigarette consumption in China soared between 1970 and 1990, but has fallen slightly since': *The Economist*, 22 September 2007, p. 73. '[About] 1.2 million people die each year from smoking-related causes': www.iht.com, 23 July 2008. 'At the moment one in three cigarettes in the world is smoked in China': www.bbc.co.uk, 4 October 2008. ' "One in every three smokers in the world is a Chinese man," the experts ... in a paper published in *The Lancet* medical journal ... wrote. They reported that cigarette consumption increased to 2,022 billion in 2006, to a level 17.4 per cent higher than in 2002. The average Chinese male smoker smoked fifteen cigarettes a day in 2002, up from thirteen in 1984': www.iht.com, 20 October 2008.)

China has indefinitely postponed the release of an environmental report on the costs of economic development. Several local governments are reported to have objected to the release of 'sensitive' information about the pollution they cause. Government officials from different departments also appear to disagree on how to calculate the figures. But despite the setback the man in charge of the scheme says the research should continue. The project – to calculate how much money pollution costs China each year, the so-called 'green GDP' – was launched in 2004 ... Figures for 2004 – which revealed pollution cost China about $86 billion or 3 per cent of GDP – were not released until late last year [2006]. Although officials have promised on a number of occasions to release the results for 2005, these figures have yet to materialize. Now Wang Jinnan, the technical head of the project, has told the *Beijing News* that the release will be 'postponed indefinitely' ... Wang Jinnan: 'Some local governments are quite sensitive about the research and calculations for their provinces' ... There also appears to be a difference of opinion between the State Environmental Protection Administration and the National Bureau of Statistics. Earlier this month [July] NBS head Xie Fuzahn seemed to cast doubt on whether a figure for the 'green GDP' could even be calculated.

(www.bbc.co.uk, 23 July 2007)

The *Beijing News* reported Monday [23 July] that the release of a 'green GDP' report computing the cost of pollution and ecological degradation in 2005 had been 'indefinitely postponed' ... Wang Jinnan, a senior expert at the Chinese Academy for Environmental Planning who was technical head of the project, said that publicly spelling out the cost of bad air, water and soil had drawn fierce opposition from local officials eager to maintain growth ... Wang Jinnan: 'Taking out the costs of environmental damage would lead to a huge fall in the quality of economic growth in some areas. At present many areas still place GDP above all else and when such thinking dominates the size of resistance to a green GDP can well be imagined' ... Wang said that some provincial governments had lobbied the State Environmental Protection Administration and the National Bureau of Statistics not to publicly release the latest data. A previous report for 2004 had calculated that environmental degradation that year cost $67.7 billion or 3.05 per cent of GDP ... That report was issued last September [2006] with official fanfare and wide media attention. The report for 2005 shows 'losses from pollution and reduction in the GDP indicator even higher than the 2004 report', the *Beijing News* said, citing a weekend seminar in the study. The report would also have computed economic losses from pollution for each province – a sensitive step in a system where economic growth can be crucial to officials' promotion prospects ... Wang said that in the bureaucratic fight over environmental data, the environmental protection agency and the statistics bureau had 'major differences' over what the report should say and how it should be distributed.

(www.iht.com, 23 July 2007)

President Hu Jintao's most ambitious attempt to change the culture of fast growth collapsed this year [2007]. The project, known as 'green GDP' was an effort to create an environmental yardstick for evaluating the performance of every official in China. It calculated GDP to reflect the cost of pollution. But the early results were so sobering – in some provinces the pollution-adjusted growth rates were reduced almost to zero – that the project was banished to China's ivory tower this spring [2007] and stripped of official influence ... In an internal address in 2004 Hu Jintao endorsed 'comprehensive environmental and economic accounting' – otherwise known as 'green GDP'. He said the 'pioneering endeavour' would produce a new performance test for government and party officials that better reflected the leadership's environmental priorities. The green GDP team sought to calculate the yearly damage to the environment and human health in each province. Their first report, released last year [2006], estimated that pollution in 2004 cost just over 3 per cent of GDP, meaning that the pollution-adjusted growth rate that year would drop to about 7 per cent from 10 per cent. Officials said at the time that their formula used low estimates of environmental damage to health and did not assess the impact on China's ecology. They would produce a more decisive formula, they said, next year. That did not happen. Hu's plan died amid intense squabbling, people involved in the effort said. The green GDP group's second report, originally scheduled for release in March [2007], never materialized. The official explanation was that the science behind the green index was immature. Wang Jinnan, the leading academic researcher on the green GDP team, said provincial leaders killed the project.

(www.iht.com, 26 August 2007; *IHT*, 27 August 2007, pp. 1, 4)

Just as the speed and scale of China's rise as an economic power have no clear parallel in history, so its pollution problem has shattered all precedents ... Growth derives now more than at any time in the recent past from a staggering expansion of heavy industry and urbanization that requires colossal amounts of energy, almost all from coal, the most readily available, and dirtiest, source ... China has entered the most robust stage of its industrial revolution, even as much of the outside world has become preoccupied with global warming ... Chinese leaders argue that the outside world is a partner in degrading the country's environment. Chinese manufacturers ... make the cheap products that fill stores in the United States and Europe. Often the manufacturers subcontract for foreign companies – or are owned by them ... Beijing insists that it will accept no mandatory limits on its carbon dioxide emissions ... It argues that rich countries cause global warming and should find a way to solve it without impinging on China's development ... The costs of pollution have mounted well before it is ready to curtail economic development. But the price of business as usual – including the predicted effects of global warming on China itself – strikes many of its own experts and some senior officials as intolerably high ... Ren Yong (a climate expert at the Centre of Environment and Economy in Beijing): 'Typically, industrial countries deal with green problems when they are rich. We have to deal with them while we are still poor. There is no model for us to follow' ... Land, water, electricity, oil and bank loans remain relatively inexpensive, even for heavy polluters ... Water remains inexpensive by global standards ... Beijing has declined to use the kind of tax policies and market-orientated incentives for conservation that have worked well in Japan and many European countries. Provincial officials, who enjoy substantial autonomy, often ignore environmental edicts, helping to reopen mines or factories closed by central authorities. Over all, enforcement is often tinged with corruption ... Energy and environmental officials have little influence in the bureaucracy. The environmental agency has only about 200 full-time employees, compared with 18,000 at the Environmental Protection Agency in the United States. China has no energy ministry. The Energy Bureau of the National Development and Reform Commission, the country's central planning agency, has 100 full-time members. The Energy Department of the United States has 110,000 employees. China does have an army of amateur regulators. Environmentalists expose pollution and press local government officials to enforce environmental law. But private individuals and non-government organizations cannot cross the line between advocacy and political agitation without risking arrest. At least two leading environmental organizers have been prosecuted in recent weeks, and several others have received sharp warnings to tone down their criticism of local officials.

(Joseph Kahn and Jim Yardley, www.iht.com, 26 August 2007; *IHT*, 27 August 2007, pp. 1, 4)

('An environmental activist accused of blackmailing polluting businesses was sentenced to three years in prison Friday [10 August 2007] ... Wu Lihong, named one of China's top environmentalists on 2005, has been collecting water samples from Lake Tai in eastern China for more than fifteen years and submitting reports on its worsening condition. He was arrested in April on what his wife and friends say were charges concocted by local officials embarrassed by Wu's whistle blowing ... Wu's arrest in April came as he and a fellow activist were planning to travel to Beijing to present evidence of pollution to the central government ... Throughout his years of advocacy Wu faced repeated harassment and detention in Yixing [where his trial took place] ... While China's leaders have called for stronger environmental protections, they remain wary of independent activists whose ranks have swelled in recent years alongside rising incomes and the spread of the internet': www.iht.com, 10 August 2007.)

'Several studies conducted both inside and outside China estimate that environmental degradation and pollution cost the Chinese economy between 8 per cent and 12 per cent of GDP annually' (Economy 2007: 46).

Pollution has reached epidemic proportions in China, in part because the ruling Communist Party still treats environmental advocates as bigger threats than the degradation of air, water and soil that prompts them to speak out. Senior officials have tried to address environmental woes mostly through the traditional levers of China's authoritarian system: issuing command quotas on energy efficiency and emissions reduction; punishing officials who shield polluters; planting billions of trees across the country to hold back deserts and absorb carbon dioxide. But they do not dare to unleash individuals who want to make China cleaner. Grassroots environmentalists arguably do more to expose abuses than any edict emanating from Beijing. But they face a political climate that varies from lukewarm tolerance to icy suppression. Fixing the environment is, in other words, a political problem. Central party officials say they need people to report polluters and hold local governments to account. They granted legal status to private citizens' groups in 1994 and have allowed environmentalism to emerge as an incipient social force. But local officials in

China get ahead mainly by generating high rates of economic growth and ensuring social order. They have wide latitude to achieve these goals, including nearly complete control over the police and the courts in their domains. They have little enthusiasm for environmentalists who appeal over their heads to higher-ups in the capital … Lake Tai … or Taihu in Chinese … [is] the country's third largest freshwater body … The crusading peasant Wu Lihong protested for more than a decade that the region's thriving chemical industry, and its powerful friends in the local government, were destroying one of the country's ecological treasures … In 2005 he was named an 'Environmental Warrior' by China's National People's Congress … [But he was arrested] on the night of 13 April [2007] … [and] in mid-August … a local court sentenced him to three years on an alchemy of charges [such as blackmail and fraud] and that smacked of official retribution.

(Joseph Kahn, www.iht.com, 14 October 2007;
IHT, 15 October 2007, pp. 1, 4)

China will spend the equivalent of $14.5 billion to clean up a famed lake inundated by so much pollution this year [2007] that it has become a symbol of the country's lax environmental regulation against polluting industry … Lake Tai [is] a major freshwater lake. The campaign would initially focus on eradicating the toxic algae bloom that choked the lake this spring and left more than 2 million people without drinking water. Lake Tai is a legendary setting in China, known as the country's ancient 'land of rice and fish' and famous for its bounty of white shrimp, whitebait and whitefish. But an industrial build-up transformed the region and more than 2,800 chemical factories arose around the lake. Industrial dumping became a severe problem and, eventually, an environmental crisis.

(*IHT*, 27 October 2007, p. 6)

Over time an industrial build-up transformed the region. More than 2,800 chemical factories arose around the lake, and industrial dumping became a severe problem and eventually a crisis. This spring [2007] urban sewage and chemical dumping caused an explosion of bright green pond scum that coated much of the lake with a foetid algal coating. Panic quickly followed in Wuxi, a nearby city that depended on the lake to supply drinking water for its 2.3 million residents. Officials were forced to shut off the drinking water supply for several days … Several local officials have been fired or demoted and state news media have reported that regulators have already closed as many as 1,000 factories in the area. But the new crackdown has not helped Wu Lihong … Wu was arrested shortly before the algae crisis and was convicted in August on questionable charges. He is now serving three years in prison, even as his direst warnings about the lake have come to pass … State news media reports have hinted that more factories might be closed or forced to suspend operations. In general the campaign includes stricter emissions standards and tighter water treatment regulations. Ultimately, though, the success or failure of the programme will depend on the sustained commitment of local officials and regulators. In other major clean-up campaigns, including one of the Huai River, corruption and the pressure for economic development have undermined environmental protection efforts.

(www.iht.com, 28 October 2007)

('The algae covered about one-third of the lake': www.bbc.co.uk, 27 October 2007.)

China has raised the stakes for companies violating environmental laws with rules to block polluters from exporting their goods ... Companies found ignoring waste-discharge limits face a ban from international trade for as long as three years to discourage exporters from cutting costs at the expense of the environment, according to a statement Friday [12 October] ... The statement: 'Some enterprises seek to reduce export costs by exceeding pollution limits ... [Export prices then] do not fully reflect social costs, aggravate trade frictions, fuel unreasonable growth in the trade surplus and damage the image of China's products.'

(*IHT*, 15 October 2007, p. 13)

In the first move of its kind, a dozen Chinese businesses ... [including] a brewer and a power plant ... have had loans blocked or withdrawn after being accused of flouting environmental laws ... The authorities threatened to get tough with persistent polluters this summer. Firms guilty of environmental breaches are currently subject to a maximum fine of just $13,500 ... The authorities plan to increase financial penalties for rule breakers and force firms to pay more towards the cost of emissions. Under China's new 'green credit policy' environmental regulators are required to pass on details of corporate offenders to the central bank. Of the thirty companies which were identified earlier this year [2007], twelve have now been sanctioned ... Earlier this year the State Environmental Protection Administration (Sepa) suspended approval of construction projects on eight provinces and autonomous regions due to environmental concerns.

(www.bbc.co.uk, 16 November 2007)

Experts ... estimate that 80 per cent of the 20 million to 50 million tonnes of electronic waste ... [such as television sets, refrigerators, washing machines, mobile phones and computers] ... produced globally each year is dumped in China, with most of the rest going to India and African nations. According to the US Environmental Protection Agency, it is ten times cheaper to export e-waste than to dispose of it at home ... International agreements and European regulations have made a dent in the export of old electronics to China, but loopholes – and sometimes bribes – allow many to skirt the requirements ... Imports slip into China despite a Chinese ban and Beijing's ratification of the Basel Convention, an international agreement that outlaws the trade ... The EU bans such exports, but ... smuggling is rife, largely due to the lack of measures to punish the rule breakers. China, meantime, allows the import of plastic waste and scrap metal, which many recyclers use as an excuse to send old electronics there. And though US states increasingly require that electronics be sent to collection and recycling centres, even from those centres American firms can send the e-waste abroad legally because the US Congress has not ratified the Basel Convention.

(www.iht.com, 18 November 2007)

Trucks burn diesel fuel contaminated with more than 130 times the pollution-causing sulphur that the United States allows in most diesel ... Trucks are by far the largest source of street-level pollution [in China] ... Tiny particles of sulphur-laden soot ... [and] nitrogen oxides [are emitted] ... Oil giants like Sinopec, losing money on every gallon of diesel they refine because of the low sales cost, upgrade refineries slowly, if at all, and seek out cheap crude with high levels of sulphur, negating the effects of higher emission standards for new vehicles ... Oil industry experts suggest that China raise diesel prices by at least 20 per cent to eliminate subsidies and fuel lines [at service stations] and to foster investment.

(*IHT*, 8 December 2007, pp. 1–2)

'China is already, by some estimates, the world's largest emitter of greenhouse gases ... Between 2000 and 2005 China accounted for more than half the increase in the world's emissions of carbon dioxide' (*IHT*, 5 January 2008, p. 7).

The government says it is banning shops from handing out free plastic bags from June this year [2008] in a bid to curb pollution. Production of ultra-thin plastic bags will also be banned ... Instead, people will be encouraged to use baskets or reusable cloth bags for their shopping ... A statement by the State Council: 'Plastic bags, due to reasons such as excessive use and inefficient recycling, have caused serious energy and resources waste and environment pollution ... The super-thin bags have especially become a main source of plastic pollution as they are easy to break and thus disposed of carelessly' ... Shops that violated the new rules could be fined or have their goods confiscated, it said. The Council also called for greater recycling efforts from rubbish collectors and suggested financial authorities should consider higher taxes on the production and sale of plastic bags.

(www.bbc.co.uk, 9 January 2008)

China will ban shops from giving out free plastic bags and has called on consumers to use baskets and cloth sacks instead to reduce environmental pollution. The regulation, effective in June [2008], was decided on about fifteen years after shopkeepers started handing out cheap, flimsy plastic bags to customers. 'White pollution', a reference to the colour of many bags, has cluttered landfills ... Beginning on 1 June all supermarkets, department stores and shops will be prohibited from giving out free plastic bags, the State Council said. Stores must clearly mark the price of plastic shopping bags and are banned from tacking that price on to products. The production, sale and use of ultra-thin bags – those less than 0.025 millimetres, or

0.00098 inches, thick – were also banned, according to the State Council notice, Dated 31 December [2007] and posted on a government website Tuesday [9 January 2008], it called for 'a return to cloth bags and shopping baskets'. It also urged waste collectors to step up recycling efforts to reduce the amount of bags burned or buried. Finance authorities were told to consider tax measures to discourage plastic bag production and sale.

(www.iht.com, 9 January 2008)

China announced new national regulations to help clean up the environment and slow the country's growing addiction to imported oil by focusing on a ubiquitous but unexpected target: the lowly plastic bag. On Tuesday the State Council banned the production of ultra-thin plastic bags and required store owners to charge customers for thicker ones. The initiative is intended not only to fight littering but also to reduce oil usage.

(*IHT*, 10 January 2008, p. 11)

The State Council statement: 'Our country consumes huge amounts of plastic bags every year. While providing convenience to customers, they have also caused serious pollution, and waste energy and resources, because of excessive use and inadequate recycling. The ultra-thin bags are the main source of "white" pollution as they can easily get broken and end up as litter … We should encourage people to return to carrying cloth bags, using baskets for their vegetables' … A pilot scheme in Shenzhen last year [2007], where 1,75 billion plastic bags are used every year and where city authorities introduced a ban on free plastic shopping bags, was not a success, as consumers struggled to get used to the idea.

(*The Independent*, 10 January 2008, p. 28)

'[In] a remote county in western Qinghai province plastic bags have been banned outright since 2005' (*The Times*, 10 January 2008, p. 35).

The government has unveiled a detailed plan to limit pollution in China's lakes by 2010 and return them to their original state by 2030. The State Council, China's cabinet, ordered strict regulation of the release of wastewater, the closing of heavily polluting factories near lakes, the improvement of sewage treatment facilities and strict limits of fish farms, the official Xinhua news agency said Tuesday [22 January]. The council also banned the use of pesticides with highly toxic residue near large lakes as well as detergents containing phosphorus … China's three main lakes – Tai, Chaohu and Dianchi – have all had algae blooms in recent years. Stimulated by high levels of phosphorus and other chemicals, algae has blanketed large areas of water, killing fish and making the water undrinkable. An algae bloom that covered a large area of Lake Tai last spring [2007] was particularly severe and received national attention … Wastewater from fish farms has become another serious problem and one that the State Council tried to address on Tuesday, ordering that all fish farms be removed from the three main lakes by the end of this year [2008]. Fish farms elsewhere are to be more tightly limited to certain designated areas within three years ... The water clean-up effort will also include the lake behind the Three Gorges Dam on the Yangtze River.

(www.iht.com, 23 January 2008)

Beijing has put into effect a 'green securities' plan aimed at making it harder for companies that pollute heavily to raise capital and requiring companies listed on stock exchanges to disclose more information about their environmental records. The plan is part of a drive by the State Environmental Protection Administration to enlist other government agencies to give consideration to ecology in financial and economic policies. China has adopted 'green credit' and 'green insurance' in recent months and has plans for 'green taxation' and 'green trade' ... One element of the agency's green securities programme is already in place. Companies in sectors including thermal power, steel, cement and aluminium need its approval before they can apply to the securities regulator to sell shares. The agency said it had checked the environmental record of thirty-seven listed companies and objected to the capital-raising plans of ten companies last year [2007]. Eight of them went on to issue shares only after improving their pollution controls, the agency said ... [The agency] said some listed companies had applied to sell shares to finance environmental protection but then used the capital to expand production. The second pillar of the programme is a requirement that listed companies provide more information about their environmental performance. The agency said fewer than half of listed companies even mentioned the environment in their 2006 annual reports.

(*IHT*, 26 February 2008, p. 17)

More than half of the water in China ... is still unfit to drink. Last year [2007] around 48 million people living there lacked sufficient drinking water ... China boasts a fifth of the world's population, yet it has only 7 per cent of global water resources ... The country's *per capita* water resources stand at a mere fifth of the world average. More than 70 per cent of China's rivers and lakes are polluted ... The country has traditionally supported its agricultural industry, which makes up over 60 per cent of total water consumption, by keeping prices low.

(www.iht.com, 27 March 2008)

A ban on smoking in most Beijing public places is expected to take effect in May, in hopes of meeting China's pledge of a smoke-free Olympics. China is home to 350 million smokers, a third of the global total. More than 150 Chinese cities already have limited restrictions, but Beijing would be the first to ban smoking in all restaurants, offices and schools ... The government estimates that 1 million Chinese die smoking-related deaths annually; that is projected to double by 2010. Beijing has had some smoking restrictions since 1995, when the municipal government prohibited lighting up in large public venues such as schools, sports arenas and movie theatres. The new rules, which were announced in state media Saturday [29 March], expand the scope to include restaurants, bars, hotels, offices, vacation resorts and indoor areas of medical facilities, according to a draft released earlier this year [2008] ... Organizers of the 8–24 August Olympics have said they want smoking bans in all hotels serving athletes and all competition venues and restaurants in the Olympic Village by June ... In 2005 China ratified WHO rules that urged it, within three years, to restrict tobacco advertising and sponsorship, put tougher health warnings on cigarettes, raise tobacco prices and taxes, curb second-hand smoke, prohibit cigarette sales to minors and clamp down on smuggling.

(www.iht.com, 31 March 2008)

(For further details of anti-pollution measures taken as a result of China hosting the 2008 Olympic Games, see the chronology in Chapter 8 of the companion volume, *Political Developments in Contemporary China*.)

'The University of California will report [in May 2008] ... that China's greenhouse gas emissions have been underestimated and probably passed those of the United States in 2006–7' (www.bbc.co.uk, 15 April 2008).

In late March [2008] blue-green blooms were again found along the southern shore [of Lake Tai] ... Such growths are rare so early in the year. Officials admit that despite their clean-up efforts the water remains at the lowest grade in China's water quality scale, unfit for human contact, and that another 'big bloom' is possible this year.

(*The Economist*, 3 May 2008, p. 71)

China on Sunday [1 June 2008] became the latest country to declare war on plastic bags in a drive to save energy and protect the environment. Under new regulations plastic bags under 0.025 millimetres thick are banned and shopkeepers must charge shoppers for any other plastic bags. Those found breaking the law face fines and could have their goods confiscated. According to China Plastics Processing Industry Association, the country uses 3 billion plastic bags a day ... Ultra-thin bags are the main target of the crackdown because they are typically used once and then thrown away, littering streets, fields and streams and creating what the Chinese call 'white pollution'.

(www.iht.com, 1 June 2008)

After rising steeply for many years, emissions of three important pollutants began to decline last year [2007], China's Ministry of Environmental Protection announced Thursday [5 June] as part of an annual report. But total levels of pollution in China's lakes, rivers and coastal waters continued to rise, the ministry said, as more pollutants continued to flow into them than their ecologies could absorb. And the air in many cities remains severely polluted. The ministry said that emissions of sulphur dioxide, mainly emitted by coal-fired power plants and the primary cause of acid rain, declined by 4.66 per cent last year. The government has been pursuing a stringent programme that requires power plants to cleanse most of the sulphur dioxide from their flue gases before they are released into the atmosphere, and environmentalists had been expecting this programme to show success. Emissions of organic pollutants into waterways, as measured by tests of chemical oxygen demand, also declined by 3.14 per cent last year, the ministry said. Industries reduced their discharges of solid waste into the air and water by 8.1 per cent ... The ministry said the percentage of coastal waters rated at the worst level of pollution rose to 25.4 per cent last year, from 24.3 per cent a year earlier. The proportion of coastal waters in good condition dropped to 62.8 per cent from 67.7 per cent. The proportion of cities with fairly good air quality was practically unchanged last year, while the number of extremely polluted cities declined ... The pollutants identified in the report as showing improvement, particularly sulphur dioxide, tended to be those emitted by relatively few factories and power plants, many of them owned or controlled by the state. That makes it easier to limit pollution. Air quality experts calculate that up to 90 per cent of deaths from air pollution are caused by tiny particles of soot. The biggest contributors in cities are trucks. The ministry provided no figures on Thursday for emissions of such particles.

(www.iht.com, 5 June 2008)

China is rapidly extending its lead over the United States as the world's largest emitter of carbon dioxide, the main greenhouse gas, according to figures released Friday [13 June 2008] by the Netherlands Environmental Assessment Agency. The agency, which tracks global annual emission, said the volume of carbon from China was 14 per cent higher than those of the United States in 2007. That compares to emissions from China that were 7 per cent higher than the United States in 2006 and 5 per cent below the United States in 2005, according to the agency. It describes its findings as more up-to-date than similar studies from bodies including the International Energy Agency. Last year [2007] the agency was the first to identify that China had overtaken the United States as the world's largest emitter of carbon. It based its latest findings on recently published information on energy use from the oil company BP and on cement production, which is a major source of carbon emissions.

(www.iht.com, 13 June 2008)

Many experts were sceptical of last year's [2007] findings. The International Energy Agency continued to say only that China was projected to overtake the United States by the end of 2007 ... China, like the United States, is heavily dependent on coal for its energy, and it has seen its most rapid growth in some of the world's most polluting sectors, like cement, aluminium and plate glass ... The Dutch researchers cautioned that there were some signs that China's emissions trajectory would be somewhat blunted this year [2008], although growth would still be rapid. Its emissions rose

8 per cent in 2007, compared to more than 11 per cent annually for the previous two years ... About 80 per cent of the world's coal demand comes from China, according to the International Energy Agency. But the United States is also a major user of coal to power its industry.

(www.iht.com, 14 June 2008)

Chinese carbon dioxide pollution rose by 8 per cent in 2007 and was responsible for two-thirds of the year's total increase in global CO_2 emissions, according to the Netherlands Environmental Assessment Agency. Cement production to meet China's demand for infrastructure to support its booming economy was a large factor: half of all global cement production now takes place in China and the industry is responsible for a fifth of Chinese CO_2. Rebuilding roads and homes after the Sichuan province earthquake is expected to increase demand further. According to the figures, China is now responsible for 24 per cent of global carbon dioxide emissions, followed by the United States with 22 per cent. The EU produces 12 per cent, India 8 per cent and the Russian Federation 6 per cent. Per head of the population China is still far behind the United States, which remains the biggest polluter per person by a large margin. US citizens produce an average of 19.4 tonnes of CO_2 each year, while those in China produce just 5.1 tonnes each. Russians produce 11.8 tonnes each, the agency says, with the figure for the EU at 8.6 tonnes and India just 1.8 tonnes per person.

(www.guardian.co.uk, 13 June 2008)

'The proportion of Chinese who own a vehicle is still only around 3 per cent' (*FT*, 21 July 2008, p. 11).

A third of the Yellow River ... the second longest in China after the Yangtze ... is heavily polluted by industrial waste and unsafe for any use, according to new scientific date. The Yellow River Conservancy Committee said that 33.8 per cent of the river's water sampled registered worse than level 5, meaning it is unfit for drinking, aquaculture, industrial use and even agriculture, according to data used by the UN Environmental Programme ... A 2007 survey covered more than 13,492 kilometres (8,385 miles) of the river ... Only 16 per cent of the river samples reached level 1 or 2 – water considered safe for household use ... The results showed pollution had gotten slightly worse since 2006, when 31 per cent of the water in the river was worse than a level 5, according to an earlier survey, although only 12,510 kilometres was measured then ... Pollution in China's waterways remains 'grave', according to a June report by the ministry of environmental protection on the state of the environment in 2007. More than 20 per cent of water tested in nearly 200 rivers was not safe to use, it said.

(www.iht.com, 25 November 2008)

A senior family planning official has noted an alarming rise in the number of babies with birth defects ... Jiang Fan, from China's National Population and Family Planning Commission, said environmental pollution was a cause of the increase. The coal mining heartland of Shanxi province had the biggest problem ... Officials blame emissions from Shanxi's large coal and chemical industry for the problems there ... China has reported the trend before and it was not clear if Mr Jiang was commenting on new or old statistics.

(www.bbc.co.uk, 1 February 2009)

China has the world's third largest coal reserves, after the United States and Russia ... China now uses more coal than the United States, Europe and Japan combined ... But China has emerged in the past two years as the world's leading builder of more efficient, less polluting coal power plants, mastering the technology and driving down costs ... China has begun requiring power companies to retire an older, more polluting power plant for each new one they build ... Only half the country's coal-fired power plants have the emissions control equipment to remove sulphur compounds that cause acid rain, and even power plants with that technology do not always use it. China has not begun regulating some of the emissions that lead to heavy smog in big cities. Even among China's newly built plants, not all are modern. Only about 60 per cent of the new plants are being built using newer technology that is highly efficient, but more expensive ... Coal supplies 80 per cent of China's electricity ... Even an efficient coal-fired power plant emits twice the carbon dioxide of a natural gas-fired plant.

(www.iht.com, 11 May 2009; *IHT*, 12 May 2009, pp. 1, 16)

China passed the United States two years ago as the world's largest emitter of greenhouse gases, and the two countries together account for 42 per cent of humanity's emissions of these gases ... [On 15 July 2009 China and the United States] announced that each country would put up $15 million for a joint research centre on clean energy, with headquarters in each country ... [The United States estimated that] Chinese emissions per person were still roughly a quarter of American emissions per person and that the United States had put more than twice as much global warming gases into the atmosphere as China since the beginning of the Industrial Revolution.

(www.iht.com, 15 July 2009; *IHT*, 16 July 2009, p. 8).

The US energy secretary, Steven Chu, concluded his first official visit to Beijing on Thursday [16 July] with a memorandum of understanding with Chinese officials for joint studies on ways to improve the energy efficiency of buildings ... China now accounts for half the square footage of buildings under construction around the world.

(www.iht.com, 16 July 2009)

'[US] energy secretary Steven Chu and commerce secretary Gary Locke [are] both Chinese Americans' (*FT*, 31 July 2009, p. 10).

The authorities in central China have suspended two environmental officials and detained a chemical plant boss after hundreds of residents protested claiming the factory polluted a river and caused at least two deaths in the area, an official said Sunday [2 August 2009]. On Saturday [1 August] the police detained the head of the Xianghe Chemical Factory in Liuyang and the government suspended the chief and deputy chief of the city's environmental protection bureau.

(*IHT*, 3 August 2009, p. 4)

Hundreds of residents near a chemical plant have been found to have high levels of a dangerous metal [cadmium] in their bodies ... Production at the Changsha Xianghe plant in Liuyang stopped earlier this year [in April 2009], shortly before the two people died [in May and June] ... Medical tests were carried out on nearly 3,000 residents of Zhentou township over the weekend following a protest on Thursday [30 July], involving about 3,000 people ... Xinhua said people had been seeking a government investigation of the plant since 2007, but that the local authorities had failed to act.

(www.bbc.co.uk, 3 August 2009)

After surpassing the United States as the world's largest producer of household garbage, China has embarked on a vast programme to build incinerators as landfills run out of space. But these incinerators have become a growing source of toxic emissions that can damage the human body's nervous system. And these pollutants, particularly long-lasting substances like dioxin and mercury, are dangerous not only in China ... The pollutants float downwind on air currents across the Pacific to American shores and beyond.

(*IHT*, 13 August 2009, p. 13)

'Su Wei (director-general of the climate change department at the National Development and Reform Commission): "China's [carbon] emissions will not continue to rise beyond 2050"' (*FT*, 15 August 2009, p. 5).

Despite a global economic slump, worldwide carbon dioxide pollution jumped 2 per cent last year [2008], most of the increase coming from China, according to a study published Tuesday [17 November] ... Worldwide emissions rose 671 million more tonnes from 2007 to 2008. Nearly three-quarters of that increase came from China ... The 2008 emissions increase was smaller than normal for this decade. Annual pollution growth has averaged 3.6 per cent. This year [2009] scientists are forecasting a nearly 3 per cent reduction, despite China, because of the massive economic slowdown ... The goal is to limit global warming to 2 degrees Centigrade (1.3 degrees Celsius).

(www.iht.com, 17 November 2009)

Pollution and public protest

'In the southern city of Xiamen ... citizens who were outraged over plans to build a $10 billion chemical plant in an urban area took to the streets last June [2007] in protest' (*IHT*, 5 January 2008, p. 2).

Demonstrations against … Shanghai's high-speed 'maglev' train … over the weakened, the city's largest public protest since thousands took part in some-times violent anti-Japanese demonstrations in 2005, present authorities with a new challenge: a growing middle class that wants a say in major decisions about development in the city … The maglev train runs without wheels, using electromagnetic forces to hover just above the tracks and to propel it … Resi-dents along the maglev's planned route are complaining about noise and elec-tromagnetic radiation, rejecting city officials' insistence that the line would be no threat to their health. Articulate, well-educated and adept at public rela-tions, the demonstrators may prove harder to handle than the farmers and factory workers who stage thousands of protests against pollution and abuse of power in more remote parts of China every year … This weekend's dem-onstrations were triggered by Shanghai's plan to extend its magnetic levitation train by 32 kilometres, or 20 miles, through the city, to near its domestic airport. A $1.4 billion, 30-kilometre line from the city outskirts to the interna-tional airport, the world's only commercial maglev operation, opened in 2003. Built with German technology, the trains reach above 400 kilometres an hour. The extension plan was promoted by Chen Liangyu, the city's former Com-munist Party boss, fond of grandiose public projects to burnish Shanghai's image as a global city. But public opposition to the plan began growing last year [2007] and increased after officials began at the end of December a three-week period for public comment. Charging that the comment period was too short and lacked transparency, protesters turned to an unauthorized method of expressing opinion – demonstrations by hundreds of people on one of Shang-hai's busiest shopping streets during the weekend … The police briefly detained dozens of people at the march on Saturday [12 January 2008] and ended the demonstration on Sunday by chasing and manhandling protesters … But the protesters appear to be calculating that Shanghai has changed enough to give them a good chance of succeeding, Chen was dismissed as the city's party boss in a corruption scandal in late 2006, casting a political shadow over projects linked to him. The protest may also benefit from national political trends. President Hu Jintao is called for a 'harmonious society' in which the government pays more attention to the cares of common people, a slogan protesters have plastered on banners hanging from their apartment buildings … [The protesters] have struck a chord with many people by asking why Shanghai should spend so much money on the maglev instead of improving the creaking public bus system or schools.

(www.iht.com, 15 January 2008; *IHT*, 16 January 2008, p. 10)

Middle-class city dwellers have marched peacefully in Xiamen and more recently in Shanghai to demand that the government reconsider big develop-ment projects being built in their midst … [Protesters are] organizing around issues like the construction of a chemical plant in Xiamen or the extension of a high-speed rail link through a densely populated middle-class area of Shanghai.

(*IHT*, 19 January 2008, p. 2)

For the last two weekends protesters opposed to plans to extend the city's fastest-on-earth magnetic levitation train – the maglev – have taken to the streets in marches that organizers dubbed 'collective walks' ... The maglev, which can rocket passengers at speeds well over 200 miles per hour, currently connects the Pudong airport at the eastern edge of the metropolis to a nearby subway station ... The first extension in the works would link Pudong's new airport to the old Hongqiao airport west of the city. This has angered residents of some largely middle-class neighbourhoods through which the new rail line would run. They claim that the path of noisy maglev trains would make their property values plummet and disturb the tranquillity of their homes ... Describing mass actions as 'collective walks' is new ... Co-ordinating actions [also include] text messages and having videos uploaded on to YouTube.

(www.iht.com, 21 January 2008; *IHT*, 22 January 2008, p. 6)

On 12 January ... a few thousand disgruntled residents [of Shanghai], many of them carrying signs, denounced the [maglev] train project in one of the largest demonstrations this city has seen in recent years ... The ordinary citizens who marched on People's Square are wary of calling their event and the anti-train movement a protest. Indeed, most even shy from the word 'march', preferring to speak instead of a 'collective walk' to the square ... Homeowners here [are coalescing] around issues like property values, environmental safety, urban planning and how their tax money is spent ... Many of the early opponents of the route seized upon objections cited in a protest last year [2007] that forced a retracing of the line in which people voiced fears about radiation from the trains' powerful electromagnets, but grievances have multiplied ... [The] smaller homeowner-led protest [in 2007] against the maglev train resulted in a change of route ... An even more recent event [took place] in the southern city of Xiamen, where civic mobilization forced the suspension of plans to build a large chemical plant in an urban area.

(www.iht.com, 27 January 2008)

'The main complaint appears to be a sharp fall in property prices along the 20-mile route' (*The Times*, 25 January 2008, p. 49).

In recent days, Zheng Enchong, one of China's best-known human rights lawyers, has been repeatedly beaten by police, according to his wife and associates of the lawyer ... Jiang said the beatings represent a sharp escalation of a recent campaign by the Shanghai authorities to quiet Zheng ... Associates of the lawyer who have spoken with him say the beatings started after he began advising residents who have mounted a campaign against a high-tech railroad project that would cut through middle-class neighbourhoods in the city. Others said Zheng had also recently spoken of details of what he calls evidence of high-level corruption in Shanghai involving real estate speculation and influence peddling ... People who have visited Zheng say the beatings follow other efforts to silence the lawyer, including what they describe as a harassment campaign based on spurious tax evasion charges.

(www.iht.com, 25 February 2008; *IHT*, 26 February 2008, p. 8)

More than 100 people are under investigation and several government officials have been detained or removed from office in central China after a dispute in early January [2008] in which a group of city officials beat a bystander to death. The government investigation ... was touched off by bloggers in China who were outraged that a forty-one-year-old man had been fatally beaten while trying to use his cellphone to photograph a dispute between villagers and city inspectors. City officials in Tianmen in Hubei province in central China are being punished and investigated for their role in the killing of the man, Wei Wenhua, the general manager of a construction company, and the beatings of five villagers during a dispute on 7 January ... The episode is the latest in which bloggers and others have used the internet to force Chinese authorities to investigate beatings and other abuses by government officials ... On 7 January the government says a dispute in a village near Tianmen broke out because villagers were angry over the dumping of heaps of garbage near their homes. Apparently, some villagers had tried to stop a truck from dumping garbage in their neighbourhood. To put down the protest, the government says, local officials called in a large group of parapolice officials, who are often used to quell uprisings or deal with unlicensed business operations in cities. Wei apparently drove by in a car and stopped to photograph the skirmish with his cellphone. He was confronted by government inspectors and beaten to death ... Soon after several large protests took place in Tianmen as residents demanded justice.

(www.iht.com, 18 January 2008)

'Wei Wenhua was set upon by members of a quasi-police force that operates in Chinese cities known as *cheng guan* ... The entire affair became a cause célèbre in the press and Chinese internet sites' (*IHT*, 19 January 2008, p. 2).

The heads of China's nationwide urban inspection force have openly criticized their officers for beating to death a bystander who filmed a protest, in rare admission of abuse of power. Over 100 local leaders of the force, known in Chinese as the *cheng guan* or 'urban administration bureau', issued a joint letter saying that the killing in the central city of Tianmen, apparently committed by *cheng guan* members, had sparked 'deep concern and reflection' ... The head of the Tianmen *cheng guan* department has been fired from all of his government and Communist Party positions, and four of his officers were arrested in the killing ... Xinhua reported that the four suspects had been stripped of their party membership, a step presaging a rapid move to prosecute ... Xinhua said the incident has prompted calls from officials nationwide for tighter oversight over *cheng guan*, a uniformed force charged with enforcing urban planning regulations and clearing streets of unlicensed traders. The role frequently brings them into conflict with

residents. While *cheng guan* are empowered to issue fines and other administrative penalties, only the police are technically allowed to deal with criminal matters or violent behaviour. In some places, however, *cheng guan*, are
used as police auxiliaries, and Xinhua cited officials it did not identify as
saying that the *cheng guan*'s powers and duties must be better defined to
avoid abuses.

(www.iht.com, 21 January 2008)

'Shanghai's local government has backed off construction work on a new
electro-magnetic train until at least next year [2009] ... Work began last May
[2007] ... The city opened its first maglev line in 2002' (*FT*, 7 March 2008,
p. 7).

Hundreds of people marched in a western provincial capital over the
weekend to protest environmental risks they say are associated with the construction of a petrochemical factory and oil refinery, witnesses said Monday
[5 May]. It was the latest in a series of rare but increasingly ambitious grassroots movements in Chinese cities aimed at derailing government-backed
industrial projects that could damage the environment and people's health
... The protesters in Chengdu, the capital of Sichuan province, walked
peacefully through the centre of the city for several hours Sunday [4 May]
to criticize the building of an ethylene plant and oil refinery in Pengzhou, a
few minutes' drive outside the city ... About 400 to 500 protesters took part
in the march ... Organizers circumvented a law that requires protesters to
apply for a permit by saying they were only out for a 'stroll' ... The chemical plant and oil refinery is a joint venture of the Sichuan provincial government and PetroChina, a publicly traded oil company that is the listed arm
of China National Petroleum Corp., the state-owned concern that is the
country's largest oil producer. The project [was] approved last year [2007]
... The protest movement in Chengdu is at least the third such groundswell
to emerge in recent years. Last year construction of a chemical plant outside
Xiamen, in Fujian province, was halted after residents held a series of street
protests. More recently residents in Shanghai protested construction of a
high-speed rail line designed to link a suburb with the airport, forcing officials to announce that the project was being delayed. In both cases residents
complained that the projects would bring significant environmental and
health risks.

(www.iht.com, 5 May 2008)

Ordinary people appear to have won a victory by forcing the government to
move a planned chemical factory. The plant was supposed to be built in the
picturesque coastal city of Xiamen, but will now be moved inland ... to the
nearby city of Zhangzhou ... Government officials seem to have changed their
minds after thousands of Xiamen residents staged protests against the factory
... The chemical plant, funded by Taiwan's Xianglu Group, was to be built
next to a new residential area in Xiamen, Fujian province ... In June 2007

local residents staged a series of protests in Xiamen city centre against the proposed plant on environmental grounds. They fear the factory, which will make the chemical paraxylene, would emit toxic fumes that could cause cancer ... Work had already started on the plant at its original location ... But after the protests, which received nationwide publicity, the local government put the project on hold. It also ordered an environmental report on the scheme ... The findings ... suggest the company agreed to limit the factory's pollution.

(www.bbc.co.uk, 14 January 2009)

'The environmental ministry has approved a petrochemical plant that drew fierce opposition over feared pollution. But the approval is based on the plant being built in another city ... [namely] Zhangzhou, about 30 miles west of Xiamen' (www.iht.com, 15 January 2009).

China has taken the unusual step of moving a $5 billion refinery and petrochemical plant, one of the country's biggest foreign investment projects, after a public outcry ... The plant was to be built in southern Guangzhou, the provincial capital, 60 kilometres upwind of Hong Kong, where the project has also come under criticism ... [It was not revealed] where Sinopec and Kuwait Petroleum had agreed to move the plant. Privately, provincial officials say it is most likely destined for the industrial port of Zhanjiang in western Guangdong, a much less populated and ecologically sensitive region.

(*FT*, 31 July 2009, p. 6)

Hundreds of villagers have broken into a factory that poisoned more than 600 children ... Villagers tore down fencing and smashed coal trucks at the lead smelting factory in Shaanxi province. Local authorities have admitted that the plant is responsible for poisoning the children. More than 150 were in hospital ... The smelting plant has now been closed down.

(www.bbc.co.uk, 17 August 2009)

'Several hundred villagers tore down fences and blocked traffic outside the Dongling Lead and Zinc Smelting Co. in Shaanxi province after news of the poisoning emerged last week' (*IHT*, 18 August 2009, p. 4).

The police clashed with residents of two villages near a smelting plant in northern China that is blamed for the lead poisoning of nearly all the children in the villages, reports said Monday [17 August]. It was another sign of growing anger over China's rampant industrial pollution ... Fighting between angry parents and scores of police officers broke out Sunday [16 August], and trucks delivering coal to the plant were stoned ... China's breakneck economic development has left much of its soil, air and waterways dangerously polluted, and environmental showdowns with enraged residents are growing more frequent. Authorities routinely pledge to close down polluting industrial operations but often back down because of their importance to the local economy. At least 615 out of 731 children in the two villages have tested positive for lead poisoning, which can damage the nervous and reproductive systems and cause high blood pressure, amnesia and memory loss. Lead levels in the children were more than ten times the level China considers safe. Air quality tests near the smelting plant found unusually high lead levels, according to the official Xinhua news agency, although officials say groundwater, surface water, soil and company waste discharge all meet national standards.

(www.iht.com, 18 August 2009)

More than 1,300 children have been sickened in a lead poisoning case in China's central Hunan province, the second such case involving a large number of children in the past month, state media said Thursday [20 August]. The official Xinhua news agency said 1,354 children who lived near a manganese processing plant in Wenping were diagnosed as having excessive lead in their blood ... [An anonymous source in] the Wenping township government office said 60 per cent to 70 per cent of the local children tested were found to have excessive levels of lead in their blood ... In Shaanxi province in northern China at least 615 out of 731 children in two villages near the Dongling smelter in the town of Changqing have tested for lead poisoning, which can damage the nervous and reproductive systems and cause high blood pressure and memory loss. In the Hunan case the children are from four villages near the Wugang Smelting Plant in Wenping ... The children still have to be tested in the provincial capital Changsha to see how serious their cases are ... The plant opened in May 2008 without the approval of the local environmental protection bureau.

(www.iht.com, 20 August 2009)

Officials in Wenping shut down the smelter, the Wugang Fine-Processed Manganese Smelting Factory, last week ... after about a thousand local residents protested the poisoning ... The plant was ordered closed on 13 August ... The smelter opened in May 2008 without required environmental permits ... Tests since then have found elevated levels of lead in the blood of 1,354 children, or about seven in ten children who were examined ... The severity of the poisoning cannot be measured without further testing; seventeen of the eighty-three children who received those tests have been hospitalized ... The report of poisoning in Wugang followed a similar incident in Shaanxi province, in north-central China, where state news reports say 851 children living near the nation's fourth largest smelter have tested positive for lead poisoning since early August. More than 170 have since been hospitalized.

(www.iht.com, 20 August 2009)

'In both cases the smelters were closed after angry parents confronted the authorities over their children's illnesses ... Lead poisoning can cause a range of health problems, from learning difficulties to seizures. Children under six are most at risk' (www.bbc.co.uk, 20 August 2009). 'Officials said 1,354 children – 70 per cent of those under fourteen living in four villages near the plant – were found to have excessive levels of lead in their blood' (www.bbc.co.uk, 23 August 2009).

Officials announced that 1,354 children under fourteen, who had been living and going to school within a few hundred metres of a manganese smelter ... had excess lead in their blood ... The smelter has not submitted to any environmental safety tests even though schools and a nursery are within 500 metres of the plant ... Zhou Shengxian, the environmental protection minister, noted an increase in the number of 'mass incidents' – the official term for riots or protests – caused by environmental problems.

(*The Times*, 21 August 2009, p. 46)

The plant ... in Wenping township, Hunan province ... is within 500 metres of a primary school, a middle school and a kindergarten ... Authorities are not obliged to conduct expensive tests for heavy metals, which tend to accumulate over time rather than be emitted in noticeable bursts.

(*Guardian*, 21 August 2009, p. 24)

China has closed a manganese smelter in the southern province of Hunan ... the case is the country's third heavy metal contamination scandal in less than a month ... The *South China Morning Post* reported the closure of another plant in Hunan earlier this month [August] that was linked to cadmium and indium poisoning among nearby villages.

(www.ft.com, 20 August 2009)

So far 1,354 children in Hunan province have tested positive for abnormal levels of lead in their blood, authorities say ... In Shaanxi's Fengxiang county 851 children recently also turned up with high lead levels along with more than 200 in Yunnan province. All of them lived near industrial plants, some only a few hundred feet away. Local officials say eight factories in Wenping and Simachong, including the plant in Hengjiang, have since been shut down, including coal, manganese and iron smelting plants ... Authorities say children living up to 20 kilometres away have been affected and more were being tested ... Lead can remain in the air, water, soil and crops even after the source of contamination is cut off ... According to the government, about 10 per cent of the nation's arable land is contaminated with lead, and annually about 12 million tonnes of food crops are contaminated with lead.

(www.cnn.com, 2 September 2009)

According to reports, up to 10,000 villagers recently rioted at a sewage plant in Fujian province, claiming it is responsible for causing cancer. The protesters reportedly clashed with 2,000 police, who fired warning shots and tear gas to break up the crowd.

(www.cnn.com, 2 September 2009)

In recent months Beijing has made increasing commitments to boosting alternative energy and energy efficiency, which will reduce the rate at which China's carbon emissions rise over the next decade. China is pouring billions of dollars into alternative energy – an investment that, as a percentage of GDP, is ten times that of the United States. Its installed wind capacity has doubled in each of the past four years. Chinese newspapers have carried a string of reports about the human costs of pollution. Indeed, the faltering response of pollution contrasts starkly with China's foresight on energy, and indicates that the country's political system is far better at envisioning solutions for the future than fixing problems already at hand ... Efforts to increase alternative energy and energy efficiency are backed by the powerful National Development and Reform Commission and usually coincide with Beijing's economic agenda ... But efforts to enforce stricter controls, which can stand in the way of economic activity, have proceeded much more slowly. The Ministry of Environmental Protection occupies a much weaker position in the political pantheon ... Since the first legal Chinese civic organization, Friends of Nature, was founded in 1994, environmental groups have been the spearhead of China's fledging non-governmental sector, with more than 5,000 groups in existence today. Ironically, even as climate change has climbed on the national agenda, the political space for domestic green groups has shrunk ... China may soon have the odd distinction of being the world's leader in alternative energy – and industrial pollution.

(Christina Larson, *IHT*, 3 September 2009, p. 6)

Medical tests have shown that at least 121 children living near a battery plant in eastern China are suffering from lead poisoning, the latest in a recent string of such cases that have affected hundreds. Two medical agencies tested 287 children younger than fourteen years of age for lead poisoning and found 121 of them had excessive levels of lead in their blood, the government of Shanghang county in Fujian province said in a statement late Saturday [26 September] ... The government ordered the Huaqiang Battery Plant to shut about ten days ago.

(www.iht.com, 27 September 2009)

Local health officials acted after parents presented test results suggesting widespread lead poisoning, and then blocked roads in protest. The authorities shut down the factory and offered free testing to 300 children ... Local officials said they would cover medical expenses for any child under fourteen living near the factory.

(www.iht.com, 28 September 2009)

Last month [August] health officials in Hunan province revealed that more than 1,300 children living near a manganese processing plant had lead poisoning. The disclosure came a few days after 850 children in rural Shaanxi province were found to have been contaminated by lead levels so high that 174 of them had to be hospitalized. The authorities in Shaanxi, in north-central China, blamed a zinc and lead smelting facility, which has since been closed, for the poisonings. Last week officials announced a $29 million relocation project to move 1,400 families who lived near the smelter to an entirely new community farther away.

(www.iht.com, 28 September 2009)

Nearly 1,000 children in a central province have tested positive for excessive lead in their blood in the latest of several poisoning cases involving thousands of children across the country. The health bureau in Jiyuan City, Henan province, conducted blood tests on 2,743 children under the age of fourteen ... Signs of poisoning were found in 968 children who live near three major lead smelters.

(*Independent*, 14 October 2009, p. 30)

'Officials in central China plan to relocate 15,000 residents after more than 1,000 children tested positive for lead poisoning ... The residents live in about ten villages around China's biggest lead smelter in Jiyuan ... The factory will keep operating' (www.bbc.co.uk, 19 October 2009).

'Fifty-one children in south-east China [in Hekou village in Jiangsu] have been found to have high levels of lead in their blood ... Authorities have linked their illnesses to a battery factory ... Xinhua reported Wednesday [6 January 2010]' (www.cnn.com, 6 January 2010).

China's government on Tuesday [9 February] unveiled its most detailed survey ever of pollution ... revealing that water pollution in 2007 was more than twice as severe as official figures that had long omitted agricultural waste ... [This is] the first-ever national pollution census ... The pollution census, scheduled to be repeated in 2010, took more than two years to complete. The comprehensiveness of the survey resulted in stark discrepancies between some of the calculations and annual figures that the government has published in the past. By far the biggest of these involved China's total discharge of chemical oxygen demand – the main gauge of water pollution. These discharges totalled 30.3 million tonnes in 2007 ... In recent years the ministry of environmental; protection has done a much narrower calculation of these discharges, excluding agricultural effluents like fertilizers and pesticides as well as fluids from landfills. By that narrower measure, discharges came to only 13.8 million tonnes in 2007, which officials described at the time as a decline of more than 3 per cent from 2006 and a 'turning point' ... The census keepers had also employed updated methodologies and reached many more parts of the countryside and industrial sites than had official statistics ... The director of the Institute of Public and Environmental Affairs, a non-profit research group in Beijing, said that government planners estimated that the country's rivers and lakes could handle only 7.4 million tonnes of chemical oxygen demand ... In terms of sulphur dioxide emissions in 2007, in fact, the census totalled only 23.3 million tonnes, compared with 24.7 million tonnes in the official data released in 2008. But census figures for other important metrics, such as soot and ammonia nitrogen, another indicator of water quality, were higher than the previous date by double-digit percentages.

(www.iht.com, 9 February 2010; *IHT*, 10 February 2010, p. 2)

Farmers' fields are a far bigger source of water contamination in China than factory effluent, the government revealed today [9 February] in its first census on pollution ... According to the study, agriculture is responsible for 43.7 per cent of the nation's chemical oxygen demand (the main measure of organic compounds in water), 67 per cent of phosphorus and 57 per cent of nitrogen discharges ... The government suggested the country's pollution problem may be close to – or even past – a peak. That claim is likely to prompt scepticism among environmental groups ... The government said the new agricultural data and other figures from the census would not be used to evaluate the success of its five-year plan to reduce pollution by 10 per cent.

(www.guardian.co.uk, 9 February 2010; *Guardian*, 10 February 2010, p. 17)

China's first national census of pollution has revealed such a dire picture that the government has mooted a new tax on its sources, according to reports ... Zhang Lijun ... vice minister of environmental protection ... painted a relatively optimistic picture, forecasting pollution would soon peak.

(*FT*, 10 February 2010, p. 8)

At least ninety-four people living near a lead factory, most of them children, have tested positive for lead poisoning, state media said Monday [15 March], prompting the authorities to order the closure of the plant in Sichuan province. Hundreds more people [745] were still waiting for test results. The authorities organized medical tests for 1,600 residents in four villages.

(*IHT*, 16 March 2010, p. 7)

Energy sources

(See Jeffries 2006a: 636–7.)

'China uses around three times as much energy per unit of GDP as the United States, and nine times as much as Japan' (www.economist.com, 12 July 2007).

In mid-1996 coal accounted for 75 per cent of energy consumption. Gas accounted for only 2 per cent (*FT*, 8 July 1996, p. 30).

'Coal provides 67 per cent of the country's energy' (www.iht.com, 21 September 2005).

'China was a net importer of coal in January 2007 for the first time ... About 78 per cent of China's electricity comes from coal. China is the world's second largest energy user after the United States' (*IHT*, 16 July 2007, p. 13).

'China became a net oil importer in 1993' (*IHT*, 3 June 1995, p. 9).

'By 2025, according to the US Energy Information Administration, foreign supplies will account for 77 per cent of China's total oil consumption, compared to the current level of less than 50 per cent' (www.economist.com, 12 July 2007).

China has found a huge offshore oil field that could become the ... biggest new oil source in a decade, a state news agency said Wednesday [28 March] ... PetroChina found the field in Bohai Bay off China's east coast ... The biggest recent domestic oil discovery, also made by PetroChina, was a field found in the mid-1990s in the Tarim Basin in China's desert northwest. Chinese oil companies have been spending heavily on exploration in the north-western and coastal areas but results have been disappointing.

(www.iht.com, 28 March 2007)

'China's biggest oil firm, PetroChina, says it has made the country's largest crude discovery in a decade ... The find [is] off China's north-east coast' (www. bbc.co.uk, 4 May 2007).

Natural gas accounts for 2.7 per cent of energy needs (*IHT*, 20 August 2003, p. 11).

'[China] wants gas to supply 8 per cent of the country's energy by 2010, up from 3 per cent today' (*FT*, 3 March 2006, p. 30).

> The government aims to raise the use of natural gas from just 2.9 per cent of primary energy consumption in 2005 to 10 per cent in 2020. Since China has just 1.3 per cent of the world's natural gas reserves, meeting this target will require a big increase in imports.
>
> (www.economist.com, 12 July 2007)

'China announced Sunday [14 December 2008] that it had found a major natural gas field ... in Xinjiang. It is the first field of its size to be discovered around the Junggar Basin' (*IHT*, 15 December 2008, p. 14).

> China's largest energy company agreed yesterday [18 August] to buy $41 billion worth of natural gas from Australia ... PetroChina agreed to buy 2.25 million metric tonnes a year of liquefied natural gas from ExxonMobil's Gorgon project off the coast of Western Australia. At current gas prices the deal will be worth $41 billion over the next twenty years and is Australia's biggest ever trade deal ... Sino-Australian trade is worth about $53 billion a year ... The Gorgon project is one of the world's largest proposed gas developments. As well as the agreement with ExxonMobil, which owns 25 per cent of Gorgon, PetroChina has a longstanding agreement with Royal Dutch Shell, which also owns 25 per cent, to source gas from the field. Chevron, the US oil group, that is 50 per cent owner and operator of Gorgon, has yet to sign off on the project, but a 'final investment decision' is thought to be only weeks away.
>
> (*FT*, 19 August 2009, p. 19)

'China, which received its first LNG [liquefied natural gas] cargo in May 2006, plans to build more than ten terminals on the east coast to meet a government target to double the use of natural gas' (*IHT*, 19 August 2009, p. 13).

> Australia gave final approval Wednesday [26 August] for a natural gas field development that will export $41 billion in energy to China over twenty years ... [The Australian environment ministry] said Chevron, a partner in the joint venture, had agreed to meet twenty-eight environmental conditions set for the development of the Gorgon gas field off the north-western coast of Australia.
>
> (www.iht.com, 26 August 2009)

'By early 1998 nuclear energy contributed only 1 per cent of total energy output. The plan was to increase this to 5 per cent by 2020 (*FEER*, 26 February 1998, p. 7).

'China needs to add two reactors a year to meet a 2020 target of getting 4 per cent of its power from nuclear energy, against about 2.3 per cent now' (*IHT*, 6 March 2007, p. 18).

'China plans to spend some $50 billion, adding about thirty reactors by 2020 ... That would be about 4 per cent of the country's power capacity ... still far behind the three-quarters in France and one-quarter in Japan' (www.iht.com, 24 July 2007).

'By 2020, starting from a miniscule base that it has established only recently, China expects to supply 10 per cent of its needs from so-called renewable energy sources, including wind, solar power and small hydroelectric dams' (www.iht.com, 26 July 2005). 'China plans to raise renewable energy to about 15 per cent of total supply by 2020, from 7 per cent' (www.iht.com, 29 September 2005). 'A law taking effect next year [2006] will require that China produces 10 per cent of its energy from renewable resources by 2020' (www.iht.com, 30 October 2005).

> China, the world's second biggest emitter of greenhouse gases, announced plans yesterday [7 November 2005] to more than double its reliance on renewable energy by 2020, which could make it a leading player in the wind, solar and hydropower industries ... [China] said it would aim to provide 15 per cent of its energy needs from non-fossil fuels within fifteen years – up from 7 per cent today, and 50 per cent more than its previously stated goal of reaching 10 per cent by 2020 ... Earlier this year the National People's Congress enacted the country's first renewable energy law, which will promote the use of alternatives to coal and oil.
>
> (*Guardian*, 8 November 2005, p. 25)

'China has imposed a requirement that power companies generate a fifth of their electricity from renewable resources by 2020. China's target calls for expanding wind power almost as much as nuclear energy over the next fifteen years' (www.iht.com, 29 September 2006).

> China is planning a vast increase in its use of wind and solar power ... and believes it can match Europe by 2020, producing a fifth of its energy needs from renewable sources ... Zhang Xiaoqiang ... vice chairman of China's National Development and Reform Commission ... said yesterday [9 June 2009] ... [He said that] Beijing would easily surpass current 2020 targets for the use of wind and solar power and was now contemplating targets that were more than three times higher. In the current development plan the goal for wind energy is 30 gigawatts, Zhang said the new goal could be 100 giga-watts by 2020 ... China generates only 120 megawatts of its electricity from solar power, so the goals represents a seventy-five-fold expansion in just over a decade ... Zhang Xiaoqiang: 'We are formulating a plan for develop-ment of renewable energy. We can be sure we will exceed the 15 per cent

target. We will at least reach 18 per cent. Personally I think we could reach the target of having renewables provide 20 per cent of total energy consumption' ... That matches the European goal.

(*Guardian*, 10 June 2009, p. 1)

In a briefing at China's foreign ministry ... [it was claimed that China] is the world's foremost user of non-polluting hydropower and solar power, and fourth in wind power. By 2020 15 per cent of China's energy will come from renewable sources ... [It was claimed that China had reduced] the amount of energy used per unit of GDP by a tenth since 2005. The government has said it will achieve a total reduction of 20 per cent by 2020.

(www.iht.com, 5 August 2009)

The still nascent-state of green power generation makes it an obvious bet for Beijing, which has placed it at the centre of its industrial policy. With a combination of subsidies and protectionism, China hopes to corner the market and leap-frog the competition – so far with success. China is overtaking the United States as a market for wind turbines; its solar cell industry is the world's largest; and Chinese 'clean coal' technology is attracting foreign customers.

(*FT*, 17 August 2009, p. 8)

Chinese government officials signed an agreement on Tuesday [8 September] with First Solar, an American solar developer, for a 2,000 megawatt photovoltaic farm to be built in the Mongolian desert. Set for completion in 2019 the First Solar project represents the world's biggest photovoltaic power plant project to date, and is part of an 11,950 megawatt renewable energy park planned for Ordos City in Inner Mongolia ... When completed the Ordos solar farm would generate enough electricity to power about 3 million Chinese homes ... First Solar expects the 2,000 megawatt power plant to cost $5 billion to $6 billion ... Plans for Ordos renewable energy park call for wind farms to generate 6,950 megawatts, photovoltaic power plants to provide 3,900 megawatts and solar thermal farms to supply 720 megawatts. Biomass operations will contribute 310 megawatts and hydro storage 70 kilowatts.

(www.iht.com, 8 September 2009; *IHT*, 9 September 2009, p. 15)

An analysis from the International Energy Agency released Tuesday [6 October] shows that China could slow the growth of its global warming gases much more quickly than is commonly assumed, thanks to huge programme of wind and nuclear energy and an emphasis on energy efficiency ... China is building more nuclear power plants and bolstering renewable energy, raising efficiency standards in new buildings and gradually moving the economy from its manufacturing base to services, the energy agency said. China's carbon emissions could reach 7.1 gigatonnes by 2030, up from 61. gigatonnes in 2007. But that would mean much less than the 11.6 gigatonnes that the agency previously expected. The agency said: 'These savings would put China at the forefront of all global efforts to combat climate change.'

(*IHT*, 7 October 2009, pp. 1, 22)

There is no national grid; instead, there are six regional ones ... Connections between the grids are weak and long-distance transmission capacity is extremely limited ... China relies heavily on rivers and canals to carry about 75 per cent of all internal freight (by volume), including a large proportion of the coal delivered to generators. Rail accounts for another 14 per cent and highways 12 per cent. But the rivers flow mostly west to east.

(www.iht.com, 13 November 2008)

('In the 1950s an average of 70,000 people died each year in coal mines, compared with 40,000 in the 1980s, 10,000 in the 1990s and roughly 6,000 since 2000': *The Economist*, 25 August 2007, p. 65. 'Nearly 3,800 people died in gas blasts, flooding and other accidents in coal mines last year [2007], according to official figures': www.bbc.co.uk, 18 November 2008. 'China's State Administration of Work Safety office has said the death toll among coal mine workers fell 15 per cent last year [2008], compared to that of 2007': www.bbc.co.uk, 28 January 2009. 'At least 3,200 people died in China's coal mines last year [2008], making them the deadliest in the world: www.bbc.co.uk, 25 August 2009. 'Government figures show that about 3,200 people died in mining accidents last year [2008], a 15 per cent decrease from 2007 ... An estimated 80 per cent of the 16,000 mines operating in China are illegal, according to the State Administration of Work Safety: www.iht.com, 8 September 2009. 'In 2008 3,215 died in China's coal mines, down about 15 per cent from 2007, the State Administration of Work Safety reported. China closed 1,054 illegal coal mines in 2008, but government figures show almost 80 per cent of the country's 16,000 mines are illegal. Luo Lin, head of the Administration of Work Safety, said Saturday [5 September] that China would take measures to close 1,000 small coal mines this year to improve work safety and mine management': www.cnn.com, 9 September 2009. 'According to official figures, 2,631 coal miners died in 1,616 mine accidents in 2009, down 18 per cent from the previous year: www.bbc.co.uk, 2 March 2010.)

Raw materials

China has ended more than a century of South African dominance of the gold mining industry to become the world's biggest producer of the ore. Chinese gold output jumped to a record high of 276 tonnes last year [2007], a 12 per cent increase over 2006, while South Africa produced 272 tonnes ... Its dominance in gold follows a 70 per cent jump in output in the past decade ... In spite of soaring prices, global gold production is falling, notably in South Africa, where output has halved in the past decade ... China is already the world's biggest producer of aluminium, zinc and lead, the second largest of tin, and among the top ten in copper, nickel and silver.

(*FT*, 18 January 2008, p. 1)

'China last year [2008] overtook South Africa as the world's largest gold producer and is estimated to have produced 282 tonnes of gold' (*FT*, 7 May 2009, p. 6).

The number of labour disputes

(See Jeffries 2006a: 636–40 for the section on labour unrest.)

According to government statistics, there were 5,600 labour disputes in 1987, with action ranging from wage conflicts to full strikes. By 2001 that number had soared to 154,600, according to the International Labour Organization [ILO]. Last year [2005] there were 300,000 disputes.

(*The Times*, 19 June 2006, p. 36)

Aid

The UN World Food Programme announced [on 20 December 2003] that China no longer required the international food aid it has been receiving for twenty-five years. Instead it will be asked to become a donor and to share its experience of lifting 400 million people out of poverty ... The World Food Programme's executive director ... announced a new partnership with the government that will see China start to provide rather than receive support from the international community: 'China has lifted as many as 400 million of its own people out of poverty in less than a generation,' he said. 'That is an extraordinary achievement.'

(*Guardian*, 23 December 2003, p. 12)

China's soaring cereal shipments to North Korea made it the world's third largest food donor last year [2005], according to the United Nations World Food Programme ... Pyongyang received more than 90 per cent of the 576,582 tonnes of cross-border food aid provided by China in 2005 ... The shipments meant China's total food donations climbed 260 per cent year-on-year and were surpassed only by those of the United States and the EU ... China's food aid in 2005 accounted for 7 per cent of the global total, comparable to the EU's 7.6 per cent but well behind the United States at 48.8 per cent ... South Korea supplied nearly 400,000 tonnes [of food aid to North Korea in 2005] ... Fears have since grown of another food crisis in North Korea after typhoons and floods that have wiped out crops in some areas ... Food aid donors to North Korea (proportion of that country's total food aid donations): China, 92.2 per cent; South Korea, 99.9 per cent; Japan, 11.9 per cent; United States, 0.7 per cent.

(*FT*, 21 July 2006, p. 5)

For poor countries like Cambodia, Laos and Myanmar, and medium-poor countries like the Philippines, China's loans are proving to be more attractive than complicated loans from the West. Chinese money usually comes unencumbered with conditions for environmental standards or community resettlement that can hold up major projects. The Chinese aid does not carry penalties for corruption that are increasingly stressed by the World Bank president, Paul Wolfowitz [of the United States] ... China's offers rarely include the extra freight of expensive consultants common to World Bank projects. For its part China benefits from infrastructure – roads, ports, bridges – in an underdeveloped but growing region that is vital for increasing trade and for moving natural resources from China's periphery to its heartland ... Beyond its no-strings approach, China is often appreciated as a donor by poor counties because it is willing to take on complicated projects in distant areas that others are not.

(*IHT*, 18 September 2006, pp. 1, 4)

China is using its reserves to hand out billions of dollars of loans to Angola, Sudan, Nigeria, Zimbabwe and increasingly in South-east Asia in a way that the West criticizes because many of these same countries have recently negotiated debt forgiveness packages and are in danger of sinking back into debt.

(*IHT*, 18 September 2006, p. 15)

Education

'Although great strides have also been made in education, President Jiang Zemin said in August 2001 that there were still 100 million illiterate Chinese (*IHT*, 10 August 2001, p. 3).

The number of people deemed to be illiterate in China grew by 30 million to 116 million in the five years to 2005, an education official has said ... [He] said that the main reason was that farmers' children were leaving school early to find work.

(www.bbc.co.uk, 2 April 2007)

The proportion of government spending on education – about 3.2 per cent of GDP – is much lower than the average for developed countries and even lags behind several developing Asian nations including Thailand and the Philippines. The government's share of overall education outlays has been falling steadily over the last two decades, a sharp departure from the decades of central planning when the state met almost all education expenses. Chinese families are now forced to meet about a third of all education costs, according to a study of China's public spending released earlier this year [2006] by the Paris-based OECD. The *China Economic Quarterly* reported late last year [2005] that South Korea was 'the only significant country with a higher reliance on private education spending than China'. Beijing has promised sharp increases in government outlays to reach about 4.5 per cent of GDP by 2010 as one of the first steps of an ambitious fifty-year plan to upgrade the education system. As the economy expands further increases are projected ... To make up the gap in their budgets government schools and universities routinely demand that families pay a raft of additional tuition fees and special charges.

(www.iht.com, 27 August 2006)

More Chinese students than ever are heading overseas to study – nearly 180,000 of them in 2008, almost 25 per cent more than in 2007. For every four who left in the past decade, only one returned ... Those who have obtained doctorates in science or engineering were among the least likely to return ... Nine in ten of those graduates remained in the United States five years after obtaining their degrees – the highest percentage of all foreign doctoral recipients in those fields ... Spending in research and development has steadily increased for a decade and now amounts to 1.5 per cent of China's GDP. That is less than the share typically allotted by developed countries – the United States, for example, devotes 2.7 per cent of its GDP to research and development – but it is far more than that of other developing countries ... No Chinese-born scientist has ever been awarded a Nobel Prize for research carried out in China though several have received one for their work in the West.

(*IHT*, 7 January 2010, p. 2)

'According to a recent study sponsored by the US Department of Energy, 92 per cent of Chinese graduate students who received doctorates in the United States in 2002 were still in the United States five years later' (www.iht.com, 15 February 2010).

Postscript

A section entitled 'Food contamination and defective goods' is to be found in the companion volume on politics.

Stock market

18 March 2010, 3,046.09;
19 March 2010, 3,067.75;
22 March 2010, 3.074.58;
23 March 2010, 3,053.13;
24 March 2010, 3,056.81;
25 March 2010, 3,019.18;
26 March 2010, 3,059.72;
29 March 2010, 3,123.80;
30 March 2010, 3,128.47;
31 March 2010, 3,109.11;
1 April 2010, 3,147.42;
2 April 2010, 3,157.96;
6 April 2010, 3,158.68;
7 April 2010, 3,148.22;
8 April 2010, 3,118.71;
9 April 2010, 3,145.35;
12 April 2010, 3,129.26;
13 April 2010, 3,161.25;
14 April 2010, 3,166.18;
15 April 2010, 3,164.87;
16 April 2010, 3,130.30;
19 April 2010, 2,980.30;
20 April 2010, 2,979.53
21 April 2010, 3,033.28;
22 April 2010, 2,999.48;
23 April 2010, 2,983.54;
26 April 2010, 2969.50;
27 April 2010, 2,907.93;

28 April 2010, 2,900.33;
29 April 2010, 2,868.43;
30 April 2010, 2,870.61;
4 May 2010, 2,835.28;
5 May 2010, 2,857.15;
6 May 2010, 2,739.70;
7 May 2010, 2,688.38;
10 May 2010, 2,698.76;
11 May 2010, 2,647.57;
12 May 2010, 2,655.71;
13 May 2010, 2,710.51;
14 May 2010, 2,696.63;
17 May 2010, 2,559.93;
18 May 2010, 2,594.78;
19 May 2010, 2,587.81;
20 May 2010, 2,555.94;
21 May 2010, 2,583.52;
22 May 2010, 2,673.42;
23 May 2010, 2,622.63;
24 May 2010, 2.673.42;
25 May 2010, 2.622.63;
26 May 2010, 2,625.79;
27 May 2010, 2,655.92;
28 May 2010, 2,655.77;
31 May 2010, 2,592.15;
1 June 2010, 2,568.28;
2 June 2010, 2,571.42;
3 June 2010, 2,552.66;
4 June 2010, 2,553.59;
7 June 2010, 2,511.73;
8 June 2010 2,513.95.

The Shanghai stock exchange is finalizing plans to create an international board this year [2010], which would allow foreign companies to sell shares to Chinese investors on the mainland for the first time. An international board, which regulators have been contemplating for years, would strengthen the development of China's capital market system, significantly bolster Shanghai's efforts to transform itself into a global financial capital, allow multinational companies to raise billions from new investors and probably force Wall Street banks and global investment firms to expand their presence in the city … [It was announced on Wednesday 15 April] that the exchange had prepared a final draft of rules for the international board and that it was being reviewed by regulators … Analysts say Shanghai is trying to persuade dozens of Chinese companies that now have shares listed on the Hong Kong stock exchange, the New York stock exchange or the Nasdaq stock market to return for separate listings

... Up to now the Shanghai stock exchange has catered largely to big, state-owned companies. Many of China's best known private companies have listed on overseas exchanges. A few multinational firms doing business in China have listed shares in Hong Kong ... In 2009 Beijing endorsed plans to make Shanghai into an international financial centre to compete with cities like New York, London and Hong Kong ... On Friday [16 April] China will begin stock-index futures, giving local investors more options. The city is also planning to introduce financial derivatives and has encouraged the Blackstone Group and the Carlyle Group – two of the world's biggest private equity firms – to establish funds here denominated in the renminbi.

(www.iht.com, 15 April 2010)

Banks and security houses in Pudong have begun recently to trade stock index futures – agreements to buy or sell an index at a pre-set value on a future date – but only if they pass a tough exam, deposit renminbi 500,000, put up funds equal to a 15 per cent to 18 per cent margin and hurdle other barriers designed to keep out most participants.

(*FT*, 24 April 2010, p. 5)

Oil

Saudi Arabia exported more oil to China than to the United States last year [2009] ... Saudi exports to the United States fell to 989,000 barrels a day, the lowest in twenty-two years, from 1.5 million barrels a day the previous year ... Meanwhile, Saudi sales to China surged above a million barrels a day last year, nearly doubling from the previous year. The kingdom now accounts for a quarter of Chinese oil imports ... China's oil demand is set to grow by 900,000 barrels a day in the next two years. Chinese oil consumption reached 8.5 million barrels a day last year, compared with 4.8 million in 2000. It will account for a third of the world's total consumption growth this year [2010]. While China is by far the fastest growing oil market in the year, the United States is still the top consumer: despite the slump, Americans consumed 18.5 million barrels a day in 2009. That amounts to twenty-two barrels of oil a year for each American, compared with 2.4 barrels for each Chinese ... Saudi officials have said they favour prices of around $80 a barrel. Despite soft demand and high levels of inventories, oil futures in New York have averaged $75 a barrel over the last six months. On Friday [19 March] they closed at $80.68 ... Saudi Aramco, the kingdom's state-owned oil giant, recently inaugurated a huge refinery in Fujian province, on the south-east coast of China, which is projected to receive 200,000 barrels a day of Saudi crude, and is looking at a second project in the north-east city of Qingdao.

(www.iht.com, 20 March 2010; *IHT*, 22 March 2010, p. 16)

'[On 5 April] US crude oil climbed to an eighteen-month high of $86.61 [a barrel]' (*FT*, 6 April 2010, p. 30). (WTI crude reached as high as $86.65 a barrel and Brent $85.77: www.ft.com, 5 April 2010.)

'US crude oil futures climbed over $86 a barrel' (*IHT*, 6 April 2010, p. 17). (US crude oil reached as high as $86.67 a barrel: www.iht.com, 5 April 2010.)

'[On 6 April] oil touched an eighteen-month high above $87 a barrel' (*FT*, 7 April 2010, p. 36).

'[On 6 April] oil climbed to an eighteen-month high, touching $86.71 a barrel' (*IHT*, 7 April 2010, p. 17). (US crude oil reached as high as $86.81 a barrel: www.iht.com, 6 April 2010.)

Agriculture

'As of last year [2009] 150 million farmers moved from farming to non-farming jobs, joining what is called *liudong renkou* or floating population of rural migrants' (www.cnn.com, 28 May 2010).

Land seizures

In a provisional move, state media revealed this week, China's cabinet issued an 'emergency notice' in recent days demanding that local governments hold officials accountable for 'vicious incidents' and, by the end of June, publicize 'reasonable' standards of compensation ... In China's seventy biggest cities government land-sale revenues leaped 140 per cent in 2009 ... Land sales provide up to 60 per cent of local government revenues, by one semi-official estimate – and much more by some private ones ... The existing loophole-ridden rules, dating from 2001, give developers wide leeway to clear property. Two years ago the National People's Congress approved a law to strengthen individual property rights and ordered new rules written to regulate urban land. But that stagnated in the legislative affairs office of the State Council ... The latest draft requires developers and officials to consult homeowners, pay market rates for homes and put off demolition until sales and relocation details are settled – and, sometimes, approved by two-thirds of homeowners. It would also prohibit governments from forcibly seizing homes ... without specific 'public interest' purposes ... The draft covers only urban property, leaving out rural city outskirts where local governments have reaped huge profits – up to 100 times the value of a home – by converting commercially zoned countryside to city land ... The public comment period ended in February.

(www.iht.com, 27 May 2010)

The *hukou* system

The relaxation of *hukou* rules in recent years has been half-hearted. Chongqing last year [2009] offered urban *hukou* to any rural resident who had graduated from senior high school and who was prepared to give up his entitlement to farm a plot of land and own a village homestead. Those are big provisos. Shanghai announced with fanfare last year that seven years' work in the city – along with the required tax and social security payments – would entitle a resident to *hukou*. But rural migrants often work without contracts and do not pay tax or contribute to welfare funds; only 3,000 of Shanghai's millions of migrant workers would qualify, said Chinese press reports. On 1 May [2010] Guangzhou, the capital of Guangdong province and a magnet for migrants, began phasing out the 'agricultural' distinction in its *hukou* documents, but the effect of this is mostly cosmetic. Beijing has been among the slowest to change … [There has been a] massive migration of rural residents in the past two decades … the biggest shift in human history, with 150 million moving so far and another 300 million predicted to do so in the next twenty to thirty years … A recent survey by Renmin University in Beijing found that about a third of migrants in their twenties aspired to build a house in their home village rather than buy one in a city. Only 7 per cent of them identified themselves as city people. Another survey recently quoted in a party journal said that nearly 30 per cent of migrants planned eventually to return to their villages … China's one-child policy is more relaxed in the countryside, where two-child families are common. Rural health care is rudimentary, but a scheme introduced in recent years provides subsidized treatment for rural *hukou*-holders who make a small annual contribution (cheaper than urban insurance) … Around half of China's migrants work in the province of their *hukou* … Chongqing … in late 2008 set up a 'country land exchange institute' … [The institute's] president … describes this as something like a market for trading carbon emissions. By cutting the amount of land used for building homes or factories and converting it into farmland, villages can gain credits known as *dipiao*, or land tickets. These can be sold to urban developers who want to build on other patches of farmland, usually far away from the city periphery. The aim is to ensure no net loss of tillable fields. Chongqing is not the only place trying this out, but it is doing so on a provincial scale. Eleven auctions held so far at the exchange have raised nearly 1.9 billion yuan for *dipiao* equivalent to 1,200 hectares (2,970 acres) of farmland. The money has been spent on repaying villages for the cost of creating new farmland, compensating those who do not want to stay and building new, more condensed housing for those who do … The Chinese government … [has a] deep-rooted fear that domestically produced grain may be insufficient to feed the country. It has decreed that a minimum of 120 million hectares of arable land be preserved for this, a 'red line' that officials say is already close to being crossed … A nationwide push has begun to issue rural households with certificates stating what land they farm and what residential property they occupy. These, potentially, could be used as proof of ownership should the government eventually decide to encourage a rural property market. The government said in December [2009] that it wanted the task to be completed within three years … Chongqing municipality, having got an early start, hopes to finish handing out its certificates next year [2011]. But in rural Chongqing change still seems slow. The village of Shuangxi in the hills north-east of

Chongqing city has been designated by local officials as a reform blazer. Its peasants were encouraged to give up their land-use rights to a dairy company, which used the fields to produce fodder. All but a dozen households agreed, in return for a share of the rent paid by the company … Li Longhui, Shuangxi's party chief, wants to go further. By persuading the farmers to move from their freestanding homes into new three-storey apartment blocks, the village has recovered 33 hectares of land (10 per cent of its total area). Ms Li would like to trade this on the *dipiao* market, but complains that the price is still too low.

(*The Economist*, 8 May 2010, pp. 25–7)

Economic developments

'The World Bank … expects inflation to be 3.5 per cent to 4 per cent in 2010' (*FT*, 18 March 2010, p. 6).

Chinese steel output in the first two months of this year [2010] was far above demand and exports may drop further this year, while a rise in inventories could weigh on the sector, a top industry executive … vice chairman of the China Iron and Steel Association … said Friday [19 March] … Rising rates of fixed asset investment in China would still have a positive effect on steel demand in 2010, but over-capacity is likely to restrict profits and a possible fall in exports would also limit growth, he said.

(*IHT*, 20 March 2010, p. 14)

'The OECD forecasts that China's economy will grow by 10.2 per cent in 2010 and 9.3 per cent in 2011' (*FT*, 22 March 2010, p. 22).

The government has outlawed property development by state-owned enterprises whose core business is not real estate and ordered them to produce plans by mid-April [2010] on how they will leave the industry. The ruling from the state-owned Assets Supervision and Administration Commission bars seventy-eight state-owned conglomerates from the property sector and orders them to speed up their restructuring and to divest related in an 'orderly' way. A surge in land prices, particularly in big centres such as Shanghai and Beijing, had been blamed partly on inexperienced state-owned companies with easy access to credit over-bidding on land auctions as a way of speculating in the property market … Property sales by all companies under the commission's control accounted for just 5 per cent of total property sales in the country, according to its figures, and analysts said the seventy-eight companies barred from the sector accounted for about 14 per cent of the total property sales by commission-controlled companies.

(*FT*, 24 March 2010, p. 7)

The profits of China's big industrial companies were 120 per cent higher in January and February [2010] than in the first two months of 2009. China's statistical bureau advised that profits had 'merely' returned to the level that prevailed before the start of the financial crisis, and that some sectors, notably steel and oil exploration, had yet to rebound.

(The Economist, 3 April 2010, p. 9)

Profit margins at Chinese industrial enterprises have recovered to pre-crisis levels ... the National Bureau of Statistics said Friday [26 March]. Industrial earnings jumped 119.7 per cent in the first two months ... from a year earlier ... But profit margins in oil exploration, steel and electronics had yet to recover to pre-crisis levels.

(IHT, 27 March 2010, p. 15)

Led by growth in China and India, world trade is projected to expand 9.5 per cent this year [2010] after shrinking 12.2 per cent last year [2009], the sharpest contraction since World War II, the WTO said Friday [26 March] ... Last year export declines were greater in the United States (13.9 per cent), in the EU (24.9 per cent) and Japan (24.9 per cent) than in the rest of the world. Chinese exports fell 10.5 per cent. The WTO confirmed that China overtook Germany as the world's top merchandise exporter in 2009, accounting for almost 10 per cent of the total. China is second in imports, with an 8 per cent share of world imports compared with 13 per cent for the United States.

(IHT, 27 March 2001, p. 15)

Last year's decline in global trade was higher than the 10 per cent drop the WTO had projected last July [2009] and was far larger than any of the most recent declines: 0.2 in 2001, 2 per cent in 1982 and 7 per cent in 1975.

(www.iht.com, 26 March 2010)

[On 30 March] five prominent members of the G-20 leading economies [the United States, the UK, France, Canada and South Korea] ... sent a letter to the rest of the G-20: 'Without co-operative action to make the necessary adjustments to achieve [strong and sustainable growth], the risk of future crises and low growth remain ... We need to design co-operative strategies and work together to ensure that our fiscal, monetary, foreign exchange, trade and structural policies are collectively consistent with strong, sustainable and balanced growth ... [We urge all G-20 members to] move quickly ... [to] report robustly on what each of us can do to contribute to strong sustainable and balanced global growth' ... Ottawa and Seoul ... will host ... G-20 summits ... in June and November respectively ... China has hampered efforts by the IMF to issue a report which Dominique Strauss-Kahn, managing director of the IMF, told the *Financial Times* in January would conclude that national strategies for growth around the world 'will not add up'.

(FT, 31 March 2010, p. 8)

The Chinese cabinet has approved major banks' requests to raise additional capital in 2010 and encouraged them to rely more on the Hong Kong market for fund raising, the *National Business Daily* reported Friday [2 April] ... The State Council also urged the four biggest listed banks in China to slow lending and use innovative ways to raise cash ... Among the four state-owned lenders, Industrial and Commercial Bank of China, Bank of China and Bank of Communications have in recent months announced fund raising plans that include selling shares in Hong Kong.

(*IHT*, 3 April 2010, p. 16)

Hainan Island [is] luring speculators ... The boom ... is being fuelled by a first-of-its-kind edict from the nation's top leaders: on 31 December [2009] the State Council, China's cabinet, issued a memorandum that said Hainan had been designated a 'test case' in developing an 'internationally competit-ive tourist destination' ... In January [2010] the provincial government announced a temporary halt to new commercial development projects ... The history of Hainan in the 1990s offers a cautionary tale ... Early that decade, after the Chinese government had designated Hainan one of the country's 'Special Economic Zones', property speculators flocked to the island. Across China, the island's freewheeling capitalism became synony-mous with corruption. The bubble burst after a few years, and the island stagnated.

(www.iht.com, 31 March 2010)

'The World Bank says that rural wages (outside farms) fell by a fifth between 2007 and 2009 as migrant workers fled back to their villages in search of work' (www.economist.com, 7 April 2010).

China is expected to report its first monthly trade deficit in nearly six years at the end of the week ... For some economists there is little reason to dismiss the Chinese trade report for March as an aberration if, as the Chinese vice commerce minister, Chen Jian, noted Friday [2 April], it con-firms a deficit that was caused by a rise in imports.

(*IHT*, 5 April 2010, p. 16)

China announced on Saturday [10 April] that it had a trade deficit of $7.24 billion ... in March ... its first monthly trade deficit ... since April 2004. China had a trade surplus of $7.6 billion in February and $14.2 billion in January ... Chinese New Year came late this year [2010], falling on 14 Feb-ruary, which hurt factory production in early March ... The March deficit was much larger than the consensus estimate of Western economists, who had been anticipating a deficit of less than $1 billion.

(www.iht.com, 10 March 2010; 12 April 2010, p. 15)

'Combining the first three months, China still recorded a trade surplus of $14.49 billion in the first quarter [of 2010], a fall of 76.7 per cent from the same period of last year [2009]' (www.cnn.com. 10 April 2010).

The officials who announced the figures ... say the deficit is likely to be a short-term phenomenon ... The deficit for March was China's first [monthly one] since a \$2.3 billion deficit in April 2004 ... Senior Chinese politicians have said it could take three years for exports to reach the levels they were at before the global economic crisis began.

(www.bbc.co.uk, 10 April 2010)

Liu Mingkang ... head of the China Banking Regulatory Commission ... has expressed concern over loans made to local government companies ... [He] said yesterday [11 April] that China's financial institutions had until the end of June [2010] to submit 'comprehensive' reviews of their loans books ... The precise size of local debts has become the focus of foreign investors concerned about a property bubble in China.

(*FT*, 12 April 2010, p. 7)

'Commercial bank lending in March slowed substantially to renminbi 511 billion (\$75 billion), well below forecasts and down from February's renminbi 700 billion increase' (*FT*, 13 April 2010, p. 8).

In a statement released last night [14 April] the State Council said that the dramatic increase in property values in some cities had become a 'prominent problem' after government figures released earlier in the day showed urban housing prices in March rose 11.7 per cent during the previous twelve months, up from 10.7 per cent the month before and the biggest increase since the index began nearly five years ago.

(*FT*, 15 April 2010, p. 5)

GDP jumped 11.9 per cent in the first quarter of this year [2010] over the same period in 2009, the government said on Thursday [15 April] ... That growth rate, the highest in three years, not only topped most economists' forecasts, but handily beat the 10.7 per cent expansion that had been recorded in the last quarter of 2009 ... The consumer price index rose 2.4 per cent in March from a year earlier ... The producer price index was up 5.2 per cent. Those figures were generally in line with analysts' expectations ... The National Bureau of Statistics repeated in a statement that China would maintain its 'appropriately loose' monetary policy and an expansionist fiscal policy ... The government said consumer prices were 'basically stable' ... The government raised retail gasoline prices by as much as 5 per cent on Wednesday [14 April], the first increase in gas prices in more than five months ... China's economy grew by only 6.2 per cent in the first quarter of 2009 ... Overall investment rose by 25.6 per cent on an annual basis in the first quarter, while urban fixed asset investment rose 26.4 per cent. Industrial production rose 18.1 per cent in March over March 2009, in line with the 20.7 per cent gain for the January–February period ... Investment in property leaped 35.1 per cent in the first quarter compared to the year-earlier period, the fastest growth in more than two years. And on Wednesday the government said housing prices had risen 11.7 per cent in March from the previous year, the fastest rise ever recorded.

(www.iht.com, 15 April 2010; *IHT*, 16 April 2010, p. 18)

The [first quarter GDP] growth figure was slightly higher than expected, while consumer price inflation was surprisingly low at 2.2 per cent ... March's consumer price inflation was 2.4 per cent versus expectations of 2.7 per cent, and producer price inflation was 5.9 per cent versus the expected 6.4 per cent.

(www.bbc.co.uk, 15 April 2010)

China unveiled restrictions on property speculation yesterday [15 April] as economic growth accelerated to 11.9 per cent in the first quarter from the same period last year [2009] ... The economy expanded at its fastest in nearly three years – and more quickly than economists had expected ... The growth was the fastest since the data series began five years ago ... The State Council said yesterday that anyone buying a second home would need to put up a 50 per cent deposit, up from 40 per cent, while the mortgage rate for second homes was also increased. The downpayment for first homes bigger than 90 square metres was set at a minimum of 30 per cent ... China does not release quarter-on-quarter figures, Royal Bank of Scotland estimated 14.5 per cent economic growth on that basis ... The median of estimates by seven economists was 11.2 per cent ... The last time China's growth accelerated to more than 11 per cent, in the first quarter of 2006, the central bank raised [interest] rates within a month ... Factory gate inflation continued to accelerate, increasing half a percentage point to 5.9 per cent.

(*FT*, 16 April 2010, p. 8)

The real estate bubbles in China are largely local, in high-end segments of cities such as Shanghai. Overall urban housing prices have risen 11.7 per cent in the past year ... It does not even keep up with the increase in the country's income.

(p. 12)

China's corporate bond market makes up a small proportion of financing for enterprises. Even with the spike issuance, bank lending still accounts for 82 per cent of corporate financing; bonds make up nearly 13 per cent and equity markets provide 5 per cent.

(*FT*, 19 April 2010, p. 17)

Members of the World Bank agreed on Sunday [25 April] to support a $5.1 billion increase in its operating capital, the largest increase in general financing since 1988, and give developing countries a greater say in running the anti-poverty institution. Under the changes China will become the World Bank's third largest shareholder, ahead of Germany, after the United States and Japan. Countries like Brazil, India, Indonesia and Vietnam will also have greater representation ... The World Bank's 186 members also agreed a reform package that calls for greater openness and disclosure of information and improvements in managing risks and measuring results. The World Bank has made $105 billion in financial commitments since July 2008 in response to the global economic turmoil ... The World Bank president ...

Robert Zoellick ... devised the capital increase and voting changes to be adopted together. The $5.1 billion in so-called paid-in capital, which the bank can use for day-to-day operations, will bring the bank's cash on hand to about $40 billion. Of the $5.1 billion, developing countries will contribute $1.6 billion in connection with a shift in representation that will give them 47.19 per cent of voting power, up from 44.06 per cent. The actions fulfil a pledge the bank's members made in Istanbul in October [2009] ... In 2008 the bank's members approved a smaller shift of 1.46 per cent of voting power to the developing countries from the wealthy ones ... All told, the cumulative shift of 4.59 per cent of voting power amounts to the greatest alignment in representation at the World Bank since 1988 ... The bank's members approved on Sunday an $86.2 billion general capital increase, bringing the bank's total subscribed capital, not counting about $26 billion in reserves, to $276.1 billion ... Mr Zoellick ... said ... that the less wealthy countries were leading the global economic recovery.

(www.iht.com, 26 April 2010)

'The United States, which holds the largest voting share in the World Bank at 16.4 per cent, would not seek any increase in that' (www.bbc.co.uk, 26 April 2010).

The World Bank increased the voting power of developing and transition countries among its 186 members, raising the total for that block to 47.2 per cent, from 44.6 per cent in 2008. China's voting share was raised to 4.42 per cent, vaulting it ahead of European countries and leaving it behind only the United States and Japan ... World Bank shareholders (2010): United States, 15.85 per cent; Japan, 6.84 per cent; China, 4.42 per cent; Germany, 4.00 per cent; France, 3.75 per cent; Britain, 3.75 per cent; India, 2.91 per cent.

(www.economist.com, 29 April 2010; *The Economist*, 1 May 2010, p. 8)

China tightened real estate financing by requiring developers to submit fund-raising plans for review ... The China Securities Regulatory Commission has sent financing requests from forty-one companies to the ministry of land and resources for reviews of land use compliance ... The latest data show property prices in seventy cities rose a record 11.7 per cent in March.

(*FT*, 26 April 2010, p. 6)

'Income from land sales makes up 40 per cent to 60 per cent of the average local government's revenues, according to Bao Zonghua, the former head of the housing ministry's policy research centre. Others say the figure is far higher' (*IHT*, 29 April 2010, p. 5).

China is expected to impose a moratorium on share sales by real estate companies in mainland markets as part of a campaign to rein in rising property prices, state media said Wednesday [28 April]. The move could delay plans by forty-five Chinese companies to raise about 110 billion renminbi ($16.1 billion) ... A China Securities Regulatory Commission official ... [said] that a formal suspension was not in place but confirmed that before approving any share issues in mainland markets, the regulator and the land and resources ministry were examining whether property companies had illegally manipulated land prices.

(IHT, 29 April 2010)

'The central bank reported last week that mortgage loans were equivalent to 66 per cent of the value of housing sold in the first quarter [of 2010], up from an average of 34 per cent in 2003–9' (FT, 30 April 2010, p. 10).

China's share of cash committed to IMF shares, known as its quota, has nearly doubled since the Asian financial crisis in 1997 and 1998, to $12.2 billion. The IMF board has approved another increase soon, which would raise China's stake to 4 per cent from 3.72 per cent. China is already the fourth largest holder of quota rights at the IMF, after the member countries of the EU (32.4 per cent), the United States (17.1 per cent) and an Asian bloc informally led by Japan (11.5 percent). China agreed last September [2009] to buy up to $50 billion worth of bonds issued by the IMF to help … strengthen its lending capacity, in the first such deal done by the IMF … Zhu Min, a deputy governor of the People's Bank of China, was named on 24 February to become the special adviser to the IMF's managing director Dominique Strauss-Kahn, and will start work on 3 May … China closely guards any details on the currency allocation of its reserves. Western bankers estimate that the Chinese reserves are about 70 per cent invested in dollar-denominated assets, mainly Treasury notes and bonds, and 20 per cent to 25 per cent invested in Euro-denominated assets, with the rest in British pounds, Japanese yen and other currencies.

(www.iht.com, 30 April 2010)

China's central bank said yesterday [2 May] that it will raise the amount banks must hold in reserve for the third time this year [2010] … The increase comes after regulators ordered China's largest banks to re-examine their loan books and provide estimates of their exposure to uncollateralized loans, especially to provincial governments … If banks are unable to find assets to collateralize their loans within the next few months they may be required to downgrade the loans, potentially leading to a spike in non-performing assets on their books … The biggest concerns for regulators are huge loans to shell companies set up by local governments to supplement their fiscal income, as well as loans to real estate developers and speculators that have helped to inflate a bubble in the property market … As part of its efforts to reduce lending, the People's Bank of China will raise the reserve requirement ratio for deposit-taking financial institutions by 0.5 percentage points, effective on 10 May, bringing the rate to 17 per cent for large Chinese banks and 15 per cent for smaller lenders. The ratio for rural credit co-operatives and village banks will not be raised.

(FT, 3 May 2010, p. 7)

China ... has made twenty-nine adjustments ... to the reserve requirement ratio or the proportion of lenders' deposits to be kept at the central bank ... during the past decade, compared with fifteen to the lending rate and thirteen to the deposit rate.

(*FT*, 4 May 2010, p. 18)

[On Monday 3 May] China ordered banks to raise their reserves, the latest in a series of moves aimed at curbing inflation and surging property prices ... The People's Bank of China said that the deposit reserve requirement ratio for most banks will be raised half a percentage point, starting on 10 May. This is the third time this year [2010] that the central bank has raised the deposit reserve minimum.

(www.iht.com, 3 May 2010)

China returned to a modest trade surplus last month [April] after recording a deficit in March ... The surplus was $1.7 billion in April following the surprise deficit of $7.2 billion in March, the first month in six years in which imports exceeded exports ... Policy-makers are watching with concern the unfolding of the Greek debt crisis. The Euro decline meant that the renminbi had appreciated by 5 per cent against a basket of currencies of its main trading partners this year [2010] ... Last night [10 May] the central bank said it would manage the renminbi 'with reference to a basket of currencies', prompting speculation of an imminent policy shift, although the wording has been used before ... Many economists expect ... China's trade surplus ... to rebound in the second half of the year.

(*FT*, 11 May 2010, p. 12)

[Consumer] inflation accelerated to 2.8 per cent in April, driven by a jump in politically sensitive food prices ... Food price inflation accelerated to 5.9 per cent over a year earlier, up from March's 5.2 per cent ... Overall April inflation was up 0.4 per cent from the previous month ... Inflation has been driven lately by surges in the cost of food and housing ... Housing prices in seventy ... large and medium-sized ... cities climbed 12.8 per cent from the same time last year [2009], despite government efforts to cool prices ... Wholesale prices climbed 6.8 per cent in April from a year earlier, a 0.9 per cent increase over March's rise.

(www.iht.com, 11 May 2010)

Retail sales and bank lending soared in April ... Retail sales climbed 18.5 per cent in April and ... banks ... issued about 774 billion renminbi (about $113 billion). In March banks issued about 510 billion renminbi in such loans ... Industrial production and fixed asset investment ... each slowed slightly in April from their pace in March but remained robust, growing 17.8 per cent and 25.6 per cent from a year earlier ... [China] recorded a $1.7 billion trade surplus for April.

(www.iht.com, 11 May 2010; *IHT*, 12 May 2010. p. 15)

April's consumer prices were up 2.8 per cent from a year ago. The highest in eighteen months ... New bank lending of 774 billion yuan ($8.4 billion) exceeded predictions. Many analysts had forecast an inflation rate of 2.7 per cent ... Industrial output rose 17.8 per cent year-on-year in April, while retail sales were up 18.5 per cent.

(www.bbc.co.uk, 11 May 2010)

The annual China–US Strategic and Economic Dialogue took place in Beijing on 23–25 May.

Secretary of State Hillary Clinton and Treasury Secretary Timothy Geithner are leading a delegation that will include nearly 200 policy-makers and advisers, one of the largest groups of Americans ever to travel to a foreign capital for a single set of meetings.

(www.iht.com, 21 May 2010)

'[There are to be] three days of high-level economic and security meetings ... Nearly 200 American officials have descended on Beijing, the largest such groups ever to come to the Chinese capital' (www.iht.com, 23 May 2010).

China is Boeing's largest market outside the United States, with 450 orders for planes from fast-growing carriers like China Eastern Airlines, which is headquartered in Shanghai. But Boeing, which buys parts from Chinese suppliers, is facing greater competition from Airbus, the European consortium. Airbus opened a final assembly plant, its first outside Europe, in the industrial city of Tianjin in 2009.

(www.iht.com, 23 May 2010)

President Hu Jintao (24 May): 'China will continue to steadily advance reform of the renminbi exchange rate mechanism following the principles of being independent, controllable and gradual' ... [He] said the two global powers needed to enhance economic policy co-ordination and work together to promote 'full economic recovery' ... He said his government wanted to expand domestic demand to create more balanced growth ... The annual US trade deficit with China fell to $226.8 billion in 2009, down from a record $280.0 billion in 2008.

(www.iht.com, 24 May 2010)

President Hu Jintao ... praised the 'mutually beneficial and win–win co-operation' between the United States and China. Such co-ordination, he said, had helped the recovery from the 2008 financial crisis ... [As regards the renminbi exchange rate mechanism] Hu said Beijing would move 'under the principle of independent decision-making, controllability, and gradual progress' ... Mr Hu [made a] pledge to 'steadily advance the reform mechanism of the renminbi exchange rate' ... without repeating his previous references to the rate being 'basically stable'.

(www.iht.com, 24 May 2010; *IHT*, 25 May 2010, pp. 1, 4)

China and the United States wrapped up two days of high-level meetings on Tuesday [25 May] with some modest trade and energy agreements but little progress on winning China's backing for international measures against North Korea over the sinking of a South Korean warship. Secretary of State Hillary Clinton said China would take 'a period of careful consideration in order to determine the best way forward in dealing with North Korea as a result of this incident' ... Treasury Secretary Timothy Geithner said: '[President Hu Jintao recognizes that moving China's currency closer to a market rate] is an important part of their broader reform agenda. This, of course, is China's choice' ... The United States did get concessions on two issues of importance to American investors in China: a change in rules governing innovation that now disadvantage foreign companies, and a pledge to submit a revised offer to join the WTO's agreement on government procurement by 2010. The two countries also signed a raft of modest agreements on issues ranging from clean energy and shale gas exploration to trade finance between the export–import banks of the United States and China. They also agreed to co-operate on nuclear safety and on preventing infectious diseases ... The Chinese government has agreed to help pay for 10,000 students to study for doctorate degrees in the United States, while President Barack Obama has set a goal of sending 100,000 American students to China over the next four years.

(www.iht.com, 25 May 2010; *IHT*, 26 May 2010, pp. 1, 8)

'China's current account surplus fell from 11 per cent of GDP in 2007 to 5.8 per cent last year [2009]' (*FT*, 24 May 2010, p. 1).

On North Korea, US Secretary of State Hillary Clinton opted for low-key encouragement of China to back the administration's criticisms of Pyongyang over the sinking of a South Korean warship [a corvette], the *Cheonan* in March [2010]. She said {24 May]: 'I can say that the Chinese recognize the gravity of the situation we face. They understand the reaction by the South Koreans and they understand our unique responsibility for peace and stability on the Korean Peninsula.'

(*FT*, 25 May 2010, p. 12)

'The *Cheonan* sank near the inter-Korean maritime border on 26 March. An international panel says a torpedo fired from a North Korean submarine sent the ship down, but Pyongyang denies this' (www.bbc.co.uk, 25 May 2010). 'The investigation itself was given an added air of impartiality by the presence of twenty-four foreign experts from American, Australia, Britain and Sweden' (www.bbc.co.uk, 24 May 2010).

South Korean military officials on Thursday [20 May] announced the results of an official investigation into the sinking of the *Cheonan*, which concluded that North Korea fired a torpedo that cut the vessel in half ... The South Korean military group that presented its report on the ship's sinking on Thursday comprises experts from South Korea, Australia, Sweden, the United Kingdom and the United States. Yoon Duk Yong (the group's chairman):

'The evidence points overwhelmingly to the conclusion that the torpedo was fired by a North Korean submarine. There is no other plausible explanation.'

(www.cnn.com, 21 May 2010)

'North Korea has denied responsibility for the sinking of the *Cheonan*, on 26 March, which left forty-six sailors dead. A growing body of evidence assembled by the South has suggested a North Korean torpedo sank the ship' (*IHT*, 25 May 2010, p. 4).

Prime minister Wen Jiabao met with President Lee Myung Bak of South Korea on Friday [28 May] before the start of three-party weekend talks [in South Korea] with Japan ... Mr Wen told Mr Lee that China will make an 'impartial judgement' on who was responsible for sinking the ship. Wen Jiabao: 'Once we have our conclusion, we will not protect anyone.'

(www.iht.com, 28 May 2010)

'The summit ... was originally meant to focus on regional economic integration' (www.iht.com, 30 May 2010). 'The talks had been scheduled before the *Cheonan* sinking to discuss greater regional co-operation and economic integration' (www.iht.com, 31 May 2010).

Prime minister Wen Jiabao (after talks in Seoul): 'China objects to and condemns any act that destroys the peace and stability of the Korean Peninsula ... The Chinese government will decide its position by objectively and fairly judging what is right and wrong about the incident while respecting the international probe and responses to it by each nation' ... China has previously called for all sides to show restraint.

(www.bbc.co.uk, 28 May 2010)

'The three-nation summit was meant to focus on trade, but the sinking of the warship overshadowed other issues' (www.bbc.co.uk, 30 May 2010).

Premier Wen Jiabao said during a visit to Seoul yesterday [28 May] that China would not protect 'whoever sank the warship' ... South Korea has given China the complete technical report on the sinking and has said it would welcome a Chinese delegation should they want to inspect the shattered hull and corroded torpedo retrieved from the seabed.

(*FT*, 29 May 2010)

'Prime minister Wen Jiabao offered condolences on Saturday to South Korea for the sinking of one of its warships' (www.iht.com, 29 May 2010).

Premier Wen Jiabao: 'The sinking of the *Cheonan* is an unfortunate incident. We understand the sorrow of the South Korean people, especially the victims' families ... If clashes flare up the worst victim will be South Korea. And China, too, cannot avoid misfortune' (www.cnn.com, 4 June 2010).

Prime minister Wen Jiabao (30 May):

We must promote peace and stability in the North-east Asian region through every effort. We should be considerate of each other on a grave issue, deal reasonably with a sensitive matter and strengthen political trust ... The urgent task for the moment is to properly handle the serious impact caused by the Cheonan incident, gradually defuse tensions over it, and avoid possible conflicts. China will continue to work with every country through aggressive negotiations and co-operation to fulfil our mission of maintaining peace and stability in the region.'

(www.cnn.com, 30 May 2010; www.bbc.co.uk, 30 May 2010)

Prime minister Wen Jiabao [30 May]: 'Most urgent is to dispel the impact of the Cheonan incident, gradually ease tension and especially avoid a clash. We must put all our efforts without fail to boost peace and stability in North-east Asia. Without this we cannot talk about development, and the achievements we have made with difficulty will evaporate' ... After Mr Wen's bilateral talks with President Lee Myung Bak on Friday [[28 May] Mr Lee's office quoted Mr Wen as saying that Beijing 'will not protect anyone' once it had concluded who was responsible after its own 'impartial judgement' ... Reading from a joint statement from the three leaders, Mr Lee said that Japan and China 'attached importance' to the 20 May report by the South Korean-led international investigative team that blamed North Korea for the sinking.

(www.iht.com, 31 May 2010)

'The three said in a joint statement issued on 30 May: "We share the view that a denuclearized Korean Peninsula would greatly contribute to enduring peace, security and economic prosperity in North-east Asia"' (www.cnn.com, 30 May 2010).

[On 31 May there was an] announcement by the State Council that it had approved reform of property taxes, the clearest indication yet that the government will impose an annual tax on some residential housing in order to rein in rising prices ... Prime minister Wen Jiabao: 'The debt crisis in some European countries may impeded Europe's economic recovery. China will make sure it maintains a sense of crisis.'

(*FT*, 1 June 2010, p. 7)

On Tuesday [1 June] the state-controlled *China Daily* reported that the government had signalled that it would 'gradually' introduce taxes on property holdings. It also cited an unnamed government official who said a tax would be levied on state-owned properties, starting with Wuhan, the capital of Hubei province, on a trial basis. Other details, including on timing, remained sketchy, but the news was fresh evidence of Beijing's determination to rein in property prices.

(www.iht.com, 1 June 2010; *IHT*, 2 June 2010, p. 20)

China has ordered developers to put more money on deposit to pay tax on sales revenue, a requirement that will reduce their cash flows, the domestic media reported Friday [4 June]. The government has not increased the final VAT, but it has instructed real estate firms to set more money aside in advance of expectations of higher capital gains as property prices surge. The General Administration of Taxation urged cities that were not collecting deposits to start doing so. It also told local tax bureaux to make examples of as many as five developments with high or fast rising prices by making sure that their owners paid the exact amount of the required tax.

(IHT, 5 June 2010, p. 19)

Agricultural Bank of China said Friday [4 June] that it would sell [in Shanghai and Hong Kong] a 15 per cent stake in what could become the world's largest initial public offering [IPO] ... The bank may seek to raise as much as $30 billion ... Agricultural Bank will compete for investors' money with publicly traded rivals that plan to raise a combined $32 billion in stock and bond sales even as bank valuations are close to record lows. The IPO coincides with a government crackdown on real estate speculation and a European sovereign debt crisis that threatens to slow China's exports.

(IHT, 5 June 2010, p. 19)

Agricultural Bank of China's IPO is likely to raise much less than the $30 billion record-setting total it had hoped for when it sells shares in Hong Kong and Shanghai as early as next month [July] ... Agricultural Bank was more likely to raise a little more than $20 billion. At that level the IPO would not be the world's largest. Industrial and Commercial Bank of China raised $22 billion in 2006. China's stock market has dropped about 20 per cent since mid-April ... Bank of Communications, China's fifth largest bank and nearly one-fifth owned by HSBC of the UK, announced a renminbi 33.07 billion ($4.8 billion) rights issue in Hong Kong and Shanghai yesterday [6 June] that was 21 per cent smaller than the amount it had earlier said it planned to raise ... Agricultural Bank is the last of China's large state-controlled banks to seek a public listing and is regarded as the weakest of the country's lenders ... Following a $19 billion bail-out from China's sovereign wealth fund at the end of 2008. Agricultural Bank's non-performing loan ratio fell from almost 24 per cent at the end of 2007 to 2.9 per cent at the end of last year [2009].

(FT, 7 June 2001, p. 22)

WTO

China started two anti-dumping investigations Thursday [22 April] and levied tariffs on some nylon products as it escalated trade disputes with the United States and the EU. The ministry of commerce said it had started investigations on a type of optical fibre and on caprolactum, a chemical compound, which are produced in the EU and the United States. The EU recently extended tariffs on Chinese shoes and the US Commerce Department said Wednesday [21 April] that it had started an investigation into Chinese aluminium products.

(IHT, 23 April 2010, p. 17)

China raised concerns by reducing its export quotas for raw rare-earth elements from 2005 to 2009. A year ago the Chinese government caused further alarm for Western corporations and governments by proposing a ban on the export of five of the seventeen rare-earth elements, although no ban has actually been imposed ... Chinese cost may be about to rise if the Chinese government follows through on recent pledges to start requiring the rare-earth industry to reduce pollution ... China now mines 97 per cent of the world's rare-earth elements.

(www.iht.com, 21 April 2010)

The EU is seeking to extend anti-dumping duties on high-tech equipment exported by ... NuTech, the only Chinese company to export such equipment ... [The] company was once run by the son of President Hu Jintao ... [The company] came to public notice last year [2009] when it was embroiled in a corruption inquiry in Namibia ... The European Commission's investigation concluded that exports from NuTech surged at the expense of its main European competitor, Smiths Detection, based in Britain ... The Commission imposed provisional duties of 36.6 per cent on imports of large-scale cargo-scanning equipment from China in December [2009]. On Wednesday [28 April] EU experts are expected to endorse a proposal to make the duties permanent at a rate of 34 per cent ... After the expert committee vote, the decision will still need to be approved by ministers from member states before taking effect ... Participants at the meeting Wednesday are also being asked to approve provisional duties of 20.6 per cent on aluminium car wheels from China.

(*IHT*, 28 April 2010, p. 14)

China announced yesterday [28 April] it would impose a second round of tariffs on imports of chicken products of as much as 31.4 per cent. The commerce ministry said the tariffs were a response to what it called unfair subsidies given to US poultry farmers. The duties come on top of charges of up to 105.4 per cent placed on poultry two months ago because of alleged dumping.

(*FT*, 29 April 2010, p. 8)

China has said it will levy duties of up to 31.4 per cent on some chicken products from the United States ... The commerce ministry ruled Wednesday [28 April] that US chicken producers have been receiving unfair subsidies and that these had hurt Chinese companies.

(*IHT*, 29 April 2010, p. 18)

'The Indian government is blocking purchases of telecoms equipment from Chinese vendors on national security grounds ... [China has a] growing trade surplus with India – about $16 billion last year [2009]' (*FT*, 30 April 2010, p. 23).

'The Indian government is banning the purchase of some Chinese-made telecommunications equipment, one of the largest private mobile operators in India said Friday [30 April 2010).

'India is the world's second largest mobile market after China with 584 million subscribers' (www.cnn.com, 30 April 2010).

China's extensive restrictions on its own exports are doing more to distort global commerce than its supposed goals of protecting the environment [by reducing the export of energy-intensive and other environmentally destructive goods] and balancing the country's trade, according to the WTO ... The area of export curbs [is] the subject of ongoing trade disputes with China's largest trading partners. The WTO report said: 'China's export barriers have not been falling at the same pace as its import barriers. It still uses various export restrictions, including prohibitions, licensing, quotas, taxes and less-than-full VAT rebates' ... The effect of the restrictions was merely to help Chinese companies by driving down the price of raw materials used as industrial inputs. The WTO said: 'Export restraints for whatever reason tend to reduce export volumes of the targeted products and divert supplies to the domestic market, leading to a downward pressure on the domestic prices of these products. The resulting gap between domestic prices and world prices constitutes implicit assistance to domestic downstream processors of the targeted products.'

(*FT*, 1 June 2010, p. 7)

China is failing to carry out its pledges to liberalize its economy and open its market to foreign companies, according to the EU, which accused the nation of protectionism to prop up its domestic industry. John Clarke (head of the EU's delegation to the WTO) said on Monday 31 May: 'Even though China reiterates its firm commitment to continued opening-up and reform, this does not duly characterize the current situation in China. In fact, our companies have reported a worsening of the business climate' Even though China reiterates its firm commitment to continued opening-up and reform ... Mr Clarke said China used a weak currency, export incentives and subsidies to bolster its economy. Trade in goods between the bloc and China was worth $364 billion last year [2009].

(www.iht.com, 1 June 2010)

'China will submit a fresh proposal by mid-July to the WTO to join its government procurement agreement, which regulates trade in public sector purchases ... China first applied to join in 2007, but its partners wanted better terms' (*FT*, 3 June 2010, p. 9).

Exchange rate policy

A rise in the yuan would be a disaster for labour-intensive Chinese exporters, a semi-official trade group said on Thursday [18 March] ... The China Council for the Promotion of International Trade was checking with more than 1,000 exporters in twelve industries on whether they could cope with a stronger exchange rate ... [The] organization was polling more than 1,000

Chinese manufacturers on how a change in exchange rates would affect their business ... [It] disclosed Thursday that it is surveying experts in twelve export-related industries to determine how badly they would be affected by a rise in the renminbi's value ... Exporters in labour-intensive sectors such as garments and furniture worked on margins as small as 3 per cent ... China's shipbuilders alone had $150 billion of orders on hand, so a stronger yuan would result in immediate losses ... Only a minority of Chinese firms hedge exchange rate risk. Exporters of telecommunications equipment and mechanical products would also be particularly vulnerable ... Several branches of government, including the ministries of commerce and industry, conducted similar currency stress tests last month. A government source familiar with one of the missions to China's coastal exporting hubs came back unconvinced that the drawbacks of a stronger yuan would outweigh the advantages because of the razor-thin margins mentioned ... He said: 'We found that these companies are quite flexible in adapting to new market conditions' ... Because they can make a steady profit on their current margins, thanks to high volume, they have little incentive to move up the value chain, the source added. He said: 'So yuan appreciation would be a nice catalyst to force these firms to change for the better, which is also what the government wants to see. It is true that jobs are a major concern. But we are also seeing labour shortages in many places. So I think it would be manageable' ... The ministry of finance might also send research teams to Guangdong, Zhejiang and Shanghai later this month [March] to test companies' ability to withstand an appreciation of the yuan ... [The China Council for the Promotion of International Trade] said that Chinese exporters, anticipating a stronger exchange rate, had been improving their product ranges and switching their attention from the United States and Europe to Africa, Latin America and the Middle East.

(www.iht.com, 18 March 2010; *IHT*, 19 March 2010, p. 19)

After meeting with officials at the [US] Treasury and Commerce Departments on Wednesday [24 March], China's deputy commerce minister, Zhing Shan, said: 'The Chinese government will not succumb to foreign pressures to adjust our exchange rate. It is wrong for the United States to jump to the conclusion that China is manipulating currency from the sheer fact that China is enjoying a trade surplus. Besides, it is wrong for the United States to press for the appreciation of the renminbi and threaten to impose punitive tariffs on Chinese exports. This is unacceptable to China ... The basic stability of the renminbi ... [is generally beneficial because] a great surge in the value of the renminbi would hurt the economies of developing countries, especially the least developed countries' ... [There is] a 15 April deadline for the Treasury to deliver its semi-annual report on foreign exchange ... The Treasury has not found China to be manipulating its currency since 1994, making the argument, among others, that manipulation involves intent. Successive administrations have argued that it would be more fruitful to convince China that its interests would be served by allowing the renminbi to appreciate, a move that could stimulate domestic consumption in China and help wean its economy off a reliance on American consumers ... Unemployment [is] near 10 per cent in the United States ... Two senators ... Lindsey Graham and Charles Schumer ... [have] pointed to a new study by the Economic Policy Institute, a labour-backed research organization, saying the growing trade deficit between China and the United States resulted in the elimination or displacement of 2.4 million American jobs between 2001 and 2008.

(www.iht.com, 25 March 2010)

Chinese leaders are engaged in a bitter and unusually public struggle over whether to allow the renminbi to rise against the dollar ... The fight [is] mainly between the central bank and the commerce ministry ... The face-off began on 6 March, when the governor of the central bank [Zhou Xiao-chuan] stunned analysts by saying that the bank's policy of keeping the renminbi at a constant exchange rate against the dollar was a 'special' response to the global financial crisis ... But other Chinese officials, particularly at the commerce ministry, have fought back in the past two weeks, stoking nationalism and anti-American sentiment by declaring that China will not be told what to do by the United States ... For decades currency policy has been the purview of the central bank, but the central bank is a politically weak institution. The People's Bank of China is just one of many economic policy ministries and even lacks independent authority over monetary policy ... The commerce ministry has long been close to the country's exporters.

(www.iht.com, 25 March 2010)

Most Western economists agree that China's currency is undervalued, meaning that the renminbi is weaker than it would be if it were allowed to float freely. But that is about all the economists agree on. Some economists argue that the currency is undervalued by an astonishing 50 per cent or more. Others contend it is about where it should be, economically speaking, saying the currency is undervalued by about 10 per cent. Still others say the renminbi might be overvalued because Beijing does not allow its people to trade freely for other currencies. If that policy were changed, Chinese savers might move money from low-interest-rate domestic accounts into foreign markets, helping drive down the value of the renminbi ... Studies of the renminbi usually reflect one of three schools of thought about the exchange rate. (1) The first is based on trade and financial transfers, known as the current account balance, of a country or a group of countries ... Scholars compare the country's actual ... current account balance (which includes its trade and financial relationship with the rest of the world) ... with the ideal balance based on the country's development status and demographics ... Researchers from the Washington-based Peterson Institute for International Economics have created a model based on equilibrium exchange rates ... China is running a current account surplus equal to about 10.5 per cent of its annual economic output. But the Peterson Institute scholars estimate that the gap should ideally be 4.2 per cent. Based on that assumption, they estimate that the renminbi is about 20 per cent undervalued against all currencies, and 40 per cent against the dollar ... (2) The second is based on worker productivity ... Scholars compare the relative productivity improvements in different countries ... As countries like China become more productive, they become more wealthy and their currencies should appreciate against those countries like the United States whose productivity is not improving as quickly. Using this method, professors at Harvard and Freie Universität Berlin estimate the renminbi is undervalued by 30 per cent to 50 per cent ... (3) The third is based on the theory of purchasing-power parity [PPP], which equalizes the PPP of different countries for a given basket of goods ... [This] group of scholars believe the concerns about the renminbi have been overplayed ... As countries become richer their prices catch up with those in developed countries ... Using regression analysis, scholars can determine whether the currency is undervalued relative to its state of development ... One variant of that model used by Helmut Reisen, who heads research for the OECD, suggest that the renminbi was undervalued by just 12 per cent in 2008. Mr Reisen, who said his comments did not represent the official view of the OECD, acknowledged that the currency was probably more undervalued now, but not much more.

(*IHT*, 2 April 2010, p. 15)

'Since October 2008 China's trade-weighted real exchange rate has depreciated by 8 per cent' (*FT*, 6 April 2010, p. 10).

The commerce ministry ... is often opposed to any move that would strengthen the renminbi and hurt domestic exporters ... the National Development and Reform Commission, China's powerful state planning agency, is thought by analysts to wield veto power over any move to break the peg. Although it opposes the concept of a floating exchange rate, it is not seen as implacably opposed to greater currency flexibility ... The People's Bank of China, under central bank governor Zhou Xiaochuan, has to manage China's huge and persistent intervention in currency markets and square that with a commitment to control inflation. Stephen Green (Standard Chartered in Shanghai): 'The People's Bank of China wants more flexibility and an additional tool to manage the economy and recognizes that a dollar peg in this day and age is not a particularly stable arrangement' ... Many foreign multinationals operating in China are ambivalent on the issue, since their exports will also be hit by any appreciation. In a business survey released Friday [2 April] by the American Chamber of Commerce in China, US companies ranked renminbi appreciation seventh in a list of risks facing foreign companies in China.

(www.ft.com, 6 April 2010; www.cnn.com, 6 April 2010)

On one side of the discussion is the People's Bank of China ... [whose] chairman is Zhou Xiaochuan ... The People's Bank of China recently appointed three scholars to advise it, two of whom, David Daokui Li and Xia Bin, have advocated currency reform … On the other side of the debate is China's Commerce Ministry and some members of its National Development and Reform Commission, which formulates the country's long-term economic strategy … Several studies suggest that China's exports fall by about 1.5 per cent when its trade-weighted exchange rate, adjusted for inflation, strengthens by 1 per cent.

(www.economist.com, 7 April 2010)

China announced on Thursday [1 April] that President Hu Jintao will attend a summit on nuclear security in Washington later this month … Beijing had not committed to attend the 12 April summit … [The Chinese] foreign ministry spokesman … [said] the nuclear summit would mainly discuss nuclear terrorism and potential counter-measures … [The United States] said on Wednesday [31 March] that Beijing had agreed in a conference call to start talks about sanctions against Iran.

(www.ft.com, 1 April 2010)

The security meeting, scheduled for 12–13 April, seeks to limit the proliferation of nuclear materials 'so that they never fall into the hands of terrorists', President Barack Obama said in announcing it in his State of the Nation speech in January [2010] … [The announcement] came less than a day after the Chinese government appeared to throw its support behind new UN sanctions aimed at pressurizing Iran over its nuclear programme. In recent months the five permanent members of the Security Council have been stymied by China's insistence on diplomacy over sanctions.

(www.iht.com, 1 April 2010)

The US ambassador to the United Nations, Susan Rice, said on Wednesday [31 March] her government, Britain, France, Russia and Germany had agreed with China to begin discussing a proposed UN Security Council resolution with new sanctions on Iran. She said: 'This is progress, but the negotiations have yet to begun in earnest.'

(www.iht.com, 1 April 2010)

On Thursday night [1 April] President Barack Obama spoke with President Hu Jintao for about an hour by telephone … For now the United States is setting aside potentially the most divisive issue in the relationship, deferring a decision on whether to accuse China of manipulating its currency until well after Mr Hu's visit, according to a senior administration official … The administration decided not to report on 15 April, one of ten deadlines set by Congress and the Treasury Department to issue a report on possible currency manipulation … An official said that if China did not take action on its own, the administration could raise the issue again at the G-20 summit meeting in June … American officials said they expected China to wrangle over the wording of a UN resolution, with a goal of watering down the measures against Tehran.

(www.iht.com, 2 April 2010)

Susan Rice, US ambassador to the United Nations, said this week that China agreed to negotiate possible sanctions against Iran. But Chinese officials were not as bold in their statements Thursday [1 April], again emphasizing the difference in priorities. Foreign ministry spokesman Qin Gang said he hoped the issue could be resolved 'through diplomatic negotiations'. The spokesman added: 'We oppose Iran's possession of nuclear weapons, and at the same time we also believe that as a sovereign state it has the right to peacefully use nuclear technology.'

(www.iht.com, 2 April 2010)

'On Wednesday [31 March] US ambassador to the United Nations, Susan Rice, said China had "agreed to sit down and begin serious negotiations in New York" over possible new sanctions against Iran ... Iran is China's third largest oil supplier' (www.cnn.com, 4 April 2010).

'The US ambassador to the UN, Susan Rice, said ... China had indicated it was ready to hold "serious" talks with Western powers on a new UN resolution' (www.bbc.co.uk, 2 April 2010).

President Hu Jintao will travel to Washington next month for a summit on nuclear issues ... The announcement comes as the United States and France are pushing for sanctions against Iran's nuclear energy programme, and as Iran's top nuclear official was heading to China to discuss his country's nuclear programme ... Chinese foreign ministry spokesman Qin Gang: '[China hopes the issue can be solved] through diplomatic negotiations. We oppose Iran's possession of nuclear weapons, and at the same time we also believe that as a sovereign state it has the right to peacefully use nuclear technology.'

(www.cnn.com, 1 April 2010)

China traditionally opposes sanctions. Although it went along with three earlier UN sanctions against Iran, Beijing has been a vocal opponent of a fourth round, insisting that further negotiations with Tehran were needed. But US officials say a Chinese representative made a commitment in a phone call on Wednesday [31 March] with officials of the United States, Russia, China, Britain, France and Germany to discuss specifics of a potential Security Council resolution ... China depends on oil- and gas-rich Iran for 11 per cent of its energy needs and last year [2009] became Tehran's biggest trading partner, according to Iranian figures.

(www.independent.co.uk, 2 April 2010)

The Obama administration said Saturday [3 April] that it would delay a decision on whether to declare China a currency valuation manipulator, but it vowed to press Chinese leaders on the politically charged issue of currency manipulation during a series of meetings through June ... US Treasury Secretary Timothy Geithner said he had decided to delay the semi-annual exchange rate report to Congress, which was to be due on 15 April ... Timothy Geithner: 'China's inflexible exchange rate has made it difficult for other emerging market economies to let their currencies appreciate. A move by China to a more market-orientated exchange rate will make an essential contribution to global rebalancing. China's continued maintenance of a currency peg has required increasingly large volumes of currency intervention' ... Mr Geithner pledged to raise the issue at a series of forums: a meeting of finance ministers and central banker governors from the G-20 nations later this month [April]; the twice-yearly Strategic and Economic Dialogue between the two countries, expected to be in China in May; and a meeting of G-20 leaders and finance ministers in June. Mr Geithner called these meetings 'the best avenue of advancing US interests at this time' ... China said on Thursday [1 April] that President Hu Jintao would attend a nuclear security summit meeting in Washington this month ... The United States has not found China to be a currency manipulator since 1994. Under successive administrations, officials have tried to persuade China that letting the renminbi appreciate would stimulate domestic demand and reduce reliance on exports ... Within the Chinese government there has been debate about the [exchange rate] issue. The central bank has signalled that a gradual appreciation is in order, but the commerce ministry, which represents the interests of the country's powerful exporters and manufacturers, has argued for maintaining the currency peg.

(www.iht.com, 4 April 2010; *IHT*, 5 April 2010, pp. 1, 15)

US Treasury Secretary Timothy Geithner has delayed a scheduled 15 April report to Congress ... Timothy Geithner, explaining the delay in a statement Saturday [3 April], said a series of upcoming meetings, including among officials of the G-20 financially influential countries and with China, countries, are 'the best avenue for advancing US interests at this time'.

(www.cnn.com, 4 April 2010)

White House spokesman Robert Gibbs: 'The president has spoken repeatedly and recently that China's currency must be market-based' ... A congressional aid speaking on condition of anonymity: 'If there's no substantive sign of action, Congress will be forced to act' ... Several Chinese economists quoted in the overseas edition of the *People's Daily*, the official newspaper of the Communist Party, maintained that the yuan was not to blame for the US trade deficit. But Li Daokui, a member of the central bank's monetary policy committee, said China could nonetheless buy more goods to ease pressure from the White House and Congress. Li Daokui (a Harvard-trained economist at Tsinghua University in Beijing): 'China can increase purchases from [US] states facing mass unemployment because of recession in the manufacturing sector.'

(www.iht.com, 5 April 2010)

'China has begun to prepare the ground publicly for a shift in exchange rate policy, days after the US Treasury said it would postpone a decision on whether to name China a "currency manipulator"' (*FT*, 7 April 2010, p. 7).

US Treasury Secretary Timothy Geithner will meet vice premier Wang Qishan in Beijing on Thursday [8 April] on his way back to the United States from India, a Treasury spokesman said on Wednesday [7 April] ... Mr Wang is an influential economic policymaker in Beijing who was the primary point of contact for Henry Paulson, the former [US] Treasury Secretary who started a strategic economic dialogue with China in part to persuade the country to allow its currency to rise against the dollar ... China has been letting the renminbi edge up almost imperceptibly in the past few days in trading in Shanghai. The currency stayed close to 6.827 per dollar since July 2008, but the official fixing for the start of trading on Wednesday [7 April] in Shanghai was 6.8259, the first time this year [2010] that the government has allowed the currency to open below 6.826. The currency has bobbed up and down lately. The government has been worried that many exporters earn revenues in dollars, and sign contracts three months or more in advance, but incur many of their costs in renminbi. By allowing even a slight variation in the currency, the government may be signalling to exporters that they should begin preparing for the possibility of a stronger renminbi ... In Asian trading before the announcement of Mr Geithner's meeting with Mr Wang, investors bid up yuan forward contracts used to speculate on the Chinese currency's value in the future. The one-year forward contracts traded up 0.1 per cent to 6.6303 per dollar ... Also on Wednesday the People's Bank of China said it would sell 15 billion renminbi, the equivalent of $2.2 billion, in three-year bills at higher interest rates than what bills are trading at now. The move suggests that policymakers may be preparing the ground for a revaluation of the currency and are trying to cool down the economy ... The thirty-member OECD reiterated its call to Beijing on Wednesday to allow the renminbi to appreciate.

(www.iht.com, 7 April 2010; *IHT*, 8 April 2010, p. 15)

The government is preparing to announce in the coming days that it will allow its currency to strengthen slightly and vary more from day to day ... people with knowledge of the emerging consensus in Beijing said on Thursday [8 April]. While any announcement could still be delayed, China's central bank appears to have prevailed with its arguments within the Chinese leadership for a stronger but more flexible currency ... these people said ... Forward contracts on the value of the renminbi surged by the most in six weeks on Thursday in response to a report on the website of *The New York Times* that China was close to a shift in currency, according to Bloomberg. One closely watched contract strengthened to 6.62 renminbi to the dollar for transactions a year from now; the spot rate is still 6.82. Xia Bin, a member of the monetary policy committee of the central bank, hinted at the new policy for the currency while attending a forum in Shanghai on Thursday. He said: 'Whether to let the yuan slowly appreciate or let it rise to a tolerable range after careful calculation, I think it is better to have that quick, prompt appreciation ... At a certain point, when necessary, it is better to have a quick, prompt appreciation in a bid to fend off speculative capital' ... But Mr Xia cautioned that no one should expect a 'large, one-time' appreciation of the renminbi of the sort that many members of [the US] Congress have sought.

(www.iht.com, 8 April 2010; *IHT*, 9 April 2010, pp. 1, 14)

'China is quietly preparing for a modest appreciation of the renminbi ... Currency markets anticipate a 3 per cent climb in the renminbi against the dollar over the next year' (www.iht.com, 11 April 2010; *IHT*, 12 April 2010, p. 17).

Allowing the yuan to strengthen against the dollar would hurt the economy in the short term, a senior Chinese official has told the BBC. But Yi Xiaozhun, a vice minister in the commerce ministry, said he expected the currency to rise in the longer term ... Mr Yi says the ... global economic crisis ... is not yet over, and so an increase in the value of the yuan now would hurt China's economy ... Yi Xiaozhun: 'Some American politicians and academics, because of hardship at home, have politicized this argument. They are blaming other countries, including China, for their own problems. This is unreasonable' ... He says the current level ... [of the] exchange rate for the yuan and the dollar ... is reasonable and has helped keep the country's trade flows stable ... He also hinted that China is likely to announce a trade deficit for March ... the first monthly deficit in more than five years.

(www.bbc.co.uk, 9 April 2010)

'Foreign exchange reserves rose by $47.9 billion to $2,447 billion by the end of the first quarter [of 2010], compared with a $126.5 billion rise in the fourth quarter of 2009' (*FT*, 13 April 2010, p. 8).

'Zhou Xiaochuan ... the governor of China's central bank ... said over the weekend that fighting inflation was the central bank's top priority' (www.iht.com, 13 April 2010; *IHT*, 14 April 2010, p. 13).

President Hu Jintao at the nuclear security summit in Washington (13 April): 'China will firmly stick to a path of reforming the yuan's exchange rate formation mechanism ... [But the move] won't be advanced by any foreign pressure ... Renminbi appreciation would neither balance Sino-US trade nor solve the unemployment problem in the United States' ... Financial markets reacted by lowering expectations for liberalization of the renminbi. Economists said a gradual rise beginning around the middle of the year was still the most likely outcome.

(*FT*, 14 April 2010, p. 7)

President Barack Obama: 'I think China rightly sees the issue of currency as ... sovereign issue. I think they are resistant to international pressure when it comes to them making decisions about their currency policy and monetary policy' (www.iht.com, 14 April 2010).

China is facing growing international pressure to begin allowing its currency to appreciate, providing unexpected allies for the United States .... Speaking ahead of a meeting of finance ministers and central bank heads from the G-20 countries which starts today [Thursday 22 April] in Washington, Indian and Brazilian central bank presidents have made the most forceful statements yet by their countries about the case for a stronger renminbi ... Lee Hsien Loong, prime minister of Singapore ... last week ... [said] it was 'in China's interests' with the financial crisis over to have a more flexible exchange rate ... The increase in criticism of China comes at a time of relative calm between Beijing and Washington over the issue, with many US officials and analysts assuming China has already decided to abandon its peg with the dollar over coming months ... Although there have been strong signs in recent weeks that China is preparing to shift policy, a number of prominent officials continue to oppose any immediate changes.

(*FT*, 22 April 2010, p. 10)

'Although India and Brazil this week joined calls by the United States for China to allow the value of the renminbi to appreciate, G-20 officials said the topic did not come up in the meetings [held 22–23 April]' (www.iht.com, 24 April 2010).

China returned to a modest trade surplus last month [April] after recording a deficit in March ... The surplus was $1.7 billion in April following the surprise deficit of $7.2 billion in March, the first month in six years in which imports exceeded exports ... Policy-makers are watching with concern the unfolding of the Greek debt crisis. The Euro decline meant that the renminbi had appreciated by 5 per cent against a basket of currencies of its main trading partners this year [2010] ... Last night [10 May] the central bank said it would manage the renminbi 'with reference to a basket of currencies', prompting speculation of an imminent policy shift, although the wording has been used before ... Many economists expect ... China's trade surplus ... to rebound in the second half of the year.

(*FT*, 11 May 2010, p. 12)

The pain of the European debt crisis is spreading, with the plummeting Euro making Chinese companies less competitive in Europe, their largest market, and complicating any move to break the Chinese currency's page to the dollar. Chinese policy-makers reached a consensus last month [April] about dropping the dollar peg. But allowing the renminbi to rise against the dollar now would mean a further increase in the renminbi's level against the Euro, creating even more problems for Chinese exporters to Europe. The Euro has plunged against the renminbi in recent weeks, at one point Monday [17 May] reaching its lowest level since late 2002 before turning higher. The steep rise of the renminbi prompted a commerce ministry official in Beijing to warn on Monday that China's exports could be threatened. The official's comments ... suggest that even China ... is not immune to the crisis that started in Greece and threatens to spread across much of Europe. Yal Jian (the ministry official) said: 'The yuan has risen about 14.5 per cent against the Euro during the past four months, which will increase cost pressure for Chinese exporters and also have a negative impact on China's exports to European countries' ... The renminbi is rising along with the dollar against the Euro. The Chinese government has continued to intervene heavily in currency markets in recent weeks to prevent the renminbi from rising against the dollar, maintaining an informal peg of 6.827 renminbi to the dollar, the level since July 2008. Because American companies compete in the Chinese market with European companies in many industries, the Euro's weakness against the renminbi is putting American companies at a disadvantage just as Gary Locke, the US commerce secretary, is leading the first cabinet-level trade mission of the administration of President Barack Obama this week ... Chinese leaders reached a consensus in April [2010] to break the renminbi's peg to the dollar, ending a dispute that spilled into public view in March when commerce ministry officials warned in speeches and interviews in Beijing and Washington about the dangers of any change in the renminbi's value. The ministry halted those warnings immediately after the consensus was reached, and Chen Deming, the commerce minister, even reversed himself publicly by saying that China's trade deficit in March was nothing to worry about. But events since then have delayed implementation of the consensus, including public attention paid to a visit to Beijing by US Treasury Secretary Timothy Geithner, followed by the earthquake in Qinghai province and then the Euro's slide.

(www.iht.com, 17 May 2010)

President Hu Jintao (24 May): 'China will continue to steadily advance reform of the renminbi exchange rate mechanism following the principles of being independent, controllable and gradual' (www.iht.com, 24 May 2010).

President Hu Jintao said Beijing would move 'under the principle of independent decision-making, controllability, and gradual progress' ... Mr Hu [made a] pledge to 'steadily advance the reform mechanism of the renminbi exchange rate' ... without repeating his previous references to the rate being 'basically stable'.

(*IHT*, 25 May 2010, pp. 1, 4)

China's State Administration of Foreign Exchange (Safe) ... holds an estimated $630 billion of Eurozone bonds in its reserves ... Beijing has been trying to diversify away from the dollar in recent years by buying a greater proportion of assets denominated in other currencies ... [It is said that] the fund ... started raising their purchases of Eurobonds last year [2009] ... An estimated 70 per cent of reserves are held in dollars ... Analysts point out that Safe rarely cuts its holdings significantly, as it has so much new money to invest every month. Instead, it reduces the proportion of new investment it devotes to a particular asset ... According to the latest figures by Safe, foreign exchange reserves totalled $2,447 billion at the end of March [2010], up $174 billion in just six months.

(*FT*, 27 May 2010, p. 8)

China's main sovereign wealth fund is 'very concerned' about short-term market fluctuations resulting from instability in the Eurozone, according to the fund's president. However, Gao Xiqing, president of China Investment Corp., told Chinese state media that the ongoing debt crisis would not seriously affect China's overseas investment in Europe. He said: '[China Investment Corp.] will keep its investment in Europe, no more, no less. Short-term fluctuations won't bring serious effect on us' ... Xinhua paraphrased Mr Gao as saying: 'CIC is very concerned about the short-term market fluctuations amid threatened Eurozone stability' ... His comments came as Safe, which manages the country's near $2,500 billion in foreign exchange reserves, said in a statement that a report in the *Financial Times* – that it was reviewing its holdings of Eurozone assets – was 'groundless'. It said: 'Safe is a responsible long-term investor and, under the principle of maintaining diversified investments, Europe has been and will continue to be one of the major markets for investing China's exchange reserves' ... Mr Gao said CIC's $300 billion fund [is] managed separately from Safe.

(*FT*, 28 May 2010, p. 9)

Safe ... put out a rare statement after a *Financial Times* story that caused the Euro and US stocks to fall in New York trading last night [26 May]. The agency said: 'This report is groundless. The European market in the past, present and future always will be one of the major investment markets for the State Administration of Foreign Exchange' ... It expressed confidence that Europe will restore 'stability and healthy development' in its financial markets with international help.

(www.guardian.co.uk, 27 May 2010)

A statement by the People's Bank of China dismissed reports that Safe ... was evaluating its investment in Eurozone debt amid concerns that some European nations might eventually default on their debts ... The central bank said it was committed to long-term investment in Europe. It also said it supported the European integration process and the stabilization measures worked out this month by the EU and the IMF, and that the Eurozone would be able to overcome its difficulties.

(www.iht.com, 27 May 2010)

'Many economists are predicting ... [that China will allow] the renminbi to appreciate against the US dollar later this year [2010]' (www.iht.com, 8 June 2010).

Outward investment

The Anglo-Australian miner Rio Tinto signed a $2.9 billion agreement with the Chinese metals group Chinalco on Friday [19 March] to jointly develop an iron ore project in the West African country of Guinea ... The venture [is] not binding at this stage ... The non-binding joint venture agreement covers rail and port infrastructure as well as the Simandou mine itself ... Under the deal, Rio Tinto would put its current holding in Simandou into the new joint venture. Chinalco would invest $1.35 billion for a 47 per cent stake in the venture, an effective 44.65 per cent interest in the project itself. Guinea has an option to buy up to 20 per cent of the project ... Rio Tinto would operate the joint venture but they would have an equal number of directors, with ore being sold to China ... Major additional capital would be required on top of Chinalco's investment to fully develop Simandou ... Rio Tinto ... says Simandou is the world's biggest undeveloped iron ore deposit.

(www.iht.com, 19 March 2010)

Chinalco holds a 9.3 per cent stake in Rio ... Four Rio Tinto employees were arrested in Shanghai in July [2009]. They were later charged with accepting bribes and stealing trade secrets. The trial of the four employees is to begin on Monday [22 March], almost nine months after they were detained ... Chinese authorities have said the portion of the trial dealing with bribery allegations will be open, but the part concerning charges of infringement of commercial secrets will be closed, even to Australian diplomats ... Rio Tinto has spent more than $600 million on exploration and evaluation work to develop the mine at Simandou.

(www.iht.com, 19 March 2010)

For the Guinea agreement, Rio Tinto said that it would put its 95 per cent stake in the project, which is in the south-eastern town of Simandou, into a new joint venture. The state-owned Chinalco, whose official name is Aluminium Corp. of China, then plans to acquire a 47 per cent stake in the venture by investing $1.35 billion over the next two to three years. That would take Chinalco's stake in the project to 44.65 per cent.

(*IHT*, 20 March 2010, p. 14)

According to Rio Tinto, Simandou is one of the world's biggest undeveloped iron ore deposits. Guinea is the world's largest producer of bauxite, from which iron is derived. The deal also covers rail and port infrastructure ... The announcement comes just two weeks after a date [27 June] was set for elections in Guinea to restore civilian rule ... Last year [2009] China was condemned by human rights groups after it signed a $7 billion mining and oil deal with the government just two weeks after some 150 protesters were allegedly killed by soldiers.

(www.bbc.co.uk, 19 March 2010)

The partnership will cover mining as well as the construction of rail and port infrastructure in a project that analysts believe could cost $12 billion. Rio believes Simandou could become the world's third most important iron ore province outside Brazil and Australia ... Rio Tinto and Chinalco ... have agreed on a non-binding joint venture despite Rio losing half of the Simandou concession area last year [2009], amid the Guinean government frustration that Rio had taken too long to develop the project ... Rio's ownership of the full deposit is still uncertain. Last year [2009] the government

of Guinea took away half of the licence area and gave it to a company con-
trolled by Beny Steinmetz, the Israeli diamond and mining entrepreneur ...
People close to the Mongolian mining industry have said they believe Rio
Tinto and Chinalco are working out a deal on Oyu Tolgoi, a copper–gold
deposit that is a joint venture between Rio Tinto and Ivanhoe Mines of
Canada.

(FT, 20 March 2010, p. 16)

China ... accounted for a quarter of ... Rio Tinto's ... revenues in 2009,
mainly because of China's voracious appetite for iron ore ... The Simandou
deal will give Chinalco a 47 per cent stake in the African mine for $1.35
billion and will guarantee a portion of its output for China ... The deal
comes soon after a report compiled for the Chinese cabinet, which blamed
economic forces and campaigning by BHP Billiton, rather than perfidy by
Rio Tinto's management, for scuppering Chinalco's proposed investment
[in 2009] in Rio ... This year's iron ore price talks have so far been as frosty
as last year's, which never reached an agreement.

(www.economist.com, 20 March 2010)

'China already accounts for 24 per cent of Rio Tinto's sales' *(FT*, 24 March
2010, p. 12).

Australian Stern Hu ... told a court in Shanghai that he took bribes ... Mr
Hu's colleagues ... Liu Caikui, Ge Minqiang and Wang Yong ... also
admitted taking bribes, but disputed the amounts ... Mr Hu was charged
with accepting bribes of about $900,000 ... An Australian diplomat attended
the court session ... Foreign reporters are not allowed to attend the trial ...
On Tuesday [23 March] the court will address the commercial espionage
charges ... [Australian] consular officials ... [will not be allowed] to attend
this part of the trial Rio Tinto had said that its four employees had done
nothing wrong.

(www.bbc.co.uk, 22 March 2010)

Stunning confessions [were made] on the opening day of the three-day trial
in Shanghai ... The employees ... admitted to having received several
million dollars in bribes ... Stern Hu admitted in court Monday [22 March]
to receiving some of the $1 million in bribes prosecutors accused him of
having taken while at Rio Tinto ... Mr Hu and his three colleagues of
having accepted about $12 million in bribes ... Each of the defendants could
face up to ten years in jail if they plead guilty to accepting bribes ... Wang
Yong agreed to plead guilty to accepting about $1 million in bribes – much
less than the $10 million he is accused of taking ... [Wang claims that] $9
million ... was legitimate profit from an iron ore deal ... For much of the
past year Rio Tinto ... has defended its employees, saying the company has
no evidence they engaged in wrongdoing ... In the nine months since the
four were detained, the Chinese authorities have announced no other arrests
of steel industry officials for bribing Rio Tinto employees or trading in gov-

ernment secrets ... On Tuesday or Wednesday [23 and 24 March] the court is expected to shift its focus to the commercial secrets charges.

(www.iht.com, 22 March 2010)

'Four defendants admitted to taking far less money than the $13 million prosecutors said they had accepted in the form of bribes ... The commercial secrets part of the proceedings .. [are] closed even to Australian consular officials' (www.iht.com, 23 March 2010).

Donald Clarke (George Washington University): 'The charges of receiving bribes are a little puzzling. If they're stealing secrets, normally they'd be giving bribes. And why aren't the bribers being charged?' (*IHT*, 24 March 2010, p. 17).

> Stern Hu had been charged with accepting 6 million yuan in bribes ... Wang Yong was charged with accepting 70 million yuan ... No foreign reporters were allowed inside [the court], although journalists from Chinese media gained entry ... Taking bribes [is] a charge that carries a maximum sentence of five years in prison ... Charges of engaging in commercial espionage ... [means] they could face [an additional] seven years in jail.
>
> (www.thetimes.co.uk, 22 March 2010)

'If found guilty the men could [each] face a maximum sentence of twenty years' (*FT*, 23 March 2010, p. 17).

> [The] court trying four employees of Rio Tinto concluded its hearing on the bribery charges against them Tuesday [23 March] and began to consider evidence of their alleged theft of [commercial secrets] ... Stern Hu is accused of receiving two bribes: one for 1 million yuan ($146,490) and another for 5.3 million yuan ($790,000).
>
> (www.cnn.com, 23 March 2010)

'The trial is scheduled to take three days' (www.bbc.co.uk, 23 March 2010).

'The trial ... has ended. The mid-day [Wednesday 24 March] end to the trial was earlier than expected because the proceedings went smoothly' (www.bbc.co.uk, 24 March 2010).

> [The] three-day trial ... ended Wednesday [24 March], but there was no verdict ... The defendants face five to fifteen years in prison, if convicted. A three-judge panel is expected to rule in days or weeks on the high profile case, which has stunned foreign companies operating in China ... [The] panel will decide how much time the four Rio Tinto employees will serve for pleading guilty to taking at least some money. Legal experts say the secretive nature of the trail raised as many questions as it answered ... What took place in the courtroom is still unclear. Lawyers involved in the case offered often contradictory accounts of who had pleaded guilty and whether their clients had accepted bribes. Prosecutors charged the four with receiving about $12 million in bribes, some of it related to iron ore contracts. But lawyers for the defence said their clients had accepted much less and that some of the money was unrelated to Rio Tinto, like a loan used to invest in

stocks. Tao Wuping, Liu Caikui's attorney, said after one court session: 'Liu Caikui pleaded guilty, but he said part of the bribery that he was accused of taking was actually commission.'

(www.iht.com, 24 March 2010; *IHT*, 25 March 2010, p. 18)

'Wang Yong's lawyer ... [said] that payments he received were legitimate bonuses ... A number of analysts have suggested that Monday's guilty pleas are in recognition of a plea bargain' (www.indpendent.co.uk, 24 March 2010).

Zhang Peihong said his client, Wang Yong, admitted guilt to all charges, but denied accepting a bribe ... At the end of the first day of the trial on Monday, Zhai Jian – the lawyer for another defendant – said his client acknowledged receiving money, but said it was gift or a loan – not a bribe.

(www.cnn.com, 24 March 2010)

On the bribery charges, Stern Hu has admitted taking money – totalling about $1 million – on two occasions from two steel mills in northern China, his lawyer said. The lawyer for another defendant also said his client acknowledged receiving money. CNN has not been able to verify whether the other two defendants also admitted taking money ... Obtaining commercial secrets carries a maximum penalty of seven years in prison.

(www.cnn.com, 29 March 2010)

Stern Hu, an executive at Rio Tinto, has said in court that he accepted two large bribes in late 2008 and early 2009 totalling about $1 million from Chinese steel mills in exchange for agreeing to sell them long-term supplies of iron ore ... Mr Hu's admission – and guilty pleas on the bribery charges from the three Rio Tinto employees – has intensified a case that began last July [2009] ... Their surprise guilty pleas have switched the focus back onto corruption in the Chinese steel industry and questions about whether Rio Tinto had proper oversight over its employees ... Steel industry experts say bribery had grown rampant in recent years as Chinese steel mills competed for valuable imports of iron ore, much of which was controlled by foreign suppliers. Analysts also said a chaotic pricing system created a two-tiered market fuelling corrupt deal-making. Many large state-run steel companies in China agree to long-term supply contracts at a set price with foreign suppliers, while small steel mills competed to buy supplies on the open market, often for higher prices ... Getting a discount on the open market could mean saving tens of millions of dollars, experts say, giving tremendous power to iron ore salesmen working for companies like Rio Tinto ... Many big steel makers made huge profits by simply reselling their contracted iron ore to smaller mills ... Jin Chunqing, a lawyer representing Stern Hu, says his client admitted to taking money in November 2008 and January 2009 from 'friends' at local mills, and that it was the only time he had ever taken bribes. Prosecutors accused Mr Hu of taking one bribe for $790,000 and another for about $147,000. Mr Jin said: 'Those two small companies bribed Stern Hu in order to get a long-term contract with Rio Tinto, which normally is not available for medium- and small-sized enterprises' ... Mr Jin said Mr Hu had agreed to repay the bribes and has pleaded for leniency from the court. A three-judge panel is expected to rule on the case on Monday [29 March].

(www.iht.com, 26 March 2010)

[On Monday 29 March] Stern Hu was given a seven year sentence for bribery and five years for commercial secrets theft, reduced to ten years in total. He also had assets worth 500,000 yuan ($73,000) confiscated and was fined the same amount. Wang Yong was given thirteen years for bribery and three years for secrets theft, reduced to fourteen years in jail. He was fined 200,000 yuan and assets worth 5 million yuan were confiscated from him. Liu Caikui was given five years for bribery and four for secrets theft, reduced to seven years. He was fined 400,000 yuan and had assets worth 300,000 yuan confiscated. Ge Minqiang was handed a six year sentence for bribery and three-and-a-half years for secrets theft, reduced to eight in total. He was fined 300,000 yuan and had 500,000 worth of assets confiscated ... All the sentences would be backdated to 5 July 2009 when the four were first arrested ... Rio Tinto described its employees' behaviour as 'deplorable' and said it had decided to dismiss them. It said it had concluded that the illegal activities were carried out 'wholly outside our systems'.

(www.bbc.co.uk, 29 March 2010)

Rio Tinto ... said the court's evidence showing that they had accepted about $13.5 million in bribes in recent years was 'beyond doubt' ... Although Rio Tinto was not charged in this case, the Shanghai No. 1 Intermediate People's Court said the company had profited from stolen information that harmed Chinese economic interests, costing steel mills in China an extra $150 million last year [2009]. Between 2003 and 2009, the court said, the four defendants had used 'improper means' to gain information that allowed Rio Tinto to 'jack up the price that China paid for its iron ore imports'. The court said that it would soon charge at least two Chinese steel industry officials with passing secrets to Rio Tinto ... Rio Tinto ... said it could not comment on the trade secrets charges because part of the trial had been closed to the public ... At a three-day trial ... the four employees all pleaded guilty to accepting some bribes, though several of the men denied having stolen commercial secrets, according to lawyers in the case.

(www.iht.com, 29 March 2010; *IHT*, 30 March 2010, p. 15)

The court said the men's actions had cost Chinese industry 'severe losses'. In an extremely unusual move it allowed foreign reporters into the building to see the verdict via a video link between courtrooms ... A defence lawyer told Reuters last week that the men had all said the company was not aware of their actions.

(www.guardian.co.uk, 29 March 2010)

'The court said: "The four have seriously damaged the interests of the Chinese steel enterprises and out those enterprises in an unfavourable place in the iron ore negotiations and led to the suspension of the negotiations in 2009"' (*FT*, 30 March 2010, p. 1)

> During the course of the trial all four employees admitted they personally took money from smaller Chinese steelmakers keen to guarantee supply of Rio Tinto's iron ore. One employee, however, claimed it was a loan and not a bribe. The trial included a closed-door session on the men's theft of so-called 'commercial secrets', which could include information important for iron ore price negotiations such as state-owned steelmakers' tonnage requirements. Rio Tinto yesterday [29 March] fired them ... The company said there was 'clear evidence presented in court that showed beyond doubt that the four convicted employees had accepted bribes' ... The company implied it was less certain about the commercial secrecy charges, saying that its internal investigation had uncovered no evidence to support the claims.
>
> (p. 16)

> The court gave few details except to say that the convicted men obtained the secret CISA [China Iron and Steel Association] memo and received advance information that Shougang, a Chinese steel company also accused in the case, was planning to cut output. A Shougang official was also due to be sentenced on Monday [29 March] in the same court. At least ten other Chinese steel firms are also understood to have been involved, paying bribes to the Rio Tinto employees in order to secure preferential access to contract iron ore supplies.
>
> (www.ft.com, 30 March 2010; www.cnn.com, 30 March 2010)

No one involved in the bribery phase of the trial knows exactly what was said in the commercial secrets phase. But court leaks imply there were different pleas at the onset. Of those sentenced Liu Caikui appears to have admitted obtaining commercial secrets, while Wang Yong and Ge Minqiang denied it. Stern Hu does not appear to have made a statement either way.

(*FT*, 6 April 2010, p. 9)

Three Chinese ... [and] an Australian of Chinese decent ... were jailed for between seven and fourteen years for bribery and theft of commercial secrets. Only one of them admitted the second charge. That the trial began with confessions came as a surprise. Rio Tinto had previously said an internal examination had turned up no wrongdoing. However, denials of guilt can lead to far harsher treatment by the Chinese courts. As a result of his confession, Stern Hu had his sentence reduced from twelve years ... to ten. Admissions are also said to enhance the prospects of being shown clemency in the future ... One of China's richest citizens, Du Shuanghua, a politically connected private steel operator, testified that he provided $9 million (either as a payment or a loan – the facts were disputed) to Wang Yong ... It is unclear how the bribery allegations were linked to those of commercial espionage, since the latter charges were heard behind closed doors ...

According to some reports, the court was told that the four had got their hands on a confidential memo from a meeting of the Chinese steelmakers' association, containing details of their negotiating position in talks with Rio Tinto and other big iron ore producers.

(www.economist.com, 30 March 2010)

The part of the trial relating to commercial espionage was held in secret … Australian prime minister Kevin Rudd (30 March): '[This leaves] serious unanswered questions about this conviction. In holding this part of the trial in secret, China I believe has missed an opportunity to demonstrate to the world at large transparency that would be consistent with its emerging global role' … [Australian] foreign minister Stephen Smith said the case could raise concerns for foreign companies doing business in China, saying it was not clear whether 'we are dealing with what the international community … would simply regard as the normal ebb and flow of commercial discussions or commercial information' … Chinese foreign ministry spokesman Qin Gang: '[The Australian comments are cause for] serious concern. The Rio Tinto case is an individual criminal case and relevant judicial authorities have issued the verdict of the first trial. The Australian side should respect that result and should stop making such irresponsible remarks.'

(www.bbc.co.uk, 30 March 2010)

'Stern Hu became an Australian citizen in 1994' (www.independent.co.uk, 30 March 2010).

Global steel prices are set to leap by up to a third … after miners and steelmakers yesterday [30 March] agreed a ground-breaking change in the iron ore pricing system. The deal by Vale of Brazil and Anglo-Australia BHP Billiton with Japanese and Chinese mills marks the end of the forty-year-old benchmark system of annual contracts and lengthy price negotiations. The industry instead agree to move to quarterly contracts linked to the nascent iron ore spot market … The new system is a response to last year's stalemate in the negotiations between miners and Chinese steelmakers, when both sides were unable to reach an agreement on annual prices.

(*FT*, 31 March 2010, p. 1)

This move is possible only because over the past ten years or so the spot market has developed to the point where it amounts to somewhere between 10 per cent and 25 per cent of trade … Asian steelmakers were paying $60 per tonne under the 2009–10 annual contracts: between April and June [2010] they can expect to pay about $100 to $120 … In 2000 China accounted for just 16 per cent of the seaborne iron ore market … By last year [2009] … China's share of it had jumped to almost 70 per cent.

(*FT*, 1 April 2010, p. 12)

In 1983 Rio Tinto opened its first China office. On 26 May 2009 Rio Tinto agreed a 33 per cent discount to the 2008–9 benchmark price with Japanese steelmakers. On 1 June 2009 the Chinese steel industry body Cisa rejected the agreement, seeking a 45 per cent cut. It never agreed a current-year contract price.

(FT, 6 April 2010, p. 9)

Rio Tinto ... said Friday [9 April] that it had joined two other global mining companies and decided to sell iron ore based on quarterly prices, a move that effectively ends a decades-old annual pricing system. The decision means that the world's three biggest exporters of iron ore – Rio Tinto, BHP Billiton and Vale of Brazil – have all decided to quit selling the raw material to global steel mills using annual contracts ... The mining companies decided to move away from annual contracts after years of acrimonious negotiations with Chinese steel producers. For several years China's state-controlled iron and steel association has fought with the mining giants, calling them a cartel and accusing them of manipulating prices and negotiating unfairly ... For decades the benchmark pricing system allowed steel companies to lock in iron ore prices for a year under annual contracts. Such deals helped miners make long-term investment decisions. But in China a dual system of both benchmark prices and spot, or market, prices led to corruption, with some steel mills paying bribes to get access to iron ore at the lower of the two prices.

(www.iht.com, 9 April 2010; *IHT*, 10 April 2010, p. 7)

The agreements with Asian steel mills in effect killed the forty-year-old benchmark system of annual contracts and long price negotiations ... The new system does not alter the long-term relationship between miners and steelmakers: Rio Tinto and other miners will continue to supply iron ore under long-term contracts, but prices will be reset every quarter.

(FT, 10 April 2010, p. 21)

Australian natural gas company Arrow Energy agreed on Monday [22 March] to accept a sweetened ... $3.2 billion ... bid by Shell and PetroChina ... [which] raised their initial offer ... transaction is subject to Australian regulatory approval, as well as approval from Arrow shareholders ... The announcement on Monday from Arrow also foresees a spin-off of Arrow's international assets – including in China, India, Vietnam and Indonesia – as well as some Australian assets into a new company ... [called] Dart Energy ... held by Arrow's existing shareholders.

(www.iht.com, 22 March 2010; *IHT*, 23 March 2010, p. 18)

BG Group, the oil and gas producer, is poised to sign a contract worth an estimated $40 billion, a record for the company, to supply natural gas to China. The twenty-year deal to supply liquefied natural gas from coal-seam gas deposits in eastern Australia is being finalized today [24 March] in Beijing with CNOOC ... As part of the agreement it will acquire 5 per cent of BG's coal-seam gas interests in the Surat Basin in south-western Queensland. The Chinese company will also hold a 10 per cent stake in an LNG processing unit.

(www.thetimes.com, 24 March 2010)

BG Group said Wednesday [24 March] that it had agreed to supply CNOOC … liquefied natural gas annually for the next twenty years … The two companies did not reveal the value of the supply deal … [but] one analyst estimated [it] to be worth up to $70 billion … [BG Group is] selling the state-run company a small stake in BG's Australian coalbed gas assets … CNOOC will also buy 10 per cent of an LNG processing train, as well as join BG in a consortium to build two LNG ships … CNOOC's proposed stake in BG's Australian assets requires regulatory approval … BG, which is based in Britain, has operations in more than twenty-five countries, and is competing with Shell and Arrow's current gas projects in Queensland. Coalbed gas is methane by coal deposits deep underground, which has to be cooled until it liquefies. The reserves can be more difficult to access than traditional natural gas deposits, and the rush to exploit them comes as global companies face limited access elsewhere.

(www.iht.com, 24 March 2010)

The World Bank's private sector arm has signed its first deal to finance Chinese investment in Africa, a move it hopes will help to discourage violations of human rights and environmental standards. The International Finance Corporation agreed yesterday [22 April] that it would help finance a commercial complex, including a fourteen-storey office block, in Dar es Salaam, Tanzania's capital. The project, run by the China Railway Jianchang Engineering Company and a local non-profit organization, is small. The IFC will provide $10 million in funding and hope to attract another $6.5 million from other investors, which together will fund about half the project. But with other deals with Chinese investors in Africa under negotiation, including the possibility of financing special industrial zones, the IFC hopes that a growing proportion of Chinese investment can be covered by internationally recognized standards. The loan follows years of foreign investor concern, particularly from the United States and Europe, that they are under-bid by Chinese companies prepared to cut corners in social and environmental standards to win contracts, particularly in the oil, gas and mining industries.

(*IHT*, 23 April 2010, p. 10)

'China has agreed to spend up to $23 billion to build oil refineries and other petroleum infrastructure in Nigeria' (*FT*, 15 May 2010, p. 8).

Inward investment

US companies feel increasingly unwelcome in China because of what they see as discrimination and inconsistent legal treatment, according to a survey. The American Chamber of Commerce in China (ACCC) found 38 per cent of its members felt unwelcome, up from 26 per cent last quarter. Inconsistent regulation and judicial treatment topped the list of concerns for American businesses, the ACCC found … Companies surveyed by the ACCC cited claims that Beijing wanted to squeeze foreign technology companies out of the multi-billion dollar market for selling computers and office equipment to government departments. New rules stipulate sellers of high-tech goods must contain Chinese intellectual property as part of an 'indigenous innovation' campaign, in order for them to be included in a government procurement catalogue. The survey said: 'The survey shows that US companies believe they face product discrimination in state-owned enterprise purchase, as well as in government procurement' ... Of the American technology companies surveyed, 57 per cent said they expected the preferential purchasing policy to have a negative impact on their operations in China while 37 per cent said they were already losing sales. Member companies believed some policies in China were 'increasingly restrictive and protectionist' ... the survey said.

(www.bbc.co.uk, 22 March 2010)

'A Monday [22 March] survey ... [involved] 203 companies ... Michael Barbalas (president of the American Chamber of Commerce in China): "By and large American companies here are profitable, but you see this growing concern about long-term potential"' (www.cnn.com, 22 March 2010).

A recent survey by the American Chamber of Commerce in China found that a high proportion of American firms doing business in the country feel that they are the victims of discriminatory or inconsistent treatment ... The Communist Party regards foreign investment as a mechanism for acquiring foreign know-how rather than just jobs and capital; hence the insistence on joint ventures ... The Chinese emphasis on personal connections (*guanxi*) makes it hard to distinguish between business as usual and corruption ... Transparency International's most recent Corruption Perception Index ranks China seventy-ninth out of 180 countries ... There is growing evidence that the Chinese market is living up to its promise. The American Chamber reported in 2008 that three-quarters of the companies that it surveyed were finally making money in China, and almost half were enjoying margins that are higher than the global average, up from 13 per cent a decade before.

(*The Economist*, 3 April 2010, p. 63)

Foreign companies say China is increasingly using discriminatory rules to reduce access to previously open areas of its economy and promote its technology industries, a US business group said Friday [2 April] ... The report by the American Chamber of Commerce in China came as companies said Beijing was violating the spirit of market-opening commitments by trying to preserve segments of its economy for domestic companies in an effort to build up Chinese global competitors. The chamber highlighted complaints about China's efforts to nurture companies that make computers and other technology – a policy dubbed 'indigenous innovation' – but favouring them in government contracts and other areas. The report said a survey of 388 companies had found for the first time that inconsistent regulation had become the most significant challenge faced by US companies in China. Previously, they cited trouble finding enough Chinese managers as the biggest problem.

(*IHT*, 3 April 2010, p. 16)

China retains a raft of non-tariff barriers, including tax rebates and quotas, that discriminate against foreign manufactured and farm goods, the US Trade Representative's office said on Wednesday [31 March] in its annual [USTR] report to the US Congress. The report, along with two new spotlights on technical barriers to manufactured goods and farm exports, comes at a time of rising economic tensions with China over Beijing's exchange rate policy and an import substitution campaign. But the trio of reports, which comprise about 600 pages of trade irritants with more than sixty countries, did not include any mention of China's currency policy ... The USTR report covered long-standing concerns by US businesses about counterfeiting, export subsidies and taxation policies that tilt the playing field to favour Chinese firms. It lays out the US case at the WTO against China's export constraints on materials used to make steel, aluminium and chemicals ... The report described the hot-button issues of internet censorship and technology policies that discriminate against firms operating in China – but removed specific references to Google Corp. that had been part of the previous year's report ... The USTR report said: 'Chinese government authorities may issue lists of banned search terms or banned sites weekly, with little justification or means of appeal, putting internet-enabled services in a precarious position' ... Echoing increasing criticism from US and other foreign businesses in China, the USTR raised alarm about government procurement policy. It said: 'A troubling trend that has emerged ... is China's willingness to encourage domestic or "indigenous" innovation at the cost of foreign innovation and technologies.'

(www.iht.com, 1 April 2010; 2 April 2010, p. 15)

Ford Motor Co. reached an agreement on Sunday [28 March] to sell its Volvo subsidiary to Zhejiang Geely Holding Co., based in Hangzhou ... [It] agreed to pay $1.8 billion for Volvo, with $1.6 billion in cash and the rest in a note payable to Ford ... Ford paid $6 billion in 1999 to acquire [Volvo] ... Zhejiang Geely said it planned to retain production of Volvo cars in Sweden, but build another assembly plant for them in China ... Ford already builds small numbers of Volvos for the Chinese market at an assembly plant in Chongqing. Most of that factory's output is Fords and Mazdas for sale in China. Zhejiang Geely's majority-owned automotive subsidiary, Geely Automobile Holdings, is China's twelfth largest automaker based on production so far this year. But it is China's second largest, after BYD Group, that is not at least partly state owned ... Zhejiang Geely owns 51 per cent of Geely Automobile Holdings, which is publicly traded in Hong Kong ... Zhejiang Geely has said repeatedly that it planned to keep Volvo as a separate unit from Geely Auto. The company has promised to retain Volvo's existing management, but said it has already hired several executives with international automotive experience to help it oversee the new subsidiary. Zhejiang Geely is dominated by its founder, Li Shufu, the son of a farmer from Taizhou, in south-eastern China, who turned a small business manufacturing motorcycle parts there into one of China's fastest growing companies ... China overtook the United States in 2009 as the world's largest auto market in terms of the number of family vehicles sold – although the value of the US market remains greater, because the typical American car sells for [more] than the typical Chinese car ... Geely Automobile ... purchased 23 per cent of Manganese Bronze of Britain two years ago, and set up a joint venture with it to make the famous boxy London taxis in Shanghai for markets around the world. Manganese Bronze announced earlier this month [March] that Geely was set to take a majority stake in the company.

(www.iht.com, 28 March 2010)

The deal is scheduled to close in the third quarter of this year [2010] ... The average car in China sold for $17,000 last year [2009] while the average price tag in the United States was close to $30,000 ... So the American car market is still bigger by value than China's.

(*IHT*, 29 March 2010, p. 16)

'The $1.8 billion deal represents the biggest ever purchase by a Chinese car manufacturer, but it is considerably less than the $6.4 billion Ford paid for Volvo in 1999' (www.cnn.com, 28 March 2010).

[The] government has laid the ground for giving foreign businesses access to government procurement contracts for technology products, a climbdown from earlier rules criticized as excluding foreign groups from this market ... Over the weekend the Ministry of Science and Technology said any company whose products conformed with Chinese laws, regulations and the country's technology policy and which possessed legal rights to the related intellectual policy could gain accreditation under rules on 'indigenous innovation' to bid for government contracts.

(*FT*, 13 April 2010, p. 8)

Global technology suppliers are facing a deadline to reveal the inner workings of computer encryption and other security products, a requirement that the United States and Europe say is Chinese protectionism. Technology suppliers must comply with the rules that take effect Saturday [1 May] or risk being shut out of billions of dollars in purchases that the Chinese government makes for smart cards, secure routers, anti-spam software and other security products. Encryption codes and other trade secrets would have to be disclosed to a government panel, and the foreign companies worry that they might be leaked to their Chinese rivals ... The demand reflects the Chinese government's unease about relying on foreign technology to manage its secrets and its desire to help fledgling Chinese high-technology companies to catch up and compete with global rivals. The rules cover thirteen types of products, including database and network security systems, secure routers and anti-spam and anti-hacking software … Acquiring such know-how would also help Beijing improve its system on internet monitoring and filtering, essentially giving security forces the keys to pry into encrypted messages and data. Beijing faced a storm of criticism after it said in November [2009] that it would favour Chinese goods in government procurement of computers and other technology in an effort to promote domestic innovation. The government backed down this month [April] and promised to make it easier for foreign companies to qualify as domestic suppliers. China announced the computer security rules in 2008. But after US complaints, they were postponed to this year and scaled back to cover only government procurement.

(www.iht.com, 30 April 2010)

China is expected to issue regulations on Saturday [1 May] requiring technology companies to disclose proprietary information like data-encryption keys and underlying software to sell a range of security-related digital technology products to government agencies, American industry officials said on Friday [30 April] … The regulations, set to take effect on Friday, largely affect sales of network routers, smart cards, firewall software and other products involved in protecting digital data. They would require software and equipment from both Chinese and foreign companies to meet new technology standards before being certified for sale to government agencies. To be certified, companies apparently would have to give government-connected testing laboratories encryption algorithms, software code and design specifications that, for many of the products, are regarded as sensitive trade secrets … American industry officials have also argued that the new rules would gut their technology exports, because few other nations would purchase technology whose essential security secrets had been shared with the Chinese government … The Chinese first planned to apply the rules to all technology purchases, but later scaled them back to apply only to purchases by local, provincial and national governments.

(www.iht.com, 1 May 2010)

In recent years Taiwan has watched as rivals like South Korea have signed free-trade deals in Asia … Taiwan has been hampered in negotiating similar agreements because Beijing views the island as a part of China and objects to other countries signing formal treaties that could strengthen Taiwan's claims to independence. The island has trade deals with only five Latin American countries, which buy a tiny slice of its exports. The Ma Ying-jeou administration argues that the … Economic Co-operation Framework Agreement being negotiated [with China] … would be a prelude to similar deals with Malaysia, Singapore and, eventually, Japan or the United States … Taiwan has invested $150 billion in China since the early 1990s, according to a Taiwan government estimate. About 40 per cent of Taiwan's exports go to China, where they face average tariffs of 9 per cent. Half of those exports to China are semi-finished goods that are shipped to factories for assembly and other value-added services and then re-exported, according to Mr Ma ... Mr Ma's government ... [insists] that the deal would not allow mainland workers into Taiwan or remove restrictions on mainland agricultural imports – at least at first.

(www.iht.com, 12 May 2010; *IHT*, 13 May 2010, p. 16)

PepsiCo Inc. has announced it will invest $2.5 billion in China over the next three years. The world's second biggest drinks maker said it would open nineteen new plants and install new production lines at existing factories ... Pepsi currently lags behind Coke in China, with less than half of its rival's market share ... In 2008 Coke held a 17.7 per cent market share, with Pepsi having 7.2 per cent ... Pepsi plans to open plants in Fujian, Gansu, Henan and Yunnan provinces. The company said it also planned to create new products aimed specifically at the Asian market.

(www.bbc.co.uk, 21 May 2010)

Add another entry to the list of worries for the global economy and financial markets: labour unrest in China ... The biggest eye-opener for multinationals in China recently has been a nine-day strike at the sprawling Honda transmission factory here [in Foshan], about 100 miles north-west of Hong Kong. The strike, which has forced Honda to suspend production at all four of its joint venture assembly plants in China, has shown that Chinese authorities are willing to tolerate work stoppages at least temporarily, even at high-tech operations on which other factories may depend. Chinese policy-makers are trying to let wages rise to create the foundations of an economy driven by domestic demand, without derailing the export machine ... Even before the strike, manufacturers and buyers of low-cost products were already actively seeking alternatives to China, like Vietnam and Cambodia ... said Richard Vuylsteke, the president of the American Chamber of Commerce in Hong Kong. 'They're looking very seriously, and we're seeing that in apparel and footwear' ... Honda has been making increasingly generous offers ... to settle the strike ... There were signs on Saturday [29 May] that the Honda strike was beginning to test the government's patience. After two days of allowing surprisingly extensive coverage by state-controlled media, the authorities imposed a blanket ban on domestic coverage, reverting to their usual policy of hushing up labour disputes ... Labour advocacy groups say that they hear of frequent strikes in China, with work stoppages occurring somewhere every day. But strikes are typically hushed up and are often resolved in a day or two by the authorities, either with the police or through pressure on employees to resolve their differences. Honda is not alone in facing intense pressure to raise wages. Foxconn, a giant [Taiwanese] electronics manufacturer in Shenzhen, said on Friday [28 May] that it would raise wages by about 20 per cent after being deeply embarrassed by a series of suicides by workers this year and criticism of working conditions ... The overall effect of wage increases on China's competitiveness is not entirely clear, because of incomplete national data on average wages and productivity. Nicholas Lardy ... said that Chinese productivity was rising so quickly that actual labour costs per unit of production appeared to be flat ... One surprise of the [Honda] strike is that it involves labourers whose wages appear to have already roughly doubled in the last five years: blue-collar workers in export factories in the Pearl River delta region around Hong Kong. By contrast, the wages of young college graduates have actually declined in recent years as China has rapidly expanded its universities and built new ones, creating a surplus of more highly educated workers ... The government has tried to respond to the glut of college graduates by ordering state-owned enterprises to hire large numbers of them and try to find tasks for them to do. But these enterprises are increasingly expected to be profitable and have not absorbed all of the graduates, with the result that big cities in China have growing numbers of unemployed or low-paid college graduates ... Partly because so many young Chinese now go to university and partly because of a declining birth rate, the number of young Chinese available for factory work is falling far short of the demand from employers. That is producing higher ages for blue-collar workers and giving them leverage to demand even more, as the Honda strike shows.

(www.iht.com, 30 May 2010)

The 1,900 workers at the Honda factory [in Foshan] have been on strike to demand higher pay since 21 May ... The resulting shortage of transmissions and engine parts has forced Honda to halt production this week at all four of its assembly plants in China, with one closing Monday [24 May] and the other three Wednesday [26 May] ... An employee of Foxconn ... fell to his death Wednesday, bringing the total of such suicides to ten this year [2010].

(*IHT*, 29 May 2010, p. 11)

'The ninth death in the past six months followed a similar pattern of behaviour – young factory workers plunging from buildings in a Foxconn industrial complex' (www.iht.com, 25 May 2010).

According to 1999 data compiled by the WHO, China has a suicide rate of about fourteen deaths per 100,000 people. That figure suggests that the rate at Foxconn is not unusually high. But the company has said that in previous years there were only one or two suicides a year at its factories in Shenzhen ... Foxconn [is] a unit of Hon Hai Precision industry of Taiwan.

(www.iht.com, 21 May 2010)

Foxconn Technology [is] the Hon Hai subsidiary that operates some of the world's biggest factories and produces a wide range of electronics for global brands ... [including] Apple, Dell and Hewlett-Packard ... Foxconn has about 420,000 employees on two campuses in Shenzhen ... Health experts say the suicide figures from Foxconn are troubling but far below the national rate of about fourteen per 100,000 in China, according to the WHO.

(www.iht.com, 26 May 2010)

'Foxconn is one of the world's top electronics manufacturers. Of its 800,000 employees in China's mainland, 420,000 are in Shenzhen, where they work in shifts and live in the sprawling factory complex' (www.cnn.com, 28 May 2010).

Workers at a strikebound Honda Motor Parts factory in Foshan continued Monday [31 May] with a drive to win higher wages even as the Japanese carmaker lured some labourers back to partially resume production. Executives at Honda's Tokyo headquarters said negotiations were proceeding with workers at the factory, leaving four other plants idle at least through Tuesday after being closed for most of last week. China has been hit with a string of labour disputes at foreign companies, whose migrant workers have begun to demand better pay and working conditions. Workers at Honda have been on strike for higher wages and more benefits since 22 May ... The Communist Party-backed All China Federation of Labour Unions discourages independent worker activism, and generally sides with management. Honda said employees were gradually returning to work at the transmission plant in Foshan in Guangdong province, and that assembly had restarted in the late afternoon ... Honda, which lags Toyota Motor and Nissan Motor in China, operates car ventures with Dongfeng Motor Group Company and Guangzhou Automobile. It also has a small plant making its Jazz model for export. It said the two plants it owned with Guangzhou Auto would close at least until Tuesday, while Dongfeng Honda's factory would remain closed until Wednesday ... More than 1,000 workers at a parts factory near Beijing that supplies South Korea's Hyundai Motor suspended work for most of Saturday [29 May] to demand higher wages. They returned to work after management promised a pay rise.

(www.iht.com, 31 May 2010)

There were signs of a resolution Tuesday [1 June] ... Honda said the majority of workers had accepted a wage increase of 24 per cent ... The strike [was] staged by local workers to protest low pay and tough working conditions ... On top of low wages, workers complained about early shifts and working conditions like the temperature of the factory's air conditioning system. The workers also voiced frustration over a wage gap of some fifty times between local Chinese workers and those dispatched by Honda from Japan.

(www.iht.com, 1 June 2010)

The right to strike was excised from the Chinese constitution in 1982, and attempts by workers to organize outside the official All China Federation of Trade Unions are frowned on by Beijing. Yet Honda's workers have achieved this, while three other car factories that rely on the plant's components have had to close as well ... At least a third of the transmission plant's employees are interns, reflecting a wider use of students and temporary employees across China's manufacturing sector as demand for labour outstrips supply. This, in turn, has increased the bargaining power of workers across southern China.

(*FT*, 1 June 2010, p. 7)

Stung by labour shortages and a rash of suicides this year at its massive factories in southern China, Foxconn Technology said Wednesday [2 June] that it would raise the salaries of many of its Chinese workers by 33 per cent immediately. The pay increase is the latest indication that labour costs are rising in China's coastal manufacturing centres and that workers are demanding higher pay to offset a jump in inflation and soaring food and property prices. On Wednesday Honda Motor said it had resolved a strike in southern China and resumed operations at a transmission plant there after agreeing to give 1,900 Chinese workers there a 24 per cent pay rise. The Honda strike, which has lasted more than two weeks, was a rare show of power by Chinese workers, who are not commonly allowed by the government to publicly strike and walk off the job for higher wages ... The announcement comes just a week after Foxconn's chairman, Terry Gou, visited its factories in the southern city of Shenzhen and promised to do everything possible to halt a spate of worker suicides and improve conditions at Foxconn, which is the world's largest contract electronics manufacturer. Police say ten Foxconn workers have committed suicide this year in Shenzhen. The company, which is based in Taiwan and employs over 800,000 workers in China, has denied that the suicides are work-related or above the national average, saying instead that they are the result of social ills and personal problems of young, migrant workers ... Foxconn, which produces electronics and computer components for Dell, Hewlett-Packard and Apple, has come under growing scrutiny in recent years because of recurring reports of harsh labour conditions at its factories, including long working hours and claims by labour rights activists that the company treats them like machines. Apple, Dell and Hewlett-Packard said last week that they were concerned about the recent suicides and were investigating the situation at Foxconn ... Southern China's manufacturing centres have been struggling with labour shortages since about 2003, and many coastal cities have raised the minimum wage in recent years. Indeed, to help offset inflation and rising food, energy and housing costs – and to spur domestic consumption among the lower classes – Beijing urged local governments early this year to raise the minimum wage in the region ... To cope with labour shortages and hold down costs, many factories in southern China expect employees to work a considerable amount of overtime. And often half of an employee's wages come from overtime pay.

(www.iht.com, 2 June 2010; *IHT*, 3 June 2010, p. 15)

Wages for production workers in all Foxconn companies were raised by 30 per cent as of 1 June ... [It has been reported that] government authorities in Shenzhen, a manufacturing centre where Foxconn operates a large factory complex, would announce a 10 per cent to 20 per cent hike in the minimum wage on 1 July [2010] ... Foxconn employs about 800,000 workers in more than twenty locations in China ... Honda said its transmission plant in Foshan had restarted production after 'a large proportion' of the factory's 1,800 workers accepted a 24 per cent wage increase to renminbi 1,900 ($280) per month.

(*FT*, 3 June 2010, p. 21)

'Striking employees at Honda ... settled for a 24 per cent increase in pay to renminbi 1,900 ($280), having initially asked for 50 per cent' (*FT*, 4 June 2010, p. 11).

Strikes are rare since independent labour unions are banned and 'official trade unions' rarely, if ever, organize industrial action ... Because of China's one-child policy, the supply of workers under forty has dwindled by as much as a fifth ... Japanese car manufacturers, such as Honda, have brought with them a network of components makers, and built ties with Chinese parts suppliers. What goes for cars goes for iPads, mobile phones, digital cameras and colour photocopiers.

(p. 13)

Manufacturers ... argue that better wages would reap other rewards, including higher worker retention rates and increased efficiency. Combined with first-rate infrastructure and dense 'clusters' of components suppliers, which tend to group around assemblers such as Foxconn, China would remain a formidable manufacturing power.

(*FT*, 4 June 2010, p. 11)

The stoppage ... that crippled Honda's car production in late May ... was one of the biggest and longest-running in an enterprise with foreign investors ... The strike over wages (which broke out briefly on 17 May and began anew on 21 May) had halted production at the Foshan facility and forced the temporary closure of all Honda's car assembly plants in China that depend on it ... Some workers remain unhappy with a settlement offered by the Japanese firm. Strikes and protests at factories are becoming more common ... At the Honda plant employees fume more about the factory's trade union than about Japanese managers. On 31 May more than a hundred high-level union members were sent to the factory by the local government. Some scuffled with workers who were trying to get to the gate to talk to reporters ... Several workers complained that despite paying membership dues ... they had received virtually nothing from the union, least of all help negotiating with managers. But their ability to keep up their strike for nearly two weeks seems to have rattled the government. Normally worker protests dissipate rapidly, with unions usually taking the side of managers. A few days into the Honda strike, however, the party's propaganda authorities secretly ordered the media to tone down their coverage. They may well have worried that the Honda workers' tenacity could inspire others (a brief strike did break out at a Hyundai car parts factory on 28 May) ... [It is said that] the

Honda workers are unusual ... because many of them are 'interns' sent by technical colleges. The bonding as fellow students means they can organize themselves more easily than can workers who are usually migrants from different rural areas.

(*The Economist*, 5 June 2010, p. 68)

'An eleventh worker recently died at another factory in northern China. In total there have been thirteen suicides and suicide attempts at Foxconn factories this year [201]' (www.bbc.co.uk, 3 June 2010).

'Beijing will increase the city's minimum wage by 20 per cent ... from 1 July ... state media reported Thursday [3 June], the latest sign of rising labour costs' (*IHT*, 4 June 2010, p. 22).

Beijing will increase the city's minimum wage by 20 per cent ... The minimum wage in the capital will be increased to renminbi 960 ($140) a month from renminbi 800 on 1 July ... Provinces and cities throughout the country have raised their minimum wage this year [2010] as companies have reported growing labour shortages with migrant workers from the interior choosing to seek jobs in small cities closer to their homes.

(www.iht.com, 4 June 2010)

Honda reported an accord Friday [4 June] with about 1,900 workers who went on strike two weeks ago ... [Honda] said the workers, who had returned to the job a few days ago pending a final deal, had accepted 'additional cash and benefits' in exchange for ending their strike. The workers had been seeking a raise of about 75 per cent. Honda offered them a 24 per cent raise earlier this week ... [One worker said] the group had won a 34 per cent pay raise as well as cash bonuses and other concessions. That would bring the base pay to more than $300 a month, well above the minimum wage in the region ... The terms of the agreement could not be verified Friday ... The strike was a show of unusual labour power in China, where the government has discouraged independent labour unions and strikes out of fear that they could lead to copycat actions and threaten social stability and foreign investment in the country. The state-controlled labour union said it had played no role in the action. The Honda workers in Foshan said they had independently organized the strike.

(www.iht.com, 4 June 2010)

'Beijing has signalled that it would like to see higher wages for migrant workers in order to close a widening income gap between the rich and poor' (*IHT*, 5 June 2010, p. 19).

For the second time in a week, Foxconn Technology, the world's largest contract electronics manufacturer, said that it planned to substantially raise the salaries of its huge Chinese work force ... In announcing the wage increase Sunday [6 June], the company ... said that within three months the basic salaries of many of its 800,000 workers in China could reach nearly $300 a month, about double what many were earning a few weeks ago ... Last week the Japanese automaker Honda settle a two-week-long strike at its transmission plant by agreeing to raises of up to 24 per cent to 34 per cent, according to people with knowledge of the negotiations. Also last week Foxconn said it would immediately raise the salaries of its Chinese workers by 33 per cent ... Labour conditions at Foxconn's factories have been widely criticized in the Chinese media for being unduly harsh ... As recently as two weeks ago, the basic salary for many workers at Foxconn's huge factories in the southern city of Shenzhen was about 900 renminbi a month, or about $134 a month. Last week Foxconn said that salaries would immediately rise to $176 a month. And now the company says that after a three-month trial period, workers will be paid $294 a month.

(www.iht.com, 7 June 2010; *IHT*, 7 June 2001, p. 14)

Foxconn ... is a $60 billion manufacturer with a reputation for military-style efficiency that includes mapping out assembly line workers' movements in great detail and monitoring tasks with a stopwatch ... Some of the families of suicide victims have reportedly received settlements of as much as $15,000 – a factor some sociologists say may have led to copycat suicides in some cases by workers hoping to help their families ... In recent interviews employees said the typical Foxconn hire lasted just a few months at the factory before leaving ... A Foxconn executive said last week that the turnover rate at its two Shenzhen campuses – which employ over 400,000 – is about 5 per cent a month, meaning that an astounding 20,000 workers are leaving every month and need to be replaced.

(www.iht.com, 7 June 2010)

Foxconn has offered workers at its Shenzhen manufacturing hub a 66 per cent performance-based pay rise ... Foxconn said production line workers would be able to earn 2,000 yuan ($292) a month if they pass a three-month performance review ... The rise comes on top of a 30 per cent across-the-board increase in the cash part of wages announced last week and means wages will have more than doubled since employee suicides were revealed last month [May]. Before the rises workers earned 900 yuan a month.

(*FT*, 7 June 2010, p. 24)

Foxconn ... said salaries would be raised to 2,000 yuan in October for workers at its plants in the city of Shenzhen. Workers elsewhere in China will get rises in July adjusted for local conditions ... The basic salary at Foxconn's China plants was about 900 yuan a month before the 30 per cent rise, and new recruits are paid 1,200 yuan a month.

(www.guardian.co.uk, 6 June 2010; *Guardian*, 7 June 2010, p. 17)

Foxconn said the second pay rise would lessen the pressure to do overtime ... It said wages for production line employees at the firm's Shenzhen plant would rise from 1,200 yuan ($176) to 2,000 yuan. To get that pay rise workers would first have to pass a performance test lasting three months. New employees will be put on probation for the same amount of time before getting the increase. Pay increases at Foxconn's other Chinese plants ... will be announced from 1 July ... Foxconn has also employed psychiatrists and installed safety nets on buildings.

(www.bbc.co.uk, 7 June 2010)

The minimum wage in southern China is close to $125 a month ... Analysts say Beijing is backing wage increases as a way to spur domestic consumption and make the country less dependent on low-priced exports. The government hopes the move will enforce some export-orientated companies to invest in more innovative or higher-value goods ... Chinese policy-makers also favour wages because they could help ease a widening income gap between the rich and the poor.

(www.iht.com, 7 June 2010)

Foxconn International Holdings said it would seek higher prices from its clients to help offset wage hikes ... Hon Hai chairman Terry Gou ... [who] founded the company in 1974 to make plastic switches for televisions ... said the company was looking for locations in Taiwan to shift some unspecified production from China to automated plants in Taiwan and wanted local authorities in China to manage its worker dormitories. Analysts said already razor thin margins at Foxconn and Hon Hai would likely suffer as they wait to pass on the cost increases, and shares in both companies continued to slide.

(www.iht.com, 8 June 2010)

Honda Motor said Tuesday [8 June] that another parts factory in southern China has stopped production after many of its 600 workers went on strike ... Workers went on strike Monday morning [7 June] at the parts factory in Foshan, Guangdong province ... The factory supplies exhaust parts for Guangqi Honda, a joint car assembly venture between Honda and Guangzhou Automobile of China.

(www.iht.com, 8 June 2010)

TPV Technology, a contract manufacturer that produces computer monitors with about 16,000 workers in five cities in China, says it raised salaries by 15 per cent in January, and plans to raise them again, perhaps as early as July ... Economists say that China's labour force is growing increasingly bold and that over the past year periodic strikes in southern China – some even involving global companies – have been resolved quietly or not reported in the media.

(www.iht.com, 8 June 2010)

The cost of doing business in China is going up. Coastal factories are increasing hourly payments to workers. Local governments are raising minimum wage standards. And if China allows its currency, the renminbi, to appreciate against the US dollar later this year [2010], as many economists are predicting, the relative cost of manufacturing in China will almost certainly rise. The salaries of factory workers in southern China are still low compared to those in the United States and Europe: the hourly wage in southern China is only about 75 cents an hour. But economists say wage increases will eventually ripple through the global economy.

(www.iht.com, 8 June 2010)

Energy

China overtook the United States during 2009 to become the leading investor in renewable energy, according to ... Pew Charitable Trusts ... China invested $34.6 billion in clean energy over the year ... [compared with the US figure of] $18.6 billion ... The United States still holds a marginal lead in the total amount of installed capacity, but will be overtaken by China during the course of this year [2010] if existing trends continue. China's target of having 30 GW of installed capacity in place by 2010 will soon be exceeded through wind alone, and new targets are in the process of being set ... The Global Wind Energy Council said: 'It is now the world's leading manufacturer of solar pho- tovoltaic cells, and more wind turbines are made in China than anywhere else' ... However, China's use of fossil fuels is also expanding fast.

(www.bbc.co.uk, 26 March 2010)

In early 1994 the International Energy Agency ... [said that China] had just become 'a net importer of oil on an annual basis for the first time since the 1960s' ... [China is now] the world's second largest importer, behind only the United States ... Last year [2009] China became a net importer of coal on an annual basis for the first time since reliable records have existed ... Last year's 104 million tonnes of imports pale in comparison to the amount of coal China mines locally, which at about 3.3 billion tonnes is the biggest annual output of any nation.

(*FT*, 14 April 2010, p. 11)

'According to China's Work Safety Administration, 2,631 people died in coal mine accidents in 2009' (www.iht.com, 28 March 2010).
    'Last year [2009] 2,631 miners died in accidents – down from 6,995 deaths in 2002, which was the most dangerous year on record, according to the state administration of coalmine safety' (www.guardian.co.uk, 5 April 2010).

Even as China has set ambitious goals for power for itself in clean-energy production and reduction of global warming gases, the country's surging demand for power from oil and coal has led to the largest six-month increase in the tonnage of human generated greenhouse gas by a single country. China's leaders are so concerned about rising energy use and declining energy efficiency that the cabinet held a special meeting this week to discuss the problem, according to a statement from the ministry of information techno- logy. Coal-fired electricity and oil sales each climbed 24 per cent from the first quarter [of 2010] from a year earlier, on the heels of similar increases in the fourth quarter. Premier Wen Jiabao promised tougher policies to enforce energy conservation, including a ban on government approval of any new projects by companies that fail to eliminate inefficient capacity, the ministry said. Mr Wen also said that China had to find a way to meet the target in its current five-year plan of a 20 per cent improvement in energy efficiency ... The nation's ravenous appetite for fossil fuels is driven by China's shifting economic base – away from light export industries like garment and shoe production and toward energy-intensive heavy industries like steel and cement manufacturing for cars and construction for the domestic market ... The shift in the composition of China's economic output is overwhelming the effects of China's rapid expansion of renewable energy and its existing energy conservation programme, energy experts say ... The shift in activity is partly because of China's economic stimulus programme, which has resulted in a surge in public works construction that requires a lot of steel and cement ... China's current five-year lane, from 2006 to 2010, already sets an efficiency target that the country may now be less likely to meet. The plan calls for the energy needed for each unit of economic output to decline by 20 per cent in 2010 compared to 2005. For a while China seemed to be on track toward that goal. According to the ministry of industry and information technology, energy efficiency actually improved by more than 14 per cent from 2005 to 2009. But it deteriorated by 3.2 per cent in the first quarter, the ministry said on Tuesday [4 May]. Mr Wen said that this deterioration would make it 'particularly difficult' for China to meet the 20 per cent target ... Wind energy effectively doubled in this year's first quarter compared with a year earlier, as China has emerged as the world's largest manufacturer and installer of wind turbines. But wind still accounts for just 2 per cent of China's electricity capacity – and only 1 per cent of actual output because the wind does not blow all the time ... To some extent China's energy consumption now might actually help limit its global emissions in the future ... For example ... China currently moves only 55 per cent of its coal by rail ... which is down from 80 per cent a decade ago ... But now, with new high-speed passenger lines leaving more room on older lines to haul coal and other freight, the percentages could begin shifting away from energy-efficient trucking.

(www.iht.com, 7 May 2010)

Monday's [21 June] 0.42 per cent rise was the biggest one-day move since 2005 and an indication that China had begun to permit a gradual rise in the renminbi against the dollar ... The renminbi [has been pegged] at around 6.827 to the dollar, permitting only the tiniest of moves within a trading band that in theory allowed for fluctuations of up to 0.5 per cent above and below the daily reference rate to the dollar ... [The moves] were widely interpreted as a precursor to a gradual and modest appreciation of the renminbi.

(www.iht.com, 22 and 23 June 2010)

Bibliography

Periodicals and reports

CDSP Current Digest of the Soviet Press (since 5 February 1992 *Post-Soviet*)
EIU Economist Intelligence Unit
FEER Far Eastern Economic Review
FT Financial Times
IHT International Herald Tribune

Books and journals

Aubert, C. (1990) 'The Chinese model and the future of rural–urban development' in K.-E. Wädekin (ed.) *Communist Agriculture: Farming in the Far East and Cuba*, London: Routledge.

Aziz, J. and Dunaway, S. (2007) 'China's rebalancing act', *Finance and Development*, September.

Bai, C., Li, D. and Wang, Y. (1997) 'Enterprise productivity and efficiency: when is up really down?' *Journal of Comparative Economics*, vol. 24, no. 3.

Bergson, A. (1985) 'A visit to China's economic reform', *Comparative Economic Studies*, vol. XXVII, no. 2.

Bideleux, R. and Jeffries, I. (1998) *A History of Eastern Europe: Crisis and Change*, London: Routledge.

—— (2007a) *A History of Eastern Europe: Crisis and Change*, second edition, London: Routledge.

—— (2007b) *The Balkans*, London: Routledge.

Bleaney, M. (1988) *Do Socialist Economies Work? The Soviet and East European Experience*, Oxford: Basil Blackwell.

Bolton, P. (1995) 'Privatization and the separation of ownership and control: lessons from Chinese enterprise reform', *Economics of Transition*, vol. 3, no. 1.

Bowles, P. and White, G. (1989) 'Contradictions in China's financial reforms: the relationship between banks and enterprises', *Cambridge Journal of Economics*, vol. 13, no. 4.

Bramall, C. (1993) 'The role of decollectivization in China's agricultural miracle, 1978–90', *Journal of Peasant Studies*, vol. 20, no. 2.

Broadman, H. (1999) 'The Chinese state as corporate shareholder', *Finance and Development*, September.

Brooks, K., Guash, L., Braverman, A. and Csaki, C. (1991) 'Agriculture and the transition to the market', *Journal of Economic Perspectives*, vol. 5, no. 4.

Cao, Y., Fan, G. and Woo, W. (1997) 'Chinese economic reforms: past successes and future challenges' in W. Woo, S. Parker and J. Sachs (eds) *Economies in Transition: Comparing Asia and Eastern Europe*, London: MIT Press.

Chai, J. (1992) 'Consumption and living standards in China', *China Quarterly*, no. 131.

Chamberlain, H. (1987) 'Party–management relations in Chinese industry: some political dimensions of economic reform', *China Quarterly*, no. 112 (December).

Chan, T. (1986) 'China's price reform in the 1980s', discussion paper no. 78, Department of Economics, University of Hong Kong.

Chang, C. and Wang, Y. (1994) 'The nature of the township-village enterprise', *Journal of Comparative Economics*, vol. 19, no. 3.

Chang, G. and Wen G. (1997) 'Communal dining and the Chinese famine of 1958–1961', *Economic Development and Cultural Change*, vol. 46, no. 1.

Chen, C., Chang, L. and Zhang, Y. (1995) 'The role of foreign direct investment in China's post-1978 economic development', *World Development*, vol. 23, no. 4.

Chen, K., Hongchang, W., Yuxin, Z., Jefferson, G. and Rawski, T. (1988) 'Productivity changes in Chinese industry', *Journal of Comparative Economics*, vol. XII.

Chen, K., Jefferson, G. and Singh, I. (1992) 'Lessons from China's economic reform', *Journal of Comparative Economics*, vol. 16, no. 2.

Cheung, S. (1986) *Will China Go Capitalist?* London: Institute of Economic Affairs (Hobart Papers).

Chow, G. (1997) 'Challenges of China's economic system for economic theory', *American Economic Review*, Papers and Proceedings, vol. 87, no. 2.

Dillon, M. (2002) 'China and the US bases in Central Asia', *The World Today*, vol. 58, no. 7.

Dipchand, C. (1994) 'The interbank market in China', *Development Policy Review*, vol. 12, no. 1.

Dittmer, L. (1989) 'The Tiananmen massacre', *Problems of Communism*, September–October.

Dollar, D. (1990) 'Economic reform and allocative efficiency in China's state-owned industry', *Economic Development and Cultural Change*, vol. 39, no. 1.

Donnithorne, A. (1967) *China's Economic System*, London: Allen & Unwin.

Economist, The (various surveys): 'China', 28 November 1992; 'Asia', 30 October 1993 'Asia'; 'China', 18 March 1995; 'China', 8 March 1997; 'Central Asia', 7 February 1998; 'China', 24 October 1998; 'China', 8 April 2000; 'China's economic power', 10 March 2001; 'China', 15 June 2002; 'Central Asia', 26 July 2003;'A survey of the world economy: the dragon and the eagle', 2 October 2004; 'India and China', 5 March 2005; 'China', 25 March 2006; 'Hong Kong', 30 June 2007; 'Technology in India and China', 10 November 2007; 'China's quest for resources', 15 March 2008; 'China and America', 24 October 2009.

Economy, E. (2007) 'The Great Leap Backward?' *Foreign Affairs*, vol. 86. no. 5.

Ellman, M. (1979) *Socialist Planning*, London: Cambridge University Press.

—— (1986) 'Economic reform in China', *International Affairs*, vol. 62, no. 3.

Feder, G., Lau, L., Lin, J. and Luo, X. (1992) 'The determinants of farm investment and residential construction in post-reform China', *Economic Development and Cultural Change*, vol. 41, no. 1.

Field, R. (1984) 'Changes in Chinese industry since 1978', *China Quarterly*, December.

Financial Times (various surveys on China): 9 December 1985; 20 August 1986; 5 September 1986; 22 September 1986; 29 September 1986; 30 September 1986; 18 December 1986; 18 December 1987; 12 December 1989; 24 April 1991; 16 June 1992; 2 June

1993; 18 November 1993; 7 November 1994; 20 November 1995; 27 June 1996; 8 December 1997; 19 May 1998 (Shanghai); 16 November 1998; 1 October 1999; 13 November 2000; 15 March 2002 (China and the WTO); 12 December 2002; 8 February 2003 (Asian Finance); 29 April 2003 (Yangtze Delta); 16 December 2003; 20 March 2004; 7 December 2004; 8 November 2005; 12 December 2006; 31 March 2007; 29 June 2007 (Hong Kong); 30 June 2008 (Hong Kong); 24 November 2008; 2 April 2009 (G-20 Summit: China and the World); 1 October 2009.

Fischer, A. (2008) 'Reaping Tibet's whirlwind', *FEER*, March.

Fischer, S. and Sahay, R. (2000) 'Taking stock', *Finance and Development*, vol. 37, no. 3.

Gallagher, M. (2005) 'China in 2004', *Asian Survey*, vol. XLV, no. 1.

Gaynor, M. and Putterman, L. (1993) 'Productivity consequences of alternative land division methods in China's decollectivization', *Journal of Development Economics*, vol. 42, no. 2.

Ge, W. (1999) 'Special Economic Zones and the opening of the Chinese economy: some lessons for economic liberalization', *World Development*, vol. 27, no. 7.

Gelb, A., Jefferson, G. and Singh, I. (1993) 'Can communist economies transform incrementally? The experience of China', *Economics of Transition*, vol. 1, no. 4.

Gold, T. (1989) 'Urban private business in China', *Studies in Comparative Communism*, vol. XXII, nos 2 and 3.

Goldman, M. and Goldman, M. (1988) 'Soviet and Chinese economic reforms', *Foreign Affairs*, vol. 66, no. 3

Gordon, R. and Li, W. (1991) 'Chinese economic reforms, 1979–89: lessons for the future', *American Economic Review*, Papers and Proceedings, May.

Granick, D. (1990) *Chinese State Enterprises: A Regional Property Rights Analysis*, Chicago: University of Chicago Press.

Gregory, P. and Stuart, R. (1990) *Soviet Economic Structure and Performance*, fourth edition, New York: Harper & Row (second edition 1981 and third edition 1986).

—— (1994) *Soviet and Post-Soviet Economic Structure and Performance*, fifth edition, New York: HarperCollins.

Groves, T., Hong, Y., McMillan, J. and Naughton, B. (1994) 'Autonomy and incentives in Chinese state enterprises' *Quarterly Journal of Economics*, vol. CIX, no. 1.

—— (1995) 'China's evolving managerial labour market', *Journal of Political Economy*, vol. 103, no. 4.

Guardian (various surveys on China): 13 October 1986; regional China – Jiangsu and Guangdong 16 October 1987; Shanghai: 19 November 1987.

Gungwu, W. (1993) 'Greater China and the Chinese overseas', *China Quarterly*, no. 136.

Halpern, N. (1985) 'China's industrial economic reform: the question of strategy', *Asian Survey*, vol. XXV, no. 10.

Harris, P. (2008) 'Tibet's legal right to autonomy', *FEER*, May.

Hartford, K. (1987) 'Socialist countries in the world food system: the Soviet Union, Hungary and China', *Food Research Institute Studies*, vol. XX, no. 3.

Hillman, B. (2008) 'Money can't buy Tibetan's love', *FEER*, April.

Hirschler, R. (2002) 'China's experience with transition: what is behind its stunning economic success?' *Transition*, vol. 13, no. 3.

Holzman, F. (1976) *International Trade under Communism*, New York: Basic Books.

Hsu, R. (1989) 'Changing conceptions of the socialist enterprise in China, 1979–88', *Modern China*, vol. 14, no. 4.

—— (1992) 'Industrial reform in China' in I. Jeffries (ed.) *Industrial Reform in Socialist Countries: from Restructuring to Revolution*, Aldershot: Edward Elgar.

Hu, Teh-wei, Li, Ming and Shi, Shuzhong (1988) 'Analysis of wages and bonus payments among Tianjin urban workers', *China Quarterly*, no. 113.

Hu, Z. and Khan, M. (1997) 'Why is China growing so fast?' *IMF Staff Papers*, vol. 44, no. 1.

Huang Yasheng (1990) 'Webs of interest and patterns of behaviour of Chinese local economic bureaucracies and enterprises during reforms', *China Quarterly*, no. 123 (September).

Huang, Y. and Duncan, R. (1997) 'How successful were China's state sector reforms?' *Journal of Comparative Economics*, vol. 24, no. 1.

Hussain, A. (1992) 'The Chinese economic reforms in retrospect and prospect', LSE, Discussion Paper CP no. 24.

Hussain, A. and Stern, N. (1991) 'Effective demand, enterprise reforms and public finance in China', *Economic Policy*, no. 12.

—— (1993) 'The role of the state, ownership and taxation in transitional economies', *Economics of Transition*, vol. 1, no. 1.

—— (1994) 'Economic transition on the other side of the Wall: China', LSE, Discussion Paper CP no. 29.

Hussain, A. and Zhuang, J. (1996) 'Pattern and causes of loss-making in Chinese state enterprises', LSE, Discussion Paper CP no. 31.

Imai, H. (1994) 'Inflationary pressure in China's consumption goods market: estimation and analysis', *The Developing Economies*, vol. XXXII, no. 2.

International Herald Tribune (various surveys on China): 15 September 1986; 9 July 1986; 11 April 1994; 30 May 1994; 13 March 1995; 24 April 1995; 28 October 1996; 25 November 1996; 12 August 1997; 1 October 1999; 27 June 2002.

Ishihara, K. (1987) 'Planning and the market in China', *The Developing Economies*, vol. XXV, no. 4.

—— (1990) 'Inflation and economic reform in China', *The Developing Economies*, vol. XXVIII, no. 2.

Jackson, S. (1986) 'Reform of state enterprise management in China', *China Quarterly*, no. 107.

Jefferson, G. and Rawski, T. (1994) 'Enterprise reform in Chinese industry', *Journal of Economic Perspectives*, vol. 8, no. 2.

Jefferson, G. and Xu, W. (1991) 'The impact of reform on socialist enterprises in transition: structure, conduct, and performance in Chinese industry', *Journal of Comparative Economics*, vol. 15, no. 1.

—— (1994) 'Assessing gains in efficient production among China's industrial enterprises', *Economic Development and Cultural Change*, vol. 42, no. 3.

Jefferson, G., Rawski, T. and Zheng, Y. (1996) 'Chinese industrial productivity: trends, measurement issues and recent developments', *Journal of Comparative Economics*, vol. 23, no. 2.

Jeffries, I. (ed.) (1981) *The Industrial Enterprise in Eastern Europe*, New York: Praeger.

—— (1990) *A Guide to the Socialist Economies*, London: Routledge.

—— (1992a) 'The impact of reunification on the East German economy' in J. Osmond (ed.) *German Reunification: A Reference Guide and Commentary*, London: Longman.

—— (ed.) (1992b) *Industrial Reform in Socialist Countries: From Restructuring to Revolution*, Aldershot: Edward Elgar.

—— (1993) *Socialist Economies and the Transition to the Market: A Guide*, London: Routledge.

—— (1996a) *A Guide to the Economies in Transition*, London: Routledge.

—— (ed.) (1996b) *Problems of Economic and Political Transformation in the Balkans*, London: Pinter.

—— (2001a) *Economies in Transition: A Guide to China, Cuba, Mongolia, North Korea and Vietnam at the Turn of the Twenty-first Century*, London: Routledge.

—— (2001b) 'Good governance and the first decade of transition' in H. Hoen (ed.) *Good Governance in Central and Eastern Europe: The Puzzle of Capitalism by Design*, Cheltenham: Edward Elgar.

—— (2002a) *Eastern Europe at the Turn of the Twenty-First Century: A Guide to the Economies in Transition*, London: Routledge.

—— (2002b) *The Former Yugoslavia at the Turn of the Twenty-First Century: A Guide to the Economies in Transition*, London: Routledge.

—— (2002c) *The New Russia: A Handbook of Economic and Political Developments*, London: RoutledgeCurzon.

—— (2003) *The Caucasus and Central Asian Republics at the Turn of the Twenty-First Century: A Guide to the Economies in Transition*, London: Routledge.

—— (2004) *The Countries of the Former Soviet Union: the Baltic and European States in Transition*, London: Routledge.

—— (2006a) *China: A Guide to Economic and Political Developments*, London: Routledge.

—— (2006b) *North Korea: A Guide to Economic and Political Developments*, London: Routledge.

—— (2006c) *Vietnam: A Guide to Economic and Political Developments*, London: Routledge.

—— (2007) *Mongolia: A Guide to Economic and Political Developments*, London: Routledge.

—— (2009) *Contemporary North Korea: A Guide to Economic and Political Developments*, London: Routledge.

Jeffries, I., Melzer, M. (eds), and Breuning, E. (advisory ed.) (1987) *The East German Economy*, London: Croom Helm.

Johnson, D. (1988a) 'Economic reforms in the People's Republic of China', *Economic Development and Cultural Change*, vol. 36, no. 3.

—— (1988b) 'Agriculture' in A. Cracraft (ed.) *The Soviet Union Today*, Chicago: University of Chicago Press.

Jones-Luong, P. and Weinthal, E. (2002) 'New friends, new fears in Central Asia', *Foreign Affairs*, vol. 81, no. 2.

Kamath, S. (1990) 'Foreign direct investment in a centrally planned developing economy: the Chinese case', *Economic Development and Cultural Change*, vol. 39, no. 1.

Kaminski, B., Wang, Z. and Winters, A. (1996) 'Export performance in transition economies', *Economic Policy*, no. 23.

Kane, P. (1988) *Famine in China (1958–1961): Demographic and Social Implications*, London: Macmillan.

Kojima, R. (1990) 'Achievements and contradictions in China's economic reform', *The Developing Economies*, vol. XXVIII, no. 4.

Koo, A. (1990) 'The contract responsibility system: transition from a planned to a market system', *Economic Development and Cultural Change*, vol. 35, no. 4.

Korzec, M. (1988) 'Contract labour, the right to work and new labour laws in the People's Republic of China', *Comparative Economic Studies*, vol. XXX, no. 2.

Kosta, J. (1987) 'The Chinese economic reform: approaches, results and prospects' in P. Gey, J. Kosta and W. Quaisser (eds) *Crisis and Reform in Socialist Economies*, London: Westview Press.

Kueh, Y. (1989) 'The Maoist legacy and China's new industrialization strategy', *China Quarterly*, no. 119.

—— (1992) 'Foreign investment and economic change', *China Quarterly*, no. 131.

Kung, J. (2000) 'Common property rights and land reallocations in rural China: evidence from a village survey', *World Development*, vol. 28, no. 4.

Lam, W. (2008) 'Hope for a better Tibet policy', *FEER*, April.

Lardy, N. (1998) 'China and the Asian contagion', *Foreign Affairs*, vol. 77, no. 4.

Lee, K. (1990) 'The Chinese model of the socialist enterprise: an assessment of its organization and performance', *Journal of Comparative Economics*, vol. 14, no. 3.

—— (1993) 'Property rights and the agency problem in China's enterprise reform', *Cambridge Journal of Economics*, vol. 17, no. 2.

Lee, P. (1986) 'Enterprise autonomy in post-Mao China: a case study of policy-making, 1978–83', *China Quarterly*, no. 105.

Li, D. (1998) 'Changing incentives for the Chinese bureaucracy', *American Economic Review*, Papers and Proceedings, May.

Li, W. (1997) 'The impact of economic reform on the performance of Chinese state enterprises, 1980–1989', *Journal of Political Economy*, vol. 105, no. 5.

Lin, C. (1995) 'The assessment: Chinese economic reform in retrospect and prospect', *Oxford Review of Economic Policy*, vol. 11, no. 4.

Lin, J. (1988) 'The household responsibility system in China's agricultural reform: a theoretical and empirical study', *Economic Development and Cultural Change*, vol. 36, no. 3 (Supplement).

—— (1990) 'Collectivization and China's agricultural crisis in 1959–61', *Journal of Political Economy*, vol. 98, no. 6.

—— (1992) 'Rural reforms and agricultural growth in China', *American Economic Review*, vol. 82, no. 1.

Lin, J., Cae, F. and Li, Z. (1998) 'Competition, policy burdens and state-owned enterprise reform', *American Economic Review*, Papers and Proceedings, May.

Ling, L. (1988) 'Intellectual responses to China's economic reforms', *Asian Survey*, vol. XXVIII, no. 5.

Ling, Z. and Zhongyi, J. (1993) 'From brigade to village community: the land tenure system and rural development in China', *Cambridge Journal of Economics*, vol. 17, no. 4.

Liu, Z. and Liu, G. (1996) 'The efficiency impact of the Chinese industrial reforms in the 1980s', *Journal of Comparative Economics*, vol. 23, no. 3.

Lockett, M. (1987) 'China's development strategy: the Seventh Five Year Plan and after', *Euro-Asia Business Review*, July.

Long, S. (1990) *China against the Tide*, London: EIU.

Lynch, D. (2008) 'Mr Ma's Taiwanese identity', *FEER*, March.

Ma, S. (1998) 'The Chinese route to privatization: the evolution of the shareholding system option', *Asian Survey*, vol. XXXVIII, no. 4.

McKinnon, R. (1992a) 'Taxation, money, and credit in a liberalizing socialist economy', *Economics of Planning*, vol. 25, no. 1.

—— (1992b) 'Taxation, money and credit in a liberalizing socialist economy' in C. Clague and G. Rausser (eds) *The Emergence of Market Economies in Eastern Europe*, Oxford: Basil Blackwell.

—— (1994) 'Financial growth and macroeconomic stability in China, 1978–92: implications for Russia and other transitional economies', *Journal of Comparative Economics*, vol. 18, no. 3.

McMillan, J. and Woodruff, C. (2002) 'The central role of entrepreneurs in transition economies', *Journal of Economic Perspectives*, vol. 16, no. 3.

McMillan, J., Whalley, J. and Lijing Zhu (1989) 'The impact of China's economic reforms on agricultural productivity growth', *Journal of Political Economy*, vol. 97, no. 4.

Mancours, K. and Swinnen, J. (2002) 'Patterns of agrarian transition', *Economic Development and Cultural Change*, vol. 50, no. 2.

Mao, Y. and Hare, P. (1989) 'Chinese experience in the introduction of a market mechanism into a planned economy: the role of pricing', *Journal of Economic Surveys*, vol. 3, no. 2.

Meng, X. and Zhang, J. (2001) 'The two-tier labour market in urban China. Occupational segregation and wage differentials between urban residents and rural migrants in Shanghai', *Journal of Comparative Economics*, vol. 29, no. 3.

Murrell, P. (1990) *The Nature of Socialist Economies: Lessons from Eastern European Foreign Trade*, Princeton, NJ: Princeton University Press.

—— (1992a) 'Evolutionary and radical approaches to economic reform', *Economics of Planning*, vol. 25, no. 1.

—— (1992b) 'Evolution in economics and in the economic reform of the centrally planned economies' in C. Clague and G. Rausser (eds) *The Emergence of Market Economies in Eastern Europe*, Oxford: Basil Blackwell.

—— (1993) 'What is shock therapy? What did it do in Poland and Russia?' *Post-Soviet Affairs*, vol. 9, no. 2.

Naughton, B. (1994) 'Chinese institutional innovation and privatization from below', *American Economic Review*, vol. 84, no. 2.

—— (1996) 'China's emergence and prospects as a trading nation', *Brookings Papers on Economic Activity*, no. 2.

Nellis, J. (1999) 'Time to rethink privatization in transition economies?', *Finance and Development*, vol. 36, no. 2.

Nolan, P. (1992) 'Transforming Stalinist systems: China's reforms in the light of Russian and East European experience', University of Cambridge, Discussion Paper on Economic Transition DPET 9203.

—— (1993) 'China's post-Mao political economy: a puzzle', *Contributions to Political Economy*, no. 12.

—— (1996a) 'Large firms and industrial reform in former planned economies: the case of China', *Cambridge Journal of Economics*, vol. 20, no. 1.

—— (1996b) 'China's rise, Russia's fall', *Journal of Peasant Studies*, vol. 24, nos 1 and 2.

Nolan, P. and Xiaoqiang, W. (1999) 'Beyond privatization: institutional innovation and growth in China's large state-owned enterprises', *World Development*, vol. 27, no. 1.

Nove, A. (1961) *The Soviet Economy*, London: Allen & Unwin.

OECD (2005) *Economic Survey of China 2005*, OECD, available www.oecd.org/documentprint/0,2744,en_2649

Pearson, M. (1991) 'The erosion of controls over foreign capital in China', *Modern China*, vol. 17, no. 1.

Perkins, D. (1988) 'Reforming China's economic system', *Journal of Economic Literature*, vol. XXVI, no. 2.

—— (1994) 'Completing China's move to the market', *Journal of Economic Perspectives*, vol. 8, no. 2.

Phillips, D. (1986) 'Special Economic Zones in China's modernisation: changing policies and changing fortunes', *National Westminster Review*, February.

Platte, E. (1994) 'China's foreign debt', *Pacific Affairs*, vol. 66, no. 4.

Pomfret, R. (1993) 'Mongolia's economic reforms: background, contents and prospects', *Economic Bulletin for Asia and the Pacific*, vol. XLIV, no. 1.

—— (2000a) 'Transition and democracy in Mongolia', *Europe–Asia Studies*, vol. 52, no. 1.

—— (2000b) 'Agrarian reform in Uzbekistan: why has the Chinese model failed to deliver?' *Economic Development and Cultural Change*, vol. 48, no. 2.

—— (2000c) 'The Uzbek model of economic development, 1991–99', *Economics of Transition*, vol. 8, no. 3.

Prasad, E. and Rumbaugh, T. (2003) 'Beyond the Great Wall', *Finance and Development*, vol. 40, no. 4.

Prybyla, J. (1985) 'The Chinese economy: adjustment of the system or systemic reform?' *Asian Survey*, vol. XXV, no. 5.

—— (1986) 'China's economic experiment: from Mao to market', *Problems of Communism*, vol. XXXV, no. 1.

—— (1987) 'On some questions concerning price reform in the People's Republic of China', University Park: Pennsylvania State University, Working Paper 9–87–16.

—— (1994) Review in *Economic Development and Cultural Change*, vol. 42, no. 3.

Pudney, S. and Wang, L. (1994) 'Housing and housing reform in urban China: efficiency, distribution and the implications for social security', LSE, EF no. 8.

Putterman, L. (1988) 'Group farming and work incentives in collective-era China', *Modern China*, vol. 14, no. 4.

Qian, Y. (1994) 'A theory of shortage in socialist economies based on the soft budget constraint', *American Economic Review*, vol. 84, no. 1.

Qian, Y. and Xu, C. (1993) 'Why China's economic reforms differ: the M-form hierarchy and entry/expansion of the non-state sector', *Economics of Transition*, vol. 1, no. 2.

Quaisser, W. (1987) 'The new agricultural reform in China: from the people's communes to peasant agriculture' in P. Gey, J. Kosta and W. Quaisser (eds) *Crisis and Reform in Socialist Economies*, London: Westview Press.

Rawski, T. (1994) 'Chinese industrial reform: accomplishments, prospects and implications', *American Economic Review*, vol. 84, no. 2.

Richman, B. (1969) *Industrial Society in Communist China*, New York: Random House.

Riskin, C. (1987) *The Political Economy of Chinese Development since 1949*, London: Oxford University Press.

Roy, D. (1990) 'Real product and income in China, Cuba, North Korea and Vietnam', *Development Policy Review*, vol. 8, no. 1.

Sachs, J. (1992) 'The economic transformation of Eastern Europe: the case of Poland', *Economics of Planning*, vol. 25, no. 1.

—— (1994) *Poland's Jump to the Market Economy*, Cambridge, MA: MIT Press.

—— (1995) 'Consolidating capitalism', *Foreign Policy*, no. 98.

—— (1996a) 'The transition at mid-decade', *American Economic Review*, Papers and Proceedings (May).

—— (1996b) 'Economic transition and the exchange rate regime', *American Economic Review*, Papers and Proceedings (May).

—— (1997) 'An overview of stabilization issues facing economies in transition' in W. Woo, S. Parker and J. Sachs (eds) (1997) *Economies in Transition: Comparing Asia and Eastern Europe*, London: MIT Press.

Sachs, J. and Woo, W. (1994) 'Structural factors in the economic reforms of China, Eastern Europe and the former Soviet Union', *Economic Policy*, no. 18.

—— (1996) 'China's transition experience reexamined', *Transition*, vol. 7, nos 3–4.

Schram, S. (1988) 'China after the 13th Congress', *China Quarterly*, no. 114.

Shakya, Tsering (2008) 'The gulf between Tibet and its exiles', *FEER*, May.

Shambaugh, D. (1989) 'The fourth and fifth plenary sessions of the 13th CCP Central Committee', *China Quarterly*, no. 120.

Shen Xiaofang (1990) 'A decade of direct foreign investment in China', *Problems of Communism*, March–April.

Sicular, T. (1988a) 'Plan and market in China's agricultural commerce', *Journal of Political Economy*, vol. 96, no. 2.

—— (1988b) 'Grain pricing: a key link in Chinese economic policy', *Modern China*, vol. 14, no. 4.

—— (1988c) 'Agricultural planning and pricing in the post-Mao period', *China Quarterly*, no. 116.

Skinner, G. (1985) 'Rural marketing in China: repression and revival', *China Quarterly*, no. 103.

Smyth, R. (1998) 'Recent developments in rural enterprise reform in China', *Asian Survey*, vol. XXXVIII, no. 8.

—— (2000) 'Should China be promoting large-scale enterprises and enterprise groups?' *World Development*, vol. 28, no. 4.

Solinger, D. (1989a) 'Urban reform and relational contracting in post-Mao China: an interpretation of the transition from plan to market', *Comparative Communism*, vol. XXII, nos 2 and 3.

—— (1989b) 'Capitalist measures with Chinese characteristics', *Problems of Communism*, vol. XXXVIII, January–February.

Stavis, B. (1989) 'The political economy of inflation in China', *Studies in Comparative Communism*, vol. XXII, nos 2 and 3.

Tam, On-Kit (1988) 'Rural finance in China', *China Quarterly*, no. 113.

Thurow, L. (1998) 'Asia: the collapse and the cure', *The New York Review of Books*, 5 February, vol. XLV, no. 2.

Tsai, K. (2008) 'China's complicit capitalists', *FEER*, January–February.

Tsang, S. (1996) 'Against "big bang" in economic transition: normative and positive arguments', *Cambridge Journal of Economics*, vol. 20, no. 2.

Ungar, E. (1987–8) 'The struggle over the Chinese community in Vietnam, 1946–86', *Pacific Affairs*, vol. 60, no. 4.

United Nations (1993) *World Economic Survey 1993*, New York: United Nations.

—— (2001) *World Economic and Social Survey 2001*, New York: United Nations.

—— (2006) *World Economic Situation and Prospects 2006*, New York: United Nations.

Wädekin, K.-E. (1982) *Agrarian Policies in Communist Europe*, Totowa, NJ: Rowman & Allanheld.

—— (1988) 'Soviet agriculture: a brighter prospect' in P. Wiles (ed.), *The Soviet Economy on the Brink of Reform*, London: Unwin Hyman.

—— (ed.) (1990a) *Communist Agriculture: Farming in the Far East and Cuba*, London: Routledge.

—— (1990b) *Communist Agriculture: Farming in the Soviet Union and Eastern Europe*, London: Routledge.

—— (1990c) 'Private agriculture in socialist countries: implications for the USSR' in E. Gray (ed.) *Soviet Agriculture: Comparative Perspectives*, Ames: University of Iowa Press.

Walder, A. (1989) 'Factory and manager in an era of reform', *China Quarterly*, no. 118.

Wall, D. (1991) 'Special economic zones and industrialisation in China', International Economics Research Centre at the University of Sussex, Discussion Paper no. 01/91.

—— (1993) 'China's economic reform and opening-up process: the Special Economic Zones', *Development Policy Review*, vol. 11, no. 3.

Wang, J. (1999) 'China's rural reform: the "rights" direction', *Transition*, vol. 10, no. 2.

Wang Jun (1989) 'The export-oriented strategy of China's coastal areas: evaluation and prospects', University of Leicester, Department of Economics, Discussion Paper no. 116 (September).

Wang, X. (1997) 'Rural empowerment of state and peasantry: grassroots democracy in rural China', *World Development*, vol. 25, no. 9.

Wang Xiao-qing (1993) ' "Groping for stones to cross the river": Chinese price reform against the "big bang" ', University of Cambridge, Discussion Paper DPET 9305.

Wang Zhonghui (1990) 'Private enterprise in China: an overview', *Journal of Communist Studies*, vol. 6, no. 3.

—— (1993) 'China's policies towards collective rural enterprises', *Small Enterprise Development*, vol. 4, no. 1.

Watson, A. (1988) 'The reform of agricultural marketing in China', *China Quarterly*, no. 113.

Weitzman, M. and Xu, C. (1993) 'Chinese township-village enterprises as vaguely defined co-operatives', LSE, CP no. 26.

—— (1994) 'Chinese township-village enterprises as vaguely defined co-operatives', *Journal of Comparative Economics*, vol. 18, no. 2.

Wen, G. (1993) 'Total factor productivity in China's farming sector, 1952–89', *Economic Development and Cultural Change*, vol. 42, no. 1.

White, G. (1987a) 'Cuban planning in the mid-1980s: centralisation, decentralisation and participation', *World Development*, vol. 15, no. 1.

—— (1987b) 'The politics of economic reform in Chinese industry: the introduction of the labour contract system', *China Quarterly*, no. 111.

—— (1988) 'State and market in China's labour reform', *Journal of Development Studies*, vol. 24, no. 4.

White, G. and Bowles, P. (1988) 'China's banking reforms: aims, methods and problems', *National Westminster Bank Quarterly Review*, November.

Wong, C. (1986) 'The economics of shortage and the problems of reform in Chinese industry', *Journal of Comparative Economics*, vol. 10, no. 4.

—— (1988) 'Interpreting rural industrial growth in post-Mao China', *Modern China*, vol. 14, no. 1.

—— (1989) 'Between plan and market: the role of the local sector in post-Mao reforms in China' in S. Gomulka, Ha Yong-Chool and Kim Cai-One (eds) *Economic Reforms in the Socialist World*, London: Macmillan.

—— (1991) 'Central–local relations in an era of fiscal decline', *China Quarterly*, no. 128 (December).

Wong, E. (1987) 'Recent developments in China's Special Economic Zones: problems and prognosis', *The Developing Economies*, vol. XXV, no. 1.

Woo, W. (1994) 'The art of reforming centrally planned economies: comparing China, Poland and Russia', *Journal of Comparative Economics*, vol. 18, no. 3.

—— (1997) 'Improving the performance of enterprises in transition' in W. Woo, S. Parker and J. Sachs (eds) *Economies in Transition: Comparing Asia and Eastern Europe*, London: MIT Press.

Woo, W., Hai, W., Jin, Y. and Fan, G. (1994) 'How successful has Chinese enterprise reform been? Pitfalls in opposite biases and focus', *Journal of Comparative Economics*, vol. 18, no. 3.

Woo, W., Parker, S. and Sachs, J. (eds) (1997) *Economies in Transition: Comparing Asia and Eastern Europe*, London: MIT Press.

World Bank (1996) *World Development Report: From Plan to Market*, New York: Oxford University Press.

—— (2002) 'The World Bank, privatization and enterprise reform in transition economies', *Transition*, vol. 13, no. 1.

Wu, H.-L. and Chen, C.-H. (2001) 'An assessment of outward foreign direct investment from China's transitional economy', *Europe-Asia Studies*, vol. 53, no. 8.

Wu, J. and Reynolds, B. (1988) 'Choosing a strategy for China's economic reform', *American Economic Review*, Papers and Proceedings, May.

Wu, Z. (1997) 'How successful has state-owned enterprise reform been in China?' *Europe–Asia Studies*, vol. 49, no. 7.

Yao, S. (2000) 'Economic development and poverty reduction in China over twenty years of reform', *Economic Development and Cultural Change*, vol. 48, no. 3.

Zhu Ling (1990) 'The transformation of the operating mechanism in Chinese agriculture', *Journal of Development Studies*, vol. 26, no. 2.

Zhu, Y. (1995) 'Major changes under way in China's industrial relations', *International Labour Review*, vol. 134, no. 1.

Zhuang, J. and Xu, C. (1996) 'Profit-sharing and financial performance in the Chinese state enterprises: evidence from panel data', *Economics of Planning*, vol. 29, no. 3.

Index

For Product Safety Concerns and Information please contact our EU
representative GPSR@taylorandfrancis.com
Taylor & Francis Verlag GmbH, Kaufingerstraße 24, 80331 München, Germany

www.ingramcontent.com/pod-product-compliance
Ingram Content Group UK Ltd.
Pitfield, Milton Keynes, MK11 3LW, UK
UKHW021837240425
457818UK00006B/219